THE MAKING OF THE WEST

PEOPLES AND CULTURES

A CONCISE HISTORY

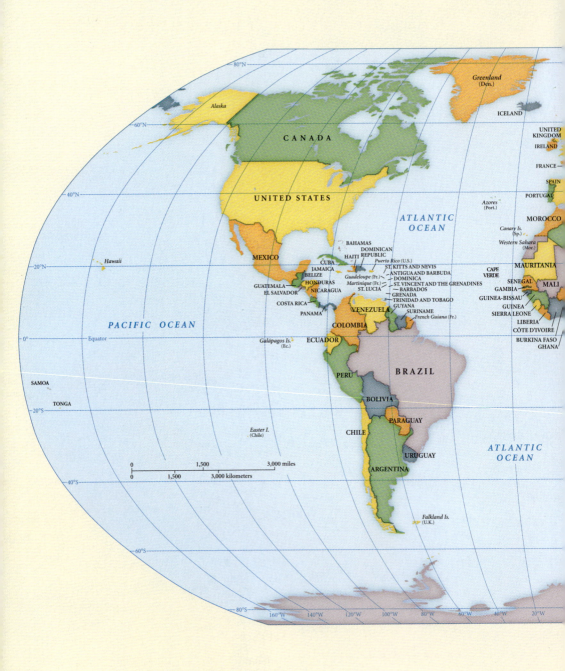

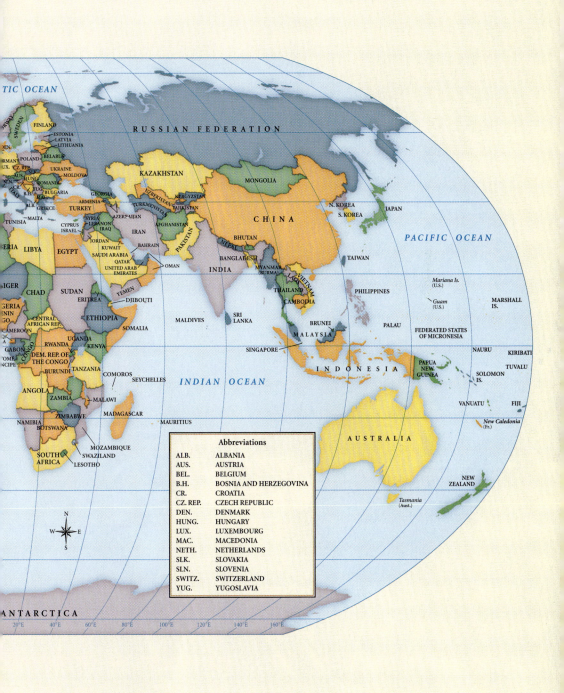

ARCTIC OCEAN

RUSSIAN FEDERATION

KAZAKHSTAN

MONGOLIA

N. KOREA
S. KOREA
JAPAN

CHINA

PACIFIC OCEAN

SWEDEN
FINLAND
NORWAY
ESTONIA
LATVIA
LITHUANIA
DEN.
BELARUS
GERMANY POLAND
LUX. CZ. REP.
AUS. SLK.
SWITZ. HUNG. UKRAINE MOLDOVA
SLN. CR.
ITALY B.H. YUG. ROMANIA
ALB. BULGARIA
MALTA GREECE TURKEY
TUNISIA CYPRUS SYRIA GEORGIA
LEBANON ARMENIA AZERBAIJAN
ISRAEL IRAQ UZBEKISTAN
JORDAN IRAN TURKMENISTAN KYRGYZSTAN
KUWAIT TAJIKISTAN
ALGERIA LIBYA EGYPT SAUDI ARABIA AFGHANISTAN
QATAR BAHRAIN PAKISTAN
UNITED ARAB NEPAL BHUTAN
EMIRATES OMAN
NIGER YEMEN INDIA BANGLADESH
CHAD SUDAN ERITREA DJIBOUTI MYANMAR
NIGERIA (BURMA)
BENIN CENTRAL ETHIOPIA TAIWAN
TOGO AFRICAN REP. MALDIVES LAOS
CAMEROON SOMALIA SRI VIETNAM
EQ. GUINEA UGANDA LANKA THAILAND
GABON RWANDA KENYA CAMBODIA
CONGO DEM. REP. OF PHILIPPINES
SAO TOME THE CONGO BURUNDI BRUNEI
& PRINCIPE TANZANIA SINGAPORE MALAYSIA PALAU
COMOROS
ANGOLA SEYCHELLES
ZAMBIA MALAWI INDONESIA
ZIMBABWE
NAMIBIA MADAGASCAR
BOTSWANA MOZAMBIQUE
SOUTH SWAZILAND MAURITIUS
AFRICA LESOTHO

Mariana Is.
(U.S.)

Guam
(U.S.)

MARSHALL
IS.

FEDERATED STATES
OF MICRONESIA

NAURU

KIRIBATI

PAPUA
NEW
GUINEA

SOLOMON
IS.

TUVALU

VANUATU

FIJI

New Caledonia
(Fr.)

INDIAN OCEAN

AUSTRALIA

NEW
ZEALAND

Tasmania
(Aust.)

Abbreviations	
ALB.	ALBANIA
AUS.	AUSTRIA
BEL.	BELGIUM
B.H.	BOSNIA AND HERZEGOVINA
CR.	CROATIA
CZ. REP.	CZECH REPUBLIC
DEN.	DENMARK
HUNG.	HUNGARY
LUX.	LUXEMBOURG
MAC.	MACEDONIA
NETH.	NETHERLANDS
SLK.	SLOVAKIA
SLN.	SLOVENIA
SWITZ.	SWITZERLAND
YUG.	YUGOSLAVIA

N
W E
S

ANTARCTICA

20°E 40°E 60°E 80°E 100°E 120°E 140°E 160°E

THE MAKING OF THE WEST

PEOPLES AND CULTURES

A CONCISE HISTORY

LYNN HUNT
University of California at Los Angeles

THOMAS R. MARTIN
College of the Holy Cross

BARBARA H. ROSENWEIN
Loyola University Chicago

R. PO-CHIA HSIA
Pennsylvania State University

BONNIE G. SMITH
Rutgers University

BEDFORD/ST. MARTIN'S   Boston   ◆   New York

FOR BEDFORD/ST. MARTIN'S

Publisher for History: Patricia A. Rossi
Director of Development for History: Jane Knetzger
Executive Editor for History: Elizabeth M. Welch
Production Editor: Lori Chong Roncka
Production Supervisor: Maria R. Gonzalez
Marketing Manager: Jenna Bookin Barry
Editorial Assistant: Brianna Germain
Production Assistants: Thomas P. Crehan, Kendra LeFleur, Courtney Jossart
Copyeditor: Patricia Herbst
Proofreaders: Mary Lou Wilshaw-Watts, Janet Cocker
Text Design: Wanda Kossak
Indexer: Maro Riofrancos
Cover Design: Donna Lee Dennison
Composition: TechBooks
Cartography: Mapping Specialists Limited
Printing and Binding: R.R. Donnelley & Sons Company

President: Joan E. Feinberg
Editorial Director: Denise B. Wydra
Director of Marketing: Karen Melton
Director of Editing, Design, and Production: Marcia Cohen
Managing Editor: Elizabeth M. Schaaf

Library of Congress Control Number: 2002102840

Manufactured in the United States of America.

7 6 5 4 3 2
f e d c b a

For information, contact: Bedford/St. Martin's, 75 Arlington Street, Boston, MA 02116
(617-399-4000)
www.bedfordstmartins.com

ISBN: 0–312–39538–8 (paperback complete edition)
      0–312–40207–4 (paperback Volume I)
      0–312–40208–2 (paperback Volume II)

Cover and Title Page Art: *The Trial of Galileo,* artist unknown. Private collection, New York. © Photograph by Erich Lessing/Art Resource.

Preface

MUCH OF OUR EXCITEMENT ABOUT THIS PROJECT arose from its very nature: textbook writing requires constant revision and updating to keep it fresh and make it better. Since publication of the full-length version of our textbook, *The Making of the West: Peoples and Cultures,* we have had the opportunity to hear from many teachers and students who have used it in their classrooms. Their comments have gratified us considerably and deepened our commitment to the project's basic goal and approach. At the same time, we learned that a shorter book would be appropriate for those instructors who need to cover the entire introduction to Western civilization in a single semester, who wish to assign extensive supplementary readings, or who find a comprehensive textbook by definition too detailed and daunting for their students.

This book—*The Making of the West: Peoples and Cultures, A Concise History*—is intended to meet their needs. We shortened our original narrative by 35 percent, combining some chapters while reducing others. For example, we rethought and rewrote two chapters on the ancient Near East and Greece and two on the French Revolution and Napoleonic era as single chapters, and we condensed and combined thematically related sections throughout the text. The result, we believe, is a concise edition that preserves the narrative flow, balance, and power of the full-length work.

Central Themes and Approach

Our title, *The Making of the West: Peoples and Cultures,* tells much about the themes and approach that we sought to preserve, and indeed strengthen, in *A Concise History.* We focus on the contributions of a multitude of peoples and cultures to the making of Western values and traditions while we show that the history of the West is the story of a process that is still ongoing, not a finished result with a fixed meaning. To understand the historical development of the West and its position in the world today, it is essential as well to place the West's emergence in a larger, global context that reveals the cross-cultural interactions fundamental to the shaping of the Western identity. Our task as authors, moreover, was to integrate the best of recent social and cultural history with the enduring developments of political, military, and diplomatic history, offering a clear, compelling narrative that sets all the key events and stages of the West's evolution in broad, meaningful context.

From our own teaching, we have learned that introductory students need a solid chronological framework, one with enough familiar benchmarks to make the material readily assimilable, but also one with enough flexibility to incorporate the new varieties of historical research. That is one reason why we present our account in a straightforward chronological manner. Each chapter treats all the main events, people, and themes of a period of time in which conditions of life in the West significantly changed; thus students are not required to learn about political events in one chapter, then backtrack to concurrent social and cultural developments in the next. The chronological organization also accords with our belief that it is important, above all else, for students to see the interconnections among varieties of historical experience—between politics and cultures; between public events and private experiences; between wars and diplomacy, on the one hand, and everyday life, on the other. Our chronological synthesis allows students to appreciate these relationships while, we hope, capturing the spirit of each age and sparking their historical imagination. For teachers, it ensures a balanced account, the flexibility to stress themes of one's own choosing, and perhaps best of all, a text that reveals history not as a settled matter but as a process that is constantly alive, subject to pressure, and able to surprise us. If we have succeeded in conveying some of the vibrancy of the past, we will not be satisfied with what we have done—history does not sit still that long—but we will be encouraged to start rethinking and revising once again.

Pedagogy and Features

To engage and inform students, we retained many of the study aids that we learned contribute to the success of the parent text. Each chapter begins with a vivid anecdote that draws readers into the atmosphere and issues of the period and raises the chapter's major themes, supplemented by a full-page reproduction of an artwork that similarly reveals the temper of the times. Chapters conclude with brief summaries that tie together the thematic strands and point the reader onward. A list of important dates at the end of each chapter helps students review key events of the period, while topic-specific timelines appear where useful to assist students' grasp of particular themes and processes. An annotated list of suggested references that combine print works and Web sites appears for each chapter to aid in research of particular topics, and an unusually comprehensive index incorporates a pronunciation guide.

We also drew on the experience of teachers throughout the United States and Canada to fashion our approach to primary sources. Learning that many instructors require a short edition with documents while others either do not elect to ask their students to work with primary sources or prefer their own choices of readings, we carefully selected three or four substantive documents per chapter that put a human face on a development central to the period and illuminate the relationship between narrative history and original sources. To preserve the narrative flow of the text and to allow teachers the flexibility to pick and choose sources, all documents appear in a separate reader, *Sources of THE MAKING OF THE WEST: PEOPLES AND CULTURES, A CONCISE HISTORY*, with cross-references in the textbook to ensure easy access.

A new full-color design and trim format give *A Concise History* the look and feel of a trade book, reinforcing visually the strong story line of the historical narrative and encouraging students to turn the page. We retain, however, many of the illustrations of the parent text, which have proved so important to the book's effectiveness in the classroom, to provide the most extensive map, graph, and artwork programs available in a brief survey. Each chapter includes, on average, three or four full-size maps showing major developments and one to three "spot maps," a first in this brief edition, intended to aid the student's understanding of single but crucial issues ranging from the structure of Old Kingdom Egypt to German reunification. "Mapping the West" summary maps, also unique, at the end of each chapter individually provide a snapshot of the West at the close of a transformative period and collectively help students visualize the West's changing contours over time. In addition to the over 160 maps, numerous graphs and charts visually support the narrative, including innovative "Taking Measure" statistical features in every chapter that introduce students to the skill of quantitative analysis by revealing how individual facts add up to broad trends. In common with all maps and graphs, "Taking Measure" features are cited in the text to prompt close study and carry informative captions.

We are proud as well of the over 240 illustrations, most in full color and all contemporaneous with the period under discussion, that directly reinforce or extend the narrative. Carefully chosen to reflect the text's broad topical coverage and geographic inclusion, the illustrations combine classics that are important for students to encounter with images new to brief texts. Unusually substantive captions accompany each picture, helping students to unlock the image and encouraging them to analyze artwork as primary sources. Together with the maps and documents, they provide instructors with a trove of teaching materials and allow students to enter the life of the past to see it from within.

Ancillaries

Because textbook ancillaries take on special importance in classrooms in which a brief survey text is assigned, we have taken care as well to assemble a comprehensive set of print and electronic resources for students and instructors. Reinforcing or extending *A Concise History,* these supplements offer a host of practical learning and teaching aids.

For Students

Sources of THE MAKING OF THE WEST: PEOPLES AND CULTURES, *A* CONCISE HISTORY—
Volumes I (to 1740) and II (since 1340)—by Katharine J. Lualdi, University of
Southern Maine. For each chapter in *A Concise History,* this companion sourcebook
features three or four important political, social, or cultural documents that am-
plify the discussion in the textbook, where they are cross-referenced to ensure easy
access and to encourage students to understand the connection between narrative
history and primary sources. Chapter introductions and headnotes further contex-
tualize the wide array of sources and perspectives represented in the documents,
while discussion questions guide students' reading and promote historical-think-
ing skills.

Online Study Guide for THE MAKING OF THE WEST: PEOPLES AND CULTURES, **A**
CONCISE HISTORY at **www.bedfordstmartins.com/huntconcise**.   Thoroughly revised to correspond to *A Concise History,* the free Online Study Guide is a uniquely
personalized learning tool that offers multimedia activities to help students master
the ideas and information in the textbook. For each chapter in *A Concise History,*
the Guide offers an initial multiple-choice test that allows students to assess their
comprehension of the material and a Recommended Study Plan that suggests
specific exercises on the subject areas students still need to master. Two follow-up
multiple-choice tests per chapter help students judge their mastery of the material. Additional exercises, including map and visual activities keyed directly to images in the textbook, encourage students to think about chapter themes as well as
help them develop skills of analysis. Results of multiple-choice tests can be e-mailed
to instructors.

LINKS LIBRARY.   Students can conduct their own online research through our comprehensive Links Library, a database of more than 350 carefully reviewed and annotated history Web links searchable by topic or by textbook chapter.

A Student's Guide to History, **Eighth Edition,** by Jules R. Benjamin, Ithaca College.
This brief yet comprehensive introduction to the study of history discusses the discipline, reviews basic study, research, and writing skills, and describes the most common history assignments. A thoroughly class-tested bestseller through eight editions,
the text has been revised to give students even more help with writing and with
conducting research online. The online edition at **www.bedfordstmartins.com/
benjamin** contains abbreviated content from the print version and is accessible to
students wherever they have a connection to the Internet.

Research and Documentation Online by Diana Hacker, Prince George's Community College, at **www.bedfordstmartins.com/resdoc**. This online version of Diana
Hacker's highly regarded handbook provides clear advice across the disciplines on

how to integrate outside material into a paper, how to cite sources correctly, and how to format in MLA, APA, CPE, or Chicago style.

Research Assistant HyperFolio. Delivered on CD-ROM, this tool for conducting research helps students collect, evaluate, and cite sources found both online and off.

After September 11: An Online Reader for Writers at **www.bedfordstmartins.com/ september11**. This free collection of more than 100 annotated links provides social, political, economic, and cultural commentary about the terrorist attacks on the United States of September 11, 2001. Thoughtful discussion questions and ideas for research and writing projects are included.

For Instructors

Instructor's Resource Manual for THE MAKING OF THE WEST: PEOPLES AND CULTURES, *A* CONCISE HISTORY by Michael D. Richards and Lynn M. Laufenberg, both of Sweet Briar College. Thoroughly revised to correlate with *A Concise History*, this well-received Instructor's Manual offers extensive teaching information for each chapter in the textbook: outlines of chapter themes, lecture and discussion topics, in-class exercises for working with maps and illustrations, writing and classroom presentation assignments, and research topic suggestions. The manual also includes eight essays for instructors, such as "What Is 'The West'?," "Teaching Western Civilization with Computers," and "Literature and the Western Civilization Classroom," and over a dozen frequently assigned primary sources for easy access and distribution.

Computerized Test Bank developed by Tamara Hunt, Loyola Marymount University, and Angela A. Kurtz, University of Maryland at College Park. User-friendly software lets instructors create and administer tests on paper or over a network, and a grade management function helps keep track of students' progress. Teachers can write their own tests or generate exams and quizzes from the test bank provided. Conversion utilities allow instructors to create exams in WebCT and Blackboard formats. In addition to twenty fill-in-the-blank, forty multiple-choice (labeled by difficulty), ten short-answer, and four essay questions, this thoughtfully designed test bank includes for each chapter in *A Concise History* a relationship-causation exercise, which asks students to place five events in chronological order and to explain a common theme that runs through them, and four map and document exercises that test students' comprehension of chapter material and their ability to use sources. An answer key is provided.

Instructor's Resource CD-ROM. This CD-ROM includes visual materials from *A Concise History* in an easy-to-use format for PowerPoint™ and other classroom presentations.

The Bedford Series in History and Culture—Advisory Editors: Natalie Zemon Davis, Princeton University; Ernest R. May, Harvard University; David W. Blight, Amherst College; and Lynn Hunt, University of California at Los Angeles. Any of the volumes from this highly acclaimed series of brief, inexpensive, document-based supplements can be packaged with *The Making of the West: A Concise History* at a reduced price. The fifteen European history titles include *Spartacus and the Slave Wars, Utopia, The Enlightenment, The French Revolution and Human Rights,* and *The Communist Manifesto.*

Using The Bedford Series with THE MAKING OF THE WEST by Maura O'Connor, University of Cincinnati. This short guide gives practical suggestions for using the volumes for Western civilization in The Bedford Series in History and Culture in conjunction with *The Making of the West.* Available online as well as in print, the guide not only supplies links between the textbook and the supplements but also provides ideas for starting discussions focused on a single primary-source volume.

Map Transparencies.   Full-color transparencies of over 145 maps in the parent textbook broaden the map program of *A Concise History* while helping instructors present the materials and teaching students important map-reading skills. A correlation guide that shows how the transparencies align with the brief text appears in the Instructor's Resource Manual and on the book companion Web site.

Map Central at **www.bedfordstmartins.com/mapcentral**.   Map Central is a searchable database of over 450 maps from Bedford/St. Martin's major history textbooks. Instructors can download maps for lectures using PowerPoint™ or other presentation software, browse maps by chapter within a specific text, or search for maps by keyword across several textbooks to find all maps related to a given topic.

E-Content for Online Learning allows teachers using *A Concise History* to develop custom Web sites with WebCT or other course-building systems.

Book Companion Web Site at **www.bedfordstmartins.com/huntconcise**.   The companion Web site for *A Concise History* gathers all the new media resources for the text at a single address.

Acknowledgments

The scholars and teachers who reviewed *The Making of the West: Peoples and Cultures* made suggestions that we gratefully incorporated into *A Concise History.* Our thanks to the following instructors, whose comments often challenged us to rethink or justify our interpretations and always provided a check on accuracy down to the smallest detail: Dorothy Abrahamse, California State University at Long Beach;

F. E. Beeman, Middle Tennessee State University; Martin Berger, Youngstown State University; Raymond Birn, University of Oregon; Charmarie J. Blaisdell, Northeastern University; Keith Bradley, University of Victoria; Paul Breines, Boston College; Caroline Castiglione, University of Texas at Austin; Carolyn A. Conley, University of Alabama; William Connell, Seton Hall University; Jo Ann H. Moran Cruz, Georgetown University; John P. Daly, Louisiana Tech University; Suzanne Desan, University of Wisconsin at Madison; Michael F. Doyle, Ocean County College; Jean C. England, Northeastern Louisiana University; Steven Epstein, University of Colorado at Boulder; Steven Fanning, University of Illinois at Chicago; Laura Frader, Northeastern University; Alison Futrell, University of Arizona; Gretchen Galbraith, Grand Valley State University; Timothy E. Gregory, Ohio State University; Katherine Haldane Grenier, The Citadel; Martha Hanna, University of Colorado at Boulder; Julie Hardwick, Texas Christian University; Kenneth W. Harl, Tulane University; Charles Hedrick, University of California at Santa Cruz; Robert L. Hohlfelder, University of Colorado at Boulder; Maryanne Horowitz, Occidental College; Gary Kates, Trinity University; Ellis L. Knox, Boise State University; Lawrence Langer, University of Connecticut; Keith P. Luria, North Carolina State University; Judith P. Meyer, University of Connecticut; Maureen C. Miller, Hamilton College; Stuart S. Miller, University of Connecticut; Dr. Frederick Murphy, Western Kentucky University; James Murray, University of Cincinnati; Phillip C. Naylor, Marquette University; Carolyn Nelson, University of Kansas; Richard C. Nelson, Augsburg College; John Nichols, University of Oregon; Byron J. Nordstrom, Gustavus Adolphus College; Maura O'Connor, University of Cincinnati; Lawrence Okamura, University of Missouri at Columbia; Dolores Davison Peterson, Foothill College; Carl F. Petry, Northwestern University; Carole A. Putko, San Diego State University; Michael D. Richards, Sweet Briar College; Barbara Saylor Rodgers, University of Vermont; Sally Scully, San Francisco State University; Jane Slaughter, University of New Mexico; Donald Sullivan, University of New Mexico; Victoria Thompson, Xavier University; Sue Sheridan Walker, Northeastern Illinois University; John E. Weakland, Ball State University; Theodore R. Weeks, Southern Illinois University at Carbondale; and Merry Wiesner-Hanks, University of Wisconsin at Milwaukee.

We thank as well the many colleagues, friends, and family members who have helped us develop this work. We also wish to express our gratitude to the publishing team who did so much to bring this book into being. Patricia A. Rossi, publisher for history, guided our efforts throughout publication. Joan E. Feinberg, president, and her predecessor, Charles H. Christensen, shared generous resources, mutual vision, and best of all, confidence in the textbook and in us. Special thanks are due to many other individuals: Lori Chong Roncka, our production editor, who with great skill and professionalism pulled all the pieces together with the help of Maria R. Gonzalez, John Amburg, Thomas P. Crehan, Courtney Jossart, and Kendra LeFleur; Carole Frohlich and Martha Shethar, who contributed their imagination and research to make possible the outstanding art program; Jenna Bookin Barry, marketing manager for history, whose strong efforts helped ensure the success of the full-length work; William J. Lombardo, associate new media editor, who ably shepherded numerous electronic supplements to completion with the help of Coleen O'Hanley and Denise Wydra; Louise Townsend, Sarah Barrash Wilson, and Brianna Germain, who helped in myriad ways on many essential editorial tasks; and our superb copyeditor, Patricia Herbst. Last and above all, we thank Elizabeth M. Welch, executive editor for history, who provided just the right doses of encouragement, prodding, and concrete suggestions for improvement. Her intelligence, skill, and determination proved to be crucial at every step of the process.

Our students' questions and concerns have shaped much of this work, and we welcome all our readers' suggestions, queries, and criticisms. Please contact us at our respective institutions or through our Web site: **www.bedfordstmartins.com/ huntconcise**.

L.H.   T.R.M.   B.H.R.   R.P.H.   B.G.S.

Brief Contents

Contents

Foundations of Western Civilization, to 500 B.C.   3

CHAPTER 2

The Greek Golden Age, c. 500–400 B.C.   53

CHAPTER 3

From the Classical to the Hellenistic World, c. 400–30 B.C. 93

The Roman Empire, c. 44 B.C.–A.D. 284   171

The Transformation of the Roman Empire, A.D. 284–c. 600   213

CHAPTER 7

The Heirs of the Roman Empire, 600–750   257

CHAPTER 11

Crisis and Renaissance, 1340–1500   429

CHAPTER 12

State Building and the Search for Order, 1648–1690   527

The Atlantic System and Its Consequences, 1690–1740   571

CHAPTER 15

The Promise of Enlightenment, 1740–1789   611

The French Revolution and Napoleon, 1789–1815   653

Industrialization and Social Ferment, 1815–1850   703

Constructing the Nation-State, c. 1850–1880   755

CHAPTER 20

War, Revolution, and Reconstruction, 1914–1929   863

An Age of Catastrophes, 1929–1945   907

The Atomic Age, c. 1945–1960   951

CHAPTER 23

Challenges to the Postindustrial West, 1960–1980   991

CHAPTER 24

The New Globalism: Opportunities and Dilemmas, 1980 to the Present   1029

Documents

The primary-source collection that accompanies this textbook—*Sources of THE MAKING OF THE WEST: PEOPLES AND CULTURES, A CONCISE HISTORY*—provides the following documents.

Maps and Figures

xlviii

FIGURES

The B.C./A.D. System for Dates

"WHEN WERE YOU BORN?" "What year is it?" We customarily answer questions like these with a number, such as "1983" or "2000." Our replies are usually automatic, taking for granted the numerous assumptions Westerners make about dates. But to what do numbers such as 1983 and 2000 actually refer? In this book, the numbers used to specify dates follow the system most common in the Western secular world. This system reckons the dates of solar years by counting backward and forward from the traditional date of the birth of Jesus Christ, over two thousand years ago.

Using this method, numbers followed by the abbreviation B.C., standing for "before Christ," indicate the number of years counting backward from the birth of Jesus. The larger the number after B.C., the earlier in history is the year to which it refers. The date 431 B.C., for example, refers to a year 431 years before the birth of Jesus and therefore comes earlier in time than the dates 430 B.C., 429 B.C., and so on. The same calculation applies to numbering other time intervals calculated on the decimal system: those of ten years (a decade), of one hundred years (a century), and of one thousand years (a millennium). For example, the decade of the 440s B.C. (449 B.C. to 440 B.C.) is earlier than the decade of the 430s B.C. (439 to 430 B.C.). "Fifth century B.C." refers to the fifth period of 100 years reckoning backward from the birth of Jesus and covers the years 500 B.C. to 401 B.C. It is earlier in history than the fourth century B.C. (400 B.C. to 301 B.C.), which followed the fifth century B.C. Because this system has no year "zero," the first century B.C. covers the years 100 B.C. to 1 B.C. As for millennia, the second millennium B.C. refers to the years 2000 B.C. to 1001 B.C., the third millennium to the years 3000 B.C. to 2001 B.C., and so on.

To indicate years counted forward from the traditional date of Jesus' birth, numbers are sometimes preceded by the abbreviation A.D., standing for the Latin phrase *anno Domini* ("in the year of the Lord"). The date A.D. 1492, for example, translates as "in the year of the Lord 1492," meaning 1492 years after the reported birth of Jesus. Writing dates with A.D. following the number, as in 1492 A.D., makes no sense because it would amount to saying "1492 in the year of the Lord." It is, however, customary to indicate centuries by placing the abbreviation A.D. after the number. Therefore "first century A.D." refers to the period from A.D. 1 to A.D. 100. For numbers indicating dates after the birth of Jesus, the smaller the number, the earlier the date in history. The fourth century A.D. (A.D. 301 to A.D. 400) comes before the fifth century A.D. (A.D. 401 to A.D. 500). The year A.D. 312 is a date in the early fourth century A.D., and A.D. 395 is a date late in the same century. When numbers are given without either B.C. or A.D., they are presumed to be dates after the birth of Jesus. For example, *eighteenth century* with no abbreviation accompanying it refers to the years A.D. 1701 to A.D. 1800.

No standard system of numbering years, such as the B.C./A.D. method, existed in antiquity. Different people in different parts of the world identified years with varying names and numbers. Consequently, it was difficult to match up the years in any particular local system with those in a different system. Each city of ancient Greece, for example, had its own method for keeping track of the years. The ancient Greek historian Thucydides therefore faced a problem in presenting a chronology for the war between Athens and Sparta, which began (by our reckoning) in 431 B.C. To try to explain to as many of his readers as possible the date the war had begun, he described its first year by three different local systems: "the year when Chrysis was in the forty-eighth year of her priesthood at Argos, and Aenesias was overseer at Sparta, and Pythodorus was magistrate at Athens."

A monk named Dionysius, who lived in Rome in the sixth century A.D., invented the system of reckoning dates forward from the birth of Jesus. Calling himself "Exiguus" (Latin for "the little" or "the small") as a mark of humility, he placed Jesus' birth 754 years after the foundation of ancient Rome. Others then and now believe his date for Jesus' birth was in fact several years too late. Many scholars today figure that Jesus was born in what would be 4 B.C. according to Dionysius's system, although a date a year or so earlier also seems possible.

Counting backward from the supposed date of Jesus' birth to indicate dates earlier than that event represented a natural complement to reckoning forward for dates after it. The English historian and theologian Bede in the early eighth century was the first to use both forward and backward reckoning from the birth of Jesus in a historical work, and this system gradually gained wider acceptance because it provided a basis for standardizing the many local calendars used in the Western Christian world. Nevertheless, B.C. and A.D. were not used regularly until the end of the eighteenth century.

The system of numbering years from the birth of Jesus is not the only one still used. The Jewish calendar of years, for example, counts forward from the date given to the creation of the world, which would be calculated as 3761 B.C. under the B.C./A.D. system. Years are designated A.M., an abbreviation of the Latin *anno mundi,* "in the year of the world under this system." The Islamic calendar counts forward from the date of the prophet Muhammad's flight from Mecca, called the *Hijra,* in what would be the year A.D. 622 under the B.C./A.D. system. The abbreviation A.H.

(standing for the Latin phrase *anno Hegirae*, "in the year of the Hijra") indicates dates calculated by this system. Today the abbreviations B.C.E. ("before the common era") and C.E. ("of the common era") are often used in place of B.C. and A.D., respectively, to allow the retention of numerical dates as reckoned by the B.C./A.D. system without the Christian reference implied by this system. Anthropology commonly reckons distant dates as "before the present" (abbreviated B.P.).

History is often defined as the study of change over time; hence the importance of dates for the historian. But just as historians argue over which dates are most significant, they disagree over which dating system to follow. Their debate reveals perhaps the most enduring fact of history—its vitality.

About the Authors

LYNN HUNT, Eugen Weber Professor of Modern European History at the University of California at Los Angeles, received her B.A. from Carleton College and her M.A. and Ph.D. from Stanford University. She is the author of *Revolution and Urban Politics in Provincial France* (1978); *Politics, Culture, and Class in the French Revolution* (1984); and *The Family Romance of the French Revolution* (1992). She is also the coauthor of *Telling the Truth about History* (1994); coauthor of *Liberty, Equality, Fraternity: Exploring the French Revolution* (2001, with CD-ROM); editor of *The New Cultural History* (1989); editor and translator of *The French Revolution and Human Rights* (1996); and coeditor of *Histories: French Constructions of the Past* (1995), *Beyond the Cultural Turn* (1999), and *Human Rights and Revolution* (2000). She has been awarded fellowships by the Guggenheim Foundation and the National Endowment for the Humanities and is a fellow of the American Academy of Arts and Sciences. She is president of the American Historical Association in 2002.

THOMAS R. MARTIN, Jeremiah O'Connor Professor in Classics at the College of the Holy Cross, earned his B.A. at Princeton University and his M.A. and Ph.D. at Harvard University. He is the author of *Sovereignty and Coinage in Classical Greece* (1985) and *Ancient Greece* (1996, 2000) and is one of the originators of *Perseus: Interactive Sources and Studies on Ancient Greece* (1992, 1996; www.perseus.tufts.edu), which, among other awards, was named the EDUCOM Best Software in Social Sciences (History) in 1992. He also wrote the lead article on ancient Greece for the revised edition of the electronic *Encarta Encyclopedia*. He serves on the editorial board of STOA (www.stoa.org) and as codirector of its DEMOS project (online resources on ancient Athenian democracy). A recipient of fellowships from the National Endowment for the Humanities and the American Council of Learned Societies, he is currently conducting research on the history and significance of freedom of speech in Athenian democracy.

BARBARA H. ROSENWEIN, professor of history at Loyola University Chicago, earned her B.A., M.A., and Ph.D. at the University of Chicago. She is the author of *Rhinoceros Bound: Cluny in the Tenth Century* (1982); *To Be the Neighbor of Saint Peter: The Social Meaning of Cluny's Property, 909–1049* (1989); *Negotiating Space: Power, Restraint, and Privileges of Immunity in Early Medieval Europe* (1999); and *A Short History of the Middle Ages* (2001). She is the editor of *Anger's Past: The Social Uses of an Emotion in the Middle Ages* (1998) and coeditor of *Debating the Middle Ages: Issues and Readings* (1998) and *Monks and Nuns, Saints and Outcasts: Religion in Medieval Society* (2000). A recipient of Guggenheim and National Endowment for the Humanities fellowships, she is currently working on a history of emotions in the early Middle Ages.

R. PO-CHIA HSIA, Edwin Erle Sparks Professor of History at Pennsylvania State University, received his B.A. from Swarthmore College and his M.A. and Ph.D. from Yale University. He is the author of *Society and Religion in Münster, 1535–1618* (1984); *The Myth of Ritual Murder: Jews and Magic in Reformation Germany* (1988); *Social Discipline in the Reformation: Central Europe, 1550–1750* (1989); *Trent 1475: Stories of a Ritual Murder Trial* (1992); and *The World of the Catholic Renewal* (1997). He has edited *The German People and the Reformation* (1998); *In and Out of the Ghetto: Jewish-Gentile Relations in Late Medieval and Early Modern Germany* (1995); *Calvinism and Religious Toleration in the Dutch Golden Age* (2002); and *The Blackwell Companion to the Worlds of the Reformation* (forthcoming). An Academician at the Academia Sinica, Taiwan, he has also been awarded fellowships by the Woodrow Wilson International Society of Scholars, the National Endowment for the Humanities, the Guggenheim Foundation, the Davis Center of Princeton University, the Mellon Foundation, the American Council of Learned Societies, and the American Academy in Berlin. Currently he is working on the cultural contacts between Europe and Asia between the sixteenth and eighteenth centuries.

BONNIE G. SMITH, Board of Governors Distinguished Professor of History at Rutgers University, earned her B.A. at Smith College and her M.A. and Ph.D. at the University of Rochester. She is the author of *Ladies of the Leisure Class* (1981); *Confessions of a Concierge: Madame Lucie's History of Twentieth-Century France* (1985); *Changing Lives: Women in European History since 1700* (1989); *The Gender of History: Men, Women, and Historical Practice* (1998); and *Imperialism* (2000). She is also the coeditor and translator of *What Is Property?* (1994); editor of *Global Feminisms since 1945* (2000); and coeditor of *Objects of Modernity: Selected Writings of Lucy Maynard Salmon* (2001) and the forthcoming Oxford series in world history and *Oxford Encyclopedia of Women in World History*. She has received fellowships from the Guggenheim Foundation, the National Endowment for the Humanities, the National Humanities Center, the Davis Center of Princeton University, and the American Council of Learned Societies. Currently she is studying the globalization of European culture and society since the seventeenth century.

The Making of the West

PEOPLES AND CULTURES

A Concise History

Foundations of Western Civilization

To 500 B.C.

A<small>CCORDING TO THE</small> M<small>ESOPOTAMIAN</small> *E<small>PIC OF</small> C<small>REATION,</small>* a violent struggle among the gods created the universe. The mighty goddess Tiamat, furious over the murder of her husband, threatened to destroy the other gods. At a raucous meeting they pledged to hail the male god Marduk as king of the universe if he could save them. The fearsome Marduk—"four were his eyes, four were his ears; when his lips moved, fire blazed forth"—crushed Tiamat and her army of snaky monsters in a gory battle. He then created human beings out of the blood of her fiercest monster so that they could serve their divine masters.

This myth made clear how important it was for people to please the gods, who could crush them at will. The precariousness of life implied by this story was real. Before civilization, in the Stone Age, tens and tens of thousands of years ago, people hunted and gathered food in the wild, using tools that they made from stone, bone, and wood. They were constantly on the move to find enough food for their families and still have some left over for offerings to the supernatural forces that they believed controlled nature. Around 10,000 or 12,000 years ago, this way of life began to change fundamentally, though slowly, when people living in the region known to us as southwestern Asia began to cultivate wild plants and domesticate wild animals and became farmers and herders.

The invention of agriculture and the domestication of animals made life in permanent settlements possible and produced surpluses of grain, fruit, vegetables, and

■ **Egyptian Painted Sarcophagus**
This brilliantly painted sarcophagus held the mummified corpse of an ancient Egyptian named Khonsu or Khons, who died in his fifties—a ripe old age for his era—and was buried alongside his family members in their tomb at Deir el Medina outside Thebes, probably in the 1200s B.C. Like his father, he was an artisan who had worked on the royal tombs in the Valley of the Kings just west of the Nile. The goddesses shown here on one end of the sarcophagus were believed to offer protection in the afterlife. The green tint of their skin—the color of healthy, growing plants— symbolizes their powers of rejuvenation. (Ken S. Graetz.)

meat that allowed some people to engage not in farming but in other occupations. Gradually, the size of settlements increased, and by 4000–3000 B.C. the first cities had come into being in Mesopotamia, the region between the Euphrates and Tigris Rivers (today southern Iraq). Thus emerged the earliest civilization: life based in cities that functioned as political states, each having its own territory, ruler, taxes, and sense of local identity.

Religious concerns permeated Mesopotamian society. Mindful of the Marduk myth about human origins, rulers believed that the gods held them responsible for maintaining order on earth and for making sure that people honored their divine masters. The Egyptians, whose civilization emerged about 3100–3000 B.C., felt the same. Piety, combined with extraordinary architectural skills, inspired them to build fabulous temples and the pyramids.

Civilizations arose at different times in different places. Starting about 2500 B.C., they emerged in India, China, and the Americas. By 2000 B.C., civilizations had appeared in Anatolia (today Turkey), on islands in the eastern Mediterranean Sea, and in Greece. The early civilizations of Mesopotamia, Egypt, the eastern Mediterranean, and Greece began the history of Western civilization by interacting with each other. Trade and war brought them into contact, and this cultural interaction provided opportunities for people to learn from one another and to adapt for their own use the traditions, beliefs, and technology of others. Civilizations developed as a result of both intended and unintended consequences of this exchange. Metallurgical technology, for example, created ever better tools and weapons but also increased social differences among people. Just as the gods insisted on their superiority to human beings, so did people develop status differences, or *hierarchy,* among themselves. The complex unfolding of early Western civilization proceeded in fits and starts until two centuries of violent upheaval threatened to end its story about 1000 B.C.

Making Civilization, to 1000 B.C.

Earth was populated by human beings for a long time before the first appearance of what we call civilization. (We refer to the people who lived before civilization as "prehistoric" because, with writing not yet invented, they left no historical records.) About 400,000 years ago, during the period that archaeologists call the "Stone Age," people whose brains and bodies resembled ours first appeared in Africa. These people, called *Homo sapiens,* or "wise human beings," by scientists, were the immediate ancestor of modern human beings, called *Homo sapiens sapiens.* From Africa, they spread out and gradually populated the rest of the earth. Anthropologists divide the Stone Age into two periods: the Paleolithic ("Old Stone") began with the appearance of *Homo sapiens*; and the Neolithic ("New Stone") began much more recently—some 10,000 to 12,000 years ago (c. 10,000–8000 B.C.). Paleolithic peoples were *hunter-gatherers.* The search for food kept them on the move. Neolithic peoples learned to farm and to domesticate animals and lived in settled communities. So radical were these changes that historians gave them the name "Neolithic Revolution." This revolution, however, unfolded gradually.

Eventually the Neolithic Revolution brought into being what historians traditionally identify as the features of civilization: cities with large buildings for community purposes (especially religion); political systems; production of textiles, pottery, and other crafts for local use and trade; and writing. In Mesopotamia, where the first cities arose about 4000 to 3000 B.C., the invention of bronze, an alloy of copper and tin, led archaeologists to call the period from approximately 4000 to 1000 B.C. the "Bronze Age." The rulers of Bronze Age cities battled one another for glory, territory, and, especially, access to copper and tin. The drive to acquire metal ores pushed the Akkadians (named after Akkad, their capital city on the Tigris River) to create the first empire, a political unit controlling formerly independent territories consolidated under a single ruler. In this and many other ways, early human history set precedents that deeply influenced later times.

Paleolithic and Neolithic Life, c. 400,000–8000 B.C.

Anthropologists reconstruct Paleolithic life from studying hunter-gatherer populations that survived into modern times, such as the !Kung in Africa, the Aborigines in Australia, and the Coahuiltecans in the American Southwest. Paleolithic peoples probably banded together in groups of twenty to fifty, hunting and foraging for food, which they shared. Even though they might return to places where they once found food, they had to roam to survive. Finding food was the responsibility of both men and women. Women of childbearing age had to nurse their young, so they usually stayed close to camp, gathering roots, nuts, and berries and trapping frogs and rabbits. Their work provided most of the group's sustenance. The labor of women beyond childbearing age was crucial because, unburdened by infants, they could help wherever needed. Men probably did most of the hunting of large, dangerous animals far from camp, although recent archaeological evidence shows that women also participated, especially when groups ensnared game in nets.

Hunter-gatherer societies may have been egalitarian, meaning all adults enjoyed a rough equality when decisions affecting the whole group needed to be made. At the same time, differences in social status probably existed. Men likely acquired prestige from their prominent role in hunting. Older women and men probably were respected because of their wisdom from long experience and because their age set them apart at a time when, according to historical demographers, illness and accidents killed most people before age thirty. Some Paleolithic grave sites contain weapons, tools, animal figurines, seashells, ivory beads, and bracelets. The individuals buried with such care and expenditure probably were especially prestigious members of their group.

The grave goods indicate that hunter-gatherer bands traded energetically with one another, sometimes acquiring objects from far away. Trade spread knowledge—especially technological advances, such as ways to start fires or make tools, and artistic techniques for creating beauty and expressing beliefs—that changed lives. The use of fire for cooking was a momentous technological innovation. Cooking expanded the human diet. It made edible food out of some plants, such as wild grain, that were indigestible raw.

Paleolithic cave paintings in Spain and France display striking artistic ability and hint at religious beliefs. Using strong, dark lines and earthy colors to depict wild animals, the paintings suggest that these powerful beasts and the dangerous hunts that killed them played a significant role in prehistoric life and religion. Paleolithic artists also sculpted statuettes of human figures, most likely for religious purposes. The care with which the dead were buried, decorated with red paint, flowers, and seashells, indicates concern with the mystery of death and perhaps some belief in an afterlife.

Farming and the domestication of animals—the so-called Neolithic Revolution—began about 10,000 to 12,000 years ago in the foothills of the Near East's Fertile Crescent, an arc of relatively well-watered territory bounded by desert and mountain ranges that curved up from what is today the Jordan Valley in Israel, through eastern Turkey, and down into the foothills and plains of Iraq and Iran

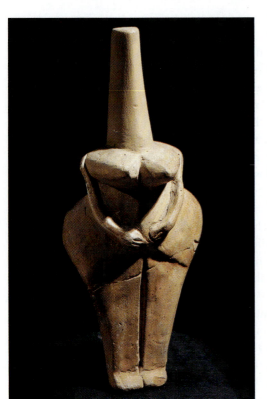

■ **Prehistoric "Venus" Figurine**
Archaeologists have discovered small female figures, like this one from Romania, in many late Paleolithic and Neolithic sites in Europe. They predate writing, so we cannot be sure of their significance, but many scholars assume that their hefty proportions are meant to signal a special concern for fertility. These female figures may represent prehistoric people's vision of rare good fortune: having enough food to become fat and produce healthy children. The statuettes are called "Venus" figurines after the Roman goddess of love. (Erich Lessing/Art Resource, NY.)

www.bedfordstmartins.com/huntconcise   See the ONLINE STUDY GUIDE for more help in analyzing this image.

(see Map 1.1).* From studying fossilized tree rings and plant materials found in excavations, scientists think that the revolution began when the climate turned milder and wetter in this region, where the right combination of wild plants and animals suitable for domestication—wheat, barley, peas, and lentils, together with sheep, goats, swine, and cattle—coexisted. Because hunting made game scarce, people increased their gathering of wild grains, which the changes in climate had made more abundant. The increased food supply spurred population growth. The more hungry mouths were born, the greater became the need to exploit the food supply efficiently. After thousands of years of trial and error, people invented agriculture by sowing seeds from one crop to produce another. Experienced in foraging for plants, Neolithic women probably played the major role in developing farming, while men continued to hunt. During this same period, people learned to domesticate animals for meat, starting with sheep about 8500 B.C. Domestication became widespread throughout the Near East by about 7000 B.C. Some bands moved around to find grazing land, living as *pastoralists,* but also for part of the year cultivated temporary plots. Others tended small herds close to their farms.

To raise crops year after year, people had to reside in a permanent location. Settling down marked a turning point in the relation between human beings and the natural environment. Farmers cut down trees and diverted streams for irrigation—essential for the development of agriculture and thus of cities throughout the Near East. By 4000 B.C., people migrating from the Fertile Crescent had spread knowledge of agriculture to the European shores of the Atlantic Ocean. Eventually, farmers were able to produce more food than they needed to feed themselves and their families. The creation of agricultural surpluses allowed some people to specialize in architecture, art, crafts, metalwork, textile production, and trade.

Trade connected Neolithic settlements, bringing in natural resources and goods not available locally, such as seashells for ornaments, flint for daggers, and obsidian, a volcanic glass prized for its luster and capacity to hold a sharp edge. Neolithic

---

*The meanings of the terms *Near East* and *Middle East* have changed over time. Both originally reflected a European geographic point of view. During the nineteenth century, *Middle East* usually meant the area from Iran to Burma, especially the Indian subcontinent (then part of the British Empire); *Near East* meant the Balkan peninsula (today the countries of Croatia, Slovenia, Bosnia-Herzegovina, Macedonia, Yugoslavia, Albania, Greece, Bulgaria, Romania, and the European portion of Turkey) and the eastern Mediterranean. The term *Far East* referred to the Asian lands that border the Pacific Ocean.

Today *Middle East* usually refers to the area encompassing the Arabic-speaking countries of the eastern Mediterranean region, Israel, Iran, Turkey, Cyprus, and much of North Africa. Ancient historians, by contrast, commonly use the term *ancient Near East* to designate Anatolia (often called Asia Minor, today occupied by the Asian portion of Turkey), Cyprus, the lands around the eastern end of the Mediterranean, the Arabian peninsula, Mesopotamia (the lands north of the Persian Gulf, today Iraq and Iran), and Egypt. Some historians exclude Egypt from this group on strict geographic grounds because it is in Africa (the rest of the region lies in Asia). In this book, we observe the common usage of the term *Near East* to mean the lands of southwestern Asia and Egypt.

trade established economic connections among far-flung communities—a pattern familiar in our world today.

The Neolithic Revolution gave rise to an increasingly layered social hierarchy because new degrees of cooperation, supervision, and management were needed to supply water for irrigation. The increased economic activity of the Neolithic Revolution also created a new division of labor by gender. Men began to dominate agriculture once heavy wooden plows pulled by oxen were invented, sometime after 4000 B.C. Not having to bear and nurse babies, they took over long-distance trade. Women and older children took on new domestic labor as they turned milk into cheese and yogurt and made their families' clothing. This gendered division of labor arose as an efficient response to the conditions and technologies of the time, but it coincidentally increased men's status in the social hierarchy.

The Birth of Cities and Empire in Mesopotamia, c. 4000–1000 B.C.

The first cities emerged in Mesopotamia because people living there figured out how to raise crops on the plentiful, but dry, flatland between and around the Tigris and Euphrates Rivers (Map 1.1). Agriculture had begun in the well-watered hills of the Fertile Crescent, but they offered too little habitable land to support the growth of cities. The plains bordering the rivers were huge but presented serious obstacles to agriculture: temperatures soaring to 120 degrees Fahrenheit, scant rainfall, and devastating, unpredictable floods. Mesopotamians turned this harsh environment into lush farmland by irrigating the plains with water channeled from the rivers. An intricate system of canals allowed these first farmers to turn the desert green with crops and helped limit flooding. The increase in food production created surpluses, which allowed the population to swell, nonagricultural occupations to flourish, and urban life to begin.

The need to construct and maintain the irrigation canals promoted central organization in Mesopotamian cities, which controlled the farmland lying outside their fortified walls. This arrangement—an urban center exercising political and economic control over the nearby countryside—is called a *city-state*. Mesopotamian city-states were independent communities competing with each other for land and resources. Travelers from one to another would first come to irrigated fields on the outskirts of the city, then villages housing agricultural workers, and then the city's walls. Outside the entrance, travelers would find a bustling center of trade, such as a harbor on the river or a marketplace along the land route leading to the city. Inside the walls, their eyes would be drawn to the royal family's palace and, above all, to the immense temples of the gods.

The people of Sumer, the name for southern Mesopotamia, built the first cities. Unlike other Mesopotamians, the Sumerians spoke a language not from the Semitic group of tongues (to which Hebrew and Arabic belong); its origins are unknown.

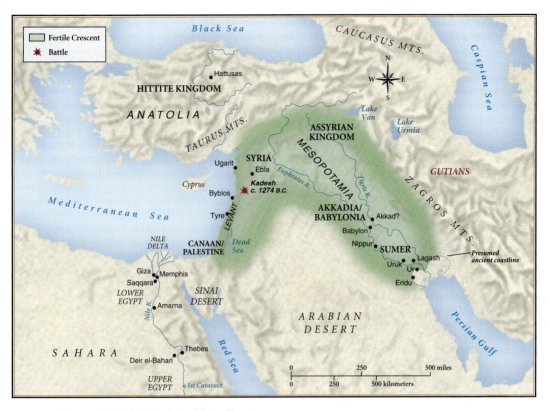

■ **MAP 1.1 The Ancient Near East**

The large region we call the ancient Near East encompassed a variety of landscapes, climates, peoples, and languages; monarchy was the usual form of government. Trade by land and sea for natural resources, especially metals, kept the peoples of the region in constant contact with one another, as did the wars of conquest that the region's kings regularly launched.

www.bedfordstmartins.com/huntconcise   See the ONLINE STUDY GUIDE for more help in analyzing this map.

By 3000 B.C., the Sumerians had created sizable walled cities, such as Uruk, Eridu, and Ur, in twelve independent city-states, which repeatedly fought wars over territory. Five centuries later, they had expanded to twenty thousand residents or more. The chambers of Sumerians' mud-brick houses surrounded open courts. Large homes had a dozen rooms or more. Everyone was in danger from contaminated water because no sewerage system existed. Pigs and dogs scavenged in the garbage dumped in the streets.

Agriculture and trade made these cities prosperous. Sumerians bartered grain, vegetable oil, woolens, and leather with one another and with foreign regions, from which they acquired natural resources such as metals, timber, and precious stones. Traders traveled as far as India, where the cities of Indus civilization emerged about

2500 B.C. Technological innovation also strengthened the Mesopotamian economy, especially around 3000 B.C. when Sumerians invented a wheel strong enough to be used on carts for transport. Temples predominated in the Sumerian economy because they controlled large farms and gangs of laborers, but some private households also amassed wealth.

Sumerian society was hierarchical. At the bottom were slaves, owned by temples and by individuals. People became enslaved by being captured in war, by being born to slaves, by voluntarily selling themselves or their children to escape starvation, or by being sold by their creditors when they could not repay loans (a practice called "debt slavery"). Children whose parents dedicated them as servants to the gods counted as slaves but could rise to prominent positions in the temple administrations. In general, however, slavery was a state of near-total dependency on other people and of exclusion from normal social relations. Slaves usually worked without compensation and lacked almost all legal rights. They could be bought, sold, beaten, or even killed by their masters because they were considered property, not human beings.

Slaves worked in domestic service, craft production, and farming, but their economic significance compared to that of free workers is disputed. Free persons performed most public tasks, paying their taxes with labor rather than with currency, which consisted of measured amounts of food or precious metal (coins were not invented until about 700 B.C., in Anatolia). Gaining freedom was only a faint possibility for most slaves. Masters' wills could liberate them, or they could purchase their freedom from the earnings they sometimes managed to accumulate.

Mesopotamian kings existed at the top of the social hierarchy. As befitted their status, Sumerian royalty lived in elaborate palaces, which served as administrative centers and treasure-houses. Archaeological excavation of the immense royal cemetery in Ur has revealed the dazzling extent of the rulers' riches—spectacular possessions crafted in gold, silver, and precious stones. These graves also yielded grisly evidence of the exalted status of the king and queen: servants sacrificed to attend to their royal masters after death. The spectacle of wealth and power that characterized Sumerian kingship reveals the breadth of the gap between the upper and lower ranks of society. *Patriarchy*—domination by men in political, social, and economic life—was already established in these first cities. Although a Sumerian queen was respected because she was the wife of the king and the mother of the royal children, the king held the supreme power.

To govern, a king formed a council of older men as his advisers and acknowledged the gods as his rulers—a notion that made the state a *theocracy* (government by gods) and gave priests and priestesses public influence. The king's supreme responsibility was to keep the gods happy and to defeat attacks from rival cities. The king extracted surpluses from the working population to support his family, court, palace, army, and officials. Otherwise, he rarely interfered in people's daily lives.

■ **The Ziggurat of Ur in Sumer**
King Ur-Nammu and his son Shulgi built this massive temple as an architectural marvel for their
city of Ur (in what is today southern Iraq) in the early twenty-first century B.C. It had three mas-
sive terraces, one above another, connected by stairways. The mud-brick core of the structure was
covered with baked bricks held in place with tar. The walls were more than seven feet thick to sup-
port the enormous weight of the terraces. The total height is uncertain, but the first terrace alone
soared some forty-five feet above ground level. (Hirmer Fotoarchiv.)

Mesopotamians believed that their lives depended on the goodwill of the gods,
whom they tried to please with sacrifices and magnificent temples. Each city-state
honored one deity as its special protector, but the Mesopotamians were *polytheists*:
worshipers of many gods, who they believed controlled different aspects of life, such
as the weather, fertility, and war. To be close to the gods they served, city dwellers
built ziggurats (temple towers), which soared as high as ten stories. They viewed
the gods as their masters, to whom they owed total devotion. If human beings offended the gods, divinities such as the sky-god Enlil and Inanna (also called Ishtar),
goddess of love and war, would punish worshipers by causing disasters ranging from
illness to floods and famine.

Mythical stories such as the *Epic of Creation* and the *Epic of Gilgamesh* emphasized the unbridgeable gap between gods and human beings. The latter epic told
the story of the hero Gilgamesh, king of the city of Uruk, who lusted to cheat death
and win immortality. He forced the young men of Uruk to toil like slaves and the
young women to sleep with him. The distressed inhabitants implored Aruru, mother
of the gods, to grant them a protector, and in response she created a man of nature, Enkidu, "hairy all over . . . dressed as cattle are." A week of sex with a prostitute tamed this brute, preparing him for civilization: "Enkidu was weaker; he ran
slower than before. But he had gained judgment, was wiser." After wrestling to a
draw, he and Gilgamesh became friends and conquered Humbaba (or Huwawa),
the ugly giant of the Pine Forest, and the Bull of Heaven. The gods doomed Enkidu
to die soon after these triumphs. In despair over human frailty, Gilgamesh sought

■ A Cuneiform Letter in Its Envelope

Written about 1900 B.C., this cuneiform text records a merchant's complaint that a shipment of copper contained less metal than he had expected. His letter, impressed on a clay tablet several inches long, was enclosed in an outer clay shell marked with the sender's private seal. This envelope protected the inner text from tampering or breakage.
(British Museum.)

the secret of immortality, only to be foiled by a thieving snake. He eventually concluded that the fame of people's achievements was their sole immortality. Only memory and gods could live forever.

A late version of the *Epic of Gilgamesh* recounted how the gods sent a huge flood over the earth. They warned one man, Utnapishtim, instructing him to build a boat. He loaded his vessel with his relatives, artisans, possessions, domesticated and wild animals, and "everything there was." After a week of torrential rains, they disembarked to repopulate the earth. This story recalled the devastating floods of Mesopotamia and foreshadowed the later biblical account of the flood and Noah's ark. Mesopotamian myths, which lived on in poetry and song, would later influence the mythology of the Greeks.

Helping to give these stories a long life was the invention of one of humanity's foremost technologies: writing. Sumerians originally invented writing to do accounting. Before this invention, people drew small pictures on clay tablets to represent objects or animals. Eventually, they devised nonpictorial symbols to represent the sounds of speech. Sumerian writing did not use an alphabet, a system in which each symbol represents a letter's sound. Instead, a mixed system of phonetic symbols and pictographs represented the sounds of syllables and entire words. The fully developed script, which other Mesopotamians adopted, is now called *cuneiform* (from *cuneus*, Latin for "wedge") because writers impressed wedge-shaped marks into clay tablets to record spoken language (Figure 1.1). For a long time, writing

					SAG Head
					NINDA bread
					GU$_7$ eat
					AB$_2$ cow
					APIN plough
					SUHUR carp
c. 3100 B.C.	c. 3000 B.C.	c. 2500 B.C.	c. 2100 B.C.	c. 700 B.C. (Neo- Assyrian)	Sumerian reading + meaning

■ **FIGURE 1.1 Cuneiform Writing**

The earliest known form of writing developed in different locations in Mesopotamia in the late 3000s B.C. when meaning and sound were associated with signs such as these. The scribes who mastered the system used sticks or reeds to press dense rows of small wedge-shaped marks into damp clay tablets or chisels to engrave them on stone. Cuneiform was used for at least fifteen Near Eastern languages and continued to be written for three thousand years.

was a professional skill mastered by only a few men and women, known as *scribes*. Schools taught them the new technology so they could write down official records.

Eventually, the scribal schools extended their curriculum to cover nature lore, mathematics, foreign languages, and literature. Written poems and stories provided a powerful new way to pass on traditions. The world's oldest written poetry by a known author was composed in the twenty-third century B.C. by Enheduanna, the daughter of King Sargon of the city of Akkad. Written in Sumerian, her poetry praised the life-giving goddess of love, Inanna: "the great gods scattered from you like fluttering bats, unable to face your intimidating gaze . . . knowing and wise queen of all the lands, who makes all creatures and people multiply." Later princesses who wrote love songs, lullabies, dirges, and prayers continued the Mesopotamian tradition of royal women becoming authors.

Metallurgy was another influential technology that developed in this period, and it indirectly fueled the creation of the world's first empire, in Akkadia (see Map 1.1). Devising innovative ways to smelt ore and forge metal alloys, Bronze Age smiths fashioned new luxury goods and better tools for agriculture, construction, and, above all, war. Pure copper had offered few advantages over stone because it easily lost its shape and edge; bronze, a copper-tin alloy hard enough to hold a razor edge, produced durable swords and spearheads. Rich men found a new way to display their status by commissioning metalworkers to decorate their weapons with ornate engravings and inlays, as on costly guns today. Ownership of metal weapons also underscored the differences between men's and women's roles in society, because it signified the masculine roles of hunter and warrior that had emerged long ago in the division of labor among hunter-gatherers.

The development of metallurgy had other social consequences as well. People now desired wealth not just in foodstuffs, animals, or land, but in metals. This desire stimulated the demand for metals and for skilled workers able to create lavishly adorned weapons for men and exquisitely crafted jewelry for both women and men. Mesopotamian monarchs constantly craved a reliable supply of metals as a sign of their royal status. Those who had no ore in their territory sought to acquire it by trade or by conquest.

The first empire arose about 2350 B.C., when Sargon, king of the city of Akkad, launched invasions north and south of his homeland in mid-Mesopotamia, seeking fame and metals. His violent campaigns conquered Sumer and the regions reaching to the Mediterranean Sea. Sargon's grandson Naram-Sin continued the family tradition of distant conquest. By 2250 B.C., he had attacked Ebla, a large city whose site was recently discovered in modern Syria. Archaeologists at Ebla have unearthed many cuneiform tablets, some in multiple languages. These discoveries suggest that Ebla thrived as an early center for learning.

Empire building indirectly helped extend Mesopotamian literature and art throughout the Near East. Although the Akkadians spoke a Semitic language unrelated to Sumerian, after conquering Sumer they adopted much of the defeated land's religion, literature, and culture. Other peoples later overrun by the Akkadians were thus exposed to Sumerian beliefs and traditions, which they in turn adapted to their own purposes. In this way, war indirectly promoted cultural interaction between peoples.

The Akkadian Empire eventually fell to attacks from neighboring hill peoples, the Gutians, around 2200 B.C. A Mesopotamian poet gave a religious explanation for this catastrophe. King Naram-Sin, enraged at the god Enlil when his capital's prosperity waned, reduced Enlil's temple in Nippur to "dust like a mountain mined for silver." In retribution, Enlil punished the Akkadians by sending the Gutians swooping down from their "land that rejects outside control, with the intelligence of human beings but with the form and stumbling words of a dog." This account reflected the Mesopotamians' deep-seated belief that human life remained extremely precarious in the face of the gods' power: no matter how large its populations or how high its city walls, the world's earliest empire could not escape a divinely ordained fate.

Mesopotamian Legacies, c. 2200–1000 B.C.

Two kingdoms, Assyria and Babylonia, emerged in the second millennium B.C. to fill the power vacuum left by the fall of the Akkadian Empire. Although they became militarily powerful for a time, their lasting legacies for Western civilization came from their innovations in commerce, law, and learning. The Assyrians, a Semitic people descended from the Akkadians, lived in northern Mesopotamia (see Map 1.1). They took advantage of their proximity to Anatolia to build an independent kingdom whose prosperity depended on long-distance trade. By acting as middlemen in the trade between Anatolia and the rest of Mesopotamia, the Assyrians became the leading merchants of the Near East. They produced woolen textiles to exchange for Anatolian copper, silver, and gold, which they in turn sold throughout Mesopotamia. In earlier Mesopotamian societies, state monopolies had regulated the redistribution of goods and had managed trade according to the king's orders. This system never totally disappeared in Mesopotamia, but by 1900 B.C. the Assyrian kings were allowing private individuals to transact large commercial deals among themselves. Assyrian investors financed donkey caravans to travel hundreds of rocky and dangerous miles to Anatolia. Regulators existed to deal with fraud and losses in transit in what was a risky mission for profits.

The expansion of commerce created a demand for fairness and reliability in contracts and other business arrangements. It was the king's sacred duty to render justice to his subjects in all sorts of cases, from commercial disputes to crime. The record of the king's decisions is today called a "law code," though the Mesopotamians did not use this term. King Hammurabi (r. c. 1792–1750 B.C.) of Babylon, a great city on the Euphrates River, instituted the most famous set of early laws. Like kings before him, Hammurabi proclaimed that his goal was to show Shamash, the Babylonian sun-god and god of justice, that he was fulfilling the social responsibility imposed on him as a divinely installed monarch—to ensure justice and the moral and material welfare of his people: "So that the powerful may not oppress the powerless, to provide justice for the orphan and the widow . . . let the victim of injustice see the law which applies to him, let his heart be put at ease."

Hammurabi's code divided society into three categories: free persons, commoners, and slaves. We do not know what made the first two categories different, but it is clear that free persons outranked commoners in Babylonian society. An attacker who caused a pregnant woman of the free class to miscarry, for example, paid twice the fine levied for the same offense against a woman in the commoner class. For social equals, the code specified "an eye for an eye." But a member of the free class who killed a commoner was fined, not executed. The people themselves assembled in courts to determine most cases.

Most of the laws concerned the king's interests as a property owner who leased innumerable tracts of land to tenants in return for rent or services. For offenses against property, the laws imposed severe penalties, including mutilation or a gruesome death for crimes as varied as theft, wrongful sales, and careless construction. In this patriarchal society, women had limited legal rights, but they could make business contracts and appear in court. A wife could divorce her husband for cruelty; a husband could divorce his wife for any reason. In practice, the inequality of the divorce laws was tempered because a woman was entitled to recover the property she had brought to the marriage; this potential loss was a considerable disincentive for a man to end the marriage.

The situations covered by Hammurabi's laws tell us much about urban life in Bronze Age Mesopotamia. Burglary and assault apparently plagued city dwellers. Marriages were arranged by the groom and the bride's father, who sealed the agreement with a legal contract. Laws on surgical practice illuminate the work of doctors. Because people believed that angry or evil spirits caused many diseases, Mesopotamian medicine included magic as well as treatment with potions and diet. Magicians offered therapy that depended primarily on spells and on interpreting signs, such as the patient's dreams or hallucinations.◆

Archaeological excavations and cuneiform records supplement the information on daily life provided by the code. Cities had many taverns and wine shops, often run by women proprietors, offering alcoholic drinks and a convivial atmosphere. Relief from the odors and crowding of the streets could be found in the open spaces set aside for parks. The oldest known map in the world, an inscribed clay tablet showing the outlines of the Babylonian city of Nippur about 1500 B.C., indicates a substantial area designated for this purpose.

Mapmaking required sophisticated calculations and spatial knowledge, which formed part of what historians widely regard as Mesopotamia's most long-lasting legacy: its achievements in mathematics and astronomy. Mathematicians used algebra to solve complex problems and knew how to derive the roots of numbers. They invented place-value notation and a system of reckoning based on sixty, still used in our division of hours and minutes and degrees of a circle. Mesopotamians' expertise in recording the paths of the stars and planets probably arose from their desire to make predictions about the future, based on the astrological belief that the movements of celestial bodies affect human life. Astrology never lost its appeal in Mesopotamia, and the charts and tables compiled by Mesopotamian stargazers laid the basis for later advances in astronomical knowledge.

Early Civilizations in Egypt, the Levant, and Anatolia, c. 3100–1000 B.C.

Africa was home to the second great civilization to shape the West: Egypt, which lay close enough to Mesopotamia to learn from its peoples but was geographically protected enough to develop its own distinct culture. Egyptians created a wealthy, profoundly religious, and strongly traditional civilization ruled by kings. Unlike Mesopotamia, Egypt was politically united under a strong central authority. The Egyptian kings' desire for immortality and interest in the afterlife motivated the construction of some of the most imposing tombs in history, the pyramids, and

---

◆ For an excerpt from these early laws, see Document 1, "The Code of Hammurabi."

Egyptian architecture and art inspired later Mediterranean peoples, especially the Greeks.

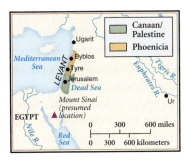

The Ancient Levant

During the height of Egyptian power under the New Kingdom (c. 1567–1085 B.C.), the Hittite kingdom loomed as Egypt's most aggressive rival. The Hittites had become the most powerful people in Anatolia by about 1750 B.C. (see Map 1.1). They flourished because they inhabited a fertile, upland plateau in the peninsula's center and controlled trade in their region and southward into the Levant* (modern Jordan, Syria, Lebanon, and Israel), the commercial crossroads of the eastern Mediterranean and the persistent site of conflict among Near Eastern powers.

Religion and Rule in Egypt, c. 3100–2181 B.C.

The first large-scale Egyptian state emerged about 3100–3000 B.C. when King Menes united Upper (southern) Egypt and Lower (northern) Egypt. (*Upper* and *Lower* derive from the direction in which the Nile River flows—from south of Egypt northward to the Mediterranean Sea.) By around 2686 B.C., Menes' successors had forged a strong, centralized state, today known as the Old Kingdom, which lasted until around 2181 B.C. (Map 1.2).[†] Egypt's people lived in a narrow stretch of land along the Nile. Their irrigated farms extended several miles away from the river's banks. Under normal weather conditions, the Nile overflowed its banks annually for several weeks, when melting snow from the mountains of central Africa swelled its flow. This predictable annual flood enriched the soil adjacent to the river with nutrients from the river's silt and diluted harmful deposits of mineral salts. Unlike the random floods in Mesopotamia, the flooding of the Nile recurred during the same season every year and benefited the land. Trouble came only if dry weather in the mountains kept the river from overflowing.

Deserts east and west of the Nile protected Egypt from invasion, except through the Nile delta in the north and on the southern frontier with Nubia. Deposits of metal ores, trade by sea, and lush agriculture made Egypt prosperous. From their ample supplies of grain, the Egyptians made bread and beer, a staple beverage. Egypt's population included a diversity of people, whose skin color ranged from

---

*The name *Levant*, French for "rising (sun)"—that is, the East—reflects the European perspective on the area's location.

[†]Scholars still dispute the precise dates for ancient Egyptian history because the evidence is often contradictory, even when related to ancient observations of celestial events. The approximate chronology given here is simply one of several reasonable schemes; it can be found conveniently tabulated in T. G. H. James, *An Introduction to Ancient Egypt* (1979), 263–66.

light to very dark. A significant proportion of ancient Egyptians would be regarded as black by modern racial classification (unknown to ancient peoples). The modern controversy over whether Egyptians were people of color is anachronistic; ancient Egyptians presumably identified themselves as an African population united by geography, language, and religion. Later peoples, especially the Greeks, admired Egyptian civilization for its great antiquity and piety. Some nineteenth-century historians minimized the Egyptian contribution to Western civilization, but ancient peoples did not.

Like everyone else in history, Egyptians learned from other peoples. For example, they probably learned the technology of writing from the Sumerians, but they developed their own scripts rather than adopting cuneiform. To write formal and official texts, they used an ornate pictographic script known as *hieroglyphs* (Figure 1.2). Looking southward, Egyptians would have seen that the Nubians had already built extensive settlements and produced complex art by Menes' time. At places such as Afyeh near the Nile's First Cataract, a Nubian social elite lived in dwellings much grander than the small huts housing most of the population. Egyptians constantly interacted with Nubians while trading for raw materials such as gold, ivory, and animal skins, and the hierarchical organization of Nubia perhaps influenced the development of centralized authority in Egypt's Old Kingdom. Eventually, however, Egypt's power overshadowed that of its southern neighbor.

The waxing and waning of central authority determined Egyptian political history. When the kings were strong, as during the Old Kingdom, the country was stable and rich and trade, especially with the Levant, flourished. However, when regional governors or prominent priests,

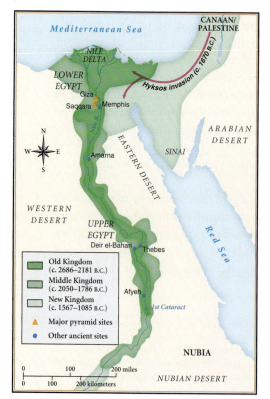

■ **MAP 1.2 Ancient Egypt**
The Nile River, closely embraced by arid deserts, provided Egyptians with water to irrigate their fields and a highway for traveling north to the Mediterranean Sea and south to Nubia. The only easy land route into and out of Egypt lay through the northern Sinai peninsula into the coastal area of the Levant; Egyptian kings therefore always fought to control these areas to secure the safety of their land.

whose status was second only to the royal family's, refused to support the king, political instability resulted.

The king's power and success depended on his properly fulfilling his religious obligations. Egyptians worshiped many gods, often depicted as creatures with both human and animal features such as the head of a jackal or a bird atop a human body. They did not worship animals; rather, they believed that associated with each god was a particular animal serving as the bearer of the god's divine soul. A picture or statue of a divinity had to include the animal so the depiction would not lack a soul. Egyptian religion told complicated stories about the daily lives of the gods to explain their powers. Deities were associated with powerful natural objects, emotions, qualities, and technologies, such as the sun-god Re; Isis, goddess of love and fertility; and Thoth, god of wisdom and the inventor of writing.

Egyptians regarded their king as a god in human form, while recognizing that the individual on the throne was mortal. Therefore, they differentiated

Hieroglyph	Meaning	Sound value
	vulture	glottal stop
	flowering reed	consonantal I
	forearm and hand	ayin
	quail chick	W
	foot	B
	stool	P
	horned viper	F
	owl	M
	water	N
	mouth	R
	reed shelter	H
	twisted flax	slightly guttural
	placenta (?)	H as in "loch"
	animal's belly	slightly softer than h
	door bolt	S
	folded cloth	S
	pool	SH
	hill	Q
	basket with handle	K
	jar stand	G
	loaf	T

■ **FIGURE 1.2 Egyptian Hieroglyphs**
Ancient Egyptians developed their own system of writing about 3100 B.C., using pictures such as these. Because this formal script was used mainly for religious inscriptions on buildings and sacred objects (such as the sarcophagus illustrated on page 2), Greeks referred to it as "the sacred carved letters" (ta hieroglyphica), from which comes the modern term hieroglyphs. *Egyptian hieroglyphs employ around seven hundred pictures in three categories: ideograms (signs indicating things or ideas), phonograms (signs indicating sounds), and determinatives (signs clarifying the meaning of the other signs). Eventually (the chronology is unsure), Egyptians also developed the handwritten cursive script called* demotic (*Greek for "of the people"), a much simpler and quicker form of writing.*
(Giraudon/Art Resource, NY.)

between the king's human existence and the divine origin of monarchy. Their system of rule was divine because it represented on earth the supernatural, eternal force that created harmony and stability in the universe. This force was called *ma'at*, often translated as "truth" or "justice" or "correct balance." It was the king's responsibility to rule according to *ma'at* by keeping the forces of nature in balance for the benefit of his people. The Egyptian kings' religious dimension distinguished them from Sumerian kings, who ruled as strictly human lords even though their cities were devoted to the gods.

An Egyptian king ensured the welfare of his country by strictly observing ritual. For example, he had to keep to a specific time to take a bath, go for a walk, or make love to his wife. Above all, the king was obliged to summon the divine power necessary to make the Nile overflow. If he failed to make the flood occur, he gravely weakened his authority. The inability to produce annual floods and keep the people well fed showed he had lost his *ma'at*, and he might then lose his kingdom.

Old Kingdom rulers used expensive building programs to demonstrate their piety and proclaim their status atop the social hierarchy. Unlike their Mesopotamian counterparts ruling independent states, they built only a few large cities. The first capital, Memphis (south of modern Cairo), grew into a metropolis packed with mammoth structures. In the suburbs of Memphis, these kings erected the most stunning manifestations of their status and piety—huge tombs in the form of pyramids. These monuments formed the centerpieces of groups of buildings for royal funerals and religious ceremonies. Although the pyramids were not the first monuments built from enormous, worked stones (that designation goes to temples on the Mediterranean island of Malta), they rank as the grandest. The Old Kingdom rulers spent vast sums of money and labor on these huge complexes because they cared so much about protecting their mummified bodies for existence in the afterlife. Around 2575 B.C., King Cheops commissioned the biggest of them all—the so-called Great Pyramid at Giza. At about 480 feet high, it stands taller than a forty-story skyscraper. Covering over thirteen acres and extending 760 feet on each side, it required more than two million blocks of limestone, some of which weighed fifteen tons apiece. Quarried in the desert, they were floated to the site on river barges and dragged on rollers and sleds up earthen ramps into position.

The kings' lavish preparations for death reflect the strong Egyptian belief in an afterlife. A prayer from about 2300 B.C. expresses that hope: "O divine Atum, put your arms around King Nefer-ka-Re, around this construction work, around this pyramid. . . . May you guard lest anything happen to him evilly throughout the course of eternity." Members of the royal family packed their tombs for their new existence with gilded furniture, sparkling jewelry, and exquisite objects of all kinds. Archaeologists uncovered two full-size cedar ships buried next to the Great Pyramid, meant to carry King Cheops on his journey into eternity.

To mobilize labor for their mammoth projects, Old Kingdom rulers centralized their administration and created a structured hierarchy. The king and queen

■ **The Pyramids at Giza in Egypt**
The kings of Old Kingdom Egypt constructed massive stone pyramids for their tombs. Pyramids were the centerpieces of large complexes of temples and courtyards stretching to the banks of the Nile or along a canal leading to the river. The burial chambers lay at the end of long, narrow tunnels snaking through the pyramids' interiors. The biggest pyramid shown here is the Great Pyramid of King Cheops, erected about 2575 B.C. (Farrell Grehean/NGS Image Collection.)

topped the social order. Brothers and sisters in the royal family could marry each other, perhaps because such matches were believed necessary to preserve the purity of the royal line or to imitate the marriages of the gods. The priests, royal administrators, regional governors, and commanders of the army came next in the hierarchy. The common people, who did all the manual labor, constituted the massive base of this figurative pyramid of free people in Egypt. (Slaves became more common after the Old Kingdom.) Free workers had heavy obligations to the state. For example, although they were not slaves, they were compelled to work on the pyramids. On occasion they received wages, but mostly their labor was a way of paying taxes. Rates of taxation reached 20 percent on the produce of free farmers.

Women generally had the same legal rights as men. They could own land and slaves, inherit property, pursue lawsuits, transact business, and initiate divorces. Old Kingdom portrait statues display the equal status of wife and husband: each figure is the same size and sits on the same kind of chair. Men dominated public life, while women devoted themselves mainly to private life, managing their households and property. When their husbands went to war, however, women often took on men's work. As a result, some women held government posts, served as priestesses, managed farms, and practiced medicine.

The formalism of Egypt's art illustrates how much its people valued piety, order, and predictability. Almost all sculptures and paintings belonged to tombs or temples, testimony to the desire to please the gods. Old Kingdom artists excelled in stonework, from carved ornamental jars to massive portrait statues of the kings. These statues represent the subject either standing stiffly with the left leg advanced or sitting on a chair or throne, stable and poised. Concern for decorum also appears in the Old Kingdom literature the Egyptians called *Instructions,* known today as *wisdom literature.* These texts conveyed instructions for appropriate behavior for high officials. In the *Instruction of Ptahhotep,* for example, the king advises his minister Ptahhotep to tell his son, who will succeed him in office, not to be arrogant or overconfident just because he is well educated and to seek advice from ignorant people as well as from the wise.

Life in the Egyptian and Hittite Kingdoms, 2181–1000 B.C.

The Old Kingdom's stability disintegrated when climate changes shrank the annual Nile flood. The ensuing starvation and civil unrest discredited the regime and by 2181 B.C. had destroyed the country's unity because regional governors seized power. King Mentuhotep II finally restored central authority, initiating what historians call the Middle Kingdom (c. 2050–1786 B.C.). Reachieving unity gave Egyptians pride in their homeland, to judge from the period's vigorous literature. The Egyptian narrator of *The Story of Sinuhe,* for example, reports that he lived luxuriously during a forced stay in Syria but still pined to return: "Whichever deity you are who ordered my exile, have mercy and bring me home! Please allow me to see the land where my heart dwells! Nothing is more important than that my body be buried in the country where I was born!"

The Middle Kingdom fell apart around 1786 B.C. when irregular Nile floods again undermined royal power. Another long period of disunity ensued, made worse by a foreign invasion. Taking advantage of the land's political weakness, a Semitic people from the Syria-Palestine region whom the Egyptians called the Hyksos took over Lower Egypt around 1670 B.C. (see Map 1.2). Recent archaeological discoveries have revealed the Hyksos transplanted elements of foreign culture to Egypt. The invaders brought bronze-making technology, horses and war chariots, more powerful bows, new musical instruments, hump-backed cattle, and olive trees, and they promoted contact with other Near Eastern states. As with the wars of the Akkadians, so, too, did the Hyksos invasion generate cultural interchange.

Eventually, the leaders of Thebes in southern Egypt once again reunited Egypt. They overthrew the Hyksos around 1567 B.C. and initiated the New Kingdom (c. 1567–1085 B.C.). Its kings, known as *pharaohs* (meaning "the Great House," that is, the royal palace and estate), rebuilt central authority by restricting the power of regional governors. Recognizing that knowledge of the rest of the world was necessary for safety, they established diplomatic contacts with foreign states, such as the Hittite kingdom in Anatolia.

The New Kingdom pharaohs also used war to promote Egypt's interests. They earned the title "warrior pharaohs" by invading Nubia and the Sudan to the south, seeking gold and other precious materials, and by fighting in Palestine and Syria to control trade routes. Of all their activities, religion remained the most important. The principal festivals of the gods, for example, involved lavish public celebrations. A calendar based on the moon governed the dates of religious ceremonies. (The Egyptians also developed a calendar for administrative and fiscal purposes that had 365 days divided into twelve months of thirty days each, with the extra five days added before the start of the next year. Our modern calendar derives from it.) The royal family in the New Kingdom also built most of Egypt's magnificent temples, whose sculpted columns set a precedent for later Greek architecture. Queen Hatshepsut in the fifteenth century B.C., for example, erected a massive complex at Deir el Bahri near Thebes. After her husband (who was also her half-brother) died, Hatshepsut had proclaimed herself "female king" as co-ruler with her young stepson. In this way, she shrewdly sidestepped Egyptian political ideology, which made no provision for a queen to reign in her own right. She therefore had herself often represented in official art as a man, sporting a king's beard and male clothing.

So fervent was religious feeling that it threatened the stability of the New Kingdom in the fourteenth century B.C. when the pharaoh Akhenaten acted to reform tradition, believing it was misguided. He made the cult of Aten, the shining disk of the sun, the centerpiece of official religion and excluded other deities and their supporters. Akhenaten's reforms did not aim at pure *monotheism* (belief in the existence of only one god, as in Judaism, Christianity, and Islam) because they did not revoke the divine status of the king. His wife, Queen Nefertiti, tried to restrain him when she realized the hostility that his changes were generating in the priesthood and the general population, but he continued undeterred, even neglecting the defense of Egypt to devote himself to religion. His religious reform died with him; during the reign of his successor Tutankhamun (r. 1361–1352 B.C.), famous today through the discovery in 1922 of his rich, unlooted tomb, the traditional solar cult of Amen-Re reclaimed its leading role.

Whether Egypt was at peace or in turmoil, Egyptians' daily lives focused on work (mainly farming and craft production) and religion. Ordinary people devoted much attention to deities outside the royal cults, especially to gods supposed to protect them. They venerated Bes, for instance, a dwarf with the features of a lion, as a protector of the household. They carved his image on amulets, beds, headrests, and the handles of mirrors. Magic also played a large role in their lives. They sought spells and charms to ward off demons, smooth the course of love, exact revenge on enemies, and find relief from disease and injury. Egyptian doctors made medicinal use of many herbs, knowledge that was passed on to later civilizations, and they could perform demanding surgeries, including opening the skull. But they could not cure infections.

Like royalty, ordinary people prepared for the afterlife. Those who could afford to do so arranged to have their bodies mummified and their tombs outfitted with

■ **The "Opening of the Mouth" Ceremony in an Egyptian Funeral**
This picture from a papyrus scroll containing the Egyptian Book of the Dead, *instructions for the afterlife, shows priests, mourners, and the god Anubis performing the Opening of the Mouth funeral ceremony. In this ritual, the deceased's mummy was touched on the mouth by sacred instruments that released the person's individual personality* (ba) *to join the rest of his or her spirit for a happy new existence in the next world.* (British Museum.)

all the goods needed for the journey to their new existence. A mummy's essential equipment included a copy of the *Book of the Dead*—a collection of magic spells to ward off danger and ensure a successful verdict in the divine judgment that every soul had to pass to avoid experiencing death a second time. The text enumerated a long list of misdeeds that the deceased had to swear to have avoided, including "I have not committed crimes against people; I have not mistreated cattle; I have not robbed the poor; I have not caused pain; I have not caused tears." Dead persons who received positive judgments experienced a mystical union with the god Osiris, the head judge of souls.

The greatest external threat of death to New Kingdom Egyptians came from the aggressive wars of the Hittite kingdom in Anatolia (see Map 1.1). Unrelated to the Egyptians, the Hittites spoke an Indo-European language, from the linguistic family that eventually populated most of Europe. The original Indo-European speakers had migrated as separate groups into Anatolia and Europe from somewhere in western Asia. Recent archaeological discoveries there of graves of women buried with weapons suggest that Indo-European women originally occupied positions of leadership alongside men; the prominence of Hittite queens in official documents perhaps sprang from that tradition.

Hittite kingship was based on religion—the worship of Indo-European gods and local Anatolian deities. The king served as high priest of the storm-god and had to maintain strict purity. His drinking water, for example, was always strained, and his water carrier was executed if so much as a hair was found in a drink. Like Egyptian kings, Hittite rulers felt responsible for maintaining divine goodwill toward their subjects. One of them, King Mursili II (r. 1321–1295 B.C.), issued a set of prayers begging the gods to end a plague: "What is this, o gods, that you have done? Our land is dying. . . . We have lost our wits, and we can do nothing right. O gods, whatever sin you behold, either let a prophet come forth to identify it . . . or let us see it in a dream!"

The Hittite rulers launched ambitious military campaigns to acquire metals and control trade routes. The Hittites did not owe their success in war to a special knowledge of making weapons from iron, as once thought, because iron weapons did not become common until well after 1200 B.C. They did excel in the use of chariots, which perhaps gave them an edge. Hittite kings particularly wanted to dominate the lucrative trade from Mesopotamia and Egypt. In 1595 B.C., therefore, their army raided as far as Babylon, destroying that kingdom.

They also invaded the Levant, the principal trade highway to Egypt. Previously, independent Canaanite city-states, such as the bustling ports of Ugarit, Byblos, and Tyre, had dominated the Levant. There, the interaction of traders and travelers from many different cultures created an overwhelmingly important innovation in writing technology about 1600 B.C.: the alphabet. In this new system, a picture—that is, a letter—stood for only one sound in the language. This was a marvelous improvement over cumbersome cuneiform and hieroglyphic scripts. The Canaanite alphabet later became the basis for the Greek and Roman alphabets and hence of modern Western alphabets.

The New Kingdom pharaohs fiercely resisted Hittite expansion in the Levant, but they could not defeat the Hittites at the climactic battle of Kadesh in Syria about 1274 B.C. Diplomacy finally created a balance of power between the kingdoms when, around 1259 B.C., the Hittite king Hattusili III signed a treaty with the Egyptian king Ramesses II and gave Ramesses his daughter in marriage to seal the agreement. Remarkably, both Egyptian and Hittite copies of this landmark in diplomatic history survive. In it the two monarchs pledged to be "at peace and brothers forever."

Shifting Empires in the Ancient Near East, to 500 B.C.

A prolonged spasm of war and unrest, apparently generated by invasions of separate bands of shipborne raiders known to us as the "Sea Peoples" (their history remains mysterious), afflicted the eastern Mediterranean region from about 1200 to 1000 B.C. The turmoil wiped out many communities, producing what scholars call a "Dark Age" because economic conditions were so gloomy for so many people and because our view of what happened is so dim. In the Near East, recent archaeological excavation suggests that this Dark Age lasted about a century. Egypt lost its international power forever during this troubled period when the New Kingdom fell apart about 1085 B.C.

By 900 B.C., a powerful and centralized Assyrian kingdom had reemerged from the Near East's Dark Age. From their Mesopotamian homeland, the Assyrians ruthlessly carved out a new empire even larger than the one their ancestors had created long before. The riches and power of this Neo-Assyrian ("New Assyrian") Empire later inspired the Babylonians and then the Persians to try to fill the void created when Assyrian power collapsed. This constant striving for imperial wealth and territory kept the Near East on the same political and military path—monarchy and empire—that the region had followed in the past.

Hebrew (or Israelite) civilization, centered in the southern Levant, lost its independence to these Near Eastern empires, but its religion—Judaism—transmitted a lasting legacy to Western civilization. The Hebrews' religion, originally reflecting influences from their polytheistic Canaanite neighbors, took a long time to consolidate as monotheism, but eventually it initiated one of the most important religious movements in Western history.

From Assyrian, to Babylonian, to Persian Supremacy, c. 900–500 B.C.

The collapse of the Egyptian and Hittite kingdoms by 1000 B.C. gave an opening to the aggressive warriors of Assyria to seize supplies of metal and control land and sea trade routes. By about 900 B.C., the armies of the Neo-Assyrian kingdom were relentlessly driving westward against the Aramaean states in Syria until they punched through to the Mediterranean coast (Map 1.3). Neo-Assyrian monarchs constantly pursued foreign expansion, and the values of violence pervaded their society, which male warriors dominated. For the first time, their armies made foot soldiers the principal striking force instead of cavalry. Trained infantrymen excelled in the use of military technology such as siege towers and battering rams; archers rode in chariots. Campaigns against foreign lands brought in booty to supplement the kingdom's agriculture and long-distance trade. Conquered peoples had to pay annual tribute to support the kingdom's prosperity, supplying raw materials and luxury goods such as incense, wine, dyed linens, glass, and ivory.

Neo-Assyrian kings treated conquered peoples brutally to keep order by instilling fear. They herded large numbers of people from their homelands to Assyria to make them build temples and palaces. One unexpected consequence of this merciless policy was that the kings undermined their native language: so many Aramaeans were deported from Canaan to Assyria that Aramaic had largely replaced Assyrian as the land's everyday language by the eighth century B.C.

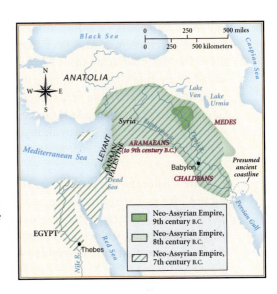

■ **MAP 1.3 Expansion of the Neo-Assyrian Empire, c. 900–650 B.C.**
Like their Akkadian, Assyrian, and Babylonian predecessors, the Neo-Assyrian kings dominated a vast region of the Near East to secure a supply of metals, access to trade routes on land and sea, and imperial glory. They built the largest empire the world had yet seen. Also like their predecessors, they treated disobedient subjects harshly and intolerantly to try to prevent their diverse territories from rebelling.

When not waging war, Neo-Assyrian men loved to hunt—the more dangerous the quarry, the better. The king hunted lions as proof of his vigor and power. Royal lion hunts provided a favorite subject for sculptors, who mastered the artistic technique of carving long relief sculptures that narrated a connected story. Although the Neo-Assyrian imperial administration devoted much effort to preserving documents in its archives, literacy apparently mattered far less to the kingdom's males than war, hunting, and practical technology. King Sennacherib (r. 704–681 B.C.), for example, boasted that he invented new irrigation equipment and a novel method of metal casting. Ashurbanipal (r. 680–626 B.C.) is the only king to proclaim his scholarly accomplishments: "I have read complicated texts, whose versions in Sumerian are obscure and in Akkadian hard to understand. I do research on the cuneiform texts on stone from before the Flood." Women of the social elite probably had a chance to become literate, but they were excluded from the male dominions of hunting and war. Public religion, which included deities adopted from Babylonia, also reflected the prominence of war in Assyrian culture: even the Assyrian cult of Ishtar (the Babylonian name for Inanna), the goddess of love and fertility, glorified warfare.

The Neo-Assyrian kings' harshness made their own people dislike their rule, especially the social elite. Rebellions were common, and in the seventh century B.C. they enfeebled the kingdom. The Medes, an Iranian people, and the Chaldeans, a Semitic people who had driven the Assyrians from Babylonia, combined forces to invade. They destroyed the Neo-Assyrian capital at Nineveh in 612 B.C. and ended its kings' dreams of empire.

Sprung from seminomadic herders along the Persian Gulf, the Chaldeans went on to establish the Neo-Babylonian Empire, which became the most powerful empire in Babylonian history and perpetuated imperial monarchy as the standard form of government in the Near East. King Nebuchadnezzar II (r. 605–562 B.C.) drove the Egyptian army from Syria at the battle of Carchemish in 605 B.C. Nebuchadnezzar spent lavishly to turn Babylon into an architectural showplace, rebuilding the great temple of its chief god, Marduk, creating the famous Hanging Gardens—so named because lush plants drooped over its terraced sides—and constructing a dazzling city gate dedicated to the goddess Ishtar. Blue-glazed bricks and lions molded in yellow, red, and white decorated the gate's walls, which soared thirty-six feet.

The Chaldeans adopted traditional Babylonian culture and preserved much ancient Mesopotamian literature, such as the *Epic of Gilgamesh* and other famous myths. They also created many new works of prose and poetry, which educated people, a minority of the population, often read aloud publicly for the enjoyment of the illiterate. Particularly popular were fables, proverbs, essays, and prophecies that taught morality and proper behavior. This so-called wisdom literature, a Near Eastern tradition going back at least to the Egyptian Old Kingdom, would greatly influence the later religious writings of the Hebrews.

The Chaldeans also passed on their knowledge to others outside their region. Their advances in astronomy became so influential that the word *Chaldean* became the Greeks' word for *astronomer*. The primary motivation for observing the stars was the belief that the gods communicated their will to humans through natural phenomena, such as celestial movements and eclipses, abnormal births, smoke curling upward from a fire, and the trails of ants. The interpretation of these phenomena as messages from the gods exemplified the mixture of science and religion characteristic of ancient Near Eastern thought and proved influential on the Greeks.

The Persian kingdom, the Near East's last and greatest empire, began when Cyrus (r. 559–530 B.C.) overthrew Median rule in Persia (today Iran). Relying on his skills as a general and a diplomat who respected others' religious beliefs, he conquered Babylon in 539 B.C. A rebellion there had weakened the Chaldean dynasty when King Nabonidus (r. c. 555–539 B.C.) provoked a revolt among Marduk's priests by promoting a different deity. Cyrus exploited this religious strife by promising to restore traditional Babylonian religion, thereby winning local support. According to an ancient inscription, he proclaimed: "Marduk, the great lord, caused Babylon's generous residents to adore me."

Drawing on the same principles of military strength and cultural tolerance, Cyrus's successors expanded Persian rule. Darius I (r. 522–486 B.C.) vastly extended Cyrus's conquests by pushing Persian power eastward to the Indus Valley and westward to Thrace (Map 1.4). Organizing this vast territory into provinces, he assigned each region taxes payable in the form best suited to its local economy—precious metals, grain, horses, or slaves. In addition, he required each region to send soldiers to staff the royal army. A network of roads and a courier system for royal mail fostered contact among the far-flung provincial centers. The Greek historian Herodotus

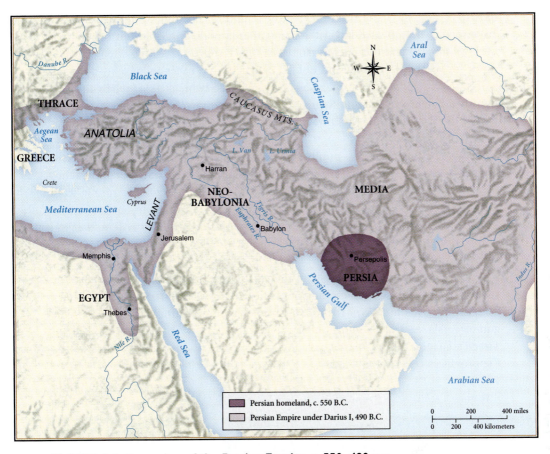

■ **MAP 1.4 Expansion of the Persian Empire, c. 550–490 B.C.**
Cyrus (r. 559–530 B.C.) initiated the Persian Empire, which his successors expanded to be even larger than the Neo-Assyrian Empire, which it replaced. By the later years of Darius's reign (r. 522–486 B.C.), the Persian Empire had expanded east as far as the western edge of India, and to the west it reached Thrace, the eastern edge of Europe. Persian kings, unlike their imperial predecessors, won their subjects' loyalty with tolerance and religious freedom, although they treated rebels harshly.

reported that neither snow, rain, heat, nor darkness slowed the couriers from completing their routes as swiftly as possible (a feat later transformed into the U.S. Postal Service motto). The kings' belief in their divine right to rule everyone everywhere would provoke great conflicts—above all, the war between Persians and Greeks that would break out around 500 B.C.

The revenue flowing into the imperial treasury made the Persian monarch wealthy beyond imagination. His purple robes were more splendid than anyone else's; the red carpets spread for him to walk on could not be used by anyone else; servants held their hands before their mouths in his presence so that he would not have to breathe the same air as they; in the sculpture adorning his immense palace at Persepolis, he appeared larger than any other human. To display his concern for his loyal subjects and the gargantuan scale of his resources, the king often provided meals for some fifteen thousand nobles, courtiers, and other followers—although he himself ate hidden from the view of his guests. Lawbreakers or rebels the king punished harshly, mutilating their bodies and executing their families. Greeks, in awe of the Persian monarch's power and his lavish style of life, referred to him as "The Great King."

So long as his subjects—numbering in the millions and of many different ethnicities—remained peaceful, the king left them alone to live and worship as they pleased. The empire's smoothly functioning administrative structure sprang from Assyrian precedents: provincial governors (*satraps*) ruled enormous territories with little if any direct interference from the king. In this decentralized system, the governors' duties included keeping order, enrolling troops when needed, and sending revenues to the royal treasury.

Ruling as absolute autocrats and therefore possessing the power to make the rules for everyone else, the Persian kings believed they were superior to all humans. They regarded themselves not as gods but as the agents of Ahura Mazda, the supreme god of Persia. As Darius said in his autobiography carved into a mountainside in three languages, "Ahura Mazda gave me kingship . . . by the will of Ahura Mazda the provinces respected my laws."

■ **The Great King of Persia**

Like their Assyrian predecessors, the Persian kings decorated their palaces with large relief sculptures emphasizing royal dignity and success. This one from Persepolis shows officials and petitioners giving the king proper respect when entering his presence. To symbolize their elevated status, the king and his son, who stands behind the throne, are depicted as larger than everyone else.

(Courtesy of the Oriental Institute of the University of Chicago.)

Based on the teachings of the legendary prophet Zarathustra and called Zoroastrianism from the Greek name for this holy man, Persian religion made Ahura Mazda the center of its devotion. It seems, however, not to have been pure monotheism. Its most important doctrine was a moral dualism: perceiving the world as the arena for an ongoing battle between the opposing forces of good and evil. Ahura Mazda's two children, according to Persian belief, made different moral choices, one choosing the way of the truth and the other the way of the lie. Like these divine beings, humans could freely decide between purity and impurity, and their judgment had consequences: Zoroastrianism promised that salvation awaited those following the way of the truth and damnation would be the fate of those electing the way of the lie. The Persian religious emphasis on ethical behavior had a lasting influence on others, most strikingly on the Hebrews.

Consolidating Hebrew Monotheism, c. 1000–539 B.C.

The enduring legacy of the Hebrews to Western civilization comes from the significance of the book that became their sacred scripture, the Hebrew Bible (known to Christians as the Old Testament). It deeply affected the formation of not only Judaism but also Christianity and, later, Islam. Unfortunately, no source provides clear information on the origins of the Hebrews or of their religion. The Bible tells stories to explain God's moral plan for the universe, not the full history of the Hebrews, and archaeology has not yielded a clear picture.

The Hebrew Bible reports that the patriarch Abraham led his followers from the Mesopotamian city of Ur to ancient Palestine, at the southeast corner of the Mediterranean Sea where the Canaanites ruled (see Map 1.1). Traditionally believed to have been divided into twelve tribes, the Hebrews never formed a political state in this period, about 1900 B.C. The biblical story of Joseph bringing Hebrews to Egypt may belong between 1600 and 1400 B.C., during the time of Hyksos rule there. By the thirteenth century B.C., the pharaohs had conscripted the male Hebrews into labor gangs for farming and construction work.

According to the book of Exodus, around 1250 B.C. the Hebrew deity Yahweh instructed Moses to lead the Hebrews out of bondage in Egypt against the will of the king. The biblical narrative then relates a seminal event in Hebrew history: the sealing of a covenant between the Hebrews and Yahweh at Mount Sinai. The covenant declared that if the Hebrews promised to worship Yahweh as their only God and to live by his laws, Yahweh would make them his chosen people and lead them into a promised land of safety and prosperity. This binding agreement demanded human obedience to divine law and promised punishment for unrighteousness. As God described himself, he was "compassionate and gracious, patient, ever constant and true . . . forgiving wickedness, rebellion, and sin, and not sweeping the guilty clean away; but one who punishes sons and grandsons to the third and fourth generation for their fathers' iniquity" (Exodus 34:6–7). The religious and moral code the Hebrews had to follow appears in the Ten Commandments and the Pentateuch (the first five books of the Hebrew Bible), or Torah.◆

Many of the Pentateuchal laws recalled earlier Mesopotamian rules, such as those of Hammurabi, but Hebrew law differed by making the same rules and punishments apply to all, regardless of their social position. Hebrew law also forbade vicarious punishment—a Mesopotamian tradition ordering, for example, that a rapist's wife be raped. Hebrew women had less extensive legal rights than men, such as in initiating divorce. Crimes against property never carried the death penalty, as they frequently did in other Near Eastern societies, and Hebrew laws protected slaves against flagrant mistreatment.

The earliest parts of the Hebrew Bible were probably composed about 950 B.C., some three centuries after the exodus from Egypt. Many uncertainties cloud our understanding of how the Hebrews acquired their distinctive religion. It seems that it took much longer to evolve than the biblical account suggests. In the time of Moses, Yahweh-religion was not yet pure monotheism because it did not deny the existence of other gods, such as Baal of Canaan. Fully developed Hebrew monotheism did not emerge until well after 1000 B.C., by which time the first Hebrew kingdom had formed. Solomon (r. c. 961–922 B.C.) brought the united nation to the height of its prosperity, largely from trade. He displayed his wealth by building in Jerusalem a temple to Yahweh richly decorated with gold leaf; it became the Hebrews' central religious monument.

After Solomon, the monarchy split into two kingdoms: Israel in the north and Judah in the south. The Assyrian king Tiglath-pileser III conquered Israel in 722 B.C. and deported its population to Assyria. In 597 B.C., the Neo-Babylonian king Nebuchadnezzar II conquered Judah; ten years later he destroyed Solomon's temple and sent most of the Hebrews into exile in Babylon. When the Persian king Cyrus overthrew the Babylonians in 539 B.C., he permitted the Hebrews to return to Palestine, which was called *Yehud* from the name of the southern Hebrew kingdom, Judah. From this geographical term came the name *Jews*, a designation for the Hebrews after their Babylonian exile. Cyrus allowed them to rebuild their Jerusalem temple and practice their religion. After returning from exile, the Jews were forever after a people subject to the political domination of various Near Eastern powers, save for a period of independence during the second and first centuries B.C.

Jewish prophets, both men and women, preached that the Hebrews' defeats were divine punishment for neglecting the Sinai covenant and mistreating the poor. Some prophets also predicted the coming end of the present world following a great crisis, a judgment by Yahweh, and salvation leading to a new and better world. This

---

◆ For an excerpt from the Hebrew Bible that describes divine law and suggests the Hebrews' way of life, see Document 2, "The Book of Exodus, Chapters 19–24."

apocalypticism ("uncovering" of the future), reminiscent of Babylonian prophetic wisdom literature, would later influence Christianity. Yahweh would save the Hebrew nation, the prophets thundered, only if Jews learned to observe divine law strictly.

To ensure proper observance, Jewish religious leaders developed firm regulations requiring people to maintain ritual and ethical purity in all aspects of life. Ethics applied not only to obvious crimes but also to financial dealings. Taxes and offerings had to be paid to support Yahweh's temple, and debts had to be forgiven every seventh year. Gradually, the Jews created the first complete monotheism, with laws based on ethics. They retained their cultural identity by following their religious laws, regardless of where they lived. A remarkable outcome of these religious developments was that Jews who did not return to their homeland could maintain their identity while living among foreigners. In this way, the Diaspora ("dispersion of population") came to characterize the history of the Jewish people.

Hebrew monotheism made the preservation and understanding of a sacred text, the Hebrew Bible, the center of religious life. Making scripture the focus of religion proved the most crucial development for the history not only of Judaism but also of Christianity and Islam, because these later religions made their own sacred texts, the Christian Bible and the Qur'an respectively, the centers of their belief and practice. The Hebrews thus passed on ideas—the belief in monotheism and the notion of a covenant bestowing a divinely ordained destiny on a people if they obey divine will—that have endured to this day.

Greek Civilization, to 750 B.C.

Neolithic settlements of Indo-European speakers dotted the mountainous terrain of the Greek mainland and the islands of the Aegean Sea by 8000 B.C. By 6000 B.C., Anatolian peoples had migrated to the large island of Crete, southeast of the Greek mainland. The type of language spoken by these early Cretans, called the Minoans, remains controversial, but they definitely created the first civilization in this part of the world in the late third millennium B.C. Eventually, they lost their preeminence and power to their warlike northern neighbors, the Mycenaean Greeks.

When Mycenaean civilization was destroyed during the tumult that affected the entire eastern Mediterranean from about 1200 to 1000 B.C., the aftermath—a prolonged Dark Age of depopulation and poverty—threatened doom for Greek civilization.

Minoan and Mycenaean Civilization, c. 2200–1000 B.C.

With its large, fertile plains, adequate rainfall, and sheltered ports for fishing and seaborne trade, Crete offered a fine home for settlers (Map 1.5). By 2200 B.C., the inhabitants of Crete had created what scholars have named a *palace society*, because

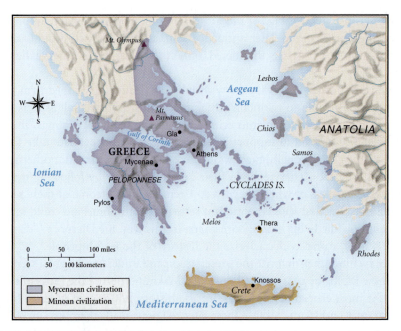

■ **MAP 1.5 Greece and the Aegean Sea, c. 1500 b.c.**
Mountains, islands, and sea defined the geography of Greece. The distances between settlements were mostly short, but rough terrain and seasonally stormy sailing made travel a chore. The distance from the mainland to the largest island in this region, Crete, where Minoan civilization arose, was sufficiently long to keep Cretans isolated from the turmoil of most of later Greek history.

of the sprawling, many-chambered buildings that appear to have been the residences of rulers and the centers of political, economic, and religious administration. The palaces seem to have been independent; no one ruler controlled Crete. We call this civilization *Minoan* because a famous archaeologist, Arthur Evans (1851–1941), believed that one of its rulers was King Minos, renowned in Greek myth because his wife bore the Minotaur ("Minos's bull").

Minoan farmers developed *Mediterranean polyculture*—the cultivation of olives, grapes, and grain simultaneously instead of only a single crop. This innovation optimized agricultural labor because these crops' different growing cycles allowed the same laborers to take care of them all. The combination of crops provided a healthy diet and thus stimulated population growth. Agriculture became both diversified and specialized. Farmers produced valuable and versatile products such as olive oil and wine.

The vast storage areas of the Cretan palaces, such as the one at Knossos, suggest that Minoan rulers, like some Mesopotamian kings, may have instituted a redistributive economic system. The Knossos palace, for example, held hundreds of gigantic jars holding 240,000 gallons of olive oil and wine. The rulers would have decided how much each farmer or crafts producer had to contribute to the palace

■ **Wall Painting from the Palace at Knossos**
Minoan artists painted with vivid colors on plaster to enliven the walls of buildings. They depicted a wide variety of subjects, from lively animals and flowering plants to young boxers and women of the court in splendid dress. Unfortunately, time and earthquakes have severely damaged most Minoan wall paintings, and the versions we see today are largely reconstructions painted around surviving fragments of the originals. The paintings from the Knossos palace, for example, were reconstructed as part of the overall plan of the original excavator, Arthur Evans, to rebuild the entire structure from fragmentary remains. (Julia M. Fair.)

storehouse and how much of those contributions would then be redistributed to each person in the community for basic subsistence or as an extra reward.

Greek civilization on the mainland certainly had a redistributive economy controlled by independent rulers. Emerging about the same time as the Hittite kingdom, in the early second millennium B.C., this civilization derives its modern designation—Mycenaean—from the hilltop site of Mycenae in the Peloponnese (the large peninsula forming southern Greece), which by 1400 B.C. had a fortified settlement dominated by a palace and dotted with rich tombs (see Map 1.5). Because Greece's mountainous terrain had little fertile land but many useful ports, settlements tended to spring up near the coast. Greeks from the earliest times depended on the sea: for food, for trade with one another and with foreign lands, and for naval raids on rich targets.

Seaborne commerce connected Greece with the rest of the eastern Mediterranean region and promoted cultural interaction, as underwater archaeology dramatically reveals. Off Uluburun in Turkey, for example, divers discovered a late-fourteenth-century B.C. ship carrying such a mixed cargo and varied personal possessions—from Greece, Egypt, Canaan, Cyprus, Babylon, and elsewhere in the Near East—that attaching a single "nationality" to this vessel would make no sense.

The sea brought Mycenaeans and Minoans into close contact. Many artifacts found on the mainland display motifs clearly inspired by Cretan designs. At the same time, the two civilizations remained different in important ways. The Mycenaeans burned offerings to the gods; the Minoans did not. The Minoans scattered sanctuaries across the landscape in caves, on mountaintops, and in country villas; the mainlanders kept their sanctuaries inside the palaces. When the Mycenaeans started building palaces in the fourteenth century B.C., unlike the Minoans they designed them around *megarons*—rooms with prominent ceremonial hearths and thrones for the rulers. Some Mycenaean palaces had more than one megaron, which could soar two stories high with columns to support a roof above the second-floor balconies.

A startling find of clay tablets in the Knossos palace shows that Mycenaeans achieved dominance over Crete, possibly in a war over international trade. These documents were written in a script that archaeologists called Linear B, a pictographic script based on an earlier script called Linear A. A brilliant twentieth-century architect named Michael Ventris proved that Linear B was used to write the Mycenaeans' language. Because the Linear B tablets dated from before the final destruction of Knossos in about 1370 B.C., they revealed that the palace administration had been keeping its records in a foreign language for some time and therefore that Mycenaeans were controlling Crete well before the end of Minoan civilization.

The Greeks later recalled this conquest in the myth about Theseus of Athens defeating the half-man, half-bull Minotaur of King Minos: when the Cretan king forced the Athenians to send youths for the monster to devour in his labyrinth, Theseus slew the beast and found his way to freedom by backtracking along the thread that the king's daughter Ariadne, who had fallen in love with the dashing hero, had told him to leave to mark his way in the maze.

By the time Mycenaeans took over Crete, war at home and abroad was the principal concern of well-off Mycenaean men. Contents of Bronze Age tombs in Greece reveal that no wealthy man went to his grave without his war equipment. The expense of these grave goods shows that armor and weapons were so central to a Mycenaean male's identity that he could not do without them even in death. Dedication to war, however, did not preserve the Mycenaeans when the calamities of the period of the Sea Peoples (c. 1200–1000 B.C.) struck.

The palace settlements of eastern Greece now constructed such massive defensive walls that later Greeks believed that giants had built them. These fortifications would have protected coastal palaces against invading Sea Peoples. But the wall around the palace at Gla, far inland where foreign sea raiders could not easily reach, suggests a land-based threat: apparently the Mycenaeans at Gla and elsewhere had to defend themselves against other Mycenaeans. Archaeologists therefore speculate that internal turmoil and earthquakes were responsible for the destruction of Mycenaean civilization by about 1000 B.C.

The failure of their redistributive economies devastated most Mycenaeans, who depended on their rulers' system for their subsistence. The catastrophic fall of Mycenaean civilization initiated the Greek Dark Age.

The Greek Dark Age, c. 1000–750 B.C.

The Dark Age created a void in Greece. Political organization disappeared, the economy collapsed, and the population declined. Even the technologies of writing and of depicting people and animals in art were lost in the depressed conditions that lasted from about 1000 to 750 B.C.

After the powerful rulers of Mycenaean Greece disappeared, competition for leadership positions in Dark Age society was wide open. The men and women who proved themselves excellent in action, words, and religious knowledge became the social elite. Excellence—*aretê* in Greek—became a competitive value: high social status stemmed from a family's men and women outdoing others. Men displayed *aretê* above all through prowess in war and persuasiveness in speech; women, through savvy management of a bustling household of children, slaves, and the family's storerooms. Members of the elite also accumulated wealth by controlling agricultural land, which people of lower status worked for them as tenants or slaves.

The rebuilding of social and political life called for the reestablishing of values. The poetry of Homer and Hesiod provided the elite with its ideals. Greeks believed that Homer was a blind poet from Ionia (today Turkey's western coast) who composed the epics the *Iliad* and the *Odyssey* in order to illuminate *aretê* as a social value. Many modern scholars believe that Homer lived in the eighth century B.C. and belonged to a long line of poets who, influenced by Near Eastern mythology, had been singing these stories for centuries. The *Iliad* tells the story of the Greek army in the Trojan War (which may have been one of the raids of the Sea Peoples period). The greatest Greek hero is Achilles, who displays his surpassing excellence by choosing to die gloriously in battle rather than return home safely but without glory. The *Odyssey* recounts the hero Odysseus's ten-year adventure finding his way home to his family after the fall of Troy, and the struggle of his wife, Penelope, to protect their household from schemes and threats in his absence. Penelope proves herself the best of women, showing her *aretê* by outwitting treacherous neighbors and thereby preserving her family's prosperity.

The *Iliad* and *Odyssey* reveal how the quest for excellence could provoke a disturbing level of inhumanity. As Achilles prepares to duel with Hector, the prince of Troy, he brutally rejects the Trojan's proposal for the winner to return the loser's corpse to his family and friends: "Do wolves and lambs agree to cooperate? No, they hate each other to the roots of their being." The victor, Achilles, mutilates Hector's body. When Hecuba, the queen of Troy, sees this outrage, she bitterly shouts, "I wish I could sink my teeth into his liver in his guts to eat it raw." The poems suggest that the gods could promote reconciliation, but the level of suffering Homer attributes to the human condition shows that excellence, though a worthy ideal, comes at a high price.

Hesiod's poetry expressed the importance of justice. A contemporary of Homer, Hesiod worked with myths influenced by Near Eastern stories, such as the Mesopotamian *Epic of Creation.* His poems make plain that existence, even for deities, entails sorrow and violence. They also insist that concern for justice is part of the divine order of the universe. In *Works and Days*, Hesiod identifies Zeus, king of the gods, as the source of justice: "Zeus ordained that fishes and wild beasts and birds should eat each other, for they have no justice; but to human beings he has given justice, which is far the best." Hesiod emphasizes that the men from the social elite, who dominated society, should demonstrate excellence by employing persuasion instead of force: "When his people in their assembly get on the wrong track, [a good leader] gently sets matters right, persuading them with soft words." Hesiod proclaims that the divine origin of justice should be a warning to "bribe-devouring chiefs" who impose "crooked judgments." The outrage that commoners felt at not receiving equal treatment stimulated gradual movement toward a new form of social and political organization in Greece.

During the Dark Age, the Greeks remained in contact with the Near East, and about 800 B.C. they learned to write again in a new way when Phoenician traders from Canaan taught them the alphabet. Eastern art inspired Greeks once more to include lively figures in their paintings. Most important, trade brought to Greece the new technology of iron metallurgy. Because iron ore was available in Greece, iron was cheaper than bronze there. The relatively low cost of iron tools helped revive farming, which in turn rebuilt the population. By the eighth century B.C., Greece's recovery was assured.

Remaking Greek Civilization, c. 750–500 B.C.

In a startling transformation, the Greeks gradually remade their civilization on new social and political principles, inventing citizenship and democracy. Kept alive economically and culturally during their Dark Age through ties with Egypt and the rest of the Near East, they created their own version of the city-state (*polis*) and new ways of expression and thinking in art, literature, philosophy, and science.

The best evidence of the improved conditions is the founding of the Olympic Games, traditionally dated to 776 B.C. Every four years, the games took place during a religious festival at Olympia, in the northwest Peloponnese, in a huge sanctuary dedicated to Zeus. There, male athletes from elite families vied in sports recalling the *aretê* needed for war: running, wrestling, jumping, and throwing. Horse and chariot racing were added to the program later, but the main event remained a two-hundred-yard sprint, the *stadion*. Women were barred on pain of death, but they had their own separate Olympic festival on a different date in honor of Hera, queen of the gods; only unmarried women could compete.

Athletes competed as individuals, not on national teams as in the modern Olympic Games. Only first prizes were awarded; winners received no financial rewards, only a garland made from wild olive leaves to symbolize the prestige of victory. Later, full-time athletes dominated the Olympics, earning their living from appearance fees and prizes at games held throughout the Greek world. The most famous winner was Milo, from Croton in Italy. Six-time Olympic wrestling champion, he stunned audiences with demonstrations of strength such as holding his breath until his veins expanded so much that they snapped a cord tied around his head.

Historians date the end of the Dark Age and the beginning of the Archaic Age (c. 750–500 B.C.) near the time when the Olympics began. The Archaic Age gave birth to the Greek *polis*—city-state—an independent community of citizens inhabiting a city and the countryside around it. Greece's geography, dominated by mountains and islands, promoted the creation of city-states that were fiercely independent communities (Map 1.6). The ancient Greeks never constituted a united nation.◆

During the Archaic Age, Greeks dispersed widely in settlements around the Mediterranean in a process traditionally called "Greek colonization." This modern term, however, is misleading because it implies that governments established and administered foreign colonies. Close study of architectural and textual evidence suggests that individuals' desire for profit from trade, especially in raw materials such as metals, and the hope of acquiring farmland on foreign shores drove the founding of new settlements. By about 580 B.C., Greeks had settled in Spain, present-day southern France, southern Italy and Sicily, North Africa, and along the Black Sea coast. Greek settlements in the east were fewer, perhaps because the monarchies there restricted foreign immigration.

Citizenship and Freedom in the City-State

The movement of Greeks outside Greece itself produced more than a thousand city-states, most with populations no greater than several hundred or a thousand. The Greek city-state was unusual because all free inhabitants were considered citizens and, usually, all free men could participate in governance. Some historians argue that the Greeks' knowledge of the older, monarchical cities of the island of Cyprus and of Phoenicia in the Levant influenced the creation of the Greek city-state, but

---

◆ For primary sources revealing the values that shaped two city-states, see Document 3, Tyrtaeus of Sparta and Solon of Athens, "Poems."

■ **MAP 1.6 Archaic Greece, c. 750–500 B.C.**

*The Greek heartland lay in and around the Aegean Sea, in what is today the nation of Greece and
the western edge of the nation of Turkey (ancient Anatolia). The "mainland," where Athens,
Corinth, and Sparta are located, is the southernmost tip of the mountainous Balkan peninsula.
The many islands of the Aegean area were home mainly to small city-states, with the exception of
the large islands just off the western Anatolian coast, which were home to populous ones.*

others conclude that the Greeks on their own originated the concept of citizenship
and the sharing of power, which were the defining characteristics of the *polis*. The
most famous ancient analyst of Greek politics and society, the philosopher Aristotle
(384–322 B.C.), insisted that the city-state was natural: "Humans are beings who by
nature live in a city-state." Anyone who existed outside such a community, Aristotle
only half-jokingly maintained, must be either a beast or a deity.

Citizenship was distinctive because it assumed a basic level of political and legal equality—above all, the expectation of equal treatment under the law for citizens regardless of their social status or wealth. Women had the protection of the
law, but they were barred from participation in politics on the assumption that female judgment was inferior to male. The most dramatic indication of political
equality in a Greek city-state was the involvement of all free, adult male citizens in
governance by attending and voting in a political assembly, where the laws and policies of the community were ratified. Not all city-states reached this level of power
sharing and participation, however. In some, the social elite kept a stranglehold on

■ **The Acropolis and Harbor of Lindos**

The topography of Lindos, one of several city-states on the large island of Rhodes (see Map 1.6), illustrates the ideal setting for a Greek settlement. A high, rocky outcropping served as the citadel (acropolis) and religious center; sheer sides made the buildings easy to defend. The nearly circular harbor below offered ships protection from storms and a safe place for loading and unloading passengers and cargo. (E. Hosking/Bruce Coleman, Inc.)

politics, and a small group or, more rarely, a single person or family dominated. Rule by a small elite group is called *oligarchy*. Rule by one person is called *tyranny*.

No matter how incomplete the Greeks' notion of equal citizenship remained in practice, the fact that it emerged at all is remarkable because legal inequality between rich and poor in the free population was the rule in the ancient Near East and in Greece itself before the emergence of the *polis*. Given the lack of precedent, how and why the poor in Greece gained citizenship and equality before the law remains a mystery. The greatest population increase in the late Dark Age and in the Archaic Age occurred in the ranks of the poor. These families raised more children to help farm more land, which otherwise would have lain idle because of the depopulation brought on by the worst of the Dark Age. (See "Taking Measure," page 42.) There was no precedent for extending even limited political and legal rights to this growing segment of the population, but the Greek city-state did so.

For a long time, historians attributed the general widening of political rights to a so-called hoplite revolution, but recent research undermines this theory.

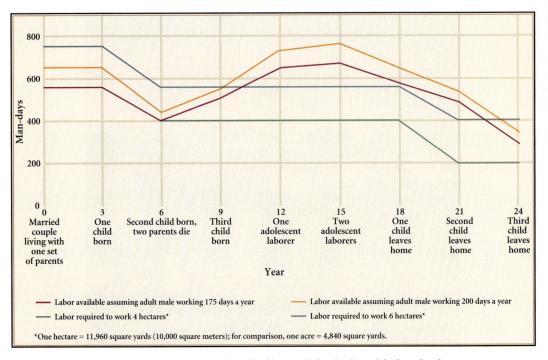

■ TAKING MEASURE Greek Family Size and Agricultural Labor in the Archaic Age

Modern demographers have calculated the changing relationship in the Archaic Age between a farm family's productive capacity to work the land and the number of people in the family over time. The graph makes it obvious why healthy teenage children were so valuable to the family's well-being. A family that had two adolescent laborers available could farm more than 50 percent more land, increasing its productivity significantly and thus making life more prosperous.

(Adapted from Thomas W. Gallant, *Risk and Survival in Ancient Greece: Reconstructing the Rural Domestic Economy* [1991], fig. 4.10. Reprinted with the permission of Stanford University Press.)

Hoplites were infantrymen who wore metal body armor, carried a metal shield in one hand, and wielded a spear with the other. They constituted the main strike force of the volunteer militia that defended each city-state. In the eighth century B.C., a growing number of men could afford to buy hoplite equipment (the use of iron had cut its cost). It seems likely that the new hoplites believed they were entitled to political rights because they bought their own equipment and voluntarily trained hard to defend their community. According to the hoplite revolution theory, the new hoplites forced the social elite to share political power by threatening to refuse to serve in the militia. The problem with that theory is that hoplites were not poor. How, then, did poor men, too, win political rights, especially the vote in the assembly? The answer is unknown. Perhaps poor men earned respect and political rights by fighting as lightly armed skirmishers, disrupting the enemy's infantry by hurling barrages of rocks. Whatever the reason for the designation of poor men as citizens with roughly the same rights as the rich, this unprecedented decision constituted the most innovative feature of Greek society in the Archaic Age.

The inclusiveness of the Greek city-state did not extend to slaves. Indeed, the more prominent the notion of freedom, the more common it became to distinguish it from unfreedom, and the practice of slavery became ever more widespread in Archaic Age Greece. Individual Greeks and the city-states themselves owned slaves. Public slaves sometimes lived on their own, performing specialized tasks such as detecting counterfeit coins. Temple slaves "belonged" to the deity of the temple, for whom they worked as servants. Private slaves totaled perhaps a third of the population by the fifth century B.C. They did all sorts of jobs, from household chores to crafts production to farm labor. Their masters controlled their lives and could punish them or demand sexual favors at will. Most owners did not brutalize their slaves because doing so would have damaged their human property. Lacking any right to family life and having no property or legal rights, slaves were completely alienated from *polis* society. As Aristotle later put it, slaves were "living tools." Sometimes owners let slaves earn money to purchase their freedom, or promised freedom at a future date to encourage hard work. Slaves who gained their freedom did not become citizens but instead mixed into the population of noncitizens (*metics*) officially allowed to live in the city-state. Despite the bitter nature of their lives, Greek slaves rarely revolted on a large scale except in Sparta, perhaps because elsewhere they were of too many different origins and nationalities to organize. No Greek is known to have called for the abolition of slavery.

Women, like slaves, lacked the right of political participation in the city-state. Women, however, did count as citizens, enjoyed the protection of the laws, and played a central role in religion. Citizen women had recourse to the courts in disputes over property, although they usually had to have a man speak for them. Before marriage, a woman's father served as her legal guardian; after marriage, her husband assumed the same role. The paternalism of Greek society—men acted as "fathers" to regulate the lives of women and safeguard their interests as men defined them—demanded that all women have male guardians to protect them physically and legally.

The expansion of slavery increased the size of households and added new responsibilities for women. While their husbands farmed, participated in politics, and met with their male friends, well-off wives managed the household: raising children, supervising the preservation and preparation of food, keeping the family's financial accounts, making cloth and clothing, directing the work of the slaves, and tending slaves and family members when they were ill. Poor women worked outside the home, hoeing and reaping in the fields and selling produce and small goods such as ribbons and trinkets in the market at the center of every settlement. Women

■ **A Greek Woman at an Altar**

This vase painting from the center of a large drinking cup shows a woman in rich clothing pouring a libation to the gods onto a flaming altar. In her other arm, she carries a religious object that we cannot identify with certainty. This scene illustrates the most important and frequent role of women in Greek public life: participating in religious ceremonies, both at home and in community festivals. This painting style is called "red figure" because the picture's details are painted over the reddish color of the baked clay, which shows through to depict the surfaces of the figures, such as skin or clothing.
(The Toledo Museum of Art, Toledo, Ohio. Purchased with funds from the Libbey Endowment, Gift of Edward Drummond Libbey.)

rich and poor attended funerals, state festivals, and public rituals, and they controlled cults reserved exclusively for them. Their religious functions gave them freedom of movement and prestige. At Athens, for example, by the fifth century B.C. they officiated as priestesses for more than forty different deities and enjoyed benefits such as salaries paid by the state.

The overriding paternalism of the Greek city-state allowed men to control human reproduction and consequently the distribution of property. Families arranged marriages, and everyone was expected to marry and produce children. The bride brought to the marriage a dowry of property (perhaps land yielding an income, if she was wealthy) that her children would inherit. Her husband was legally obligated to preserve this dowry and to return it to the woman in case of a divorce. A husband could expel his wife from his home. In theory, a wife could leave her husband on her own initiative to return to the guardianship of her male relatives, but in reality her husband could force her to stay. Except in certain cases in Sparta, monogamy was the rule, as was a nuclear family (that is, husband, wife, and children living together without other relatives in the same house). Citizen men could have sexual relations without penalty with slaves, foreign concubines, female prostitutes, or willing preadult citizen males. Citizen women, single or married, had no such freedom. Sex between a wife and anyone other than her husband carried harsh penalties for both parties.

Sparta differed from other city-states because it ranked every other value second to military readiness. Citizens of Sparta were required to place obedience to the state before personal concerns because their state's survival was threatened by their society's economic foundation: the great mass of slaves called *helots*, who were owned by the community and did almost all the work. Helots were Greeks from neighboring towns and regions that the Spartans had conquered, especially the fertile plain of Messenia, to the west, which Sparta overran by about 700 B.C. The helots outnumbered the citizen population. They toiled as farmers and servants so that Spartans would not have to stoop to ordinary tasks. Spartan men wore their hair very long to show that they were "gentlemen," not laborers.

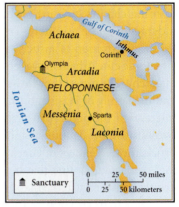

Sparta and the Peloponnese, c. 750–500 B.C.

The helots faced constant humiliation and the threat of violence. Every year Spartan officials formally declared war on them so that a citizen could kill without penalty any helot thought to be disobedient or dangerous. To control the helots and intimidate other city-states, Spartans devoted their lives to communal preparation for war. Boys left home at age seven to live in barracks, drilling and eating together to learn discipline. Any youth unable to handle the harsh training fell into disgrace and lost citizen rights.

Adolescent boys often were involved in homosexual relationships. A boy would be chosen as a special favorite by an older male to build bonds of affection, often including sexual relations, for a fellow soldier at whose side he would one day march into battle. The elder partner was supposed to help educate the young man in politics and community values and not just exploit him for physical pleasure. Both were expected to marry. Homoerotic sex between adult males was considered disgraceful, as it was between women of all ages.

Spartan women were known throughout the Greek world for their relative liberty. They could own property, including land. Women were expected to use their freedom from farm labor, provided by the helot system, to keep themselves physically fit so they could bear healthy children to sustain the Spartan population. Women also were expected to teach their children Spartan values. One mother became legendary for handing her son his shield on the eve of battle and admonishing him, "Come back with it or on it."

Athens stood in stark contrast with Sparta. During the Archaic Age, it took the first steps toward democracy and a much freer way of life. In 594 B.C., an economic crisis that pitted rich against poor unexpectedly promoted this development when Solon, appointed as a mediator, outlawed debt slavery and created a council to guide the legislative work of the assembly. The council's four hundred members were chosen by lottery and could serve only two annual terms (not in succession), ensuring wide participation. Equally important was Solon's decision to empower any citizen to bring charges in court on behalf of any victim and to appeal any magistrate's judgments to the assembly. These measures gave ordinary citizens a real share in the administration of justice.

Some elite Athenians vehemently opposed Solon's reforms because they wanted oligarchy. The unrest they caused opened the door temporarily to tyranny at Athens, and the family of Peisistratus held power from 546 to 510 B.C. by championing the interests of the poor. A rival elite family, the Alcmaeonids, finally got the tyranny overthrown by denouncing it as unjust and inducing the Spartans, the self-proclaimed defenders of Greek freedom, to "liberate" Athens. Cleisthenes, the leading Alcmaeonid, found that he could become a political success only by promising greater democracy to the masses. Beginning in 508 B.C., he delivered on his promises and came to be remembered as the "father of Athenian democracy" for his reforms. His complex political reorganization achieved its goal of promoting participation in governance by as many male citizens as possible. He expanded Solon's council to five hundred members. It would take another fifty years of controversy before Athens's democracy reached its fullest form, but Cleisthenes' changes paved the road for the success of this unprecedented way of life based on people persuading, not compelling, each other to achieve common goals.

New Ways of Thought and Expression

The idea that persuasion, rather than force or social status, should propel political decision making fit well with the spirit of intellectual change rippling through Greece in the late Archaic Age. In city-states all over the Greek world, new ways of thought were inspiring artists, poets, and philosophers. Ongoing contacts with the Near East exposed the Greeks to new traditions to learn from and, in some cases, to alter dramatically. Artists became expert at rendering fully three-dimensional figures—whether goddesses, warriors, or monsters from myth—in an increasingly realistic style. Sculptors made their statues less stiff and more varied, from gracefully clothed young women to muscular male nudes, and made them come alive with gleaming paint.

Poets expanded the Near Eastern tradition of using poetry to express personal emotions by devising the *lyric*, a new type of verse that developed from popular song. Enlivened by rhythmic diversity and performed to the accompaniment of a lyre (a kind of harp that gives its name to the poetry), Greek lyric poems could

■ Vase Painting of a Music Lesson

This sixth-century B.C. red-figure vase shows a young man (seated on the left, without a beard) holding a lyre and watching an older, bearded man also play a lyre while an adolescent boy and an older man listen. The youth is evidently a pupil learning to play. Instruction in performing music and singing lyric poetry was considered an essential part of the education of an upper-class Greek male. The soundboard of the teacher's lyre is made from a turtle shell, as was customary. (Staatliche Antikensammlungen und Glypothek.)

be short monologues or extended choral songs. Sappho, a lyric poet from Lesbos born about 630 B.C., became renowned for her poems on love, writing, "Some would say the most beautiful thing on our dark earth is an army of cavalry, others of infantry, others of ships, but I say it's whatever a person loves." In this poem Sappho was expressing her longing for a woman she loved, who was far away.

Archilochus of Paros, who probably lived in the early seventh century B.C., became infamous for his unheroic lines about throwing down his shield in battle so he could run away to save his life: "Oh, the hell with it; I can get another one just as good."◆

In this same period, Greek philosophers developed radically new explanations of the human world and its relation to the gods. Most of these thinkers came from Ionia. This location placed them in close contact with Near Eastern knowledge, especially astronomy, mathematics, and myth. Because there were no formal schools, pupils who studied privately with these philosophers helped spread the new ideas. Inspired by

Ionia and the Aegean, c. 750–500 B.C.

◆ For more examples of Greek lyric poetry, see Document 4, Sappho of Lesbos, "Poems."

Babylonian astronomy, Ionian Greek philosophers such as Thales (c. 625–545 B.C.) and Anaximander (c. 610–540 B.C.) of Miletus expressed the boldly novel view that the universe was regulated by a set of laws of nature rather than by the arbitrary intervention of divine beings. Pythagoras, who emigrated from the island of Samos to the Greek city-state Croton in southern Italy about 530 B.C., taught that patterns and relationships of numbers explained the entire world and began the systematic study of mathematics and the numerical aspects of musical harmony.

Ionian philosophers insisted that the workings of the universe could be discovered because natural phenomena were neither random nor arbitrary. They named the universe *cosmos,* meaning an orderly arrangement that is beautiful. The order of the cosmos encompassed not only the motions of heavenly bodies but also the weather, the growth of plants and animals, human health and well-being, and so on. Because the universe was ordered, it was intelligible; because it was intelligible, events could be explained by thought and research. They therefore looked for the first or universal cause of things, a problem that scientists still pursue. The philosophers who deduced this view of the cosmos believed they needed to give reasons for their conclusions and to persuade others by arguments based on evidence. They believed, in other words, in *logic.* This mode of thought, called *rationalism,* represented a crucial first step toward science and philosophy as these disciplines endure today. The rule-based view of the causes of events and physical phenomena developed by these philosophers contrasted sharply with the traditional mythological view of causation. Naturally, many people had difficulty accepting such a startling change in their understanding of the world, and the older tradition explaining events as the work of deities lived on alongside the new approach.

The idea that people must give reasons to explain their beliefs, rather than just make assertions that others must believe without evidence, was the Ionian philosophers' most important achievement. This insistence on rationality, coupled with the belief that the world could be understood as something other than the plaything of divine whims, gave people hope that they could improve their lives through their own efforts. As Xenophanes from Colophon (c. 580–480 B.C.) put it, "The gods have not revealed all things from the beginning to mortals, but, by seeking, human beings find out, in time, what is better." This saying well expressed the value Archaic Age Greek philosophers attached to intellectual freedom, corresponding to the value given to political freedom in the city-state, unequally distributed though it may have been.

Conclusion

Fundamental characteristics of Western civilization slowly emerged in the lengthy period from the Stone Age to 1000 B.C. The Neolithic Revolution transformed human life into a settled existence, culminating in cities arising in Mesopotamia by

IMPORTANT DATES

c. 400,000 B.C.	*Homo sapiens*, the immediate ancestors of modern human beings, appear in Africa	c. 1250 B.C.	Exodus of Hebrews from Egypt
c. 10,000–8000 B.C.	Development of agriculture and domestication of animals	c. 1200–1000 B.C.	The Near East's Dark Age; disturbances across the eastern Mediterranean region end many kingdoms
c. 4000–1000 B.C.	Bronze Age in southwestern Asia, Egypt, and Europe	c. 1000–750 B.C.	Greece's Dark Age
c. 4000–3000 B.C.	First cities established and writing developed in Mesopotamia	c. 900 B.C.	Neo-Assyrians create an empire
c. 3000 B.C.	The wheel invented in Sumer	776 B.C.	Traditional date of first Olympic Games in Greece
c. 2686–2181 B.C.	Old Kingdom in Egypt	c. 775–500 B.C.	Greeks establish many new settlements around the Mediterranean
c. 2350 B.C.	Sargon establishes the first empire in Akkadia in Mesopotamia	c. 750 B.C.	Greeks begin to create city-states
c. 2200 B.C.	Earliest Minoan palaces on Crete	605–562 B.C.	Nebuchadnezzar II creates the Neo-Babylonian Empire and exiles most Hebrews to Babylon
c. 2050–1786 B.C.	Middle Kingdom in Egypt	594 B.C.	Athenians appoint Solon to recodify their laws to try to end social unrest
c. 1792–1750 B.C.	Reign of Hammurabi, king of Babylon, in Mesopotamia	559 B.C.	Cyrus founds the Persian Empire
c. 1750 B.C.	Beginning of Hittite kingdom in Anatolia	539 B.C.	Cyrus allows exiled Hebrews to return from Babylon to Palestine
c. 1600–1400 B.C.	Hebrews migrate into Egypt	508 B.C.	Cleisthenes begins to reform Athenian democracy
c. 1567–1085 B.C.	New Kingdom in Egypt		
c. 1400 B.C.	Earliest Mycenaean palaces in Greece; Mycenaeans take over Minoan Crete		

4000 to 3000 B.C. Trade and war were pervasive, generating constant cultural interaction. The development of metallurgy, monumental architecture, mathematics, and alphabetic writing in the eastern Mediterranean region during the Bronze Age profoundly affected later ages.

After the devastation wrought by the Sea Peoples (1200–1000 B.C.), the traditional pattern of empire under a strong central authority was revived in the Near East. The Neo-Assyrians, then the Neo-Babylonians, and then the Persians

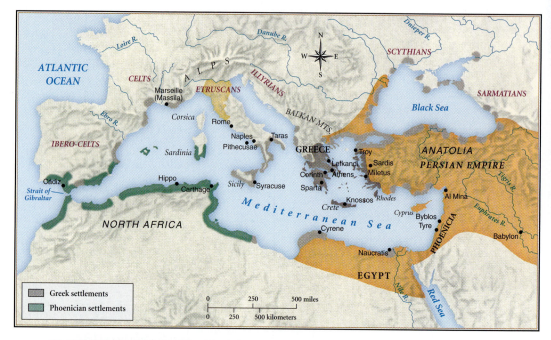

▪ **MAPPING THE WEST** Mediterranean Civilizations, c. 500 B.C.

At the end of the sixth century B.C., the Persian Empire was far and away the most powerful civilization touching the Mediterranean. Its vast territory and riches gave it resources that no Phoenician or Greek city could match. The Phoenicians dominated economically in the western Mediterranean, while the Greek city-states in Sicily and southern Italy rivaled the power of those in the heartland. In Italy, the Etruscans were the most powerful civilization; the Romans were still a small community struggling to replace monarchy with a republic.

succeeded one another as rulers of enormous territories. The moral dualism of Persian Zoroastrianism influenced later religions, most importantly Hebrew monotheism, whose expression in the Torah created the first religion based on scripture.

The destruction of the Mycenaean palaces about 1000 B.C. opened the way to remaking Greek civilization. Recovering from economic and population decline, Greeks invented the *polis* (city-state) as a new form of social and political organization based on the notions of citizenship and equal protection of the laws as essential components of justice. The Greek city-state treasured the notion of personal freedom for men, but only in limited ways for women and not at all for slaves. Equally revolutionary were new ways of thought. By arguing that the universe was based on laws of nature that humans could discover through reason and research, Greek philosophers established rationalism as the conceptual basis for science and philosophy.

Thus it was in Archaic Age Greece that ideals with a lasting significance for Western civilization began to emerge. But the Greek world and its new values would soon face a grave threat from the awesome empire of Persia.

Suggested References for further reading and online research appear on page SR-1 at the back of the book.

www.bedfordstmartins.com/huntconcise   See the ONLINE STUDY GUIDE to assess your mastery of the material covered in this chapter.

The Greek Golden Age

c. 500–400 B.C.

A DIPLOMATIC FIASCO set in motion the gravest danger ever to threaten ancient Greece. In 507 B.C., the Athenians sent ambassadors to the Persian king, Darius I (r. 522–486 B.C.), to request a protective alliance against the Spartans. The Persian Empire was then the greatest power in the ancient world. The diplomats met with one of the king's governors at Sardis, the Persian regional headquarters in western Anatolia (modern Turkey). After the royal administrator heard their plea, he reportedly replied, "But who in the world are you and where do you live?"

This incident reveals the background to the conflicts that would dominate the military and political history of mainland Greece during the fifth century B.C. First, the two major powers in mainland Greece—Athens and Sparta—distrusted each other. Second, the Persian kingdom had taken over Ionia (today western Turkey), including the Greek city-states there. Yet neither the Persians nor the mainland Greeks knew much about each other. Their mutual ignorance sparked explosive wars.

Although the fifth century B.C. saw almost continuous warfare, first between Greeks and Persians and then between Greek city-states themselves, it also was the period of Greece's most enduring cultural and artistic achievements. Athenian accomplishments of the fifth century B.C. had such a profound impact that historians call this period a Golden Age. This Golden Age opens the Classical Age of Greek history, a modern designation that covers the period from about 500 B.C. to the death of Alexander the Great in 323 B.C.

■ **The Sculptural Style of the Greek Golden Age**
This sculpture of a male nude was cast in bronze in the fifth century B.C.; bronze was preferred over marble for top-rank statues. The relaxed pose displays the asymmetry—the head looking to one side, the arms in different positions, the torso tilted—that made statues from the Classical period appear less stiff than those of the Archaic period. The lifelike body, however, displays an idealized physique. Complete bronze statues rarely survived because they usually were melted down for their metal in the medieval and early modern periods. (Erich Lessing/Art Resource, NY.)

Despite the pressures of war, Athenians in the Golden Age created Greece's pre-eminent society, developing their fullest democracy at home while establishing an empire abroad. They generated enormous prosperity and world-famous artistic and cultural accomplishments. More than any other city-state, Golden Age Athens was home to innovations in drama, art, architecture, and thought that have had a lasting influence on Western civilization. Some of these changes created tensions, however, because they conflicted with ancient traditions, especially people's religious fear that abandoning ancestral beliefs and practices would offend the gods and bring disaster.

The Peloponnesian War, a protracted struggle between Athens and Sparta that dragged on from 431 to 404 B.C., ended the Golden Age in the closing decades of the fifth century B.C. This period of cultural blossoming therefore both began and finished with destructive wars, with Greeks standing together in the first one and tearing each other apart in the concluding one.

Clash between Persia and Greece, 499–479 B.C.

The most famous series of wars in ancient Greek history had its roots in the Athenian-Persian meeting at Sardis in 507 B.C. There the Athenian ambassadors acceded to the customary Persian terms for an alliance: acknowledging Persian superiority by presenting symbolic tokens of earth and water to the king's representative. Although the Athenian assembly expressed outrage when they learned that their diplomats had submitted to a foreign power, they never explicitly rejected the alliance. King Darius therefore believed that Athens had become an obedient ally. This misunderstanding initiated a chain of events culminating in two invasions of Greece by Persia's enormous military. The Persian kingdom outstripped Greece in every category of material resources, from precious metals to soldiers. The clash between Persia and Greece pitted the equivalent of an elephant against a small swarm of mosquitoes. Greek victory in such a mismatch seemed unthinkable. It even seemed improbable—given the city-states' proclivity for quarreling—that they could work together to resist the threat.

The Ionian Revolt and the Battle of Marathon, 499–490 B.C.

Hostilities commenced in 499 B.C. with a revolt of the Ionian Greek city-states against their Persian-installed tyrants. Athenian troops dispatched to aid the rebels burned Sardis, but a Persian counterattack sent them fleeing and crushed the revolt by 494 B.C. (Map 2.1).

King Darius erupted when he learned that the Athenians had aided the Ionian revolt: not only had they dared attack his kingdom, but they had done it after, as

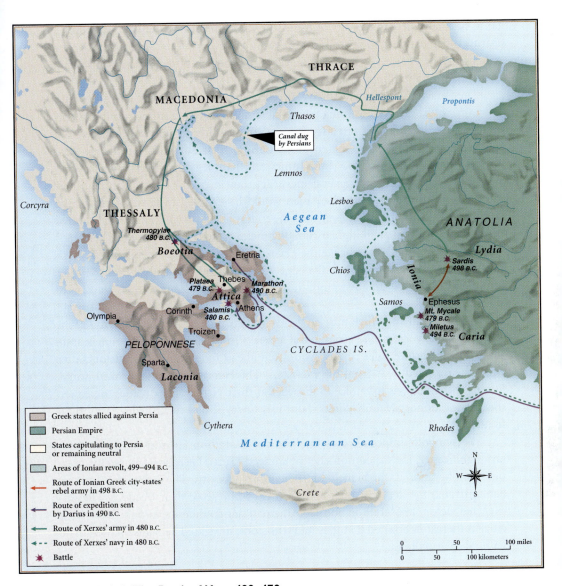

THRACE

MACEDONIA

Hellespont

Propontis

Thasos

Canal dug by Persians

Lemnos

Corcyra

THESSALY

Thermopylae 480 B.C.

Boeotia

Eretria

Plataea 479 B.C.

Thebes

Marathon 490 B.C.

Attica

Corinth

Salamis 480 B.C.

Athens

Olympia

Troizen

PELOPONNESE

Sparta

Laconia

Aegean Sea

Lesbos

Chios

Samos

CYCLADES IS.

ANATOLIA

Lydia

Sardis 498 B.C.

Ionia

Ephesus

Mt. Mycale 479 B.C.

Miletus 494 B.C.

Caria

Cythera

Mediterranean Sea

Rhodes

Crete

Legend:

- ☐ Greek states allied against Persia
- ☐ Persian Empire
- ☐ States capitulating to Persia or remaining neutral
- ☐ Areas of Ionian revolt, 499–494 B.C.
- → Route of Ionian Greek city-states' rebel army in 498 B.C.
- → Route of expedition sent by Darius in 490 B.C.
- → Route of Xerxes' army in 480 B.C.
- ◄- - Route of Xerxes' navy in 480 B.C.
- ✸ Battle

N / S / E / W compass

0   50   100 miles
0   50   100 kilometers

■ **MAP 2.1 The Persian Wars, 499–479 B.C.**

Following the example of the founder of the Persian kingdom, Cyrus the Great (d. 530 B.C.), Cambyses (r. 530–522 B.C.) and Darius (r. 522–486 B.C.) energetically worked to expand their empire eastward and westward. Darius invaded Thrace more than fifteen years before the conflict against the Greeks known as the Persian Wars. The Persians' unexpected defeat in Greece put an end to their attempt to extend their power into Europe.

www.bedfordstmartins.com/huntconcise   See the ONLINE STUDY GUIDE for more help in analyzing this map.

far as he knew, pledging loyalty to him. To remind himself to punish this betrayal, Darius ordered a slave to say to him three times at every meal, "Sire, remember the Athenians." In 490 B.C., he launched a fleet with orders to punish them by installing their exiled tyrant, Hippias, as his puppet.

The Persians anticipated Athens surrendering without a fight. The Athenians, however, confronted the seemingly invincible invaders at Marathon, on the northeastern coast of Athenian territory. The Athenian soldiers, who had never before seen Persians, grew anxious merely at the sight of their outlandish (to Greek eyes) outfits—pants instead of the short tunics and bare legs that Greeks regarded as manly dress. The Athenian generals never let their men lose heart. Planning their tactics to minimize the time their men would be exposed to Persian arrows, the commanders sent their hoplites against the enemy at a dead run. The Greeks dashed across the Marathon plain in their clanking metal armor (seventy pounds per man) under a hail of missiles to engage the Persians in hand-to-hand combat. The hoplites' heavier weapons gave them the edge. After a furious struggle, they drove their opponents backward into a swamp; those who failed to escape to their ships were slaughtered.

The Athenian army then hurried the twenty-six miles from Marathon to Athens to guard the city against a Persian naval attack. (Today's marathons commemorate the legendary exploit of a runner who raced ahead to announce the victory, after which he dropped dead from the exertion.) The Persians thereupon sailed home, leaving the Athenians to rejoice in disbelief at their victory. For decades thereafter, the greatest honor a family could claim was to say it had furnished a "Marathon fighter."

The symbolic importance of the battle of Marathon far outweighed its military significance. His expedition's defeat enraged Darius because it injured his prestige, not because it threatened his kingdom's security. The Athenians' success demonstrated the depth of their commitment to preserve their freedom. The unexpected victory at Marathon boosted Athenian self-confidence, and the city-state's citizens thereafter boasted that they had withstood the feared Persians on their own, without Sparta's help.

The Great Invasion of 480–479 B.C.

The Marathon victory spurred Greeks to find the will to resist the gigantic Persian invasion of Greece in 480 B.C., led by Darius's son Xerxes I (r. 486–465 B.C.). So immense was his army, the Greeks claimed, that it required seven days and seven nights of continuous marching to cross a pontoon bridge over the Hellespont strait, the narrow passage of sea between Anatolia and mainland Greece. Xerxes expected the Greek city-states to surrender immediately once they learned the size of his forces. Some did, but thirty-one city-states allied to fight the Persians. This coalition, known as the Hellenic League, accomplished the incredible: protecting their independence from the world's strongest power. They succeeded without the aid of the city-states in Italy and Sicily, such as Syracuse, the powerful ruler of a regional empire. Those western Greeks declined to join the league because they were occupied fighting Carthage, a Phoenician settlement in North Africa that was aggressively trying to monopolize commerce in the west.

The Greek coalition chose Sparta as its leader because of its renowned hoplite army. The Spartans demonstrated their courage when three hundred of their men held off Xerxes' huge army for several days at the narrow pass called Thermopylae ("warm gates") in central Greece. A hoplite summed up the Spartans' bravery with his reputed response to the observation that the Persian archers were so numerous that their arrows darkened the sky in battle. "That's good news," said the Spartan warrior. "We'll fight in the shade." They all died fighting.

When the Persians marched south, the Athenians evacuated their population instead of surrendering. They believed their city-state and its freedom would survive so long as its people survived, regardless of what happened to their property. The Persians promptly burned the empty city. In the summer of 480 B.C., Themistocles of Athens maneuvered the other, less aggressive Greek leaders into facing the larger Persian navy in a sea battle in the narrow channel between the island of Salamis and the west coast of Athenian territory. The narrowness of the channel prevented the Persians from using all their ships at once and let the heavier Greek ships win victory by ramming the flimsier Persian craft. When Xerxes observed that the most energetic of his naval commanders appeared to be the one woman among them, Artemisia, ruler of Caria (the southwest corner of Anatolia), he remarked, "My men have become women, and my women, men." In 479 B.C., the Greek infantry headed by the Spartans defeated the remaining Persian land forces at Plataea (see Map 2.1).

■ **Leonidas, Hero of the Battle of Thermopylae**

One of the two kings of Sparta at the time, Leonidas in 480 B.C. led the small force of Spartans and other Greeks sent to block the advance of the Persian army at the narrow pass of Thermopylae in central Greece. According to the Greek historian Herodotus, a contemporary of the Persian Wars, this heroic action was meant to inspire wavering Greek city-states to remain in the Hellenic alliance against Persia. The defenders fell and were buried where they fought, inspiring the lines of poetry inscribed over the graves of Leonidas's men:

> *Go tell the Spartans, you strangers who pass by,*
> *That here obeying their orders we lie.*

(Deutsches Archaeologisches Institut—Athens.)

The Greeks' superior weapons and resourceful use of Greece's topography to counterbalance the Persians' greater numbers help explain their military victories. But most remarkable is the decision of the thirty-one Greek city-states to unite in a coalition. They could easily have agreed to become Persian subjects to save themselves; for most of them, Persian rule would have meant only minimal interference in their internal affairs. Instead, they chose to fight for absolute independence against seemingly overwhelming odds. Because the Greek forces included not only the social elite and hoplites but also thousands of poorer men who rowed the warships, the effort against the Persians cut across social and economic divisions. The Hellenic League's decision to fight the Persian Wars demonstrated both courage and a commitment to the ideal of political freedom that had emerged in the Archaic Age.

Athenian Confidence in the Golden Age, 479–431 B.C.

Victory undid the alliance that the Persian threat had forged between Sparta and Athens. Out of this fractured partnership arose the so-called Athenian Empire, a modern label to describe the Athenians' new vision of grander international power that emerged following the Persian Wars. The growth of Athens's power internationally went hand in hand with more democracy and vast spending on public buildings, art, and festivals.

The Establishment of the Athenian Empire, 479–c. 460 B.C.

After the Persian Wars, Sparta and Athens both built up their own alliances to strengthen their positions against each other. Relying on long-standing treaties with city-states located mainly in the Peloponnese, Sparta headed forces stronger in infantry than in warships, with the notable exception of Corinth, a naval power. The Spartan allies, called the Peloponnesian League, met in a representative assembly, but no action could be taken unless the Spartan leaders approved.

By 477 B.C., under the leadership of the Athenian aristocrat Aristides (c. 525–465 B.C.), Athens allied with city-states exposed to possible Persian retaliation—in northern Greece, on the islands of the Aegean Sea, and along the western coast of Anatolia. Most Athenian allies had strong navies, and all solemnly swore never to desert the coalition. This alliance, called the Delian League because its treasury was originally located on the island of Delos, also had an assembly. Theoretically, every ally had an equal say in making decisions, but in practice Athens was in charge.

The special arrangements for financing the alliance's naval operations allowed the Athenians to dominate. Each ally paid annual "dues" based on its size and pros-

perity. Because compulsory, these dues were actually "tribute." Larger member states supplied
entire triremes (warships) complete with crews
and their pay; smaller states could share the cost
of a ship and crew or contribute cash instead.

**The Delian and
Peloponnesian Leagues**

Over time, more and more members paid
cash. It proved beyond their capacities to build
warships and to train crews (170 rowers each);
the recent reconstruction of a full-size trireme
has shown how difficult it was to build one and
train an effective crew. Athens, far larger than
most league members, possessed the necessary
shipyards, as well as many men eager to earn pay
as rowers. Many oarsmen came from Athens's
poor, and they earned not only money but also
political influence in Athenian democracy as naval strength became the city-state's
principal source of military power. Without them, Athens had no navy.

The decision of many Delian League allies to let Athens supply warships eventually left them without any navies of their own. Therefore, they had no power if
they disagreed with Athens's policy. The Athenian assembly could simply order its
fleet to compel discontented allies to comply and continue paying their tribute. As
the Athenian historian Thucydides observed, rebellious allies "lost their independence," and the Athenians became "no longer as popular as they used to be." This
unpopularity was the price Athenians paid for making themselves the preeminent
naval power in the eastern Mediterranean. They insisted that their dominance of
the Delian League was justified because it kept the alliance strong enough to protect Greece from the Persians.

By about 460 B.C., their fleet had expelled almost all the Persian garrisons that
had held out along the northeastern Aegean coast. The alliance drove the enemy
fleet from the Aegean Sea, quashing any Persian threat to Greece for the next fifty
years. Athens meanwhile grew rich off spoils captured from Persian outposts and
the league's tribute.

The Athenian assembly decided how to spend this revenue. Rich and poor alike
had a stake in keeping the fleet active and the league members paying for it. The
poor men who rowed the ships came to depend on the pay they earned on league
expeditions. Members of the social elite enhanced their social status by commanding
campaigns and spending their portion of the booty on public festivals and buildings.
Wealthy Athenians were expected to make financial contributions to the common
good to win popular support. They did not form political parties but gathered informal circles of friends and followers to support their agendas. Arguments about
policy tended to revolve around how Athens should exercise its growing power
internationally, not whether it was right to treat allies as subjects.

■ **A Modern Reconstruction of a Greek Warship**
This full-scale reconstruction of an ancient trireme (the largest warship of the Classical period, with three banks of oars on each side) has been commissioned in today's Royal Greek Navy. Attached to the bow of each ship and projecting just below the water line was a bronze ram for puncturing enemy vessels. Sea trials with volunteer rowers indicate that ancient oarsmen must have had very high levels of aerobic fitness and muscular strength to propel a trireme forward at full ramming speed, more than nine knots. (Trireme Trust.)

Radical Democracy and Pericles' Leadership, 461–445 B.C.

As the Delian League grew, the poorer men who powered the Athenian fleet came to recognize that they provided a cornerstone of Athenian security and prosperity. They felt the time had come to increase their political power by making the judicial system of Athens just as democratic as the process of passing laws in the assembly, which was open to all male citizens over eighteen years of age. The leaders of this initiative were members of the elite, who competed for popular support to win elective office. One of Athens's most socially prominent citizens, Pericles (c. 495–429 B.C.), became the leading Golden Age politician by supporting the masses' desire for greater democracy.

Golden Age Athenian democracy gradually became so sweeping, compared with most ancient governments, that today it is called "radical." Its principles were clear: direct and widespread participation by male citizens in the assembly to make laws and policy by majority rule; random selection and rotation for members of the Council of 500, most magistrates, and jurors; elaborate precautions to prevent corruption; and equal protection under the law for citizens regardless of wealth. At the same time, excellence was recognized by making the top public offices—the board of ten "generals," who managed the city-state's military and financial affairs—elective annually and without limits on how many terms a man could serve.

Reforming the judicial system was essential to radical democracy. Ever since Cleisthenes' reforms, archons (magistrates) and the Areopagus Council of ex-archons had rendered most judicial verdicts. Although archons were now chosen annually by lottery to make their selection democratic, they and the Areopagus members were still susceptible to bribery and pressure from the social elite. Since even democratically enacted laws meant little if applied unfairly, the masses demanded reforms to halt corruption.

The opportunity for change arose in 461 B.C. when a prominent member of the elite, Ephialtes, sought the people's political support by sponsoring a reformed court system. Ephialtes' reforms made it nearly impossible to bribe or pressure jurors. They were selected by lottery from male citizens over thirty years old, the selection was made only on the day of the trial, all trials were concluded in one day, and juries were large (from several hundred to several thousand). No judges presided; only one official was present—to stop fistfights. Jurors voted after hearing speeches from the accuser and the accused, who had to speak for themselves although they might pay someone else to compose their speeches and ask others to speak in support. A majority vote of the jurors ruled, and no appeals were allowed.

Majority rule was the operative principle for enforcing accountability in Athenian radical democracy. Any citizen could call for a trial to judge an official's conduct in office, but the most striking example of this principle was the procedure called *ostracism* (from *ostracon*, meaning a "piece of broken pottery," the material used for casting ballots). Once a year, all male citizens could scratch on a ballot the name of one man they thought should be ostracized (exiled for ten years). If at least six thousand ballots were cast, the man who received the most "votes" was expelled from Athenian territory. He suffered no other penalty, and his family and property remained behind undisturbed. Ostracism was not a criminal penalty, and ostracized men recovered their citizen rights after their exile.

This process was meant to protect radical democracy, so a man could be ostracized if the majority perceived his prominence as a threat to their interests. An anecdote about the politician Aristides illustrates this possibility. He was nicknamed "the Just" because he had proved himself so fair-minded in setting the dues for Delian League members. On the day of the balloting, an illiterate farmer handed Aristides a pottery fragment and asked him to scratch the name of the man's choice for ostracism on it.

"Certainly," said Aristides. "Which name shall I write?"

"Aristides," replied the countryman.

"Very well," remarked Aristides as he proceeded to inscribe his own name. "But tell me, why do you want to ostracize Aristides? What has he done to you?"

"Oh, nothing. I don't even know him," sputtered the man. "I just can't stand hearing everybody refer to him as 'the Just.'"

True or not, this tale demonstrates that Athenians assumed that the right way to protect democracy was always to trust the majority vote of freeborn, adult male citizens, without any restrictions on a man's ability to decide what he thought was best for democracy. It also shows that men seeking political success in Athenian democracy had to be ready to pay the price that envy or scapegoating could exact.

Like his distant relative Cleisthenes before him, Pericles became the most influential Athenian politician of his era by devising innovations to strengthen the egalitarian tendencies of Athenian democracy. The Golden Age's most spellbinding public speaker, Pericles repeatedly persuaded the assembly to pass laws increasing its political power. In return, he gained such popularity that he was regularly elected as a general.

Pericles' most important democratic innovation was pay for service in public offices filled by lottery. This allowed poorer men to leave their regular work to serve in government. Early in the 450s b.c., he convinced the assembly to use state revenues to pay a daily stipend to men who served in the Council of 500, on juries, and in numerous other posts. The amount was approximately what an unskilled worker could earn in a day. The generals received no pay because the prestige of their position was considered its own reward.

In 451 b.c., Pericles strengthened citizen identity, which even the poor possessed under democracy, by sponsoring a law making citizenship more exclusive and enhancing the status of Athenian mothers. This law mandated that citizenship would be conferred only on children whose mother and father were both Athenian by birth. Thereafter, men avoided seeking wives outside the citizen body.

Finally, Pericles supported the interests of poorer men by recommending frequent naval campaigns against Spartan and Corinthian interests in Greece and against Persian control of Cyprus, Egypt, and the eastern Mediterranean. The assembly's confidence reached such a fever pitch that they voted to carry on as many as three different major expeditions simultaneously. The Athenians' ambitions at last outstripped their resources, however, and by 450 b.c. they had to pull back from the eastern Mediterranean and stop fighting the Peloponnesian League. In the winter of 446–445 b.c., Pericles engineered a peace treaty with Sparta designed to freeze the balance of power in Greece for thirty years and thus preserve Athenian control of the Delian League. Pericles dropped his aggressive foreign policy because he realized that preserving radical democracy at home depended on Athens not losing its power over its allies.

The Urban Landscape of Golden Age Athens

The Delian League's fleet protected seaborne trade, and Athens became a flourishing commercial center for cargo, merchants, and crafts producers from around the Mediterranean world. The city's new riches flowed mainly into public building projects, art, and festivals rather than private luxury. People's homes in the city and the countryside remained modest. Farmhouses usually clustered in villages, while homes in the city wedged higgledy-piggledy against one another along narrow, winding streets. All residences grouped bedrooms, storerooms, and dining rooms around small, open-air courtyards. Wall paintings or art works were not yet common as decorations, and sparse furnishings were the rule. Sanitary facilities usually consisted of a pit dug outside the front door, which was emptied by collectors paid to dump the contents outside the city at a distance set by law. Poorer people rented small apartments.

Generals who won enormous booty leading Delian League forces against Persian outposts in the eastern Mediterranean used this wealth to beautify the city, not to build themselves mansions. In this way, Athens acquired landscaping with shade trees, running tracks for exercise, and gathering places such as the renowned Painted Stoa. A *stoa* was a narrow building open along one side whose purpose was to provide shelter from sun or rain. One successful general's family built the Painted Stoa in the heart of the city, on the edge of the central market square, the *agora*. The crowds who came to the agora daily to shop and chat about politics would cluster inside this shelter. There they could gaze on its bright paintings, which depicted the glorious exploits of the general's family and thus publicized its dedication to the city-state. Wealthy citizens also paid for other major public expenses, such as equipment for warships and entertainment at city festivals. This custom was essential because Athens, like most Greek city-states, had no regular direct taxes on income or property.

Huge buildings paid for by public funds constituted the most conspicuous new architecture in Golden Age Athens (Map 2.2). In 447 B.C., Pericles instigated the city's greatest building project ever, on the rocky hill at the center of the city called the *acropolis*. The project's centerpieces were a mammoth gate building with columns straddling the western entrance of the acropolis and a new temple of Athena housing a huge statue of the goddess. Comparing the value of a day's wage then and now, we can calculate that these buildings easily cost more than the modern equivalent of a billion dollars, a phenomenal sum for a Greek city-state. Pericles' political rivals railed at him for squandering public funds. Scholars disagree about whether the assembly used Delian League dues to help finance the program; it is certain that substantial funds were taken from sales taxes, harbor taxes, and the financial reserves of the sanctuaries of the goddess Athena, which derived from private donations and public support.

The vast new temple built for Athena—the Parthenon ("the house of the virgin goddess")—became Greece's most famous building. As the patron goddess of Athens, Athena had long had another sanctuary on the acropolis. Its focus was an

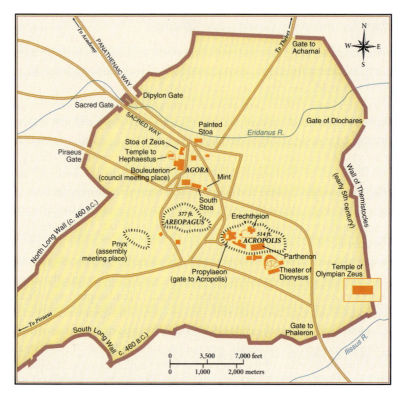

■ **MAP 2.2 Fifth-Century B.C. Athens**

The urban center of Athens with the agora and acropolis at its heart measured about one square mile, surrounded by a stone wall with a perimeter of some four miles. Fifteen large gates flanked by towers and various smaller doors allowed traffic in and out of the city; much of the Athenian population lived in the many villages (demes) of the surrounding countryside. Most of the city's water supply came from wells and springs inside the walls, but, unusually for a Greek city, Athens also had water piped in from outside. Most streets were narrow (no more than fifteen or twenty feet wide) and winding, with houses crowding in on both sides. Recent research suggests ruins of an Athena temple torched in the Persian invasion were left as a memorial between the Parthenon and the Erechtheion on the acropolis.

olive tree regarded as the goddess's sacred symbol as protector of the city-state's economic health. The Parthenon honored her in a different capacity: as the divine champion of Athenian military power. Inside the temple stood a gold and ivory statue nearly forty feet high depicting the goddess in battle armor, holding in her outstretched hand a six-foot statue of Victory (Nike in Greek).

Like all Greek temples, the Parthenon was meant as a house for its divinity, not as a gathering place for worshipers. Its design followed standard temple architecture: a rectangular box on a raised platform, a plan the Greeks probably derived from Egyptian temples. The box, which had only one small door at the front, was fenced in by columns all around. The Parthenon's columns were carved in the

■ The Acropolis of Athens

Like most Greek city-states, Athens grew up around a prominent hill (acropolis) whose summit served as a special sanctuary for the gods and as a fortress to which the population could retreat when an enemy attacked. The invading Persians burned the buildings on the Athenian acropolis in 480 B.C. The Athenians left the charred remains in place for thirty years to remind themselves of the sacrifice they had made for their freedom. In the 440s B.C., they began erecting the magnificent temples and other public buildings that have made the city famous for its monumental marble architecture. (Michael Freeman/Bruce Coleman, Ltd.)

simple style called Doric, in contrast to the more elaborate Ionic and Corinthian styles, often imitated in modern buildings (Figure 2.1). Only priests and priestesses could enter the temple usually; public religious ceremonies took place out front.

The Parthenon proclaimed the self-confidence of Golden Age Athens. Constructed from twenty thousand tons of Attic marble, it stretched nearly 230 feet in length and 100 feet wide, with eight columns across the ends instead of the six normally found in Doric style and seventeen instead of thirteen along the sides. Its massive size conveyed an impression of power. The temple's sophisticated architecture demonstrated Athenian ability to construct order that was both apparent and real: because perfectly rectilinear architecture appears curved to the human eye,

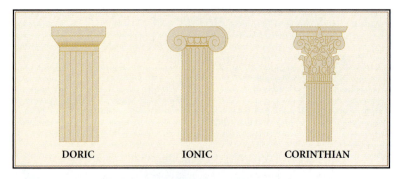

■ **FIGURE 2.1 Styles of Greek Capitals**
The capital is the top part of a column. The Greeks decorated capitals in these three styles to fit the different architectural "canons" (their word for precise mathematical systems of proportions) that they devised for designing buildings. The "pillow" atop Doric columns evolved into the Ionic style sporting "ears" (volutes). Corinthian capitals with their elaborately carved leaves were a later outgrowth of Ionic.

subtle curves and inclines were built into the Parthenon to produce an illusion of completely straight lines and emphasize its massiveness.

The elaborate sculptural frieze of the Parthenon announced the temple's most innovative and confident message: Athens's citizens possessed the special goodwill of the gods. The frieze, a continuous band of figures, was carved in relief around the top of the walls inside the porch along the edges of the building's platform. This sort of decoration usually appeared only on Ionic-style buildings. Adding it to a Doric-style temple was a striking departure meant to attract attention. The Parthenon's frieze portrayed Athenian men, women, and children in a parade in the presence of the gods. Depicting the procession in motion, like a filmstrip in stone, the frieze included youths riding spirited horses and women carrying sacred implements. As usual on Greek temples, brightly colored paint and shiny metal attachments enlivened the figures of people and animals.

No other city-state had ever gone beyond the traditional function of temples—glorifying and paying homage to the community's special deities—by adorning a temple with representations of its citizens. The Parthenon frieze made a unique statement about how Athenians perceived their relationship to the gods. A temple adorned with pictures of citizens being viewed by the gods amounted to a claim of special intimacy between the city-state and the gods. This assertion reflected the Athenians' interpretation of their success in helping turn back the Persians, in achieving leadership of a powerful naval alliance, and in amassing wealth that made Athens richer than all its neighbors in mainland Greece. Their success, the Athenians believed, proved that the gods were on their side.

Like the Parthenon frieze, the changes that Golden Age artists made in free-standing sculpture broke with tradition. Archaic male statues had only one pose:

arms pressed to their sides and left leg striding forward, imitating the unchanging posture of Egyptian statuary. This style gave them an appearance of stability; even a hard shove seemed unlikely to budge them. By the time of the Persian Wars, Greek sculptors began to express motion in their art. Male statues could have bent arms and the body's weight on either leg. Female statues, too, had more relaxed poses and clothing that hung in a way that hinted at the shape of the curves underneath. The faces of Golden Age sculptures were self-confidently calm rather than smiling like Archaic figures. This spirited new style suggested the confident energy of the times but also hinted at the possibility of instability: Golden Age sculptors took more chances with the balance of their statues.

Whether private individuals or the city-state paid for statues, they were meant to be displayed in public to broadcast a message. Art was not yet used to decorate homes. Instead, wealthy families would commission statues of gods to be housed in a sanctuary as symbols of devotion. They also placed statues of their deceased members, especially if they had died young in war or in childbirth, above their graves as memorials of their virtue.

Tradition and Innovation in Athens's Golden Age

Fifth-century B.C. Athens hosted unprecedented accomplishments in architecture, art, drama, and intellectual life, but many central aspects of its social and religious life remained unchanged. The simultaneous love for innovation and for tradition created social tensions, especially concerning religion. Women's role in public life did not change, and women continued to make essential contributions by managing the household, participating in religious ceremonies, and, if they were poor, working in commerce and agriculture to help support their families. The severest tension arose from the startling ideas of teachers called *sophists* and the ethical views of the philosopher Socrates. The most visible response to the tension produced by new developments was the increased importance of tragic and comedic drama as publicly supported art forms examining problems in city-state life.

Religious Tradition in a Period of Change

Greeks maintained their polytheistic religious traditions with sacrifices and public festivals and by seeking a personal relationship with the gods in the rituals of hero cults and mystery cults. City-states were officially religious communities: each honored a particular god or goddess, such as Athena at Athens, as its protector and patron, while also worshiping many other deities. The twelve most important gods were envisioned assembling for banquets atop Mount Olympus, the highest peak in mainland Greece. Zeus headed this immortal pantheon; joining him were Hera, his wife; Aphrodite, goddess of love; Apollo, sun god; Ares, war god; Artemis, moon goddess; Athena, goddess of wisdom and war; Demeter, goddess of agriculture and fertility; Dionysus, god of pleasure, wine, and disorder; Hephaestus, god of fire and technology; Hermes, messenger god; and Poseidon, sea god.

Like the peoples of the ancient Near East, the Greeks believed that humans, as individuals and as communities, must honor the gods to thank them for blessings received and to receive blessings in return. The idea of reciprocity between gods and humans underlay the Greeks' understanding of the nature of the gods. Deities did not love humans, though in some mythological stories they took earthly lovers and produced half-divine children. Rather, they supported humans who paid them honor and did not offend them. Gods offended by humans could punish them by sending calamities such as famine, earthquake, epidemic disease, or defeat in war. The Greeks did not expect to reach paradise at some future time when evil forces would finally be vanquished forever.

Each god's cult—the set of prayers and rituals for worshiping a particular divinity—had its own practices, but sacrifice provided the focus. Sacrifices ranged from the bloodless offering of fruits, vegetables, and small cakes to the slaughter of large animals. The speechwriter Lysias (c. 445–380 B.C.), a Syracusan residing in Athens, explained the necessity for public sacrifice in an address composed for an Athenian official: "Our ancestors handed down to us the most powerful and prosperous community in Greece by performing the prescribed sacrifices. It is therefore proper for us to offer the same sacrifices as they, if only for the sake of the success which has resulted from those rites." The sacrifice of a large animal provided an occasion for the community to assemble and reaffirm its ties to the divine world and, by sharing the roasted meat of the sacrificed beast, for the worshipers to benefit personally from a good relationship with the gods. The feasting that followed a large-animal sacrifice was especially significant because meat was rare in the diet of most Greeks.

The bloody killing of the victim followed strict rules to avoid ritual contamination. The victim had to be an unblemished domestic animal, specially decorated with garlands and induced to approach the altar as if of its own free will. The assembled crowd maintained strict silence to avoid possibly impure remarks. The sacrificer sprinkled water on the victim's head so it would shake its head and appear to consent to die. After washing his hands, the sacrificer scattered barley grains on the altar fire and on the animal's head and then cut a lock of the animal's hair and threw it on the fire. Following a prayer, he swiftly cut the animal's throat while musicians played flutelike pipes and female worshipers screamed, presumably to express the group's ritual sorrow at the victim's death. The carcass was then butchered, and some portions of it were thrown on the altar fire so their aromatic smoke could waft its way upward to the cult's god. The rest of the meat was cooked for the worshipers to eat.

Public festivals featured not just sacrifices but also elaborate rituals, such as parades, open to the entire community. Athens boasted of having the most festivals, with nearly half the days of the year featuring one. Its biggest festival, the Panathenaia, honored Athena with sacrifices, parades, and contests with valuable prizes for music, dancing, poetry, and athletics. Some occasions were for women only, such as the three-day festival for married women in honor of Demeter.

Greek religion encompassed many activities besides the civic cults of the twelve Olympian gods. People took a keen interest in religious actions meant to improve their personal relations with the divine. Families marked significant moments such as birth, marriage, and death with prayers, rituals, and sacrifices. They honored their ancestors with offerings made at their tombs, consulted seers about the meanings of dreams and omens, and sought out magicians for spells to improve their love lives or curses to harm their enemies. Particularly important were hero cults and mystery cults. The former were rituals performed at the tomb of an extraordinarily famous man or woman. Local heroes' remains were thought to retain special power to reveal the future through oracles, to heal illnesses and injuries, and to provide protection in battle. The only hero to whom cults were established all over the Greek world was the strongman Heracles (or Hercules, as his name was later spelled by the Romans). His superhuman feats gave him an appeal as a protector in many city-states.

The Athenian mystery cult of Demeter and her daughter Kore (also called Persephone), headquartered in the village of Eleusis, attracted men and women from all over the Mediterranean world because it offered the hope of protection in this life and the afterlife. The central rite of this cult was the Mysteries: a series of initiation ceremonies into the secret knowledge of the cult. The main initiation occurred during an annual festival lasting nearly two weeks, which culminated in the revelation of Demeter's central secret after a day of fasting. The most eloquent proof of the sanctity attached to these Mysteries is that no one ever revealed the secret

■ **Cup with Symbols to Avert Evil**
Ancient Greeks had a healthy respect for the ability of nature and their fellow human beings to do them harm. Like prayer, magical symbols were thought to have power to ward off bad luck and other evils. Sometimes items from everyday life, such as this cup, were decorated with these symbols as a way of providing the object's owner with some hope of averting evil fortune both large and small. Here the god Dionysus is seated between two large eyes as sources of magical power. (Kannellopoulos Museum/Archaeological Receipts Fund.)

throughout the thousand years during which the rites were celebrated. Indirect reports reveal that it promised initiates a better life on earth and a better fate after death.

Other mystery cults also emphasized protection for initiates in their current lives, whether against ghosts, illness, poverty, shipwrecks, or the countless other dangers of life. Divine protection was accorded, however, as a reward for appropriate worship, not for any abstract faith. The ancient Greeks believed that the gods expected honors and rites, and their religion required action from worshipers. Greeks had to pray and sing hymns honoring the gods, perform sacrifices, and undergo ritual purification. Preserving religious tradition mattered deeply to most people because it offered a safeguard against the precarious conditions of human life in a world in which early death from disease, accident, or war was commonplace.

Women, Slaves, and Metics in Traditional Society

The power and status of Athenian women came from their roles in the family and in religion. Upper-class women devoted their lives to running their households, meeting female friends, and participating in the city-state's religious cults. Poorer women helped support themselves and their families, often as small-scale merchants and crafts producers.

Women's exclusion from politics meant that their contributions to the city-state might be overlooked by men. In his play *Medea* of 431 B.C., the Athenian dramatist Euripides had his heroine insist that women who bear children are owed respect at least commensurate with that granted hoplites, a plausible claim given the high risks of childbirth under the medical conditions of antiquity:

> *People say that we women lead a safe life at home, while men have to go to war. What fools they are! I would much rather fight in the army three times than give birth to a child even once.*

Women, like men, could own property, including land (the most valued possession in Greek society), and they were supposed to preserve it to hand down to their children. A daughter's share in her father's estate usually came to her in her dowry at marriage. Husband and wife co-owned the household's common property, which was apportioned to its separate owners if the marriage dissolved. The husband was legally responsible for preserving the dowry and using it for the support and comfort of his wife and any children she bore. Upon her death, her children inherited the dowry.

Athenian laws concerning heiresses reveal the society's goal of enabling males to establish and maintain households. If a father died leaving only a daughter, his

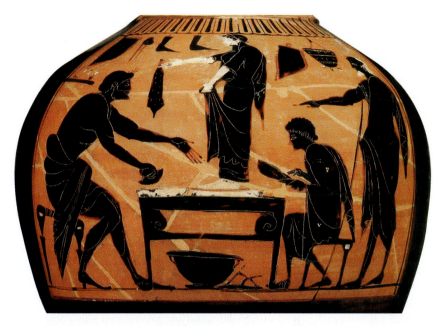

■ **Vase Painting of a Woman Buying Shoes**

Greek vases were frequently decorated with scenes from daily life instead of mythological stories.
Here, a woman is being fitted for a pair of custom-made shoes by a craftsman and his apprentice.
As was customary, her husband has accompanied her on the expedition and, to judge from his
gesture, is participating in the discussion of the purchase. This vase was painted in so-called black-
figure technique, in which the figures are rendered as black outlines, with their details incised into
a background of red clay. Painters later reversed this technique on red-figure vases (see pages 44
and 47) so that they could draw pictures with greater precision and elegance of line.
(H. L. Pierce Fund. Courtesy Museum of Fine Arts, Boston.)

www.bedfordstmartins.com/huntconcise   See the ONLINE STUDY GUIDE for more help in
analyzing this image.

property went to her, but she could not dispose of it as she pleased. Instead, her
father's closest male relative—her official guardian after her father's death—was required to marry her, with the aim of producing a son. This child inherited the property when he reached adulthood. This rule applied regardless of whether the heiress
was already married (without any sons) or whether the male relative already had a
wife. The heiress and the male relative were both supposed to divorce their present
spouses and marry each other (although in practice the rule could be circumvented
by legal subterfuge) to preserve the father's line and keep the property in his family.

Athenian women from the urban propertied class were expected to avoid close
contact with men who were not family members or good friends. They were supposed to spend much of their time in their own homes or the homes of women
friends. Women dressed and slept in rooms set aside for them, which opened onto

a walled courtyard where they could walk in the open air, talk, supervise the family's slaves, and interact with other members of the household, male and female. Here in her "territory" a woman would spin wool for clothing while chatting with visiting friends, play with her children, and give her opinions on various matters to the men of the house as they came and went. Poor women had little time for such activities because they, like their husbands, sons, and brothers, had to leave their homes, usually crowded rental apartments, to work. They often set up small stalls to sell bread, vegetables, simple clothing, or trinkets.

A woman with servants who answered the door herself would be reproached as careless of her reputation. A proper woman left her home only for an appropriate reason. Fortunately, Athenian life offered many occasions for women to get out: religious festivals, funerals, childbirths at the houses of relatives and friends, and trips to workshops to buy shoes or other domestic articles. Sometimes her husband escorted her, but more often a woman was accompanied only by a servant and could act independently. Social protocol required men not to speak the names of respectable women in public conversations or in court speeches unless absolutely necessary.

Because rich women stayed out of the sun, they maintained pale complexions. This pallor was much admired as a sign of an enviable life of leisure and wealth. Women regularly used powdered white lead to give themselves a suitably pallid look. Presumably, many upper-class women viewed their limited contact with men outside the household as a badge of superior social status. In a gender-segregated society such as that of upper-class Athens, a woman's primary personal relationships were probably with her children and other women.

Men restricted women's freedom of movement partly to reduce uncertainty about the paternity of their children and to protect their daughters' virginity from seducers and rapists. Since citizenship guaranteed the city-state's political structure and a man's personal freedom, Greeks felt it crucial to ensure that a boy truly was his father's son and not the offspring of a foreigner or a slave. Women who bore legitimate children earned higher status and greater freedom in the family, as an Athenian man explained in this excerpt from a court case:

When I decided to marry and had brought a wife home, at first my attitude towards her was this: I did not wish to annoy her, but neither was she to have too much of her own way. . . . I kept an eye on her as was proper. But later, after my child had been born, I came to trust her, and I handed all my possessions over to her, believing that this was the greatest possible proof of affection.◆

_____

◆ For further testimony from this revealing court case, see Document 5, Lysias, "A Husband Speaks in His Own Defense."

Bearing male children brought special honor to a woman because sons meant security for parents. Sons could appear in court in support of their parents in lawsuits and protect them in the streets of Athens, which for most of its history had no police force. By law, sons were required to support elderly parents. So intense was the pressure to produce sons that stories of women who smuggled in male babies born to slaves and passed them off as their own were common. Such tales, whose truth is hard to gauge, were credible because husbands customarily stayed away at childbirth.

A small number of Athenian women were able to flaunt traditional restrictions because they gave up the usual expectations of marrying or were too rich to be cowed by men. The most renowned of the former group were called *companions.* Often foreigners, they were physically attractive, witty in conversation, and able to sing and play musical instruments. They often entertained at a symposium (a male dinner party without wives), and sometimes they sold sexual favors for a high price. Their independent existence distinguished companions from citizen women, as did the freedom to control their own sexuality. Equally distinctive was their cultivated ability to converse with men in public. Companions charmed men with their witty, bantering conversation. Their characteristic skill at clever taunts and verbal snubs allowed companions a freedom of speech denied to "proper" women.

■ Vase Painting of a Symposium

Upper-class Greek men often spent their evenings at symposia, drinking parties that always included much conversation and usually featured music and entertainers; wives were not included. The discussions could range widely, from literature to politics to philosophy. Here, a female musician, whose nudity shows she is a hired prostitute, entertains the guests, who recline on couches, as was customary. The man on the right is about to fling the dregs of his wine, playing a messy game called kottabos. (Master and Fellows of Corpus Christi College, Cambridge, The Parker Library.)

Some companions lived precarious lives subject to exploitation and even violence at the hands of their male customers, but the most accomplished could attract lovers from the highest levels of society and live in luxury on their own. The most famous such woman was Aspasia from Miletus, who became Pericles' lover and bore him a son. She dazzled Athens's upper-class males with her brilliant conversation and confidence. Ironically, Pericles' desire to marry her was blocked by his own law of 451 B.C. restricting citizenship.

Only the very wealthiest citizen women could speak to men publicly with the frankness of companions. One such was Elpinike, a member of a super-rich Athenian family of great military distinction. She once openly rebuked Pericles for having boasted about the Athenian conquest of a rebellious ally. When some other Athenian women praised Pericles for his success, Elpinike sarcastically remarked, "This really is wonderful, Pericles, . . . that you have caused the loss of many good citizens, not in battle against Phoenicians or Persians, like my brother Cimon, but in suppressing an allied city of fellow Greeks." Ancient sources confirm that ordinary women, too, remained engaged and interested in issues affecting the city-state as a whole. They often had strong opinions on politics and public policy, but they had to express their views privately to their husbands, children, and relatives.

In contrast to citizen women, slaves and *metics* (foreigners granted permanent residency) had no political influence because they were "outsiders" living inside Greek society. Individuals and the city-state alike owned slaves, who could be purchased from traders or bred in the household. Unwanted newborns abandoned by their parents (the practice called *infant exposure*) were often picked up by others and raised as slaves. Athens's commercial growth in this period increased the demand for slaves. Although no reliable statistics survive, slaves probably made up 100,000 or more of the city-state's estimated 250,000 residents in Pericles' time. (This population made Athens an extraordinarily large city-state.) Slaves worked in homes, on farms, in crafts shops and, if they were truly unfortunate, in the cramped and dangerous silver mines whose riches boosted Athens's prosperity. Unlike Sparta's helots, Athens's slaves never rebelled, probably because they originated from too many different places to be able to unite.

Golden Age Athens's wealth and cultural vitality attracted numerous metics, who flocked to the city as importers, crafts producers, entertainers, and laborers. By the start of the Peloponnesian War in 431 B.C., they constituted perhaps half the free population. Metics had to pay for the privilege of working in Athens through a special foreigners' tax and military service. Citizens had ambivalent feelings about metics, valuing their contributions to the city's prosperity but almost never offering them citizenship.

Metics therefore sometimes found themselves relegated to ways of life outside the mainstream, such as prostitution. Men, unlike women, were not penalized for sexual activity outside marriage. "Certainly you don't think men beget children out of sexual desire?" wrote the upper-class author Xenophon. "The streets and the

brothels are swarming with ways to take care of that." Men could have sex with female or male slaves, who could not refuse their masters, or they could patronize
various classes of prostitutes, depending on how much money they wanted to spend.

Education and Intellectual Innovation

Athenians learned the rules of respectable behavior in the family and in the course
of everyday life. Public schools did not exist. Only well-to-do families could afford
to pay private teachers, to whom they sent their sons to learn to read, write, perhaps sing or play a musical instrument, and train for athletics and military service.
Physical fitness was considered vital for men, who could be called up for military
service from ages eighteen to sixty. Therefore, men exercised daily in public open-
air facilities paid for by wealthy families. Men frequently discussed politics and exchanged news at these *gymnasia*. The daughters of wealthy families usually learned
to read, write, and do simple arithmetic; a woman with these skills would be better prepared to manage a household and help her future husband run their estate.

Poorer girls and boys learned a trade and perhaps some rudiments of literacy
by assisting their parents in their daily work or, if they were fortunate, by being ap-
prenticed to skilled crafts producers. Scholars disagree about the level of literacy,
but most likely it was low outside the ranks of the prosperous. The predominance
of oral rather than written communication meant that people usually absorbed information by ear: songs, speeches, narrated stories, and lively conversation were
central to Greek life.

Young men from prosperous families traditionally acquired the skills to participate successfully in the public life of Athenian democracy by observing their fathers, uncles, and other older men as they debated in the Council of 500 and the
assembly, served as magistrates, and spoke in court. In many cases, an older man
would choose an adolescent boy as his special favorite to educate. The boy would
learn about public life by spending his time in the company of the older man and
his adult friends. During the day, the boy would observe his mentor talking politics in the agora, help him perform his duties in public office, and work out with
him in a gymnasium. Their evenings would be spent at a symposium, which would
encompass a range of behavior from serious political and philosophical discussion
to riotous partying.

Such a mentor-protégé relationship could lead to sexual relations between the
boy and the older male, who would normally be married. Although both male homosexuality outside a mentor-protégé relationship and female homosexuality in
general were regarded as wrong throughout the Greek world, sexual relations between older mentors and younger protégés were considered acceptable in many,
though not all, city-states. These differing attitudes about homosexual behavior reflected the complexity of Greek ideas of masculinity, about what made a man a man
and what unmade him. In any case, a mentor was never supposed to exploit his

younger companion physically or neglect his political education. If this ideal was observed, Athenian society accepted the relationship as part of a complicated range of bonds among males, from political and military activity, to training of mind and body, to sexual activity.

By the time radical democracy was established in Athens, young men eager to become adept political speakers had access to a new kind of teacher. These experts in public speaking and argumentation were called *sophists* ("wise men"), a label that later acquired a negative connotation (preserved in the English word *sophistry*), because they were so clever in debate. Sophists created controversy because they taught unprecedented skills in public speaking and ideas about the nature of human existence and religion that challenged traditional beliefs. The earliest sophists were not Athenians, but beginning about 450 B.C. these foreigners began arriving in Athens, then at the height of its prosperity, to attract pupils who could pay the hefty prices they charged for instruction.

Sophists primarily taught what every ambitious young man needed to become influential in Athens's radical democracy: powerful public speaking for the political debates in the assembly and the councils or lawsuits in court. Wealthy men therefore flocked to the dazzling demonstrations these itinerant teachers put on to showcase their techniques of persuasion. In some cases, the sophists charged stiff fees to write speeches the purchasers could deliver as their own compositions.

The sophists alarmed traditionalists, who feared their seductive eloquence might undermine communal social and political traditions in favor of individual interests. In ancient Greek culture, where codes of proper behavior, moral standards, and religious ideals were transmitted orally from generation to generation, a persuasive and charismatic speaker could potentially wield as much power as an army of warriors. Sophists made people nervous because political leaders, such as Pericles, flocked to hear them. Many citizens feared that selfish politicians would use the silver-tongued style of the sophists to mislead the assembly and the councils.

The sophists' novel ideas about human existence and religion deeply upset many people. One especially controversial sophist was Protagoras, a contemporary of Pericles from Abdera in northern Greece. He immigrated to Athens around 450 B.C., when he was about forty, and spent most of his career there. His views proved extremely controversial, especially his agnosticism (the belief that supernatural phenomena are unknowable): "Whether the gods exist I cannot discover, nor what their form is like, for there are many impediments to knowledge, [such as] the obscurity of the subject and the brevity of human life." Statements like this implied that conventional religion had no meaning, and people worried that they might provoke divine anger.

Equally controversial was Protagoras's denial of any absolute standard of truth, his assertion that every issue had two, irreconcilable sides. For example, if one person feeling a breeze thinks it warm, whereas another person thinks it cool, neither judgment can be absolutely correct because the wind simply is warm to one and cool to the other. Protagoras summed up his subjectivism—the belief that there is no absolute reality behind and independent of appearances—in the much-quoted opening of his work *Truth*: "Man is the measure of all things, of the things that are that they are, and of the things that are not that they are not." *Man* (*anthropos* in Greek, hence our word *anthropology*) in this passage refers to the individual human, male or female, whom Protagoras makes the sole judge of his or her own impressions.

These ideas, which other sophists expressed in different ways, aroused special concerns: that human institutions and values were only matters of convention, custom, or law (*nomos*) and not products of nature (*physis*), and that because truth was subjective, speakers should be able to argue either side of a question with equal persuasiveness. The first view implied that traditional human institutions were arbitrary rather than grounded in nature, and the second made morality irrelevant to politics. The combination of the two ideas amounted to moral relativism, which threatened the shared public values of the democratic city-state.

Protagoras, however, insisted that his doctrines were not hostile to democracy, arguing that every person had an innate capability for "excellence" and that human survival depended on the rule of law based on a sense of justice. Members of the community, he explained, must be persuaded to obey the laws not because they are based on absolute truth, which does not exist, but because it was advantageous for people to live by them. A thief, for example, would have to be persuaded that the law forbidding theft was to his advantage because it protected his own property and the city-state in which he, like others, had to live in order to survive.

Other sophists taught other unsettling ideas. Anaxagoras of Clazomenae, for example, offended believers in traditional religion by arguing that the sun was nothing more than a lump of flaming rock, not a deity. Leucippus of Miletus, whose doctrines were made famous by his pupil Democritus of Abdera, invented an atomic theory of matter to explain how change was constant. Everything, he argued, consisted of tiny, invisible particles in eternal motion. Their random collisions caused them to combine and recombine in an infinite variety of forms. This physical explanation of the source of change, like Anaxagoras's theory about the sun, implied that traditional religion, which explained events as the outcome of divine forces, was invalid.

Because only wealthy men could afford instruction from sophists, this new education worked against the egalitarian principles of Athenian democracy by giving an advantage to the rich. In addition, moral relativism and the physical explanation of the universe struck many Athenians as dangerous: they feared that the teachings of the sophists could bring down divine punishment on the whole community.

The provocative ideas of Socrates of Athens (469–399 B.C.), the most famous philosopher of the Golden Age, added to the consternation that the sophists provoked. He was not a sophist and offered no courses, but his views became well known because his lifestyle was so distinctive. Socrates devoted his life to conversation combating the notion that justice should be equated with the power to work one's will. His passionate concern to discover valid guidelines for leading a just life and to prove that justice is better than injustice under all circumstances gave a new direction to Greek philosophy: an emphasis on ethics. Although other thinkers before him had dealt with moral issues, especially the poets and dramatists, Socrates was the first philosopher to make ethics and morality his central concern.

Socrates lived a life that attracted attention. He paid so little heed to his physical appearance and clothes that he seemed eccentric. Sporting a stomach, in his words, "somewhat too large to be convenient," he wore the same nondescript cloak summer and winter and went barefoot in all weather. His tirelessness as a hoplite and his ability to outdrink anyone at a symposium amazed his companions. Unlike the sophists, he lived in poverty and disdained material possessions, somehow managing to support a wife and several children. He may have inherited some money, but he certainly received gifts from wealthy admirers.

Socrates spent his time in conversations: participating in a symposium, strolling in the agora, or watching young men exercise in a gymnasium. He wrote nothing; our knowledge of his ideas comes from others' writings, especially those of his pupil Plato (c. 428–348 B.C.). Plato portrays Socrates as a relentless questioner of his fellow citizens, foreign friends, and leading sophists. Socrates' questions

■ **Statuette of the Philosopher Socrates**

The controversial Socrates, the most famous philosopher of Athens in the fifth century B.C., joked that he had a homely face and a bulging stomach. This small statue is an artist's impression of what Socrates looked like; we cannot be sure of the truth. Socrates was renowned for his irony, and he may have purposely exaggerated his physical unattractiveness to show his disdain for ordinary standards of beauty and his own emphasis on the quality of one's soul as the true measure of a person's worth.

(British Museum.)

aimed at making his conversational partners examine the basic assumptions of their way of life. Giving few answers, Socrates never directly instructed anyone; instead, he led them to draw conclusions in response to his probing questions and refutations of their unexamined assumptions.◆

This indirect method of searching for the truth often left people uncomfortably baffled because they were forced to conclude that they were ignorant of what they had assumed they knew very well. Socrates' questions showed that accepted careers—pursuing success in politics or business or art—were excuses for avoiding genuine virtue. Socrates insisted that he was ignorant of the best definition of virtue but that his wisdom consisted of knowing that he did not know. He vowed that he was trying to improve, not undermine, people's beliefs in morality, even though, as a friend put it, a conversation with Socrates made a man feel numb—just as if he had been stung by a stingray. Socrates especially wanted to use reasoning to discover universal standards justifying individual morality. He fiercely attacked the sophists, who proclaimed conventional morality to be the "fetters that bind nature." This view, he protested, equated human happiness with power and "getting more."

Socrates passionately believed that just behavior was better for people than injustice and that morality was invaluable because it created happiness. Essentially, he argued that just behavior, or virtue, was identical to knowledge and that true knowledge of justice would inevitably lead people to choose good over evil. They would therefore live truly happy lives, regardless of how rich or poor they were. Since Socrates believed that moral knowledge was all a person needed for the good life, he argued that no one knowingly behaved unjustly and that behaving justly was always in the individual's interest. It was simply ignorant to believe that the best life was the life of unlimited power to pursue whatever one desired. The most desirable human life was concerned with virtue and guided by reason, not by dreams of personal gain.

Socrates' effect on many people was as disturbing as the relativistic doctrines of the sophists. His refutation of his fellow citizens' ideas about the importance of wealth and public success made some men extremely upset. Unhappiest of all were the fathers whose sons, after listening to Socrates reduce someone to utter bewilderment, came home to try the same technique on their parents by arguing that the accomplishments their family held dear were old-fashioned, even worthless. Men who experienced this reversal of the traditional educational hierarchy—fathers were supposed to educate sons—felt that Socrates was undermining the stability of society by making young men question Athenian traditions. The ancient sources fail to reveal what Athenian women thought of Socrates or he of them. His thoughts

---

◆ For an account from Plato of his renowned teacher's philosophy, see Document 6, "The Apology of Socrates."

about human capabilities and behavior could be applied to women as well as to men, and he probably believed that women and men both had the same basic capacity for justice.

The feeling that Socrates presented a danger to conventional society gave the playwright Aristophanes the inspiration for his comedy *Clouds* (423 B.C.). He portrayed Socrates as a cynical sophist operating a Thinking Shop who, for a fee, offered instruction in Protagorean techniques of making the weaker argument the stronger. When Socrates' curriculum transforms a youth into a public speaker arguing that a son has the right to beat his parents, his father burns down Socrates' school. None of these plot details was real; what was genuine was the fear that Socrates' uncompromising views on individual morality endangered the traditional practices of the community at a time when new ways of thought were springing up fast and furiously.

One especially significant intellectual innovation that emerged in the Golden Age was historical writing as a critical vision of the past. Herodotus of Halicarnassus (c. 485–425 B.C.) and Thucydides of Athens (c. 455–399 B.C.) became Greece's most famous historians and established Western civilization's tradition of history writing. By 428–425 B.C., Herodotus had finished his groundbreaking work called *Histories* (meaning "inquiries" in Greek) to explain the Persian Wars as a clash between East and West; by Roman times he had been christened "Father of History." Herodotus achieved an unprecedented depth for his book by giving it a wide geographical scope, an investigative approach to evidence, and a lively narrative. Herodotus searched for the origins of the Persian-Greek conflict both by delving deep into the past and by examining the cultural traditions of all the peoples involved. He recognized the relevance and the delight of studying other cultures as a component of historical investigation.

Thucydides took another giant step in this process by writing contemporary history influenced by what today is called political science. His *History of the Peloponnesian War* made power politics, not divine intervention, history's primary force. Deeply affected by the war's brutality, he brilliantly used his personal experiences as a politician and military commander to make his narrative vivid and frank in describing human moral failings. His insistence that historians should spare no effort in seeking out the most reliable sources and evaluating their testimony with objectivity set a high standard for later writers.

Equally innovative were the medical doctrines of Hippocrates of Cos, a fifth-century B.C. contemporary of Thucydides, who became Greece's most famous physician. He is remembered today in the oath bearing his name that doctors swear at the beginning of their professional careers. Hippocrates made great strides in putting medical diagnosis and treatment on a scientific basis. Earlier medicine had depended on magic and ritual. Hippocrates viewed the human body as an organism whose parts must be understood as segments of the whole. Some attributed to him the view, profoundly influential in later times, that four humors (fluids) made up the human body: blood, phlegm, black bile, and yellow bile. Health depended on keeping the proper balance among them; being healthy was to be in "good humor." This intellectual system corresponded to philosophers' division of the inanimate world into four parts: the elements earth, air, fire, and water.

Hippocrates taught that the physician's most important duty was to base his knowledge on careful observation of patients and their response to remedies. Clinical experience, not theory, he insisted, was the best guide to effective treatments. Although various cults in Greek religion offered healing to petitioners, Hippocratic medical doctrine apparently made little or no mention of any role for the gods in illnesses and their treatments.

The Development of Tragedy and Comedy

The complex relationship between gods and humans formed the basis of Golden Age Athens's most influential cultural innovation: tragic drama. Greek plays, still read and produced onstage today, were presented over three days at the major annual festival of the god Dionysus, which was held in the spring and included a drama contest, in keeping with the competitive spirit characteristic of many events honoring the gods. By presenting shocking stories relevant to tensions in the city-state, tragedy inspired its large audiences to ponder the danger that ignorance, arrogance, and violence presented to Athens's democratic society. Following the tradition of Homer and Hesiod, Golden Age playwrights explored topics ranging from individual freedom and responsibility in the *polis* to the underlying nature of good and evil.

Every year, one of Athens's magistrates chose three competing authors to present four plays each: three tragedies in a row (a trilogy), followed by a semicomic play featuring satyrs (mythical half-man, half-animal beings) to end the day on a lighter note. The term *tragedy*—derived, for reasons now lost, from the Greek words for "goat" and "song"—referred to plays with plots that involved fierce conflict and characters who represented powerful forces. Tragedies were written in verse and used solemn language; they were often based on stories about the violent consequences of interaction between gods and humans told in myth. The plots often ended with a resolution to the trouble—but only after considerable suffering.

The performance of Athenian tragedies bore little resemblance to modern theater productions. They took place during the daytime in an outdoor theater sacred to Dionysus, built into the southern slope of Athens's acropolis. This theater held about fourteen thousand spectators overlooking an open, circular area in front of a slightly raised stage. Every tragedy had to have eighteen cast members, all of whom were men: three actors to play the speaking roles (both male and female

■ **Theater of Dionysus at Athens**

*Tragedies, satyr plays, and comedies produced at this theater in daytime festivals riveted the atten-
tion of the city. In the Classical period, the seating, the stage, and scenery were not yet permanent
installations. The seating and stone stage building foundations are remnants of much later
changes.* (John Elk III/Bruce Coleman, Inc., New York.)

characters) and fifteen chorus members. Although the chorus leader sometimes
engaged in dialogue with the actors, the chorus primarily performed songs and
dances in the circular area in front of the stage, called the *orchestra*.

Scenery on the stage was sparse, but a good tragedy presented a vivid spectacle. The chorus wore decorative costumes and performed intricate dance routines. The actors wore masks and used broad gestures and booming voices to
reach the upper tier of seats. A powerful voice was crucial to a tragic actor because
words represented the heart of a tragedy, in which dialogue and long speeches
were far more common than physical action. Special effects, however, were part of
the spectacle. For example, a crane allowed actors playing the roles of gods to
fly suddenly onto the stage. The actors playing lead roles, called the *protagonists*
("first competitors"), competed against one another for the designation of best
actor. So important was a first-rate protagonist to a successful tragedy that actors
were assigned by lottery to the playwrights to give all three an equal chance to have
the finest cast. Great protagonists became enormous celebrities.

Most playwrights came from the social elite because only men of property could afford the amount of time and learning their work demanded: as author, director, producer, musical composer, choreographer, and sometimes even actor. The prizes awarded in the tragedy competition were modest. As citizens, playwrights also fulfilled the normal military and political obligations of Athenian men. The best-known Athenian tragedians—Aeschylus (525–456 B.C.), Sophocles (c. 496–406 B.C.), and Euripides (c. 485–406 B.C.)—all served in the army, held public office at some point in their careers, or did both.

Athenian tragedy was a public art form. Its performances were subsidized with public funds, and its plots explored the ethical quandaries of humans in conflict with the gods and with one another in a city-state. Even though most tragedies were based on stories that referred to a legendary time before city-states existed, such as tales of the Trojan War, the moral issues the plays illuminated always pertained to the society and obligations of citizens in a city-state. To take only a few examples: Aeschylus in his trilogy *Oresteia* (458 B.C.) reworks the story of how the gods stopped the murderous violence in the family of Orestes, son of the Greek leader against Troy, to explain the necessity and the sanctity of democratic Athens's court system. The plays suggest that human beings have to learn by suffering but that the gods will provide justice in the long run. Sophocles' *Antigone* (441 B.C.) presents the sad story of the family of Oedipus of Thebes as a drama of harsh conflict between a courageous woman, Antigone, who insists on her family's moral obligation to bury its dead in obedience to divine command, and her uncle Creon, the city-state's stern male leader, who defends the need to preserve order and protect community values by prohibiting the burial of traitors. In a horrifying story of anger and suicide centered on one of the most famous heroines of Western literature, Sophocles deliberately exposes the right and wrong on each side of the conflict, and the play offers no easy resolution of the competing interests of divinely sanctioned moral tradition and the political rules of the state. Euripides' *Medea* (431 B.C.) implies that the political order of a city-state depends on men treating their wives and families with honor and trust: when Medea's husband betrays her for a younger woman, she takes revenge by destroying their children and the community's political leadership with her magical power.

We cannot reconstruct precisely how the audiences of the drama competition of the Dionysian festival understood the messages of tragedies. At the very least, however, they must have been aware that the central characters of the plays were figures who fell into disaster from positions of power and prestige. The characters' reversals of fortune came about not because they were absolute villains but because, as humans, they were susceptible to a lethal mixture of error, ignorance, and *hubris* (violent arrogance). The Athenian Empire was at its height when audiences at Athens attended the tragedies of these three great playwrights. Thoughtful spectators may have reflected on the possibility that Athens's current power and prestige, managed as they were by humans, remained hostage to the same forces that controlled the fates of the heroes and heroines of tragedy. Tragedies certainly appealed to audiences because they were compelling, but they also had an educational function: to remind male citizens, who made policy for the city-state, that success engendered complex moral problems that could not be solved casually or arrogantly.

Athens developed theatrical comedy as another innovative form of public art. Like tragedies, comedies were written in verse, were performed in a competition in the city's large outdoor theater during festivals honoring the god Dionysus, and were subsidized with public funds. Unlike tragedies, comedies made direct comments about public policy, criticized current politicians and intellectuals by name, and devised plots of outrageous fantasy to make their points. Comic choruses of twenty-four actors, for example, could feature characters colorfully dressed as talking birds or dancing clouds.

The immediate goal of a comic playwright was to win the award for the festival's best comedy by creating beautiful poetry, raising laughs with constant jokes and puns, and skewering political leaders. Much of the humor concerned sex and bodily functions, delivered in a stream of imaginative profanity. Well-known male citizens were targets for insults as cowardly or sexually effeminate. Women characters portrayed as figures of fun and ridicule, however, seem to have been fictional.

Comedy's remarkable freedom of speech promoted frank, even brutal, commentary on current issues and personalities. Even during the Peloponnesian War, comic playwrights presented plays that criticized the city-state's policy, for example by recommending an immediate peace settlement. It was no accident that this energetic, critical drama emerged in Athens at the same time as radical democracy, in the mid-fifth century B.C. The feeling that all citizens should have a stake in determining their government's policies evidently fueled a passion for using biting humor to keep the community's leaders from becoming arrogant and aloof.

Athenian comedies often blamed particular political leaders for government policies that had been approved by the assembly, similar to the way ostracism singled out individuals for punishment. As the leading politician of radical democracy, Pericles came in for fierce criticism in comedy. Comic playwrights mocked his policies, his love life, and his looks ("Old Tuber Head" was a favorite insult). Cleon, the most prominent politician after Pericles, was so outraged by the way that he was parodied on stage by Aristophanes (c. 455–385 B.C.), Athens's most famous comic playwright, that he sued him. When Cleon lost the case, Aristophanes responded by pitilessly mocking him as a slavish foreign slob in *The Knights* (424 B.C.).

The most remarkable of Aristophanes' comedies are those in which the main characters are powerful women who compel the men of Athens to change their policy to preserve family life and the city-state. Most famous is *Lysistrata* (411 b.c.), named after the female lead character of the play. In it, the women of Athens and Sparta unite to force their husbands to end the Peloponnesian War. To make the men agree to a peace treaty, they first seize the acropolis, where Athens's financial reserves are kept, to prevent the men from squandering them further on the war. They then beat back an attack on their position by the old men who have remained in Athens while the younger men are out on campaign. When their husbands return from battle, the women refuse to have sex with them. This strike, which is portrayed in a series of risqué episodes, finally coerces the men of Athens and Sparta to agree to a treaty.

Lysistrata presents women acting bravely and aggressively against men who seem bent on destroying their traditional family life—they are staying away from home for long stretches while on military campaigns and are ruining the city-state by prolonging a pointless war. Lysistrata insists that women have the intelligence and judgment to make political decisions: "I am a woman, and, yes, I have brains. And I'm not badly off for judgment. Nor has my education been bad, coming as it has from my listening often to the conversations of my father and the elders among the men." Her old-fashioned training and good sense allow her to see what needs to be done to protect the community. Like the heroines of tragedy, Lysistrata is a reactionary; she wants to put things back the way they were. To do that, however, she has to act like an impatient revolutionary. That irony well sums up the challenge that Golden Age Athens faced in trying to balance its reliance on tradition with the dynamism of the period's innovation in so many fields.

■ **Statuettes of Comic Actors**

These little statues portray comic actors wearing the kinds of masks and costumes that came into vogue after Aristophanes and his contemporaries wrote their comedies in the fifth century b.c., but they give a vivid sense of the exaggerated buffoonery that characterized the acting in Greek comedy. In Aristophanes' day, the grotesque unreality of comic costumes would have been even more striking because attached below the waists of the male actors were large leather phalluses that were props for all sorts of ribald jokes.
(Staatliche Museen zu Berlin-Preußicher Kulturbesitz Antikensammlung.)

The End of the Golden Age, 431–403 B.C.

A war between Athens and Sparta that lasted a generation (431–404 B.C.) ended the Athenian Golden Age. Called "Peloponnesian" today because it pitted Sparta's Peloponnese-based alliance against Athens's alliance, it arose at least in part as a result of Pericles' policies. The most powerful politician in Athens—he won election as a general for fifteen years in a row beginning in 443 B.C.—Pericles nevertheless had to withstand severe criticism of the huge public spending on his building program and harsh measures against Delian League allies that his rivals said sullied Athens's reputation. He faced his greatest challenge, however, when relations with Sparta worsened in the mid-430s B.C. over Athenian actions against Corinth and Megara, crucial Spartan allies. Finally, Corinth told Sparta to attack Athens or Corinth would change sides to the Athenian alliance. Sparta's leaders therefore gave Athens an ultimatum—stop mistreating our allies—which Pericles convinced the Athenian assembly to reject as unfair because Sparta was refusing arbitration of the disputes. In this way, the relations of Athens and Sparta with lesser city-states propelled the two powers over the brink into war. Pericles' critics claimed he was insisting on war against Sparta to revive his fading popularity. By 431 B.C., the thirty-year peace made in 446–445 B.C. had been shattered beyond repair.

The Peloponnesian War, 431–404 B.C.

Dragging on longer than any previous war in Greek history, the Peloponnesian War took place above all because Spartan leaders feared that the Athenians would use their superior long-distance offensive weaponry—the naval forces of the Delian League—to destroy Spartan control over the Peloponnesian League. (See "Taking Measure," page 87.) The duration of the struggle reflects the unpredictability of war and the consequences of the repeated reluctance of the Athenian assembly to negotiate peace terms instead of dictating them.

Thucydides dramatically revealed the absolute refusal of the Athenians to find a compromise solution with these words of Pericles to the assembly:

> If we do go to war, harbor no thought that you went to war over a trivial affair. For you this trifling matter is the assurance and the proof of your determination. If you yield to their demands, they will immediately confront you with some larger demand, since they will think that you only gave way on the first point out of fear. But if you stand firm, you will show them that they have to deal with you as equals. . . . When our equals, without agreeing to arbitration of the matter under dispute, make claims on us as neighbors and state those claims as commands, it would be no better than slavery to give in to them, no matter how large or how small the claim may be.

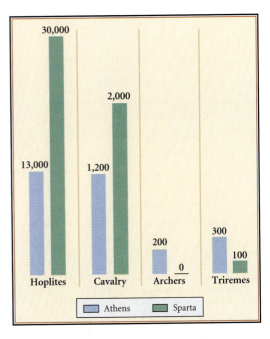

■ **TAKING MEASURE Military Forces of Athens and Sparta at the Beginning of the Peloponnesian War**
These figures give estimates of the relative strengths of the military forces of the Athenian side and the Spartan side when the Peloponnesian War broke out in 431 B.C. The numbers come from ancient historical sources—above all, the Athenian general and historian Thucydides, who fought in the war. The bar graphs reveal the different characteristics of the competing forces: Athens relied on its navy of triremes and its archers (the fifth-century B.C. equivalent of artillery and snipers). Sparta was preeminent in the forces needed for pitched land battles—hoplites (heavily armed infantry) and cavalry (shock troops used to disrupt opposing infantry). These differences dictated the strategies and tactics of each side. Athens tried to launch surprise raids from the sea, and Sparta tried to force decisive confrontations on the battlefield.
(From Pamela Bradley, *Ancient Greece: Using Evidence* [Melbourne: Edward Arnold, 1990], 229.)

Pericles advised Athens to use its superior navy to raid enemy lands while avoiding pitched battles with the Spartan infantry, even when they invaded the Athenian countryside and destroyed citizens' property there. In the end, he predicted, the superior resources of Athens would enable it to win a war of attrition.◆ With his unyielding leadership, this strategy might have prevailed, but chance intervened. From 430 to 426 B.C., an epidemic disease ravaged Athens's population, killing thousands—including Pericles in 429 B.C. The Athenians fought on, but they lost the clear direction that Pericles' costly strategy had required. The generals after him followed increasingly risky plans, culminating in an overambitious campaign against Sparta's allies in Sicily, far to the west. Dazzling the assembly in 415 B.C. with the dream of conquering that rich island, Alcibiades, the most innovative and brashest commander of the war, persuaded the Athenians to launch their largest naval expedition ever. His political rivals got him recalled from his command, however, and the invasion force suffered a catastrophic defeat in 413 B.C. (Map 2.3).

◆ For a primary source that reflects the confidence of Pericles in particular and Golden Age Greece in general, see Document 7, Thucydides, "The Funeral Oration of Pericles."

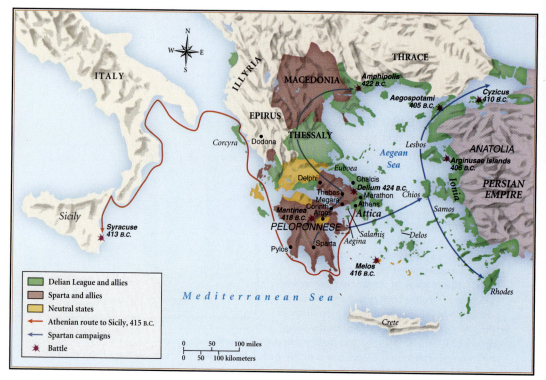

■ MAP 2.3 The Peloponnesian War, 431–404 B.C.
During the first ten years of the war, most of the battles took place in mainland Greece. Sparta, whose armies usually avoided distant campaigns, shocked Athens when its general Brasidas led successful attacks against Athenian forces in northeast Greece. In the war's next phase, Athens stunned the entire Greek world by launching a naval expedition against Spartan allies in Sicily. In the last ten years of the war, the action moved to the east, on and along the western coast of Anatolia and its islands, on the boundary of the Persian Empire, which helped the Spartans build a navy to defeat the Athenian fleet.

The Spartans then launched the final phase of the war by establishing a permanent base of operations in the Athenian countryside for year-round raids. The agricultural economy was devastated, and revenues fell drastically when twenty thousand slave workers crippled production in Athens's publicly owned silver mines by deserting to the enemy. Distress over the war's course led to an oligarchic coup that briefly overturned the democracy in 411 B.C., but the citizens soon restored traditional government and fought on. The end came when Persia sent money to help the Spartans finally build a strong navy. Aggressive Spartan action at sea forced Athens to surrender in 404 B.C. After twenty-seven years of near-continuous war, the Athenians were at the mercy of their enemies.

IMPORTANT DATES

c. 499–494 B.C.	Ionian revolt against Persian control	446–445 B.C.	Athens and Sparta sign a peace treaty meant to last thirty years
490 B.C.	Darius I sends Persian force against Athens; battle of Marathon	431 B.C.	Peloponnesian War between Athens and Sparta begins
480 B.C.	Xerxes leads Persian invasion of Greece; battles of Thermopylae and Salamis	c. 428–425 B.C.	Herodotus finishes the *Histories*
		415–413 B.C.	Alcibiades leads Athenian expedition against Sparta's allies in Sicily
477 B.C.	Athens assumes leadership of Delian League		
469–399 B.C.	Life of Socrates	411 B.C.	Aristophanes presents the comedy *Lysistrata*
461 B.C.	Ephialtes' political and judicial reforms strengthen Athenian democracy	404 B.C.	Athens surrenders to Sparta, ending the Peloponnesian War
		404–403 B.C.	Thirty Tyrants suspend democracy at Athens and conduct a reign of terror
458 B.C.	Aeschylus presents the trilogy *Oresteia*		
450 B.C.	The sophist Protagoras comes to Athens	403 B.C.	Athenians overthrow the Thirty Tyrants and restore democracy
447 B.C.	Pericles starts construction of the Parthenon		

Athens Humbled, 404–403 B.C.

The Spartans soon imposed a regime of antidemocratic Athenians, members of the social elite who became known as the Thirty Tyrants. Brutally suppressing democratic opposition, these oligarchs embarked on an eight-month period of terror in 404–403 B.C. The speechwriter Lysias, for example, reported that Spartan henchmen seized his brother for execution as a way of stealing the family's valuables, down to the gold earrings ripped from the ears of his brother's wife. An Athenian democratic resistance movement soon arose and in 403 B.C. expelled the Thirty Tyrants after a series of bloody street battles. Fortunately for the democrats, a split in the Spartan leadership, fueled by the competing ambitions of its two most prominent men, prevented effective Spartan military support for the tyrants.

To settle the internal strife that threatened to tear Athens apart, the newly restored democracy proclaimed the first known amnesty in Western history, a truce agreement forbidding any official charges or recriminations stemming from the crimes of 404–403 B.C. Athens's government was once again a functioning democracy, but its financial and military strength was shattered. Worse, its society

■ **MAPPING THE WEST Greece, Europe, and the Mediterranean, c. 400 B.C.**
No single power controlled the Mediterranean region at the end of the fifth century B.C. In the west, the Phoenician city of Carthage and the Greek cities of Sicily and southern Italy were rivals for the riches to be won by trade. In the east, the Spartans, emboldened by their recent victory over Athens in the Peloponnesian War, tried to become an international power outside the mainland for the first time in their history by sending campaigns into Anatolia. This aggressive action aroused stiff opposition from the Persians because it was a threat to their westernmost imperial provinces. There was to be no peace and quiet in the Mediterranean even after the twenty-seven years of the Peloponnesian War.

harbored the memory of a bitter divisiveness that no amnesty could dispel. The end of the Golden Age left Athenians worriedly wondering how to remake their lives and restore the luster that their city-state's innovative accomplishments had produced in that wondrous period.

Conclusion

Athens's Golden Age in the fifth century B.C. was a time of prosperity, political stability, international power, and artistic and cultural accomplishment. Its citizens had won great glory in the unexpected victory of the Greek alliance against the Persians at the beginning of the century. This stunning triumph occurred, the Athenians believed, because the gods smiled upon them with special favor and because they displayed superior courage, intelligence, and virtue.

Athens soon rivaled Sparta for the leadership of the Greek world, and by the mid-fifth century B.C. it was enjoying unprecedented confidence and prosperity. As the money poured in, the city-state built glorious temples, instituted pay for service in many government offices, and assembled the Mediterranean's most powerful navy. The poorer men who rowed the ships demanded greater democracy, leading to a judicial system guaranteeing fair treatment for all. Pericles became the most famous politician of the Golden Age by leading the drive for radical democracy.

Religious practice and women's lives maintained their traditional boundaries, but the scale of intellectual change was as dramatic as that in politics. Art and architecture broke out of old forms, promoting an impression of precarious motion rather than stability. Tragedy and comedy developed at Athens as public art forms commenting on contemporary social and political issues. Sophists' relativistic views of the universe and morality disturbed traditionally minded people, as did Socrates' strict ethics denying the value of the ordinary pursuit of wealth and success.

Wars framed the Golden Age. The Persian Wars sent the Athenians soaring to imperial power and prosperity, but their high-handed treatment of allies and enemies helped bring on the disastrous Peloponnesian War. Nearly three decades of battle brought the stars of the Greek Golden Age thudding back to earth: the Athenians in 400 B.C. found themselves in the same situation as in 500 B.C., fearful of Spartan power and worried whether the world's first democracy could survive. As it turned out, the next great threat to Greek stability and independence would once again come from outside, not from the east this time but from the north.

Suggested References for further reading and online research appear on page SR-3 at the back of the book.

www.bedfordstmartins.com/huntconcise   See the ONLINE STUDY GUIDE to assess your mastery of the material covered in this chapter.

From the Classical to the Hellenistic World

c. 400–30 B.C.

A BOUT 255 B.C., AN EGYPTIAN CAMEL TRADER in Syria paid a bilingual scribe to pen a letter to his Greek employer, Zeno, back in Egypt, to complain about his treatment by Zeno's Greek assistant, Krotos: "You know that when you left me in Syria with Krotos I followed all your instructions concerning the camels and behaved blamelessly towards you. But Krotos has ignored your orders to pay me my salary; I've received nothing despite asking him for my money over and over. He just tells me to go away. I waited a long time for you to come, but when I no longer had the necessities of life and couldn't get help anywhere, I had to run away to keep from starving to death. . . . I am desperate summer and winter. . . . They have treated me with contempt because I am not a Greek. I therefore beg you, please, command them to pay me my salary so that I won't go hungry just because I don't know how to speak Greek."

The camel trader's name has been lost, but his desperate plea reveals that not being Greek contributed to his mistreatment. His plight—having to communicate persuasively with a foreigner holding power in his homeland—reveals the challenges facing the eastern Mediterranean world as it moved from the Classical period (500–323 B.C.) to the Hellenistic period (323–30 B.C.). These challenges were created by the large-scale movement of Greeks into the Near East and the resulting interaction between the local cultures and the culture of the newcomers. War initiated these changes. The Peloponnesian War (431–404 B.C.) had accustomed many Greeks to making a living as soldiers, and after the war thousands of them became mercenaries serving Near Eastern rulers. The migration of Greeks to the

■ **Dancing Figure on Gilded Bowl**
The large metal crater (wine bowl) on which this exuberant dancer appears was found at Derveni in Macedonia. Fashioned from gilded bronze, it probably dates from the 330s B.C. The intricate detail shows the high level of skill of Greek metalworkers; bowls and vases crafted in precious metals were favorite luxury items for the social elite. The imagery on this bowl—worshipers of Dionysus, the god of wine, in a state of ecstatic joy—was appropriate for wine drinking, a prominent feature of Macedonian life. (Thessalonike, Archaeological Museum, © Archaeological Receipts Fund.)

Near East accelerated when the Macedonian king Alexander the Great (356–323 B.C.) conquered the Persian Empire and left colonies of Greeks from Egypt and the Near East to present-day Afghanistan.

Nineteenth-century scholars coined the term *Hellenistic* to designate the period of Greek and Near Eastern history from Alexander's death in 323 B.C. to the death of Cleopatra VII, the last Macedonian queen of Egypt, in 30 B.C. The term conveys the idea that a mixed, cosmopolitan form of social and cultural life combining Hellenic (that is, Greek) and indigenous traditions emerged in the aftermath of Alexander's conquest of the Persian Empire.

His successors revived monarchy in the Greek world by carving Macedonian and Near Eastern territory into kingdoms whose wealth made them dominant and reduced Greece's city-states to second-rate powers. The city-states retained their local political and social institutions but lost their independence in foreign policy. Hellenistic kings decided international politics. However, they imported Greeks to fill royal offices, man their armies, and run businesses; the result was tension with their non-Greek subjects. Immigrant Greeks, such as Zeno in Egypt, formed a social and political elite dominating the kingdoms' local populations. Egyptians or Syrians or Mesopotamians who wanted to rise in society had to win the support of these Greeks and learn their language. Otherwise, they might find themselves as powerless as the hungry camel trader.

Over time, however, the enduring local cultures of the Near East interacted with the culture of the Greek overlords. The result was a new, multicultural synthesis. Locals married Greeks, shared their religious traditions with the newcomers, taught them their agricultural and scientific knowledge, and sometimes learned Greek to win administrative jobs. Although Hellenistic society always remained hierarchical, with Greeks at the top, and tension between rulers and ruled persisted, Hellenistic society did achieve a cohesion that promoted innovation in art, science, philosophy, and religion based on a blend of Greek and Near Eastern traditions.

The end of the Hellenistic kingdoms came in the first century B.C., after the Romans expanded beyond their home base in Italy and overthrew them all. The complex mixing of peoples and ideas that occurred in the Hellenistic period greatly influenced Roman civilization and thus later Western civilization. Hellenistic religious developments, for example, provided the background for Christianity. The period's cultural legacy remained visible long after the glories of Greece's Golden Age had faded away.

The Decline of Classical Greece, c. 400–350 B.C.

The fifth century B.C. was Greece's Golden Age, but the Peloponnesian War brought a violent end to that prosperous part of the Classical period. After Sparta defeated Athens in the war, Athens's economy gradually recovered, but the stability of daily life could not conceal the bitterness that democratic Athenians felt toward those whom they blamed for the violent rule of the Thirty Tyrants. This tension provoked the execution of Socrates in 399 B.C. His fate spurred Plato and Aristotle to create Greece's most famous philosophies about right and wrong and how human beings should live.

The Spartans tried to use their victory to turn Sparta into an international power, but their high-handed behavior and collaboration with the Persian king stirred up fierce resistance from Greek city-states, especially Thebes and Athens. By the 350s B.C., bloody squabbling had so weakened the Greeks that they lacked the strength and will to prevent the expansion of their ambitious northern neighbors, the Macedonians. This failure ensured the decline of Classical Greece.

The Aftermath of War and the Case of Socrates

Spartan invaders during the Peloponnesian War wrecked the homes of many Athenians living in the countryside and devastated Athens's agriculture and trade. Especially hard hit were moderately well-off women whose husbands and brothers died during the conflict. Such women traditionally did weaving at home and supervised household slaves while the men earned the family's income by farming or commerce. Deprived of their providers, these widows had to find work outside the home. The jobs open to them were low-paying occupations, some traditional for women, such as wet nurses or weavers, or some for which not enough men were available, such as vineyard laborers.

Resourceful Athenians found ways to profit from women's skills. Socrates' friend Aristarchus, for example, became poverty-stricken supporting several widowed sisters, nieces, and female cousins. Socrates reminded his friend that his relatives knew how to make cloaks, shirts, capes, and smocks, "the work considered the best and most fitting for women." The women had been making clothing only for family members. Socrates suggested that they sell it for profit. The plan succeeded financially, but the women complained that Aristarchus was the only member of the household who ate without working. Socrates advised his friend to reply that the women should think of him as sheep viewed a guard dog—earning his food by keeping the wolves away.

Economic recovery stumbled when revenue fell in Athens's biggest enterprise—the state-owned silver mines, which were leased to private citizens exploiting gangs of slave miners. But economic conditions improved when business owners and households energetically revived trade and produced manufactured goods in their homes and in small shops, such as metal foundries and pottery workshops. Businesses, usually family run, were small; the largest known was a shield-making company owning 120 slaves. The return of prosperity, coupled with the flexible work roles resulting from the needs of war, apparently led to changes in gender-defined occupations. The earliest evidence for men working alongside women in cloth production occurs in this period, when commercial weaving shops sprang up for the first time. Previously, only women made cloth and did so at home. Later in the fourth century B.C., there is also evidence that a few women made careers in the arts, especially painting and music, which men traditionally dominated.

In the improved postwar economy, most workers earned just enough to feed and clothe their families. They customarily ate two meals a day, a light lunch in midmorning and a heavier evening meal. Bread baked from barley provided the main part of their diet; only rich people could afford wheat bread. A family bought its bread from small bakery stands, often run by women, or made it at home. Most people ate greens, beans, onions, garlic, olives, fruit, and cheese with their bread; they had meat only at animal sacrifices paid for by the state. Everyone drank wine, diluted with water. Water was fetched from public fountains in jugs by women or slaves. All but the poorest families owned at least one or two slaves to do household chores and look after the children.

The restored stability of their everyday lives did not make Athenians forget the murderous reign of the Thirty Tyrants. Socrates became the most renowned victim of the lingering bitterness dividing Athenians when he was blamed for the violent crimes of his follower Critias, one of the Thirty. In fact, Socrates put himself at risk by refusing to cooperate with the tyrants, but some prominent Athenians believed his philosophy turned Critias into a traitor. Since the amnesty blocked prosecution for wartime offenses, Socrates' opponents charged him with impiety in 399 B.C. They accused him of not believing in the city-state's gods and of introducing new divinities and also of turning young men away from Athenian moral traditions. When Socrates spoke in his own defense, he repeated his unyielding dedication to goading his fellow citizens into examining their preconceptions. He vowed to remain their stinging gadfly.

■ **Vase Painting of Women Fetching Water**

This painting depicts a scene from everyday life in a well-appointed city-state: women filling water jugs to take back to their homes from the gushing spouts at an elaborate public fountain. Practically no Greek homes had running water, so it was the duty of freeborn and slave women in a household to gather water for drinking, cooking, washing, and cleaning. Prosperous cities built attractive fountain houses, such as the one shown here, where a regular supply of fresh water was available from springs or was piped in through aqueducts. These fountains were popular spots for women's conversations outside the house. The women in this scene wear the long robes and hair coverings characteristic of the time. (William Francis Warden Fund. Courtesy of the Museum of Fine Arts, Boston.)

After the jury narrowly voted to convict, the prosecutors proposed death. In such instances, the defendant was then expected to propose exile as an alternative, which the jury usually accepted. Socrates, however, said that he deserved a reward rather than a punishment, until his friends at the trial prevailed upon him to propose a fine as his penalty. The jury, however, chose death. Socrates accepted his sentence calmly because, as he put it, "no evil can befall a good man either in life or in death." He was executed in the customary way, with a poisonous drink concocted from powdered hemlock. Ancient sources report that many Athenians soon came to regret the execution of Socrates as a tragic mistake and a severe blow to their reputation.

The Philosophy of Plato and Aristotle

Socrates' fate turned the world upside down for his most famous follower, Plato (c. 429–348 B.C.). After Socrates' death, Plato turned his back on marriage and a public career and devoted himself to pondering the nature of the world in which an evil fate could befall such a good man as Socrates. He established a philosophical school, the Academy, in Athens around 386 B.C. An informal association of people who studied philosophy, mathematics, and theoretical astronomy, the Academy attracted intellectuals to Athens for the next nine hundred years.

Plato's highly abstract ideas on ethics and politics have remained central to philosophy and political science since his day. He presented his ideas in dialogues, which

■ **Mosaic of Plato's Academy**
This mosaic from the Roman period depicts philosophers—identified by their beards—at Plato's school in Athens holding discussions among themselves. The Academy, founded around 386 B.C., became one of Greece's most famous and long-lasting institutions, attracting scholars and students until it closed around A.D. 530. The columns and tree express the harmonious blend of the natural and built environment of the Academy, which was meant to promote productive and pleasant discussions.
(Erich Lessing/Art Resource, NY.)

were intended to provoke readers into thoughtful reflection rather than to prescribe a predetermined set of beliefs. His views apparently changed over time—nowhere did he present one cohesive set of doctrines. Nevertheless, he always maintained one essential idea: moral qualities in their ultimate reality are universal and absolute, not relative.

In some of his works, Plato proposed that absolute virtues, such as Goodness, Justice, Beauty, and Equality, existed as metaphysical realities he called Forms (or Ideas). He argued that the Forms are invisible, invariable, and eternal entities located in a higher realm beyond the daily world. According to Plato, the Forms are the only true reality; what we experience through our senses in everyday life are only dim and imperfect representations of these flawless realities, as if, he said, we were watching their shadows cast on the wall of a cave. His theory of Forms elevated metaphysics—the consideration of the ultimate nature of reality beyond the reach of the human senses—to a central and enduring issue for philosophers.

Plato's idea that humans possess immortal souls distinct from their bodies established the concept of *dualism,* a separation between spiritual and physical being. This notion influenced much of later philosophical and religious thought. Plato believed the proper goal for humans is to seek order and purity in their own souls by using rational thoughts to control their irrational desires, which are harmful. The desire to drink wine to excess, for example, is irrational because the drinker fails to consider the hangover to come the next day. Finally, because the soul is immortal and the body is not, our present, impure existence is only one part of our true existence.

Plato presented the most famous version of his utopian political vision in his dialogue *The Republic.* This work, whose Greek title means "system of government," primarily concerns the nature of justice and the reasons people should be just. According to Plato, justice is unattainable in a democracy and requires hierarchy. The condemnation of Socrates convinced him that most citizens were incapable of rising above self-interest. He therefore ranked people in his ideal society by their ability to grasp the truth of the Forms.

Women could rank as high as men because they possess the same virtues. To minimize distraction, the highest-ranking members of Plato's utopia are to have neither private property nor individual families. These men and women are to live together in barracks, eat in mess halls, and exercise in the same gymnasiums. They are to have sexual relations with various partners so that the best women can mate with the best men to produce the best children, who will be raised in a common environment by special caretakers. Those who achieve the highest level of knowledge in Plato's ideal society qualify to rule over it as philosopher-kings. Plato did not think such a society was truly possible, but he did believe that imagining it was an important way to help people teach themselves to live justly. For this reason above all, he passionately believed the study of philosophy mattered to human life.

Plato's legacy included inspiring his most famous pupil, Aristotle (384–322 B.C.). From 342 to 335 B.C., Aristotle tutored the young Alexander the Great in

Macedonia. He then created his own practical philosophy for living a happy life and founded his own school in Athens, the Lyceum, in 335 B.C. Later called the Peripatetic School after the covered walkway (*peripatos*) where students conversed protected from the sun, his school became world famous. He lectured with dazzling intelligence and energy on nearly every branch of learning: biology, medicine, anatomy, psychology, meteorology, physics, chemistry, mathematics, music, metaphysics, rhetoric, political science, ethics, and literary criticism.

Aristotle's vast writings made him one of the most influential scientists and philosophers in Western history. His great reputation rests on his development of rigorous systems of logical argument as well as his emphasis on scientific investigation of the natural world. Creating a sophisticated system of logic to identify the forms of valid arguments, Aristotle established grounds for distinguishing a logically sound case from a merely persuasive one. Furthermore, Aristotle insisted on explanations based on common sense rather than metaphysics. He denied the validity of Plato's theory of Forms, for example, on the grounds that the separate existence Plato postulated for them did not make sense. As for scientific investigation, Aristotle believed that the best way to understand objects and beings was to observe them in their natural settings. The first scientist to try to collect all available information on animals, Aristotle recorded facts about more than five hundred different species, including insects. His recognition that whales and dolphins are mammals, which later writers on animals overlooked, was not rediscovered for another two thousand years.

Like Plato, Aristotle criticized democracy because it allowed uneducated instead of "better" people to control politics. Some of Aristotle's views justified inequalities characteristic of his time. He regarded slavery as natural, arguing that some people were by nature bound to be slaves because their souls lacked the rational part that should rule in a human. He also concluded, based on faulty notions of biology, that women were by nature inferior to men, a conclusion with disastrous influence on later thought.

In ethics, Aristotle emphasized the need to develop habits of just behavior. People should achieve self-control by training their minds to win out over instincts and passions. Self-control did not mean denying human desires and appetites; rather, it meant striking a balance between suppressing and heedlessly indulging physical yearnings, of finding "the mean." Aristotle claimed that the mind should rule in finding this balance because the intellect is the finest human quality and the mind is the true self—indeed, the godlike part of a person.

The Disunity of Greece

During the fifty years following the Peloponnesian War, Sparta, Thebes, and Athens each in turn tried to dominate Greece. None succeeded. Their struggles with one another left Greece susceptible to outside interference and undermined the political independence of the Classical city-states. In the 390s to 370s B.C., the Spartans did the most to provoke this fatal disunity by trying to conquer other city-states. Thebes, Athens, Corinth, and Argos responded by forming an anti-Spartan coalition because Spartan aggression threatened their interests at home and abroad. The Spartans checkmated the alliance by coming to terms with the Persian king. Blatantly renouncing their commitment to defend Greek freedom, the Spartans acknowledged the Persian ruler's right to control the Greek city-states of Anatolia—in return for permission to pursue their own interests in Greece without Persian interference. This agreement of 386 B.C., called the King's Peace, deprived the Anatolian Greeks of the freedom won in the Persian Wars. The Athenians rebuilt their military strength to combat Sparta. By 377 B.C., Athens had again become the leader of a naval alliance. This time, league members insisted that their rights be specified in writing to prevent any imperialistic Athenian behavior.

The Thebans became Greece's main land power in the 370s B.C. They decisively defeated a Spartan invasion at the battle of Leuctra in Boeotia in 371 B.C. and then attacked the Spartan homeland, destroying Sparta's power forever by freeing many helots. This Theban success so frightened the Athenians, whose city lay only forty miles from Thebes, that they made a temporary alliance with the Spartans. Their combined armies confronted the Thebans in the battle of Mantinea in the Peloponnese in 362 B.C. Thebes won the battle but lost the war when its best general was killed and no capable replacement could be found.

The battle of Mantinea left the Greek city-states in impotent disunity. The contemporary historian Xenophon succinctly summed up the situation: "Everyone had supposed that the winners of this battle would be Greece's rulers and its losers their subjects; but there was only more confusion and disturbance in Greece after it than before." By the 350s B.C., then, the Greek city-states' struggle for supremacy over one another had petered out in a stalemate of exhaustion. Failing to cooperate, they opened the way for the rise of a new power—the kingdom of Macedonia, which would threaten their cherished independence.

The Rise of Macedonia, 359–323 B.C.

The kingdom of Macedonia took advantage of the Greek city-states' disunity to make itself an international superpower. That this previously minor kingdom would seize the leadership of Greece and conquer the Persian Empire ranks as one of the greatest surprises in ancient political and military history. Two aggressive and charismatic kings produced this amazing transformation: Philip II (r. 359–336 B.C.) and his son Alexander the Great (r. 336–323 B.C.). Their conquests marked the end of the Classical period and paved the way for the cultural interactions of the Hellenistic age.

Philip II and the Background of Macedonian Power

The Macedonians' power sprang from the characteristics of their monarchy and their ethnic pride. The Macedonian people demanded the freedom to tell their monarchs what needed to be improved, and a king could govern effectively only as long as he maintained the support of the most powerful nobles, who were the king's social equals and controlled large bands of followers. Fighting, hunting, and heavy drinking were these men's favorite pastimes. The king was expected to excel in these activities to show he was capable of ruling. Queens and royal mothers received respect in this male-dominated society because they came from powerful families in the nobility or the ruling houses of lands bordering Macedonia.

Macedonians thought of themselves as Greek by blood and took pride in their identity. They had their own language, but the nobles routinely learned to speak Greek. Macedonians looked down on their southern relatives as too soft for the adversities of northern life. The Greeks reciprocated this scorn. The famed Athenian orator Demosthenes (384–322 B.C.) lambasted Philip II as "not only not a Greek nor related to the Greeks, but not even a barbarian from a land worth mentioning; no, he's a pestilence from Macedonia, a region where you can't even buy a slave worth his salt."

■ **Statue of the Orator Demosthenes**

The Athenian political leader Demosthenes (384–322 B.C.) became the most famous orator in the Greek world by opposing the expansionist actions of the Macedonian king Philip and his son Alexander the Great. This statue is a marble copy from the Roman period of a Greek original that was cast in bronze and showed Demosthenes holding a scroll to symbolize his great learning. Demosthenes delivered his speeches, whether before the democratic assembly or in a court case, without reading from a text. The statue shows him in fine physical condition; he reportedly practiced delivering speeches while jogging to improve his lung power.

(Scala/Art Resource, NY.)

Until Philip II's reign, strife between the king and the nobles kept Macedonia from mobilizing its full military strength. Indeed, kings so feared violence from their own countrymen that they stationed bodyguards outside the royal bedroom. A military disaster brought Philip to the throne at a desperate moment. The Illyrians, hostile neighbors to the north, had slaughtered Philip's predecessor and four thousand troops. Philip restored the army's confidence by teaching the infantry an unstoppable new tactic with their thrusting spears, which extended fourteen to sixteen feet long and took two hands to wield. Arranging his hoplites in a phalanx formation, he created deep blocks of soldiers bristling with outstretched spears like a lethal porcupine. Deploying cavalry as a strike force to protect the infantry's flanks, Philip's reorganized army promptly routed the Illyrians.

Philip soon embarked on a whirlwind of diplomacy, bribery, and military action that made Macedonia into an international power. A Greek contemporary, the historian Theopompus of Chios, labeled Philip "insatiable and extravagant; he did everything in a hurry . . . he never spared the time to reckon up his income and expenditure." By the late 340s B.C., Philip had cajoled or coerced most of northern Greece to follow his lead in foreign policy. Seeking the glory of avenging Greece and fearing the potentially destabilizing effect his reinvigorated army would have on his kingdom if the soldiers had nothing to do, Philip planned to lead a united Macedonian and Greek army against the Persian Empire. To launch this grandiose invasion, he needed to control the forces of southern Greece.

Expansion of Macedonia under Philip II, r. 359–336 B.C.

Philip found in Greek history the justification for attacking Persia: revenge for the Persian Wars. But some Greeks remained unconvinced. Demosthenes used stirring rhetoric to criticize Greeks for their failure to resist Philip. They stood by, he thundered, "as if Philip were a hailstorm, praying that he would not come their way, but not trying to do anything to head him off." Finally, Athens and Thebes headed a coalition of southern Greek city-states to try to block Philip, but in 338 B.C. the king and his Greek allies trounced the coalition's forces at the battle of Chaeronea in Boeotia. The defeated city-states retained their internal freedom, but Philip compelled them to join his alliance. The course of later history showed the battle of Chaeronea to be a turning point in Greek history: never again would the city-states of Greece make foreign policy for themselves without the interference of outside powers. Although the city-states no longer were independent actors in international politics, they did remain the basic economic and social units of Greece.

Exploits of Alexander the Great, 336–323 B.C.

Alexander III stepped onto center stage in 336 B.C. when a Macedonian assassinated his father. Unconfirmed rumors speculated that Alexander's mother, Olympias, had instigated the murder to procure the throne for her twenty-year-old son. He promptly murdered potential rivals for the crown and, in several lightning-fast wars, subdued Macedonia's enemies on the west and north. Then Alexander compelled the southern Greeks, who had defected from the alliance after Philip's death, to rejoin. To demonstrate the price of disloyalty, in 335 B.C. Alexander destroyed Thebes for rebelling.

The following year he embarked on the most astonishing military campaign in ancient history by leading a Macedonian and Greek army against the Persian Empire to fulfill his father's dream of avenging Greece. Alexander's astounding success in conquering everything from Turkey to Egypt to Uzbekistan while still in his twenties earned him the title "the Great" in later ages and inspired countless legends. His greatness consisted of his ability to inspire his men to follow him into unknown lands and to lead cavalry charges against the enemy's infantry. Alexander regularly rode his warhorse Bucephalus ("Oxhead") into the heart of the enemy's front line, sharing the danger of the common soldier. No one could miss him in his plumed helmet, vividly colored cloak, and armor polished to reflect the sun. He alarmed his principal adviser by giving away nearly all his property to create new landowners who would furnish troops. "What," the adviser asked, "do you have left for yourself?" "My hopes," Alexander replied. Those hopes centered on being a warrior as splendid as the incomparable Achilles of Homer's *Iliad*; he always slept with a copy of the *Iliad* and a dagger under his pillow.

Alexander displayed his heroic ambitions as his army advanced relentlessly eastward through Persian territory (Map 3.1). In Anatolia, he visited Gordion, where an oracle had promised the lordship of Asia to whoever could loosen a seemingly impenetrable knot of rope tying the yoke of an ancient chariot preserved in the city. The young king, so the story goes, cut the knot with his sword. When his army later forced the Persian king, Darius III, to abandon his wives and daughters, Alexander treated the captured women with honor. His chivalrous behavior toward the royal women enhanced his reputation among the peoples of the Persian Empire.

Alexander complemented his bravery and chivalry with a keen eye for innovative military technology. When Tyre, a fortified city on an island off the coast of the Levant, refused to surrender in 332 B.C., he built a massive stone pier as a platform for armored battering rams and catapults flinging boulders to breach the walls of the city. The capture of Tyre rang the death knell of impregnable walled city-states; furthermore, the knowledge that a well-equipped army could penetrate fortification walls made it difficult for populations to remain united in the face of attacks.

■ **Mosaic of Alexander the Great at the Battle of Issus**
This large mosaic, which served as a floor in an upscale Roman house, was a copy of a famous earlier painting of the battle of Issus of 333 B.C. It shows Alexander the Great on his warhorse Bucephalus confronting the Persian king Darius in his chariot. Darius reaches out in compassion for his warriors who are sacrificing themselves to protect him. The original artist was an extremely skilled painter. Notice the dramatic foreshortening of the horse directly in front of Darius and the startling effect of the face of the dying warrior reflected in the polished shield just to the right of the horse. (Erich Lessing/Art Resource, NY.)

Alexander's actions after he conquered Egypt and the Persian heartland revealed his strategy for ruling a vast empire: establishing colonies of Greeks and Macedonians in conquered territory while retaining the traditional administrative system. The first new city he established, in 331 B.C., was in Egypt, on the Mediterranean coast to the west of the Nile River. He named it Alexandria after himself. In Persia, he proclaimed himself king of Asia but left the existing governing units intact, even retaining some high-ranking Persian administrators. The succession of a Macedonian to the Persian throne changed the lives of the local populations of the Persian Empire very little. They continued to send the same taxes to a still-remote master, whom they rarely if ever saw.

Alexander's goal seems to have been to outdo even the heroes of legend by marching to the end of the world. Paring his army to reduce the need for supplies, he led his forces northeast into the trackless steppes of Bactria and Sogdiana (modern Afghanistan and Uzbekistan). On the Jaxartes River (Syr Darya), he founded a

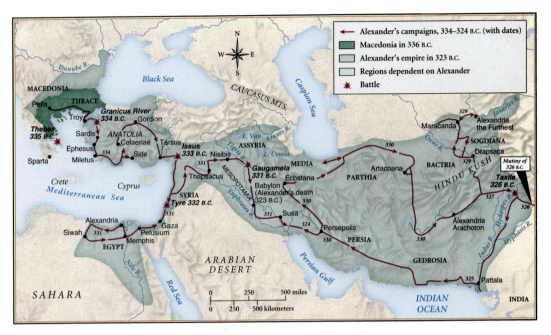

■ **MAP 3.1 Conquests of Alexander the Great, 336–323 B.C.**

The scale of Alexander's military campaigns in Asia made him a legend. From the time he led his army out of Macedonia and Greece in 334 B.C. until his death in Babylon in 323 B.C., he was on the move. His careful intelligence gathering combined with his charismatic and brilliant generalship produced an unbroken string of victories. His skillful choice of regional administrators, founding of garrison cities, and preservation of local governing structures kept his conquests stable after he moved on.

www.bedfordstmartins.com/huntconcise   See the ONLINE STUDY GUIDE for more help in analyzing this map.

city called Alexandria the Furthest to show that he had penetrated deeper into this region than even Cyrus, founder of the Persian Empire. When it proved impossible to subdue the highly mobile locals, however, Alexander settled for an alliance sealed by his marriage to the Bactrian princess Roxane. He then headed east into India. Seventy days of marching through monsoon rains extinguished his soldiers' fire for conquest. In the spring of 326 B.C., they mutinied on the banks of the Hyphasis River in western India and forced Alexander to turn back. A difficult march brought him back to Persia by 324 B.C.; he immediately began planning an invasion of the Arabian peninsula and, after that, North Africa.

By this time, Alexander had dropped all pretense of keeping his promise to respect the internal freedom of the Greek city-states. He ordered them to restore citizenship to the many war-created exiles whose status as wandering, stateless persons was creating unrest. Even more striking was his announcement that he wished to receive the honors due a god. Initially dumbfounded by these instructions, most

Greek city-states soon complied by sending honorary religious delegations to him. The Spartan Damis pithily expressed the only prudent position on Alexander's deification: "If Alexander wishes to be a god, then we'll agree that he be called a god." Personal rather than political motives best explain Alexander's wish. He almost certainly had come to believe he was actually the son of Zeus; after all, Greek mythology contained many stories of Zeus mating with a human female and producing children. Alexander's feats exceeded the bounds of human possibility, demonstrating that he had achieved godlike power; he therefore must be a god himself.

Alexander's premature death in Babylon in 323 b.c. from a fever and heavy drinking ended his plan to conquer the western Mediterranean. Roxane was to bear their first child a few months after Alexander's death, but, like Pericles, Alexander had made no plans about what should happen if he died unexpectedly. The story goes that when his commanders asked him on his deathbed to whom he bequeathed his kingdom, he replied, "To the most powerful."

Modern scholars disagree on almost everything about Alexander. They offer varying assessments of his character, ranging from bloodthirsty monster interested solely in endless conquest to romantic visionary intent on creating a multiethnic world open to all cultures. The ancient sources suggest that Alexander's overall aims can best be explained as interlinked goals: the conquest and administration of the known world and the exploration and possible colonization of new territory beyond. Conquest through military action was a time-honored pursuit for Macedonian aristocrats like Alexander and suited his restless, ruthless, and incredibly energetic nature. He included non-Macedonians in his administration and army because he needed their expertise. Alexander's explorations benefited numerous scientific fields, from geography to botany, because he took along scientifically minded writers to collect and catalog the new knowledge they acquired; he regularly sent reams of new scientific information to his old tutor Aristotle. The far-flung cities that Alexander founded served as outposts to warn headquarters about local uprisings. They also created new opportunities for trade in valuable goods such as spices that were not produced in the Mediterranean region.

The Athenian orator Aeschines (c. 397–322 b.c.) summed up the bewildered reaction of many people to Alexander's exploits: "What strange and unexpected event has not occurred in our time? The life we have lived is no ordinary human one, but we were born to be an object of wonder to posterity." Aeschines predicted correctly. Stories of fabulous deeds attributed to Alexander became popular folk tales throughout the world, reaching even distant regions where Alexander had never set foot, such as southern Africa. The popularity of his legend as a warrior-hero was one of his most persistent legacies to later ages. That the worlds of Greece and the Near East had been brought into closer contact than ever before represented another long-lasting effect of his astonishing career, which drew the curtain on the Classical period and opened the next act in the drama of Western history, the Hellenistic period.

The Hellenistic Kingdoms, 323–30 B.C.

The innovative political, cultural, and economic developments of the Hellenistic period arose from the interaction of Greek and Near Eastern civilizations. The process, set in motion by war, was filled with tension between conquerors and subjects and produced uneven results. Greek ideas and practices had their greatest impact on the urban populations of Egypt and southwestern Asia. The many people who farmed in the countryside had much less contact with Greek ways of life. Still, the legacy of the Hellenistic world would be decisive in its influence on the Romans.

The dominant Hellenistic political structures were new kingdoms, which reintroduced monarchy into Greek history; kings had been rare in Greece since the fall of Mycenaean civilization nearly a thousand years earlier. The new kingdoms were created by commanders from Alexander's army who seized portions of his empire for themselves after his death and proclaimed themselves kings. Between 306 and 304 B.C., after more than twenty years of struggle, their families established themselves as the dynasties ruling the Hellenistic kingdoms.

The Structure of Hellenistic Kingdoms

Alexander's army commanders divided his conquests among themselves (Map 3.2): Antigonus (c. 382–301 B.C.) took over in Anatolia, the Near East, Macedonia, and Greece; Seleucus (c. 358–281 B.C.), in Babylonia and the East as far as India; and Ptolemy (c. 367–282 B.C.), in Egypt. These new rulers—historians call them "successor kings"—had to create their own form of kingship because they did not inherit their positions legitimately: they were self-proclaimed monarchs with neither blood ties to any traditional royal family line nor any personal relationship to a particular territory. For this reason, historians often characterize their type of rule as "personal monarchy."

By the middle of the third century B.C., the three Hellenistic kingdoms had reached a balance of power that precluded their expanding much beyond their core territories. The Antigonids had been reduced to a kingdom in Macedonia, but they also controlled mainland Greece, whose city-states had to follow royal foreign policy even though they retained their internal freedom. The Seleucids ruled in Syria and Mesopotamia, but they had been forced to cede their easternmost territory to the Indian king Chandragupta (r. 323–299 B.C.), founder of the Mauryan dynasty. They also lost most of Persia to the Parthians, a northern Iranian people. The Ptolemies retained control of the rich land of Egypt.

Conflicts frequently arose over contested border areas. The armies of the Ptolemaic and Seleucid kingdoms, for example, periodically engaged in a violent tug-of-war over the lands of the Levant, just as the Egyptians and Hittites had done a thousand years earlier. Sometimes the struggles between the major kingdoms left openings for smaller, regional kingdoms to establish themselves. The most famous

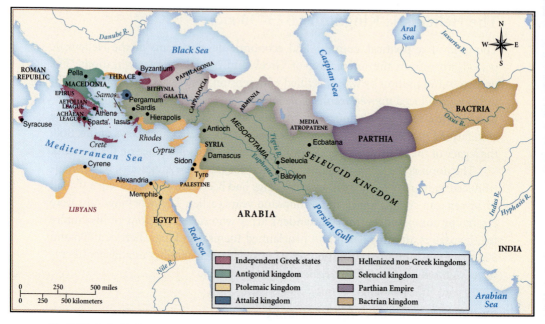

■ **MAP 3.2 Hellenistic Kingdoms, c. 240 B.C.**
*Although the traditional Greek city-states retained their formal independence in the Hellenistic pe-
riod, monarchy became the dominant political system in the areas of Alexander's former conquests.
By about eighty years after his death in 323 B.C., the most striking changes to the three major
kingdoms originally established by his successors were that the Seleucids had given up their easternmost territories and the Attalid kingdom had carved out an independent local reign in western
Anatolia.*

of these was the kingdom of the Attalids in western Anatolia, with the wealthy city
of Pergamum as its capital. In Central Asia (in modern Afghanistan), Greek colonists
settled by Alexander broke off from the Seleucid kingdom in the mid-third century

Attalid Kingdom

B.C. to found their own regional kingdom in Bactria. Between 239 and 130 B.C., it flourished from
the trade in luxury goods between India and
China and the Mediterranean world.

The Hellenistic kings realized that establishing the legitimacy of their rule was essential if
their royal lines were to endure. In seeking stability, they tried to incorporate local traditions
into their rule. For the Seleucids, for example,
this meant combining Macedonian with Near
Eastern royal customs; for the Ptolemies, Macedonian with Egyptian. The strength of successor
kings ultimately rested on their personal ability

and power. A letter from the city of Ilion (on the site of ancient Troy) summed up the situation in its praise of the Seleucid king Antiochus I (c. 324–261 B.C.): "His rule depends mostly on his own excellence [*aretê*], and on the goodwill of his friends and on his forces." In the end, then, Hellenistic monarchy amounted to foreign rule over indigenous populations by kings and queens of Macedonian descent. Seleucus, for one, claimed this right as a universal truth: "It is not the customs of the Persians and other people that I impose upon you, but the law which is common to everyone, that what is decreed by the king is always just."

The survival of Hellenistic dynasties depended on their ability to create strong armies, effective administrations, and cooperative urban elites. Hellenistic militaries provided security against internal unrest as well as external enemies. To develop their forces, the Seleucid and Ptolemaic kings vigorously promoted immigration by Greeks and Macedonians, who received land grants in return for service as professional soldiers. When this source of manpower gave out, the kings had to employ more local men as troops. Military expenditures eventually became a problem because the kings faced continual pressure to pay large numbers of mercenaries and because military technology had become so expensive. To compete effectively, a Hellenistic king had to provide giant artillery, such as catapults capable of flinging a projectile weighing 170 pounds a distance of nearly two hundred yards.

Hellenistic kings had to create large administrations to collect the revenues they needed. They recruited Greeks, Macedonians, and local people to be officials. Immigrants held the top jobs. Local men who aspired to a government career bettered their chances if they learned to read and write Greek in addition to their native language. This bilingualism qualified them to communicate official orders, especially tax laws, to the indigenous farmers and crafts producers. Greeks and Macedonians generally saw themselves as too superior to mix with the locals, so Greeks and non-Greeks tended to live in separate communities.

Agriculture and trade generated the wealth of the kingdoms, and cities old and new were their economic and social hubs. Many Greeks and Macedonians lived in new cities founded by Alexander and his successors in Egypt and the Near East, and they also moved to old cities. Hellenistic kings promoted this urban emigration to build a supportive constituency for their reigns. These rulers adorned their new cities with the traditional features of classical Greek city-states, such as gymnasiums and theaters. Although these cities often retained the political institutions of the *polis*, such as councils and assemblies for citizen men, the requirement to follow royal policy limited their freedom. The kings treated the cities considerately because they needed the Greek and Macedonian urban elites to keep order and ensure a steady flow of tax revenues.♦ Wealthy people had the crucial responsibility of collecting taxes from the surrounding countryside, as well as from their city, and

---

♦ For a primary source that reveals the vibrant urban culture and economy of the Hellenistic world, see Document 8, Zenon, Egyptian Official, "Records."

■ **Mosaic Floor from Ai Khanoum**

*This mosaic floor was excavated at the site of a city founded by Greeks and Macedonians in Af-
ghanistan about 300 B.C. The city's original name is unknown; its modern name is Ai Khanoum.
Like the other cities that Alexander the Great and the successor kings founded in the Near East
and Asia, this one was built to serve as a defense point and an administrative center. To make the
immigrant Greek population feel more at home, buildings were designed to replicate the Greek
way of life. Decorating floors with designs constructed from pebbles or colored pieces of stone was
a favorite technique for giving visual interest to a room while providing a durable surface.*
(Paul Bernard/Hellenisme et Civilizations Orientales.)

sending the money on to the royal treasury. In turn, the kings honored and flattered members of the cities' social elites.

This mutual dependence led the kings to establish cordial relationships with
well-to-do non-Greeks living in the old cities of Anatolia and the Near East, such
as Sardis, Tyre, and Babylon. In addition, non-Greeks and non-Macedonians from
eastern regions began moving westward to the new Hellenistic Greek cities in
increasing numbers. Jews in particular moved from Palestine to Anatolia, Greece,
and Egypt. The Jewish community eventually became an influential minority in
Egyptian Alexandria, the most important Hellenistic city.

All the Hellenistic kingdoms eventually fell to the Romans. The Ptolemaic kingdom survived the longest. The end came when Queen Cleopatra VII, a descendant
of Ptolemy and the last Macedonian to rule Egypt, chose the losing side in the Roman civil war between Mark Antony, her lover at that time, and the future emperor
Augustus in the late first century B.C. In 30 B.C., an invading Roman army ended
her reign and three centuries of Hellenistic monarchy.

The Layers of Hellenistic Society

Hellenistic society in the eastern Mediterranean world was divided into separate layers. The royal family and the king's friends topped the hierarchy. The Greek and Macedonian elites of the major cities ranked next. Just under them came the indigenous wealthy elites of the cities, the leaders of large minority urban populations, and the traditional lords and princes of local groups who maintained their ancestral domains in rural regions. Lowest of the free population were the masses of small merchants, artisans, and laborers. Slaves remained outside the bounds of society. (See "Taking Measure," below.)

The growth of the kingdoms apparently increased the demand for slave labor throughout the eastern Mediterranean. The centrally located island of Delos established a market where up to ten thousand slaves a day were bought and sold. The fortunate ones would become servants at court and live physically comfortable lives; the luckless ones would toil, and soon die, in the mines. Enslaved children often were taken far from home and set to work. A sales contract from 259 B.C. shows

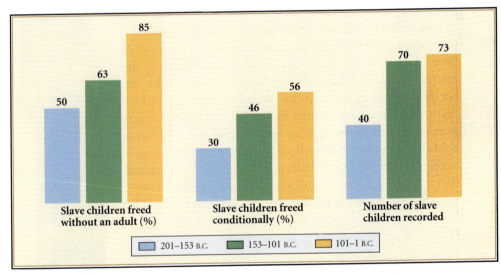

■ **TAKING MEASURE** Records of Slave Children Freed at Delphi, 201–1 B.C.
Inscriptions from the temple of Apollo in Delphi in central Greece in the Hellenistic period record the prices that slaves paid to obtain their freedom, either fully or conditionally. Conditional freedom, the less expensive option, obliged the former slave to work for his or her former owner until the latter's death. The records reveal that from 201 to 1 B.C. more and more children remained in slavery even after their parents had bought their own freedom. In this period, the increasing demand for slaves to work on large estates in Italy made prices for slaves rise. Many slave parents probably could not afford to buy their children's freedom until years after they had purchased freedom for themselves.
(Adapted from Keith Hopkins, *Conquerors and Slaves: Sociological Studies in Roman History* [Cambridge: Cambridge University Press, 1978], 166, Table III.6. Reprinted with the permission of Cambridge University Press.)

that Zeno, to whom the camel trader wrote, bought a girl about seven years old named Sphragis ("Gemstone") to work in an Egyptian textile factory. This was not her first job. Originally from Sidon in the Levant, she had previously been the slave of a Greek mercenary soldier employed by Toubias, a Jewish cavalry commander in the Transjordan region.

Even with power based in the cities, most of the population continued to live in small villages. Most farmers were compulsory tenants who were not allowed to move away or stop working. Free peasants still worked their own small plots as well as the farms of wealthy landowners. Perhaps 80 percent of all adult men and women had to work the land to produce enough food to sustain the population. In the cities, the poor worked as small merchants, peddlers, and artisans. Men could sign on as deckhands on the merchant ships that sailed the Mediterranean Sea and Indian Ocean.

Women's status in the Hellenistic world depended on the social layer to which they belonged. Like their Macedonian predecessors, Hellenistic queens enjoyed enormous riches and high honor. Because the Ptolemaic royal family observed the Egyptian royal tradition of brother-sister marriage, daughters could rule alongside sons. For example, Arsinoe II (c. 316–270 B.C.), the daughter of Ptolemy I, first married the Macedonian successor king Lysimachus, who gave her four towns as her personal domain. After Lysimachus's death she married her brother Ptolemy II and exerted at least as much influence on Egyptian policy as he did. The virtues publicly praised in a queen reflected traditional Greek values for women. When the city of Hierapolis around 165 B.C. passed a decree honoring Queen Apollonis of Pergamum, for example, it praised her piety toward the gods, her reverence toward her

■ **Egyptian-Style Statue of Queen Arsinoe II**

Arsinoe II (c. 316–270 B.C.), daughter of Ptolemy I and widow of the Macedonian successor king Lysimachus, married her brother Ptolemy II to unify the monarchy. Hailed as Philadelphoi ("Brother-Loving"), the couple set a precedent for brother-sister marriages in the Ptolemaic dynasty. One of the most remarkable women of the Hellenistic period, Arsinoe was the first Ptolemaic ruler whose image was placed in Egyptian temples as a "temple-sharing goddess." This eight-foot-tall, red granite statue portrays her in the traditional sculptural style of the pharaohs. (Vatican Museums.)

parents, her distinguished conduct toward her husband, and her harmonious relations with her "beautiful children born in wedlock."

Elite women continued to live separated from nonfamily males; poor women still worked in public. Greeks continued to abandon infants they could not or would not raise—girls more often than boys. Other populations, such as the Egyptians and the Jews, did not practice abandonment, or *exposure*, as it is often called. Exposure differed from infanticide because the parents expected someone else to find the child and rear it, albeit usually as a slave.

In some limited ways, women achieved greater control over their own lives in the Hellenistic period. A woman of exceptional wealth could enter public life by making donations or loans to her city and being rewarded with an official post in local government. Such positions were less prestigious than in the days of the independent city-states because the king and his top administrators now controlled the real power. In Egypt, women acquired greater say in the family because marriage contracts, the standard procedure, gradually evolved from an agreement between the groom and the bride's parents to one in which the bride made her own arrangements with the groom.◆

During this period, it became more common for the wealthy to follow the example of royalty and show concern for the poor. On the island of Samos, for example, prosperous citizens funded a foundation to distribute free grain. Donor-sponsored schools sprang up in various cities, and sometimes girls as well as boys could attend. Many cities also began sponsoring doctors. Donors were repaid by the respect and honor they earned from their fellow citizens. In this system, the welfare of the masses depended on the generosity of the rich; without democracy, the poor had no political power to demand reforms. This strongly hierarchical arrangement reflected the top-down structure of Hellenistic society.

Hellenistic Culture

Hellenistic culture reflected three principal characteristics of the age: royal wealth, a concentration on private rather than public matters, and the increased interaction of diverse peoples. In keeping with the era's hierarchical trends, the kings almost single-handedly determined developments in literature, art, science, and philosophy by deciding which fields and which scholars and artists to support financially. The kings' status as sole rulers and the source of law meant that authors and artists did not have freedom to criticize public policy and thus concentrated on individual emotions and aspects of private life. Nevertheless, royal patronage did produce an expansion and diversification of knowledge. Cultural interaction between Greek

---

◆ For a primary source that illuminates women's roles in the Classical and Hellenistic periods, see Document 9, "Funerary Inscriptions and Epitaphs."

and Near Eastern traditions happened most prominently in language and religion. These developments eventually became extremely influential in Roman culture; in this way, "captive Greece captured its fierce victor," as the Roman poet Horace (65–8 B.C.) expressed the effect of Hellenistic culture on his own.

The Arts under Royal Patronage

The Hellenistic kings became patrons of scholarship and the arts on a vast scale, competing with one another to lure the best scholars and artists to their capitals with magnificent salaries and benefits. These expenditures paid for many intellectual innovations but for little applied technology except for military use. The Ptolemies assembled the Hellenistic world's most intellectually distinguished court by turning Alexandria into the Mediterranean's leading center of the arts. There they established the first scholarly research institute. Its massive library had the ambitious goal of trying to collect all the books (that is, manuscripts) in the world; it grew to hold a half-million scrolls, an enormous number for the time. Linked to it was a building in which the hired scholars dined together and produced encyclopedias of knowledge such as *The Wonders of the World* and *On the Rivers of Europe* by Callimachus, a learned prose writer as well as a poet. The name of this building, the Museum (meaning "place of the Muses," the Greek goddesses of learning and the arts), is still used to designate institutions that preserve and promote knowledge. The output of the Alexandrian scholars was prodigious. Their champion was Didymus (c. 80–10 B.C.), nicknamed "Brass Guts" for his tireless writing of nearly four thousand learned books; it is a sad commentary on the preservation of ancient sources that not a single one has survived.

The writers and artists whom Hellenistic kings paid had to please their employers with their works. The poet Theocritus (c. 300–260 B.C.), for example, relocated from his home in Syracuse to the Ptolemaic court. In a poem expressly praising his patron, Ptolemy II, he spelled out the quid pro quo of their professional relationship: "The spokesmen of the Muses [that is, poets] celebrate Ptolemy in return for his benefactions." Theocritus and other poets succeeded by avoiding political subjects and stressing the division in society between the intellectual elite—to which the kings belonged—and the uneducated masses. Their poetry centered on individual emotions and broke new ground in demanding great intellectual effort as well as emotional engagement from the audience. Only people with a deep literary education could appreciate the allusions and complex references to mythology that these poets employed in their elegant poems.

Theocritus was the first Greek poet to express the divide between town and countryside, a poetic stance corresponding to a growing Hellenistic reality. The *Idylls,* his pastoral poems, emphasized the discontinuity between the environment of the city and the bucolic life of the country dweller, reflecting the fundamental social division of the Ptolemaic kingdom between the food consumers of the town and the food producers of the countryside. He presented a city dweller's idealized dream that country life must be peaceful and stress free; this fiction deeply influenced later literature.

Women poets made important contributions to literature in the Hellenistic period, apparently without any support from royal patronage. They excelled in writing epigrams, a style of short poem originally used for funeral epitaphs. Elegantly worded poems written by women from diverse regions of the Hellenistic world—Anyte of Tegea in the Peloponnese, Nossis of Locri in southern Italy, Moero of Byzantium—still survive. Women, from courtesans to respectable matrons, figured as frequent subjects in their work and expressed a wide variety of personal feelings, love above all. Nossis's poem on the power of Eros (Greek for "Love"), for example, proclaimed, "Nothing is sweeter than Eros. All other delights are second to it—from my mouth I spit out even honey. And this Nossis says: whoever Aphrodite has not kissed knows not what sort of flowers are her roses." No Hellenistic literature better conveys the depth of human emotion than the epigrams of women poets.

The Hellenistic theater, too, largely shifted its focus to stories of individual emotion; no longer did dramatists offer open critiques of politics or contemporary leaders, as they had in Golden Age comedy. Comic playwrights such as Menander (c. 342–289 B.C.) presented plays with timeless plots concerning the trials and tribulations of fictional lovers. These comedies of manners, as they are called, proved enormously popular because, like modern situation comedies, they offered a humorous view of situations and feelings that occur in daily life and a slyly satirical look at social conditions. Recent papyrus finds have allowed us to recover almost complete plays of Menander, the most famous Hellenistic playwright, and to appreciate his subtle skill in depicting personality. He presented his first comedy at Athens in 324 or 323 B.C. No tragedies written in this period have survived intact, but we know that they could involve the interaction among peoples and cultures at this time. Ezechiel, for example, a Jew living in Alexandria, wrote *Exodus*, a tragedy in Greek about Moses leading the Hebrews out of captivity in Egypt.

Like their literary counterparts, Hellenistic sculptors and painters featured human emotions prominently in their works. Classical-era artists had imbued their subjects' faces with a serenity that represented an ideal rather than reality. Numerous examples, usually surviving only in later copies, show that Hellenistic artists depicted individual emotions more naturally in a variety of types. In portrait sculpture, Lysippus's widely copied bust of Alexander the Great captured the young commander's passionate dreaminess. A sculpture from Pergamum by an unknown artist commemorated the third-century B.C. Attalid victory over the plundering Gauls (one of the Celtic peoples, called Galatians) by showing a defeated Gallic warrior stabbing himself after killing his wife to prevent her enslavement by the victors. A large-scale painting of Alexander battling the Persian king Darius (see page 104) portrayed Alexander's intense concentration and Darius's horrified expression. The artist, probably either Philoxenus of Eretria or a Greek woman from Egypt named

Helena (one of the first female artists known), used foreshortening and strong contrasts between shadows and highlights to accentuate the emotional impact of the picture.

To appreciate fully the appeal of Hellenistic sculpture, we must recognize that, like earlier Greek sculpture, it was painted in bright colors. But Hellenistic art differed from classical art in its social context. Works of classical art had been commissioned by the city-states for public display or by wealthy individuals to donate to their city-state as a work of public art. Now sculptors and painters created their works primarily as commissions from royalty and from the urban elites who wanted to show they had artistic taste like the royal family. The increasing diversity of subjects that emerged in Hellenistic art presumably represented a trend approved by kings, queens, and the elites. Sculpture best reveals this new preference for depiction of humans in a wide variety of poses, mostly from private life (in contrast with classical art). Hellenistic sculptors portrayed subjects never before shown: foreigners (such as the dying Celt, opposite page), drunkards, battered athletes, wrinkled old people. The female nude became a particular favorite. A statue of Aphrodite, which Praxiteles sculpted completely nude as an innovation in depicting this goddess, became so renowned as a religious object and tourist attraction in the city of Cnidos, which had commissioned it, that the king of Bithynia later offered to pay off the citizens' entire public debt if he could have the work of art. They refused.

Philosophy for a New Age

New philosophies arose in the Hellenistic period, all asking the same question: what is the best way for humans to live? They recommended different paths to the same answer: individual humans must attain personal tranquility to achieve freedom from the turbulence of outside forces, especially chance. For Greeks in particular, the changes in political and social life accompanying the rise to dominance of the Macedonian and, later, the Hellenistic kings made this focus necessary. Outside forces—aggressive kings—had robbed the city-states of their freedom of action internationally, and the fates of entire communities as well as individuals rested in the hands of distant, often capricious monarchs. More than ever before, human life and opportunities for free choice seemed poised to career out of individuals' control. It therefore made sense, at least for those wealthy enough to spend time philosophizing, to look for personal, private solutions to the unsettling new conditions of life in the Hellenistic age.

Few Hellenistic thinkers concentrated on metaphysics. Instead they focused on philosophical materialism, a doctrine asserting that only things made up of matter truly exist. It denied the concept of soul that Plato described and ignored any suggestion that nonmaterial phenomena could exist. Hellenistic philosophy was regularly divided into three related areas: *logic,* the process for discovering truth; *physics,* the fundamental truth about the nature of existence; and *ethics,* the way humans

■ Dying Celts

Hellenistic artists excelled in portraying deeply emotional scenes such as this murder-suicide scene of a Celtic warrior who is in the act of slaying himself after killing his wife, to prevent their capture by the enemy after defeat in battle. Celtic women followed their men to the battlefield and willingly exposed themselves to the same dangers. The original of this composition was in bronze, forming part of a large sculptural group that Attalus I, king of Pergamum from 241 to 197 B.C., set up on his acropolis to commemorate his defeat around 230 B.C. of the Celts, called Galatians, who had moved into Anatolia in the 270s B.C. to conduct raids throughout the area. It is striking that Attalus celebrated his victory by erecting a monument that portrayed the defeated enemy as brave and noble.
(Erich Lessing/Art Resource, NY.)

www.bedfordstmartins.com/huntconcise
See the ONLINE STUDY GUIDE for more help in analyzing this image.

should achieve happiness and well-being as a consequence of logic and physics. The era's philosophical thought greatly influenced Roman thinkers and many important Western philosophers who followed them.

One of the two most significant new philosophical schools of thought was Epicureanism. It took its name from its founder, Epicurus (341–271 B.C.), who settled his followers in Athens in a house about 307 B.C. amid a verdant park (hence "The Garden" as his school's name). Under Epicurus the study of philosophy assumed a social form that broke with tradition because he admitted women and slaves as regular members of his group. His lover, the courtesan Leontion, became well known for her treatise criticizing the views of Theophrastus (c. 370–285 B.C.), Aristotle's most famous pupil.

People should above all be free of worry about death, Epicurus taught, because all matter consists of microscopic atoms in random movement and death is nothing more than the painless separating of the body's atoms. Moreover, all human knowledge must be empirical—that is, derived from experience and perception. Thunder, drought, and other phenomena that most people perceive as the work of the gods do not result from divine intervention. The gods live far away in perfect tranquility, paying no attention to human affairs. People therefore have nothing to fear from the gods, in life or in death.

Epicurus believed people should pursue pleasure, but his notion of true pleasure had a special definition: he insisted that it consists of the "absence of disturbance" from pain and everyday turbulence, passions, and desires. A sober life spent in the society of friends apart from the cares of the common world could best provide this essential peace of mind. His teaching represented a serious challenge to the traditional ideal of Greek citizenship, which required men of means to participate in local politics and citizen women to engage in public religious cults.

The other important new Hellenistic philosophy, Stoicism, recommended a less isolationist path for individuals. Its name derived from the Painted Stoa in Athens, where Stoic philosophers discussed their doctrines. Zeno (c. 333–262 B.C.) from Citium on Cyprus founded Stoicism, but Chrysippus (c. 280–206 B.C.) from Cilicia in Anatolia did the most to make it a comprehensive guide to life. Stoics believed that life is fated but that people should still make the pursuit of virtue their goal. Virtue, they said, consists of putting oneself in harmony with the divine, rational force of universal Nature by cultivating the virtues of good sense, justice, courage, and temperance. These doctrines applied to women as well as men. In fact, the Stoics advocated equal citizenship for women and doing away with the conventions of marriage and families as the Greeks knew them. Zeno even proposed unisex clothing as a way to obliterate unnecessary distinctions between women and men.

The belief that fate determines everything created the question of whether humans truly have free will. Employing some of the subtlest reasoning ever applied to this fundamental issue, Stoic philosophers concluded that purposeful human actions do have significance. Nature, itself good, does not prevent vice from occurring, because virtue would otherwise have no meaning. What matters in life is the striving for good, not the result. A person should therefore take action against evil by, for example, participating in politics. To be a Stoic also meant to shun desire and anger while enduring pain and sorrow calmly, an attitude that yields the modern meaning of the word *stoic*. Through endurance and self-control, adherents of Stoic philosophy attained tranquility. They did not fear death because they believed that people live over and over again infinitely in identical fashion to their present lives.◆

Numerous other philosophies emerged in the Hellenistic period to compete with Epicureanism and Stoicism. Some of them carried on the work of earlier giants such as Plato and Pythagoras. Still others struck out in idiosyncratic directions.

◆ For a primary source that reflects the influence of Stoicism, see Document 10, Polybius, "The Histories."

Skeptics, for example, aimed at the same state of personal imperturbability as did Epicureans, but from a completely different premise. Pyrrho (c. 360–270 B.C.) of Elis in the Peloponnese established the principles of Skepticism; his ideas were influenced by the Indian ascetic wise men (the magi) he met while a member of Alexander the Great's expedition. Skeptics believed that secure knowledge about anything is impossible because the human senses yield contradictory information about the world. All that people can do, they insisted, is depend on appearances while suspending judgment about their reality. This basic premise of Skepticism inevitably precluded any unity of doctrine.

The philosophers called Cynics ostentatiously rejected every convention of ordinary life, especially wealth and material comfort. They believed that humans should aim for complete self-sufficiency. Whatever is natural is good, they said, and can be done without shame before anyone. According to this idea, public defecation and fornication were acceptable, and women and men alike were free to follow their sexual inclinations. Above all, Cynics disdained the pleasures and luxuries of a comfortable life. The most famous early Cynic, Diogenes (d. 323 B.C.) from Sinope on the Black Sea, had a reputation for wearing borrowed clothes and sleeping in a giant storage jar. Almost as notorious was Hipparchia, a Cynic of the late fourth century B.C. She once bested an obnoxious philosophical opponent named Theodorus the Atheist with the following argument: "That which would not be considered wrong if done by Theodorus would also not be considered wrong if done by Hipparchia. Now if Theodorus strikes himself, he does no wrong. Therefore, if Hipparchia strikes Theodorus, she does no wrong." The name *Cynic*, which meant "like a dog," reflected the common evaluation of this ascetic and unconventional way of life.

In the Hellenistic period, Greek philosophy reached a wider audience than ever before. Although the working poor had neither the leisure nor the resources to attend philosophers' lectures, affluent members of society studied philosophy in growing numbers. Theophrastus lectured to crowds of up to two thousand in Athens. Most philosophy students continued to be men, but women could join the groups attached to certain philosophers. Kings competed to attract famous thinkers to their courts, and Greek settlers took their interest in philosophy with them, even to the most remote Hellenistic cities. Archaeologists excavating a Hellenistic city located thousands of miles from Greece on the Oxus River in Afghanistan, for example, turned up a Greek philosophical text as well as inscriptions of moral advice imputed to Apollo's oracle at Delphi.

Innovation in the Sciences

Science first became a pursuit separate from philosophy during the Hellenistic period. Scientific investigation of the physical world so benefited from this divorce that historians have dubbed this era the Golden Age of ancient science. Various factors contributed to this flourishing of thought and discovery: the expeditions of Alexander had encouraged curiosity and increased knowledge about the extent and differing features of the world, royal patronage supported scientists financially, and the concentration of scientists in Alexandria promoted a fertile exchange of ideas that could not have taken place otherwise.

The greatest advances came in geometry and mathematics. Euclid, who taught at Alexandria around 300 B.C., made revolutionary progress in the analysis of two- and three-dimensional space. The utility of Euclidean geometry endures today. Archimedes of Syracuse (287–212 B.C.) was a mathematical genius who calculated the approximate value of *pi* and devised a way to manipulate very large numbers. He also invented hydrostatics (the science of the equilibrium of a fluid system) and mechanical devices such as a screw for lifting water to a higher elevation. Archimedes' shout of delight "I have found it" (*heureka* in Greek) when he solved a problem while soaking in his bathtub has been immortalized in the modern expression "Eureka!"

The sophistication of Hellenistic mathematics affected other fields that also required complex computation. Aristarchus of Samos early in the third century B.C. became the first to propose the correct model of the solar system: he argued that the earth revolves around the sun, which he also identified as being far larger and far more distant than it appeared. Later astronomers rejected Aristarchus's heliocentric model in favor of the traditional geocentric one (with the earth at the center) because calculations based on the orbit he calculated for the earth failed to correspond to the observed positions of celestial objects. Aristarchus had made an unfortunate mistake: assuming a circular orbit instead of an elliptical one. Eratosthenes of Cyrene (c. 275–194 B.C.) pioneered mathematical geography. He calculated the circumference of the earth with astonishing accuracy by simultaneously measuring the length of the shadows of widely separated but identically tall structures. The basic ideas and procedures of these Hellenistic researchers gave Western scientific

■ **Bronze Astronomical Calculator**

These fragments were discovered underwater in an ancient shipwreck off Anticythera, south of the Peloponnese. The device was being transported to Italy in the early first century B.C. as part of a shipment of metalwork and other valuable objects. The product of sophisticated applied engineering and astronomical knowledge, the calculator consisted of a complex set of intermeshed gears, turned by hand, that controlled rotating dials that indicated the position of celestial phenomena.

(National Archaeological Museum, Athens. Archaeological Receipts Fund.)

thought an important start toward the essential process of reconciling theory with observed data through measurement and experimentation.

Hellenistic science maintained a spirit of discovery despite the enormous difficulties imposed by technical limitations. Rigorous scientific experimentation was not possible because no technology existed for the precise measurement of very short intervals of time. Measuring tiny quantities of matter was also next to impossible. The science of the age was as quantitative as it could be given these limitations. Ctesibius of Alexandria (b. c. 310 B.C.), a contemporary of Aristarchus, invented the scientific field of pneumatics by creating machines operated by air pressure. He also built a working water pump, an organ powered by water, and the first accurate water clock. A later Alexandrian, Hero, continued the Hellenistic tradition of mechanical ingenuity by building a rotating sphere powered by steam. As in most of Hellenistic science, these inventions did not lead to viable applications in daily life. The scientists and their royal patrons were more interested in new theoretical discoveries than in practical results, and the metallurgical technology to produce the pipes, fittings, and screws needed to build powerful machines did not yet exist.

Military technology was the one area in which Hellenistic science produced noteworthy applications. The kings hired engineers to design powerful catapults and wheeled siege towers many stories high to batter down the defenses of walled cities. The most famous large-scale application of technology for nonmilitary purposes was the construction of a lighthouse three hundred feet tall (the Pharos) for the harbor at Alexandria. Using polished metal mirrors to reflect the light from a large bonfire, it shone many miles out over the sea. Awestruck sailors regarded it as one of the wonders of the world.

Medicine also benefited from the thirst for new knowledge characteristic of Hellenistic science. The increased contact between Greeks and people of the Near East in this period made the medical knowledge of the ancient civilizations of Mesopotamia and Egypt better known in the West and gave an impetus to the study of human health and illness. Around 325 B.C., Praxagoras of Cos discovered the value of measuring the pulse in diagnosing illness. A bit later, Herophilus of Chalcedon (b. c. 300 B.C.), working in Alexandria, became the first scientist in the West to study anatomy by dissecting human cadavers and, it was rumored, the bodies of condemned criminals while they were still alive; he had access to these subjects because the king authorized his research. Some of the anatomical terms Herophilus invented are still used. Other Hellenistic advances in understanding anatomy included the discovery of the nerves and nervous system.

As in science, however, Hellenistic medicine was limited by its inability to measure and observe phenomena not visible to the naked eye. Unable to see what really occurred under the skin in living patients, for example, doctors thought many illnesses in women were caused by displacements of the womb, which they wrongly believed could move around in the body. These mistaken ideas could not be corrected because the technology to evaluate them was absent.

A New East-West Culture

Wealthy non-Greeks increasingly adopted Greek habits as they adapted to the new social hierarchy of the Hellenistic world. To give only one example: Diotimus of Sidon in the Levant adopted a Greek name and pursued the premier Greek sport, chariot racing. He traveled to Nemea in the Peloponnese to enter his chariot in the race at the prestigious festival of Zeus. He announced his victory in an inscription written in Greek, which had become the language of international commerce and culture in the Hellenistic world. The explosion in the use of the Greek language in the form called *koine* ("shared" or "common") reflected the emergence of an international culture based on Greek models; this was why the Egyptian camel trader stranded in Syria had to communicate in Greek with a high-level official such as Zeno. The most striking evidence of this cultural development comes from Afghanistan. There, King Ashoka (r. c. 268–232 B.C.), who ruled most of the Indian subcontinent, used Greek as one of the languages in his public inscriptions to announce his efforts to introduce his subjects to Buddhist traditions of self-control, such as abstinence from eating meat. Local languages did not disappear in the Hellenistic kingdoms, however. In one region of Anatolia, for example, people spoke twenty-two different languages.

The diversity of Hellenistic religion matched the variety of many other areas of life in this period of cultural interaction. The traditional cults of Greek religion remained very popular, but new cults, such as those that deified ruling kings, responded to changing political and social conditions. Preexisting cults that previously had only local significance, such as that of the Greek healing deity Asclepius or the mystery cult of the Egyptian goddess Isis, grew prominent all over the Hellenistic world. In many cases, Greek cults and local cults from the eastern Mediterranean influenced each other. Their beliefs meshed well because these cults shared many assumptions about how to remedy the troubles of human life. In other instances, local cults and Greek cults existed side by side, with some overlap. The inhabitants of villages in the Fayum district of Egypt, for example, continued worshiping their traditional crocodile god and mummifying their dead according to the old ways but also paid homage to Greek deities. In the tradition of polytheistic religion, people could worship in both old and new cults.

New cults picked up a prominent theme of Hellenistic thought: a concern for the relationship between the individual and what seemed the controlling, unpredictable power of the divinities Luck and Chance. Although Greek religion had always addressed randomness at some level, the chaotic course of Greek history since the Peloponnesian War had made human existence appear more unpredictable than ever. Since advances in astronomy revealed the mathematical precision of the celestial sphere of the universe, religion now had to address the seeming disconnect between that heavenly uniformity and the shapeless chaos of life on earth. One increasingly popular approach to bridging that gap was to rely on astrology for advice deduced from the movement of the stars and planets, thought of as divinities. Another very common choice was to worship Tyche (Chance) as a god in the hope of securing good luck in life.

The most revolutionary approach in seeking protection from the capricious tricks of Chance or Luck was to pray for salvation from deified kings, who enjoyed divine status in what are known as *ruler cults*. Various populations established these cults to honor generous benefactors. The Athenians, for example, deified the Macedonians Antigonus and his son Demetrius as savior gods in 307 B.C., when these commanders liberated the city and bestowed magnificent gifts on it. Like most ruler cults, this one expressed both spontaneous gratitude and a desire to flatter the rulers in the hope of obtaining additional favors. Many cities in the Ptolemaic and Seleucid kingdoms instituted ruler cults for their kings and queens. An inscription put up by Egyptian priests in 238 B.C. concretely described the qualities appropriate for a divine king and queen:

> *King Ptolemy III and Queen Berenice, his sister and wife, the Benefactor Gods, . . . have provided good government . . . and [after a drought] sacrificed a large amount of their revenues for the salvation of the population, and by importing grain . . . they saved the inhabitants of Egypt.*

As these words make clear, the Hellenistic monarchs' tremendous power and wealth gave them the status of gods to the ordinary people who depended on their generosity and protection in times of danger. The idea that a human being could be a god, present on earth to be a "savior" delivering people from evils, was firmly established and would prove influential later in Roman imperial religion and Christianity.

Healing divinities offered another form of protection to anxious individuals. Scientific Greek medicine had rejected the notion of supernatural causes and cures for disease ever since Hippocrates had established his medical school on the Aegean island of Cos in the late fifth century B.C. Nevertheless, the cult of the god Asclepius, who offered cures for illness and injury at his many shrines, grew popular during the Hellenistic period. Suppliants seeking Asclepius's help would sleep in special dormitories at his shrines to await dreams in which he prescribed healing treatments. These prescriptions emphasized diet and exercise, but numerous inscriptions set up by grateful patients also testified to miraculous cures and surgery performed while the sufferer slept. The following example is typical:

> *Ambrosia of Athens was blind in one eye. . . . She . . . ridiculed some of the cures [described in inscriptions in the sanctuary] as being incredible and impossible. . . . But when she went to sleep, she saw a vision; she thought the god was standing next to her. . . . He split open the diseased eye and poured in a medicine. When day came she left cured.*

■ Bust of the Greco-Egyptian God Sarapis

Sarapis was originally an Egyptian divinity incorporating aspects of Osiris, the consort of Isis, and the sacred Apis bull. In the early Hellenistic period, the Ptolemaic royal family adopted Sarapis as its patron god. Eventually, groups of devotees who met for worship and feasting spread the cult of Sarapis around the Hellenistic world. They identified Sarapis as a transcendent god combining the powers of Zeus with those of other divinities, and they looked to him for miracles. He was commonly portrayed with a food container or measure on his head, as here, to signify his concern for human prosperity in this world and in the afterlife. The fact that this marble head was found in a Roman-era temple in Britain indicates the enduring and widespread appeal of this deity.

(Museum of London Photographic Library.)

People's faith in divine healing gave them hope that they could overcome the constant danger of illness, which seemed to them to strike at random.

Mystery cults proffered secret knowledge as a key to worldly and physical salvation. The cults of the Greek god Dionysus and, in particular, the Egyptian goddess Isis gained many followers in this period. The popularity of Isis, whose powers extended over every area of human life, received a boost from King Ptolemy I, who established a headquarters for her cult in Alexandria. He also promoted the cult of the Egyptian deity Sarapis, Isis's consort, as his dynasty's patron; Sarapis reportedly performed miracles of rescue from shipwreck and illness. The cult of Isis, who became the most popular female divinity in the Mediterranean, involved extensive rituals and festivals incorporating features of Egyptian religion mixed with Greek elements. Disciples of Isis apparently hoped to achieve personal purification as well as the aid of the goddess in overcoming the sometimes demonic influence of Chance on human life. That an Egyptian deity like Isis could achieve enormous popularity among Greeks (and Romans in later times) alongside the traditional gods of Greek religion is the best evidence of the cultural cross-fertilization of the Hellenistic world.

IMPORTANT DATES

399 B.C.	Trial and execution of Socrates at Athens	331 B.C.	Alexander takes Egypt and founds Alexandria
390s–370s B.C.	Sparta attacks city-states in Anatolia and Greece	326 B.C.	Alexander's army mutinies at the Hyphasis River in India
386 B.C.	Sparta makes a peace with Persia ceding control over the Anatolian Greek city-states; Plato founds the Academy in Athens	324 or 323 B.C.	Menander presents his first comedy at Athens
		323 B.C.	Alexander dies in Babylon
371 B.C.	Thebes defeats Sparta at the battle of Leuctra	c. 307 B.C.	Epicurus founds "the Garden" in Athens
359 B.C.	Philip II becomes Macedonian king	306–304 B.C.	Alexander's successors declare themselves kings
338 B.C.	Philip II defeats Greek alliance at Chaeronea to become the leading power in Greece	263–241 B.C.	Eumenes I founds the independent Attalid kingdom in Anatolia
		239–130 B.C.	Independent Greek kingdom in Bactria
336 B.C.	Philip II is murdered; Alexander becomes king	167 B.C.	Jewish revolt in Jerusalem
335 B.C.	Aristotle founds the Lyceum in Athens	30 B.C.	Death of Cleopatra VII and takeover of the Ptolemaic kingdom by Rome
334 B.C.	Alexander leads an army of Greeks and Macedonians against the Persian Empire		

The history of Judaism in the Hellenistic period shows especially striking evidence of cultural interaction. King Ptolemy II had the Hebrew Bible translated into Greek (the Septuagint) in Alexandria in the early third century B.C. Many Jews, especially those living in the large Jewish communities that had grown up in Hellenistic cities outside Palestine, adopted the Greek language and many aspects of Greek culture. Nevertheless, these Hellenized Jews largely retained the ritual practices and habits of life that defined traditional Judaism, and they refrained from worshiping Greek gods. Hellenistic politics also affected the Jewish community in Palestine, which was controlled militarily and politically first by the Ptolemies and then by the Seleucids. Both allowed the Jews to live according to their ancestral tradition under the political leadership of a high priest in Jerusalem.

Internal dissension among Jews erupted in second-century B.C. Palestine over the amount of Greek influence that was compatible with traditional Judaism. The Seleucid king Antiochus IV (r. 175–163 B.C.) intervened in the conflict in support of an extreme Hellenizing faction of Jerusalem Jews, who had taken over the high priesthood. In 167 B.C., Antiochus converted the main Jewish temple there into a Greek temple and outlawed the practice of Jewish religious rites, such as observing the Sabbath and circumcision. A revolt led by Judah the Maccabee eventually won Jewish independence from the Seleucids after twenty-five years of war. The most famous episode of this revolt was the retaking of the Jerusalem temple and its rededication to the worship of the Jewish god, Yahweh—a triumphant moment commemorated by Jews ever since on the holiday of Hanukkah. That Greek culture attracted some Jews in the first place, however, provides a striking example of the transformations that affected many—though far from all—people of the Hellenistic world. By the time of the Roman Empire, one of those transformations would be Christianity, whose theology had roots in the cultural interaction of Hellenistic Jews and Greeks and their ideas on apocalypticism and divine human beings.

Conclusion

Between about 400 and 323 B.C., Greece's Classical period came to an end. The violence and bitterness of the Peloponnesian War and its aftermath led ordinary people as well as philosophers to question the basis of morality. The characteristic disunity of Greek international politics proved disastrous because the Macedonian kingdom developed aggressive leaders, Philip II and Alexander the Great, who made themselves masters of the squabbling city-states to their south. Inspired by Greek heroic ideas, Alexander conquered the entire Persian Empire and set in motion the momentous political, social, and cultural changes of the Hellenistic period.

When Alexander's generals transformed themselves into Hellenistic kings, they not only made use of the governmental structures they found already established in the lands they conquered but also added an administrative system staffed by Greeks and Macedonians. Local elites as well as Greeks and Macedonians cooperated with the Hellenistic monarchs in governing and financing their society, which was divided along hierarchical ethnic lines. To enhance their image of magnificence, the kings and queens of the Hellenistic world supported writers, artists, scholars, philosophers, and scientists, thereby encouraging the distinctive energy of Hellenistic intellectual life. The traditional city-states continued to exist in Hellenistic Greece, but their freedom extended only to local affairs; their foreign policy was constrained by the need to stay on good terms with powerful monarchs.

The diversity of the Hellenistic world encompassed much that was new, especially because cultural interaction between different peoples became more common than ever before. An outgrowth of the greater opportunities created by this interaction and change was anxiety about the role of chance in life. In response, people looked to new religious experiences to satisfy their yearning for protection from perils. In the midst of so much novelty, however, the most fundamental elements of the ancient world remained unchanged—the labor, the poverty, and the necessarily limited horizons of the mass of ordinary people working in fields, vineyards, and pastures.

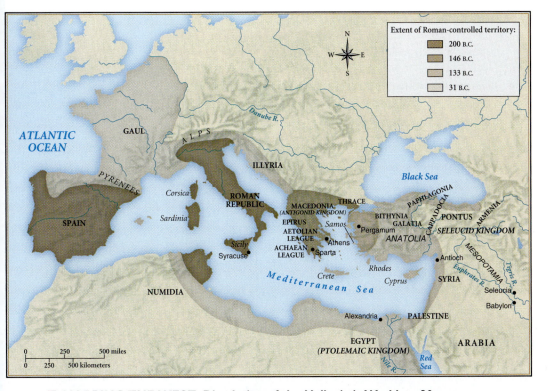

■ MAPPING THE WEST Dissolution of the Hellenistic World, to 30 B.C.

By 30 B.C. (the death of Cleopatra VII, the last Ptolemaic monarch of Egypt), the Roman republic had conquered or absorbed the Hellenistic kingdoms of the eastern Mediterranean. Competition for the tremendous wealth that this expansion captured helped fuel bitter and divisive feuds between Rome's most ambitious generals and political leaders. This territory became the eastern half of the Roman Empire, with only minor changes in extent over time.

What did change was the culture of Rome once it came into close contact with the fertile traditions of the Hellenistic kingdoms that it replaced as the Mediterranean's dominant political state. That rise to power, however, took centuries because Rome originated as a tiny, insignificant place that no one except Romans ever expected to amount to anything on the world stage.

Suggested References for further reading and online research appear on page SR-5 at the back of the book.

www.bedfordstmartins.com/huntconcise   See the ONLINE STUDY GUIDE to assess your mastery of the material covered in this chapter.

The Rise of Rome

c. 753–44 B.C.

R OMANS TREASURED THE LEGENDS describing their state's long and often violent transformation from a tiny village to a world power. They especially loved stories about their legendary first king, Romulus, who was remembered as a passionate leader. According to the legend later known as the "Rape of the Sabine Women," Romulus's Rome was a community so tiny that it lacked enough women to bear children to increase the population and help defend it. The king therefore beseeched the surrounding peoples of central Italy to allow Romans to intermarry with them. Everyone turned him down, scorning Rome's poverty and weakness. Enraged, Romulus hatched a shrewd plan. Inviting the neighboring Sabines to a festival honoring the gods, he had his men kidnap the unmarried women and fight off their relatives' frantic attempts at rescue. The kidnappers promptly married the women, fervently promising to cherish them as beloved wives and new citizens. When the neighbors' armies returned to attack Rome, the women rushed into the midst of the bloody battle, begging their brothers, fathers, and new husbands either to stop slaughtering one another or to kill them to end the war. The men immediately made peace and agreed to merge their populations under Roman rule.

This legend emphasizes that Rome, unlike the city-states of Greece, expanded by absorbing outsiders into its citizen body, sometimes violently, sometimes peacefully. Rome's growth became the ancient world's most dramatic expansion of population and territory, as a people originally housed in a few huts gradually created

■ **Temple of Castor and Pollux in the Roman Forum**
One of the most prominent temples in the center of Rome, this building was originally constructed in the forum in the fifth century B.C. to honor the divine twins, Castor and Pollux, for their help in battle. It was rebuilt several times; the remains seen today date to the time of Augustus (c. 27 B.C.– A.D. 14). The temple served important state functions: the Senate often met inside, and it held the official standards for weights and measures as well as treasuries for the emperors and wealthy individuals. Its architectural detail is famous for its elegance. Notice the sculpted capitals atop the forty-foot-high columns. (Sonia Halliday Photographs.)

a state that encompassed most of Europe, North Africa, Egypt, and the eastern Mediterranean. The social, cultural, political, legal, and economic traditions that the Romans developed in ruling this vast area created closer connections between its diverse peoples than ever before or since. Unlike the Greeks and Macedonians, the Romans maintained the unity of their state for centuries. Alexander the Great's conquests won him everlasting fame as the ancient world's most fearless hero, but even he failed to equal the Romans in affecting the course of Western civilization: the history of Europe and its colonies, including the United States, has deep roots in Rome.

Roman culture sprang from the traditions of ancient Italy's many peoples, but Greek literature, art, and thought profoundly influenced Romans as they gained international power. Of course, they did not just passively absorb the other civilization's traditions or change them only in superficial ways, such as giving Latin names to Greek gods. As always happens in cultural interaction, whatever they took over from others they adapted to their own purposes in complex ways. The cross-cultural contact that so deeply influenced Rome was a kind of competition in innovation rather than an "advanced" Greek culture improving a "primitive" Roman culture.

The kidnapping legend belongs to the earliest period of Rome, when kings ruled (c. 753–509 B.C.), but the majority of Roman history falls into two periods of about five hundred years each—the republic and the empire. These terms refer to the system of government in each period: under the republic (founded 509 B.C.), an oligarchy dominated by the elite governed; under the empire, monarchs (the Roman emperors) once again ruled. Rome's greatest expansion came during the republic. The confidence that fueled this amazing growth rested in Romans' faith that the gods willed them to rule the world by military might and law and improve it through social and moral values. Belief in their divine destiny is illustrated by the foundation legend, in which Romulus's Romans employed a religious festival as a ruse for kidnapping. Their firm belief that values should drive politics showed in their determination to persuade the captives that loyalty and love would wipe out the crime that had forcibly turned them into wives and Romans.

In addition to the devotion to family implied by this story, Roman values under the republic emphasized selfless service to the community, individual honor and public status, the importance of the laws, and shared decision making. By the first century B.C., however, the inherent tension between these values had erupted into open conflict because powerful individuals were placing their personal and family interests ahead of the common good. Blinded by ambition, Rome's politician-generals plunged into a civil war that would destroy the republic.

Social and Religious Traditions

Romans regulated their lives by values that stressed personal connections, education for public service, religious duties, and hierarchy. In society, people connected with one another as patron or client, each with obligations to the other. In families, power was distributed unequally. In religion, the magnificent superiority of the gods meant that people had to pray for divine favor to protect the family and the community.

Roman Values

Romans believed that their values had been handed down from ancient times. They therefore referred to them as *mos maiorum,* "the way of the ancestors." The Romans treasured their values' antiquity because, for them, *old-fashioned* meant "good," while *newfangled* suggested "dangerous." Roman morality made honor the reward for right conduct, which required uprightness, faithfulness, and respect for others. Uprightness specified how a person related to others. In the second century B.C., the poet Lucilius defined it as *virtue:*

> *Virtue is to know the human relevance of each thing,*
> *To know what is humanly right and useful and honorable,*
> *And what things are good and what are bad, useless, shameful, and*
>   *dishonorable. . . .*
> *Virtue is to pay what in reality is owed to honorable status,*
> *To be an enemy and a foe to bad people and bad values*
> *But a defender of good people and good values. . . .*
> *And, in addition, virtue is putting the country's interests first,*
> *Then our parents', with our own interests third and last.*

Faithfulness (*fides,* from which the English word *fidelity* derives) had many forms, for women as well as for men. Basically, it meant to keep one's obligations, no matter the cost. Failing to meet an obligation offended the community and the gods. Faithful women remained virgins before marriage and monogamous afterward. Faithful men kept their word, paid their debts, and treated everyone justly—which did not mean treating everyone the same, but rather treating people appropriately according to whether they were equals, superiors, or inferiors.

Faithfulness was one aspect of respect, a very complex value. Demonstrating devotion to the gods and to one's family, especially elders, was respect's supreme form. Maintaining divine favor required regular worship and sacrifices. Respect for one's self meant maintaining self-control and displaying emotion with dignity. So strict was this expectation that not even wives and husbands could kiss in public without seeming emotionally out of control. Respect also required never giving up no matter the difficulties. Persevering and overcoming all obstacles to do one's duty were thus fundamental Roman values.

The reward for living by these values was honor. Women earned their honor—a good reputation—by bearing legitimate children and educating them morally. Honor for men also brought concrete rewards, especially election to public office and commemoration of military bravery and other contributions to the common good. A man who had gained the status bestowed by honor commanded so much respect that others would obey him regardless of whether he exercised formal power over them. A man earning this much prestige was said to possess "authority."

Finally, Romans believed that family lineage influenced a person's values. High birth was therefore a two-edged sword. It automatically carried greater status, but at the same time it imposed a stricter demand to behave morally. Originally, wealth had nothing to do with moral virtue. Over time, however, it became overwhelmingly important to the Roman elite to spend money in displays of conspicuous consumption, social entertainments, and gifts to the community. By the later centuries of the Roman republic, ambitious men required vast fortunes to buy honor, and they became willing to trample on other values to acquire riches.

The Patron-Client System

The hierarchy of Roman society was made concrete in the patron-client system, an interlocking network of personal relationships obligating people to one another morally and legally. A patron was a man of superior status who was obliged to provide *benefits* to people of lower status who paid special attention to him. These were his clients, who in return owed him *duties*. Both sets of obligations centered on financial and political help. The system had multiple levels: a patron of others was often himself the client of a more distinguished man. The Romans called this hierarchy "friendship"—with clearly defined roles for each party. A sensitive patron would greet a social inferior as "my friend," not as "my client." A client, however, showed respect by addressing his superior as "my patron."

Benefits and duties took various forms. A patron benefited his clients by providing gifts or loans in hard times, supporting them when they started political careers, and backing them in lawsuits. Clients' duties included lending money when patrons needed it to pay for public works or their daughters' lavish dowries and aiding their campaigns for public office by soliciting votes. Furthermore, because it was a mark of great status to have numerous clients thronging around like a swarm of bees, a patron expected them to gather at his house early in the morning and accompany him to the forum, the city's public center. A Roman leader needed a large, fine house to accommodate this throng and to entertain his social equals; a crowded house signified social success.

These mutual obligations endured over generations. Ex-slaves, for example, who automatically became the clients of the masters who freed them, passed on this relationship to their children. Wealthy Romans could acquire clients among foreigners, sometimes even entire communities. With its emphasis on duty and permanence, the system epitomized the Roman view that social stability and well-being were achieved by faithfully maintaining people's obligations to one another.

■ **Sculpted Tomb of a Family of Ex-Slaves**

The husband and wife depicted on this tomb, which may date to the first century B.C., started life as slaves but gained their freedom and thus became Roman citizens. Their son, in the background holding a pet pigeon, was a free person. One of the remarkable features of Roman civilization, and a source of its demographic strength, was the wholesale incorporation of ex-slaves into the citizen body. This family had done well enough financially to afford a sculpted tomb. The tablets the man is holding and the carefully groomed hairstyle of the woman are meant to show that their family was literate and stylish. (German Archeological Institute/Madeline Grimoldi.)

The Roman Family

The family was the bedrock institution of Roman society because it taught values and determined the ownership of property. Men and women shared the duty of teaching values to their children, though by law the father possessed the *patria potestas* ("power of a father") over his children, no matter how old, and over his slaves. This power gave him legal ownership of all the property acquired by his dependents. As long as he was alive, no son or daughter could own anything, accumulate money, or possess any independent legal standing—in theory at least. In practice, adult children controlled personal property and money, and favored slaves might accumulate savings. Fathers also held legal power of life and death over these members of their households, but they rarely exercised it on anyone except unwanted or deformed newborns. Abandoning babies so that they would die, be adopted, or be raised as slaves by strangers was an accepted practice to control the size of families and dispose of physically imperfect infants. Baby girls probably suffered this fate more often than boys—a family enhanced its power by investing its resources in its sons.

In keeping with the communal aspect of their values, Roman fathers regularly conferred with others on important family issues. Each Roman man identified a circle of friends and relatives, his "council," whom he consulted before making significant decisions. A man contemplating the drastic decision to execute an adult member of his household, for example, would never have made the decision on his own. His council would recommend this violent exercise of a father's power only in the direst circumstances, as in 63 B.C. when a father had his son executed because the youth had committed treason by joining a conspiracy to overthrow the government.

Patria potestas did not allow a husband to control his wife because "free" marriages—in which the wife formally remained under her father's power as long as he lived—eventually became prevalent. But in the ancient world, few fathers lived long enough to oversee the lives of their married daughters or sons; four out of five parents died before their children reached thirty. A Roman woman without a living father was relatively independent. Legally she needed a male guardian to conduct business for her, but guardianship became an empty formality by the first century B.C. Upper-class women could on occasion express their opinions; in 195 B.C., for example, they blocked Rome's streets for days, until the men rescinded a wartime law meant to reduce tensions between rich and poor by limiting the amount of gold jewelry and fine clothing women could wear and where they could ride in carriages.◆ A later jurist commented on women's freedom of action: "The common belief, that because of their instability of judgment women are often deceived and that it is only fair to have them controlled by the authority of guardians, seems more specious than true. For women of full age manage their affairs themselves."

Roman women had to grow up fast to assume their duties as teachers of values to children and managers of their household's resources. Tullia (c. 79–45 B.C.), daughter of the renowned politician and orator Marcus Tullius Cicero (106–43 B.C.), was engaged at twelve, married at sixteen, and widowed by twenty-two. As a typical married Roman woman of wealth, she oversaw the household slaves, including wet nurses for infants, kept account books for the property she personally owned, and accompanied her husband to dinner parties—something Greek wives never did.

Roman mothers won public honor for managing their households well and shaping their children's moral outlook. Cornelia, an aristocrat of the second century B.C., won extraordinary fame after her husband died by refusing an offer of mar-

---

◆ For a source that details this early women's protest while revealing Romans' veneration of tradition, see Document 11, Livy, "Roman Women Demonstrate against the Oppian Law."

riage from the Ptolemaic king of Egypt so she could instead oversee the family estate and educate her surviving daughter and two sons. (Her other nine children had died.) The boys, Tiberius and Gaius Gracchus, grew up to be among the most influential and controversial officials of the late republic. Wealthy women such as Cornelia wielded political influence, if only indirectly, by expressing their opinions privately to the male members of their families. Marcus Porcius Cato (234–149 B.C.), a famous politician and author, hinted at the behind-the-scenes reality of women's power with a biting comment directed at his fellow leaders: "All mankind rule their wives, we rule all mankind, and our wives rule us."

Women accumulated property in diverse ways, from inheritance to entrepreneurship; recent archaeological discoveries suggest that by the late republic some women owned large businesses. Poor women, like poor men, toiled to help support their families, by selling vegetables or amulets or colorful ribbons from a stand. Slightly more prosperous families crafted furniture or clothing at home, the location of most Roman production, with the men cutting, fitting, and polishing the wood, leather, and metal. The poorest women could earn money only as prostitutes, which was legal but disgraceful. Prenuptial agreements to outline the rights of both partners in the marriage were common, and divorce was a simple matter, with fathers usually keeping the children.

■ **Sculpture of a Woman Running a Store**
This relief sculpture portrays a woman selling food from behind the counter of a small shop, while customers make purchases or converse with each other. Roman women could own property, so the woman may be the store owner. The man immediately to her right behind the counter could be her husband or a servant. Market areas in Roman towns were packed with small family-run stores like this that sold everything imaginable, much like malls of today. (Art Resource, NY.)

Education for Public Life

The education of both women and men had the goal of making them exponents of traditional values and, for different purposes, effective speakers. As in Greece, most children received their education in the family; only the well-to-do could afford to pay teachers. Wealthy parents bought literate slaves to tend their children and help with their education. By the late republic, they often chose Greek slaves so their children could be taught to speak Greek and read its literary classics, which most Romans regarded as the world's best. Parents might also send their children, from about seven years old, to classes offered by independent schoolmasters in their lodgings. Repetition was the usual teaching technique. Corporal punishment frequently was used to keep pupils attentive.

In upper-class families, both daughters and sons learned to read. The girls were also taught literature, perhaps some music, and, especially, how to make educated conversation at dinner parties. Another principal aim of the education of women was to prepare them for the important role of instilling traditional social and moral values in their children.

Fathers instilled masculine traits in their sons, especially physical training, fighting with weapons, and courage, but the pinnacle of an upper-class boy's education was rhetoric—skill in persuasive public speaking. Rhetorical training was crucial to a successful public career. A boy would accompany his father to public meetings and court sessions. By listening to speeches, he would learn to imitate winning techniques. Cicero, Rome's most famous orator, agreed with his brother's advice that young men must learn to "excel in public speaking. It is the tool for controlling men at Rome, winning them over to your side, and keeping them from harming you. You fully realize your own power when you are a man who can cause your rivals the greatest fears of meeting you [as a speaker] in a trial." Roman rhetoric owed much to Greek techniques. This was only one of the crucial ways in which Greek culture influenced Rome.

Religion for Public and Private Interests

Romans followed Greek models in religion, too, worshiping many divinities identified directly with those of Greece. Romans viewed their chief god, Jupiter, who corresponded to the Greek god Zeus, as a powerful, stern father. Juno (Greek Hera), queen of the gods, and Minerva (Greek Athena), goddess of wisdom, joined Jupiter to form the central triad of the state cults. These three deities shared Rome's most revered temple on its acropolis, the Capitoline hill.

Preserving Rome's safety and prosperity was the goal of Roman religion: above all, the gods were supposed to ensure victory in war and support agriculture. Many official prayers implored divine aid for growing crops, preventing disease, and spurring healthy reproduction for animals and people. In times of crisis, Romans sought foreign gods to protect them, such as when the government brought the cult of the healing god Asclepius from Greece in 293 B.C. to fight a plague. In 204 B.C., officials imported the pointed black stone representing Cybele ("the Great Mother"), whose chief sanctuary was in Phrygia in Asia Minor (the Roman term for Anatolia), to promote fertility.

Romans supported many other cults with special guardian responsibilities. The shrine of Vesta (Greek Hestia), goddess of the hearth and a protector of the family, housed the official eternal flame of Rome, which guaranteed the state's permanent existence. Vestal Virgins, six unmarried women sworn to chastity at age six to ten for terms of thirty years, tended Vesta's shrine. Their chastity symbolized Roman family values and thus the preservation of the republic itself. As Rome's only female priesthood, the Vestals garnered high status and freedom from their fathers' control by performing their most important duty: keeping the flame from going out. As the Greek historian Dionysius of Halicarnassus reported in the first century B.C., "The Romans dread the extinction of the fire above all misfortunes, looking upon it as an omen which portends the destruction of the city." Should the flame happen to go out, the Romans assumed that one of the women had broken her vow of chastity and that a Vestal had to be buried alive as the penalty.

At home, families maintained a sacred space for small shrines housing statuettes of their *Penates* (spirits of the household) and *Lares* (spirits of the ancestors), protectors of their well-being and moral traditions. Upper-class families hung death masks of distinguished ancestors in the main room in their homes and wore them at funerals to express the current generation's responsibility to live up to the family's virtuous past. In sum, tradition represented the principal source of Roman morality. The shame of losing public esteem by tarnishing one's reputation, not the fear of divine punishment, was the strongest deterrent to immoral behavior.

Romans performed many rituals to combat life's precariousness, in activities as diverse and commonplace as breast-feeding babies and fertilizing crops. Many public religious gatherings promoted the community's health and stability. For example, during the February 15 Lupercalia festival (whose name recalled the wolf, *luper* in Latin, which legend said had reared Romulus), naked young men streaked around the Palatine hill, lashing any woman they met with strips of goat skin. Women who had not yet borne children would run out to be struck, believing this would make them fertile. The December 17 Saturnalia festival, honoring the Italian deity of liberation, Saturnus, temporarily turned the social order topsy-turvy to release tensions caused by the inequalities between masters and slaves. As the playwright and scholar Accius (c. 170–80 B.C.) described the occasion, "People joyfully hold feasts all through the country and the towns, each owner acting as a waiter to his slaves." This reversal of roles reinforced slaves' ties to their owners by symbolizing patrons' benefits, which had to be repaid with faithful service.

Rome's principal deities had few direct connections with human morality because Roman tradition did not regard the gods as the guarantors of their moral

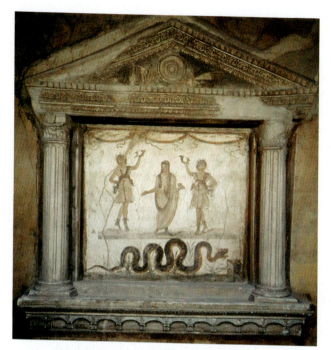

■ **Household Shrine from Pompeii**

This colorfully painted shrine stood inside the entrance to a house at Pompeii known as the House of the Vettii from the name of its owners. Successful businessmen, they spared no expense in decorating their home: with 188 frescoes (paintings done by applying pigments to damp plaster) adorning its walls, the interior blazed in a riot of color. This type of shrine, found in every Roman home, is called a lararium *because it housed the* Lares *(spirits of the ancestors), who are shown here flanking a central figure, who represents the spirit (genius) of the father of the family. The snake, poised to drink from a bowl probably holding milk set out for it, also symbolizes a protective force ("the good daimon"). The scene sums up the role Romans expected their gods to play: staving off harm and bad luck.* (Scala/Art Resource, NY.)

code. Like the Greek gods, Roman gods were more connected to national security and prosperity, as Cicero explains: "We call Jupiter the Best (*Optimus*) and Greatest (*Maximus*) not because he makes us just or sober or wise but, rather, healthy, unharmed, rich, and prosperous." Therefore, every official action was preceded by "taking the auspices"—seeking Jupiter's approval by observing natural "signs" such as the direction of the flights of birds, their eating habits, or the presence of thunder and lightning. Romans gave their values a religious dimension by hailing moral qualities such as faithfulness as divine forces. Also regarded as divine was piety (*pietas*), the sense of devotion and duty to family, friends, and the republic. Rome's temple to *pietas* housed a statue personifying it as a female divinity. The religious aura attached to the cults of moral qualities emphasized that they were ideals to which every Roman should aspire.

Roman government and public religion were inextricably intertwined: both were intended to preserve the community. Priests were to ensure the gods' goodwill toward the state, a crucial relationship the Romans called the *pax deorum* ("peace of/with the gods"). Men from the top of the social hierarchy served as priests by conducting sacrifices, festivals, and other rituals conforming strictly to ancestral tradition. They were not professionals devoting their lives solely to religious activity but, rather, citizens performing public service. The most important official, the *pontifex maximus* ("highest priest"), served as the head of state religion and the ultimate authority on religious matters affecting government; Rome's most prominent men sought this priesthood for its political influence.

Disrespect for religious tradition brought punishment. Naval commanders, for example, took the auspices by feeding sacred chickens on their ships: if the birds ate energetically before a battle, Jupiter favored the Romans and an attack could begin. In 249 B.C., the commander Publius Claudius Pulcher grew frustrated when his chickens, probably seasick, refused to eat. Determined to attack, he finally hurled them overboard in a rage, sputtering, "Well then, let them drink!" When he suffered a huge defeat, he was fined very heavily.

From Monarchy to Republic, c. 753–287 B.C.

Rome's communal values provided the unity necessary for its astounding growth from a minuscule settlement into the Mediterranean's greatest power. This process took centuries, while the Romans reinvented their government and expanded their territory and population. From the eighth through the sixth century B.C., they lived under a monarchy, the most common regime in the ancient world. Provoked by the later kings' violence, members of the social elite overthrew the monarchy to create a new political system—the republic—that lasted from the fifth through the first century B.C. The republic, from the Latin *res publica* ("the people's matter" or "the public business"), elected political officials in open meetings of male citizens, but the elite dominated. Rome acquired land and population by winning aggressive wars and by absorbing other peoples. Its economic and cultural growth depended on contact with peoples around the Mediterranean.

The Monarchy, c. 753–509 B.C.

Legend taught that Rome's original government had seven kings in succession from 753 (the most commonly given date for the city's founding) to 509 B.C.; in truth, little reliable evidence exists for this period. The kings probably created the Senate, a body of advisers chosen from the city's leading men to serve as the ruler's council, in keeping with the Roman principle that decisions should be made by consensus. This institution advised government leaders for two thousand years, as Rome changed from a monarchy to the republic and back to a monarchy under the empire.

Rome's policy of taking in conquered outsiders produced tremendous expansion, promoted ethnic diversity, and contrasted sharply with the exclusionary citizenship policy of Greek city-states. Another important Roman policy—also different from Greek tradition—was to grant citizenship to freed slaves. These "freedmen" and "freedwomen," as ex-slaves were called, became clients of their former owners.

They were barred from elective offices or military service but in all other ways possessed full civil rights, such as legal marriage. Their children enjoyed citizenship without any limitations. By the late republic, many Roman citizens were descendants of freed slaves.

By around 550 b.c., the Romans controlled three hundred square miles of the area around Rome, called Latium—enough agricultural land to support a population of thirty thousand to forty thousand people. Geography and contact with other cultures, especially Greek, helped propel Rome's growth. The city lay at the natural center of both Italy and the Mediterranean world. As the historian Livy (59 b.c.–a.d. 17), our source for the heroic legends of early Rome, expressed it, "With reason did gods and men choose this site: all its advantages make it of all places in the world the best for a city destined to grow great." Those advantages were fertile farmland, control of a river crossing on the major north-south route in the peninsula, a nearby harbor on the Mediterranean Sea, and accessible terrain that made political expansion easier. Most important, Rome was ideally situated for contact with the outside world. The peninsula of Italy stuck so far out into the Mediterranean that east-west traffic naturally encountered it (Map 4.1).

■ **MAP 4.1 Ancient Italy, c. 500 b.c.**

When the Romans ousted the monarchy to found a republic in 509 b.c., they inhabited a relatively small territory in central Italy between the western coast and the mountain range that bisects the peninsula from north to south. Numerous different peoples lived in Italy at this time. The most prosperous occupied fertile agricultural land and sheltered harbors on the peninsula's west side. The early republic's most urbanized neighbors were the Etruscans to the north and the Greek city-states to the south and on the island of Sicily.

Ancient Italy was home to a diverse population, and contact with their neighbors profoundly influenced Romans' cultural development. The people of Latium were poor villagers like the Romans and spoke the same Indo-European language, an early form of Latin. To the south, however, lived Greeks, and contact with them had the greatest effect on Rome. Greeks had established colonies in the Campanian plain, such as Naples, from the 700s B.C. These settlements grew prosperous thanks to their ideal location for participating in international trade. Romans developed a love-hate relationship with Greeks, admiring their literature and art but despising their lack of military unity. They adopted many elements from Greek culture—from ethical values to deities, from the model for their poetry and prose to architectural design and style.

The Etruscans, a people north of the Tiber River, also influenced the Romans. They lived in prosperous, independent towns nestled on central Italian hilltops. Vividly colored wall paintings, which survive in some tombs, portray funeral banquets and games testifying to their society's splendor. They crafted their own fine artwork, jewelry, and sculpture but also had a passion for importing luxurious objects from Greece and other Mediterranean lands. Most of the intact Greek vases known today, for example, were found in Etruscan tombs. Etruscans' international contacts encouraged cultural interaction: gold tablets inscribed in Etruscan and

■ **Banquet Scene Painted in an Etruscan Tomb**
Painted about 480–470 B.C., this brightly colored fresco decorated a wall in an Etruscan tomb (known today as the "Tomb of the Leopards" from the animals painted just above this scene) at Tarquinia. Wealthy Etruscans filled their tombs with pictures such as these, which simultaneously represented the funeral feasts held to celebrate the life of the dead person and the social pleasures experienced in this life and expected in the next. The banqueters recline on their elbows in Greek style. The Greeks themselves probably adopted their dining customs from Near Eastern precedents.
(Scala/Art Resource, NY.)

Phoenician and discovered in 1964 at the port of Pyrgi (thirty miles northwest of Rome) reveal that at about 500 B.C. the Etruscans dedicated a temple to the Phoenician goddess Astarte, whom they had learned about by trading with Carthage. That rich city, founded in western North Africa (modern Tunisia) by Phoenicians about 800 B.C., dominated seaborne commerce in the western Mediterranean.

The extent of Etruscan influence on Rome remains controversial. Until recently, scholars speculated that Etruscans conquered Rome and dominated it politically in the sixth century B.C. The Etruscans were also seen as more culturally refined, mainly because so much Greek art has been found at Etruscan sites; they were therefore assumed to have reshaped Roman culture during this period of supposed domination. New scholarship, however, stresses the independence of Romans in developing their own cultural traditions: they borrowed from Etruscans, as from Greeks, whatever appealed to them and adapted it to fit their local circumstances. Romans took over the Etruscans' procedures for religious rituals, magistrates' elaborate garments, and musical instruments. They also learned their divination techniques for discerning the gods' will by identifying clues in the shapes of the internal organs of slaughtered animals. Romans may also have adopted from Etruscan society the tradition of wives joining husbands at dinner parties.

Many features of Roman culture formerly seen as deriving from Etruscan influence were probably part of the ancient Mediterranean's shared cultural environment. The organization of the Roman army, a citizen militia of heavily armed infantry troops (hoplites) fighting in formation, reflected not just Etruscan precedent but that of other peoples. The Romans' alphabet, which they first learned from the Etruscans, was Greek; the Greeks had acquired it through their contact with the Levant. The engineering necessary to urbanize Rome has been said to have been done by the Etruscans, but it is too simplistic to assume that cultural developments of this breadth resulted from one superior culture "instructing" another, less-developed one. Rather, at this time in Mediterranean history, similar cultural developments were under way in many places. The Romans, like so many others, found their own way in navigating through this common cultural sea.

The Early Roman Republic, 509–287 B.C.

The social elite's distrust of kings motivated the creation of the Roman republic. Their fear that monarchy must inevitably become tyranny was enshrined in Livy's story of the rape of Lucretia, the most famous legend about the birth of the republic. Like most of Livy's stories, it stressed the role of moral virtue in Roman history. The assault on Lucretia, a chaste wife in the social elite, took place when the swaggering son of King Tarquin the Proud violently raped her to demonstrate his superior power. Despite pleas from her husband and father not to blame herself, she committed suicide after denouncing her attacker.

Declaring themselves Rome's liberators from tyranny, her relatives and friends, led by Lucius Junius Brutus, expelled Tarquin in 509 B.C. They then created a new political system—the republic—to ensure the sharing of power by the elite and to block rule by one man or family. Thereafter, the Romans prided themselves on living under a freer political system than that of their neighbors. The legend of the warrior Horatius at the bridge, for example, advertised the republic's dedication to national freedom. As Livy told the story, Horatius single-handedly blocked the Etruscan army's access to Rome when they tried to reimpose a monarch on the city. While hacking at his opponents, Horatius berated them as slaves who had lost their freedom because they were ruled by haughty kings. Horatius's legend made clear that Romans founded the republic to prevent a ruler's overt abuse of power.

Conflict over how to achieve this ideal persisted for over two hundred years, a period called "the struggle of the orders." Bitter turmoil between a closed circle of elite families (called the *patricians*) and the rest of Rome's citizen population (the *plebeians*), the two "orders" of the republic's hierarchy, centered on social and economic issues. The patricians inherited their status by being born to about 130 wealthy families controlling important religious activities. Some plebeians, however, were also rich, and they resented the patricians' arrogance in monopolizing political offices, banning intermarriage with plebeians, and advertising their social superiority by sporting red shoes (later they changed to black footwear adorned with a shiny metal crescent).

Poor plebeians clamored for relief from crushing debts and a more equitable distribution of farmland. To pressure the patricians, plebeians periodically resorted to the drastic measure of physically withdrawing from the city to a temporary settlement and refusing to serve in the militia. This tactic worked because Rome's army was minuscule without plebeians. A secession provoked by a patrician's violence against a plebeian woman led to the earliest Roman laws, called the Twelve Tables, from the bronze tablets on which they were engraved for display between 451 and 449 B.C. In Livy's words, these laws prevented the patrician public officials who judged most legal cases from "arbitrarily giving the force of law to their own preferences." So important did the Twelve Tables become as a symbol of the Roman commitment to justice for all citizens that children were required to memorize them for the next four hundred years.◆

These laws were, however, only a first step toward greater sharing of political power; that process occurred mainly through hammering out the different and sometimes overlapping responsibilities of Rome's assemblies. These outdoor meetings of adult male citizens elected officials, passed laws, decided government policies, and held some trials. Assemblies were only for voting, not discussion, but every

◆ For a passage from these seminal laws, see Document 12, "The Twelve Tables."

session was preceded by a public gathering to hear speeches. Everyone, including women and noncitizens, could listen to these addresses. The crowd would loudly express its agreement or disagreement by applauding or hissing. Speakers therefore had to pay close attention to public opinion in forming the proposals that they put before the male citizens who then voted them up or down in the assemblies.

A significant restriction on the democratic aspect of assemblies was that each one was divided into groups, whose membership was determined by status and wealth. Voting took place by groups. Each group, not each individual, had a vote, and a small group had the same vote as a large group. The hierarchy of the voting groups in the Centuriate Assembly, which elected the major officials (consuls and praetors), reflected the organization of the army: it confined the huge population of men too poor to afford military weapons, the *proletarians*, to one group casting only one out of the total of 193 votes. The Plebeian Assembly excluded patricians and grouped itself into thirty-five tribes based on where voters lived; it elected special officials (tribunes) responsible for protecting plebeians, and it passed resolutions called *plebiscites*. The conflict of the orders finally ended when plebiscites gained the status of laws in 287 B.C. Finally, patricians joined plebeians in the Tribal Assembly, which also grouped voters by residence. This assembly, in which plebeians greatly outnumbered patricians, eventually became the republic's most important institution for making policy, passing laws, and, until separate courts were created, conducting judicial trials.

Annually elected officials ran the republic's government; they served in groups, numbering from two to more than a dozen, to ensure shared rule. The highest officials were *consuls*; two were elected each year, and their foremost duty was commanding the military. Winning a consulship was the greatest political honor a Roman man could achieve, and it bestowed high status on his descendants forever, entitling them to be called "nobles." To be elected consul, a man traditionally had to work his way up a "ladder" of offices. After ten years of military service beginning about age twenty, he would seek election as a *quaestor*, a financial administrator. Continuing to climb the ladder, he would next be elected to the board of *aediles*, officials overseeing the city's streets, sewers, aqueducts, temples, and markets. Each rung up the ladder was more competitive, and few men reached the next office, that of *praetor*, which performed judicial and military command duties. The most successful praetors then reached for the gold ring of Roman public office, the consulship.

Ex-consuls could also compete to become one of the *censors*, prestigious senior officials elected very five years to conduct censuses of the citizen body and select new members of the three-hundred-man Senate, which advised the consuls (as it had the kings). The role of the Senate in the republic's government expressed the supreme embodiment of the Roman principle of making decisions by consensus. The Senate had no authority to pass laws; it could only give advice. But its prestige was so enormous that no high official or assembly would disregard the senators' advice, unless they wished to provoke a crisis. Following the Roman tradition that prestige should be visible, the senators proclaimed their status by wearing special black high-top shoes and robes embroidered with a broad purple stripe.

The struggle of the orders extended to control of these offices. The patricians tried to monopolize the highest ones, but the plebeians resisted fiercely. Through violent struggle from about 500 to 450 B.C., they forced the patricians to yield another important concession besides the Twelve Tables: the creation of a special panel of ten annually elected officials, called *tribunes*, whose original responsibility was to stop actions that would harm the plebeians and their property. The tribunate's focus made it stand apart from regular ladder offices. Tribunes, who had to be plebeians, derived their power from the sworn oath of the other plebeians to protect them against all attacks; this inviolability, called *sacrosanctity*, allowed tribunes the right to use a *veto* (a Latin word meaning "I forbid") to block the actions of officials, suspend elections, and even counter the advice of the Senate. The tribunes' extraordinary power to halt government action could make them the sources of bitter political disputes.

Roman values motivated men to compete for honor, not money, in pursuing a public career. By 367 B.C., the plebeians had pushed their way fully into this competition by requiring that at least one consul every year must be a plebeian. Only well-off men could run for election because officials earned no salaries. On the contrary, they were expected to spend large sums to win popular support by entertaining the electorate with, for example, lavish shows that featured gladiators (trained fighters) and wild beasts, such as lions imported from Africa. Once elected, a magistrate had to benefit the people by paying for public works, such as roads, aqueducts, and temples.

As the Romans won control of more and more overseas territory through warfare, the desire for the status that money could buy in financing successful election campaigns overcame the values of faithfulness and honesty. By the second century B.C., military officers could enrich themselves by seizing booty from enemies in successful foreign wars and by extorting bribes from the local people while administering conquered territory. They could then use these profits of war to finance their political careers at home. In this way, acquiring money became more important in the late republic than winning honor through upright public service.

Controversy over how to bring corrupt officials to justice eventually led to the creation of a court system with jury trials in the second century B.C. Since most officials were also senators, the Senate self-interestedly tried to have these juries be manned only by its members, while non-senators agitated to be included. Both accusers and accused had to speak for themselves in court or have friends speak for them. Prominent men, usually senators with expertise in law, played a central role as advisers in the Roman judicial system. These jurists, as they were called (from the Latin *jus, juris*, "law"), operated as private citizens, not officials, in providing legal advice. This reliance on jurists reflected the Roman tradition of consulting councils of advisers to reach decisions. Roman law developed over centuries, some-times incorporating laws from other peoples, and became the basis for many later European legal codes still in use today.

The republic's political and judicial systems, with their jumbled network of in-stitutions, lacked an overall integration. Many different political bodies voted laws or, in the Senate's case, opinions that guided lawmaking, and legal cases could be heard by magistrates, assemblies, or juries. Rome had no highest judicial authority, such as the U.S. Supreme Court, to resolve disputes about conflicting laws or ver-dicts. The republic's stability therefore depended on a reverence for tradition, the "way of the ancestors." This reliance on tradition ensured that the most socially prominent and the richest Romans dominated government and society—because they defined the "way of the ancestors."

Consequences of Roman Imperialism, Fifth to Second Centuries B.C.

Expansion through war made conquest and military service central to the lives of Romans under the republic. During the fifth, fourth, and third centuries B.C., they fought war after war in Italy until they became the most powerful state on the peninsula. In the third and second centuries B.C., they began warring far from home in the west, the north, and the east, but above all they battled Carthage to the south. Their success in these campaigns made Rome the premier power in the Mediterranean.

Fear and ambition motivated this imperialism. Worries about national security made the senators recommend preemptive attacks against others perceived as en-emies of Rome, and everyone longed to capture wealth on foreign military cam-paigns. Poorer soldiers hoped their gains would pull their families out of poverty. The elite longed to increase their riches and acquire glory as commanders, to pro-mote their public careers.

The consequences of repeated wars in Italy and abroad transformed Romans culturally and socially. Astonishingly, they had no literature before about 240 B.C. The cultural interaction with others that expansion brought stimulated their first history and poetry and deeply influenced their art, especially portraiture. Endless military campaigns far from home created stresses on family life and small farm-ers in the army, while the novel demands of ruling conquered territory undermined the government's equilibrium. The importation of huge numbers of war captives to work as slaves on the estates of the rich put free laborers out of work. The con-quests and spoils of war from Rome's great victories in the third and second cen-turies B.C. thus turned out to be a two-edged sword: they brought expansion and wealth, but their unexpected social and political consequences disrupted traditional values and the community's stability.

Expansion in Italy

The Romans believed they were successful militarily because they respected the will of the gods. Cicero claimed, "We have overcome all the nations of the world, because we have realized that the world is directed and governed by the gods." Believing that the gods supported defensive wars as just, the Romans always insisted they fought only in self-defense, even when they attacked first. After a victory over their Latin neighbors in the 490s B.C., the Romans spent the next hundred years warring with the Etruscan town of Veii, a few miles north of the Tiber River. Their 396 B.C. victory doubled Roman territory. A devastating sack of Rome in 387 B.C. by Gauls (a Celtic group) from beyond the Alps proved only a temporary military setback, but it made Romans forever fearful of foreign invasion. By around 220 B.C., Rome controlled all of the peninsula south of the Po River.

Rome and Central Italy, Fifth Century B.C.

The Romans sometimes forced defeated opponents to give up large parcels of land or even enslaved them, yet they also often struck generous peace terms with former enemies. Some defeated Italians immediately became Roman citizens; others gained limited citizenship without the right to vote; still other communities received treaties of alliance. No conquered Italian peoples had to pay taxes to Rome. All, however, had to render military aid in future wars. These new allies then received a share of the booty, chiefly slaves and land, from victorious campaigns against a new crop of enemies. In this way, the Romans adroitly co-opted their former opponents by making them partners in the spoils of conquest, an arrangement that in turn enhanced Rome's wealth and authority.

To buttress Italy's security, the Romans planted colonies of citizens and constructed roads up and down the peninsula to allow troops to march faster. These roads also connected the diverse peoples of Italy, hastening the creation of a more unified culture dominated by Rome. Latin, for example, came to be the common language, although local tongues lived on, especially Greek in the south. The wealth flowing from the first two centuries of expansion attracted hordes of people to the capital because it financed new

Roman Roads, c. 110 B.C.

■ **Aqueduct at Nîmes in France**

Like the Greeks, the Romans met the challenge of supplying towns with drinkable water by constructing aqueducts. They excelled at building complex systems of tunnels, channels, and bridges to move water over great distances. One of the best-preserved sections of a major aqueduct is the so-called Pont-du-Gard near present-day Nîmes in France, erected in the late first century B.C. to serve the flourishing town of Nemausus. Built of stones fitted together without clamps or mortar, the span soars 160 feet high and is 875 feet long, carrying water from thirty-five miles away in a channel constructed to fall only one foot in height for every three thousand feet in length, so that the flow would remain steady but gentle. (Hubertus Kanus/Photo Researchers, Inc.)

www.bedfordstmartins.com/huntconcise   See the ONLINE STUDY GUIDE for more help in analyzing this image.

aqueducts to provide fresh, running water—a rarity in the ancient world—and a massive building program employing poor laborers. By around 300 B.C., perhaps 150,000 people lived within Rome's walls. Outside the city, about 750,000 free Roman citizens inhabited various parts of Italy on land taken from local peoples. Much conquered territory was declared public land, open to any Roman to use for grazing herds of cattle.

Rich patricians and plebeians cooperated to exploit the expanding Roman territories; the old hierarchy separating the orders had become a technicality. This merged elite derived its wealth mainly from agricultural land and plunder acquired during military service. Since Rome levied no regular income or inheritance taxes, families could pass down this wealth from generation to generation.

Wars with Carthage

The republic fought three wars against the powerful and wealthy North African city of Carthage. Governed, like Rome, as a republic, by the third century B.C. Carthage controlled an empire encompassing the northwest African coast, part of Libya, Sardinia, Corsica, Malta, and the southern portion of Spain. Geography therefore ensured that an expansionist Rome would sooner or later infringe on Carthage's interests, which depended on the sea; the Carthaginians fielded a strong fleet but had to hire mercenaries to field a sizable infantry. To Romans, remembering the invasion by the Gauls, Carthage seemed a dangerous rival, as well as a fine prize because of its riches. Roman hostility was also fueled by horror at the Carthaginian tradition of incinerating infants in times of trouble in the belief this would placate their gods.

A coincidence ignited open conflict with Carthage, taking Roman troops outside Italy and across the sea for the first time; the three wars that ensued are called the Punic Wars, from the Roman term *Punici*, meaning "Phoenicians" (the ancestors of the Carthaginians). The First Punic War (264–241 B.C.) began when a band of mercenaries embroiled in a local war at Messana, on Sicily's northeastern tip, appealed for help to Rome and Carthage simultaneously. Both states sent troops. The Carthaginians wanted to protect their revenue from Sicilian trade; the Romans wanted to keep Carthaginian troops from moving close to their territory and to reap the rewards of conquest. The clash between their forces exploded into a war that lasted a generation. Its agonizing battles revealed why the Romans so consistently conquered their rivals. In addition to being able to draw on the Italian population for reserves of manpower, they were prepared to spend as much money, sacrifice as many troops, and fight as long as necessary to prevail. Previously unskilled at naval warfare, they expended vast sums to build warships to combat Carthage's experienced navy; they lost more than five hundred ships and 250,000 men while learning how to win at sea. (See "Taking Measure," page 150.)

Victory in the First Punic War made the Romans masters of Sicily, where they set up their first province (a foreign territory ruled and taxed by Roman officials). This innovation proved so profitable that they soon seized the islands of Sardinia and Corsica from the Carthaginians to create another province. These successful foreign conquests whetted their appetite for more, and they also feared a renewal of Carthage's power (Map 4.2). Pressing their advantage, they next made alliances with local peoples in Spain, where the Carthaginians were expanding from their original trading posts in the south.

A Roman ultimatum to Carthage against further expansion convinced the Carthaginians that another war was inevitable, so they decided to strike back. In the Second Punic War (218–201 B.C.), the daring Carthaginian general Hannibal (247–182 B.C.) flabbergasted the Romans by marching troops and war elephants

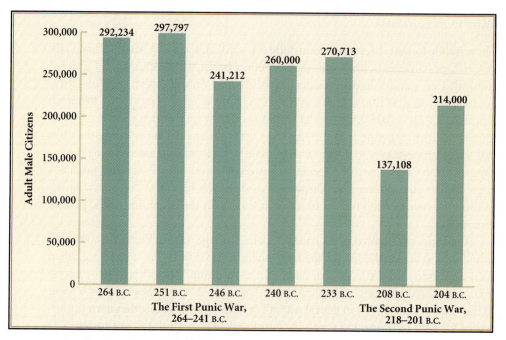

■ TAKING MEASURE Census Records of Adult Male Roman Citizens during the First and Second Punic Wars

Livy (59 B.C.–A.D. 17) and Jerome (c. A.D. 347–420) provide these numbers from Roman censuses conducted during and between the first two wars against Carthage. Only adult male citizens (the men eligible for Rome's regular army) were counted. The drop in the total for 246 B.C., compared with the total for 264 B.C., reflects losses in the First Punic War. The low total for 208 B.C. reflects losses in battle and defections by communities such as Capua in 216 B.C. Because the censuses did not include the Italian allies fighting on Rome's side, the numbers understate the wars' total casualties. Scholars estimate that the first two Punic Wars took the lives of nearly a third of Italy's adult male population—perhaps a quarter of a million soldiers killed.

(Tenney Frank, *An Economic Survey of Ancient Rome, Vol. I* [New York: Farrar, Straus, and Giroux, 1959], 56.)

from Carthaginian territory in Spain over the snowy Alps into Italy. Slaughtering more than thirty thousand at Cannae in 216 B.C. in the bloodiest defeat in Roman history, he tried to provoke widespread revolts among the Italian cities allied to Rome. Disastrously for him, most Italians remained loyal to Rome. Hannibal's alliance in 215 B.C. with King Philip V of Macedonia (238–179 B.C.) forced the Romans to fight on a second front in Greece (their first presence in that region), but they refused to crack despite Hannibal's ravaging Italy from 218 to 203 B.C. The Romans finally won by turning the tables: invading the Carthaginians' homeland, the Roman general Scipio crushed Carthage at the battle of Zama in 202 B.C. and was dubbed "Africanus" to commemorate the victory. The Senate imposed a punishing settlement on the Carthaginians in 201 B.C., forcing them to scuttle their

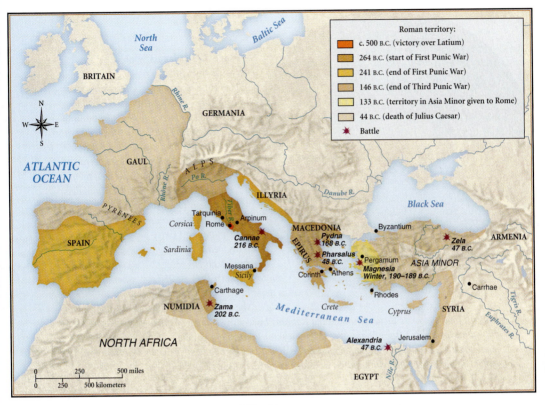

MAP 4.2 Roman Expansion, c. 500–44 B.C.

During the first two centuries of its existence, the Roman republic used war and diplomacy to extend its power north and south on the Italian peninsula. In the third and second centuries B.C., conflict with Carthage to the south and west and with the Hellenistic kingdoms to the east extended Roman power far outside Italy and led to the creation of provinces from Spain to Greece. The first century B.C. saw the conquest of the Levant by Pompey and of Gaul by Julius Caesar.

navy, pay huge war indemnities for fifty years, and hand over their lucrative holdings in Spain, which Rome made into provinces famous for their mines.

The Third Punic War (149–146 B.C.) broke out when the Carthaginians, who had finally revived financially, retaliated against the aggression of their neighbor and Roman ally the Numidian king Masinissa. After winning the war, the Romans heeded the advice "We must destroy Carthage," which the crusty senator Cato repeatedly intoned: they razed the city and converted its territory into a province. This disaster did not obliterate Punic social and cultural ways, however, and under the Roman Empire this part of North Africa became renowned for its economic and intellectual vitality, which emerged from a synthesis of Roman and Punic traditions.

The conquests of the Punic Wars spurred the extension of Roman power beyond Spain and North Africa to Macedonia, Greece, and part of Asia Minor. After

■ **Plate Decorated with a War Elephant**

This third-century B.C. plate from southern Italy depicts an Indian elephant followed by her calf. The adult animal carries on its back a fortified compartment holding archers. War elephants were introduced to the Mediterranean after Alexander the Great saw them in his campaigns in India. Commanders used them to frighten and confuse the enemy with their size and loud bellowing. This plate most likely depicts one of the twenty beasts that the mercenary general Pyrrhus of Epirus (319–272 B.C.) transported by sea to southern Italy in 280 B.C. when the Greek cities there hired him to fight the Romans on their behalf. In 218 B.C., the Carthaginian general Hannibal, who had studied Pyrrhus's tactics, shocked the Romans by leading a force of thirty-seven elephants (and thousands of troops) from Spain over the treacherous passes of the Alps to invade Italy. In the long run, however, armies gave up on elephants because they were too expensive to maintain and too difficult to control when confused or wounded in battle. (Scala/Art Resource, NY.)

thrashing Philip in Macedonia for revenge and to prevent any threat of his invading Italy, the Roman commander Flamininus had proclaimed the "freedom of the Greeks" in 196 B.C. to show respect for Greece's distinguished past. The Greek cities and federal leagues naturally interpreted the proclamation to mean they could behave as they liked. They misunderstood. The Romans meant them to behave as clients and follow their new patrons' advice; the Greeks thought, as "friends" of Rome, that they were truly free. Trouble then developed because the two parties failed to realize that common and familiar words like *freedom* and *friendship* could carry very different implications in different societies. The Romans continued military intervention to make the kingdom of Macedonia and the Greeks observe their obligations as clients. Frustrated by continuing Greek resistance, the Senate in 146 B.C. ordered the destruction of Corinth for asserting its independence and converted Macedonia and Greece into a province. In 133 B.C., the Attalid king Attalus III of Pergamum boosted Roman power with an astonishing gift: he left his Asia Minor kingdom to Rome in his will. In 121 B.C., the lower part of Gaul across the Alps (modern France) was made into a province. By this date, then, Rome governed and profited from two-thirds of the Mediterranean region; only the easternmost Mediterranean lay outside its control (see Map 4.2).

Greece's Influence on Rome's Literature and Art

Although Romans looked down on Greeks for their military impotence, they felt awe before Greece's literature and art. Roman authors and artists looked to Greek models in all that they did. In about 200 B.C., the first Roman historian, Fabius Pictor, published his narrative of Rome's foundation and the Punic Wars—in Greek. Greece also directly inspired the earliest literature in Latin: an adaptation of Homer's *Odyssey* by a Greek ex-slave, Livius Andronicus, written sometime after the First Punic War. Unfortunately, very little of these works has survived.

Like Livius, many of the most famous early Latin authors were not native Romans; their widespread origins testified to the intermingling of cultures under the republic. The poet Naevius (d. 201 B.C.) came from Campania; the poet Ennius (d. 169 B.C.) from even farther south, in Calabria; the comic playwright Plautus (d. 184 B.C.) from north of Rome, in Umbria; his fellow comedy writer Terence (c. 190–159 B.C.) from North Africa. They all found inspiration in Greek literature. Roman comedies, for example, took their plots and stock characters from Hellenistic Greek comedy, which raised laughs from family life and stereotyped personalities, such as the braggart warrior and the obsessed lover.

Not all Romans applauded Greek influence. Cato, although he studied Greek himself, repeatedly thundered against the deleterious effect the "effete" Greeks had on the "sturdy" Romans. He established Latin as an appropriate language for prose by publishing a history of Rome, *The Origins* (written between 168 and 149 B.C.), and instructions for running a large farm, *On Agriculture* (published about 160 B.C.). He glumly predicted that if the Romans ever became infected with Greek literature, they would lose their dominions. In fact, as usual in cultural interactions, early Roman authors employed foreign models to express their own values in new ways. Ennius, for example, was inspired by Greek epic poetry to compose his path-breaking Latin epic *Annals*, a poetic version of Roman history. Its contents praised ancestral tradition, as a much-quoted line demonstrated: "On the ways and the men of old rests the Roman commonwealth."

Later Roman writers also took inspiration from Greek literature. Lucretius (c. 94–55 B.C.), for example, published a long poem entitled *On the Nature of Things* to argue that people should have no fear of death, which only inflamed "the running sores of life." His work's content followed closely the "atomic theory" of the nature of existence of the Greek philosopher Epicurus (341–270 B.C.) and explained matter as composed of tiny, invisible particles. Dying, the poem taught, simply meant the dissolution of the union of atoms, which had united temporarily to create a person's body. There could be no eternal punishment or pain after death, indeed no existence at all, because a person's soul, itself made up of atoms, perished along with the body.

Hellenistic authors inspired Catullus (c. 84–54 B.C.), whose concise and witty poems savaged prominent politicians for their sexual behavior and lamented his

■ **Wall Painting Depicting Actors in a Roman Comedy**
This painting found in the excavation of Pompeii dates to the second or first century b.c. It shows actors wearing masks associated with stock comic characters that Plautus borrowed from the Greek playwright Menander (c. 342–289 b.c.). As in Greek comedy, the actors were men, who strove for broad, farcical humor. The plots were often burlesques of famous mythological stories.
(Scala/Art Resource, NY.)

own disastrous love life. His most notorious erotic poems detailed his passion for a married woman named Lesbia, whom he begged to think only of immediate pleasures: "Let us live, my Lesbia, and love; the gossip of stern old men is not worth a cent. Suns can set and rise again; we, when once our brief light has set, must sleep one never-ending night. Give me a thousand kisses, then a hundred, then a thousand more."

The orator Cicero wrote not only speeches and letters but also many essays on political science, philosophy, ethics, and theology that built on the work of Greek philosophers. He adapted their ideas to Roman life and infused his thoughts with a deep understanding of the need to appreciate the uniqueness of each human personality. He wrote his most influential philosophical works in one period of furious activity while in political exile in 45 and 44 b.c. His doctrine of *humanitas* ("humanness, the quality of humanity") combined various strands of Greek philosophy, especially Stoicism, to express an ideal for human life based on generous and honest treatment of others and an abiding commitment to morality derived from natural law (the right that exists for all people by nature, independent of the differing laws and customs of different societies). What he passed on to later ages was perhaps the most attractive ideal to come from republican Rome: the spirit of *humanitas.*◆

Greece deeply influenced Rome not only in literature but also in art and architecture, from the style of sculpture and painting to the design of public buildings. Typically, Romans adapted Greek models to their own purposes, most strikingly in portrait sculpture. Hellenistic artists had pioneered the sculpting of realistic statues that showed the ravages of age and infirmity on the human body. Such works, however, portrayed human stereotypes (the "old man," the "drunken woman"), not specific people. Greek portrait sculpture tended to present real individuals in the best possible light, much like a retouched photograph today.

Roman artists in the later republic transferred the Greek tradition of realistic sculpture to portraiture busts, as contemporary Etruscan sculptors did also. Roman sculptures of specific men did not conceal unflattering features: protruding noses, receding chins, fissured wrinkles, bald heads, careworn eyes. Portraits of women, by contrast, were generally more idealized, perhaps to represent the traditional vision of married bliss. Portraits of children were not popular during the republic, perhaps because offspring were not seen as contributing to public life until they were grown. Because either the men depicted in the portraits or their families paid for the busts, they presumably wanted the faces sculpted realistically—showing the toll of age and effort—to emphasize how hard the men had worked to serve "the people's matter" that was the republic.

Stresses on Society

Before the protracted campaigns required to defeat Carthage, Macedonia, and Greece in the third and second centuries B.C., Roman warfare, like Greek, had followed a pattern of short campaigns timed not to interfere with the fluctuating labor needs of farming. Rome's long wars abroad had the unintended consequence of disrupting the traditional rhythm of Roman agricultural life and forcing many poor people to move to the capital. Furthermore, the years of conquest ruined many small farmers in Italy, who constituted the principal source of soldiers. A farmer absent on prolonged military expeditions had two choices: relying on a hired hand or slave to manage his crops and animals or having his wife take on what was traditionally man's work in the fields in addition to her usual domestic tasks. The story of the consul Regulus, who led a Roman army to victory in

---

◆ For an excerpt from this renowned lawyer, statesman, author, and orator, see Document 13, Cicero, "On the Commonwealth."

Africa in 256 B.C., revealed the severe problems a man's absence could cause. When the man who managed his 4⅓-acre farm died while the consul was away fighting Carthage, a hired hand ran off with all the farm's tools and livestock. Regulus begged the Senate to send a general to replace him so he could return home to save his wife and children from starving. The senators preserved Regulus's family and property from ruin because they wanted to retain him as a commander in the field.

Ordinary soldiers could expect no such special aid, and these troubles hit the poor particularly hard. Many farmers and their families fell so far into debt that they were forced to sell their land. Not all regions of Italy suffered as severely as others, and some impoverished farmers and their families managed to remain in the countryside by working as day laborers for others. Many homeless people, however, migrated to Rome, where the men looked for work as menial laborers and women sought piecework making cloth but often were forced into prostitution.

This influx of desperate, landless people swelled the poverty-level urban population. The difficulty they experienced just surviving made them a swing element in Roman politics, as ambitious politicians jockeyed for their support by promising to improve their plight. The state had to feed them to avert riots, and by the late second century B.C. Rome was importing food to support this swollen population of urban poor. Their demand for rations of low-priced (and eventually free) grain distributed at the state's expense became one of the most contentious issues in late republican politics.

At the other end of the social hierarchy, Rome's elite reaped abundant rewards from imperialism. The increased need for commanders to lead military campaigns abroad created opportunities for successful generals to enrich themselves and their families. By using their gains to finance public buildings, the elite enhanced their reputations while benefiting the general population. Building new temples, for example, was thought to increase everyone's security by pleasing the gods. In 146 B.C., a victorious general, Caecilius Metellus, paid for Rome's first temple built of marble, finally bringing this Greek style to the capital city.

The distress of small farmers suited rich landowners because they could buy bankrupt plots to create large estates. They further increased their holdings by illegally occupying public land carved out of the territory of defeated peoples. The rich worked their large estates, called *latifundia*, with slaves as well as free laborers. Many of Italy's small farmers were ruined because of the large number of slaves taken captive during the wars. The victories won by poor Roman soldiers had produced a workforce with which they could not compete. The growing size of the slave crews working on *latifundia* was a mixed blessing for their wealthy owners because the presence of so many slave workers in one place led to periodic revolts that required the army to suppress.

The elite also profited from Rome's expansion by filling the governing offices in the new provinces; they could enrich themselves if they ignored the traditional value of uprightness. Since provincial officials ruled by martial law, no one in the provinces could curb a greedy governor's appetite for graft, extortion, and plunder. Not all governors were corrupt, of course, but some did use their unsupervised power to extort everything they could from the provincials. Normally such offenders faced no punishment because their colleagues in the Senate, who controlled the judicial system, excused one another's crimes.

The new desire for luxury, financed by the fruits of expansion abroad, fractured the traditional values of moderation and frugality. Before, a general like Manius Curius (d. 270 B.C.) represented the ideal: despite his glorious military victories, he was said to have boiled turnips for his meals in a humble hut. Now, the elite acquired ostentatious luxuries, such as large and showy country villas for entertaining friends and clients, to proclaim their social superiority. Money had become more valuable to them than the good of "the people's matter."

Upheaval in the Late Republic, c. 133–44 B.C.

Placing their own interests ahead of traditional communal values, some ambitious men in the Roman elite propelled the republic to war with itself. When the tribunes Tiberius and Gaius Gracchus agitated for reforms to help impoverished farmers, their opponents in the Senate resorted to murder to curb them. When a would-be member of the elite, Gaius Marius, opened army service to the poor to boost his personal status, his creation of "client armies" undermined faithfulness to the republic. When the people's unwillingness to share citizenship with Italian allies sparked a war in Italy and the clashing ambitions of the "great men" Sulla, Pompey, and Julius Caesar burst into civil war, the republic shattered beyond repair.

The Gracchi and Factional Politics

The aristocratic brothers Tiberius and Gaius Sempronius Gracchus won election as tribunes by advocating that rich landowners make concessions to aid the poor. This policy set them at odds with many of the elite into whose order they had been born: their grandfather Scipio had defeated Hannibal, and their mother was the Cornelia whom the king of Egypt had courted after their father died. Tiberius, the older of the Gracchi (the plural of *Gracchus*), eloquently dramatized the tragic circumstances that motivated them politically, according to the biographer Plutarch (c. A.D. 50–120):

> *The wild beasts that roam over Italy have their dens. . . . But the men who*
> *fight and die for Italy enjoy nothing but the air and light; without house or*
> *home they wander about with their wives and children. . . . They fight and*
> *die to protect the wealth and luxury of others; they are styled masters of the*
> *world, and have not a clod of earth they call their own.*

In 133 B.C., when the Senate blocked Tiberius's proposed reforms, he outflanked his opponents by having the Plebeian Assembly pass laws redistributing public land to landless Romans. He further shattered tradition by circumventing the senators' will on financing his agrarian reform: before the Senate could decide whether to accept the bequest of the Attalid kingdom from the ruler of Pergamum, Tiberius had the plebeians pass another law specifying that the gift's proceeds pay to equip the new farms being established on the redistributed land.

Tiberius then announced his intention to run for reelection as tribune, violating the tradition against consecutive terms. His senatorial enemies boiled over: Tiberius's own cousin, Scipio Nasica, led a band of senators and their clients in an ambush against him to, as they shouted, "save the republic." Pulling their togas up over their left arms so they would not trip in the attack, they clubbed to death the tribune and many of his followers. Their assault began the bloody history of murder as a political tactic in the republic.

Gaius, elected tribune for 123 B.C. and, contrary to precedent, elected again the next year, followed his brother's lead by pushing measures that outraged the elite: more agrarian reform, greatly subsidized prices for grain, public works projects throughout Italy to provide employment for the poor, and colonies abroad with farms for the landless. His most revolutionary proposals were to grant Roman citizenship to many Italians and to establish new courts that would try senators accused of corruption as provincial governors. The new juries would be manned not by senators but by *equites* ("equestrians" or "knights"). These were landowners from outside the city, wealthy businessmen whose choice of commerce over a public career set them apart from senators. Because they did not serve in the Senate, equestrians could convict corrupt senators without fear of peer pressure. Gaius's proposal marked the emergence of the equestrians as a political force in Roman politics, to the dismay of the Senate. When the senators stymied his plans, Gaius in 121 B.C. assembled an armed group to threaten them. They responded by instructing the consuls "to take all measures necessary to defend the republic," meaning the use of force. To escape arrest and certain execution, Gaius had one of his slaves cut his throat; hundreds of his supporters were then killed by the senators and their supporters.

The violent deaths of the Gracchi and so many of their followers introduced factions into Roman politics. From now on, members of the elite positioned themselves either as supporters of the people, referred to as *populares,* or of "the best," referred to as *optimates*. Some identified with one faction or the other from genuine allegiance to its policies; others based their choice on political expediency, supporting whichever side better promoted their own political advancement. This division of the elite persisted as a source of friction and violence until the end of the republic.

Gaius Marius and the First Client Armies

The split in the elite broke the stranglehold of the "nobles" on political power, allowing a new kind of leader to arise: men with no consul among their ancestors. These members of the elite relied on sheer ability to force their way to fame, fortune, influence, and—their ultimate goal—the consulship. The most controversial of them was Gaius Marius (c. 157–86 B.C.), an equestrian from Arpinum in central Italy. Ordinarily, a man from this background had no chance of cracking the ranks of Rome's ruling elite. Fortunately for Marius, however, Rome at the end of the second century B.C. direly needed a first-rate general. His military prowess won him election as a consul for 107 B.C. In Roman terms this election made him a "new man"—that is, the first man in the history of his family to become consul. Marius's success in great crises, first in North Africa and next against German tribes who attacked southern France and then Italy, led the people to elect him consul for an unprecedented six terms, including consecutive service, by 100 B.C.

Marius became so celebrated that the Senate voted him a triumph, Rome's ultimate military honor. On the day of the ceremony, the general paraded through Rome in a chariot. His face was painted red for reasons Romans could no longer remember. Huge crowds cheered him, while his army teased him with off-color jokes to avert the evil eye at this moment of supreme glory. For a similar reason, a slave rode with him to keep whispering in his ear, "Look behind you, and remember that you are a mortal."

The optimates faction never accepted Marius, scorning him as a dangerous upstart. His support came mainly from the common people, who loved him for his reform of military service. Previously, only men with property could enroll as soldiers. Marius opened enlistment to proletarians, men who owned almost nothing. For them, serving in the army meant an opportunity to better their lot by acquiring booty and a grant of land to retire on.

This change had a momentous consequence: creating armies more loyal to their commander than to the republic. Proletarian troops felt immense goodwill toward a commander who led them to victory and then divided the spoils with them generously. Impoverished soldiers thus began to behave like an army of clients following their patron—their general. They naturally supported his personal ambitions. Marius was the first to promote his own career in this way, but he lost his political importance after 100 B.C. because he stopped commanding armies and tried to win favor with the optimates. Other generals after him used client armies to advance

their political careers more ruthlessly than ever Marius had, with appalling consequences for the republic.

Sulla and Civil War

Taking Marius's lesson to heart, an unscrupulous noble named Lucius Cornelius
Sulla (c. 138–78 B.C.) exploited the dirty secret of politics in the late republic: traditional values no longer restrained commanders who prized their own advancement and the enrichment of their troops above peace and the good of the community. Sulla wielded his client army as a weapon to extort the consulship and cow
the Senate, perverting the Roman notion of honor. His opportunity came when
Rome's Italian allies rebelled in frustration at their being denied citizenship by the
elite. The Italians' discontent finally erupted in 91–87 B.C. in the Social War (so
named because the Latin word for *ally* is *socius*). The allies lost the war and 300,000
men, but they won the political battle: Romans granted citizenship to all freeborn
peoples of Italy south of the Po River. Most important, their men were now entitled to vote in Rome's assemblies.

Sulla's successful command in the Social War won him election as consul for
88 B.C. His luck continued when, in that same year, the king of Pontus on the southern coast of the Black Sea, Mithridates VI (120–63 B.C.), organized a murderous
rebellion against Rome's control of Asia Minor, especially its rapacious tax collectors, who squeezed provincials to pay much more than they owed. Denouncing Romans as "the common enemies of all mankind," Mithridates persuaded the locals
to slaughter all the Italians they could locate—tens of thousands of them—in a
single day. As retaliation for this treachery, the Senate advised a military expedition;
victory would mean unimaginable booty because Asia Minor held many wealthy
cities.

Born to a patrician family that had lost most of its status and all of its money,
Sulla craved the command against Mithridates. When the Senate advised giving
Sulla the appointment, his jealous rival Marius, now an old man, immediately plotted to have it transferred to himself by plebiscite. Outraged, Sulla marched his client
army against Rome itself. All his officers except one deserted him in horror at this
unthinkable outrage. But common soldiers united behind him; neither they nor
their commander shrank from civil war. Capturing Rome, Sulla murdered or exiled his opponents and let his men rampage through the city. He then led them off
to fight Mithridates, ignoring a summons to stand trial and sacking Athens on the
way to Asia Minor.

Sulla's unprecedented violence raised the stakes. In Sulla's absence, Marius
and his friends embarked on their own reign of terror in Rome. In 83 B.C., Sulla
returned after defeating Mithridates and allowing his soldiers to plunder Asia
Minor. Civil war recommenced for two years until Sulla crushed his enemies and

their Italian allies. The climactic battle took place in 82 B.C. before the gates of Rome. An Italian general whipped his troops into a frenzy by shouting, "The last day is at hand for the Romans! These wolves that have made such ravages upon our liberty will never vanish until we have cut down the forest that harbors them."

This passionate cry for freedom failed. Sulla won and destroyed everyone who had opposed him. To speed the extermination, he devised a merciless procedure called *proscription*—posting a list of those supposedly guilty of treasonable crimes so that anyone could hunt them down and execute them. Because the property of those proscribed was confiscated, the victors listed the name of anyone whose wealth they desired. The Senate in terror appointed Sulla dictator—an emergency office supposed to be held only temporarily—without any limitation of term. He promptly reorganized the government in the interest of "the best"—his social class—by making senators the only ones allowed to judge cases against their colleagues and forbidding tribunes to offer legislation on their own or hold any other office after their term.

Convinced by an old prophecy that he had only a short time to live, Sulla surprised everyone by retiring to private life in 79 B.C. and indeed dying the next year. His murderous career revealed the sad fate of the traditional values of the republic.

■ **Bust of Lucius Cornelius Sulla**
This bust, now in the Venice Archaeological Museum, is usually identified as Sulla; its harsh gaze corresponds to what the ancient sources reported of his personality. When Sulla (c. 138–78 B.C.) marched on Rome in 88 B.C., he smashed beyond repair the Roman tradition that leading citizens put the interests of the commonwealth ahead of their own private goals.
(Scala/Art Resource, NY.)

First, success in war had long ago changed its meaning from defense of the community to acquiring profits for commanders and common soldiers alike. Second, the patron-client system had mutated to make poor soldiers feel stronger ties of obligation to their generals than to the republic; Sulla's men obeyed his order to attack Rome because they owed obedience to him as their patron and could expect benefits from him in return. He fulfilled his obligations to them by permitting the plundering of domestic and foreign opponents alike.

Finally, the traditional desire to win honor now worked both for and against political stability. So long as that value motivated men from distinguished families to seek office to promote the welfare of the population as well as the status of their families—the traditional ideal of a public career—it exerted a powerful force for social peace and general prosperity. But pushed to its extreme, the concern for prestige and wealth could overshadow all considerations of public service, even to the point of unleashing civil war. The republic was doomed once its leaders and followers forsook the "way of the ancestors" that valued respect for the peace, prosperity, and traditions of the republic above personal gain.

Pompey, Caesar, and the Downfall of the Republic

The great generals whose names dominate the history of the republic after Sulla all took him as their model: while professing allegiance to the state, they unscrupulously pursued their own advancement. Their motivation—the belief that a Roman noble could never have too much glory or too much wealth—was a corruption of the republic's finest ideals. Their fevered pursuit of self-aggrandizement scorned the tradition of public service to the commonwealth. Two Roman nobles, Pompey and Julius Caesar, especially fanned the flames of internal discord with their ambitious conflicts. The protracted civil war they eventually fought ruined the republic. In its aftermath, monarchy returned to Rome after an absence of nearly five hundred years.

The career of Gnaeus Pompey (106–48 B.C.) shows how weak the traditional restraints on an individual's power became in the aftermath of Sulla. At only twenty-three years of age, Pompey gathered a private army from his father's clients to fight for Sulla in 83 B.C. So splendid were his victories that his astonishing demand for a triumph could not be refused. Awarding the supreme honor to such a young man, who had held not a single public office, shattered precedent, but Pompey's personal power made him irresistible. As he told Sulla, "People worship the rising, not the setting, sun."

Pompey went from victory to victory. After helping suppress a renegade Roman commander in Spain, in 71 B.C. he piggybacked onto the final victories over a massive slave rebellion led by Spartacus, a fugitive gladiator who had terrorized southern Italy for two years and defeated consuls with his army of 100,000 escaped slaves. Stealing the glory from the real victor, the commander Marcus Licinius Crassus (c. 115–53 B.C.), Pompey demanded and won election to the consulship in 70 B.C., without climbing the ladder of offices or reaching the legal age of forty-two. Three years later, he received unlimited powers to eradicate the pirates infesting the Mediterranean. He smashed them in a matter of months. This success made him wildly popular with the urban poor, who depended on a steady flow of imported grain; with wealthy shippers, who depended on safe sea lanes; and with coastal communities that had suffered from the pirates' raids. In 66 B.C., he won the first Roman victories in the Levant. By annexing Syria as a province in 64 B.C., he ended the Seleucid kingdom and extended Rome's power to the eastern edge of the Mediterranean. He marched as far south as Jerusalem, capturing it in 63 B.C. Jews had lived in Rome since the second century B.C., but most Romans knew little about their religion; Pompey inspected the Jerusalem temple to satisfy his curiosity and remove its treasures.

Pompey's victories were so spectacular that people compared him to Alexander the Great and referred to him as *Magnus* ("the Great"). No fan of modesty, he boasted that he had increased Rome's provincial revenues by 70 percent and distributed spoils equal to twelve and a half years' pay to his soldiers. He treated foreign policy as his personal business: in the east he operated on his own initiative and ignored the tradition of commanders consulting the Senate to decide on new political arrangements for conquered territories. For all practical purposes, he behaved abroad more like an independent king than a Roman magistrate. He pithily expressed his attitude when replying to some foreigners after they objected to his actions as unjust: "Stop quoting the laws to us," he told them. "We carry swords."

Fearing his power, Pompey's enemies at Rome tried to strengthen their own positions by proclaiming their concern for the plight of the common people. By the 60s B.C., Rome's population had soared to over half a million people. Hundreds of thousands of them lived crowded together in shabby apartment buildings no better than slums and depended on subsidized food. Work was hard to find. Danger haunted the crowded streets because the city had no police force. Even the propertied class was in trouble: Sulla's confiscations had produced a credit crunch by flooding the real estate market with properties for sale and caused land values to plummet. Overextended investors were trying to borrow their way back to liquidity, with no success.

Pompey's return to Rome in 62 B.C. lit the fuse to this political powder keg. The Senate, eager to bring "the Great" down a notch, shortsightedly refused to approve his arrangements in the Levant or his grants of land to his veterans. This setback forced Pompey to negotiate with his fiercest political rivals, Crassus and Julius Caesar (100–44 B.C.). In 60 B.C., these three allied in an unofficial arrangement designated the "First Triumvirate" ("coalition of three men"). Their combined influence proved unstoppable: Pompey rammed through laws confirming his eastern arrangements and guaranteeing land for his troops, thus affirming his status as a generous patron; Caesar gained the consulship for 59 B.C. along with a special command in Gaul, allowing him to build his own client army financed with booty; and Crassus received financial breaks for the Roman tax collectors in Asia Minor, whose support gave him political clout and in whose business he had invested.

This unprecedented alliance of former political enemies shared no common philosophy of governing; its only cohesion came from personal connections. To cement his bond with Pompey, Caesar married his daughter, Julia, to him in 59 B.C., even though she had been engaged to another man. Pompey soothed Julia's jilted fiancé by having him marry his own daughter, who had been engaged to yet somebody else. Through these marital machinations, the two powerful antagonists now had a common interest: the well-being of Julia, Caesar's only daughter and Pompey's new wife. (Pompey had earlier divorced his second wife after Caesar allegedly seduced her.) Pompey and Julia apparently fell deeply in love in their arranged marriage. As long as Julia lived, Pompey's affection for her restrained him from an outright break with her father. During the triumvirate, these private relationships blatantly replaced communal values as the glue of republican politics.

Caesar won the affection of his client army with years of victories and plunder in central and northern Gaul, which he added to the Roman provinces; he awed his troops with his daring by crossing the channel to Britain for brief campaigns. His political enemies at Rome dreaded him even more as his military suc-

■ **Coin Portrait of Julius Caesar**
Julius Caesar (100–44 B.C.) was the first living Roman to have his portrait appear on a Roman coin. Roman republican coinage had annually changing types—the images and words stamped on the front and back of coins—chosen by the officials in charge of minting. Tradition mandated that only persons who had died could be shown (the same rule applies to United States currency), but after Caesar won the civil war in 45 B.C., he broke that tradition, as he did many others, to show that he was Rome's supreme leader. Here, he wears the laurel wreath of a conquering general. The realistic portrait conforms to late republican style. Caesar's wrinkled neck and careworn expression emphasize the suffering he endured—and imposed on others—to reach the pinnacle of success. (Bibliothèque Nationale, Paris.)

cesses mounted, and the bond linking him to Pompey vanished in 54 B.C. when Julia died in childbirth. With Caesar's followers agitating to win the masses' support for his return to the capital, the two sides' rivalry exploded into violence. By the mid-50s B.C., political gangs of young men combed the alleys of Rome searching for opponents to beat up or murder. Street fighting reached such a pitch in 53 B.C. that it prevented elections; no consuls could be chosen until the year was half over. The triumvirate completely dissolved that same year with the death of Crassus in battle at Carrhae in northern Mesopotamia. In an attempt to win the military glory he felt Pompey had stolen from him, Crassus—without authorization—had taken a Roman army across the Euphrates River to fight the Parthians, an Iranian people who ruled a vast territory stretching from the Euphrates to the Indus River. A year later, Caesar's enemies took the extraordinary step of having Pompey appointed sole consul. The traditions of republican government had crumbled.

When the Senate ordered Caesar to surrender his command and thus open himself to prosecution by his enemies, he led his army against Rome. As he crossed the Rubicon River, the official northern boundary of Italy, in early 49 B.C., he uttered the famous words signaling that he had made an irrevocable choice for civil war: "The die is cast." His troops followed him unhesitatingly, and the people of Italy cheered him on enthusiastically. He had many backers in Rome, too, from the masses who looked forward to his legendary generosity and from impoverished members of the elite hoping to recoup their fortunes through proscriptions.

The enthusiasm for Caesar induced Pompey and most senators to flee to Greece to prepare resistance. Caesar entered Rome peacefully but soon departed to defeat the army his enemies had raised in Spain; he then sailed to Greece in 48 B.C. There he nearly lost the war when his supplies ran out, but his soldiers remained loyal even when they were reduced to eating bread made from roots. When Pompey saw what his opponent's troops were willing to subsist on, he lamented, "I am fighting wild beasts." Caesar exploited the high morale of his army and Pompey's weak generalship to gain a stunning victory at the battle of Pharsalus in 48 B.C. Pompey fled to Egypt, where the ministers of the boy-king Ptolemy XIII (63–47 B.C.) treacherously murdered him.

Caesar then invaded Egypt, winning a difficult campaign that ended when the young pharaoh drowned in the Nile and Caesar restored Cleopatra VII (69–30 B.C.) to the Egyptian throne. As intelligent as she was ruthless, Cleopatra charmed the invader into sharing her bed and supporting her rule. This attachment shocked Caesar's friends and enemies alike: they believed Rome should seize power from foreigners, not yield it to them. Still, so effective were Cleopatra's powers of persuasion that Caesar maintained the love affair and guaranteed her rule over a rich land that his army otherwise would have ransacked.

IMPORTANT DATES		
753 B.C.	Traditional date of Rome's founding as a monarchy	**149–146 B.C.** Third Punic War
509 B.C.	Roman republic established	**146 B.C.** Destruction of Carthage and Corinth
509–287 B.C.	Struggle of the orders	**133 B.C.** Tiberius Gracchus elected tribune and then assassinated
451–449 B.C.	Creation of the Twelve Tables, Rome's first written law code	
396 B.C.	Defeat of the Etruscan city of Veii; first great expansion of Roman territory	**91–87 B.C.** Social War between Rome and its Italian allies
		60 B.C. First Triumvirate (Caesar, Pompey, and Crassus)
387 B.C.	Sack of Rome by Gauls	**49–45 B.C.** Civil war, with Caesar the victor
264–241 B.C.	First Punic War	
c. 220 B.C.	Rome controls Italy south of the Po River	**45–44 B.C.** Cicero writes his philosophical works on *humanitas*
218–201 B.C.	Second Punic War	**44 B.C.** Caesar appointed dictator for life and then assassinated
168–149 B.C.	Cato writes *The Origins*, the first history of Rome in Latin	

By 45 B.C., Caesar had won the civil war but faced the predicament of ruling a shattered republic. Sad experience had shown that only a sole ruler could end the chaotic violence of factional politics, but the oldest tradition of the republic's elite was its hatred of monarchy. The second-century B.C. senator Cato, notorious for his advice about destroying Carthage, had best expressed this horror of royalty: "A king," he quipped, "is an animal that feeds on human flesh." Caesar's solution was to rule as king in everything but name. First, he had himself appointed dictator in 48 B.C.; his term in this temporary office was extended to a lifetime tenure around 44 B.C. "I am not a king," he insisted, but the distinction was meaningless. As dictator, he controlled the government despite the appearance of normal procedures. Elections for offices continued, for example, but Caesar manipulated the results by recommending candidates to the assemblies, which his supporters dominated. Naturally his recommendations were followed.

Caesar's policies were wide-ranging: a moderate cancellation of debts; a limitation on the number of people eligible for subsidized grain; a large program of public works, including the construction of public libraries; colonies for his veterans in Italy and abroad; the rebuilding of Corinth and Carthage as commercial centers; and a revival of the ancient policy of strengthening the state by giving citizenship to non-Romans, such as the Cisalpine Gauls (those on the Italian side of the Alps). He also admitted non-Italians to the Senate when he expanded its membership from six hundred (the number after Sulla) to nine hundred.

Unlike Sulla, he did not proscribe his enemies. Instead he prided himself on his clemency, the recipients of which were, by Roman custom, bound to be his grateful clients. In return, he received unprecedented honors, such as a special golden seat in the Senate house and the renaming of the seventh month of the year after him (July). He also regularized the Roman calendar by having each year include 365 days, a calculation based on an ancient Egyptian calendar that roughly forms the basis for our modern one.

His rule pleased most Romans but outraged the optimates. They resented being dominated by one of their own, a "traitor" who had deserted to the people's faction. A band of senators formed a conspiracy, led by Caesar's former close friend Marcus Junius Brutus and inspired by the legend about Brutus's ancestor Lucius Junius Brutus having led the violent expulsion of Rome's original monarchy. They cut Caesar to pieces with daggers in the Senate house on March 15 (the Ides of March on the Roman calendar), 44 B.C. When his friend Brutus stabbed him, Caesar, according to some ancient reports, gasped his last words—in Greek: "You, too, child?"

The "liberators," as they styled themselves, had no concrete plans for reviving the republic. They apparently believed that it would automatically reconstitute itself; in their profound naiveté, they ignored the grisly reality of the previous forty years and the distortion of Roman values, with ambitious individuals honoring their own interests and those of their clients above the community's. Distraught at the loss of their patron, the masses rioted at Caesar's funeral to vent their anger against the elite that had robbed them of their benefactor. Failing to form a united front, the elite resumed their vendettas with one another to secure personal political power. By 44 B.C., the republic was a lost cause.

Conclusion

From its beginnings in 509 B.C., Rome's republic flourished because its values stressed the common good, it incorporated outsiders, and its small farmers produced agricultural surpluses. These surpluses supported a growing population to supply soldiers for a strong army. Romans' willingness to endure tremendous losses of life and property—the proof that they valued faithfulness—helped make them invincible: Rome might lose battles but never wars. Because warfare brought profits, peace seemed a wasted opportunity. Elite commanders craved victories because they brought glory and riches to enhance their status in Rome's social hierarchy.

■ MAPPING THE WEST The Roman World at the End of the Republic, c. 44 B.C.

When Octavius (the future Augustus) finished Julius Caesar's plan for expansion by conquering Egypt in 30 B.C., the territory that would form the Roman Empire was essentially complete. Geography and distance were the primary factors inhibiting further expansion, which Romans never stopped thinking of as desirable even when practical difficulties rendered this goal purely theoretical. The deserts of Africa and the Near East worked against expansion southward or eastward against the often formidable powers located beyond, and trackless forests and fierce resistance from local inhabitants made expansion into central Europe and the British Isles impossible to sustain.

The protracted wars against Carthage, Macedonia, and Greece, however, had unexpected consequences that spelled disaster. Long military service ruined many of the small farmers on whom Italy's prosperity depended. When the dispossessed flocked to Rome, they created an unstable political force: the urban mob demanding subsidized food. Members of the elite escalated their competition with each other for the increased career opportunities presented by constant war. These rivalries became unmanageable when successful generals began to extort advantages for themselves by acting as patrons to their client armies of poor troops. In this hypercompetitive environment, force became the preferred means of settling political disputes. But violent actions provoked violent responses; communal values were drowned in the blood of civil war. No reasonable Roman could have been optimistic about the chances for an enduring peace in the aftermath of Caesar's assassination in 44 B.C. That another "great man" would forge such a peace less than fifteen years later would have seemed an impossible dream.

Suggested References for further reading and online research appear on page SR-7 at the back of the book.

www.bedfordstmartins.com/huntconcise   See the ONLINE STUDY GUIDE to assess your mastery of the material covered in this chapter.

The Roman Empire

c. 44 B.C.–A.D. 284

I N A.D. 203, VIBIA PERPETUA, wealthy and twenty-two years old, nursed her infant in a Carthage jail while awaiting execution. She had received a death sentence for refusing to offer a sacrifice to the gods for the Roman emperor's health and safety. One morning, the jailer dragged her off to the city's main square, where a crowd gathered. Perpetua described in a journal what happened next when the local governor attempted to persuade her to save her life: "My father came carrying my son, crying 'Perform the sacrifice; take pity on your baby!' Then the governor pleaded, 'Think of your old father; show pity for your little child! Offer the sacrifice for the welfare of the imperial family.' 'I refuse,' I answered. 'Are you a Christian?' asked the governor. 'Yes.' When my father would not stop trying to change my mind, the governor ordered him flung to the earth and whipped with a rod. I felt sorry for my father; it seemed they were beating me. I pitied his pathetic old age." Nevertheless, she did not give in. Later, gored by a bull and stabbed by a gladiator, she died professing her faith.

The clash of traditional Roman values of faithfulness and loyalty doomed Perpetua: she believed that her faith in Christ required her to refuse the state's demand for allegiance to the "way of the elders" in public religion and her father's pleas to preserve her family. This conflict echoed the division of loyalty that had destroyed the Roman republic in the first century B.C., when ambitious commanders started civil war because they valued their private interests over the

■ **Portrait of a Married Couple from Pompeii**
This twenty-six-inch-high wall painting of a wife and her husband was found in an alcove off the central room of a comfortable house in Pompeii, the town near Naples in southern Italy buried by a volcanic eruption in A.D. 79. The couple's names are unknown. They may have owned the bakery that adjoined the house. Both hold items indicating that they were fashionable and educated. She has the note pad of the time, a hinged wooden tablet filled with wax on which she would write with the stylus (thin stick) that she touches to her lips. He has a scroll, the standard form for books in the early Roman Empire. Her hairstyle, popular in the middle of the first century A.D., hints that this picture was painted not so many years before Mount Vesuvius erupted.
(Scala/Art Resource, NY.)

171

community's interests. A bloodbath followed Julius Caesar's assassination in 44 B.C.: seventeen more years of Roman fighting Roman. Augustus (63 B.C.–A.D. 14) finally restored peace in 27 B.C. by devising a special kind of monarchy—the *principate*—that reoriented communal loyalty toward the ruling family. His new system opened the pivotal period in Western civilization known to us as the Roman Empire.

Augustus ingeniously disguised his government as a restoration of the republic because official abandonment of the tradition of shared rule never would have won the support of Roman citizens. He retained old institutions—the Senate, the consuls and other officials, the courts—while fundamentally reshaping political power by making himself sole ruler in practice. He masked his monarchy with deft propaganda: instead of calling himself "king" (Latin *rex*), he used "first man" (*princeps*, hence the term *principate*), a traditional honorary title designating the leading senator. The *princeps* was what today we call the "emperor" (from Latin *imperator*, "commander").

Augustus's innovation transformed Rome into a monarchy on the Hellenistic model, without the name but with an untested principle of succession calling for the *princeps* to groom a successor approved by the Senate. This system of government brought stability for two hundred years, except during a few brief struggles over who should become the next *princeps*. Ever mindful of the way the republic had fallen, Augustus's successors were always fearful of anything that suggested disloyalty. Perpetua's refusal to sacrifice, for example, was considered treason and impiety because it threatened the entire community by angering the gods.

Romans welcomed the principate's tranquility, which historians call the *Pax Romana* ("Roman peace"). In the third century A.D., however, rivalry over the succession reignited civil war, leading to economic crisis. By the 280s, Roman imperial government again desperately needed to refocus and transform its political institutions to restore traditional values of loyalty and public service. Diocletian, a military commander from the provinces, would begin that process by winning the throne in A.D. 284.

Creating "Roman Peace"

Inventing tradition takes time. Augustus developed his new political system gradually; as the biographer Suetonius (c. 70–130) expressed it, Augustus "made haste slowly." In the long run, the principate produced an extended period of peace, although its rulers periodically fought to expand imperial territory, suppress rebellions, and repel invaders. Augustus succeeded in reinventing monarchy as an effective form of Roman government because he won the civil war and during his long reign found new ways to inspire loyalty by promoting an image of himself as a dedicated leader.

From Republic to Principate, 44–27 B.C.

The principate was born in blood. Julius Caesar's assassination in 44 B.C. spawned gruesome infighting to fill the political vacuum. The leading contenders were Mark Antony and Octavian (the future Augustus), Caesar's ambitious eighteen-year-old grandnephew and heir. The inexperienced Octavian won the loyalty of Caesar's soldiers by promising them rewards from their murdered general's wealth. Marching these veterans to Rome, the teenager, who had never held any post on the ladder of offices, intimidated the Senate into declaring him a consul in 43 B.C. As it had with Pompey, the threat of force overrode tradition to grant the demand of an ambitious army leader.

Octavian, Antony, and a general named Lepidus joined forces to eliminate potential rivals, especially Caesar's assassins—the self-styled liberators of the republic. In late 43 B.C., the trio formed the so-called Second Triumvirate, which they forced the Senate to recognize as an official emergency panel for "reconstituting the state." With no check on their power, they began to murder their enemies and confiscate their property. Octavian and Antony soon forced Lepidus into retirement and, too ambitious to cooperate, began civil war anew with each other.

Antony made the eastern Mediterranean his base, joining forces with Cleopatra VII (69–30 B.C.), the remarkable Ptolemaic queen of Egypt who had earlier allied with Caesar. Beguiled by Cleopatra's wit and intelligence, Antony became her ally and lover. Skillfully playing on Romans' fear of foreign attack, Octavian rallied support by claiming that Antony planned to make Cleopatra queen of Rome. He shrewdly persuaded the residents of Italy and the western provinces to swear a personal oath of allegiance to him, effectively making them all his clients. Octavian's victory at the naval battle of Actium in northwest Greece in 31 B.C. won the war (see Map 5.1). Cleopatra and Antony fled to Egypt, where they both committed suicide in 30 B.C., following the ancient tradition of choosing one's own death to deprive a victorious enemy of a celebrity hostage. The general first stabbed himself, bleeding to death in his lover's embrace. The queen then ended her life by allowing a poisonous serpent, a symbol of Egyptian royal authority, to bite her. Octavian's capture of Egypt made him Rome's richest citizen and its unrivaled leader.

Augustus's "Restoration," 27 B.C.–A.D. 14

After distributing land to the soldiers who had fought with him, and after creating colonies in the provinces, Octavian announced in 27 B.C. that he had restored the republic. It was now the task of the Senate and the Roman people, he proclaimed, to preserve it. Awed by Octavian's power in this brilliant bit of political theater, the Senate promptly implored him to do whatever was necessary to safeguard the restored republic, granted him special civil and military powers, and bestowed on him the honorary name *Augustus,* meaning "divinely favored." Octavian had considered changing his name to Romulus, after Rome's legendary first king, but as the historian Cassius Dio (c. 164–230) later wrote, "When he realized the people thought this preference meant he longed to be their king, he accepted the other title instead, as if he were more than human; for everything that is most treasured and sacred is called *augustus.*"

In the years following 27 B.C., Augustus maintained the façade of republican government by continuing the annual election of consuls and other officials, the passing of legislation in public assemblies, and respect for the Senate. Periodically, he served as consul, the republic's premier official. To preserve the tradition that no official should hold more than one post at a time, he had the Senate grant him the powers of the tribunate without actually holding the office of tribune. He possessed the authority to act and to compel as if he were a tribune protecting the rights of the people, but he left the tribunate itself open for members of the plebeian elite to occupy, as they had done under the republic. The ceremony of rule also remained republican: Augustus dressed and acted like a regular citizen, not a haughty monarch.

Augustus's choosing *princeps* as his only title of office was a cleverly calculated move. In the republic, the "first man" had guided Rome because of the respect (*auctoritas*) he commanded; he had no more formal power (*potestas*) than any other leader. By appropriating the title *princeps,* Augustus appeared to carry on this valued tradition, but in fact he revised the basic power structure. Previously, no one could have exercised the powers of both consul and tribune simultaneously. The principate in effect was a monarchy disguised as a corrected and improved republic, headed by an emperor cloaked as the *princeps.*

Augustus and his successors exercised supreme power because they controlled the army and the treasury. By turning the republican army—a part-time militia— into a full-time professional force, Augustus made the military a buttress for his moral authority as restorer of the republic. He completed the transformation of the *princeps* into the troops' patron by establishing regular lengths of enlistment, regular pay, and substantial benefits upon retirement. To cover the added costs, Augustus imposed an inheritance tax on citizens. The rich vehemently opposed this innovation, but the grateful army obeyed and protected the emperor. Another change Augustus made was to station soldiers—the *praetorian cohorts*—in Rome itself for the first time. These troops prevented rebellion in the capital and provided an imperial bodyguard, a visible reminder of the emperor's dominance.

To promote political stability, Augustus brilliantly communicated his image as patron and protector on objects as small as coins and as large as buildings. As the only mass-produced source of official messages, coins functioned like modern political advertising. They proclaimed slogans such as "Father of his Country" to remind Romans of their emperor's moral authority over them, or "Roads have been built" to emphasize his personal generosity in paying for highway construction.

■ **Priests on the Altar of Augustan Peace**

After four years of construction, Augustus dedicated the Altar of Augustan Peace in northwest Rome on his wife's birthday in 9 B.C. The altar itself resided inside a four-walled enclosure measuring about thirty-four feet long, thirty-eight feet wide, and twenty-three feet high and open to the sky. Relief sculptures covered the walls. This section shows a religious procession. The figures wearing leather caps with spikes are priests called flamines, *who had to wear this headgear whenever they went outside; the man holding a staff is their attendant. The hooded man at the right is probably Marcus Agrippa, Augustus's greatest general. The laurel wreaths worn on bare heads signify both piety and victory; as Augustus commented in his* Res Gestae *("Accomplishments") 13, "Peace was achieved through victories." The altar can be seen today in its original form because it was reconstructed by Benito Mussolini, Fascist dictator of Italy from 1926 to 1943, who wanted to associate his regime with Augustan glory.* (Art Resource, NY.)

Grandly fulfilling the traditional expectation that rich politicians and generals should spend money for the public good, Augustus erected huge buildings in Rome paid for by the fortune he had inherited and increased in the civil wars. The huge Forum of Augustus best illustrates his skill at communicating through bricks and stone. Its plaza centered on a temple to Mars, Rome's god of war. Two-story colonnades stretched out from the temple like wings, sheltering statues of famous Roman heroes as inspirations to future leaders. Augustus's Forum provided gathering space for religious rituals and ceremonies marking the passage into adulthood of upper-class boys, but it also stressed the themes Augustus wanted to communicate about his regime: peace restored through victory, the foundation of a new age, devotion

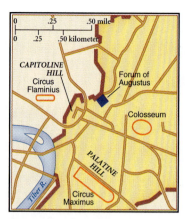

Central Rome and the Forum of Augustus

to the gods who led Rome to victory, respect for tradition, and unselfishness in spending money for the community. These messages constituted Augustus's justification for his rule.

Augustus never revealed his deepest motives in establishing the principate. Was he a cynical despot bent on suppressing the freedoms of the republic? Did he have no choice but to impose a veiled monarchy to stabilize a society crippled by anarchy? Or did his motives lie somewhere in between? Perhaps it is best to see him as a revolutionary bound by tradition. His problem had been the one always facing Roman politicians— how to balance his own personal ambitions, the need for peace, and Rome's reverence for shared rule. Augustus's goal was stability and order, not political freedom, and his strategy was to employ traditional values to justify changes, as in his inspired reinvention of the meaning of "first man." Above all, he extended the patron-client system to politics by making the emperor everyone's most important patron, possessing the moral authority to guide the lives of all. This process culminated with the Senate proclaiming him "Father of his Country" in 2 B.C. He declared that this title was the greatest honor Rome could grant, emphasizing that the principate provided Romans with a leader to govern them like a father: stern but caring, requiring obedience and loyalty from his children but obligated to nurture them in return.

Despite frequent bouts of poor health, Augustus ruled as emperor until he died at seventy-five in A.D. 14. The length of his reign—forty-one years—gave his innovations time to become tradition. As the Roman historian Tacitus (c. 56–120) remarked, by the time Augustus died, "almost no one was still alive who had seen the republic." Through his longevity, command over the army and the empire's revenues, rapport with the capital's urban masses, and crafty manipulation of the traditional vocabulary of politics to disguise his power, Augustus restored stability to society and transformed republican Rome into imperial Rome.◆

Life in Augustan Rome

A crucial factor in Augustus's success was caring for the lives of ordinary people. Life in ancient times was always and everywhere precarious, but Augustus's most pressing problems arose in Rome. From archaeological and literary sources we can

---

◆ For Augustus's own description of his reign, see Document 14, "The Accomplishments of Augustus."

sketch a composite picture of life in Augustus's Rome. Although some of the sources refer to times after Augustus and to cities other than the capital, they nevertheless help us understand this period; economic and social conditions were essentially the same in all larger cities throughout the early centuries of the empire.

The population of Augustan Rome—probably far over half a million—was vast for the ancient world. Indeed, no European city would have nearly as many people again until London in the 1700s. The streets were packed: "One man jabs me with his elbow, another whacks me with a pole; my legs are smeared with mud, and from all sides big feet step on me" was the poet Juvenal's description of walking in Rome in the early second century. To ease congestion in the narrow streets, the city banned carts and wagons in the daytime. This regulation made nights noisy with the creaking of axles and the shouting of drivers caught in traffic jams.

Most urban residents lived in small apartments in multistoried buildings called *insulae* ("islands," so named because before the city became crowded each building had an open strip around it). Outnumbering private houses by more than twenty to one, the apartment buildings usually housed shops, bars, and simple restaurants on the first floor. Graffiti—political endorsements, personal insults, advertising, messages of all kinds—festooned the outside walls. The higher the floor, the cheaper were the apartments; the poorest people lived on the top floors in single rooms that they rented by the day. Aqueducts delivered plentiful fresh water to public fountains, but because apartments had no plumbing, residents had to lug buckets up the stairs. The wealthy few had piped-in water at ground level. Most tenants lacked bathrooms and had to use public latrines or pots for toilets at home. Some buildings had cesspits, or buckets could be carried down to the streets to be emptied by people who made their living collecting excrement. Careless tenants haphazardly flung the foul-smelling contents of these containers out the window.

Because the city generated about sixty tons of human waste every day, sanitation presented an enormous challenge. Roman officials made Herculean efforts to keep the city clean. By 33 B.C., Augustus's general Marcus Agrippa had vastly improved the city's main sewer, but its untreated contents emptied directly into the Tiber River, which ran through the city. The technology for sanitary disposal of waste simply did not exist. People regularly left human and animal corpses in the streets, to be gnawed by vultures and dogs. The poor were not the only people affected by such conditions: a stray mutt once brought a human hand to the table where Vespasian, who would be emperor from 69 to 79, was eating lunch. Flies buzzing everywhere and a lack of mechanical refrigeration contributed to frequent gastrointestinal ailments: the most popular jewelry of the time was supposed to ward off stomach trouble. Although the wealthy could not eliminate such discomforts, they made their lives more pleasant with luxuries such as snow rushed from the mountains to ice their drinks and slaves to clean their airy houses, which were built around courtyards and gardens.

Public baths helped residents keep clean. Because admission fees were low, almost everyone could afford to go daily. Scores of baths dotted the city, serving like modern health clubs as centers for exercising and socializing as well as washing. Bathers progressed through a series of increasingly warm, humid areas until they reached a sauna-like room. They swam naked in their choice of hot or cold pools. Women had full access to the public baths, but the genders bathed apart, either in separate rooms or at different times of the day. Since bathing was thought to be particularly valuable for sick people but no one understood the danger of propagating infections, communal bathers unwittingly contributed to the spread of communicable diseases.

City residents faced hazards beyond infectious disease. Broken crockery and other debris were routinely hurled out of the upper stories of apartment buildings, falling like missiles on unwary pedestrians. "If you are walking to a dinner party in Rome," Juvenal warned, "you would be foolish not to make out your will first. For every open window is a source of potential disaster." The *insulae* could be dangerous to their inhabitants as well as to passersby because they were in constant danger of collapsing. Roman engineers, despite their expertise in using concrete, brick, and stone as building materials, lacked the technology to calculate precisely how much stress their constructions could stand. Builders trying to cut costs paid little

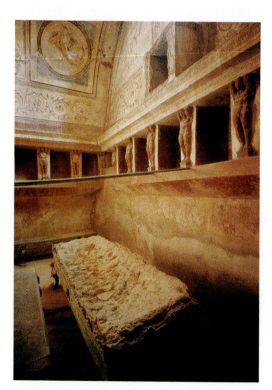

■ **The Warm Room of a Public Bath**

By the first century B.C., near the centers of most sizable Roman towns were public bath buildings. Wealthy houses had private baths, but large public bathing establishments served the rest of the urban population. This vaulted room from a bath at Herculaneum displays the artful decoration that upper-class patrons in this luxury suburb of Naples expected. Outfitted with couches on which bathers could rest on cushions, this so-called warm room was the middle room in a set of linked chambers kept at differing temperatures ranging from cold to hot and often equipped with pools for immersion, through which patrons proceeded as they warmed up. Bathing was a daily activity in Roman social life; at the public baths, socializing was as important a goal as cleanliness.

(Erich Lessing/Art Resource, NY.)

attention to engineering safeguards in any case. Augustus upgraded public safety by imposing a height limit of seventy feet on new apartment buildings. Fire presented the greatest risk; one of Augustus's most important innovations to improve people's lives was to provide Rome with the first public fire department in Western history. He also established the first permanent police force, despite his reported fondness for stopping to watch the frequent brawls that the crowding in Rome's streets incited.

Many city dwellers had too little to eat and few chances for jobs. Augustus benefited these masses by ensuring them an adequate food supply. This service was his responsibility as Rome's foremost patron, and he freely drew upon his personal fortune to pay for imported grain. Distributing free grain to the capital's poor citizens had been a tradition for decades, but his dole system reached the unprecedented scale of 250,000 recipients. Counting their families, this statistic suggests that between 600,000 and 700,000 people depended on the government for their daily sustenance. Poor Romans usually boiled this grain and made a watery porridge, which they washed down with cheap wine. If they were lucky, they might have some beans, leeks, or cheese on the side. The rich, as we learn from an ancient cookbook, ate more delectable dishes, such as spiced roast pork or crayfish, often flavored with sweet-and-sour sauce concocted from honey and vinegar.

Some wealthy Romans had come to prefer spending money on luxuries and costly political careers rather than on families. Fearing that lack of offspring would destroy the elite on which Rome relied for leadership, Augustus passed laws to strengthen marriage and encourage more births by granting special legal privileges to the parents of three or more children. Adultery became a criminal offense. So seriously did Augustus support these reforms that he exiled his own daughter—his only child—and a granddaughter after extramarital scandals. His legislation had little effect, however, and the prestigious old families dwindled over the coming centuries. Recent research suggests that up to three-quarters of senatorial-rank families lost their official status (by losing the wealth required for that designation) or died out every generation. Equestrians and provincials who won imperial favor took their places in the social hierarchy and in the Senate.

Slaves occupied the lowest rung of society's hierarchy and provided the basis of the imperial workforce. Unlike Greece, however, Rome gave citizenship to freed slaves, a policy that deeply affected Roman society in the long term. All slaves could hope to acquire the rights of a free citizen, and their descendants, if they became wealthy, could become members of the social elite. This arrangement gave slaves reason to persevere and cooperate with their masters. Conditions of slavery varied widely according to occupation. Slaves in agriculture and manufacturing had a grueling existence. Most such workers were men, although women might assist the foremen who managed gangs of rural laborers. The second-century novelist Apuleius penned this grim description of slaves at work in a flour mill: "Through the holes in their ragged clothes you could see all over their bodies the scars from whippings. Some wore only loincloths. Letters had been branded on their foreheads and irons manacled their ankles." Worse than the mills were the ore mines, where the foremen constantly flogged the miners to keep them working in a perilous environment.

Household slaves had an easier physical existence. Most Romans owned slaves to work in their homes, from one or two in modestly well-off families to hordes of them in rich houses and, above all, the imperial palace. Domestic slaves were often women, working as nurses, maids, kitchen help, and clothes makers. Some male slaves ran businesses for their masters, and they, as an incentive to hard work, were often allowed to keep part of the profits to save toward purchasing their freedom someday. Women had less opportunity to earn money. Masters sometimes granted tips for sexual favors, and female prostitutes (many of whom were slaves) could earn money for themselves. Slaves who managed to acquire funds would sometimes buy slaves themselves, thereby creating their own hierarchy. A male slave might buy a woman for a mate. They could then have a semblance of family life, though a normal marriage was impossible because they remained their master's property, as did their children. If truly fortunate, slaves could slowly accumulate enough to buy themselves from their masters or could be freed by their masters' wills. Some epitaphs on tombs testify to masters' affectionate feelings for slaves, but even household servants had to endure violent treatment if their masters were cruel. Slaves had no recourse; if they attacked their owners because of inhumane treatment, their punishment was death.

While slaves always faced potential violence, actual violence held a prominent place in Roman public entertainment. The emperors regularly provided mass spectacles featuring hunters killing fierce beasts, wild African animals such as lions mangling condemned criminals, mock naval battles in flooded arenas, gladiatorial combats, and chariot races. Spectators jammed stadiums for these shows, seated according to their social rank and gender following an Augustan law; the emperor and senators sat close to the action, while women and the poor were relegated to the upper tiers. These shows communicated a political message: the emperors were generous in providing expensive entertainment for their subjects, powerful enough to command life-and-death exhibitions, and dedicated to preserving the social hierarchy.

Gladiators were men and, rarely, women who fought with a variety of weapons in expensive shows; war captives, criminals, slaves, and free volunteers performed as gladiators. Gladiatorial combats, which originated under the republic as part of the ceremony at extravagant funerals, became so popular under Augustus that they attracted crowds numbering tens of thousands. Gladiatorial fights were bloody but usually contested to the death only for captives and criminals; professional fighters could have extended careers. To make the fights more exciting, gladiators brandished different weapons. One favorite bout pitted a lightly armored fighter, called a "net man" because he used a net and a trident, against a more heavily armored

■ Violent Shows

This section of a ninety-one-foot-long mosaic from about A.D. 300 was found in the atrium (open-roofed entrance hall) of a large country home near Tusculum outside Rome, was restored, and now is displayed in Rome's Villa Borghese Museum. It shows animals and gladiators in combat. Such giant pictures reminded the guests of the wealthy homeowner that their host was a virtuous citizen able to pay for spectacular entertainments for the benefit of his community. (CORBIS/Roger Woods.)

"fish man," so named from the design of his helmet crest. Betting was a great attraction, and spectators could be rowdy. As the Christian theologian Tertullian (c. 160–240) lamented: "Look at the mob coming to the show—already they're out of their minds! Aggressive, heedless, already in an uproar about their bets! They all share the same suspense, the same madness, the same voice."

Champion gladiators won riches and celebrity but not social respectability. Early in the first century A.D., the senators became alarmed at what they regarded as the disgrace of members of the upper class becoming gladiators. They therefore forbade the elite and all freeborn women under twenty from appearing in gladiatorial shows. Daughters trained by their gladiator fathers had first competed during the republic, and women continued to compete until the emperor Septimius Severus (r. 193–211) banned their appearance.

Festivals featuring gladiatorial shows, chariot races, and theater productions became a venue for ordinary citizens to express their wishes to the emperors, who were expected to attend. On more than one occasion, for example, poorer Romans rioted at shows to protest a shortfall in the free grain supply. In this way, public entertainment served as a two-way form of communication between ruler and ruled.

Arts and Letters Fit for an Emperor

Elite culture adapted under Augustus to serve the same goal as public entertainment: to legitimize and strengthen the transformed system of government. In particular, oratory—the highest attainment of Roman arts and letters—lost its bite. Under the republic, rhetorical skill in making stinging speeches to criticize political opponents had been such a powerful weapon that it could catapult a "new man" like Cicero, who lacked social and military distinction, to international fame. Under the principate, the emperor's supremacy ruled out freewheeling debate and open decision making; political criticism was now out of bounds. Prudent men turned their rhetorical skills to praising the emperor at public festivals meant to advance his image as a competent and compassionate ruler.

Education for oratory remained a privilege of the wealthy. Rome had no free public schools, so the poor were lucky to pick up even rudimentary learning from their harried parents. Most people had time only for training in practical skills. A character in *Satyricon,* a satirical literary work of the first century by Petronius, expressed this utilitarian attitude toward education: "I didn't study geometry and literary criticism and worthless junk like that. I just learned how to read the letters on signs and how to work out percentages, and I learned weights, measures, and the values of the different kinds of coins."

Although the Roman ideal called for mothers to teach children right from wrong, servants usually looked after the offspring of rich families. These children attended private elementary schools from age seven to eleven to learn reading, writing, and basic arithmetic. Teachers used rote methods in the classroom and physical punishment for mistakes. Some children went on to the next three years of school, in which they were introduced to literature, history, and grammar. Only a few boys then proceeded to the study of oratory.

Advanced studies focused on literature, history, ethical philosophy, law, and dialectic (reasoned argument). Mathematics and science were rarely studied as discrete disciplines, but engineers and architects trained at calculation. Much reading was done aloud. The rich owned educated slaves to read to them. Books consisted of continuous scrolls made from papyrus or animal skin, not bound pages. Reading required manual dexterity as well as literacy because the reader had to unroll the scroll with one hand while simultaneously rolling it up with the other.

So much literature blossomed at this time that modern critics call Augustus's reign the Golden Age of Latin literature. The emperor himself dabbled in composing verse and prose and supported the flourishing arts by serving as the patron of a circle of writers and artists. His favorites were Horace (65–8 B.C.) and Virgil (70–19 B.C.). Horace entranced audiences with the supple rhythms and subtle irony of his short poems on public and private subjects. His poem celebrating Augustus's victory over Antony and Cleopatra at Actium became famous for its opening line "Now it's time to drink!"

Virgil later became the most popular Augustan poet because of his epic poem, the *Aeneid,* in which he deftly intertwined praise and subtle criticism of Augustus. He composed so painstakingly that the epic remained unfinished at his death. He wanted it burned, but Augustus preserved it. Inspired by Homer's *Iliad* and *Odyssey,* the *Aeneid* told the legend of the Trojan Aeneas, the most distant ancestor of the Romans. Virgil tempered his praise of the principate with a profound recognition of the price to be paid for success. The *Aeneid* therefore underscored the complex mix of gain and loss that followed Augustus's transformation of politics and society. Above all, it expressed a moral code for all Romans: no matter how tempting the emotional pull of revenge and pride, be merciful to the conquered but lay low the haughty.

Authors with a more independent streak had to be careful. The historian Livy (54 B.C.–A.D. 17) composed a lengthy chronicle of Rome in which he refused to ignore the ruthless actions of Augustus and his supporters. The emperor chided but did not punish him because Livy did show that success and stability depended on traditional values of loyalty and self-sacrifice. The poet Ovid (43 B.C.–A.D. 17) fared worse. An irreverent wit, in *Art of Love* and *Love Affairs* he implicitly mocked the emperor's moral legislation with tongue-in-cheek tips for conducting love affairs and picking up other men's wives at festivals. His *Metamorphoses*

■ **Marble Statue of Augustus from Prima Porta**

At six feet eight inches high, this statue stood a foot taller than its subject, Rome's first emperor. Found at his wife's country villa at Prima Porta ("First Gate") just outside the capital, the statue was probably a copy of a bronze original sculpted about 20 B.C., when Augustus was in his early forties. The sculptor depicted him as a younger man, using the idealizing techniques of Greek art of the fifth and fourth centuries B.C. to emphasize the emperor's dignity. The sculpture is crowded with symbols that convey the impression of Augustus that he wanted to communicate. His bare feet hint that he is a near-divine hero, and the statue of Cupid alludes to the Julian family's descent from the goddess Venus. The carving on the breastplate shows a Parthian surrendering to a Roman soldier under the gaze of personified cosmic forces basking in the peace of Augustus's reign. (Scala/Art Resource, NY.)

www.bedfordstmartins.com/huntconcise
See the ONLINE STUDY GUIDE for more help in analyzing this image.

("Transformations") undermined the idea of hierarchy as natural through bizarre stories of supernatural shape-changes, with people becoming animals and confusion between the human and the divine. In 8 B.C., after Ovid was embroiled in a scandal involving Augustus's daughter, the emperor exiled the poet to a bleak town on the Black Sea.

Public sculpture also reflected the emperor's preferences. When Augustus was growing up, portraits were starkly realistic, portraying the strain of human experience. The sculpture that Augustus commissioned displayed a more idealized style, reminiscent of classical Greek and Hellenistic portraiture. In renowned works of art such as the *Prima Porta* ("First Gate") statue of himself or the sculpted frieze on his Altar of Peace (finished in 9 B.C.), Augustus had himself portrayed as serene and dignified, not careworn and sick as he often was (see page 183). As with his monumental architecture, Augustus used sculpture to project a calm and competent image of himself as "restorer of the world" and founder of a new age for Rome.

Maintaining "Roman Peace"

A serious problem confronted Augustus's "restored republic": how to prevent the violent struggles for power that ruined the republic. His solution was to train an heir to take over as *princeps* at his death, with the Senate's blessing and awarding of the same powers conferred on Augustus. This strategy kept the throne in his family, called the Julio-Claudians, until the death of the infamous Nero in 68. Thus was established the tradition that family dynasties ruled imperial Rome.

Under the Augustan system, the *princeps's* goals were building loyalty, preventing unrest, and financing the administration while governing a vast territory of diverse provinces. Augustus set a pattern for effective rule that some of his successors emulated better than others: taking special care of the army, communicating the image of the *princeps* as a just and generous ruler, and promoting Roman law and culture as universal standards while allowing as much local freedom in the provinces as possible. The citizens, in return for their loyalty, expected the emperors to be generous patrons, but the difficulties of long-range communication imposed practical limits on imperial intervention in the lives of the empire's residents, for better or worse.

Making Monarchy Permanent, A.D. 14–180

Augustus wanted to make monarchy the permanent government to avoid civil war, but his fiction that Rome remained a republic required the Senate's cooperation to give legitimacy to his plan. During the 20s B.C. he began looking for a male relative to designate as his heir (he had no son), but one after another the young men he chose died before he did. Finally, in A.D. 4, he adopted someone who would survive him, his stepson Tiberius (42 B.C.–A.D. 37). Because Tiberius had a distinguished record as a general, the army supported recommending him to the Senate as the next "first man." The senators prudently accepted this recommendation when Augustus died in A.D. 14; the Julio-Claudian succession thus began.

The stern and irascible Tiberius (r. 14–37) ruled for twenty-three years because he had the most important qualification for succeeding as *princeps*: the army's respect. His long reign provided the stable transition period that the principate needed to establish the compromise between the elite and the emperor that made the monarchy workable. On the one hand, the traditional offices of consul, senator, and others continued, filled by the elite; on the other hand, the emperor decided who held office and determined law and policy. In this way, everyone could pretend that the vestiges of republican government still mattered.

Tiberius's reign also revealed the problems that a disaffected *princeps* could create. A reluctant emperor, Tiberius paid a steep personal price for becoming "first man." To strengthen their family ties, Augustus had forced him to divorce his beloved wife Vipsania and marry Augustus's daughter, Julia, a marriage that proved disastrously unhappy. His personal torments and fear of rivals led him to spend the last decade of his rule away from Rome as a virtual recluse. His lack of involvement in governing opened the way for abuses by subordinates in Rome and kept him from preparing a successor.

Tiberius designated Gaius (12–41), better known as Caligula, as the next *princeps* because he was Augustus's great-grandson and a fawning supporter. He ignored Caligula's lack of the personal qualities and training that a worthy ruler needed. Still, the young emperor (r. 37–41) might have been successful because he knew about soldiering. *Caligula* means "baby boots." Soldiers gave him that nickname as a child because he wore little leather shoes like theirs while growing up in the military garrisons his father commanded. Unfortunately, he lacked strength of character; what he did possess were enormous appetites. Ruling through cruelty and violence, Caligula drained the treasury to humor his whims. Suetonius labeled him a "monster." He frequently defied convention by fighting mock gladiatorial combats and appearing in public in women's clothing or costumes imitating gods. His abuses knit his doom: two praetorian commanders murdered him in 41 to avenge personal insults.

After Caligula's assassination, the Senate debated the possibility of refusing to choose a new emperor in order to restore a real republic. They capitulated, however, when Claudius (r. 41–54), Augustus's grandnephew and Caligula's uncle, secured the backing of the praetorian guard with promises of money. The succession of Claudius under the threat of force made one thing clear: the genuine republic would never return because the soldiers would always insist on having an emperor— a patron—to promote their interests. Claudius buttressed the stability of imperial rule by enrolling men from Gaul (today France), a province outside Italy, in the Senate. This change opened the way for provincial inhabitants to expand their participation in governing the principate. In return for their help in keeping their

regions peaceful and prosperous, they received offices at Rome and imperial patronage. Claudius also changed imperial government by employing freed slaves as
powerful administrators. Because these men owed their great advancement to the
emperor, they could be expected to be loyal.

When Claudius died under suspicious circumstances at sixty-four, the temp-
tations of power corrupted his teenage stepson and successor. Only sixteen, Nero
(r. 54–68) passionately loved music and theater, not governing. The spectacular
public festivals he sponsored and the cash he distributed to the masses in Rome
kept him popular with the poor. Among the wealthy, however, a giant fire in 64
(the incident that led to the legend of Nero "fiddling while Rome burned")
aroused suspicions that he had ordered the conflagration to clear space for imperial building projects. Nero scandalized the senatorial class by repeatedly appearing onstage to sing to captive audiences, while he bankrupted the treasury
by spending outrageous sums on a sumptuous palace (the Golden House) and
a lavish trip to Greece. His unsavory methods of raising money included trump-
ing up charges of treason against senators and equestrians to seize their property. When rebellious commanders in the provinces toppled his regime, he had
a servant help him cut his own throat, after wailing, "To die! And such a great
artist!"

A year of civil war ensued in 69; four rival generals vied for the throne in this
"Year of the Four Emperors." Vespasian (r. 69–79) won. With his accession, the dynasty of the Flavian family began. The new emperor took two steps to minimize
resistance. First, he had the Senate publicly recognize him as *princeps* even though
he was not a Julio-Claudian. Second, he encouraged the spread of the imperial cult
(worship of the emperor as a living god and sacrifices for the welfare of the emperor's household) in the provinces outside Italy, where most of the empire's population resided.

In promoting emperor worship, Vespasian was building on local traditions. In
the eastern provinces, the Hellenistic kingdoms had long before established the
precedent of worshiping royalty; provincials there had treated Augustus as a living
god. The imperial cult communicated the same image of the emperor to the
people of the provinces as Rome's architecture and sculpture did to the people of
the city: he was larger than life, worthy of loyal respect, and the source of aid and
gifts as their patron. Because emperor worship was already well established in Greece
and the ancient Near East, Vespasian concentrated on spreading it in the provinces
of Spain, southern France, and North Africa. Italy, however, still had no temples to
the living emperor. Traditional Romans scorned the imperial cult as a provincial
aberration. Vespasian, known for his wit, even muttered as he lay dying in 79, "Oh
me! I think I'm becoming a god."

Vespasian's sons Titus (r. 79–81) and Domitian (r. 81–96) strengthened the
principate with hardheaded fiscal policy, professional administration, and high-
profile military campaigns on the frontiers to forestall threats. Titus, for ex-

ample, completed his father's effort to suppress a revolt in Judaea by capturing Jerusalem in 70. He sent relief to the populations of Pompeii and Herculaneum after their towns were buried by a massive volcanic eruption of Mount Vesuvius in 79, and he provided a state-of-the-art site for huge public entertainments by finishing Rome's Colosseum, outfitted with giant awnings to shade the crowd.◆ This soaring amphitheater was deliberately constructed on the site of the former fish pond in Nero's Golden House to demonstrate the public-spiritedness of the new Flavian dynasty. Domitian balanced the budget and led the army north to hold the line against Germanic tribes threatening the empire's frontier regions along the Rhine and Danube Rivers—an area destined for sporadic wars for centuries to come.

Domitian handled his success poorly, and his arrogance inspired hatred among the senators, to whom he once sent a letter announcing, "Our lord god, myself, orders you to do this." Embittered by the rebellion of a general in Germany, he executed numerous upper-class citizens as conspirators. Fearful they, too, would become victims, his wife and members of his court murdered him in 96. As Domitian's fate showed, the principate had not solved monarchy's enduring weakness: rivalry for rule that was likely to explode into murderous conspiracy and destabilize the succession. The danger of civil war always existed, whether generated by ambitious generals or by competition among the emperor's heirs. As Tacitus acidly commented, emperors became like the weather: "We just have to wait for bad ones to pass and hope for good ones to appear."

Fortunately for Rome, fair weather dawned with the next five emperors—Nerva (r. 96–98), Trajan (r. 98–117), Hadrian (r. 117–138), Antoninus Pius (r. 138–161), and Marcus Aurelius (r. 161–180). Historians have dubbed these reigns the empire's political Golden Age because they provided peaceful transfers of power for nearly a century (the first four of these men, lacking surviving sons, used adoption to pick capable successors). This period, however, was full of war and strife, as Roman history always was. Trajan fought fierce campaigns expanding Roman power northward across the Danube River into Dacia (today Romania) and eastward into Mesopotamia (Map 5.1). Hadrian earned the hatred of the Senate by executing several senators as alleged conspirators and punished a Jewish revolt by turning Jerusalem into a military colony. Aurelius spent many miserable years at war protecting the Danube region from outside attacks.

Still, there is validity to the idea of a Golden Age under the "five good emperors." They succeeded one another without murder or conspiracy, the economy continued strong, and the army remained obedient. Their reigns marked the longest stretch in Roman history without a civil war since the second century B.C.

◆ For a primary source that illuminates daily life in Pompeii before the volcanic eruption of 79, see Document 15, "Notices and Graffiti from Pompeii."

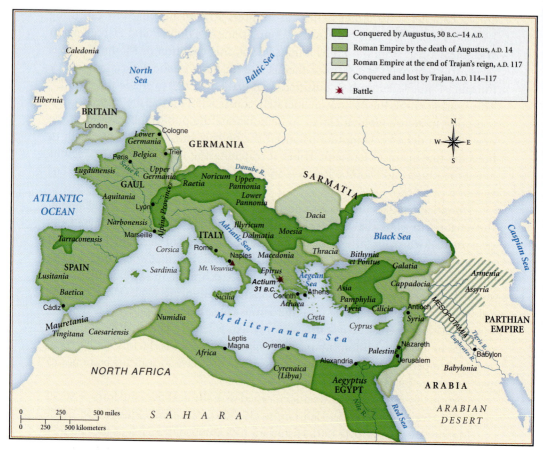

MAP 5.1 Expansion of the Roman Empire, 30 B.C.–A.D. 117

When Octavian (the future Augustus) captured Egypt in 30 B.C. after the suicides of Mark Antony and Cleopatra, he made a significant contribution to the economic strength of Rome because the land of the Nile yielded prodigious amounts of grain and gold. Roman power now effectively encircled the Mediterranean Sea (although Mauretania remained technically under the rule of indigenous kings with Roman approval until c. A.D. 44 in the reign of Claudius). When the emperor Trajan took over the southern part of Mesopotamia in A.D. 114–117, imperial conquest reached its height: Rome's control had never before extended so far east. Egypt remained part of the empire until the Arab conquest in A.D. 642. Hadrian, Trajan's successor, abandoned Mesopotamia, probably because it seemed too far away from Rome to defend.

Life in the Golden Age, A.D. 96–180

The peace and prosperity of the second century A.D. depended on effective defense, public-spiritedness among provincial elites, the spread of common laws and culture throughout the provinces, and a healthy population reproducing itself. The empire's size and the limited technology of the times meant that emperors had only modest control over these factors.

In theory, Rome's military goal remained infinite expansion because conquest brought glory to the emperor. Virgil in the *Aeneid* had expressed this ambition by portraying Jupiter, king of the gods, as promising "imperial rule without limit." In reality, the emperors were usually satisfied if neighboring peoples left the frontier regions undisturbed. Imperial territory never expanded permanently much beyond the area that Augustus had controlled. Stable and peaceful in the first two centuries after Augustus, most provinces had no need for garrison troops during this era; soldiers were a rare sight in many places. Even Gaul, which had originally resisted Roman control with a lethal frenzy, was, according to a contemporary witness, "kept in order by 1,200 troops—hardly more soldiers than it has towns." Most legions (a legion was a unit of five thousand to six thousand troops) were stationed on the empire's northern and eastern frontiers, where hostile neighbors threatened and the distance from the capital weakened the provincials' loyalty.

The policy of not conquering new lands made paying for the army difficult. In the past, victories abroad had fueled Roman prosperity by bringing in huge amounts of booty, prisoners of war sold into slavery, and additional taxes from conquered peoples. These sources of revenue had dried up, but the standing army still had to be paid to maintain discipline. To fulfill their obligations as patrons of the army, emperors on their accession and on other special occasions supplemented soldiers' regular pay with large bonuses. These rewards made a legionary career desirable, and enlistment counted as a privilege restricted to free male citizens. The army, however, also included auxiliary units of noncitizens from the provinces. Serving under Roman officers, they could pick up some Latin and Roman customs, and they improved life in the provinces by constructing public works. Upon discharge, they received Roman citizenship. In this way, the army served as an instrument for spreading a common way of life.

The Roman peace guaranteed by the army allowed commerce to operate smoothly in imperial territory. The Golden Age's prosperity promoted long-distance trade for luxury goods, such as spices and silk, from as far away as India and China. Still, taxation of agricultural land in the provinces (Italy was exempt) provided the government's principal source of revenue. The administration itself cost relatively little because it was small compared with the size of the population it governed: several hundred top officials governed about fifty million people. Most taxes collected in the provinces stayed there for local expenditures. Senatorial and equestrian governors with small staffs ran the provinces, which eventually numbered about forty. In Rome, the emperor employed a substantial palace staff, while equestrian officials called *prefects* managed the city itself.

The decentralized tax system required public service by the provincial elites; the central and provincial governments' financial well-being absolutely depended on it. Local officials called *decurions* (members of a municipal senate, later called *curiales*) collected taxes and personally guaranteed that their town's expenses were covered. If there was a shortfall in tax collection or local finances, these wealthy men had to make up the difference from their own pockets. Most emperors under the early principate attempted to keep taxes low. As Tiberius put it when refusing a request for tax increases from provincial governors, "I want you to shear my sheep, not skin them alive."

The financial obligations of civic office could make public service expensive, but the prestige that the positions bestowed made the elite willing to take the risk. Some received priesthoods in the imperial cult as a reward, an honor open to both men and women. All could hope to catch the emperor's ear for special help for their area—for example, after an earthquake or a flood. The system worked because it sprang from Roman tradition: the local social elites were the patrons of their communities but the clients of the emperors. As long as there were enough rich, public-spirited provincials participating in this system for its nonmonetary rewards, the principate could function effectively by fostering the republican ideal of communal values.

The principate changed the Mediterranean world profoundly but not evenly. Within the provinces lived a wide diversity of peoples speaking different languages, observing different customs, dressing in different styles, and worshiping different divinities (Map 5.2). In the remote countryside, Roman conquest had only a modest effect on local customs. Where new cities sprang up, however, Roman influence prevailed. These communities sprouted around Roman forts or grew from the settlements of army veterans the emperors had sprinkled throughout the provinces. They became particularly influential in western Europe, permanently rooting Latin (and the languages that would emerge from it) and Roman law and customs there. Prominent modern cities such as Trier and Cologne in Germany started as Roman towns. As time passed, social and cultural distinctions between the provinces and Italy lessened. Eventually, emperors came from the provinces; Trajan, from Spain, was the first.

Romanization, as historians call the spread of Roman culture in the provinces, raised the standard of living as roads and bridges improved, trade increased, and agriculture flourished under the peaceful conditions secured by the army. Supplying the troops brought new business to farmers and merchants. Greater prosperity under Roman rule made Romanization easier for provincials to embrace. In addition, Romanization was not a one-way process of cultural change. In western areas as different from each other as Gaul, Britain, and North Africa, interactions among the local people and Romans produced new, mixed cultural traditions, especially evident in religion and art. Romanization led not to the imposition of the conquerors' way of life but to the gradual merging of Roman and local western cultures.

Romanization affected the eastern provinces less; they retained their Greek and Near Eastern character. In much of this region, daily life continued to follow traditional Greek models. When the Romans took over these areas during the second and first centuries B.C., they found urban cultures that had been flourishing for hundreds of years. Huge Hellenistic cities such as Alexandria in Egypt and Antioch in Syria rivaled Rome in size and splendor (see Map 5.1). In fact, compared with

■ MAP 5.2 Natural Features and Languages of the Roman World

In topography, climate, and languages, the Roman world was an area of great variety. People living there, estimated to have numbered as many as 55 million, spoke dozens of languages, many of which survived until the last years of the empire. The two predominant languages spoken by Roman citizens were Latin in the western part of the empire and Greek in the eastern. Latin remained the language of law even in the eastern empire. Fields suitable for growing grain were the most crucial topographical feature for agriculture because wheat and barley were the mainstays of the ancient diet. Vineyards and olive groves also were important. Wine was regarded as an essential beverage, and olive oil was the main source of fat in the diets of most people and the principal ingredient in soap, perfume, and other products for daily life.

■ The Arch at Thamugadi, a Roman Military Colony in North Africa

The emperors fueled the process of Romanization in the provinces by building new settlements for military veterans. The best preserved such town is Thamugadi (today Timgad in Algeria). Founded by Emperor Trajan in A.D. 100, it was laid out like a Roman military camp, a perfect square with a grid of straight streets and rectangular houses. The new town's architecture imitated Rome's. A capacious theater provided space for public entertainments, and this mammoth arch, probably built toward the end of the second century A.D., provided a spectacular entrance to a colonnaded boulevard. Romanization was a two-way process: local peoples influenced the Roman settlers and vice versa. At Thamugadi, indigenous African religious cults, lightly adapted to Roman traditions, flourished alongside ancient Roman cults and attracted worshipers of all kinds. (SEF/Art Resource, NY.)

Rome, they boasted more single-family houses, fewer blocks of high-rise tenements, and equally magnificent temples. While retaining their local languages and customs, the eastern social elites easily accepted the nature of Roman governance: the emperor was their patron, and they were his clients, with the mutual obligations this traditional relationship required. Provincial elites were long accustomed to such a system because of the paternalistic relationships that had underlain Hellenistic rule. Their willing cooperation in the task of governing the provinces was crucial for imperial stability and prosperity.

The continuing vitality of Greek culture and language in bustling eastern cities contributed to the flourishing of literature. New genres, often harking back to classical literature, blossomed in Greek. Authors of the second century, such as Chariton and Achilles Tatius, wrote romantic adventure novels, making that literary form popular. Lucian (c. 117–180) composed satirical dialogues fiercely mocking both stuffy people and superstitious religiosity. As part of his enormous and varied literary output, the essayist and philosopher Plutarch (c. 50–120) wrote *Parallel Lives,* paired biographies of illustrious Greek and Roman men. His keen moral sense and lively taste for anecdotes made him favorite reading for centuries; the great English dramatist William Shakespeare (1564–1616) would base several of his plays on Plutarch's work.

Latin literature thrived as well; in fact, scholars rank the late first and early second centuries A.D. as its Silver Age, second only to the masterpieces of Augustan literature. Its most famous authors wrote with acid wit, verve, and imagination. Tacitus (c. 56–120) composed his *Annals* as a biting narrative of the Julio-Claudians, laying bare the ruthlessness of Augustus and the personal weaknesses of his successors. The satiric poet Juvenal (c. 65–130) skewered pretentious Romans and grasping provincials while hilariously bemoaning the indignities of being broke in the city. Apuleius (c. 125–170) intrigued readers with *The Golden Ass,* a lusty novel about a man turned into a donkey who regains his body and his soul through the power of the Egyptian goddess Isis.

Unlike Augustus, later emperors never worried that titillating literature posed a threat to social order. They did, however, share his belief that law was essential. Indeed, Romans prided themselves on their ability to order their society through law. As Virgil said, their mission was "to establish law and order within a framework of peace." Even today, the influence of Roman law is still evident in most systems of law in much of Europe. One distinctive characteristic of Roman law was its recognition of the principle of equity, which meant accomplishing what was "good and fair" even if the letter of the law had to be disregarded. This principle led legal thinkers to insist, for example, that the intent of parties in a contract outweighed the words of their agreement and that the burden of proof lay with the accuser rather than the accused. The emperor Trajan ruled that no one should be convicted on the grounds of suspicion alone because it was better for a guilty person to go unpunished than for an innocent person to be condemned.

Roman notions of fairness required formal distinctions among the "orders" in which it was believed people naturally belonged. As always, the elites constituted a tiny portion of the population. Only about one person in every fifty thousand had enough money to qualify for the senatorial order, the highest-ranking class, while about one in a thousand belonged to the equestrian order, the second-ranking class. Different purple stripes on clothing identified these orders. The third-highest order consisted of decurions, the local officials in provincial towns.

Those outside the social elite faced greater disadvantages than mere snobbery. An old republican distinction between the "better people" and the "humbler people" hardened under the principate, and by the third century it pervaded Roman law. Law institutionalized such distinctions because an orderly existence was thought to depend on them. The "better people" included senators, equestrians, decurions, and retired army veterans. Everybody else—except slaves, who counted as property, not people—made up the vastly larger group of "humbler people." The latter faced their gravest disadvantage in court: the law imposed harsher penalties on them than were imposed on the "better people" who committed the same crimes. "Humbler people" convicted of capital crimes were regularly executed by being crucified or torn apart by wild animals before a crowd of spectators. "Better people" rarely suffered the death penalty. But if they were condemned, they received a quicker and more dignified execution by the sword. "Humbler people" could also be tortured in criminal investigations, even if they were citizens. Romans regarded these differences as fair on the grounds that a person's higher status created a higher level of responsibility for the common good. As one provincial governor expressed it, "Nothing is less equitable than mere equality itself."

Law was crucial in maintaining order, but nothing mattered more to the stability and prosperity of the empire than steady population levels. Concern about reproduction therefore permeated marriage. The upper-class government official Pliny, for example, sent the following report to the grandfather of his third wife, Calpurnia: "You will be very sad to learn that your granddaughter has suffered a miscarriage. She is a young girl and did not realize she was pregnant. As a result she was more active than she should have been and paid a high price."◆ Roman medicine could do little to promote healthy childbirth and reduce infant mortality. Complications at birth could easily lead to the mother's death because doctors could not stop internal bleeding or cure infections. They possessed carefully crafted instruments for surgery and physical examinations but were seriously misinformed about reproduction. Gynecologists such as Soranus, who practiced in Rome during the reigns of Trajan and Hadrian, erroneously recommended the days just after menstruation as the best time to become pregnant, when the woman's body was "not congested." As in Hellenistic medicine, treatments were mainly limited to potions, poultices, and bleeding; Soranus recommended treating exceptionally painful menstruation by drawing blood "from the bend of the arm." Doctors, often freedmen from Greece and other provinces, were considered of low status, unless they served the upper class.

As in earlier times, girls often wed in their early teens to have as many years as possible to bear children. Because so many babies died, families had to produce numerous offspring to keep from disappearing. The tombstone of Veturia, a soldier's wife married at eleven, tells a typical story: "Here I lie, having lived for twenty-seven years. I was married to the same man for sixteen years and bore six children, five of whom died before I did." The propertied classes usually arranged marriages between spouses who hardly knew each other, although they could grow to love each other in a partnership devoted to family.

The emphasis on childbearing in marriage brought many health hazards to women, but to remain single and childless represented social failure for Romans. Once children were born, they were cared for by their mothers and by servants. Wealthy women routinely hired "wet nurses" to attend to and breastfeed their babies. When Romans wanted to control family size, they used female contraception by obstructing the female organs or by administering drugs. Like the Greeks, they practiced exposure, more frequently for infant girls than for boys because sons were considered more valuable than daughters as future supporters and protectors of families.

◆ For more correspondence that reveals conditions in the empire during Trajan's reign, see Document 16, Pliny the Younger, "Letters."

■ **Midwife's Sign Depicting Childbirth**
Childbirth was an exceptionally perilous experience for women because of the likelihood of bleeding to death from an internal hemorrhage. This terra-cotta sign from Ostia, the ancient port city of Rome, probably hung outside a midwife's rooms to announce her expertise in aiding women in giving birth. It shows a pregnant woman clutching the sides of her chair and supported by another woman while the midwife crouches in front to help deliver the baby. The meaning of the sign was clear to people who were illiterate; a person did not have to be able to read to understand the services that the specialist inside could provide. (Scala/Art Resource, NY.)

The emperors and some members of the social elite did their best to support reproduction. The emperors aided needy children to encourage larger families, and wealthy people often adopted children in their communities. One North African man gave enough money to support three hundred boys and three hundred girls each year until they grew up. The differing value afforded male and female children was also evident in these humanitarian programs: boys often received more aid than girls.

The Emergence of Christianity

Christianity began as a splinter group within Judaism in Judaea, where, as elsewhere under Roman rule, Jews were allowed to practice their ancestral religion. The new faith did not soon attract many converts; three centuries after the death of Jesus, Christians remained a small minority. Christianity grew, if only gradually, because it had an appeal based in the charismatic career of Jesus, its message of salvation, its believers' sense of mission, and the strong bonds of community it inspired. Ultimately, the emergence of Christianity proved the most significant and enduring development during the Roman Empire.

Jesus of Nazareth and the Spread of His Teachings

The new religion sprang from the life and teachings of Jesus (c. 4 B.C.–A.D. 30; see "The B.C./A.D. System for Dates" at the beginning of this book for an explanation of the apparent anomaly of the date of Jesus' birth "before Christ"). Its context, however, belonged to Jewish history. By the time of Jesus' boyhood, some Jews in Judaea were agitating for independence from Roman rule, making provincial authorities anxious about rebellion. Jesus' career, therefore, developed in an unsettled environment. His execution reflected Roman readiness to eliminate perceived threats to peace and social order. In the two decades after his crucifixion, his devoted followers, particularly Paul of Tarsus, developed a new religion—Christianity— stretching beyond the Jewish community of Palestine.

Christianity offered an answer to a difficult question about divine justice that the Jews' long history of defeat and exile raised: how could a just God allow the wicked to prosper and the righteous to suffer? The question had become pressing some two centuries before Jesus' birth, when persecution by the Seleucid king Antiochus IV (r. 175–164 B.C.) had provoked the Jews into a bloody revolt. This protracted struggle gave birth to a complex of ideas called *apocalypticism* (from the Greek for "revealing what is hidden"). According to this worldview, evil powers, divine and human, controlled the present world. Their regime would soon end, however, when God and his agents revealed their plan to conquer the forces of evil by sending an "anointed one" (Hebrew, *Mashia* or *Messiah;* Greek, *Christ*) to win the great battle. A final judgment would follow, to bestow eternal punishment on the wicked and eternal reward on the righteous. Apocalypticism proved compelling, especially among many Jews living in Judaea under Roman rule. Eventually, it inspired not only Jews but Christians and Muslims.

Apocalyptic doctrines gained special appeal around the time of Jesus' birth because most Judaean Jews were angry about Rome's control but disagreed about what form Judaism should take in such troubled times. Some favored accommodation with their overlords, while others preached rejection of the non-Jewish world and its spiritual corruption. Their local ruler, installed by the Romans, was Herod the Great (r. 37–4 B.C.). His flamboyantly Greek style of life flouted Jewish law, making him unpopular with his subjects despite his magnificent rebuilding of the holiest Jewish shrine, the great temple in Jerusalem. When a decade of unrest followed his death, Augustus responded to local petitions for help by installing a provincial government to deal with squabbling dynasts and competing religious factions. Jesus' homeland thus turned into a powder keg during his lifetime.

Born in Nazareth, Jesus began his career as a teacher and healer in his native Galilee, the northern region of Palestine, during the reign of Tiberius. The books that would later become the Gospels, or the first four books of the Christian New Testament, offer the earliest accounts of his life and teachings, yet they were composed between about 70 and 90, decades after Jesus' death. Jesus himself wrote nothing down, and others' accounts of his words and deeds are varied and controversial. He taught largely not by direct instruction but by telling parables, stories with a moral or religious message, that challenged his followers to ponder what he meant.

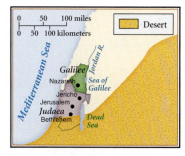

Palestine in the Time of Jesus, A.D. 30

All of the Gospels begin the narrative of his public ministry with his baptism by John the Baptist, who preached a message of repentance before the approaching final judgment. John was executed by the Jewish ruler Herod Antipas, a son of Herod the Great whom the Romans supported; Herod feared that John's apocalyptic preaching might instigate riots. After John's death, Jesus continued his mission by traveling around Judaea's countryside proclaiming the imminence of God's kingdom and the need to prepare spiritually for its coming. Many saw Jesus as the Messiah, but his complex apocalypticism did not preach immediate revolt against the Romans. Instead, he taught that God's true kingdom was to be sought not on earth but in heaven. He stressed that this kingdom was open to believers regardless of their social status or apparent sinfulness. His emphasis on God's love for humanity and people's overriding responsibility to love one another reflected Jewish religious teachings, as in the first-century scholar Hillel's interpretation of the Hebrew Bible.

An educated Jew who probably knew Greek as well as Aramaic, the local language, Jesus realized that he had to reach the urban crowds to make an impact. Therefore, leaving the Galilean villages where he had started, he took his message to the Jewish population of Jerusalem, the region's main city. His miraculous healings and exorcisms and his powerful preaching created a sensation. His popularity attracted the attention of the Jewish authorities, who automatically assumed he aspired to political power. Fearing he might ignite a Jewish revolt, the Roman governor Pontius Pilate (r. 26–36) ordered his crucifixion, the usual punishment for rebellion, in Jerusalem in 30.

After Jesus' death, his followers reported that they had seen him in person. They proclaimed that God had miraculously raised him from the dead, and they set about convincing other Jews that he was the promised savior and would soon return to judge the world and impose God's kingdom. His closest disciples, twelve Apostles (Greek for "messengers"), still considered themselves faithful Jews and continued to follow the commandments of Jewish law.

A radical change took place with the conversion of Paul of Tarsus (c. 10–65), a pious Jew of the Diaspora and a Roman citizen who had violently opposed those who accepted Jesus as the Messiah. Around three years after Jesus' death, a spiritual vision on the road to Damascus in Syria, which Paul interpreted as a divine revelation, inspired him to become a follower of Jesus as the Messiah or Christ—a

■ **Catacomb Painting of Christ as the Good Shepherd**
Catacombs (underground tombs), cut into soft rock outside various cities of the Roman Empire, served as vast burial chambers for Jews and Christians. Rome alone had 340 miles of catacombs. Painted in the third century A.D. on the wall of a Christian catacomb outside Rome, this fresco depicts Jesus as the Good Shepherd (see John 10:10–11). In addition to the tired or injured sheep, Jesus carries a pot of milk and perhaps honey, which new Christians received after their baptism as a symbol of their entry into the Promised Land of the Hebrew Bible. Such catacomb paintings were the earliest Christian art. By the fifth century A.D., the emperors' adoption of the new religion meant that Christians no longer had to make their tombs inconspicuous, and catacombs became sites of pilgrimage instead of burial. (Scala/Art Resource, NY.)

www.bedfordstmartins.com/huntconcise   See the ONLINE STUDY GUIDE for more help in analyzing this image.

Christian, as members of the movement came to be known. Paul taught that accepting Jesus as divine and his crucifixion as the ultimate sacrifice for the sins of humanity was the only way of becoming righteous in the eyes of God. In this way alone, Paul said, could one expect to attain salvation in the world to come.

Seeking to win converts outside Judaea, in about 46 Paul began to travel to preach to Jews of the Diaspora and to Gentiles (non-Jews) who had adopted some Jewish practices in Syria, Asia Minor, and Greece (see Map 5.3). Although he stressed the necessity of ethical behavior along traditional Jewish lines, especially the rejection of sexual immorality and polytheism, he also taught that converts need not keep all the provisions of Jewish law. To make conversion easier, Paul did not require the males who entered the movement to undergo the Jewish initiation rite of circumcision. This tenet and his teachings that his congregations did not have to observe Jewish dietary restrictions or festivals led to tensions with Jewish authorities in Jerusalem as well as with the followers of Jesus living there, who still believed that Christians had to follow Jewish law. Roman authorities then arrested Paul as a criminal troublemaker; he was executed in about 65.

Paul's mission was only one part of the turmoil afflicting the Jewish community in this period; hatred of Roman rule in Palestine finally provoked the Jews to revolt in 66, with disastrous results. After defeating the rebels in 70, Titus destroyed the Jerusalem temple and sold most of the city's population into slavery. In the aftermath of this catastrophe, the Jewish community lost its religious center, and the distancing of Christianity from Judaism begun by Paul gained momentum, giving birth to a separate religion. Paul's impact on the movement can be gauged by the number of letters—thirteen—attributed to him in the twenty-seven Christian writings brought together as the New Testament by around 200. Followers of Jesus came to regard the New Testament as having equal authority with the Hebrew Bible, which they then called the Old Testament. Because teachers like Paul preached mainly in the cities to reach large crowds, congregations of Christians mostly sprang up in urban areas. Women could sometimes be leaders in the movement, but not without arousing controversy; many people believed that men should teach and women only listen. Still, early Christianity was diverse enough that the first head of a congregation named in the New Testament was a woman.

Growth of a New Religion

Christianity faced serious obstacles in developing as a new religion separate from Judaism. Roman officials, suspecting it of being politically subversive, sporadically persecuted its adherents, such as Perpetua, as traitors, especially for refusing to participate in the imperial cult. Christian leaders had to build an organization from scratch to administer their growing congregations. Also, they had to address the controversial question of the leadership role of women in the movement.

Most Romans found early Christians baffling and irritating. First, in contrast to Jews, Christians espoused a novel faith rather than a traditional religion handed down from their ancestors; they therefore enjoyed no special treatment under Roman law. Next, people feared that tolerating Christians would offend the gods of official religion; their denial of the old gods and of the emperor's divine associations seemed sure to provoke natural catastrophes. Christians furthermore aroused contempt because they proclaimed as their divine king a man whom the imperial government had crucified as a criminal. Finally, their secret rituals led to accusations of cannibalism amid sexual promiscuity because they symbolically ate the body and drank the blood of Jesus during communal dinners called "Love Feasts," which men and women attended together. In short, Christians seemed a threat to social order and peace with the gods.

Not surprisingly, then, Romans were quick to blame Christians for disasters. When a large portion of Rome burned in 64, Nero punished them for arson. As Tacitus reports, the emperor had innocent Christians "covered with the skins of wild animals and mauled to death by dogs, or fastened to crosses and set on fire to provide light at night." The cruelty of their arbitrary punishment reportedly earned Christians some sympathy from Rome's population. After Nero, the government persecuted Christians only intermittently. No law specifically forbade their religion, but they made easy prey for officials, who were prepared to punish them to maintain public order.

In response to persecution, defenders of Christianity, such as Tertullian (c. 160–240) and Justin (c. 100–165), argued that Romans had nothing to fear from Christianity. Far from spreading immorality and subversion, these writers insisted, their faith taught an elevated moral code and respect for authority. It was not a foreign superstition but the true philosophy that combined the best features of Judaism and Greek thought and was thus a fitting religion for their diverse world. Tertullian pointed out that, although Christians could not worship the emperors, they did "pray to the true God for their [the emperors'] safety. We pray for a fortunate life for them, a secure rule, . . . a courageous army, a loyal Senate, a virtuous people, a world of peace."

Persecution did not stop Christianity. Tertullian indeed proclaimed that "the blood of the martyrs is the seed of the Church." Christians like Perpetua regarded public trials and executions as an opportunity to become witnesses (*martyrs* in Greek) to their faith and thus to strengthen Christians' sense of identity. Their firm conviction that their deaths would lead directly to heavenly bliss allowed them to face excruciating tortures with courage; some even sought martyrdom. Ignatius (c. 35–107), bishop of Antioch, begged Rome's congregation, which was becoming the most prominent Christian group, not to ask the emperor to show him mercy after his arrest: "Let me be food for the wild animals [in the arena] through whom I can reach God," he pleaded. "I am God's wheat, to be ground up by the teeth of beasts so that I may be found pure bread of Christ." Most Christians tried their best to avoid becoming martyrs by keeping a low profile, but stories recounting the martyrs' courage helped shape the identity of this new religion as a creed that gave its believers the spiritual strength to overcome great suffering.

Many first-century Christians expected their troubles would cease during their lifetime because Jesus would return to pass judgment on the world and hence overturn the Roman Empire. When this hope was not met, believers began transforming their faith from an apocalyptic Jewish sect predicting the immediate end of the world into a religion organized to survive indefinitely. Most important, they tried to achieve unity in their beliefs and to create a hierarchical organization to impose order on congregations.

Unity proved an elusive goal because early Christians constantly and fiercely disagreed about what they should believe, how they should live, and who had the authority to decide these questions. Some insisted that it was necessary to withdraw from the everyday world to escape its evil, even abandoning their families and shunning sex and reproduction. Others believed they could observe Christ's teachings while retaining their jobs and ordinary lives. Many Christians questioned whether they could serve in the army without betraying their religion because soldiers worshiped in the imperial cult. Controversy over such matters raged in the many congregations that arose in the early empire around the Mediterranean, from Gaul to Africa to the Near East (Map 5.3).

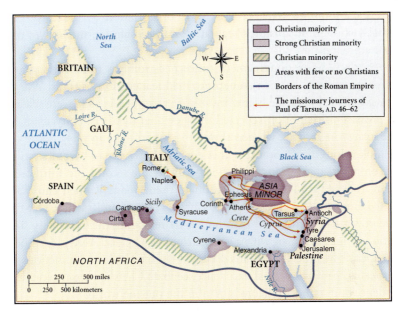

■ **MAP 5.3 Christian Populations in the Late Third Century** A.D.
Christians remained a minority in the Roman world three hundred years after the crucifixion of Jesus. Certain areas of the empire, however, especially Asia Minor (western Turkey), where Paul had preached, had a concentration of Christians. Most Christians lived in cities and towns, where missionaries had gone to spread their message to crowds of curious listeners. Paganus, a Latin word for "country person" or "rural villager," was appropriated to mean a believer in traditional polytheistic cults—hence the term pagan, *meaning "non-Christian," often found in modern works on this period.*

The emergence of bishops with authority to define doctrine and conduct became the most important institutional development to counter Christian disunity in the later first and second centuries. Bishops received their positions through the principle later called *apostolic succession*, which declares that Jesus' Apostles appointed the first bishops as their successors, granting these new officials the powers Jesus had originally given to the Apostles. Those men designated bishops by the Apostles in turn appointed their own successors, and so on. Bishops had the authority to ordain priests with the holy power to administer the sacraments, above all baptism and communion, which believers regarded as necessary for achieving eternal life. Bishops also controlled their congregations' memberships and finances (the money financing early churches came from members' gifts).

The bishops held the authority to define what was true doctrine (*orthodoxy*) and what was not (*heresy*), but they had limited success in combating the splintering effect of the differing versions of the new religion. For all practical purposes, the meetings of the bishops of different cities constituted the church's organization.

Today it is common to refer to this loose organization as the early Catholic ("universal") church; but bishops regularly disagreed among themselves on what beliefs were proper.

A particularly bitter disagreement concerned women's roles in the church. In the first congregations, women sometimes held leadership positions. When bishops were established atop the hierarchy, however, women usually were relegated to inferior posts. This demotion reflected the view that in Christianity, as in Roman imperial society in general, women should be subordinate to men. Some congregations took a long time to accept this change, however, and women still occasionally commanded positions of authority during the second and third centuries.

When leadership roles were closed off to them, many women chose a life of celibacy to demonstrate their devotion to Christ. Their commitment to chastity gave them the power to control their own bodies by removing their sexuality from the domination of men. Women with a special closeness to God were judged holy and socially superior by other Christians. By rejecting the traditional functions of wife and mother in favor of spiritual excellence, celibate Christian women achieved an independence and authority denied them in the outside world.

Parallel Belief Systems

Three centuries after Jesus' death, the overwhelming majority of the population still practiced traditional polytheism. Polytheists never sought a unity of beliefs (as the modern term *paganism,* under which diverse cults are often grouped, might suggest). They did agree, however, that the old gods favored and protected them and that the imperial cult added to their safety; the success and prosperity of the principate was the proof. Even those who found a more intellectually satisfying understanding of the world in philosophies, such as Stoicism, respected the traditional cults for this reason.

Polytheistic worship therefore had as its goal gaining the favor of all the divinities who could affect human life. Its deities ranged from the stalwarts of the state cults, such as Jupiter and Minerva, to spirits traditionally thought to inhabit local groves and springs. Famous old cults, such as the initiation rituals of Demeter and Persephone at Eleusis outside Athens, remained popular; the emperor Hadrian was initiated at Eleusis in 125.

The Hellenized cult of the Egyptian goddess Isis reveals how polytheism could provide believers with a religious experience arousing strong personal emotions and demanding a moral way of life. Her cult had already attracted Romans by the time of Augustus. He tried to suppress it because it was Cleopatra's religion, but Isis's reputation as a kind, compassionate goddess who alleviated her followers' suffering made her cult too popular to crush. The Egyptians believed that her tears for famished humans caused the Nile to flood every year and bring them good harvests. Her image was that of a loving mother, and in art she is often shown nurs-

■ **Mithras Slaying the Bull**

Hundreds of shrines to the mysterious god Mithras have been found in the Roman Empire, but the cult remains poorly known because almost no texts exist to explain it. To judge from the many representations in art, such as this wall painting of about A.D. 200 from the shrine at Marino south of Rome, the story of Mithras slaying a bull was a central part of the cult's identity. Scholars strenuously debate the symbolic meaning of the bull slaying, in which a snake and a dog lick the animal's blood while a scorpion pinches its testicles. Most agree, however, that Mithras was derived, perhaps as late as the early imperial period, from the ancient Persian divinity Mithra. Only men could be worshipers, and many were soldiers. Earlier scholarly claims of the cult's popularity were exaggerated; its members numbered no more than 1 or 2 percent of the population. Mithraism probably involved complex devotion to astrology, with devotees ranked in grades, each grade protected by a different celestial body. (Scala/Art Resource, NY.)

ing her son. A central doctrine of her cult concerned the death and resurrection of her husband, Osiris; Isis promised her followers a similar hope for life after death.

Isis required her adherents to behave righteously. Inscriptions put up for all to read declared her standards by referring to her own civilizing accomplishments: "I broke down the rule of tyrants; I put an end to murders; I caused what is right to be mightier than gold and silver." The dissolute hero of Apuleius's novel *The Golden Ass*, whom Isis rescues from torturous enchantment, expresses his intense joy after being spiritually reborn: "O holy and eternal guardian of the human race, who always cherishes mortals and blesses them, you care for the troubles of miserable humans with a sweet mother's love. Neither day nor night, nor any moment of time, ever passes by without your blessings." Other cults also required their adherents to lead ethically upright lives. Inscriptions from remote villages in Asia Minor, for example, record the confessions of peasants to sins such as sexual transgressions for which their local god had imposed severe penance.

Many upper-class Romans found ethical guidance in philosophy. Stoicism, derived from the teachings of the Greek Zeno (335–263 B.C.), was the most popular. Stoics believed in self-discipline above all, and their code of personal ethics left no room for riotous conduct. As the philosopher Seneca (4 B.C.–A.D. 65) explained, "It is easier to prevent harmful emotions from entering the soul than it is to control them once they have entered." Stoicism taught that the universe is directed by a single creative force incorporating reason, nature, and divinity. Humans share in the essence of this universal force and find happiness and patience by living in accordance with it and always doing their duty. The emperor Marcus Aurelius, in his memoirs entitled *Meditations*, emphasized the Stoic belief that people exist for each other: "Either make them better, or just put up with them," he advised.

Christian and polytheistic intellectuals energetically debated Christianity's relationship to traditional Greek philosophy. The theologian Origen (c. 185–255), for example, argued that Christianity was both true and superior to Hellenic philosophical doctrines as a guide to correct living. At about the same time, however, philosophic belief achieved its most intellectual formulation in the works of Plotinus (c. 205–270). Plotinus's spiritual philosophy, called *Neo-Platonism* because it developed new doctrines based on Plato's philosophy, influenced many educated Christians as well as polytheists. Its religious ideas focused on a human longing to return to the universal Good from which human existence derives. By turning away from the life of the body through the intellectual pursuit of philosophy, individual souls could ascend to the level of the universal soul, becoming the whole of what as individuals they formed a potential part. This mystical union with what the Christians would call God could be achieved only through strenuous self-discipline in personal morality as well as intellectual life. Neo-Platonism's stress on spiritual purity gave it a powerful appeal to Christian intellectuals. Like the cult of Isis or Stoicism, Neo-Platonism provided guidance, comfort, and hope through good times or bad.

The Crisis of the Third Century

Bad times arrived for the empire in the middle of the third century. Several factors combined to create the crisis. Attacks by outsiders on the northern and eastern frontiers forced the emperors to expand the army for defense, and their ill-conceived measures to fight inflation and raise money to pay their troops crippled the economy and infuriated the public. The ensuing unrest encouraged ambitious generals to engage in the behavior that had destroyed the republic: placing themselves in command of personal armies and once again plunging Rome into civil war. Earthquakes and scattered epidemics added to the destruction caused by this turmoil. By the end of the third century, this conglomeration of troubles had shredded the "Roman peace."

Defending the Frontiers

Emperors since Domitian (r. 81–96) had been fighting campaigns to repel invaders from the frontier regions. The most aggressive attackers were loosely organized Germanic bands that often crossed the Danube and Rhine Rivers for raiding. The constant fighting against Roman troops forged these northern warriors into formidable armies, and they mounted especially dangerous invasions during the reign of Marcus Aurelius (r. 161–180). A major threat also loomed over the empire's eastern edge when a new dynasty, the Sassanids, defeated the Parthian Empire and reenergized the ancient Persian kingdom. By 227, Persia's military resurgence compelled the emperors to concentrate forces in the rich eastern provinces, at the expense of the defense of the northern frontiers.

Recognizing the courage of Germanic warriors, Domitian and his successors began hiring them as auxiliary soldiers for the Roman army and settling them on the frontiers as buffers against invasion. By around 200, the army had enrolled perhaps as many as 450,000 legionary and auxiliary troops (the size of the navy remains unknown). As always in the Roman military, existence was demanding. Training constantly, soldiers had to be fit enough to carry forty-pound packs up to twenty miles in five hours, swimming rivers en route. Since the reign of Hadrian (r. 117–138), the emperors had built many stone camps for permanent garrisons, but an army on the march constructed its own fortified camp every night. Soldiers transported all the makings of a wooden-walled city everywhere they went. As one ancient commentator noted during the republic, "Infantrymen were little different from loaded pack mules." At one temporary fort in a frontier area, archaeologists found a supply of a million iron nails—ten tons' worth. The same encampment required seventeen miles of timber for its barracks walls. To outfit a single legion with tents required 54,000 calves' hides.

The increased requirement for pay and supplies strained imperial finances because successful conquests had dwindled over time. The army had become a source of negative instead of positive cash flow to the treasury, and the economy had not expanded sufficiently to make up the difference. To make matters worse, inflation had driven up prices. A principal cause of inflation under the principate may have been, ironically, the long period of peace that promoted increased demand for the economy's relatively static production of goods and services.

Some emperors responded to rising prices by the desperate scheme of debasing imperial coinage in a vain attempt to cut government costs. By putting less silver in each coin without changing its face value, emperors hoped to create more cash with the same amount of precious metal. (See "Taking Measure," below.) Merchants, however, raised prices to make up for the diminished value of the debased currency. By 200, the debased coinage and inflation were ruining the imperial balance sheet and undermining public confidence in the imperial currency. Because the soldiers kept demanding that their patrons, the emperors, pay them well, the stage was set for a crisis. The financial system fell into full collapse in the 250s and 260s.

The Severan Emperors and Catastrophe

Decisions by Septimius Severus (r. 193–211) and his sons made the crisis inevitable: the father drained the treasury to satisfy the army, and his sons' murderous rivalry and reckless spending destroyed the government's stability. A soldier's soldier who came from the large North African city of Leptis Magna in what is today Libya, Severus became emperor in 193 after sparking a civil war to replace his hopelessly incompetent predecessor. To restore imperial prestige and acquire money through foreign conquest, Severus vigorously pursued successful campaigns beyond the frontiers of the provinces, in Mesopotamia and northern Britain.

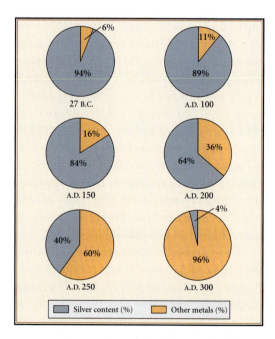

■ **TAKING MEASURE**
The Value of Roman Imperial Coinage, 27 B.C.–A.D. 300
Ancient silver coinage derived its value from its metallic content; the less silver in a coin, the less it was worth. Emperors facing rising government and military expenses but flat or falling revenues tried to cut costs by debasing the coinage: they reduced the amount of silver in each coin and increased the amount of other, cheaper metals. These pie charts reveal the gradual debasement of the Roman imperial coinage until the third century, when military expenses apparently skyrocketed. By A.D. 300, coins contained only trace amounts of silver. Merchants and producers had to raise their prices for goods and services when they were being paid with currency that was increasingly less valuable. Thus debasement fueled inflation.

(Adapted from Kevin Greene, *The Archeology of the Roman Empire* [London: B. T. Batsford Ltd., 1986], 60. Reprinted with permission of Salamander Books Limited.)

By this time, the soldiers were desperate because inflation had eroded the value of their wages to practically nothing after they bought themselves basic supplies and clothing. They therefore routinely expected the emperors to favor them with gifts of extra money. Severus expended large sums for this purpose, then tried to improve conditions fundamentally by raising the soldiers' pay by one-third. The expanded size of the army made this raise more expensive than the treasury could handle and further stoked the fires of inflation. The dire financial consequences of his policy, however, concerned Severus not at all. His deathbed advice to his sons in 211 was to "stay on good terms with each other, be generous to the soldiers, and pay no attention to anyone else."

Sadly for the principate, Severus's sons followed only the last two points of his advice. Caracalla (r. 211–217) seized the throne for himself by murdering his brother Geta, and his violent and profligate reign signaled the end of the peace and prosperity of the Roman Golden Age. He increased the soldiers' pay by another 40 to 50 percent and spent gigantic sums on grandiose building projects, including the largest public baths Rome had ever seen, covering blocks and blocks of the city. His extravagant spending put unbearable pressure on the provincial elites responsible for collecting taxes and on the citizens whom they squeezed for ever greater amounts.

In 212, Caracalla took his most famous step to try to fix the budget crisis: he granted Roman citizenship to almost every man and woman in imperial territory except slaves. His goal was to increase revenues from inheritance taxes and from fees for freeing slaves, which only citizens paid (noncitizens paid other levies): the more citizens, the more money (most of it earmarked for the army). Caracalla, who contemporaries whispered was insane, spent wildly and soon wrecked the imperial budget, paving the way for the absolutely ruinous inflation of the coming decades. Once when his mother upbraided him for his excesses, he replied as he drew his sword, "Never mind, we shall not run out of money as long as I have this."

The empire's financial weakness spawned political instability. When Macrinus, commander of the praetorians, murdered Caracalla in 217 to make himself emperor, Caracalla's female relatives bribed the army to overthrow Macrinus in favor of a young male relative. The restored Severan dynasty did not last long, however, and the assassination of the last Severan emperor in 235 opened a half-century of civil wars that, compounded by natural disasters, broke the principate's back. For the next fifty years, a parade of emperors and pretenders fought over power. During this period of near anarchy, over two dozen men, often several at a time, held or claimed the throne. Their only qualification was their ability to command a frontier army and to reward the troops for loyalty to their general instead of to the state.

The almost constant civil war of the mid-third century exacted a tremendous toll on the population and the economy. Violence and hyperinflation made life miserable in many regions. Crops withered as farmers found it impossible to keep up normal agricultural production while battling armies trampled their fields searching for food. Members of city councils faced constantly escalating demands for tax

IMPORTANT DATES

44 B.C.	Julius Caesar's assassination reignites civil war	**A.D. 69**	Civil war in the "Year of the Four Emperors"
30 B.C.	Ptolemaic Egypt falls to Roman army	**A.D. 70**	Titus captures Jerusalem and destroys the Jewish temple
27 B.C.–A.D. 14	Augustus's principate	**C. A.D. 70–90**	Texts that become the first four books of the New Testament are written
19 B.C.	The poet Virgil dies, leaving the *Aeneid* unfinished		
9 B.C.	Altar of Augustan Peace is completed	**A.D. 79**	Eruption of Mount Vesuvius
2 B.C.	Senate proclaims Augustus "Father of his Country"	**A.D. 80s**	Domitian leads campaigns against Germanic invaders on northern frontiers
A.D. 8	Augustus exiles the poet Ovid	**A.D. 161–180**	Germanic bands attack northern frontiers
A.D. 30	Jesus of Nazareth crucified in Jerusalem	**A.D. 212**	Caracalla extends Roman citizenship to almost all free inhabitants of the provinces
C. A.D. 35	Paul of Tarsus becomes a Christian	**A.D. 249–251**	Decius persecutes Christians
A.D. 41	Praetorian guard forces Senate to accept Claudius as emperor	**A.D. 250s–260s**	Imperial finances collapse from civil war, debased coinage, and inflation
C. A.D. 46	Paul begins travels seeking converts to Christianity	**A.D. 260**	Shapur I of Persia captures the Roman emperor Valerian
A.D. 64	Much of Rome burns; Nero blames Christians	**A.D. 284**	Diocletian assumes the throne

revenues from every new emperor, and the financial pressure destroyed their commitment to serving their communities.

Foreign enemies took advantage of the Roman civil wars, invading from the east and north. Roman fortunes hit bottom in 260 when Shapur I, king of the Sassanid Empire of Persia, captured the emperor Valerian (r. 253–260) while assaulting the province of Syria. Imperial territory was in danger of splintering into breakaway principalities. Even the tough and experienced emperor Aurelian (r. 270–275) could do no more to reduce the danger than to recover Egypt and Asia Minor from Zenobia, the warrior queen of Palmyra in Syria. He also had to encircle Rome with a massive wall to ward off surprise attacks by Germanic tribes smashing their way into Italy from the north.

Historians dispute how severely these troubles were worsened by natural disasters, but devastating earthquakes and virulent epidemics did strike some of the

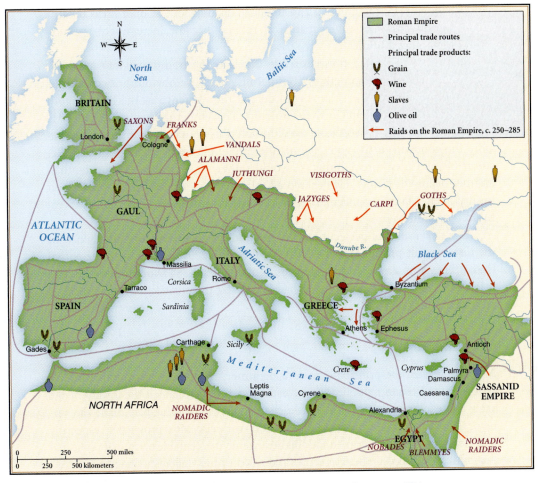

■ **MAPPING THE WEST**   **The Roman Empire in Crisis, c. A.D. 284**

By the early 280s, the principate had been wracked by the fifty years of civil war that followed the end of the Severan dynasty. Imperial territory retained the general outline in existence since the time of Augustus (see Map 5.1), except for the loss of Dacia during the reign of Aurelian (r. A.D. 270–275). Attacks from the north and east had repeatedly penetrated the frontier regions, however. The Sassanid king Shapur I (r. c. A.D. 240–270) for example, temporarily held Antioch and captured the emperor Valerian in 260. The public humiliation and death in captivity of the elderly imperial ruler indicate the depths to which Roman fortunes sank in the third century.

www.bedfordstmartins.com/huntconcise   See the ONLINE STUDY GUIDE for more help in analyzing this map.

provinces around the middle of the century. The population declined significantly as food supplies became less dependable, civil war killed soldiers and civilians alike, and infection flared over large regions. The loss of population meant fewer soldiers for the army, whose efficiency as a defense and police force had already deteriorated seriously because of the political and financial chaos. More frontier areas became vulnerable to raids, and roving bands of robbers became increasingly common within the imperial borders.

Polytheists explained these horrible times in the traditional way: the state gods were angry about something. But about what? The obvious answer seemed to be the presence of Christians, who denied the existence of the Roman gods and refused to participate in their worship. The emperor Decius (r. 249–251) launched systematic persecutions to eliminate this contaminated group and restore the goodwill of the gods. He justified the violence by styling himself "Restorer of the Cults," proclaiming, "I would rather see a rival to my throne than another bishop of Rome." He ordered all inhabitants of the empire to prove their loyalty to the state by participating in a sacrifice to its gods. Christians who refused to join in were killed.

This new round of persecutions did not end the civil war, economic failure, or the diseases that precipitated the crisis. By the early 280s, no one could deny that the empire was in danger of fragmenting. Remarkably, in 284 Diocletian would drag it back to safety in the same way it had begun: by the creation of a new form of authoritarian leadership.

Conclusion

Augustus created the principate by devising a monarchy while insisting that he was restoring the Roman republic. He succeeded because he retained the loyalty of the army and exploited the familiar patron-client system. The principate made the emperor the patron of the army and, indeed, of everyone else. Most provincials, especially in the eastern Mediterranean, found this arrangement acceptable because it replicated the familiar relationship between ruler and ruled of the Hellenistic kingdoms.

Stability prevailed as long as the emperors had enough revenue to keep their millions of clients satisfied. They spent money to provide food to the poor, build baths and arenas for public entertainment, and pay their troops. The emperors of the first and second centuries enlarged the military to protect distant territories stretching from Britain to North Africa to Syria. By the second century, peace and prosperity had created an imperial Golden Age. Long-term fiscal difficulties set in, however, because the army, concentrated on defense rather than conquest, no longer brought money into the treasury. Severe inflation and debasement of the currency worsened the situation. The wealthy elites found they could no longer meet the demand for increased taxes without draining their personal fortunes, and they lost their public-spiritedness and avoided their communal responsibilities. Loyalty to the state became too expensive.

The emergence of Christians added to the uncertainty. Imperial officials doubted their loyalty to the state. Their new religion evolved from Jewish apocalypticism to an increasingly hierarchical organization. Its adherents disputed with each other and with the authorities; martyrs such as Perpetua worried the imperial government with the depth of their convictions. Citizens' placing loyalty to a divinity ahead of loyalty to the state was a new and troubling phenomenon for Roman officialdom.

When financial ruin, civil war, and natural disasters combined to weaken the imperial system in the mid-third century, the emperors lacked the money and the popular support to end the crisis. Not even the persecution of Christians could convince the gods to restore Rome's good fortunes. The empire instead had to be transformed politically and religiously. Against all expectations, Diocletian began that process in 284.

Suggested References for further reading and online research appear on page SR-9 at the back of the book.

www.bedfordstmartins.com/huntconcise See the ONLINE STUDY GUIDE to assess your mastery of the material covered in this chapter.

The Transformation of the Roman Empire

A.D. 284–c. 600

A N EGYPTIAN WOMAN NAMED ISIS wrote a letter to her mother in the third century that modern archaeologists found at the site of a village near the Nile River. Written in Greek on papyrus, the letter hints at the unsettling changes that affected people during that tumultuous period.

> *Every day I pray to the lord Sarapis and his fellow gods to watch over you. I want you to know that I have arrived in Alexandria safely after four days. I send fond greetings to my sister and the children and Elouath and his wife and Dioscorous and her husband and children and Tamalis and her husband and son and Heron and Ammonarion and . . . Sanpat and her children. And if Aion wants to be in the army, let him come. For everybody is in the army.*

The letter leaves us with tantalizing questions unanswered: What was the relationship between Isis and most of the people she mentions, with their mixture of Greek and Semitic names? Did Isis know how to write or, as was common, had she hired a scribe? Why had she gone to Alexandria? Why did Aion want to become a soldier? Why was "everybody" in the army?

These questions correspond to many dimensions of the third-century crisis in the Roman Empire. Perhaps economic troubles forced Isis to leave her village to seek

■ **Justinian and His Court in Ravenna**
This mosaic scene dominated by the Byzantine emperor Justinian (r. 527–565) stands across the chancel from Theodora's mosaic (see page 247) in St. Vitale's Church in Ravenna. Justinian and Theodora had finished building the church, which the Ostrogothic king Theodoric had started, to commemorate their successful campaign to restore Italy to the Roman Empire and reassert control of the western capital, Ravenna. The soldiers at left remind viewers of the monarchs' aggressive military policy in service of imperial unity. The inclusion of the portrait of Maximianus, bishop of Ravenna, standing on Justinian's left and identified by name, stresses the theme of cooperation between bishops and emperors in ruling the world. (Scala/Art Resource, NY.)

work in the city. Perhaps Aion wanted to join the army to earn wages. Perhaps everybody seemed to be in the army because political turmoil was generating continuous civil war. These answers reflect the desperate challenge facing imperial government by the 280s, after half a century of Roman armies fighting Roman armies over who should be emperor: how to reorganize the empire to restore peace and order through military force, government administration, ancestral religion, and economic prosperity. Diocletian, emperor beginning in A.D. 284, turned out to be a leader tough enough to meet this challenge and delay the political fragmentation of the empire.

Restoring social calm proved difficult because religious tensions were growing between Christians and followers of traditional polytheistic cults like Isis the letter writer, whose faith was visible in her namesake, an Egyptian goddess. Polytheist emperors, believing that Christians provoked divine anger, conducted brutal persecutions. Then, unexpectedly, early in the fourth century the emperor Constantine stopped the violence by converting to Christianity and officially favoring it. By the end of the fourth century, the new faith had become the state religion. The persistence of pre-Christian traditions and Christians' fierce disputes over doctrine kept this transformation turbulent.

Ending the civil wars postponed but did not prevent the splintering of imperial territory. At the end of the fourth century, the empire fragmented permanently into western and eastern sections. In the west, Germanic peoples began migrating into the region, transforming it—and themselves—socially, culturally, and politically by replacing Roman provincial government with their own new kingdoms. They lived side by side with Romans, the different groups often merging their customs. By the fifth century, the decentralization of authority had transformed western Europe politically, foreshadowing its modern divisions. In the east, the Roman provinces remained economically vibrant and politically united, becoming (in modern terminology) the Byzantine Empire in the sixth century. Despite financial pressures and diminishing territory, this Christian continuation of the Roman Empire would endure for centuries, until Turkish invaders finally conquered it in 1453.

Reorganizing the Empire

During the third-century crisis, attacks by foreign enemies had weakened the Roman Empire's defenses and stymied tax collection. The emperors also faced a significant religious problem: the growing influence of the Christian church. Diocletian (r. 284–305) and Constantine (r. 306–337) met these challenges by restoring strong central authority in the empire.

Imperial Reform and Fragmentation

Diocletian was an uneducated military man from the rough region of Dalmatia (in what is now Croatia), but his exceptional leadership and intelligence propelled him through the ranks until the army made him emperor in 284. He ended the third-

■ **Miniature Portrait of Emperor Constantine**

This eight-inch-high bust of Constantine is carved from chalcedony, a crystalline mineral prized for its milky translucence. The first Christian emperor is shown gazing upward, to link himself to his hero and model Alexander the Great, who had ordered his portrait done in this posture. Constantine also appears without a beard, a style made popular by Alexander and imitated by Augustus and Trajan, successful emperors with whose memory Constantine also wished to be associated. The cross visible at the top center of Constantine's breastplate makes the statuette one of the relatively few pieces of fourth-century Roman art to display overtly Christian symbols. The position of this unmistakable sign of the emperor's religious choice recalls the sculpture on the armor on the Prima Porta statue of Augustus (see page 183); like the founder of the principate, Constantine communicated his image through art.
(Bibliothèque Nationale.)

century anarchy by imposing the most autocratic system of rule the Roman world had yet seen. With the military's support, Diocletian proclaimed himself *dominus*— "master," what slaves called their owners—to replace Augustus's republican title, *princeps* ("first man"). Roman imperial rule from Diocletian onward is therefore called the *dominate*. It was autocracy—rule by absolute power. Senators, consuls, and other traditional republican offices continued to exist, but the emperors held all the power. To find loyal supporters, they increasingly chose their administrators from lower ranks of society.

The emperors of the dominate emphasized their supremacy by holding court from a raised platform (a dais), wearing jeweled robes, and surrounding themselves with courtiers and ceremony. Constantine wore a diadem—a purple headband sparkling with gems, a symbol of kingship that earlier emperors had avoided. To demonstrate the ruler's superiority, a series of veils separated palace waiting rooms from the inner space where the emperor heard petitioners. High-ranking officials received grandiose titles such as "most perfect" and sported distinctive shoes and belts. The court of the dominate resembled the court of the Great King of Persia a thousand years earlier. The emperors of the dominate abandoned the first Roman emperors' claim that the ruler was merely the *princeps*, the most distinguished citizen. Diocletian and his successors embraced the notion that citizens were their subjects. The architecture of the dominate reflected the all-powerful status of its rulers. Diocletian's public bath in Rome rivaled earlier emperors' buildings in the capital; its soaring vaults and domes covered a space more than three thousand feet long on each side.

The dominate also used religious language to mark the emperor's special status. The emperors added *et deus* ("and God") to *dominus* as their title. Diocletian also adopted the title *Jovius,* claiming Jupiter (Jove), the chief Roman god, as his ancestor. His titles signaled the sense of awe he now expected from his subjects and asserted that Rome's government replicated divine hierarchy.

The emperors alone made law and did not consider themselves bound by the decisions of their predecessors. Relying on a loyal personal staff that isolated them from the outside world, they rarely sought advice from the elite, as earlier rulers had done. Their desire to maintain order led them to impose brutal punishments for crimes. For example, Constantine mandated that officials who did not keep their "greedy hands" off bribes would have their hands "cut off by the sword," and the guardians of a young girl who allowed a lover to seduce her were punished by having molten lead poured into their mouths. Punishments grew especially harsh for the large segment of the population legally designated as "humbler people," but the laws excused the "better people" from most of the harshest penalties for comparable offenses. In this way, autocracy strengthened the divisions between poor and rich.

Diocletian decided that the empire could not be administered and defended from a single center (that is, Rome). In 293, he therefore subdivided imperial territory into two administrative districts in the west and two in the east (Map 6.1). Having no sons, he appointed three "partners" so he and they could govern cooperatively in two pairs, both consisting of a senior "Augustus" with a junior "Caesar" as his adopted son and designated successor. Each emperor controlled one of the four districts. To prevent disunity, the most senior partner—in this case Diocletian—served as supreme ruler and was supposed to receive the loyalty of the others. This *tetrarchy* ("rule by four"), as modern scholars call it, was Diocletian's attempt to keep imperial government from being isolated at the center and to prevent civil war over the succession.

Diocletian also subdivided the provinces, nearly doubling their number to almost a hundred. He grouped them into twelve dioceses under the jurisdiction of regional administrators, who reported to the four emperors' first assistants, the praetorian prefects. To prevent rebellion, Diocletian began to separate civil from military authority, giving administrators control only of legal and financial affairs and generals only of defense. Constantine completed this process.

Although the tetrarchy later lapsed, Diocletian's hierarchical system of provincial administration endured. It also ended Rome's thousand years as the empire's capital city. Diocletian lived in Nicomedia, in Asia Minor, and did not even visit Rome until 303, nearly twenty years after becoming emperor. He chose four new capitals for their utility as military command posts closer to the frontiers: Milan in northern Italy, Sirmium near the Danube River border, Trier near the Rhine River border, and Nicomedia. Italy became just another section of the empire, on an equal footing with the other provinces and subject to the same taxation system, except

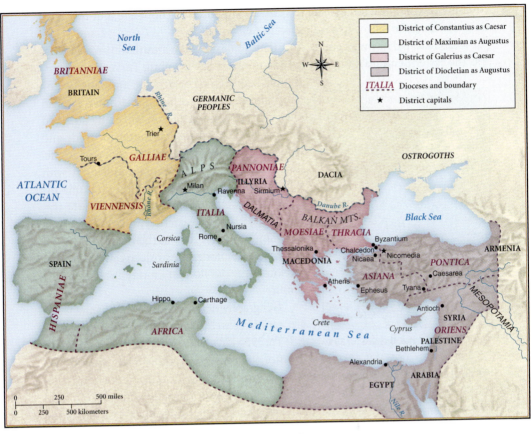

■ MAP 6.1 Diocletian's Reorganization of 293

To try to prevent civil war and tighten imperial control, Emperor Diocletian reorganized the Roman Empire. He created four administrative districts, each one governed by a separate emperor. He subdivided the preexisting provinces into smaller units and grouped them into twelve dioceses, each overseen by a regional administrator. This map shows the four districts as the imperial official Sextus Aurelius Victor described them in his book On the Caesars, *a biographically oriented history of the empire inspired by the famous biographies of Suetonius from the early second century. Victor published his book around 360.*

for the district of Rome itself—the last vestige of the city's former primacy and prestige.

Despite Diocletian's reforms, civil war broke out soon after he abdicated in 305. It took Constantine (r. 306–337) until 324 to eliminate rivals from outside his family. Near the end of his reign, he designated his three sons as joint heirs, admonishing them to rule as co-emperors. They failed as bloodily as had the sons of Septimius Severus a century earlier, plunging into war with one another. Their gory rivalry informally split the empire on a north-south line along the Balkan peninsula. In 395, it was formally divided into a western and an eastern empire, with a co-emperor ruling each half. The rulers were supposed to cooperate, but this division launched the halves toward different fates.

Each half had its own capital. Constantinople, near the mouth of the Black Sea, was the eastern empire's. Originally Byzantium (today Istanbul, Turkey), Constantinople had been reconstructed and renamed by Constantine in 324 as his "new Rome." He had chosen it because it lay on an easily fortified peninsula astride principal routes for trade and troop movements. To recall the glory of Rome, Constantine had graced his refounded city with a forum, an imperial palace, a hippodrome for chariot races, and monumental statues of the traditional gods. The eastern emperors inherited Constantine's "new" city as their capital; from its ancient name modern historians call the eastern section of the old Roman Empire the "Byzantine Empire."

The Division of the Empire, c. 395

Geography determined the site of the western capital as well. The western emperor Honorius (r. 395–423) wanted to keep the protective mass of the Alps between his territory and marauding Germanic bands to the north. In 404, he made Ravenna, a port on Italy's northeastern coast, the western capital because it was a naval base and an important commercial city. Walls and marshes protected it from attack by land, while access to the sea kept it from being starved out in a siege. Ravenna never rivaled Constantinople in size or splendor, but it did receive churches gleaming with multicolored mosaics.

Financial Reform and Social Consequences

Diocletian's rescue of the empire called for vast revenues, which the hyperinflation of the third century had made hard to acquire. He tried to improve imperial finances by issuing new money, price controls, and a new taxation system. Unfortunately, Diocletian miscalculated in mandating values for the new currency and sparked a financial panic that fueled inflation in many regions after 293. High prices caused people to hoard whatever goods they could buy, and hoarding drove prices ever higher. "Hurry and spend all my money you have; buy me any kinds of goods at whatever prices they are available," wrote one official to his servant, fearing yet another decline in the value of the currency.

In 301, Diocletian tried to curb inflation with price and wage controls in the worst-hit areas. His Edict on Maximum Prices blamed high prices on profiteers' "unlimited and frenzied avarice," forbade hoarding, and set ceilings on the prices that could legally be charged for about a thousand goods and services. Promulgated only in the eastern part of the empire, the edict soon became ineffective because merchants refused to cooperate and government officials were unable to enforce it despite the threat of death or exile as the penalty for violations. In his final years, Diocletian revalued the currency to restore sound money and stable prices, but the civil war under Constantine again weakened it.

With the currency losing value, the emperors began collecting taxes not only in coins but also in goods. Recent research disputes whether this form of revenue actually displaced taxes paid in coin, as previous scholars believed, or only served as a way to impose higher property taxes, which had to be paid in coin as much as possible. By the end of the fourth century, it is clear, the government expected payment in gold and silver. Whatever the details, taxes rose, especially on the local elites. Taxes went mostly to support the army, which required enormous amounts of grain, meat, wine, horses, camels, and mules. The major sources of revenue were a tax on land, assessed according to its productivity, and a head tax on individuals.

The empire was too large to enforce consistency in tax rates. In some areas, both men and women from about the age of twelve to sixty-five paid the full tax; in others, women paid only one-half the tax assessment or none at all. Workers in cities probably owed taxes only on their property. They periodically paid "in kind"— laboring without pay on public works projects such as cleaning municipal drains or repairing buildings. Urban businesspeople, from shopkeepers to prostitutes, paid taxes in money. Members of the senatorial class were exempt from ordinary taxes but had to pay special levies.

The new tax system would work only if agricultural production remained stable and the government controlled the people liable for the head tax. (See "Taking Measure," page 220.) Diocletian therefore restricted the movement of tenant farmers (*coloni*), the empire's economic base. *Coloni* had traditionally been free to move to different farms under different landlords. Now tenant farmers and their children were increasingly tied to a particular plot, and agriculture became a hereditary occupation.

The government also restricted workers in other occupations deemed essential. State bakers, for example, could not leave their jobs, and anyone who acquired a baker's property had to assume that occupation. The bakers were essential in producing free bread for Rome's poor, a tradition begun under the republic to prevent food riots. Also, from Constantine's reign on, military service became a lifetime, hereditary career: the sons of military veterans had to serve in the army.

The emperors decreed equally oppressive regulations for the propertied class in the empire's towns, the *curiales*. Almost all men in the *curial* class were obliged sooner or later to serve as unsalaried city council members, who had to use their own funds if necessary to support the community. Their financial responsibilities ranged from maintaining the water supply to feeding troops, but their most expensive duty was covering shortfalls in tax collection. The emperors' demands for increased revenue made this a crushing burden, compounding the damage to the *curiales* that the third-century crisis had begun.

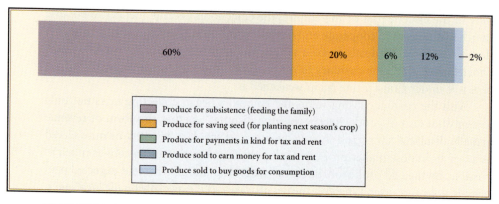

| 60% | 20% | 6% | 12% | —2% |

■ Produce for subsistence (feeding the family)
■ Produce for saving seed (for planting next season's crop)
■ Produce for payments in kind for tax and rent
■ Produce sold to earn money for tax and rent
■ Produce sold to buy goods for consumption

■ **TAKING MEASURE** **Peasants' Use of Farm Produce in the Roman Empire**
This graph offers a hypothetical model of how peasants during the Roman Empire may have used what they produced as farmers and herders to maintain their families and pay their expenses for rent, taxes, and the things they needed but did not produce themselves. The amounts are necessarily speculative because reliable and comprehensive statistics of this kind do not exist for the ancient world. Naturally, individual families would have had widely varying experiences, and this estimate applies only to the population of peasant producers as a whole. Still, it is very likely that most families did have to use the majority of their production just to keep themselves alive at the subsistence level and, by modern standards, were living in poverty.
(Adapted from Keith Hopkins, *Conquerors and Slaves: Sociological Studies in Roman History* [New York: Cambridge University Press, 1978], 17. Reprinted with permission of Cambridge University Press.)

For centuries, the empire's welfare had depended on a steady supply of public-spirited members of the social elite enthusiastically filling these crucial posts to win the admiration of their neighbors. Now this tradition broke down as wealthy people avoided public service to escape financial ruin. So distorted was the situation that compulsory service on a city council became one of the punishments for a minor crime. Eventually, to prevent *curiales* from escaping their obligations, the emperors forbade them to move away from the town where they had been born; they even had to ask official permission to travel. These laws made members of the elite feverish to win exemptions from public service by exploiting their connections to petition the emperor, by bribing high-ranking officials, or by taking up an occupation that freed them from such obligations (the military, imperial administration, or church governance). The most desperate simply fled, abandoning home and property.

The restrictions on freedom caused by the vise-like pressure for higher taxes thus eroded the communal values that had motivated wealthy Romans for so long. The attempt to stabilize the empire by increasing its revenues also produced social discontent among poorer citizens. The tax rate on land eventually reached one-third of its gross yield. This intolerable burden impoverished the rural population. Conditions became so bad in fifth-century Spain, for example, that peasants openly revolted against imperial control. Financial troubles, especially severe in the west, kept the empire from ever regaining the prosperity of its Golden Age and worsened the friction between government and citizens.

Religious Reform: From Persecution to Conversion

Traditional belief required religious explanations for disasters. Accordingly, Diocletian concluded that the gods' anger had caused the third-century crisis. To restore divine goodwill, he instructed citizens to follow the traditional gods who had guided Rome to power and virtue: "Through the providence of the immortal gods, eminent, wise, and upright men have in their wisdom established good and true principles. It is wrong to oppose these principles or to abandon the ancient religion for some new one." Christianity was the new faith he meant.

Blaming Christians' hostility to traditional religion for the empire's troubles, Diocletian in 303 launched a massive attack remembered as the Great Persecution. He expelled Christians from his administration, seized their property, tore down churches, and executed them for refusing to participate in official religious rituals. As often, policy was applied differently in different regions. In the western empire, the violence stopped after about a year; in the east, it continued for a decade. So gruesome were the public executions of martyrs that they aroused the sympathy of some polytheists.

Constantine changed the empire's religious history forever by converting to the new faith. He chose Christianity for the same reason that Diocletian had persecuted it: in the belief that he was securing divine protection for himself and the empire. During the civil war that he fought to succeed Diocletian, Constantine experienced a dream-vision promising him the support of the Christian God. His biographer, Eusebius (c. 260–340), later reported that Constantine had also seen a vision of Jesus' cross in the sky surrounded by the words "In this sign you shall be the victor." When Constantine triumphed over his rival Maxentius by winning the battle of the Milvian Bridge in Rome in 312, he proclaimed that God's miraculous power and goodwill needed no further demonstration and declared himself a Christian emperor.

After his conversion, Constantine did not outlaw polytheism or make Christianity the official religion. Instead, he decreed religious toleration. The best statement of this new policy survives in the Edict of Milan of 313. It proclaimed free choice of religion for everyone and referred to the empire's protection by "the highest divinity"—an imprecise term meant to satisfy both polytheists and Christians.

Constantine wanted to avoid angering polytheists because they still greatly outnumbered Christians, but he nevertheless did all he could to promote his newly chosen religion. These goals called for a careful balancing act. For example, he returned all property seized during the Great Persecution to its Christian owners, but he had the treasury compensate those who had bought the confiscated property at auction. When in 321 he made Lord's Day a holy occasion each week on which no official business or manufacturing work could be performed, he called it "Sunday" to blend Christian and traditional notions in honoring two divinities, God and the sun. To adorn his new capital, Constantinople, he erected numerous statues of traditional gods around the city. He also conspicuously respected tradition by holding the office of *pontifex maximus* ("chief priest"), which emperors had filled ever since Augustus.

Christianizing the Empire

Constantine's brilliantly crafted religious policy of toleration and compromise set the empire on the path to Christianization. The process proved to be slow and sometimes violent. Not until the end of the fourth century was Christianity proclaimed the official religion, and even thereafter many people long kept worshiping the traditional gods in private. Christianity eventually became the religion of the overwhelming majority in the empire because it solidified its hierarchical organization, drew believers from women as well as men of all classes, assured them of personal salvation, nourished a strong sense of community, and offered the social advantages of belonging to the emperors' religion. The transformation from polytheist empire into Christian state became by far the most influential legacy of Greco-Roman antiquity to later history.

■ **Relief Sculpture of Saturn from North Africa**

This sculpted and inscribed pillar depicts the divinity known to the Romans as Saturn and to the Carthaginians as Ba'al Hammon, from the cult of the Phoenician founders of Carthage. This syncretism (identifying deities as the same even though they carried different names in different places) was typical of ancient polytheism and allowed Roman and non-Roman cults to merge. The smaller figure below the god is sacrificing a sheep before an altar. The inscription dates the pillar to 323, a decade later than Constantine's conversion to Christianity. Such objects testifying to the prevalence of polytheistic cults remained common until the end of the fourth century, when the Christian emperors succeeded in suppressing most public manifestations of traditional religion.

(Copyright Martha Cooper/Peter Arnold, Inc.)

The Spread of Christianity

The empire's Christianization provoked passionate responses because ordinary people cared fervently about religion. It provided their best hope for private salvation in a dangerous world over which they had little control. In this regard, polytheists and Christians held some similar beliefs. Both assigned a potent role to spirits and demons as ever-present influences on daily life. For some, it seemed safest to ignore neither faith. For example, a silver spoon used in the worship of the polytheist forest spirit Faunus has been found engraved with a fish, the common symbol whose Greek spelling (*ichthys*) was taken as an acronym for the Greek words "Jesus Christ the Son of God, the Savior."

The differences between polytheists' and Christians' beliefs far outweighed their similarities. People debated earnestly whether there was one God or many and about what actions the divinity (or divinities) performed in the human world. Polytheists still participated in festivals and sacrifices to many different gods. Why, they asked, did these joyous occasions not satisfy Christians' yearnings for contact with divinity?

Equally incomprehensible to polytheists was belief in a savior who had failed to overthrow Roman rule and been executed as a common criminal. The traditional gods, they insisted, had bestowed a world empire on their worshipers. Moreover, they pointedly argued, cults such as that of the goddess Isis, after whom the worried

■ **Mosaic of Christ as Sun God**
This heavily damaged mosaic comes from a burial chamber in Rome that is now in the Vatican, under the basilica of St. Peter built by Constantine. It perhaps dates to the mid-third century. Christ appears in a guise traditional for polytheistic representations of the Sun god, especially the Greek Apollo: riding in a chariot pulled by horses, with rays of light shining forth around his head. This symbolism—God is light—had a long history, reaching back to ancient Egypt. Christian artists portrayed Jesus in this way because he had said, "I am the light of the world" (John 8:12). The cloak flaring from Christ's shoulder suggests the spread of his motion across the heavens. (Scala/Art Resource, NY.)

www.bedfordstmartins.com/huntconcise
See the ONLINE STUDY GUIDE for more help in analyzing this image.

Egyptian letter writer had been named, and philosophies such as Stoicism insisted that only the pure of heart could be admitted to their fellowship. Christians, by contrast, embraced the impure. Why, perplexed polytheists wondered, would anyone want to associate with sinners? In short, as the Greek philosopher Porphyry (c. 234–305) remarked, Christians had no right to claim they possessed the sole version of religious truth, for no doctrine that provided "a universal path to the liberation of the soul" had ever been devised.

The slow pace of religious change revealed how strong polytheism remained in the fourth century, especially at the highest social levels. In fact, the emperor Julian (r. 361–363) rebelled against his family's Christianity—hence he was known as Julian the Apostate—and tried to impose his philosophical brand of polytheism as the official faith. Deeply religious, he believed in a supreme deity corresponding to the aspirations of Greek philosophers: "This divine and completely beautiful universe, from heaven's highest arch to earth's lowest limit, is tied together by the continuous providence of god, has existed ungenerated eternally, and is imperishable forever." Julian's restoration of the traditional gods ended with his unexpected death while invading Persia.

The Christian emperors succeeding Julian undermined polytheism by slowly removing governmental support. In 382, Gratian (r. 375–383 in the west), who had shunned the title *pontifex maximus,* took the highly symbolic step of removing from the Senate house in Rome the Altar of Victory, which Augustus had placed there to remind senators of Rome's success under its ancestral religion; he also took the practical step of cutting off public funding for traditional sacrifices. Aurelius Symmachus (c. 340–402), a polytheist senator who held the prestigious post of prefect ("mayor") of Rome, objected to what he saw as an outrage against Rome's custom of religious diversity. Protesting eloquently against the new religious conformity, he argued: "We all have our own way of life and our own way of worship. . . . So vast a mystery cannot be approached by only one path."

Christianity replaced traditional polytheism as the state religion in 391 when the emperor Theodosius (r. 379–395 in the east) succeeded where his predecessors had failed: he enforced a ban on polytheist sacrifices, even if private individuals paid for the animals. Following Gratian in rejecting the emperor's traditional role as chief priest of the state's polytheist cults, he made divination by the inspection of entrails punishable as high treason and ordered that all polytheist temples be closed. But many shrines, such as the Parthenon in Athens, remained in use for a long time; only gradually were temples converted to churches during the fifth and sixth centuries. Christian emperors outlawed what they perceived as offensive beliefs, just as their polytheist predecessors had done, but they lacked the means to enforce religious uniformity. Non-Christian schools were not forced to close—the Academy, founded by Plato in Athens in the early fourth century B.C., endured for 140 years after Theodosius's reign—but Christians received advantages in government careers. Non-Christians became outsiders in an empire whose monarchs were devoted to the Christian deity.

Jews posed a special problem for the Christian emperors. Like polytheists, Jews rejected the new official religion. Yet they seemed entitled to special treatment because Jesus had been a Jew and because previous emperors had allowed Jews to practice their religion, even after Hadrian's refounding of Jerusalem as a Roman colony after putting down a fierce revolt there (132–135). Fourth-century and later emperors imposed legal restrictions on Jews. For example, they eventually banned Jews from holding government posts but still required them to assume the financial burdens of *curiales* without receiving the honor of curial status. By the late sixth century, they barred Jews from making wills, receiving inheritances, or testifying in court, increasing the pressure on Jews to convert.

Although these developments began the long process that made Jews into second-class citizens in later European history, they did not disable their faith. Magnificent synagogues continued to exist in Palestine, where a few Jews still lived (most had been dispersed throughout the cities of the empire and the lands beyond the eastern border). The study of Jewish law and lore flourished in this period, culminating in the learned texts known as the Palestinian and the Babylonian Talmuds (collections of scholarly opinions on Jewish law) and the scriptural commentaries of the Midrash (explanation of the meaning of the Hebrew Bible). These works of religious scholarship laid the foundation for later Jewish life and practice.

Christianity's official status attracted new believers, especially in the military. Soldiers now found it comfortable to convert and still serve in the army. Previously, Christian soldiers had sometimes created disciplinary problems. As one senior infantryman had said at his court-martial in 298 for abandoning his duties, "A Christian serving the Lord Christ should not serve the affairs of this world." Once the emperors had become Christians, however, soldiers could justify military duty as supporting Christ.

The main sources of Christianity's appeal were its religious and social values. Christianity offered believers a strong sense of community in this world as well as the promise of salvation in the next. Wherever they traveled or migrated, they could find a warm welcome in the local congregation (Map 6.2). The faith also won adherents by performing charitable works—in the tradition of Jews and some polytheist cults—especially for the poor, widows, and orphans. By the mid-third century, for example, Rome's congregation was supporting fifteen hundred widows and other impoverished persons. Christians' practice of fellowship and philanthropy was enormously important because people at that time had to depend mostly on friends and relatives for help; state-sponsored social services were rare and limited.

Scholars continue to debate the role of women in early Christianity, but it is clear that they were deeply involved. Augustine (354–430), bishop of Hippo in North Africa and perhaps the most influential theologian in Western history, eloquently recognized women's contribution to the strengthening of Christianity in a letter he wrote to the unbaptized husband of a baptized woman: "O you men, who fear all the burdens imposed by baptism. You are easily bested by your women. Chaste and devoted to the faith, it is their presence in large numbers that causes the church to

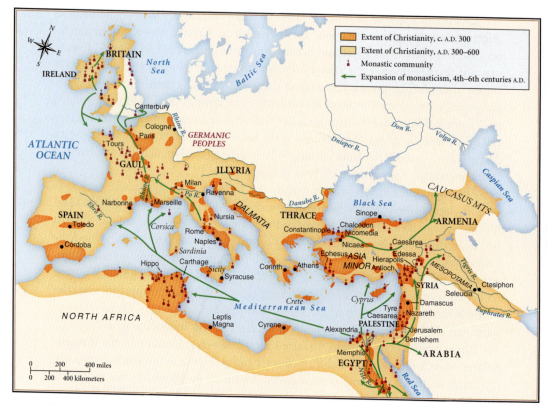

■ MAP 6.2 The Spread of Christianity, 300–600

Christians were distinctly a minority in the population of the Roman Empire in 300, although congregations existed in many cities and towns, especially in the eastern provinces. The emperor Constantine's conversion to Christianity in the early fourth century gave a boost to the new religion; it gained further strength during that century as the Christian emperors gave it imperial financial support and eliminated subsidies for the polytheist cults that had previously made up the religion of the state. By 600, the preaching of the church's missionaries and the money of the emperors had spread Christianity from one end of the empire's huge expanse of territory to the other. (Adapted from Henry Chadwick and G. R. Evans, *Atlas of the Christian Church* [Oxford: Andromeda Oxford Ltd., 1987], 28. Reproduced by permission of Andromeda Oxford Limited.)

grow." Some women earned exceptional renown and status by giving their property to their congregation or by renouncing marriage to dedicate themselves to Christ. Consecrated virgins and widows who chose not to remarry thus joined large donors as especially respected women. These women challenged the traditional social order, in which women were supposed to devote themselves to raising families. But even these sanctified women were excluded from leadership positions as the church's organization evolved into a hierarchy more and more resembling the male-dominated world of imperial rule.

The most crucial boost to Christianity's expansion came from its constructing a leadership hierarchy of male bishops, who replaced early Christianity's communal organization in which women could be leaders. Bishops had the authority to certify priests to conduct the church's sacraments, above all baptism and communion—rituals guaranteeing eternal life. Bishops also controlled their congregations' memberships and finances; much of the funds came from believers' gifts and bequests. Over time, bishops replaced *curiales* as the emperors' partners in local rule, deciding which towns received imperial subsidies. Regional councils of bishops exercised supreme authority in appointing new bishops and settling the doctrinal disputes that increasingly arose. The bishops in the largest cities became the most powerful leaders in the church. The main bishop of Carthage, for example, oversaw at least one hundred local bishops in the surrounding area. But it was the bishop of Rome who eventually emerged as the church's supreme leader in the western empire. The eastern church never agreed that this status entitled the bishop of Rome to control the entire Christian world, but his dominance in the west won him preeminent use there of the title previously applied to many bishops: *pope* (from *pappas*, Greek for "father"), the designation still used for the head of the Roman Catholic church.

The bishops of Rome identified a scriptural basis for their leadership over other bishops in the New Testament, where Jesus speaks to the Apostle Peter: "You are Peter, and upon this rock I will build my church. . . . I will entrust to you the keys of the kingdom of heaven. Whatever you bind on earth shall be bound in heaven. Whatever you loose on earth shall be loosed in heaven" (Matt. 16:18–19). Because Peter's name in Greek means "rock" and because Peter was believed to have been the first bishop of Rome, later bishops there claimed that this passage recognized their direct succession from Peter and thus their supremacy in the church.

Competing Visions of Religious Truth

Christians urgently disagreed about what they should believe. The church's expanding hierarchy struggled to create uniformity in belief and worship to ensure its members' spiritual purity and to maintain its authority over them. The bishops clashed over theology, however, and Christians never achieved doctrinal unity.

Disputes flared over what constituted *orthodoxy* (the official doctrines voted in by councils of bishops, from the Greek for "correct thinking") as opposed to *heresy* (dissent from official thinking, from the Greek for "private choice"). After Christianity became official, the emperor was ultimately responsible for enforcing orthodox creed (a summary of beliefs) and could use force to compel agreement if disputes became so serious that they provoked violence.

Questions about the nature of the Trinity of Father, Son, and Holy Spirit—seen by the orthodox as a unified, co-eternal, and identical divinity—caused the deepest divisions. *Arianism*, for example, generated fierce controversy for centuries. Named after its founder, Arius (c. 260–336), a priest from Alexandria in Egypt, this doctrine maintained that Jesus as God's son had not existed eternally; rather, God the Father had "begot" (created) his son from nothing and bestowed on him his special status. Thus Jesus was not co-eternal with God and not identical in nature with his father. This view implied that the Trinity was divisible and that Christianity's monotheism was not absolute. Arianism found widespread support, perhaps because it eliminated the difficulty of understanding how a son could be as old as his father and because its subordination of son to father corresponded to the norms of family life. Arius used popular songs to make his views known, and people everywhere became engrossed in the controversy. "When you ask for your change from a shopkeeper," one observer remarked in describing Constantinople, "he harangues you about the Begotten and the Unbegotten. If you inquire how much bread costs, the reply is that 'the Father is superior and the Son inferior.'"

Many Christians became so incensed over this apparent demotion of Jesus that Constantine had to intervene. In 325, he convened 220 bishops at the Council of Nicaea to settle the dispute. The majority of bishops voted to crack down on Arianism: they banished Arius to Illyria, a rough Balkan region, and declared that the Father and the Son were indeed "of one substance" and co-eternal. So complicated were the issues, however, that Constantine later changed his mind twice, first recalling Arius from exile and then reproaching him again not long after. The doctrine lived on: Constantine's third son, Constantius II (r. 337–361), favored Arianism, and his missionaries converted many of the Germanic peoples who later came to live in the empire.

Numerous other disputes about the nature of Christ fractured Christian unity, especially in the east. The orthodox position held that Jesus' divine and human natures commingled within his person but remained distinct. Monophysites (a Greek term for "single-nature believers") argued that the divine took precedence over the human and that Jesus had essentially only a single nature. They split from the orthodox hierarchy in the sixth century to found independent churches in Egypt (the Coptic church), Ethiopia, Syria, and Armenia.

Nestorius, who became bishop of Constantinople in 428, disagreed with the orthodox version of how Jesus' human and divine natures were related to his birth, insisting that Mary gave birth to the human that became the temple for the indwelling divine. Nestorianism enraged orthodox Christians by rejecting the designation *theotokos* (Greek for "bearer of God") as an appellation of Mary. The bishops of Alexandria and Rome had Nestorius deposed and his doctrines officially rejected at councils held in 430 and 431; they condemned his writings in 435. Nestorian bishops in the eastern empire refused to accept these decisions, however, and they formed a separate church centered in Persia, where for centuries Nestorian Christians flourished under the benign tolerance of non-Christian rulers. They later became important agents of cultural diffusion by establishing communities that still endure in Arabia, India, and China.

No heresy better illustrates the ferocity of Christian disunity than Donatism. A dispute arose in North Africa in the fourth century over whether to readmit to their old congregations those Christians who had cooperated with imperial au-

■ **Mosaic of a Family from Edessa**
This mosaic, found in a cave tomb, depicts an upper-class family of Edessa in the late Roman imperial period. Their names are given in Syriac, the dialect of Aramaic spoken in their region, and their colorful clothing reflects local Iranian traditions. Edessa was the capital of the small kingdom of Osrhoëne, which lay on the east bank of the Euphrates River between the Taurus Mountains and the Syrian desert. Rome annexed the kingdom in 216, and it became famous in Christian history because its king, Agbar (r. 179–216), was remembered as the first monarch to convert to Christianity, well before Constantine. By the early fourth century, the story had emerged that after

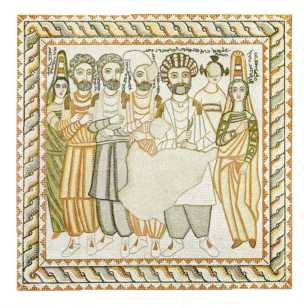

his death and resurrection, Jesus sent one of his disciples to Edessa, where the disciple painted a picture of Jesus that served as a talisman to protect the city from its enemies. The Byzantine emperors proclaimed themselves the heirs of King Agbar and the city's grant of divine protection.
(Photo courtesy Thames and Hudson Ltd., London, from *Vanished Civilizations.*)

thorities and had thus escaped martyrdom during the Great Persecution. Some North African Christians felt these lapsed members should be forgiven, but the Donatists (followers of the North African priest Donatus) insisted that the church should not be polluted with such "traitors." Most important, Donatists insisted, unfaithful priests and bishops could not administer the sacraments. So bitter was the clash that it even sundered Christian families. A son threatened his mother thus: "I will join Donatus's followers, and I will drink your blood."

These fiery emotions made it difficult for bishops to impose orthodoxy as religious truth. The Council of Chalcedon (an outskirt of Constantinople), at which the empress Pulcheria and her consort Marcian brought together more than five hundred bishops in 451, was the most important attempt to forge agreement. Its conclusions form the basis of what many Christians still accept as doctrine. At the time, it failed to create unanimity, especially in the eastern empire, where Monophysites were many.

No one person had a stronger impact on the establishment of the western church's orthodoxy and therefore on later Catholicism than Augustine (354–430). Born in North Africa to a Christian mother and a polytheist father, he began his career by teaching rhetoric at Carthage, where he fathered a son by a mistress; he was later befriended by the prominent polytheist noble Aurelius Symmachus after moving to Italy. In 386, he converted to Christianity under the influence of his mother and Ambrose (c. 339–397), the powerful bishop of Milan. In 395, he himself was appointed bishop of Hippo, but his reputation rests on his writings. By around 500, Augustine and other influential theologians such as Ambrose and Jerome (c. 345–420) had earned the informal title "church fathers" because their views were cited as authoritative in disputes over orthodoxy. Augustine became the most famous of this group of patristic (from the Greek for "father," *pater*) authors, and for the next thousand years his works would be the most influential texts in western Christianity besides the Bible. He wrote so prolifically in Latin about religion and philosophy that a later scholar was moved to declare: "The man lies who says he has read all your works."

Augustine's most influential exposition of Christianity's role in the world came in his *City of God,* a "large and arduous work," as he called it, written between 413 and 426. The book's immediate purpose was to refute those who expected that Christianity, like the traditional cults it had replaced, would guarantee Christians earthly success. For example, some polytheists asserted that the sack of Rome by Germanic marauders in 410 was divine retribution for abandoning Rome's traditional gods; Augustine sought to reassure Christians that their faith had not caused Rome's defeat. His larger aim, however, was to redefine the ideal state as a society of Christians. Not even Plato's doctrines offered a true path to purification, Augustine insisted, because the real opposition for humans was not between emotion and reason but between desire for earthly pleasures and spiritual purity. Emotion, especially love, was natural and desirable, but only when directed toward God. Humans were misguided to look for value in life on earth. Earthly life was transitory. Only life in God's city had meaning.

Nevertheless, Augustine wrote, secular law and government were required because humans are inherently imperfect. God's original creation in the Garden of Eden was full of goodness, but humans lost their initial perfection by inheriting a permanently flawed nature after Adam and Eve had disobeyed God. The doctrine of original sin—a subject of theological debate since at least the second century—meant that people suffered from a hereditary moral disease that turned the human will into a disruptive force. This corruption required governments to use coercion to suppress vice. Although desperately inferior to the divine ideal, civil government was necessary to impose moral order on the chaos of human life after the fall from grace in the Garden of Eden. The state therefore had a right to compel people to remain united to the church, by force if necessary.

Order in society was essential, Augustine argued; it could even turn to comparatively good purposes such inherently evil practices as slavery. Social institutions like slavery, in his view, were lesser evils than the violent troubles that would follow if disorder were to prevail. Moreover, it was Christians' duty to obey the emperor and participate in political life. Soldiers, too, had to follow their orders. Torture and capital punishment, however, were ruled out because the purpose of secular authority was to maintain a social order based on a moral order.

In *City of God,* Augustine sought to show a divine purpose, not always evident to humans, in the events of history. All that Christians could know with certainty was that history progressed toward an ultimate goal, but only God could know the meaning of each day's events. What could not be doubted was God's guiding power:

> To be truthful, I myself fail to understand why God created mice and frogs, flies and worms. Nevertheless, I recognize that each of these creatures is beautiful in its own way. For when I contemplate the body and limbs of any living creature, where do I not find proportion, number, and order exhibiting the unity of concord? Where one discovers proportion, number, and order, one should look for the craftsman.

The repeated *I* in this passage exemplifies the intense personal engagement Augustine brought to matters of faith and doctrine.

Next to the nature of Christ, the question of how to understand and regulate sexual desire presented Christians with the thorniest problem in the quest for religious truth. Augustine became the most influential source of the doctrine that sex automatically enmeshed human beings in evil and that they should therefore practice *asceticism* (self-denial, from the Greek *askesis,* meaning "training"). Augustine knew from personal experience how difficult it was to accept this doctrine. In fact, he revealed in his autobiographical work *Confessions,* written about 397, that he felt a deep conflict between his sexual desire and his religious philosophy. Only after a long period of doubt, he explained, did he find the inner strength to pledge his future chastity as part of his conversion to Christianity.

He advocated sexual abstinence as the purest choice for Christians because he believed that Adam and Eve's disobedience in the Garden of Eden had forever ruined the original harmony God created between human will and human passions. According to Augustine, God punished his disobedient children by making sexual desire a disruptive force that humans could never completely control through will. Although he reaffirmed the value of marriage in God's plan, he added that sexual intercourse even between loving spouses carried the melancholy reminder of humanity's fall from grace. A married couple should "descend with a certain sadness" to the task of procreation, the only acceptable reason for sex; sexual pleasure could never be a human good.

This doctrine ennobled virginity and sexual renunciation as the highest virtues; in the words of Jerome, they counted as "daily martyrdom." Such self-chosen holiness earned women benefits beyond status in the church: they could, for example, demand more education in Hebrew and Greek to read the Bible. By the end of the fourth century, virginity had become so significant for Christian virtue that congregations began to demand virgin priests and bishops.

The Beginning of Christian Monasticism

Christian asceticism reached its peak in monasticism. The word *monk* (from Greek *monos*, "single, solitary") described the essential experience of monasticism: men and women withdrawing from society to live a life of extreme self-denial imitating Jesus' suffering, demonstrating their devotion to God, and praying for divine mercy on the world. The earliest monks lived alone, but soon they formed communities for mutual support in the pursuit of ascetic holiness (see Map 6.2).

Polytheist and Jewish ascetics, motivated by philosophy and religion, had long existed. What made Christian monasticism distinctive were the huge numbers of people it attracted and the high status that monks garnered. Leaving their families and congregations, they renounced sex, worshiped frequently, wore the roughest clothes, and ate barely enough to survive, aiming to win an inner peace detached from daily concerns. They reported, however, that they constantly struggled against fantasies of earthly delights, dreaming of plentiful, tasty food more often than of sex.

The earliest Christian ascetics emerged in the late third century in Egypt. Antony (c. 251–356), from a well-to-do family, was among the first. One day, he abruptly abandoned all his property after hearing a sermon based on Jesus' admonition to a rich young man to sell his possessions and give the proceeds to the poor (Matt. 19:21). Forsaking his duty to see his sister married, he placed her in a home for unmarried women and spent his life alone in barren territory, demonstrating his excellence through worshiping God.

Monasticism appealed for many reasons, but above all because it gave ordinary people a way to achieve excellence and recognition. This opportunity seemed all the more valuable after Constantine's conversion and the end of the persecutions. Becoming a monk—a living martyrdom—served as the substitute for a martyr's death and emulated the sacrifice of Christ. Individual or *eremetic* (hence *hermit*) monks spared no pains in securing fame. In Syria, for example, "holy women" and "holy men" attracted great attention with feats of pious endurance. Symeon the Stylite (390–459) lived atop a tall pillar (*stylos* in Greek) for thirty years, preaching to people gathered below his perch. Egyptian Christians believed that their monks' wondrous piety made them living heroes ensuring the annual flooding of the Nile, the duty once associated with the pharaohs' divine power. Exceptionally famous ascetics exercised even greater influence after death. Their relics—body parts or clothing—became treasured sources of protection and healing. Expressing the living power of saints (people venerated after their deaths for their special holiness), relics gave believers faith in divine favor.

The earliest monks followed the example of Antony in living alone. In about 323, Pachomius in Upper Egypt organized the first monastic community. This "coenobitic," or "life in common," monasticism—single-gender settlements of men or women bringing monks together to encourage one another along the hard road to holiness—dominated Christian asceticism ever after. Monasteries were often

■ **Monastery of St. Catherine at Mount Sinai**

The Byzantine emperor Justinian (r. 527–565) built a wall to enclose the building of this monastery in the desert at the foot of the twin peaks of Mount Sinai (on the peninsula between Egypt and Arabia). Jews and Christians regarded this spot as holy because Moses had received the Ten Commandments there during the Hebrews' wanderings after their exodus from Egypt. Justinian supported the monastery to promote orthodoxy in a region dominated by Monophysite Christians. The monks at St. Catherine's developed a reputation for exceptional piety, expressed by their near-constant repetition of a simple prayer to Jesus. The monastery gained its name in the ninth century when the story was circulated that angels had recently brought the body of Catherine of Alexandria there. Catherine was said to have been martyred in the fourth century for refusing to marry the emperor because, in her words, she was the bride of Christ; no contemporary sources record her story. (Erich Lessing/Art Resource, NY.)

built close together to divide their labor, with women making clothing, for example, while men farmed.

All monasteries imposed military-style discipline, but they differed in the harshness of their austerity and contact with the outside world. The most isolationist groups arose in the eastern empire, but the followers of Martin of Tours (c. 316–397), an ex-soldier famed for his pious deeds, founded communities in the west as austere as any eastern ones. Basil ("the Great") of Caesarea in Asia Minor (c. 330–379) started a different tradition: monasteries serving society. He required monks to perform charitable deeds, leading to the foundation of the first hospitals, attached to monasteries.

A relatively mild code of monastic conduct became the standard in the west, influencing almost every area of Catholic worship. Called the Benedictine rule after its creator, Benedict of Nursia in central Italy (c. 480–553), this code prescribed a daily routine of prayer, scriptural readings, and manual labor. The rule divided the day into seven parts, each with a compulsory service of prayers and lessons, the *office*. Unlike harsher codes, Benedict's did not isolate the monks from the outside world or deprive them of sleep, adequate food, or warm clothing. Although it gave the abbot (the head monk) full authority, it instructed him to listen to what every member of the community, even the youngest monk, had to say before deciding important matters. He was not allowed to beat them for lapses in discipline, as sometimes happened under other, stricter systems. Communities of women, such as those founded by Basil's sister Macrina and Benedict's sister Scholastica, usually followed the rules of the male monasteries, with an emphasis on the decorum thought necessary for women.

The thousands of Christians who became monks from the fourth century onward joined monasteries for social as well as theological reasons. Some had been given as babies to monasteries by parents who could not raise them or were fulfilling pious vows, a practice called *oblation*. Jerome once gave this advice to a mother about her daughter:

> Let her be brought up in a monastery, let her live among virgins, let her learn to avoid swearing, let her regard lying as an offense against God, let her be ignorant of the world, let her live the angelic life, while in the flesh let her be without the flesh, and let her suppose that all human beings are like herself.

When she reaches adulthood as a virgin, he added, she should avoid the baths so she would not be seen naked or give her body pleasure by dipping in the warm pools. Jerome enunciated traditional values favoring males when he promised that God would reward the mother with the birth of sons in compensation for the dedication of her daughter. But he also said, "[As monks] we evaluate people's virtue not by their gender but by their character, and deem those to be worthy of the greatest glory who have renounced both status and riches."◆

The monasteries' prickly independence threatened the church's hierarchy. Bishops resented devoted members of their congregations withdrawing into monasteries, not least because they bestowed their gifts and bequests on their new community rather than on their local churches. Moreover, monks challenged bishops' authority because holy men and women earned their special status not by having it bestowed by the church's leaders but through their own actions. At bottom, how-

---

◆ For a primary source that further reveals Jerome's ideas on gender roles, see Document 17, "Letter 107."

ever, bishops and monks did share a spiritual goal—salvation and service to God. While polytheists had enjoyed immediate access to their gods, who were thought to visit the earth constantly, Christians worshiped a transcendent God removed from this world. Monks bridged the chasm between the human and the divine by interceding with God to show mercy on the faithful.

Germanic Kingdoms in the West

The regional differences between western and eastern monasticism found a parallel in the diverging social and political characteristics of the divided empire. The fragmentation of the empire was especially significant in western Europe. The migrations of Germanic peoples transformed politics, society, and the economy there. Two strong desires drew these diverse groups into Roman territory: to flee the brutal attacks of the Huns (nomads from the steppes of central Asia) and to benefit from the empire's prosperity. By the 370s, their influx had swollen to a flood, provoking widespread violence in the western empire. As the imperial government's ability to maintain order weakened, Germanic peoples underwent a remarkable transition, transforming themselves from vaguely defined and organized tribes into kingdoms with separate ethnic identities. By the 470s, one of their commanders ruled Italy. That political change has been said to mark the "fall of the Roman Empire." In fact, the lasting effects of the interactions of these Germanic peoples with the diverse peoples of western Europe and North Africa are better understood as a political, social, and cultural transformation that made them the heirs of the western Roman Empire and led to the formation of medieval Europe.

Germanic Migrations

At first, the fourth-century emperors encouraged the migrations. Like their predecessors, they recruited Germanic warriors for the Roman army. By the late fourth century, a flood of noncombatants had followed these warriors into the empire (Map 6.3). The western government's failure either to absorb the newcomers or expel them proved its undoing.

Economic failure rooted in the third-century political crisis hampered the emperors in dealing with the migrations. They had demanded higher taxes during the crisis, forcing landowners to demand higher payments from their *coloni*. Many of these tenants responded by illegally running away. Eventually, landowners also had to run away if they could not pay their taxes. This flight left farms deserted; as much as 20 percent of arable territory lay unfarmed in the most seriously affected areas. The government squeezed the farmers who remained to pay even more, but financial weakness crippled its ability to hire soldiers to prevent more Germanic peoples from entering the empire.

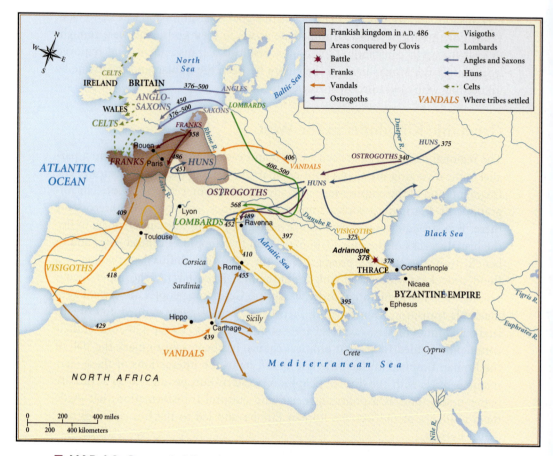

■ **MAP 6.3 Germanic Migrations and Invasions of the Fourth and Fifth Centuries**

The movements of Germanic peoples into imperial territory transformed the Roman Empire. This phenomenon began as early as the reign of Domitian (r. 81–96), but in the fourth century it became a pressing problem for the emperors when the Huns' attacks pushed Germanic bands from their homelands in eastern Europe into the empire's northern provinces. Maps offer only schematic representations of dynamic processes such as the Germanic migrations and invasions, but this map does indicate the variety of peoples involved, the wide extent of imperial territory that they affected, and the concentration of their effects in the western section of the empire.

Germanic bands crossed into imperial territory not in carefully planned invasions but often fleeing for their lives. Fourth-century raids by the Huns drove them from their traditional homelands east of the Rhine and north of the Danube. Groups of men, women, and children crossed the Roman border as refugees. Their prospects looked grim because they came with no political or military unity, no clear plan, and not even a shared sense of identity.

Loosely organized as vaguely democratic and often warring tribes, they shared only the Germanic origins of their languages (hence the use of *Germanic* to designate them as a whole) and their terror of the Huns. The migrating Germanic peoples developed their respective ethnic identities, by which we designate them today, only after they were unable to assimilate into Roman society, instead settling in groups forming new states within the imperial frontiers. The quest for new homes forced them to develop a more tightly structured society to govern their new lands.

Previously, these peoples lived in small settlements as farmers, herders, and ironworkers; they had no experience running kingdoms. The groups were dominated by men averse to strong central authority. Even groups with clearly defined leaders operated as chiefdoms, whose members could be only persuaded, not compelled, to follow the chief. Chiefs maintained their leadership by giving gifts to their followers and by leading warriors on frequent raids to seize cattle and slaves.

Germanic society was patriarchal: men headed households and exercised authority over women, children, and slaves. Germanic women were valued for their ability to bear children, and rich men could have more than one wife and perhaps concubines as well. A clear division of labor made women responsible for agriculture, pottery making, and the production of textiles, while men worked iron and herded cattle. Warfare and its accompaniments preoccupied Germanic men, as their ritual sacrifices of weapons—preserved in northern European bogs—have shown. Women had certain rights of inheritance and could control property, and married women received a dowry of one-third of their husbands' property.

Households were grouped into clans on kinship lines based on maternal as well as paternal descent. The members of a clan were supposed to keep peace among themselves, and violence against a fellow clan member was the worst possible offense. Clans in turn grouped themselves into tribes, multiethnic coalitions that non-Germans could join. Different tribes identified themselves primarily by their clothing, hairstyles, jewelry, weapons, religious cults, and oral stories.

Assemblies of free male warriors provided the tribes' only traditional form of political organization. Tribal leaders' functions were mostly religious and military. Tribes tended to be unstable groupings prone to interclan conflict. Clans frequently feuded, with bloody consequences. Tribal law tried to set limits to the violence acceptable in seeking revenge, but Germanic law was oral, not written, and thus open to wide dispute.

The Germanic migrations increased when the Huns invaded eastern Europe in the fourth century. Distantly related to the Hiung-nu people who had attacked China and Persia, these Turkish-speaking nomads arrived on the Russian steppes shortly before 370. They excelled as raiders, launching cavalry attacks far and wide. Their victims were aghast at their skulls, elongated from having been bound between boards in infancy, their faces grooved with decorative scars, and their arms fearsome with elaborate tattoos. Huns' prowess as horsemen made them legendary. They could shoot their powerful bows while riding full tilt, and they could remain on horseback for days, sleeping atop their horses and securing snacks of raw meat between their thighs and the animal's back.

The emperors in Constantinople bribed the Huns to spare eastern territory. The Huns then abandoned their nomadic lifestyle and became landlords, cooperating among themselves to create an empire north of the Danube that subjugated local farmers and siphoned off their agricultural surplus. The Huns' most ambitious leader, Attila (r. c. 440–453), extended their domains from the Caspian Sea to the Alps and even farther west. He led his forces as far as Paris in 451 and into northern Italy the next year. At Attila's death in 453, the Huns lost their fragile cohesiveness and faded from history. By this time, however, the pressure that they had put on the Germanic peoples had already begun the migrations that would transform the western empire.

The people who, after entering imperial territory, coalesced to create an identity as Visigoths were the first to experience what became the common pattern of the migrations: some desperate Germanic people in barely organized groups would petition for asylum, and the empire would accept them in return for military service. Shredded by constant Hunnic raids, in 376 the Visigoths begged the eastern emperor Valens (r. 364–378) to let them migrate into the Balkans. They received permission on condition that their warriors enlist in the Roman army to help repel the Huns.

As events proved, the final part of the pattern was for such deals to fall apart disastrously. The plight of the Visigoths started this dismal trend. When greedy and incompetent Roman officers charged with helping the refugees neglected them, they starved; the officials forced them to sell some of their own people into slavery in return for dogs to eat. In desperation, the Visigoths rebelled. In 378, they defeated and killed Valens in battle at Adrianople in Thrace (see Map 6.3). His successor, Theodosius I (r. 379–395), then had to renegotiate the deal from a position of weakness. His concessions established the terms that other bands would seek for themselves and that would create new, self-conscious identities for them: permission to settle permanently inside the imperial borders, freedom to establish a kingdom under their own laws, large annual payments from the emperors, and designation as "federates" (allies) expected to help protect the empire.

Soon realizing they could not afford to keep this agreement, the eastern emperors decided to force the migrating bands westward. They cut off the subsidies and threatened full-scale war unless the refugees decamped. Following the path of least resistance, the disgruntled Visigoths entered the western empire; neither the western empire nor they would ever be the same. In 410, they stunned the world by sacking Rome itself. When their commander Alaric demanded all the city's gold, silver, movable property, and foreign slaves, the Romans asked, "What will be left to us?" "Your lives," he replied.

Too weak to defeat the invaders, the western emperor Honorius (r. 395–423) in 418 reluctantly agreed to settle the Visigoths in southwestern Gaul (present-day France), saving face by calling them federates. The Visigoths then completed their transition from tribal society to formal kingdom by doing what no Germanic group

■ Eagle *Fibulae* (Brooches) from Visigothic Spain

Visigothic women in their new kingdom in Spain signaled their ethnic identity by their style of dress, in particular through the old Germanic tradition of fastening their clothing at the shoulders with brooches. These expensive examples, fashioned from gold inlaid with semiprecious stones, also expressed elite status. The choice of eagles as a frequent Gothic brooch design reveals how ethnic identity can be constructed through cultural interaction: Goths probably adopted the eagle as a symbol of power from Hunnic and Roman traditions.
(Walters Art Gallery, Baltimore.)

had done before: establishing an ethnic identity and organizing a state. They followed the model of Roman emperors by emphasizing mutually beneficial relations with the social elite. Romans could join that elite and use time-tested ways of flattering their superiors to gain advantages. Sidonius Apollinaris, for example, a well-connected noble from Lyon (c. 430–479), once purposely lost a backgammon game to the Visigothic king as a way of gaining a favor from the ruler. Honorius tried, without much success, to limit Germanic influence on Roman citizens by ordering them not to adopt Visigothic clothing styles.

How the new Germanic kingdoms such as that of the Visigoths financed their states has become a much debated question. The older view is that the newcomers became landed proprietors by forcing Roman landowners to turn over a portion of their lands, slaves, and movable property to them. Recent scholarship argues that Roman taxpayers in the kingdoms did not have to give up their lands but were instead made directly responsible for paying the expenses of the Germanic soldiers, who lived mostly in urban garrisons. Whatever the new arrangements were, the Visigoths found them profitable enough to expand into Spain within a century of establishing themselves in southwestern Gaul.

The western imperial government's settlement with the Visigoths emboldened other groups to seize territory and create kingdoms and identities (see Map 6.4). An especially dramatic episode began in 406 when the Vandals, fleeing the Huns, cut a swath through Gaul all the way to the Spanish coast. (The modern word

■ Mosaic of Upper-Class Country Life

This fourth-century mosaic, measuring fourteen-by-eighteen feet, covered a floor in a country villa at Carthage in North Africa. It portrays the life of an elite couple on their estate at different seasons of the year. Their house, resplendent with towers and a second-story colonnade, stands as a fortified retreat at the center. The top third of the mosaic shows the lady of the house sitting in parklike surroundings while her servants and tenants tend to animals; winter activities are shown at the left, summer activities at the right. In the middle third, hunters pursue game. The bottom section shows the lady in a springtime setting (on the left) and her husband sitting (on the right) amid activities characteristic of autumn. A servant is handing the husband a roll addressed "to the master Julius," revealing his name. Such estates provided security and prosperity for their owners but also made desirable prizes for the Vandal invaders of North Africa. (Le Musée du Bardo, Tunis.)

vandal, meaning "destroyer of property," perpetuates their reputation for warlike ruthlessness.) In 429, eighty thousand Vandals ferried to North Africa, where they soon broke their agreement to become federates and captured the region. Their kingdom caused tremendous hardship for local Africans by confiscating property rather than allowing owners to make regular payments to "ransom" their land. The Vandals further weakened the western emperors by seizing the region's traditional tax payments of grain and vegetable oil and disrupting the importation of grain to Rome; they also built a navy strong enough to threaten the eastern empire. In 455, they set the western government tottering by plundering Rome.

Other small groups also managed to break off distant pieces of the weakened western empire. The most significant such band for later history was the Anglo-Saxons. Composed of Angles from what is now Denmark and Saxons from northwestern Germany, this mixed group invaded Britain in the 440s after the Roman army had been recalled from the province to defend Italy against the Visigoths. They established their kingdoms by wresting territory away from the indigenous Celtic peoples and the remaining Roman inhabitants. Gradually, Anglo-Saxon culture replaced the local traditions of the island's eastern regions: the Celts there lost most of their language, and Christianity survived only in Wales and Ireland.

By the time Theodoric (r. 493–526) established the Ostrogothic kingdom in Italy, there was no longer a formally recognized western Roman emperor and never would be again. This political change has traditionally, but simplistically, been called the "fall of Rome" from the best-selling, multivolume work that made it famous—*The Decline and Fall of the Roman Empire* by the English historian Edward Gibbon (1737–1794). The real story's details, however, reveal the complexity of the political transformation of the western empire under new Germanic regimes. The weakness of the imperial army in the west had obliged the western emperors to employ Germanic officers to lead the defense of Italy. By the middle of the fifth century, one Germanic general after another decided who would serve as puppet emperor under his control. The last such unfortunate "emperor" was a usurper; his father, Orestes, a former aide to Attila, had rebelled against the emperor Julius Nepos in 475 and raised his young son to the throne. He gave the boy emperor the name Romulus Augustulus, meant to recall Rome's founder and its first emperor. In 476, after a dispute over pay, the Germanic soldiers murdered Orestes and deposed the boy; pitied as an innocent child, Romulus was provided with safe refuge and a generous pension. The rebels' leader, Odoacer, did not appoint another emperor. Instead, seeking to block Nepos's campaign to regain the throne, he had the Roman Senate petition Zeno, the eastern emperor, to recognize his leadership in return for his acknowledging Zeno as sole emperor. Odoacer thereafter oversaw Italy nominally as the eastern emperor's viceroy, but in fact he ruled as he liked.

In 488, Zeno plotted to rid himself of another ambitious Germanic general living in Constantinople—Theodoric—by sending him to fight Odoacer, whom the emperor had found too independent. Eliminating Odoacer by 493, Theodoric went on to establish his own state to rule Italy from the traditional capital at Ravenna until his death in 526. Thus the Ostrogothic kingdom was founded. Theodoric and his Ostrogothic nobles wanted to enjoy the empire's luxury and prestige, not destroy them. They therefore left the Senate and consulships intact. An Arian Christian, Theodoric followed Constantine's example by announcing a policy of religious toleration: "No one can be forced to believe against his will." In sum, like other Germanic rulers, he appropriated the traditions of the Roman past that would support the stability of his own rule. For this reason, modern scholars consider it more accurate to speak of the western empire's "transformation" than its "fall" (Map 6.4).

The Franks were the Germanic people who transformed Roman Gaul into Francia (from which the name *France* comes). Roman emperors had allowed some

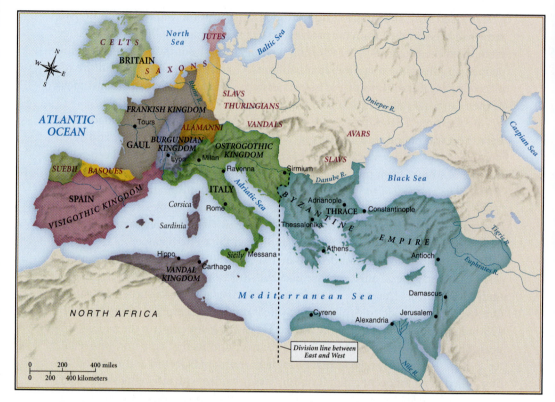

■ **MAP 6.4 Peoples and Kingdoms of the Roman World, c. 526**

The provinces of the Roman Empire had always been home to a population diverse in language and ethnicity. By the early sixth century, the territory of the western empire had become a welter of diverse political units as well. Italy and most of the former western provinces were kingdoms organized and ruled by Germanic peoples who had moved into former imperial territory over the past several centuries. The eastern empire (the Byzantine Empire) remained under the political control of the emperor in Constantinople. Justinian, who ascended the Byzantine throne in 527, made it his mission to try to reunite the eastern and western halves of the empire by force.

www.bedfordstmartins.com/huntconcise   See the ONLINE STUDY GUIDE for more help in analyzing this map.

of them to settle in a northern border region (now in the Netherlands) in the early fourth century; by the late fifth century, they were a major presence in Gaul. Their king Clovis (r. 485–511) in 507 overthrew the Visigothic king in southern Gaul with support from the eastern Roman emperor. When the emperor named him an honorary consul, Clovis celebrated this ancient honor by having himself crowned with a diadem in the style of the dominate's emperors. He carved out western Europe's largest Germanic kingdom in what is today mostly France, overshadowing the neighboring and rival kingdoms of the Burgundians and Alamanni in eastern Gaul. Probably persuaded by his wife Clotilda, a Christian, to believe that God had helped him defeat the Alamanni, Clovis proclaimed himself an orthodox Christian and renounced Arianism. To build stability, he carefully fostered good relations with the bishops as the regime's intermediaries with the population.

Clovis's dynasty, called *Merovingian* after the legendary Frankish ancestor Merovech, foreshadowed the kingdom that would emerge much later as the forerunner of modern France. The dynasty endured for another two hundred years, far longer than most other Germanic royalty in the west. The Merovingians survived so long because they created a workable combination between Germanic military might and Roman social and legal traditions.

Mixing Roman and Germanic Traditions

Western Europe's political transformation—the replacement of imperial government by Germanic kingdoms—fueled equally innovative social and cultural transformations. The Germanic newcomers and the former Roman provincials created new ways of life combined from the old. This process proved particularly potent in developing new law codes and altering the economic landscape.

Some of these changes were intentional. The Visigoth king Athaulf (r. 410–415), having married a Roman noblewoman, reflected on his goals:

> At the start I wanted to erase the Romans' name and turn their land into a Gothic empire, doing myself what Augustus had done. But I have learned that the Goths' free-wheeling wildness will never accept the rule of law, and that state with no law is no state. Thus, I have more wisely chosen another path to glory: reviving the Roman name with Gothic vigor. I pray that future generations will remember me as the founder of a Roman restoration.

Roman law was the most influential precedent for Germanic kings in their efforts to build stable new states. They had never before had written laws; now that they had transformed themselves into monarchs ruling Romans as well as their own people, they wanted legal codes to promote justice and order. The Visigothic kings were the first Germanic leaders to create a written law code. Composed in Latin and heavily influenced by Roman legal traditions, it made the payment of fines and compensation the primary method for resolving disputes.◆

Clovis also emphasized written law for the Merovingian kingdom. His code, published in Latin, promoted social order through clear penalties for specific crimes. In particular, he formalized a system of fines intended to defuse feuds and vendettas between individuals and between clans. The most prominent component of this system was *Wergild*, the payment a murderer had to make as compensation for his

---

◆ For excerpts from one of the most comprehensive early Germanic law codes, see Document 18, "The Burgundian Code."

crime. Most of the money was paid to the victim's kin, but the king received perhaps one-third of the amount.

Because law codes enshrine social values, the differing payments offer a glimpse of the relative social value of different categories of people in Clovis's kingdom. The penalty for murdering a woman of childbearing age, a boy under twelve, or a man in the king's retinue was a massive fine of six hundred gold coins, enough to buy six hundred cattle. The fine for murdering a woman past childbearing age (specified as sixty years), a young girl, or a freeborn man was two hundred gold coins; for murdering ordinary slaves, thirty-five.

The migrations that transformed the west harmed its already weak economy. The Vandals damaged many towns in Gaul, hastening the decline of urban areas. In the countryside, now outside the control of any central government, wealthy Romans built sprawling villas on extensive estates staffed by tenants bound to the land like slaves. The owners of these establishments strove to operate them as self-sufficient units by producing all they needed, defending themselves against raids, and keeping their distance from any authorities. Craving isolation, the owners shunned membership on city councils and tax collection—the public services that had supplied the lifeblood of Roman administration—although the wealthiest boasted an annual income rivaling that of an entire region in the old western empire. In short, Roman provincial government withered, but the new kingdoms never matured sufficiently to replace its services.

A few provincial Romans helped transmit ancient learning to later ages. Cassiodorus (c. 490–585), for one, founded a monastery on his ancestral estate in Italy in the 550s after a career in imperial administration. He gave the monks the task of copying manuscripts to keep their contents alive as old texts disintegrated. His own book *Institutions,* composed in the 550s to guide his monks, encapsulated the respect for tradition that kept classical traditions alive: in prescribing the works a person of superior education should read, it included ancient secular texts as well as Scripture and Christian literature. The most strenuous effort to perpetuate the Roman past, however, came from the eastern empire.

The Byzantine Empire in the East

The eastern Roman Empire avoided the massive transformations that reshaped western Europe. Trade routes and diverse agriculture kept the east richer than the west, and the eastern emperors minimized the effect of the Hunnic and Germanic migrations on their territory and blunted the aggression of the Sassanid kingdom in Persia with force, diplomacy, and bribery. By the early sixth century, the empire's eastern half had achieved such power, riches, and ambition that historians have given it a new name, the Byzantine Empire; its emperors continued until 1453.

These rulers saw themselves as perpetuating the Roman Empire and guarding its culture against barbarism. Justinian (r. 527–565), the most famous of the early

Byzantine emperors, took this mission seriously: he nearly bankrupted the east with wars to recover the west, and he sought to impose religious orthodoxy as a guarantee of divine favor in unsettled times. One especially significant contribution of the early Byzantine Empire to later history was its crucial role in preserving classical literature and learning, which nearly disappeared in the west.

Byzantine Society

The sixth-century Byzantine Empire enjoyed an economic vitality that western Europe had lost. Members of the elite spent freely on luxury goods imported from China and India: silk, precious stones, and prized spices such as pepper. The largest cities—Constantinople, Damascus, and Alexandria—teemed with merchants from far and wide, and their churches' soaring domes testified to Byzantine confidence in God's power.

Continuing a Roman imperial tradition, the Byzantine emperors sponsored massive religious festivals and entertainments to rally public support. Rich and poor alike crowded city squares, theaters, and hippodromes on these spirited occasions; chariot racing aroused the hottest passions. Constantinople's residents, for example, divided themselves into competitive factions—called Blues and Greens after the racing colors of their favorite charioteers—that combined religious and sports rivalries: orthodox Christians became Blues, Monophysites Greens. They brawled with one another as frequently over theological arguments as over race results.

The eastern emperors did everything they could to preserve "Romanness." They feared that contact with Germanic peoples would "barbarize" their empire, as it had done in the west. Like the western emperors, they employed Germanic and Hunnic mercenaries, but they tried to keep Germanic and Hunnic customs from influencing the empire's residents. Clothing styles were a sore point. Like the western emperor Honorius in the early fifth century, eastern emperors forbade the capital's residents to wear Germanic-style outfits (especially heavy boots and clothing made from animal furs) instead of traditional Roman garb (sandals or light shoes and robes).

Most people in Byzantine society saw themselves as heirs to ancient Roman culture, and they called themselves "Romans." At the same time, they spoke Greek as their native language and used Latin only for government and military communication. (The Latin-speaking western empire referred to them as "Greeks.") In fact, Byzantine society was deeply multilingual and multiethnic, so preserving an unchanging Roman identity was a hopeless goal. Many people spoke their traditional languages, such as Phrygian and Cappadocian in western Asia Minor, Armenian farther east, and Syriac and other Aramaic dialects in the Levant. Travelers around the empire heard a potpourri of languages, saw varying styles of dress, and encountered numerous ethnic groups.

For the Byzantines, Romanness presupposed Christianity, but their theological diversity rivaled their ethnic variety. Bitter controversies over doctrine divided eastern Christians, and emperors joined forces with bishops to impose orthodoxy. They generally preferred words to swords to pressure heretics to accept orthodox theology, but they resolutely employed violence when persuasion failed. Resorting to such extreme measures was necessary, they believed, to save lost souls and preserve the empire's divine goodwill. The persecution of nonorthodox Christian subjects by Christian emperors demonstrated the passions that the quest for a unitary identity sometimes ignited.

In the patriarchal society of the Byzantine Empire, most women followed ancient Mediterranean precedent by concentrating on the support of their households and minimizing contact with men outside that circle. Law barred women from fulfilling many public functions, such as witnessing wills. Subject to the authority of their fathers and husbands, women veiled their heads (though not their faces) to show modesty. Christian theology made divorce more difficult and discouraged remarriage, even for widows. Stiffer legal penalties for sexual offenses also developed. Female prostitution remained legal, but emperors raised the penalties for people forcing women (children or slaves) to become prostitutes.

As always, women in the imperial family lived by different rules: they could sometimes achieve a prominence unattainable for their workaday contemporaries. Theodora (d. 548), wife of the emperor Justinian, exemplified the influence women could achieve in Byzantine monarchy. Undeterred by her ignoble background (daughter of a bear trainer and then an actress with a scandalous reputation), she rose to rival anyone in influence and wealth. Some ancient sources suggest that she had a hand in every aspect of Justinian's rule, advising him on personnel choices for his administration, pushing for her religious views in the continuing disputes over Christian doctrine, and rallying his courage at time of crisis. John Lydus, a high-ranking administrator, judged her "superior in intelligence to any man."

Byzantine government aggravated social divisions because it provided services according to people's wealth. Its complicated hierarchy required reams of paperwork and fees for countless transactions, from commercial permits to legal grievances. Without bribery, nothing got done. People with status and money found this process easy: they relied on their social connections to get a hearing from the right official and on their wealth to pay bribes to move matters along quickly. Whether seeking preferential treatment or just spurring administrators to do what they were supposed to do, the rich could make the system work.

The poor, by contrast, could not afford the large bribes that government officials routinely expected. Interest rates were high, and people could incur backbreaking debt to raise the cash needed to persuade officials to carry out their duties. This system saved the emperors money: they could pay civil servants paltry salaries because bribes from the public supplemented their incomes. John Lydus, for example, reported that he earned thirty times his annual salary in payments from petitioners during his first year in office. To keep unlimited extortion from destroying the system, the emperors published an official list of the maximum bribes

■ Theodora and Her Court in Ravenna

This colorful mosaic shows the empress Theodora (c. 500–548) and her court. It was placed on one wall of the chancel of the church of St. Vitale in Ravenna, facing the matching scene of her husband, Justinian, and his attendants (see page 212). Theodora wears the jewels, pearls, and rich robes characteristic of Byzantine monarchs. She extends in her hands a gem-encrusted bowl, evidently a present to the church; her gesture imitates the gift-giving of the Magi to the baby Jesus, the scene illustrated on the hem of her garment. The circle around her head, called a nimbus *(Latin for "cloud"), indicates special holiness.* (Scala/Art Resource, NY.)

that employees could exact. Overall, however, their approach to government service generated enormous hostility among poorer subjects and did nothing to encourage public morale for the emperors' plans for glory and conquest.

The Reign of Justinian, 527–565

Justinian dreamed of resurrecting the empire as it had been under Augustus. Born to a Latin-speaking family in a small Balkan town, he rose rapidly in imperial service until 527, when he succeeded his uncle as emperor. During his reign he launched military expeditions to try to reclaim western Europe and North Africa. His desire to build imperial glory led him to embellish Constantinople with magnificent and costly architecture. He was also an intellectual—the first on the throne since Julian in the 360s—whose passion for the law and theology drove him to push reforms with the same goals as all his predecessors, whether Christian or polytheist: to preserve social order based on hierarchy and maintain heaven's favor for himself and his subjects.

Instead, unfortunately, Justinian's bold projects created social unrest, not least because of their cost. So heavy and unpopular were his taxes and so ruthless was his tax collector, John of Cappadocia, that they provoked a major riot in 532. Known as the "Nika Riot," it arose when the Blue and Green factions gathering in Constantinople's hippodrome to watch chariot races unexpectedly united against the emperor, shouting "Nika! Nika!" ("Win! Win!"). After nine days of violence that left much of the capital in ashes, a panicky Justinian prepared to abandon his throne and flee. But Theodora sternly rebuked him: "Once born, no one can escape dying, but for one who has held imperial power it would be unbearable to be a fugitive. May I never take off my imperial robes of purple, nor live to see the day when those who meet me will not greet me as their sovereign." Shamed, Justinian dispatched troops, who quelled the disturbance by slaughtering thirty thousand rioters trapped in the racetrack.

Justinian's most ambitious plan was to reunite the eastern and western empires. His brilliant generals Belisarius and Narses defeated the Vandals and Ostrogoths after campaigns that in some cases took decades to complete. At enormous expense, imperial armies reoccupied Italy, the Dalmatian coast, Sicily, Sardinia, Corsica, part of southern Spain, and western North Africa by 562. These successes restored the old empire's geography temporarily: Justinian's territory stretched from the Atlantic to the western edge of Mesopotamia (see "Mapping the West" on page 253).

But these triumphs came at a tragic price: they destroyed the west's infrastructure and the east's finances. Italy endured the greatest damage; the war there against the Goths inflicted death and destruction on a massive scale. The east suffered because Justinian squeezed ever more taxes out of his already overburdened population to finance the western wars and bribe the Sassanids in Mesopotamia not to attack while his eastern defenses were depleted. The tax burden crippled the economy, leading to constant banditry in the countryside. Crowds poured into the capital from rural areas, seeking relief from poverty and robbers.

Natural disaster compounded Justinian's troubles. In the 540s, a horrific epidemic killed a third of the empire's inhabitants; a quarter of a million succumbed in Constantinople alone, half the capital's population. This was only the first onslaught in a long series of pandemics that erased millions of people in the eastern empire over the next two centuries. The loss of so many people created a shortage of army recruits, required the hiring of expensive mercenaries, and left countless farms vacant, reducing tax revenues.

The strains threatening his regime made Justinian crave stability; to strengthen his authority he emphasized the emperor's closeness to God and intensified imperial autocracy, which became characteristics of Byzantine monarchy. His artists brilliantly recast the symbols of rule in a Christian context. A gleaming mosaic in his church at San Vitale in Ravenna, for example, displayed a dramatic vision of the emperor's role: Justinian standing at the center of the cosmos shoulder to shoulder with both the ancient Hebrew patriarch Abraham and Christ. In legal matters, Justinian proclaimed the emperor the "living law," reviving a Hellenistic royal doctrine.

His building program in Constantinople concretely communicated an image of his religiosity and power. Most spectacular of all was his magnificent reconstruction of Constantine's Church of the Holy Wisdom (Hagia Sophia).◆ Its location facing the palace announced Justinian's interlacing of imperial and Christian authority. Creating a new design for churches, the architects erected a huge building on a square plan capped by a dome 107 feet across and soaring 160 feet above the floor. Its interior walls glowed like the sun from the light reflecting off their four acres of gold mosaics. Imported marble of every color added to the sparkling effect. When he first entered his masterpiece, dedicated in 538, Justinian exclaimed, "Solomon, I have outdone you," boasting that he had bested the glorious temple the ancient king built for the Hebrews.

Constantinople during the Rule of Justinian

The new autocracy concentrated attention on the capital to the detriment of the provinces. Most seriously, it reduced the autonomy of the empire's cities. Their councils ceased to govern; imperial officials took over instead. Provincial elites still had to ensure full payment of their area's taxes, but they lost the compensating reward of deciding local matters. Now the imperial government determined all aspects of decision making and social status. Men of property from the provinces who aspired to a public career knew they could satisfy their ambitions only by joining the imperial administration.

To solidify his control, Justinian had the empire's laws codified to bring uniformity to the confusing welter of enactments by earlier emperors; the final edition of his *Codex* appeared in 534. A team of scholars also condensed millions of words

◆ For a contemporary account of the Hagia Sophia's reconstruction, see Document 19, Procopius, "Buildings."

to produce the *Digest* in 533, a collection of past decisions intended to expedite legal cases and provide a syllabus for law schools. This collection, written like the others in Latin and therefore readable in the western empire, influenced legal scholars for centuries. Justinian's experts also compiled a textbook for students in 533, the *Institutes*, which proclaimed the principles of a just life: "live honorably, harm no one else, and give to each his own"; it remained on law school reading lists until modern times.

To fulfill his sacred duty to protect the empire, Justinian enacted reforms to guarantee religious orthodoxy. Like the emperors before him, he believed his world would suffer if its divine protector became angered by the presence of religious offenders. Zealously enforcing laws against polytheists, he compelled them to be baptized or forfeit their lands and official positions. Three times he purged heretical Christians whom he could not reconcile to his version of orthodoxy. In pursuit of sexual purity, his laws made male homosexual relations illegal for the first time in Roman history. Homosexual marriage, apparently not uncommon earlier, had been officially prohibited in 342, but civil sanctions had never before been imposed on men engaging in homosexual activity. All the previous emperors, for example, had simply taxed male prostitutes. The legal status of homosexual activity between women is less clear; it probably counted as criminal adultery for married women.

A brilliant theologian in his own right, Justinian hoped to reconcile orthodox and Monophysite Christians by revising the creed of the Council of Chalcedon. But the church leaders in Rome and Constantinople had become too bitterly divided to agree on a unified church. The church's eastern and western divisions were by now embarked on the diverging courses that would climax in formal schism five hundred years later. Justinian's own ecumenical council in Constantinople dissolved in disaster in 553 when he jailed Rome's defiant Pope Vigilius and estranged the Monophysite bishops. Perhaps no emperor could have done better, but Justinian's drive for religious unity only propelled Christians farther apart and undermined his vision of a restored Roman world.

Preserving Classical Literature

The empire's Christianization endangered classical literature—from plays and histories to speeches and novels—because these works were polytheist and therefore potentially subversive of Christian belief. The real danger to the classical tradition's survival, however, stemmed less from active censorship than from simple neglect. As Christians became authors in great numbers, their works displaced the ancient texts of Greece and Rome as the most important literature of the age. Fortunately for later times, however, the Byzantine Empire helped preserve these brilliant intellectual legacies.

Above all, classical texts survived because elite Christian culture was rooted in traditional polytheist learning, Greek and Roman. Latin literature continued to be read in the eastern empire because the administration was bilingual; official documents were published in Rome's ancient tongue along with Greek translations. Latin scholarship in the east received a boost when Justinian's Italian wars impelled Latin-speaking scholars to flee for safety to Constantinople. Their work there helped conserve many works that might otherwise have disappeared in the turmoil in the west.

Byzantine scholars valued classical literature because they regarded it as a crucial part of a high-level education. Many of the classical works available today survived because they served as school texts in the eastern empire. A rudimentary knowledge of famous pre-Christian classics was a requirement for a good career in government service, the goal of most ambitious students. In the words of an imperial decree from 360, "No person shall obtain a post of the first rank unless it shall be shown that he excels in long practice of liberal studies, and that he is so polished in literary matters that words flow from his pen faultlessly."

What also helped classical literature survive was the use of the principles of ancient rhetoric as guidelines for the most effective presentation of Christian theology. When Ambrose, bishop of Milan from 374 to 397, composed the first systematic description of Christian ethics for young priests, he consciously imitated the great classical orator Cicero. Theologians employed the dialogue form pioneered by Plato to refute heretical Christian doctrines, and polytheist traditions of laudatory biography survived in the hugely popular genre of saints' lives. Similarly, Christian artists incorporated polytheist traditions to communicate their beliefs in paintings, mosaics, and carved reliefs. A favorite artistic motif of Christ with a sunburst surrounding his head, for example, took its inspiration from polytheist depictions of the radiant Sun as a god (see page 223).

Ironically, a technological innovation promoted by the proliferation of Christian literature also helped preserve classical polytheist texts. Previously, scribes had written books on sheets made of thin animal skin or paper made from papyrus, gluing the sheets together and attaching rods at both ends to form a scroll. Readers faced a burdensome task in unrolling them to read. For ease of use, Christians produced their literature in the form of the *codex*—a book with bound pages. Eventually the codex became the standard form of book production in the Byzantine world. Because it was less susceptible to damage from rolling and unrolling and could contain text more efficiently than scrolls, which were cumbersome for long works, the codex aided the preservation of all forms of literature.

Despite the continuing importance of classical Greek and Latin literature in Byzantine education and rhetoric, its survival remained precarious in a war-torn world dominated by Christians. Knowledge of Greek in the turbulent west faded so drastically that almost no one could read the original versions of Homer's *Iliad*

IMPORTANT DATES

284	Diocletian assumes the throne	418	Western emperor settles Visigoths in southwestern Gaul
293	Diocletian creates the tetrarchy		
303	Diocletian's Great Persecution of Christians begins	429	Vandals capture Roman North Africa after invading Spain
312	Constantine converts to Christianity	440s	Anglo-Saxons take over Roman Britain
c. 323	Pachomius in Upper Egypt establishes the first monasteries for men and women	451	Council of Chalcedon
		476	German commander Odoacer deposes the final western emperor, Romulus Augustulus
324	Constantine refounds Byzantium as Constantinople, the "new Rome"	c. 480–553	Life of Benedict of Nursia, who devises the Benedictine rule
325	Council of Nicaea	493–526	Theodoric establishes Ostrogothic kingdom in Italy
361–363	Julian attempts to restore polytheism as the state religion	507	Clovis establishes Frankish kingdom in Gaul
382	Removal of the Altar of Victory from the Senate house in Rome	c. 530	Plato's Academy in Athens closes
391	Theodosius bans pagan sacrifice and closes polytheist temples	534	Final edition of the *Codex*, Justinian's codification of Roman law
395	Roman Empire is split into western and eastern sections		
404	Western emperor makes Ravenna his capital	538	Justinian dedicates Church of the Holy Wisdom
410	Visigoths sack Rome	540s	Epidemic kills a third of the eastern empire's population
c. 413–426	Augustine writes *City of God*	565	Death of Justinian

and *Odyssey*, the traditional foundations of a polytheist literary education. Latin fared better, and scholars such as Augustine and Jerome knew Rome's ancient literature extremely well. But they also saw its classics as potentially too seductive because the pleasure of reading them could distract Christians from worshiping God. Jerome once had a nightmare of being condemned on Judgment Day for having been a Ciceronian instead of a Christian.

The closing around 530 of the Academy founded in Athens by Plato more than nine hundred years earlier vividly demonstrated the dangers for classical learning in the Byzantine world. This most famous of classical schools finally shut its doors

■ MAPPING THE WEST The Byzantine Empire and Western Europe, c. 600
*Justinian employed brilliant generals and spent huge sums of money to reconquer Italy, North
Africa, and part of Spain to reunite the western and eastern halves of the old Roman Empire. His
wars to regain Italy and North Africa eliminated the Ostrogothic and Vandal kingdoms, respectively, but at a huge cost in effort, time—the war in Italy took twenty years—and expense. The resources of the eastern empire were so depleted that his successors could not maintain the reunification. By the early seventh century, the Visigoths had taken back all of Spain. Africa, despite serious
revolts by indigenous Berber tribes, remained under imperial control until the Arab conquest of the
seventh century, but within five years of Justinian's death, the Lombards set up a new kingdom
controlling a large section of Italy. Never again would anyone attempt to reestablish a universal
Roman Empire.*

when many of its scholars emigrated to Persia to escape harsher restrictions on
polytheists and its revenues dwindled because the Athenian elite, its traditional supporters, were increasingly Christianized. The Neo-Platonist school at Alexandria,
by contrast, continued; its leader John Philoponus (c. 490–570) was a Christian. In
addition to Christian theology, Philoponus wrote commentaries on Aristotle's
works; some of his ideas anticipated those of Galileo a thousand years later. John's

work achieved the kind of synthesis of old and new that was one fruitful possibility of the ferment of the late Roman world—that is, he was a Christian subject of
the Byzantine Empire in Egypt, heading a school founded long before by polytheists, studying the works of an ancient Greek philosopher as the inspiration for his
innovative scholarship. The strong possibility that the present could learn from the
past would continue as Western civilization once again remade itself in medieval
times.

Conclusion

Tension between unity and division characterized the late Roman Empire. Diocletian's autocratic reorganization delayed the empire's fragmentation but opened the
way to its eventual separation in 395 into western and eastern halves. From then
on, its history increasingly divided into two regional streams, even though emperors as late as Justinian in the sixth century retained the dream of reuniting it and
restoring the glory of its Golden Age.

The eastern empire fared better economically and avoided the worst of the vi-
A complex of forces interacted to destroy the Roman Empire's unity, beginning
with the catastrophic losses of property and people during the third-century crisis,
which hit the west harder than the east. The late-fourth-century migrations of Germanic peoples fleeing the Huns further undermined centralized rule. When Roman
authorities failed to absorb the Germanic tribes peacefully, the newcomers created
kingdoms that eventually replaced imperial government in the west. This change
transformed not only the west's politics, society, and economy but also the Germanic tribes, who had to develop ethnic identities while organizing themselves in
a new way politically. The economic deterioration accompanying these transformations drove a stake into the heart of the elite public-spiritedness that had been
one of the foundations of imperial stability. Wealthy nobles in the west retreated to
self-sufficient country estates and shunned municipal office.

The eastern empire fared better economically and avoided the worst of the violent effects from the Germanic migrations, as the Byzantine emperors sought to
preserve an idealized "Romanness" that they believed would strengthen their rule.
Unfortunately, the financial drain of pursuing unity through war against the
Germanic kingdoms fueled social discontent by raising tax rates to punitive levels,
while the concentration of power in the capital weakened the local communities,
the traditional foundation of stability and revenue.

In religion, Constantine's conversion in 312 marked an epochal turning point
in Western history. Christianization of the Roman world proceeded slowly, and
Christians fiercely disagreed among themselves over doctrine, even to the point of
violence. The church developed a hierarchy to fight heresy, but believers proved remarkably recalcitrant. Many of them abandoned everyday society to live as monks,
to come closer to God personally and to pray for mercy for the world. Monastic

life redefined the meaning of holiness by creating communities of God's heroes who withdrew from this world to devote their service to glorifying the next.

In the end, then, the imperial vision of unity faded before the divisive forces of the human spirit combined with the powerful dynamics of political and social transformation. Nevertheless, the memory of Roman power and culture remained potent and present, providing an influential inheritance to the peoples and states that would become Rome's heirs.

Suggested References for further reading and online research appear on page SR-10 at the back of the book.

www.bedfordstmartins.com/huntconcise   See the ONLINE STUDY GUIDE to assess your mastery of the material covered in this chapter.

The Heirs of the Roman Empire

600–750

ACCORDING TO A WRITER who was not very sympathetic to the Byzantines, one night Emperor Heraclius (r. 610–641) had a dream: "Verily [he was told] there shall come against thee a circumcised nation, and they shall vanquish thee and take possession of the land." Heraclius thought the vision foretold an uprising of the Jews, and he ordered mass baptisms into the Christian faith in all his provinces. "But," continued the story,

> after a few days there appeared a man of the Arabs, from the southern districts, that is to say, from Mecca or its neighborhood, whose name was Muhammad; and he brought back the worshipers of idols to the knowledge of the One God. . . . And he took possession of Damascus and Syria, and crossed the Jordan and dammed it up. And the Lord abandoned the army of the Romans before him.

This tale, however fanciful, recalls the most astonishing development of the seventh century: the Arabs conquered much of the Roman Empire and became one of its heirs. The western and eastern parts of the empire, both diminished, were now joined by yet a third power—Arab and Muslim. The resulting triad has endured in various guises to the present day: the western third of the old Roman Empire became western Europe; the eastern third, occupying what is now Turkey, Greece, and some of the Balkans, became part of eastern Europe and helped to create Russia; and North Africa, together with the ancient Near East (now called the Middle East), remains the Arab world.

■ **Mosque at Damascus (detail)**
Islam conquered the Byzantines; then Islam was "conquered" in turn by Byzantine culture. For the grand mosque at Damascus, his capital city, the Umayyad caliph al-Walid employed Byzantine-trained mosaicists, who depicted classical motifs—buildings, animals, vegetation—in a style that harked back to the classical past. However, the artists scrupulously avoided depicting human beings, in this way conforming to one strain of Islamic thought that argued against figural representations. (Jean-Louis Nou.)

As diverse as these cultures are today, they share many of the same roots. All were heirs of Hellenistic and Roman traditions. All adhered to monotheism. The western and eastern halves of the empire had Christianity in common, although they differed at times in interpreting it. The Arab world's religion, Islam, accepted the same one God that Christians did but considered Jesus a prophet of God rather than his son.

The history of the seventh and eighth centuries is a story of adaptation and transformation. Historians consider the changes important enough to signal the end of one era—antiquity—and the beginning of another—the Middle Ages.* During this period, all three heirs of the Roman Empire combined elements of their heritage with new values, interests, and conditions. The divergences among them resulted from disparities in geographical and climatic conditions, material and human resources, skills, and local traditions. But these differences should not obscure the fact that the Byzantine, Muslim, and western European worlds were sibling cultures.

Byzantium: A Christian Empire under Siege

Emperor Justinian (r. 527–565) had tried to re-create the old Roman Empire. On the surface he succeeded. His empire once again included Italy, North Africa, and the Balkans. Vestiges of old Roman society persisted: an educated elite maintained its prestige, town governments continued to function, and old myths and legends were retold in poetry and depicted on silver plates and chests. By 600, however, the eastern empire began to undergo a transformation as striking as the one that had earlier remade the western half. Historians call this reorganized empire the Byzantine Empire, or Byzantium, after the Greek name for the city of Constantinople. From the last third of the sixth century, Byzantium was almost constantly at war, and its territory shrank drastically. Cultural and political change came as well. Cities—except for a few such as Constantinople—decayed, and the countryside became the focus of government and military administration. Following these shifts, the old elite largely disappeared, and classical learning gave way to new forms of education, mainly religious in content. The traditional styles of urban life, dependent on public gathering places and community spirit, faded away.

Wars on the Frontiers, c. 570–750

From about 570 to 750, the Byzantine Empire waged war against invaders on all fronts. Its first major challenge came from the east, from the Sassanid Empire of Persia. Its second came from new groups—Lombards, Slavs, Avars, Bulgars, and Muslims—who pushed into the empire. In the wake of these onslaughts, Byzantium was transformed.

---

*The term *Middle Ages* was coined in the sixteenth century to refer to the period "in between"—in the middle of—the ancient and modern periods.

The Persian challenge was the most predictable: since the third century, the Sassanid kings and Roman emperors had fought sporadically but never with decisive effect on either side. But in the middle of the sixth century, the Sassanids chose to concentrate their activities on their western half, Mesopotamia (today Iraq), nearer the Byzantine border (Map 7.1). Reforming the army, which previously had depended on nobles who could provide their own arms, the Sassanid kings began to pay and arm new warriors drawn from the lower nobility. With the army more fully their own, the Sassanid kings tried to re-create the Persian Empire of Xerxes and Darius (see page 54). Under Chosroes II (r. 591–628), the Persians invaded the Byzantine Empire in 603. By 613, they had taken Damascus; by 619, they were masters of Egypt. But after reorganizing his own army, Byzantine emperor Heraclius regained all of Byzantium's lost territory by 627. The chief outcome of these confrontations was the exhaustion of both sides.

The Byzantines could ill afford this weakness. From every side, new groups were pushing into their empire. The Lombards, a Germanic people, arrived in northern Italy in 568 and by 572 were masters of the Po valley and some inland regions in Italy's south, leaving the Byzantines only Bari, Calabria, and Sicily as well as Rome and a narrow swath of land through Italy's middle called the Exarchate of Ravenna.

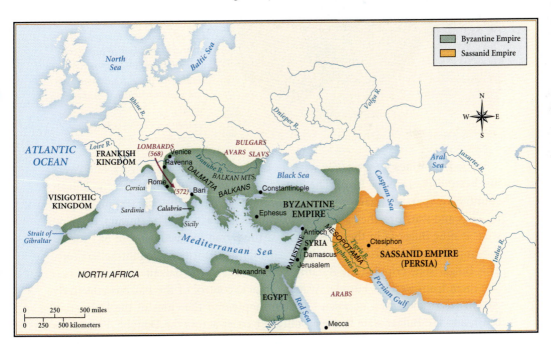

■ **MAP 7.1 Byzantine and Sassanid Empires, c. 600**

Justinian's grand design to regain the Roman Empire produced something new: the Byzantine Empire, with a capital at Constantinople and heartlands in the Balkans and Asia Minor. To its east was the Sassanid Empire, equally powerful and ambitious. In 600, the two faced one another uneasily. Three years later, the Sassanid king attacked Byzantine territory. The resulting wars, which lasted until 627, exhausted both empires and left them open to invasion by the Arabs.

■ **A Sassanid King**

His head topped by a mighty horned headdress, this representation of a Sassanid ruler evokes the full majesty of the Kings of Kings. Despite the enmity between Sassanid Persia and Byzantium (heir of Greece and Rome), the influence of Greek and Roman classical styles is evident in this sixth- or seventh-century bronze figure. Unlike this piece, traditional Persian sculpture was not in the round.

(Louvre/Agence Photographique de la réunion des musées nationaux.)

The Byzantines were equally weak in the face of the Slavs, Bulgars, and Avars just beyond the Danube River. The Slavs conducted lightning raids on the Balkan countryside (part of Byzantium at the time) and, joined by the Avars, nomadic pastoralists and warriors, they attacked Byzantine cities as well. The Bulgars, entering what is now Bulgaria in the 670s, defeated the Byzantine army and in 681 forced the emperor to recognize the state they carved out of formerly Byzantine territory. This Bulgar state crippled the Byzantines' influence in the Balkans and helped isolate them from western Europe. Avar and Slavic control of the Balkans effectively cut off trade and travel between Constantinople and the cities of the Dalmatian coast, and the Bulgar state threw a political barrier across the Danube. Perhaps as a result of this physical separation, Byzantine historians ceased to be interested in the West, and eastern scholars no longer bothered to learn Latin. The two halves of the Roman Empire, once united, communicated very little in the seventh century.

While fighting these groups on their northern frontier, the Byzantines at the same time had to contend with the Arabs, whose military prowess was creating a new empire and spreading a new religion, Islam. In the hundred years between 630 and 730, the Muslim Arabs succeeded in conquering much of the Byzantine Empire, at times attacking the walls of Constantinople itself. No wonder the patriarch of Jerusalem, chief bishop of the entire Levant, saw in the Arab onslaught the impending end of the world: "Behold," he said, "the Abomination of Desolation, spoken of by the Prophet Daniel, that standeth in the Holy Place."

From an Urban to a Rural Way of Life

As Byzantine borders shrank, Byzantines confronted new rulers and learned to accommodate to them. Slavs and Avars settling in the Balkans intermingled with the indigenous population, gradually absorbing local agricultural techniques and burial practices while contributing the Slavic language and religious cults. When Byzantine subjects in Syria and Egypt found themselves under Arab rule, they learned to adjust, paying a special tax to their conquerors but continuing to practice their Christian and Jewish religions in peace. In the countryside they were permitted to keep and farm their lands, and their cities remained centers of government, scholarship, and business. For these former Byzantines, daily life remained essentially unchanged.

■ **The Walls of Constantinople**
The thick walls and stone forts built by Emperor Theodosius II (r. 408–450) are still visible at Istanbul. The walls enclosed not only the urban center but rural fields and gardens as well. Thus the city could support and feed itself even when under siege. For over a thousand years, the walls helped protect Constantinople from the onslaughts of invaders. (Sonia Halliday Photographs.)

Ironically, the most radical transformations for seventh- and eighth-century Byzan-tines occurred not in the territories conquered but in the shrunken empire itself. Un-der the ceaseless barrage of invaders, many towns, formerly bustling nodes of trade and centers of the imperial bureaucratic network, vanished or became unrecognizable in their changed way of life. The public activity of marketplaces, theaters, and town squares gave way to the private pursuits of table and hearth. City baths, once places where people gossiped, made deals, and talked politics and philosophy, disappeared in most Byzantine towns—with the significant exception of Constantinople. Warfare reduced some cities to rubble, and when they were rebuilt, the limited resources available went to construct thick city walls and solid churches instead of large open marketplaces and baths. Markets moved to overcrowded streets that looked much like the open-air bazaars of the modern Middle East. People under siege sought protection rather than com-munity pastimes. In the Byzantine city of Ephesus, for example, the citizens who built the new walls in the seventh century enclosed not the old public edifices but rather their homes and churches. Despite the new emphasis on church buildings, many cities were too impoverished even to repair their churches. (See "Taking Measure," below.)

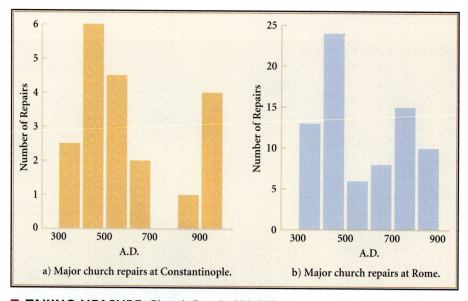

a) Major church repairs at Constantinople.   b) Major church repairs at Rome.

■ **TAKING MEASURE** Church Repair, 600–900

The impoverishment of the period 600–750 is clear from graph a, which shows a major slump in church repair at Constantinople during the period. If there had been any money to spend on building repairs, it undoubtedly would have gone to the churches first. By contrast, graph b shows that Rome was not so hard hit as Constantinople, even though it was part of the Byzantine Empire. There was, to be sure, a clear diminution in the number of church repairs in the period 500–600. But between 700 and 800, there was a clear, though small, increase. Taken together, the two graphs help show the toll taken by the invasions, diseases, and financial hardships of the period 600–750.

(Data adapted from Klavs Randsborg, "The Migration Period: Model History and Treasure," *The Sixth Century: Production, Distribution and Demand,* eds. Richard Hodges and William Bowden [Leiden: Brill, 1998].)

The pressures of war against the Arabs brought a change in Byzantine society parallel to the change in the West a few centuries before, spelling the end of the class of *curiales* (town councilors), the elite that for centuries had mediated between the emperor and the people. But an upper class nevertheless remained: as in the West, bishops and their clergy continued to form a rich and powerful upper stratum even within declining cities.

Despite the general urban decline, Constantinople and a few other urban centers retained much of their old vitality. Some industry and trade continued, particularly the manufacture of silk textiles. These were the prestige items of the time, and their production and distribution were monitored by the government. State-controlled factories produced the finest fabrics, which legally could be worn only by the emperor, his court, and his friends. In private factories, merchants, spinners, and weavers turned raw silk into slightly less luxurious cloth for both internal consumption and foreign trade. Even though Byzantium's economic life became increasingly rural and barter-based in the seventh and eighth centuries, the skills, knowledge, and institutions of urban workers made possible long-distance trade and the domestic manufacture of luxury goods.

As urban life declined, agriculture, always the basis of the Byzantine economy, became the center of its social life as well. But unlike the West, where an extremely rich and powerful elite dominated the agricultural economy, the Byzantine Empire of the seventh century was principally a realm of free and semifree peasant farmers, who grew food, herded cattle, and tended vineyards on small plots of land. In the shadow of decaying urban centers, the social world of the farmer was narrow. Two or three neighbors were enough to ratify a land transfer. Farmers interacted mostly with their families or with local monasteries. The buffer once provided by the curial class was gone; these families now felt directly the impact of imperial rule.

Eager to strengthen these social developments, the emperors of the seventh and eighth centuries tried to give ordinary family life new institutional importance. Imperial legislation narrowed the grounds for divorce and set new punishments for marital infidelity. Husbands and wives who committed adultery were whipped and fined, and their noses were slit. Abortion was prohibited, and new protections were set in place against incest with children. Mothers were given equal power with fathers over their offspring and, if widowed, became the legal guardians of their minor children and controlled the household property.

The transformations of the countryside went hand in hand with military, political, and cultural changes. On the military front, the Byzantine navy found a potent weapon in "Greek fire," a combustible oil that floated on water and burst into flames upon hitting its target. Determined to win wars on land as well, the imperial government exercised greater autocratic control, hastening the decline of the curial class, wresting power from other elite families, and encouraging the formation of a middle class of farmer-soldiers.

In the seventh century, an emperor, possibly Heraclius, divided the empire into military districts called *themes* and put all civil matters in each district into the hands of one general, a *strategos* (plural, *strategoi*). Landless men were lured to join the army with the promise of land and low taxes; they fought side by side with local farmers, who provided their own weapons and horses. The new organization effectively countered frontier attacks.

The new emphasis on the rural world affected Byzantine education and culture. The old curial elite had cultivated the study of classical literature, sending their children (above all, their sons) to city schools or tutors to learn to read the works of Greek poets and philosophers. In contrast, eighth-century parents showed far more interest in giving their children, both sons and daughters, a religious education. Even with the decay of urban centers, cities and villages often retained an elementary school. There teachers used the Book of Psalms (the Psalter) as their primer. Throughout the seventh and eighth centuries, secular, classical learning remained decidedly out of favor, and dogmatic writings, saints' lives, and devotional works took center stage.

Religion, Politics, and Iconoclasm

The importance placed on religious learning and piety complemented both the autocratic imperial ideal and the powers of the bishops in the seventh century. Since the spiritual and secular realms were understood to be inseparable, the bishops wielded political power in their cities, while Byzantine emperors ruled as religious as well as political figures. In theory, imperial and church power were separate but interdependent. In fact, the emperor functioned as the head of the church hierarchy: he appointed the chief religious official, the patriarch of Constantinople; formulated Christian doctrine; called church councils to determine dogma; and set out the criteria for bishops to be ordained.

Bishops and monks were important as well. Bishops functioned as administrators, acting as judges and tax collectors in their cities. They distributed food in times of famine or siege, provisioned troops, and set up military fortifications. As part of their charitable work, they cared for the sick and the needy. In theory, they controlled the monasteries in their region (diocese). However, in fact, monasteries were enormously powerful institutions that often defied the authority of bishops and even emperors. Monks commanded immense prestige as the holiest of God's faithful, and they were the chief sponsors of icons.

Icons were (and are still considered by some) images of holy people—Christ, the Virgin, and the saints. To many Byzantine Christians, they were far more than mere representations: they were believed to possess holy power that directly affected people's daily lives as well as their chances for salvation. Many seventh-century Byzantines followed the monks in making icons the focus of their religious devotion. To them, icons were like the incarnation of Christ; they turned spirit into material substance. Thus an icon manifested in physical form the holy person it depicted.

■ Icon of Virgin and Child

*With two angels behind them and a sol-
dier saint at either side, the Virgin Mary
and the Christ Child display a still, otherworldly dignity. Working with hot pig-
mented beeswax, the sixth-century artist
gave the angels transparent halos to emphasize their incorporeality but depicted
the saints as earthly men, with hair and
beard, feet planted firmly on the ground.
Icons such as this were used in private
worship as well as in the religious life of
Byzantine monasteries.*

Other Byzantines, however, abhorred icons. Most numerous of these were soldiers on the frontiers. Shocked by Arab triumphs, they thought that they discovered
the cause of their misfortunes in the biblical injunction against graven images. When
they compared their defeats to Muslim successes, they could not help but notice that
Islam prohibited all representations of the divine. To these soldiers and others who
shared their view, icons revived pagan idolatry and desecrated Christian divinity. As
iconoclastic (anti-icon or, literally, icon-breaking) feeling grew, some churchmen became outspoken in their opposition to icons, and some church councils condemned
icons outright.

Byzantine emperors shared these religious objections, but they also had important political reasons for opposing icons. In fact, the issue of icons became a test
of their authority. Icons diffused loyalties, setting up between worshipers and God
intermediaries that undermined the emperor's exclusive place in the divine and
temporal order. In addition, the emphasis on icons in monastic communities made
the monks potential threats to imperial power; the emperors hoped to use this issue to break the power of the monasteries. Above all, though, the emperors opposed
icons because the army did, and they needed the support of their troops.

The controversy climaxed in 726, after Emperor Leo III the Isaurian (r. 717–741)
had defeated the Arabs besieging Constantinople in 718 and turned his attention

to consolidating his political position. In the wake of the victory, officers of the imperial court tore down the great golden icon of Christ at the gateway of the palace and replaced it with a cross. In protest, a crowd of women went on a furious rampage in support of icons. This event marked the beginning of the period of *iconoclasm*; soon afterward, Leo ordered all icons destroyed, a ban that remained in effect, despite much opposition, until 787. A modified ban would be revived in 815 and last until 843.

Iconoclasm had an enormous impact on daily life. At home, where people had their own portable icons, it forced changes in private worship: the devout had to destroy their icons or worship them in secret. Iconoclasm meant ferocious attacks on the monasteries: splendid collections of holy images were destroyed, vast properties were confiscated, and monasteries were disbanded. With their power now consolidated, Byzantine rulers were able to maintain themselves against the onslaught of the Arabs, who attacked under the banner of Islam.

Islam: A New Religion and a New Empire

Islam, which means "submission," called for all to submit to the will of one God. It demanded a revolutionary change—the conversion to one community—of the disunited Bedouin tribal society from which it sprang. Islam was founded by Muhammad, a merchant turned holy man from the Arabian city of Mecca, a major oasis near the Red Sea. He recognized only one God, that of the Jews and the Christians. He saw himself as God's last prophet, the person to receive and in turn repeat God's final words to humans. Invited by the city of Medina to come and mediate disputes there, Muhammad exercised the powers of both a religious and a secular leader. This dual role became the model for his successors (the caliphs) as well. Through a combination of persuasion and force, Muhammad and his coreligionists, the Muslims, converted most of the Arabian peninsula. By the time he died in 632, Islamic conquest and conversion had begun to move northward, into Byzantine and Persian territories. In the next generation, the Muslims took over most of Persia and all of Egypt and were on their way across North Africa to Spain. Yet within the territories they conquered with such lightning speed, daily life went on much as before.

The Rise and Development of Islam, c. 610–632

In the seventh century, the Arabian peninsula, a desert punctuated by a few oases, was largely inhabited by nomadic Bedouin tribes made up of loose confederations of clans, or kin groups. Herding their flocks of sheep or camels for meat and milk, the Bedouins traded—or raided—more settled areas as well as one another for grain, dried fruit, and slaves. Small settled oases dotted the desert here and there, but the *polis*-centered life so crucial to Greece and Rome was unknown. Nor could the inhabitants, unlike the Greeks and Romans, take the Mediterranean Sea for granted. In fact, water was precious in Arabia, the very source of life: "The heavens and the earth were an integrated mass, then We split them and made every living thing from water," says God in the Qur'an, the holy book of Islam that serves Muslims much as the Bible does Christians and Jews.

Arabia in Muhammad's Lifetime

The Bedouins spoke the same language and transmitted their traditions orally in poetry of extraordinary delicacy, precision, and beauty. Their tribes shared as well a common culture that prized "manliness," which meant far more than sexual prowess. Bedouin men strove to be brave in battle and feared being shamed. Manliness also entailed an obligation to be generous, to give away the booty that was the goal of intertribal warfare. Women were often part of this booty; a counterpart to Bedouin manliness was therefore the practice of polygyny (having more than one wife at the same time). Thus, although the tribes were rivalrous and almost constantly fighting, Bedouin wars rarely involved much bloodshed; their main purpose was to capture and take belongings. It was not a big step from this booty-gathering to trading and from that to the establishment of commercial centers.

Mecca was one such commercial center. Meccan caravans were organized to sell Bedouin products—mainly leather goods and raisins—to more urbanized areas in the north. More important, Mecca played an important religious role because it contained a shrine, the Ka'ba, which served as a sacred place within which war and violence were prohibited. The tribe that dominated Mecca, the Quraysh, controlled access to the shrine and was able to tax the pilgrims who flocked there as well as sell them food and drink. In turn, plunder was transformed into trade as the visitors bartered on the sacred grounds, assured of their security.

This center of both religion and culture was the birthplace of Muhammad (c. 570–632). His early years were inauspicious: orphaned at the age of six, he spent two years with his grandfather and then came under the care of his uncle, a leader of the Quraysh tribe. Eventually, Muhammad became a trader. At the age of twenty-five, he married Khadija, a rich widow who had once employed him. They had at least four daughters and lived (to all appearances) happily and comfortably. Yet Muhammad sometimes left home and spent a few days in a nearby cave in prayer and contemplation, practicing a type of piety also pursued by early Christians.

Beginning in 610 and continuing until he died in 632, Muhammad heard a voice. "Recite!" it commanded. Muhammad recited not what he understood as his own words but rather the words of God, or Allah (*Allah* means "God" in Arabic).

■ **Qur'an**

More than a "holy book," the Qur'an represents the very words of God. Usually the text appeared on pages that were wider than they were long, perhaps to differentiate the Qur'an from other books. This particular example dates from the seventh or eighth century. It is written in Kufic script, a formal and majestic form of Arabic that scribes used for the Qur'an until the eleventh century. The round floral decoration on the right-hand page marks a new section of the text.

Muhammad submitted, the first believer in the new faith. He saw himself as entrusted with a prophet's mission: to speak God's words, to live by them, eventually to preach them, and to convert others to follow them. The name of the holy book of Islam, the Qur'an, means "recitation"; each chapter, or *sura,* of the Qur'an is understood to be God's revelation. The beginning of the Qur'an emphasizes the greatness, mercy, and goodness of God; the obligations of the rich to the poor; and the certainty of Judgment Day, the day when the world will end and God will determine who goes to heaven and who to hell. Later *suras* cover the gamut of human experience and the life to come. For Muslims the Qur'an contains the sum total of history, prophecy, and the legal and moral code by which men and women should live: "Do not set up another god with God. . . . Do not worship anyone but Him, and be good to your parents. . . . Give to your relatives what is their due, and to those who are needy, and the wayfarers."

The Qur'an emphasizes the nuclear family—a man, his wife, and children— as the basic unit of Muslim society. With the family given new importance, larger tribal affiliations were downgraded. However, everyone did have a wider identity as part of the *ummah,* the community of believers, who shared both a belief in one God and a set of religious practices. Islam depends entirely on individual belief and adherence to the Qur'an. Muslims have leaders, but they have no priests to mediate between the divine and the individual. Instead, Islam stresses the relationship between each person and God, a relationship characterized by gratitude to and worship of God, by the promise of reward or punishment on Judgment Day "when the sky is cleft asunder," and by exhortations to human kindness—"Do not oppress the orphan. And do not drive the beggar away." The Ka'ba, with its many idols, had attracted tribes from the surrounding vicinity. Muhammad, with his beliefs in one God, forged an even more universal religion.

First to convert to Muhammad's faith were his wife, Khadija, and a few friends and members of his immediate family. As it found more converts, however, the new faith polarized Meccan society. Muhammad's insistence that all polytheistic cults be abandoned in favor of his one faith brought him into conflict with leading members of the Quraysh tribe, whose positions of leadership and livelihood were threatened. Lacking political means to expel him, they insulted Muhammad and harassed his adherents.

Disillusioned and angry with his own tribe and with Mecca, where he had failed to make much of an impact, Muhammad tried to find a place and a population receptive to his message. Most important, he expected support from Jews, whose monotheism, in Muhammad's view, prepared them for his own faith. When a few of Muhammad's converts from Medina promised to protect him if he would join them there, he eagerly accepted the invitation, in part because Medina had a significant Jewish population. In 622, Muhammad emigrated to Medina, an oasis about two hundred miles north of Mecca. This journey, known as the *Hijra,* proved a crucial event for the fledgling movement. At Medina, Muhammad found followers ready to listen to his religious message and to regard him as the leader of their community. They expected him, for example, to act as a neutral and impartial judge in their interclan disputes. Muhammad's political position in the community set the pattern by which Islamic society would be governed afterward; rather than add a church to political and cultural life, Muslim political and religious institutions were inseparable. After Muhammad's death, the year of the Hijra was named the first year of the Islamic calendar; it marked the beginning of the new Islamic era.*

Successful at Medina, the Muslims were not content to confine themselves to this minor outpost alone. Above all, they needed to control Mecca, still a potent holy place. In 624, Muhammad led a small contingent to ambush a huge Meccan caravan brimming with goods; at the battle of Badr, aided by their position near an oasis, he and his followers killed forty-nine of the Meccan enemy, took numerous prisoners, and confiscated rich booty. This was a major turning point in the history of Islam. With the battle of Badr, traditional Bedouin plundering was grafted onto the Muslim duty of *jihad* (literally "striving" but often translated as "holy war").

---

*Thus 1 A.H. (1 *anno Hegirae,* "year of the Hijra") on the Muslim calendar is equivalent to A.D. 622 (*anno Domini,* "year of the Lord," 622) on the Christian calendar.

The battle of Badr was a great triumph for Muhammad, who was now able to consolidate his position at Medina, gaining new adherents and silencing all doubters. When Jews at Medina remained unreceptive to his message, Muhammad attacked them, expelling, executing, or enslaving many. At the same time Muhammad instituted new practices to define Islam as a unique religion. Among these were the *zakat,* a tax on possessions to be used for alms; the fast of Ramadan, which took place during the ninth month of the Islamic year, the month in which the battle of Badr had been fought; the *hajj,* a yearly pilgrimage to Mecca; and the *salat,* formal worship at least three times a day (later increased to five), which could include the *shahadah,* or profession of faith—"There is no god but God, and Muhammad is his Messenger." Soon Muhammad had Muslims direct their prayer away from Jerusalem, the center of Jewish worship, toward Mecca and the Ka'ba. Detailed regulations for these practices, sometimes called the "five pillars of Islam," were worked out in the eighth and early ninth centuries.

Meanwhile, the fierce rivalry between Mecca's clans and Medina's Muslims began to spill over into the rest of the Arabian peninsula as both sides strove to win converts. Muhammad sent troops to subdue Arabs north and south. In 630, he entered Mecca with ten thousand men and took over the city, assuring the Quraysh of leniency and offering alliances with tribal leaders. By this time the prestige of Islam was enough to convince clans elsewhere to convert. Through a combination of force, conversion, and negotiation, Muhammad was able to unite many, though by no means all, Arabic-speaking tribes under his leadership by the time of his death two years later (Map 7.2).

In so doing, Muhammad brought about important social transformations. As Muhammad's converts "submitted" to Islam, they formed not a clan or tribe but rather a community bound together by the worship of God. Women were accepted into this community, and their status was enhanced. Islam prohibited all infanticide, a practice that had long been used largely against female infants. Men were allowed to have up to four wives at one time, but they were obliged to treat them equally; wives received dowries and had certain inheritance rights. At first, Muslim women joined men during the salat, the prayer periods that punctuated the day. Beginning in the eighth century, however, women began to pray apart from the men. Like Judaism and Christianity, Islam retained the practices of a patriarchal society in which women's participation in community life was circumscribed.

Even though Islamic society was a new sort of community, in many ways it did function as a tribe, or rather a "supertribe," obligated to fight common enemies, share plunder, and resolve peacefully any internal disputes. Muslims participated in group rituals, such as the salat and public recitation. The Qur'an was soon publicly sung by professional reciters, much as the old tribal poetry had been. Most significant for the eventual spread of Islam, Muslim men continued to be warriors. They took up where Meccan traders had been forced to leave off; along the routes once

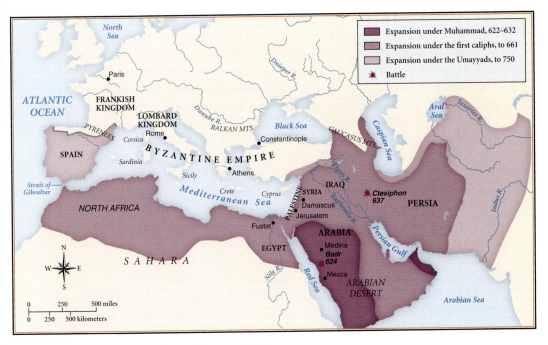

■ MAP 7.2 Expansion of Islam to 750
In little more than a century, Islamic armies conquered a vast region that included numerous different peoples, cultures, climates, and living conditions. Under the Umayyads, these disparate territories were administered by one ruler from his capital city at Damascus. The uniting force was the religion of Islam itself, which gathered all believers into one community, the ummah.

taken by caravans to Syria, their armies reaped profits at the point of a sword. But this differed from intertribal fighting; it was the "striving" (jihad) of people who were carrying out the injunction of God against unbelievers. "Strive, O Prophet," says the Qur'an, "against the unbelievers and the hypocrites, and deal with them firmly. Their final abode is Hell: And what a wretched destination!"

Muhammad's Successors, 632–750

Following his death, Muhammad's successors, the caliphs, assaulted the Roman and Persian worlds, taking them by storm. To the west, the Muslims attacked Byzantine territory in Syria with ease and moved into Egypt in the 640s (see Map 7.2). To the east, they invaded the Sassanid Empire, defeating the Persians at the gates of their capital, Ctesiphon, in 637. The whole of Persia was in Muslim hands by 661. During the last half of the seventh and the beginning of the eighth century, Islamic warriors extended their sway from Spain to India.

How were such conquests possible, especially in so short a time? First, the Islamic forces came up against weakened empires. The Byzantine and Sassanid states were exhausted from fighting each other. The cities of the Middle East that had been taken by the Persians and retaken by the Byzantines were depopulated, their few survivors burdened with heavy taxes. Second, the Muslims were welcomed into both Byzantine and Sassanid territories by discontented groups. Many Monophysite Christians in Syria and Egypt had suffered persecution by the Byzantines and were glad to have new, Islamic overlords. In Persia, Jews, Monophysites, and Nestorian Christians were at best irrelevant to the Zoroastrian King of Kings and his regime. These were the external reasons for Islamic success. There were also internal reasons. Arabs had long been used to intertribal warfare; now, under the banner of jihad, Muslims exercised their skills as warriors not against one another but rather against unbelievers. Fully armed, on horseback, and employing camels in convoys, they seemed almost a force of nature. Where they conquered, the Muslims built garrison cities from which soldiers requisitioned taxes and goods. Sometimes whole Arab tribes, including women and children, were imported to settle conquered territory, as happened in parts of Syria. In other regions, such as Egypt, a small Muslim settlement at Fustat sufficed to gather the spoils of conquest.

These successes hid tensions that developed within the Muslim leadership. Muhammad's death in 632 marked a crisis in the government of the new Islamic state, as different groups sought to promote their own man as his successor. The first caliphs came not from the traditional tribal elite but rather from a new inner circle of men close to Muhammad and participants in the Hijra. The first two caliphs ruled without serious opposition, but the third, Uthman (r. 644–656), a member of the Umayyad family and Muhammad's son-in-law, aroused discontent among other clan members of the inner circle and soldiers unhappy with his distribution of high offices and revenues. Accusing Uthman of favoritism, they supported his rival, Ali, a member of the Hashim clan (to which Muhammad had belonged) and the husband of Muhammad's only surviving child, Fatimah. After a group of discontented soldiers murdered Uthman, civil war broke out between the Umayyads and Ali's faction. It ended in 661 when Ali was killed by one of his own former supporters, and the caliphate remained in Umayyad hands from 661 to 750.

Nevertheless, the *Shi'at Ali*, the faction of Ali, did not fade away. Ali's memory lived on among groups of Muslims, Shi'ites, who saw in him a symbol of justice and righteousness. For them, Ali's death was the martyrdom of the only true successor to Muhammad. They remained faithful to his dynasty, shunning the caliphs of the other Muslims (Sunni Muslims, from Arabic *sunna*, "custom" or "the way"). The Shi'ites awaited the arrival of the true leader—the *imam*—who in their view could come only from the house of Ali.

Under the Umayyads, the Muslim world became a state with its capital at Damascus. Borrowing from the institutions well known to the civilizations they had just conquered, the Muslims issued coins and hired former Byzantine and Persian officials. They made Arabic a tool of centralization, imposing it as the language of government on regions not previously united linguistically. For Byzan-

■ Arab Coin

The Arabs learned coinage and minting from peoples whom they conquered—the Persians and the Byzantines. The ruler depicted on this silver coin is wearing a headdress that echoes the one worn in the bronze image of the Sassanid ruler depicted on page 260. But dirham, *the word for this type of coin, is not Persian but rather Greek, from* drachma. *The Umayyad Islamic fiscal system retained the old Roman land tax and was administered by Syrians who had served Byzantine rulers in the same capacity.*

(The British Museum.)

tium this period was one of unparalleled military crisis, the prelude to iconoclasm. For the Islamic world, now a diverse society of Muslim Arabs, Syrians, Egyptians, Iraqis, and other peoples, it was a period of settlement, new urbanism, and literary and artistic flowering.

Peace and Prosperity in Islamic Lands

Ironically, the Islamic warriors brought peace. While the conquerors stayed within their fortified cities or built magnificent hunting lodges in the deserts of Syria, the conquered went back to work, to study, to play, and—in the case of Christians and Jews, who were considered "protected subjects"—to worship as they pleased in return for the payment of a special tax (*jizya*).◆ At Damascus, local artists and craftspeople worked on the lavish decorations for a mosque in a neoclassical style at the very moment Muslim armies were storming the walls of Constantinople (see page 261). Leaving the Byzantine institutions in place, the Muslim conquerors allowed Christians and Jews to retain their posts and even protected dissidents.

During the seventh and eighth centuries, Muslim scholars wrote down the hitherto largely oral Arabic literature. They determined the definitive form for the Qur'an and compiled pious narratives about Muhammad (*hadith* literature). Scribes composed these works in exquisite handwriting, Arab calligraphy, which was a real art form. A literate class, composed mainly of the old Persian and Syrian elite now converted to Islam, created new forms of prose writing in Arabic—official documents as well as essays on topics ranging from hunting to ruling. Umayyad poetry explored new worlds of thought and feeling. Patronized by the caliphs, who found in written poetry an important source of propaganda and a buttress for their power,

---

◆ For a primary source that illuminates the Muslims' methods of conquest and rule in the decade following Muhammad's death, see Document 20, "Islamic Terms of Peace."

the poets also reached a wider audience that delighted in their clever use of words, their satire, and their invocations of courage, piety, and sometimes erotic love:

> I spent the night as her bed-companion,
>   each enamored of the other,
> And I made her laugh and cry, and stripped
>   her of her clothes.
> I played with her and she vanquished me;
>   I made her happy and I angered her.
> That was a night we spent, in my sleep,
>   playing and joyful,
> But the caller to prayer woke me up.

Such poetry scandalized conservative Muslims, brought up on the ascetic tenets of the Qur'an. But this love poetry was a product of the new urban civilization of the Umayyad period, where wealth, cultural mix, and the confidence born of conquest inspired diverse and experimental literary forms. By the close of the Umayyad period in 750, Islamic civilization was multiethnic, urban, and sophisticated, a true heir of Roman and Persian traditions.

The Western Kingdoms

With the demise of Roman imperial government in the West, the primary foundations of power and stability in Europe were kinship networks, church patronage, royal courts, and wealth derived from land and plunder. In contrast to Byzantium, where an emperor still ruled as the successor to Augustus and Constantine, drawing upon an unbroken chain of Roman legal and administrative traditions, political power in the West was more diffuse. Churchmen and rich magnates, sometimes one and the same person, held sway. Power derived as well from membership in royal dynasties, such as that of the Merovingian kings of the Franks. In addition, people believed that power lodged in the tombs and relics of saints, who represented and wielded the divine forces of God. Although the patterns of daily life and the procedures of government in the West remained recognizably Roman, they were undergoing change, borrowing from and adapting local traditions.

Frankish Kingdoms with Roman Roots

The core of the Frankish kingdoms was Roman Gaul. During the sixth century, the Franks had established themselves as dominant in Gaul, and by the seventh century the limits of their kingdoms roughly approximated the eastern borders of present-day France, Belgium, Switzerland, and Luxembourg (Map 7.3). Moreover, their kings, the Merovingians (c. 485–751), had subjugated many of the peoples beyond the Rhine, foreshadowing the contours of modern Germany. These north-

■ **MAP 7.3 The Merovingian Kingdoms in the Seventh Century**
By the seventh century, there were three powerful Merovingian kingdoms: Neustria, Austrasia, and Burgundy. The important cities of Aquitaine were assigned to one or another of these major kingdoms, and Aquitaine as a whole was assigned to a duke or other governor. Kings did not establish capital cities; they did not even stay in one place. Rather, they continually traveled throughout their kingdoms, making their power felt in person.

ern and eastern regions were little Romanized, but the inhabitants of the rest of the Frankish kingdoms lived with the vestiges of Rome at their door.

Travel was difficult in this world of decaying roads and few amenities. Yet there were many travelers, such as pilgrims on their way to Rome and traders with slaves—precious human cargo captured on the borders of the Christian world and sold to wealthy aristocrats within. Most seventh-century voyagers would have relied on river routes, for land travel was very slow, and even large groups of travelers on the roads were vulnerable to attacks by robbers. Returning north via the Rhône River from a pious trip to Rome, voyagers would have passed Roman amphitheaters and farmland neatly and squarely laid out by Roman land surveyors. The great stone palaces of villas would still have dotted the countryside. All this would have seemed quite classical and Roman. But if the travelers had been very observant, they would have

■ **Amphitheater at Arles**
In what is today the south of France, the ruins of an amphitheater built by the Romans still dwarf the surrounding buildings of the modern city of Arles. This huge stadium was even more striking in the seventh century, when the city was impoverished and depopulated. Plague, war, and the dislocation of Roman trade networks forced most people to abandon the cities to live on the land. Only the bishop and his clergy—and individuals who could make a living servicing them—stayed in the cities. At Arles there were monasteries as well, and some of them were thriving. In the mid-sixth century there were perhaps two hundred nuns at one of the female convents there. (Jean Dieuzaide.)

noticed what was missing: thriving cities. By the seventh century, Roman cities were mere hulks, serving as the centers of church administration but no longer boasting commercial or cultural vitality. Depopulated, many survived as mere skeletons, with the exception of such busy commercial centers as Arles and Marseille.

Continuing their journey north along the Moselle, our travelers would pass through dense, nearly untouched forests and land more often used as pasture for animals than for cereal cultivation. Not much influenced by the Romans, these areas represented far more the farming and village settlement patterns of the Germans. Yet even here some structures of the Roman Empire remained. Fortresses were still standing at Trier, and large stone villas, such as the one excavated by archaeologists near Douai, loomed over the humble wooden dwellings of the countryside.

In the south, gangs of slaves still might occasionally be found cultivating the extensive lands of wealthy estate owners, as they had done since the days of the late Roman Republic. Scattered here and there, independent peasants worked their own small plots as they had for centuries. But for the most part, seventh-century travelers found semifree peasant families settled on small holdings, their *manse*—including a house, a garden, and cultivable land—for which they paid dues and owed labor services to a landowner. Some of these peasants were descendants of the *coloni* (tenant farmers) of the late Roman Empire; others were the sons and daughters of slaves, now provided with a small parcel of land; and a few were people of free Germanic origin who for various reasons had come down in the world. At the lower end of the social scale, the status of Germans and Romans had become identical.

At the upper end of the social scale, Romans (or, more precisely, Gallo-Romans) and Germans had also merged. Although people south of the Loire River continued to be called "Romans" and people to the north "Franks," their cultures were strikingly similar: they shared languages, settlement patterns, and religious sensibilities. Many dialects were spoken in the western kingdoms in the seventh century, many deriving from Latin, though no longer the Latin of Cicero. "Though my speech is rude," Gregory, bishop of Tours (r. 573–c. 594), wrote at the end of the sixth century,

> I have been unable to be silent as to the struggles between the wicked and the upright; and I have been especially encouraged because, to my surprise, it has often been said by men of our day, that few understand the learned words of the rhetorician but many the rude language of the common people.

Thus Gregory began his *Histories*, a valuable source for the Merovingian period (c. 485–751). He was trying to evoke the sympathies of his readers, a traditional Roman rhetorical device; but he also expected that his "rude" Latin—the plain Latin of everyday speech—would be understood and welcomed by the general public.

In the fourth and fifth centuries Gallo-Roman aristocrats had lived in isolated villas with their *familia*—family members, slaves, and servants. In the seventh century aristocrats lived in more populous settlements: in small villages surrounded by the huts of peasants, shepherds, and artisans. The early medieval village, constructed mostly out of wood or baked clay, was generally built near a waterway or forest or around a church for protection.

The cities, too, were transformed. At Tours, Bishop Gregory and his household and clerics still lived in the old Roman city center. But Tours's main focus was now outside the city walls, where a church had been built. The population of the surrounding countryside was pulled to this church as if to a magnet, for it housed the remains of the most important and venerated person in the locale: St. Martin. This saint, a fourth-century soldier-turned-monk, was long dead, but his relics—his bones, teeth, hair, and clothes—could be found at Tours, where he had served as bishop. There, in the succeeding centuries, he remained a supernatural force: a protector, healer, and avenger through whom God manifested divine power. In Gregory's view, for example, Martin's relics (or rather God *through* Martin's relics) had prevented armies from plundering local peasants. Martin was not the only human thought to have great supernatural power; all of God's saints were miracle workers.

In the classical world, the dead had been banished from the presence of the living; in the medieval world, the holy dead held the place of highest esteem. The church had no formal procedures for proclaiming saints in the early Middle Ages, but influential community leaders, including the local bishop, "recognized" holiness. When, for example, miracles were observed at the site of a tomb in Dijon, the common people went there regularly to ask for help. The nearby bishop, however, was convinced that St. Benignus inhabited the tomb only after the martyr himself visited the bishop in a vision. At St. Illidius's tomb in Clermont, it was reported that "the blind are given light, demons are chased away, the deaf receive hearing, and the lame the use of their limbs." Even a few women were so esteemed: "[Our Savior] gave us

■ Reliquary

The cult of relics necessitated housing the precious parts of the saints in equally precious containers. This reliquary, made of cloisonné enamel (bits of enamel framed by metal), garnets, glass gems, and a cameo, is in the shape of a miniature sarcophagus. On the back is the inscription "Theuderic the priest had this made in honor of Saint Maurice." Theuderic must have given the reliquary to the monastery of Saint Maurice d'Agaune (today in Switzerland), which was renowned for its long and elaborate liturgy—its daily schedule of prayer—in the late seventh century.
(Photo courtesy Thames and Hudson Ltd., London, from *The Dark Ages*, 1975.)

as models [of sanctity] not only men, who fight [against sinfulness] as they should, but also women, who exert themselves in the struggle with success," wrote Gregory as a preface to his story of the nun Monegund, who lived with a few other ascetic women and whose miracles included curing tumors and prompting paralyzed limbs to work again. No one at Tours doubted that Martin was a saint, and to tap into the power of his relics one of Gregory's predecessors as bishop had constructed his church in the cemetery directly over Martin's tomb. For a man like Gregory of Tours and his flock, the church building was above all a home for the relics of the saints.

Economic Activity in a Peasant Society

As a bishop, Gregory was aware of some of the sophisticated forms of economic activity in seventh- and eighth-century Europe, such as long-distance trade. Yet most people lived on the edge of survival. Studies of Alpine peat bogs show that from the fifth to the mid-eighth century glaciers advanced and the average temperature in Europe dropped. This climatic change spelled shortages in crops. Chronicles, histories, and saints' lives also describe crop shortages, famines, and diseases as a normal part of life. For the year 591 alone, Gregory reported that

> *a terrible epidemic killed off the people in Tours and in Nantes. . . . In the town of Limoges a number of people were consumed by fire from heaven for having profaned the Lord's day by transacting business. . . . There was a terrible drought which destroyed all the green pasture. As a result there were great losses of flocks and herds.*

An underlying reason for these calamities was the weakness of the agricultural economy. The dry, light soil of the Mediterranean region was easy to till, and wooden implements were no liability there. But in the north of Europe, where the soil was heavy, wet, and difficult to turn and aerate, the limitations of wooden implements meant a meager food supply. At the same time, agricultural work was not equitably or efficiently allocated and managed. A leisure class of landowning warriors and churchmen lived off the work of peasant men, who tilled the fields, and peasant women, who gardened, brewed, baked, and wove cloth.

Occasionally surpluses developed, either from peaceful agriculture or plunder in warfare, and these were traded, though rarely in an impersonal, commercial manner. Most economic transactions of the seventh and eighth centuries were part of a *gift economy,* a system of give-and-take: booty was taken, tribute was demanded, harvests were hoarded, and coins were minted, all to be redistributed to friends, followers, and dependents. Kings and other rich and powerful men and women amassed gold, silver, ornaments, and jewelry in their treasuries and grain in their storehouses to mark their power, add to their prestige, and demonstrate their generosity. Those benefiting from this largesse included religious people and institutions: monks, nuns, and bishops, monasteries and churches. We still have a partial gift economy today. At holidays, for example, goods change hands for social purposes: to consecrate a holy event, to express love and friendship, to show off wealth and status. In the Merovingian world, the gift economy was the dynamic behind most of the moments when goods and money changed hands.

Some economic activity in the seventh century was purely commercial and impersonal. In the north of Europe, a thriving North Sea trade was beginning. Older networks still tied the West—which supplied slaves and raw materials such as furs and honey—to the East, which provided luxuries and manufactured goods such as silks and papyrus. Trade was a way for the Byzantine, Islamic, and western European descendants of the Roman Empire to keep in tenuous contact with one another. Seventh- and eighth-century sources speak of Byzantines, Syrians, and Jews as the chief intermediaries, many of them living in the still-thriving port cities of the Mediterranean. Gregory of Tours associated Jews with commerce, complaining that they sold things "at a higher price than they were worth."

Contrary to Gregory's view, Jews were not involved only, or even primarily, in trade but were almost entirely integrated into every aspect of secular life in many regions of Europe. They used Hebrew in worship, but otherwise they spoke the same languages as Christians and used Latin in their legal documents. Their children were often given the same names as Christians (and, in turn, Christians often took Old Testament biblical names); they dressed like everyone else; and they engaged in the same occupations. Many Jews planted and tended vineyards, in part because of the importance of wine in synagogue services, in part because the surplus could easily be sold. Some Jews were rich landowners, with slaves and dependent peasants working for them; others were independent peasants of modest means. Some Jews lived in towns with a small Jewish quarter where their homes and synagogues were located. However, most Jews, like their Christian neighbors, lived on the land. Only much later, in the tenth century, would their status change, setting them markedly apart from Christians.

Nor were women as noticeably set apart from men in the Merovingian period as they had been in Roman times. As in the Islamic world, western women received dowries and could inherit property. In the West, they could be entrepreneurs as well: documents reveal at least one enterprising peasant woman who sold wine at Tours to earn additional money.

The Powerful in Merovingian Society

Monarchs and aristocrats were the powerful people in Merovingian society. Aristocrats included monks and bishops as well as laypeople. Holding power through hereditary wealth, status, and political influence, they lived in leisurely abundance. At the end of the sixth century, for example, one of them, Bishop Nicetius, inhabited a palace that commanded a view of his estates overlooking the Moselle River:

> From the top [of the palace] you can see boats gliding by on the surface of the river in summertime; orchards with fruit-trees growing here and there fill the air with the perfume of their flowers.

Besides tending their estates, male aristocrats of the period spent their time honing their skills as warriors. To be a great warrior in Merovingian society, just as in the otherwise very different world of the Bedouin, meant more than just fighting: it meant perfecting the virtues necessary for leading armed men. Aristocrats affirmed their skills and comradeship in the hunt; they proved their worth in the regular taking of booty; and they rewarded their followers afterward at generous banquets. At these feasts, following the dictates of the gift economy, the lords combined fellowship with the redistribution of wealth, as they gave abundantly to their retainers.

Merovingian aristocrats also spent a good deal of time in bed. The bed—and the production of children—was the focus of their marriage. Because of its importance to the survival of aristocratic families and to the transmission of their property and power, marriage was an expensive institution, especially the most formal kind, in which the husband paid a dowry to his bride—a generous gift of livestock and land—and gave her a smaller morning gift after the marriage was consummated. Very wealthy men might also support "lesser wives," to whom they gave a morning gift but no dowry. In this period, churchmen had many ideas about the value of marriages, but in practice they had little to do with the matter: no one was married in a church.

Sixth-century aristocrats with wealth and schooling like Nicetius patterned their lives on those of Romans, teaching their children Latin poetry and writing to one another in phrases borrowed from Virgil. Less than a century later, however, aristocrats no longer adhered to the traditions of the classical past. Some still learned Latin, but they cultivated it mainly to read the Psalms. A religious culture emphasizing Christian piety over the classics was developing in the West at the same time as in Byzantium.

The new religious sensibility was given powerful impetus by the arrival (c. 591) on the European continent of the Irish monk St. Columbanus (d. 615). The Merovingian aristocracy was much taken by Columbanus's brand of monasticism, which stressed exile, devotion, and discipline. The monasteries St. Columbanus established from Gaul to Italy attracted local recruits from the aristocracy, some of them grown men and women. Others were young children, given to the monastery by their parents. This practice, called *oblation*, was not only accepted but also often considered essential for the spiritual well-being of both the children and their families. Irish monasticism introduced aristocrats on the continent to a deepened religious devotion. Those aristocrats who did not join or patronize a monastery still often read (or listened to others read) books about penitence, and they chanted the Psalms.

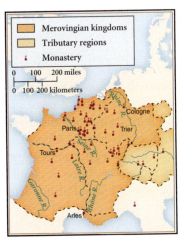

The Growth of Columbanian Monasticism

Bishops, generally aristocrats, ranked among the most powerful men in Merovingian society. Gregory of Tours, for example, considered himself the protector of "his citizens" at Tours. When representatives of the king came to collect taxes, Gregory stopped them in their tracks, warning them that St. Martin would punish anyone who tried to tax his people. "That very day," Gregory reported, "the man who had produced the tax rolls caught a fever and died." Gregory then obtained a letter from the king, "confirming the immunity from taxation of the people of Tours, out of respect for Saint Martin."

Like other aristocrats, many bishops were married. Church councils demanded celibacy, however, and as the overseers of priests, bishops were expected to be moral supervisors and refrain from sexual relations with their wives. Since bishops were ordinarily appointed late in life, long after they had raised a family, this restriction did not threaten the ideal of a procreative marriage.

Because unions bound together extended families rather than simply husbands and wives, noble parents determined whom their daughters were to marry. But women had some control over their lives. If they were widowed without children, they were allowed to sell, give away, exchange, or rent out their dowry estates as they wished. Moreover, men could give their women kinfolk property outright in written testaments. Fathers so often wanted to share their property with their daughters that an enterprising author created a formula for scribes to follow when drawing up such wills. It began:

For a long time an ungodly custom has been observed among us that forbids sisters to share with their brothers the paternal land. I reject this impious law:

I make you, my beloved daughter, an equal and legitimate heir in all my patrimony [inheritance].

Because of such bequests, dowries, and other gifts, many aristocratic women were very rich. Childless widows frequently gave grand and generous gifts to the church from their vast possessions. But a woman need not have been a widow to control enormous wealth: in 632, for example, the nun Burgundofara, who had never married, drew up a will giving her monastery the land, slaves, vineyards, pastures, and forests she had received from her two brothers and her father. In the same will, she gave other property near Paris to her brothers and sister. Aristocratic women maintained close ties with their relatives. They tried to find powerful husbands for their sisters and prestigious careers for their brothers; in turn, they relied on their relatives for support.

Though legally under the authority of her husband, a Merovingian woman often found ways to assert control over her life and her husband's life as well. Tetradia, wife of Count Eulalius, left her husband, taking all his gold and silver, because

he was in the habit of sleeping with the women-servants in his household . . . [and] neglected his wife. . . . As a result of his excesses, he ran into serious debt, and to meet this he stole his wife's jewelry and money.

In a court of law, Tetradia was sentenced to repay Eulalius four times the amount she had taken from him, but she was allowed to keep and live on her own property. Other women were able to exercise behind-the-scenes control through their sons. Nicetius's mother, Artemia, used the prophecy that her son would become a bishop to prevent her husband from taking the bishopric himself. Although the prophecy eventually came to pass, Nicetius remained at home with his mother well into his thirties, working alongside the servants and teaching the younger children of the household to read the Psalms.

Occasionally women exercised direct power. Some women were abbesses, rulers in their own right over female monasteries and sometimes over "double monasteries," with separate facilities for men and women. These could be very substantial centers of population: the convent at Laon, for example, had three hundred nuns in the seventh century. Because women lived in populous convents or were monopolized by rich men able to support several wives or mistresses at one time, unattached aristocratic women were scarce in society and therefore valuable.

Atop this aristocracy of men and women were the Merovingian kings, rulers of the Frankish kingdoms from about 485 to 751.♦ The dynasty owed its longevity to good political sense: it had allied itself with local lay aristocrats and ecclesiasti-

---

♦ For a primary source that focuses on the important role of the queen in Merovingian society, see Document 21, "The Life of Lady Balthild, Queen of the Franks."

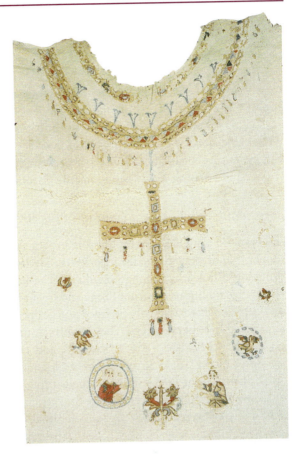

■ Relic of Queen Balthild

The slave Balthild, purchased in England by a Frankish mayor of the palace, caught the eye of the Frankish king himself, who made her his queen. This seventh-century Cinderella story did not end with marriage. When her husband died, Balthild played an important role as regent (caretaker ruler) for her young son. Later, she retired to a monastery, where she was revered as a saint. This shirt is one of her relics. Tradition has it that instead of wearing real jewels, Balthild distributed them to the poor and contented herself with their images in embroidery.

(Musée de Chelles/photographers: E. Mittard and N. Georgieff.)

cal authorities. The kings relied on these men to bolster their power derived from other sources: their tribal war leadership and access to the lion's share of plunder and their takeover of the taxation system, public lands, and the legal framework of Roman administration. The kings' courts functioned as schools for the sons of the aristocracy, tightening the bonds between royal and aristocratic families and loyalties. And when kings sent officials—counts and dukes—to rule in their name in various regions of their kingdoms, these regional governors worked with and married into the aristocratic families who had long controlled local affairs.

Aristocrats as well as kings had good reason to want a powerful royal authority. The king acted as arbitrator and intermediary for the competing interests of the aristocrats while taking advantage of local opportunities to appoint favorites and garner prestige by giving out land and privileges to supporters and religious institutions. Gregory of Tours's history of the sixth century is filled with stories of bitter battles between Merovingian kings, as royal brothers fought continuously over territories, wives, and revenues. Yet what seemed like royal weakness and violent chaos to the bishop was in fact one way the kings focused local aristocratic enmities, preventing them from spinning out of royal control. By the beginning of the seventh century, three relatively stable kingdoms had emerged: Austrasia to the northeast; Neustria to the west, with its capital city at Paris; and Burgundy, incorporating the southeast (see Map 7.3). These divisions were so useful to local aristocrats and to the Merovingian dynasty alike that even when royal power was united in the hands of one king, Clothar II (r. 613–623), he made his son the independent king of Austrasia.

The very power of the kings in the seventh century, however, gave greater might to their chief court official, the mayor of the palace. In the following century, allied with the Austrasian aristocracy, one mayoral family would displace the Merovingian dynasty and establish a new royal line, the Carolingians.

Christianity and Classical Culture in the British Isles

The Frankish kingdoms exemplify some of the ways in which Roman and non-Roman traditions combined. Anglo-Saxon England shows still another way in its formation of a learned monastic culture. The impetus for this culture came not from native traditions but from Rome and Ireland. After the Anglo-Saxon conquest (440–600), England gradually emerged politically as a mosaic of about a dozen kingdoms ruled by separate kings. They were surrounded by Christian cultures in the rest of the British Isles (Wales, Scotland, and Ireland), and slowly the quadrant conquered by the Anglo-Saxons became Christian as well.

In the north of England, Irish monks brought their own brand of Christianity. Converted in the fifth century by St. Patrick and other missionaries, the Irish had rapidly evolved a church organization that corresponded to its rural clan organization. Abbots and abbesses, generally from powerful dynasties, headed monastic *familiae*, communities composed of blood relatives, servants, and slaves as well as monks or nuns. Bishops were often under the authority of abbots, and the monasteries rather than cities were the centers of population settlement in Ireland. The Irish missionaries to England were monks, and they set up monasteries on the model of those at home.

In the south of England, Christianity came by way of missionaries sent by Gregory the Great (r. 590–604) in 596–597. The missionaries, under the leadership of Augustine (not the same Augustine as the bishop of Hippo), intended to convert the king and people of Kent, the southernmost kingdom, and then work their way northward. But Augustine and his party brought with them Roman practices at odds with those of Irish Christianity, stressing ties to the pope and the organization of the church under bishops rather than abbots.◆ Using the Roman model, they divided England into *dioceses*, territorial units headed by an archbishop and bishops. Augustine, for example, became archbishop of Canterbury. Because he was a monk, he set up a monastery right next to his cathedral, and it became a unique characteristic of the English church to have a community of monks attached to the bishop's church.

◆ For a primary source that describes the missions from Rome to England, see Document 22, Pope Gregory the Great, "Letters."

A major bone of contention between the Roman and Irish churches involved the calculation of the date of Easter. The Roman church insisted that Easter fall on the first Sunday after the spring equinox. The Irish had a different method of determining when Easter should fall, and therefore they celebrated on a different day. As everyone agreed that believers could not be saved unless they observed Christ's resurrection properly and on the right day, the conflict over dates was bitter. It was resolved by Oswy, king of Northumbria. In 664, he organized a meeting of churchmen, the Synod of Whitby, which chose the Roman calculation. Oswy was convinced that Rome spoke with the voice of St. Peter, who, according to the New Testament, held the keys of the Kingdom of Heaven. Oswy's decision paved the way for the triumph of the Roman brand of Christianity in England.

St. Peter was not the only reason the Anglo-Saxons favored Rome. To many English churchmen, Rome had great prestige because it was a treasure trove of knowledge, piety, and holy objects. Benedict Biscop (c. 630–690), the founder of two important English monasteries, made many arduous trips to Rome, bringing back relics, liturgical vestments, and even a cantor to teach his monks the proper melodies in a time before written musical notation. Above all, he went to Rome to get books. At his monasteries in the north of England, he built up a grand library. In Anglo-Saxon England as in Ireland, both of which lacked a strong classical tradition from Roman times, a book was considered a precious object, to be decorated as finely as a garnet-studded brooch.

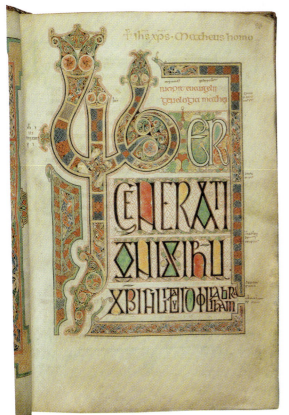

■ **Page from the Lindisfarne Gospels**
At the end of the seventh century, the monks of Lindisfarne, in the extreme north of England, produced a lavishly illuminated manuscript of the Gospels. For the Lindisfarne brethren and many others of the time, the book was a precious object, to be decorated much like a piece of jewelry. To introduce each of the four Gospels, the artist, the monk Eadfrith, produced three elaborate pages: the first was a "portrait" of the evangelist, the second a decorative "carpet" page, and the third the beginning of the text itself. The page depicted here is the beginning of the Gospel according to St. Matthew, which opens with the words "Liber generationis." Notice how elaborately Eadfrith treated the first letter, L, and how the decoration gradually recedes, so that the last line, though still very embellished, is quite plain in comparison with the other lines. In this way, Eadfrith led the reader slowly and reverently into the text. (British Library.)

The Anglo-Saxons and Irish Celts had a thriving oral culture but extremely limited uses for writing. The ability to write and read became valuable only when these societies converted to Christianity. Just as Islamic reliance on the Qur'an made possible a literary culture under the Umayyads, so Christian dependence on the Bible, written liturgy, and patristic thought helped make England and Ireland centers of literature and learning in the seventh and eighth centuries. Archbishop Theodore (r. 669–690), who had studied at Constantinople and was one of the most learned men of his day, founded a school at Canterbury where students mined Latin and even some Greek manuscripts to comment on biblical texts. Men like Benedict Biscop soon sponsored other centers of learning, using texts from the classical past. Although women did not establish famous schools, many abbesses ruled over monasteries that stressed Christian learning. Here as elsewhere, Latin writings, even pagan texts, were studied diligently, in part because Latin was so foreign a language that mastering it required systematic and formal study. One of Benedict Biscop's pupils was Bede (673–735), an Anglo-Saxon monk and a historian of extraordinary breadth. Bede in turn taught a new generation of monks who became advisers to eighth-century rulers.

After the Synod of Whitby, the English church was tied by doctrine, friendship, and conviction to the church of Rome. An influential Anglo-Saxon monk and bishop, Wynfrith, even changed his name to the Latin "Boniface" to symbolize his loyalty to the Roman church. Preaching on the continent, Boniface (680–754) worked to set up churches in Germany and Gaul that, like those in England, looked to Rome for leadership and guidance. His zeal would give the papacy new importance in the West.

Unity in Spain, Division in Italy

In contrast to England, southern Gaul, Spain, and Italy had long been part of the Roman Empire and preserved many of its traditions. Nevertheless, as new peoples settled and fought over them, their histories diverged dramatically. When the Merovingian king Clovis defeated the Visigoths in 507, their vast kingdom, which had sprawled across southern Gaul and into Spain, was dismembered. By midcentury, the Franks came into possession of most of the Visigothic kingdom in southern Gaul.

In Spain the Visigothic king Leovigild (r. 569–586) established territorial control by military might. But no ruler could hope to maintain power there without the support of the Hispano-Roman population, which included both the great landowners and the leading bishops; and their backing was unattainable while the Visigoths remained Arian. Leovigild's son Reccared (r. 586–601) took the necessary step in 587, converting to Catholic Christianity. Two years later, at the Third Council of Toledo, most of the Arian bishops followed their king by announcing their conversion to Catholicism, and the assembled churchmen enacted decrees for a united church in Spain.

Thereafter the bishops and kings of Spain cooperated to a degree unprecedented in other regions. The king gave the churchmen free rein to set up their own hierarchy (with the bishop of Toledo at the top) and to meet regularly at synods to regulate and reform the church. The bishops in turn supported their Visigothic king, who ruled as a minister of the Christian people. Rebellion against him was tantamount to rebellion against Christ. The Spanish bishops reinforced this idea by anointing the king, daubing him with holy oil in a ritual that paralleled the ordination of priests and demonstrated divine favor. Toledo, the city where the highest bishop presided, was also where the kings were "made" through anointment. While the bishops in this way made the king's cause their own, their lay counterparts, the great landowners, helped supply the king with troops, allowing him to maintain internal order and repel his external enemies.

Ironically, it was precisely the centralization and unification of the Visigothic kingdom that proved its undoing. When the Arabs arrived in 711, they needed only to kill the king, defeat his army, and capture Toledo to deal it a crushing blow.

By contrast, in Italy the Lombard king constantly faced a hostile papacy in the center of the peninsula and virtually independent dukes in the south. Theoretically royal officers, in fact the dukes of Benevento and Spoleto ruled on their own behalf. Although many Lombards were Catholics, others, including important kings and dukes, were Arian. The official religion varied with the ruler in power. Rather than signal a major political event, the conversion of the Lombards to Catholic Christianity occurred gradually, ending only around the mid-seventh century. Partly as a result of this slow development, the Lombard kings, unlike the Visigoths, Franks, or even the Anglo-Saxons, never enlisted the wholehearted support of any particular group of churchmen.

Lacking strong and united ecclesiastical favor, Lombard royal power still had bulwarks. Chief among these were the traditions of leadership associated with the royal dynasty, the kings' military ability and their control over large estates in northern Italy, and the Roman institutions that survived in Italy. Although the Italian peninsula had been devastated by the wars between the Ostrogoths and the Byzantine Empire, the Lombard kings took advantage of the still-urban organization of Italian society and economy, assigning dukes to city bases and setting up a royal capital at Pavia. Recalling emperors like Constantine and Justinian, the kings built churches, monasteries, and other places of worship in the royal capital, maintained the walls, and minted coins. Revenues from tolls, sales taxes, port duties, and court fines filled their coffers. Like other Germanic kings, the Lombards issued law codes that

**Lombard Italy,
Early Eighth Century**

revealed a great debt to Roman legal collections, such as those commissioned by Justinian. While individual provisions of the law code promulgated by King Rothari (r. 636–652), for example, reflected Lombard traditions, the code also suggested the Roman idea that the law should apply to all under his rule, not just Lombards. "We desire," Rothari wrote,

> that these laws be brought together in one volume so that everyone may lead a secure life in accordance with the law and justice, and in confidence thereof will willingly set himself against his enemies and defend himself and his homeland.

Unfortunately for the Lombard kings, the "homeland" that they hoped to rule was fractured, not only by the duchies of Spoleto and Benevento but, more importantly, by the papacy, which dominated central Italy.

By 600, the pope's position was ambiguous: he was both a ruler and a subordinate. On the one hand, believing he was the successor of St. Peter and head of the church, he wielded real secular power. Pope Gregory the Great (r. 590–604) in many ways laid the foundations for the papacy's later spiritual and temporal ascendancy. During his tenure, the pope became the greatest landowner in Italy; he organized the defenses of Rome and paid for its army; he heard court cases, made treaties, and provided welfare services. The missionary expedition he sent to England was only a small part of his involvement in the rest of Europe. For example, Gregory maintained close ties with the churchmen in Spain who were working to convert the Visigoths from Arianism to Catholicism. A prolific author of spiritual works and biblical commentaries, Gregory digested and simplified the ideas of church fathers like St. Augustine of Hippo, making them accessible to a wider audience. His practical handbook for the clergy, *Pastoral Rule*, was matched by practical reforms within the church: he tried to impose in Italy regular elections of bishops and to enforce clerical celibacy.

On the other hand, the pope was not independent. He was only one of many bishops in the Roman Empire, which was now ruled from Constantinople; and he was therefore subordinate to the emperor and Byzantium. Imperial authority did not begin to unravel in Rome until the late seventh century. In 691, Emperor Justinian II convened a council that determined 102 rules for the church, and he sent them to Rome for papal endorsement. Most of the rules were unobjectionable, but Pope Sergius I (r. 687 or 689–701) was unwilling to agree to the whole because it permitted priestly marriages (which the Roman church did not want to allow) and it prohibited fasting on Saturdays in Lent (which the Roman church required). Outraged by Sergius's refusal, Justinian tried to arrest the pope, but Italian armies (theoretically under the emperor) came to the pontiff's aid, while Justinian's arresting officer cowered under the pope's bed. The incident reveals that some local forces

IMPORTANT DATES			
c. 570–632	Life of Muhammad, prophet of Islam	630–730	Period of Islamic conquests
590–604	Papacy of Gregory the Great	661	Death of Ali; origins of Sunni/Shi'ite split
c. 591	Columbanus, an Irish monk, arrives on the European continent	661–750	Umayyad caliphate
596–597	Augustine sent to England by Pope Gregory the Great to convert the Anglo-Saxons	664	Synod of Whitby; English king opts for Roman Christianity
610–641	Reign of Emperor Heraclius	718	Major Arab attack on Constantinople repulsed
622	Muhammad's Hijra to Medina and beginning of Islamic calendar	726–843	Period of iconoclasm at Byzantium

were already willing to rally to the side of the pope against the emperor. By now Constantinople's influence and authority over Rome was tenuous at best. Sheer distance, as well as diminishing imperial power in Italy, meant the popes were in effect the leaders of the parts of Italy not controlled by the Lombards.

The gap between Byzantium and the papacy widened in the early eighth century as Emperor Leo III tried to increase the taxes on papal property to pay for his all-consuming war against the Arab invaders. The pope responded by leading a general tax revolt. Meanwhile, Leo's fierce policy of iconoclasm collided with the pope's tolerance of images. In the West, Christian piety focused not so much on icons as on relics, but the papacy was not willing to allow sacred images and icons to be destroyed. The pope argued that holy images could and should be venerated—but not worshiped. His support of images reflected popular opinion as well. A later commentator wrote that iconoclasm so infuriated the inhabitants of Ravenna and Venice that "if the pope had not prohibited the people, they would have attempted to set up a [different] emperor over themselves."

These difficulties with the emperor were matched by increasing friction between the pope and the Lombards. The Lombard kings had gradually managed to bring under their control the duchies of Spoleto and Benevento as well as part of the Exarchate of Ravenna. By the mid-eighth century, the popes feared that Rome would fall to the Lombards, and Pope Zachary (r. 741–752) looked northward for friends. He created an ally by sanctioning the deposition of the last Merovingian king and his replacement by the first Carolingian king, Pippin III the Short (r. 751–768). In 753, Zachary's successor, Pope Stephen II (r. 752–757), called on Pippin to march to Italy with an army to fight the Lombards. Thus events at Rome had a major impact on the history not only of Italy but of the Frankish kingdom as well.

Conclusion

The three heirs of the Roman Empire—Byzantines, Muslims, and the peoples of western Europe—built upon three distinct legacies. Byzantium directly inherited the central political institutions of Rome; its people called themselves Romans; its emperor was the Roman emperor; and its capital, Constantinople, was the new Rome. Sixth-century Byzantium also inherited the cities, laws, and religion of Rome. The changes of the seventh and eighth centuries—contraction of territory, urban decline, disappearance of the old elite, a ban on sacred images—whittled away at this Roman character. By 750, Byzantium was less Roman than it was a new, resilient political and cultural entity, a Christian polity on the borders of the new Muslim empire.

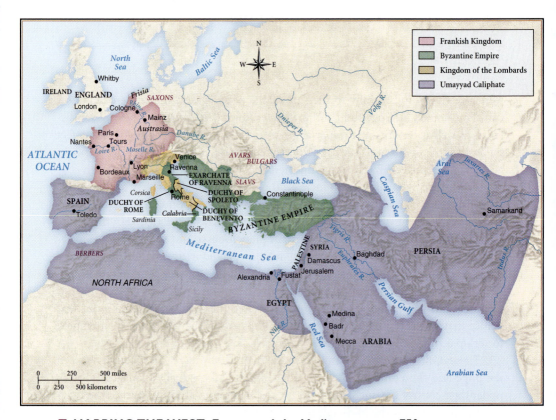

■ **MAPPING THE WEST** Europe and the Mediterranean, c. 750
The major political fact of the period 600–750 was the emergence of Islam and the conquest of an Islamic state that reached from Spain to the Indus River. The Byzantine Empire, once a great power, was dwarfed—and half swallowed up—by its Islamic neighbor. To the west were fledgling barbarian kingdoms, mere trifles on the world stage. The next centuries, however, would prove their resourcefulness and durability.

www.bedfordstmartins.com/huntconcise   See the ONLINE STUDY GUIDE for more help in analyzing this map.

Muslims were the newcomers to the Roman world, with Islam influenced by Jewish monotheism and only indirectly by Roman Christianity. Under the guidance of the Prophet Muhammad, Islam became both a coherent theology and a tightly structured way of life with customs based on Bedouin tribal traditions and defined in the Qur'an. But once the Muslim Arabs embarked on military conquests, they, too, became heirs of Rome, preserving its cities, hiring its civil servants, and adopting its artistic styles. Drawing upon Roman and Persian traditions, the Muslims created a powerful Islamic state, with a capital city in Syria, regional urban centers elsewhere, and a culture that tolerated a wide variety of economic, religious, and social institutions so long as the conquered paid taxes to their Muslim overlords.

Western Europe also inherited Roman institutions but changed them in many diverse ways. Merovingian Gaul built on Roman traditions that had long been transformed by provincial and Germanic custom. In Italy and at Rome itself, the traditions of the classical past remained living parts of the fabric of life. The roads remained, the cities of Italy (though depopulated) survived, and both the popes and the Lombard kings ruled in the traditions of Roman government. In Spain, the Visigothic kings allied themselves with a Hispano-Roman elite that maintained elements of the organization and vigorous intellectual traditions of the late empire. However, in England, once the far-flung northern summit of the Roman Empire, the Roman legacy had to be "reimported" in the seventh century by Anglo-Saxon churchmen seeking what they took to be a more authentic Christianity.

All three heirs to Rome suffered the ravages of war. In all three societies the social hierarchy became simpler, with the loss of "middle" groups like the *curiales* at Byzantium, the decline of city dwellers in western Europe, and the near suppression of tribal affiliations among Muslims. As each of the three heirs shaped Roman institutions to its own uses and advantages, each also strove to create a religious polity. In Byzantium, the emperor was a religious force, presiding over the destruction of images. In the Islamic world, the caliph was the successor to Muhammad, a religious and political leader. In the West, the kings allied with churchmen in order to rule. Despite their many differences, all these leaders had a common understanding of their place in a divine scheme: they were God's agents on earth, ruling over God's people.

Suggested References for further reading and online research appear on page SR-12 at the back of the book.

www.bedfordstmartins.com/huntconcise   See the ONLINE STUDY GUIDE to assess your mastery of the material covered in this chapter.

Unity and Diversity in Three Societies

750–1050

I N 841, A FIFTEEN-YEAR-OLD BOY NAMED WILLIAM went to serve at the court of Charles the Bald, king of the Franks. William's father was Bernard, an extremely powerful noble. His mother was Dhuoda, a well-educated, pious, and able woman who administered the family's estates in the south of France while her husband occupied himself in court politics and royal administration. In 841, however, politics had become a dangerous business. King Charles, named after his grandfather Charlemagne, was fighting with his brothers over his portion of the Carolingian Empire, and Bernard (who had been a supporter of Charles's father, Louis the Pious) held a precarious position at the young king's court. In fact, William was sent to Charles's court as a kind of hostage, to ensure Bernard's loyalty. Anxious about her son, Dhuoda wanted to educate and counsel him, so she wrote a handbook of advice for William, outlining what he ought to believe about God, about politics and society, about obligations to his family, and, above all, about his duties to his father, which she emphasized even over loyalty to the king:

> In the human understanding of things, royal and imperial appearance and power seem preeminent in the world, and the custom of men is to account those men's actions and their names ahead of all others. . . . But despite all this . . . I caution you to render first to him whose son you are special, faithful, steadfast loyalty as long as you shall live.

■ **Ivory Situla**

A situla is a bucket. This one, carved out of ivory, held the holy water used in the consecration of an emperor—probably Otto III, whose imperial rule began in 996. The carving depicts important personages. At the center of the upper panel sits the crowned emperor, holding the symbols of his universal power: the scepter and orb. On the left sits the pope, raising his hand in blessing. The other niches of the upper panel are occupied by archbishops, bishops, and an abbot. Below stand armed guards. The ensemble as a whole suggests equality and amity between the emperor and the church. (Ann Munchow/Das Domkapital.)

William heeded his mother's words, with tragic results: when Bernard ran afoul of Charles and was executed, William died in a failed attempt to avenge his father.

Dhuoda's handbook reveals the volatile political atmosphere of the mid-ninth century, and her advice to her son points to one of its causes: a crisis of loyalty. Loyalty to emperors, caliphs, and kings—all of whom were symbols of unity cutting across regional and family ties—competed with allegiances to local authorities; and those, in turn, vied with family loyalties. The period 600–750 had seen the startling rise of Islam, the whittling away of Byzantium, and the emergence of stable political and economic institutions in an impoverished West. The period 750–1050 would see all three societies contend with internal issues of diversity even as they became increasingly conscious of their unity and uniqueness. At the beginning of this period, rulers built up and dominated strong and united polities. By the end, these realms had fragmented into smaller, more local, units. Although men and women continued to feel some loyalty toward faraway kings, caliphs, or emperors, their most powerful allegiances often focused on authorities closer to home.

At Byzantium, military triumphs brought the emperors enormous prestige. A renaissance of culture and art took place at Constantinople. Yet at the same time newly powerful families began to dominate the Byzantine countryside. In the Islamic world, a dynastic revolution in 750 ousted the Umayyads from the caliphate and replaced them with a new family, the Abbasids. The new caliphs moved their capital eastward—shifting from Damascus to Baghdad—and adopted some elements of the persona of the Sassanid King of Kings of Persia. Yet their power, too, began to ebb as regional Islamic rulers came to the fore. In the West, Charlemagne—a Frankish king from a new dynasty, the Carolingians—forged an empire that embraced most of Europe. But this new state, like the others, turned out to be fragile, disintegrating within a generation of Charlemagne's death. Indeed, in the West even more than in the Byzantine and Islamic worlds, power fell into the hands of local strongmen.

All along the fringes of these realms, new political entities began to develop, conditioned by the religion and culture of their more dominant neighbors. Russia grew up in the shadow of Byzantium, as did Bulgaria and Serbia. The West was more crucial in the development of central Europe. By the year 1050, the contours of modern Europe and the Middle East were dimly visible.

Byzantium: Renewed Strength and Influence

In the hundred years between 750 and 850, Byzantium staved off Muslim attacks in Asia Minor and began to rebuild itself. After 850 it went on the attack, and by 900 it had reconquered some of the territory it had lost. Military victory brought new wealth and power to the imperial court, and the emperors supported a vast program of literary and artistic revival—the Macedonian renaissance—at Constantinople. But while the emperor dominated at the capital, a new landowning elite began to control the countryside. On its northern front, Byzantium helped create new Slavic realms.

Imperial Might

The seventh-century imperial reorganization of the Byzantine army into *themes* proved effective against Islamic armies. Avoiding battles in the field, the Byzantines allowed Muslim warriors to enter their territory, but they evacuated the local populations and burned any extra food. Then they waited in their fortified strongholds for the Muslims to attack. In this way they fought from a position of strength. If the Muslims decided to withdraw, other Byzantine troops were ready at the border to ambush them.

Beginning around 850 and lasting until 1025, the Byzantines turned the tables. They began advancing on all fronts, employing new-style mobile forces along with the *theme* soldiers. By the 1020s, they had regained Antioch, Crete, and Bulgaria (Map 8.1). They had not controlled so much territory since their wars with the Sassanid Persians four hundred years earlier.

■ **MAP 8.1 The Expansion of Byzantium, 860–1025**

In 860, the Byzantine Empire was a shrunken hourglass. To the west, it had lost most of Italy; to the east, it held only part of Asia Minor. On its northern flank, the Bulgarians had set up an independent state. By 1025, however, the empire had become a barbell, its western half embracing the whole Balkans, its eastern arm reaching around the Black Sea, and its southern fringe reaching nearly to Tripoli. It even encroached on the Duchy of Benevento in Italy. The year 1025 marked the Byzantine Empire at its greatest extent after the rise of Islam.

Victories such as these gave new prestige to the army and to the imperial court. New wealth matched this prestige. The emperors drew revenues from vast and growing imperial estates. They could tax and demand services from the general population at will—requiring them to build bridges and roads, to offer lodging to the imperial retinue, and to pay taxes in cash. These taxes increased over time, partly because of fiscal reforms and partly because of population increases (the approximately seven million people who lived in the empire in 780 had swelled to about eight million less than a century later).

The emperor's power extended over both civil administration and military command. Fearing potential rivals, whether from the court or in the army, emperors surrounded themselves with eunuchs—castrated men who were believed unfit to rule as emperors themselves and who were unable to have sons to challenge the imperial dynasty. Eunuchs were employed in the civil service; they held high positions in the army; and they were important palace officials.

Supported by their wealth and power, emperors negotiated with other rulers from a position of strength. Ambassadors were exchanged, and the Byzantine court received and entertained diplomats with elaborate ceremonies. One such diplomat, Liutprand, bishop of the northern Italian city of Cremona, reported on his audience with Emperor Constantine VII Porphyrogenitos (r. 913–959):

> Leaning upon the shoulders of two eunuchs I was brought into the emperor's presence. At my approach [mechanical] lions began to roar and birds to cry out, each according to its kind. . . . After I had three times made obeisance to the emperor with my face upon the ground, I lifted my head, and behold! the man whom just before I had seen sitting on a moderately elevated seat had now changed his raiment and was sitting on the level of the ceiling. How it was done I could not imagine, unless perhaps he was lifted up by some such sort of device as we use for raising the timbers of a wine press.

Although this elaborate court ceremonial clearly amused Liutprand, its real function was to express the serious, sacred, concentrated power of imperial majesty. Liutprand missed the point because he was a westerner unaccustomed to such displays.

The emperor's wealth relied on the prosperity of an agricultural economy organized for trade. State regulation and entrepreneurial enterprise were delicately balanced in Byzantine commerce. Although the emperor controlled craft and commercial guilds (such as those of the silk industry) to ensure imperial revenues and a stable supply of valuable and useful commodities, entrepreneurs organized most of the fairs held throughout the empire. Foreign merchants traded within the empire, either at Constantinople or in some border cities. Because this international trade intertwined with foreign policy, the Byzantine government considered trade a political as well as an economic matter. Emperors issued privileges to certain "nations" (as, for example, the Venetians, Russians, and Jews were called), regulating the fees they were obliged to pay and the services they had to render. At the end of the tenth century, for example, the Venetians bargained to reduce their customs dues per ship from thirty *solidi* (coins) to two; in return they promised to transport Byzantine soldiers to Italy whenever the emperor wished.

Imperial authority was not absolute, however. In the countryside, particularly in Anatolia, powerful families—often army generals but also members of the civil service and the church—bought up lands and dominated huge tracts of land. Many peasants became dependents of these great landlords, tilling the soil without owning it. Although the new magnates were a potential counterweight to imperial power, they ordinarily considered their interests to coincide with that of the emperor. They were glad to profit from imperial victories and the expansion of Byzantine territory.◆

The Macedonian Renaissance, c. 870–c. 1025

Flush with victory, which reminded them of Rome's glory, the emperors revived classical intellectual pursuits. Basil I (r. 867–886) from Macedonia founded the imperial dynasty that presided over the so-called Macedonian renaissance (c. 870–c. 1025). The *renaissance* (French for "rebirth") was made possible by an intellectual elite, members of families who, even in the anxious years of the eighth century, had persisted in studying the classics in spite of the trend toward a simple religious education.

Now, with the empire slowly regaining its military eminence and with icons permanently restored in 843, this scholarly elite thrived again. Emperors and other members of the new court society, liberated from sober taboos, sponsored sumptuous artistic productions. Emperor Constantine Porphyrogenitos wrote books of geography and history and financed the work of other scholars and artists. He even supervised the details of his craftspeople's products, insisting on exacting standards: "Who could enumerate how many artisans the Porphyrogenitos corrected? He corrected the stonemasons, the carpenters, the goldsmiths, the silversmiths, and the blacksmiths," wrote a historian supported by the same emperor's patronage.

Other members of the imperial court also sponsored writers, philosophers, and historians. Scholars wrote summaries of classical literature, encyclopedias of ancient knowledge, and commentaries on classical authors. Others copied manuscripts of religious and theological commentaries, such as homilies, liturgical texts, Bibles, and Psalters. They hoped to revive the intellectual and artistic achievements of the heyday of imperial Roman rule. But the Macedonian renaissance could not possibly succeed in this endeavor: too much had changed since the time of Justinian. Nevertheless, the renaissance permanently integrated classical forms into Byzantine political and religious life.

◆ For a primary source that reveals the prestige and power of the Byzantine aristocracy, see Document 23, the epic poem "Digenis Akritas."

New States under the Influence of Byzantium

The shape of modern eastern European states—Bulgaria, Serbia, and Russia—grew out of the Slavic polities created during the period 850–950. By 800, Slavic settlements dotted the area from the Danube River down to Greece and from the Black Sea to Croatia. The Bulgar khagan ruled over the largest realm, populated mostly by Slavic peoples and situated northwest of Constantinople. Under Khagan Krum (r. c. 803–814) and his son, Slavic rule stretched west all the way to the Tisza River in modern Hungary. At about the same time as Krum's triumphant expansion, however, the Byzantine Empire began its own campaigns to conquer, convert, and control these Slavic regions.

The Byzantine offensive began under Emperor Nicephorus I (r. 802–811), who waged war against the Slavs of Greece in the Peloponnese, set up a new Christian diocese there, organized it as a new military *theme*, and forcibly resettled Christians in the area to counteract Slavic paganism. The Byzantines followed this pattern of conquest as they pushed northward. By 900, Byzantium ruled all of Greece.

Still under Nicephorus, the Byzantines launched a massive attack against the Bulgarians, took the chief city of Pliska, plundered it, burned it to the ground, and then marched against Krum's encampment in

■ **The Crowning of Constantine Porphyrogenitos**

This ivory plaque was carved at Constantinople in the middle of the tenth century. The artist wanted to emphasize hierarchy and symbolism, not nature. Christ is shown placing the imperial crown on the head of Emperor Constantine Porphyrogenitos (r. 913–959). What message do you suppose the artist wanted to convey by making Christ higher than the emperor and by having the emperor slightly incline his head and upper torso to receive the crown?

(Hirmer Fotoarchiv, München.)

www.bedfordstmartins.com/huntconcise
See the ONLINE STUDY GUIDE for more help in analyzing this image.

the Balkan mountains. Krum took advantage of his position, however, attacked the imperial troops, killed Nicephorus, and brought home the emperor's skull in triumph. Cleaned out and lined with silver, the skull served as the victorious Krum's drinking goblet. In 816, the two sides agreed to a peace that lasted for thirty years. But hostility remained, and wars between the Bulgarians and Byzantines broke out with increasing intensity. Intermittent skirmishes gave way to longer wars throughout the tenth century. The Byzantines advanced, at first taking Bulgaria's eastern territory. Then, in a slow and methodical

The Balkans, c. 850–950

conquest (1001–1018) led by Emperor Basil II (r. 976–1025), aptly called the "Bulgar-Slayer" (Bulgaroctonos), they subjected the entire region to Byzantine rule and forced its ruler to accept the Byzantine form of Christianity. Similarly the Serbs, encouraged by Byzantium to oppose the Bulgarians, began to form the state that would become Serbia, in the shadow of Byzantine interest and religion.

Religion played an important role in the Byzantine offensive. In 863, two brothers, Cyril and Methodius, were sent as missionaries from Byzantium to the Slavs. Well-educated Greeks, they spoke one Slavic dialect fluently and devised an alphabet for Slavic (until then an oral language) based on Greek forms. It was the ancestor of the modern Cyrillic alphabet used in Bulgaria, Serbia, and Russia.

Russia in the ninth and tenth centuries lay outside the sphere of direct Byzantine rule, but like Serbia and Bulgaria, it came under increasingly strong Byzantine cultural and religious influence. Vikings—Scandinavian adventurers who ranged over vast stretches of ninth-century Europe seeking trade, booty, and land—had penetrated Russia from the north and imposed their rule over the Slavs inhabiting the broad river valleys connecting the Baltic Sea with the Black Sea and thence with Constantinople. Like the Bulgars in Bulgaria, the Scandinavian Vikings gradually blended into the larger Slavic population. At the end of the ninth century, one Dnieper valley chief, Oleg, established control over most of the tribes in southwestern Russia and forced peoples farther away to pay tribute. The tribal association he created formed the nucleus of Kievan Russia, named for the city that had become the commercial center of the region and is today the capital of Ukraine (see "Mapping the West," page 334).

Kievan Russia and Byzantium began their relationship with war, developed it through trade agreements, and finally sustained it by religion. Around 905, Oleg launched a military expedition to Constantinople, forcing the Byzantines to pay a large indemnity and open their doors to Russian traders in exchange for peace. At the time only a few Christians lived in Russia, along with Jews and probably some Muslims. The Russians' conversion to Christianity was spearheaded by a Russian ruler later in the century. Vladimir (r. c. 980–1015), the grand prince of Kiev and all Russia, and the Byzantine emperor Basil II agreed that Vladimir should adopt the Byzantine form of Christianity. Vladimir took a variant of the name Basil in honor of the emperor and married the emperor's sister Anne; then he reportedly had all the people of his state baptized in the Dnieper River.

Vladimir's conversion represented a wider pattern. Along with the Christianization of Slavic realms such as Old Moravia, Serbia, and Bulgaria under the Byzantine church, the rulers and peoples of Poland, Hungary, Denmark, and Norway were converted under the auspices of the Roman church. Russia's conversion to Christianity was especially significant, because Russia was geographically as close to the Islamic world as to the Christian and could conceivably have become an Islamic land. By converting to Byzantine Christianity, Russians made themselves heirs to Byzantium and its church, customs, art, and political ideology. Adopting Christianity linked Russia to the Christian world, but choosing Byzantine rather than

■ **Four Daughters of Iaroslav the Wise**

Imitating the Byzantines, who had a church of St. Sophia (Holy Wisdom) in their capital at Constantinople, Iaroslav the Wise built his own church of Holy Wisdom at Kiev. Iaroslav was in contact with Europe as well as with Byzantium, and his church contains a hint of those interests. On its walls are frescoes (paintings on fresh plaster) of his daughters. Here they are portrayed as pious members of the church. But they were also pawns of diplomacy. Iaroslav had his oldest daughter marry the king of Norway; the second married the king of France, Henry I; and the third married the king of Hungary. (Photo courtesy Thames and Hudson Ltd., London, from *The Dark Ages*, 1975.)

Roman Christianity served to isolate Russia later from western Europe, because in time the Greek and Roman churches would become estranged.

Under Prince Iaroslav the Wise (r. 1019–1054), Russia forged links through Iaroslav's own marriage and the marriages of his sons and daughters to rulers and princely families in France, Hungary, and Scandinavia. His ideal of rulership came directly from Roman traditions; he encouraged intellectual and artistic developments that would connect Russian culture to the classical past. But after his death, civil wars broke out, shredding what unity Russia had known. Massive invasions by outsiders, particularly from the east, further weakened Kievan rulers, who were eventually displaced by princes from northern Russia. At the crossroads of East and West, Russia could meet and adopt a great variety of traditions; but its situation also opened it to unremitting military pressures.

From Unity to Fragmentation in the Islamic World

A new dynasty of caliphs—the Abbasids—first brought unity and then, in their decline, fragmentation to the Islamic world. Caliphs continued to rule in name only, while regional rulers took over the real business of government in Islamic lands. Local traditions based on religious and political differences played an increasingly important role in people's lives. Yet even in the eleventh century, the Islamic world had a clear sense of its own unity, based on language, commercial life, and vigorous intellectual give-and-take across regional boundaries.

The Abbasid Caliphate, 750–c. 950

In 750, a civil war ousted the Umayyads and raised the Abbasids to the caliphate. The Abbasids found support in an uneasy coalition of Shi'ites (the faction loyal to Ali's memory) and non-Arabs who had been excluded from Umayyad government and now demanded a place in political life. The new regime signaled a revolution. The center of the Islamic state shifted from Damascus, with its roots in the Roman tradition, east to Baghdad, a new capital city built by the Abbasids right next to Ctesiphon, which had been the Sassanid capital. At first the caliphs were powerful: commanding a large centralized civil service, they also controlled the appointment of regional governors.

The Abbasid caliph Harun al-Rashid (r. 786–809), for example, presided over a flourishing empire from Baghdad.♦ (He and his court are immortalized in *A Thousand and One Nights,* a series of anonymous stories about Scheherezade's efforts to keep her husband from killing her by telling him a story each night for 1,001 nights.)

♦ For a primary source that details life in the Abbasid capital, see Document 24, Ahmad al-Yaʿqūbī, "Kitāb al-buldān."

Charlemagne, Harun's contemporary, was very impressed with the elephant Harun sent him as a gift, along with monkeys, spices, and medicines. But these items were mainstays of everyday commerce in Harun's Iraq. For example, a mid-ninth-century list of imports inventoried "tigers, panthers, elephants, panther skins, rubies, white sandal, ebony, and coconuts" from India and "silk, chinaware, paper, ink, peacocks, racing horses, saddles, felts [and] cinnamon" from China.

The Abbasid dynasty began to decline after Harun's death, mostly because of economic problems. Obliged to support a huge army and an increasingly complex civil service, the Abbasids found their tax base inadequate. They needed to collect revenues from their provinces, such as Syria and Egypt, but the governors of those regions were often able to refuse to send the revenues. After Harun's caliphate, ex-soldiers, seeking better salaries, recognized different caliphs and fought for power in savage civil wars. The caliphs tried to bypass the regular army, made up largely of free Muslim foot soldiers, by turning to slaves, bought and armed to serve as mounted cavalry. But the caliphate's dwindling revenues could not sustain a loyal or powerful military force, and in the tenth century the caliphs became figureheads only, as independent rulers established themselves in the various Islamic regions. To support themselves militarily, many of these new rulers turned to independent military commanders who led armies of Mamluks—Turkish slaves or freedmen trained as professional mounted soldiers. Mamluks were well paid to maintain their mounts and arms, and many gained renown and high positions at the courts of regional rulers.

■ **Minaret of the Great Mosque at Samarra**
From 836 to 892, the Abbasid caliphs had their capital at Samarra, about seventy miles north of Baghdad. In part, the choice of this location was a response to the very tensions that eventually produced the separate Islamic states of the tenth century. At Samarra itself, the Abbasid court created a cultural center. The Great Mosque, begun in 847, is the largest mosque ever built. Shown here is its minaret (the tower from which Muslims are summoned to prayer), which looms over the mosque some distance from its outer wall. Scholars are still debating the reasons for its spiral shape.
(Bildarchiv Preußischer Kulturbesitz.)

Regional Diversity

A faraway caliph could not command sufficient allegiance from local leaders once he demanded more in taxes than he gave back in favors. The forces of fragmentation were strong in the Islamic world: it was, after all, based on the conquest of many diverse regions, each with its own deeply rooted traditions and culture. The Islamic religion, with its Sunni/Shi'ite split, also became a source of polarization. Western Europeans knew almost nothing about Muslims and called them all *Saracens* (from the Latin for "Arabs") without distinction. But, in fact, Muslims were of different ethnicities, practiced different customs, and identified with different regions. With the fragmentation of political and religious unity, each of the tenth- and early-eleventh-century Islamic states built on local traditions under local rulers (Map 8.2).

The most important and successful of these new states was formed by the Fatimids, a group of Shi'ites who took their name after Fatimah, wife of Ali and Muhammad's only surviving child. Allying with the Berbers in North Africa, the Fatimids established themselves in 909 as rulers in the region now called Tunisia. The Fatimid Ubayd Allah claimed to be not only the true imam, descendant of Ali, but also the *mahdi*, the "divinely guided" messiah, come to bring justice on earth.

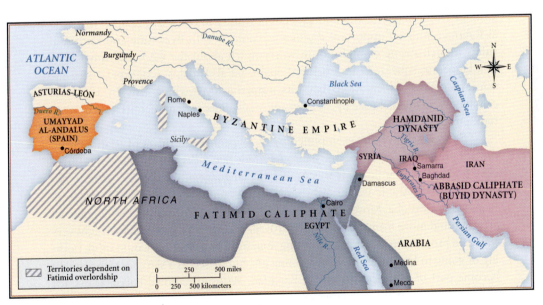

■ **MAP 8.2 Islamic States, c. 1000**

A glance back at Map 7.2 (see page 271) will quickly demonstrate the fragmentation of the once united Islamic caliphate. In 750, one caliph ruled territory stretching from Spain to India. In 1000, there was more than one caliphate as well as several other ruling dynasties. The most important were the Fatimids, who began as organizers of a movement to overthrow the Abbasids. By 1000, they had conquered Egypt and claimed hegemony over all of North Africa and even Sicily.

In 969, the Fatimids declared themselves rulers of Egypt, and eventually they controlled North Africa, Arabia, and even southern Syria. Their dynasty lasted for about two hundred years.

While the Shi'ite Fatimids were dominating Egypt, Sunni Muslims ruled al-Andalus, the Islamic central and southern heart of Spain. Unlike the other independent Islamic states forged during the ninth and tenth centuries, the Spanish emirate of Córdoba (so called because its ruler took the secular title *emir*, "commander," and fixed his capital at Córdoba) was created near the start of the Abbasid caliphate, in 756. During the Abbasid revolution, Abd al-Rahman—a member of the Umayyad family—fled to North Africa, gathered an army, invaded Spain, and was declared emir after only one battle. He and his Umayyad successors ruled a broad range of peoples, including many Jews and Christians. After the initial Islamic conquest of Spain, the Christians adopted so much of the new language and so many of the customs that they were called *Mozarabs*, "would-be Arabs," by Christians elsewhere. Their rulers allowed them freedom of worship and let them live according to their own laws. Some Mozarabs were content with their status; others converted to Islam; still others intermarried—most commonly, Christian women married Muslim men and raised their children as Muslims.

Under Abd al-Rahman III (r. 912–961), who took the title *caliph* ("successor" to Muhammad) in 929, members of all religious groups in al-Andalus were given absolute freedom of worship and equal opportunity to rise in the civil service. Abd al-Rahman initiated important diplomatic contacts with Byzantine and European rulers. He felt strong enough not to worry much about the weak and tiny Christian kingdoms squeezed into northern Spain. Yet al-Andalus, too, experienced the same political fragmentation that was occurring everywhere else. In 1031, the caliphate of Córdoba broke up, as rulers of small, independent regions, called *taifas*, took power.

The regional diversity exemplified by the Fatimids and rulers of Islamic Spain did not prevent a measure of unity through trade networks and language. The principal bond of all Islamic lands was Arabic, the language of the Qur'an. At once poetic and sacred, Arabic was also the language of commerce and government from Baghdad to Córdoba. Moreover, despite political differences, borders were open: an artisan could move from Córdoba to Cairo; a landowner in North Africa might very well own property in al-Andalus; a young man from North Africa would think nothing of going to Iran to find a wife; a young girl purchased as a slave in Mecca might become part of a prince's harem in Baghdad. With no national barriers to trade and few regulations (though every city and town had its own customs dues), traders regularly dealt in far-flung, various, and often exotic goods.

Although the primary reason for this internationalism was Islam itself, open borders extended to non-Muslims as well. The Tustari brothers, Jewish merchants from southern Iran, typified the commercial activity in the Arabic-speaking world. By 1026, they had established a flourishing business in Egypt. The Tustaris did not have "branch offices," but informal contacts allowed them many of the same advantages and much flexibility: friends and family in Iran shipped them fine textiles to sell in Egypt, and the Tustaris exported Egyptian fabrics to sell in Iran. But the sophisticated Islamic society of the tenth and eleventh centuries supported networks even more vast than those represented by the Tustari family. Muslim merchants brought tin from England; salt and gold from Timbuktu in west-central Africa; amber, gold, and copper from Russia; and slaves from every region.

The Islamic Renaissance, c. 790–c. 1050

The dissolution of the caliphate into separate political entities multiplied the centers of learning and intellectual productivity. Unlike the Macedonian renaissance of Byzantium, which was concentrated in Constantinople, a "renaissance of Islam" occurred throughout the Islamic world. It was particularly dazzling in urban court centers such as Córdoba, where tenth-century rulers presided over a brilliant court culture. They patronized scholars, poets, and artists, and their library at Córdoba contained the largest collection of books in Europe.

Elsewhere, already in the eighth century, the Abbasid caliphs endowed research libraries and set up centers for translation where scholars culled the writings of the ancients, including the classics of Persia, India, and Greece. Scholars read, translated, and commented on the works of Neo-Platonists and Aristotle. Others worked

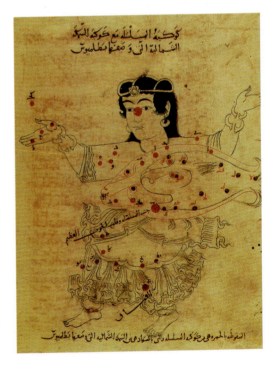

■ **Andromeda C**

The study of medicine, physics, astronomy, and other sciences flourished in the tenth and eleventh centuries in the cosmopolitan Islamic world. This whimsical depiction of Andromeda C, a constellation visible in the Northern Hemisphere, illustrates the Book of Images of the Fixed Stars *(c. 965), an astronomical treatise written by al-Sufi at the request of his "pupil," the ruler of Iran. Knowledge of astronomy was important for both secular and religious reasons: the Muslim calendar was lunar, and the times of Muslim prayer were calculated from the movement of the sun. Al-Sufi drew from classical treatises, particularly the Almagest by Ptolemy. This copy of the* Book of Images, *probably made by al-Sufi's son in 1009, also draws on classical models for the illustrations, although instead of Greek clothing, Andromeda wears the pantaloons and skirt of an Islamic dancer.*

(Bodleian Library, Oxford.)

on mathematical matters. Al-Khwarizmi wrote a book on equation theory in about 825 that became so well known in the West that the word *al-jabr* in the title of his book became the English word *algebra*. Other scholars, such as Ali al-Hasan (d. 1038) (known as "Alhazen" in the West) wrote studies on cubic and quadratic equations. Muhammad ibn Musa (d. 850) used a numeral system devised in India in his treatise on arithmetical calculations, introducing as well the crucial number zero. No wonder that the numbers 1, 2, 3, and so on, were known as "Arabic numerals" when they were introduced into western Europe in the twelfth century.

The newly independent Islamic rulers supported science as well as mathematics. Unusual because she was a woman was al-Asturlabi, who followed her father's profession as a maker of astrolabes for the Syrian court. Astrolabes measured the altitude of the sun and stars to calculate time and latitude. More typical were men like Ibn Sina (980–1037), known in the West as Avicenna, who wrote books on logic, the natural sciences, and physics. His *Canon of Medicine* systematized earlier treatises and reconciled them with his own experience as a physician. Active in the centers of power, he served as vizier (prime minister) to various rulers.

Long before there were universities in the West, there were important institutions of higher learning in the Islamic world. In Islam all law and literature was understood to derive from God's commands as contained in the Qur'an or as revealed to the ummah, the community of believers. For this reason, the study of the Qur'an and related texts held a central place in Islamic life. In the tenth and eleventh centuries, rich Muslims, generally of the ruling elite, demonstrated their piety and charity by establishing schools for professors and their students. Each school, or *madrasa*, was located within or attached to a mosque. Visiting scholars often arrived at the madrasas to dispute, in a formal and rational way, with the professors there. Such events of intellectual sparring attracted huge audiences. On ordinary days, though, the professors held regular classes. A professor might begin his day with a class interpreting the Qur'an, following it with a class on other interpretations, and ending with a class on literary or legal texts. Students, all male, attended the classes that suited their achievement level and interest. Most students paid a fee for learning, but there were also scholarship students, such as one group of lucky students who were given annual funds by a tenth-century vizier. He was so solicitous for the welfare of all scholars that each day he set out for them iced refreshments, candles, and paper in his own kitchen.

The use of paper, made from flax and hemp or rags and vegetable fiber, points up a major difference among the Islamic, Byzantine, and (as we shall see) Carolingian renaissances. Byzantine scholars worked to enhance the prestige of the ruling classes. Using expensive parchment, their manuscripts could serve only the very rich. This was true of scholarship in the West as well. By contrast, Islamic scholars had goals that cut across all classes: to be physicians to the rich, teachers to the young, and contributors to passionate religious debates. Their writings, on less expensive paper, were widely available.

The Creation and Division of a New Western Empire

Just as in the Byzantine and Islamic worlds, so, too, in the West, the period 750–1050 saw first the formation of a strong empire, ruled by one man, and then its fragmentation, as local rulers took power into their own hands. A new dynasty, the Carolingians, came to rule in the Frankish kingdom at almost the very moment that the Abbasids gained the caliphate. Charlemagne, the most powerful Carolingian monarch, conquered new territory, took the title of emperor, and initiated the revival of Christian classical culture known as the "Carolingian renaissance" (c. 790–c. 900). He ruled at the local level through counts and other military men who were faithful to him—he called them his *fideles*, or "loyal men." Nevertheless, the unity of this empire, based largely on conquest, a measure of prosperity, and personal allegiance to Charlemagne, was shaky. Its weaknesses were exacerbated by attacks from invaders—Vikings, Muslims, and Magyars. Charlemagne's successors divided his empire among themselves and saw it divided further as local strongmen took over the defense—and rule—of the land.

The Rise of the Carolingians

The Carolingians were among many aristocratic families on the rise during the Merovingian period. Like the others, they were important landowners, but unlike the others they gained exceptional power by monopolizing the position of "palace mayor" in the kingdom of Austrasia and, after 687, the kingdom of Neustria as well (see Map 7.3). As mayors, the Carolingians traveled with the Merovingian kings, signed their documents, and helped them formulate and carry out policies. They also cemented alliances with other aristocrats on their own behalf and, by patronizing monasteries and supporting churchmen in key positions, they garnered additional prestige and influence. In the first half of the eighth century, many of the Merovingian kings were children, and the mayors took over much of the responsibility and power of kings themselves.

Charles Martel gave the name "Carolingian" (from *Carolus*, Latin for "Charles") to the dynasty. As palace mayor from 714 to 741, Charles Martel spent most of his time fighting vigorously against opposing aristocratic groups, although later generations would recall with nostalgia his defeat of a contingent of Muslims between Poitiers and Tours in about 733. In contending against regional aristocrats who were trying to carve out independent lordships for themselves, Charles Martel and his successors turned aristocratic factions against one another, rewarded supporters while crushing enemies, and brought both lay and clerical aristocrats into alliance with him.

The Carolingians chose their allies well. Anglo-Saxon missionaries like Boniface, who went to Frisia (today the Netherlands) and Germany, helped them expand their control, converting the population as a prelude to conquest. Many of the areas Boniface reached had long been Christian, but the churches there had followed local or Irish models rather than Roman. Boniface, who came to Germany from England as the pope's ambassador, set up a hierarchical church organization and founded monasteries dedicated to the rule of St. Benedict. His newly appointed bishops were loyal to Rome and the Carolingians, not to regional aristocracies. They knew that their power came from papal and royal fiat rather than from local power centers.

Charles Martel's son Pippin III (d. 768) and his supporters cemented the Carolingian partnership with the pope by deposing the Merovingian king in 751 and petitioning Pope Zachary to legitimize their actions. He agreed. The Carolingians readily returned the favor a few years later when the pope asked for their help in defense against hostile Lombards. The request signaled a major shift. Before 754, the papacy had been part of the Byzantine Empire; after that it turned to the West. Pippin launched a successful campaign against the Lombard king that ended in 756 with the so-called Donation of Pippin, a peace accord between the Lombards and the pope. The treaty gave back to the pope cities that had been ruled by the Lombard king. The new arrangement recognized what the papacy had long ago created: a territorial "republic of St. Peter" ruled by the pope, not by the Byzantine emperor. Henceforth the fate of Italy would be tied largely to the policies of the pope and the Frankish kings to the north, not to the emperors of the East.

The Carolingian partnership with the Roman church gave the dynasty a Christian aura, expressed in symbolic form by anointment. Carolingian kings, as Visigothic kings had been, were rubbed with holy oil on their foreheads and on their shoulders in a ceremony that, to contemporaries, harked back to the Old Testament kings who had been anointed by God.

Charlemagne and His Kingdom, 768–814

The most famous Carolingian king was Charles (r. 768–814), called "the Great" (*le Magne* in Old French) by his contemporaries. Epic poems portrayed Charlemagne as a just, brave, wise, and warlike king. In a biography written by Einhard, his friend and younger contemporary, Charlemagne was the model of a Roman emperor. Some scholars at his court described him as another David, the anointed Old Testament king. Modern historians are less dazzled than his contemporaries were, noting that he was complex, contradictory, and sometimes brutal. He loved listening to St. Augustine's *City of God* and supported major scholarly enterprises, yet he never learned to write. He was devout, building a beautiful chapel at his major residence at Aachen in Austrasia, yet he flouted the advice of churchmen when they told him to convert pagans rather than force baptism on them. He waged many successful wars, yet he thereby destroyed the buffer states surrounding the Frankish kingdoms, unleashing a new round of invasions even before his death.

Behind these contradictions, however, lay a unifying vision. Charlemagne dreamed of an empire that would unite the martial and learned traditions of the Roman and Germanic worlds with the legacy of Christianity. In the early years of his reign, he emphasized the martial tradition, conquering lands in all directions and subjugating the conquered peoples (Map 8.3). He invaded Italy, seizing the crown of the Lombard kings and annexing northern Italy in 774. He then moved northward and began a long and difficult war against the Saxons, concluded only after more than thirty years of fighting, during which he forcibly annexed Saxon territory and converted the Saxon people to Christianity through mass baptisms at the point of the sword. To the southeast, Charlemagne waged a campaign against

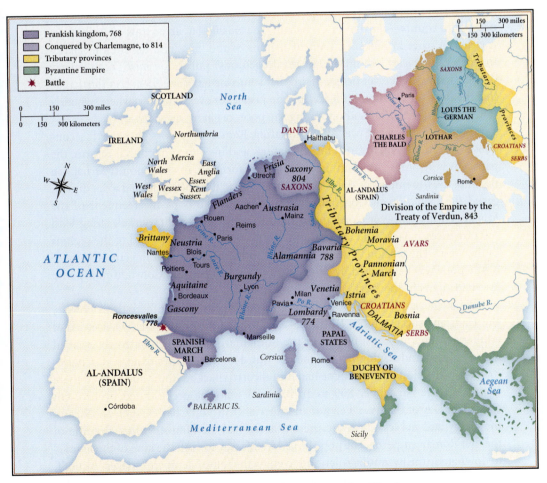

■ **MAP 8.3 Expansion of the Carolingian Empire under Charlemagne**
The conquests of Charlemagne temporarily united almost all of western Europe under one government. Although this great empire broke apart (the inset shows the divisions resulting from the Treaty of Verdun), the legacy of that unity remained and is, even today, one of the inspirations behind the European Union.

the Avars, the people who had fought the Byzantines almost two centuries before. To the southwest, Charlemagne led an expedition to Spain, setting up a *march,* or military buffer region, between al-Andalus and his own realm. By the 790s, Charlemagne's kingdom stretched eastward to the Saale River (today in eastern Germany), southeast to what is today Austria, and south to Spain and Italy.

Such hegemony in the West was unheard of since the time of the Roman Empire, and Charlemagne began to act according to the old Roman imperial model. He sponsored building programs to symbolize his authority, standardized weights and measures, and became a patron of intellectual and artistic efforts, building at Aachen a capital city that included a church patterned on one built by Justinian at Ravenna. To discourage corruption, Charlemagne appointed special officials, called *missi dominici* (meaning "those sent out by the lord king"), to oversee his regional governors—the counts—on the king's behalf. The *missi*—lay aristocrats or bishops— traveled in pairs to make a circuit of regions of the kingdom. As one of Charlemagne's capitularies (summaries of royal decisions) put it, the *missi* "are to make diligent inquiry wherever people claim that someone has done them an injustice, so that the *missi* fully carry out the law and do justice for everyone everywhere, whether in the holy churches of God or among the poor, orphans, or widows."◆

While Charlemagne was busy imitating Roman emperors through his conquests, his building programs, his legislation, and his efforts at church reform, the papacy was beginning to claim imperial power for itself. At some point, perhaps in the mid-750s, members of the papal chancery, or writing office, forged a document, called the Donation of Constantine, that declared the pope the recipient of the fourth-century emperor Constantine's crown, cloak, and military rank along with "all provinces, palaces, and districts of the city of Rome and Italy and of the regions of the West." The tension between the imperial claims of the Carolingians and those of the pope was heightened by the existence of an emperor at Constantinople who also had rights in the West.

Pope Hadrian I (r. 772–795) maintained a balance among these three powers. But Hadrian's successor, Leo III (r. 795–816), tipped the balance. In 799, accused of adultery and perjury by a faction of the Roman aristocracy, Leo narrowly escaped being blinded and having his tongue cut out. He fled northward to seek Charlemagne's protection. Charlemagne had him escorted back to Rome and arrived there himself in late November 800 to an imperial welcome orchestrated by Leo. On Christmas Day of that year, Leo put an imperial crown on Charlemagne's head, and the clergy and nobles who were present acclaimed the king *Augustus,* the title of the first Roman emperor. The pope hoped in this way to exalt the king of the Franks, to downgrade the Byzantine ruler, and to enjoy the role of "emperor maker" himself.

About twenty years later, when Einhard wrote about this coronation, he said that the imperial title at first so displeased Charlemagne "that he stated that, if he had

◆ For the text of one of Charlemagne's capitularies, see Document 25, "General Capitulary for the *Missi.*"

known in advance of the pope's plan, he would not have entered the church that day." In fact, Charlemagne did not use any title but king for more than a year afterward. But it is unlikely that he was completely surprised by the imperial title; his advisers certainly had been thinking about claiming it. He might have hesitated adopting it because he feared the reaction of the Byzantines, as Einhard went on to suggest, or he might well have objected to the papal role in his crowning rather than to the crown itself. When he finally did call himself emperor, after establishing a peace with the Byzantines, he used a long and revealing title: "Charles, the most serene Augustus, crowned by God, great and peaceful Emperor who governs the Roman Empire and who is, by the mercy of God, king of the Franks and the Lombards." According to this title, Charlemagne was not the Roman emperor crowned by the pope but rather God's emperor, who governed the Roman Empire along with his many other duties.

Charlemagne's Successors, 814–911

Charlemagne's son Louis the Pious (r. 814–840) was also crowned emperor, and he took his role as guarantor of the Christian empire even more seriously. He brought the monastic reformer Benedict of Aniane to court and issued a capitulary in 817 imposing on all the monasteries of the empire a uniform way of life based on the rule of St. Benedict. Although some monasteries opposed this legislation, and in the years to come the king was unable to impose his will directly, this moment marked the effective adoption of the Benedictine rule as the monastic standard in the West. Louis also standardized the practices of his notaries, who issued his documents and privileges, and he continued to use *missi* to administer justice throughout the realm.

In a new development of the coronation ritual, Louis's first wife, Ermengard, was crowned empress by the pope in 816. In 817, their firstborn son, Lothar, was given the title emperor and made coruler with his father. Their other sons, Pippin and Louis (later called "the German"), were made subkings under imperial rule. Louis the Pious hoped in this way to ensure the unity of the empire while satisfying the claims of his and Ermengard's three sons. But Louis's plans were thwarted by events.

Ermengard died, and Louis married Judith, the daughter of one of the most powerful families in the kingdom. In 823, Judith and Louis had a son, Charles (later known as "the Bald," to whose court Dhuoda's son William was sent). The three sons of Ermengard, bitter over the birth of another royal heir, rebelled against their father and fought one another. A chronicle written during this period suggests that nearly every year was filled with family tragedies. In 830, for example, Pippin and his brother Lothar plotted to depose their father and shut Judith up in a convent. Louis the Pious regained control, but three years later his sons by Ermengard once again banded together and imprisoned him. Louis was lucky that the brothers began quarreling among themselves. Their alliance broke apart, and he was released.

Family battles such as these continued, both during Louis's lifetime and, with great vigor, after his death in 840. In 843, the Treaty of Verdun divided the empire among the three remaining brothers (Pippin had died in 838) in an arrangement that would roughly define the future political contours of western Europe (see Map 8.3, inset). The western third, bequeathed to Charles the Bald (r. 843–877), would eventually become France; the eastern third, handed to Louis the German (r. 843–876), would become Germany. The "Middle Kingdom," which was given to Lothar (r. 840–855) along with the imperial title, had a different fate: parts of it were absorbed by France and Germany, and the rest eventually formed the modern states of the Netherlands, Belgium, Luxembourg, Switzerland, and Italy.

In 843, the European-wide empire of Charlemagne dissolved. Forged by conquest, it had been supported by a small group of privileged aristocrats with lands and offices stretching across the whole realm. Their loyalty, based on shared values, real friendship, expectations of gain, and sometimes formal ties of vassalage and fealty (see page 321), was crucial to the success of the Carolingians. The empire had also been supported by an ideal, shared by educated laymen and churchmen alike, of Christian belief and imperialism working together to bring good order to the earthly state. But powerful forces operated against the Carolingian Empire. Once the empire stopped expanding, the aristocrats could no longer hope for new lands and offices. They put down roots in particular regions and began to gather their own followings. Powerful local traditions such as different languages also undermined imperial unity. Finally, as Dhuoda revealed, some people disagreed with the imperial ideal. Asking her son to put his father before the emperor, she demonstrated her belief in the primacy of the family and the intimate and personal ties that bound it together. Dhuoda's ideal did not eliminate the emperor (European emperors would continue to reign until World War I), but it represented a new sensibility that saw real value in the breaking apart of Charlemagne's empire into smaller, more intimate local units.

Land and Power

The Carolingian economy, based on trade and agriculture, contributed to both the rise and the dissolution of the Carolingian Empire. At the onset its wealth came from land and plunder. After the booty from war ceased to pour in, the Carolingians still had access to money and goods. To the north, in Viking trading stations such as Haithabu (today Hedeby, in northern Germany), archaeologists have found Carolingian glass and pots alongside Islamic coins and cloth, which tells us that the Carolingian economy intermingled with that of the Abbasid caliphate. Silver from the Islamic world probably came north up the Volga River through Russia to the Baltic Sea. There the coins were melted down, the silver traded to the Carolingians in return for wine, jugs, glasses, and other manufactured goods. The Carolingians turned the silver into coins of their own, to be used throughout the empire for small-scale local trade. The weakening of the Abbasid caliphate in the mid-ninth century, however, disrupted this far-flung trade network and contributed to the weakening of the Carolingians at about the same time.

Land provided the most important source of Carolingian wealth and power. Like the landholders of the late Roman Empire and the Merovingian period, Carolingian aristocrats held many estates, scattered throughout the Frankish empire. But in the Carolingian period these estates were reorganized, and their productivity was carefully calculated. Modern historians often call these estates *manors*.

Typical was the manor called Villeneuve St.-Georges, which belonged to the monastery of St.-Germain-des-Prés (today in Paris) in the ninth century. Villeneuve consisted of arable fields, vineyards, meadows where animals could roam, and woodland, all scattered about the countryside rather than connected in a compact unit. The land was not tilled by slave gangs, as had been the custom on great estates of the Roman Empire, but rather by peasant families, each one settled on its own *manse*, consisting of a house, a garden, and small pieces of the arable land. The peasants farmed the land that belonged to them and also worked the *demesne*, the very large manse of the lord (in this case the abbey of St.-Germain). These peasant farms marked a major social and economic development. Slaves had not been allowed to live in family units. By contrast, the peasants on Villeneuve and on other Carolingian estates could not be displaced from their manses or separated involuntarily from their families. In this sense, the peasant household of the Carolingian period was the precursor of the modern nuclear family.

Peasants at Villeneuve practiced the most progressive sort of plowing, known as the *three-field system*. At any one time, they farmed two-thirds of the arable land. They plowed one third and planted winter wheat; they plowed another third and planted summer crops; and they plowed the final third but left the land fallow, to restore its fertility. The fields sown with crops and the field left fallow were then rotated, so that land use was repeated only every three years. Because two-thirds of the arable land was cultivated each year, this system produced larger yields than did the still prevalent two-field system, in which only half of the arable land was cultivated in any one year.

All the peasants at Villeneuve were dependents of the monastery and owed dues and services to St.-Germain. Peasants' obligations varied enormously, depending on their status and on the manse they held. One family, for example, owed four silver coins, wine, wood, three hens, and fifteen eggs every year, and the men had to plow the fields of the demesne land. Another family owed the intensive labor of working the vineyards. One woman was required to weave cloth and feed the chickens. Peasant women spent much time at the lord's house in the *gynaeceum*—the women's workshop, where they made and dyed cloth and sewed garments—or in the kitchens, as cooks. Peasant men spent most of their time in the fields.

Like other lords, the Carolingians benefited from their extensive estates. Nevertheless, farming was still too primitive to return great surpluses. Further, as the lands belonging to the king were divided up in the wake of the partitioning of the empire and new invasions, Carolingian dependence on manors scattered throughout the kingdom proved to be a source of weakness.

The Carolingian Renaissance

At the height of their power, when wealth was coming in from trade and profits from their estates, the Carolingians supported a revival of learning designed to enhance their glory, educate their officials, reform the liturgy, and purify the faith. The revival began in the 790s and continued for about a century. Like the renaissances of the Byzantine and Islamic worlds, the Carolingian renaissance resuscitated the learning of the past. Scholars studied Roman imperial writers such as Suetonius and Virgil; they read and commented on the works of the church fathers; and they worked to establish complete and accurate texts of everything they read and prized.

The English scholar Alcuin (c. 732–804), a member of the circle of scholars whom Charlemagne recruited to form a center of study, brought with him the traditions of Anglo-Saxon scholarship that had been developed by men such as Benedict Biscop and Bede. Invited to Aachen, Alcuin became Charlemagne's chief adviser, writing letters on the king's behalf, counseling him on royal policy, and tutoring the king's household, including the women. Charlemagne's sister and daughter, for example, often asked Alcuin to explain passages from the Gospel to them. Charlemagne entrusted Alcuin with the task of preparing an improved edition of the Vulgate, the Latin Bible read in all church services.

The Carolingian renaissance depended on an elite staff of scholars such as Alcuin, yet its educational program had broader appeal. In one of his capitularies, Charlemagne ordered that the cathedrals and monasteries of his kingdom teach reading and writing to all who were able to learn. Some churchmen expressed the hope that schools for children (perhaps they were thinking also of girls) would be established even in small villages and hamlets. Although this dream was never realized, it shows that even before the Islamic world was organizing the madrasa system of schools, the Carolingians were thinking about the importance of religious education for more than a small elite.

Scholarship complemented the alliance between the church and the king symbolized by Charlemagne's anointment. In the Carolingian world, much as in the Islamic and Byzantine, there was little distinction between politics and religion: kings considered themselves appointed by the grace of God, often based their laws on biblical passages, involved themselves in church reform, appointed churchmen on their own initiative, and believed their personal piety a source of power.

Art, like scholarship, served Carolingian political and religious goals. Just as in the Byzantine renaissance, Carolingian artists illuminated texts—often lavish Gospels meant for the royal family or liturgical books commissioned by bishops and abbots—using earlier pictures as models. But their imitation was not slavish. To their models Carolingian artists added exuberant decoration and design, often rendering architectural elements as bands of color and portraying human figures with great liveliness. Some models came from Byzantium, and perhaps some Carolingian artists themselves came from there, refugees from Byzantium during its iconoclastic period. Pictorial models from Italy provided the kings' artists with examples of the sturdy style of the late Roman Empire.

The Carolingian program was ambitious and lasting, even after the Carolingian dynasty had faded to a memory. The work of locating, understanding, and transmitting models of the past continued in a number of monastic schools. In the materials they studied, the questions they asked, and the answers they suggested, the Carolingians offered a mode of inquiry fruitful for subsequent generations. In the twelfth century, scholars would build on the foundations laid by the Carolingian renaissance. The very print of this textbook depends on one achievement of the period: modern letter fonts are based on the clear and beautiful letter forms, called *Caroline minuscule*, invented in the ninth century to standardize manuscript handwriting and make it more readable.

Vikings, Muslims, and Magyars Invade

Like the Roman emperors they emulated, Carolingian kings and counts confronted new groups along their borders (Map 8.4). The new peoples—Vikings to the north, Muslims to the south, and Magyars to the east—were feared and hated; but like the Germanic tribes that had entered the Roman Empire, they also served as military allies. As royal sons fought one another and as counts and other powerful men

■ **St. Matthew**

The Carolingian renaissance produced art of extraordinary originality. The creator of this picture was certainly inspired by the same sort of classical models that interested Byzantine artists, but his frenetic, emotional lines and uncanny colors are something new. This depiction of St. Matthew, holding an ink horn in his left hand and writing with a quill pen, precedes the text of the Gospel according to St. Matthew in a book of Gospels made around 820 for Ebbo of Reims. Ebbo had been born a serf but was freed and educated by Charlemagne. Later he was appointed to one of the highest positions in the empire, the archbishopric of Reims. Artistic patronage by a former serf was very unusual.

(La Médiathèque, Ville d'Epernay.)

■ MAP 8.4 Viking, Muslim, and Magyar Invasions of the Ninth and Tenth Centuries

Bristling with multicolored arrows, this map suggests that western Europe was continually and thoroughly pillaged by outside invaders for almost two centuries. That impression is only partially true and must be offset by several factors. First, not all the invaders came at once. The Viking raids were about over when the Magyar attacks began. Second, the invaders were not entirely unwelcome. The Magyars were for a time enlisted as mercenaries by the king of Italy, and some Muslims were allied to local lords in Provence. Third, the invasions, though widespread, were local in effect. Notice, for example, that the Viking raids were largely limited to rivers and coastal areas.

sought to carve out their own principalities, their alliances with the newcomers helped integrate the outsiders swiftly into European politics. The impact of these foreign groups hastened, but did not cause, the dissolution of the empire. The Carolingian kings could not muster troops quickly or efficiently enough to counter the lightning attacks of the raiders. Defense fell into the hands of local authorities who, building on their new prestige and the weakness of the king, became increasingly independent rulers themselves.

The first of the new groups to attack the Carolingian Empire was the Vikings. The Franks called them "Northmen"; the English called them "Danes." They were, in fact, much less united than their victims thought. When they began their voyages at the end of the eighth century, they did so in independent bands. Merchants and pirates at the same time, Vikings followed a chief, seeking profit, prestige, and land. Many traveled as families: husbands, wives, children, and slaves.

The Vikings perfected the art of navigation. In their longships they crossed the Atlantic, settling Iceland and Greenland and (about A.D. 1000) landing on the coast of North America. Other Viking bands navigated the rivers of Europe. The Vikings were pagans, and to them monasteries and churches—with their reliquaries, chalices, and crosses—were storehouses of booty. "Never before," wrote Alcuin, who experienced one attack, "has such terror appeared in Britain as we have now suffered from a pagan race. . . . Behold the church of St. Cuthbert spattered with the blood of the priests of God, despoiled of all its ornaments."

The British Isles confronted sporadic attacks by the Vikings from the eighth to the tenth century. From their fortified bases along the coast of Ireland they attacked and plundered churches and monasteries. But they also established Dublin as a commercial center and, in the tenth century, began to intermarry with the Irish and

■ **Oseberg Ship**
Excavated in 1904 from a burial mound at Oslofjord, Norway, this ninth-century ship, here shown reconstructed and displayed at the Viking Ship Museum at Bygdøy, is much finer and more highly carved than the typical longships used by the Vikings in their far-flung voyages across the seas. This must have been a ceremonial ship, and it is therefore not surprising that in its center was the burial chamber of a royal lady.
(Universitetet: Oslo, Oldsakimlingen, Oslo, Norway.)

convert to Christianity. In Scotland, the Scandinavians settled on the west coast. Meanwhile, by the 870s, they had settled the east coast of England, plowing the land and preparing to live on it. The region where they settled and imposed their own laws was later called the *Danelaw*. (See "Taking Measure," below.)

In Wessex, the southernmost kingdom of England, King Alfred the Great (r. 871–899) bought time and peace by paying tribute and giving hostages. Such tribute, later called *Danegeld*, was collected as a tax that eventually became the basis of a relatively lucrative taxation system in England. Then in 878, Alfred led an army that, as his biographer put it, "gained the victory through God's will. He destroyed the Vikings with great slaughter and pursued those who fled . . . hacking them down." Thereafter, the pressures of invasion eased as Alfred reorganized his army, set up strongholds, and deployed new warships.

On the continent of Europe, too, the invaders set up trading emporia and settled where originally they had raided. Beginning about 850, their attacks became well-organized expeditions for regional control. At the end of the ninth century, one contingent settled in the region of France that soon took the name Normandy, land of the Northmen. The new inhabitants converted to Christianity during the tenth century. Rollo, the Viking leader in Normandy, accepted Christianity in 911

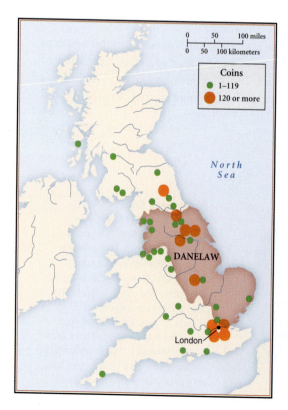

■ **TAKING MEASURE** Viking Coin Hoards, c. 865–895

From chronicles and other texts, we know that the Vikings invaded and settled in England. But from such sources it is very hard to know exactly where they settled and how many Vikings there were. Counting buried coins from the period can help answer these questions. Before safe-deposit boxes and banks, people buried their money in times of trouble. Archaeologists counting Viking coin hoards in England believe that the area called Danelaw was fairly thickly populated by Vikings, with a scattering in other regions as well. The Viking impact on England was not so much political—no Viking king took it over—as demographic. After 900, England was as much Scandinavian as it was Anglo-Saxon. Interestingly, although the Vikings also attacked Ireland, the lack of Viking coin hoards suggests that the Scandinavians did not settle there permanently.

(From David Hill, *An Atlas of Anglo-Saxon England* [Toronto, 1981].)

when the Frankish king Charles the Simple (or Straightforward) formally ceded Normandy to him.

Normandy was not the only new Christian state formed in the north during the tenth and eleventh centuries. Scandinavia itself was transformed with the creation of the powerful kingdom of Denmark. There had been kings in Scandinavia before the tenth century, but they had been weak, their power challenged by nearby chieftains. The Vikings had been led by these chieftains, each competing for booty to win prestige, land, and power back home. During the course of their raids, they and their followers came into contact with new cultures and learned from them. Meanwhile the Carolingians and the English supported missionaries in Scandinavia. By the middle of the tenth century, the Danish kings and their people had become Christian. Following the model of the Christian kings to their south, the Danish kings built up an effective monarchy, with a royal mint and local agents who depended on them. By about 1000, the Danes had extended their control to parts of Sweden, Norway, and even, under King Cnut (r. 1017–1035), England.

Far from Denmark, Muslims were taking advantage of Byzantium's early weakness. In 827 one group unconnected to the caliphate began the slow conquest of Sicily, which took nearly one hundred years. During the same century, Muslim pirates set up bases on Mediterranean islands and strongholds in Provence (in southern France) and near Naples (in southern Italy). Liutprand of Cremona reported on the activities of one such group:

> [*Muslim pirates from al-Andalus*], *disembarking under cover of night, entered the manor house unobserved and murdered—O grievous tale!—the Christian inhabitants. They then took the place as their own . . . [fortified it, and] started stealthy raids on all the neighboring country.*

The Muslims at this base, set up in 891, robbed, took prisoners, and collected ransoms. But they were so useful to their Christian neighbors, who called on them to support their own feuds, that they were not ousted until 972. Only then, when they caused a scandal by capturing the holiest man of his era, Abbot Maieul of Cluny, did the count of Provence launch a successful attack against their lair.

Farther to the east, the Magyars, latecomers to the West, arrived around 899 in the Danube basin. Until then the region had been predominantly Slavic, but the Magyars came from the East and spoke a language unrelated to any other in Europe (except Finnish). Their entry drove a wedge between the Slavs near the Frankish kingdom and those bordering on Byzantium; those near Byzantium, such as the Bulgarians, Serbs, and Russians, were driven into the Byzantine orbit, while those nearer the Frankish kingdom came under the influence of Germany.

From their bases in present-day Hungary, the Magyars raided far to the west, attacking Germany, Italy, and even southern Gaul frequently between 899 and 955. Then in the summer of 955, one marauding party of Magyars was met at the Lech

River by the German king Otto I (r. 936–973), whose army decimated them in the battle of Lechfeld. Otto's victory, his subsequent military reorganization of his eastern frontiers, and the cessation of Magyar raids around this time made Otto a great hero to his contemporaries. Today, however, historians think the containment of the Magyars had more to do with their internal transformation from nomads to farmers than with their military defeat.

The Viking, Muslim, and Magyar invasions were the final onslaught western Europe experienced from outsiders. In some ways they were a continuation of the invasions that had rocked the Roman Empire in the fourth and fifth centuries. Loosely organized in warbands, the new groups entered western Europe looking for wealth but, apart from the Muslims, stayed on to become absorbed in its new postinvasion society.

The Emergence of Local Rule in the Post-Carolingian Age

The Carolingian Empire was too diverse to cohere. Latin was a universal language, but few people spoke it; instead they used a wide variety of languages and dialects. The king demanded loyalty from everyone, but most people knew only his representative, the local count. As the empire ceased to expand and was instead attacked by outsiders, the counts and other powerful men stopped looking to the king for new lands and offices and began to develop and exploit what they already had. They became powerful lords, commanding warriors and peasants, building castles, setting up markets, collecting revenues, keeping the peace, and seeing themselves as independent regional rulers. In this way, a new warrior class of lords and vassals came to dominate post-Carolingian society.

Yet it would be wrong to imagine that all of Europe came under the control of rural warlords. In Italy, where cities had never lost their importance, urban elites ruled over the surrounding countryside. Everywhere, kings retained a certain amount of power; indeed, in some places, such as Germany and England, they were extremely effective. Central European monarchies formed under the influence of Germany.*

Public Power and Private Relationships

The key way in which both kings and less powerful men commanded others was by ensuring personal loyalty. In the ninth century, the Carolingian kings had their *fideles,* their "faithful men." Among these were the counts. In addition to a share in the revenues of their administrative district, the *county,* the counts received

---

*Terms such as "Germany," "France," and "Italy" are used here for the sake of convenience. They refer to regions, not to the nation-states that would eventually become associated with those names.

benefices, later also called *fiefs,* temporary grants of land given in return for service. These short-term arrangements often became permanent, however, once a count's son inherited the job and the fiefs of his father. By the end of the ninth century, fiefs were often properties that could be passed on to heirs.

In the wake of the invasions, more and more warriors were drawn into similar networks of dependency, but not with the king: they became the faithful men—the *vassals*—of local lords. From the Latin word for *fief* comes the word *feudal,* and historians often use the term *feudalism* to describe the social and economic system created by the relationship among vassals, lords, and fiefs.*

It was frequently said by medieval people that their society consisted of three groups: those who prayed, those who fought, and those who worked. All of these people were involved in hierarchies of dependency and were linked by personal bonds, but the upper classes—the prayers (monks) and the fighters (the knights)—were free. Their brand of dependency was honorable, whether they were vassals, lords, or both. In fact, a typical warrior was lord of several vassals and the vassal of another lord. Monasteries normally had vassals to fight for them, and their abbots in turn were likely to be vassals of a king or other powerful lord.

Vassalage grew up as an alternative to public power and at the same time as a way to strengthen what little public power there was. Given the impoverished economic conditions of the West, its primitive methods of communication, and its lack of unifying traditions, kings came to rely on vassals personally loyal to them to muster troops, collect taxes, and administer justice. When in the ninth century the Frankish Empire broke up politically and power fell into the hands of local lords, they, too, needed "faithful men" to protect them and carry out their orders. And vassals needed lords. At the low end of the social scale, poor vassals looked to their lords to feed, clothe, house, and arm them. They hoped that they would be rewarded for their service with a fief of their own, with which they could support themselves and a family. At the upper end of the social scale, vassals looked to lords to enrich them further.

A few women were vassals and some were lords (or, rather, "ladies," the female counterpart); many upper-class laywomen participated in the society of fighters and prayers as wives and mothers of vassals and lords. Other aristocratic women entered convents and became members of the social group that prayed. Through its abbess or a man standing in for her, a convent was likely to have vassals as well.

Becoming the vassal of a lord often involved both ritual gestures and verbal promises. In a ceremony witnessed by others, the vassal-to-be knelt and, placing his hands between the hands of his lord, said, "I promise to be your man." This act,

---

*Many historians, however, regard *feudalism* as a problematic term. Does it mean "anarchy"? Some historians have used it that way. Does it mean "a hierarchical scheme of lords and knights"? This is another common definition. And there are others. This imprecision has led some historians to drop the word altogether. Moreover, *feudalism* implies that one way of life dominated the Middle Ages, when in fact there were numerous social, political, and economic arrangements. For these reasons, *feudalism* rarely appears in *The Making of the West.*

known as *homage*, was followed by the promise of *fealty*—fidelity, trust, and service—which the vassal swore with his hand on relics or a Bible. Then the vassal and the lord kissed. In an age when many people could not read, a public ceremony such as this represented a visual and verbal contract. Vassalage bound the lord and vassal to one another with reciprocal obligations, usually military. Knights, as the premier fighters of the day, were the most desirable vassals.

At the bottom of the social scale were those who worked—the peasants. In the Carolingian period, many peasants were free; they did not live on a manor, or if they did, they owed very little to its lord. But as power fell into the hands of local rulers, fewer and fewer peasants remained free. Rather, they were made dependent on lords, not as vassals but as serfs. Serfdom was a dependency separate from and completely unlike that of a vassal. It was not voluntary but inherited. No serf did homage or fealty to his lord; no serf kissed his lord as an equal. And the serf's work as a laborer was not considered honorable. Unlike knights, who were celebrated in song, peasants, who constituted the majority of the population, were nevertheless barely noticed by the upper classes—except as a source of revenue.

New methods of cultivation and a burgeoning population helped transform the rural landscape and make it more productive. With a growing number of men and women to work the land, the lower classes now had more mouths to feed and faced the hardship of food shortage. Landlords began reorganizing their estates to run more efficiently. In the tenth century, the three-field system became more prevalent; heavy plows that could turn the heavy northern soils came into wider use; and horses (more effective than oxen) were harnessed to pull the plows. The result was surplus food and a better standard of living for nearly everyone.

In search of greater profits, some lords lightened the dues and services of peasants temporarily to allow them to open up new lands by draining marshes and cutting down forests. Some landlords converted dues and labor services into money payments, a boon for both lords and peasants. Lords now had money to spend on what they wanted rather than hens and eggs they might not need or want. Peasants benefited because their tax was fixed despite inflation. Thus, as the prices of their hens and eggs went up, they could sell them, reaping a profit in spite of the dues they owed their lords.

By the tenth century, many peasants lived in populous rural settlements, true villages. In the midst of a sea of arable land, meadow, wood, and wasteland, these villages developed a sense of community. Boundaries—sometimes real fortifications, sometimes simple markers—told nonresidents to keep out and to find shelter in huts located outside the village limits.

The church often formed the focal point of local activity. There people met, received the sacraments, drew up contracts, and buried their parents and children. Religious feasts and festivals joined the rituals of farming to mark the seasons. The church dominated the village in another way: men and women owed it a tax called a *tithe* (equivalent to one-tenth of their crops or income, paid in money or in kind), which was first instituted on a regular basis by the Carolingians.

Village peasants' sense of common purpose grew out of their practical interdependence, as they shared oxen or horses for the teams that pulled the plow or turned to village craftsmen to fix their wheels or shoe their horses. Their feeling of solidarity sometimes encouraged villagers to band together to ask for privileges as a group. Near Verona, in northern Italy, for example, twenty-five men living around the castle of Nogara in 920 joined together to ask their lord, the abbot of Nonantola, to allow them to lease plots of land, houses, and pasturage there in return for a small yearly rent and the promise to defend the castle. The abbot granted their request.

Village solidarity could be compromised, however, by conflicting loyalties and obligations. A peasant in one village might very well have one piece of land connected with a certain manor and another bit of arable field on a different estate; and he or she might owe several lords different kinds of dues. Even peasants of one village working for one lord might owe him varied services and taxes.

Layers of obligations were even more striking across the regions of Europe than in particular villages. The principal distinction was between free peasants, such as small landowners in Saxony and other parts of Germany, and unfree peasants, who were especially common in France and England. In Italy, peasants ranged from small independent landowners to leaseholders (like the tenants at Nogara); most were both, owning a parcel in one place and leasing another nearby.

Once the power of kings began to weaken, this system of peasant obligations became part of a larger system of local rule. As landlords consolidated their power over their manors, they collected not only dues and services but also fees for the use of their flour mills, bake houses, and breweries. Some built castles, fortified strongholds, and imposed the even wider powers of the *ban*: the rights to collect taxes, hear court cases, levy fines, and muster men for defense.

In France, for example, as the king's power waned, political control fell into the hands of counts and other princes. By 1000, castles had become the key to their power. In the south of France, power was so fragmented that each man who controlled a castle—a *castellan*—was a virtual ruler, although often with a very limited reach. In northwestern France, territorial princes, basing their rule on the control of *many* castles, dominated much broader regions. For example, Fulk Nera, count of Anjou (987–1040), built more than thirteen castles and captured others from rival counts. By the end of his life, he controlled a region extending from Blois to Nantes along the Loire valley.

Castellans extended their authority by subjecting everyone near their castle to their ban. Peasants, whether or not they worked on a castellan's estates, had to pay him a variety of dues for his "protection" and judicial rights over them. Castellans also established links with the better-off landholders in the region, tempting or coercing them to become vassals. Lay castellans often supported local monasteries and controlled the appointment of local priests. But churchmen themselves sometimes held the position of territorial lord: a good example is the archbishop of Milan in the eleventh century.

The development of nearly independent local political units, dominated by a castle and controlled by a military elite, marked an important turning point for western Europe. Although this development did not occur everywhere simultaneously (and in some places it hardly occurred at all), the social, political, and cultural life of the West was now dominated by landowners who saw themselves as military men and regional leaders.

War and Peace

All warriors were not alike. At the top of the elite were the kings, counts, and dukes. Below them, but "on the rise," were the castellans. Still farther down the social scale were ordinary knights. Yet all shared in a common lifestyle.

Knights and their lords fought on horseback. High astride his steed, wearing a shirt of chain mail and a helmet of flat metal plates riveted together, the knight marked a military revolution. The war season started in May, when the grasses were

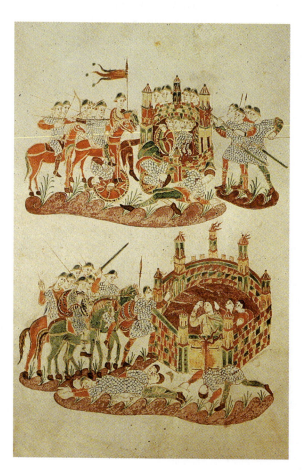

■ Two Cities Besieged

In about 900 the monks of the monastery of St. Gall produced a Psalter with numerous illuminations. To illustrate Psalm 59, which tells of King David's victories, they made a four-page spread. This is the fourth page. In the upper scene, David's army besieges a fortified city from two directions. On the right are foot soldiers, one of whom holds a burning torch to set the city afire. On the left are horsemen—led by their standard-bearer—armed with lances and bows and arrows. Notice their chain-mail coats and their horses' stirrups. Within the city, four soldiers protect themselves with shields. A fallen soldier hangs upside down from the city wall. The dead and wounded on the ground are bleeding. Four other men seem to be cowering behind the city. In the lower scene, a different city burns fiercely (notice the burning towers). This city lacks defenders because the people within it are unarmed. Although this illumination purports to show David's victories, in fact it nicely represents the equipment and strategies of ninth-century warfare.

(Stiftsbibliothek St. Gallen, Switzerland.)

high enough for horses to forage. Horseshoes allowed armies to move faster than ever before and to negotiate rough terrain previously unsuitable for battle. Stirrups, probably invented by Asiatic nomadic tribes, allowed the mounted warrior to hold his seat. This made it possible for knights to thrust at their enemy with heavy lances. The light javelin of ancient warfare was abandoned.

Lords and their vassals often lived together. In the lord's great hall they ate, listened to entertainment, and bedded down for the night. They went out hunting together, competed with one another in military games called *tournaments*, and went off to the battlefield as a group as well. Of course there were powerful vassals—counts, for example. They lived on their own fiefs and hardly ever saw their lord (probably the king), except when doing homage and fealty—once in their lifetime—or serving him in battles, for perhaps forty days a year. But they themselves were lords of knightly vassals who were not married and who lived and ate and hunted with them.

No matter how old they might be, unmarried knights who lived with their lords were called "youths" by their contemporaries. Such perpetual bachelors were something new, the result of a profound transformation in the organization of families and inheritance. Before about 1000, noble families had recognized all their children as heirs and had divided their estates accordingly. In the mid-ninth century, Count Everard and his wife, for example, willed their large estates, scattered from Belgium to Italy, to their four sons and three daughters (although they gave the boys far more than they gave the girls, and the oldest boy far more than the others).

By 1000, however, adapting to diminished opportunities for land and office and wary of fragmenting the estates they had, French nobles changed both their conception of their family and the way property passed to the next generation. Recognizing the overriding claims of one son, often the eldest, they handed down their entire inheritance to him. (In cases where the heir is indeed the eldest son, this system of inheritance is called *primogeniture*.) The heir, in turn, traced his lineage only through the male line, backward through his father and forward through his own eldest son. Such *patrilineal* families left many younger sons without an inheritance and therefore without the prospect of marrying and founding a family; instead, the younger sons lived at the courts of the great as "youths," or they joined the church as clerics or monks. The development of territorial rule and patrilineal families went hand in hand, as fathers passed down to one son undiminished not only manors but titles, castles, and the authority of the ban.

Patrilineal inheritance tended to bypass daughters and so tended to work against aristocratic women. In families without sons, however, widows and daughters did inherit property. And wives often acted as lords of estates when their husbands were at war. Moreover, all aristocratic women played an important role in this warrior society, whether in the monastery (where they prayed for the souls of their families) or through their marriages (where they helped forge alliances between their own families and the families of their husbands).

This highly militarized society was almost constantly at war. Warfare benefited territorial rulers in the short term, but in the long run their revenues suffered as armies plundered the countryside and sacked walled cities. Bishops, who were themselves from the class of lords and warriors, worried about the dangers to church property. Peasants cried out against wars that destroyed their crops or forced them to join regional infantries. Monks and religious thinkers were appalled at violence that was not in the service of an anointed king. By the end of the tenth century, all classes clamored for peace.

Sentiment against local violence was united in a movement called the Peace of God, which began in the south of France and by 1050 had spread over a wide region. Meetings of bishops, counts, and lords and often crowds of lower-class men and women set forth the provisions of this peace: "No man in the counties or bishoprics shall seize a horse, colt, ox, cow, ass, or the burdens which it carries. . . . No one shall seize a peasant, man or woman," ran the decree of one council held in 990. Anyone who violated this peace was to be excommunicated: cut off from the community of the faithful, denied the services of the church and the hope of salvation.

The peace proclaimed at local councils like this limited some violence but did not address the problem of conflict between armed men. A second set of agreements, the Truce of God, soon supplemented the Peace of God. The truce prohibited fighting between warriors at certain times: on Sunday because it was the Lord's Day, on Saturday because it was a reminder of Holy Saturday, on Friday because it symbolized Good Friday, and on Thursday because it stood for Holy Thursday. Enforcement of the truce fell to the local knights and nobles, who swore over saints' relics to uphold it and to fight anyone who broke it.

The Peace of God and Truce of God were only two of the mechanisms that attempted to contain or defuse violent confrontations in the tenth and eleventh centuries. At times, lords and their vassals mediated wars and feuds in assemblies called *placita*. In other instances, monks or laymen tried to find solutions to disputes that would leave the honor of both parties intact. Rather than try to establish guilt or innocence, winners or losers, these methods of adjudication often resulted in compromises on both sides.

Political Communities in Italy, England, and France

The political systems that emerged in the wake of the breakup of the Carolingian Empire were as varied as the regions of Europe. In Italy, cities were the centers of power, still reflecting, though feebly, the political organization of ancient Rome. In England, strong kings came to the fore. In France, as we have seen, great lords dominated the countryside; there the king was relatively weak.

Whereas in France great landlords built their castles in the countryside, in Italy they often constructed their family seats within the walls of cities such as Milan and

Lucca. Churches, as many as fifty or sixty, were also built within the city walls, the proud work of rich laymen and laywomen or of bishops. From their perches within the cities, the great landholders of Italy, both lay and religious, dominated the countryside.

Italian cities also functioned as important marketplaces. Peasants sold their surplus goods there; artisans and merchants lived within the walls; foreign traders offered their wares. These members of the lower classes were supported by the noble rich, who in Italy even more than elsewhere depended on cash to satisfy their desires. In the course of the ninth and tenth centuries, both servile and free tenants became renters who paid in currency.

Social and political life in Italy favored a familial organization somewhat different from the patrilineal families of France. To stave off the partitioning of their properties among heirs, families organized themselves by formal contract into *consorteria*, in which all male members shared the profits of the family's inheritance and all women were excluded. The consorterial family became a kind of blood-related corporation, a social unit on which early Italian businesses and banks would later be modeled.

Where Italy was urban, England was rural. In the face of the Viking invasions in England, King Alfred of Wessex (r. 871–899) developed new mechanisms of royal government, instituting reforms that his successors continued. He fortified settlements throughout Wessex and divided the army into two parts. The duty of one was to defend the fortifications (or *burhs*); the other operated as a mobile unit. Alfred also started a navy. These military innovations cost money, and the assessments fell on peasants' holdings.

England in the Age of King Alfred, r. 871–899

Alfred sought to strengthen his kingdom's religious integrity as well as its regional fortifications. In the ninth century, people interpreted invasions as God's punishment for sin, which therefore was the real culprit. Thus Alfred began a program of religious reform by bringing scholars to his court to write and to educate others. Above all, Alfred wanted to translate key religious works from Latin into Anglo-Saxon (or Old English). He was determined to "turn into the language that we can all understand certain books which are the most necessary for all men to know." Alfred and scholars under his guidance translated works by church fathers such as Gregory the Great and St. Augustine. Even the Psalms, until now sung only in Hebrew, Greek, and Latin, were rendered into Anglo-Saxon. In most of ninth- and

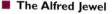

■ The Alfred Jewel

About two and a half inches long, this jewel consists of a gold drop-shaped frame surrounding an enamel plaque that depicts a man enthroned and holding two flowering rods. Rock crystal encloses the plaque within the frame. Along the side of the frame are gold letters in Anglo-Saxon; translated, they mean "Alfred had me made." The snout of the beast at the bottom was hollowed out, probably to hold a wooden or ivory pointer. If this jewel belonged to King Alfred, as is likely, it may be like the pointers that Alfred wanted distributed to all the bishops in his kingdom along with the Anglo-Saxon translation of Gregory the Great's Pastoral Care. *Such pointers were used to point to passages in manuscripts. Why did Alfred have the* Pastoral Care *translated? Why did he want copies sent to the bishops? And why did he want the bishops to have pointers?*
(Ashmolean Museum, Oxford.)

tenth-century Europe, Latin remained the language of scholarship and writing, separate from the language people spoke. In England, however, the vernacular—the common spoken language—was also a literary language. With Alfred's work giving it greater legitimacy, Anglo-Saxon came to be used alongside Latin for both literature and royal administration.

Alfred's reforms strengthened not only defense, education, and religion but also royal power. He consolidated his control over Wessex and fought the Danish kings, who by the mid-870s had taken Northumbria, northeastern Mercia, and East Anglia. Eventually, as he harried the Danes who were pushing south and westward, he was recognized as king of all the English not under Danish rule. He issued a law code, the first by an English king since 695. Unlike earlier codes, drawn up for each separate kingdom of England, Alfred drew up his laws from and for all of the English kingdoms. In this way, Alfred became the first king of all the English.

Alfred's successors rolled back Danish rule in England. "Then the Norsemen departed in their nailed ships, bloodstained survivors of spears," wrote one poet about a battle the Vikings lost in 937. But many Vikings remained. Converted to Christianity, their great men joined Anglo-Saxons in attending the English king at court. As peace returned, new administrative subdivisions—*shires* (counties) and *hundreds* (districts)—were established throughout England for judicial and taxation purposes. The powerful men of the kingdom swore fealty to the king, promising to be enemies of his enemies, friends of his friends. England was united and organized to support a strong ruler.

Alfred's grandson Edgar (r. 957–975) commanded all the possibilities early medieval kingship offered. He was the sworn lord of all the great men of the kingdom. He controlled appointments to the English church and sponsored monastic reform. In 973, following the continental fashion, he was anointed. The fortifications of the kingdom were in his hands, as was the army, and he took responsibility for keeping the peace by proclaiming certain crimes—arson and theft—to be under his special jurisdiction and mobilizing the machinery of the shire and the hundred to find and punish thieves.

Despite its apparent centralization, England was not a unified state in the modern sense, and the king's control was often tenuous. Many royal officials were great landowners who (as on the continent) worked for the king because doing so was in their best interest. When it was not, they allied with different claimants to the throne. This political fragility may have helped the Danish king Cnut (or Canute) to conquer England. King there from 1017 to 1035, Cnut reinforced the already strong connections between England and Scandinavia while keeping intact much of the administrative, ecclesiastical, and military apparatus already established in England by the Anglo-Saxons. By Cnut's time Scandinavian traditions had largely merged with those of the rest of Europe, and the Vikings were no longer an alien culture.

French kings had a harder time than the English coping with the invasions because their realm was much larger. They had no chance to build up their defenses slowly from one powerful base. During most of the tenth century, Carolingian kings alternated on the throne with kings from a family that would later be called "Capetian." As the Carolingian dynasty waned, the most powerful men of the kingdom—dukes, counts, and important bishops—came together to elect Hugh Capet (r. 987–996), a lord of considerable prestige yet relatively little power. His choice marked the end of Carolingian rule and the beginning of the new Capetian dynasty, which would hand down the royal title from father to son until the fourteenth century.

In the eleventh century, the reach of the Capetian kings was limited by territorial lordships in the vicinity. The king's scattered but substantial estates lay in the north of France, in the region around Paris—the Île-de-France (literally "island of France"). His castles and his vassals were there. Independent castellans, however, controlled areas nearby. In the sense that he was a neighbor of castellans and not much more powerful militarily than they, the king of the Franks—who would only later take the territorial title of king of France—was just another local strongman. Yet the Capetian kings enjoyed considerable prestige. They were anointed with holy oil, and they represented the idea of unity inherited from Charlemagne. Most of the counts, at least in the north of France, became their vassals. They did not promise to obey the king, but they did vow not to try to kill or depose him.

Emperors and Kings in Central and Eastern Europe

In contrast with the development of territorial lordships in France, Germany's fragmentation hardly began before it was reversed. Five *duchies* (regions dominated by dukes) emerged in Germany in the late Carolingian period, each much larger than the counties and castellanies of France. With the death in 911 of the last Carolingian king in Germany, Louis the Child, the dukes elected one of themselves as king. Then, as the Magyar invasions increased, the dukes gave the royal title to the duke of Saxony, Henry I (r. 919–936), who proceeded to set up fortifications and reorganize his army, crowning his efforts with a major defeat of a Magyar army in 933.

Otto I, the son of Henry I, was an even greater military hero. His defeat of the Magyar forces in 955 gave him prestige and helped solidify his dynasty. In 951, he marched into Italy and took the Lombard crown. Against the Slavs, with whom the Germans shared a border, Otto set up marches from which he could make expeditions and stave off counterattacks. After the pope crowned him emperor in 962, he claimed the Middle Kingdom carved out by the Treaty of Verdun and cast himself as the agent of Roman imperial renewal.

The Ottonian Empire, 936–1002

Otto's victories brought tribute and plunder, ensuring him a following but also raising the German nobles' expectations for enrichment. He and his successors, Otto II (r. 973–983), Otto III (r. 983–1002)—not surprisingly the dynasty is called the "Ottonian"—and Henry II (r. 1002–1024), were not always able or willing to provide the gifts and inheritances their family members and followers expected. To maintain centralized rule, for example, the Ottonians did not divide their kingdom among their sons: like castellans in France, they created a patrilineal pattern of inheritance. But the consequence was that younger sons and other potential heirs felt cheated, and disgruntled royal kin led revolt after revolt against the Ottonian kings. The rebels found followers among the aristocracy, where the trend toward the patrilineal family prompted similar feuds and thwarted expectations.

Relations between the Ottonians and the German clergy were more harmonious. With a ribbon of new bishoprics along his eastern border, Otto I appointed bishops, gave them extensive lands, and subjected the local peasantry to their overlordship. Like Charlemagne, Otto believed that the well-being of the church in his kingdom depended on him. The Ottonians placed the churches and many monas-

■ Otto III Receiving Gifts

This triumphal image is in a book of Gospels made for Otto III. The crowned women on the left are personifications of the four "parts" of Otto's empire: Sclavinia (the Slavic lands), Germania (Germany), Gallia (Gaul), and Roma (Rome). Each holds a gift in tribute and homage to the emperor, who sits on a throne, holding the symbols of his power (orb and scepter) and flanked by representatives of the church (on his right) and of the army (on his left). Why do you suppose the artist separated the image of the emperor from that of the women? What does the body language of the women tell you about the relations that Otto wanted to portray between himself and the parts of his empire? Can you relate this manuscript, which was made in 997–1000, to Otto's conquest over the Slavs in 997? (Pro Biblioteca Academiae Scientiarum, Hungaricae.)

teries of Germany under their control. They gave bishops the powers of the ban, allowing them to collect revenues and call men to arms. Answering to the king and furnishing him with troops, the bishops became royal officials, while also carrying out their pastoral and religious duties. German kings claimed the right to select bishops, even the pope at Rome, and to "invest" them by participating in the ceremony that installed them in office. The higher clergy joined royal court society. Most came to the court to be schooled; in turn, they taught the kings, princes, and noblewomen there.

Like all the strong rulers of the day, whether in the West or in the Byzantine and Islamic worlds, the Ottonians presided over a renaissance of learning. For example, the tutor of Otto III was Gerbert, the best-educated man of his time. Placed on the papal throne as Sylvester II (r. 999–1003), Gerbert knew how to use the abacus and to calculate with Arabic numerals. He spent "large sums of money to pay

IMPORTANT DATES			
750	Abbasid caliphate begins	843	End of iconoclasm at Byzantium; Treaty of Verdun divides Frankish kingdom
751	Pippin III deposes the last Merovingian king; beginning of the Carolingian monarchy	c. 870–c. 1025	Macedonian renaissance at Byzantium
756	Spanish emirate at Córdoba begins	871–899	Reign of King Alfred the Great in England
768–814	Charlemagne rules as king of the Franks	955	Otto I defeats Magyars
786–809	Caliphate of Harun al-Rashid	969–1171	Fatimid dynasty in Egypt
c. 790–c. 900	Carolingian renaissance	976–1025	Reign of Byzantine emperor Basil II Bulgaroctonos
c. 790–c. 1050	Islamic renaissance		
800	Charlemagne crowned emperor by Pope Leo III	c. 1000	Age of the castellans in France

copyists and to acquire copies of authors," as he put it. He studied the classics as models of rhetoric and argument, and he reveled in logic and debate. Not only did churchmen and kings support Ottonian scholarship, but to an unprecedented extent noblewomen in Germany also acquired an education and participated in the intellectual revival. Aristocratic women spent much of their wealth on learning. Living at home with their kinfolk and servants or in convents that provided them with comfortable private apartments, noblewomen wrote books and occasionally even Roman-style plays. They also supported other artists and scholars.

Despite their military and political strength, the kings of Germany faced resistance from dukes and other powerful princes, who hoped to become regional rulers themselves. The Salians, the dynasty that succeeded the Ottonians, tried to balance the power among the German dukes but could not meld them into a corps of vassals the way the Capetian kings tamed their counts. In Germany, vassalage was considered beneath the dignity of free men. Instead of relying on vassals, the Salian kings and their bishops used *ministerials*, men who were legally serfs, to collect taxes, administer justice, and fight on horseback. Ministerials retained their servile status even though they often rose to wealth and high position. Under the Salian kings, ministerials became the mainstay of the royal army and administration.

Supported by their prestige, their churchmen, and their ministerials, the German kings expanded their influence eastward, into the region from the Elbe River to Russia. Otto I was so serious about expansion that he created an extraordinary "elastic" archbishopric: it had no eastern boundary, so it could increase as far as future conquests and conversions to Christianity would allow. Hand in hand with the papacy, the German kings fostered the emergence of Christian monarchies aligned with the Roman church in the regions that today constitute the Czech and Slovak Republics, Poland, and Hungary.

The Czechs, who lived in the region of Bohemia, converted under the rule of Václav (r. 920–929), who thereby gained recognition in Germany as the duke of Bohemia. He and his successors did not become kings, remaining politically within the German sphere. Václav's murder by his younger brother made him a martyr and the patron saint of Bohemia, a symbol around which later movements for independence rallied.

The Poles gained a greater measure of independence than the Czechs. In 966, Mieszko I (r. 963–992), the leader of the Slavic tribe known as the Polanians, accepted baptism to forestall the attack that the Germans were already mounting against pagan Slavic peoples along the Baltic coast and east of the Elbe River. Busily engaged in bringing the other Slavic tribes of Poland under his control, he adroitly shifted his alliances with various German princes to suit his needs. In 991, Mieszko placed his realm under the protection of the pope, establishing a tradition of Polish loyalty to the Roman church. Mieszko's son Boleslaw the Brave (r. 992–1025) greatly extended Poland's boundaries, at one time or another holding sway from the Bohemian border to Kiev. In 1000, he gained a royal crown with papal blessing.

Hungary's case is similar to that of Poland. The Magyars settled in the region known today as Hungary. They became landowners, using the native Slavs to till the soil and imposing their language. At the end of the tenth century, the Magyar ruler Stephen I (r. 997–1038) accepted Christianity. In return, German knights and monks helped him consolidate his power and convert his people. According to legend, the crown placed on Stephen's head in 1001, like Boleslaw's crown, was sent to him by the pope. To this day, the crown of St. Stephen remains the most hallowed symbol of Hungarian nationhood.

Symbols of rulership such as crowns, consecrated by Christian priests and accorded a prestige almost akin to saints' relics, were among the most vital institutions of royal rule in central Europe. The economic basis for the power of central European rulers gradually shifted from slave raids to agriculture. This change encouraged a proliferation of regional centers of power that challenged monarchical rule. From the eleventh century onward, all the medieval Slavic states would face a constant problem of internal division.

Conclusion

In 800, the three heirs of the Roman Empire all appeared to be organized like their "parent": centralized, monarchical, imperial. Byzantine emperors writing their learned books, Abbasid caliphs holding court in their resplendent new palace at Baghdad, and Carolingian emperors issuing their directives for reform to the *missi dominici* all mimicked the Roman emperors. Yet they confronted tensions and regional pressures that tended to decentralize political power. Byzantium felt this

■ **MAPPING THE WEST** Europe and the Mediterranean, c. 1050

In 1050, the future seemed to lie with the four great political entities that dominated the west. In Europe the German king presided over an empire reaching from Rome to the North Sea. To the east a new state, Kievan Russia, was being forged from a mix of Scandinavian and Slavic populations, leavened by Byzantine Orthodox Christianity. To the south was the Byzantine Empire, still celebrating its successes over the Bulgarians. And on the other side of the Mediterranean was the Muslim world, united by religion if not by rulers. The next centuries would show how weak these large states actually were.

www.bedfordstmartins.com/huntconcise   See the ONLINE STUDY GUIDE for more help in analyzing this map.

fragmentation least, yet even there the emergence of a new elite led to decentralization and the emperor's loss of control over the countryside. In the Islamic world, economic crisis, religious tension, and the ambitions of powerful local rulers decisively weakened the caliphate and opened the way to separate successor states. In the West, powerful independent landowners strove with greater or lesser success (depending on the region) to establish themselves as effective rulers. By 1050, the states that would become those of modern Europe began to form.

In Europe, local conditions determined political and economic organizations. Between 900 and 1000, for example, French society was transformed by the development of territorial lordships, patrilineal families, and ties of vassalage. These factors figured less prominently in Germany, where a central monarchy remained, buttressed by churchmen, ministerials, and conquests to the east. We shall see in the next chapter, however, how fragile this centralization was to be.

Suggested References for further reading and online research appear on page SR-13 at the back of the book.

www.bedfordstmartins.com/huntconcise   See the ONLINE STUDY GUIDE to assess your mastery of the material covered in this chapter.

Renewal and Reform

1050–1200

Bruno of Cologne was engaged in a promising career in the church. He was an esteemed teacher at the prominent French cathedral school of Reims and a likely choice for promotion to bishop or even archbishop. But around 1084, he abandoned it all. He was disgusted with the new archbishop of Reims, Manasses, who had purchased his office and was so uninterested in religious matters that he once reportedly said, "The archbishopric of Reims would be a good thing, if one did not have to sing Mass for it." Bruno quit his post at the school and left the city. But he did not do what ethical and morally outraged men of the time were expected to do—join a monastery. Rejecting both the worldly goals of secular clerics like Manasses and the communal goals of Benedictine monks, Bruno set up a hermitage at Chartreuse, high in the Alps. The hermits who gathered there lived in isolation and poverty. One of Bruno's contemporaries marveled: "They do not take gold, silver, or ornaments for their church from anyone." This unworldliness was matched, however, by keen interest in learning: for all its poverty, Chartreuse had a rich library.

Thus began La Chartreuse, the chief house of the Carthusian order, an order still in existence. The Carthusian monks lived as hermits, eschewed material wealth, and emphasized learning. In some ways their style of life was a reaction against the monumental changes rumbling through their age: their reclusive solitude ran counter to the burgeoning cities, and their austerity contrasted sharply with the opulence and power of princely courts. Their reverence for the written word, however, reflected the growing interest in scholarship and learning.

The most salient feature of the period 1050–1200 was increasing wealth. Cities, trade, and agricultural production swelled. The resulting worldliness met with a

---

■ **Church over State**

Around 1140, Gratian, an expert in canon law, wrote a concordance of church laws that soon became authoritative. A late-twelfth-century artist decorated this capital H in one copy of Gratian's book. Above the crossbar, he put a saint, symbolizing the church; below the crossbar, he placed a king. The scroll, which represents the voice of the church, says "I am the King of kings; I make you king." (Berlin, Staatsbibliothek zu Berlin—Preußischer Kulturbesitz-Handschriftenabteilung.)

wide variety of responses. Some people, like Bruno, fled the world; others tried to reform it; and still others embraced, enjoyed, or tried to understand it.

Within one century, the development of a profit economy transformed western European communities. Many villages and fortifications became cities where traders, merchants, and artisans conducted business. Although most people still lived in less-populated, rural areas, their lives were touched in many ways by the new cash economy. Economic concerns drove changes within the church, where a movement for reform gathered steam. Money helped redefine the role of the clergy, and popes, kings, and princes came to exercise new forms of power.

At the same time, city dwellers began to demand their own governments. Monks and clerics reformulated the nature of their communities and, like Bruno of Cologne, sought intense spiritual lives. All of these developments inspired (and in turn were inspired by) new ideas, new forms of scholarship, and new methods of inquiry. The rapid pace of religious, political, and economic change was matched by new developments in thought, learning, and artistic expression.

The Commercial Revolution

As the population of Europe continued to expand in the eleventh century, cities, long-distance trade networks, local markets, and new business arrangements meshed to create a profit-based economy. With improvements in agriculture and more land in cultivation, the great estates of the eleventh century produced surpluses that helped feed—and therefore make possible—a new urban population.

Centers of Commerce and Commercial Life

The new commercial centers developed around castles and monasteries and within the walls of ancient towns. Great lords in the countryside—including monasteries —were eager to take advantage of the profits that their estates generated. In the late tenth century, they had reorganized their lands for greater productivity, encouraged their peasants to cultivate new land, and converted services and dues to money payments. Now with ready cash, they not only fostered the development of sporadic markets where they could sell their surpluses and buy luxury goods, but even encouraged traders and craftspeople to settle down near them. The lords gained at each step: their purchases brought them an enhanced lifestyle and greater prestige, while they charged merchants tolls and sales taxes, in this way profiting even more from trade. At Bruges (today in Belgium), for example, the local lord's castle became the magnet around which a city formed. At Conques, it was the church of Ste. Foy that attracted pilgrims and the merchants to serve them. Some markets formed just outside the walls of older cities; these gradually merged into new and enlarged urban communities as town walls were built around them to protect the inhabitants. Sometimes informal country markets came to be housed in permanent structures. To the north, in places like Frisia, the Vikings had already established centers of wealth and trade, and these settlements became permanent, thriving towns. Along the Rhine and in other river valleys, cities sprang up to service the merchants who traversed the route between Italy and the north (Map 9.1).

By the mid-twelfth century even rural life was increasingly organized for the marketplace in many regions of western Europe. The commercialization of the countryside opened up opportunities for both peasants and lords, but it also

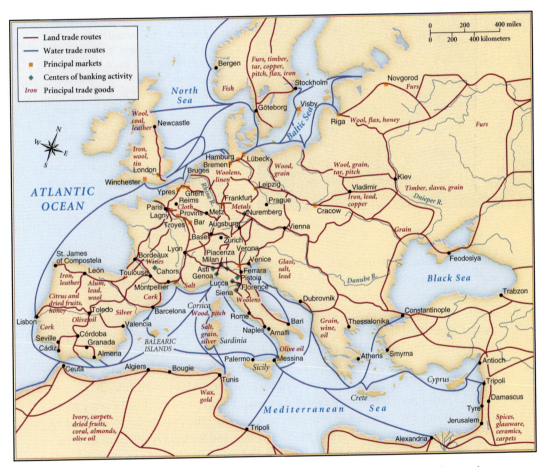

■ **MAP 9.1 Medieval Trade Routes in the Eleventh and Twelfth Centuries**
This spider's web of lines obscures the simple pattern: bulk goods from the north (furs, fish, wood) were traded for luxury goods from the south (ivory and spices—a category that included medicines, perfumes, and dyes). Already regions were beginning to specialize. England, for example, supplied raw wool, and Flanders (Ypres, Ghent) specialized in turning that wool into cloth and shipping it farther south, to the fairs of Champagne (whose capital was Troyes) or Germany. Italian cities served as the funnels that channeled goods from the Muslim and Byzantine worlds northward and exported European goods south and eastward.

■ **Medieval Conques**

Conques was a major pilgrimage center. Housed in its monastery church was the powerful relic of Ste. Foy (St. Faith), whose miracle-working cures were famous across Europe. People went directly to Conques to seek help from Ste. Foy, or they stopped there on a journey that took them across the south of France and the north of Spain to Santiago da Compostella, where they sought the relics of St. James. A whole city of shopkeepers, hoteliers, and craftspeople grew up around the monastery at Conques to serve the throngs of pilgrims. The church of Conques dominates the center of this photograph. Does the placement of buildings around it suggest careful town planning? (Jean Dieuzaide.)

burdened some with unwelcome obligations. Great lords hired trained, literate agents to administer their estates, calculate profits and losses, and make marketing decisions. Aristocrats needed money not only because they relished luxuries such as fine wines, spices, and soft, glowing fabrics, but also because their honor and authority continued to depend on their personal generosity, patronage, and displays of wealth. In the late twelfth century, when some townsmen could boast fortunes that rivaled the riches of the landed aristocracy, economic pressures on the nobles increased as their extravagance exceeded their income. Many went into debt.

The lord's need for money changed peasant life, as peasants, too, became more integrated into the developing commercial economy. The population continued to increase in the twelfth century, and the greater demand for food required more farmland. By the middle of the century, isolated and sporadic attempts to cultivate new land had become a regular and coordinated activity. Great lords offered special privileges to peasants who would do the backbreaking work of plowing marginal land. In Flanders, where land was regularly inundated by seawater, the great monasteries sponsored drainage projects, and newly dug canals linking the cities to the agricultural regions let boats ply the waters to nearly every nook and cranny of the region.

Sometimes, free peasants acted on their own to clear land and relieve the pressure of overpopulation. For example, small freeholders in England's Fenland region cooperated to build banks and dikes to reclaim land that led out to the North Sea. Villages were founded on the drained land, and villagers shared responsibility for repairing and maintaining the dikes even as each peasant family farmed its new holding individually.

On old estates the rise in population strained the manse organization that had developed in Carolingian Europe, where each household was settled on the land that supported it. In the twelfth century, twenty peasant families might live on what had been, in the tenth century, the manse of one family. With the manse supporting so many more people, labor services and dues had to be recalculated, and peasants and their lords often turned services and dues into money rents, payable once a year. With this change, peasant men gained more control over their plots—they could sell them, will them to their sons, or even designate a small portion for their daughters. However, for these privileges, they had to pay high fees. In addition, the revived monarchies of the twelfth century required taxes that were passed along to the lowest classes either directly or indirectly. In Italy the cities themselves often imposed and enforced dues on the peasants, normally tenant farmers who leased their plots in the *contado*, the countryside surrounding each city. Thus peasants' gains from rising prices, access to markets, greater productivity, and increased personal freedom were partially canceled out by their cash burdens. Peasants of the late twelfth century ate better than their forebears, but they also had more responsibilities.

Looming over the rural landscape were the walled towns that made the new economy possible. Their look and feel varied enormously, though nearly all included a marketplace, a castle, and several churches. Most had to adapt to increasingly crowded conditions. Archaeologists have discovered that at the end of the eleventh century in Winchester, England, city plots were still large enough to accommodate houses parallel to the street; but the swelling population soon necessitated destroying these houses to build instead long, narrow, hall-like tenement houses, constructed at right angles to the thoroughfare. These were built on a frame made from strips of wood filled with wattle and daub—twigs woven together and covered with clay. If they were like the stone houses built in the late twelfth century (a period about which historians know a good deal), they had two stories: a shop or warehouse on the lower floor and living quarters above. Behind this main building was the kitchen and perhaps also enclosures for livestock, as archaeologists have found at Southampton, England. Even city dwellers clung to rural pursuits, living largely off the food they raised themselves.

The construction of wattle and daub houses, churches, castles, and markets was part of a building boom that began in the tenth century and continued at an accelerated pace through the thirteenth. Specialized buildings for trade and city government were put up—charitable houses for the sick and indigent, community houses, and warehouses. In addition to individual buildings, the new construction involved erecting massive walls, which ringed most medieval cities. By 1100, Speyer (today in Germany) had three: one around its cathedral, the next just beyond the parish church of St. Moritz, the third still farther out to protect the marketplace. Within the walls lay a network of streets—usually narrow, dirty, dark, and winding—made of packed clay or gravel. In English towns the main street broadened as it approached a rectangular or V-shaped marketplace. Bridges spanned the rivers; on the Meuse, for example, six new bridges were built during the eleventh century alone. Before the eleventh century, Europeans had depended on boats and waterways for bulky long-distance transport; now carts could haul items overland because new roads through the countryside linked the urban markets.

Although commercial centers developed throughout western Europe, they grew fastest and became most dense in regions along key waterways: the Mediterranean coasts of Italy, France, and Spain; northern Italy along the Po River; the river system of the Rhône-Saône-Meuse; the Rhineland; the English Channel; the shores of the Baltic Sea. During the eleventh century, these waterways became part of a single interdependent economy.◆

Business Arrangements

The development of commercial centers reflected changing attitudes toward money. The new mode of commerce transformed the social relations involved in economic transactions. In the gift economy, exchanges of coins, gold, and silver were components of ongoing relationships. Kings offered treasures to their followers, peasants gave dues to their lords, and pious donors presented land to the saintly patrons of churches, all in the expectation of long-term relationships. In the new market economy, which thrived on the profit motive, arrangements were less personal. They often relied on written contracts and calculations of the profitability of a particular business venture.

Although all the new business agreements took many forms, they had the common purpose of bringing people together to pool their resources and finance larger enterprises. The *commenda*, for example, an Italian invention, was a partnership established for commerce by sea. In a common arrangement, one or more investors furnished the money, and the other partners undertook the risks of the actual voyage. If a trip proved successful, the investors received three-quarters of the profit and the travelers the rest. But if the voyage failed, the investors lost their outlay, and the travelers expended their time and labor to no profit. The impermanence of such partnerships (they lasted for only one voyage) meant that capital could be shifted easily from one venture to another and could therefore be used to support a variety of enterprises.

◆ For a pair of sources that illuminate the rise of medieval urbanism and its economic and social implications, see Document 26, "Urban Charters of Jaca, Spain, and Lorris, France."

Land trade often involved a more enduring partnership. In Italy this took the form of a *compagnia*, formed when family property was invested in trade. Unlike the *commenda*, in which the partners could lose no more than they had put into the enterprise, the *compagnia* left its members with joint and unlimited liability for all losses and debts. This provision enhanced family solidarity, because each member was responsible for the debts of all the others; but it also risked bankrupting entire households.

The commercial revolution also fostered the development of contracts for sales, exchanges, and loans. Loans were the most problematic. In the Middle Ages, as now, interest payments were the chief inducement for an investor to supply money. To circumvent the church's ban on usury (profiting from loans), interest was often disguised as a penalty for "late payment" under the rules of a contract. The new willingness to finance business enterprises with loans signaled a changed attitude toward credit: risk was acceptable if it brought profit.

Contracts and partnerships made large-scale productive enterprises possible. In fact, light industry began in the eleventh century. Just as in the Industrial Revolution of the eighteenth and nineteenth centuries, one of the earliest products to benefit from new industrial technologies was cloth. Water mills powered machines such as flails to clean and thicken cloth and presses to extract oil from fibers. Machines were also used to exploit raw materials more efficiently: new deep-mining technology provided Europeans with hitherto untapped sources of metals. At the same time, forging techniques improved, and iron was for the first time regularly used for agricultural tools and plows. This, in turn, made for better farming, and better farming fed the commercial revolution. Metals were also used for weapons and armor or made into ornaments or coins.

Whether fashioned by machines or handworkers, production relied on the expertise of artisans able to finish the cloth, mint the coins, and forge the weapons. To regulate and protect their products and trades, craftspeople and others involved in commerce formed *guilds*: local social, religious, and economic associations whose members plied the same trade. By the late twelfth century, they had become corporations defined by statutes and rules. They controlled their membership, determining dues, working hours, wages, and standards for materials and products. Sometimes they came into conflict with town government, as for example in Italy, where some cities considered bread too important a commodity to allow bakers to form a guild. At other times, city governors supported guild efforts to control wages, reinforcing guild regulations with statutes of their own.

Guilds often had to cooperate with one another. Producing wool cloth involved numerous guilds—shearers, weavers, fullers (people who beat the cloth to make it bulkier), dyers—generally working under the supervision of the merchant guild that imported the raw wool. Some guilds were more prestigious than others: in Florence, for example, professional guilds of notaries and judges ranked above craft guilds.

Within each guild of artisans or merchants existed another kind of hierarchy. Apprentices were at the bottom, journeymen and -women in the middle, and masters at the top. Apprentices were boys and occasionally girls placed under the tutelage of a master for a number of years to learn a trade. (See "Taking Measure," page 345.) Journeymen and -women were simple day laborers; they did not live with the guild master but rather worked for a wage. As for the masters, these men (but almost never women) dominated the offices and policies of the guild, hired journeymen, and recruited and educated apprentices. They drew up the guild regulations and served as chief overseers, inspectors, and treasurers. Because the number of masters was few and the turnover of official posts frequent, most masters eventually had a chance to serve as guild officers. Occasionally officers were elected, but more often the rulers of the city appointed them from among the masters of the craft.

During the late twelfth century, women's labor in some trades gradually declined in importance. In Flanders, for example, as the manufacture of woolen cloth shifted from rural areas to cities, women participated less in the process. In cities like Ypres and Ghent, men working in pairs ran new-style large looms. They produced a heavyweight cloth superior to the fabric made on the lighter looms that women had worked. Similarly, women had ground grain into flour tediously by hand, but water mills and animal-powered mills gradually took the place of female labor, and most millers who ran the new machinery were male. Some women were certainly artisans and traders, and their names occasionally appeared in guild memberships. But they did not become guild officers, and they played no official role in town government.

Self-Government for the Towns

Guilds were one way townspeople expressed their mutual concerns and harnessed their collective energies. Movements for self-government were another. Townspeople banded together for protection and freedom.

Both to themselves and to outsiders, townspeople seemed different. Tradespeople, artisans, ship captains, innkeepers, and moneychangers did not fit into the old categories of medieval types—those who pray, those who fight, and those who labor. Just knowing they were different gave townspeople a sense of solidarity with one another. But practical reasons also contributed to their feeling of common purpose: they lived in close quarters with one another, and they shared a mutual interest in reliable coinage, laws to facilitate commerce, freedom from servile dues and services, and independence to buy and sell as the market dictated. Already in the early twelfth century, the king of England granted to the citizens of Newcastle-upon-Tyne the privilege that any unfree peasant who lived there unclaimed by his lord for a year and a day would thereafter be a free person. To townspeople, freedom meant having their own officials and law courts. They petitioned the political powers that ruled them—bishops, kings, counts, castellans—for the right to gov-

Lengths of Apprenticeships (years)	Occupation: Paris	Occupation: Genoa
4	Baker, carpenter	Draper, spinner
5	Fur hatter	Horseshoer, barber, cobbler, mason
6	Hatter, cutler, mason	Dyer, tailor
7	Felt hatter	Turner, smith, carpenter, coppersmith, carder
8	Tanner, locksmith, lace and silk maker	Locksmith, cutler, butcher
9		Harness maker
10	Buckle maker, tapestry maker, crucifix maker, table maker, goldsmith	Silversmith, armorer, saddler, cooper
11	Harness maker	Chest maker

■ **TAKING MEASURE** Lengths of Apprenticeships in the Thirteenth Century

An apprenticeship was a form of schooling, and, as this table makes clear, many apprenticeships lasted up to eleven years and none lasted less than four. The table also shows how local standards differed. To be a harness maker in Paris required eleven years of apprenticeship, but the same skills were considered to have been acquired in only nine years in Genoa.

(From *Wage Labor and Guilds in Medieval Europe* by Steven A. Epstein. Copyright © 1991 by the University of North Carolina Press. Used by permission of the publisher.)

ern themselves. Often they formed *communes*, sworn associations of townspeople that generally cut across the boundaries of rich and poor, merchants and craftspeople, clergy and laity.

Collective movements for urban self-government emerged especially in Italy, France, and Germany. Italian cities were centers of regional political power even before the commercial revolution. Castellans constructed their fortifications, and bishops ruled the countryside from such cities. The commercial revolution swelled the Italian cities with tradespeople, whose interest in self-government was often fueled by religious as well as economic concerns. At Milan in the second half of the eleventh century, popular discontent with the archbishop, who effectively ruled the city, led to numerous armed clashes. In 1097, the Milanese succeeded in transferring political power from the archbishop and his clergy to a government of leading men of the city who called themselves "consuls." The title recalled the government of the ancient Roman republic, affirming the consuls' status as representatives of the people. Like the archbishop's power before, the consuls' rule extended beyond the town walls, into the *contado*, the outlying countryside.

Outside of Italy, movements for city independence took place within the framework of larger kingdoms or principalities. Such movements were sometimes violent, as at Milan, but at other times they were peaceful. For example, William Clito, who claimed the county of Flanders (today in Belgium), willingly granted the citizens of Saint-Omer the rights they asked for in 1127 in return for their support of his claims: he recognized them as legally free, gave them the right to mint coins, allowed them their own laws and courts, and lifted certain tolls and taxes. Although the merchant guild profited the most, as it alone gained freedom from tolls throughout Flanders, all the citizens of Saint-Omer benefited from these privileges. Here, as elsewhere, the men and women who created new forms of business and political associations to meet their needs gained a measure of self-rule in towns and cities.

Church Reform and Its Aftermath

The commercial revolution affected the church because the church, too, was part of the world. Bishops ruled over many cities. Kings appointed many bishops. Local lords installed priests in their parish churches. Churchmen gave gifts and money to these secular powers for their offices. The impulse to free the church from "the world" was as old as the origins of monasticism, but, beginning in the tenth century and increasing to fever pitch in the eleventh, reformers demanded that the church as a whole remodel itself and become free of secular entanglements.

This freedom was from the start as much a matter of power as of religion. Most people had long believed that their ruler—whether king, duke, count, or castellan—reigned by the grace of God and had the right to control the churches in his territory. But by the second half of the eleventh century, more and more people saw a great deal wrong with secular power over the church. They looked to the papacy to lead the movement of church reform. The most important moment came in 1075, when Pope Gregory VII called on the emperor, Henry IV, to end his appointment of churchmen. This request ushered in a major civil war in Germany and a great upheaval in the distribution of power everywhere. By the early 1100s, a reformed church—with the pope at its head—had become institutionalized, penetrating into areas of life never before touched by churchmen. Church reform began as a way to free the church from the world; but in the end, the church was equally involved in the new world it had helped to create.

Beginnings of the Reform Movement

The idea of freeing the church from the world began in the tenth century with no particular program and only a vague idea of what it might mean. At the Benedictine monastery of Cluny, for example, which was founded in 910, there was no organized program of reform. Nevertheless, the founders of the monastery, the duke and duchess of Aquitaine, wanted to "free" it from the world. They achieved this goal by endowing the monastery with property but then giving it and its worldly possessions to Saints Peter and Paul. In this way, they put control of the monastery into the hands of the two most powerful heavenly saints. They designated the pope, as the successor of St. Peter, to be the monastery's worldly protector if anyone should bother or threaten it. The whole notion of "freedom" at this point was very vague. But Cluny's prestige was great because of its status as St. Peter's property and because of the elaborate round of prayers that its monks carried out with scrupulous devotion. The Cluniac monks fulfilled the role of "those who pray" in a way that dazzled their contemporaries. Through their prayers they seemed to guarantee the salvation of all Christians. Rulers, bishops, rich landowners, and even serfs (if they could) gave Cluny donations of land, joining their contributions to the land of St. Peter. Powerful men and women called on the Cluniac monks to reform new monasteries along the Cluniac model.

The abbots of Cluny came to see themselves as reformers of the world as well. They believed in clerical celibacy, preaching against the prevailing norm that let parish priests and even bishops marry. They also thought that the laity could be reformed, become more virtuous, and cease its oppression of the poor. In the eleventh century, the Cluniacs began to link their program of internal monastic and external worldly reform to the papacy. They asked the popes to help them when Cluniac lands were encroached upon by bishops and laypeople at the same time as the papacy itself was becoming interested in reform.

Around the time the Cluniacs were joining their fate to that of the popes, a small group of clerics and monks in the empire began calling for systematic reform within the church. They buttressed their arguments with new interpretations of *canon law*—the laws decreed over the centuries at church councils and by bishops and popes. They concentrated on two breaches of those laws: nicolaitism (clerical marriage) and simony (buying church offices). Most of the men who promoted these ideas lived in the most commercialized regions of the empire: the Rhineland (the region along the northern half of the Rhine River) and Italy. Their familiarity with the impersonal practices of a profit economy led them to interpret as crass purchases the gifts that churchmen were used to giving in return for their offices.

Emperor Henry III (r. 1039–1056) supported the reformers. Taking seriously his position as the anointed of God, Henry felt responsible for the well-being of the church in his empire. He denounced simony and personally refused to accept money or gifts when he appointed bishops to their posts. When in 1046 three men, each representing a different faction of the Roman aristocracy, claimed to be pope, Henry, as ruler of Rome, traveled to Italy to settle the matter. The Synod of Sutri (1046), over which he presided, deposed all three popes and elected another. In 1049, Henry appointed Leo IX (r. 1049–1054), a bishop from the Rhineland, to the papacy. This appointment marked an unanticipated turning point for the emperor when Leo set out to reform the church under papal, rather than imperial, control. During Leo's tenure, the pope's role expanded. He traveled to France and Germany, holding councils to condemn simoniac bishops. He sponsored the creation of a canon law textbook—the *Collection in 74 Titles*—that emphasized the pope's power. To the papal court, Leo brought the most zealous reformers of his day: Humbert of Silva Candida, Peter Damian, and Hildebrand (later Pope Gregory VII).

At first, Leo's claims to new power over the church hierarchy were complacently ignored by clergy and secular rulers alike. The Council of Reims, which he called in 1049, for example, was attended by only a few bishops and boycotted by the king of France. Nevertheless, Leo made it into a forum for exercising his authority. Placing the relics of St. Remegius (the patron saint of Reims) on the altar of the church, he demanded that the attending bishops and abbots say whether or not they had purchased their offices. A few confessed they had; some did not respond; others gave excuses. The new and extraordinary development was that all present felt accountable to the pope and accepted his verdicts.

In 1054, Leo sent Humbert of Silva Candida to Constantinople on a diplomatic mission to argue against the patriarch of Constantinople on behalf of the new, lofty claims of the pope. Furious at the contemptuous way he was treated, Humbert ended his mission by excommunicating the patriarch. In retaliation, the Byzantine emperor and his bishops excommunicated Humbert and his party, threatening them with eternal damnation. Clashes between the two churches had occurred before and had been patched up, but this one, called the Great Schism, proved insurmountable.* Thereafter, the Roman Catholic and the Greek Orthodox churches were largely separate.

The popes who followed Leo continued his program to expand papal power. When military adventurers from Normandy began carving out states for themselves in southern Italy, the popes in nearby Rome felt threatened. After waging unsuccessful war against the interlopers, the papacy made the best of a bad situation by granting the Normans Sicily and parts of southern Italy as a fief, turning its former enemies into vassals.

As leader of the Christian people, the papacy also participated in wars in Spain, where it supported Christians against the dominant Muslims. The political fragmentation of al-Andalus into small and weak *taifas* (see page 304) made it fair game to the Christians to the north. Slowly the idea of the *reconquista*, the Christian reconquest of Spain, took shape, fed by religious fervor as well as worldly ambition.

---

*Despite occasional thaws and liftings of the sentences, the mutual excommunications of pope and patriarch largely remained in effect until 1965, when Pope Paul VI and the Greek Orthodox patriarch, Athenagoras I, publicly deplored them.

Gregorian Reform and the Investiture Conflict, 1073–1085

The papal reform movement is above all associated with Pope Gregory VII (r. 1073–1085). He began as a lowly Roman cleric—Hildebrand—with the job of administering the papal estates and rose slowly in the hierarchy. A passionate advocate of papal primacy (the theory that the pope was head of the church), he was not afraid to clash with Emperor Henry IV (r. 1056–1106) over leadership of the church. In his view—and it was astonishing at the time, given the religious and spiritual roles associated with rulers—the emperor was just a layman who had no right to meddle in church affairs.

Gregory was and remains an extraordinarily controversial figure. He certainly thought that he was acting as the vicar, or representative, of St. Peter on earth. Describing himself, he declared, "I have labored with all my power that Holy Church, the bride of God, our Lady Mother, might come again to her own splendor and might remain free, pure, and Catholic." He thought the reforms he advocated and the upheavals he precipitated were necessary to free the church from the Satanic rulers of the world. His great nemesis, Henry IV, had a very different view. He considered Gregory an ambitious and evil man who "seduced the world far and wide and stained the Church with the blood of her sons." Not surprisingly, modern historians are only a bit less divided in their assessment of Gregory. Few deny his sincerity and deep religious devotion, but many speak of his pride, ambition, and single-mindedness. He was not an easy man.

The World of the Investiture Conflict, c. 1070–1122

Henry IV was less complex. He was brought up in the traditions of his father, Henry III, a pious church reformer who considered it part of his duty to appoint bishops and even popes to ensure the well-being of church and state together. The emperor believed that he and his bishops—who were, at the same time, his most valuable supporters and administrators—were the rightful leaders of the church. He had no intention of allowing the pope to become head of the church.

The great confrontation between Gregory and Henry began over the appointment of the archbishop of Milan. Gregory disputed Henry's right to "invest" the archbishop (put him into office). In the investiture ritual, the emperor or his representative symbolically gave the church and the land that went with it to the priest or bishop or archbishop chosen for the job. In 1075, Gregory prohibited lay investiture, thereby denying the emperor's right to invest churchmen. When Henry defied this prohibition and invested a new archbishop of Milan, the two men hurled unceasing denunciations at each other. The next year Henry called a council of German bishops who demanded that Gregory, that "false monk," resign. In reply, Gregory called a synod that both excommunicated and suspended Henry from office:

> *I deprive King Henry, son of the emperor Henry, who has rebelled against [God's] Church with unheard-of audacity, of the government over the whole kingdom of Germany and Italy, and I release all Christian men from the allegiance which they have sworn or may swear to him, and I forbid anyone to serve him as king.*

The last part of this decree gave it a secular punch because it authorized anyone in Henry's kingdom to rebel against him.◆ Henry's enemies, mostly German princes (as German aristocrats were called), now threatened to elect another king. Responding to this attack, Henry traveled to intercept Gregory, who was journeying northward to visit the rebellious princes. In early 1077, king and pope met at Canossa, high in central Italy's snowy Apennine Mountains. Gregory was inside a fortress there; Henry stood outside as a penitent. This posture was an astute move by Henry because no priest could refuse absolution to a penitent; Gregory had to lift the excommunication and receive Henry back into the church. But Gregory now had the advantage of the king's humiliation before the majesty of the pope.

Although Henry was technically back in the fold, nothing of substance had been resolved, and civil war began. The princes elected an antiking (a king chosen illegally), and Henry and his supporters elected an antipope. From 1077 until 1122, papal and imperial armies waged intermittent war. Long after the original antagonists, Gregory and Henry, had died, the Concordat of Worms of 1122 ended the fighting with a compromise that relied on a conceptual distinction between two parts of the investiture ceremony—the spiritual (in which a man received the symbols of his clerical office) and the secular (in which he received the symbols of the material goods that would allow him to function). Under the terms of the concordat, the ring and staff, the symbols of church office, would be given by a churchman in the first part of the ceremony. In the second part, the emperor or his representative would touch the bishop with a scepter, a symbolic gesture that stood for the land and other possessions that went with his office. Elections of bishops in

---

◆ For primary sources that reveal the competing arguments of Emperor Henry IV and Pope Gregory VII, see Document 27, "Letters of the Investiture Conflict."

Germany would take place "in the presence" of the emperor—that is, under his influence. In Italy, the pope would have a comparable role.

Superficially, nothing much had changed; secular rulers would continue to have a part in choosing and investing churchmen. In fact, however, almost no one any longer would claim that the king was head of the church. Just as the new investiture ceremony broke the ritual into spiritual and secular parts, so, too, it implied a new notion of kingship that separated it from priesthood. The Investiture Conflict did not produce the modern distinction between church and state—that would develop only very slowly—but it set the wheels in motion.

The most important changes brought about by the Investiture Conflict, however, were on the ground: the political landscape in both Italy and Germany was irrevocably transformed. In Germany, the princes consolidated their lands and their positions at the expense of royal power. They became virtual monarchs within their own principalities; the emperor, though retaining his title, became a figurehead. In Italy, the emperor lost power to the cities. The Italian communes were formed in the crucible of the war between the pope and the emperor. In fierce communal struggles, city factions, motivated in part by local grievances but often claiming to fight on behalf of the papal or the imperial cause, created their own governing bodies. In the course of the twelfth century, northern Italian cities became used to self-government.

The Sweep of Reform

Church reform involved much more than the clash of popes, emperors, and their supporters. It penetrated deeply into the daily lives of ordinary Christians, in part through the church's new emphasis on the sacraments—the regular means (according to the Catholic church) by which God's heavenly grace infused mundane existence. But this did not mean that Christians were clear about how many sacraments there were, how they worked, or even their significance. Eleventh-century church reformers began the process—which would continue into the thirteenth century—of emphasizing the importance of the sacraments and the special nature of the priest, whose chief role was to administer them.

In the sacrament of marriage, for example, the effective involvement of the church in the wedding of man and woman came only after the Gregorian reform. Not until the twelfth century did people regularly come to be married by a priest in church, and only then did churchmen assume jurisdiction over marital disputes, not simply in cases involving royalty but also in those of lesser aristocrats. The clergy's prohibition of marriage partners as distant as seventh cousins (marriage between such cousins was considered incest) had the potential to control dynastic alliances. Because many noble families kept their inheritance intact through a single male heir, the heirs' marriages took on great significance.

At the same time, churchmen began to stress the sanctity of marriage. Hugh of St. Victor, a twelfth-century scholar, dwelled on the sacramental meaning of marriage:

Can you find anything else in marriage except conjugal society which makes it sacred and by which you can assert that it is holy? . . . Each shall be to the other as a same self in all sincere love, all careful solicitude, every kindness of affection, in constant compassion, unflagging consolation, and faithful devotedness.

Hugh saw marriage as a matter of love.

The reformers also proclaimed the special importance of the sacrament of the Mass, holy communion through the body and blood of Christ. Gregory VII called the Mass "the greatest thing in the Christian religion." No layman, no matter how powerful, and no woman of any sort at all could perform anything equal to it, for the Mass was the key to salvation.

The new emphasis on the difference between the priest (who could celebrate Mass) and the laity (who could not) led to vigorous enforcement of an old element of church discipline: the celibacy of priests. The demand for a celibate clergy had far-reaching significance for the history of the church. It distanced western clerics even further from their eastern Orthodox counterparts (whose priests did not practice celibacy), exacerbating the Great Schism of 1054. It also broke with traditional local practices, for clerical marriage was customary in many places. Gregorian reformers exhorted every cleric in higher orders, from the humble parish priest to the exalted bishop, to refrain from marriage or to abandon his wife. Many churchmen resisted. The historian Orderic Vitalis (1075–c. 1142) reported that one zealous archbishop

fulfilled his duties as metropolitan with courage and thoroughness, continually striving to separate immoral priests from their mistresses [wives]: on one occasion when he forbade them to keep concubines he was stoned out of the synod.

Undaunted, the reformers persisted, and in 1123 the pope proclaimed all clerical marriages invalid. With its new power, the papacy was largely able to enforce the rule.

The rule about clerical marriages was only one in a veritable explosion of canon law. Canon law had begun simply as rules determined at church councils. These were then coupled with papal declarations. Some attempts to gather together and organize these laws had been made before the eleventh century. But the proliferation of rules during that century, along with the desire of Gregorians to clarify church law as they saw it, made a systematic collection even more necessary. This was supplied in about 1140 by a landmark in canon law jurisprudence: the *Concordance of Discordant Canons*, also known as the *Decretum*, by Gratian, a monk who taught law at Bologna in northern Italy. Gratian gathered thousands of passages from the decrees of popes and councils with the intention of showing their harmony. To make conflicting canons conform to one another, he adopted the principle that papal pronouncements superseded the laws of church councils and all secular laws.

At the time Gratian was writing, the papal *curia*, or government, centered in Rome, resembled a court of law with its own collection agency. The papacy had developed a bureaucracy to hear cases and rule on petitions, such as disputed elections of bishops. Hearing cases cost money: lawyers, judges, and courtroom clerks had to be paid. Churchmen not involved in litigation went to Rome for other sorts of benefits: to petition for privileges for their monasteries or to be consecrated by the pope. These services were also expensive, requiring hearing officers, notaries, and collectors. The lands owned by the papacy were not sufficient to support the growing administrative apparatus, and the petitioners and litigants themselves had to pay, a practice they resented. A satire written about 1100, in the style of the Gospels, made bitter fun of papal greed:

> *There came to the court a certain wealthy clerk, fat and thick, and gross, who in the sedition [rebellion] had committed murder. He first gave to the dispenser, second to the treasurer, third to the cardinals. But they thought among themselves that they should receive more. The Lord Pope, hearing that his cardinals had received many gifts, was sick, nigh unto death. But the rich man sent to him a couch of gold and silver and immediately he was made whole. Then the Lord Pope called his cardinals and ministers to him and said to them: "Brethren, look, lest anyone deceive you with vain words. For I have given you an example: as I have grasped, so you grasp also."*

The pope, with his law courts, bureaucracy, and financial apparatus, had become a monarch.

Early Crusades and Crusader States

Asserting itself as head of the Christian church and leader of its reform movement, the papacy sometimes supported and proclaimed holy wars to advance the cause of Christianity. The most important of these were the crusades. Combinations of war and pilgrimage—the popular practice of making a pious voyage to a sacred shrine to petition for help or cure—the early crusades sent armed European Christians into battle against Muslims in the Holy Land, the place where Christ had lived and died. The crusaders established several tiny states in the Levant, holding on to them precariously until 1291. Although the crusades ultimately "failed" in the sense that the crusaders did not succeed in permanently retaining the Holy Land for Christendom, they were a pivotal episode in Western civilization. They marked the first stage of European overseas expansion, of what later would become imperialism.

The First Crusade began with the entry of the Seljuk Turks in Asia Minor (Map 9.2). In the 900s, the Muslim world had splintered into numerous small states; by the 1050s, the fierce, nomadic Sunni Muslim Seljuks had captured Baghdad, subjugated the caliphate, and begun to threaten Byzantium. The difficulties the Byzantine emperor Romanus IV had in pulling together an army to attack the Turks in 1071 reveal how weak his position had become. Unable to muster Byzantine troops—the *strategoi* were busy defending their own districts, and provincial nobles were wary of sending support to the emperor—Romanus had to rely on a merce-

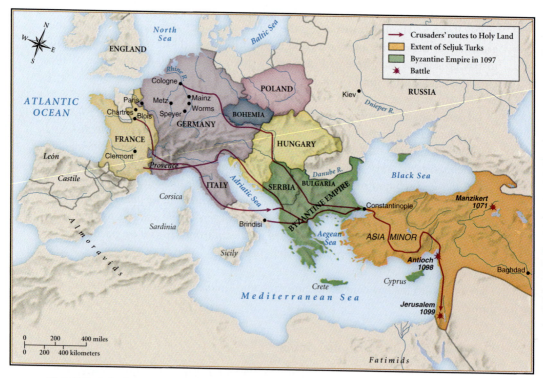

■ **MAP 9.2 The First Crusade, 1096–1098**

The First Crusade was a major military undertaking that required organization, movement over both land and sea, and enormous resources. Four main groups were responsible for the conquest of Jerusalem. One set out from Cologne, in northern Germany; a second group started from Blois, in France; the third originated to the west of Provence; and the fourth launched ships from Brindisi, at the heel of Italy. All joined up at Constantinople, where their leaders negotiated with Alexius for help and supplies in return for a pledge of vassalage to the emperor.

www.bedfordstmartins.com/huntconcise   See the ONLINE STUDY GUIDE for more help in analyzing this map.

nary army made up of Normans, Franks, Slavs, and even Turks. This motley force met the Seljuks under Sultan Alp Arslan at Manzikert in what is today eastern Turkey. The battle was a disaster for Romanus: the Seljuks routed his army and captured him. Manzikert marked the end of Byzantine domination in the region.

The Turks, gradually settling in Asia Minor, extended their control across the empire and beyond, all the way to Jerusalem, which had been under Muslim control since the seventh century. In 1095, the Byzantine emperor Alexius I appealed for help to Pope Urban II (r. 1088–1099), hoping to get new mercenary troops for a fresh offensive.

Urban II chose to interpret the request in his own way. At the Council of Clermont (in France) in 1095, after finishing the usual business of proclaiming the Truce of God (prohibition of fighting on various days of the week for various reasons) and condemning simony among the clergy, Urban moved outside the church and addressed an already excited throng:

> *Oh, race of Franks, race from across the mountains, race beloved and chosen by God. . . . Let hatred depart from among you, let your quarrels end, let wars cease, and let all dissensions and controversies slumber. Enter upon the road to the Holy Sepulcher; wrest that land from the wicked race, and subject it to yourselves.*

The crowd reportedly responded with one voice: "God wills it."

■ **A Crusader and His Wife**
How do we know that the man on the left is a crusader? On his shirt is a cross, the sign worn by all men going on the crusades. In his right hand is a pilgrim's staff, a useful reminder that the crusades were sometimes considered less a matter of war than of penance and piety. What does the embrace of the crusader's wife imply about marital love in the twelfth century?
(Musée Lorrain, Nancy/photo: P. Mignot.)

Historians remain divided over Urban's motives for his massive call to arms. Certainly he hoped to win Christian control of the Holy Land. He was also anxious to fulfill the goals of the Truce of God by turning the entire "race of Franks" into a peace militia dedicated to holy purposes, an army of God. Just as the Truce of God mobilized whole communities to fight against anyone who broke the truce, so the First Crusade mobilized armed groups sworn to free the Holy Land of its enemies. Finally, Urban's call placed the papacy in a new position of leadership, one that complemented in a military arena the position the popes had gained in the church hierarchy.

Both men and women, rich and poor, young and old, heeded Urban's call. They abandoned their homes and braved the rough journey to the Holy Land to fight for their God. They also went—especially younger sons of aristocrats, who could not expect an inheritance because of the practice of primogeniture—because they wanted land. Some knights went on the expedition because in addition to their pious duty they were obligated to follow their lord. Others hoped for plunder. Although women were discouraged from going on the crusades (one, who begged permission from her bishop, was persuaded to stay home and spend her wealth on charity instead), some crusaders were accompanied by their wives. Other women went as servants; a few may have been fighters. Children and old men and women, not able to fight, made the cords for siege engines—giant machines used to hurl stones at enemy fortifications. As more crusades were undertaken during the twelfth century, the transport and supply of these armies became a lucrative business for the commercial classes of maritime Italian cities such as Venice.

The main objective of the First Crusade—to wrest the Holy Land from the Muslims and subject it to Christian rule—was accomplished largely because of Muslim disunity. After nearly a year of ineffectual attacks, the crusaders took Antioch on June 28, 1098, killing every Turk in the city; on July 15, 1099, they seized Jerusalem. Carving out several tiny states in the Holy Land by 1109 (when they won a major battle in Tripoli), the crusaders set up a western European outpost where foreign knights imposed their rule on indigenous populations with vastly different customs and religions. In Europe, peasants clearly differed from knights and nobles by occupation, dress, and style of life, but they were not separate from the upper classes because the two classes lived on the same estates and shared the same religion. By contrast, in the crusader states, Europeans lived in towns and had little in common with the Muslims, Jews, and even native Arab-speaking Christians who tilled the soil.

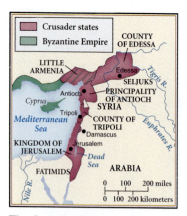

The Crusader States in 1109

■ **Krak-des-Chevaliers**

*The Hospitallers, a religious military order much like the Templars, built this imposing castle in
1142 on the site of a Muslim fortification in Syria. A large community of perhaps fifty monk-
knights and their hired mercenaries lived there. To the northeast (in back of the complex seen here)
was a fortified village that served the needs of the castle. Peasants raised grain, which was ground
by a windmill on one wall of the castle. For water, there were reservoirs to catch the rain, wells,
and an aqueduct (visible on the right). Twelve toilets connected to a common drain. The monks
worshiped in a chapel within the inner walls. The outer walls, built of masonry, completely enclosed the inner buildings, making Krak one of the most important places for refuge and defense in
the crusader states.* (Maynard Williams/NGS Image Collection.)

These states largely kept themselves aloof not only from the peasants at their
doorstep but also from the Islamic states that surrounded them. Good trade relations and numerous declared truces reveal times of peaceful and neighborly coexistence. However, the settlers of the crusader states thought of themselves as living
on a slender beach threatened by a vast Islamic sea. Their leaders feared attack at
any time, and the countryside bristled with their defensive stone castles and towers.

So organized for war was this society that it produced a new and militant kind
of monasticism: the Knights Templar. Like Bruno's Carthusians, the Templars vowed
themselves to poverty and chastity. But rather than withdraw to a hermitage on a
mountaintop, the Templars, whose name came from their living quarters in the area
of the former Jewish Temple at Jerusalem, devoted themselves to warfare. Their first
mission—to protect the pilgrimage routes from Palestine to Jerusalem—soon diversified. They manned the town garrisons of the crusader states, and they transported money from Europe to the Holy Land.

The presence of the Templars did not prevent a new Seljuk chieftain, Zengi,
from taking Edessa in 1144. The slow but steady shrinking of the crusader states

began. The Second Crusade (1147–1149) came to a disastrous end. After besieging the walls of Damascus for only four days, the crusaders, whose leaders could not keep the peace among themselves, gave up and went home. Soon the Muslim hero Nur al-Din united Syria under his command and presided over a renewal of Sunni Islam. His successor, Saladin (1138–1193), took Jerusalem in 1187, galvanizing the pope to call the Third Crusade (1189–1192). Led by the greatest rulers of Europe— Emperor Frederick I Barbarossa, Philip II of France, Leopold of Austria, and Richard I of England—the Third Crusade nevertheless accomplished little, and the crusader states were reduced to a few tiny outposts.

The Jews as Strangers

The same militant piety that inspired the crusades was turned against the Jews. Sentiment against Jews grew over time. Ever since the Roman Empire had become Christian, Jews had been seen as separate from Christians. Imperial law, for example, prohibited them from owning Christian slaves or marrying Christian women. Church laws added to these restrictions. Socially isolated and branded as outcasts, Jews served as scapegoats who helped define the larger society as orthodox. But only at the end of the eleventh century did severe persecution begin.

Forced out of the countryside during the eleventh century by castellans and other regional rulers, most Jews ended up in the cities as craftsmen, merchants, or moneylenders. They provided capital for the developing commercial society, whose Christian members were prohibited from charging interest by the Bible's constraints against usury. Many Jews lived in the flourishing commercial region of the Rhineland. Under Henry IV, the Jews in Speyer and elsewhere in the empire gained a place within the government system by receiving protection from the local bishop (an imperial appointee) in return, of course, for paying a tax. Within these cities, the Jews lived in their own neighborhoods—Bishop Rudiger even built walls around the Jewish section of Speyer. Their tightly knit communities focused on local synagogues, which served as schools and community centers as well as places of worship. Nevertheless, Jews also participated in the life of the larger Christian community. Archbishop Anno of Cologne dealt with Jewish moneylenders, and other Jews in Cologne were allowed to trade their wares at the fairs there.

It was against these Rhineland Jews that some of the earliest anti-Jewish attacks were directed. Some of the crusaders of the First Crusade declared it ridiculous to attack Muslims when other infidels lived in their own backyards: "That's doing our work backward," they said, as they moved into the Rhineland to force conversions or to kill. Some Jews found refuge with bishops or in the houses of Christian friends, but in many cities—Metz, Speyer, Worms, Mainz, and Cologne—they were massacred.

In the course of the twelfth century, the growing monopoly of the guilds, which prohibited Jewish members, pushed Jews out of the crafts and trades. In effect, Jews were compelled to become "usurers" because other fields were closed to them. Even with Christian moneylenders available (for some existed despite the prohibitions), lords, especially kings, borrowed from Jews and encouraged others to do so because, along with their newly asserted powers, European rulers claimed the Jews as their serfs and Jewish property as their own. In England, a special royal financial bureau—the exchequer of the Jews—was created in 1194 to collect unpaid debts due after the death of a Jewish creditor.

Even before 1194, King Henry II of England had imposed new and arbitrary taxes on the Jewish community. Similarly in France, persecuting Jews and confiscating their property benefited both the treasury and the authoritative image of the king. For example, early in the reign of the French king Philip Augustus (r. 1180–1223), royal agents surprised Jews at Sabbath worship in their synagogues and seized their goods, demanding that they redeem their own property for a large sum of money. Shortly thereafter, Philip declared forfeit 80 percent of all debts owed to Jews; the remaining 20 percent was to be paid directly to the king. About a year later, in 1182, Philip expelled the Jews from the Île-de-France:

> *The king gave them leave to sell each his movable goods. . . . But their real estate, that is, houses, fields, vineyards, barns, winepresses, and such like, he reserved for himself and his successors, the kings of the French.*

■ The Jew as the Other

Medieval artists often portrayed people not as individuals but rather as "types" that could be identified by physical markers. In the second half of the twelfth century, Jews were increasingly portrayed as looking different from Christians. This illustration shows clerics borrowing money from a Jew. What physical features do all the clerics have in common? (Be sure to look at the clothes as well as the hairstyle.) What distinguishes the layman from the clerics? How do you know who is meant to be the Jew? In fact, Jews did not regularly wear this type of pointed hat until they were forced to do so in some regions of Europe in the late thirteenth century.

(Bayerische Staatsbibliothek.)

When he allowed the Jews to return in 1198, he intended for them to be money-lenders or moneychangers exclusively, and their activities were to be taxed and monitored by officials.

Limiting Jews to moneylending in an increasingly commercial economy also served the interests of lords in debt to Jewish creditors. For example, in 1190, local nobles orchestrated a brutal attack on the Jews of York (in England). Their purpose was to rid themselves of their debts—and of the Jews to whom they owed money. Churchmen, too, used credit in a money economy but resented the fiscal obligations it imposed. With their drive to create centralized territorial states and their desire to make their authority known and felt, powerful rulers of Europe—churchmen and laymen alike—exploited and coerced the Jews while drawing upon and encouraging widespread anti-Jewish feeling. Although Jews must have looked exactly like Christians in reality, Jews now became clearly identified in sculpture and in drawings by markers such as conical hats and, increasingly, by demeaning features.

Attacks against Jews were inspired by more than resentment against Jewish money and the desire for power and control. They also grew out of the codification of Christian religious doctrine and Christians' anxiety about their own institutions. For example, in the twelfth century, church leaders promulgated a newly rigorous definition of the Eucharist, declaring that when the bread and wine were blessed by the priest during Mass, they became the true body and blood of Christ. For some believers this meant that Christ, wounded and bleeding, lay on the altar. Miracle tales sometimes reported that the elements of the Eucharist bled. Reflecting Christian anxieties about the presence of real flesh on the altar, sensational stories, originating in clerical circles but soon widely circulated, told of Jews who secretly sacrificed Christian children in a morbid revisiting of the crucifixion of Jesus. This charge, called "blood libel" by historians, led to massacres of Jews in cities in England, France, Spain, and Germany. Jews had no rituals involving blood sacrifice at all, but they were convenient and vulnerable scapegoats for Christian guilt and anxiety.

The Revival of Monarchies

Attacks on the Jews reveal the ugly side of a wider development: kings and other rulers were enhancing and consolidating their power. They created new and revived old ideologies to justify their hegemony; they hired officials to work for them; and they found vassals and churchmen to support them. The money that flowed into their treasuries from the new urban economy increased their effectiveness.

Byzantium in Its Prime

The First Crusade itself was an unanticipated result of a monarchical revival at Byzantium. In 1081, ten years after the disastrous battle at Manzikert, the energetic soldier Alexius Comnenus seized the throne. He faced considerable unrest in Constantinople, whose populace suffered from a combination of high taxes and rising living costs. In addition, the empire was under attack on every side—by Normans in southern Italy, Seljuk Turks in Asia Minor, and new groups in the Balkans. But Alexius I (r. 1081–1118) managed to turn actual and potential enemies against one another, staving off immediate defeat.

When Alexius asked Pope Urban II to supply him with some western troops to fight his enemies, he was shocked and disappointed to learn that crusaders rather than mercenaries were on the way. His daughter, Anna Comnena (1083–c. 1148), later wrote an account of the crusades from the Byzantine perspective in a book about her father, the *Alexiad*. To her, the crusaders were barbarians and her father the consummate statesman and diplomat:

> The emperor sent envoys to greet them as a mark of friendship. . . . It was typical of Alexius: he had an uncanny prevision [foresight] and knew how to seize a point of vantage before his rivals. Officers appointed for this particular task were ordered to provide victuals on the journey—the pilgrims must have no excuse for complaint for any reason whatever.

To wage all the wars he had to fight, Alexius relied less on the peasant farmers and the *theme* system than on mercenaries and great magnates armed and mounted like western knights and accompanied by their own troops. In return for their services he gave these nobles *pronoia* grants, lifetime possession of large imperial estates and their dependent peasants. The *theme* system, under which peasant soldiers in earlier centuries had been settled on imperial lands, gradually disappeared. Alexius conciliated the great families by giving the provincial nobility *pronoia* grants and satisfied members of the urban elite by granting them new offices. The emperor normally got on well with the patriarch and Byzantine clergy, for emperor and church depended on each other to suppress heresy and foster orthodoxy. The emperors of the Comnenian dynasty (1081–1185) thus gained a measure of increased imperial power, but at the price of important concessions to the nobility.

In the eleventh and twelfth centuries, Constantinople remained a rich, sophisticated, and highly cultured city. Sculptors and other artists strove to depict ideals of human beauty and elegance. Churches built during the period were decorated with elaborate depictions of the cosmos. Significant innovations occurred in Byzantine scholarship and literature. The Neo-Platonic tradition of late antiquity had always influenced Byzantine religious and philosophical thought, but now scholars renewed their interest in the wellsprings of classical Greek philosophy, particularly Plato and Aristotle. The rediscovery of ancient culture inspired Byzantine writers to reintroduce old forms into the grammar, vocabulary, and rhetorical style of Greek literature. Anna Comnena wrote her *Alexiad* in this newly learned Greek and prided herself on "having read thoroughly the treatises of Aristotle and the dialogues of Plato." The revival of ancient Greek writings, especially Plato's, in eleventh- and twelfth-century Byzantium would have profound consequences for both eastern and western European civilization in centuries to come as their ideas slowly penetrated European culture.

Norman and Angevin England

In Europe, the twelfth-century kings of England were the most powerful monarchs before 1200 because they ruled the whole kingdom by right of conquest. When

the Anglo-Saxon king Edward the Confessor (r. 1042–1066) died childless in 1066, the duke of Normandy, William (1027–1087), claimed the throne of England. Gathering a force recruited from many parts of France, he launched an invasion. His armies clashed with those of another claimant to the throne, Harold, at Hastings on October 14, 1066. In one of history's rare decisive battles, William won and took over the realm.

Some people in England gladly supported William, considering his victory a verdict from God and hoping to be granted a place in the new order themselves. But William—known to posterity by the epithet "the Conqueror"—wanted to replace, not assimilate, the Anglo-Saxons. In the course of William's reign, families from continental Europe almost totally supplanted the English aristocracy. And although the English peasantry remained—now with new lords—the peasants were severely shaken. A twelfth-century historian claimed to record William's deathbed confession:

Norman Conquest of England, 1066

> *I have persecuted [England's] native inhabitants beyond all reason. Whether gentle or simple, I have cruelly oppressed them; many I unjustly disinherited; innumerable multitudes, especially in the county of York, perished through me by famine or the sword.*

Modern historians estimate that one out of five people in England died as a result of the Norman conquest and its immediate aftermath.

Although the Normans destroyed a generation of English men and women, they preserved and extended some Anglo-Saxon institutions, retaining the old administrative divisions and legal system of shires (counties) and hundreds (see page 328). The Normans also, of course, drew from continental institutions. They set up a political hierarchy, culminating in the king and buttressed by his castles, just as French kings were trying to do at about the same time (see page 368). But because all of England was the king's by conquest, he could treat it as his booty; William kept about 20 percent of the land for himself and divided the rest, distributing it

■ **Bayeux "Tapestry"**

This famous "tapestry" is misnamed; it is really an embroidery, 231 feet long and 20 inches wide, created to tell the story of William's conquest of England from his point of view. In this detail, Norman archers are lined up at the bottom. Above them, Norman knights on horseback attack English foot soldiers wielding long battle-axes. Who seems to be winning? Compare the armor and fighting gear shown here with the equipment shown on page 324. (Tapisserie de Bayeux.)

www.bedfordstmartins.com/huntconcise   See the ONLINE STUDY GUIDE for more help in analyzing this image.

in large but scattered fiefs to a relatively small number of his barons and family members, lay and ecclesiastical, as well as to some lesser men, such as personal servants and soldiers. In turn these men and their vassals owed the king military service along with certain dues, such as reliefs (money paid upon inheriting a fief) and aids (payments made on important occasions).

Those were the revenues expected from the nobles, but the king of England commanded the peasantry as well. In 1086, twenty years after his conquest, William ordered a survey and census of England, popularly called "Domesday" because, like the records of people judged at doomsday, it provided facts that could not be appealed. It was the most extensive inventory of land, livestock, taxes, and population that had ever been compiled in Europe. The king

> sent his men over all England into every shire and had them find out how many hundred hides [a measure of land] there were in the shire, or what land and cattle the king himself had in the country, or what dues he ought to receive every year from the shire. . . . So very narrowly did he have the survey to be made that there was not a single hide or yard of land, nor indeed . . . an ox or a cow or a pig left out.

The king's men conducted local surveys by consulting Anglo-Saxon tax lists and by taking testimony from local jurors, men sworn to answer a series of formal questions truthfully. From these inquests scribes wrote voluminous reports filled with facts and statements from villagers, sheriffs, priests, and barons. These reports were then summarized in Domesday itself, a concise record of England's resources that supplied the king and his officials with information such as how much and what sort of land England had, who held it, and what revenues—including the lucrative Danegeld, which was now in effect a royal tax—could be expected from it.

The Norman conquest tied England to the languages, politics, institutions, and culture of France and Flanders. Modern English is an amalgam of Anglo-Saxon and Norman French, the language the Normans spoke. English commerce was linked to the wool industry in Flanders. St. Anselm (1033–1109), the archbishop of Canterbury (England), was born in Italy and was the abbot of a monastery in Normandy before crossing the Channel. The barons of England retained their estates in Normandy and elsewhere, and the kings of England often spent more time on the continent than they did on the island. When William's son Henry I (r. 1100–1135) died without male heirs, civil war soon erupted: the throne of England was fought over by two French counts, one married to Henry's daughter, the other to his sister.

The ultimate outcome of that civil war was the accession to the English throne of Henry II (r. 1154–1189).* He was not only count of Anjou but also, by an astute marriage to Eleanor of Aquitaine in 1152, duke of Aquitaine. His father, who had conquered Normandy, named him duke there, and he also exercised hegemony over Poitou and Brittany. Although technically a vassal of the king of France for his continental lands, in effect Henry ruled a territory that stretched from England to the south of France (Map 9.3).

The marriage to Eleanor brought Henry both a huge duchy and a feisty queen, who, however, bore him the sons he needed to maintain his dynasty. Before her marriage to Henry, Eleanor was married to King Louis VII of France. Louis had the marriage annulled because she bore him only daughters. Nevertheless, as queen of France, Eleanor enjoyed an important position: she disputed with St. Bernard, the Cistercian abbot who was the most renowned churchman of the day; and she accompanied her husband on the Second Crusade, bringing more troops than he did. She determined to separate from Louis even before he considered leaving her. Married to Henry, she had much less power, for he dominated her as he dominated his barons. Turning to her offspring in 1173, Eleanor, disguised as a man, tried to join

---

* Henry II is known as the first *Angevin* (from *Anjou*) king of England because by inheritance he was count of Anjou. But he also has another name: his father, Count Geoffrey of Anjou, was nicknamed "Plantagenet," from *genet*, a shrub he liked, and historians sometimes use that name to refer to the entire dynasty. Thus Henry II was the first *Plantagenet* as well as the first *Angevin* king of England.

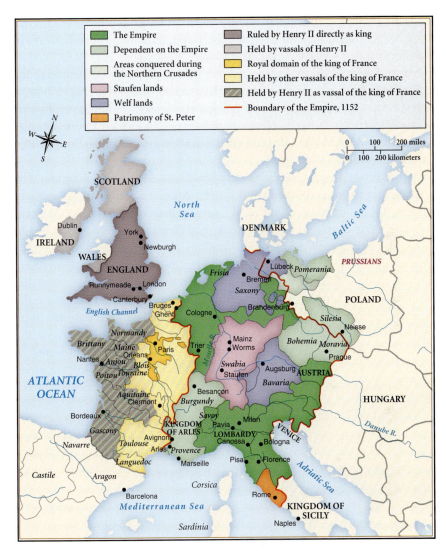

MAP 9.3 Europe in the Age of Frederick Barbarossa and Henry II, 1150–1190

The second half of the twelfth century was dominated by two men, Emperor Frederick Barbarossa and King Henry II. Not just king of England, Henry also held northwestern France by inheritance and southwestern France through his wife, Eleanor of Aquitaine. A few hundred miles to the east were the borders of Frederick Barbarossa's empire, a huge territory but much of it held by him only weakly. Only the Staufen lands were directly under his control.

her eldest son, Henry the Younger, in a plot against his father. But the rebellion was put down, and she spent most of her years thereafter, until her husband's death in 1189, confined under guard at Winchester Castle.

As king of England, Henry immediately set to work to undo the damage to the monarchy caused by the civil war of 1139–1153, during which the English barons and high churchmen had gained new privileges and powers, building private castles as symbols of their strength. Henry destroyed or confiscated the new castles and regained crown lands. Then he proceeded to further extend monarchical power, above all by imposing royal justice.

Henry's judicial reforms built on an already well-developed English system. The Anglo-Saxon kings had established royal district courts and appointed sheriffs to police the shires, call up men to fight, and haul criminals into court. The Norman kings retained these courts, which all the free men of the shire were summoned to attend. To these already well-developed institutions, Henry II added a system of judicial visitations called *eyres* (from the Latin *iter*, "journey"). Under this system, royal justices made regular trips to every locality in England. Henry declared that some crimes, such as murder, arson, and rape, were so heinous as to violate the "king's peace," no matter where they were committed. The king required local representatives of the knightly class to meet during each eyre and either give the sheriff the names of those suspected of committing crimes in the vicinity or arrest the suspects and hand them over to the royal justices.

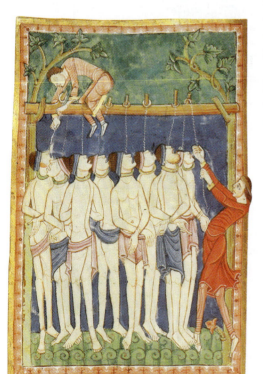

During the eyres, the justices also heard cases between individuals, now called civil cases. Free men and women (that is, people of the knightly class or

▪ **Hanging Thieves**
The development of common law in England meant mobilizing royal agents to bring charges and make arrests. In 1124, the royal justice Ralph Basset hanged forty-four thieves. This miniature from around 1130 shows the hanging of eight thieves for breaking into the shrine of St. Edmund. Under Henry II, all cases of murder, arson, and rape were considered crimes against the king himself. The result, in addition to the enhancement of the king's power, was new definitions of crime, more thorough policing, and more systematic punishments.
(Pierpont Morgan Library/Art Resource, NY.)

above) could bring their disputes over such matters as inheritance, dowries, and property claims to the king's justices. Earlier courts had generally relied on duels between litigants to determine verdicts. Henry's new system offered a different option, an inquest under royal supervision.

The new system was praised for its efficiency, speed, and conclusiveness by a contemporary legal treatise known as *Glanvill* (after its presumed author): "This legal institution emanates from perfect equity. For justice, which after many and long delays is scarcely ever demonstrated by the duel, is advantageously and speedily attained through this institution." *Glanvill* might have added that the king also speedily gained a large treasury. The exchequer, as the financial bureau of England was called, recorded all the fines paid for judgments and the sums collected for writs. The amounts, entered on parchment sewn together and stored as rolls, became the Receipt Rolls and Pipe Rolls, the first of many such records of the English monarchy and an indication that writing had become a mechanism for institutionalizing royal power in England.

The stiffest opposition to Henry's extension of royal courts came from the church, where a separate system of trial and punishment had long been available to the clergy and to others who enjoyed church protection. The punishments that these courts meted out were generally quite mild. Jealous of their prerogatives, churchmen refused to submit to the jurisdiction of Henry's courts, and the ensuing contest between Henry II and his appointed archbishop, Thomas Becket (1118–1170), became the greatest battle between the church and the state in the twelfth century. The conflict over jurisdiction simmered for six years, until Henry's henchmen murdered Thomas, unintentionally turning him into a martyr. Although Henry's role in the murder remained ambiguous, he had to do public penance for the deed largely because of the general outcry. In the end, both church courts and royal courts expanded to address the concerns of an increasingly litigious society.

Praising the King of France

The twelfth-century kings of France were much less obviously powerful than their English and Byzantine counterparts. Yet they, too, took part in the monarchical revival. Louis VI the Fat (r. 1108–1137), so heavy that he had to be hoisted onto his horse by a crane, was a tireless defender of royal power. We know a good deal about him and his reputation because a contemporary and close associate, Suger (1081–1152), abbot of St. Denis, wrote Louis's biography. When Louis set himself the task of consolidating his rule in the Île-de-France, Suger portrayed the king as a righteous hero. He thought of the king as the head of a political hierarchy in which Louis had rights over the French nobles because they were his vassals or because they broke the peace.

Suger also believed that Louis had a religious role: to protect the church and the poor. He viewed Louis as another Charlemagne, a ruler for all society, not merely an overlord of the nobility. Louis waged war to keep God's peace. Of course, the Gregorian reform had made its mark: Suger did not claim Louis was head of the church. Nevertheless, he emphasized the royal dignity and its importance to the papacy. When a pope happened to arrive in France, Louis, not yet king, and his father, Philip I (r. 1052–1108), bowed low, but (recalled Suger) "the pope lifted them up and made them sit before him like devout sons of the apostles. In the manner of a wise man acting wisely, he conferred with them privately on the present condition of the church." Here the pope was shown needing royal advice. Meanwhile, Suger stressed Louis's piety and active defense of the faith:

> *Helped by his powerful band of armed men, or rather by the hand of God, he abruptly seized the castle [of Crécy] and captured its very strong tower as if it were simply the hut of a peasant. Having startled those criminals, he piously slaughtered the impious.*

When Louis VI died in 1137, Suger's notion of the might and right of the king of France reflected reality in an extremely small area. Nevertheless, Louis laid the groundwork for the gradual extension of royal power in France. As the lord of vassals, the king could call upon his men to aid him in times of war (though the great ones sometimes disregarded his wishes and chose not to help). As a king and landlord, he could obtain many dues and taxes. He also drew revenues from Paris, a thriving city not only of commerce but also of scholarship. Officials called *prévôts* enforced his royal laws and collected taxes. With money and land, Louis could dispense the favors and give the gifts that added to his prestige and his power. Louis VI and Suger together created the territorial core and royal ideal of the future French monarchy.

Remaking the Empire

The Investiture Conflict and the civil war it generated (1075–1122) strengthened the German princes and weakened the kings Henry IV and Henry V, who were also the emperors. For decades, the princes enjoyed near independence, building castles on their properties and establishing control over whole territories. To ensure that the emperors who succeeded Henry V (r. 1106–1125) would be weak, the princes supported only rulers who agreed to give them new lands and powers. A ruler's success depended on his ability to juggle the many conflicting interests of his own royal and imperial offices, his family, and the German princes. He also had to contend with the increasing influence of the papacy and the Italian communes, which forged alliances with one another and with the German princes, preventing the consolidation of power under a strong German monarch during the first half of the twelfth century.

Weakness at the top, however, meant constant warfare among princely factions. Eventually the German princes became exhausted by conflict and in 1152 elected

Frederick I Barbarossa (r. 1152–1190) as the first Hohenstaufen king of Germany. He was an impressive man with a striking red-blond beard (hence *Barbarossa*, or "red-beard") and a firm sense of his position. Frederick affirmed royal rights even when he handed out duchies and allowed others to name bishops, because in return for these political powers he required the princes to concede formally and publicly that they held their rights and territories from him as their lord. By making them his vassals, though with nearly royal rights within their principalities, Frederick defined the princes' relationship to the German king: they were powerful yet personally subordinate to him. In this way, Frederick hoped to save the monarchy and to coordinate royal and princely rule, thus ending Germany's chronic civil wars. Frederick used the lord-vassal relationship to give himself a free hand to rule while placating the princes.

Since the Investiture Conflict, the emperor had ruled Italy in name only. The communes of the northern cities guarded their liberties jealously, and the pope considered Italy his own sphere of influence. Frederick's territorial base north of Italy (in Swabia) and his designs on northern Italy threatened those interests (see Map 9.3).

Some historians have criticized Frederick for "entangling" himself in Italy, but Frederick's title was *emperor*, a position that demanded he intervene there. To fault him for not concentrating on Germany is to blame him for lacking modern wisdom, which knows from hindsight that European polities developed into nation-states, such as France, Germany, and Italy. There was nothing inevitable about the development of nation-states, however, and Frederick should not be condemned for failing to see into the future. In addition, control of Italy made sense even for Frederick's effectiveness in Germany. His base in Swabia together with northern Italy would give him a compact and central territory. Moreover, the flourishing commercial cities of Italy would make him rich. Taxes on agricultural production there alone would yield thirty thousand silver talents annually, an incredible sum.

By alternately negotiating with and fighting against the great cities of northern Italy, especially Milan, Frederick achieved military control there in 1158. No longer able to make Italian bishops royal governors, as German kings had done earlier— the Investiture Conflict had effectively ended that practice—Frederick insisted that the communes be governed by magistrates (called *podestà*) from outside the commune who were appointed (or at least authorized) by the emperor and who would collect revenues on his behalf. Here is where Frederick made his mistake: the heavy hand of these officials, many of them from Germany, created enormous resentment. By 1167, most of the cities of northern Italy had joined with Pope Alexander III (r. 1159–1181) to form the Lombard League against Frederick. Defeated at the battle of Legnano in 1176, Frederick made peace with Alexander and withdrew most of his forces from Italy. The battle marked the triumph of the city over the crown in Italy, which would not have a centralized government until the nineteenth century; Italy's political history would instead be that of its various regions and their dominant cities.

The Courtly Culture of Europe

With the consolidation of territory, wealth, and power in the last half of the twelfth century, kings, barons, princes, and their wives and daughters created a newly opulent court culture. For the first time on the European continent, poems and songs were written in the vernacular, the spoken language, rather than in Latin. They celebrated the lives of the nobility and were meant to be read aloud or sung. Already at the beginning of the twelfth century, Duke William IX of Aquitaine (1071–1126), the grandfather of Eleanor of Aquitaine, had written lyric poems in Occitan, the vernacular spoken in southern France. Perhaps influenced by love poetry in Arabic and Hebrew from al-Andalus, his own poetry in turn provided a model for poetic forms that gained popularity through repeated performances. The final four-line stanza of one such poem demonstrates the composer's skill with words:

Per aquesta fri e tremble,	*For this one I shiver and tremble,*
quar de tan bon' amor l'am;	*I love her with such a good love;*
qu'anc no cug qu'en nasques	*I do not think the like of her was ever*
* semble*	* born*
en semblan de gran linh n'Adam.	*in the long line of Lord Adam.*

The rhyme scheme of this poem appears to be simple—*tremble* rhymes with *semble, l'am* with *n'Adam.* But the poem has five earlier verses, all six lines long and all containing the *-am, -am* rhyme in the fourth and sixth lines, while every other line within each verse rhymes as well. The whole scheme is dazzlingly complex.

William was followed by other *troubadours*—lyric poets who wrote in Occitan. Whether male or female, their subject was love. The Contessa de Dia (flourished c. 1160), probably the wife of the lord of Die in France, wrote about her unrequited love for a man:

> *So bitter do I feel toward him*
> *whom I love more than anything.*
> *With him my mercy and fine manners [cortesia] are in vain.*

The key to troubadour verse is the notion of *cortesia*—courtesy—which refers to the refinement of people living at court and to their struggle to achieve an ideal of virtue.

Historians and literary critics used to use the term *courtly love* to emphasize one of the themes of courtly literature: the poet expresses overwhelming love for a beautiful married noblewoman who is far above him in status and utterly unattainable. But this was only one of many aspects of love that the troubadours sang about. Some boasted of sexual conquests; others played with the notion of equality between lovers; still others preached that love was the source of virtue. The real

■ **Troubadour Song**

Raimon de Miraval flourished between 1191 and 1229, very late for a troubadour. He was a petty knight who became a poet and was welcomed at the courts of rulers such as those of Toulouse, Aragon, and Castile. More than forty of his poems have survived, twenty-two with written music. The song here, beginning "A penas," is set to music with a five-line staff. Notice that some of the notes are single and others are in groups. The grouped notes are to be sung, one right after the other, on the same syllable or word.

overall theme of this literature was not courtly love but the power of women. No wonder Eleanor of Aquitaine and other aristocratic women patronized the troubadours: they enjoyed the image that the poetry gave them of themselves. Nor was that image a delusion. There were many powerful female lords in southern France. They owned property, had vassals, led battles, decided disputes, and entered into and broke political alliances as their advantage dictated. Both men and women appreciated troubadour poetry, which recognized and praised women's power even as it eroticized it.

From southern France the lyric love song spread to Italy, northern France, England, and Germany—regions in which Occitan was a foreign language. Similar poetry appeared in other vernacular languages: the *minnesingers* (literally, "love singers") sang in German; the *trouvères* sang in the Old French of northern France. One *trouvère* was the English king Richard the Lion-Hearted, son of Henry II and Eleanor of Aquitaine and king of England for a short time (r. 1189–1199). Taken prisoner on his return from the Third Crusade, Richard wrote a poem expressing his longing not for a lady but for the good companions of war, the knightly "youths" he had joined in battle:

> *They know well, the men of Anjou and Touraine,*
> *those bachelors, now so magnificent and safe,*
> *that I am arrested, far from them, in another's hands.*
> *They used to love me much, now they love me not at all.*
> *There's no lordly fighting now on the barren plains,*
> *because I am a prisoner.*

Richard's yearning for the battlefield was not as common a topic in lyric poetry as love, but long narrative poems about heroic deeds (*chansons de geste*) written in the vernacular sang of war. Such poems followed a long oral tradition and appeared at about the same time as love poems. Like the songs of the troubadours, these vernacular narrative poems, later called *epics*, implied a code of behavior for aristocrats, in this case on the battlefield.

By the end of the twelfth century, warriors wanted a guide for conduct and a common class identity. Nobles and knights had begun to merge into one class because they felt threatened from below by newly rich merchants and from above by newly powerful kings. Their ascendancy on the battlefield, where they unhorsed one another with lances and long swords and took prisoners rather than kill their opponents, was beginning to wane in the face of mercenary infantrymen who wielded long hooks and knives that ripped easily through chain mail. A knightly ethos and sense of group solidarity emerged in the face of these social, political, and military changes. Thus the protagonists of heroic poems yearned not for love but for battle:

> *The armies are in sight of one another. . . . The cowards tremble as they march, but the brave hearts rejoice for the battle.*

Examining the moral issues that made war both tragic and inevitable, poets played on the contradictory values of their society, such as the conflicting loyalties of friendship and vassalage or a vassal's right to a fief versus a son's right to his father's land.

Those long, heroic poems focused on war. Other long poems, later called *romances*, explored relationships between men and women. Romances reached the zenith of their popularity during the late twelfth and early thirteenth centuries. The legend of King Arthur inspired a romance by Chrétien de Troyes (c. 1150–1190) in which a heroic knight, Lancelot, in love with Queen Guinevere, the wife of his lord, comes across a comb bearing some strands of her radiant hair:

> *Never will the eye of man see anything receive such honour as when [Lancelot] begins to adore these tresses. . . . Even for St. Martin and St. James he has no need.*

At one level Chrétien is evoking the familiar imagery of relics, such as bits of hair or the bones of saints, as items of devotion. Making Guinevere's hair an object of adoration not only conveys the depth of Lancelot's feeling but also pokes a bit of fun at him. Like the troubadours, the romantic poets delighted in the interplay between religious and amorous feelings. Just as the ideal monk merged his will in God's will, Chrétien's Lancelot loses his will to Guinevere. When she sees Lancelot—the greatest knight in Christendom—fighting in a tournament, she tests him by asking him to do his "worst." The poor knight is obliged to lose all his battles until she changes her mind.

Lancelot was the perfect chivalric knight. The word *chivalry* derives from the French word *cheval* ("horse"); the fact that the knight was a horseman marked him as a warrior of the most prestigious sort. Perched high on his mount, his heavy lance couched in his right arm, the knight was an imposing and menacing figure. Chivalry made him gentle—except to his enemies on the battlefield. The chivalric hero was a knight constrained by a code of refinement, fair play, piety, and devotion to an ideal. Historians debate whether real knights lived up to the codes implicit in epics and romances. But there is no doubt that real knights liked to imagine themselves that way. They were the poets' audience. Sometimes they were the poets' subject as well. For example, when the knight William the Marshal died, his son commissioned a poet to write his biography. In it, William was depicted as a model knight, courteous with the ladies and brave on the battlefield.

New Forms of Scholarship and Religious Experience

The commercial revolution, the newly organized church, and the revived monarchies of the twelfth century set the stage for the growth of schools and for new forms of scholarship. Money and career opportunities attracted unheard-of numbers of young men to city schools. Worldly motivations, however, were equaled by spiritual ones. The movement for church reform stressed the importance of the church and its beliefs. Many students and teachers in the twelfth century sought knowledge to make their faith clearer and deeper. "Nothing can be believed unless it is first understood," said one of the period's greatest scholars, Peter Abelard (1079–1142).

Other people in the twelfth century, however, sought to avoid the cities and the schools. Some found refuge in the measured ceremonies and artistic splendor of Benedictine monasteries such as Cluny. Others considered these vast monastic complexes to be ostentatious and worldly. Rejecting the opulence of cities and the splendor of well-endowed monasteries alike, some pursued a monastic life of poverty, while others, like St. Francis, rejected even the shelter of the cloister.

Schools, Scholars, and the New Learning

Schools had been connected to monasteries and cathedrals since the Carolingian period. They served to train new recruits to become either monks or priests. Some were better endowed with books and masters (or teachers) than others; a few developed a reputation for a certain theological approach or specialized in a certain branch of learning, such as literature, medicine, or law. By the end of the eleventh century, the best schools were generally in the larger cities: Reims, Paris, Bologna, Montpellier.

Eager students sampled nearly all of them. The young monk Gilbert of Liège was typical: "Instilled with an insatiable thirst for learning, whenever he heard of somebody excelling in the arts, he rushed immediately to that place and drank whatever delightful potion he could draw from the master there." For Gilbert and other students, a good lecture had the excitement of theater. Teachers at cathedral schools found themselves forced to find larger halls to accommodate the crush of students. Other teachers simply declared themselves "masters" and set up shop by renting a room. If they could prove their mettle in the classroom, they had no trouble finding paying students.

"Wandering scholars" like Gilbert were probably all male, and because schools had hitherto been the training ground for clergymen, all students were considered clerics, whether or not they had been ordained. Wandering became a way of life as the consolidation of castellanies, counties, and kingdoms made violence against travelers less frequent. Urban centers soon responded to the needs of transients with markets, taverns, and lodgings. Using Latin, Europe's common language, students could drift from, say, Italy to Spain, Germany, England, and France, wherever a noted master had settled. Along with crusaders, pilgrims, and merchants, students made the roads of Europe very crowded indeed.

■ **A Teacher and His Students**
This miniature expresses the hierarchical relationship between students and teachers in the twelfth century. But there is more. The miniature appears in a late-twelfth-century manuscript of a commentary written by Gilbert (d. 1154), bishop of Poitiers. Gilbert's ideas in this commentary provoked the ire of St. Bernard, who accused Gilbert of heresy. But Gilbert escaped condemnation. Here, in pictorial form, the artist asserts Gilbert's orthodoxy by depicting him with a halo, in the full dress of a bishop, speaking from his throne. Below Gilbert are three of his disciples, also with halos. The artist's positive view of Gilbert is echoed by modern historians, who recognize Gilbert as a pioneer in his approach to scriptural commentary.
(Bibliothèque Municipale de Valenciennes.)

What the students sought, above all, was knowledge of the seven liberal arts. Grammar, rhetoric, and logic (or dialectic) belonged to the "beginning" arts, the so-called *trivium*. Logic, involving the technical analysis of texts as well as the application and manipulation of mental constructs, was a transitional subject leading to the second, higher part of the liberal arts, the *quadrivium*. This comprised four areas of study that we might call theoretical math and science: arithmetic, geometry, music (theory rather than practice), and astronomy. Of all these, logic excited the most intense interest. Medieval students and masters were convinced that logic clarified every issue, even questions about the nature of God. With logic, they thought, one could prove that what one believed on faith was in fact true. At the end of the twelfth century, some western scholars took advantage of Islamic achievements; they traveled to Islamic centers in Spain and Sicily, where the Greek texts of Aristotle, with their sophisticated logic, had already been translated into Arabic and closely commented on. Translating these Arabic texts into Latin, western scholars made Aristotle their own.

After studying the liberal arts, students went on to study medicine (the great school for that was at Montpellier), theology, or law. Schools of law, for example, began in Italy in the eleventh century. At Bologna, Irnerius (d. c. 1129) was the guiding light of a law school where students studied Lombard, Roman, or canon law. Men skilled in canon law served popes and bishops; popes, kings, princes, and communes all found that Roman law, which claimed the emperor as its fount, justified their claims to power.

The remarkable renewal of scholarship in the twelfth century had an unexpected benefit: we know a great deal about the men involved in it—and a few of the women—because they wrote so much, often about themselves. Three important figures typify the scholars of the period: Abelard and Heloise, who embraced the new learning wholeheartedly and retired to monasteries only when forced to do so, and Hildegard of Bingen, who spent most of her life happily in a cloister yet wrote knowingly about the world.

Peter Abelard (1079–1142) was one of the twelfth century's greatest thinkers. Turning his back on an expected career as a warrior and lord, he studied in Paris and soon began to write influential works on ethics, logic, and theology. Around 1122–1123, he prepared a textbook for his students, the *Sic et Non* (*Yes and No*), unusual because it arranged side-by-side opposing positions on various subjects without reconciling them. Instead, Abelard challenged his students to make sense of the conflicts and resolve the contradictions themselves. In Abelard's view, the inquiring student would follow the model of Christ himself, who as a boy sat among the rabbis, questioning them.

Abelard's fame as a teacher was such that a Parisian cleric named Fulbert gave him room and board and engaged him as tutor for Heloise (c. 1100–c. 1163/1164), Fulbert's niece. Brought up under Fulbert's guardianship, Heloise had been sent as a young girl to a convent school, where she received a thorough grounding in

■ **Hildegard of Bingen**
*The illustrations that Hildegard com-
missioned for her* Scivias *were lost after
World War II, but a hand-drawn copy
made in 1920 survives. This image from
the copy shows Hildegard at the beginning of the book, where, she writes,
"Heaven was opened and a fiery light
. . . came and permeated my whole
brain. . . . And immediately I knew the
meaning of the . . . Scriptures." In this
miniature, the fiery light, resembling giant fingers, descends to cover Hildegard's
head, while she uses a stylus to write on
a wax tablet. The monk peeking through
the doorway is Volmar, who served as
Hildegard's secretary.*
(Photograph by Erich Lessing/Art Resource.)

literary skills. Her uncle hoped to continue her education at home by hiring
Abelard. Abelard, however, became her secret lover as well as her tutor. "Our desires left no stage of love-making untried," wrote Abelard in his *Historia calami-
tatum* (*Story of My Calamities*), his autobiographical account. When Heloise became pregnant, Abelard insisted they marry. They did so clandestinely, informing
only a very few, such as Fulbert, for the new emphasis on clerical celibacy meant
that Abelard's professional success and prestige would have been compromised if
news of his marriage were made public. After they were married, Heloise and
Abelard rarely saw one another. Suspecting that Abelard had abandoned his niece,
Fulbert plotted a cruel punishment: he paid a servant to castrate Abelard. Soon
after, husband and wife entered separate monasteries.

For Heloise, separation from Abelard was a lasting misfortune. For Abelard,
however, the loss of Heloise and even his castration were not the worst disasters of
his life. The cruelest blow came later, and it was directed at his intellect. He wrote
a book that applied "human and logical reasons" (as he put it) to the Trinity; the
book was condemned at the Council of Soissons in 1121, and he was forced to
throw it, page by page, into the flames. Bitterly weeping at the injustice, Abelard
lamented, "This open violence had come upon me only because of the purity of
my intentions and love of our Faith which had compelled me to write."

Abelard had written the treatise on the Trinity for his students, maintaining that "words were useless if the intelligence could not follow them, [and] that nothing could be believed unless it was first understood." For Abelard, logic was the key to knowledge, and knowledge the key to faith.

Unlike Abelard and Heloise, Hildegard of Bingen (1098–1179) did not attend the city schools or learn under one of their scholars. Placed in a German convent at age eight, she received her schooling there and took vows as a nun. In 1136, she was elected abbess of the convent. Shortly thereafter, very abruptly, she began to write and to preach. She was probably the only woman authorized by the church to preach in her day.

Writing and preaching were the sudden external manifestations of an inner life that had been extraordinary from the beginning. Even as a child, Hildegard had had visions—of invisible things, of the future, and (always) of a special kind of light. These visions were intermingled with pain and sickness. Only in her forties did Hildegard interpret her sickness and her visions as gifts from God. In her *Scivias* ("Know the Ways of the Lord," 1151), Hildegard describes some of her visions and explains what they mean. She interprets them as containing nothing less than the full story of creation and redemption, a *summa*, or compendium, of church doctrine.◆

Benedictine Monks and Artistic Splendor

Hildegard's contentment within the confines of her cloister was characteristic of many. Known as "black monks"—so called because they dyed their robes black— the Benedictines reached the height of their popularity in the eleventh century. Monasteries often housed hundreds of monks; convents for nuns were usually less populated. Cluny was one of the largest monasteries, with some four hundred brothers in the mid-eleventh century.

The chief occupation of the monks, as befitted (in their view) citizens of heaven, was prayer. The black monks and nuns devoted themselves to singing Psalms and other prayers specified in the rule of St. Benedict, adding to them still more Psalms. The rule called for chanting the entire Psalter—150 psalms—over the course of a week, but some monks, like those at Cluny, chanted that number in a day. Such prayer was neither private nor silent. Black monks had to know not only the words but also the music that went with their prayers; they had to be musicians. The music of the Benedictine monastery was *plainchant*, also known as *Gregorian chant*, which consisted of melodies, each sung in unison, without accompaniment. Although chant was rhythmically free, lacking a regular beat, its melodies ranged from extremely simple to highly ornate and embellished. By the twelfth century, a large repertoire of melodies had grown up, at first through oral composition and transmission and then in written notation, which first appeared in manuscripts of the ninth century.

◆ For other examples of Hildegard's many works, see Document 28, "Selected Writings."

Musical notation was first developed in the ninth century to help monks remember unfamiliar melodies and to ensure that the tunes were sung in approximately the same way in all parts of the Carolingian realm. The melodies were further mastered and organized at this time by fitting them into the Byzantine system of eight *modes*, somewhat like modern scales. This music survived the dissolution of the Carolingian Empire and remained the core music of the Catholic church into the twentieth century. At Cluny, where praying and singing occupied nearly the entire day and part of the night, the importance of music was made visible—the modes were personified and depicted in sculpture on some of the columns circling the choir of the church.

That church, so finely decorated, was part of a twelfth-century building boom that saw the construction or repair of town walls, dwellings, mills, castles, monasteries, and churches. The style of many of these buildings, like the church of Cluny, rebuilt around 1100, was Romanesque. Cluny was particularly enormous. Constructed of stone, it must have reverberated with the voices of the hundreds of monks who sang there. Although they varied greatly, most Romanesque churches, like Cluny, had massive stone and masonry walls decorated on the interior with paintings in bright colors. The various parts of the church—the chapels in the *chevet*, or apse (at the east end of the building), for example—were handled as discrete units, retaining the forms of cubes, cones, and cylinders (Figure 9.1). Inventive sculptural reliefs,

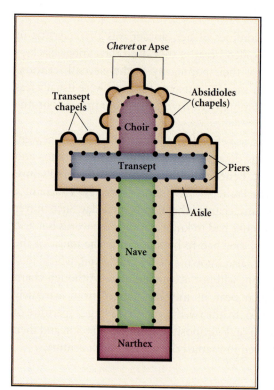

■ **FIGURE 9.1 Floor Plan of a Romanesque Church**

As churchgoers entered a Romanesque church, they passed through the narthex, an anteroom decorated with sculptured depictions of important scenes from the Bible. Walking through the portal of the narthex, they entered the church's nave, at the east end of which—just after the crossing of the transept and in front of the choir—was the altar, the focus of the Mass. Walking down the nave, they passed massive and tall piers leading up to the vaulting (the roof) of the nave. Each of these piers was decorated with sculpture, and the walls were brightly painted. Romanesque churches were both lively and colorful (because of their decoration) and solemn and somber (because of their heavy stones and massive scale).

both inside and outside the church, enlivened these pristine geometrical forms. Emotional and sometimes frenzied, Romanesque sculpture depicted themes ranging from the beauty of Eve to the horrors of the Last Judgment.

In such a setting, gilded reliquaries and altars made of silver, precious gems, and pearls were the fitting accouterments of worship. Prayer, liturgy, and music in this way complemented the gift economy: richly clad in vestments of the finest materials, intoning the liturgy in the most splendid of churches, monks and priests offered up the gift of prayer to God; in return they begged for the gift of salvation of their souls and the souls of all the faithful.

New Monastic Orders of Poverty

Not everyone agreed that such opulence pleased or praised God. At the end of the eleventh century, the new commercial economy and the profit motive that fueled it led many to reject wealth and to embrace poverty as a key element of religious life. The Carthusian order founded by Bruno of Cologne was one such group. Each monk took a vow of silence and lived as a hermit in his own small hut. Monks occasionally joined others for prayer in a common prayer room, or *oratory*. When not engaged in prayer or meditation, the Carthusians copied manuscripts. They considered this task part of their religious vocation, a way to preach God's word with their hands rather than their mouths. The Carthusian order grew slowly. Each monastery was limited to only twelve monks, the number of the Apostles.

The Cistercians, in contrast, expanded rapidly. Rejecting even the conceit of blackening their robes, they left them the original color of wool (hence their nickname, "white monks"). The Cistercian order began as a single monastery, Cîteaux (in Latin, *Cistercium*) in France, founded in 1098. It grew rapidly under the leadership of St. Bernard (d. 1153), abbot of the important Cistercian monastery Clairvaux. Despite the Cistercian order's official repudiation of female houses, many convents followed its lead and adopted its customs. Women were as eager as men to live the life of simplicity and poverty that they believed the Apostles had enjoyed and endured.

Although they held up the rule of St. Benedict as the foundation of their customs, the Cistercians elaborated a style of life all their own, largely governed by the goal of simplicity. Cistercian churches, though built of stone, were initially unlike the great Romanesque churches of the Benedictines. They were remarkably standardized; the church and the rest of the buildings of any one Cistercian monastery were almost exactly like those of any other (Figure 9.2). The churches were small, made of smoothly hewn, undecorated stone. Wall paintings and sculpture were prohibited. Illuminated by the pure white light that came through clear glass windows, Cistercian houses were luminous, cool, and serene.

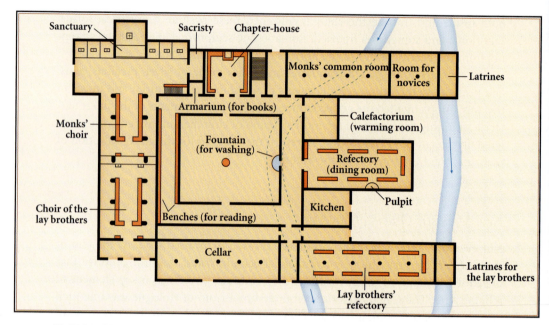

■ FIGURE 9.2 Floor Plan of a Cistercian Monastery

Cistercian monasteries seldom deviated much from this standard plan, which perfectly suited their double lifestyle: one half for the lay brothers, who worked in the fields, the other half for the monks, who performed the prayers. This plan shows the first floor. Above were dormitories: the lay brothers slept above their cellar and refectory; the monks slept above their chapter-house (where the rule of St. Benedict was read to them), common room, and room for novices. No one had a private bedroom, just as the rule prescribed.

(From Wolfgang Braunfels, *Monasteries of Western Europe: The Architecture of the Orders* [Princeton, N.J.: Princeton University Press, 1972], 75.)

There were two sorts of white monks: *conversi* or "lay brothers" toiled in the fields; "choir monks" dedicated themselves to private prayer and contemplation and to monastic administration. By the end of the twelfth century, the Cistercians had a closely monitored network of houses, and each year the Cistercian abbots met to hammer out legislation for all of them. The abbot of the mother house (or founding house) visited the daughter houses annually to make sure the legislation was being followed. Each house, whether mother or daughter, had large and highly organized farms and grazing lands called *granges*. Cistercian monks spent much of their time managing their estates and flocks, both of which were yielding handsome profits by the end of the twelfth century. Clearly part of the agricultural and commercial revolutions of the Middle Ages, the Cistercian order made managerial expertise a part of the monastic life.

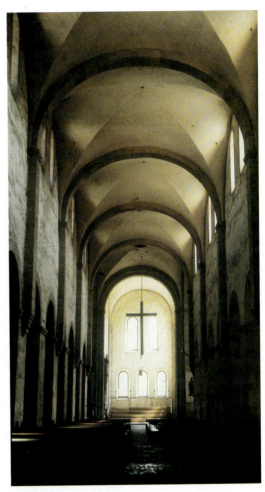

■ St.-Savin-sur-Gartempe

The nave of the church of St.-Savin was built between 1095 and 1115. Its barrel (or tunnel) vault is typical of Romanesque churches, as is its sense of liveliness, variety, and color. The columns, decorated with striped or wavy patterns, are topped by carved capitals, each one different from the next. The entire vault is covered with frescoes painted in shades of brown, ocher, and yellow depicting scenes from the Old Testament. What were the purposes of such decorations?

(Giraudon/Art Resource, NY.)

■ Eberbech

Compare the nave of Eberbech, a Cistercian church built between 1170 and 1186, with the nave of St.-Savin. What at St.-Savin appears full of variety and color is here subdued by order and calm. There are no wall paintings in a Cistercian church, no variegated columns— nothing that might distract the worshiper. Yet a close look reveals subtle points of interest. How has the architect played with angles, planes, and light in the vaulting? Are the walls utterly smooth? What decorative elements can you see on the massive piers between the arches? (AKG London/Stefan Drechsel.)

At the same time, the Cistercians elaborated a spirituality of intense personal emotion. As Bernard said:

Often enough when we approach the altar to pray our hearts are dry and luke-warm. But if we persevere, there comes an unexpected infusion of grace, our breast expands as it were, and our interior is filled with an overflowing love.

The Cistercians emphasized not only human emotion but also Christ's and Mary's humanity. While pilgrims continued to stream to the tombs and reliquaries of saints, the Cistercians dedicated all their churches to the Virgin Mary (for whom they had no relics) because for them she signified the model of a loving mother. Indeed, the Cistercians regularly used maternal imagery (as Bernard's description invoking the metaphor of a flowing breast illustrates) to describe the nurturing care provided to humans by Jesus himself. The Cistercians' God was approachable, human, protective, even mothering.

Similar views of God were held by many who were not members of the Cistercian order; their spirituality signaled wider changes. For example, around 1099, St. Anselm wrote a theological treatise entitled *Why God Became Man* in which he argued that since man had sinned, only a sinless man could redeem him. St. Anselm's work represented a new theological focus on the redemptive power of human charity, including that of Jesus as a human being.

Religious Fervor and Dissent

The emphasis on a common humanity in Christ beckoned to men and women of every age and every walk of life. Fervent piety spread beyond the convent, punctuating the routines of daily life with scriptural reading, fasting, and charity. The new religious groups of the late twelfth century embraced urban populations. Rich and poor, male and female joined these movements. Many criticized the existing church as too wealthy, ritualistic, and impersonal. Intensely and personally focused on the life of Christ, men and women in the late twelfth century made his childhood, agony, death, and presence in the Eucharist—the bread and wine that became the body and blood of Christ in the Mass—the most important experiences of their own lives. Some of this intense religious response developed into official, orthodox movements within the church; other religious movements so threatened established doctrine that church leaders declared them heretical.

St. Francis (c. 1182–1226) founded the most famous orthodox religious movement—the Franciscans. Francis was a child of the commercial revolution. Expected to follow his well-to-do father in the cloth trade at Assisi in Italy, Francis experienced doubts, dreams, and illnesses, which spurred him to religious self-examination. Eventually he renounced his family's wealth, dramatically marking the decision by casting off all his clothes and standing naked before his father, a crowd of spectators, and the bishop of Assisi. Francis then put on a simple robe and went about preaching penance to anyone who would listen. He accepted no money, walked without shoes, wore only one coarse tunic, and refused to be cloistered. Intending to follow the model of Christ, he received, as his biographers put it, a miraculous gift of grace: the stigmata, bleeding sores corresponding to the wounds Christ suffered on the cross.

By all accounts Francis was a spellbinding speaker, and he attracted many followers. Recognized as a religious order by the pope, the Brothers of St. Francis (or friars, from the Latin term for "brothers") spent their time preaching, ministering to lepers, and doing manual labor. Eventually they dispersed, setting up fraternal groups throughout Italy and then in France, Spain, the Holy Land, Germany, and England. Unlike Bruno of Cologne and the Cistercians, who had rejected cities, the friars sought town life, preaching to urban crowds and begging for their daily bread. St. Francis converted both men and women. In 1212, a young noblewoman, Clare, formed the nucleus of a community of pious women, which became the Order of the Sisters of St. Francis. At first the women worked alongside the friars; but the church disapproved of their activities in the world, and soon Franciscan sisters were confined to cloisters under the rule of St. Benedict.◆

Clare was one of many women who sought a new kind of religious expression. In northern Europe at the end of the twelfth century, laywomen who lived together in informal pious communities were called Beguines. Without permanent vows or an established rule, the Beguines chose to be celibate (though they were free to leave and marry) and often made their living by weaving cloth or working with the sick and old. Although their daily occupations were ordinary, the Beguines' private, internal lives were often emotional and ecstatic, infused with the combined imagery of love and religion so pervasive in both monasteries and courts. One renowned Beguine, Mary of Oignies (1177–1213), who like St. Francis was said to have received stigmata, felt herself to be a pious mother entrusted with the Christ child. As her biographer, Jacques de Vitry, wrote:

> Sometimes it seemed to her that for three or more days she held [Christ] close to her so that He nestled between her breasts like a baby, and she hid Him there lest He be seen by others.

More hardheaded was St. Dominic (1170–1221), founder of an order of friars—the Dominicans—that was patterned very closely on the Franciscans. Like Francis, Dominic and his followers rejected material riches and instead went about

---

◆ For a pair of sources that reveal the fundamental principles guiding the Order of the Sisters of St. Francis, see Document 29, Saints Francis and Clare of Assisi, "Selected Writings."

IMPORTANT DATES

1054	Great Schism between Roman Catholic and Greek Orthodox churches	c. 1122	Abelard writes *Sic et Non*
1066	Norman conquest of England; battle of Hastings	1139–1153	Civil war in England
1077	Emperor Henry IV does penance before Pope Gregory VII at Canossa	c. 1140	Gratian's *Decretum* published
		1151	Hildegard of Bingen's *Scivias* published
1086	Domesday survey commissioned by William I of England	1152–1190	Reign of Emperor Frederick Barbarossa
c. 1090–1153	Life of St. Bernard, leader of Cistercian order	1154–1189	Reign of Henry II of England
1095	Urban II preaches the First Crusade at Clermont	1176	Battle of Legnano; Frederick Barbarossa defeated in northern Italy
1122	Concordat of Worms ends the Investiture Conflict	1182–1226	Life of St. Francis

on foot, preaching and begging. Their initial audience was not the men and women of the Italian cities, however, but rather the people of southern France, where new doctrines that contradicted those officially accepted by the church—and were therefore labeled "heretical"—had become very popular.

Dominic and his friars were responding to an unprecedented explosion of heresies, part of the ferment of ideas and experiments in social life that were characteristic of medieval city growth. Among the most visible of the heretics were *dualists*, who saw the world torn between two great forces, one good, the other evil. Already important in Bulgaria and Asia Minor, dualism became a prominent ingredient in religious life in Italy and the Rhineland by the end of the twelfth century. Another center of dualism was Languedoc, an area of southern France; there the dualists were called Albigensians, a name derived from the Languedoc town of Albi.

Described collectively as Cathars, or "Pure Ones," these dualists believed that the devil had created the material world. Therefore they renounced the world, abjuring wealth, sex, and meat. Their repudiation of sex reflected some of the attitudes of eleventh-century church reformers (whose orthodoxy, however, was never in doubt); their rejection of wealth echoed the same concerns that moved Bruno of Cologne to forswear city life and St. Francis to embrace poverty. In many ways the dualists simply took these attitudes to an extreme; but unlike orthodox reformers, they also challenged the efficacy and value of the church hierarchy. Cathars

■ **MAPPING THE WEST** **Major Religions in the West, c. 1200**
The broad washes of colors on this map tell a striking story: by 1150, there were three major religions, each corresponding to a broad region. To the west, north of the Mediterranean Sea, Catholic Christianity held sway; to the east, the Greek Orthodox Church was ascendant; all along the southern Mediterranean, Islam triumphed. Only a few places defied this logic: one was the crusader states, a tiny outpost of Catholics who ruled over a largely Muslim population. What this map does not show, however, are the details: Jewish communities in many cities; lively varieties of Islamic beliefs within the Muslim world; communities of Coptic Christians in Egypt; and scattered groups of heretics in Catholic lands.

considered themselves followers of Christ's original message. But the church called them heretics.

The church also condemned other, nondualist groups as heretical, not on doctrinal grounds but because these groups allowed their lay members to preach, challenging the authority of the church hierarchy. In Lyon (in southeastern France) in the 1170s, for example, a rich merchant named Waldo decided to take literally the Gospel message "If you wish to be perfect, then go and sell everything you have, and give to the poor" (Matt. 19:21). The same message had inspired countless monks and would worry the church far less several decades later, when St. Francis established his new order. But when Waldo went into the street and gave away his belongings, announcing, "I am not really insane, as you think," he scandalized not only the bystanders but the church as well. Refusing to retire to a monastery, Waldo and his followers, men and women called Waldensians, lived in poverty and went about preaching, quoting the Gospel in the vernacular so that everyone would understand. But the papacy rebuffed Waldo's bid to preach freely; and the Waldensians—denounced, excommunicated, and expelled from Lyon—wandered to Languedoc, Italy, northern Spain, and the Moselle valley (in Germany).

Conclusion

The commercial revolution and the building boom it spurred profoundly changed the look of Europe. Thriving cities of merchants and artisans brought trade, new wealth, and new institutions to the West. Mutual and fraternal organizations like the commune, the *compagnia*, and the guilds expressed and reinforced the solidarity and economic interest of city dwellers.

Political consolidation accompanied economic growth, as kings and popes exerted their authority and tested its limits. The Gregorian reform pitted the emperor against the pope, and two separate political hierarchies emerged: the secular and the ecclesiastical. The two might cooperate, as Suger and Louis VI showed in their mutual respect, admiration, and dependence. But they might also clash, as Becket did with Henry II. Secular and religious leaders developed new and largely separate systems of administration, reflecting in political life the new distinctions that separated clergy from laity, such as clerical celibacy and allegiance to the pope. Although in some ways growing apart, the two groups never worked together so closely as in the crusades, military pilgrimages inspired by the pope and led by lay lords.

The commercial economy, political stability, and ecclesiastical needs fostered the growth of schools and the achievements of new scholarship. Young men sought learning to enhance their careers and bring personal fulfillment; women gained excellent educations in convents. Logic fascinated some students because it seemed to clarify the nature of both the world and God. But others, such as St. Bernard, felt that faith could not be analyzed.

While Benedictine monks added to their hours of worship, built lavish churches, and devoted themselves to the music of the plainchant, the white monks insisted on an intense, interior spiritual life in a monastery shorn of decoration. Other reformers, such as Bruno of Cologne, sought the high mountaintop for its isolation and hardship. These reformers repudiated urban society yet unintentionally reflected it: the Cistercians were as anxious as any tradesman about the success of their granges, and the Carthusians were dedicated to their books. With the Franciscans and Dominicans—as well as heretical groups such as the Cathars—laypeople were drawn to participate actively in a deeply felt imitation of Christ's life and sufferings. Yet this new piety, paired with new power, contributed to the persecution of Jews and the periodic call for Crusades against the Muslims.

Suggested References for further reading and online research appear on page SR-15 at the back of the book.

www.bedfordstmartins.com/huntconcise   See the ONLINE STUDY GUIDE to assess your mastery of the material covered in this chapter.

An Age of Confidence
1200–1340

I N ABOUT 1220, CHINGIZ KHAN (c. 1162–1227), leader of a confederation of horseback warriors in Mongolia, conquered northern China. By 1240, his successors had conquered Russia and were attacking Poland and Hungary. Europeans were galvanized. Some considered the Mongols a new incarnation of the Devil. But others looked forward to converting the newcomers to Christianity and hoped for new ports of call for their ships, caravans, and traders. The brothers Niccolò and Maffeo Polo, merchants from Venice, were among the first Western adventurers who saw an opportunity to make a profit. According to Niccolò's son Marco, early in their travels the brothers met the Mongol ruler of the Volga region in Russia, "gave him all the jewels they had brought; and [the ruler] took [the jewels] willingly . . . and gave them goods of fully twice the value in return." After making a tidy profit, the brothers moved on, eventually finding their way to China. On a second trip, they brought with them the young Marco, whose later account of his travels dazzled his contemporaries.

Niccolò and Maffeo's intrepid self-confidence in the face of the "inhuman Tartars," as Pope Alexander IV called the Mongols in 1260, was characteristic of an age in which participants in emerging institutions of government, commerce, and religion were unafraid to assert themselves, their rights, and their interests. In the thirteenth century, merchants, kings, princes, popes, city dwellers, and even heretics were acutely conscious of themselves as individuals and as members of like-minded groups with identifiable objectives and plans to promote and perpetuate their aims. Students and teachers created the permanent institution called the university; staffs of literate government officials now preserved

■ **Man at the Center of the Universe**
In this thirteenth-century miniature, a man representing humankind stands with arms outstretched at the center of the universe. The universe, in turn, is embraced by nature (her arms encircle the globe), and crowning nature is the head of wisdom. The whole image expresses confidence in human capacity and its harmony with nature. (Biblioteca Statale di Lucca.)

official documents and other important papers; lords reckoned their profits with the help of accountants; craft guilds and religious associations defined and regulated their membership with increased exactitude.

The period 1200–1340 was characterized by confidence buttressed by new organizations and institutions. Well-prepared rulers exercised control over whole territories through institutions of government that could—if need be—function without them. As monarchs gained power, so, too, did the popes, and this period witnessed the height of the medieval church. In the cultural arena, vernacular poets wrote literature of astonishing beauty and increasing complexity and sophistication. Musicians, like poets, developed forms that bridged sacred and secular subjects, and Gothic churches sprang up in cities throughout Europe, dazzling observers with their light-filled expression of a universe of order and harmony.

With greater confidence and more clearly defined group and individual identities came conflict as well as unity. Kings and popes disputed about the limits of their power, while theologians fought over the place of reason in matters of faith. The church created tribunals of inquisition to root out religious dissidents, and kings and other rulers extended their influence over their subjects. Yet these tribunals did not end heresy, and kings did not gain all the power that they wanted. Diversity and opposition continually threatened expectations of harmony and order.

War, Conquest, and Colonization

In the thirteenth and early fourteenth centuries, Europeans aggressively moved outward in nearly all directions. While one group of armies pushed north and east on the Baltic coast, another was assailing Constantinople itself, while still a third was pursuing the *reconquista* of Spain. In the south of France and in Sicily, crusaders, with the pope's blessing, waged war against people whom the church declared to be heretics, including a Christian king. Far beyond Europe's eastern fringes, merchants like Marco Polo traveled to and settled in lands ruled by the Mongols.

The Northern Crusades

Long before the twelfth century, the peoples living along the Baltic coast—partly pagan, mostly Slavic- or Baltic-speaking—had learned to glean a living and a profit from the inhospitable soil and climate. Through fishing and trading, they supplied the rest of Europe and Russia with slaves, furs, amber, wax, and dried fish. Like the Vikings, they combined commercial competition with outright raiding. The Danes and the Saxons (that is, the Germans in Saxony) both benefited and suffered from their presence.

When St. Bernard began to preach the Second Crusade in Germany, he discovered that the Germans were indeed eager to attack the infidels—the ones right next door to them. St. Bernard pressed the pope to add these northern heathens to the list of those against whom holy war should be launched, and he urged their conversion or extermination. Thus began the Northern Crusades, which continued intermittently until the early fifteenth century.

The king of Denmark and the duke of Saxony launched the first phase of the Northern Crusades. Their initial attacks were uncoordinated—in some instances they even fought each other. Then, in key raids in the 1160s and 1170s, the two leaders worked together briefly to bring much of the region west of the Oder River under their control. They took some land outright—the Saxon duke apportioned conquered territory to his followers, for example—but more often the Slavic princes surrendered and had their territories reinstated once they became vassals of the Christian rulers.

In 1198, Pope Innocent III (r. 1198–1216) declared a crusade against the Livs, even farther to the north and east. A military order—the Order of Sword Brothers, later supplanted by the Teutonic Knights—was set up to lead crusading armies, and a bishopric, the "see of Riga," was established at the mouth of the Dvina River. The native populations were obliged to submit, whether by material inducements (the crusaders helped the Livs raid the Estonians, for example) or by sheer force. Repeatedly they agreed to truce and baptism, and just as repeatedly they rebelled. In some areas, the crusaders resorted to scorched-earth tactics. By 1300, they had secured Livonia, Prussia, Estonia, and Finland. Only Lithuania managed to resist conquest and conversion (Map 10.1).

Though less well known than the crusades to the Holy Land, the Northern Crusades had far more lasting effects: they settled the Baltic region with German-speaking lords and peasants, and they forged a permanent relationship between the very north of Europe and its neighbors to the south and west. With the Baltic dotted with churches and monasteries and its peoples dipped into baptismal waters, the region would gradually adopt the institutions of western medieval society—cities, guilds, universities, castles, and manors.

The Capture of Constantinople

Four years after calling for the crusade against the Livs, Pope Innocent III declared the Fourth Crusade (1202–1204) to the Holy Land. He hoped to reverse the failures of the Second and Third Crusades, but attitudes and circumstances beyond his control took over the new enterprise. Prejudices, religious zeal, and self-confidence had become characteristic of western European dealings with the Byzantine Greeks.

These attitudes help explain what happened from 1202 to 1204. The crusading army turned out to be far smaller than had been expected. Its leaders could not pay the Venetians, who had fitted out a large fleet of ships in anticipation of carrying multitudes of warriors across the Mediterranean to Jerusalem. The Venetians seized the opportunity to exact a different form of payment by convincing the crusade's leaders to attack Zara, a Christian city that was Venice's competitor in the Adriatic

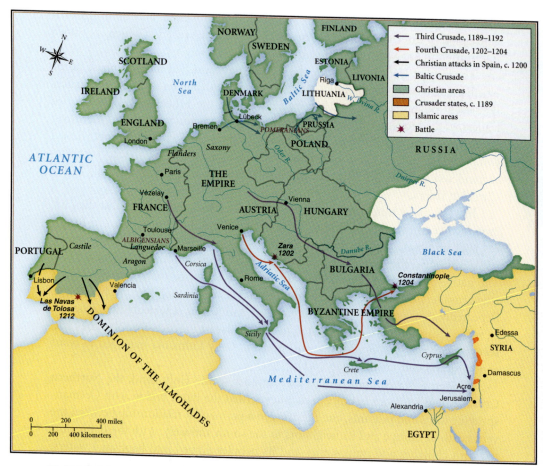

■ **MAP 10.1 Crusades and Anti-Heretic Campaigns, 1150–1300**
*Europeans aggressively expanded their territory from the second half of the twelfth century to the
end of the thirteenth. To the north, German knights pushed into the lands bordering the Baltic
Sea; to the south, Spanish warriors moved into most of Islamic Iberia; to the east, new crusades
were undertaken to shore up the tiny European outpost in the Holy Land. Although most of these
aggressive activities had the establishment of Christianity as at least one motive, the conquest of
Constantinople in 1204 had no such justification. It occurred in part because of general European
hostility toward Byzantium but mainly because of Venice's commercial ambitions.*

(see Map 10.1). The Venetians then turned their sights toward Constantinople, hoping to control it and gain a commercial monopoly there. They persuaded the crusaders to join them on behalf of Alexius, a member of the ousted imperial family.
Alexius claimed the Byzantine throne and promised the crusaders that he would
reunite the eastern with the western church and fund the expedition to the Holy
Land. Most of the crusaders convinced themselves that the cause was noble. "Never,"
wrote a contemporary, "was so great an enterprise undertaken by any people since
the creation of the world."

The siege of Constantinople lasted nearly a year. Finally, on April 12, 1204, the city fell to the crusaders. The deal with Alexius had broken down, and the crusaders brutally sacked Constantinople, killing residents and plundering treasure and relics. When one crusader discovered a cache of relics, a chronicler recalled, "he plunged both hands in and, girding up his loins, he filled the folds of his gown with the holy booty of the Church." The loss of that "holy booty" was, for the Byzantines, a great tragedy. The bishop of Ephesus wrote:

> *And so the streets, squares, houses of two and three stories, sacred places, nun-neries, houses for nuns and monks, sacred churches, even the Great Church of God and the imperial palace, were filled with men of the enemy, all of them maddened by war and murderous in spirit. . . . [T]hey tore children from their mothers and mothers from their children, and they defiled the virgins in the holy chapels, fearing neither God's anger nor man's vengeance.*

Pope Innocent decried the looting of Constantinople but also took advantage of it, ordering the crusaders to stay there for a year to consolidate their gains. The crusade leaders chose one of themselves—Baldwin of Flanders—to be Byzantine emperor, and he, the other princes, and the Venetians parceled out the empire among themselves. This new Latin empire of Constantinople lasted until 1261, when the Byzantines recaptured the city and some of its outlying territory. No longer a strong heir to the Roman Empire, Byzantium in 1204 became overshadowed and hemmed in by the military might of the Muslims and the Europeans.

Popes continued to call crusades to the Holy Land until the mid-fifteenth century, but the Fourth Crusade marked the last major mobilization of men and leaders. Working against these expeditions were the new values of the late twelfth century, which placed a premium on the *interior* pilgrimage of the soul and valued rulers who stayed

■ **Innocent III**

The pope appears young, aristocratic, and impassive in this thirteenth-century fresco in the lower church of Sacro Speco, Subiaco, about thirty miles east of Rome and not far from Innocent's birthplace. Innocent claimed full power over the whole church, in any region. Moreover, he thought the pope had the right to intervene in any issue where sin might be involved—and that meant most matters. Although these were only theoretical claims, difficult to put into practice given his meager resources and inefficient staff, Innocent was a major force through his sometimes deadly dealings with secular leaders, through his calling of the Fourth Crusade, and above all through the Fourth Lateran Council, which set the standard for the behavior of all Christians.

(Scala/Art Resource, NY.)

home to care for their people. The crusades to the Holy Land served as an outlet for religious fervor, self-confidence, ambition, prejudice, and aggression. But they had very little lasting positive effect. They managed to stimulate the European economy slightly, and they inspired a vast literature of songs and chronicles. Such achievements must be weighed against the lives lost on both sides and the religious polarization and prejudices that the crusades fed upon and fortified. The bitterest fruit of the crusades was the destruction of Byzantium. The Latin conquest of Constantinople in 1204 irrevocably weakened the one buffer state standing between Europe and Islam.

The Spanish Reconquista Advances

By 1200, Christian Spain had achieved the political configuration that would last for centuries: to the east was the kingdom of Aragon; to the west was Portugal; and in between was Castile, which in 1230 merged with León (see Map 10.2). The leaders of these kingdoms competed for territory and power, but above all they sought an advantage against the Muslims still ruling a strip of southern Spain.

The *reconquista,* which had begun against the Muslim *taifas,* continued in full force, aided by Muslim disunity. For the *taifas* not only were in competition with one another but were beset from the south by the Almoravids and, after 1147, the Almohades, Muslims from North Africa. Claiming religious purity, these Berber groups declared their own holy war against the Andalusians. These simultaneous threats caused alliances within Spain to be based on political as well as religious considerations. The Muslim ruler of Valencia, for example, declared himself a vassal of the king of Castile and bitterly opposed the Berber expansion.

The crusading ideal, however, held no room for such subtleties. During the 1140s, armies under the command of the Christian kings of Portugal, Castile, and Aragon scored resounding victories against Muslim cities. Enlisting the aid of crusaders on their way to the Holy Land in 1147, the king of Portugal promised land, plunder, and protection to all who would help him attack Muslim-controlled Lisbon. His efforts succeeded, and Lisbon's Muslim inhabitants fled or were slain, its Mozarabic bishop (the bishop of the Christians living under Muslim rule) was killed, and a crusader from England was set up as bishop.

In the 1170s, the Almohades conquered the Muslim south and advanced toward the cities taken by the Christians, but their exertions had no lasting effect. In 1212, a Christian crusading army of Spaniards led by the kings of Aragon and Castile defeated the Almohades decisively at Las Navas de Tolosa. "On their side 100,000 armed men or more fell in the battle," the king of Castile wrote afterward, "but of the army of the Lord . . . incredible though it may be, unless it be a miracle, hardly 25 or 30 Christians of our whole army fell. O what happiness! O what thanksgiving!" The turning point in the *reconquista* had been reached (Map 10.2). The Almohades continued to lose strength, and Christian armies marched from victory to victory. Mérida fell in 1230. Córdoba was taken six years later, Seville in 1248. All that remained of Muslim-controlled Spain was a thin wedge of territory around Granada.

■ **MAP 10.2 The *Reconquista* Triumphs, 1212–1275**

A major turning point in the recon-quista was the battle of Las Navas de Tolosa (1212). This marked not only the defeat of the Muslims but also the triumph of Castile, which had origi-nally been a tributary of León. In the course of the twelfth century, Castile became a power in its own right; in 1230, León and Castile merged into one kingdom. During the thirteenth century, Castile-León (and, to a lesser extent, Portugal and Aragon) conquered most of the rest of the Iberian peninsula, leaving only Granada under Islamic rule.

Putting Down the Heretics in Their Midst

In the thirteenth century, the church and secular powers combined not only to con-quer pagans and Muslims on the borders of Europe but also to stamp out heresy in their midst. The papacy declared crusades against the Albigensians of southern France and even against a reigning emperor, Frederick II.

The church initially hoped that sending missionaries to Languedoc would end the Albigensian heresy there (see Map 10.1). But it did not bargain for the impres-sion made by the Catholic preachers, who arrived on horseback, wearing fine clothes and followed by a crowd of servants. These men had no moral leverage with their audience. This was immediately apparent to St. Dominic (1170–1221), founder of the Dominican order. Like his adversaries the Albigensians, Dominic rejected material riches. Instead he and his followers went about on foot, preaching and begging. The Dominicans resembled the Franciscans both organizationally and spir-itually; they, too, were called friars. But their first calling was to the heretics of Languedoc rather than to the city dwellers of Italy.

Even with St. Dominic's preachers at the forefront, missionary work was slow and frustrating. In 1208, the murder of a papal legate in southern France prompted Pope Innocent III to demand that princes from the north of France take up the sword, invade Languedoc, wrest the land from the heretics, and populate it with orthodox Christians. This Albigensian Crusade (1209–1229) marked the first time the pope offered warriors fighting an enemy in Christian Europe all the spiritual and temporal benefits of a crusade to the Holy Land. Innocent suspended the crusaders' monetary debts and promised that their sins would be forgiven after forty days' service.

Like all crusades, the Albigensian Crusade had political as well as religious dimensions. It pitted southern French princes with Cathar connections, like Raymond VI, count of Toulouse, against northern leaders like Simon IV de Montfort l'Amaury, a castellan from the Île-de-France eager to demonstrate piety and win new possessions. After twenty years of fighting, leadership of the crusade was taken over in 1229 by the Capetian kings of France. Southern resistance was broken, and Languedoc was brought under the French crown.

Meanwhile, the papacy set up the Inquisition in southern France to ferret out undetected heretics. The Inquisition was a legal proceeding. First the inquisitors typically called the people of a district to a "preaching," where they gave a sermon and promised clemency to those who confessed their heresy promptly. Then, at a general inquest, they questioned each man and woman who seemed to know something about heresy: "Have you ever seen any heretics . . . ? Have you heard them preach? Attended any of their ceremonies? Adored heretics?" The judges assigned relatively lenient penalties to those who were not aware that they held heretical beliefs and to heretics who quickly recanted. But unrepentant heretics were burned at the stake, because the church believed that such people threatened the salvation of all. Anyone who died while still a heretic could not be buried in consecrated ground. Raymond VII, count of Toulouse, saw the body of his father—who died excommunicated—rot in its coffin as the pope denied all requests for its burial. Houses where heretics had resided or even simply entered were burned, and the sites were turned into garbage dumps. Children of heretics could not inherit any property or become priests, even if they adopted orthodox views.

In the thirteenth century, for the first time, long-term imprisonment became a tool to repress heresy, even if the heretic confessed. "It is our will," wrote one tribunal, "that [Raymond Maurin and Arnalda, his wife,] because they have rashly transgressed against God and holy church . . . be thrust into perpetual prison to do [appropriate] penance, and we command them to remain there in perpetuity." The inquisitors also used imprisonment to force people to recant, to give the names of other heretics, or to admit a plot. Guillaume Agasse, for example, confessed to participating in a wicked (and imaginary) meeting of lepers who planned to poison all the wells. As the quest for religious control spawned wild fantasies of conspiracy, the inquisitors pinned their paranoia on real people.

The Inquisition also created a new group—penitent heretics—who lived on as marginal people. Forced to wear badges as a mark of disgrace, penitent heretics were stigmatized by huge yellow fabric crosses sewn on the front and back of their shirts. So that the crosses would be visible, penitents were forbidden to wear yellow clothing. Moreover, every Sunday and every feast day penitent heretics had to attend church twice; and during religious processions these men and women were required to join with the clergy and the faithful, carrying large branches in their hands as a sign of their penance. (See "Taking Measure," below.)

One "heretic" was an emperor. Innocent III—the pope who called the Fourth Crusade, the crusade against the Livs, and the Albigensian Crusade—had given the imperial crown to Frederick II (r. 1212–1250). Innocent's successors would rue the day. Like his grandfather Frederick Barbarossa, Frederick II, who was king of Sicily as well as Germany, sought to control Italy. This policy was intolerable to the papacy, which had its own ambitions on the peninsula.

Frederick was an amazing ruler: "*stupor mundi*"—"wonder of the world"—his contemporaries called him. Heir to two cultures, Sicilian on his mother's side and German on his father's, he cut a worldly and sophisticated figure. In Sicily, he moved easily within a diverse culture of Jews, Muslims, and Christians. There he could play the role of all-powerful ruler. In Germany, where Christian princes—often churchmen with ministerial retinues—were acutely aware of their rights and privileges, he was less at home.

■ **TAKING MEASURE**
Sentences Imposed by an Inquisitor, 1308–1323

How harsh was the Inquisition? Did its agents regularly burn people alive? How frequently did they imprison people or order them to wear crosses on their clothing? Statistical data to answer these sorts of questions are normally lacking for the medieval period. But there are exceptions. One comes from a register of offenses and punishments kept by the Languedocian inquisitor Bernard Gui from 1308 to 1323. Of 633 punishments handed down by Gui's tribunal, only a relatively small number of people were burned alive. (Those "burned posthumously" would have been burned alive, but they died be-

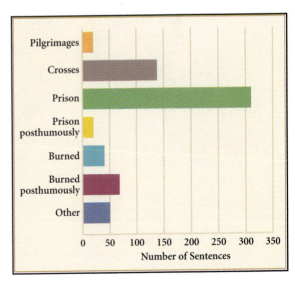

fore that could happen.) Nearly half of the guilty were sentenced to prison, usually for life. (Some were sent to prison posthumously—that is, they would have gone to prison had they not died in the meantime.) Many historians conclude that the Inquisition was not particularly harsh, for capital punishment at the time was regularly meted out to criminals under secular law.

(From J. Given, "A Medieval Inquisitor at Work," in S. K. Cohn Jr. and S. A. Epstein, *Portraits of Medieval and Renaissance Living* [Ann Arbor: University of Michigan Press, 1996], 215.)

Frederick had a three-pronged imperial strategy. First, to ensure that opponents in Germany would not hound him, he granted the princes important concessions, finalized in 1232. These privileges allowed the German princes to turn their principalities into virtually independent states. Second, Frederick revamped the government of Sicily to give himself more control and yield greater profits. His *Constitutions of Melfi* (1231), an eclectic body of laws, called for nearly all court cases to be heard by royal courts, regularized commercial privileges, and set up a system of taxation. Third, Frederick sought to enter Italy through Lombardy, as his grandfather had done (Map 10.3).

■ **MAP 10.3 Europe in the Time of Frederick II, r. 1212–1250**
King of Sicily and Germany and emperor as well, Frederick ruled over territory that encircled—and threatened—the papacy. Excommunicated several times, Frederick spent much of his career fighting the pope's forces. In the process, he conceded so many powers to the German princes that the emperor thenceforth had little power in Germany. Meanwhile, rulers of smaller states, such as England, France, and Castile-León, were increasing their power and authority.

www.bedfordstmartins.com/huntconcise See the ONLINE STUDY GUIDE for more help in analyzing this map.

The papacy followed Frederick's every move, excommunicating the emperor a number of times. The most serious of these came in 1245, when the pope and other churchmen, assembled at the Council of Lyon, excommunicated and deposed Frederick, absolving his vassals and subjects of their fealty to him and, indeed, forbidding anyone to support him. "He has deservedly become suspect of heresy," the council intoned, explaining that "he has despised and continues to despise the keys of the church [the symbol of St. Peter and thus of the pope], causing the sacred rites to be celebrated or rather . . . to be profaned. . . . Besides, he is joined in odious friendship with the Saracens [Muslims]." By 1248, papal legates were preaching a crusade against Frederick and all his followers. Two years later, Frederick died.

The fact that Frederick's vision of the empire failed is of less long-term importance than the way it failed. His concessions to the German princes meant that Germany would remain divided under numerous regional princes until the nineteenth century. In fact, between 1254 and 1273, the princes kept the German throne empty. Splintered into factions, they elected two different foreigners, who spent their time fighting each other. In one of history's strange twists, it was during this low point of the German monarchy that the term "Holy Roman Empire" was coined. In 1273, the princes at last united and elected a German, Rudolph (r. 1273–1291), whose family, the Habsburgs, was new to imperial power. Rudolf used the imperial title to help him gain Austria for his dynasty, but he did not try to fulfill the meaning of the imperial title in Italy. For the first time, the word *emperor* was freed from its association with Italy and Rome. For the Habsburgs, the title "Holy Roman Emperor" was a prestigious but otherwise meaningless honorific.

Frederick's failure in Italy meant that the Italian cities would continue their independent course. In Sicily, the papacy ensured that the heirs of Frederick would not continue their rule. Instead, the popes called successively on other dynasts to take over the island—first Henry III of England and then Charles of Anjou. Forces loyal to Frederick's family turned to the king of Aragon (Spain). That move left two enduring claimants to Sicily's crown: the kings of Aragon and the house of Anjou. And it spawned a long war impoverishing the region.

In the struggle between pope and emperor, the pope had clearly won. The moment marked a high point in the political power of the medieval papacy. Nevertheless, some agreed with Frederick II's view that by tampering with secular matters the popes had demeaned and sullied

Italy at the End of the Thirteenth Century

their office: "These men who feign holiness," Frederick sneered, referring to the popes, are "drunk with the pleasures of the world." Scattered throughout Germany were people who believed that Frederick was a divine scourge sent to overpower a materialistic papacy. The papacy won the war against Frederick, but at a cost. Even the king of France criticized the popes for doing "new and unheard of things." By making its war against Frederick part of its crusade against heresy, the papacy came under attack for using religion as a political tool.

The Mongol Takeover

Europeans were not the only warring society in the thirteenth century: to the east, the Mongols (sometimes called Tatars or Tartars) created an aggressive army under the leadership of Chingiz Khan and his sons. In part, economic necessity impelled them out of Mongolia: climatic change had reduced the grasslands that sustained their animals and their nomadic way of life. But they were also inspired by Chingiz's hope of conquering the world. In the 1230s, the Mongols began concerted attacks in Europe—in Russia, Poland, and Hungary, where weak native princes were no match for the Mongols' formidable armies and tactics. Only the death of their Great Khan, Chingiz's son Ogodei (1186–1241)—styled the *khagan,* or "Khan of Khans"—and disputes over his succession prevented a concentrated assault on Germany. In the 1250s, the Mongols took Iran, Baghdad, and Damascus.

The Mongols' sophisticated and devastating military tactics contributed to their overwhelming success. Organizing their campaigns at meetings held far in advance of a planned attack, they devised two- and three-flank operations. The invasion of Hungary, for example, was two-pronged: one division of the Mongol army arrived from Russia while the other moved through Poland and Germany. Many Hungarians perished in the assault as the Mongols, fighting mainly on horseback and wielding heavy lances and powerful bows whose arrows traveled far and penetrated deeply, crushed the Hungarian force of mixed infantry and cavalry (Map 10.4).

The Mongols' attacks on Russia had the most lasting impact. At Vladimir, in the north, they broke through the walls of the city and burned the people huddled for protection in the cathedral. The Mongols' most important victory in Russia was the capture of Kiev in 1240. Making the mouth of the Volga River the seat of their power in Russia, the Mongols dominated Russia's principalities for about two hundred years.

The Mongol Empire in Russia, later called the Golden Horde (*golden* probably from the color of their leader's tent; *horde* from a Turkish word meaning "camp"), adopted much of the local government apparatus. The Mongols standardized the collection of taxes and the recruitment of troops by basing them on a population census, and they allowed Russian princes to continue ruling as long as they paid homage and tribute to the khan. Mongol overlords even exempted the Russian church from taxes.

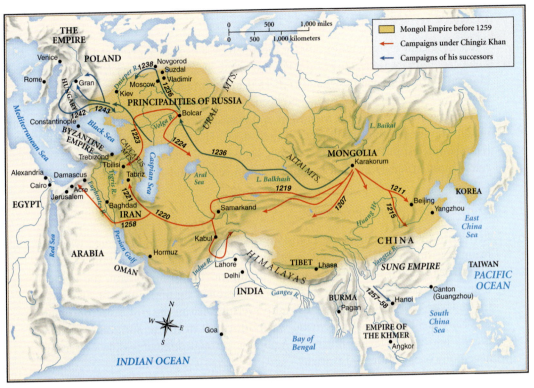

■ **MAP 10.4 The Mongol Invasions to 1259**

The Mongols were the first people to tie the Eastern world to the West. Their conquest of China, which took place at about the same time as their invasions of Russia and Iran, opened up trade relations across regions formerly separated by language, religion, and political regimes.

The Mongol invasion changed the political configuration of Europe and Asia. Because the Mongols were willing to deal with westerners such as the Polo family, one effect of their conquests was to open China to Europeans for the first time. For example, an entire community of Venetian traders—women, men, and children— lived in the city of Yangzhou in the mid-fourteenth century. Some missionaries, diplomats, and merchants traveled overland to China; others made the difficult journey from the Persian Gulf (controlled by the Mongols), rounding India before arriving in China.

The long-term effect of the Mongols on the West was to open up new land routes to the East that helped bind together the regions of the known world. Travel stories such as Marco Polo's stimulated others to seek out the fabulous riches— textiles, ginger, ceramics, copper—of China and other places in the East. In a sense, the Mongols initiated the search for exotic goods and missionary opportunities that culminated in the European "discovery" of a new world, the Americas.

Politics of Control

In the thirteenth century, Europeans for the first time spoke of their rulers not as kings of a people (for example, king of the Franks) but as kings of a territory (for example, king of France). This new designation reflected an important change in medieval ruler-ship. However strong earlier rulers had been, their political power had been personal (depending on ties of kinship, friendship, and vassalage) rather than territorial (touching all who lived within the borders of their state). That new conception, along with renewed interest in Roman legal concepts, served as a foundation for strong, central rule—most strikingly in western Europe but in central and eastern Europe as well.

France: From Acorn to Oak

Even with the achievements of Louis VI, the French monarchy remained weak, a realm surrounded by powerful neighbors. This changed under Philip II (r. 1180–1223). When Philip first came to the throne, the royal domain, the Île-de-France, was sandwiched between territory controlled by the counts of Flanders, Champagne, and Anjou. By far the most powerful ruler on the European continent was King Henry II of England, who was both count of Anjou and duke of Normandy and also held the duchy of Aquitaine through his wife while exercising hegemony over Poitou and Brittany.

Henry and the counts of Flanders and Champagne vied to control the young king of France. Philip, however, quickly learned to play them off against one another. Contemporaries were astounded when Philip successfully gained territory: he wrested Vermandois and Artois from Flanders in the 1190s and Normandy, Anjou, Maine, Touraine, and Poitou from Henry II's son King John of England in 1204, making good his claim at the decisive battle of Bouvines in 1214. No wonder a contemporary chronicler dubbed him Philip Augustus, the "augmenter."

Pivotal forces led to the extension of the French king's power and the territorial integrity of France. The Second Crusade (1147–1149) had brought together many French lords as vassals of the king and united them against a common foe. The language they spoke was becoming increasingly uniform and "French." Nevertheless, this in itself did not create a larger French kingdom. That came about through royal strategy. Rather than give his new territories out as fiefs, Philip

Consolidation of France under Philip Augustus, r. 1180–1223

determined to govern them himself.* In Normandy, for example, he demanded that the aristocrats become his vassals, and he sent his officials to collect taxes and hear cases. Philip also instituted a new kind of French administration, based on writing. Before his day, most royal arrangements were committed to memory rather than to parchment. If decrees were written at all, they were saved by the recipient, not by the government. For example, when a monastery wanted a confirmation of its privileges from the king, its own scribes wrote the document for its archives to preserve the monastery against possible future challenges. The king did keep some documents, which generally followed him in his travels like personal possessions. But in 1194, in a battle with the king of England, Philip lost his meager cache of documents along with much treasure when he had to abandon his baggage train. After 1194, the king had all his decrees written down, and he established permanent repositories in which to keep them.

To do the daily work of government, Philip relied on members of the lesser nobility—knights and clerics, many of whom were "masters" educated in the city schools of France. They served as officers of his court; as *prévôts* (provosts), who oversaw the king's estates and collected his taxes; and as *baillis* (bailiffs; *sénéchaux* in the south), who supervised the provosts and functioned as regional judges, presiding over courts that met monthly and making the king's power felt locally as never before.

Under Philip's grandson, Louis IX (r. 1226–1270), the Capetian monarchy reached the height of its prestige if not its power. Louis was revered, not because he was a military leader but because he was an administrator, judge, and "just father" of his people. On warm summer days, he would sit under a tree in the woods near his castle at Vincennes on the outskirts of Paris, hearing disputes and dispensing justice personally. He used his administrators to impose royal law and justice throughout his kingdom. Over the city of Paris he appointed a salaried officer who could be supervised and fired if necessary. During his reign, the influence of the *Parlement* of Paris, the royal court of justice, increased significantly. Originally a changeable and movable body, part of the king's personal entourage when he dealt with litigation, it was now permanently housed in Paris and staffed by professional judges who heard cases and recorded their decisions.

Unlike his grandfather Philip Augustus, Louis did not try to expand his territory. He inherited a large kingdom that included Poitou and Languedoc (Map 10.5), and he was content. Although the king of England attacked him continually to try to regain territory lost under Philip Augustus, Louis remained unprovoked. Rather than prolong the fighting, he conceded a bit and made peace in 1259. At the same time, Louis was a zealous crusader. He took seriously the need to defend the Holy Land when most of his contemporaries were weary of the idea.

---

*Philip was particularly successful in imposing royal control in Normandy; later French kings gave most of the other territories to collateral members of the royal family.

Louis was respectful of the church and the pope; he accepted limits on his power in relation to the church and never claimed power over spiritual matters. Nevertheless, Louis vigorously maintained the dignity of the king and his rights. He expected royal and ecclesiastical power to work in harmony, and he refused to let the church dictate how he should use his temporal authority. For example, French bishops wanted royal officers to support the church's sentences of excommunication. But Louis declared that he would authorize his officials to do so only if he were able to judge each case for himself, to see whether the excommunication had been justly pronounced. The bishops refused, but Louis held his ground. Royal and ecclesiastical power would work side by side, neither subservient to the other.

Many modern historians fault Louis for his policies toward the Jews. His hatred of them was well known. He did not exactly advocate violence against them, but he sometimes subjected them to arrest, canceling debts owed to them (but collecting part into the royal treasury) and confiscating their belongings. In 1253, he ordered them to live "by the labor of their hands" or leave France. He meant that they should no longer lend money, in effect taking away their one means of livelihood. Louis's contemporaries did not criticize him for his Jewish policies. If anything, his hatred of Jews enhanced his reputation.

In fact, many of Louis's contemporaries considered him a saint, praising his care for the poor and sick, the pains and penances he inflicted on himself, and his regular participation in church services. In 1297, Pope Boniface VIII canonized him as St. Louis. The result was enormous prestige for the French monarchy. This prestige, joined with the renown of Paris as the center of scholarship and the repute of French courts as the hubs of chivalry, made France the cultural model of Europe.

■ **MAP 10.5 France under Louis IX, r. 1226–1270**

Louis IX did not expand his kingdom as dramatically as his grandfather Philip Augustus had done. He was greatly admired nevertheless, for he was seen by contemporaries as a model of Christian charity, piety, and justice. After his death, Louis IX was recognized as a saint and thus posthumously enhanced the prestige of the French monarchy in a new way.

England: Crisis and Consolidation

What the French king gained the English king lost. Henry II had been very strong, and his son Richard I (r. 1189–1199) was called "Lion-Hearted" for his boldness. Under these men, the English monarchy was omnipresent and rich. Its omnipresence derived largely from its judicial and administrative apparatus. Its wealth came from court fees, income from numerous royal estates both in England and on the continent, taxes from cities, and customary feudal dues (called *aids*) collected from barons and knights. These aids were paid on such occasions as the knighting of the king's eldest son and the marriage of the king's eldest daughter. Enriched by the commercial economy of the late twelfth century, the English kings encouraged their knights and barons not to serve them personally in battle but instead to pay the king a tax called *scutage* in lieu of service. The monarchs preferred to hire mercenaries both as troops to fight external enemies and as policemen to enforce the king's will at home.

But Richard died young, and his brother and heir, John (r. 1199–1216), lost badly to Philip Augustus. John was widely disliked by his contemporaries, who accused him of asserting his will in a high-handed way. But to understand John, it is necessary to appreciate how desperate he was to keep his continental possessions. After he lost his northern French territories to Philip, John did everything he could to add to the crown revenues so he could pay for an army to fight the French. He forced his vassals to pay ever-increasing scutages and extorted money in the form of new feudal aids. He compelled the widows of his vassals to marry men of his choosing or pay him a hefty fee if they refused. John's heavy investment in this war effort, however, could not prevent defeat of his army in 1214 at the battle of Bouvines, and this defeat caused discontented English barons to rebel openly against

■ **John's Seal on Magna Carta**

When the rebels at Runnymede got John to assent to their charter, later known as Magna Carta, he did not sign it; he sealed it. From the thirteenth through the fifteenth century, kings, queens, aristocrats, guilds, communes, and many other people at all levels of society used seals to authenticate their charters, or legal documents. The seal itself was made of melted wax or lead, which was dropped onto the document and pressed with a gold or brass matrix carved with an image in the negative. These images reminded the public of the status as well as the name of the sealer. Notice the image that John chose to place on his seal.

(British Museum.)

the king. At Runnymede in June 1215, John was forced to agree to the charter of baronial liberties that has come to be called *Magna Carta*, "Great Charter."

The English barons intended Magna Carta (so named to distinguish it from a smaller charter issued around the same time concerning the royal forests) to be a conservative document defining the "customary" obligations and rights of the nobility and forbidding the king to break from these customs without consulting his barons. "No widow shall be forced to marry so long as she wishes to live without a husband," it declares, continuing:

> *No scutage or aid shall be imposed in our kingdom unless by common counsel of our kingdom, except for [the customary purposes:] ransoming our person, for making our eldest son a knight, and for once marrying our eldest daughter.*

In its most famous clause, Magna Carta provided that

> *No free man shall be arrested or imprisoned or disseised [deprived of his property] or outlawed or exiled or in any way victimized, neither will we attack him or send anyone to attack him, except by the lawful judgment of his peers or by the law of the land.*

Thus Magna Carta established that all free men in the land had certain customs and rights in common and that the king must uphold those customs and rights. In this way, it documented the subordination of the king to custom; it implied that the king was not above the law. Magna Carta shows that the growth of royal power was matched by the self-confidence of the English barons, certain of their rights and eager to articulate them. Although in the thirteenth century the "free men" of the realm were a tiny elite, in time, as the definition of "free men" expanded to include all the king's subjects, Magna Carta came to be seen as a guarantee of the rights of Englishmen in general.

Papal Monarchy

As the kings of France and England were gaining newly precise roles, so, too, were the popes. Innocent III was the most powerful, respected, and prestigious of the medieval popes. The first pope to be trained at the city schools, Innocent had studied theology at Paris and law at Bologna. From theology, he learned to tease new meaning out of the pope's position: he thought of himself as ruling in the place of Christ the King. In his view, secular kings and emperors existed to help the pope. From law, Innocent gained his conception of the pope as lawmaker and of law as an instrument of moral reformation.

Utilizing the traditional method of declaring church law, Innocent convened and presided over a council in 1215 at the pope's Lateran Palace in Rome. Known as the Fourth Lateran Council, it aimed to reform not only the clergy but also the laity. Innocent and the other assembled churchmen hoped to create a society united under the authority of the church.

For laymen and laywomen, perhaps the most important canons of the Fourth Lateran concerned the sacraments, the rites the church believed Jesus had instituted to confer sanctifying grace. One canon required Christians to attend Mass and confess their sins to a priest at least once a year. At the same time, the council explained with new precision the transformation of bread and wine (the Eucharist) in the Mass. In the twelfth century, a newly rigorous understanding of this transformation had already been promulgated, according to which Christ's body and blood were truly contained in the sacrament that looked like bread and wine on the altar. The Fourth Lateran Council not only declared this to be dogma (authoritative) but also explained it by using a technical term coined by twelfth-century scholars. The bread and wine were *transubstantiated*: although the Eucharist continued to *look* like bread and wine, with its consecration during the Mass the bread became the actual flesh and the wine the real blood of Christ. The council's emphasis on this potent event strengthened the role of the priesthood, for only a priest could celebrate this mystery (that is, transform the bread and wine into Christ's body and blood), through which God's grace was transmitted to the faithful.

Innocent III wanted the council to condemn Christian men who had intercourse with Jewish women and then claimed "ignorance" as their excuse. But the council went even further, requiring all Jews to advertise their religion by some outward sign: "We decree that [Jews] of either sex in every Christian province at all times shall be distinguished from other people by the character of their dress in public." Like all church rules, this canon took effect only when local rulers enforced it. In many instances, they did so with zeal, not so much because they were eager to humiliate Jews but rather because they could make money selling exemptions to Jews who were willing to pay to avoid the requirements. Nonetheless, sooner or later Jews almost everywhere had to wear a badge as a sign of their second-class status. In southern France and in a few places in Spain, Jews were supposed to wear round badges. In England, the city of Salisbury demanded that they wear special clothing. In Vienna, they were told to put on pointed hats.

The Fourth Lateran Council's longest decree blasted heretics: "Those condemned as heretics shall be handed over to the secular authorities for punishment." If the secular authority did not "purge his or her land of heretical filth," the heretic was to be excommunicated. If he had vassals, they were to be released from their oaths of fealty, and the heretic's land was to be taken over by orthodox Christians. Rulers heeded these rules. Already some had taken up arms against heretics in the Albigensian Crusade (1209–1229). The Fourth Lateran Council was also responsible for setting up the Inquisition.

The Fourth Lateran was the high-water mark of the medieval papacy. However, the growing prestige and actual jurisdiction of secular rulers changed the balance of power between church and state in the course of the thirteenth century. At the end of that century, when the pope clashed with the kings of France and England, the kings were the clear winners, and the papacy lost both prestige and power.

The clash began over taxing the clergy. The French king Philip IV (r. 1285–1314), known as Philip the Fair, and the English king Edward I (r. 1272–1307) financed their wars (mainly against one another) by taxing the clergy along with everyone else. The new principle of national sovereignty that they were claiming led them to assert jurisdiction over all people, even churchmen, who lived within their borders. For the pope, however, the principle at stake was his role as head of the clergy. In response to clerical taxation, Boniface VIII (r. 1294–1303) declared that only the pope could authorize such taxes. Threatening to excommunicate kings who taxed prelates without papal permission, he called upon clerics to disobey any such royal orders.

Edward and Philip reacted swiftly. Taking advantage of the important role that English courts played in protecting the peace, Edward declared that all clerics who refused to pay their taxes would be considered outlaws—literally "outside the law." Clergymen who were robbed, for example, would have no recourse against their attackers; if accused of crimes, they would have no defense in court. Relying on a different strategy, Philip forbade the exportation of precious metals, money, or jewels, effectively sealing the French borders. Immediately the English clergy cried out for legal protection, while the papacy itself clamored for the revenues it had long enjoyed from French pilgrims, litigants, and travelers. Boniface was forced to back down, conceding in 1297 that kings had the right to tax the clergy of their kingdoms in emergencies.

But the crisis was not over. In 1301, Philip the Fair tested his jurisdiction in southern France by arresting Bernard Saisset, the bishop of Pamiers, on a charge of treason for slandering the king by comparing him to an owl, "the handsomest of birds which is worth absolutely nothing." Saisset's imprisonment violated the principle, maintained both by the pope and by French law, that a clergyman was not subject to lay justice. Boniface reacted angrily, and Philip seized the opportunity to deride and humiliate the pope, orchestrating a public relations campaign against him. Boniface's reply, the bull* *Unam Sanctam* (1302), intensified the situation to fever pitch by declaring bluntly "that it is altogether necessary to salvation for every human creature to be subject to the Roman Pontiff." At meetings of the king's inner circle, Philip's agents declared Boniface a false pope, accusing him of sexual perversion, various crimes, and heresy. In 1303, royal agents, acting under Philip's orders, invaded Boniface's palace at Anagni (southeast of Rome) to capture the pope, bring him to France, and try him. Fearing for the pope's life, however, the people of Anagni joined forces and drove the French agents out of town. Yet even

---

*An official papal document is called a *bull,* from the *bulla,* or seal, that was used to authenticate it.

after such public support for the pope, the king made his power felt. Boniface died very shortly thereafter, and the next two popes quickly pardoned Philip and his agents for their actions.

Just as Frederick II's defeat showed the weakness of the empire, so Boniface's humiliation showed the limits of papal control. The two powers that claimed "universal" authority had very little weight in the face of the new, limited, but tightly controlled national states. After 1303, popes continued to fulminate against kings, but their words had less and less impact. In the face of newly powerful medieval states such as France, Spain, and England—undergirded by vast revenues, judicial apparatuses, representative institutions, and even the loyalty of churchmen—the papacy could make little headway. The delicate balance between church and state, a hallmark of the years of Louis IX, broke down by the end of the thirteenth century.

In 1309, forced from Rome by civil strife, the papacy settled at Avignon, a city technically in the Holy Roman Empire but very close to, and influenced by, France (see Map 10.5). Here the popes remained until 1378. The period from 1309 to 1378 came to be called the "Babylonian Captivity" by Europeans sensitive

■ **Boniface VIII**

For the sculptor who depicted Pope Boniface VIII, Arnolfo di Cambio (d. 1302), not much had changed since the time of Innocent III. Look at the picture of Innocent on page 393 and compare the two popes: both are depicted as young, majestic, authoritative, sober, and calm. Yet Boniface could not have been very calm, for his authority was challenged at every turn. He was forced to withdraw his opposition to royal taxation of the clergy. He tried to placate the French king, Philip the Fair, by canonizing Philip's grandfather, Louis IX. Even so, Philip arrested the bishop of Pamiers and brought him to trial. When Boniface protested, he was proclaimed a heretic by the French. A few months later he was dead. (Scala/Art Resource, NY.)

to having the popes live far from Rome, on the Rhône River. The Avignon popes, many of them French, established a sober and efficient organization that took in regular revenues and gave the papacy more say than ever before in the appointment of churchmen. They would, however, slowly abandon the idea of leading all of Christendom and would tacitly recognize the growing power of the secular states to regulate their internal affairs.

Power Shift in the Italian Communes

During the thirteenth century, the Italian communes continued to extend their control over the surrounding countryside as independent city-states. While generally presenting a united front to outsiders, factions within the communes fought for control and its spoils. In the early thirteenth century, these factions represented noble families. However, in the course of the century, newer groups, generally from the nonnoble classes, attempted to take over the reins of power in the communes. The *popolo* ("people"), as such groups were called, incorporated members of city associations such as craft and merchant guilds, parishes, and the commune itself. In fact, the *popolo* was a kind of alternative commune, a sworn association in each city that dedicated itself to upholding the interests of its members. Armed and militant, the *popolo* demanded a share in city government, particularly to gain a voice in matters of taxation. In 1222 at Piacenza, for example (see map on page 399), the *popolo*'s members won half the government offices; a year later they and the nobles worked out a plan to share the election of their city's *podestà*, or chief executive. Such power sharing often resulted from the *popolo*'s struggle, though in some cities, nobles overcame and dissolved the *popolo,* while in others, the *popolo* virtually excluded the nobles from government. Constantly confronting one another, quarreling, feuding, and compromising, such factions turned Italian cities into centers of civil discord.

Weakened by this constant friction, the communes were tempting prey for great regional nobles who, allying with one or another faction, established themselves as *signori* (singular *signore,* "lord") of the cities, keeping the peace at the price of repression. In these circumstances, the commune gave way to the *signoria* (a state ruled by a *signore*), and one family began to dominate the government. The communes ceased to exist, and many Italian cities fell under control of despots. The fate of Piacenza over the course of the thirteenth century was typical. First dominated by nobles, its commune granted the *popolo* a voice by 1225; but then by midcentury the *signore*'s power eclipsed both the nobles and the *popolo.*

New-Style Associations amid the Monarchies

Although the thirteenth century was the age of newly strong *signori* or monarchs, there were some exceptions. Under the leadership of Lübeck, the cities of northern Germany trading between the Baltic and the North Seas banded together to form the Hanseatic League. It was one fruit of the Northern Crusades: even the Teutonic Knights were members. Merchants in these cities dominated the northern grain trade, and their control over this commodity gave them power. They were able to declare embargos against enemies and monopolies for themselves. Throughout the thirteenth and fourteenth centuries, the Hanse dominated the Baltic region.

Similarly independent were the self-governing peasant and town communes in the high Alpine valleys that became a united Swiss Confederation. In 1291, the peasants of Uri, Schwyz, and Unterwalden swore a perpetual alliance against their oppressive Habsburg over-lord. After defeating a Habsburg army in 1315, these free peasants took the name "Confederates" and developed a new alliance that would become Switzerland. In the process, the Swiss enshrined their freedom in the legend of William Tell, their national hero, who was forced by a Habsburg official to prove his archery skills by shooting an apple placed on the head of his own son. This act so outraged the citizens that they rose up in arms against Habsburg rule. By 1353, the important cities of Lucerne, Zurich, and Bern had joined the confederation. The Swiss Confederation continued to acquire new members into the sixteenth century, defeating armies sent by different princes to undermine its liberties.

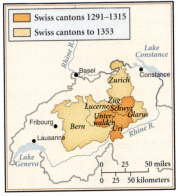

Growth of the Swiss Confederation to 1353

The Birth of Representative Institutions

Even monarchies found it useful to embrace groups beyond the narrow elite of the aristocracy. One of the ways in which Philip the Fair orchestrated his public rela-tions campaign against Pope Boniface was to convene representatives of the clergy, nobles, and townspeople to explain, justify, and propagandize his position. This new assembly, which met at Paris in 1302, was the ancestor of the Estates General, which would meet sporadically for centuries thereafter—for the last time in 1789, at the beginning of the French Revolution. (In France, the various orders—clergy, nobles, and commoners—were called "estates.") After Philip's agents declared Boniface a false pope, the king sent his commissioners to the various provinces of France to convene local meetings to popularize his charges against Boniface and gain sup-port. Clergy, local nobles, townspeople, and even villagers attending these meetings almost unanimously denounced the pope.

As in France, representative institutions elsewhere began as political tools with which rulers hoped to broaden their support. All across Europe—from Spain to Poland, from England to Hungary—rulers summoned parliaments. These assemblies grew out of the ad hoc advisory sessions kings customarily held with their nobles and clergy, men who informally represented the two most powerful classes, or "orders," of medieval society. Although these bodies differed from place to place, the impulse behind their creation was similar. They began (as in France) as assemblies where kings celebrated their royal power and prestige and where the "orders" simply assented to royal policy. In the thirteenth century, the advisory sessions became solemn, formal meetings of representatives of the "orders" to the kings' chief councils—the precursor of parliamentary sessions. Eventually these bodies became organs through which people not ordinarily at court could articulate their wishes.

In practice, thirteenth-century kings did not so much command representatives of the orders to come to court as they simply summoned the most powerful members of their realm—whether clerics, nobles, or important townsmen—to support their policies. In thirteenth-century León (part of present-day Spain), for example, the king sometimes called only the clergy and nobles; sometimes he sent for representatives of the towns, especially when he wanted the help of town militias. As townsmen gradually began to participate regularly in advisory sessions, kings came to depend on them and their support. In turn, commoners became more fully integrated into the work of royal government.

The *cortes* of Castile-León were among the earliest representative assemblies called to the king's court and the first to include townsmen. Enriched by plunder from the *reconquista*, fledgling villages soon burgeoned into major commercial centers. Like the cities of Italy, Spanish towns dominated the countryside. Their leaders—called *caballeros villanos*, or "city horsemen," because they were rich enough to fight on horseback—monopolized municipal offices. In 1188, when King Alfonso IX (r. 1188–1230) summoned townsmen to the *cortes*, the city *caballeros* served as their representatives, agreeing to Alfonso's plea for military and financial support and for help in consolidating his rule. Once convened at court, these wealthy townsmen joined bishops and noblemen in formally counseling the king and assenting to royal decisions. Beginning with Alfonso X (r. 1252–1284), Castilian monarchs regularly called on the *cortes* to participate in major political and military decisions and to assent to new taxes to finance them.

The English Parliament* also developed as a new tool of royal government. In this case, however, the king's control was complicated by the power of the barons, manifested, for example, in Magna Carta. In the twelfth century, King Henry II had

---

*Although *parliament* and *parlement* are very similar words, both deriving from the French word *parler* ("to speak"), the institutions they named were very different. The Parlement of France was a law court, whereas the English Parliament, although beginning as a court to redress grievances, had by 1327 become above all a representative institution. The major French representative assembly, the Estates General, first convened at the beginning of the fourteenth century.

consulted prelates and barons at Great Councils, using these parliaments as his tool to ratify and gain support for his policies. Although Magna Carta had nothing to do with such councils, the barons thought the document gave them an important and permanent role in royal government as the king's advisers and a solid guarantee of their customary rights and privileges. When Henry III (r. 1216–1272) was crowned at the age of nine, he was king in name only for the first sixteen years of his reign. During that period, England was governed by a council consisting of a few barons, professional administrators, and a papal legate. Though not quite "government by Parliament," this council set a precedent for baronial participation in government.

An English parliament that included commoners came into being in the midst of war and as a result of political weakness. Henry so alienated nobles and commoners alike by his wars, debts, choice of advisers, and demands for money that the barons threatened to rebel. At a meeting at Oxford in 1258, they forced Henry to dismiss his foreign advisers; to rule with the advice of a Council of Fifteen chosen jointly by the barons and the king; and to limit the terms of his chief officers. However, this new government itself was riven by strife among the barons, and civil war erupted in 1264. At the battle of Lewes in the same year, the leader of the baronial opposition, Simon de Montfort (c. 1208–1265), routed the king's forces, captured the king, and became England's de facto ruler. Because only a minority of the barons followed Simon, he sought new support by convening a parliament in 1265. He summoned not only the earls, barons, and churchmen who backed him but also representatives from the towns—the "commons"—and he appealed for their help. Thus, for the first time, the commons were given a voice in government. Simon's brief rule ended that very year, and Henry's son Edward I (r. 1272–1307) became a rallying point for royalists. Yet the idea of representative government in England had emerged, born out of the interplay between royal initiatives and baronial revolts.

Religious and Cultural Life in an Age of Expansion

In the course of the thirteenth century, the religious life, originally associated with monks, nuns, priests, and bishops, became possible—and officially recognized—for laypeople as well. There was a clear connection between this development and the rise of universities, for the ethical teachings of "scholastics" (the scholars of medieval universities) were preached to the people. But the scholastics were also occupied with subjects that ranged far beyond ethics. Outside of the schools, poets well aware of scholastic teachings wrote vernacular works of great sophistication. And architects and artists elaborated the soaring structures of "Gothic" style in which much of this activity took place.

Lay Religious Fervor

The Fourth Lateran's mission to regulate and Christianize lay behavior was carried forward by the friars. Both orders—the Dominican and the Franciscan—insisted on travel, preaching, and poverty—vocations that brought friars into cities and towns. Soon their members dominated the fledgling city universities and were sending into the community friar-preachers trained by the scholastics. Townspeople flocked to such preachers because they wanted to know how the Christian message applied to their daily lives. They were concerned, for example, about the ethics of moneymaking, sex in marriage, and family life. In turn, the preachers represented the front line of the church. They met the laity on their own turf and taught them to bend their activities to church teachings.

The friars further tied their members to the lay community through "tertiaries," affiliated laymen and -women who adopted many Franciscan practices—prayer and works of charity, for example—while continuing to live in the world, raising families and tending to the normal tasks of daily life, whatever their occupation. Even kings became tertiaries.

All across Europe, women too sought outlets for their piety. As in previous centuries, powerful families founded new nunneries, especially within towns and

■ Friars and Usurers

As the illustration on page 359 indicates, clerics sometimes borrowed money. The friars had a different attitude. St. Francis, son of a merchant, refused to touch money altogether. Franciscans begged for food and shelter. Even when their numbers grew and they began forming communities and living in monasteries, the friars still insisted on personal poverty, while ministering to city dwellers, who had to deal with money in some way to make a living. In this illumination from about 1250, a Franciscan (in light-colored robes) and a Dominican (in black) reject offers from two usurers, whose profession they are thus shown to condemn. Other friars, including Thomas Aquinas, worked out justifications for some kinds of moneymaking professions.

(Bibliothèque Nationale, Paris.)

cities. On the whole, these were set up for the daughters of the very wealthy. Ordinary women found different modes of religious expression. Some sought the lives of quiet activity and rapturous mysticism of the Beguines, others the lives of charity and service of women's mendicant orders, and still others domestic lives of marriage and family punctuated by religious devotions.♦ Elisabeth of Hungary, who married a German prince at the age of fourteen, raised three children. At the same time, she devoted her life to fasting, prayer, and service to the poor.

Of course, many women were not as devout as Elisabeth. In the countryside, they cooked their porridge, brewed their ale, and raised their children. They attended church regularly, on major feast days or for churching—the ritual of purification after a pregnancy—but not extravagantly. In the cities, workingwomen scratched out a meager living. They sometimes made pilgrimages to relic shrines to seek help or cures. Religion was part of these women's lives but did not dominate them.

For some women, however, religion was the focus of life, and the church's attempt to define and control the Eucharist had some unintended results. The new emphasis on the holiness of the transformed wine and bread induced some of these pious women to eat nothing but the Eucharist. One such woman, Angela of Foligno, reported that the consecrated bread swelled in her mouth, tasting sweeter than any other food. In the minds of these holy women, Christ's crucifixion was the literal sacrifice of his body, to be eaten by sinful men and women as the way to redeem themselves. Renouncing all other foods became part of a life of service to others, because many of these devout women gave to the poor the food that they refused to eat. Even if not engaged in community service, holy women felt their suffering itself was a work of charity, helping to release souls from purgatory, the place where (the church taught) souls were cleansed of their sins.

Universities and the Scholastics

The city schools of the twelfth century became real institutions—universities—in the thirteenth. The university was a type of guild (one word for guild in Latin is *universitas*). The universities regulated student discipline, scholastic proficiency, and housing while determining the masters' behavior in equal detail. For example, at the University of Paris the masters were required to wear long black gowns, follow a particular order in their lectures, and set the standards by which students could become masters themselves. The University of Bologna was unique in having two guilds, one of students and one of masters. At Bologna, the students participated in the appointment of masters and paid their salaries.

♦ For a primary source that reveals the religious beliefs of many Beguines, see Document 30, Hadewijch of Brabant, "Letters and Poems of a Female Mystic."

The University of Bologna was unusual because it was principally a school of law, where the students were often older men, well along in their careers (normally in imperial service) and used to wielding power. The University of Paris, however, attracted younger students, drawn particularly by its renown in the liberal arts and theology. The Universities of Salerno and Montpellier specialized in medicine. Oxford, once a sleepy town where students clustered around one or two masters, became a center of royal administration, and its university soon developed a reputation for teaching the liberal arts, theology, science, and mathematics.

The curriculum at each university differed in content and duration. At the University of Paris in the early thirteenth century, for example, a student had to spend at least six years studying the liberal arts before he could begin to teach. If he wanted to continue his studies with theology, he had to attend lectures on the subject for at least another five years. Lectures were clearly the most important way in which material was conveyed to students. Books were very expensive and not readily available, so students often committed their teachers' lectures to memory. The lectures were organized around important texts: the master read an excerpt aloud, delivered his commentary on it, and disputed any contrary commentaries that rival masters might have proposed.

Within the larger association of the university, students found more intimate groups with which to live. These groups, called *nations,* were linked to students' places of origin. At Bologna, for example, students incorporated themselves into two nations: Italians and non-Italians. Each nation protected its members, wrote statutes, and elected officers.

With few exceptions, masters and students were considered clerics. This had two important consequences. First, there were no university women. And second, university men were subject to church courts rather than to the secular jurisdiction of towns or lords. Many universities could also boast generous privileges from popes and kings, who valued the services of scholars. The combination of clerical status and special privileges made universities nearly self-governing corporations within the towns. Their autonomy sometimes led to friction. For example, when a student at Oxford was suspected of killing his mistress and the townspeople tried to punish him, the masters protested by refusing to teach and leaving town. Such incidents explain why historians speak of the hostility between "town" (the city) and "gown" (the students and masters). Yet university towns depended on scholars to patronize local restaurants, shops, and hostels. Town and gown normally learned to negotiate with one another to their mutual advantage.♦

University scholars used a form of inquiry and exposition called "scholasticism," based on the logical method pioneered by Abelard in his *Sic et Non* and extended by other twelfth-century teachers. In the thirteenth century, the method was used to

---

♦ For a set of sources that portray official and student attitudes toward this new institution of learning, see Document 31, "Medieval University Life."

summarize and reconcile all knowledge. Many of the thirteenth-century "scholastics" (the name given to the scholars who used this method) were members of the Dominican and Franciscan orders, who dominated some of the faculties of the universities. Most were sure that knowledge obtained through the senses and by logical reasoning was compatible with the knowledge known through faith and revelation. One of their goals was to demonstrate this harmony. The scholastic *summa*, or summary of knowledge, was a systematic exposition of the answer to every possible question about human morality, the physical world, society, belief, action, and theology.

The *summa* was an orderly presentation of various positions that were then "reconciled" by the author. Both the presentation and the arguments borrowed much of the vocabulary and rules of logic long ago outlined by Aristotle. Even though Aristotle was a pagan, scholastics considered his coherent and rational body of thought the most perfect that human reason alone could devise. Because they had the benefit of Christ's revelations, the scholastics considered themselves able to take Aristotle's philosophy one necessary step further and reconcile human reason with Christian faith. Full of confidence in their method and conclusions, scholastics embraced the world and its issues.

Some scholastics considered questions about the natural world. Albertus Magnus (c. 1200–1280), a major theologian, also contributed to the fields of biology, botany, astronomy, and physics. His reconsideration of Aristotle's views on motion led the way to distinctions that helped scientists in the sixteenth and seventeenth centuries arrive at the modern notion of inertia.

One of Albertus's students was St. Thomas Aquinas (c. 1225–1274), perhaps the most famous scholastic. Huge of build, renowned for his composure in debate, Thomas came from a noble Neapolitan family that had hoped to see him become a powerful bishop rather than a poor university professor. When he was about eighteen years old, he thwarted his family's wishes and joined the Dominicans. Soon he was studying at Cologne with Albertus. At thirty-two he became a master at the University of Paris.

Like many other scholastics, Thomas considered Aristotle "the Philosopher," the authoritative voice of human reason, which he sought to reconcile with divine revelation in a universal and harmonious scheme. In 1273, he published his monumental *Summa Theologiae* (sometimes called the *Summa Theologica*), which covered all important topics, human and divine. He divided these topics into questions, exploring each one thoroughly and systematically, and concluding each question with a decisive position and a refutation of opposing views.

Many of Thomas's questions spoke to the keenest concerns of his day. He asked, for example, whether it was lawful to sell something for more than its worth. Thomas arranged his argument systematically, quoting first authorities that seemed to declare every sort of selling practice, even deceptive ones, to be lawful. This was the *sic* (or "yes") position. Then he quoted an authority that opposed selling something for more than its worth. This was the *non*. Following that, he gave his own argument, prefaced by the words *I answer that*. Unlike Abelard, whose method left differences unresolved, Thomas wanted to harmonize the two points of view, so he pointed out that price and worth depended on the circumstances of the buyer and seller, and he concluded that charging more than a seller had originally paid could be legitimate at times.

For townspeople engaged in commerce and worried about biblical prohibitions on moneymaking, Thomas's ideas about selling practices addressed burning questions. Hoping to go to heaven as well as reap the profits of their business ventures, laypeople listened eagerly to preachers who delivered their sermons in the vernacular but who based their ideas on the Latin *summae* of Thomas and other scholastics. Thomas's conclusions aided townspeople in justifying their worldly activities.

In his own day, Thomas Aquinas was a controversial figure, and his ideas, emphasizing reason, were by no means universally accepted. In Thomas's view, God, nature, and reason were in harmony, so Aristotle's arguments could be used to explore both the human and the divine orders. The work of the thirteenth-century scholastics to unite the secular with the sacred continued for another generation after Thomas. Yet at the beginning of the fourteenth century, fissures began to appear. In the *summae* of John Duns Scotus (c. 1266–1308), for example, the world and God were less compatible. John, whose name "Duns Scotus" betrays his Scottish origin, was a Franciscan who taught at both Oxford and Paris. For John, human reason could know truth only through the "special illumination of the uncreated light"—that is, by divine illumination. But unlike his predecessors, John believed that this illumination came

■ **Thomas Aquinas in Glory**

In this fourteenth-century painting (probably by Francesco Traini) from Santa Caterina, Pisa, Thomas Aquinas is pictured as a philosopher-saint. Flanking him to his right is Aristotle, who holds up a book, symbol of the philosophy that Thomas has harvested; to his left is Plato, the second great influence behind scholastic philosophy. Above are other learned saints, and at the top is Christ, source of the Word and hence of all philosophy. Compare this representation of a great teacher with that of Gilbert of Poitiers on page 374. (Scala/Art Resource, NY.)

not as a matter of course but only when God chose to intervene. John—and others—now sometimes experienced God as willful rather than reasonable. Human reason could not soar to God; God's will alone determined whether a person could know God. In this way, John separated the divine and secular realms.

Like John, William of Ockham (c. 1285–1349), an English Franciscan who was one of the most eminent theologians of his age, rejected any confident synthesis of Christian doctrine and Aristotelian philosophy. Ockham believed that universal concepts had no reality in nature but instead existed only as mere representations, names in the mind—a philosophy that came to be called *nominalism*. Perceiving and analyzing such concepts as "man" or "papal infallibility" offered no assurance that the concepts expressed truth. Observation and human reason were limited as the means to understand the universe and to know God. Ockham's insistence that the simplest explanation is the best came to be known as "Ockham's razor." Where human reason left off, God's covenant with his faithful took over.

New Syntheses in Writing and Music

Thirteenth-century writers and musicians, as confident in their powers as any king or scholastic, presented complicated ideas and feelings as harmonious and unified syntheses. Writers explored the relations between this world and the next; musicians found ways to bridge sacred and secular forms of music.

Dante Alighieri (1265–1321), perhaps the greatest medieval vernacular poet, harmonized the scholastic universe with the mysteries of faith and the poetry of love. Born in Florence in a time of political turmoil, Dante incorporated the heroes and villains of his day into his most famous poem, the *Commedia,* written between 1313 and 1321. Later known as the *Divine Comedy,* Dante's poem describes the poet taking an imaginary journey from Hell to Purgatory and finally to Paradise.

The poem is an allegory in which every person and object must be read at more than one level. At the most literal level, the poem is about Dante's travels. At a deeper level, it is about the soul's search for meaning and enlightenment and its ultimate discovery of God in the light of divine love. Just as Thomas Aquinas thought that Aristotle's logic could lead to important truths, so Dante used the pagan poet Virgil as his guide through Hell and Purgatory. And just as Thomas believed that faith went beyond reason to even higher truths, so Dante found a new guide representing earthly love to lead him through most of Paradise. This guide was Beatrice, a Florentine girl with whom Dante had fallen in love as a boy and whom he never forgot. But only the Virgin Mary, representing faith and divine love, could bring Dante to the culmination of his journey—a blinding and inexpressibly awesome vision of God:

> *What I then saw is more than tongue can say.*
> *Our human speech is dark before the vision.*
> *The ravished memory swoons and falls away.*

■ **The Last Judgment**

Satan sits in the center of hell devouring souls in this mid-thirteenth-century mosaic on the vault of the baptistery at Florence. The horrors of hell are graphically depicted, partly because mosaics allow for greater detail than stone carving and partly because of the vivid and expressive visions of the afterlife that poets like Dante, a Florentine, were promulgating around the time this mosaic was made. (Scala/Art Resource, NY.)

Dante's poem electrified a wide audience. By elevating one dialect of Italian— the language that ordinary Florentines used in their everyday life—to a language of exquisite poetry, Dante was able to communicate the scholastics' harmonious and optimistic vision of the universe in an even more exciting and accessible way. So influential was his work that it is no exaggeration to say that modern Italian is based on Dante's Florentine dialect.◆

Other writers of the period used different methods to express the harmony of heaven and earth. The anonymous author of *Quest of the Holy Grail* (c. 1225), for example, wrote about the adventures of some of the knights of King Arthur's Round Table to convey the doctrine of transubstantiation and the wonder of the vision of God. In *The Romance of the Rose*, begun by one author (Guillaume de Lorris, a poet in the romantic tradition) and finished by another (Jean de Meun, a poet in the scholastic tradition), a lover seeks the rose, his true love. In the long dream that the poem describes, the narrator's search for the rose is thwarted by personifications of love, shame, reason, abstinence, and so on. They present him with arguments for and against love, not incidentally commenting on people of the poets' own day. In the end, sexual love is made part of the divine scheme—and the lover plucks the rose.

Musicians, like poets, developed new forms that bridged sacred and secular subjects in the thirteenth and fourteenth centuries. This connection appears in the most distinctive musical form of the thirteenth century, the *motet* (from the French *mot*,

---

◆ For further excerpts from Dante's writings, see Document 32, Dante Alighieri, "Human and Divine Love."

meaning "word"). The motet is an example of polyphony, music that consists of two or more melodies performed simultaneously. Before about 1215, most polyphony was sacred; purely secular polyphony was not common before the fourteenth century. The motet, a unique merging of the sacred and the secular, evidently originated in Paris, the center of scholastic culture as well.

The typical thirteenth-century motet has three melody lines (or "voices"). The lowest, usually from a liturgical chant melody, has no words and may have been played on an instrument rather than sung. The remaining melodies have different texts, either Latin or French (or one of each), which are sung simultaneously. Latin texts are usually sacred, whereas French ones are secular, dealing with themes such as love and springtime. In one example, the top voice chirps in quick rhythm about a lady's charms ("Fair maiden, lovely and comely; pretty maiden, courteous and pleasing, delicious one"); the middle voice slowly and lugubriously laments the "malady" of love; and the lowest voice sings a liturgical melody. The motet thus weaves the sacred (the chant melody in the lowest voice) and the secular (the French texts in the upper voices) into a sophisticated tapestry of music. Like the scholastic *summae,* the motets were written by and for a clerical elite. Yet they incorporated the music of ordinary people, such as the calls of street vendors and the boisterous songs of students. In turn, they touched the lives of everyone, for polyphony influenced every form of music, from the Mass to popular songs that entertained and diverted laypeople and churchmen alike.

Complementing the motet's complexity was the development of a new notation for rhythm. By the eleventh century, musical notation could indicate pitch but had no way to denote the duration of the notes. Music theorists of the thirteenth century, however, developed increasingly precise methods to indicate rhythm. Franco of Cologne, for example, in his *Art of Measurable Song* (c. 1280), used different shapes to mark the number of beats each note should be held. His system became the basis of modern musical notation. Because each note could now be allotted a specific duration, written music could express new and complicated rhythms. The music of the thirteenth century reflected both the melding of the secular and the sacred and the possibilities of greater order and control.

The Order of High Gothic

Just as polyphonic music united the sacred with the secular, so Gothic architecture, sculpture, and painting expressed the order and harmony of the universe. The term *Gothic* refers to much of the art and architecture of the twelfth to fifteenth centuries. Gothic style is characterized by pointed arches, which began as architectural motifs but were soon adopted in every art form. Gothic churches appealed to the senses the way that scholastic argument appealed to human reason: both were designed to lead people to knowledge that touched the divine. Being in a Gothic church was a foretaste of heaven.

Gothic architecture began around 1135, with the project of Abbot Suger, the close associate of King Louis the Fat (see page 367), to remodel portions of the church of St. Denis. Suger's rebuilding of St. Denis was part of the fruitful melding of royal and ecclesiastical interests and ideals in the north of France. At the west end of his church, the point where the faithful entered, Suger decorated the portals with figures of Old Testament kings, queens, and patriarchs, signaling the links between the present king and his illustrious predecessors. Within the church, Suger rebuilt the *chevet,* or choir area, using pointed arches and stained glass to let in light, which Suger believed would transport the worshiper from the "slime of earth" to the "purity of Heaven." Suger thought that the Father of lights, God himself, "illuminated" the minds of the beholders via the light that filtered through the stained-glass windows.

Soon the style that Suger pioneered was taken up across northern France and then, in the 1250s, as French culture gained enormous prestige under Louis IX, all across Europe. Gothic was an urban architecture, reflecting—in its towering heights, jewel-like windows, and bright ornaments—the aspirations, pride, and confidence of rich and powerful merchants, artisans, and bishops. A Gothic church, usually a cathedral (the bishop's principal church), was the focal point of a city.

Building Gothic cathedrals was a community project, enlisting the labor and support of an entire urban center. New cathedrals required a small army of quarrymen, builders, carpenters, and glass cutters. Bishops, papal legates, and clerics planned and helped pay for these grand churches, but townspeople also generously financed them and filled them to attend Mass and visit relics. Guilds raised money to pay for stained-glass windows that depicted and celebrated their own patron saints. In turn, towns made money when pilgrims came to visit relics, and sightseers arrived to marvel at their great churches. At Chartres, near Paris, for example, which had the relic of the Virgin's robe, crowds thronged the streets, the poor buying small lead figures of the Virgin, the rich purchasing wearable replicas of her robe. Churches were centers of commercial activity. In their basements, wine merchants plied their trade, while other vendors sold goods outside.

The technologies that made Gothic churches possible were all known before the twelfth century. But Suger's church showed how they could be used together to achieve a particularly dazzling effect. Gothic techniques included ribbed vaulting, which gave a sense of precision and order; pointed arches, which produced a feeling of soaring height; and flying buttresses, which took the weight of the vault off the walls (Figure 10.1). The buttresses permitted much of the wall to be cut away and the open spaces to be filled with glass.

Unlike Romanesque churches, whose exteriors prepare visitors for what they will see within, Gothic cathedrals surprise. The exterior of a Gothic church has an opaque, bristling, and forbidding look owing to the dark surface of its stained glass and its flying buttresses. The interior, however, is just the opposite. It is all soaring lightness, harmony, and order. Just as a scholastic presented his argument with utter clarity, so the interior of a Gothic church revealed its structure through its skeleton of ribbed

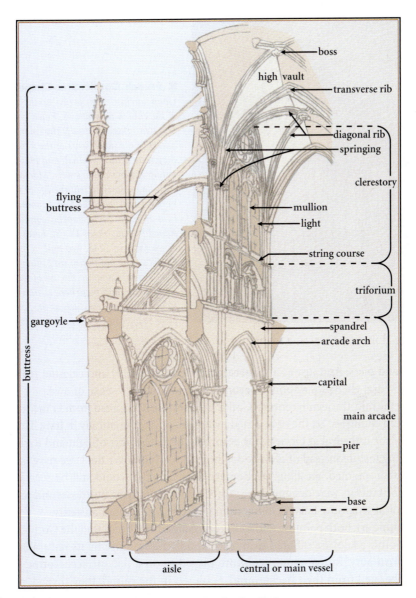

■ **FIGURE 10.1 Elements of a Gothic Cathedral**

Bristling on the outside with stone flying buttresses, Gothic cathedrals were lofty and serene on the inside. The buttresses, which held the weight of the vault, allowed Gothic architects to pierce the walls with windows running the full length of the church. Within, thick piers anchored on sturdy bases became thin columns as they mounted over the triforium and clerestory, blossoming into ribs at the top. Whether plain or ornate, the ribs gave definition and drew attention to the high pointed vault. (Figure adapted from Michael Camille, *Gothic Art: Glorious Visions* [New York: Abrams, 1996].)

■ **French Gothic: Ste.-Chapelle**
Gothic architecture opened up the walls of the church to windows. Filled with "stained" glass—actually the colors were added to the ingredients of the glass before they were heated, melted, and blown—the windows glowed like jewels. Moreover, each had a story to tell: the life of Christ, major events from the Old Testament, the lives of saints. Ste.-Chapelle, commissioned by King Louis IX (St. Louis) and consecrated in 1248, was built to house Christ's crown of thorns and other relics of the Passion. Compare the use of windows, walls, vault, and piers here to that of a Romanesque church such as St.-Savin (see page 381). (Giraudon/Art Resource, NY.)

vaults and piers. And just as a scholastic bridged the earthly and celestial realms, so the cathedral elicited a response beyond reason, evoking a sense of awe.

By the mid-thirteenth century, Gothic architecture had spread from France to other European countries. Yet the style varied by region, most dramatically in Italy. The outer walls of the cathedral at Orvieto, for example, alternate bricks of light and dark color, providing texture instead of glass and light; and the vault over the large nave is round rather than pointed, recalling the Roman aqueducts that could still be seen in Italy when the builders were designing the cathedral. With no flying buttresses and relatively little portal sculpture, Italian Gothic churches convey a spirit of austerity.

Gothic art, both painting and sculpture, echoed and decorated the Gothic cathedral. Gothic sculpture differed from earlier church sculpture by its naturalism and monumentality. Romanesque sculpture played upon a flat surface; Gothic figures were liberated from their background. Sculpted in the round, they turned, moved, and interacted with one another. The positions of the figures, the people they represented, and the ways in which they interacted were meant to be "read" like a scholastic *summa,* for Gothic sculpture often depicted complex stories or scenes. The south portal complex of Chartres cathedral is a good example. Each massive doorway tells a separate story through sculpture: the left depicts the martyrs, the right the confessors, and the center the Last Judgment. Like Dante's *Divine Comedy,* these portals taken together show the soul's pilgrimage from the suffering of this world to eternal life.

Gothic sculpture began in France and was adopted, with many variations, elsewhere in Europe during the thirteenth century. The Italian sculptor Nicola Pisano

■ **German Gothic: Strasbourg**

The Virgin is mourned in this tympanum over the portal of the Strasbourg cathedral's south transept (the arm that crosses the church from north to south). Here, in German Gothic, the emphasis is on emotion and expressivity. Notice the depiction of Mary, with her bedclothes agitated and her body contorted. Why do you suppose that Christ stands in the center of the tympanum, as if he is one of the mourners? What is he holding in the crook of his arm? (Hint: The souls of the dead are often shown as miniature people.) (Bildarchiv Foto Marburg.)

(c. 1220–1278?), for example, was very interested in classical forms. German sculptors, in contrast, created excited, emotional figures that sometimes gestured dramatically to one another.

By the early fourteenth century, the expansive sculptures so prominent in architecture were reflected in painting as well. This new style is evident in the work of Giotto (1266–1337), a Florentine artist who helped change the emphasis of painting, which had been predominantly symbolic, decorative, and intellectual. For example, Giotto filled the walls of a private chapel at Padua with paintings depicting scenes of Christ's life. Here he experimented with the illusion of depth. Giotto's figures, appearing weighty and voluminous, express a range of emotions as they seem to move across interior and exterior spaces. In bringing sculptural realism to a flat surface, Giotto stressed three-dimensionality, illusional space, and human emotion. By melding earthly sensibilities with religious themes, Giotto found yet another way to bring together the natural and divine realms.

Conclusion

In the thirteenth and early fourteenth centuries, western Europeans aggressively expanded outward, from the Baltic to the Strait of Gibraltar. When they sacked Constantinople in 1204, they joined the Muslims as the dominant political forces in the

IMPORTANT DATES

1180–1223	Reign of Philip II ("Philip Augustus") of France	1250s	Gothic becomes a European-wide style
1198–1216	Papacy of Innocent III	1265	English Parliament called by Simon de Montfort includes representatives of the commons
1202–1204	Fourth Crusade; sack of Constantinople		
1209–1229	Albigensian Crusade	1265–1321	Life of Dante Alighieri
1212–1250	Reign of Frederick II	1273	*Summa Theologiae* of Thomas Aquinas
1215	Magna Carta; Fourth Lateran Council	1285–1314	Reign of Philip IV ("the Fair") of France
1216–1272	Reign of Henry III of England	1294–1303	Papacy of Boniface VIII
c. 1225–1274	Life of Thomas Aquinas	1302	Meeting of the estates at Paris; Boniface issues *Unam Sanctam*
1226–1270	Reign of Louis IX ("St. Louis") of France		
1230s	Mongols begin attacks on the West	1309–1378	Avignon papacy ("Babylonian Captivity")
		1313–1321	Dante's *Divine Comedy*

West. They treated the Mongol hegemony in the East as an opportunity for trade and missionary work.

Powerful territorial kings and princes expressed their new self-confidence through bureaucratic institutions. They hired staffs to handle their accounts, record acts, collect taxes, issue writs, and preside over courts. Flourishing cities, a growing money economy, and trade and manufacturing provided the finances necessary to support the personnel now used by medieval governments. The universities became the training grounds for the new administrators as well as for urban preachers.

Both the church and the state became more assertive. The Fourth Lateran Council was an attempt to regulate intimate aspects of the lives of all, even laypeople and non-Christians. The conflict between Boniface and Philip showed how the French king could galvanize his subjects—even his clergy—on behalf of the interests of the state. In England, where John agreed to Magna Carta, it was the barons who helped forge a notion of government that transcended the king.

New power, new piety, and new exclusivity arose in a society both more confident and less tolerant. Crusaders fought against an increasing variety of foes, not only in the Holy Land but in Spain, in southern France, and on Europe's northern frontiers. With heretics voicing criticisms and maintaining their beliefs, the church, led by the papacy, now defined orthodoxy and declared dissenters its enemies. The Jews, who had once been fairly well integrated into the Christian community, were treated ambivalently, alternately used and abused. Balts became targets for new

■ **MAPPING THE WEST** Europe, c. 1340

The empire, now called the Holy Roman Empire, still dominated the map of Europe in 1340, but the emperor himself had little power. Each principality—often each city—was ruled separately and independently. To the east, the Ottoman Turks were beginning to make themselves felt. In the course of the next century, they would disrupt Mongol hegemony and become a great power.

evangelical and armed zeal; the Greeks became the butt of envy, hostility, and finally enmity.

Confident and aggressive, the leaders of Christian Europe in the thirteenth and early fourteenth centuries attempted to impose their rule, legislate morality, and create a unified worldview impregnable to attack. But their drive for order would be countered by political crises and epidemic disease.

Suggested References for further reading and online research appear on page SR-16 at the back of the book.

www.bedfordstmartins.com/huntconcise See the ONLINE STUDY GUIDE to assess your mastery of the material covered in this chapter.

Tandē p̄ stragem lpim maximā luct̄ reiuuia et
pīnas graues ip̄ proceffionalr eunt̄ p̄ romā cum
tnuīla plebe et clero apparet angelus languino
lentū enfe̅ inagna repones̄ sup̄ palacui̅ magr̄

Crisis and Renaissance

1340–1500

I N 1453, THE CANNONS OF OTTOMAN RULER MEHMED II breached the walls of Constantinople. A Byzantine historian mourned "the city deserted, lying lifeless, naked, soundless, without either form or beauty." The pope at Rome preached a crusade against the Turks. There was a clear sense of crisis. Yet a very few years later, Mehmed was writing to the *signore* of Rimini, asking the Italian prince to lend him the Rimini court painter and architect Matteo de Pasti. The Ottoman sultan was planning to build a new palace at Constantinople (modern Istanbul), as a fitting symbol of his imperial dominion, and he had heard of Matteo de Pasti's reputation. When Pasti was unable to help him, Mehmed turned to several Venetian painters instead. The palace came to be called the Topkapi Saray and still stands today looking across the Bosporus, the strait that divides European and Asian Turkey.

Mehmed sums up in one personage the twin themes of the period 1340–1500. His conquest of Constantinople was one of many crises that rocked the West from the Bosporus to the Atlantic: his age saw disease, war, economic contraction, and religious upheaval. At the same time, his tastes and culture aligned him with the Renaissance, a movement that was rediscovering the arts and worldview of classical antiquity. His interest in Italian art reflected the connection between power and culture characteristic of his era. In the fourteenth and fifteenth centuries, much new

■ **The Last Days of the Plague**
This scene from Les Très Riches Heures du Duc de Berry *(the book of hours of the duke of Berry) depicts the burial of Roman victims of the plague. Books of hours were prayer books for individual use. They contained prayers appropriate for the months of the year, days of the week, and hours of the day. This scene reminds Christians of the imminence of death and the importance of leading a pious life: sudden death does not spare even those in the holy city of Rome. The miniature paintings in this book of hours were created for the duke of Berry around 1415 by the Limbourg brothers, three Flemish miniaturists.*
(The Metropolitan Museum of Art, The Cloisters Collection, 1954. [54.1.1] Photograph © 1987 The Metropolitan Museum of Art [detail].)

artistic, architectural, and musical work was created in praise of personal and public lives. Portraits, palaces, and poetry commemorated the glory of the rich and powerful, while a new cultural movement called *humanism* advocated classical learning and argued for the active participation of the individual in civic affairs. Family, honor, social status, and individual distinction—these were the goals that fueled the ambitions of Renaissance men and women.

Their quest for glory duplicated on a smaller scale the enhanced power of the state, shored up by new military technologies—firearms, siege equipment, fortifications, and well-equipped soldiers. Commoners, criminals, and adventurers often joined the ranks of the fighters. To maintain their social eminence, many nobles were forced to take on new roles as officials or officers in the service of the state. By appointing nobles to the royal household, as military commanders and councilors, kings and princes consolidated their power.

Like individuals, these states, too, competed for wealth, glory, and honor. While warfare and diplomacy channeled the restless energy of the Italian states, monarchies and empires outside of Italy also expanded their power through conquests and institutional reforms. The European world changed dramatically as new powers such as the Ottoman Empire and Muscovy rose to prominence in the east, while the Iberian kingdoms of Portugal and Spain expanded European domination to Africa, Asia, and the Americas.

A Multitude of Crises

Beginning in the fourteenth century and extending to the middle of the fifteenth, Europeans confronted crises of both nature and human design. The plague wracked the cities and hurt the countryside. The Hundred Years' War devastated France. To the east, the rise of the Ottomans had a cataclysmic impact on the politics of eastern and central Europe. Everywhere economic contraction made for material hard times, while spiritual well-being seemed threatened by a long papal schism. Minorities—religious dissenters, heretics, Jews, and Muslims in Spain—suffered the effects of pent-up anxieties.

The Black Death and Its Consequences

Bad weather and overpopulation contributed to a series of famines at the beginning of the fourteenth century. Having cleared forests and drained swamps, peasants divided their plots into ever smaller parcels and farmed marginal land; their income and the quality of their diet eroded. In the great urban centers, where thousands depended on steady employment and cheap bread, a bad harvest, always followed by sharply rising food prices, meant hunger and eventual famine. A cooling of the European climate also contributed to the crisis in the food supply. Modern studies of tree rings indicate that fourteenth-century Europe entered a colder period, with a succession of severe winters beginning in 1315 and extending to 1317. Crop failures were widespread. In many cities of northwestern Europe, the price of bread tripled in a month, and thousands starved to death. Some Flemish cities, for example, lost 10 percent of their population. Many who survived were badly weakened, prime quarry for disease.

In midcentury, the bubonic plague passed from its breeding ground in central Asia eastward into China, where it decimated the population and wiped out the remnants of the tiny Italian merchant community in Yangzhou. Bacteria-carrying fleas living on black rats transmitted the disease. They traveled back to Europe alongside valuable cargoes of silk, porcelain, and spices. In 1347, the Genoese colony in Caffa in the Crimea contracted the plague. Fleeing by ship in a desperate but futile attempt to escape the disease, the Genoese in turn communicated the plague to other Mediterranean seaports. By January 1348, the plague had infected Sicily, Sardinia, Corsica, and Marseille. Six months later, it had spread to Aragon, all of Italy, the Balkans, and most of France. The disease then crept northward to Germany, England, and Scandinavia, reaching the Russian city of Novgorod in 1351 (Map 11.1).

Nothing like the Black Death, as this epidemic came to be called, had struck Europe since the great plague of the sixth century. The Italian writer Giovanni Boccaccio (1313–1375) reported that the plague

> *first betrayed itself by the emergence of certain tumors in the groin or the armpits, some of which grew as large as a common apple, others as an egg.... From the two said parts of the body this . . . began to propagate and spread itself in all directions indifferently; after which the form of the malady began to change, black spots or livid making their appearance in many cases on the arm or the thigh or elsewhere, now few and large, now minute and numerous.*◆

Inhabitants of cities, where crowding and filth increased the chances of contagion, died in massive numbers. Florence lost almost two-thirds of its population of ninety thousand; Siena, like most cities visited by the plague, lost half its people. Rural areas suffered fewer deaths, but regional differences were pronounced. (See "Taking Measure," page 433.) Nor was the toll over after 1350. Further outbreaks of the plague occurred in Europe in 1361, 1368–1369, 1371, 1375, 1390, and 1405; they continued, with longer dormant intervals, into the eighteenth century.

Although the Black Death took a horrible human toll, the disaster actually profited some people. In an overpopulated society with limited resources, massive death opened the ranks for advancement. For example, after 1350, landlords had difficulty acquiring new tenant farmers without making concessions in land contracts,

---

◆ For further contemporary accounts of the plague, see Document 33, "The Black Death."

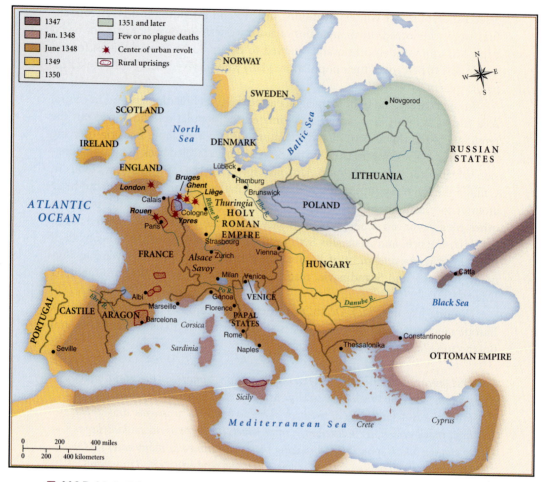

■ MAP 11.1 Advance of the Plague

The gradual but deadly spread of the plague followed the roads and rivers of Europe. Note the earlier transmission by sea from the Crimea to the ports of the Mediterranean before the general spread to northern Europe.

www.bedfordstmartins.com/huntconcise   See the ONLINE STUDY GUIDE for more help in analyzing this map.

fewer priests competed for the same number of benefices (ecclesiastical offices funded by an endowment), and workers received much higher wages because the supply of laborers had plummeted. The Black Death and the resulting decline in urban population meant a lower demand for grain relative to the supply and thus a drop in cereal prices.

All across Europe noble landlords, whose revenues fell as prices dropped, had to adjust to these new circumstances. Some revived seigneurial demands for labor

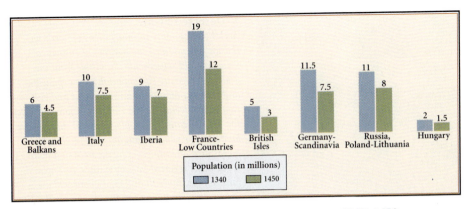

■ **TAKING MEASURE** Population Losses and the Plague, 1340–1450

The bar chart represents dramatically the impact of the Black Death and the recurrent plagues between 1340 and 1450. More than a century after the Black Death, none of the regions of Europe had made up for the losses of population. The population of 1450 stood at between 75 and 80 percent of the pre-plague population. The hardest-hit areas were France and the Low Countries, which also suffered from the devastations of the Hundred Years' War.

(From Carlo M. Cipolla, ed., *Fontana Economic History of Europe: The Middle Ages* [Great Britain: Collins/Fontana Books, 1974], 36.)

services. Others looked to their central government for legislation to regulate wages. Still others granted favorable terms to peasant proprietors, often after bloody peasant revolts. Many noblemen lost a portion of their wealth and a measure of their autonomy and political influence. Consequently, European nobles became more dependent on their monarchs and on war to supplement their incomes and enhance their power.

For the peasantry and the urban working population, higher wages generally meant an improvement in living standards. To compensate for the lower demand and price for grain, many peasants and landlords turned to stock breeding and grape and barley cultivation. As European agriculture diversified, peasants and artisans consumed more beer, wine, meat, cheese, and vegetables, a better and more varied diet than their thirteenth-century forebears had eaten.

Because of the shrinking population and decreased demand for food, cultivating marginal fields was no longer profitable, and many settlements were simply abandoned. By 1450, for example, some 450 large English villages and many small hamlets had disappeared. In central Europe east of the Elbe River, where German peasants had migrated, large tracts of cultivated land reverted to forest. Estimates suggest that some 80 percent of all villages in parts of Thuringia (Germany) vanished.

In the cities, production shifted from manufacturing for a mass market to a highly lucrative, though small, luxury market. The drastic loss in urban population had reduced the demand for such mass-manufactured goods as cloth. Fewer people

■ **Deserted Fields**

Aerial photography in many areas of northern Europe has revealed the outlines of cultivated fields and old settlements not visible from the ground. These are signs marking the expansion and contraction of human settlement and cultivation in fourteenth-century Europe before and after the Black Death. As the plague swept through the land, and as whole populations of small settlements died off, villages were deserted and cultivated fields reverted back to nature. In England, for example, more than 225 of about 900 medieval churches were abandoned, and nearly 250 were in ruins in the second half of the fourteenth century. This photograph shows the former cultivated fields of the village of Tusmore, Oxfordshire, whose inhabitants all died of the plague.

(Copyright reserved Cambridge University, Collection of Air Photographs.)

now possessed proportionately greater concentrations of wealth. In the southern French city of Albi, for example, the proportion of citizens possessing more than 100 livres in per capita income doubled between 1343 and 1357, while the number of poor people, those with less than 10 livres, declined by half.

Faced with the possibility of imminent and untimely death, some of the urban populace sought immediate gratification. The Florentine Matteo Villani described the newfound desire for luxury in his native city in 1351. "The common people . . . wanted the dearest and most delicate foods . . . while children and common women clad themselves in all the fair and costly garments of the illustrious who had died." Those with means increased their consumption of luxuries such as silk clothing, hats, doublets (snug-fitting men's jackets), and expensive jewelry. Whereas agricultural prices continued to decline, the prices of manufactured goods, particularly luxury items, remained constant and even rose as demand for them outstripped supply. The middle class sought new material comforts, such as fireplaces and private latrines, beds, chests, and curtains. Members of the new peasant elite must have lived in simpler style, but perhaps they no longer shared their house with animals, as they had in the thirteenth century.

The long-term consequences of this new consumption pattern spelled the end for the traditional woolen industry that had produced for a mass market. Diminishing demand for wool caused hardships for woolworkers, and social and political unrest shook many older industrial centers dependent on the cloth industry, such as Flanders. At Ypres, for example, production figures fell from a high of ninety thousand pieces of cloth in 1320 to fewer than twenty-five thousand by 1390. In Ghent, where 44 percent of all households were woolworkers and where some 60 percent of the working population depended on the textile industry, the woolen market's slump meant constant labor unrest.

The new labor market tended to undermine women's economic position. In the German city of Cologne, for example, more and more artisan guilds excluded women from their ranks. Everywhere, fathers favored sons and sons-in-law to succeed them in their crafts. Daughters and widows resisted this patriarchal regime in the urban economy, but they were most successful in industries with the least regulations, such as beer-brewing.

The Hundred Years' War, 1337–1453

In France, the misery wrought by the plague was compounded by the devastation of war. Conflicting French and English interests in southwestern France sparked the Hundred Years' War. As part of the French royal policy of centralizing jurisdiction, Philip VI in 1337 confiscated the southwestern province of Aquitaine, which had been held by the English monarchs as a fief of the French crown. To recover his lands, Edward III of England in turn laid claim to the French throne. Some of his soldiers were nobles and knights, who brought with them the expectations of chivalry. But many were yeomen (free farmers) eager for booty, hostages, and amorous conquests. Mercenary companies came to replace levies of freemen archers in the English army, remaining to wreak havoc on the French countryside when not employed in war.

Ruling over a more populous realm and commanding far larger armies than the English, the French kings were, nevertheless, hindered in the war by the independent actions of their powerful barons. Against the accurate and deadly English freemen archers, the French knights met repeated defeats. Yet the French nobility despised their own peasants, perhaps fearing them and the urban middle classes more than they feared their noble English adversaries.

The war may be divided into three periods: the first was marked by English triumphs, the second saw France slowly gaining the upper hand, and the third ended in the English expulsion from France (Map 11.2). The final, most important phase saw two key developments: the rise of Burgundy, a hodgepodge of territories held together only by the political machinations of its dukes; and the rise of France as a distinct nation. This phase began when the English king Henry V (r. 1413–1422) launched a full-scale invasion of France and crushed the French at Agincourt (1415). Three parties then struggled for domination in France. Henry occupied Normandy and claimed the French throne; the dauphin (heir apparent to the French throne), Charles VII of France (r. 1422–1461),* ruled central France; and the duke of

---

*Although the dauphin was not crowned until 1429, he assumed the title Charles VII in 1422, after the death of his father.

1337 (before the Battle of Crécy)
- English holdings
- French holdings

1360 (after the Battle of Poitiers)
- English holdings
- French holdings
- ✴ Battle

c.1429 (after the Siege of Orléans)
- English holdings
- French holdings
- Burgundian lands allied with England to 1435
- ✴ Battle
- → Route taken by Joan of Arc, 1429–31

1453 (end of war)
- English holdings
- French holdings
- Burgundian lands reconciled with France after 1435

■ **MAP 11.2 The Hundred Years' War, 1337–1453**

As rulers of Aquitaine and claimants to the throne of France, English kings contested the French monarchy for domination of France. Squeezed between England and Burgundy, the holdings of the French kings were vastly reduced after the battle of Poitiers in 1356.

■ **The Spoils of War**
This illustration from Jean Froissart's Chronicles *depicts soldiers pillaging a conquered city. During the Hundred Years' War, looting became the main source of income for mercenary troops and contributed to the general misery of late-medieval society. Food, furniture, even everyday household items were taken.* (Bibliothèque Nationale de France.)

Burgundy held a vast territory in the northeast that included the Low Countries. Burgundy was thus able to broker war or peace by shifting support first to the English and then to the French. But even with Burgundian support, the English could not establish firm control. In Normandy, a savage guerrilla war harassed the English army. Driven from their villages by pillaging and murdering soldiers, Norman peasants retreated into forests, formed armed bands, and attacked the English. The miseries of war inspired prophecies of miraculous salvation; among the predictions was that a virgin would deliver France from the English invaders.

At the court of the dauphin, in 1429, a sixteen-year-old peasant girl presented herself and her vision to save France. Born in a village in Lorraine, Joan of Arc, La Pucelle ("the Maid"), as she always referred to herself, grew up in a war-ravaged country that longed for divine deliverance. She had first presented herself as God's messenger to the local noble, who was sufficiently impressed to equip Joan with horse, armor, and a retinue to send her to the dauphin's court. Joan of Arc's extraordinary appearance inspired the beleaguered French to trust in divine providence. In 1429, she accompanied the French army that laid a prolonged but successful siege on Orléans, was wounded, and showed great courage in battle. Upon her urging, the dauphin traveled deep into hostile Burgundian territory to be anointed King Charles VII of France at Reims cathedral, thus strengthening his legitimacy by following the traditional ritual of coronation.

Although Joan's fortunes declined after Reims and she was burned as a heretic by the English in 1431, she had helped undermine the English position, which slowly crumbled thereafter. The duke of Burgundy recognized Charles VII as king of France, and Charles entered Paris in 1437. Skirmish by skirmish, the English were driven from French soil.

The Hundred Years' War profoundly altered the economic and political landscape of western Europe. It aggravated the demographic and economic crises of the fourteenth century by further ravaging the countryside. Constant insecurity caused by marauding bands of soldiers prevented the cultivation of fields even in times of truce. City and countryside united in 1358, unhappy with the heavy war taxes and the incompetence of the warrior nobility. The movement, called the Jacquerie, began when the townspeople of Paris, led by Étienne Marcel, the provost of the merchants there, sought to take over control of the city. His rebellion was put down and Marcel was killed, but meanwhile rebels in the countryside began their own revolt, de-

■ **Joan the Warrior**

Joan of Arc's career as a military leader was an extraordinary occurrence in fifteenth-century France. In this manuscript illumination, the charismatic Joan, in full armor, directs French soldiers as they besiege the English at Orléans. The victory she gained there amazed and emboldened the French people.

(Erich Lessing/Art Resource, NY.)

stroying manor houses and castles near Paris and massacring entire noble families in a savage class war. The chronicler Jean Froissart, sympathetic to the nobility, reflected the views of the ruling class in describing the rebels as "small, dark, and very poorly armed." Repression by nobles was swift, as thousands of rebels died in battles or were executed.◆

In England, the war brought discontent to the rural and urban classes as well. The trigger for outright rebellion by the peasantry was the imposition of a poll tax passed by Parliament in 1377 to raise money for the war against France, a war that peasants believed benefited only the king and the nobility. Unlike traditional subsidies to the king, the poll tax was levied on everyone. In May 1381, a revolt broke out to protest the taxes. Rebels in Essex and Kent joined bands in London to confront the king. The famous couplet of the radical preacher John Ball, who was executed after the revolt, expresses the rebels' egalitarian, anti-noble sentiment:

> *When Adam delved [dug] and Eve span [spun]*
> *Who was then the gentleman?*

Forced to address the rebels, young King Richard II (r. 1377–1399) agreed to abolish serfdom and impose a ceiling on land rent, but he immediately rescinded these concessions after the rebels' defeat.

Richard was not the only monarch to pay little attention to the pains of the war. In France, the ruler benefited from it: under Charles VII, a standing army was established to supplement the feudal noble levies, an army financed by increased taxation and expanded royal judicial claims. Steadily increasing in power and pretensions, in the 1470s the French monarchy dismantled and absorbed Burgundy, and in the 1490s it entered Italy with conquest in mind. By 1500, it was clear that the French monarchy was one of the leading powers of Europe.

Defeated in war, the English monarchy suffered more. From the 1460s to 1485, England was torn by civil war—the War of the Roses between the red rose of Lancaster and the rival white rose of York. A deposed king (Henry VI), a short reign (Edward IV), and the murder of two princes by their uncle (Richard III) followed in quick succession in a series of conflicts that decimated the leading noble families of England. When Henry Tudor succeeded to the throne as Henry VII in 1485, England was tired of civil war. Henry ended the fighting and united the houses of Lancaster and York. By the early sixteenth century, the English monarchy was poised to take advantage of the general prosperity and war-weariness to enhance its position and power.

◆ For a primary source that offers a view of France's ruling class different from Froissart's, see Document 34, Christine de Pisan, "Lament on the Evils of Civil War."

Ottoman Conquest and New Political Configurations in the East

The rise of the Ottoman Turks was the most astonishing fact of the late thirteenth century, when the Islamic Ottomans began a holy war against Byzantium. Under Osman I (r. 1280–1324), who gave the dynasty its name, and his son, the Ottomans became a formidable force in Anatolia and the Balkans, where political disunity opened the door for their advances (Map 11.3). By the end of the fourteenth century, they had reduced the Byzantine Empire to the city of Constantinople, Thessalonika, and a narrow strip of land in modern-day Greece.

Although the empire's fortunes were declining, Byzantium experienced a religious and cultural ferment as the elites compensated for their loss of power in a search for past glory. The majority asserted the superiority of the Greek Orthodox faith and opposed the reunion of the Roman and Greek churches, the political price for western European military aid. Many adhered to tradition, attacking any departures from ancient literary models and Byzantine institutions. A handful, such as the scholar George Gemistos (1353–1452), abandoned Christianity and embraced Platonic philosophy. The scholar Manuel Chrysoloras became professor of Greek in Florence in 1397, thus establishing the study of ancient Greece in western Europe, an important aspect of Renaissance culture.

Meanwhile, the Ottomans continued to expand. In 1364, they defeated a joint Hungarian-Serbian army at the Maritsa River, alerting Europe for the first time to the threat of an Islamic invasion. Pope Urban V called vainly for a crusade. In the Balkans, the Ottomans skillfully exploited Christian disunity, playing local interests against one another. An Ottoman army allied with the Bulgarians and some Serbian princes won the battle of Kosovo (1389), destroying the last organized Christian

■ **MAP 11.3 Ottoman Expansion in the Fourteenth and Fifteenth Centuries**
The Balkans were the major theater of expansion for the Ottoman Empire, whose conquests also included Egypt and the North African coast. The Byzantine Empire was long reduced to the city of Constantinople and surrounded by the Ottomans before its final fall in 1453.

resistance south of the Danube. The Ottomans secured control of southeastern Europe after 1396, when at Nicopolis they crushed a crusading army summoned by Pope Boniface IX.

When Mehmed II (r. 1451–1481) ascended the throne, he proclaimed a holy war and laid siege to Constantinople in 1453. A city of 100,000, the Byzantine capital could muster only 6,000 defenders (including a small contingent of Genoese) against an Ottoman force estimated at between 200,000 and 400,000 men. The city's fortifications, many of which dated from Emperor Justinian's rule in the sixth century, were no match for fifteenth-century cannons. The defenders held out for fifty-three days. While the Christians confessed their sins and prayed for divine deliverance, in desperate anticipation of the Second Coming, the Muslim besiegers pressed forward, urged on by the certainty of rich spoils and Allah's promise of a final victory over the infidel Rome. Finally the defenders were overwhelmed, and the last Byzantine emperor, Constantine Palaeologus, died in battle. Some 60,000 residents were carried off in slavery, and the city was sacked. Mehmed entered Constantinople in triumph, rendered thanks to Allah in Justinian's Church of St. Sophia, which had been turned into a mosque, and was remembered as "the Conqueror."

At the same time, however, as we have seen, the Muslim ruler was ready to ask Italian court painter Matteo de Pasti to help create his Topkapi palace, intended to communicate Ottoman power. The Ottoman conquest was more than a continuation of the struggle between Christendom and Islam. The battle for territory transcended the boundaries of faith. Christian princes also served the Ottoman Empire as vassals to the sultan. The Janissaries, Christian slave children raised by the sultan as Muslims, constituted the fundamental backbone of the Ottoman army. They formed a service class, the *devshirme*, which was both dependent on and loyal to the ruler. At the sultan's court, Christian women were prominent in the harem; thus many Ottoman princes had Greek or Serbian mothers. In addition to the Janissaries, Christian princes and converts to Islam served in the emerging Ottoman administration. In areas conquered, existing religious and social structures remained intact when local people accepted Ottoman overlordship and paid taxes. Only in areas of persistent resistance did the Ottomans drive out or massacre the inhabitants, settling Turkish tribes in their place. A distinctive pattern of Balkan history was thus established at the beginning of the Ottoman conquest: the extremely diverse ethnic and religious communities were woven together into the fabric of an efficient central state.

The rise of strong, new monarchies—represented by France, England, and the Ottoman sultanate—contrasted sharply with the weakness of state authority in central and eastern Europe, where Hungary, Bohemia, and Poland were held together, like Burgundy, by personal dynastic authority alone (Map 11.4). Under Matthias Corvinus (r. 1456–1490), the Hungarian king who briefly united the Bohemian and Hungarian crowns, a central-eastern European empire seemed to be emerging. A patron of the arts and a humanist, Matthias created a great library in Hungary. He repeatedly defeated the encroaching Austrian Habsburgs and even occupied Vienna in 1485. However, his empire did not outlast his death in 1490. The powerful Hungarian magnates, who enjoyed the constitutional right to elect the king, ended it by refusing to acknowledge his son's claim to the throne.

In the mid-fourteenth century, two large monarchies—Poland and Lithuania— began to take shape in northeastern Europe. King Casimir III (r. 1333–1370) won recognition in most of Poland's regions. A problem that persisted throughout his reign, however, was conflict with the neighboring princes of Lithuania, Europe's last pagan rulers, who for centuries had fiercely resisted the Christianization demanded by the Teutonic Knights. After the Mongols conquered Russia, Lithuania extended its rule southward, offering western Russian princes protection against Mongol and Muscovite rule. By the late fourteenth century, a vast Lithuanian principality had arisen, embracing modern Lithuania, Belarus, and Ukraine.

Casimir III died in 1370 without a son; the failure of a new dynasty to take hold opened the way for the unification of Poland and Lithuania. In 1386, the Lithuanian prince Jogaila (Jagiellon) accepted Roman Catholicism, married the young queen of Poland, and assumed the Polish crown as Wladyslaw II. Under the Jagiellonian dynasty, Poland and Lithuania kept separate legal systems. Catholicism and Polish culture prevailed among the principality's upper class, while most native Lithuanian village folk remained pagan for several centuries. With only a few interruptions, the Polish-Lithuanian federation would last for five centuries.

North of the Black Sea and east of Poland-Lithuania, a different polity was taking shape. In the second half of the fifteenth century, the

■ MAP 11.4 Eastern Europe in the Fifteenth Century

The rise of Muscovy and the Ottomans shaped the map of eastern Europe. Some Christian monarchies, such as Serbia, lost their independence. Others, such as Hungary, held off the Ottomans until the early sixteenth century.

princes of Muscovy embarked on a spectacular path of success that would make their state the largest on earth. Subservient to the Mongols in the fourteenth century, the Muscovite princes began to assert their independence with the collapse of Mongol power. Ivan III (r. 1462–1505) was the first Muscovite prince to claim an imperial title, referring to himself as *tsar* (or *czar,* from the name *Caesar*). Expanding his power to Novgorod in 1471, Ivan then moved to the south and east, pushing back the Mongols to the Volga River. Unlike monarchies in western and central-eastern Europe, whose powers were bound by collective rights and laws, Ivan's Russian monarchy claimed absolute property rights over all lands and subjects.

The expansionist Muscovite state was shaped by two traditions: religion and service. After the fall of the Byzantine Empire, the tsar was the Russian Orthodox church's only defender of the faith against Islam and Catholicism. Orthodox propaganda thus legitimized the tsar's rule by proclaiming Moscow the "Third Rome" (the first two being Rome and Constantinople) and praising the tsar's autocratic power as essential to protect the faith. The Mongol system of service to rulers also deeply informed Muscovite statecraft. Ivan III and his descendants considered themselves heirs to the empire of the Mongols. In their conception of the state as private dominion, their emphasis on autocratic power, and their division of the populace into a landholding elite in service to the tsar and a vast majority of taxpaying subjects, the Muscovite princes created a state more in the despotic political tradition of the central Asian steppes and the Ottoman Empire than of western Europe.

Economic Contraction

The wars of the fourteenth and fifteenth centuries brought hard times to many members of the commercial classes. During the Hundred Years' War, the English king Edward III borrowed heavily from the largest Italian banking houses, the Bardi and Peruzzi of Florence. With many of their assets tied up in loans to the English monarchy, the Italian bankers had no choice but to extend new credits, hoping vainly to recover their initial investments. In the early 1340s, however, Edward defaulted, and the once-illustrious houses went bankrupt. Meanwhile, diminished production and trade eventually caused turmoil in northern Europe and a crisis for financiers in the Low Countries. Bruges, the financial center for northwestern Europe, saw its power fade during the fifteenth century when a succession of its money changers went bankrupt.

This breakdown in the most advanced economic sector reflected the general recession in the European economy. Merchants were less likely to take risks and more willing to invest their money in government bonds than in production and commerce. Fewer merchants traveled to Asia, partly because of the danger of attack by Ottoman Turks on the overland routes that had once been protected by the Mongols. Italians, while still exporting luxuries north and obtaining raw materials and silver in return, now tended to invest in the arts rather than in trade and industry. The Medici, who dominated Florence in the fifteenth century, are good examples. They stayed close to home, investing part of their banking profits in art and politics and relying on business agents to conduct their affairs in other European cities.

At the lower end of the economic ladder, this war-torn society rested on a broad base of underclass—poor peasants and laborers in the countryside, workers and servants in the cities. Lower still were the marginal elements of society, straddling the line between legality and criminality. Organized gangs prowled the larger cities, their members mostly artisans vacillating between work and crime. Paris, for example, teemed with thieves, thugs, beggars, prostitutes, and vagabonds. Some disguised themselves as clerics to escape the law, and others were bona fide clerics who turned to crime to make ends meet during an age of steadily declining clerical income. "Decent society" treated these marginal elements with suspicion and hatred.

Often the underclass served as soldiers as well. War was no longer mainly for knights; it absorbed young men from poor backgrounds. Initiated into a life of plunder and killing, soldiers adjusted poorly to civilian life after discharge; between wars, these men turned to crime, adding to the misery.

Women featured prominently in the underclass, reflecting the unequal distribution of power between the sexes. Urban domestic service was the major employment for girls from the countryside, who worked to save money for their dowries. In addition to the usual household chores, women also worked as wet nurses. Some women, unable to find other means of support, became prostitutes. In Mediterranean Europe, some 90 percent of slaves were women in domestic servitude. They came from Muslim or Greek Orthodox countries and usually served in upper-class households in the great commercial city republics of Venice, Florence, and Ragusa. Their actual numbers were small—several hundred in fourteenth-century Florence, for example—because only rich households could afford slaves.

The Crisis of the Papacy

By the second half of the fourteenth century, the Avignon papacy had taken on a definitive French character. All five popes elected between 1305 and 1378 were natives of southern France. Subjected to pressure from the French monarchy and turning increasingly secular in its opulence and splendor, the papacy was lambasted by the Italian poet Francesco Petrarch as being "in Babylonian Captivity," like the Jews of ancient Israel who were exiled by their Babylonian conquerors.

The popes did not see themselves as captives. Lawyers by training, they concentrated on consolidating the financial and legal powers of the church, mainly through appointments and taxes. Claiming the right to assign all benefices (the properties or income that supported clerical positions), the popes gradually secured authority over the clergy throughout western and central Europe. Under the skillful guidance of John XXII (r. 1316–1334), papal rights increased incrementally without causing much protest. By 1350, the popes had secured the right to grant all major benefices and many minor ones. To gain these lucrative positions, potential candidates often made gifts to the papal court. The imposition of papal taxes on all benefice holders originated in taxes to finance the crusades. Out of these precedents, the papacy instituted a regular system of papal taxation that produced the money it needed to consolidate papal government.

That government—the curia—consisted of the pope's personal household, the College of Cardinals, and the church's financial and judicial apparatuses. Combining elements of monarchy and oligarchy, the curia developed a bureaucracy that paralleled the organization of secular government. The pope's relatives often played a major role in his household; many popes came from extended noble lineages, and they often gave their family members preferential treatment.

After the pope, the cardinals as a collective body were the most elevated entity in the church. Like great nobles in royal courts, the cardinals, many of them nobles themselves, advised and aided the pope. They maintained their own households, employing scores of scribes, servants, and retainers. The papal army also expanded at the same time, as the popes sought to restore and control the Papal States in Italy.

This growing papal monarchy was sharply criticized by members of the Franciscan and Dominican orders, who denounced the papal pretension to worldly power and wealth. The scholastic William of Ockham, for example, believed that church power derived from the congregation of the faithful, both laity and clergy, not from the pope or church councils. Imprisoned by Pope John XXII for heresy, Ockham escaped in 1328 and found refuge with Emperor Louis of Bavaria.

Another antipapal refugee at the imperial court was Marsilius of Padua, a citizen of an Italian commune, a physician and lawyer by training, and rector of the University of Paris. Marsilius attacked the very basis of papal power in *The Defender of the Peace* (1324). The true church, Marsilius argued, was constituted by the people, who had the right to select the head of the church, either through the body of the faithful or through a "human legislator." Papal power, Marsilius asserted, was the result of historical usurpation, and its exercise represented tyranny. In 1327, John XXII, the living target of the treatise, decreed the work heretical.

Successes in Italy emboldened Gregory XI, elected pope in 1371, to return to Rome. When he died in 1378, sixteen cardinals—one Spanish, four Italian, and eleven French—met in Rome to elect the new pope. Although many in the curia were homesick for Avignon, the Roman people, determined to keep the papacy and its revenues in Rome, clamored for the election of a Roman. An unruly crowd rioted outside the conclave, drowning out the cardinals' discussions. Fearing for their lives, the cardinals elected the archbishop of Bari, an Italian, who took the title Urban VI. If the cardinals thought they had elected a weak man who would do their bidding and satisfy the Romans, they were wrong: Urban immediately tried to curb the cardinals' power. In response, thirteen cardinals elected another pope, Clement VII, and returned to Avignon.

Thus began the "Great Schism," which was perpetuated by political divisions in Europe (Map 11.5). Charles V of France, who did not want the papacy to return to Rome, immediately recognized Clement, his cousin, as did the rulers of Sicily, Scotland, Castile, Aragon, Navarre, Portugal, Ireland, and Savoy. An enemy of Charles V, Richard II of England, professed allegiance to Urban and was followed by the rulers of Flanders, Poland, Hungary, most of the Holy Roman Empire, and central and northern Italy. Faithful Christians were equally divided in their loyalties. Even the greatest mystic of the age—Catherine of Siena (1347–1380), who told of her mystical unions with God and spiritual ecstasies in more than 350 letters and was later can-

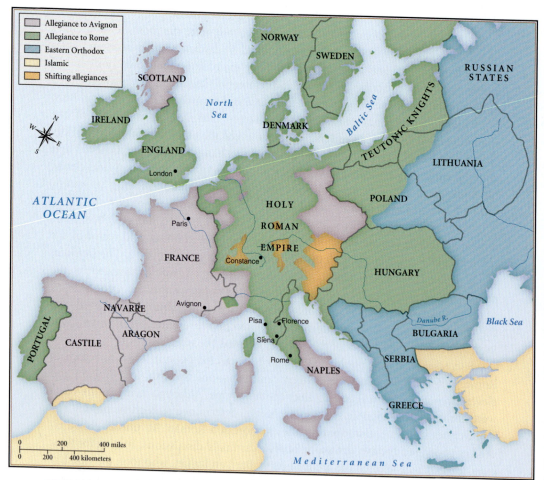

■ MAP 11.5 The Great Schism, 1378–1417

Allegiance to Roman and Avignon popes followed the political divisions among the European monarchs. The Great Schism weakened the Latin West during a period of Islamic expansion through the Ottoman Empire.

onized a saint—found herself forced to take sides. Catherine supported Urban. But another holy man, Vincent Ferrer (1350–1419), a popular Dominican preacher, supported Clement. All Christians theoretically found themselves deprived of the means of salvation, as bans from Rome and Avignon each placed part of Christian Europe under interdict, which deprived them of most sacraments and Christian burial.

Because neither pope would step down willingly, the leading intellectuals in the church tried to end the schism another way. Many of them became "conciliarists." According to canon law, only a pope could summon a general council of the church—a sort of parliament of all Christians. But given the state of confusion in Christendom, many intellectuals argued that the crisis justified calling a general council to represent the body of the faithful, over and against the head of the church. Jean Gerson, chancellor of the University of Paris, asserted that "the pope can be removed by a general council celebrated without his consent and against his will." He justified his claim by reasoning that "normally a council is not legally . . . celebrated without papal calling. . . . But, as in grammar and in morals, general rules have exceptions. . . . Because of these exceptions a superior law has been ordained to interpret the law."

The first attempt to resolve the question of church authority came in 1409, at the Council of Pisa, attended by cardinals who had defected from the two popes. The council asserted its supremacy by declaring both popes deposed and electing a new pontiff, Alexander V. When the popes at Rome and Avignon refused to yield to the authority of the council, Christian Europe found itself in the embarrassing position of choosing among three popes. Pressure to hold another council then came from central Europe, where a new heretical movement, ultimately known as Hussitism, undermined orthodoxy from Bohemia to central Germany. Threatened politically by challenges to church authority, Emperor Sigismund pressed Pope John XXIII, the successor to Alexander (who had died ten months after being elected), to convene a church council at Constance in 1414.

The cardinals, bishops, and theologians assembled in Constance felt compelled to combat heresy, heal the schism, and reform the church. They ordered Jan Hus, the Prague professor and inspiration behind the Hussite movement, burned at the stake in spite of an imperial safe conduct he had been promised, but this act failed to suppress dissent. They deposed John XXIII, the "Pisan pope," because of tyrannical behavior, condemning him as an antipope. The Roman pope, Gregory XII, accepted the council's authority and resigned in 1415 (having been elected in 1406). At its closing in 1417, the council also deposed Benedict XIII (Clement's successor), the "Spanish mule," who refused to abdicate the Avignon papacy and lived out his life in a fortress in Spain, still regarding himself as pope and surrounded by his own curia. The rest of Christendom, however, hailed Martin V, the council's appointment, as the new pope, thus ending the Great Schism. The council had taken a stand against heresy and had achieved unity under one pope. But the papacy's prestige had suffered a lasting blow.

Stamping Out Dissenters, Heretics, Jews, and Muslims

The stand against Hus was part of a wider movement. Everywhere church and state moved to stamp out groups that, in their view, did not fit within the established church. The church condemned the Free Spirits, for example. These groups, often associated with the Beguines (see page 415), were found mostly in northern Europe. They practiced an extreme form of mysticism, asserting that humans and God were of the same essence and that individual believers could attain salvation, even sanctity, without the church and its sacraments. In the 1360s, Emperor Charles IV and Pope Urban V extended the Inquisition to Germany in a move to crush this heresy. In the cities of the Rhineland, fifteen mass trials took place, most around the turn of the fifteenth century. By condemning the "heretics" and requiring beguinages to be under the control of the mendicant orders, the church contained potential dissent.

In England, intellectual dissent, social unrest, and nationalist sentiment combined to create a powerful anticlerical movement that the church hierarchy labeled Lollardy (from *lollar*, meaning "idler"). John Wycliffe (c. 1330–1384), who inspired the movement, was an Oxford professor who challenged the very foundations of the Roman church. His treatise *On the Church*, composed in 1378, advanced the view that the true church was a community of believers rather than a clerical hierarchy. In other writings, Wycliffe repudiated monasticism, excommunication, the Mass, and the priesthood, substituting reliance on Bible reading and individual conscience in place of the official church as the path to salvation. Responsibility for church reform, Wycliffe believed, rested with the king, whose authority he claimed exceeded that of the pope. In spite of persistent persecutions, Lollardy survived underground during the fifteenth century, to resurface during the convulsive religious conflict of the early sixteenth century known as the Reformation.

The most profound challenge to papal authority in the later Middle Ages came from Bohemia. Here the spiritual, intellectual, political, and economic criticisms of the papacy that sprang up in other countries fused in one explosive spark. Religious dissent quickly became the vehicle for a nationalist uprising and a social revolution.

Under Emperor Charles IV, the pace of economic development and social change in the Holy Roman Empire had quickened in the mid-fourteenth century. Prague, the capital, became one of Europe's great cities: the new silver mine at Kutná Hora boosted Prague's economic growth, and the first university in the empire was founded there in 1348. Prague was located in Bohemia, a part of the Holy Roman Empire settled by a Slavic people, the Czechs, since the early Middle Ages. Later, many German merchants and artisans migrated to Bohemian cities, and Czech peasants, uprooted from the land, flocked to the cities in search of employment. This diverse society became a potentially explosive mass when heightened expectations of commercial and intellectual growth collided with the grim realities of the plague and economic problems in the late fourteenth century. Tax protests, urban riots, and ethnic conflicts signaled growing unrest, but it was religious discontent that became the focus for popular revolt.

■ **Burning of a Heretic**
Execution by fire was the usual method of killing heretics. This illustration shows the burning of a Lollard, a follower of the teachings of Wycliffe, who opposed the established church. Although heretics were condemned by the church, their executioners were secular authorities, who are present here. (Hulton Getty/Liaison Agency.)

Critics of the clergy, often clergy themselves, decried the moral conduct of priests and prelates who held multiple benefices, led dissolute lives, and ignored their pastoral duties. How could the clergy, living in a state of mortal sin, legitimately perform the sacraments? critics asked. Advocating greater lay participation in the Mass and in the reading of Scripture, religious dissenters drew some of their ideas from the writings of Wycliffe. Among those influenced by Wycliffe's ideas were Jan Hus (d. 1415) and his follower Jerome of Prague (d. 1416), both Prague professors, ethnic Czechs, and leaders of a reform party in Bohemia. Although the reform party attracted adherents from all Czech-speaking social groups, the German minority, who dominated the university and urban elites in Prague, opposed it out of ethnic rivalry. The Bohemian nobility protected Hus; the common clergy rebelled against the bishops; and the artisans and workers in Prague were ready to back the reform party by force. These disparate social interests all focused on one symbolic but passionately felt religious demand: the ability to receive the Eucharist as both bread and wine at Mass. In traditional Roman liturgy, the chalice was reserved for the clergy; the Utraquists, as their opponents called them (from *utraque*, Latin for "both"), wanted to drink wine from the chalice as well, to achieve a measure of equality between laity and clergy.

When Hus was burned at the stake by the Council of Constance in 1415, his death caused a national uproar. The reform movement, which had thus far focused only on religious issues, burst forth as a national revolution. Sigismund's initial repression of the revolt in the provinces was brutal, and many dissenters were massacred. To organize their defense, Hussites gathered at a mountain in southern Bohemia, which they called Mount Tabor after the mountain in the New Testament where the transfiguration of Christ took place. Now called Taborites, they began to restructure their community according to biblical injunctions. Like the first Christian church, they initially practiced communal ownership of goods and thought of themselves as the only true Christians awaiting the return of Christ and the end of the world. As their influence spread, the Taborites compromised with the surrounding social order, collecting tithes from peasants and retaining magistrates in towns under their control. Taborite leaders were radical priests who ministered to the community in the Czech language, exercised moral and judicial leadership, and even led the people into battle. Resisting all attempts to crush them, the Czech revolutionaries eventually gained the right from the papacy to receive the Eucharist as both bread and wine, a practice that continued until the sixteenth century.

A still different group of heretics grew out of the anguish of the Black Death. Believing that the plague was God's way of chastising a sinful world, bands of men and women sought to save themselves by repenting their sins in a dramatic manner: wearing tattered clothes, they visited local churches and sang hymns while publicly whipping themselves until blood flowed. The flagellants, as they soon came to be called, cried out to God for mercy and called upon the congregation to repent their sins. But the clergy distrusted this lay movement that did not originate within the church hierarchy.

In some communities, the religious fervor aroused by the flagellants spawned violence against Jews. From 1348 to 1350, anti-Semitic persecutions, beginning in southern France and spreading through Savoy to the Holy Roman Empire, destroyed many Jewish communities in central and western Europe. Sometimes the clergy incited the attacks against the Jews, calling them Christ-killers, accusing them of poisoning wells and kidnapping and ritually slaughtering Christian children. In towns throughout Europe, economic resentment fueled anti-Semitism as those in debt turned on creditors, often Jews who had become rich from the commercial revolution of the thirteenth century.

Many anti-Semitic incidents were spontaneous, with mobs plundering Jewish quarters and killing anyone who refused baptism. But it is equally true that sometimes authorities orchestrated the violence. For example, the magistrates of Nuremberg obtained approval from Emperor Charles IV before organizing the 1349 persecution directed by the city government. Thousands of German Jews were slaughtered. Many fled to Poland, where the incidence of plague was low and where the authorities welcomed Jews as productive taxpayers. In western and central Europe, however, the persecutions destroyed the financial power of the Jews.

End of the Reconquista and Expulsion of the Jews in Spain, 1492

Like France and England, war wracked Spain as dynasties fought over the royal succession in the various kingdoms. But again, as in France and England, the end result was a strengthened monarchy. In 1469, Queen Isabella of Castile and King Ferdinand of Aragon married. Retaining their separate titles, the two monarchs ruled jointly over their dominions, each of which adhered to its traditional laws and privileges. Their union represented the first step toward the creation of a unified Spain out of two medieval kingdoms. Isabella and Ferdinand limited the privileges of the nobility and allied themselves with the cities, relying on the Hermandad (civic militia) to enforce justice and on lawyers to staff the royal council.

The united strength of Castile and Aragon brought the *reconquista* to a close with a final crusade against the Muslims. After more than a century of peace, war broke out in 1478 between Granada, the last Iberian Muslim state, and Catholic royal forces. Weakened by internal strife, Granada finally fell in 1492. Two years later, in recognition of the crusade, Pope Alexander VI bestowed the title "Catholic monarchs" on Isabella and Ferdinand, ringing in an era in which militant Catholicism became an instrument of state authority and shaped the national consciousness.

Unification of Spain, Late Fifteenth Century

In this climate, it no longer seemed possible for Iberian Muslims, Jews, and Christians to live side by side. The practice of Catholicism became a test of one's loyalty to the church and to the Spanish monarchy. In 1478, the king and queen introduced the Inquisition to Spain, primarily as a means to control the *conversos* (Jewish converts to Christianity), whose elevated positions in the economy and the government aroused widespread resentment from the so-called Old Christians. *Conversos* often were suspected of practicing Judaism, their ancestral religion, in secret while pretending to adhere to their new Christian faith. Appointed by the monarchs, the inquisitors presided over tribunals set up to investigate those suspected of religious deviancy. The accused, who were arrested on charges often based on anonymous denunciations and information gathered by the inquisitors, could defend themselves but not confront their accusers. The wide spectrum of punishments ranged from monetary fines to the *auto da fé* (a ritual of public confession) to burning at the stake. After the fall of Granada, many Muslims were forced to convert or resettle in Castile. At the same time, Ferdinand and Isabella ordered all Jews in their kingdoms to choose between exile and conversion. Many chose exile.

The expulsion of the Jews from Spain had far greater consequences than their earlier banishments from France and England. Spain had had the largest and most vibrant Jewish communities of Europe. On the eve of the expulsion, approximately 200,000 Jews and 300,000 *conversos* were living in Castile and Aragon. Faced with the choice to convert or leave, well over 100,000 Jews dispersed, some settling in North Africa, more in Italy, and many in the Ottoman Empire, Greek-speaking Thessalonika, and Palestine. Conversant in two or three languages, these Jews often served as intermediaries between the Christian West and Muslim East.

New Forms of Thought and Expression: The Renaissance

The Renaissance had its medieval roots in vernacular literature like Dante's *Divine Comedy* and the humanism of the Gothic sculptors who portrayed figures in the round, interacting with one another. But it grew far beyond those roots, to discover and embrace the classical past and to use classical themes to celebrate human glory. Fostered by the printing press, Renaissance writings spread far and wide to a literate middle class eager to absorb every sort of text. Meanwhile, Renaissance artists celebrated the newly powerful republics, principalities, and kingdoms of their age. Flush with power, these states intruded into the most intimate personal matters, such as sexuality, marriage, and childbirth.

Renaissance Humanism

From the epics and romances of the twelfth and thirteenth centuries, vernacular writings blossomed into a full-blown literature in the fourteenth. Poetry, stories, and chronicles composed in Italian, French, English, and other national languages helped articulate a new sense of aesthetics. The great writers of late medieval Europe were of urban middle-class origins, from families that had done well in government, church service, or commercial enterprises. Unlike the medieval troubadours, with their aristocratic backgrounds, the men and women who wrote vernacular literature in this age typically came from the cities, and their audience was the literate laity. Francesco Petrarch (1304–1374), the poet laureate of Italy's vernacular literature, and his younger contemporary and friend Giovanni Boccaccio (1313–1375) were both from the Florentine professional classes. Geoffrey Chaucer (c. 1342–1400), an important vernacular poet of medieval England, came from a family of wine merchants. Even writers who celebrated the life of the nobility were children of commoners. Though born in Valenciennes to a family of moneylenders and merchants, Jean Froissart (1333?–c. 1405), whose chronicle vividly describes the events of the Hundred Years' War, was an ardent admirer of chivalry. Christine de Pisan (1364–c. 1430), a poet and prose writer of great range, was the daughter of a Venetian municipal counselor.

Life in all its facets found expression in the new vernacular literature, as writers told of love, greed, and salvation. Boccaccio's *Decameron* popularized the short story, as the characters in this novella tell sensual and bizarre tales in the shadow of the Black Death. Members of different social orders parade themselves in Chaucer's *Canterbury Tales,* journeying together on a pilgrimage.

Noble patronage was crucial to the growth of vernacular literature, a fact reflected in the careers of the most famous writers. Perhaps closest to the model of an independent man of letters, Petrarch nonetheless relied on powerful patrons at various times. His early career began at the papal court in Avignon, where his father worked as a notary; during the 1350s, Petrarch enjoyed the protection and patronage of the Visconti duke of Milan. Boccaccio started out in the Neapolitan world of commerce. The court of King Robert of Naples initiated him into the realm of letters. Chaucer served in administrative posts and on many diplomatic missions, during which he met his two Italian counterparts. Noble patronage also shaped the literary creations of Froissart and Christine de Pisan. Christine would have been unable to produce most of her writings without the patronage of women in the royal household. She presented her most famous work, *The Book of the City of Ladies* (1405), a defense of women's reputation and virtue, to Isabella of Bavaria, the queen of France and wife of Charles VI.

Vernacular literature blossomed not at the expense of Latin but alongside a classical revival. In spite of the renown of their Italian writings, Petrarch and Boccaccio, for example, took great pride in their Latin works. In the second half of the fourteenth century, writers began to imitate the antiquated "classical" Latin of Roman literature. In the forefront of this literary and intellectual movement, Petrarch traveled to many monasteries in search of long-ignored Latin manuscripts. For writers like Petrarch, medieval church Latin was an artificial, awkward language, whereas classical Latin and, after its revival, Greek were the mother tongues of the ancients, even more authentic, vivid, and glorious than the poetry and prose written in Italian and other contemporary European languages. Classical allusions and literary influences abound in the works of Boccaccio, Chaucer, Christine de Pisan, and others. The new intellectual fascination with the ancient past also stimulated translations of classical works into the vernacular.

This attempt to emulate the virtues and learning of the ancients gave impetus to an intellectual movement: humanism. For humanists the study of history and literature was the chief means of identifying with the glories of the ancient world. By the early fifteenth century, the study of classical Latin had become fashionable among a small intellectual elite, first in Italy and gradually throughout Europe. Reacting against the painstaking logic and abstract language of the scholastic philosophy that predominated in the medieval period, the humanists of the Renaissance preferred eloquence and style in their discourse, imitating the writings of Cicero and other great Roman authors.

Gradually the imitation of ancient Roman rhetoric led to the absorption of ancient ideas. In the writings of Roman historians such as Livy and Tacitus, fifteenth-

■ **Poet and Queen**

Christine de Pisan, kneeling, presents a manuscript of her poems to Isabella of Bavaria, the queen of France. Isabella's royal status is indicated by the royal French emblem, the fleur-de-lis, which decorates the bedroom walls. The sumptuous interior (chairs, cushions, tapestry, paneled ceiling, glazed and shuttered windows) was typical of aristocratic domestic architecture. Even in the intimacy of her bedroom, Queen Isabella, like all royal personages, was constantly attended and almost never alone (notice her ladies-in-waiting).

(The British Library Picture Library, London.)

century Italian civic elites (many of them lawyers) found echoes of their own devout patriotism. Between 1400 and 1430 in Florence, a time of war and crisis, the study of the humanities evolved into a republican ideology that historians call "civic humanism." In the early fifteenth century, the Florentines waged a highly successful propaganda war on behalf of virtuous republican Florence against tyrannical Milan, invoking the memory of the overthrow of Etruscan tyrants by the first Romans. Thus, the study of ancient civilization was not only an antiquarian quest but a call to public service and political action.

The fall of Constantinople in 1453 sent Greek scholars to Italy for refuge, giving extra impetus to the revival of Greek learning in the West. Venice and Florence assumed leadership in this new field—the former by virtue of its commercial and political ties to the eastern Mediterranean, the latter thanks to the patronage of Cosimo de' Medici, who sponsored the Platonic Academy, a discussion group dedicated to the study of Plato and his followers under the intellectual leadership of Marsilio Ficino (1433–1499).

Most humanists did not consider the study of ancient cultures to be in conflict with their Christian faith. In "returning to the sources"—a famous slogan of the time—philosophers attempted to harmonize the disciplines of Christian faith and ancient learning. Ficino, the foremost Platonic scholar of the Renaissance, was deeply attracted to natural magic and was also a priest. He argued that the immortality of the soul, a Platonic idea, was perfectly compatible with Christian doctrine and that much of ancient wisdom actually foreshadowed later Christian teachings.◆

Through their activities as educators and civil servants, professional humanists gave new vigor to the humanist curriculum of grammar, rhetoric, poetry, history,

---

◆ For a primary source that expresses the ideals of Renaissance humanism, see Document 35, Giovanni Pico della Mirandola, *Oration on the Dignity of Man.*

and moral philosophy. By the end of the fifteenth century, European intellectuals considered a good command of classical Latin, with perhaps some knowledge of Greek, as one of the requirements of an educated person.

The invention of mechanical printing aided greatly in making the classical texts widely available. Printing from movable type—a revolutionary departure from the old practice of copying by hand—was invented in the 1440s by Johannes Gutenberg, a German goldsmith. Mass production of identical books and pamphlets made the world of letters more accessible to a literate audience.

The advent of mass printed books depended on paper production. The art of papermaking came to Europe from China via Arab intermediaries. By the fourteenth century, paper mills were operating in Italy, producing paper that was more fragile but much cheaper than parchment or vellum, the animal skins that Europeans had previously used for writing. To produce paper, old rags were soaked in a chemical solution, beaten by mallets into a pulp, washed with water, treated, and dried in sheets—a method that still produces good-quality paper today.

Even before the printing press, a brisk industry in manuscript books had been flourishing in Europe's university towns and major cities. Production was in the hands of stationers, who organized workshops known as *scriptoria*, where the manuscripts were copied, and acted as retail booksellers. Demand was high. The stationer for Cosimo de' Medici, for example, employed forty-five copyists to complete two hundred volumes in twenty-two months.

Nonetheless, bookmaking in *scriptoria* was slow and expensive, and the invention of movable type was an enormous technological breakthrough. It took bookmaking out of the hands of human copyists. Movable type consisted of reusable metal molds of letters, numbers, and various other characters. The typesetter arranged the characters by hand, page by page, to create a printable text. The surface of the type was inked, and sheets of paper pressed against the type picked up an impression of the text. Numerous copies could be made with only a small amount of human labor. In 1467, two German printers established the first press in Rome and produced twelve thousand volumes in five years, a feat that in the past would have required one thousand scribes working full-time.

After the 1440s, printing spread rapidly from Germany to other European countries. In Germany, Cologne, Strasbourg, Nuremberg, and Augsburg all had major presses; many Italian cities had established their own by 1480. In the 1490s, the German city of Frankfurt-am-Main became an international meeting place for printers and booksellers. The Frankfurt Book Fair, where printers from different nations exhibited their newest titles, represented a major international cultural event and remains an unbroken tradition to this day.

The invention of mechanical printing gave rise to a "communications revolution" as significant as the widespread use of the personal computer today. The multiplication of standardized texts altered the thinking habits of Europeans by freeing individuals from having to memorize everything they learned; it made possible the relatively speedy and inexpensive dissemination of knowledge; and it created a wider community of scholars, no longer dependent on personal patron-age or church sponsorship for texts. Printing facilitated the free expression and exchange of ideas, and its disruptive potential did not go unnoticed by political and ecclesiastical authorities. Emperors and bishops in Germany, the homeland of the printing industry, moved quickly to issue censorship regulations.

New Perspectives in Art and Music

New techniques in painting, architecture, and musical performance fostered origi-nal styles and subjects. Artists paid close attention to the human figure and strove to depict the world from nature rather than from pictorial models. Musicians enhanced polyphony with new harmonies and more versatile instruments.

As individual talent and genius were recognized by a society hungry for culture, artists themselves gained prestige. In exalting the status of the artist, Leonardo da Vinci (1452–1519), painter, architect, and inventor, described himself as a creative genius. He was not alone; Renaissance artists intended to convince society that their works were unique and their talents priceless. They exalted the artist above the "mere artisan," claiming to be independent of the blueprints of a patron. During the fifteenth century, as artists began to claim the respect and recognition of soci-ety, however, the reality was that most relied on wealthy patrons for support. And although they wished to create as their genius dictated, not all patrons of the arts allowed artists to work without restrictions. While the duke of Milan appreciated Leonardo's genius, the duke of Ferrara paid for his art by the square foot.

A successful artist who did fit the new vision of unfettered genius was the Florentine sculptor Donatello (1386–1466). Not only did Donatello's sculptures evoke classical Greek and Roman models, but the grace and movement of his work inspired Cosimo de' Medici, the ruler of Florence, to excavate antique works of art and put them on display. Donatello was one artist who enjoyed the long-term, high-status patronage of a prince. Others, like Andrea Mantegna (1431–1506), worked more precariously. Treated more as a skilled worker in service to the prince than as an independent artist, he was once even required to adorn his majestic Gonzaga tapestries with life sketches of farm animals.

The workshop—the normal place of production in Renaissance Italy and in northern European cities such as Nuremberg and Antwerp—afforded the artist greater autonomy. As heads of workshops, artists trained apprentices and negoti-ated contracts with clients. The most famous artists fetched good prices for their work. Famous artists developed followings, and wealthy consumers were willing to pay a premium for work done by a master instead of apprentices. Studies of art contracts show that in the course of the fifteenth century artists gained greater control over their work. Early in the century, clients routinely stipulated detailed conditions for works of art—specifying, for instance, gold paint or "ultramarine blue," which were among the most expensive pigments. Clients might also determine the arrangement of figures in a picture, leaving to the artist little more than the execution. After midcentury, such specific directions became less common. In 1487, for example, the Florentine painter Filippo Lippi (1457–1504), in his contract to paint frescoes in the Strozzi chapel, specified that the work should be "all from his own hand and particularly the figures." The shift underscores the increasing recognition of the unique skills of individual artists.

A market system for the visual arts emerged during the Renaissance, initially in the Low Countries. In the fifteenth century, most large-scale work was commissioned by specific patrons, but the art market, for which artists produced works without prior arrangement for sale, was to develop into the major force for artistic creativity, a force that prevails in contemporary society. The commercialization of art celebrated the new context of artistic creation itself: artists working in an open, competitive, urban civilization.

If the individual artist was a man of genius, what greater subject for the expression of beauty was there than the human body itself? Taking their cue from fourteenth-century painters such as Giotto (see page 425), Renaissance artists learned to depict ever more expressive human emotions and movements. The work of the short-lived but brilliant painter Masaccio (1401–1428) exemplifies this development. His painting *St. Peter Baptizing* shows the recipient of the baptism trembling in the cold water. In addition to rendering homage to classical and biblical

■ **Masaccio's *St. Peter Baptizing***
This detail from a cycle of frescos about the life of St. Peter painted by Masaccio in the church of Santa Maria del Carmine in Florence shows the artist's interest in the nude body. The man receiving baptism is portrayed in the round, light playing on his flesh and revealing its contours. This emphasis on human nakedness may have reflected an egalitarian strain in republican Florence. It also echoes what Masaccio found in ancient art and sculpture.
(Erich Lessing/Art Resource, NY.)

figures, Renaissance artists painted their contemporaries as well. For the first time after classical antiquity, sculptors again cast the human body in bronze, in life-size or bigger freestanding statues. Free from fabric and armor, the human body was idealized in the eighteen-foot marble sculpture *David,* the work of the great Michelangelo Buonarroti (1475–1564).

The increasing number of portraits in Renaissance painting illustrates the new, elevated view of human existence. Portraiture initially was limited to representations of pontiffs, monarchs, princes, and patricians, but soon portraits of middle-class people became more widespread. Painters from the Low Countries such as Jan van Eyck (1390?–1441) distinguished themselves in this genre; their portraits achieved a sense of detail and reality unsurpassed until the advent of photography.

All of this art was distinguished from its predecessors by its depiction of the world as the eye perceives it. The use of *visual perspective*—an illusory three-dimensional space on a two-dimensional surface and the ordered arrangement of painted objects from one viewpoint—became one of the distinctive features of Western art. Underlying the idea of perspective was a new Renaissance worldview: humans asserting themselves over nature in painting and design by controlling space. Optics became the organizing principle of the natural world in that it detected the "objective" order in nature. The Italian painters were keenly aware of their new technique, and they criticized the Byzantine and the northern Gothic stylists for "flat" depictions of the human body and the natural world. The highest accolade for a Renaissance artist was to be described as an "imitator of nature": this

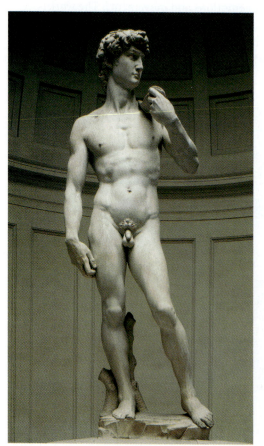

■ **Michelangelo's** *David*

Michelangelo realized a synthesis of the ancient nude statue and the biblical figure of David in this larger-than-life sculpture of the young David, his body poised for action against the giant Goliath. The figure's easy slouch recalls depictions of Greek athletes, but this sculpture was commissioned by the administrators of the cathedral at Florence and was placed in front of the Florentine town hall. Both church and state thus garnered prestige from the artist and his work.
(Nimatallah/Art Resource, NY.)

■ **Mantegna's Frescoes in the Camera degli Sposi**

For the "marital bedchamber" of the duke of Mantua, Mantegna painted scenes that integrated inside and out in a new way. To the right of the open doorway is the ducal family, portrayed as if outdoors, yet with their feet resting on the mantel of the fireplace. The painted curtain mimicked curtains that once decorated the interior of the room. To the left of the doorway is the duke greeting his son; behind them is a landscape. Thus Mantegna's paintings gave the illusion of the outside coming in, as if the walls were windows onto the world. (Scala/Art Resource, NY.)

epithet meant that the artist's teacher was nature, not design books or master painters. For the frescoes of the bridal chamber of the Gonzaga Palace (executed 1465–1474), Mantegna created an illusory extension of reality: the actual living space in the chamber "opened out" to the painted landscape on the walls.

Perhaps even more than visual artists, fifteenth-century architects embodied the Renaissance ideals of uniting artistic creativity and scientific knowledge. The Florentine architect Leon Battista Alberti (1404–1472) made such ideas explicit in *On Architecture* (1415). Alberti argued for large-scale urban planning, with monumental buildings set on open squares, harmonious and beautiful in their proportions. His ideas were put into action by Pope Sixtus IV (r. 1471–1484) and his successors in the urban renewal of Rome, and they served to transform the city into a geometrically constructed monument to architectural brilliance by recalling the grandeur of its ancient origins.

Musicians and composers, too, worked for wealthy patrons at court. Developments in polyphony were led by Guillaume Dufay (1400–1474), whose musical training began in the cathedral choir of his hometown, Cambrai, in the Low Countries. His successful career took him to all the cultural centers of the Renaissance, where nobles sponsored new compositions and maintained a corps of musicians for court and religious functions. In 1438, Dufay composed festive music to cele-brate the completion of the cathedral dome in Florence designed by Filippo Brunelleschi (1377–1446) and modeled on Roman ruins. Dufay expressed the har-monic relationship among four voices in ratios that matched the mathematically precise dimensions of Brunelleschi's architecture. After a period of employment at the papal court, Dufay returned to his native north and composed music for the Burgundian and French courts.

Josquin des Prez (1440–1521), another Netherlander, wrote music in Milan, Ferrara, Florence, and Paris and at the papal court. Music was an integral part of courtly life: Lorenzo de' Medici sent Dufay a love poem to set to music, and the great composer maintained a lifelong relationship with the Medici family. Com-posers often adapted familiar folk melodies for sacred music, expressing religious feeling primarily through human voices instead of instruments. The tambourine and the lute were indispensable for dances, however, and small ensembles of wind and string instruments with contrasting sounds performed with singers in the fash-ionable courts of Europe. Also in use in the fifteenth century were new keyboard instruments—the harpsichord and clavichord—which could play several harmonic lines at once.

Republics and Principalities in Italy

In his book *The Prince*, the Florentine political theorist Niccolò Machiavelli (1469–1527) argued that the state was an artifice of human creation to be conquered, shaped, and administered by princes according to the principles of power politics. Whether a republic—which preserved the traditional institutions of the medieval commune by allowing a civic elite to control political and economic life—or a principality, ruled by one dynasty, each Italian Renaissance state was as centralized and controlling as the new monarchies of France and England.

Venice and Florence were republics. Venice, built on a lagoon, ruled an extensive colonial empire that extended from the Adriatic to the Aegean Sea. Venetian mer-chant ships sailed the Mediterranean, the Black Sea, and, increasingly, the Atlantic coast. Whether threatened by competing Italian states or by the Turks, Venice drew strength from its internal social cohesion. Under the rule of an oligarchy of aristo-cratic merchants, Venice enjoyed stability. Its maritime empire benefited citizens of all social classes, who joined efforts to defend the interests of the "Most Serene Republic," a contemporary name that reflected Venice's lack of social strife.

Compared with serene Venice, the republic of Florence was in constant agita-tion, as social classes and political factions engaged in ongoing conflict. By 1434, a single family had emerged dominant in this fractious city: the Medici. Cosimo de' Medici (1388–1464), head of the family, "disposed of his rivals, proceeded to ad-minister the state at his pleasure and amassed wealth. . . . In Florence he built a palace fit for a king," as Pope Pius II put it. Head of one of the largest banks of

Europe, Cosimo de' Medici used his immense wealth to influence politics. Even though he did not hold any formal political office, he wielded influence in government through business associates and clients indebted to him for loans, political appointments, and other favors. Cosimo became the arbiter of war and peace, the regulator of law, more master than citizen. Yet the prosperity and security that Florence enjoyed made him popular as well. At his death, Cosimo was lauded as "father of his country."

Cosimo's grandson Lorenzo (called "the Magnificent"), who assumed power in 1467, bolstered the regime's legitimacy with his lavish patronage of the arts. But opponents were not lacking. In 1478, Lorenzo narrowly escaped an assassination attempt. Two years after Lorenzo's death in 1494, partisans who opposed the Medici drove them from Florence. The Medici returned to power in 1512, only to be driven out again in 1527. In 1530, the republic fell and the Medici once again seized control, declaring themselves dukes of Florence.

Milan had been a principality long before then. Since the fourteenth century, it had been a military state, relatively uninterested in supporting the arts but with first-class armaments and textile industries in the capital city and rich farmlands in Lombardy. Until 1447, the duchy was ruled by the Visconti dynasty, a group of powerful lords whose plans to unify all of northern and central Italy failed from the combined opposition of Venice, Florence, and other Italian powers. After a brief republican interlude (1447–1450) during which Milan fought against its neighbors, its ruling nobility appointed Francesco Sforza, who had married the illegitimate daughter of the last Visconti duke, to the post of general. Sforza promptly turned against his employers, claiming the duchy as his own. A bitter struggle between the nobility and the townspeople in Milan further undermined the republican cause, and in 1450 Sforza entered Milan in triumph.

The power of the Sforza dynasty reached its height during the 1490s. In 1493, Duke Ludovico married his niece Bianca Maria to Maximilian, the newly elected Holy Roman Emperor, promising an immense dowry in exchange for the emperor's legitimization of his rule. But the newfound Milanese glory was soon swept aside by France's invasion of Italy in 1494, and the duchy itself eventually came under Spanish rule.

In the violent arena of Italian politics, the papacy, an uneasy mixture of worldly splendor and religious authority, was a player like the other states. The popes' concern with politics stemmed from their desire to restore papal authority, greatly undermined by the Great Schism and the conciliar movement. To that end, the popes used both politics and culture. Politically, they curbed local power, expanded papal government, increased taxation, enlarged the papal army and navy, and cultivated diplomacy. Culturally, the popes renovated churches, created the Vatican Library, sponsored artists, and patronized writers to glorify their role and power. In undertaking these measures, the Renaissance papacy merely exemplified the larger trend toward the centralization of power evident everywhere else.

Concentrated power, competition between states, and the extension of warfare all raised the practice of diplomacy to nearly an art form. The first diplomatic handbook, composed in 1436, emphasized ceremonies, elegance, and eloquence. These masked the complex game of diplomatic intrigue and spying. In the fifteenth century, a resident ambassador was expected to keep a continuous stream of foreign political news flowing to the home government, not just to conduct temporary diplomatic missions, as earlier ambassadors had done. In some cases, the presence of semiofficial agents developed into full-fledged ambassadorships: the Venetian embassy to the sultan's court in Constantinople developed out of the merchant-consulate that had represented all Venetian merchants, and Medici Bank branch managers eventually acted as political agents for the Florentine republic.

Foremost in the development of diplomacy was Milan. Under the Visconti dukes, Milan sent ambassadors to Aragon, Burgundy, the Holy Roman Empire, and the Ottoman Empire. Under the Sforza dynasty, Milanese diplomacy continued to function as a cherished form of statecraft. For generations, Milanese diplomats at the French court sent home an incessant flow of information on the rivalry between France and Burgundy. Francesco Sforza, founder of the dynasty, also used his diplomatic corps to extend his political patronage. In letters of recommendation to the papacy, Francesco commented on the political desirability of potential ecclesiastical candidates by using code words, sometimes supplemented with instructions to his ambassador to indicate his true intent regardless of the coded letter of recommendation. Ciphers were used in more sensitive diplomatic reports to hide their real meaning from hostile powers.

The most outstanding achievement of Italy's Renaissance diplomacy was the negotiation of a general peace treaty that settled the decades of warfare engendered by Milanese expansion and civil war. The Treaty of Lodi (1454) established a complex balance of power among the major Italian states and maintained relative stability on the peninsula for half a century. Renaissance diplomacy eventually failed, however, when more powerful northern European neighbors invaded in 1494, bringing on the collapse of the whole Italian state system.

Intimate Matters

To deal with a mounting fiscal crisis, in 1427 the government of Florence ordered that a comprehensive tax record of households in the city and territory be compiled. Completed in 1430, this survey represented the most detailed population census then taken in European history. From the resulting mass of fiscal and demographic data, historians have been able to reconstruct a picture of Florentine society.

The state of Florence, roughly the size of Massachusetts, had a population of more than 260,000. Tuscany, the area in which the Florentine state was located, was one of the most urbanized regions of Europe. With 38,000 inhabitants, the capital city of Florence claimed 14 percent of the total population and an enormous 67 percent of the state's wealth. Straddling the Arno River, Florence was a beautiful, thriving city with a defined social hierarchy. In describing class divisions, the Florentines themselves referred to the "little people" and the "fat people." Some 60 percent of all households belonged to the "little people"—workers, artisans, small merchants. The "fat people" (roughly our middle class) made up 30 percent of the urban population and included the wealthier merchants, the leading artisans, notaries, doctors, and other professionals. At the very bottom of the hierarchy were slaves and servants, most of them women employed in domestic service. Whereas the small number of slaves were of Balkan origin, the much larger population of domestic servants came to the city from the surrounding countryside as contracted wage earners. At the top, a tiny elite of patricians, bankers, and wool merchants controlled the state with their enormous wealth. In fact, the richest 1 percent of urban households (approximately one hundred families) owned more than one-quarter of the city's wealth and one-sixth of Tuscany's total wealth. The patricians in particular owned almost all government bonds, a lucrative investment guaranteed by a state they dominated.

Surprisingly, men seem to have outnumbered women in the 1427 survey. For every 100 women there were 110 men, unlike most past and present populations, in which women are the majority. In addition to female infanticide, which was occasionally practiced, the survey itself reflected the society's bias against women: persistent underreporting on women probably explained the statistical abnormality; and married daughters, young girls, and elderly widows frequently disappeared from the memories of householders. Most people, men and women alike, lived in households with at least six inhabitants, although the form of family unit—nuclear or extended—varied, depending mainly on wealth. Poor people rarely were able to support extended families. Among urban patricians and landowning peasants, the extended family held sway. The number of children in a family, it seems, reflected class differences as well. Wealthier families had more children; childless couples existed almost exclusively among the poor, who were also more likely to abandon the infants they could not feed.

Wealth and class clearly determined family structure and the pattern of marriage and childbearing. In a letter to her eldest son, Filippo, dated 1447, Alessandra Strozzi announced the marriage of her daughter Caterina to the son of Parente Parenti. She described the young groom, Marco Parenti, as "a worthy and virtuous young man, and . . . the only son, and rich, 25 years old, and keeps a silk workshop; and they have a little political standing." The dowry was set at one thousand florins, a substantial sum—but for four to five hundred florins more, Alessandra admitted to Filippo, Caterina would have fetched a husband from a more prominent family.

The Strozzi belonged to one of Florence's most distinguished traditional families, but at the time of Caterina's betrothal the family had fallen into political disgrace. Alessandra's husband, an enemy of the Medici, was exiled in 1434; Filippo, a rich merchant in Naples, lived under the same political ban. Although Caterina was clearly marrying beneath her social station, the marriage represented an alliance in which money, political status, and family standing all balanced out. More an alliance between families than the consummation of love, an Italian Renaissance marriage was usually orchestrated by the male head of a household. In this case, Alessandra, as a widow, shared the matchmaking responsibility with her eldest son and other male relatives. Eighteen years later, when it came time to find a wife for Filippo, who had by then accumulated enough wealth to start his own household, Marco Parenti, his brother-in-law, would serve as matchmaker.◆

The upper-class Florentine family was patrilineal, tracing descent and determining inheritance through the male line. Because the distribution of wealth depended on this patriarchal system, women occupied an ambivalent position in the household. A daughter could claim inheritance only through her dowry, and she often disappeared from family records after her marriage. A wife seldom emerged from the shadow of her husband, and consequently the lives of many women have been lost to history.

Women's subordination in marriages often reflected the age differences between spouses. The Italian marriage pattern, in which young women married older men, contrasted sharply with the northern European model, in which partners were much closer in age. Significant age disparity also left many women widowed in their twenties and thirties, and remarriage often proved a hard choice. A widow's father and brothers frequently pressed her to remarry to form a new family alliance. A widow, however, could not bring her children into her new marriage because they belonged to her first husband's family. Faced with the choice between her children and her paternal family, not to mention the question of her own happiness, a widow could hope to gain greater autonomy only in her old age, when, like Alessandra, she might assume matchmaking responsibilities to advance her family's fortunes.

In northern Europe, however, women enjoyed a relatively more autonomous position. In England, the Low Countries, and Germany, for example, women played a significant role in the economy—not only in the peasant household, in which everyone worked, but especially in the town, serving as peddlers, weavers, seamstresses, shopkeepers, midwives, and brewers. In Cologne, for example, women could join one of several artisans' guilds, and in Munich they ranked among some of the richest brewers. Women in northern Europe shared inheritances with their brothers, retained control of their dowries, and had the right to represent themselves before the law. Italian men who traveled to the north were appalled at the differences in gender relations, criticizing English women as violent and brazen and disapproving of the mixing of the sexes in German public baths.

Child care and attitudes toward sexuality also reflected class differences in Renaissance life. Florentine middle- and upper-class fathers arranged business con-

---

◆ For more excerpts from Alessandra Strozzi's revealing correspondence, see Document 36, "Letters from a Widow and Matriarch of a Great Family."

tracts with wet nurses to breast-feed their infants; babies thus spent prolonged periods of time away from their families. Such elaborate child care was beyond the reach of the poor, who often abandoned their children to strangers or to public charity.

By the beginning of the fifteenth century, Florence's two hospitals were accepting large numbers of abandoned children in addition to the sick and infirm. In 1445, the government opened the Ospedale degli Innocenti to deal with the large number of abandoned children from poor families or from women who had given birth out of wedlock. Many of the latter were domestic slaves or servants impregnated by their masters; in 1445, one-third of the first hundred foundlings at the new hospital were children of the unequal liaisons between masters and women slaves. For some women, the foundling hospital provided an alternative to infanticide. Over two-thirds of abandoned infants were girls. Although Florence's government employed wet nurses to care for the foundlings, the large number of abandoned infants overtaxed the hospital's limited resources. The hospital's death rate for infants was much higher than the already high infant mortality rate of the time.

Illegitimacy in itself did not necessarily carry a social stigma in fifteenth-century Europe. Most upper-class men acknowledged and supported their illegitimate children as a sign of virility, and illegitimate children of noble lineage often rose to social and political prominence. Any social stigma was borne primarily by the woman, whose ability to marry became compromised. Shame and guilt drove some poor single mothers to kill their infants, a crime for which they paid with their own lives.

In addition to prosecuting infanticide, the public regulation of sexuality focused on prostitution and homosexuality. Intended "to eliminate a worse evil by a lesser one," a 1415 statute established government brothels in Florence. Concurrent with its higher tolerance of prostitution, the Renaissance state had a low tolerance of homosexuality. In 1432, the Florentine state appointed magistrates "to discover—whether by means of secret denunciation, accusations, notification, or any other method—those who commit the vice of sodomy, whether actively or passively." The government set fines for homosexual acts and carried out death sentences against pederasts (men who have sex with boys).

Fifteenth-century European magistrates took violence against women less seriously than illegal male sexual behavior, as the different punishments indicate. In Renaissance Venice, for example, the typical jail sentence for rape and attempted rape was only six months. Magistrates often treated noblemen with great leniency and handled rape cases according to class distinctions. For example, Agneta, a young girl living with a government official, was abducted and raped by two millers, who were sentenced to five years in prison; several servants who abducted and raped a slave woman were sentenced to three to four months in jail; and a nobleman who abducted and raped Anna, a slave woman, was freed. Whether in marriage, inheritance, illicit sex, or sexual crime, the Renaissance state regulated the behavior of men and women according to differing concepts of gender. The brilliant civilization of the Renaissance was experienced very differently by men and women.

On the Threshold of World History

The fifteenth century constituted the first time that Europe was a major player in world history. Before the maritime explorations of Portugal and Spain, Europe had remained at the periphery of world events. Fourteenth-century Mongols had been more interested in conquering China and Persia—lands with sophisticated cultures—than in invading Europe; Persian historians of the early fifteenth century dismissed Europeans as "barbaric Franks"; and China's Ming dynasty rulers, who sent maritime expeditions to Southeast Asia and East Africa around 1400, seemed unaware of the Europeans, even though Marco Polo and other Italian merchants had appeared at the court of the preceding Mongol Yuan dynasty. In the fifteenth century, Portuguese and Spanish vessels, followed a century later by English, French, and Dutch ships, sailed across the Atlantic, Indian, and Pacific Oceans, bringing with them people, merchandise, crops, and diseases in a global exchange that would shape the modern world. For the first time, the people of the Americas were brought into contact with a larger historical force that threatened to destroy not only their culture but their existence. European exploitation, conquest, and racism defined this historical era of transition from the medieval to the modern world, as Europeans left the Baltic and the Mediterranean for wider oceans.

The Divided Mediterranean

In the second half of the fifteenth century, the Mediterranean Sea, which had dominated medieval maritime trade, began to lose its preeminence to the Atlantic Ocean. To win control over the Mediterranean, the Ottomans embarked on an ambitious naval program to transform their empire into a major maritime power. War and piracy disrupted the flow of Christian trade: the Venetians mobilized all their resources to fight off Turkish advances, and the Genoese largely abandoned the eastern Mediterranean for trade opportunities presented by the Atlantic.

Mediterranean trade used ships made with relatively backward naval technology. The most common ship, the galley—a flat-bottom vessel propelled mainly by oarsmen with the help of a sail—dated from the time of ancient Rome. Most galleys could not withstand open-ocean voyages, although Florentine and Genoese galleys did make long journeys to Flanders and England, hugging the coast for protection. The galley's dependence on human labor was a more serious handicap. Because prisoners of war and convicted criminals toiled as oarsmen in both Christian and Muslim ships, victory in war or the enforcement of criminal penalties was crucial to a state's ability to float large numbers of galleys. Slaves, too, sometimes provided the necessary labor.

Portuguese Confrontations

The exploration of the Atlantic began with the Portuguese (Map 11.6). By 1415, they had captured Ceuta on the Moroccan coast, establishing a foothold in Africa. Thereafter, Portuguese voyages sailed farther still down the West African coast.

By midcentury, a chain of Portuguese forts reached Guinea, protecting the trade in gold and slaves. At home, the royal house of Portugal financed the fleets, with crucial roles played by Prince Peter, regent between 1440 and 1448; his more famous younger brother Prince Henry the Navigator; and King John II (r. 1481–1495). As a governor of the noble crusading Order of Christ, Henry financed many voyages out of the order's revenues. Private monies also helped, as leading Lisbon merchants participated in financing the gold and slave trades off the Guinea coast.

In 1455, Pope Nicholas V (r. 1447–1455) sanctioned Portuguese overseas expansion, commending King John II's crusading spirit and granting him and his successors the monopoly on trade with inhabitants of the newly "discovered" regions. In 1478–1488, Bartholomeu Dias took advantage of the prevailing winds in the South Atlantic to reach the Cape of Good Hope. A mere ten years later (1497–1499), under the captainship of Vasco da Gama, a Portuguese fleet rounded the cape and reached Calicut, India, center of the spice trade. In 1512, Ferdinand Magellan, a Portuguese sailor in Spanish service, led the first expedition to circumnavigate the globe. By 1517, a chain of Portuguese forts dotted the Indian Ocean.

In many ways a continuation of the struggle against Muslims on the Iberian peninsula, Portugal's maritime voyages displayed that country's mixed motives of piety, glory, and greed. The sailors dreamed of finding gold mines in West Africa and a mysterious Christian kingdom established by Prester John (actually the Coptic Christian kingdom of Abyssinia, or Ethiopia, in East Africa). The Portuguese hoped to reach the spice-producing lands of South and Southeast Asia by sea to bypass the Ottoman Turks, who controlled the traditional land routes between Europe and Asia.

The new voyages depended for their success on several technological breakthroughs. The lateen (triangular) sail permitted ships to tack against headwinds. Light caravels and heavy galleons, however different in size, were alike in using more than one mast and sail, harnessing wind—rather than human—power to move them. Better charts, maps, and instruments made long-distance voyages less risky.

After the voyages of Christopher Columbus, Portugal's interests clashed with Spain's. Mediated by Pope Alexander VI, the 1494 Treaty of Tordesillas reconciled Portugal and Spain by dividing the Atlantic world between the two royal houses. A demarcation 370 leagues west of the Cape Verdes Islands divided the Atlantic Ocean, reserving for Portugal the western coast of Africa and the route to India and giving Spain the oceans and lands to the west (see Map 11.6). Unwittingly, this agreement also allowed Portugal to claim Brazil in 1500, which Pedro Álvares Cabral (1467–1520) accidentally "discovered" on his voyage to India.

The Voyages of Columbus

Historians agree that Christopher Columbus (1451–1506) was born of Genoese parents; beyond that, we have little accurate information about this man who brought together the history of Europe and the Americas. In 1476, he arrived in Portugal,

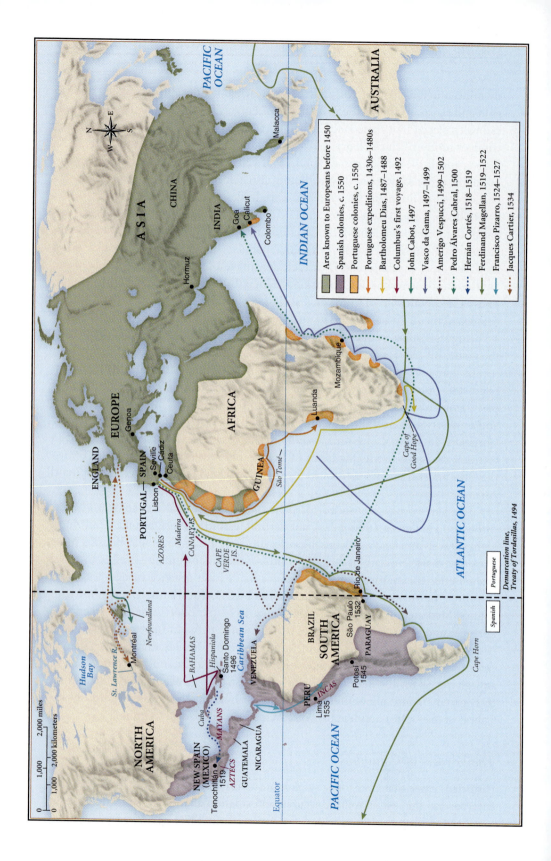

PACIFIC OCEAN

AUSTRALIA

Malacca

ASIA

CHINA

INDIA
Goa
Calicut

Colombo

INDIAN OCEAN

Hormuz

Area known to Europeans before 1450
Spanish colonies, c. 1550
Portuguese colonies, c. 1550
Portuguese expeditions, 1430s–1480s
Bartholomeu Dias, 1487–1488
Columbus's first voyage, 1492
John Cabot, 1497
Vasco da Gama, 1499–1502
Amerigo Vespucci, 1499–1502
Pedro Álvares Cabral, 1500
Hernán Cortés, 1518–1519
Ferdinand Magellan, 1519–1522
Francisco Pizarro, 1524–1527
Jacques Cartier, 1534

EUROPE

Genoa

PORTUGAL — SPAIN
Lisbon — Seville
Cádiz
Ceuta

AFRICA

Mozambique

Luanda

São Tomé

GUINEA

Cape of Good Hope

ATLANTIC OCEAN

ENGLAND

AZORES

Madeira

CANARIES

CAPE VERDE IS.

Newfoundland

Montréal

St. Lawrence R.

Hudson Bay

NORTH AMERICA

Cuba

BAHAMAS

Hispaniola
1496
Santo Domingo

Caribbean Sea

VENEZUELA

Rio de Janeiro

São Paulo
1532

BRAZIL

SOUTH AMERICA

PARAGUAY

PERU
Lima
1535
INCAS

Potosí
1545

Cape Horn

PACIFIC OCEAN

Equator

| Spanish | | Portuguese |

Demarcation line,
Treaty of Tordesillas, 1494

NEW SPAIN (MEXICO)
Tenochtitlán
1519
AZTECS
GUATEMALA
NICARAGUA
MAYANS

0   1,000   2,000 miles
0 1,000 2,000 kilometers

N E
W S

■ **MAP 11.6 Exploitation and Exploration in the Sixteenth Century**

At the end of the fifteenth century, Europeans began moving aggressively across the globe. Beginning with initial forays along the African coast, their voyages soon widened out to transatlantic crossings and, by 1522, the circumnavigation of the world. The web of arrows on this map suggests an earth bound together by many threads, and this is partly true, for never again would the two halves of the globe be isolated. At the same time, the threads pulled in one direction only—toward the Europeans. Africa was exploited for gold and slaves, while the discovery of precious metals fueled the explorations and settlements of Central and South America.

apparently a survivor in a naval battle between a Franco-Portuguese and a Genoese fleet; in 1479, he married a Portuguese noblewoman. He spent the next few years mostly in Portuguese service, gaining valuable experience in regular voyages down the west coast of Africa. In 1485, after the death of his wife, Columbus settled in Spain.

Fifteenth-century Europeans already knew that Asia lay beyond the vast Atlantic Ocean, and *The Travels of Marco Polo,* written more than a century earlier, still exerted a powerful hold on European images of the East. Columbus read it many times, along with other travel books, and proposed to sail west across the Atlantic to reach the lands of the khan, unaware that the Mongol Empire had already collapsed in eastern Asia. Vastly underestimating the distances, he dreamed of finding a new route to the East's gold and spices and partook of the larger European vision that had inspired the Portuguese voyages. (His critics had a much more accurate idea of the globe's size and of the difficulty of the venture.) But after the Portuguese and French monarchs rejected his proposal, Columbus found royal patronage with the recently proclaimed Catholic monarchs Isabella of Castile and Ferdinand of Aragon.

In August 1492, equipped with a modest fleet of three ships and about ninety men, Columbus set sail across the Atlantic. His contract stipulated that he would claim Castilian sovereignty over any new land and inhabitants and share any profits with the crown. Reaching what is today the Bahamas on October 12, Columbus mistook the islands to be part of the East Indies, not far from Japan and "the lands of the Great Khan." As the Castilians explored the Caribbean islands, they encountered communities of peaceful Indians, the Arawaks, who were awed by the Europeans' military technology, not to mention their appearance. Exchanging gifts of beads and broken glass for Arawak gold—an exchange that convinced Columbus of the trusting nature of the Indians—the crew established peaceful relationships with many communities. Yet in spite of many positive entries in the ship's log referring to Columbus's personal goodwill toward the Indians, the Europeans' objectives were clear: find gold, subjugate the Indians, and propagate Christianity.

Excited by the prospect of easy riches, many flocked to join Columbus's second voyage. When Columbus departed Cádiz in September 1493, he commanded seventeen ships that carried between 1,200 and 1,500 men, many believing all they had to do was "to load the gold into the ships." Failing to find the imaginary gold mines and spices, however, the colonial enterprise quickly switched its focus to finding slaves. Columbus and his crew first enslaved the Caribs, enemies of the Arawaks; in 1494, Colum-bus proposed a regular slave trade based in Hispaniola. The Spaniards exported en-slaved Indians to Spain, and slave traders sold them in Seville. Soon the Spaniards be-gan importing sugarcane from Madeira, forcing large numbers of Indians to work on plantations to produce enough sugar for export to Europe. Columbus himself was edged out of this new enterprise. When the Spanish monarchs realized the vast po-tential for material gain that lay in their new dominions, they asserted direct royal au-thority by sending officials and priests to the Americas, which were named after the Italian Amerigo Vespucci, who led a voyage across the Atlantic in 1499–1502.

Columbus's place in history embodies the fundamental transformations of his age. A Genoese in the service of Portuguese and Spanish employers, Columbus had a career illustrating the changing balance between the Mediterranean and the Atlantic. The voyages of 1492–1493 would eventually draw a triangle of exchange among Europe, the Americas, and Africa, an exchange gigantic in its historical impact and its human cost.

A New Era in Slavery

During the Middle Ages and Renaissance, female slaves served as domestic servants in wealthy Mediterranean homes, and male slaves toiled in the galleys of Ottoman and Christian fleets. Some were captured in war or by piracy; others—Africans—were sold by other Africans and Bedouin traders to Christian buyers. In western Asia, parents sold their children into servitude out of poverty. Many people in the Balkans became slaves when their land was devastated by Ottoman invasions. Slaves were Greek, Slav, European, African, and Turk.

The Portuguese maritime voyages changed this picture. From the fifteenth cen-tury, Africans increasingly filled the ranks of slaves. Exploiting warfare in West Africa, the Portuguese traded in gold and "pieces," as African slaves were called, a practice condemned at home by some conscientious clergy. Critical voices, however, could not deny the enormous profits that the slave trade brought to Portugal. Most slaves toiled in the sugar plantations of the Portuguese Atlantic islands and in Brazil. A for-tunate few labored as domestic servants in Portugal, where African freedmen and slaves, some 35,000 in the early sixteenth century, constituted almost 3 percent of the population, a percentage that was much higher than in other European coun-tries. In the Americas, slavery would truly flourish as an institution of exploitation.

Europeans in a New World

In 1500, on the eve of European invasion, the native peoples of the Americas were divided into many sedentary and nomadic societies. Among the settled peoples, the largest political and social organizations centered in the Mexican and Peruvian high-lands. The Aztecs and the Incas ruled over subjugated Indian populations in their

■ **Dürer's Engraving of Katharina, an African Woman**
Like other artists in early-sixteenth-century Europe, Albrecht Dürer would have seen in person Africans who went to Portugal and Spain as students, servants, and slaves. Notice Katharina's noble expression and dignified attire. Before the rise of the slave trade in the seventeenth century, most Africans in Europe were household servants of the aristocracy. Considered symbols of prestige, such servants generally were not used for economic production.
(Foto Marburg/Art Resource, NY.)

respective empires. With an elaborate religious culture and a rigid social and political hierarchy, the Aztecs and Incas based their civilizations in large urban capitals.

The Spanish explorers organized their expeditions to the mainland from a base in the Caribbean (see Map 11.6). Two prominent leaders, Hernán Cortés (1485–1547) and Francisco Pizarro (c. 1475–1541), gathered men and arms and set off in search of gold. Catholic priests accompanied the fortune hunters to bring Christianity to allegedly uncivilized peoples and thus to justify brutal conquests. His small band swelled by peoples who had been subjugated by the Aztecs, Cortés captured the Aztec capital, Tenochtitlán, in 1519. To the south, Pizarro conquered the Andean highlands, exploiting a civil war between rival Incan kings.

By the mid-sixteenth century, the Spanish Empire stretched unbroken from Mexico to Chile. Not to be outdone by the Spaniards, other European powers joined the scramble for gold in the New World. In 1500, a Portuguese fleet led by Pedro Álvares Cabral landed at Brazil, but Portugal did not begin colonizing there until 1532, when it established a permanent fort on the coast. In North America, the French went in search of a "northwest passage" to China. By 1504, French fishermen had appeared in Newfoundland. Thirty years later, Jacques Cartier led three voyages that explored the St. Lawrence River as far as Montreal. An early attempt in 1541 to settle Canada failed because of the harsh winter and Indian hostility, and

IMPORTANT DATES			
1337–1453	Hundred Years' War	c. 1450–1500	Height of Florentine Renaissance
1347–1350	First outbreak of the Black Death in Europe; anti-Jewish persecutions in the empire	1453	Fall of Constantinople; end of Byzantine Empire
1358	Jacquerie uprising in France	1460s–1485	Wars of the Roses in England
1378	Beginning of the Great Schism; Ciompi rebellion in Florence; John Wycliffe's treatise *On the Church*	1462	Ivan III of Muscovy claims imperial title "tsar"
1381	English peasant uprising	1477	Death of Charles the Bold; end of Burgundy
1389	Ottomans defeat Serbs at Kosovo	1478	Inquisition established in Spain
1414–1417	Council of Constance ends the Great Schism	1492	Columbus's first voyage; Christians conquer Muslim Granada and expel Jews from Spain
1415	Execution of Jan Hus; Portugal captures Ceuta, establishing foothold in Africa	1499	Vasco da Gama reaches India
1440s	Gutenberg introduces the printing press	1500	Portugal claims Brazil

John Cabot's 1497 voyage to find a northern route to Asia also failed. More permanent settlements in Canada and the present-day United States would succeed only in the seventeenth century.

Conclusion

Confronted by war, plague, peasant uprisings, turbulence in the cities, anti-Jewish pogroms, and a disgraced papacy, Europe's ruling classes grasped the reins of power ever more tightly, creating more centralized and institutionalized states. Surrounding themselves with artists, musicians, and humanists, these new-style rulers supported the "Renaissance"—an attempt to resuscitate the classical past for the purposes of the present. The Renaissance, which emphasized human potential and achievement, was one of Europe's most brilliant periods in artistic activity, one that glorified both God and humanity. Overwhelming confidence spurred Renaissance artists to a new appreciation for the human body and a new visual perspective in art and to apply mathematics and science to architecture, music, and artistic composition.

This intense cultural production both resulted from and fueled the competition among the burgeoning Renaissance states and between Christian Europe and

■ **MAPPING THE WEST** Renaissance Europe, c. 1500

By 1500, the shape of early modern Europe was largely set. It would remain stable until the eighteenth century, except for the disappearance of an independent Hungarian kingdom after 1529.

the Muslim Ottoman Empire. The competition also fostered an expansion of the frontiers of Europe first to Africa and then across the Atlantic Ocean to the Americas, ushering in the first period of global history. Few at the time would have guessed that Europe would soon enter yet another period of turmoil, one brought about not by demographic and economic collapse but by a profound crisis of conscience that the brilliance of Renaissance civilization had tended to obscure.

Suggested References for further reading and online research appear on page SR-17 at the back of the book.

www.bedfordstmartins.com/huntconcise　See the ONLINE STUDY GUIDE to assess your mastery of the material covered in this chapter.

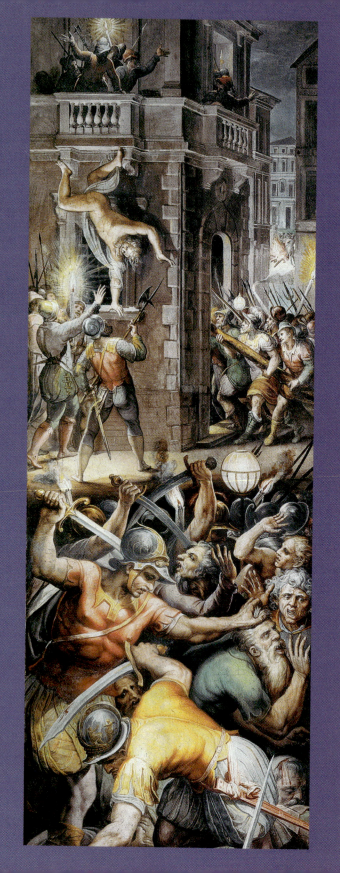

Struggles over Beliefs

1500–1648

H ILLE FEIKEN LEFT THE NORTHERN GERMAN TOWN of Münster on June 16, 1534, elegantly dressed, bedecked with jewels, and determined to kill. Münster, which religious radicals had declared a holy city, lay under siege by armies loyal to the local Catholic bishop—her intended victim. Hille crossed enemy lines and tried to persuade the commander of the besieging troops to take her to the bishop, promising to reveal a secret means of recapturing the city. When a defector from her camp recognized Hille and betrayed her, she was beheaded.

Hille Feiken belonged to the religious group known as Anabaptists, who wanted to form a holy community separate from the rest of society. Anabaptists organized in response to the Protestant Reformation, which was set in motion by the German friar Martin Luther in 1517 and quickly became a sweeping movement to uproot church abuses and restore early Christian teachings. Supporters of Luther were called "protestants," those who protested. Inspired by Luther and then by other reformers, ordinary men and women attempted to remake their heaven and earth. Their stories intertwined with bloody struggles among princes for domination in Europe, an age-old conflict now complicated by the clash of rival faiths.

Struggles over religious beliefs spread from the Holy Roman Empire northward into Scandinavia; westward into France, the Spanish-ruled Netherlands, and England; and eastward into Poland-Lithuania. These conflicts frequently erupted into armed confrontation, culminating in the Thirty Years' War of 1618–1648, which devastated much of central Europe. The orgy of mutual destruction in the Thirty Years' War left no winners in the religious struggle, and the cynical manipulation of religious issues by both Catholic and Protestant leaders showed that political interests eventually outweighed those of religion. The extreme violence of religious

■ **Massacre Motivated by Religion**
The Italian artist Giorgio Vasari (1511–1574) painted St. Bartholomew's Night: The Massacre of the Huguenots *for a public room in Pope Gregory XIII's residence. The pope and his artist intended to celebrate a Catholic victory over Protestant heresy.* (Scala/Art Resource.)

475

conflict pushed rulers and political thinkers to seek other, nonreligious grounds for governmental authority. Few would argue for genuine toleration of religious differences, but many began to insist that the interests of states had to take priority over the desire for religious conformity.

Although particularly dramatic and deadly, the church-state crisis was only one of a series of upheavals that shaped this era. After decades of rapid economic and population growth in the sixteenth century, a major economic downturn led to food shortages, famine, and disease in the first half of the seventeenth century. An upheaval in worldviews was also in the making, catalyzed by increasing knowledge of the new worlds discovered overseas and in the heavens. The development of new scientific methods of research would ultimately reshape Western attitudes toward religion and state power, as Europeans desperately sought alternatives to wars over religious beliefs.

The Protestant Reformation

Since the mid-fifteenth century, many clerics had tried to reform the church from within, criticizing clerical abuses and calling for moral renewal, but their efforts came up against the church's inertia and resistance. At the beginning of the sixteenth century, widespread popular piety and anticlericalism existed side by side, fomenting a volatile mixture of need and resentment. A young German friar, tormented by his own religious doubts, was to become the spokesman for a generation. From its origins as a theological dispute, Martin Luther's reform movement sparked explosive protests. By the time he died in 1546, half of western Europe had renounced allegiance to the Roman Catholic church. Christian unity fractured, opening the way not only to widespread turmoil but also to a host of new attitudes about the nature of religious and political authority.

Popular Piety and Christian Humanism

Numerous signs pointed to an intense spiritual anxiety among the laity. New shrines sprang up, reports of miracles multiplied, and prayer books printed in vernacular languages as well as Latin sold briskly. Expressions of piety could turn violent. In 1510, a priest in the German state of Brandenburg accused local Jews of stealing and stabbing the host, the consecrated bread that Catholics believed was the body of Christ. When, according to legend, the host bled, the Jews were killed. A shrine dedicated to the bleeding host attracted thousands of pilgrims.

Critics complained that the church gave external behavior more weight than spiritual intentions. In receiving the sacrament of penance—one of the central pillars of Christian morality and of the Roman church—sinners were expected to examine their consciences, sincerely confess their sins to a priest, and receive forgiveness. In practice, however, some priests abused their authority by demanding sexual or monetary favors in return for forgiveness. Priests also sold *indulgences,* which according to doctrine could alleviate suffering in purgatory after death. The faithful were supposed to earn indulgences by performing certain religious tasks— going on pilgrimage, attending mass, doing holy works. The sale of indulgences as a substitution for performing good works suggested that the church was more in- terested in making money than in saving souls.

Another way to diminish time in purgatory was to collect and venerate holy relics. A German prince, Frederick the Wise of Saxony, amassed the largest collec- tion of relics outside of Italy. By 1518, his castle church contained 17,443 holy relics, including what were thought to be a piece of Moses' burning bush, parts of the holy cradle and Jesus' swaddling clothes, and thirty-five fragments of the True Cross. A diligent and pious person who rendered appropriate devotion to each of these relics could earn exactly 127,799 years and 116 days of remission from purgatory.

Dissatisfaction with the official church prompted some Christian intellectuals to link their scholarship to the cause of social reform and to dream of ideal societies based on peace and morality. The Dutch scholar Desiderius Erasmus (c. 1466–1536) and the English lawyer Thomas More (1478–1535) stood out as representatives of these Christian humanists, who, unlike Italian humanists, placed their primary emphasis on Christian piety. Each established close links to the powerful. Erasmus was on intimate terms with kings and popes, and his fame spread across all Europe. More became lord chancellor to England's king Henry VIII.

Erasmus advocated a simple piety devoid of greed and the lust for power, but he also promoted the new humanist learning. To this end he devoted years to trans- lating a new Latin edition of the New Testament from the original Greek. He ar- gued ironically in *The Praise of Folly* (1509) that the wise appeared foolish, because modesty, humility, and poverty had few adherents in this world. Although Erasmus mocked the clergy's corruption and Christian princes' bloody ambitions, he em- phasized the role of education in reforming individuals and through them society as a whole. Even ordinary table manners drew his attention. In the *Colloquies* (1523), a compilation of Latin dialogues intended as language-learning exercises, he ad- vised his cultivated readers not to pick their noses at meals, not to share half-eaten chicken legs, and not to speak while stuffing their mouths. Challenged by angry younger men and radical ideas once the Reformation took hold, Erasmus chose Christian unity over reform and schism. He died in the Swiss city of Basel, isolated from the Protestant community and condemned by many in the Catholic church, who found his writings too critical of the church's authority.

Erasmus's good friend Thomas More, to whom *The Praise of Folly* was dedi- cated,* met with even greater suffering for his beliefs. He would later pay with his

---

*The Latin title *Encomium Moriae* ("The Praise of Folly") was a pun on More's name and the Latin word for *folly.*

life for upholding conscience over political expediency. Inspired by the recent voyages of discovery, More's best-known work, *Utopia* (1516), describes an imaginary ideal place that offered a stark contrast to his own society. Because Utopians enjoyed public schools, communal kitchens, hospitals, and nurseries, they had no need for money. Greed and private property disappeared in this world. Dedicated to the pursuit of knowledge and natural religion, with equal distribution of goods and few laws, Utopia knew neither crime nor war (Utopia means both "no place" and "best place" in Greek). More believed that politics, property, and war fueled human misery, whereas for his Utopians, "fighting was a thing they absolutely loathe. They say it's a quite subhuman form of activity, although human beings are more addicted to it than any of the lower animals." Despite a few oddities—voluntary slavery, for instance, and strictly controlled travel—Utopia seemed a paradise compared with the increasing violence in a Europe divided by religion.

Martin Luther and the German Nation

Like Erasmus and More, Martin Luther (1483–1546) pursued a life of scholarship, but a personal crisis of faith led him to break with the Roman church and establish a competing one. The son of a miner, Luther abandoned his studies in the law to enter the Augustinian order. The choice of a monastic life did not resolve Luther's doubts about his own salvation. Appalled at his own sense of sinfulness and the weakness of human nature, he lived in terror of God's justice in spite of frequent confessions and penance. A pilgrimage to Rome only deepened his unease with the institutional church. Sent to study theology by a sympathetic superior, Luther gradually came to new insights through his study of Scripture. He later described his breakthrough experience:

> At last, by the mercy of God, meditating day and night, I gave heed to the context of the words [in Romans 1:17], namely, "In [the gospel] the righteousness of God is revealed, as it is written, 'He who through faith is righteous shall live.'" There I began to understand that the righteousness of God is that by which the righteous live by a gift of God, namely by faith.

Luther soon came into conflict with the church authorities. In 1516, the new archbishop ordered the sale of indulgences to help cover the cost of constructing St. Peter's Basilica in Rome and also to defray his expenses in pursuing his election. Such blatant profiteering outraged many, including Luther, who now served as professor of theology at the University of Wittenberg. In 1517, Luther composed ninety-five theses—propositions for an academic debate—that questioned indulgence peddling and the purchase of church offices. Once they became public, the theses unleashed a torrent of pent-up resentment and frustration among the laypeople. This apparently ordinary academic dispute soon engulfed the Holy Roman Empire in conflict.

■ **Luther as Monk, Doctor, Man of the Bible, and Saint, 1521**

This woodcut by an anonymous artist appeared in a volume that the Strasbourg printer Johann Schott published in 1521. In addition to being one of the major centers of printing, Strasbourg was also a stronghold of the reform movement. Notice the use of traditional symbols to signify Luther's holiness: the Bible in his hands, the halo, the Holy Spirit in the form of a dove, and his friar's robes. Although monasticism and the cult of saints came under severe criticism during the Reformation, the representation of Luther with traditional symbols of sanctity stressed his conservative values instead of his radical challenge to church authorities. (The Granger Collection.)

Initially, Luther presented himself as the pope's "loyal opposition," but in 1520, he composed three treatises that laid out his theological position, attacked the papacy in Rome as the embodiment of the Antichrist, and called upon the German princes to reform the church themselves. He insisted that faith alone, not good works or penance, could save sinners from damnation. Faith came from the believer's personal relationship with God, which he or she cultivated through individual study of Scripture. Ordinary laypeople thus made up "the priesthood of all believers," who had no need of a professional caste of clerics to show them the way to salvation. The attack on the church's authority could not have been more dramatic.

From Rome's perspective, the "Luther Affair," as church officials called it, was essentially a matter of clerical discipline. Rome ordered Luther to obey his superiors and keep quiet. But the church establishment had seriously misjudged the extent of Luther's influence. Luther's ideas, published in numerous German and Latin editions, spread rapidly throughout the Holy Roman Empire, unleashing forces that Luther himself could not control. Social, nationalist, and religious protests fused into an explosive mass very similar to the Czech revolution that Jan Hus had inspired a century earlier. Like Hus, Luther appeared before an emperor: in 1521, he defended his faith before Charles V (r. 1520–1558), the newly elected Holy Roman Emperor who at the age of nineteen was the ruler of the Low Countries, Spain,

Spain's Italian and New World dominions, and the Austrian Habsburg lands. At the Imperial Diet of Worms, the formal assembly presided over by this powerful ruler, Luther shocked Germans by declaring his admiration for the Czech heretic. But unlike Hus, Luther did not suffer martyrdom because he enjoyed the protection of Frederick the Wise, the elector of Saxony (one of the seven German princes entitled to elect the Holy Roman Emperor) and Luther's lord.

What began as an urban movement turned into a war in the countryside in 1525. Lutheran propaganda radiated outward from the German towns, where local officials had appointed clerics sympathetic to reform. Luther's anticlerical message struck home with merchants and artisans who resented the clergy's tax-exempt status, but peasants had even more reason for discontent because they paid taxes to both their lord and the church. The church was the largest landowner in the Holy Roman Empire: about one-seventh of the empire's territory consisted of ecclesiastical principalities in which bishops and abbots exercised both secular and churchly power. In the spring of 1525, many peasants in southern and central Germany rose in rebellion, sometimes inspired by wandering preachers. Some urban workers and artisans joined the peasant bands, plundering monasteries, refusing to pay church taxes, and demanding village autonomy, the abolition of serfdom, and the right to appoint their own pastors. In Thuringia, the rebels were led by an ex-priest, Thomas Müntzer (1468?–1525), who promised to chastise the wicked and thus clear the way for the Last Judgment.

The uprising of 1525, known as the Peasants' War, split the reform movement. In Thuringia, Catholics and reformers joined hands to crush Müntzer and his supporters. All over the empire, princes rallied their troops to defeat the peasants and hunt down their leaders. By the end of 1525, more than 100,000 rebels had been killed and others maimed, imprisoned, or exiled. Luther had tried to mediate, criticizing the princes for their brutality toward the peasants but also warning the rebels against mixing religion and social protest. Luther believed that rulers were ordained by God and thus must be obeyed even if they were tyrants. The Kingdom of God belonged not to this world but to the next. When the rebels ignored Luther's appeal and continued to follow radical preachers like Müntzer, Luther called on the princes to destroy "the devil's work" and slaughter the rebels. Fundamentally conservative in its political philosophy, the Lutheran church would henceforth depend on established political authority for its protection.

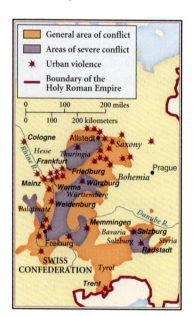

The Peasants' War of 1525

Emerging as the champions of an orderly religious reform, many German princes eventually confronted Emperor Charles V, who supported Rome. In 1529, Charles declared the Roman Catholic faith the empire's only legitimate religion. Proclaiming their allegiance to the reform cause, the Lutheran German princes protested and thus came to be called Protestants.

Huldrych Zwingli and John Calvin

While Luther provided the religious leadership for northern Germany, the south soon came under the influence of reformers based in Switzerland. In 1520, Huldrych Zwingli (1484–1531), the son of a Swiss village leader, broke with Rome and established his reform headquarters in German-speaking Zurich. In 1541, the Frenchman John Calvin (1509–1564) made French-speaking Geneva his center for reform campaigns in western Europe (see Map 12.1). Like Luther, Zwingli and Calvin began their careers as priests, but in contrast to their predecessor, they demanded an even more radical break with the Roman Catholic church.

Zwingli served as an army chaplain before declaring himself a reformer, and he brought to his version of church reform a stern disciplinarian's emphasis on a theocratic (church-directed) society in which religious values infused every aspect of politics and social life. Unlike Luther, who believed that his new church must accommodate to the established political powers and rely on their support, Zwingli refused to draw any distinction between the ideal citizen and the perfect Christian. Luther and Zwingli also differed in their views of the role of the Eucharist, or holy communion. Luther insisted that Christ was both truly and symbolically present in this central Christian sacrament; Zwingli, influenced by Erasmus, viewed the Eucharist as simply a ceremony symbolizing Christ's union with believers. In 1529, troubled by these disagreements, princes and magistrates who supported reform called a meeting at Marburg, in the center of the German lands. After several days of intense discussions, the north German and Swiss reformers managed to resolve many doctrinal differences, but Luther and Zwingli failed to agree on the meaning of the Eucharist.

In Zurich, Zwingli tolerated no dissent. When laypeople secretly set up their own new sect, called Anabaptists, Zwingli immediately attacked them. The Anabaptists believed that only adults had the free will to truly understand and accept baptism and therefore had to be rebaptized (*anabaptism* means "rebaptism"). How could a baby knowingly choose Christ? Rebaptism symbolized the Anabaptists' determination to withdraw from a social order corrupted, as they saw it, by power and evil. They therefore rejected the authority of courts and magistrates and refused to bear arms or swear oaths of allegiance. When persuasion failed to convince them, Zwingli urged Zurich magistrates to impose the death sentence.

Anabaptism spread quickly from Zurich to many cities in southern Germany, despite the Holy Roman Empire's general condemnation of the movement in 1529.

In 1534, one incendiary Anabaptist group, believing that the end of the world was imminent, seized control of the northwestern German town of Münster. Proclaiming themselves a community of saints and imitating the ancient Israelites, they were initially governed by twelve elders and later by Jan of Leiden, a Dutch Anabaptist tailor who claimed to be the prophesied leader—a second "King David." The Münster Anabaptists abolished private property and dissolved traditional marriages, allowing men, like Old Testament patriarchs, to have multiple wives, to the chagrin of many women. In 1535, besieged by a combined Protestant and Catholic army, many Münster Anabaptists died in battle or—like Hille Feiken—were executed. The remnants of the Anabaptist movement survived under the determined pacifist leadership of the Dutch reformer Menno Simons (1469–1561).

Yet another wave of reform surged forward under the leadership of John Calvin. As a young priest, Calvin believed it might be possible to reform the Roman Catholic church from within, but gradually he came to share Luther and Zwingli's conviction that only fundamental change could reestablish the true religion. While Calvin moved toward the Protestant position, his homeland of France experienced increasing turmoil over religion. On Sunday, October 18, 1534, in the so-called Affair of the Placards, Parisians found church doors posted with ribald broadsheets denouncing the Catholic Mass. Rumors of a Protestant conspiracy and massacre circulated, and magistrates swiftly organized repression of reform groups. The government arrested hundreds of French Protestants and executed scores of them, precipitating the flight into exile of many others, including Calvin.

Calvin did not intend to settle in Geneva, but when he stopped there, a local reformer threatened him with God's curse if he did not stay and help organize reform in the city. After intense conflict between the supporters of reform, many of whom were French refugees, and the opposition, led by the traditional elite families, the Calvinists triumphed in 1541. Geneva soon followed the precepts laid out in Calvin's great work, *The Institutes of the Christian Religion*, first published in 1536. Calvin took the reform doctrines to their logical conclusion. If God is almighty and humans cannot earn their salvation by good works, as all Protestants argued, then no Christian can be certain of salvation. Developing the doctrine of *predestination*, Calvin insisted that God had foreordained every man, woman, and child to salvation or damnation—even before the creation of the world. Only God knew who was among the "elect."

In practice, however, Calvinist doctrine demanded rigorous discipline: the knowledge that a small group of "elect" would be saved should guide the actions of the godly in an uncertain world. Fusing church and society into what followers named the "Reformed church," Geneva became a single theocratic community, in which dissent was not tolerated. The Genevan magistrates arrested the Spanish physician Michael Servetus when he passed through in 1553 because he had published books attacking Calvin and questioning the doctrine of the Trinity, the belief that God exists in three persons—the Father, Son (Christ), and Holy Spirit. Calvin urged the authorities to execute him, though he did not approve of their decision to burn him at the stake. Although critics cited Servetus's execution as an example of Calvinist despotism, Geneva quickly became the new center of the Reformation, the place where pastors trained for mission work and from which books propagating Calvinist doctrines were exported. The Calvinist movement spread to France, the Netherlands, England, Scotland, the German states, Poland, Hungary, and eventually New England, becoming the established form of the Reformation in many of these countries (Map 12.1).

The Progress of the Reformation	
1517	Martin Luther disseminates ninety-five theses attacking the sale of indulgences and other church practices
1520	Reformer Huldrych Zwingli breaks with Rome
1525	Radical reformer Thomas Müntzer killed in Peasants' War
1529	Lutheran German princes protest the condemnation of religious reform by Charles V; genesis of the term *Protestants*
1529	The English Parliament establishes King Henry VIII as head of the Anglican church, severing ties to Rome
1534–1535	Anabaptists control the city of Münster, Germany, in a failed experiment to create a holy community
1541	John Calvin and his followers take control in Geneva, making that city the center for Calvinist reforms

Reshaping Society through Religion

For all their differences over doctrine and church organization, the Protestant reformers shared a desire to instill greater discipline in Christian worship and in social behavior. As a consequence, they advocated changes in education, poor relief, and marriage to create a God-fearing, pious, and orderly Christian society. Some of these efforts grew out of developments that stretched back to the Middle Ages, but others, such as an emphasis on literacy and a new work ethic, appeared first in Protestant Europe.

Prior to the Reformation, the Latin Vulgate was the only Bible authorized by the church, though many vernacular translations of parts of the Bible circulated. In 1522, Martin Luther translated Erasmus's Greek New Testament into German, the first full translation in that language. Within twelve years, printers published more than 200,000 copies of it, an immense number for the time. In 1534, Luther completed a translation of the Old Testament. Peppered with witty phrases and colloquial expressions, Luther's Bible offered a treasure chest of the German language. In the same year that Luther's German New Testament appeared in print, the French humanist Jacques Lefèvre d'Étaples (c. 1455–1536) translated the Vulgate New Testament into French. Sponsored by the bishop of Meaux, who wanted to distribute free copies of the New Testament to the poor of the region, Lefèvre's translation represented an early attempt to reform the French church without breaking with Rome. By contrast, England's church hierarchy reacted swiftly

■ MAP 12.1 Spread of Protestantism in the Sixteenth Century

The Protestant Reformation divided northern and southern Europe. From its heartland in the Holy Roman Empire, the Reformation won the allegiance of Scandinavia, England, and Scotland and made considerable inroads in the Low Countries, France, eastern Europe, the Swiss Confederation, and even parts of northern Italy. While the Mediterranean countries remained loyal to Rome, a vast zone of confessional divisions and strife characterized the religious landscape of Europe from Britain in the west to Poland in the east.

against English-language Bibles, sensing in them the threat of heresy. Inspired by Luther's example during a visit to Wittenberg, the Englishman William Tyndale (1495–1536) translated the Bible into English. After he had his translation printed in Germany and the Low Countries, Tyndale smuggled copies into England. He paid for his boldness by being burned at the stake as a heretic. Because vernacular Bibles soon took pride of place in urban households as prized family heirlooms, especially in the German lands, Catholics could counter Protestant success only by printing their own translations.

Although the vernacular Bible occupied a central role in Protestantism, Bible reading did not become widespread until the 1600s. To increase literacy, educate children in the new religious principles, and replace the late medieval church schools, the Protestant reformers set up state school systems. Luther urged the German princes to use the proceeds of confiscated church properties to establish primary schools in every parish for children between six and twelve. The ordinance for a girls' school in Göttingen spelled out the emphasis on Christian discipline: "To fear God, they must learn their catechism, beautiful psalms, sayings, and other fine Christian and holy songs and little prayers." In addition to reading and writing, girls' schools included domestic skills in their curriculum. The Protestant churches developed a secondary system of humanist schools to train future pastors, scholars, and officials. These higher schools for boys, called *gymnasia* (from the Greek *gymnasion*), relied on the study of Greek and Latin classics and religious instruction to prepare students for university study.

To compete with the Protestant *gymnasia,* the new Catholic religious order, the Society of Jesus (known as the Jesuits), founded hundreds of colleges in Spain, Portugal, France, Italy, the German states, Hungary, Bohemia, and Poland. Among their alumni would be princes, philosophers, lawyers, churchmen, and officials— the elite of Catholic Europe. Except in the northern and central Italian cities, where most girls and boys received some education, Catholics nonetheless lagged behind Protestants in promoting primary education. The existence of competing Christian schools helped to perpetuate the religious divisions of Reformation Europe for many generations.

In their efforts to reshape society, Protestant reformers focused on poor relief as well as education. Although secular governments began to take over charity institutions from the church in both Protestant and Catholic regions, public poor relief quickly became more prevalent in Protestant areas. Among Protestants, private charity had ceased to be considered a good work necessary to earn salvation. In Protestant Nuremberg (1522) and Strasbourg (1523), for example, magistrates centralized poor relief with church funds; they appointed officials to head urban agencies that certified the genuine poor and distributed welfare funds to them. National measures soon followed. In 1531, Henry VIII asked justices of the peace (unpaid local magistrates) to license the poor in England and to differentiate between those capable of working and those who could not. In 1540, Charles V (who ruled Spain as Charles I) imposed a welfare tax in Catholic Spain to augment that country's in-adequate system of private charity. Despite the efforts of Catholic cities and states to prohibit begging and institute public charity, the new work ethic acquired a dis-tinctly Protestant cast. Protestants linked hard work and prosperity with piety and divine providence and considered laziness a sign of immorality—and frequently as-sociated laziness with Catholics. Collective charity persisted in Catholic lands, sup-ported by a theology of good works and by the elites' sense of social responsibility.

Like the reforms of education and poor relief, Protestant efforts to reshape mar-riage reflected their concern to discipline individual behavior and institute an or-derly Christian society. Protestant magistrates established marital courts, promul-gated new marriage laws, closed brothels, and inflicted harsher punishments for sexual deviance. Under canon law, the Catholic church recognized any promise made between two consenting adults (with the legal age of twelve for females, fourteen for males) as a valid marriage. In rural areas and among the urban poor, most couples simply lived together as common-law husband and wife, and some couples never even registered with the church. Sometimes young men promised marriage in a mo-ment of passion only to renege later. Protestant governments declared a marriage il-legitimate if the partners failed to register their marriage with a local official and a pastor. They usually also required parental consent, thus giving householders im-mense power in regulating marriage and the transmission of family property.

Enjoined to become obedient spouses and affectionate companions in Christ, women approached this new sexual regime with ambivalence. The new laws stipu-lated that women could seek divorce for desertion, impotence, and flagrant abuse, although in practice the marital courts encouraged reconciliation. These improve-ments came at a price, however: Protestant women were expected to be obedient wives, helpful companions, and loving mothers, but they could no longer join the convent and pursue their own religious paths outside the family. Luther's wife, Katharina von Bora, typified the new ideal Protestant woman. A former nun, she accepted her prescribed role in a patriarchal household: once married, Katharina ran the couple's household, feeding their children, relatives, and student boarders. Although she deferred to Luther—she addressed him as "Herr Doktor"—she nonetheless defended a woman's right as an equal in marriage. Other Protestant women spoke out even more decisively. Katharina Zell, wife of the reformer Matthew Zell, wrote hymns, fed the sick and imprisoned, and denounced the in-tolerance of the new Protestant clergy. Rebuking one for his persecution of dis-senters, she wrote, "You young fellows tread on the graves of the first fathers of this church in Strasbourg and punish all who disagree with you, but faith cannot be forced." She also insisted that women should have a voice in religious affairs.◆

◆ For several primary sources that reveal the impact of the Reformation on women's lives, see Document 37, Argula von Grumbach and John Hooker, "Women's Actions in the Reformation."

■ **Twelve Characteristics of an Insanely Angry Wife**
This 1530 broadsheet depicts with a woodcut and accompanying text "the twelve properties of an insanely angry wife." The negative representation of female anger reflects the values dominant in Reformation society: a harmonious household ruled by a patriarch. (Schlossmuseum, Gotha.)

State Power and Religious Conflict, 1500–1618

Even as religious disputes heightened the potential for conflict within Europe, the European powers continued to fight their traditional dynastic wars and still faced the military threat posed by the Muslim Ottoman Turks in the east. But these wars did not long deflect attention from increasing divisions within European countries. Rulers viewed religious divisions as a dangerous challenge to the unity of their realms and the stability of their regimes; a subject could very well swear greater allegiance to God than to his lord. Yet rulers often proved powerless to stem the rising tide of religious strife. Lutheranism flourished in the northern German states and Scandinavia; Calvinism spread from its headquarters in the Swiss city of Geneva all the way to England and Poland-Lithuania. The rapid expansion of Lutheranism and Calvinism created deadly political conflicts between Protestants and Catholics.

Wars among Habsburgs, Valois, and Ottomans

While the Reformation was taking hold in the German states, the great powers of Spain and France fought each other for the domination of Europe (Map 12.2). French claims over Italian territories sparked conflict in 1494, but the ensuing

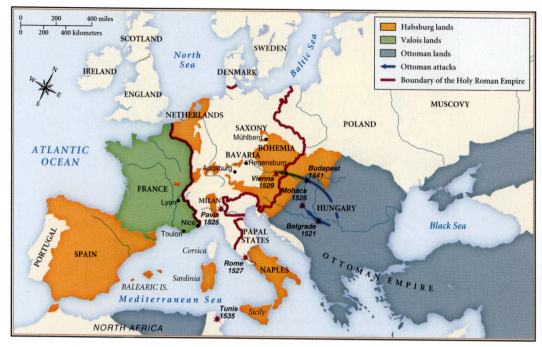

■ **MAP 12.2 Habsburg-Valois-Ottoman Wars, 1494–1559**

As the dominant European power, the Habsburg dynasty fought on two fronts: a religious war against the Islamic Ottoman Empire and a political war against the French Valois, who challenged Habsburg hegemony. The Mediterranean, the Balkans, and the Low Countries all became theaters of war.

Italian Wars soon involved most Christian monarchs and the Muslim Ottoman sultan as well. Despite some spectacular and bloody turns of fortune, no one power ultimately emerged victorious. In 1525, the troops of Emperor Charles V crushed the French army at Pavia, Italy, and captured the French king, Francis I (r. 1515–1547). Charles treated Francis as an honored guest but held him in Spain until he agreed to renounce his claims to Italy. Furious at this humiliation, Francis repudiated the agreement the moment he returned to France, reigniting the conflict. In 1527, Charles's troops invaded and then pillaged Rome to punish the pope for allying with the French. Among the imperial troops were German Protestant mercenaries, who delighted in tormenting the Catholic clergy. The sack of Rome shocked the Catholic church hierarchy and turned it toward reform.

Charles could not crush the French in one swift blow because he also had to counter the Muslim Ottomans in Hungary and along the Mediterranean coastline. The Ottoman Empire reached its height of power under Sultan Suleiman I, "the Magnificent" (r. 1520–1566). In 1526, a Turkish force destroyed the Hungarian army at Mohács. Three years later, the Ottoman army laid siege to Vienna; though unsuccessful, the siege set off alarms throughout Christian Europe. In 1535, Charles V tried to capture Tunis, the lair of North African pirates under Ottoman suzerainty. Desperate to overcome Charles's superior forces in Europe, Francis I eagerly forged an alliance with the Turkish sultan. The Turkish fleet besieged Nice, on the southern coast of France, to help the French wrest it from imperial occupiers. Francis even ordered all inhabitants of nearby Toulon to vacate their town so that he could turn it into a Muslim colony for eight months, complete with a mosque and slave market. Although the Turks eventually left Toulon, many Christians denounced the French alliance with the Turks against another Christian king. This brief Franco-Turkish alliance nonetheless showed that the age-old idea of Christian crusade against Islam had to make way for a new political strategy that considered religion as but one factor in power politics.

In 1559, the French king finally acknowledged defeat and signed the peace treaty of Cateau-Cambrésis. By then, years of conflict had drained the treasuries of all monarchs. Fueled by warfare, all armies grew in size, firepower became ever more deadly, and costs soared. For example, heavier artillery pieces meant that the rectangular walls of medieval cities had to be transformed into fortresses with jutting forts and gun emplacements. Charles V boasted the largest army in Europe— but he could not make ends meet with the proceeds from taxation, the sale of offices, and even outright confiscation.

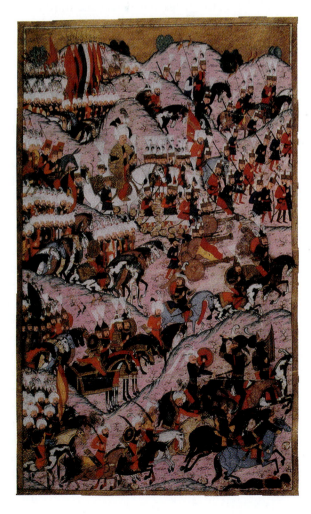

■ **The Battle at Mohács**

This Ottoman painting shows the 1529 victory of the sultan's army over the Hungarians at Mohács. The battle resulted in the end of the Hungarian kingdom, which would be divided into three realms under Ottoman, Habsburg, and Transylvanian rule. Notice the prominence of artillery and the Ottoman fighting force (the Janissaries) with muskets. The Ottomans commanded a vast army with modern equipment, a key to their military prowess in the sixteenth century. (Topkapi Palace Museum.)

Like other rulers, Charles V looked to private bankers for funds. Charles relied on the Fugger bank, based in the southern German imperial city of Augsburg. Jakob Fugger (1459–1525), nicknamed "the Rich," had loaned money to Charles V's grandfather, Maximilian I, in exchange for mining and minting concessions as well as hefty interest payments. In 1519, Fugger assembled a consortium of German and Italian bankers to secure the election of Charles V as Holy Roman Emperor. The assets of the Fuggers more than doubled between 1527 and 1547; Charles V's debts nearly doubled, too. The French kings fared no better. On his death in 1547, Francis owed the bankers of Lyon nearly 7 million pounds—approximately the entire royal income for that year. As a result, the Valois and the Habsburgs had to pay 14 to 18 percent interest on their loans.

French Wars of Religion

During the 1540s and 1550s, one-third of the French nobles converted to Calvinism, usually influenced by noblewomen who protected pastors, provided money and advice, and helped found schools and establish relief for the poor. With this noble backing, the Reformed church organized openly and held synods (church meetings), especially in southern and western France. The Catholic Valois monarchy tried to maintain a balance of power between Catholics and Calvinists. Francis I and his successor, Henry II (r. 1547–1559), both succeeded to a degree. But when Henry was accidentally killed during a jousting tournament, the weakened monarchy could no longer hold together the fragile realm.

Henry's fifteen-year-old son Francis II died in 1560, and he was succeeded by his brother, ten-year-old Charles IX (r. 1560–1574). His mother, Catherine de Medicis (1519–1589), acted as regent. Catherine, an Italian and a Catholic, urged limited toleration for the Calvinists—called Huguenots in France—in an attempt to maintain political stability, but her influence was severely limited. As one ambassador commented, "It is sufficient to say that she is a woman, a foreigner, and a Florentine to boot, born of a simple house, altogether beneath the dignity of the Kingdom of France." She could not prevent the eruption of civil war between Catholics and Huguenots in 1562.

Although a Catholic herself, Catherine aimed to preserve the throne for her son by playing the Catholic and Huguenot factions off each

Protestant Churches in France, 1562

Map legend:
- Protestant church with several pastors
- Protestant church
- Boundary of the Holy Roman Empire

0   100   200 miles
0   100   200 kilometers

North Sea
English Channel
NETH.
Paris
Nantes
ATLANTIC OCEAN
FRANCE
Geneva
Lyon
Navarre
SPAIN
Avignon
Marseille
Mediterranean Sea

other. To this end, she arranged the marriage of the king's Catholic sister Marguerite de Valois to Henry of Navarre, head of the Bourbon family, which had converted to Calvinism. Just four days after the wedding in August 1572, assassins tried but failed to kill one of the Huguenot nobles allied with the Bourbons, Gaspard de Coligny. Panicked at the thought of Huguenot revenge and perhaps herself implicated in the botched plot, Catherine convinced her son to order the killing of leading Huguenots. On St. Bartholomew's Day, August 24, a bloodbath began, fueled by years of growing animosity between Catholics and Protestants. In three days, Catholic mobs murdered three thousand Huguenots in Paris. Ten thousand died in the provinces over the next six weeks. The pope joyfully ordered the church bells rung throughout Catholic Europe; Spain's Philip II wrote Catherine that it was "the best and most cheerful news which at present could come to me." Protestants and Catholics alike now saw the conflict as an international struggle for survival that required aid to coreligionists in other countries. In this way, the French Wars of Religion paved the way for wider international conflicts over religion in the future.

The religious division in France grew even more dangerous when Charles IX died and his brother Henry III (r. 1574–1589) became king. Like his brothers before him, Henry III failed to produce an heir. Next in line to succeed the throne was none other than the Calvinist Bourbon leader Henry of Navarre. Because Henry III saw an even greater threat to his authority in a newly formed Catholic League, which had requested Spain's help in rooting out Protestantism in France, he took action against the league. In 1588, he summoned two prominent league leaders to a meeting and had his men kill them. A few months later a fanatical monk stabbed Henry III to death, and Henry of Navarre became Henry IV (r. 1589–1610), despite Spain's attempt to block his way with military intervention.

The new king soon concluded that to establish control over the war-weary country he had to place the interests of the French state ahead of his Protestant faith. In 1593, Henry IV publicly embraced Catholicism, reputedly explaining his conversion with the phrase "Paris is worth a Mass." In 1598, he made peace with Spain and issued the Edict of Nantes, in which he granted the Huguenots a large measure of religious toleration.◆ The approximately 1.25 million Huguenots became a legally protected minority within an officially Catholic kingdom of some 20 million people. Protestants were free to worship in specified towns and were allowed their own troops, fortresses, and even courts. Few believed in religious toleration, but Henry IV followed the advice of those neutral Catholics and Calvinists called *politiques* who urged him to give priority to the development of a durable state. Although their opponents hated them for their compromising spirit, the *politiques* believed that religious disputes could be resolved only in the peace provided by strong government.

◆ For excerpts from Henry IV's proclamation, see Document 38, "Edict of Nantes."

The Edict of Nantes ended the French Wars of Religion, but Henry still needed to reestablish monarchical authority. He used court festivities and royal processions to rally subjects around him, and he developed a new class of royal officials to counterbalance the fractious nobility. In exchange for an annual payment, officials who had purchased their offices could pass them on to heirs or sell them to someone else. By buying offices that eventually ennobled their holders, rich middle-class merchants and lawyers could become part of a new social elite known as the "nobility of the robe" (named after the robes that magistrates wore, much like those judges wear today). New income raised by the increased sale of offices reduced the state debt and helped Henry build the base for a strong monarchy. His efforts did not, however, prevent his own assassination in 1610 after nineteen unsuccessful attempts.

Challenges to Habsburg Power and the Rise of the Dutch Republic

Charles V proved more successful at fending off the Turks and subduing the French than he did at resolving growing religious conflicts inside his empire. After an Imperial Diet at Regensburg in 1541 failed to patch up the theological differences between Protestants and Catholics, Charles secured papal support for a war against the Schmalkaldic League, a powerful alliance of Lutheran princes and cities. Charles's army occupied the German imperial cities in the south, restoring Catholic patricians and suppressing the Reformation wherever they triumphed. In 1547, Charles defeated the Schmalkaldic League armies at Mühlberg and captured the leading Lutheran princes. Jubilant, Charles proclaimed a decree, the "Interim," which restored Catholics' right to worship in Protestant lands while still permitting Lutherans to celebrate their own services. Riots broke out in many cities as resistance to the Interim spread. Charles's victory proved ephemeral, for after one of his former allies, Duke Maurice of Saxony, joined the other side, the princes revived the war in 1552 and chased a surprised, unprepared, and practically bankrupt emperor back to Italy.

Forced to negotiate, Charles V agreed to the Peace of Augsburg in 1555. The settlement recognized the Evangelical (Lutheran) church in the empire, accepted the secularization of church lands but "reserved" the existent ecclesiastical territories (mainly the bishoprics) for Catholics, and, most important, established the principle that all princes, whether Catholic or Lutheran, enjoyed the sole right to determine the religion of their lands and subjects. Significantly, the Peace excluded Calvinist, Anabaptist, and other dissenting groups from the settlement. The Peace of Augsburg preserved a fragile peace in central Europe until 1618, but the exclusion of Calvinists would plant the seeds for future conflict.

Exhausted by constant war and depressed by the disunity in Christian Europe, Charles V resigned his many thrones in 1555 and 1556, leaving his Netherlandish-Burgundian and Spanish dominions to his son, Philip II, and his Austrian lands to his brother, Ferdinand, who was also elected Holy Roman Emperor to succeed Charles. Retiring to a monastery in southern Spain, the once powerful Christian monarch spent his last years quietly seeking salvation. Although Philip II of Spain (r. 1556–1598) ruled over fewer territories than his father, his inheritance still left him the most powerful ruler in Europe (Map 12.3). In addition to the western Habsburg lands in Spain and the Netherlands, he had inherited all the Spanish colonies recently settled in the New World of the Americas. In 1580, when the king of Portugal died without a direct heir, Philip took over this neighboring realm with its rich empire in Africa, India, and the Americas. Gold and silver funneled from the colonies supported his campaigns against the Ottoman Turks and French and English Protestants.

A deeply devout Catholic, Philip II came to the Spanish throne at age twenty-eight determined to restore Catholic unity in Europe and lead the Christian defense against the Muslims. His brief marriage to Mary Tudor (Mary I of England) did not produce an heir, but it and his subsequent marriage to Elisabeth de Valois, the sister of Charles IX and Henry III of France, gave him reason enough to oppose the spread of Protestantism in England and France. In 1571, Philip joined with Venice and the papacy to defeat the Turks in a great sea battle off the Greek coast at Lepanto. But Philip could not rest on his laurels. Between 1568 and 1570, the Moriscos—Muslim converts to Christianity who remained secretly faithful to Islam—had revolted in the south of Spain, killing 90 priests and 1,500 Christians. The victory at Lepanto destroyed any prospect that the Turks might come to their aid, yet Philip nonetheless forced 50,000 Moriscos to leave their villages and resettle in other regions. In 1609, his successor, Philip

■ **Titian, *Gloria* (detail)**

All military glory and earthly power is doomed to fade away, as the Venetian painter Titian (1477–1576) vividly depicted in Gloria. Among the multitude turning to the Trinity in the heavens is the Emperor Charles V, dressed in a white robe. Painted after his abdication in 1556, Gloria *is a reminder to Charles of the transience of earthly glory, for white is both the color of newborn innocence and that of the burial shroud.*

(Institut Amatller d'Art Hispanic.)

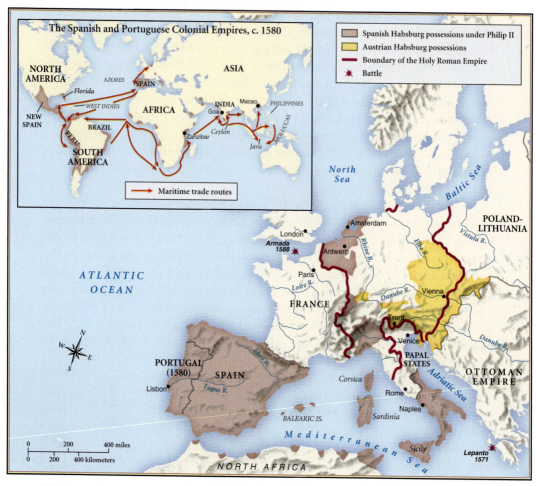

■ **MAP 12.3 The Empire of Philip II, r. 1556–1598**
Spanish king Philip II drew revenues from a truly worldwide empire. In 1580, he was the richest European ruler, but the demands of governing such far-flung territories eventually drained many of his resources.

III, ordered their expulsion, and by 1614 some 300,000 Moriscos had been forced to relocate to North Africa.

The Calvinists of the Netherlands were less easily intimidated than the Moriscos: they were far from Spain and accustomed to being left alone. In 1566, Calvinists in the Netherlands attacked Catholic churches, smashing stained-glass windows and statues of the Virgin Mary. Philip sent an army, which executed more than 1,100 people during the next six years. When resistance revived, the Spanish responded with more force, culminating in November 1576 when Philip's long-unpaid mercenary armies sacked Antwerp, then Europe's wealthiest commercial city.

In eleven days of horror known as the Spanish Fury, the Spanish soldiers slaughtered seven thousand people. Shocked into response, the ten largely Catholic southern provinces formally allied with the seven largely Protestant northern provinces and expelled the Spaniards. In 1579, however, the Catholic southern provinces returned to the Spanish fold. Despite the assassination in 1584 of William of Orange, the leader of the anti-Spanish forces, Spanish troops never regained control in the north.

The Netherlands during the Revolt, c. 1580

Spain would not formally recognize the independence of the United Provinces until 1648, but by the end of the sixteenth century the Dutch Republic was a self-governing state sheltering a variety of religious groups. The princes of Orange (whose name came from family lands in southern France) resembled a ruling family in the Dutch Republic, but their powers paled next to those of local interests. Urban merchant and professional families known as "regents" controlled the towns and provinces. Each province (Holland was the most populous of the seven provinces) governed itself and sent delegates to the one common institution, the States General. Well situated for maritime commerce, the Dutch Republic developed a thriving economy based on shipping and shipbuilding. By 1670, the Dutch commercial fleet was larger than the English, French, Spanish, Portuguese, and Austrian fleets combined.

Since the Dutch traded with anyone anywhere, it is perhaps not surprising that Dutch society tolerated more religious diversity than the other European states. One-third of the Dutch population remained Catholic, and the secular authorities allowed Catholics to worship as they chose in private. Because Protestant sects could generally count on toleration from local regents, they remained peaceful. The Dutch Republic also had a relatively large Jewish population because many Jews had settled there after being driven out of Spain and Portugal; from 1597, Jews could worship openly in their synagogues. This openness to various religions helped make the Dutch Republic one of Europe's chief intellectual and scientific centers in the seventeenth and eighteenth centuries.

England Goes Protestant

Until 1527, England's king Henry VIII (r. 1509–1547) firmly opposed the Reformation, even receiving the title "Defender of the Faith" from Pope Leo X for a treatise Henry wrote against Luther. Henry's family problems changed his mind. Henry had married Catherine of Aragon (d. 1536), the daughter of Ferdinand and Isabella of Spain and the aunt of Charles V, and the marriage had produced a daughter, Princess Mary (known as Mary Tudor). Henry wanted a male heir to consolidate the rule of his Tudor dynasty, and he had fallen in love with Anne Boleyn, a lady-in-waiting at court and a strong supporter of the Reformation. In 1527, Henry asked the reigning pope, Clement VII, to declare his eighteen-year marriage to Catherine invalid on the grounds that she was the widow of his older brother, Arthur. Arthur and Catherine's marriage, which apparently was never consummated, had been annulled by Pope Julius II.

Around "the king's great matter" unfolded a struggle for political and religious control. When Henry failed to secure a papal dispensation for his divorce, he chose two Protestants as his new loyal servants: Thomas Cromwell (1485–1540) as chancellor and Thomas Cranmer (1489–1556) as archbishop of Canterbury. Under their leadership the English Parliament passed a number of acts between 1529 and 1536 that severed ties between the English church and Rome. The Act of Supremacy of 1529 established Henry as the head of the so-called Anglican church (the Church of England), invalidated the claims of Catherine and Princess Mary to the throne, recognized Henry's marriage to Anne Boleyn, and allowed the English crown to confiscate the properties of the monasteries.

By 1536, Henry had grown tired of Anne Boleyn, who had given birth to the future Queen Elizabeth I but had produced no sons. The king, who would go on to marry four other wives but father only one son, Edward (by his third wife, Jane Seymour), had Anne beheaded on the charge of adultery, an act that he defined as treason. Thomas More, once Henry's chancellor, had been executed in 1535 for treason—in his case, for refusing to recognize Henry as "the only supreme head on earth of the Church of England"—and Cromwell suffered the same fate in 1540 when he lost favor. After Henry's death in 1547, the Anglican church, nominally Protestant, still retained much traditional Catholic doctrine and ritual. But the principle of royal supremacy in religious matters would remain a lasting feature of Henry's reforms.

Under Edward VI (r. 1547–1553) and Mary Tudor (r. 1553–1558), official religious policies oscillated between Protestant reforms and Catholic restoration. The boy-king Edward welcomed prominent Protestant refugees from continental Europe. When Mary succeeded him, however, she restored Catholicism and executed three hundred Protestants. Hundreds more fled. Finally, after Anne Boleyn's daughter, Elizabeth, came to the throne in 1558, the Anglican cause again gained momentum. As Elizabeth I (r. 1558–1603) moved to solidify her personal power and the authority of the Anglican church, she had to squash uprisings by Catholics in the north and at least two serious plots against her life. She also had to hold off Calvinist Puritans who pushed for more reform and Spain's Philip II, who first wanted to be her husband then, failing that, planned to invade her country to restore Catholicism.

The Puritans were strict Calvinists who opposed all vestiges of Catholic ritual in the Church of England. After Elizabeth became queen, many Puritans returned from exile abroad, but Elizabeth resisted their demands for drastic changes in Anglican ritual and governance. She had assumed control as "supreme governor" of the Church of England, replacing the pope as the ultimate religious authority, and she appointed all bishops. The Church of England's Thirty-Nine Articles of Religion, issued in 1563, incorporated elements of Catholic ritual along with Calvinist doctrines. Puritan ministers angrily denounced the Church of England's "popish attire and foolish disguising, . . . tithings, holy days, and a thousand more abominations." Puritans tried to undercut the bishops' authority by placing control of church administration in the hands of a local presbytery made up of the minister and the elders of the congregation. Elizabeth rejected this Calvinist "presbyterianism." The Puritans nonetheless steadily gained influence. Known for their emphasis on strict moral lives, the Puritans tried to close the theaters and Sunday fairs and insisted that every father "make his house a little church" by teaching the children to read the Bible. At Puritan urging, a new translation of the Bible, known as the King James Bible after Elizabeth's successor, James I, was authorized in 1604. Believing themselves God's elect and England an "elect nation," the Puritans also urged Elizabeth to help Protestants in Europe.

Spain's Philip II had been married to Elizabeth's half-sister Mary Tudor and had enthusiastically seconded Mary's efforts to return England to Catholicism. When Mary died, Elizabeth rejected Philip's proposal of marriage and eventually provided funds and troops to the Dutch rebels. Philip II bided his time as long as she remained unmarried and her Catholic cousin Mary Stuart, better known as Mary, Queen of Scots, stood next in line to inherit the English throne. In 1568, Scottish Calvinists forced Mary to abdicate the throne of Scotland in favor of her year-old son James (eventually James I of England), who was then raised as a Protestant. The Scottish Calvinists feared Mary's connections to Catholic France; her mother was French and devoutly

■ **Glorifying the Ruler**

This exquisite miniature (c. 1560) attributed to Levina Teerlinc, a Flemish woman who painted for the English court, shows Queen Elizabeth I, dressed in purplish blue, participating in an Easter Week ceremony at which the monarch washed the feet of poor people before presenting them with money, food, and clothing. The ceremony was held to imitate Christ's washing of the feet of his disciples; it showed that the queen could exercise every one of the ruler's customary roles. (Private collection.)

Catholic, and Mary Stuart had earlier been married to France's Francis II (he died in 1560). After her abdication, Mary spent nearly twenty years under house arrest in England, fomenting plots against Elizabeth. In 1587, when Mary's letter offering her succession rights to Philip was discovered, Elizabeth overcame her reluctance to execute a fellow monarch and ordered Mary's beheading.

In response, Pope Sixtus V decided to subsidize a Catholic crusade under Philip's leadership against the heretical queen, "the English Jezebel." At the end of May 1588, Philip II sent his *armada* (Spanish for "fleet") of 130 ships from Lisbon toward the English Channel. The English scattered the Spanish Armada by sending blazing fire ships into its midst. A great gale then forced the Spanish to flee around Scotland. When the Armada limped home in September, half the ships had been lost and thousands of sailors were dead or starving. Protestants throughout Europe rejoiced. A Spanish monk lamented, "Almost the whole of Spain went into mourning."

By the time Philip II died in 1598, his great empire had begun to lose its luster. The costs of fighting the Dutch, the English, and the French mounted, and an overburdened peasantry could no longer pay the taxes required to meet rising expenses. In his novel *Don Quixote* (1605), the Spanish writer Miguel de Cervantes captured the sadness of Spain's loss of grandeur. Cervantes himself had been wounded at Lepanto, held captive in Algiers, and then served as a royal tax collector. His hero, a minor nobleman, wants to understand "this thing they call reason of state," but he reads so many romances and books of chivalry that he loses his wits and wanders the countryside hoping to re-create the heroic deeds of times past. He refuses to believe that these books are only fantasies: "Books which are printed under license from the king . . . can such be lies?" Don Quixote's futile adventures incarnated the thwarted ambitions of a declining military aristocracy.

England could never have defeated Spain in a head-to-head battle on land, but Elizabeth made the most of her limited means and consolidated the country's position as a Protestant power. In her early years, she held out the prospect of marriage to many political suitors but never married. She cajoled Parliament with references to her female weaknesses, but she showed steely-eyed determination in protecting the monarchy's interests. Her chosen successor, James I (r. 1603–1625), came to the throne as king of both Scotland and England. Elizabeth left James secure in a kingdom of growing weight in world politics.

Catholic Renewal and Missionary Zeal

Reacting to the waves of Protestant challenge, the Catholic church mobilized for defense in a movement that is sometimes called the Counter-Reformation. Pope Paul III (r. 1534–1549) convened a general church council to codify church doctrine, and he personally approved the founding of new religious orders to undertake aggressive missionary efforts. The Council of Trent (Trent sat on the border between the Holy Roman Empire and Italy) met intermittently between 1545 and

1563, when it concluded its work. Its decisions shaped the essential character of Catholicism until the 1960s. Emphatically rejecting the major Protestant positions, the council reasserted the supremacy of clerical authority over the laity and reaffirmed the doctrine known as *transubstantiation*—that in the sacrament of the Eucharist, the bread of communion actually becomes Christ's body. But the council also undertook reforms; it insisted that bishops reside in their dioceses and ordered every diocese to establish a seminary to train priests. It also stipulated that all weddings take place in churches and be registered by the parish clergy. It further declared that all marriages remain valid, explicitly rejecting the Protestant authorization of divorce. All hopes of reconciliation between Protestants and Catholics faded.

The Counter-Reformation found its shock troops in the Society of Jesus, the new Catholic religious order that would prove the most important of the sixteenth century. Its founder was Ignatius of Loyola (1491–1556), a Spanish nobleman and charismatic former military officer, who abandoned his quest for military glory in favor of serving the church. Ignatius soon attracted other young men to his side, and in 1540 the pope recognized his small band of "Jesuits." By the time of Ignatius's death, Europe had one thousand Jesuits. Together with other new religious orders, the Jesuits restored the confidence of the faithful in the dedication and power of the Catholic church.◆

Jesuit missionaries set sail throughout the globe in order to bring Roman Catholicism to Africans, Asians, and Native Americans. They saw their effort as proof of the truth of Roman Catholicism and the success of their missions as a sign of divine favor, both particularly important in the face of Protestant challenge. To ensure rapid Christianization, European missionaries focused initially on winning over local elites. A number of young African nobles went to Portugal to be trained in theology—among them Dom Henry, a son of King Afonso I of Kongo, a Portuguese ally. Catholic missionaries preached the Gospel to Confucian scholar-officials in China and to the samurai (the warrior aristocracy) in Japan. Measured in numbers alone, the missionary enterprise seemed highly successful: by the second half of the sixteenth century, vast multitudes of Native Americans had become Christians at least in name, and thirty years after Francis Xavier's 1549 landing in Japan the Jesuits could claim over 100,000 Japanese converts.

After an initial period of relatively little racial discrimination, the Catholic church in the Americas and Africa adopted strict rules based on color. For example, the first Mexican Ecclesiastical Provincial Council in 1555 declared that holy orders were not to be conferred on Indians, *mestizos* (people of mixed European-Indian parentage), and *mulattos* (people of mixed European-African heritage), groups deemed "inherently unworthy of the sacerdotal [priestly] office." Europeans

---

◆ For several letters that express Ignatius's convictions and goals, see Document 39, St. Ignatius of Loyola, "A New Kind of Catholicism."

■ The Portuguese in Japan

In this sixteenth-century Japanese black-lacquer screen painting of Portuguese missionaries, the Jesuits are dressed in black and the Franciscans in brown. At the lower right corner is a Portuguese nobleman depicted with exaggerated "Western" features. The Japanese considered themselves lighter in skin color than the Portuguese, whom they classified as "barbarians." In turn, the Portuguese classified Japanese (and Chinese) as "whites." The perception of ethnic differences in the sixteenth century depended less on skin color than on clothing, eating habits, and other cultural signals. Color classifications were unstable and changed over time: by the late seventeenth century, Europeans no longer regarded Asians as "white." (Laurie Platt Winfrey, Inc.)

reinforced their sense of racial superiority with their perception of the "treachery" that Native Americans and Africans exhibited whenever they resisted domination. Frustrated in his efforts to convert Brazilian Indians, a Jesuit missionary wrote to his superior in Rome in 1563 that "for this kind of people it is better to be preaching with the sword and rod of iron." The Dominican Bartolomé de Las Casas (1474–1566) criticized the treatment of the Indians in Spanish America, yet even he argued that Africans should be imported in order to relieve the indigenous peoples, who were being worked to death.

The Thirty Years' War and the Balance of Power, 1618–1648

In 1618, a new series of violent conflicts between Catholics and Protestants erupted in the Holy Roman Empire. The final and most deadly of the wars of religion, the Thirty Years' War eventually drew in most European states. By the end of the war in 1648, many central European lands lay in ruins and many rulers were bankrupt. Reformation and Counter-Reformation had shattered the Christian humanist dream of peace and unity. The Thirty Years' War brought the preceding religious conflicts to a head and by its very violence effectively removed religion from future European disputes. Although religion still divided people *within* various states, after 1648 religion no longer provided the rationale for wars *between* European states. Out of the carnage would emerge centralized and powerful states that made increasing demands on ordinary people.

Origins and Course of the War

The fighting that devastated central Europe had its origins in religious, political, and ethnic divisions within the Holy Roman Empire. The Austrian Habsburg emperor and four of the seven electors who chose him were Catholic; the other three electors were Protestants. The Peace of Augsburg of 1555 was supposed to maintain the balance between Catholics and Lutherans, but it had no mechanism for resolving conflicts. Tensions rose as the Jesuits won many Lutheran cities back to Catholicism and as Calvinism, unrecognized under the Peace, made inroads into Lutheran areas. By 1613, two of the three Protestant electors had become Calvinists. When the Catholic Habsburg heir Archduke Ferdinand was crowned king of Bohemia in 1617, he began to curtail the religious freedom previously granted to Protestants. Protestants wanted to build new churches; Ferdinand wanted to stop them. Tensions boiled over when two Catholic deputy-governors tried to dissolve the meetings of Protestants.

On May 23, 1618, a crowd of angry Protestants surged up the stairs of the royal castle in Prague, trapped the two Catholic deputies, dragged them screaming for mercy to the windows, and hurled them to the pavement below. One of the rebels jeered: "We will see if your [Virgin] Mary can help you!" But because they landed in a dung heap, the Catholic deputies survived. Although no one died, this "defenestration" (from the French for "window," *la fenêtre*) of Prague touched off a new cycle of conflict. The Czechs, the largest ethnic group in Bohemia, established a Protestant assembly to spearhead resistance. A year later, when Ferdinand was elected emperor (as Ferdinand II, r. 1619–1637), the rebellious Bohemians deposed him and chose in his place the young Calvinist Frederick V of the Palatinate (r. 1616–1623). A quick series of clashes ended in 1620 when the imperial armies defeated the outmanned Czechs at the Battle of White Mountain, near Prague (see Map 12.4). Like the martyrdom of the religious reformer Jan Hus in 1415, White

Mountain became an enduring symbol of the Czechs' desire for self-determination. They would not gain their independence until 1918.

White Mountain did not end the war. Private mercenary armies (armies for hire) began to form during the fighting, and the emperor had virtually no control over them. In 1625, a Czech Protestant, Albrecht von Wallenstein (1583–1634), offered to raise an army for the Catholic emperor and soon had in his employ 125,000 soldiers, who occupied and plundered much of Protestant Germany with the emperor's approval. In response, the Lutheran king of Denmark Christian IV (r. 1596–1648) invaded to protect the Protestants and to extend his own influence. Wallenstein's forces defeated him. Emboldened by his general's victories, Ferdinand issued the Edict of Restitution in 1629, which outlawed Calvinism in the empire and reclaimed Catholic church properties confiscated by the Lutherans.

With Protestant interests in serious jeopardy, Gustavus Adolphus (r. 1611–1632) of Sweden marched into Germany in 1630. A Lutheran by religion, he also hoped to gain control over trade in northern Europe, where he had already ejected the Poles from present-day Latvia and Estonia. Poland and Lithuania had joined in a commonwealth in 1569, and many Polish and Lithuanian nobles converted to Lutheranism or Calvinism, but this did not ensure common cause with Sweden. Gustavus's highly trained army of some 100,000 soldiers made Sweden, with a population of only one million, the supreme power of northern Europe, even more powerful than Russia, which had barely recovered from the "Time of Troubles" that followed on the rule of Tsar Ivan IV (r. 1533–1584). Ivan "the Terrible" initiated Russian expansion eastward into Siberia but his moves westward ran up against the Poles and the Swedes.

Although Gustavus had religious motives for intervention in German affairs, events soon showed that power politics trumped religious interests. The Catholic French government under the leadership of Louis XIII (r. 1610–1643) and his chief minister Cardinal Richelieu (1585–1642) offered to subsidize Gustavus—and the Lutheran ruler accepted. The French hoped to counter Spanish involvement in the war and win influence and perhaps territory in the Holy Roman Empire. Gustavus defeated the imperial army and occupied the Catholic parts of southern Germany before he was killed at the battle of Lützen in 1632 (see Map 12.4). Once again the tide turned, but this time it swept Wallenstein with it. Because Wallenstein was rumored to be negotiating with Protestant powers, Ferdinand dismissed his general and had his henchmen assassinate him.

France openly joined the fray in 1635 by declaring war on Spain and soon after forged an alliance with the Calvinist Dutch to aid them in their struggle for independence from Spain. The two Catholic powers, France and Spain, pummeled each other. The Swedes kept up their pressure in Germany, the Dutch attacked the Spanish fleet, and a series of internal revolts shook the cash-strapped Spanish crown. In 1640, peasants in the rich northeastern province of Catalonia rebelled, overrunning Barcelona and killing the viceroy; the Catalans resented government confiscation of their crops and demands that they house and feed soldiers on their way to the French frontier. The Portuguese revolted in 1640 and proclaimed independence like the Dutch. In 1643, the Spanish suffered their first major defeat at French hands. Although the Spanish were forced to concede independence to Portugal (part of Spain only since 1580), they eventually suppressed the Catalan revolt.

France, too, faced exhaustion after years of rising taxes and recurrent revolts. In 1642, Richelieu died. Louis XIII followed him a few months later and was succeeded by his five-year-old son Louis XIV. With the queen mother, Anne of Austria, serving as regent and depending on the Italian cardinal, Mazarin, for advice, French politics once again moved into a period of instability, rumor, and crisis. All sides were ready for peace.

The Effects of Constant Fighting

When peace negotiations began in the 1640s, they did not come a moment too soon for the ordinary people of Europe. Some towns faced up to ten or eleven prolonged sieges during the fighting. In 1648, as negotiations dragged on, a Swedish army sacked the rich cultural capital Prague, plundered its churches and castles, and effectively eliminated it as a center of culture and learning.

Even worse suffering took place in the countryside. One of the earliest German novels, *The Adventures of a Simpleton* (1669) by Hans Grimmelshausen, recounts the horror of the war in detail. In one scene, the boy Simplicius has to watch while unidentified enemy cavalrymen ransack the house; rape the maid, his mother, and his sister; and hold the feet of his father to the fire until he tells where he hid his gold and jewels. Peasants fled their villages, which were often burned down. War and intermittent outbreaks of plague cost some German towns one-third or more of their population. One-third of the inhabitants of Bohemia also perished.

Soldiers did not fare all that much better. Governments increasingly short of funds often failed to pay the troops, and frequent mutinies, looting, and pillaging resulted. Armies attracted all sorts of displaced people desperately in need of provisions. In the last year of the Thirty Years' War, the Imperial-Bavarian Army had 40,000 men entitled to draw rations—and more than 100,000 wives, prostitutes, servants, children, maids, and other camp followers forced to scrounge for their own food. The bureaucracies of early-seventeenth-century Europe simply could not cope with such demands: armies and their hangers-on had to live off the countryside. The result was scenes like those witnessed by Simplicius.

The Peace of Westphalia, 1648

The comprehensive settlement finally provided by the Peace of Westphalia—named after the German province where negotiations took place—would serve as a model for resolving conflict among warring European states. For the first time, a diplomatic

■ The Horrors of the Thirty Years' War

The French artist Jacques Collot produced this engraving of the Thirty Years' War as part of a series called The Miseries and Misfortunes of War *(1633). The actions depicted resemble those in Hans Grimmelshausen's novel* The Adventures of a Simpleton, *based on Grimmelshausen's personal experience of the Thirty Years' War.* (The Granger Collection.)

congress addressed international disputes, and the signatories to the treaties guaranteed the resulting settlement. A method still in use, the congress was the first to bring *all* parties together, rather than two or three at a time.

France and Sweden gained most from the Peace of Westphalia. Although France and Spain continued fighting until 1659, France acquired parts of Alsace and replaced Spain as the prevailing power on the European continent. Baltic conflicts would not be resolved until 1661, but Sweden took several northern territories from the Holy Roman Empire (Map 12.4).

The Habsburgs lost the most. The Spanish Habsburgs recognized Dutch independence after eighty years of war. The Swiss Confederation and the German princes demanded autonomy from the Austrian Habsburg rulers of the Holy Roman Empire. Each German prince gained the right to establish Lutheranism, Catholicism, or Calvinism in his state, a right denied to Calvinist rulers by the Peace of Augsburg in 1555. The independence ceded to German princes sustained political divisions that would remain until the nineteenth century and prepared the way for the emergence of a new power, the Hohenzollern Elector of Brandenburg, who increased his territories and developed a small but effective standing army. After losing considerable territory in the west, the Austrian Habsburgs turned eastward to concentrate on restoring Catholicism to Bohemia and wresting Hungary from the Turks.

The Peace of Westphalia permanently settled the distributions of the main religions in the Holy Roman Empire: Lutheranism would dominate in the north, Calvinism in the area of the Rhine River, and Catholicism in the south (see "Map-

MAP 12.4 The Thirty Years' War and the Peace of Westphalia, 1648

The Thirty Years' War involved many of the major continental European powers. The arrows marking invasion routes show that most of the fighting took place in central Europe in the lands of the Holy Roman Empire. The German states and Bohemia sustained the greatest damage during the fighting. None of the combatants emerged unscathed because even ultimate winners such as Sweden and France depleted their resources of men and money.

ping the West," page 524). Most of the territorial changes in Europe remained intact until the nineteenth century. In the future, warfare between European states would be undertaken for reasons of national security, commercial ambition, or dynastic pride rather than to enforce religious uniformity. As the *politiques* of the late sixteenth century had hoped, state interests now outweighed motivations of faith in political affairs.

Growth of State Authority

Warfare increased the reach of states: as the size of armies increased, governments needed more men, more money, and more supervisory officials. Most armies in the 1550s had fewer than 50,000 men, but Gustavus Adolphus had 100,000 men under arms in 1631. In France, the rate of land tax paid by peasants doubled in the eight years after France joined the Thirty Years' War. In addition to raising taxes, governments deliberately depreciated the value of the currency, which often resulted in inflation and soaring prices; sold new offices; and manipulated the embryonic stock and bond markets. When all else failed, they declared bankruptcy. The Spanish government, for example, did so three times in the first half of the seventeenth century.

As the demand for soldiers and for the money to supply them rose, the number of state employees multiplied, paperwork proliferated, and appointment to office began to depend on university education in the law. Monarchs relied on advisers who began to take on the role of modern prime ministers. Continuity in Swedish affairs, especially after the death of Gustavus Adolphus, largely depended on Axel Oxenstierna, who played a central part in Swedish governments between 1611 and 1654. As Louis XIII's chief minister, Richelieu arranged support for the Lutheran Gustavus even though Richelieu was a cardinal of the Catholic church. His priority was *raison d'état* ("reason of state")—that is, the state's interest above all else. Richelieu silenced Protestants within France because they had become too independent, and he crushed noble and popular resistance to Louis's policies. He set up *intendants*—delegates from the king's council dispatched to the provinces— to oversee police, army, and financial affairs.

To justify the growth of state authority and the expansion of government bureaucracies, rulers carefully cultivated their royal images. James I of England explicitly argued that he ruled by divine right and was accountable only to God: "kings are not only God's lieutenant on earth, but even by God himself they are called gods." But words rarely sufficed to make the point, and rulers used displays at court to overawe their subjects. Already in the 1530s, the French court of Francis I numbered 1,600 people. Included were officials to handle finances, guard duty, clothing, and food as well as physicians, librarians, musicians, dwarfs, animal trainers, and a multitude of hangers-on. When the court changed residence, which it did frequently, no fewer than eighteen thousand horses were required to transport the people, furniture, and documents—not to mention the dogs and falcons for the royal hunt. Hunting and mock battles honed the military skills of the male courtiers. Francis once staged a mock combat at court involving twelve hundred "warriors," and he led a party to lay siege to a model town during which several players were accidentally killed.

Just as soldiers had to learn new drills for combat, courtiers had to learn to follow precise rituals. Court etiquette or "courtesy" had first been elaborated in Italy and spread from there to France, Spain, and other countries. In his influential treatise, *The Courtier* (1528), the Italian diplomat Baldassare Castiglione (1478–1529) depicted the ideal courtier as a gentleman who speaks in a refined language and carries himself with nobility and dignity in the service of his prince and his lady. Spain's king Philip IV (r. 1621–1665) translated this notion of courtesy into detailed regulations that set the wages, duties, and ceremonial functions of every courtier. At his new palace near Madrid, the courtiers lived amid extensive parks and formal gardens, artificial ponds and grottoes, an iron aviary (which led some critics to call the whole thing a "chicken coop"), a wild animal cage, a courtyard for bullfights, and rooms filled with sculptures and paintings. State funerals, public festivities, and court display, like the acquisition of art and the building of sumptuous palaces, served to underline the power and glory of the ruler.

Economic Crisis and Realignment

The devastation caused by the Thirty Years' War deepened an economic crisis that was already under way. After a century of rising prices, caused partly by massive transfers of gold and silver from the New World and partly by population growth, in the early 1600s prices began to level off and even to drop, and in most places population growth slowed. With fewer goods being produced, international trade fell into recession. Agricultural yields also declined. Just when states attempted to field ever-expanding standing armies, peasants and townspeople alike were less able to pay the escalating taxes needed to finance the wars. Famine and disease trailed grimly behind economic crisis and war, in some areas causing large-scale uprisings and revolts. Behind the scenes, the economic balance of power gradually shifted as northwestern Europe began to dominate international trade and broke the stranglehold of Spain and Portugal in the New World.

From Growth to Recession

By 1500, the cycle of demographic collapse and economic depression triggered by the Black Death of 1348 had passed. Even though religious and political turbulence led to population decline in some cities, such as war-torn Antwerp, other places grew rapidly: parts of Spain doubled in population, and England's population grew by 70 percent. The supply of precious metals swelled, too. Improvements in mining techniques in central Europe raised the output of silver and copper mines, and in the 1540s new silver mines had been discovered in Mexico and Peru. Spanish gold imports peaked in the 1550s, silver in the 1590s. (See "Taking Measure," page 508.) This flood of precious metals combined with population growth to fuel an astounding inflation in food prices in western Europe—400 percent in the sixteenth century—and a more moderate rise in the cost of manufactured goods. Wages rose much more slowly, at about half the rate of the increase in food prices, putting those at the bottom of the social scale in jeopardy.

When recession struck again after 1600, all the economic indicators slumped. After 1625, silver imports to Spain declined, in part because so many of the Native Americans who worked in Spanish colonial mines died from disease and in part because the ready supply of precious metals was progressively exhausted. Textile

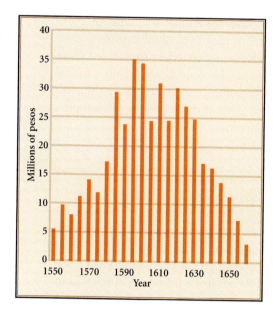

■ TAKING MEASURE **The Rise and Fall of Silver Imports to Spain, 1550–1660**

Gold and silver from the New World enabled the king of Spain to pursue aggressive policies in Europe and around the world. At what point did silver imports reach their highest level? Was the fall in silver imports precipitous or gradual? What can we conclude about the resources available to the Spanish king?

(From Earl J. Hamilton, *American Revolution and the Price Revolution in Spain, 1501–1650* [Cambridge: Harvard University Press, 1934].)

production fell in many countries and in some places nearly collapsed, largely because of decreased demand and a shrinking labor force. Even the relatively limited trade in African slaves stagnated, though its growth would resume after 1650 and skyrocket after 1700. African slaves were first transported to the new colony of Virginia in 1619, foreshadowing a major transformation of economic life in the New World colonies.

Demographic slowdown also signaled economic trouble. Overall, Europe's population may actually have declined, from 85 million in 1550 to 80 million in 1650. In the Mediterranean, growth apparently stopped in the 1570s. The most sudden reversal occurred in central Europe as a result of the Thirty Years' War: one-fourth of the inhabitants of the Holy Roman Empire perished in the 1630s and 1640s. The population continued to increase only in England and Wales, the Dutch Republic and the Spanish Netherlands, and Scandinavia.

Where the population stagnated or declined, agricultural prices dropped because of less demand, and farmers who produced for the market suffered. The price of grain fell most precipitously, causing many farmers to convert grain-growing land to pasture or vineyards. Interest in improvement of the land diminished. In some places, peasants abandoned their villages and left land to waste, as had happened during the plague epidemic of the late fourteenth century. The only country that emerged unscathed from this downturn was the Dutch Republic, principally because it had long excelled in agricultural innovation. Inhabiting Europe's most densely populated area, the Dutch developed systems of field drainage, crop rotation, and animal husbandry that provided high yields of grain for both people and animals. Their foreign trade, textile industry, crop production, and population all grew. After the Dutch, the English fared best; unlike the Spanish, the English never depended on New World gold and silver, and unlike most continental European countries, England escaped the direct impact of the Thirty Years' War.

Historians have long disagreed about the causes of the early-seventeenth-century recession. Some cite the inability of agriculture to support a growing population by the end of the sixteenth century; others blame the Thirty Years' War, the states' demands for more taxes, the irregularities in money supply resulting from rudimentary banking practices, or the waste caused by middle-class expenditures in the desire to emulate the nobility. To this list of causes, recent researchers have added climate change. Global cooling translated into advancing glaciers, falling temperatures, and great storms, like the one that blocked the escape of the Spanish Armada. Bad harvests, food shortages, and famine followed in short order.

Consequences of Economic Crisis

When grain harvests fell short, peasants immediately suffered because outside of England and the Dutch Republic, grain had replaced more expensive meat as the essential staple of most Europeans' diets. Peasants lived on bread, soup with a little fat or oil, peas or lentils, garden vegetables in season, and only occasionally a piece of meat or fish. Usually the adverse years differed from place to place, but from 1594 to 1597 most of Europe suffered from shortages that triggered revolts from Ireland to Muscovy. To head off social disorder, the English government drew up a new Poor Law in 1597 that required each community to support its poor. Many other governments also increased relief efforts.

Most people, however, did not respond to their dismal circumstances by rebelling or mounting insurrections. They simply left their huts and hovels and took to the road in search of food and charity. Overwhelmed officials recorded pitiful tales of suffering. Women and children died while waiting in line for food at convents or churches. Husbands left their wives and families to search for better conditions in other parishes or even other countries. Those left behind might be reduced to eating chestnuts, roots, bark, and grass. In eastern France in 1637, a witness reported, "The roads were paved with people. . . . Finally it came to cannibalism." Eventually compassion gave way to fear as these hungry vagabonds, who sometimes banded together to beg for bread, became more aggressive, occasionally threatening to burn a barn if they were not given food.

Successive bad harvests led to malnutrition, which weakened people and made them more susceptible to such epidemic diseases as the plague, typhoid fever, typhus, dysentery, smallpox, and influenza. Disease did not spare the rich, although many epidemics hit the poor hardest. The plague was feared most: in one year it could cause the death of up to half of a town's or village's population, and it struck with no discernible pattern. Nearly 5 percent of France's entire population died in the plague of 1628–1632.

Economic crisis heightened the contrast between prosperity and poverty. In England, the Dutch Republic, northern France, and northwestern Germany, the peasantry was disappearing: improvements gave some peasants the means to become farmers who rented substantial holdings, produced for the market, and in good times enjoyed relative comfort and higher status. Those who could not afford to plant new crops such as buckwheat or to use techniques that ensured higher yields became simple laborers with little or no land of their own. One-half to four-fifths of the peasants in Europe did not have enough land to support a family. They descended deeper into debt during difficult times and often lost their land to wealthier farmers or to city officials intent on developing rural estates. In the towns, widows who had been able to take over their late husbands' trade now found themselves excluded by the urban guilds or limited to short tenures.

Demographic historians have shown that European families reacted almost immediately to economic crisis. During bad harvests, they postponed marriages and had fewer children. When hard times passed, more people married and had more children. But even in the best of times, one-fifth to one-quarter of all children died in their first year, and half died before age twenty. Ten percent of women died in childbirth, and even in the richest homes, childbirth often occasioned an atmosphere of panic.

It might be assumed that families would have more children to compensate for high death rates, but from around 1600 to 1800, families in all ranks of society started to limit the number of children. Because methods of contraception were not widely known, they did this for the most part by marrying later; the average age at marriage during the seventeenth century rose from the early twenties to the late twenties. The average family had about four children. Poorer families seem to have had fewer children, wealthier ones more. Peasant couples, especially in eastern and southeastern Europe, had more children than urban couples because cultivation still required intensive manual labor.

The consequences of late marriage were profound. Young men and women were expected to put off marriage (*and* sexual intercourse) until their mid-to-late twenties—if they were among the lucky 50 percent who lived that long and not among the 10 percent who never married. Because both the Reformation and the Counter-Reformation stressed sexual fidelity and abstinence before marriage, the number of births out of wedlock was relatively small (2–5 percent of births); premarital intercourse was generally tolerated only after a couple had announced their engagement.

■ **The Life of the Poor**

This mid-seventeenth-century painting by the Dutch artist Adriaen Pietersz van de Venne depicts the poor peasant weighed down by his wife and child. An empty food bowl signifies their hunger. In retrospect, this painting seems unfair to the wife of the family; she is shown in clothes that are not nearly as tattered as her husband's and is portrayed entirely as a burden, rather than as a help in getting by in hard times. In reality, many poor men abandoned their homes in search of work, leaving their wives behind to cope with hungry children and what remained of the family farm.

(Allen Memorial Art Museum, Oberlin College, Oberlin, Ohio, Mrs. F. F. Prentiss Fund, 1960.)

The Economic Balance of Power

Just as the recession produced winners and losers among ordinary people, so, too, it created winners and losers among the competing states of Europe. The seventeenth-century downturn ended the dominance of Mediterranean economies, which had endured since the time of the Greeks and Romans, and ushered in the new powers of northwestern Europe with their growing Atlantic economies. With expanding populations and geographical positions that promoted Atlantic trade, England and the Dutch Republic vied with France to become the leading mercantile powers. Northern Italian industries were eclipsed; Spanish commerce with the New World dropped. Amsterdam replaced Seville, Venice, Genoa, and Antwerp as the center of European trade and commerce. The plague also had differing effects. Whereas central Europe and the Mediterranean countries took generations to recover from its ravages, northwestern Europe quickly replaced its lost population, no doubt because this area's people had suffered less from the effects of the Thirty Years' War and from the malnutrition related to the economic crisis.

All but the remnants of serfdom had disappeared in western Europe, but in eastern Europe nobles reinforced their dominance over peasants, and the burden of serfdom increased. The price rise of the sixteenth century had prompted Polish and eastern German nobles to expand their holdings and step up their production of grain for western markets. To raise production, they demanded more rent and dues from their peasants, who the government decreed had to stay in their villages. Although noble landlords lost income in the economic downturn of the first half of the seventeenth century, their peasants gained nothing. Those who were already dependent became serfs—completely tied to the land. In Muscovy, the complete enserfment of the peasantry would eventually be recognized in the Code of Laws in 1649. Although enserfment produced short-term profits for landlords, in the long run it retarded economic development in eastern Europe and kept most of the population in a stranglehold of illiteracy and hardship.

Competition for colonies overseas intensified because many European states, including Sweden and Denmark, considered it a branch of mercantilist policy. According to the doctrine of mercantilism, governments should sponsor policies to increase national wealth. To this end, they chartered private joint-stock companies to enrich investors by importing fish, furs, tobacco, and precious metals, if they could be found, and to develop new markets for European products. Because Spain and Portugal had divided among themselves the rich spoils of South America, other prospective colonizers had to carve niches in seemingly less hospitable places, especially North America and the Caribbean. Eventually the English, French, and Dutch would dominate commerce with these colonies (see Map 14.1, page 574).

In establishing permanent colonies, the Europeans created whole new communities across the Atlantic. Careful plans often fell afoul of the hazards of transatlantic shipping, however. Originally, the warm climate of Virginia made it an attractive destination for the Pilgrims, a small English sect that, unlike the Puritans, attempted to separate from the Church of England. But the *Mayflower,* which had sailed for Virginia with Pilgrim emigrants, landed far to the north in Massachusetts, where in 1620 the settlers founded New Plymouth Colony. As the religious situation for English Puritans worsened, wealthier people became willing to emigrate, and in 1629 a prominent group of Puritans incorporated themselves as the Massachusetts Bay Company. They founded a virtually self-governing colony headquartered in Boston.

Colonization gradually spread. Migrating settlers, including dissident Puritans, soon founded new settlements in Connecticut and Rhode Island. Catholic refugees from England established a much smaller colony in Maryland. By the 1640s, the British North American colonies had more than fifty thousand people—not including the Indians, whose numbers had been decimated in epidemics and wars—and the foundations of representative government in locally chosen colonial assemblies. By contrast, French Canada had only about three thousand European inhabitants by 1640. Because the French government refused to let Protestants emigrate from France and establish a foothold in the New World, it denied itself a ready population for the settling of permanent colonies abroad. Both England and France turned their attention to the Caribbean in the 1620s and 1630s when they occupied the islands of the West Indies after driving off the native Caribs. These islands would prove ideal for a plantation economy of tobacco and sugarcane.

A Clash of Worldviews

The countries that moved ahead economically in this period—England, the Dutch Republic, and to some extent France—turned out to be the most receptive to new secular worldviews. Although *secularization* did not entail a loss of religious faith, it did prompt a search for nonreligious explanations for political authority and natural phenomena. During the late sixteenth and early seventeenth centuries, art, political theory, and science all began to break some of their bonds with religion. A "scientific revolution" was in the making. Yet traditional attitudes such as belief in magic and witchcraft did not disappear. People of all classes accepted supernatural explanations for natural phenomena, a view only gradually and partially undermined by new ideas.

The Arts in an Age of Religious Conflict

A new form of artistic expression—professional theater—developed to express secular values in this age of conflict over religious beliefs. In previous centuries, traveling companies made their living by playing at major religious festivals and by repeating their performances in small towns and villages along the way. In London, Seville, and Madrid, the first professional acting companies performed before paying audiences in the 1570s. A huge outpouring of playwriting followed. The Spanish playwright Lope de Vega (1562–1635) alone wrote more than fifteen hundred plays. Between 1580 and 1640, three hundred English playwrights produced works for a hundred different acting companies. Theaters did a banner business despite Puritan opposition in England and Catholic objections in Spain. Shopkeepers, apprentices, lawyers, and court nobles crowded into open-air theaters to see everything from bawdy farces to profound tragedies.

The most enduring and influential playwright of the time was the Englishman William Shakespeare (1564–1616), son of a glovemaker, who wrote three dozen plays and acted in one of the chief troupes. Shakespeare never referred to religious disputes in his plays and did not set the action in contemporary England. Yet his works clearly reflected the political concerns of his age: the nature of power and the crisis of authority. Three of his greatest tragedies—*Hamlet* (1601), *King Lear* (1605), and *Macbeth* (1606)—show the uncertainty and even chaos that result when power is misappropriated or misused. In each play, family relationships are linked to questions about the legitimacy of government, just as they were for Elizabeth I herself. Hamlet's mother marries the man who murdered his royal father and usurped the crown; two of Lear's daughters betray him when he tries to divide his kingdom; Macbeth's wife persuades him to murder the king and seize the throne. One character in the final act describes the tragic story of Prince Hamlet as one "Of carnal, bloody, and unnatural acts; / Of accidental judgments, casual slaughters; / Of deaths put on by cunning and forced cause." Like many real-life people, Shakespeare's tragic characters found little peace in the turmoil of their times.

Although many rulers commissioned paintings on secular subjects for their own uses, religion still played an important role in painting, especially in Catholic Europe. The popes competed with secular rulers to hire the most talented painters and sculptors. Pope Julius II, for example, engaged the Florentine Michelangelo Buonarroti (1475–1564) to paint the walls and ceiling of the Sistine Chapel and to prepare a tomb and sculpture for himself. Michelangelo's talents served to glorify a papacy under siege, just as other artists burnished the image of secular rulers.

In the late sixteenth century, the artistic style known as Mannerism departed abruptly from the Renaissance perspective of painters like Michelangelo. An almost

theatrical style, Mannerism allowed painters to distort perspective to convey a message or emphasize a theme. The most famous Mannerist painter, called El Greco because he was of Greek origin, trained in Venice and Rome before he moved to Spain in the 1570s. El Greco crowded figures or objects into every available space, used larger-than-life or elongated figures, and created new and often strange visual effects. The religious intensity of El Greco's pictures shows that faith still motivated many artists, as it did much political conflict.

■ **Mannerist Painting**

With its distortion of perspective, crowding of figures, and mysterious allusions, El Greco's painting The Dream of Philip II *(1577) is a typical Mannerist painting. Philip II can be seen in his usual black clothing with a lace ruffle as his only decoration.*

(© National Gallery, London.)

The most important new style was the baroque, which, like Mannerism, originated in the Italian states. Like many historical categories, *baroque* was not used as a label by people living at the time; in the eighteenth century, art critics coined the word to mean shockingly bizarre, confused, and extravagant, and until the late nineteenth century, art historians and collectors largely disdained the baroque. In place of the Renaissance emphasis on harmonious design, unity, and clarity, the baroque featured exaggerated lighting, intense emotions, release from restraint, and even a kind of artistic sensationalism.

Closely tied to the Counter-Reformation, the baroque melodramatically reaffirmed the emotional depths of the Catholic faith and glorified both church and monarchy. The style spread from Rome to other Italian states and then into central Europe. The Catholic Habsburg territories, including Spain and the Spanish Netherlands, embraced the style. The Spanish built baroque churches in their American colonies as part of their massive conversion campaign. Within Europe, Protestant countries largely resisted the baroque, as we can see by comparing Flemish painters from the Spanish Netherlands with Dutch artists. The first great baroque painter was an Italian-trained Fleming, Peter Paul Rubens (1577–1640). A devout Catholic, Rubens painted vivid, exuberant pictures on religious themes, packed with figures. His was an extension of the theatrical baroque style, conveying ideas through broad gestures and dramatic poses. The great Dutch Protestant painters of the next generation, such as Rembrandt van Rijn (1606–1669), sometimes used biblical subjects, but their pictures were more realistic and focused on everyday scenes. Many of them suggested the Protestant concern for an inner life and personal faith rather than the public expression of religiosity.

Differences in musical style also reflected religious divisions. The new Protestant churches developed their own distinct music, which differentiated their worship from the Catholic Mass and also marked them as Lutheran or Calvinist. Unlike Catholic services, for which professional musicians sang in Latin, Protestant services invited the entire congregation to sing, thereby encouraging participation. Martin Luther, an accomplished lute player, composed many hymns in German, including "Ein' feste Burg" ("A Mighty Fortress"). Protestants sang hymns before going into battle, and Protestant martyrs sang before their executions. Lutheran composers developed a new form, the strophic hymn, or chorale, a religious text set to a tune that is then enriched through harmony. Calvinist congregations, in keeping with their emphasis on simplicity and austerity, often sang in unison and avoided harmony.

A new secular musical form, the opera, grew up parallel to the baroque style in the visual arts. First influential in the Italian states, opera combined music, drama, dance, and scenery in a grand sensual display, often with themes chosen to please the ruler and the aristocracy. Operas could be based on typically baroque sacred subjects or on traditional stories. Like Shakespeare, opera composers often turned to familiar stories their audiences would recognize and readily follow. One of the

■ **Baroque Painting**

The Flemish baroque painter Peter Paul Rubens used monumental canvases to glorify the French queen Marie de Medici, wife of Henry IV and mother of Louis XIII. Between 1622 and 1625, Rubens painted twenty-four panels like this one to decorate Marie's residence in Paris (some were more than twenty feet wide). Baroque style is evident in its gigantic size, the imposing figures captured in rich colors, and the epic setting to exalt a secular ruler. In this scene, Henry is shown handing over government to his wife on behalf of his young son (Henry was assassinated in 1610). (Giraudon/Art Resource, NY.)

most innovative composers of opera was Claudio Monteverdi (1567–1643), whose work contributed to the development of both opera and the orchestra. His earliest operatic production, *Orfeo* (1607), was the first to require an orchestra of about forty instruments and to include instrumental as well as vocal sections.

The Natural Laws of Politics

In reaction to the wars over religious beliefs, jurists and scholars not only began to defend the primacy of state interests over those of religious conformity but also insisted on secular explanations for politics. Machiavelli had pointed in this direction with his prescriptions for Renaissance princes in the early sixteenth century, but the intellectual movement gathered steam in the aftermath of the religious violence unleashed by the Reformation. Religious toleration could not take hold until government could be organized on some principle other than one king, one faith. The French *politiques* Michel de Montaigne and Jean Bodin and the Dutch jurist Hugo Grotius started the search for those principles.

Michel de Montaigne (1533–1592) was a French magistrate who resigned his office in the midst of the wars of religion to write about the need for tolerance and open-mindedness. Although himself a Catholic, Montaigne painted on the beams of his study the words "All that is certain is that nothing is certain." To capture this need for personal reflection in an age of religious turmoil, he invented the essay as a short and thoughtful form of expression. He revived the ancient doctrine of skepticism, which held that total certainty is never attainable—a doctrine, like toleration of religious differences, that was repugnant to Protestants and Catholics alike, both of whom were certain that their religion was the right one. Montaigne also questioned the common European habit of calling newly discovered peoples in the New World barbarous and savage: "Everyone gives the title of barbarism to everything that is not in use in his own country."

The French Catholic lawyer Jean Bodin (1530–1596) sought systematic secular answers to the problem of disorder in *The Six Books of the Republic* (1576). Comparing the different forms of government throughout history, he identified three basic types of sovereignty: monarchy, aristocracy, and democracy. Only strong monarchical power offered hope for maintaining order, he insisted. Bodin rejected any doctrine of the right to resist tyrannical authority: "I denied that it was the function of a good man or of a good citizen to offer violence to his prince for any reason, however great a tyrant he might be" (and, it might be added, whatever his ideas on religion). Bodin's ideas helped lay the foundation for absolutism, the idea that the monarch should be the sole and uncontested source of power. Nonetheless, the very discussion of types of governments in the abstract implied that they might be subject to choice rather than simply being God-given, as most rulers maintained.

During the Dutch revolt against Spain, the jurist Hugo Grotius (1583–1645) gave new meaning to the notion of "natural law"—laws of nature that give legitimacy to government and stand above the actions of any particular ruler or religious group. Grotius argued that natural law stood beyond the reach of either secular or divine authority; it would be valid even if God did not exist. Natural law should govern politics, by this account, not Scripture, religious authority, or tradition. Such ideas got Grotius into trouble with both Catholics and Protestants. When the Dutch Protestant government arrested him, his wife helped him escape prison by hiding him in a chest of books. Grotius was one of the first to argue that international conventions should govern the treatment of prisoners of war and the making of peace treaties.

At the same time that Grotius expanded the principles of natural law, many jurists worked on codifying the huge amount of legislation and jurisprudence devoted to legal forms of torture. Most states and the courts of the Catholic church used torture when the crime was very serious and the evidence seemed to point to a particular defendant but no definitive proof had been established. The judges ordered torture—hanging the accused by the hands with a rope thrown over a beam, pressing the legs in a leg screw, or just tying the hands very tightly—to extract a confession, which had to be given with a medical expert and notary present and had to be repeated without torture. Children, pregnant women, the elderly, aristocrats, kings, and even professors were exempt.

Grotius's conception of natural law directly challenged the use of torture. To be in accord with natural law, Grotius argued, governments had to defend natural rights, which he defined as life, body, freedom, and honor. Grotius's ideas would influence John Locke and the American revolutionaries of the eighteenth century: although Grotius did not encourage rebellion in the name of natural law or rights, he did hope that someday all governments would adhere to these principles and stop killing their own and one another's subjects in the name of religion. Natural law and natural rights would play an important role in the founding of constitutional governments from the 1640s forward and in the establishment of various charters of human rights in our own time.

Origins of the Scientific Revolution

Although the Catholic and Protestant churches encouraged the study of science and many prominent scientists were themselves clerics, the search for a secular, scientific method of determining the laws of nature eventually challenged the traditional accounts of natural phenomena. Christian doctrine had incorporated the scientific teachings of ancient philosophers, especially Ptolemy and Aristotle; now these came into question. A revolution in astronomy challenged the Ptolemaic view, endorsed by the Catholic church, which held that the sun revolved around the earth. Remarkable advances took place in medicine, too, which laid the foundations for modern anatomy and pharmacology. By the early seventeenth century, a new scientific method had been established based on a combination of experimental observation and mathematical deduction. Conflicts between the new science and religion followed almost immediately.

The "new science" began with the first subject ever studied by scientists, astronomy. The traditional account of the movement of the heavens derived from the second-century Greek astronomer Ptolemy, who put the earth at the center of the cosmos. Above the earth were fixed the moon, the stars, and the planets in concentric crystalline spheres; beyond these fixed spheres dwelt God and the angels. The planets revolved around the earth at the command of God. In this view, the sun revolved around the earth; the heavens were perfect and unchanging, and the earth was "corrupted." Ptolemy insisted that the planets revolved in perfectly circular orbits (because circles were more "perfect" than other figures). To account for the actual elliptical paths that could be observed and calculated, he posited orbits within orbits, or epicycles.

In 1543, the Polish clergyman Nicolaus Copernicus (1473–1543) attacked the Ptolemaic account in his treatise *On the Revolution of the Celestial Spheres*. He argued that the earth and planets revolved around the sun, a view known as *heliocentrism* (a sun-centered universe). Copernicus discovered that by placing the sun instead of the earth at the center of the system of spheres, he could eliminate many epicycles from the calculations. In other words, he claimed that the heliocentric view simplified the mathematics.

Copernicus's views began to attract widespread attention in the early seventeenth century, when astronomers systematically collected evidence that undermined the Ptolemaic view. A leader among them was the Danish astronomer Tycho Brahe (1546–1601), whose observations of a new star in 1572 and a comet in 1577 called into question the Aristotelian view that the universe was unchanging. Brahe still rejected heliocentrism, but the assistant he employed when he moved to Prague in 1599, Johannes Kepler (1571–1630), was converted to the Copernican view. Kepler continued Brahe's collection of planetary observations and used the evidence to develop his three laws of planetary motion, published between 1609 and 1619. Kepler's laws provided mathematical backing for heliocentrism and directly challenged the claim long held, even by Copernicus, that planetary motion was circular. Kepler's first law stated that the orbits of the planets are ellipses, with the sun always at one focus of the ellipse.

The Italian Galileo Galilei (1564–1642) provided more evidence to support the heliocentric view and also challenged the doctrine that the heavens were perfect and unchanging. In 1609, he developed an improved telescope and then observed the earth's moon, four satellites of Jupiter, the phases of Venus (a cycle of changing physical appearances), and sunspots. The moon, the planets, and the sun were no more perfect than the earth, he insisted, and the shadows he could see on the moon could only be the product of hills and valleys like those on earth. Galileo portrayed the earth as a moving part of a larger system, only one of many planets revolving around the sun, not as the fixed center of a single, closed universe. Because he recognized the utility of the new science for everyday projects and hoped to appeal to a lay audience of merchants and aristocrats, Galileo was the first scientist to publish his studies in the vernacular (Italian) rather than in Latin.◆

◆ For a primary source that focuses on the new science, see Document 40, Galileo Galilei, "Letter to the Grand Duchess Christina."

Since his discoveries challenged the Bible as well as the commonsensical view that the sun rises and sets while the earth stands still, Galileo's work alarmed the Catholic church. In 1616, the church forbade Galileo to teach that the earth moves and in 1633 accused him of not obeying the earlier order. Forced to appear before the Inquisition, he agreed to publicly recant his assertion that the earth moves to save himself from torture and death. Afterward he lived under house arrest and could publish his work only in the Dutch Republic, which had become a haven for iconoclastic scientists and thinkers.

Startling breakthroughs took place in medicine, too. Until the mid-sixteenth century, medical knowledge in Europe had been based on the writings of the second-century Greek physician Galen, a contemporary of Ptolemy. In the same year that Copernicus challenged the traditional account in astronomy (1543), the Flemish scientist Andreas Vesalius (1514–1564) did the same for anatomy. He published a new illustrated anatomical text, *On the Construction of the Human Body*, that revised Galen's work by drawing on public dissections in the medical faculties of European universities. Theophrastus Bombastus von Hohenheim, better known as Paracelsus (1493–1541), went even further than Vesalius. He burned Galen's text at the University of Basel, where he was a professor of medicine. Paracelsus experimented with new drugs, performed operations (at the time most academic physicians taught medical theory, not practice), and pursued his interests in magic, alchemy, and astrology. He helped establish the modern science of pharmacology.

The Englishman William Harvey (1578–1657) also used dissection to examine the circulation of blood within the body, demonstrating how the heart worked as a pump. The heart and its valves were "a piece of machinery," Harvey claimed. They obeyed mechanical laws just as the planets and earth revolved around the sun in a mechanical universe. Nature could be understood by experiment and rational deduction, not by following traditional authorities.

In the 1630s, the European intellectual elite began to accept the new scientific views. Ancient learning, the churches and their theologians, and even cherished popular beliefs seemed to be undermined by a new standard of truth—scientific method, which was based on systematic experiments and rational deduction. Two men were chiefly responsible for spreading the prestige of scientific method, the English politician Sir Francis Bacon (1561–1626) and the French mathematician and philosopher René Descartes (1596–1650). Respectively, they represented the two essential processes of scientific method: (1) inductive reasoning through observation and experimental research and (2) deductive reasoning from self-evident principles.

In *The Advancement of Learning* (1605), Bacon attacked reliance on ancient writers and optimistically predicted that scientific method would lead to social progress. The minds of the medieval scholars, he said, had been "shut up in the cells of a few authors (chiefly Aristotle, their dictator) as their persons were shut up in the cells of monasteries and colleges." Knowledge, in Bacon's view, must be empirically based—that is, gained by observation and experiment. Bacon ardently supported the scientific method over popular beliefs, which he rejected as "fables and popular errors." Claiming that God had called the Catholic church "to account for their degenerate manners and ceremonies," Bacon looked to the Protestant English state, which he served as lord chancellor, for leadership on the road to scientific advancement.

Although Descartes agreed with Bacon's denunciation of traditional learning, he saw that the attack on tradition might only replace the dogmatism of the churches with the skepticism of Montaigne—that nothing at all was certain. A Catholic who served in the Thirty Years' War, Descartes insisted that human reason could not only unravel the secrets of nature but also prove the existence of God. He aimed to establish the new science on more secure philosophical foundations, those of mathematics and logic. Not coincidentally, Descartes invented analytic geometry. In his *Discourse on Method* (1637), he argued that mathematical and mechanical principles provided the key to understanding all of nature, including the actions of people and states. All prior assumptions must be repudiated in favor of one elementary principle: "I think, therefore I am." Everything else could—and should—be doubted, but even doubt showed the certain existence of someone thinking. Begin with the simple and go on to the complex, he asserted, and believe only those ideas that present themselves "clearly and distinctly." Although Descartes hoped to secure the authority of both church and state, his reliance on human reason alone irritated authorities, and his books were banned in many places. He moved to the Dutch Republic to work in peace. Scientific research, like economic growth, became centered in the northern, Protestant countries, where it was less constrained by church control.

Magic and Witchcraft

Despite the new emphasis on clear reasoning, observation, and independence from past authorities, science had not yet become separate from magic. Paracelsus and other scholars studied alchemy alongside other scientific pursuits: magic and science were still closely linked. In a world in which most people believed in astrology, magical healing, prophecy, and ghosts, it is hardly surprising that many of Europe's learned people also firmly believed in witchcraft, the exercise of magical powers gained by a pact with the devil. The same Jean Bodin who argued against religious fanaticism insisted on death for witches—and for those magistrates who would not prosecute them. In France alone, 345 books and pamphlets on witchcraft appeared between 1550 and 1650. Trials of witches peaked in Europe between 1560 and 1640, the very time of the celebrated breakthroughs of the new science.

■ **Persecution of Witches**
This engraving from a pamphlet account of witch trials in England in 1589 shows three women hanged as accused witches. At their feet are frogs and toads, which were supposed to be the witches' "familiars," sent by the devil to help them ruin the lives of their neighbors by causing disease or untimely deaths among people and livestock. The ferret on the woman's lap was reported to be the devil himself in disguise.
(Lambeth Palace Library.)

Montaigne was one of the few to speak out against executing accused witches: "It is taking one's conjectures rather seriously to roast someone alive for them," he wrote in 1580.

Belief in witches was not new in the sixteenth century. Witches had long been thought capable of almost anything: passing through walls, flying through the air, destroying crops, and causing personal catastrophes from miscarriage to demonic possession. What was new was the official persecution, justified by the notion that witches were agents of Satan whom the righteous must oppose. In a time of economic crisis, plague, warfare, and the clash of religious differences, witchcraft trials provided an outlet for social stress and anxiety, legitimated by state power. At the same time, the trials seem to have been part of the religious-reform movement itself. Denunciation and persecution of witches coincided with the spread of reform, both Protestant and Catholic. The trials concentrated especially in the German lands of the Holy Roman Empire, the boiling cauldron of the Thirty Years' War.

The victims of the persecution were overwhelmingly female: women accounted for 80 percent of the accused witches in about 100,000 trials in Europe and North America during the sixteenth and seventeenth centuries. About one-third were sentenced to death. Before 1400, when witchcraft trials were rare, nearly half of those accused had been men. What explains the gender difference? Some historians argue that the trials expressed a fundamental hatred of women that came to a head dur-

IMPORTANT DATES			
1517	Martin Luther criticizes sale of indulgences and other church practices; the Reformation begins	1598	French Wars of Religion end with Edict of Nantes
		1618	Thirty Years' War begins
1529	Henry VIII is declared head of the Anglican church	1619	First African slaves arrive in the colony of Virginia
1545–1563	Council of Trent	1629	English Puritans set up the Massachusetts Bay Company and begin to colonize New England
1555	Peace of Augsburg		
1571	Battle of Lepanto marks victory of West over Ottomans at sea	1633	Galileo Galilei is forced to recant his support of heliocentrism
1572	St. Bartholomew's Day massacre (August 24)	1648	Peace of Westphalia ends the Thirty Years' War
1588	Defeat of the Spanish Armada by England		

ing conflicts over the Reformation. Official descriptions of witchcraft oozed lurid details of sexual orgies, incest, homosexuality, and cannibalism, in which women acted as the devil's sexual slaves. Yet a social dimension also helps explain the prominence of women. The poorest and most socially marginal people in most communities were elderly spinsters and widows. Because they were thought likely to hanker after revenge on those more fortunate, they were singled out as witches. Another commonly accused woman was the midwife, who was a prime target for suspicion when a baby or mother died in childbirth.

Witchcraft trials declined when scientific thinking about causes and effects raised questions about the evidence used in court: how could judges or jurors be certain that someone was a witch? The tide turned everywhere at about the same time, as physicians, lawyers, judges, and even clergy came to suspect that accusations were based on popular superstition and peasant untrustworthiness. In 1682, a French royal decree treated witchcraft as fraud and imposture, meaning that the law did not recognize anyone as a witch. In 1693, the jurors who had convicted twenty witches in Salem, Massachusetts, recanted, claiming: "We confess that we ourselves were not capable to understand. . . . We justly fear that we were sadly deluded and mistaken." The Salem jurors had not stopped believing in witches; they had simply lost confidence in their ability to identify them. When physicians and judges had believed in witches and persecuted them officially, with torture, witches had gone to their deaths in record numbers. But when the same groups distanced themselves from popular beliefs, the trials and the executions stopped.

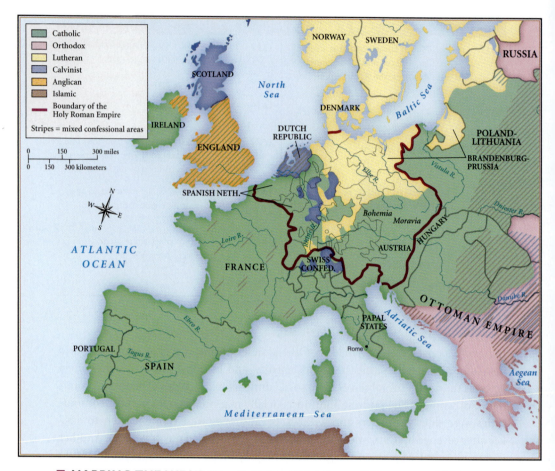

■ **MAPPING THE WEST The Religious Divisions of Europe, c. 1648**

The Peace of Westphalia recognized major religious divisions within Europe that have endured for the most part to the present day. Catholicism dominated in southern Europe, Lutheranism had its stronghold in northern Europe, and Calvinism flourished along the Rhine River. In southeastern Europe, the Islamic Ottoman Turks accommodated the Greek Orthodox Christians under their rule but bitterly fought the Catholic Austrian Habsburgs for control of Hungary.

Conclusion

The witchcraft persecutions reflected the traumas of these times of religious war and economic decline. Marauding armies combined with economic depression, disease, and the threat of starvation to shatter the lives of many ordinary Europeans, while religious conflicts shaped the destinies of every European power in this period. These conflicts began with the Protestant Reformation, which dispelled forever the Christian humanist dream of peace and unity, and came to a head from

1618 to 1648 in the Thirty Years' War, which cut a path of destruction through central Europe and involved most of the European powers. Shocked by the effects of religious violence, European rulers agreed to a peace that effectively removed disputes between Catholics and Protestants from the international arena.

The growing separation of political motives from religious ones did not mean that violence or conflict had ended, however. Struggles for religious uniformity within states would continue, though on a smaller scale. Bigger armies required more state involvement, and almost everywhere rulers emerged from these decades of conflict with expanded powers. The growth of state power directly changed the lives of ordinary people: more men went into the armies, and most families paid higher taxes. The constant extension of state power is one of the defining themes of modern history; religious warfare gave it a jump-start.

For all their increased power, rulers could not control economic, social, or intellectual trends, much as they often tried. The economic downturn of the seventeenth century produced unexpected consequences for European states even while it made life miserable for many ordinary people. Economic power and vibrancy shifted from the Mediterranean world to the northwest because the countries of northwestern Europe—England, France, and the Dutch Republic especially—suffered less from the fighting of the Thirty Years' War and recovered more quickly from the loss of population and production during bad times.

In the face of violence and uncertainty, some began to look for secular alternatives in art, politics, and science. Although it would be foolish to claim that everyone's mental universe changed because of the clash between religious and secular worldviews, a truly monumental shift in attitudes had begun. Secularization combined a growing interest in nonreligious forms of art, such as theater and opera, the search for nonreligious foundations of political authority, and the establishment of scientific method as the standard of truth. Proponents of these changes did not renounce their religious beliefs or even hold them less fervently, but they did insist that attention to state interests and scientific knowledge could serve as a brake on religious violence and popular superstitions. The search for order in the aftermath of religious warfare would continue in the decades to come.

Suggested References for further reading and online research appear on page SR-18 at the back of the book.

www.bedfordstmartins.com/huntconcise   See the ONLINE STUDY GUIDE to assess your mastery of the material covered in this chapter.

State Building and the Search for Order

1648–1690

I N ONE OF HER HUNDREDS OF LETTERS TO HER DAUGHTER, the French noblewoman Marie de Sévigné (1626–1696) told a disturbing story about a well-known cook. The cook got upset when he did not have enough roast for several unexpected guests at a dinner for King Louis XIV. Early the next morning, when the fish he had ordered did not arrive, the cook rushed up to his room, put his sword against the door, and, on the third try, ran it through his heart. The fish arrived soon after. The king regretted the trouble his visit had caused, but others soon filled in for the dead cook. That evening, Sévigné wrote, there was "a very good dinner, light refreshments later, and then supper, a walk, cards, hunting, everything scented with daffodils, everything magical."

It is difficult now for us to comprehend how anyone could care that much about a shipment of fish. The story nonetheless reveals an important aspect of state building in the seventeenth century: to extend state authority, which had been challenged during the wars over religion and threatened by economic recession, many rulers created an aura of overwhelming power and brilliance around themselves. Louis XIV, like many rulers, believed that he reigned by divine right. He served as God's lieutenant on earth and even claimed certain godlike qualities. The great gap between the ruler and ordinary subjects accounts for the extreme reaction of Louis's cook, and even leading nobles such as Sévigné came to see the king and his court as somehow "magical."

Louis XIV's model of state building was known as *absolutism,* a system of government in which the ruler claimed sole and uncontestable power. Although absolutism exerted great influence, especially in central and eastern Europe, it faced

■ **Louis XIV in Roman Splendor**
Images of Louis appear everywhere in his chateau at Versailles. This plaster relief by Antoine Coysevox in the Salon de la Guerre *(War Hall) represents Louis as Mars, the Roman god of war, riding roughshod over his enemies.* (Giraudon/Art Resource, NY.)

competition from *constitutionalism,* a system in which the ruler had to share power with parliaments made up of elected representatives. Constitutionalism led to weakness in Poland-Lithuania, but it provided a strong foundation for state power in England, the English North American colonies, and the Dutch Republic. Constitutionalism triumphed in England, however, only after one king had been executed as a traitor and another had been deposed.

These two methods of state building faced similar challenges in the mid-seventeenth century. Competition in the international arena required resources, and all states raised taxes, provoking popular protests and rebellions. The wars over religion that had culminated in the Thirty Years' War (1618–1648) left many economies in dire straits, and, even more significant, they created a need for new explanations of political authority. Monarchs still relied on religion to justify their divine right to rule, but they increasingly sought secular defenses of their powers, too.

The search for order took place not only at the level of states and rulers but also in intellectual, cultural, and social life. In science, the Englishman Isaac Newton explained the regular movement of the universe with the law of gravitation and thereby consolidated the scientific revolution. Artists sought means of glorifying power and expressing order and symmetry in new fashion. As states consolidated their power, elites endeavored to distinguish themselves more clearly from the lower orders. The upper classes emulated the manners developed at court and tried in every way to distance themselves from anything viewed as vulgar or lower class. Officials, clergy, and laypeople all worked to reform the poor, now seen as a major source of disorder. Whether absolutist or constitutionalist, seventeenth-century states all aimed to extend control over their subjects' lives.

Louis XIV: Model of Absolutism

French king Louis XIV (r. 1643–1715) personified the absolutist ruler who shared his power with no one. Louis personally made all important state decisions and left no room for dissent. In 1651, he reputedly told the Paris high court of justice, "*L'état, c'est moi*" ("I am the state"), emphasizing that state authority rested in him personally. Louis cleverly manipulated the affections and ambitions of his courtiers, chose as his ministers middle-class men who owed everything to him, built up Europe's largest army, and snuffed out every hint of religious or political opposition. Yet the absoluteness of his power should not be exaggerated. Like all rulers of his time, Louis depended on the cooperation of many others: local officials who enforced his decrees, peasants and artisans who joined his armies and paid his taxes, creditors who loaned crucial funds, and nobles who rather than stay home and cause trouble joined court festivities organized to glorify the king.

The Fronde, 1648–1653

Louis XIV built on a long French tradition of increasing centralization of state authority, but before he could extend it, he had to weather a series of revolts known as the *Fronde*. Derived from the French word for a child's slingshot, the term was used by critics to signify that the revolts were mere child's play. In fact, they posed an unprecedented threat to the French crown. Louis was only five when he came to the throne in 1643 upon the death of his father, Louis XIII. Louis XIV's mother, Anne of Austria, and her Italian-born adviser and rumored lover Cardinal Mazarin (1602–1661) ruled in the young monarch's name. To meet the financial pressure of fighting the Thirty Years' War, Mazarin sold new offices, raised taxes, and forced creditors to extend loans to the government. In 1648, a coalition of his opponents presented him with a charter of demands that, if granted, would have given the parlements (high courts) a form of constitutional power with the right to approve new taxes. Mazarin responded by arresting the coalition's leaders. He soon faced a series of revolts that at one time or another involved nearly every social group in France.

The Fronde posed an immediate menace to the young king. Fearing for his safety, his mother and members of his court took Louis and fled Paris. As civil war threatened, Mazarin and Anne agreed to compromise with the parlements. The nobles then tried to reassert their own claims to power by raising private armies. The middle and lower classes chafed at the constant tax increases and in some places organized revolts. Conflicts erupted throughout the kingdom, and rampaging soldiers devastated rural areas and disrupted commerce.

Neither the nobles nor the judges of the parlements really wanted to overthrow the king; they simply wanted a greater share in power. But Louis XIV never forgot the humiliation and uncertainty that marred his childhood. Years later he recalled an incident in which a band of Parisians invaded

The Fronde, 1648–1653

his bedchamber to determine whether he had fled the city, and he declared the event an affront not only to himself but also to the state. His own policies as ruler would be designed to prevent the repetition of any such revolts.

Court Culture as a Form of State Power

When Cardinal Mazarin died in 1661, Louis XIV decided to rule without a first minister. He described the dangers of his situation in memoirs he wrote later for his son's instruction: "Everywhere was disorder. My Court as a whole was still very far removed from the sentiments in which I trust you will find it." Louis listed many other problems in the kingdom, but none occupied him more than his attempts to control France's leading nobles. Typically quarrelsome, the French nobles had long exercised local authority by maintaining their own fighting forces, meting out justice on their estates, arranging jobs for underlings, and resolving their own conflicts through dueling.

Louis set out to domesticate the warrior nobles by replacing violence with court ritual. Using a systematic policy of bestowing pensions, offices, honors, gifts, and the threat of disfavor or punishment, he made himself the center of French power and culture. The aristocracy vied for his favor, attended the ballets and theatricals he put on, and learned the rules of etiquette he supervised. Great nobles competed for the honor of holding his shirt when he dressed; foreign ambassadors squabbled for places near him; and royal mistresses basked in the glow of his personal favor. In a typically acerbic comment, Louis de Rouvroy, duke of Saint-Simon (1675–1755) complained, "There was nothing he [Louis XIV] liked so much as flattery . . . the coarser and clumsier it was, the more he relished it."◆ Madame de Lafayette described the effects on court life in her novel *The Princess of Clèves* (1678): "The Court gravitated around ambition. Nobody was tranquil or indifferent—everybody was busily trying to better his or her position by pleasing, by helping, or by hindering somebody else." Occasionally the results were tragic, as in the suicide of the cook recounted by Marie de Sévigné.

Louis XIV appreciated the political uses of every form of art. Mock battles, extravaganzas, theatrical performances, even the king's dinner—Louis's daily life was a public performance designed to enhance his prestige. Calling himself the Sun King, Louis adorned his court with statues of Apollo, Greek god of the sun, and emulated the style of ancient Roman emperors. Sculpture and paintings adorned his palace; commissioned histories vaunted his achievements; and coins and medals spread his likeness throughout the realm.

The king's officials treated the arts as a branch of government. Louis's ministers set up royal academies of dance, painting, architecture, and music and took control of the Académie française (French Academy), which to this day decides on correct usage of the French language. A royal furniture workshop at the Gobelins tapestry works on the outskirts of Paris turned out the delicate and ornate pieces whose style bore the king's name. Louis's government also regulated the number and locations of theaters and closely censored all forms of publication.

Music and theater enjoyed special prominence. Louis commissioned operas to celebrate royal marriages, baptisms, and military victories. The king himself danced in ballets if a role seemed especially important. Playwrights presented their new plays directly to the court. Pierre Corneille and Jean-Baptiste Racine wrote tragedies

---

◆ For a firsthand account of life in Louis XIV's court, see Document 41, Louis de Rouvroy, duke of Saint-Simon, "Memoirs."

set in Greece or Rome that celebrated the new aristocratic virtues that Louis aimed to inculcate: a reverence for order and self-control.

Louis glorified his image as well through massive public works projects. Military facilities, such as veterans' hospitals and new fortified towns on the frontiers, represented his military might. Urban improvements, such as the reconstruction of the Louvre palace in Paris, proved his wealth. But his most ambitious project was the construction of a new palace at Versailles, twelve miles from the turbulent capital. Building began in the 1660s, and by 1685, the frenzied effort engaged thirty-six thousand workers, not including the thousands of troops who diverted a local river to supply water for pools and fountains. Even the gardens designed by landscape architect André Le Nôtre reflected the spirit of Louis XIV's rule: their geometrical arrangements and clear lines showed that art and design could tame nature and that order and control defined the exercise of power. Versailles symbolized Louis's success in reining in the nobility and dominating Europe, and other monarchs eagerly mimicked French fashion and often conducted their business in French.

■ **Palace of Versailles**

In this defining statement of his ambitions, Louis XIV emphasized his ability to impose his personal will even on nature itself. The sheer size and precise geometrical design of the palace underlined the presence of an all-powerful personality—that of the Sun King. The palace became a national historical monument in 1837 and was used for many momentous historical occasions, including the signing of the peace treaty after World War I. (Giraudon/Art Resource, NY.)

By the time Louis actually moved from the Louvre to Versailles in 1682, he had reigned as monarch for thirty-nine years. Fifteen thousand people crowded into the palace's apartments, including all the highest military officers, the ministers of state, and the separate households of each member of the royal family. After the death of his queen in 1683, Louis secretly married his mistress, Françoise d'Aubigné, marquise de Maintenon, and conducted most state affairs from her apartments at the palace. De Maintenon's opponents at court complained that she controlled all the appointments, but her efforts focused on her own projects, including her favorite: the founding in 1686 of a royal school for girls from impoverished noble families. She also inspired one of Louis XIV's most critical decisions—to pursue his devotion to Catholicism.

Enforcing Religious Orthodoxy

Louis believed that he ruled by divine right. As Bishop Jacques-Benigne Bossuet (1627–1704) explained, "We have seen that kings take the place of God, who is the true father of the human species. We have also seen that the first idea of power which exists among men is that of the paternal power; and that kings are modeled on fathers." The king, like a father, should instruct his subjects in the true religion, or at least make sure that others did so.

Louis's campaign for religious conformity first focused on the Jansenists, Catholics whose doctrines and practices resembled some aspects of Protestantism. Following the posthumous publication of the book *Augustinus* (1640) by the Flemish theologian Cornelius Jansen (1585–1638), the Jansenists stressed the need for God's grace in achieving salvation. They emphasized the importance of original sin and insisted on an austere religious practice. Prominent among the Jansenists was Blaise Pascal (1623–1662), a mathematician of genius, who wrote his *Provincial Letters* (1656–1657) to defend Jansenism against charges of heresy. Many judges in the parlements likewise endorsed Jansenist doctrine.

Some questioned Louis's understanding of the finer points of doctrine: according to his German-born sister-in-law, Louis himself "has never read anything about religion, nor the Bible either, and just goes along believing whatever he is told." But Louis rejected any doctrine that gave priority to considerations of individual conscience over the demands of the official church hierarchy. He preferred teachings that stressed obedience to authority. Therefore, in 1660 he began enforcing various papal bulls (decrees) against Jansenism and closed down Jansenist theological centers. Jansenists were forced underground for the rest of his reign.

After many years of escalating pressure on the Calvinist Huguenots, Louis revoked the Edict of Nantes in 1685 and eliminated all of the Calvinists' rights. Louis considered the edict (1598), by which his grandfather Henry IV granted the Protestants religious freedom and civil rights, a temporary measure, and he fervently hoped to reconvert the Huguenots to Catholicism. He closed their churches and schools, banned all their public activities, and exiled those who refused to embrace the state religion. Thousands of Huguenots emigrated to England, Brandenburg-Prussia, or the Dutch Republic. Many now wrote for publications attacking Louis XIV's absolutism. Protestant European countries were shocked by this crackdown on religious dissent and would cite it when they went to war against Louis.

Extending State Authority at Home and Abroad

Louis XIV could not have enforced his religious policies without the services of a nationwide bureaucracy. *Bureaucracy*—a system of state officials carrying out orders according to a regular and routine line of authority—comes from *bureau*, the French word for "desk," which came to mean "office," in the sense of both a physical space and a position of authority. Louis extended the bureaucratic forms his predecessors had developed, especially the use of intendants, officials who held their positions directly from the king rather than owning their offices. Louis handpicked them to represent his will against entrenched local interests such as the parlements, provincial estates, and noble governors. The intendants reduced local powers over finances and insisted on more efficient tax collection. Despite the doubling of taxes in Louis's reign, the local rebellions that had so beset the crown from the 1620s to the 1640s subsided in the face of these better-organized state forces.

Louis's success in consolidating his authority depended on hard work, an eye for detail, and an ear to the ground. In his memoirs he explained his priorities:

> *to be well-informed on an infinite number of matters about which we are supposed to know nothing; to elicit from our subjects what they hide from us with the greatest care; to discover the most remote opinions of our courtiers and the most hidden interests of those who come to us with quite contrary professions [claims].*

To gather all this information, Louis relied on a series of talented ministers, usually of modest origins, who gained fame, fortune, and even noble status from serving the king. Most important among them was Jean-Baptiste Colbert (1619–1683), the son of a wool merchant turned royal official. Colbert had managed Mazarin's personal finances and worked his way up under Louis XIV to become controller-general, the head of royal finances, public works, and the navy. He founded a family dynasty that eventually produced five ministers of state, an archbishop, two bishops, and three generals.

Colbert used the bureaucracy to establish a new economic doctrine, *mercantilism*. According to mercantilist policy, governments must intervene to increase national wealth by whatever means possible. Such government intervention inevitably increased the role and eventually the number of bureaucrats needed. Under Colbert, the French government established overseas trading companies, granted manufacturing monopolies, and standardized production methods for textiles, paper, and soap. A government inspection system regulated the quality of finished goods and compelled all craftsmen to organize into guilds, in which masters could supervise the work of the journeymen and apprentices. To protect French production, Colbert rescinded many internal customs fees while enacting high foreign tariffs, which effectively cut imports of competing goods. To compete more effectively with England and the Dutch Republic, Colbert also subsidized shipbuilding, a policy that dramatically expanded the number of seaworthy vessels. Such mercantilist measures aimed to ensure France's prominence in world markets and to provide the resources needed to fight wars against the increasingly long list of enemies. Although later economists questioned the value of this state intervention in the economy, nearly every government in Europe embraced mercantilism.

Colbert's mercantilist projects extended to Canada, where in 1663 he took control of the trading company that had founded New France. He transplanted several thousand peasants from western France to the present-day province of Quebec, which France had claimed since 1608, and he sent fifteen hundred soldiers to fend off the Iroquois, who regularly raided French fur-trading convoys. Shows of French military force, including the burning of Indian villages and winter food supplies, forced the Iroquois to make peace, and from 1666 to 1680, French traders moved westward with minimal interference. In 1672, fur trader Louis Jolliet and Jesuit missionary Jacques Marquette reached the upper Mississippi River and traveled downstream as far as Arkansas. In 1684, French explorer Sieur de La Salle ventured all the way down to the Gulf of Mexico, claiming a vast territory for Louis XIV and calling it Louisiana after him. Louis and Colbert encouraged colonial settlement as part of their rivalry with the English and the Dutch in the New World.

Colonial settlement occupied only a small portion of Louis XIV's attention, however, for his main foreign policy goal was to extend French power in Europe. In pursuing this purpose, he inevitably came up against the Spanish and Austrian Habsburgs, whose lands encircled his. To expand French power, Louis needed the biggest possible army. The ministry of war centralized the organization of French troops. Barracks built in major towns received supplies from a central distribution system. The state began to provide uniforms for the soldiers and to offer veterans some hospital care. A militia draft instituted in 1688 supplemented the army in times of war and enrolled 100,000 men. Louis's wartime army could field a force as large as that of all his enemies combined.

Absolutist governments always tried to increase their territorial holdings, and as Louis extended his reach, he gained new enemies. In 1667–1668, in the first of his major wars after assuming personal control of French affairs, Louis defeated the Spanish armies but had to make peace when England, Sweden, and the Dutch Republic joined the war. In the Treaty of Aix-la-Chapelle in 1668, he gained control of towns on the border of the Spanish Netherlands. Pamphlets sponsored by the Habsburgs accused Louis of aiming for "universal monarchy," or domination of Europe.

In 1672, Louis XIV opened hostilities against the Dutch because they stood in the way of his acquisition of more territory in the Spanish Netherlands. He declared war again on Spain in 1673. By now the Dutch had allied themselves with their former Spanish masters to hold off the French. Louis also marched his troops into territories of the Holy Roman Empire, provoking many of the German princes to join with the emperor, the Spanish, and the Dutch in an alliance against Louis, now denounced as a "Christian Turk" for his imperialist ambitions. But the French armies more than held their own. Faced with bloody yet inconclusive results on the battle-field, the parties agreed to the Treaty of Nijmegen of 1678–1679, which ceded several Flemish towns and Franche-Comté to Louis (Map 13.1). These territorial additions were costly: French government deficits soared, and increases in taxes touched off the most serious antitax revolt of Louis's reign, in 1675.

■ **MAP 13.1 Louis XIV's Acquisitions, 1668–1697**

Every ruler in Europe hoped to extend his or her territorial control, and war was often the result. Louis XIV steadily encroached on the Spanish Netherlands to the north and the lands of the Holy Roman Empire to the east. Although coalitions of European powers reined in Louis's grander ambitions, he incorporated many neighboring territories into the French crown.

Louis had no intention of standing still. Heartened by the Habsburgs' seeming weakness, he pushed eastward, seizing the city of Strasbourg in 1681 and invading the province of Lorraine in 1684. In 1688, he attacked some of the small German cities of the Holy Roman Empire and was soon involved again in a long war against a Europe-wide coalition. Between 1689 and 1697, a coalition made up of England, Spain, Sweden, the Dutch Republic, the Austrian emperor, and various German princes fought Louis XIV to a stalemate. When hostilities ended in the Peace of Rijswijk in 1697, Louis returned many of his conquests made since 1678 with the exception of Strasbourg (see Map 13.1). Louis never lost his taste for war, but his allies learned how to set limits on his ambitions.

Louis was the last French ruler before Napoleon to accompany his troops to the battlefield. In later generations, as the military became more professional, French rulers left the fighting to their generals. Although Louis had managed to suppress the private armies of his noble courtiers, he constantly promoted his own military prowess in order to keep his noble officers under his sway. He had miniature battle scenes painted on his high heels and commissioned tapestries showing his military processions into cities, even those he did not take by force. He seized every occasion to assert his supremacy, insisting that other fleets salute his ships first.

War required money and men, which Louis obtained by expanding state control over finances, conscription into the army, and military supply. Thus absolutism and warfare fed each other, as the bureaucracy created new ways to raise and maintain an army and the army's success in war justified the expansion of state power. But constant warfare also eroded the state's resources. Further administrative and legal reform, the elimination of the buying and selling of offices, and the lowering of taxes—all were made impossible by the need for more money.

The playwright Corneille wrote, no doubt optimistically, "The people are very happy when they die for their kings." What is certain is that the wars touched many peasant and urban families. The people who lived on the routes leading to the battlefields had to house and feed soldiers; only nobles were exempt from this requirement. Everyone, moreover, paid the higher taxes that were necessary to support the army. By the end of Louis's reign, one in six Frenchmen had served in the military.

Absolutism in Central and Eastern Europe

Central and eastern European rulers saw in Louis XIV a powerful model of absolutist state building. Yet they did not blindly emulate the Sun King, in part because they confronted conditions peculiar to their regions. The ruler of Brandenburg-Prussia had to rebuild lands ravaged by the Thirty Years' War and unite far-flung territories. The Austrian Habsburgs needed to govern a mosaic of ethnic and religious groups while fighting off the Ottoman Turks. The Russian tsars wanted to extend their power over a far-flung but relatively impoverished empire. The great exception to absolutism in eastern Europe was Poland-Lithuania, where a long crisis virtually destroyed central authority and sucked much of eastern Europe into its turbulent wake.

Brandenburg-Prussia and Sweden: Militaristic Absolutism

Brandenburg-Prussia began as a puny state on the Elbe River, but it would have a remarkable future. In the nineteenth century, it would unify the disparate German states into modern-day Germany. The ruler of Brandenburg was an elector, one of the seven German princes entitled to select the Holy Roman Emperor. Since the sixteenth century, the ruler of Brandenburg had also controlled the duchy of East Prussia; after 1618, the state was called Brandenburg-Prussia. Despite meager resources, Frederick William of Hohenzollern, the Great Elector of Brandenburg-Prussia (r. 1640–1688), succeeded in welding his scattered lands into an absolutist state.

Pressured first by the necessities of fighting the Thirty Years' War and then by the demands of reconstruction, Frederick William determined to force his territories' estates (representative institutions) to grant him a dependable income. The Great Elector struck a deal with the Junkers (nobles) of each land: in exchange for allowing him to collect taxes, he gave them complete control over their enserfed peasants and exempted them from taxation. The tactic worked. By the end of his reign the estates met only on ceremonial occasions.

Supplied with a steady income, Frederick William could devote his attention to military and bureaucratic consolidation. Over forty years he expanded his army from eight thousand to thirty thousand men. (See "Taking Measure," below.) The

State	Soldiers	Population	Ratio of soldiers/ total population
France	300,000	20 million	1:66
Russia	220,000	14 million	1:64
Austria	100,000	8 million	1:80
Sweden	40,000	1 million	1:25
Brandenburg-Prussia	30,000	2 million	1:66
England	24,000	10 million	1:410

*Figures for the end of the seventeenth century, ranging from 1688 for Prussia to 1710 for France

■ **TAKING MEASURE** **The Seventeenth-Century Army**
The figures in this chart are only approximate but tell an important story. What conclusions can be drawn about the relative weight of the military in the different European states? Why did England have such a smaller army than the others? Is the absolute or the relative size of the military the more important indicator?

(From André Corvisier, *Armées et sociétés en Europe de 1494 à 1789* [Paris: Presses Universitaires de France, 1976], 126.)

army mirrored the rigid domination of nobles over peasants that characterized Brandenburg-Prussian society: peasants filled the ranks, and Junkers became officers. Nobles also took positions as bureaucratic officials, but military needs always had priority. The elector named special war commissars to take charge not only of military affairs but also of tax collection. To hasten military dispatches, he also established one of Europe's first state postal systems.

As a Calvinist ruler, Frederick William avoided the ostentation of the French court, even while following the absolutist model of centralizing state power. He boldly rebuffed Louis XIV by welcoming twenty thousand French Huguenot refugees after Louis's revocation of the Edict of Nantes. In pursuing foreign and domestic policies that promoted state power and prestige, Frederick William adroitly switched sides in Louis's wars and would stop at almost nothing to crush resistance at home. In 1701, his son Frederick I (r. 1688–1713) persuaded Holy Roman Emperor Leopold I to grant him the title "king in Prussia." Prussia had arrived as an important power (Map 13.2).

Across the Baltic, Sweden also stood out as an example of absolutist consolidation. In the Thirty Years' War, King Gustavus Adolphus's superb generalship and highly trained army had made Sweden the supreme power of northern Europe. The huge but sparsely populated state included not only most of present-day Sweden but also Finland, Estonia, half of Latvia, and much of the Baltic coastline of modern Poland and Germany. The Baltic, in short, was a Swedish lake. After Gustavus Adolphus died, his daughter Queen Christina (r. 1632–1654) conceded much authority to the estates. Absorbed by religion and philosophy, Christina eventually abdicated and converted to Catholicism. Her successors temporarily made Sweden an absolute monarchy.

In Sweden (as in neighboring Denmark-Norway), absolutism meant simply the estates standing aside while the king led the army in lucrative foreign campaigns. The aristocracy went along because it staffed the bureaucracy and reaped war profits. Intrigued by French culture, Sweden also gleamed with national pride. In 1668, the nobility demanded the introduction of a distinctive national costume: should Swedes, they asked, "who are so glorious and renowned a nation . . . let ourselves be led by the nose by a parcel of French dancing-masters"? Sweden spent the forty years after 1654 continuously warring with its neighbors. By the 1690s, war expenses began to outrun the small Swedish population's ability to pay, threatening the continuation of absolutism.

An Uneasy Balance: Austrian Habsburgs and Ottoman Turks

Holy Roman Emperor Leopold I (r. 1658–1705) ruled over a variety of territories of different ethnicities, languages, and religions, yet in ways similar to his French and Prussian counterparts, he gradually consolidated his power. Like all the Holy Roman emperors since 1438, Leopold was an Austrian Habsburg. He was simulta-

Legend:
- Brandenburg-Prussian territory in 1640
- Brandenburg-Prussian territory acquired to 1688
- Austrian Habsburg territory in 1648
- Lands taken from Turks by Austrian Habsburgs, to 1699
- Polish-Lithuanian territory lost to Russia, 1667
- Swedish territory in 1648
- Swedish territory acquired to 1699
- Boundary of the Holy Roman Empire

■ **MAP 13.2 State Building in Central and Eastern Europe, 1648–1699**

Brandenburg-Prussia emerged from relative obscurity after the Thirty Years' War to begin an aggressive program of expanding its military and its territorial base. The Austrian Habsburgs had long contested the Ottoman Turks for dominance of eastern Europe, and by 1699, they had pushed the Turks out of Hungary. Poland-Lithuania lost territory to Russia. Sweden still dominated the Baltic Sea.

neously duke of Upper and Lower Silesia, count of Tyrol, archduke of Upper and Lower Austria, king of Bohemia, king of Hungary and Croatia, and ruler of Styria and Moravia (see Map 13.2). Some of these territories were provinces in the Holy Roman Empire; others were simply ruled from Vienna as Habsburg family holdings.

Leopold needed to build up his armies and state authority in order to defend the Holy Roman Empire's international position, which had been weakened by the Thirty Years' War, and to push back the Ottoman Turks who steadily encroached from the southeast. The emperor and his closest officials took control over recruiting, provisioning, and strategic planning and worked to replace the mercenaries hired during the Thirty Years' War with a permanent standing army that promoted professional discipline. To pay for the army and to staff his growing bureaucracy, Leopold had to gain the support of local aristocrats and chip away at provincial institutions' powers. Intent on replacing Bohemian nobles who had supported the 1618 revolt against Austrian authority, the Habsburgs promoted a new nobility made up of Czechs, Germans, Italians, Spaniards, and even Irish, who used German as their common tongue, professed Catholicism, and loyally served the Austrian dynasty. Bohemia became a virtual Austrian colony. "You have utterly destroyed our home, our ancient kingdom, and have built us no new one in its place," lamented a Czech Jesuit in 1670, addressing Leopold. "Woe to you! . . . The nobles you have oppressed, great cities made small. Of smiling towns you have made straggling villages." Austrian censors prohibited publication of this protest for over a century.

In addition to holding Louis XIV in check on his western frontiers, Leopold confronted the ever-present challenge of the Ottoman Turks to his east. Hungary was the chief battle zone between Austria and the Turks for more than 150 years. In 1682, when war broke out again, Austria controlled the northwest section of Hungary; the Turks occupied the center; and in the east, the Turks demanded tribute from the Hungarian princes who ruled Transylvania. In 1683, the Turks pushed all the way to the gates of Vienna and laid siege to the Austrian

■ **The Siege of Vienna, 1683 (detail)**
In this stylized rendition by Frans Geffels, the Ottoman Turks bombard the city, which they have surrounded for two months, as cavalry forces commanded by Polish king Jan Sobieski arrive in the foreground to help lift the siege.
(Museen der Stadt, Wien.)

capital; after reaching this high-water mark, however, Turkish power ebbed. With the help of Polish cavalry, the Austrians finally broke the siege and turned the tide in a major counteroffensive. By the Treaty of Karlowitz of 1699, the Ottoman Turks surrendered almost all of Hungary to the Austrians.

Hungary's "liberation" from the Turks came at a high price. The fighting laid waste vast stretches of Hungary's central plain, and the population may have declined as much as 65 percent since 1600. To repopulate the land, the Austrians settled large communities of foreigners: Romanians, Croats, Serbs, and Germans. Magyar (Hungarian) speakers became a minority, and the seeds were sown for the poisonous nationality conflicts in nineteenth- and twentieth-century Hungary, Romania, and Yugoslavia.

Once the Turks had been beaten back, Austrian rule over Hungary tightened. In 1687, the Habsburg dynasty's hereditary right to the Hungarian crown was acknowledged by the Hungarian diet, a parliament revived by Leopold in 1681 to gain the support of Hungarian nobles. The diet was dominated by nobles who had amassed huge holdings in the liberated territories. They formed the core of a pro-Habsburg Hungarian aristocracy that would buttress the dynasty until it fell in 1918. As the Turks retreated from Hungary, Leopold systematically rebuilt churches, monasteries, roadside shrines, and monuments in the flamboyant Austrian baroque style.

The Ottoman Turks also pursued state consolidation but in a very different fashion from the Europeans. The Ottoman state centralized its authority through negotiation with and incorporation of bandit armies, which European rulers typically suppressed by armed force. In the seventeenth century, mutinous army officers often deposed the Ottoman ruler, or sultan, in a palace coup, but because the Ottoman state had learned to manage constant crises, the state itself survived and rarely faced popular revolts. Rather than remaining in their villages and resisting state authorities, Ottoman peasants often left to become bandits who periodically worked for the state as mercenaries. Leaders of bandit gangs entered into negotiation with the Ottoman sultan, sometimes providing thousands of bandit mercenaries to the sultan's armies and even taking major official positions. This constantly shifting social and political system explains how the coup-ridden Ottoman state could appear "weak" in Western eyes and still pose a massive military threat on Europe's southeastern borders. In the end, the Ottoman state lasted longer than Louis XIV's absolute monarchy.

Russia: Foundations of Bureaucratic Absolutism

Superficially, seventeenth-century Russia seemed a world apart from the Europe of Louis XIV. Straddling Europe and Asia, it stretched across Siberia to the Pacific Ocean. Western visitors either sneered or shuddered at the "barbarism" of Russian life, and Russians reciprocated by nursing deep suspicions of everything foreign. But under the surface, Russia was evolving along paths much like the rest of absolutist Europe; the tsars wanted to claim unlimited autocratic power, but they had to surmount internal disorder and come to an accommodation with noble landlords.

When Tsar Alexei (r. 1645–1676) tried to extend state authority by imposing new administrative structures and taxes in 1648, Moscow and other cities erupted in bloody rioting. The government immediately doused the fire. In 1649, Alexei convoked the Assembly of the Land (consisting of noble delegates from the provinces) to consult on a sweeping law code to organize Russian society in a strict social hierarchy that would last for nearly two centuries. The code of 1649 assigned all subjects to a hereditary class according to their current occupation or state needs. Slaves and free peasants were merged into a serf class. As serfs they could not change occupations or move; they were tightly tied to the soil and to their noble masters. To prevent tax evasion, the code also forbade townspeople to move from the community where they resided. Nobles owed absolute obedience to the tsar and were required to serve in the army, but in return no other group could own estates worked by serfs. Serfs became the chattel of their lord, who could sell them like horses or land. Their conditions of life differed little from those of the slaves on the plantations in the Americas.

Some peasants resisted enserfment. In 1667, Stenka Razin, a Cossack from the Don region in southern Russia, led a huge rebellion that promised liberation from "the traitors and bloodsuckers of the peasant communes"—the great noble landowners, local governors, and Moscow courtiers. Captured four years later by the tsar's army, Razin was dismembered, his head and limbs publicly displayed, and his body thrown to the dogs. Thousands of his followers also suffered grisly deaths, but his memory lived on in folk songs and legends.◆ Landlords successfully petitioned for the abolition of the statute of limitations on runaway serfs, the use of state agents in searching for runaways, and harsh penalties against those who harbored runaways. The increase in Russian state authority went hand in hand with the enforcement of serfdom.

To extend his power and emulate his western rivals, Tsar Alexei wanted a bigger army, exclusive control over state policy, and a greater say in religious matters. The size of the army increased dramatically from 35,000 in the 1630s to 220,000 by the end of the century. The Assembly of the Land, once an important source of noble consultation, never met again after 1653. Alexei also imposed firm control over the Russian Orthodox church. In 1666, a church council reaffirmed the tsar's role as God's direct representative on earth. The state-dominated church took action against a religious group called the Old Believers, who rejected church efforts to bring Russian worship in line with Byzantine tradition. Whole communities of Old

---

◆ For a contemporary account of the uprising, see Document 42, Ludwig Fabritius, "The Revolt of Stenka Razin."

■ **Stenka Razin in Captivity**
*After leading a revolt of thousands of serfs, peasants, and members of non-Russian tribes of
the middle and lower Volga region, Razin was captured by Russian forces and led off to
Moscow, as shown here, where he was executed in 1671. He has been the subject of songs,
legends, and poems ever since.* (Novosti Photo Library, London.)

Believers starved or burned themselves to death rather than submit. Religious
schism opened a gulf between the Russian people and the crown.

Nevertheless, modernizing trends prevailed. As the state bureaucracy expanded,
the government intervened more and more in daily life. Decrees regulated tobacco
smoking, card playing, and alcohol consumption and even dictated how people
should leash and fence their pet dogs. Western ideas began to seep into educated
circles in Moscow. Nobles and ordinary citizens commissioned portraits of themselves instead of only buying religious icons. Tsar Alexei set up the first Western-
style theater in the Kremlin, and his daughter Sophia translated French plays. The
most adventurous nobles began to wear German-style clothing. A long struggle over
Western influences had begun.

Poland-Lithuania Overwhelmed

Unlike the other eastern European powers, Poland-Lithuania did not follow the
absolutist model. Decades of war weakened the monarchy and made the great nobles
into practically autonomous warlords. They used the parliament and demands for
constitutionalism to stymie monarchical power. The result was a precipitous slide
into political disarray and weakness.

In 1648, Ukrainian Cossack warriors revolted against the king of Poland-Lithuania, inaugurating two decades of tumult known as the Deluge. Cossack bands had formed from runaway peasants and poor nobles in the no man's land of southern Russia and Ukraine. The Polish nobles who claimed this potentially rich land scorned the Cossacks as troublemakers, but to the Ukrainian peasant population they were liberators. In 1654, the Cossacks offered Ukraine to Russian rule, provoking a Russo-Polish war that ended in 1667 when the tsar annexed eastern Ukraine and Kiev (see Map 13.2). Neighboring powers tried to profit from the chaos in Poland-Lithuania; Sweden, Brandenburg-Prussia, and Transylvania sent armies to seize territory.

Many towns were destroyed in the fighting, and as much as a third of the Polish population perished. The once prosperous Jewish and Protestant minorities suffered greatly: some fifty-six thousand Jews were killed either by the Cossacks, Polish peasants, or Russian troops, and thousands more had to flee or convert to Christianity. One rabbi wrote, "We were slaughtered each day, in a more agonizing way than cattle: they are butchered quickly, while we were being executed slowly." Surviving Jews moved from towns to *shtetls* (Jewish villages), where they took up petty trading, moneylending, tax gathering, and tavern leasing—activities that fanned peasant anti-Semitism. Desperate for protection amid the war, most Protestants backed the violently anti-Catholic Swedes, and the victorious Catholic majority branded them as traitors. Some Protestant refugees fled to the Dutch Republic and England. In Poland-Lithuania—once an outpost of religious toleration—it came to be assumed that a good Pole was a Catholic.

The commonwealth revived briefly when a man of ability and ambition, Jan Sobieski (r. 1674–1696), was elected king. He gained a reputation throughout Europe when he led twenty-five thousand Polish cavalrymen into battle in the siege of Vienna in 1683. His cavalry helped rout the Turks and turned the tide against the Ottomans. Married to a politically shrewd French princess, Sobieski openly admired Louis XIV's France. Despite his efforts to rebuild the monarchy, he could not halt Poland-Lithuania's decline into powerlessness.

Elsewhere the ravages of war had created opportunities for kings to increase their power, but in Poland-Lithuania the great nobles gained all the advantage. They dominated the Sejm (parliament), and to maintain an equilibrium among themselves, they each wielded an absolute veto power. This "free veto" constitutional system soon deadlocked parliamentary government. The monarchy lost its room to maneuver, and with it much of its remaining power. An appalled Croat visitor in 1658 commented, "Among the Poles there is no order in the state. . . . Everybody who is stronger thinks to have the right to oppress the weaker, just as the wolves and bears are free to capture and kill cattle. . . . Such abominable depravity is called by the Poles 'aristocratic freedom.'" The Polish version of constitutionalism fatally weakened the state and made it prey to its neighbors.

Constitutionalism in England

In the second half of the seventeenth century, western and eastern Europe began to move in different directions. In general, the farther east one traveled, the more absolutist the style of government (with the exception of Poland-Lithuania) and the greater the gulf between landlord and peasant. In eastern Europe, nobles lorded over their serfs but owed almost slavish obedience in turn to their rulers. In western Europe, even in absolutist France, serfdom had almost entirely disappeared and nobles and rulers alike faced greater challenges to their control. The greatest challenges of all would come in England.

This outcome might seem surprising, for the English monarchs enjoyed many advantages compared with their continental rivals: they needed less money for their armies because they had stayed out of the Thirty Years' War, and their island kingdom was in theory easier to rule because they governed a population only one-fourth the size of France's and of relatively homogeneous ethnicity. Yet the English rulers failed in their efforts to install absolutist policies. The English revolutions of 1642–1660 and 1688–1689 overturned two kings, confirmed the constitutional powers of an elected parliament, and laid the foundation for the idea that government must guarantee certain rights under the law.

England Turned Upside Down, 1642–1660

Disputes about the right to levy taxes and the nature of authority in the Church of England had long troubled the relationship between the English crown and Parliament. For over a hundred years, wealthy English landowners had been accustomed to participating in government through Parliament and expected to be consulted on royal policy. Although England had no one constitutional document, a variety of laws, judicial decisions, charters and petitions granted by the king, and customary procedures all regulated relations between king and Parliament. When Charles I tried to assert his authority over Parliament, a civil war broke out. It set in motion an unpredictable chain of events, which included an extraordinary ferment of religious and political ideas. Some historians view the English civil war of 1642–1646 as the last great war of religion because it pitted Puritans against those trying to push the Anglican church toward Catholicism, but it should be considered the first modern revolution because it gave birth to democratic political and religious movements.

When Charles I (r. 1625–1649) succeeded his father, James I, he faced an increasingly aggressive Parliament that resisted new taxes and resented the king's efforts to extend his personal control. In 1628, Parliament forced Charles to agree to a Petition of Right by which he promised not to levy taxes without its consent. Charles hoped to avoid further interference with his plans by simply refusing to call

Parliament into session between 1629 and 1640. Without it, the king's ministers had to find every loophole possible to raise revenues. They tried to turn "ship money," a levy on seaports in times of emergency, into an annual tax collected everywhere in the country. The crown won the ensuing court case, but many subjects still refused to pay what they considered to be an illegal tax.

Religious tensions brought conflicts over the king's authority to a head. The Puritans had long agitated for the removal of any vestiges of Catholicism, but Charles, married to a French Catholic, moved in the opposite direction. With Charles's encouragement, the archbishop of Canterbury, William Laud (1573–1645), imposed increasingly elaborate ceremonies on the Anglican church. Angered by these moves toward "popery," the Puritans poured forth vituperative pamphlets and sermons. In response Laud hauled them before the feared Court of Star Chamber, which the king personally controlled. The court ordered harsh sentences for Laud's Puritan critics; they were whipped, pilloried, and branded, and even had their ears cut off and their noses split. When Laud tried to apply his policies to Scotland, however, they backfired completely: the stubborn Presbyterian Scots rioted against the imposition of the Anglican prayer book—the Book of Common Prayer—and in 1640 they invaded the north of England. To raise money to fight the war, Charles called Parliament into session and unwittingly opened the door to a constitutional and religious crisis.

The Parliament of 1640 did not intend revolution, but reformers in the House of Commons (the lower house of Parliament) wanted to undo what they saw as the royal tyranny of the 1630s. Parliament removed Laud from office, ordered the execution of an unpopular royal commander, abolished the Court of Star Chamber, repealed recently levied taxes, and provided for a parliamentary assembly at least once every three years, thus establishing a constitutional check on royal authority. Moderate reformers expected to stop there and resisted Puritan pressure to abolish bishops and eliminate the Anglican prayer book. But their hand was forced in January 1642, when Charles and his soldiers invaded Parliament and tried unsuccessfully to arrest those leaders who had moved to curb his power. Faced with mounting opposition within London, Charles quickly withdrew from the city and organized an army.

The ensuing civil war between king and Parliament lasted four years (1642–1646) and divided the country. The king's army of royalists, known as Cavaliers, enjoyed most support in northern and western England. The parliamentary forces, called Roundheads because they cut their hair short, had their stronghold in the southeast, including London. Although Puritans dominated on the parliamentary side, they were divided among themselves about the proper form of church government: the Presbyterians wanted a Calvinist church with some central authority, whereas the Independents favored entirely autonomous congregations free from other church government (hence the term *congregationalism*, often associated with the Independents). Putting aside their differences for the sake of military unity, the Puritans united under an obscure member of the House of Commons, the country gentleman Oliver Cromwell (1599–1658), who sympathized with the Independents. After Cromwell skillfully reorganized the parliamentary troops, his New Model Army defeated the Cavaliers at the battle of Naseby in 1645. Charles surrendered in 1646.

Although the civil war between king and Parliament had ended in victory for Parliament, divisions within the Puritan ranks now came to the fore: the Presbyterians dominated Parliament, but the Independents controlled the army. The disputes between elites drew lower-class groups into the debate. When Parliament tried to disband the New Model Army in 1647, disgruntled soldiers protested. Called Levellers because of their insistence on leveling social differences, the

England during the Civil War

soldiers took on their officers in a series of debates about the nature of political authority. The Levellers demanded that Parliament meet annually, that members be paid so as to allow common people to participate, and that all male heads of households be allowed to vote. Their ideal of political participation excluded servants, the propertyless, and women but offered access to artisans, shopkeepers, and modest farmers. Cromwell and other army leaders rejected the Levellers' demands as threatening to property owners. Cromwell insisted, "You have no other way to deal with these men but to break them in pieces. . . . If you do not break them they will break you."

Just as political differences between Presbyterians and Independents helped spark new political movements, so, too, their conflicts over church organization fostered the emergence of new religious doctrines. The new sects had in common only their emphasis on the "inner light" of individual religious inspiration and a disdain for hierarchical authority. Their emphasis on equality before God and greater participation in church governance appealed to the middle and lower classes. The Baptists, for example, insisted on adult baptism because they believed that Christians should choose their own church and that every child should not automatically become a member of the Church of England. The Quakers demonstrated their beliefs in equality and the inner light by refusing to doff their hats to men in authority. Manifesting their religious experience by trembling, or "quaking," the Quakers believed that anyone—man or woman—inspired by a direct experience of God could preach.

Parliamentary leaders feared that the new sects would overturn the whole social hierarchy. Rumors abounded, for example, of naked Quakers running through the streets waiting "for a sign." Some sects did advocate sweeping change. The Diggers promoted rural communism—collective ownership of all property. Seekers and Ranters questioned just about everything. One notorious Ranter, John Robins, even claimed to be God. A few men advocated free love. These developments convinced the political elite that tolerating the new sects would lead to skepticism, anarchism, and debauchery.

In keeping with their notions of equality and individual inspiration, many of the new sects provided opportunities for women to become preachers and prophets. One Quaker prophet, Anna Trapnel, explained her vocation: "For in all that was said by me, I was nothing, the Lord put all in my mouth, and told me what I should say." Women presented petitions, participated prominently in street demonstrations, distributed tracts, and occasionally even dressed as men, wearing swords and joining armies. The duchess of Newcastle complained in 1650 that women were "affecting a Masculinacy . . . practicing the behaviour . . . of men." The outspoken women in new sects like the Quakers underscored the threat of a social order turning upside down.

At the heart of the continuing political struggle was the question of what to do with the king, who tried to negotiate with the Presbyterians in Parliament. In late 1648, Independents in the army purged the Presbyterians from Parliament, leaving a "rump" of about seventy members. This Rump Parliament then created a high court to try Charles I. The court found him guilty of attempting to establish "an unlimited and tyrannical power" and pronounced a death sentence. On January 30, 1649, Charles was beheaded before an enormous crowd, which reportedly groaned as one when the axe fell. Although many had objected to Charles's autocratic rule, few had wanted him killed. For royalists, Charles immediately became a martyr, and reports of miracles, such as the curing of blindness by the touch of a handkerchief soaked in his blood, soon circulated.

The Rump Parliament abolished the monarchy and the House of Lords (the upper house of Parliament) and set up a Puritan republic with Oliver Cromwell as chairman of the Council of State. Cromwell did not tolerate dissent from his policies. He saw the hand of God in events and himself as God's agent. Pamphleteers and songwriters ridiculed his red nose and accused him of wanting to be king, but few challenged his leadership. When his agents discovered plans for mutiny within the army, they executed the perpetrators; new decrees silenced the Levellers. Although Cromwell allowed the various Puritan sects to worship rather freely and permitted Jews with needed skills to return to England for the first time since the thirteenth century, Catholics could not worship publicly, nor could Anglicans use the Book of Common Prayer. The elites—many of whom were still Anglican—were troubled by Cromwell's religious policies but pleased to see some social order reestablished.

The new regime aimed to extend state power just as Charles I had before. Cromwell laid the foundation for a Great Britain made up of England, Wales, Ireland, and Scotland by reconquering Scotland and subduing Ireland. Anti-English

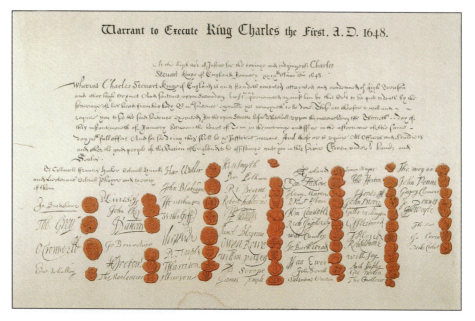

■ **Death Warrant of Charles I**

Parliament voted to try Charles I for treason, and the trial began in January 1649. A week later, the court found Charles to be a "tyrant, traitor, murderer, and public enemy" and ordered his execution. When the monarchy was restored in 1660, everyone who signed Charles I's death warrant was hunted down and executed. (Mary Evans Picture Library.)

rebels in Ireland had seized the occasion of troubles between king and Parliament to revolt in 1641. When Cromwell's position was secured in 1649, he went to Ireland with a large force and easily defeated the rebels, massacring whole garrisons and their priests. He encouraged expropriating the lands of the Irish "barbarous wretches," and Scottish immigrants resettled the northern county of Ulster. This seventeenth-century English conquest left a legacy of bitterness that the Irish even today call "the curse of Cromwell." In 1651, Parliament turned its attention overseas, putting mercantilist ideas into practice in the first Navigation Act, which allowed imports only if they were carried on English ships or came directly from the producers of goods. The Navigation Act was aimed at the Dutch, who dominated world trade; Cromwell tried to carry the policy further by waging naval war on the Dutch from 1652 to 1654.

At home, however, Cromwell faced growing resistance. His wars required a budget twice the size of Charles I's, and his increases in property taxes and customs duties alienated landowners and merchants. The conflict reached a crisis in 1653: Parliament considered disbanding the army, whereupon Cromwell abolished the Rump Parliament in a military coup and made himself Lord Protector. He now silenced his critics by banning newspapers and using networks of spies and mail readers to keep tabs on his enemies. Cromwell's death in 1658 revived the prospect

■ **Oliver Cromwell**

Shown here preparing for battle, Cromwell lived an austere life but believed fiercely in his own personal righteousness. As leader he tolerated no opposition. When he died, he was buried in Westminster Abbey, but in 1661 his body was exhumed and hanged in its shroud. His head was cut off and displayed outside Westminster Hall for nearly twenty years. (Courtesy of the National Portrait Gallery, London.)

of civil war and political chaos. In 1660, a newly elected, staunchly Anglican Parliament invited Charles II, the son of the executed king, to return from exile.

The "Glorious Revolution" of 1688

The traditional monarchical form of government was reinstated in 1660, restoring the king to full partnership with Parliament. Charles II (r. 1660–1685) promised "a liberty to tender consciences" in an attempt to extend religious toleration, especially to Catholics, with whom he sympathized. Yet in the first years of his reign more than a thousand Puritan ministers lost their positions, and after 1664, attending a service other than one conforming with the Anglican prayer book was illegal. Natural disasters also marred the early years of Charles II's reign. The plague stalked London's rat-infested streets in May 1665 and claimed more than thirty thousand victims by September. Then in 1666, the Great Fire swept the city, causing cataclysmic destruction. The crown now had a city as well as a monarchy to rebuild.

The restoration of monarchy made some in Parliament fear that the English government would come to resemble French absolutism. This fear was not unfounded. In 1670, Charles II made a secret agreement, soon leaked, with Louis XIV in which he promised to announce his conversion to Catholicism in exchange for money for a war against the Dutch. Charles never proclaimed himself a Catholic, but in his Declaration of Indulgence (1673) he did suspend all laws against Catholics and Protestant dissenters. Parliament refused to continue funding the Dutch war unless Charles rescinded his Declaration of Indulgence. Asserting its authority further, Parliament passed the Test Act in 1673, requiring all government officials to profess

■ **Great Fire of London, 1666**

This painting shows the three-day fire at its height. The writer John Evelyn described the scene in his diary: "All the sky was of a fiery aspect, like the top of a burning oven, and the light seen above 40 miles round about for many nights. God grant mine eyes may never behold the like, who now saw above 10,000 houses all in one flame; the noise and cracking and thunder of people, the fall of towers, houses, and churches, was like an hideous storm." Everyone in London at the time felt overwhelmed by the catastrophe, and many attributed it to God's punishment for the upheavals of the 1640s and 1650s. (Museum of London Photographic Library.)

allegiance to the Church of England and in effect disavow Catholic doctrine. Then in 1678, Parliament precipitated the so-called Exclusion Crisis by explicitly denying the throne to a Roman Catholic. This action was aimed at the king's brother and heir, James, an open convert to Catholicism. Charles refused to allow it to become law.

The dynastic crisis over the succession of a Catholic gave rise to two distinct factions in Parliament: the Tories, who supported a strong, hereditary monarchy and the restored ceremony of the Anglican church, and the Whigs, who advocated parliamentary supremacy and toleration for Protestant dissenters such as Presbyterians. Both labels were originally derogatory: *Tory* meant an Irish Catholic bandit; *Whig* was the Irish Catholic designation for a Presbyterian Scot. The Tories favored James's succession despite his Catholicism, whereas the Whigs opposed a Catholic monarch. The loose moral atmosphere of Charles's court also offended some Whigs, who complained tongue in cheek that Charles was father of his country in much too literal a fashion (he had fathered more than one child by his mistresses but produced no legitimate heir).

Upon Charles's death, James succeeded to the throne as James II (r. 1685–1688). James pursued pro-Catholic and absolutist policies even more aggressively than his brother. When a male heir—who would take precedence over James's two adult Protestant daughters and be reared a Catholic—was born, Tories and Whigs banded together. They invited the Dutch ruler William, prince of Orange and the husband of James's older daughter, Mary, to invade England. James fled to France, and hardly any blood was shed. Parliament offered the throne jointly to William (r. 1689–1702) and Mary (r. 1689–1694) on the condition that they accept a bill of rights guaranteeing Parliament's full partnership in a constitutional government.

In the Bill of Rights (1689), William and Mary agreed not to raise a standing army or to levy taxes without Parliament's consent. They also agreed to call meetings of Parliament at least every three years, to guarantee free elections to parliamentary seats, and to abide by Parliament's decisions and not suspend duly passed laws. The agreement gave England's constitutional government a written, legal basis by formally recognizing Parliament as a self-contained, independent body that shared power with the rulers.♦ Victorious supporters of the coup declared it the "Glorious Revolution." Constitutionalism had triumphed over absolutism in England.

The propertied classes who controlled Parliament prevented any resurgence of the popular turmoil of the 1640s. The Toleration Act of 1689 granted all Protestants freedom of worship, though non-Anglicans were still excluded from the universities; Catholics got no rights but were more often left alone to worship privately. When the Catholics in Ireland rose to defend James II, William and Mary's troops brutally suppressed them. With the Whigs in power and the Tories in opposition, wealthy landowners now controlled political life throughout the realm. Differences between the factions had become minor; essentially, the Tories had less access to the king's patronage.

Constitutionalism in the Dutch Republic and the Overseas Colonies

When William and Mary came to the throne in England in 1689, the Dutch and the English put aside the rivalries that had brought them to war against each other in 1652–1654, 1665–1667, and 1672–1674. Under William, the Dutch Republic and England together led the coalition that blocked Louis XIV's efforts to dominate continental Europe. The two states had much in common: oriented toward commerce, especially overseas, they were the successful exceptions to absolutism in Europe. Also among the few outposts of constitutionalism in the seventeenth century were the British North American colonies, which developed representative government while the English were preoccupied with their revolutions at home. Constitution-

---

♦ For the complete text of the English Bill of Rights, see Document 43.

alism was not the only factor shaping this Atlantic world; as constitutionalism developed in the colonies, so, too, did the enslavement of black Africans as a new labor force.

The Dutch Republic

When the Dutch Republic gained formal independence from Spain in 1648, it had already established a decentralized, constitutional state. Rich merchants called *regents* effectively controlled the internal affairs of each province and through the Estates General (an assembly made up of deputies from each province) named the *stadholder*, the executive officer responsible for defense and for representing the state at all ceremonial occasions. They almost always chose one of the princes of the house of Orange, but the prince of Orange resembled a president more than a king.

The decentralized state encouraged and protected trade, and the Dutch Republic soon became Europe's financial capital. The Bank of Amsterdam offered interest rates less than half those available in England and France. Praised for their industriousness, thrift, and cleanliness—and maligned as greedy, dull "butterboxes"—the Dutch dominated overseas commerce with their shipping (Map 13.3). They imported products from all over the world: spices, tea, and silk from Asia; sugar and tobacco from the Americas; wool from England and Spain; timber and furs from Scandinavia; grain from eastern Europe. A widely reprinted history of Amsterdam that appeared in 1662 described the city as "risen through the hand of God to the peak of prosperity and greatness. . . . The whole world stands amazed at its riches and from east and west, north and south they come to behold it."

The Dutch rapidly became the most prosperous and best-educated people in Europe. Middle-class people supported the visual arts, especially painting, to an unprecedented degree. Artists and engravers produced thousands of works, and Dutch artists were among the first to sell to a mass market. Whereas in other countries, kings, nobles, and churches bought art, Dutch buyers were merchants, artisans, and shopkeepers. Engravings, illustrated histories, and oil paintings, even those of the widely acclaimed Rembrandt van Rijn (1606–1669), were relatively inexpensive. The pictures reflected the Dutch interest in familiar daily details: children at play, winter landscapes, and ships in port.

The family household, not the royal court, determined the moral character of this intensely commercial society. Dutch society fostered public enterprise in men and work in the home for women, who were expected to filter out the greed and materialism of commercial society by maintaining domestic harmony and virtue. Relative prosperity decreased the need for married women to work, so Dutch society developed the clear contrast between middle-class male and female roles that would become prevalent elsewhere in Europe and in America more than a century later. As one contemporary Dutch writer explained, "The husband must be on the street to practice his trade; the wife must stay at home to be in the kitchen."

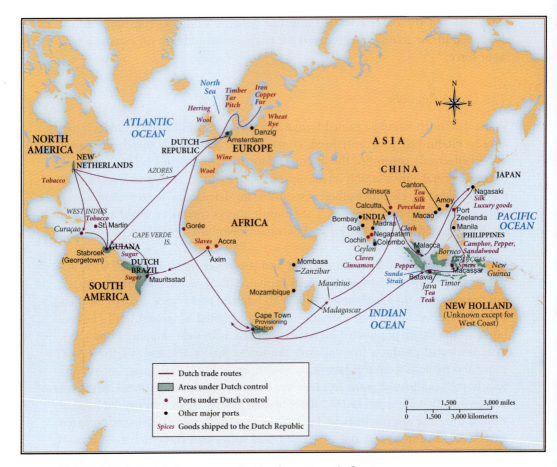

■ MAP 13.3 Dutch Commerce in the Seventeenth Century

Even before gaining formal independence from the Spanish in 1648, the Dutch had begun to compete with the Spanish and Portuguese all over the world. In 1602, a group of merchants established the Dutch East India Company, which soon offered investors an annual rate of return of 35 percent on the trade in spices with countries located on the Indian Ocean. Global commerce gave the Dutch the highest standard of living in Europe and soon attracted the envy of the French and the English.

Extraordinarily high levels of urbanization and literacy created a large reading public. Dutch presses printed books censored elsewhere (printers or authors censored in one province simply shifted operations to another), and the University of Leiden attracted students and professors from all over Europe. Dutch tolerance extended to the works of Benedict Spinoza (1633–1677), a Jewish philosopher and biblical scholar who was expelled by his synagogue for alleged atheism but was left alone by the Dutch authorities. Spinoza strove to reconcile religion with science and mathematics, but his work scandalized many Christians and Jews because he seemed to equate God and nature. Like nature, Spinoza's God followed unchangeable laws and could not be influenced by human actions, prayers, or faith.

■ **A Typical Dutch Scene from Daily Life**

Jan Steen painted The Baker Arent Oostward and His Wife *in 1658. Steen ran a brewery and tavern in addition to painting, and he was known for his interest in the details of daily life. Dutch artists popularized this kind of "genre" painting, which showed ordinary people at work and play.* (Rijksmuseum, Amsterdam.)

www.bedfordstmartins.com/huntconcise
See the ONLINE STUDY GUIDE for more help in analyzing this image.

Dutch learning, painting, and commerce all enjoyed wide renown in the seventeenth century, but this luster proved hard to maintain. The Dutch lived in a world of international rivalries in which strong central authority gave their enemies an advantage. Though inconclusive, the naval wars with England drained the state's revenues. Even more dangerous were the land wars with France, which continued into the eighteenth century. The Dutch survived these challenges but increasingly depended on alliances with other powers, such as England. By the end of the seventeenth century, the regent elite had become more exclusive, more preoccupied with ostentation, less tolerant of deviations from strict Calvinism, and more concerned with imitating French styles than with encouraging their own.

Freedom and Slavery in the New World

The French and English also increasingly overshadowed the Dutch in the New World colonies. While the Dutch concentrated on shipping, including the slave trade, the seventeenth-century French and English established settler colonies that would eventually provide fabulous revenues to the home countries. Many European governments encouraged private companies to vie for their share of the slave trade, and slavery began to take clear institutional form in the New World in this period. Even while slavery offered only a degrading form of despotism to black Africans, whites found in the colonies greater political and religious freedom than in Europe.

After the Spanish and Portuguese had shown that African slaves could be transported and forced to labor in South and Central America, the English and French endeavored to set up similar labor systems in their new Caribbean island colonies. White planters with large tracts of land bought African slaves to work fields of sugarcane, and as they gradually built up their holdings, the planters displaced most of the original white settlers, who moved to mainland North American colonies. After 1661, when Barbados instituted a slave code that stripped all Africans of rights under English law, slavery became codified as an inherited status that applied only to blacks. The result was a society of extremes: the very wealthy whites, about 7 percent of the population in Barbados; and the enslaved, powerless black majority. The English brought little of their religious or constitutional practices to the Caribbean. Other Caribbean colonies followed a similar pattern of development. Louis XIV promulgated a "black code" in 1685 to regulate the legal status of slaves in the French colonies. Although one of his aims was to prevent non-Catholics from owning slaves in the French colonies, the code had much the same effect as the English codes on the slaves themselves: they had no legal rights.

The highest church and government authorities in Catholic and Protestant countries alike condoned the gradually expanding slave trade; the governments of England, France, Spain, Portugal, the Dutch Republic, and Denmark all encouraged private companies to traffic in black Africans. The Dutch West India Company was the most successful of them. In 1600, about 9,500 Africans were exported from Africa to the New World every year; by 1700, this figure had increased nearly fourfold to 36,000 annually. Historians advance several different factors for the increase in the slave trade: some claim that improvements in muskets made European slavers more formidable; others cite the rising price for slaves, which made their sale more attractive for Africans; still others focus on factors internal to Africa, such as the increasing size of African armies and their use of muskets in fighting and capturing other Africans for sale as slaves. Whatever the reason, the way had been prepared for the development of an Atlantic economy based on slavery.

Virtually left to themselves during the upheavals in England, the fledgling English colonies in North America developed representative government on their own. Almost every colony had a governor and a two-house legislature. The colonial legislatures constantly sought to increase their power and resisted the efforts of Charles II and James II to reaffirm royal control. William and Mary reluctantly allowed emerging colonial elites more control over local affairs. The social and political elite among the settlers hoped to impose an English social hierarchy dominated by rich landowners. Ordinary immigrants to the colonies, however, took advantage of plentiful land to carve out their own farms using white servants and, later, in some colonies, African slaves.

For Native Americans, the expanding European presence meant something else altogether. They faced death through disease and warfare and the accelerating loss of their homelands. Unlike white settlers, Native Americans believed that land was a divine gift provided for their collective use and not subject to individual ownership. As a result, Europeans' claims that they owned exclusive land rights caused frequent skirmishes. In 1675–1676, for instance, three tribes allied under Metacomet (called King Philip by the English) threatened the survival of New England settlers, who savagely repulsed the attacks and sold their captives as slaves. Whites portrayed Native Americans as conspiring villains and sneaky heathens, akin to Africans in their savagery.

The Search for Order in Elite and Popular Culture

The early success of constitutionalism in England, the Dutch Republic, and the English North American colonies would help to shape a distinctive Atlantic world in the eighteenth century. Just how constitutionalism was linked to the growing commerce with the colonies remains open to dispute, however, because the constitutional governments, like the absolutist ones, avidly pursued profits in the burgeoning slave trade. Freedom did not mean liberty for everyone. One of the great debates of the time—and of much of the modern period that followed—concerned the meaning of freedom: for whom, under what conditions, with what justifiable limitations could freedom be claimed?

There was no freedom without order to sustain it, and most Europeans feared disorder above all else. Political theories, science, poetry, painting, and architecture all reflected in some measure the attempts to ground authority—to define the relation between freedom and order—in new ways. Authority concerned not just rulers and subjects but also the hierarchy of groups in society. As European states consolidated their powers, elites worked to distinguish themselves from the lower classes. They developed new codes of correct behavior for themselves and tried to teach order and discipline to their social inferiors.

Social Contract Theory: Hobbes and Locke

The turmoil of the times prompted a major rethinking of the foundations of all authority. Two figures stood out prominently amid the competing voices: Thomas Hobbes and John Locke. Their writings fundamentally shaped the modern subject of political science. Hobbes justified absolute authority; Locke provided the rationale for constitutionalism. Yet both argued that all authority came not from divine right but from a "social contract" between citizens.

Thomas Hobbes (1588–1679) was a royalist who sat out the English civil war of the 1640s in France, where he tutored the future king Charles II. Returning to England in 1651, he published his masterpiece, *Leviathan* (1651), in which he argued for unlimited authority in a ruler. Absolute authority could be vested in either a king or a parliament; it had to be absolute, he insisted, in order to overcome the defects of human nature. Believing that people are essentially self-centered and driven by the "right to self-preservation," Hobbes made his case by referring to science, not religion. To Hobbes, human life in a state of nature—that is, any situation without firm authority—was "solitary, poor, nasty, brutish, and short." He believed that the desire for power and natural greed would inevitably lead to unfettered competition. Only the assurance of social order could make people secure enough to act according to law; consequently, giving up personal liberty, he maintained, was the price of collective security. Rulers derived their power, he concluded, from a contract in which absolute authority protects people's rights.

Hobbes's notion of rule by an absolute authority left no room for political dissent or nonconformity, and it infuriated both royalists and supporters of Parliament. He enraged royalists by arguing that authority came not from divine right but from the social contract between citizens. Parliamentary supporters resisted Hobbes's claim that rulers must possess absolute authority to prevent the greater evil of anarchy; they believed that a constitution should guarantee shared power between king and parliament and protect individual rights under the law. Like Machiavelli before him, Hobbes became associated with a cynical, pessimistic view of human nature, and future political theorists often began their arguments by refuting Hobbes.

Rejecting both Hobbes and the more traditional royalist defenses of absolute authority, John Locke (1632–1704) used the notion of a social contract to provide a foundation for constitutionalism. Locke experienced political life firsthand as physician, secretary, and intellectual companion to the earl of Shaftesbury, a leading English Whig. In 1683, during the Exclusion Crisis, Locke fled with Shaftesbury to the Dutch Republic. There he continued work on his *Two Treatises of Government*, which, when published in 1690, served to justify the Glorious Revolution of 1688. Locke's position was thoroughly anti-absolutist. He denied the divine right of kings and ridiculed the common royalist idea that political power in the state mirrored the father's authority in the family. Like Hobbes, he posited a state of nature that applied to all people. Unlike Hobbes, however, he thought people were reasonable and the state of nature peaceful.

Locke insisted that government's only purpose was to protect life, liberty, and property, a notion that linked economic and political freedom. Ultimate authority rested in the will of a majority of men who owned property, and government should be limited to its basic purpose of protection. A ruler who failed to uphold his part of the social contract between the ruler and the populace could be justifiably resisted, an idea that would become crucial for the leaders of the American Revolution a century later. For England's landowners, however, Locke helped validate a revolution that consolidated their interests and ensured their privileges in the social hierarchy. Although he himself owned shares in the Royal African Company and justified slavery, Locke's writings were later used by abolitionists in their campaign against slavery.

Locke defended his optimistic view of human nature in the immensely influential *Essay Concerning Human Understanding* (1690). He denied the existence of any innate ideas and asserted instead that each human is born with a mind that is a *tabula rasa* (blank slate). Everything humans know, he claimed, comes from sensory experience, not from anything inherent in human nature. Locke's views promoted the belief that "all men are created equal," a belief that challenged absolutist forms of rule and ultimately raised questions about women's roles as well. Not surprisingly, Locke devoted considerable energy to rethinking educational practices; he believed that education crucially shaped the human personality by channeling all sensory experience.

Newton and the Consolidation of the Scientific Revolution

New breakthroughs in science lent support to Locke's optimistic view of human potential. Building on the work of Copernicus, Kepler, and Galileo (see Chapter 12), the English scientist Isaac Newton (1642–1727) finally synthesized astronomy and physics with his law of gravitation, further enhancing the prestige of the new science. A Cambridge University student at the time of Charles II's restoration, Newton was a pious Anglican who aimed to reconcile faith and science. By proving that the physical universe followed rational principles, Newton argued, scientists could prove the existence of God and so liberate humans from doubt and the fear of chaos. Newton applied mathematical principles to formulate three physical laws: (1) in the absence of force, motion continues in a straight line; (2) the rate of change in the motion of an object is a result of the forces acting on it; and (3) the action and reaction between two objects are equal and opposite. The basis of Newtonian physics thus required understanding mass, inertia, force, velocity, and acceleration—all key concepts in modern science.

Extending these principles to the entire universe in his masterwork, *Principia Mathematica* (1687), Newton united celestial and terrestrial mechanics—astronomy and physics—with his law of gravitation. This law held that every body in the universe exerts over every other body an attractive force directly proportional to the product of their masses and inversely proportional to the square of the distance between them. The law of gravitation explained Kepler's elliptical planetary orbits just as it accounted for the motion of ordinary objects on earth. Once set in motion, the universe operated like clockwork, with no need for God's continuing intervention. Gravity, though a mysterious force, could be expressed mathematically. In Newton's words, "From the same principles [of motion] I now demonstrate the frame of the System of the World." The English poet Alexander Pope later captured the intellectual world's appreciation of Newton's accomplishment:

> *Nature and Nature's laws lay hid in night*
> *God said, Let Newton be! and all was light.*

Newton's science was not just mathematical and deductive; he experimented with light and helped establish the science of optics. Even while making these fundamental contributions to scientific method, Newton carried out alchemical experiments in his rooms at Cambridge University and spent long hours trying to calculate the date of the beginning of the world and of the second coming of Jesus. Not all scientists accepted Newton's theories immediately, especially on the continent of Europe, but within a couple of generations his work was preeminent, partly because of experimental verification. His "frame of the System of the World" remained the basis of all physics until the advent of relativity theory and quantum mechanics in the early twentieth century.

Although not all Newton's peers immediately accepted the validity of his work, absolutist rulers quickly saw the potential of the new science for enhancing their prestige and glory. Frederick William, the Great Elector of Brandenburg-Prussia, for example, set up agricultural experiments in front of his Berlin palace, and various German princes supported the work of Gottfried Wilhelm Leibniz (1646–1716), one of the inventors of calculus. A lawyer, diplomat, and scholar who wrote about metaphysics, cosmology, and history, Leibniz helped establish scientific societies in the German states. Government involvement in science was greatest in France, where it became an arm of mercantilist policy; in 1666, Colbert founded the Royal Academy of Sciences, which supplied fifteen scientists with government stipends.

Constitutional states supported science less directly but nonetheless provided an intellectual environment that encouraged its spread. The English Royal Society, the counterpart to the Royal Academy of Sciences in France, grew out of informal meetings of scientists at London and Oxford rather than direct government involvement. It received a royal charter in 1662 but maintained complete independence. The society's secretary described its business to be "in the first place, to scrutinize the whole of Nature and to investigate its activity and powers by means of observations and experiments; and then in course of time to hammer out a more solid philosophy and more ample amenities of civilization." Whether the state was directly involved or not, thinkers of the day now tied science explicitly to social progress.

Because of their exclusion from most universities, women only rarely participated in the new scientific discoveries. In 1667, nonetheless, the English Royal Society invited Margaret Cavendish, a writer of poems, essays, letters, and philosophical treatises, to attend a meeting to watch the exhibition of experiments. She attacked the use of telescopes and microscopes because she detected in the new experimentalism a mechanistic view of the world that exalted masculine prowess and challenged the Christian belief in freedom of the will. She also urged the formal education of women, complaining that "we are kept like birds in cages to hop up and down in our houses." "Many of our Sex may have as much wit, and be capable of Learning as well as men," she insisted, "but since they want Instructions, it is not possible they should attain to it."

Freedom and Order in the Arts

Even though Newtonian science depicted an orderly universe, most artists and intellectuals had experienced enough of the upheavals of the seventeenth century to fear the prospect of chaos and disintegration. The French mathematician Blaise Pascal vividly captured their worries in his *Pensées* ("Thoughts") of 1660: "I look on all sides, and I see only darkness everywhere. Nature presents to me nothing which is not a matter of doubt and concern. . . . It is incomprehensible that God should exist, and incomprehensible that He should not exist." Poets, painters, and architects all tried to make sense of the individual's place within what Pascal called "the eternal silence of these infinite spaces."

The English Puritan poet John Milton (1608–1674) responded to the turmoil of the times by giving priority to individual liberty. In 1643, in the midst of the civil war between king and Parliament, he published writings in favor of divorce. When Parliament enacted a censorship law aimed at such literature, Milton countered in 1644 with one of the first defenses of freedom of the press, *Areopagitica* ("Tribunal of Opinion"). Forced into retirement after the restoration of the monarchy, Milton published in 1667 his epic poem *Paradise Lost*. He used Adam and Eve's Fall to meditate on human freedom and the tragedies of rebellion. Although Milton wanted to "justify the ways of God to man," his Satan, the proud angel who challenges God, is so compelling as to be heroic. In the end, Adam and Eve learn to accept moral responsibility. Individuals learn the limits to their freedom, yet personal liberty remains essential to their definition as human.

The dominant artistic styles of the time—the baroque and the classical—both submerged the individual in a grander design. The baroque style proved to be especially suitable for public displays of faith and power that overawed individual

■ **Gian Lorenzo Bernini,** *Ecstasy of St. Teresa of Ávila* **(c. 1650)**

In this baroque sculpture, Bernini captures the drama and sensationalism of a mystical religious faith. He based his figures on a vision of an angel reported by St. Teresa: "In his hands I saw a great golden spear, and at the iron tip there appeared to be a point of fire. This he plunged into my heart several times so that it penetrated my entrails. When he pulled it out I felt that he took them with it, and left me utterly consumed by the great love of God." (Scala/Art Resource, NY.)

beholders. The combination of religious and political purposes in baroque art is best exemplified in the architecture and sculpture of Gian Lorenzo Bernini (1598–1680), the papacy's official artist. His architectural masterpiece was the gigantic square facing St. Peter's Basilica in Rome (1656–1671). His use of freestanding colonnades and a huge open space is meant to impress the individual observer with the power of the popes and the Catholic religion. Bernini also sculpted tombs for the popes and a large statue of Constantine, the first Christian emperor of Rome— perfect examples of the marriage of power and religion. In 1665, Louis XIV hired Bernini to plan the rebuilding of the Louvre palace in Paris but then rejected his ideas as incompatible with French tastes.

Although France was a Catholic country, French painters, sculptors, and architects, like their patron Louis XIV, preferred the standards of classicism to those of the baroque. French artists developed classicism to be a national style, distinct from the baroque style that was closely associated with France's enemies, the Austrian and Spanish Habsburgs. As its name suggests, classicism reflected the ideals of the art of antiquity; geometric shapes, order, and harmony of lines took precedence over the sensuous, exuberant, and emotional forms of the baroque. Rather than being overshadowed by the sheer power of emotional display, in classicism the individual could be found at the intersection of converging, symmetrical, straight lines. These influences were apparent in the work of the leading French painters of the period, Nicolas Poussin (1594–1665) and Claude Lorrain (1600–1682), both of whom worked in Rome and tried to re-create classical Roman values in their mythological scenes and Roman landscapes.

Dutch painters found the baroque and classical styles less suited to their private market, where buyers sought smaller-scale works with ordinary subjects. Dutch artists came from common stock themselves—Rembrandt's father was a miller, and the father of his renowned contemporary, Jan Vermeer (1632–1675), was a silk worker. Their clients were people like themselves who purchased paintings much as they bought tables and chairs. Rembrandt occasionally worked on commission for the prince of Orange, but he often painted ordinary people, suffusing his canvases with a radiant, otherworldly light that made the plainest people and objects appear deeply spiritual. Vermeer's best-known paintings show women working at home, and, like Rembrandt, he made ordinary activities seem precious and beautiful. In Dutch art, ordinary individuals had religious and political significance.

Art might also serve the interests of science. One of the most skilled illustrators of insects and flowers was Maria Sibylla Merian (1646–1717), a German-born painter-scholar whose engravings were widely celebrated for their brilliant realism and microscopic clarity. Merian eventually separated from her husband and joined a sect called the Labadists (after their French founder, Jean de Labadie), who did not believe in formal marriage ties and established a colony in the northern Dutch province of Friesland. After moving there with her daughters, Merian went with missionaries from the sect to the Dutch colony of Surinam in South America and

■ European Fascination with Products of the New World

In this painting of a banana plant, Maria Sibylla Merian offers a scientific study of one of the many exotic plants and animals found by Europeans who traveled to the colonies overseas. Merian was fifty-one when she traveled to the Dutch South American colony of Surinam.

(Courtesy of Hunt Institute for Botanical Documentation, Carnegie Mellon University, Pittsburgh, PA.)

painted watercolors of the exotic flowers, birds, and insects she found in the jungle around the cocoa and sugarcane plantations. In the seventeenth century, many women became known for their still lifes and especially their paintings of flowers. Paintings by the Dutch artist Rachel Ruysch, for example, fetched higher prices than those received by Rembrandt.

Women and Manners

Poetry and painting imaginatively explored the place of the individual within a larger whole, but real-life individuals had to learn to navigate their own social worlds. Manners—the learning of individual self-discipline—were essential skills of social navigation, and women usually took the lead in teaching them. Under the tutelage of their mothers and wives, nobles learned to hide all that was crass and to maintain a fine sense of social distinction. In some ways, aristocratic men were expected to act more like women. Just as women had long been expected to please men, now aristocratic men had to please their monarch or patron by displaying proper manners and conversing with elegance and wit. Men as well as women had to master the art of pleasing—foreign languages (especially French), dance, a taste for fine music, and attention to dress.

As part of the evolution of new aristocratic ideals, nobles learned to disdain all that was lowly. The upper classes began to reject popular festivals and fairs in favor of private theaters, where seats were relatively expensive and behavior was formal. Clowns and buffoons now seemed vulgar; the last king of England to keep a court fool was Charles I. Chivalric romances that had entranced the nobility down to the time of Cervantes's *Don Quixote* (1605) now passed into popular literature.

The greatest French playwright of the seventeenth century, Molière (the pen name of Jean-Baptiste Poquelin, 1622–1673), wrote sparkling comedies of manners that revealed much about the new aristocratic behavior. Son of a tradesman, Molière left law school to form a theater company, which eventually gained the support of Louis XIV. His play *The Middle-Class Gentleman,* first performed at the royal court in 1670, revolves around the yearning of a rich, middle-class Frenchman, Monsieur Jourdain, to learn to act like a *gentilhomme* (meaning both "gentleman" and "nobleman" in French). The women in the family, including the servant girl Nicole, are reasonable, sincere, and keenly aware of what behavior is appropriate to their social station, whereas Jourdain stands for social ambition gone wild. The message for the court seemed to be a reassuring one: only true nobles by blood can hope to act like nobles. But the play also showed how the middle classes were learning to emulate the nobility; if one could learn to *act* nobly through self-discipline, could not anyone with some education and money pass himself off as noble?

As Molière's play demonstrated, new attention to manners trickled down from the court to the middle class. A French treatise on manners from 1672 explained:

> *If everyone is eating from the same dish, you should take care not to put your hand into it before those of higher rank have done so. . . . Formerly one was permitted . . . to dip one's bread into the sauce, provided only that one had not already bitten it. Nowadays that would be a kind of rusticity. Formerly one was allowed to take from one's mouth what one could not eat and drop it on the floor, provided it was done skillfully. Now that would be very disgusting.*

The key words *rusticity* and *disgusting* reveal the association of unacceptable social behavior with the peasantry, dirt, and repulsion. Ironically, however, once the elite had successfully distinguished itself from the lower classes through manners, scholars became more interested in studying popular expressions. They avidly collected proverbs, folktales, and songs—all of these now curiosities. In fact, many nobles at Louis XIV's court read fairy tales.

Courtly manners often permeated the upper reaches of society by means of the *salon,* an informal gathering held regularly in private homes and presided over by a socially eminent woman. In 1661, one French author claimed to have identified

■ Music and the Refinement of Manners

In Woman at the Clavecin, *the artist Emanuel de Witte celebrates the importance of music in the Dutch home. The woman herself remains a mystery, but the sumptuous setting of heavy draperies, mirrors, and chandeliers signals the association of keyboard music with refinement.*

(The Netherlands Institute of Cultural Heritage, Rijswijk, the Netherlands; Museum Boijmans–Van Beuningen, Rotterdam.)

251 Parisian women as hostesses of salons. Although the French government occasionally worried that these gatherings might be seditious, the three main topics of conversation were love, literature, and philosophy. Hostesses often worked hard to encourage the careers of budding authors. Before publishing a manuscript, many authors would read their compositions to a salon gathering. Corneille, Racine, and even Bishop Bossuet sought female approval for their writings.

Some women went beyond encouraging male authors and began to write on their own, but they faced many obstacles. Marie-Madeleine de La Vergne, known as Madame de Lafayette, wrote several short novels that were published anonymously because it was considered inappropriate for aristocratic women to appear in print. After the publication of *The Princess of Clèves* in 1678, she denied having written it. Hannah Wooley, the English author of many books on domestic conduct, published under the name of her first husband. Women were known for writing wonderful letters (Marie de Sévigné was a prime example), many of which circulated in handwritten form; hardly any appeared in print during their authors' lifetimes. In the 1650s, despite these limitations, French women began to turn out best-sellers in a new type of literature, the novel. Their success prompted the philosopher Pierre Bayle to remark in 1697 that "our best French novels for a long time have been written by women."

The new importance of women in the world of manners and letters did not sit well with everyone. Although the French writer François Poulain de la Barre (1647–1723), in a series of works published in the 1670s, used the new science to assert the equality of women's minds, most men resisted the idea. Clergy, lawyers, scholars, and playwrights attacked women's growing public influence. Women, they complained, were corrupting forces and needed restraint. Only marriage, "this salutary yoke," could control their passions and weaknesses. Women were accused of raising "the banner of prostitution in the salons, in the promenades, and in the streets." Molière wrote plays denouncing women's pretension to judge literary merit. English playwrights derided learned women by creating characters with names such as Lady Knowall, Lady Meanwell, and Mrs. Lovewit. A real-life target of the English playwrights was Aphra Behn (1640–1689), one of the first professional woman authors, who supported herself by journalism and wrote plays and poetry. Her short novel *Oroonoko* (1688) told the story of an African prince wrongly sold into slavery. The story was so successful that it was adapted by playwrights and performed repeatedly in England and France for the next hundred years. Behn responded to her critics by arguing that there was "no reason why women should not write as well as men."

Reforming Popular Culture

The illiterate peasants who made up most of Europe's population had little or no knowledge of the law of gravitation, upper-class manners, or novels, no matter who authored them. Their culture had three main elements: the knowledge needed to work at farming or in a trade; popular forms of entertainment such as village fairs and dances; and their religion, which shaped every aspect of life and death. What changed most noticeably in the seventeenth century was the social elites' attitude toward lower-class culture. The division between elite and popular culture widened as elites insisted on their difference from the lower orders and tried to instill new forms of discipline in their social inferiors.

In the seventeenth century, Protestant and Catholic churches alike pushed hard to change popular religious practices. Their campaigns against popular "paganism" began during the sixteenth-century Protestant Reformation and Catholic Counter-Reformation but reached much of rural Europe only in the seventeenth century. Puritans in England tried to root out maypole dances, Sunday village fairs, gambling, taverns, and bawdy ballads because they interfered with sober observance of the Sabbath. In Lutheran Norway, pastors denounced a widespread belief in the miracle-working powers of St. Olaf. *Superstition* previously meant "false religion" (Protestantism was a superstition for Catholics, Catholicism for Protestants). In the seventeenth century, it took on its modern meaning of irrational fears, beliefs, and

IMPORTANT DATES			
1642–1646	Civil war between King Charles I and Parliament in England	1678	Marie-Madeleine de La Vergne (Madame de Lafayette) anonymously publishes her novel *The Princess of Clèves*
1648	Peace of Westphalia ends Thirty Years' War; the Fronde revolt challenges royal authority in France; Ukrainian Cossack warriors rebel against the king of Poland-Lithuania	1683	Austrian Habsburgs break the Turkish siege of Vienna
1649	Execution of Charles I of England; new Russian legal code	1685	Louis XIV revokes toleration for French Protestants granted by the Edict of Nantes
1651	Thomas Hobbes publishes *Leviathan*	1687	Isaac Newton publishes *Principia Mathematica*
1660	Monarchy restored in England	1688	Parliament deposes James II and invites his daughter, Mary, and her husband, William of Orange, to take the throne
1661	Slave code set up in Barbados		
1667	Louis XIV begins the first of many wars that continue throughout his reign	1690	John Locke's *Two Treatises of Government* and *Essay Concerning Human Understanding*
1670	Molière's play *The Middle-Class Gentleman*		

practices, which anyone educated or refined would avoid. *Superstition* became synonymous with popular or ignorant beliefs.

The Catholic campaign against superstitious practices found a ready ally in Louis XIV. While he reformed the nobles at court through etiquette and manners, Catholic bishops in the French provinces trained parish priests to reform their flocks by using catechisms in local dialects and insisting that parishioners attend Mass. The church faced a formidable challenge. One bishop in France complained in 1671, "Can you believe that there are in this diocese entire villages where no one has even heard of Jesus Christ?" In some places, believers sacrificed animals to the Virgin, prayed to the new moon, and worshiped at the sources of streams as in pre-Christian times.

Like its Protestant counterpart, the Catholic campaign against ignorance and superstition helped extend state power. Clergy, officials, and local police worked together to limit carnival celebrations, to regulate pilgrimages to shrines, and to replace "indecent" images of saints with more restrained and decorous ones. In Catholicism, the cult of the Virgin Mary and devotions closely connected with Jesus, such as the Holy Sacrament and the Sacred Heart, took precedence over the celebration of more popular saints who seemed to have pagan origins or were credited with unverified miracles. Reformers everywhere tried to limit the number of feast days on the grounds that they encouraged lewd behavior.

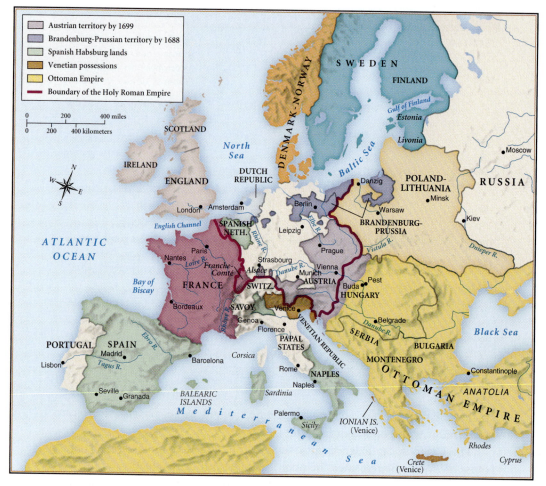

■ **MAPPING THE WEST** Europe at the End of the Seventeenth Century

A map can be deceiving. Size does not always spell advantage. Poland-Lithuania looks like a large country, but it had been fatally weakened by internal conflicts and in the next century would disappear entirely. The Ottoman Empire still controlled an extensive territory, but outside of Anatolia, Ottoman rule depended on intermediaries. The Austrian Habsburgs had pushed the Turks out of Hungary and back into the Balkans. At the other end of the scale, the very small Dutch Republic had become very rich through international commerce.

www.bedfordstmartins.com/huntconcise   See the ONLINE STUDY GUIDE for more help in analyzing this map.

The campaign for more disciplined religious practices helped generate a new attitude toward the poor. Poverty previously had been closely linked with charity and virtue in Christianity: it was a Christian duty to give alms to the poor, and Jesus and many of the saints had purposely chosen lives of poverty. In the sixteenth and seventeenth centuries, the upper classes, the church, and the state increasingly regarded the poor as dangerous, deceitful, and lacking in character. "Criminal laziness is the source of all their vices," wrote a Jesuit expert on the poor. The courts had previously expelled beggars from cities; now local leaders, both Catholic and Protestant, tried to reform their character. Municipal magistrates collected taxes for poor relief, and local notables organized charities; together they transformed hospitals into houses of confinement for beggars. In Catholic France, upper-class women's religious associations, known as *confraternities,* set up asylums that confined prostitutes (by arrest if necessary) and rehabilitated them. Confraternities also founded hospices where orphans learned order and respect. Such groups advocated harsh discipline as the cure for poverty.

Although hard times had increased the numbers of poor people and the rates of violent crime as well, the most important changes were attitudinal. The elites wanted to separate the very poor from society either to change them or to keep them from contaminating others. Hospitals became holding pens for society's unwanted members, where the poor joined the disabled, the incurably diseased, and the insane. The founding of hospitals demonstrates the connection between these attitudes and state building. In 1676, Louis XIV ordered every French city to establish a hospital, and his government took charge of their finances. Other rulers soon followed the same path.

Conclusion

The search for order in the wake of religious warfare and political upheaval took place on various levels, from the reform of the disorderly poor to the establishment of more regular bureaucratic routines in government. The biggest factor shaping the search for order was the growth of state power. Whether absolutist or constitutionalist in form, seventeenth-century states all aimed to penetrate more deeply into the lives of their subjects. They wanted more men for their armed forces, higher taxes to support their projects, and more control over foreign trade, religious dissent, and society's unwanted.

Some tearing had begun to appear, however, in the seamless fabric of state power. In England, the Dutch Republic, and the English North American colonies, property owners successfully demanded constitutional guarantees of their right to participate in government. In the eighteenth century, moreover, new levels of economic growth and the appearance of new social groups would exert pressures on the European state system. The success of seventeenth-century rulers created the political and economic conditions in which their critics would flourish.

Suggested References for further reading and online research appear on page SR-20 at the back of the book.

www.bedfordstmartins.com/huntconcise   See the ONLINE STUDY GUIDE to assess your mastery of the material covered in this chapter.

The Atlantic System and Its Consequences

1690–1740

JOHANN SEBASTIAN BACH (1685–1750), composer of mighty organ fugues and church cantatas, was not above amusing his Leipzig audiences, many of them university students. In 1732 he produced a cantata about a young woman in love— with coffee. Her old-fashioned father rages that he won't find her a husband unless she gives up the fad. She agrees, secretly vowing to admit no suitor who will not promise in the marriage contract to let her brew coffee whenever she wants. Bach offers this conclusion:

> *The cat won't give up its mouse,*
> *Girls stay faithful coffee-sisters*
> *Mother loves her coffee habit,*
> *Grandma sips it gladly too—*
> *Why then shout at the daughters?*

Bach's era might well be called the age of coffee. European travelers at the end of the sixteenth century had noticed Middle Eastern people drinking a "black drink," *kavah.* Few Europeans sampled it at first, and the Arab monopoly on its production kept prices high. This changed around 1700 when the Dutch East India Company introduced coffee plants to Java and other Indonesian islands. Coffee production then spread to the French Caribbean, where African slaves provided the plantation labor. In Europe, imported coffee spurred the development of a new kind of meeting place: the first coffeehouse opened in London in 1652, and the idea spread quickly

■ **London Coffeehouse**
This gouache (a variant on water-color painting) from about 1725 depicts a scene from a London coffeehouse located in the courtyard of the Royal Exchange (merchants' bank). Middle-class men (wearing wigs) read newspapers, drink coffee, smoke pipes, and discuss the news of the day. The coffeehouse draws them out of their homes into a new public space.
(British Museum, Bridgeman Art Library, NY.)

to other European cities. Coffeehouses became gathering places for men to drink, read newspapers, and talk politics. As a London newspaper commented in 1737, "There's scarce an Alley in City and Suburbs but has a Coffeehouse in it, which may be called the School of Public Spirit, where every Man over Daily and Weekly Journals, a Mug, or a Dram . . . devotes himself to that glorious one, his Country."

European consumption of coffee, tea, chocolate, and other novelties increased dramatically as European nations forged worldwide economic links. At the center of this new world economy was an "Atlantic system" that bound together western Europe, Africa, and the Americas. Europeans bought slaves in western Africa, transported and sold them in their colonies in North and South America and the Caribbean, bought the commodities such as coffee and sugar that were produced by the new colonial plantations, and then sold the goods in European ports for refining and reshipment. This Atlantic system first took clear shape in the early eighteenth century; it was the hub of European expansion all over the world.

Coffee drinking was one example among many of the new social and cultural patterns that took root between 1690 and 1740. Improvements in agricultural production at home reinforced the effects of trade overseas; Europeans now had more disposable income for "extras," and they spent their money not only in the new coffeehouses and cafés that sprang up all over Europe but also on newspapers, musical concerts, paintings, and novels. A new middle-class public began to make its presence felt in every domain of culture and social life.

Although the rise of the Atlantic system gave Europe new prominence in the global context, European rulers still focused most of their political, diplomatic, and military energies on their rivalries within Europe. A coalition of countries succeeded in containing French aggression, and a more balanced diplomatic system emerged. In eastern Europe, Prussia and Austria had to contend with the rising power of Russia under Peter the Great. In western Europe, both Spain and the Dutch Republic declined in influence but continued to vie with Britain and France for colonial spoils in the Atlantic. The more evenly matched competition among the great powers encouraged the development of diplomatic skills and drew attention to public health as a way of encouraging population growth.

In the aftermath of Louis XIV's revocation of the Edict of Nantes in 1685, a new intellectual movement known as the Enlightenment began to germinate. French Protestant refugees began to publish works critical of absolutism in politics and religion. Increased prosperity, the growth of a middle-class public, and the decline in warfare after Louis XIV's death in 1715 all fostered the development of this new critical spirit. Fed by the popularization of science and the growing interest in travel literature, the Enlightenment encouraged greater skepticism about religious and state authority. Eventually the movement would question almost every aspect of social and political life in Europe. The Enlightenment began in western Europe in those countries—Britain, France, and the Dutch Republic—most affected by the new Atlantic system. It, too, was a product of the age of coffee.

The Atlantic System and the World Economy

Although their ships had been circling the globe since the early 1500s, Europeans did not draw most of the world into their economic orbit until the 1700s. Western European trading nations sent ships loaded with goods to buy slaves from local rulers on the western coast of Africa; then transported the slaves to the colonies in North and South America and the Caribbean and sold them to the owners of plantations producing coffee, sugar, cotton, and tobacco; and bought the raw commodities produced in the colonies and shipped them back to Europe, where they were refined or processed and then sold to other parts of Europe and the world. The Atlantic system and the growth of international trade helped create a new consumer society.

Slavery and the Atlantic System

Spain and Portugal had dominated Atlantic trade in the sixteenth and seventeenth centuries, but in the eighteenth century European trade in the Atlantic rapidly expanded and became more systematically interconnected (Map 14.1, inset). By 1630, Portugal had already sent 60,000 African slaves to Brazil to work on the new plantations (large tracts of lands farmed by slave labor), which were producing some 15,000 tons of sugar a year. Realizing that plantations producing staples for Europeans could bring fabulous wealth, the European powers grew less interested in the dwindling trade in precious metals and more eager to colonize. Large-scale planters of sugar, tobacco, and coffee displaced small farmers who relied on one or two servants. Planters and their plantations won out because slave labor was cheap and therefore able to produce mass quantities of commodities at low prices.

State-chartered private companies from Portugal, France, Britain, the Dutch Republic, Prussia, and even Denmark exploited the 3,500-mile coastline of West Africa for slaves. Before 1675, most blacks taken from Africa had been sent to Brazil, but by 1700 half of the African slaves landed in the Caribbean (Figure 14.1). Thereafter, the plantation economy began to expand on the North American mainland. The numbers stagger the imagination. Before 1650, slave traders transported about 7,000 Africans each year across the Atlantic; this rate doubled between 1650 and 1675, nearly doubled again in the next twenty-five years, and kept going until the 1780s. In all, more than 11 million Africans, not counting those who died at sea or in Africa, were transported to the Americas before the slave trade began to wind down after 1850. Many traders gained spectacular wealth, but companies did not always make profits. The English Royal African Company, for example, delivered 100,000 slaves to the Caribbean, imported 30,000 tons of sugar to Britain, yet lost money after the few profitable years following its founding in 1672.

The balance of white and black populations in the New World colonies was determined by the staples produced. New England merchants and farmers bought few

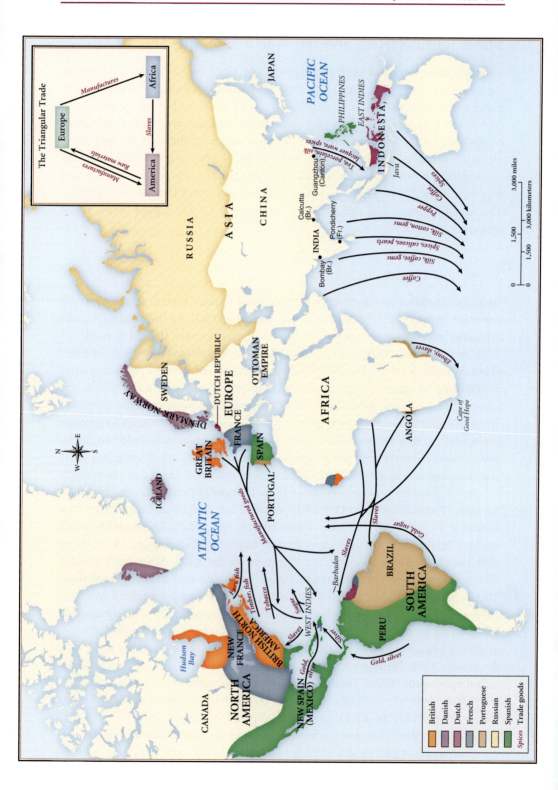

The Triangular Trade

Europe — Manufactures → Africa
Africa — Slaves → America
America — Raw materials ⇄ Manufactures — Europe

PACIFIC OCEAN

JAPAN
PHILIPPINES
EAST INDIES
INDONESIA
Java
Tea, porcelain, silk, lacquer ware, spices
Guangzhou (Canton)
Calcutta (Br.)
INDIA
Pondicherry (Fr.)
Bombay (Br.)

Coffee, Spices
Pepper
Silk, cotton, tea
Spices, calicoes, pearls
Silk, coffee, gems
Coffee

3,000 miles
3,000 kilometers
1,500
1,500

RUSSIA
ASIA
CHINA
SWEDEN
DENMARK–NORWAY
DUTCH REPUBLIC
EUROPE
OTTOMAN EMPIRE
FRANCE
AFRICA
ANGOLA
Cape of Good Hope
Ebony, slaves

GREAT BRITAIN
SPAIN
PORTUGAL
ICELAND

ATLANTIC OCEAN

Manufactured goods
Slaves
Gold, sugar
BRAZIL
SOUTH AMERICA
PERU

Barbados
Slaves
WEST INDIES
Sugar
Tobacco
Timber, fish
Furs, fish
Slaves
Gold, silver
Silver

Hudson Bay
NEW FRANCE
BRITISH NORTH AMERICA
NEW SPAIN (MEXICO)
NORTH AMERICA
CANADA

N E S W

Gold, silver

British
Danish
Dutch
French
Portuguese
Russian
Spanish
Spices Trade goods

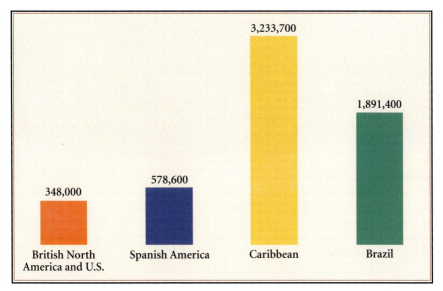

■ FIGURE 14.1 African Slaves Imported into American Territories, 1701–1810
During the eighteenth century, planters in the newly established Caribbean colonies imported millions of African slaves to work the new plantations. The vast majority of African slaves transported to the Americas ended up either in the Caribbean or in Brazil.
(Adapted from Philip D. Curtin, *The Atlantic Slave Trade: A Census* [Madison: University of Wisconsin Press, 1969].)

slaves because they did not own plantations. Blacks—both slave and free—made up only 3 percent of the population in eighteenth-century New England, compared with 60 percent in South Carolina. On the whole, the British North American colonies contained a higher proportion of African Americans from 1730 to 1765 than at any other time in American history. The imbalance of whites and blacks was even more extreme in the Caribbean; in the early 1700s, the British sugar islands had a population of about 150,000 people, only 30,000 of them Europeans. The remaining 80 percent were African slaves, as most indigenous people died fighting Europeans or the diseases brought by them.

Enslaved women and men suffered terribly. Most had been sold to European traders by Africans from the west coast who acquired them through warfare or kidnapping. The vast majority were between fourteen and thirty-five years old.

■ MAP 14.1 European Trade Patterns, c. 1740
By 1740, the European powers had colonized much of North and South America and incorporated their American colonies into a worldwide system of commerce centered on the slave trade and plantation production of staple crops. Europeans still sought spices and luxury goods in China and the East Indies, but outside of Java, few Europeans had settled permanently in these areas.

www.bedfordstmartins.com/huntconcise   See the ONLINE STUDY GUIDE for more help in analyzing this map.

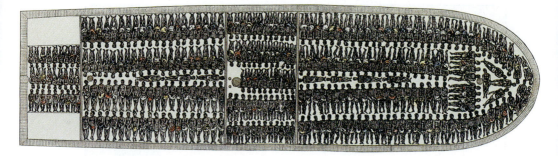

■ **Conditions on Slave Ships**
Although the viewer cannot tell whether the enslaved Africans are lying down or standing, this engraving, inspired by the campaign to abolish slavery, has a clear message: slaves endured desperately crowded conditions on the long voyage across the Atlantic. Many (like crew members, who also died in large numbers) fell victim to dysentery, yellow fever, measles, or smallpox; a few committed suicide by jumping overboard. (North Wind Picture Archive.)

Before they were crammed onto the ships for the three-month trip, their heads were shaved, they were stripped naked, and some were branded with red-hot irons. Men and women were separated. Men were shackled with leg irons. Sailors and officers raped the women whenever they wished and beat those who refused their advances. In the cramped and appalling conditions aboard ship, as many as one-fourth of the slaves died in transit.◆

Once they landed, slaves were forced into degrading and oppressive conditions. As soon as masters bought slaves, they gave them new names, often only first names, and in some colonies branded them as personal property. Slaves had no social identities of their own; they were expected to learn their master's language and to do any job assigned. Slaves worked fifteen- to seventeen-hour days and were fed only enough to keep them on their feet. Brazilian slaves consumed more calories than the poorest Brazilians do today, but that hardly made them well fed. The death rate among slaves was high, especially in Brazil, where quick shifts in the weather, lack of clothing, and squalid living conditions made them susceptible to a variety of deadly illnesses.

Not surprisingly, despite the threat of torture or death on recapture, slaves sometimes ran away. In Brazil, runaways hid in *quilombos* (hideouts) in the forests or backcountry. When it was discovered and destroyed in 1695, the *quilombo* of Palmares had thirty thousand fugitives who had formed their own social organization complete with elected kings and councils of elders. Outright revolt was uncommon, especially before the nineteenth century, but other forms of resistance included

◆ For a personal account of the eighteenth-century Atlantic slave trade, see Document 44, *The Interesting Narrative of the Life of Olaudah Equiano, Written by Himself.*

stealing food, breaking tools, and feigning illness or stupidity. Slaveholders' fears about conspiracy and revolt lurked beneath the surface of every slave-based society. In 1710, the royal governor of Virginia reminded the colonial legislature of the need for unceasing vigilance: "We are not to Depend on Either Their Stupidity, or that Babel of Languages among 'em; freedom Wears a Cap which Can Without a Tongue, Call Togather all Those who Long to Shake off the fetters of Slavery." Masters defended whipping and other forms of physical punishment as essential to maintaining discipline. Laws called for the castration of a slave who struck a white person.

Plantation owners often left their colonial possessions in the care of agents and collected the revenue to live as wealthy landowners back home, where they built opulent mansions and gained influence in local and national politics. William Beckford, for example, had been sent from Jamaica to school in England as a young boy. When he inherited sugar plantations and shipping companies from his father and older brother, he moved the headquarters of the family business to London in the 1730s to be close to the government and financial markets. His holdings formed the single most powerful economic interest in Jamaica, but he preferred to live in England, where he could collect art for his many luxurious homes, hold political office (he served as lord mayor of London and in Parliament), and even lend money to the government.

The slave trade permanently altered consumption patterns for ordinary people. Sugar had been prescribed as medicine before the end of the sixteenth century, but the development of plantations in Brazil and the Caribbean made it a standard food item. By 1700, the British sent home 50 million pounds of sugar a year, a figure that doubled by 1730. During the French Revolution of the 1790s, sugar shortages would become a cause for rioting in Paris. Equally pervasive was the spread of tobacco; by the 1720s, Britain imported two hundred shiploads of tobacco from Virginia and Maryland every year, and men of every country and class smoked pipes or took snuff.

The traffic in slaves disturbed many Europeans. As a government memorandum to the Spanish king explained in 1610: "Modern theologians in published books commonly report on, and condemn as unjust, the acts of enslavement which take place in provinces of this Royal Empire." Between 1667 and 1671, the French Dominican monk Father Du Tertre published three volumes in which he denounced the mistreatment of slaves in the French colonies.

In the 1700s, however, slaveholders began to justify their actions by demeaning the mental and spiritual qualities of the enslaved Africans. White Europeans and colonists sometimes described black slaves as animal-like, akin to apes. A leading New England Puritan asserted about the slaves: "Indeed their *Stupidity* is a *Discouragement*. It may seem, unto as little purpose, to *Teach,* as to *wash an Aethiopian* [Ethiopian]." One of the great paradoxes of this time was that talk of liberty and self-evident rights, especially prevalent in Britain and its North American colonies, coexisted with the belief that some people were meant to be slaves. Although Christians believed in principle in a kind of spiritual equality between blacks and whites, the churches often defended or at least did not oppose the inequities of slavery.

World Trade and Settlement

The Atlantic system helped extend European trade relations across the globe. The textiles that Atlantic shippers exchanged for slaves on the west coast of Africa, for example, were manufactured in India and exported by the British and the French East India Companies. As much as one-quarter of the British exports to Africa in the eighteenth century were actually re-exports from India. To expand its trade in the rest of the world, Europeans seized territories and tried to establish permanent settlements. The eighteenth-century extension of European power prepared the way for western global domination in the nineteenth and twentieth centuries.

In contrast to the sparsely inhabited trading outposts in Asia and Africa, the colonies in the Americas bulged with settlers. The British North American colonies, for example, contained about 1.5 million nonnative (that is, white settler and black slave) residents by 1750. While the Spanish competed with the Portuguese for control of South America, the French competed with the British for control of North America. Spanish and British settlers came to blows over the boundary between the British colonies and Florida, which was held by Spain.

Local economies shaped colonial social relations; men in French trapper communities in Canada, for example, had little in common with the men and women of the plantation societies in Barbados or Brazil. Racial attitudes also differed from place to place. The Spanish and Portuguese tolerated intermarriage with the native populations in both America and Asia. Sexual contact, both inside and outside marriage, fostered greater racial variety in the Spanish and Portuguese colonies than in the French or the English territories (though mixed-race people could be found everywhere). By 1800, *mestizos*, children of Spanish men and Indian women, accounted for more than a quarter of the population in the Spanish colonies, and many of them aspired to join the local elite. Greater racial diversity seems not to have improved the treatment of slaves, however, which was probably harshest in Portuguese Brazil.

Where intermarriage between colonizers and natives was common, conversion to Christianity proved most successful. Although the Indians maintained many of their native religious beliefs, the majority of Indians in the Spanish colonies had come to consider themselves devout Catholics by 1700. Indian carpenters and artisans in the villages produced innumerable altars, retables (painted panels), and sculpted images to adorn their local churches, and individual families put up domestic shrines. Yet the clergy remained overwhelmingly Spanish: the church hierarchy concluded that the Indians' humility and innocence made them unsuitable for the priesthood.

In the early years of American colonization, many more men than women emigrated from Europe. At the end of the seventeenth century, the sex imbalance began to decline but remained substantial; two and one-half times as many men as women were among the immigrants leaving Liverpool, England, between 1697 and 1707, for example. Women who emigrated as indentured servants ran great risks: if they did not die of disease during the voyage, they might end up giving birth to illegitimate children (the fate of at least one in five servant women) or being virtually sold into marriage.

The uncertainties of life in the American colonies provided new opportunities for European women and men willing to live outside the law, however. In the 1500s and 1600s, the English and Dutch governments had routinely authorized pirates to prey on the shipping of their rivals, the Spanish and Portuguese. Then, in the late 1600s, English, French, and Dutch bands made up of deserters and crews from wrecked vessels began to form their own associations of pirates, especially in the Caribbean. Called *buccaneers* from their custom of curing strips of beef, called *boucan* by the native Caribs of the islands, the pirates governed themselves and preyed on everyone's shipping without regard to national origin. After 1700, the colonial governments tried to stamp out piracy. As one British judge argued in 1705, "A pirate is in perpetual war with every individual and every state. . . . They are worse than ravenous beasts."

White settlements in Africa and Asia remained small and almost insignificant, except for their long-term potential. Europeans had little contact with East Africa and almost none with Africa's vast interior. A few Portuguese trading posts in Angola and Dutch farms on the Cape of Good Hope provided the only toeholds for future expansion. In China, the emperors had welcomed Catholic missionaries at court in the seventeenth century, but the priests' credibility diminished as they squabbled among themselves and associated with European merchants, whom the Chinese considered pirates. "The barbarians [Europeans] are like wild beasts," one Chinese official concluded. In 1720, only one thousand Europeans resided in Guangzhou (Canton), the sole place where foreigners could legally trade for spices, tea, and silk (see Map 14.1).

Europeans exercised more influence in Java in the East Indies and in India. Dutch coffee production in Java and nearby islands increased phenomenally in the early 1700s, and many Dutch settled there to oversee production and trade. In India, Dutch, English, French, Portuguese, and Danish companies competed for spices, cotton, and silk; by the 1740s the English and French had become the leading rivals in India, just as they were in North America. Both countries extended their power as India's Muslim rulers lost control to local Hindu princes, rebellious Sikhs, invading Persians, and their own provincial governors. A few thousand Europeans lived in India, though many thousand more soldiers were stationed there to protect them. The staple of trade with India in the early 1700s was calico—lightweight, brightly colored cotton cloth that caught on as a fashion in Europe.

■ **India Cottons and Trade with the East**
This brightly colored cotton cloth was painted and embroidered in Madras in southern India in the late 1600s. The male figure with a mustache may be a European, but the female figures are clearly Asian. Europeans—especially the British—discovered that they could make big profits on the export of Indian cotton cloth to Europe. They also traded Indian cottons in Africa for slaves and sold large quantities in the colonies.
(Victoria and Albert Museum, London.)

Europeans who visited India were especially struck by what they viewed as exotic religious practices. In a book published in 1696 of his travels to western India, an Anglican minister described beggars of alms, "some of whom show their devotion by a shameless appearance, and walking naked." Such writings increased European interest in the outside world, but they also fed a European sense of superiority that helped excuse violent forms of colonial domination.

The Birth of Consumer Society

Worldwide colonization produced new supplies of goods, from coffee to calico, and population growth in Europe fueled demand for them. Beginning first in Britain, then in France and the Italian states, and finally in eastern Europe, population surged, growing by about 20 percent between 1700 and 1750. The gap between a fast-growing northwest and a more stagnant south and central Europe now diminished as regions that had lost population during the seventeenth-century downturn recovered. Cities, in particular, grew. Between 1600 and 1750, London's population more than tripled, and Paris's more than doubled.

Although contemporaries could not have realized it then, this was the start of the modern "population explosion." It appears that a decline in the death rate, rather than a rise in the birthrate, explains the turnaround. Three main factors contributed to this decline in the death rate: better weather and hence more bountiful harvests, improved agricultural techniques, and the plague's disappearance after 1720.

By the early eighteenth century, the effects of economic expansion and population growth brought about a consumer revolution. The British East India Company began to import into Britain huge quantities of calicoes. British imports of tobacco doubled between 1672 and 1700; at Nantes, the center of the French sugar trade, imports quadrupled between 1698 and 1733. Tea, chocolate, and coffee became virtual necessities. In the 1670s, only a trickle of tea reached London, but by 1720 the East India Company sent 9 million pounds to England—a figure that rose to 37 million pounds by 1750. By 1700, England had two thousand coffeehouses; by 1740, every English country town had at least two. Paris got its first cafés at the end of the seventeenth century; Berlin opened its first coffeehouse in 1714; Bach's Leipzig boasted eight by 1725.

The birth of consumer society did not go unnoticed by eyewitnesses. In the English economic literature of the 1690s, writers began to express a new view of humans as consuming animals with boundless appetites. Such opinions gained a wide audience with the appearance of Bernard Mandeville's poem *Fable of the Bees* (1705), which argued that private vices might have public benefits. Mandeville insisted that pride, self-interest, and the desire for material goods (all Christian vices) in fact promoted economic prosperity: "every part was full of Vice, Yet the whole mass a Paradise." Many authors attacked the new doctrine of consumerism, and the French government banned the poem's publication. But Mandeville had captured the essence of the emerging market for consumption.

New Social and Cultural Patterns

The impact of the Atlantic system and world trade was most apparent in the cities, where people had more money for consumer goods. But rural changes also had significant long-term influence, as a revolution in agricultural techniques made it possible to feed more and more people with a smaller agricultural workforce. As population increased, more people moved to the cities, where they found themselves caught up in innovative urban customs such as attending musical concerts and reading novels. Along with a general increase in literacy, these activities helped create a public that responded to new writers and artists. Social and cultural changes were not uniform across Europe, however; as usual, people's experiences varied depending on whether they lived in wealth or poverty, in urban or rural areas, or in eastern or western Europe.

Agricultural Revolution

Although Britain, France, and the Dutch Republic shared the enthusiasm for consumer goods, Britain's domestic market grew most quickly. In Britain, as agricultural output increased 43 percent over the course of the 1700s, the population increased by 70 percent. The British imported grain to feed the growing population, but they also benefited from the development of techniques that together constituted an agricultural revolution. No new machinery propelled this revolution—just more aggressive attitudes toward investment and management. The Dutch and the Flemish had pioneered many of these techniques in the 1600s, but the British took them further.

Four major changes occurred in British agriculture that eventually spread to other countries. First, farmers increased the amount of land under cultivation by draining wetlands and by growing crops on previously uncultivated common lands (acreage maintained by the community for grazing). Second, farmers who could afford to do so consolidated smaller, scattered plots into larger, more efficient units. Third, livestock raising became more closely linked to crop growing, and the yields of each increased. (See "Taking Measure," below.) For centuries, most farmers had rotated their fields in and out of production to replenish the soil. Now farmers

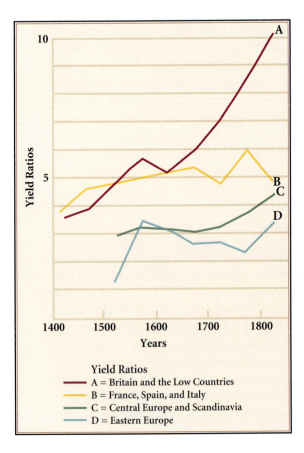

■ TAKING MEASURE
Relationship of Crop Harvested to Seed Used, 1400–1800

The impact and even the timing of the agricultural revolution can be determined by this figure, based on yield ratios (the number of grains produced for each seed planted). Britain, the Dutch Republic, and the Austrian Netherlands all experienced huge increases in crop yields after 1700. Other European regions lagged behind right into the 1800s.

(From Peter J. Hugill, *World Trade since 1431: Geography, Technology, and Capitalism* [Baltimore: Johns Hopkins University Press, 1995], 56. Reprinted by permission of Johns Hopkins University Press.)

planted carefully chosen fodder crops such as clover and turnips that added nutrients to the soil, thereby eliminating the need to leave a field fallow (unplanted) every two or three years. With more fodder available, farmers could raise more livestock, which in turn produced more manure to fertilize grain fields. Fourth, selective breeding of animals combined with the increase in fodder to improve the quality and size of herds. New crops had only a slight impact; potatoes, for example, were introduced to Europe from South America in the 1500s, but because people feared they might cause leprosy, tuberculosis, or fevers, they were not grown in quantity until the late 1700s. By the 1730s and 1740s, agricultural output had increased dramatically, and prices for food had fallen because of these inter-connected innovations.

Changes in agricultural practices did not benefit all landowners equally. The biggest British landowners consolidated their holdings in the "enclosure movement." They put pressure on small farmers and villagers to sell their land or give up their common lands. The big landlords then fenced off ("enclosed") their property. Because enclosure eliminated community grazing rights, it frequently sparked a struggle between the big landlords and villagers, and in Britain it normally required an act of Parliament. Such acts became increasingly common in the second half of the eighteenth century, and by the century's end six million acres of common lands had been enclosed and developed. "Improvers" produced more food more efficiently and thus supported a growing population.

Contrary to the fears of contemporaries, small farmers and cottagers (those with little or no property) were not forced off the land all at once. But most villagers could not afford the litigation involved in resisting enclosure, and small landholders consequently had to sell out to landlords or farmers with larger plots. Landlords with large holdings leased their estates to tenant farmers at constantly increasing rents, and the tenant farmers in turn employed the cottagers as salaried agricultural workers. In this way the English peasantry largely disappeared, replaced by a more hierarchical society of big landlords, enterprising tenant farmers, and poor agricultural laborers.

The new agricultural techniques spread slowly from Britain and the Low Countries (the Dutch Republic and the Austrian Netherlands) to the rest of western Europe. Outside a few pockets in northern France and the western German states, however, subsistence agriculture (producing just enough to get by rather than surpluses for the market) continued to dominate farming in western Europe and Scandinavia. In southwestern Germany, for example, 80 percent of the peasants produced no surplus because their plots were too small. Unlike the populations of the highly urbanized Low Countries (where half the people lived in towns and cities), most Europeans, western and eastern, eked out their existence in the countryside.

In eastern Europe, the condition of peasants worsened in the areas where landlords tried hardest to improve their yields. To produce more for the Baltic grain market, aristocratic landholders in Prussia, Poland, and parts of Russia drained wetlands, cultivated moors, and built dikes. They also forced peasants off lands the

■ **Treatment of Serfs in Russia**
Visitors from western Europe often re-marked on the cruel treatment of serfs in Russia. This drawing by one such visitor shows the punishment that could be in-flicted by landowners. Serfs could be whipped for almost any reason, even for making a soup too salty or neglecting to bow when the lord's family passed by. Their condition actually deteriorated in the 1700s, as landowners began to sell serfs much like slaves. New decrees made it illegal for serfs to contract loans, enter into leases, or work for anyone other than their lord. Some landlords kept harems of serf girls. Although the Russian landlords' treatment of serfs was more brutal than the treatment they experienced in the Ger-man states and Poland, upper classes in every country regarded the serfs as dirty, deceitful, brutish, and superstitious.
(New York Public Library Slavonic Division.)

peasants worked for themselves, increased compulsory labor services (the critical element in serfdom), and began to manage their estates directly. Some eastern landowners grew fabulously wealthy. The Potocki family in the Polish Ukraine, for example, owned three million acres of land and had 130,000 serfs. In parts of Poland and Russia, the serfs hardly differed from slaves in status, and their "masters" ran their huge estates much like American plantations.

Social Life in the Cities

Because of emigration from the countryside, cities grew in population and consequently exercised more influence on culture and social life. Between 1650 and 1750, cities with at least ten thousand inhabitants increased in population by 44 percent. From the eighteenth century onward, urban growth would be continuous. Along with the general growth of cities, an important south-to-north shift occurred in the pattern of urbanization. Around 1500, half of the people in cities of at least ten thousand residents could be found in the Italian states, Spain, or Portugal; by 1700, the urbanization of northwestern and southern Europe was roughly equal. Eastern Europe, despite the huge cities of Istanbul and Moscow, was still less urban than western Europe. London was by far the most populous European city, with 675,000 inhabitants in 1750; Berlin had 90,000 people, Warsaw only 23,000.

Many landowners kept a residence in town, so the separation between rural and city life was not as extreme as might be imagined, at least not for the very rich.

At the top of the ladder in the big cities were the landed nobles. Some of them filled their lives only with conspicuous consumption of fine food, extravagant clothing, coaches, books, and opera; others held key political, administrative, or judicial offices. However they spent their time, these rich families employed thousands of artisans, shopkeepers, and domestic servants. Many English peers (highest-ranking nobles) had thirty or forty servants at each of their homes.

The middle classes of officials, merchants, professionals, and landowners occupied the next rung down on the social ladder. London's population, for example, included about twenty thousand middle-class families (constituting, at most, one-sixth of the city's population). In this period, the middle classes began to develop distinctive ways of life that set them apart from both the rich noble landowners and the lower classes. Unlike the rich nobles, the middle classes lived primarily in the cities and towns, even if they owned small country estates. They ate more moderately than nobles but much better than peasants or laborers. For breakfast, the British middle classes ate toast and rolls and, after 1700, drank tea. Dinner, served midday, consisted of roasted or boiled beef or mutton, poultry or pork, and vegetables. Supper was a light meal of bread and cheese with cake or pie. Beer was the main drink in London, and many families brewed their own. Even children drank beer because of the lack of fresh water.

In contrast to the gigantic and sprawling country seats of the richest English peers, middle-class houses in town had about seven rooms, including four or five bedrooms and one or two living rooms, still many more than the poor agricultural worker. New household items reflected society's increasing wealth and its exposure to colonial imports: by 1700, the middle classes of London typically had mirrors in every room, a coffeepot and coffee mill, numerous pictures and ornaments, a china collection, and several clocks. Life for the middle classes on the European continent was quite similar, though wine replaced beer in France.

Below the middle classes came the artisans and shopkeepers (most of whom were organized in professional guilds), then the journeymen, apprentices, servants, and laborers. At the bottom of the social scale were the unemployed poor, who survived by intermittent work and charity. Women married to artisans and shop-keepers often kept the accounts, supervised employees, and ran the household as well. Every home from the middle classes to the upper classes employed servants; artisans and shopkeepers frequently hired them, too. Women from poorer families usually worked as domestic servants until they married. Four out of five domestic servants in the city were female. In large cities such as London, the servant population grew faster than the population of the city as a whole.

Social status in the cities was readily visible. Wide, spacious streets graced rich districts; the houses had gardens and the air was relatively fresh. In poor districts, the streets were narrow, dirty, dark, humid, and smelly, and the houses were damp and crowded. The poorest people were homeless, sleeping under bridges or in abandoned homes. A Neapolitan prince described his homeless neighbors as "lying like filthy animals, with no distinction of age or sex." In some districts, rich and poor lived in the same buildings; the poor clambered up to shabby, cramped apartments on the top floors.

Like shelter, clothing was a reliable social indicator. The poorest workingwomen in Paris wore woolen skirts and blouses of dark colors over petticoats, bodice, and corset. They also donned caps of various sorts, cotton stockings, and shoes (probably their only pair). Workingmen dressed even more drably. Many occupations could be recognized by their dress: no one could confuse lawyers in their dark robes with masons or butchers in their special aprons, for example. People higher on the social ladder were more likely to sport a variety of fabrics, colors, and unusual designs in their clothing and to own many different outfits. Social status was not an abstract idea; it permeated every detail of daily life.

The Growing Public for Culture

The ability to read and write also reflected social differences. People in the upper classes were more literate than those in the lower classes; city people were more literate than peasants. Protestant countries appear to have been more successful at promoting education and literacy than Catholic countries, perhaps because of the Protestant emphasis on Bible reading. Widespread popular literacy was first achieved in the Protestant areas of Switzerland and in Presbyterian Scotland, and rates were also very high in the New England colonies and the Scandinavian countries. In France, literacy doubled in the eighteenth century thanks to the spread of parish schools, but still only one in two men and one in four women could read and write. Despite the efforts of some Protestant German states to encourage primary education, primary schooling remained woefully inadequate almost everywhere in Europe: few schools existed, teachers received low wages, and no country had yet established a national system of control or supervision.

Despite the deficiencies of primary education, a new literate public arose, especially among the middle classes of the cities. More books and periodicals were published than ever before. Britain and the Dutch Republic led the way in this powerful outpouring of printed words. The trend began in the 1690s and gradually accelerated. In 1695, the British government allowed the licensing system, through which it controlled publications, to lapse, and new newspapers and magazines appeared almost immediately. The first London daily newspaper came out in 1702, and in 1709 Joseph Addison and Richard Steele published the first literary magazine, *The Spectator*. They devoted their magazine to the cultural improvement of the increasingly influential middle class. By the 1720s, twenty-four provincial newspapers were published in England. In the London coffeehouses, an edition of a single newspaper might reach ten thousand male readers. Women did their reading at home. Newspapers on the continent lagged behind and often consisted mainly of advertising with little critical commentary. France, for example, had no daily paper until 1777.

The new literate public did not just read newspapers; its members now pursued an interest in painting, attended concerts, and besieged booksellers in search of popular novels. Because increased trade and prosperity put money into the hands of the growing middle classes, a new urban audience began to compete with the churches, rulers, and courtiers as chief patrons for new work. As the public for the arts expanded, printed commentary on them emerged, setting the stage for the appearance of political and social criticism. New artistic tastes thus had effects far beyond the realm of the arts.

Developments in painting reflected the tastes of the new public. The rococo style challenged the hold of the baroque and classical schools, especially in France. Like the baroque, the rococo emphasized irregularity and asymmetry, movement and curvature, but it did so on a much smaller, subtler scale. Many rococo paintings depicted scenes of intimate sensuality rather than the monumental, emotional grandeur favored by classical and baroque painters. Personal portraits and pastoral paintings took the place of heroic landscapes and large ceremonial canvases. Rococo paintings adorned homes as well as palaces and served as a form of interior decoration rather than as a statement of piety. Its decorative quality made rococo art an ideal complement to newly discovered materials such as stucco and porcelain, especially the porcelain vases now imported from China.

Rococo, like *baroque*, was an invented word (from the French word *rocaille*, meaning "shellwork") and originally a derogatory label, meaning "frivolous decoration." But the great French rococo painters, such as Antoine Watteau (1684–1721) and François Boucher (1703–1770), were much more than mere decorators. Although both emphasized the erotic in their depictions, Watteau captured the melancholy side of a passing

■ Rococo Painting

In this painting, the Venetian artist Rosalba Carriera (1675–1757) reveals Europeans' growing interest in the outside world and their misunderstanding of the actual experience of colonized peoples. Africa (the title of the work) is represented by a young black woman wearing a bejewelled turban and calmly holding a handful of writhing snakes; the scorpion that dangles from her necklace competes with an enormous pearl earring for the fascinated viewer's attention. Known for her use of pastels, Carriera journeyed in 1720 to Paris, where she became an associate of Antoine Watteau and helped inaugurate the rococo style in painting.

(Staatliche Kunstsammlungen Dresden, Gemaldegalerie Alte Meister.)

aristocratic style of life, and Boucher painted middle-class people at home during their daily activities. Both painters thereby contributed to the emergence of new sensibilities in art that increasingly attracted a middle-class public.

Music as well as art grew in popularity. The first public music concerts were performed in England in the 1670s, becoming much more regular and frequent in the 1690s. City concert halls typically seated about two hundred, but the relatively high price of tickets limited attendance to the better-off. Music clubs provided entertainment in smaller towns and villages. In continental Europe, Frankfurt organized the first regular public concerts in 1712; Hamburg and Paris began holding them within a few years. Opera continued to spread in the eighteenth century; Venice had sixteen public opera houses by 1700, and in 1732 Covent Garden opera house opened in London.

The growth of a public that appreciated and supported music had much the same effect as the extension of the reading public: like authors, composers could now begin to liberate themselves from court patronage and work for a paying audience. This development took time to solidify, however, and court or church patrons still commissioned much eighteenth-century music. Bach, a German Lutheran, wrote his *St. Matthew Passion* for Good Friday services in 1729 while he was organist and choirmaster for the leading church in Leipzig. He composed secular works (like the "Coffee Cantata") for the public and a variety of private patrons.

The composer George Frederick Handel (1685–1759) was among the first to grasp the new directions in music. He began his career playing second violin in the Hamburg opera orchestra and then moved to Britain in 1710, where he eventually turned to composing oratorios, a form he introduced in Britain. The oratorio combined the drama of opera with the majesty of religious and ceremonial music and featured the chorus over the soloists. Handel's most famous oratorio, *Messiah* (1741), reflected his personal, deeply felt piety but also his willingness to combine musical materials into a dramatic form that captured the enthusiasm of the new public. In 1740, a poem published in the *Gentleman's Magazine* exulted: "His art so modulates the sounds in all,/Our passions, as he pleases, rise and fall." Music had become an integral part of the new middle-class public's culture.

But nothing captured the imagination of the new public more than the novel, the literary genre whose very name underscored the eighteenth-century taste for novelty. Over three hundred French novels appeared between 1700 and 1730. During this unprecedented explosion, the novel took on its modern form and became more concerned with individual psychology and social description than with the picaresque adventures popular earlier (such as Cervantes's *Don Quixote*). The novel's popularity was closely tied to the expansion of the reading public, and novels were available in serial form in periodicals or from the many booksellers who popped up to serve the new market.

Women figured prominently in novels as characters, and women writers abounded. The English novel *Love in Excess* (1719) quickly reached a sixth printing, and its author, Eliza Haywood (1693?–1756), earned her living turning out a stream of novels with titles such as *Persecuted Virtue, Constancy Rewarded,* and *The History of Betsy Thoughtless*—all showing a concern for the proper place of women as models of virtue in a changing world. Haywood had first worked as an actress when her husband deserted her and her two children, but she soon turned to writing plays and novels. In the 1740s, she began publishing a magazine, *The Female Spectator,* which argued in favor of higher education for women.

Haywood's male counterpart was Daniel Defoe (1660?–1731), a merchant's son who had a diverse and colorful career as a manufacturer, political spy, novelist, and social commentator. Defoe's novel about a shipwrecked sailor, *Robinson Crusoe* (1719), portrayed the new values of the time: to survive, Crusoe had to meet every challenge with fearless entrepreneurial ingenuity. He had to be ready for the unexpected and be able to improvise in every situation. He was, in short, the model for the new man in an expanding economy. Crusoe's patronizing attitude toward the black man Friday now draws much critical attention, but his discovery of Friday shows how the fate of blacks and whites had become intertwined in the new colonial environment.

Religious Revivals

Despite the novel's growing popularity, religious books and pamphlets still sold in huge numbers, and most Europeans remained devout, even as their religions were changing. In this period, a Protestant revival known as Pietism rocked the complacency of the established churches in the German Lutheran states, the Dutch Republic, and Scandinavia. Pietists believed in a mystical religion of the heart; they wanted a more deeply emotional, even ecstatic religion. They urged intense Bible study, which in turn promoted popular education and contributed to the increase in literacy. Many Pietists attended catechism instruction every day and also went to morning and evening prayer meetings in addition to regular Sunday services.

Catholicism also had its versions of religious revival. A French woman, Jeanne Marie Guyon (1648–1717), attracted many noblewomen and a few leading clergymen to her own Catholic brand of Pietism, known as Quietism. Claiming miraculous visions and astounding prophecies, she urged a mystical union with God through prayer and simple devotion. Despite papal condemnation and intense controversy within Catholic circles in France, Guyon had followers all over Europe.

Even more influential were the Jansenists, who gained many new adherents to their austere form of Catholicism despite Louis XIV's harassment and repeated condemnation by the papacy. Under the pressure of religious and political persecution, Jansenism took a revivalist turn in the 1720s. At the funeral of a Jansenist priest in Paris in 1727, the crowd who flocked to the grave claimed to witness a series of miraculous healings. Within a few years, a cult formed around the priest's tomb, and clandestine Jansenist presses reported new miracles to the reading public. When the French government tried to suppress the cult, one enraged wit placed a sign at the tomb that read "By order of the king, God is forbidden to work miracles here." Some believers fell into frenzied convulsions, claiming to be inspired by the Holy Spirit through the intercession of the dead priest. After midcentury, Jansenism became even more politically active as its adherents joined in opposition to crown policies on religion.

Consolidation of the European State System

The spread of Pietism and Jansenism reflected the emergence of a middle-class public that now participated in every new development, including religion. The middle classes could pursue these interests because the European state system gradually stabilized. Warfare settled three main issues between 1690 and 1740: a coalition of powers held Louis XIV's France in check on the continent; Great Britain emerged from the wars against Louis as the preeminent maritime power; and Russia defeated Sweden in the contest for supremacy in the Baltic. After Louis XIV's death in 1715, Europe enjoyed the fruits of a more balanced diplomatic system, in which warfare became less frequent and less widespread. States could then spend their resources establishing and expanding control over their own populations, both at home and in their colonies.

The Limits of French Absolutism

Lying on his deathbed in 1715, the seventy-six-year-old Louis XIV watched helplessly as his accomplishments continued to unravel. Not only had his plans for territorial expansion been thwarted, but his incessant wars had exhausted the treasury, despite new taxes. In 1689, Louis's rival, William III, prince of Orange and king of England and Scotland (r. 1689–1702), had set out to forge a European alliance that eventually included Britain, the Dutch Republic, Sweden, Austria, and Spain. The allies fought Louis to a stalemate in the War of the League of Augsburg, sometimes called the Nine Years' War (1689–1697), and when hostilities resumed four years later, they finally put an end to Louis's expansionist ambitions.

The War of the Spanish Succession (1701–1713) broke out when the mentally and physically feeble Charles II (r. 1665–1700) of Spain died without a direct heir. The Spanish succession could not help but be a burning issue. Even though Spanish power had declined steadily since Spain's golden age in the sixteenth century, Spain still had extensive territories in Italy and the Netherlands and colonies overseas. Before Charles died, he named Louis XIV's second grandson, Philip, duke of Anjou, as his heir, but the Austrian emperor Leopold I refused to accept Charles's deathbed will. In the ensuing war, the French lost several major battles and had to accept disadvantageous terms in the Peace of Utrecht of 1713–1714 (Map 14.2). Although Philip was recognized as king of Spain, he had to renounce any future claim to the

■ MAP 14.2 Europe, c. 1715

Although Louis XIV succeeded in putting his grandson Philip on the Spanish throne, France emerged considerably weakened from the War of the Spanish Succession. France ceded large territories in Canada to Britain, which also gained key Mediterranean outposts from Spain as well as a monopoly on providing slaves to the Spanish colonies. Spanish losses were catastrophic: Philip had to renounce any future claim to the French crown and give up considerable territories in the Netherlands and Italy to the Austrians.

French crown, thus barring unification of the two kingdoms. Spain surrendered its territories in Italy and the Netherlands to the Austrians and Gibraltar to the British; France ceded possessions in North America (Newfoundland, the Hudson Bay area, and most of Nova Scotia) to Britain. France no longer threatened to dominate European power politics.

At home, Louis's policy of absolutism had fomented bitter hostility. Nobles fiercely resented his promotions of commoners to high office. The duke of Saint-Simon complained that "falseness, servility, admiring glances, combined with a dependent and cringing attitude, above all, an appearance of being nothing without him, were the only ways of pleasing him." On his deathbed, Louis XIV gave his blessing and some sound advice to his five-year-old great-grandson and successor, Louis XV (r. 1715–1774): "My child, you are about to become a great King. Do not imitate my love of building nor my liking for war."

After being named regent, the duke of Orléans (1674–1723), nephew of the dead king, revived some of the parlements' powers and tried to give leading nobles a greater say in political affairs. Financial problems plagued the Regency as they would beset all succeeding French regimes in the eighteenth century. In 1719, the regent appointed the Scottish adventurer and financier John Law to the top financial position of controller-general. Law founded a trading company for North America and a state bank that issued paper money and stock (without them, trade depended on the available supply of gold and silver). The bank was supposed to offer lower interest rates to the state, thus cutting the cost of financing the government's debts. The value of the stock rose rapidly in a frenzy of speculation, only to crash a few months later. With it vanished any hope of establishing a state bank or issuing paper money for nearly a century.

France finally achieved a measure of financial stability under the leadership of Cardinal Hercule de Fleury (1653–1743), the most powerful member of the government after the death of the regent. Fleury aimed to avoid adventure abroad and keep social peace at home; he balanced the budget and carried out a large project for road and canal construction. Colonial trade boomed. Peace and the acceptance of limits on territorial expansion inaugurated a century of French prosperity.

British Rise and Dutch Decline

The British and the Dutch had formed a coalition against Louis XIV under their joint ruler William III, who was simultaneously stadtholder of the Dutch Republic and, with his English wife, Mary (d. 1694), ruler of England, Wales, and Scotland. After William's death in 1702, the British and Dutch went their separate ways. Over the next decades, England incorporated Scotland and subjugated Ireland, becoming "Great Britain." At the same time Dutch imperial power declined, even though Dutch merchants still controlled a substantial portion of world trade. English relations with Scotland and Ireland were complicated by the problem of succession: William and Mary had no children. To ensure a Protestant succession, Parliament ruled that Mary's sister, Anne, would succeed William and Mary and that the Protestant House of Hanover in Germany would succeed Anne if she had no surviving heirs. Catholics were excluded. When Queen Anne (r. 1702–1714) died leaving no children, the elector of Hanover, a Protestant great-grandson of James I, consequently became King George I (r. 1714–1727). The House of Hanover—renamed the House of Windsor during World War I in response to anti-German sentiment—still occupies the British throne.

Support from the Scots and Irish for this solution did not come easily because many in Scotland and Ireland supported the claims to the throne of the deposed Catholic king, James II, and, after his death in 1701, his son James Edward. Out of fear of this "Jacobitism" (from the Latin *Jacobus* for "James"), Scottish Protestant leaders agreed to the Act of Union of 1707, which abolished the Scottish Parliament and affirmed the Scots' recognition of the Protestant Hanoverian succession. The Scots agreed to obey the Parliament of Great Britain, which would include Scottish members in the House of Commons and the House of Lords. A Jacobite rebellion in Scotland in 1715, aiming to restore the Stuart line, was suppressed. The threat of Jacobitism nonetheless continued into the 1740s (Map 14.2).

The Irish—90 percent of whom were Catholic—proved even more difficult to subdue. When James II had gone to Ireland in 1689 to raise a Catholic rebellion against the new monarchs of England, William III responded by taking command of the joint English and Dutch forces and defeating James's Irish supporters. James fled to France, and the Catholics in Ireland faced yet more confiscation and legal restrictions. By 1700, Irish Catholics, who in 1640 had owned 60 percent of the land in Ireland, owned just 14 percent. The Protestant-controlled Irish Parliament passed a series of laws limiting the rights of the Catholic majority: Catholics could not bear arms, send their children abroad for education, establish Catholic schools at home, or marry Protestants. Catholics could not sit in Parliament, nor could they vote for its members unless they took an oath renouncing Catholic doctrine. These and a host of other laws reduced Catholic Ireland to the status of a colony; one English official commented in 1745, "The poor people of Ireland are used worse than negroes." Most of the Irish were peasants who lived in primitive housing and subsisted on a meager diet that included no meat.

The Parliament of Great Britain was soon dominated by the Whigs. In Britain's constitutional system, the monarch ruled with Parliament. The crown chose the ministers, directed policy, and supervised administration, while Parliament raised revenue, passed laws, and represented the interests of the people to the crown. The powers of Parliament were reaffirmed by the Triennial Act in 1694, which provided that Parliaments meet at least once every three years (this was extended to seven years in 1716, after the Whigs had established their ascendancy). Only 200,000 propertied men could vote, out of a population of more than five million people, and not surprisingly, most members of Parliament came from the landed gentry. In fact, a few hundred families controlled all the important political offices.

■ **Sir Robert Walpole at a Cabinet Meeting**

Sir Robert Walpole and George II developed government by means of a cabinet, which consisted of Walpole as first lord of the treasury, the two secretaries of state, the lord chancellor, the chancellor of the exchequer, the lord privy seal, and the lord president of the council. Walpole's cabinet was the predecessor of modern cabinets in both Great Britain and the United States. Its similarities to modern forms should not be overstated, however. The entire staff of the two secretaries of state, who had charge of all foreign and domestic affairs other than taxation, numbered twenty-four in 1726. (The Fotomas Index, U.K.)

George I and George II (r. 1727–1760) relied on one man, Sir Robert Walpole (1676–1745), to help them manage their relations with Parliament. From his position as First Lord of the Treasury, Walpole made himself into first or "prime" minister, leading the House of Commons from 1721 to 1742. Although appointed initially by the king, Walpole established an enduring pattern of parliamentary government in which a prime minister from the leading party guided legislation through the House of Commons. Walpole also built a vast patronage machine that dispensed government jobs to win support for the crown's policies. Walpole's successors relied more and more on the patronage system and eventually alienated not only the Tories but also the middle classes in London and even the North American colonies.

The partisan division between the Whigs, who supported the Hanoverian succession and the rights of dissenting Protestants, and the Tories, who had backed the Stuart line and the Anglican church, did not hamper Great Britain's pursuit of economic, military, and colonial power. In this period, Great Britain became a great power on the world stage by virtue of its navy and its ability to finance major military involvement in the wars against Louis XIV. The founding in 1694 of the Bank of England—which, unlike the French bank, endured—enabled the government to raise money at low interest for foreign wars. By the 1740s, the government could borrow more than four times what it could in the 1690s.

By contrast, the Dutch Republic, one of the richest and most influential states of the seventeenth century, saw its power eclipsed in the eighteenth. When William of Orange (William III of England) died in 1702, he left no heirs, and for forty-five years the Dutch lived without a stadtholder. The merchant ruling class of some two thousand families dominated the Dutch Republic more than ever, but they presided over a country that counted for less in international power politics. In some areas, Dutch decline was only relative: the Dutch population was not growing as fast as populations elsewhere, for example, and the Dutch share of the Baltic trade decreased from 50 percent in 1720 to less than 30 percent by the 1770s. After 1720, the Baltic countries—Prussia, Russia, Denmark, and Sweden—began to ban imports of manufactured goods to protect their own industries, and Dutch trade in particular suffered. The output of Leiden textiles dropped to one-third of its 1700 level by 1740. Shipbuilding, paper manufacturing, tobacco processing, salt refining, and pottery production all dwindled as well. The biggest exception to the downward trend was trade with the New World, which increased with escalating demands for sugar and tobacco. The Dutch shifted their interest away from great-power rivalries toward those areas of international trade and finance where they could establish an enduring presence.

Russia's Emergence as a European Power

The commerce and shipbuilding of the Dutch and British so impressed Russian tsar Peter I (r. 1689–1725) that he traveled incognito to their shipyards in 1697 to learn their methods firsthand. Known to history as Peter the Great, he dragged Russia kicking and screaming all the way to great-power status. Although he came to the throne while still a minor (on the eve of his tenth birthday), grew up under the threat of a palace coup, and enjoyed little formal education, his accomplishments soon matched his seven-foot-tall stature. Peter transformed public life in Russia and established an absolutist state on the western model. His westernization efforts ignited an enduring controversy: did Peter set Russia on a course of inevitable westernization required to compete with the West, or did he forever and fatally disrupt Russia's natural evolution into a distinctive Slavic society?

Peter reorganized government and finance on western models and, like other absolute rulers, strengthened his army. With ruthless recruiting methods, which included branding a cross on every recruit's left hand to prevent desertion, he forged an army of 200,000 men and equipped it with modern weapons. He created schools for artillery, engineering, and military medicine and built the first navy in Russian history. Not surprisingly, taxes tripled.

The tsar allowed nothing to stand in his way. He did not hesitate to use torture and executed thousands. He allowed a special guards regiment unprecedented power to expedite cases against those suspected of rebellion, espionage, pretensions to the throne, or just "unseemly utterances" against him. Opposition to his policies reached into his own family: because his only son, Alexei, had allied himself with Peter's critics, he threw him into prison, where the young man mysteriously died.

To control the often restive nobility, Peter insisted that all noblemen engage in state service. A Table of Ranks (1722) classified them into military, administrative, and court categories, a codification of social and legal relationships in Russia that would last for nearly two centuries. All social and material advantages now depended on serving the crown. Because the nobles lacked a secure independent status, Peter could command them to a degree that was unimaginable in western Europe. State service was not only compulsory but also permanent. Moreover, the male children of those in service had to be registered by the age of ten and begin serving at fifteen. To increase his authority over the Russian Orthodox church, Peter allowed the office of patriarch (supreme head) to remain vacant, and in 1721 he replaced it with the Holy Synod, a bureaucracy of laymen under his supervision. To many Russians, Peter was the Antichrist incarnate.

With the goal of westernizing Russian culture, Peter set up the first greenhouses, laboratories, and technical schools and founded the Russian Academy of Sciences. He ordered translations of Western classics and hired a German theater company to perform the French plays of Molière. He replaced the traditional Russian calendar with the Western one,* introduced Arabic numerals, and brought out the first public newspaper. He ordered his officials and the nobles to shave their beards and dress in Western fashion, and he even issued precise regulations about the suitable style of jacket, boots, and cap (generally French or German). He published a book on manners for young noblemen and experimented with dentistry on his courtiers.

Peter built a new capital city, named St. Petersburg after him. It symbolized Russia's opening to the West. Construction began in 1703 in a Baltic province that had been recently conquered from Sweden. By the end of 1709, forty thousand recruits a year found themselves assigned to the work. Peter ordered skilled workers to move to the new city and commanded all landowners possessing more than forty serf households to build houses there. In the 1720s, a German minister described the city "as a wonder of the world, considering its magnificent palaces, . . . and the short time that was employed in the building of it." By 1710, the permanent population of St. Petersburg reached eight thousand. At Peter's death in 1725, it had forty thousand residents.

As a new city far from the Russian heartland around Moscow, St. Petersburg represented a decisive break with Russia's past. Peter widened that gap by every means possible. At his new capital, he tried to improve the traditionally denigrated, secluded status of women by ordering them to dress in European styles and appear publicly at his dinners for diplomatic representatives. Imitating French manners, he decreed that women attend his new social salons of officials, officers, and merchants for conversation and dancing. A foreigner headed every one of Peter's new technical and vocational schools, and for its first eight years the new Academy of

---

*Peter introduced the Julian calendar, then still used in Protestant but not Catholic countries. Later in the eighteenth century, Protestant Europe abandoned the Julian for the Gregorian calendar. Not until 1918 was the Julian calendar abolished in Russia, at which point it had fallen thirteen days behind Europe's Gregorian calendar.

■ **Peter the Great Modernizes Russia**
In this popular print, a barber forces a protesting noble to conform to Western fashions (the barber is sometimes erroneously identified as Peter himself). Peter ordered all nobles, merchants, and middle-class professionals to cut off their beards or pay a huge tax to keep them. An early biographer of Peter, the French writer Jean Rousset de Missy (1730), claimed that those who lost their beards saved them to put in their coffins, fearing that they would not enter heaven without them.
(Carole Frohlich Archive.)

Sciences included no Russians. Every ministry was assigned a foreign adviser. Upper-class Russians learned French or German, which they often spoke even at home. Such changes affected only the very top of Russian society, however; the mass of the population had no contact with the new ideas and ended up paying for the innovations either in ruinous new taxation or by building St. Petersburg, a project that cost the lives of thousands of workers. Serfs remained tied to the land, completely dominated by their noble lords.

Despite all his achievements, Peter could not ensure his succession. In the thirty-seven years after his death in 1725, Russia endured six different rulers: three women, a boy of twelve, an infant, and an imbecile. Recurrent palace coups weakened the monarchy and enabled the nobility to loosen Peter's rigid code of state service. In the process, the status of the serfs only worsened. They ceased to be counted as legal subjects; the criminal code of 1754 listed them as property. They not only were bought and sold like cattle but also had become legally indistinguishable from them. Westernization had not yet touched their lives.

The Balance of Power in the East

Peter the Great's success in building up state power changed the balance of power in eastern Europe. Overcoming initial military setbacks, Russia eventually defeated Sweden and took its place as the leading power in the Baltic region. Russia could then turn its attention to eastern Europe, where it competed with Austria and Prussia. Formerly mighty Poland-Lithuania became the playground for great-power rivalries.

Sweden had dominated the Baltic region since the Thirty Years' War and did not easily give up its preeminence. When Peter the Great joined an anti-Swedish coalition in 1700 with Denmark, Saxony, and Poland, Sweden's Charles XII (r. 1697–1718) stood up to the test. Still in his teens at the beginning of the Great Northern War, Charles first defeated Denmark, then destroyed the new Russian army, and quickly marched into Poland and Saxony. After defeating the Poles and occupying Saxony, Charles invaded Russia. Here Peter's rebuilt army finally defeated him at the battle of Poltava (1709).

The Russian victory resounded everywhere. The Russian ambassador to Vienna reported, "It is commonly said that the tsar will be formidable to all Europe, that he will be a kind of northern Turk." Prussia and other German states joined the anti-Swedish alliance, and when Charles XII died in battle in 1718, the Great Northern War finally came to an end. By the terms of the Treaty of Nystad (1721), Sweden ceded its eastern Baltic provinces—Livonia, Estonia, Ingria, and southern Karelia—to Russia. Sweden also lost territories on the north German coast to Prussia and the other allied German states (Map 14.3). An aristocratic reaction against Charles XII's incessant demands for war supplies swept away Sweden's absolutist regime, essentially removing Sweden from great-power competition.

■ **MAP 14.3 Russia and Sweden after the Great Northern War, 1721**
After the Great Northern War, Russia supplanted Sweden as the major power in the north. Although Russia had a much larger population from which to draw its armies, Sweden made the most of its advantages and gave way only after a great military struggle.

Prussia had to make the most of every military opportunity, as it did in the Great Northern War, because it was much smaller in size and population than Russia, Austria, or France. King Frederick William I (r. 1713–1740) doubled the size of the Prussian army; though much smaller than the armies of his rivals, it was the best-trained and most up-to-date force in Europe. By 1740, Prussia had Europe's highest proportion of men at arms (1 of every 28 people, versus 1 in 157 in France and 1 in 64 in Russia) and the highest proportion of nobles in the military (1 in 7 noblemen, as compared with 1 in 33 in France and 1 in 50 in Russia).

The army so dominated life in Prussia that the country earned the label "a large army with a small state attached." So obsessed was Frederick William with his soldiers that the five-foot-five-inch-tall king formed a regiment of "giants," the Grenadiers, composed exclusively of men over six feet tall. Royal agents scoured Europe trying to find such men and sometimes kidnapped them right off the street. Frederick William, the "Sergeant King," was one of the first rulers to wear a military uniform as his everyday dress. He subordinated the entire domestic administration to the army's needs. He also installed a system for recruiting soldiers by local district quotas. He financed the army's growth by subjecting all the provinces to an excise tax on food, drink, and manufactured goods and by increasing rents on crown lands. Prussia was now poised to become one of the major players on the continent of Europe.

During the War of the Polish Succession (1733–1735), Prussia stood on the sidelines, content to watch the bigger powers fight each other. The war showed how the balance of power had changed since the heyday of Louis XIV: France had to maneuver within a complex great-power system that now included Russia, and Poland-Lithuania no longer controlled its own destiny. When the king of Poland-Lithuania died in 1733, France, Spain, and Sardinia went to war against Austria and Russia, each side supporting rival claimants to the Polish throne. After Russia drove the French candidate out of Poland-Lithuania, France agreed to accept the Austrian candidate; in exchange, Austria gave the province of Lorraine to the French candidate, the father-in-law of Louis XV, with the promise that the province would pass to France on his death. France and Britain went back to pursuing their colonial rivalries. Prussia and Russia concentrated on shoring up their influence within Poland-Lithuania.

Austria did not want to become mired in a long struggle in Poland-Lithuania because its armies still faced the Turks on its southeastern border. Even though the Austrians had forced the Turks to recognize their rule over all of Hungary and Transylvania in 1699 and occupied Belgrade in 1717, the Turks did not stop fighting. In the

Austrian Conquest of Hungary, 1657–1730

1730s, the Turks retook Belgrade, and Russia now claimed a role in the struggle against the Turks. Moreover, Hungary, though "liberated" from Turkish rule, proved less than enthusiastic about submitting to Austria. In 1703, the wealthiest Hungarian noble landlord, Ferenc Rákóczi (1676–1735), raised an army of seventy thousand men who fought for "God, Fatherland, and Liberty" until 1711. They forced the Austrians to recognize local Hungarian institutions, grant amnesty, and restore confiscated estates in exchange for confirming hereditary Austrian rule.

The Power of Diplomacy and the Importance of Numbers

No single power emerged from the wars of the first half of the eighteenth century clearly superior to the others, and the idea of maintaining a balance of power guided both military and diplomatic maneuvering. The Peace of Utrecht had explicitly declared that such a balance was crucial to maintaining peace in Europe, and in 1720 a British pamphleteer wrote, "There is not, I believe, any doctrine in the law of nations, of more certain truth . . . than this of the balance of power." It was the law of gravity of European politics. This system of equilibrium often rested on military force, such as the leagues formed against Louis XIV or the coalition against Sweden. All states counted on diplomacy, however, to resolve issues even after fighting had begun.

To meet the new demands placed on it, the diplomatic service, like the military and financial bureaucracies before it, had to develop regular procedures. The French set a pattern of diplomatic service that the other European states soon imitated. By 1685, France had embassies in all the important capitals. Nobles of ancient families served as ambassadors to Rome, Madrid, Vienna, and London, whereas royal officials were chosen for Switzerland, the Dutch Republic, and Venice. Most held their appointments for at least three or four years, and all went off with elaborate written instructions that included explicit statements of policy as well as full accounts of the political conditions of the country to which they were posted. The ambassador selected and paid for his own staff. This practice could make the journey to a new post very cumbersome, because the staff might be as large as eighty people, and they brought along all their own furniture, pictures, silverware, and tapestries. It took one French ambassador ten weeks to get from Paris to Stockholm.

By the early 1700s, French writings on diplomatic methods were read everywhere. François de Callières's manual *On the Manner of Negotiating with Sovereigns* (1716) insisted that sound diplomacy was based on the creation of confidence, rather than deception: "The secret of negotiation is to harmonize the real interests of the parties concerned." Callières believed that the diplomatic service had to be professional—that young attachés should be chosen for their skills, not their family connections. These sensible views did not prevent the development of a dual system of diplomacy, in which rulers issued secret instructions that often negated the official ones sent by their own foreign offices. Secret diplomacy had some advantages because it allowed rulers to break with past alliances, but it also led to confusion and, sometimes, scandal, for the rulers often employed unreliable adventurers as their confidential agents. Still, the diplomatic system in the early eighteenth century proved successful enough to ensure a continuation of the principles of the Peace of Westphalia (1648); in the midst of every crisis and war, the great powers would convene and hammer out a written agreement detailing the requirements for peace.

Adroit diplomacy could smooth the road toward peace, but success in war still depended on sheer numbers—of men and muskets. Because each state's strength depended largely on the size of its army, the growth and health of the population increasingly entered into government calculations. The publication in 1690 of the Englishman William Petty's *Political Arithmetick* quickened the interest of government officials everywhere. Petty offered statistical estimates of human capital—that is, of population and wages—to determine Britain's national wealth. In 1727, Frederick William I of Prussia founded two university chairs to encourage population studies, and textbooks and handbooks advocated state intervention to improve the population's health and welfare.

Public Hygiene and Health Care

Physicians used the new population statistics to explain the environmental causes of disease, another new preoccupation in this period. Petty devised a quantitative scale that distinguished healthy from unhealthy places largely on the basis of air quality, an early precursor of modern environmental studies. Cities were the unhealthiest places because excrement (animal and human) and garbage accumulated where people lived densely packed together. Paris seemed to a visitor "so detestable that it is impossible to remain there" because of the smell; even the façade of the Louvre palace in Paris was soiled by the contents of night commodes that servants routinely dumped out of windows every morning. Only the wealthy could escape walking in mucky streets, by hiring men to carry them in sedan chairs or to drive them in coaches.

After investigating specific cities, medical geographers urged government campaigns to improve public sanitation. Everywhere, environmentalists gathered and analyzed data on climate, disease, and population, searching for correlations to help direct policy. As a result of these efforts, local governments undertook such measures as draining low-lying areas, burying refuse, and cleaning wells, all of which eventually helped lower the death rates from epidemic diseases.

Hospitals and medical care underwent lasting transformations. Founded originally as charities concerned foremost with the moral worthiness of the poor, hospitals gradually evolved into medical institutions that defined patients by their diseases. The process of diagnosis changed as physicians began to use specialized Latin terms for illnesses. The gap between medical experts and their patients increased, as physicians now also relied on postmortem dissections in the hospital to gain better knowledge, a practice most patients' families resented. Press reports of body snatching and grave robbing by surgeons and their apprentices outraged the public well into the 1800s.

Despite the change in hospitals, individual health care remained something of a free-for-all in which physicians competed with bloodletters, itinerant venereal-disease doctors, bonesetters, druggists, midwives, and "cunning women," who specialized in home remedies. The medical profession, with nationwide organizations and licensing, had not yet emerged, and no clear line separated trained physicians from quacks. Physicians often followed popular prescriptions for illnesses because they had nothing better to offer. Patients were as likely to die of diseases caught in the hospital as to be cured there. Antiseptics were nearly unknown.

The various "medical" opinions about childbirth highlight the confusion people faced. Midwives delivered most babies, though they sometimes encountered criticism even from within their own ranks. One consulting midwife complained that ordinary midwives in Bristol, England, made women in labor drink a mixture of their husband's urine and leek juice. By the 1730s, female midwives faced competition from male midwives, who were known for using instruments such as forceps to pull the baby out of the birth canal. Women rarely sought a physician's help in giving birth, however; they preferred the advice and assistance of trusted local midwives. In any case, trained physicians were few in number and almost nonexistent outside cities.

Hardly any infectious diseases could be cured, though inoculation against smallpox spread from the Middle East to Europe in the early eighteenth century, thanks largely to the efforts of Lady Mary Wortley Montagu, who learned about the technique while living in Constantinople. After 1750, physicians developed successful procedures for wide-scale vaccination, although even then many people resisted the idea of inoculating themselves with a disease. Other diseases spread quickly in the unsanitary conditions of urban life. Ordinary people washed or changed clothes rarely, lived in overcrowded housing with poor ventilation, and got their water from contaminated sources, such as refuse-filled rivers.

Until the mid-1700s, most people considered bathing dangerous. Public bathhouses had disappeared from cities in the sixteenth and seventeenth centuries because they seemed a source of disorderly behavior and epidemic illness. In the eighteenth century, even private bathing came into disfavor because people feared the effects of contact with water. Fewer than one in ten newly built private mansions in Paris had baths. Bathing was hazardous, physicians insisted, because it opened the body to disease. One manners manual of 1736 admonished, "It is correct to clean the face every morning by using a white cloth to cleanse it. It is less good to wash with water, because it renders the face susceptible to cold in winter and sun in summer." The upper classes associated cleanliness not with baths but with frequently changed linens, powdered hair, and perfume, which was thought to strengthen the body and refresh the brain by counteracting corrupt and foul air.

The Birth of the Enlightenment

Economic expansion, the emergence of a new consumer society, and the stabilization of the European state system all generated optimism about the future. The intellectual corollary was the *Enlightenment*, a term used later in the eighteenth century to describe the loosely knit group of writers and scholars who believed that human beings could apply a critical, reasoning spirit to every problem they encountered in this world. The new secular, scientific, and critical attitude first emerged in the 1690s, scrutinizing everything from the absolutism of Louis XIV to the traditional role of women in society. After 1740, criticism took a more systematic turn as writers provided new theories for the organization of society and politics, but even by the 1720s and 1730s, established authorities realized they faced a new set of challenges.

Popularization of Science and Challenges to Religion

The writers of the Enlightenment glorified the geniuses of the new science and championed scientific method as the solution for all social problems. One of the most influential popularizations was the French writer Bernard de Fontenelle's *Conversations on the Plurality of Worlds* (1686). Presented as a dialogue between an aristocratic woman and a man of the world, the book made the Copernican, sun-centered view of the universe available to the literate public. By 1700, mathematics and science had become fashionable pastimes in high society, and the public flocked to lectures explaining scientific discoveries. Journals complained that scientific learning had become the passport to female affection: "There were two young ladies in Paris whose heads had been so turned by this branch of learning that one of them declined to listen to a proposal of marriage unless the candidate for her hand undertook to learn how to make telescopes." Such writings poked fun at women with intellectual interests, but they also demonstrated that women now participated in discussions of science.

Interest in science spread in literate circles because it offered a model for all forms of knowledge. As the prestige of science increased, some developed a skeptical attitude toward attempts to enforce religious conformity. A French Huguenot refugee from Louis XIV's persecutions, Pierre Bayle (1647–1706), launched an internationally influential campaign against religious intolerance from his safe haven in the Dutch Republic. His *News from the Republic of Letters* (first published in 1684) bitterly criticized the policies of Louis XIV and was quickly banned in Paris and condemned in Rome. After attacking Louis XIV's anti-Protestant policies, Bayle took a more general stand in favor of religious toleration. No state in Europe officially offered complete tolerance, though the Dutch Republic came closest with its tacit acceptance of Catholics, dissident Protestant groups, and open Jewish communities. In 1697, Bayle published the *Historical and Critical Dictionary*, which cited all the errors and delusions that he could find in past and present writers of all

■ A Budding Scientist

In this engraving, Astrologia, *by the Dutch artist Jacob Gole (c. 1660–1723), an upper-class woman looks through a telescope to do her own astronomical investigations. Women were not allowed to attend university classes in any European country, yet the Italian Laura Bassi (1711–1778) still managed to become professor of physics at the University of Bologna. Because many astronomical observatories were set up in private homes rather than public buildings or universities, wives and daughters of scientists could make observations and even publish their own findings.*
(Bibliothèque Nationale de France.)

www.bedfordstmartins.com/huntconcise
See the ONLINE STUDY GUIDE for more help in analyzing this image.

religions. Even religion must meet the test of reasonableness: "Any particular dogma, whatever it may be, whether it is advanced on the authority of the Scriptures, or whatever else may be its origins, is to be regarded as false if it clashes with the clear and definite conclusions of the natural understanding [reason]."

Although Bayle claimed to be a believer himself, his insistence on rational investigation seemed to challenge the authority of faith. As one critic complained, "It is notorious that the works of M. Bayle have unsettled a large number of readers, and cast doubt on some of the most widely accepted principles of morality and religion." Bayle asserted, for example, that atheists might possess moral codes as effective as those of the devout. Bayle's *Dictionary* became a model of critical thought in the West.

Other scholars challenged the authority of the Bible by subjecting it to historical criticism. Discoveries in geology in the early eighteenth century showed that marine fossils dated immensely farther back than the biblical flood. Investigations of miracles, comets, and oracles, like the growing literature against belief in witchcraft, urged the use of reason to combat superstition and prejudice. Comets, for example, should not be considered evil omens just because such a belief had been passed on from earlier generations. Defenders of church and state published books warning of the dangers of the new skepticism. The spokesman for Louis XIV's absolutism, Bishop Bossuet, warned that "reason is the guide of their choice, but reason only brings them face to face with vague conjectures and baffling perplexities." Human beings, the traditionalists held, were simply incapable of subjecting everything to reason, especially in the realm of religion.

State authorities found religious skepticism particularly unsettling because it threatened to undermine state power, too. The extensive literature of criticism was not limited to France, but much of it was published in French, and the French government took the lead in suppressing the more outspoken works. Forbidden books were then often published in the Dutch Republic, Britain, or Switzerland and smuggled back across the border to a public whose appetite was only whetted by censorship.

The most influential writer of the early Enlightenment was a Frenchman born into the upper middle classes, François-Marie Arouet, known by his pen name, Voltaire (1694–1778). In his early years, Voltaire suffered arrest, imprisonment, and exile, but he eventually achieved wealth and acclaim. His tangles with church and state began in the early 1730s, when he published his *Letters Concerning the English Nation* (the English version appeared in 1733), in which he devoted several chapters to Newton and Locke and used the virtues of the British as a way to attack Catholic bigotry and government rigidity in France. Impressed by British toleration of religious dissent (at least among Protestants), Voltaire spent two years in exile in Britain when the French state responded to his book with yet another order for his arrest.

Voltaire also popularized Newton's scientific discoveries in his *Elements of the Philosophy of Newton* (1738). The French state and many European theologians considered Newtonianism threatening because it glorified the human mind and seemed to reduce God to an abstract, external, rationalistic force. So sensational was the success of Voltaire's book on Newton that a hostile Jesuit reported, "The great Newton, was, it is said, buried in the abyss, in the shop of the first publisher who dared to print him. . . . M. de Voltaire finally appeared, and at once Newton is understood or is in the process of being understood; all Paris resounds with Newton, all Paris stammers Newton, all Paris studies and learns Newton." The success was international, too. Before long, Voltaire was elected a fellow of the Royal Society in London and in Edinburgh, as well as to twenty other scientific academies. Voltaire's fame continued to grow, reaching truly astounding proportions in the 1750s and 1760s (see Chapter 15).

Travel Literature and the Challenge to Custom and Tradition

Just as scientific method could be used to question religious and even state authority, a more general skepticism also emerged from the expanding knowledge about the world outside of Europe. During the seventeenth and eighteenth centuries, accounts of travel to exotic places dramatically increased as travel writers used the contrast between their home societies and other cultures to criticize the customs of European society.

In their travels to the new colonies, visitors sought something resembling "the state of nature"—that is, ways of life that preceded sophisticated social and political organization—although they often misinterpreted different forms of society and politics as having no organization at all. Travelers to the Americas found "noble savages" (native peoples) who appeared to live in conditions of great freedom and equality; they were "naturally good" and "happy" without taxes, lawsuits, or much organized government. In China, in contrast, travelers found a people who enjoyed prosperity and an ancient civilization. Christian missionaries made little headway in China, and visitors had to admit that China's religious systems had flourished for four or five thousand years with no input from Europe or from Christianity. The basic lesson of travel literature in the 1700s, then, was that customs varied: justice, freedom, property, good government, religion, and morality all were relative to the place. One critic complained that travel encouraged free thinking and the destruction of religion: "Some complete their demoralization by extensive travel, and lose whatever shreds of religion remained to them. Every day they see a new religion, new customs, new rites."

Travel literature turned explicitly political in Montesquieu's *Persian Letters* (1721). Charles-Louis de Secondat, baron of Montesquieu (1689–1755), the son of an eminent judicial family, was a high-ranking judge in a French court. He published *Persian Letters* anonymously in the Dutch Republic, and the book went into ten printings in just one year—a best-seller for the times. Montesquieu tells the story of two Persians, Rica and Usbek, who leave their country "for love of knowledge" and travel to Europe. They visit France in the last years of Louis XIV's reign, writing of the king: "He has a minister who is only eighteen years old, and a mistress of eighty. . . . Although he avoids the bustle of towns, and is rarely seen in company, his one concern, from morning till night, is to get himself talked about." Other passages ridicule the pope. Beneath the satire, however, was a serious investigation into the foundation of good government and morality. Montesquieu chose Persians for his travelers because they came from what was widely considered the most despotic of all governments, in which rulers had life-and-death powers over their subjects. In the book, the Persians constantly compare France to Persia, suggesting that the French monarchy itself might verge on despotism.◆

The paradox of a judge publishing an anonymous work attacking the regime that employed him demonstrates the complications of the intellectual scene in this period. Montesquieu's anonymity did not last long, and soon Parisian society lionized him. In the late 1720s, he sold his judgeship and traveled extensively in Europe, including an eighteen-month stay in Britain. In 1748, he published a widely influential work on comparative government, *The Spirit of Laws*. The Vatican soon listed both *Persian Letters* and *The Spirit of Laws* in its index of forbidden books.

Raising the Woman Question

Many of the letters exchanged in *Persian Letters* focused on women, marriage, and the family because Montesquieu considered the position of women a sure indicator of the

---

◆ For an excerpt from Montesquieu's classic work, see Document 45, "Persian Letters: Letter 37."

IMPORTANT DATES

1690s	Beginning of rapid development of plantations in Caribbean	1714	Elector of Hanover becomes King George I of England
1694	Bank of England established; Mary Astell's *A Serious Proposal to the Ladies* argues for the founding of a private women's college	1715	Death of Louis XIV
		1719	Daniel Defoe publishes *Robinson Crusoe*
1697	Pierre Bayle publishes *Historical and Critical Dictionary*, detailing errors of religious writers	1720	Last outbreak of bubonic plague in western Europe
		1721	Treaty of Nystad; Montesquieu publishes *Persian Letters* anonymously in the Dutch Republic
1699	Turks forced to recognize Habsburg rule over Hungary and Transylvania		
		1733	War of the Polish Succession; Voltaire's *Letters Concerning the English Nation* attacks French intolerance and narrow-mindedness
1703	Peter the Great of Russia begins construction of St. Petersburg, founds first Russian newspaper		
		1741	George Frederick Handel composes the *Messiah*
1713–1714	Peace of Utrecht		

nature of government and morality. Although he was not a feminist, his depiction of Roxana, the favorite wife in Usbek's harem, struck a chord with many women. Roxana revolts against the authority of Usbek's eunuchs and writes a final letter to her husband announcing her impending suicide: "I may have lived in servitude, but I have always been free, I have amended your laws according to the laws of nature, and my mind has always remained independent." Women writers used the same language of tyranny and freedom to argue for concrete changes in their status. Feminist ideas were not entirely new, but they were presented systematically for the first time and represented a fundamental challenge to the ways of traditional societies.

The most systematic of these women writers was the English author Mary Astell (1666–1731), the daughter of a businessman and herself a supporter of the Tory party and the Anglican religious establishment. In 1694, she published *A Serious Proposal to the Ladies,* in which she advocated founding a private women's college to remedy women's lack of education. Addressing women, she asked, "How can you be content to be in the World like Tulips in a Garden, to make a fine *shew* [show] and be good for nothing?" Astell argued for intellectual training based on Descartes's principles, in which reason, debate, and careful consideration of the issues took priority over custom or tradition. Her book was an immediate success: five printings appeared by 1701. In later works such as *Reflections upon Marriage* (1706), Astell criticized the relationship between the sexes within marriage: "If Absolute Sovereignty be not necessary in a State, how comes it to be so in a family? . . . *If all Men*

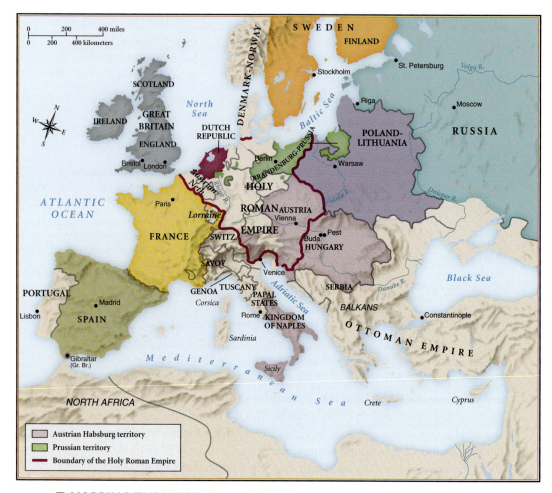

▪ MAPPING THE WEST Europe in 1740

By 1740, Europe had achieved a kind of diplomatic equilibrium in which no one power predominated. But the relative balance should not deflect attention from important underlying changes: Spain, the Dutch Republic, Poland-Lithuania, and Sweden had all declined in power and influence while Great Britain, Russia, Prussia, and Austria had solidified their positions, each in a different way. France's ambitions had been thwarted, but the combination of a big army and rich overseas possessions made France a major player for a long time to come.

are born free, how is it that all Women are born slaves?"◆ Her critics accused her of promoting subversive ideas and of contradicting the Scriptures.

Astell's work inspired other women to write in a similar vein. The anonymous *Essay in Defence of the Female Sex* (1696) attacked "the Usurpation of Men; and the

---

◆ For an extended passage from Mary Astell's *Reflections upon Marriage,* see Document 46.

Tyranny of Custom," which prevented women from getting an education. In 1709, Elizabeth Elstob published a detailed account of the prominent role women played in promoting Christianity in English history. She criticized men who "would declare openly they hated any Woman who knew more than themselves."

Most male writers unequivocally stuck to the traditional view of women, which held that women were less capable of reasoning than men and therefore did not need systematic education. Such opinions often rested on biological suppositions. The long-dominant Aristotelian view of reproduction held that only the male seed carried spirit and individuality. At the beginning of the eighteenth century, however, scientists began to undermine this belief. More physicians and surgeons began to champion the doctrine of *ovism*—that the female egg was essential in making new humans. During the decades that followed, male Enlightenment writers would continue to debate women's nature and appropriate social roles.

Conclusion

Europeans crossed a major threshold in the first half of the eighteenth century. They moved silently but nonetheless momentously from an economy governed by scarcity and the threat of famine to one of ever increasing growth and the prospect of continuing improvement. Expansion of colonies overseas and economic development at home created greater wealth, longer life spans, and higher expectations for the future. In these better times for many, a spirit of optimism prevailed. People could now spend money on newspapers, novels, and travel literature as well as on coffee, tea, and cotton cloth. The growing literate public avidly followed the latest trends in religious debates, art, and music. Everyone did not share equally in the benefits: slaves toiled in abjection in the Americas; serfs in eastern Europe found themselves ever more closely bound to their noble lords; and rural folk almost everywhere tasted few fruits of consumer society.

Politics, too, changed as population and production increased and cities grew. Experts urged government intervention to improve public health, and states found it in their interest to settle many international disputes by diplomacy, which itself became more regular and routine. The consolidation of the European state system allowed a tide of criticism and new thinking about society to swell in Great Britain and France and begin to spill throughout Europe. Ultimately, the combination of the Atlantic system and the Enlightenment would give rise to a series of Atlantic revolutions.

Suggested References for further reading and online research appear on page SR-22 at the back of the book.

www.bedfordstmartins.com/huntconcise   See the ONLINE STUDY GUIDE to assess your mastery of the material covered in this chapter.

The Promise of Enlightenment

1740–1789

I N THE SUMMER OF 1766, Empress Catherine II ("the Great") of Russia wrote to Voltaire, one of the leaders of the Enlightenment:

> It is a way of immortalizing oneself to be the advocate of humanity, the defender of oppressed innocence. . . . You have entered into combat against the enemies of mankind: superstition, fanaticism, ignorance, quibbling, evil judges, and the powers that rest in their hands. Great virtues and qualities are needed to surmount these obstacles. You have shown that you have them: you have triumphed.

Over a fifteen-year period Catherine corresponded regularly with Voltaire, a writer who, at home in France, found himself in constant conflict with church and state authorities. Her admiring letter shows how influential Enlightenment ideals had become by the middle of the eighteenth century.

Catherine's letter aptly summed up Enlightenment ideals: progress for humanity could be achieved only by rooting out the wrongs left by superstition, religious fanaticism, ignorance, and outmoded forms of justice. Enlightenment writers used every means at their disposal—from encyclopedias to novels to personal interaction with rulers—to argue for reform. Everything had to be examined

■ **Catherine the Great**

At the time of this portrait (1793) by Johann Baptist Edler von Lampi, the Russian empress had ruled for thirty-one years and was only three years from her death. Born Sophia Augusta Frederika of Anhalt-Zerbst in 1729, she was the daughter of a minor German prince. When she married the future tsar Peter III in 1745, she promptly learned Russian and adopted Russian Orthodoxy. Peter, physically and mentally frail, proved no match for her, and she took his place on his death in 1762. The painter of this portrait was a native of northern Italy who had worked at the Austrian court in Vienna before being summoned to St. Petersburg. He painted many portraits of the Russian court and royal family between 1792 and 1797. (Art Resource, NY.)

611

in the clear light of reason, and anything that did not promote the improvement of humanity was to be jettisoned. As a result, Enlightenment writers attacked the legal use of torture to extract confessions, favored the spread of education to eliminate ignorance, supported religious toleration, and criticized censorship by state or church. The book trade and new places for urban socializing, such as coffeehouses and Masonic lodges (social clubs organized around the rituals of masons' guilds), spread these ideas within a new elite of middle- and upper-class men and women.

The lower classes had little contact with Enlightenment ideas. Their lives were shaped more profoundly by the continuing rise in population, the start of industrialization, and wars among the great powers. States had to balance conflicting social pressures: rulers pursued Enlightenment reforms that they believed might enhance state power, but they feared changes that might unleash popular discontent. For example, Catherine aimed to bring Western ideas, culture, and reforms to Russia, but when faced with a massive uprising of the serfs, she not only suppressed the revolt but also increased the nobles' powers over their serfs. All reform-minded rulers faced similar potential challenges to their authority.

Even though the movement for reform had its limits, governments now needed to respond to a new force: public opinion. Rulers wanted to portray themselves as modern, open to change, and responsive to the segment of the public that was reading newspapers and closely following political developments. Enlightenment writers appealed to public opinion, but they still looked to rulers to effect reform. Writers such as Voltaire expressed little interest in the future of peasants or lower classes; they favored neither revolution nor political upheaval. Yet their ideas paved the way for something much more radical and unexpected. The American Declaration of Independence in 1776 showed how Enlightenment ideals could be translated into democratic political practice. After 1789, democracy would come to Europe as well.

The Enlightenment at Its Height

The Enlightenment emerged as an intellectual movement before 1740 but reached its peak only in the second half of the eighteenth century. The writers of the Enlightenment called themselves *philosophes* (French for "philosophers"), but that term is somewhat misleading. Whereas philosophers concern themselves with abstract theories, the philosophes were public intellectuals dedicated to solving the real problems of the world. They wrote on subjects ranging from current affairs to art criticism, and they wrote in every conceivable format. The Swiss philosophe Jean-Jacques Rousseau, for example, wrote a political tract, a treatise on education, a constitution for Poland, an analysis of the effects of the theater on public morals, a best-selling novel, an opera, and a notorious autobiography. The philosophes wrote for a broad educated public of readers who snatched up every Enlightenment book they could find at their local booksellers', even when rulers or churches tried to forbid publication. Between 1740 and 1789, the Enlightenment acquired its name and, despite heated conflicts between the philosophes and state and religious authorities, gained support in the highest reaches of government.

The Men and Women of the Republic of Letters

Although *philosophe* is a French word, the Enlightenment was distinctly cosmopolitan; philosophes could be found from Philadelphia to Moscow. The philosophes considered themselves part of a grand "republic of letters" that transcended national political boundaries. They were not republicans in the usual sense, that is, people who supported representative government and opposed monarchy. What united them were the ideals of reason, reform, and freedom. In 1784, the German philosopher Immanuel Kant summed up the program of the Enlightenment in two Latin words: *sapere aude*, "dare to know"—have the courage to think for yourself.

The philosophes used reason to attack superstition, bigotry, and religious fanaticism, which they considered the chief obstacles to free thought and social reform. Voltaire took religious fanaticism as his chief target: "Once fanaticism has corrupted a mind, the malady is almost incurable. . . . The only remedy for this epidemic malady is the philosophical spirit." Enlightenment writers did not necessarily oppose organized religion, but they strenuously objected to religious intolerance. They believed that the systematic application of reason could do what religious belief could not: improve the human condition by pointing to needed reforms. Reason meant critical, informed, scientific thinking about social issues and problems. Many Enlightenment writers collaborated on a new multivolume *Encyclopedia* that aimed to gather together knowledge about science, religion, industry, and society. The chief editor of the *Encyclopedia*, Denis Diderot (1713–1784), explained the goal: "All things must be examined, debated, investigated without exception and without regard for anyone's feelings."

The philosophes believed that the spread of knowledge would encourage reform in every aspect of life, from the grain trade to the penal system. Chief among their desired reforms was intellectual freedom, the freedom to use one's own reason and to publish the results. The philosophes wanted freedom of the press and freedom of religion, which they considered "natural rights" guaranteed by "natural law." In their view, progress depended on these freedoms. As Voltaire asserted, "I quite understand that the fanatics of one sect slaughter the enthusiasts of another sect . . . [but] that Descartes should have been forced to flee to Holland to escape the fury of the ignorant . . . these things are a nation's eternal shame."

Most philosophes, like Voltaire, came from the upper classes, yet Rousseau's father was a modest watchmaker in Geneva, and Diderot was the son of a cutlery maker. Although it was a rare phenomenon, some women were philosophes, such as the French noblewoman Émilie du Châtelet (1706–1749), who wrote extensively about the mathematics and physics of Leibniz and Newton. (Her lover Voltaire

■ Madame Geoffrin's Salon in 1755

This 1812 painting by Anicet Charles Lemonnier claims to depict the best-known Parisian salon of the 1750s. Lemonnier was only twelve years old in 1755 and so could not have based his rendition on firsthand knowledge. Madame Geoffrin is the figure in blue on the right, facing the viewer. The bust is of Voltaire. Rousseau is the fifth person to the left of the bust (facing right) and behind him (facing left) is Raynal. (Giraudon/Art Resource, NY.)

learned much of his science from her.) Few of the leading writers held university positions, except those who were German or Scottish. Universities in France were dominated by the clergy and unreceptive to Enlightenment ideals.

Enlightenment ideas developed instead through personal contacts; through letters that were hand copied, circulated, and sometimes published; through informal readings of manuscripts; and through letters to the editor and book reviews in periodicals. Salons (*salon* is French for "living room") gave intellectual life an anchor outside the royal court and the church-controlled universities. Best known was the Parisian salon of Madame Marie-Thérèse Geoffrin (1699–1777), a wealthy middle-class widow who had been raised by her grandmother and married off at fourteen to a much older man. She brought together the most exciting thinkers and artists of the time; her social gatherings provided a forum for new ideas and an opportunity to establish new intellectual contacts. In the salon, the philosophes could discuss ideas they might hesitate to put into print and thus test public opinion and even push it in new directions. Madame Geoffrin corresponded extensively with influential people across Europe, including Catherine the Great. One Italian visitor commented, "There is no way to make Naples resemble Paris unless we find a woman to guide us, organize us, *Geoffrinize* us."◆

◆ For two primary sources that reveal Geoffrin's remarkable personality and influence, see Document 47, Marie-Thérèse Geoffrin and Monsieur d'Alembert, "The Salon of Madame Geoffrin."

Women's salons helped galvanize intellectual life and reform movements all over Europe. Wealthy Jewish women created nine of the fourteen salons in Berlin at the end of the eighteenth century, and in Warsaw, Princess Zofia Czartoryska gathered around her the reform leaders of Poland-Lithuania. Middle-class women in London used their salons to raise money to publish women's writings. Salons could be tied closely to the circles of power: in France, for example, Louis XV's mistress, Jeanne-Antoinette Poisson, first made her reputation as hostess of a salon frequented by Voltaire and Montesquieu. When she became Louis XV's mistress in 1745, she gained the title Marquise de Pompadour and turned her attention to influencing artistic styles by patronizing architects and painters.

Conflicts with Church and State

Madame Geoffrin did not approve of discussions that attacked the Catholic church, but elsewhere voices against organized religion could be heard. Criticisms of religion required daring because the church, whatever its denomination, wielded enormous power in society, and most influential people considered religion an essential foundation of good society and government. Defying such opinion, the Scottish philosopher David Hume (1711–1776) boldly argued in *The Natural History of Religion* (1755) that belief in God rested on superstition and fear rather than on reason.

Before the scientific revolution, nearly every European believed in God. After Newton, however, and despite Newton's own deep religiosity, people could conceive of the universe as an eternally existing, self-perpetuating machine in which God's intervention was unnecessary. In short, such people could become either *atheists*, who did not believe in any kind of God, or *deists*, who believed in God but gave him no active role in earthly affairs. For the first time, writers claimed the label *atheist* and disputed the common view that atheism led inevitably to immorality.

Deists continued to believe in a benevolent, all-knowing God who had designed the universe and set it in motion. But deists usually rejected the idea that God directly intercedes in the functioning of the universe, and they often criticized the churches for their dogmatic intolerance of dissenters. Voltaire was a deist, and in his popular *Philosophical Dictionary* (1764) he attacked most of the claims of organized Christianity, both Catholic and Protestant. Christianity, he argued, had been the prime source of fanaticism and brutality among humans. Throughout his life, Voltaire's motto was *Écrasez l'infâme*—"Crush the infamous thing" (the "thing" being bigotry and intolerance). French authorities publicly burned his *Philosophical Dictionary*.

Criticism of religious intolerance involved more than simply attacking the churches. Critics also had to confront the states to which churches were closely tied. In 1761, a judicial case in Toulouse provoked throughout France an outcry that Voltaire soon joined. When the son of a local Calvinist was found hanged (he probably committed suicide), authorities accused the father, Jean Calas, of murdering him to prevent his conversion to Catholicism. (Since Louis XIV's revocation of the Edict of Nantes in 1685, it had been illegal to practice Calvinism publicly in France.) The all-Catholic parlement of Toulouse tried to extract a confession using torture— breaking all Calas's bones—and then executed him when he still refused to confess. Voltaire launched a successful crusade to rehabilitate Jean Calas's good name and to restore the family's properties, which had been confiscated after his death. Voltaire's efforts eventually helped bring about the extension of civil rights to French Protestants and encouraged campaigns to abolish the legal use of torture.

Critics also assailed state and church support for European colonization and slavery. One of the most popular books of the time was the *Philosophical and Political History of European Colonies and Commerce in the Two Indies,* published in 1770 by Abbé Guillaume Raynal (1713–1796), a French Catholic clergyman. Raynal and his collaborators described in excruciating detail the destruction of native populations by Europeans and denounced the slave trade. Although Raynal was forced into exile and his work was banned by both the Catholic church and the French government, the Enlightenment belief in natural rights led many others to denounce slavery. An article in the new *Encyclopedia* proclaimed, "There is not a single one of these hapless souls . . . who does not have the right to be declared free . . . since neither his ruler nor his father nor anyone else had the right to dispose of his freedom." Some Enlightenment thinkers, however, took a more ambiguous or even negative view. Hume judged blacks to be "naturally inferior to the whites," concluding, "There never was a civilized nation of any other complexion than white."

Enlightenment critics of church and state advocated reform, not revolution. Although he lived near the French-Swiss border in case he had to flee arrest, Voltaire, for example, made a fortune from financial speculations, wrote a glowing history called *The Age of Louis XIV* (1751), and lived to be celebrated in his last years as a national hero even by many former foes. Other philosophes also lived respectably, believing that published criticism, rather than violent action, would bring about necessary reforms. As Diderot said, "We will speak against senseless laws until they are reformed; and, while we wait, we will abide by them." Those few who lived long enough to see the French Revolution in 1789 resisted its radical turn, for the philosophes generally regarded the lower classes—"the people"—as ignorant, violent, and prone to superstition, hence in need of leadership from above. They pinned their hopes on educated elites and enlightened rulers.

Despite the philosophes' preference for reform, in the long run their books often had a revolutionary impact. For example, Montesquieu's widely reprinted *Spirit of the Laws* (1748) warned against the dangers of despotism, opposed the divine right of kings, and favored constitutional government. In his somewhat rosy view, Great Britain was "the one nation in the world which has political liberty as the direct object of its constitution." His analysis of British constitutionalism inspired French critics of absolutism and would greatly influence the American revolutionaries.

The Individual and Society

The controversy created by the most notorious conflicts between the philosophes and the various churches and states of Europe drew attention away from a subtle but profound transformation in worldviews. In previous centuries, questions of theological doctrine and church organization had been the main focus of intellectual and even political interest. The Enlightenment writers shifted attention away from religious questions toward the secular study of society and the individual's role in it. Religion did not drop out of sight, but the philosophes tended to make religion a private affair of individual conscience, even while rulers and churches still considered religion very much a public concern.

The Enlightenment interest in secular society produced two major results: it advanced the secularization of European political life that had begun after the Wars of Religion of the sixteenth and seventeenth centuries, and it laid the foundations for the social sciences of the modern era. Not surprisingly, then, many historians and philosophers consider the Enlightenment to be the origin of "modernity," which they define as the belief that human reason, rather than theological doctrine, should set the patterns of social and political life. This belief in reason as the sole foundation for secular authority has often been contested, but it has also proved to be a powerful force for change.

Although most of the philosophes believed that human reason could understand and even remake society and politics, they disagreed about what that reason revealed. Among the many different approaches were two that proved enduringly influential, those of the Scottish philosopher Adam Smith and the Swiss writer Jean-Jacques Rousseau. Smith provided a theory of modern capitalist society and devoted much of his energy to defending free markets as offering the best way to maximize individual efforts. The modern discipline of economics took shape around the questions raised by Smith. Rousseau set out the principles of a more communitarian philosophy, one that emphasized the needs of the community over those of the individual. His work led both toward democracy and toward communism and continues to inspire heated debate in political science and sociology. A closer look at these two thinkers will demonstrate the breadth and depth of Enlightenment thought.

Adam Smith (1723–1790) optimistically believed that individual interests naturally harmonized with those of the whole society. To explain how this natural harmonization worked, he published *An Inquiry into the Nature and Causes of the Wealth of Nations* in 1776. Smith insisted that individual self-interest, even greed, was quite compatible with society's best interest: the laws of supply and demand served as an "invisible hand" ensuring that individual interests would be synchronized with those of the whole society. Market forces—"the propensity to truck, barter, and exchange one thing for another"—naturally brought individual and social interests in line.

Smith rejected the prevailing mercantilist views that the general welfare would be served by accumulating national wealth through agriculture or the hoarding of gold and silver. Instead, he argued that the division of labor in manufacturing would increase productivity and generate more wealth for society and well-being for the individual. To maximize the effects of market forces and the division of labor, Smith endorsed a concept called *laissez-faire* (that is, "to leave alone") to free the economy from government intervention and control. He insisted that governments eliminate all restrictions on the sale of land, remove restraints on the grain trade, and abandon duties on imports. He believed that free international trade would stimulate production everywhere and thus ensure the growth of national wealth. He argued:

> *The natural effort of every individual to better his own condition, when suffered to exert itself with freedom and security, is so powerful a principle, that it is alone, and without any assistance, not only capable of carrying the society to wealth and prosperity, but of surmounting a hundred impertinent obstructions with which the folly of human laws too often encumbers its operations.*

Governments should restrict themselves to providing "security"—that is, national defense, internal order and a secure framework for market activity, and public works.

Much more pessimistic about the relation between individual self-interest and the good of society was Jean-Jacques Rousseau (1712–1778). In Rousseau's view, society itself threatened natural rights or freedoms: "Man is born free, and everywhere he is in chains." Rousseau first gained fame by writing a prize-winning essay in 1749 in which he argued that the revival of science and the arts had corrupted social morals, not improved them. This startling conclusion seemed to oppose some of the Enlightenment's most cherished beliefs. Rather than improving society, he claimed, science and art raised artificial barriers between people and their natural state. Rousseau's works extolled the simplicity of rural life over urban society. Although he participated in the salons, Rousseau always felt ill at ease in high society, and he periodically withdrew to live in solitude far from Paris. Paradoxically, his "solitude" was often paid for by wealthy upper-class patrons, who lodged him on their estates, even as his writings decried the upper-class privilege that made his efforts possible.

Rousseau explored the tension between the individual and society in various ways, including his widely influential work on education, *Émile* (1762), in which a boy develops practical skills and independent thinking under the guidance of his tutor. In *The Social Contract* (1762), Rousseau proposed a political solution to the tension between the individual and society. Whereas earlier he had argued that society corrupted the individual by taking him out of nature, in this work Rousseau

■ Rousseau's Worries

Jean-Jacques Rousseau's novel The New Heloise *(1761) sold better than any other work in French in the second half of the eighteenth century. But Rousseau himself was deeply concerned about the effects of novel reading, especially on young women. The first of these illustrations for the novel (on the left) by Moreau the Younger, was rejected by Rousseau because the couple (Julie and Saint Preux) are shown in direct physical contact. He accepted the engraving on the right, by Gravelot, because it only hinted at passion.* (Bibliothèque Nationale.)

insisted that individual moral freedom could be achieved only by learning to sub-ject one's individual interests to "the general will"—that is, to the good of the com-munity. Individuals did this by entering into a social contract, not with their rulers but with one another. If everyone followed the general will, then all individuals would be equally free and equally moral because they lived under a law to which they had all consented.

These arguments threatened the legitimacy of eighteenth-century governments. Rousseau derived his social contract from human nature, not from history, tradi-tion, or the Bible. He implied that people would be most free and moral under a republican form of government with direct democracy, and his abstract model included no reference to differences in social status. He roundly condemned slav-ery: "To decide that the son of a slave is born a slave is to decide that he is not born a man." Not surprisingly, authorities in both Geneva and Paris banned *The Social*

Contract for undermining political authority. Rousseau's works would become a kind of political bible for the French revolutionaries of 1789, and his attacks on private property would inspire the communists of the nineteenth century such as Karl Marx. Rousseau's rather mystical concept of the general will remains controversial. The "greatest good of all," according to Rousseau, was liberty and equality, but he also insisted that the individual could be "forced to be free" by the terms of the social contract. He provided no legal protections for individual rights. In other words, Rousseau's particular version of democracy did not guarantee the individual freedoms so important to Adam Smith.

Spreading the Enlightenment

The Enlightenment flourished in places where an educated middle class provided an eager audience for ideas of constitutionalism and reform. Where constitutionalism and the guarantee of individual freedoms were most advanced, as in Great Britain and the Dutch Republic, the movement had less of an edge because there was, in a sense, less need for it. Scottish and English writers concentrated on economics, philosophy, and history rather than politics or social relations. Dutch printers made money publishing the books that were forbidden in France. In British North America, Enlightenment ideas helped stiffen growing colonial resistance to British rule after 1763. In places with small middle classes, such as Spain, the Italian states, and Russia, governments successfully suppressed writings they did not like. Italian philosophes, such as the Milanese penal reformer Cesare Beccaria (1738–1794), got moral support from their French counterparts in the face of stern censorship at home.

The hot spot of the Enlightenment was France. French writers published the most daring critiques of church and state and suffered the most intense harassment and persecution. Voltaire, Diderot, and Rousseau all faced arrest, exile, or even imprisonment. The Catholic church and royal authorities routinely forbade the publication of their books, and the police arrested publishers who ignored their warnings. Yet the French monarchy was far from the most autocratic in Europe, and Voltaire, Diderot, and Rousseau all ended their lives as cultural heroes. France seems to have been curiously caught in the middle during the Enlightenment: with fewer constitutional guarantees of individual freedom than Great Britain, it still enjoyed much higher levels of prosperity and cultural development than most other European countries. In short, French elites had reason to complain, the means to make their complaints known, and a government torn between the desires to censor dissident ideas and to appear open to modernity and progress. The government in France controlled publishing—all books had to get official permissions—but not as tightly as in Spain, where the Catholic Inquisition made up its own list of banned books, or in Russia, where Catherine the Great allowed no opposition.

By the 1760s, the French government regularly ignored the publication of many works once thought offensive or subversive. In addition, a growing flood of works printed abroad poured into France and circulated underground. In the Dutch Republic and Swiss cities, private companies made fortunes smuggling illegal books into France over mountain passes and back roads. Foreign printers provided secret catalogs of their offerings and sold their products through booksellers who were willing to market forbidden texts for a high price—among them, not only philosophical treatises of the Enlightenment but also pornographic works and pamphlets (some by Diderot) lampooning the Catholic clergy and leading members of the royal court. In the 1770s and 1780s, lurid descriptions of sexual promiscuity at the French court helped undermine the popularity of the throne.

Whereas the French philosophes often took a violently anticlerical and combative tone, their German counterparts avoided direct political confrontations with authorities. Gotthold Lessing (1729–1781) complained in 1769 that Prussia was still "the most slavish society in Europe" in its lack of freedom to criticize government policies. As a playwright, literary critic, and philosopher, Lessing promoted religious toleration for Jews and spiritual emancipation of Germans from foreign, especially French, models of culture, which still dominated. Lessing also introduced the German Jewish writer Moses Mendelssohn (1729–1786) into Berlin salon society. Mendelssohn labored to build bridges between German and Jewish culture by arguing that Judaism was a rational and undogmatic religion. He believed persecution and discrimination against the Jews would end as reason triumphed.

Reason was also the chief focus of the most influential German thinker of the Enlightenment, Immanuel Kant (1724–1804). A university professor who lectured on everything from economics to astronomy, Kant wrote one of the most important works in the history of Western philosophy, *The Critique of Pure Reason* (1781). He admired Adam Smith and especially Rousseau, whose portrait he displayed proudly in his lodgings. Just as Smith founded modern economics and Rousseau modern political theory, Kant in *Critique of Pure Reason* set the foundations for modern philosophy. In this complex book, Kant established the doctrine of *idealism*, the belief that true understanding can come only from examining the ways in which ideas are formed in the mind. Ideas are shaped, Kant argued, not just by sensory information (a position central to *empiricism*, a philosophy based on John Locke's writings) but also by the operation on that information of mental categories such as space and time. In Kant's philosophy, these "categories of understanding" were neither sensory nor supernatural; they were entirely ideal and abstract and located in the human mind. For Kant the supreme philosophical questions—Does God exist? Is personal immortality possible? Do humans have free will?—were unanswerable by reason alone. But like Rousseau, Kant insisted that people could achieve true moral freedom only by living in society and obeying its laws.

The Limits of Reason: Roots of Romanticism and Religious Revival

In reaction to what some saw as the Enlightenment's excessive reliance on the authority of human reason, a new artistic movement called *romanticism* took root. Although it would not fully flower until the early nineteenth century, romanticism traced its emphasis on individual genius, deep emotion, and the joys of nature to thinkers like Rousseau who had scolded the philosophes for ignoring those aspects of life that escaped and even conflicted with the power of reason. Rousseau's autobiographical *Confessions*, published posthumously in 1782, caused an immediate sensation because it revealed so much about his inner emotional life, including his sexual longings and his almost paranoid distrust of other Enlightenment figures.

The appeal to feelings and emotions also increased interest in the occult. In the 1780s, a charismatic Austrian physician turned "experimenter," Franz Mesmer, awed crowds of aristocrats and middle-class admirers with his Paris demonstrations of "animal magnetism." He passed a weak electrical current through tubs filled with water or iron filings, around which groups of his disciples sat, holding hands; with this process of "mesmerism" he claimed to cure their ailments. (The word *mesmerize*, meaning "hypnotize" or "hold spellbound," is derived from Mesmer's name.)

A novel by the German writer Johann Wolfgang von Goethe (1749–1832) captured the early romantic spirit with its glorification of emotion. *The Sorrows of Young Werther* (1774) tells of a passionate youth who reveres nature and rural life and is unhappy in love. When the woman he loves marries someone else, he falls into deep melancholy and eventually kills himself. Reason cannot save him. The book spurred a veritable Werther craze: there were Werther costumes, Werther engravings and embroidery, Werther medallions, and a perfume called Eau de Werther. Tragically, there were even a few imitations of Werther's suicide. The young Napoleon Bonaparte, who was to build an empire for France, claimed to have read Goethe's novel seven times.

Religious revivals underlined the limits of reason in a different way. Much of the Protestant world experienced an "awakening" in the 1740s. In the German states, Pietist groups founded new communities; and in the British North American colonies, revivalist Protestant preachers drew thousands of fervent believers in a movement called the Great Awakening. In North America, bitter conflicts between revivalists and their opponents in the established churches prompted the leaders on both sides to set up new colleges to support their beliefs. These included Princeton, Columbia, Brown, and Dartmouth, all founded between 1746 and 1769.

Revivalism also stirred eastern European Jews at about the same time. Israel ben Eliezer (c. 1700–1760), later known as Ba'al Shem Tov (or the Besht, from the initials), laid the foundation for the Hasidic sect in the 1740s and 1750s. Teaching outside the synagogue system, Ba'al Shem Tov traveled the Polish countryside offering to cure men of their evil spirits. He invented a new form of popular prayer,

■ **A Hasid and His Wife**

The followers of Ba'al Shem Tov were known as Hasidim *("most pious Jews"). They insisted on wearing Polish peasant-style clothing even if they themselves were not peasants. The Hasidim stressed devotion to the* rebbe *("teacher and spiritual guide").*
(Encyclopedia of Jewish History.)

in which the believer aimed to annihilate his own personality in order to let the supernatural speak through him. His followers, the *Hasidim* (Hebrew for "most pious" Jews), often prayed at the top of their lungs, joyfully swaying and clapping their hands. They scorned the formality of the regular synagogues in favor of their own prayer houses, where they gathered in rustic clothing and broad fur hats to emphasize their piety and simplicity. Their practices soon spread all over Poland-Lithuania.

Most of the waves of Protestant revivalism ebbed after the 1750s, but in Great Britain the movement known as *Methodism* continued to grow through the end of the century. John Wesley (1703–1791), the Oxford-educated son of an Anglican cleric, founded Methodism, a term evoked by Wesley's insistence on strict self-discipline and a methodical approach to religious study and observance. In 1738, Wesley began preaching a new brand of Protestantism that emphasized an intense personal experience of salvation and a life of thrift, abstinence, and hard work. Traveling all over the British Isles, Wesley would mount a table or a box to speak to the ordinary people of the village or town. He slept in his followers' homes, ate their food, and treated their illnesses with various remedies, including small electric shocks for nervous diseases (Wesley eagerly followed Benjamin Franklin's experiments with electricity). In fifty years, Wesley preached forty thousand sermons, an average of fifteen a week. Not surprisingly, his preaching disturbed the Anglican authorities, who refused to let him preach in the churches. In response, Wesley began to ordain his own clergy. Nevertheless, during Wesley's lifetime the Methodist leadership remained politically conservative; Wesley himself denounced political agitation in the 1770s because, he said, it threatened to make Great Britain "a field of blood" ruled by "King Mob."

Society and Culture in an Age of Enlightenment

Religious revivals and the first stirrings of romanticism show that all intellectual currents did not flow in the same channel. Similarly, some social and cultural developments manifested the influence of Enlightenment ideas, but others did not. The traditional leaders of European societies—the nobles—responded to Enlightenment ideals in contradictory fashion: many simply reasserted their privileges and resisted the influence of the Enlightenment, but an important minority embraced change and actively participated in reform efforts. The expanding middle classes saw in the Enlightenment a chance to make their claim for joining society's governing elite. They bought Enlightenment books, joined Masonic lodges, and patronized new styles in art, music, and literature. The lower classes were more affected by economic growth. Continuing population increases contributed to a rise in prices for basic goods, but the industrialization of textile manufacturing, which began in this period, made cotton clothing more accessible to those at the bottom of the social scale.

The Nobility's Reassertion of Privilege

Nobles made up about 3 percent of the European population, but their numbers and way of life varied greatly from country to country. At least 10 percent of the population in Poland was noble and 7 to 8 percent in Spain, in contrast to only 2 percent in Russia and between 1 and 2 percent in the rest of western Europe. Many Polish and Spanish nobles lived in poverty; titles did not guarantee wealth. The wealthiest European nobles luxuriated in almost unimaginable opulence. Many of the English peers, for example, owned more than ten thousand acres of land (the average western European peasant owned about five acres), invested widely in government bonds and trading companies, kept several country residences with scores of servants as well as houses in London, and occasionally even had their own private orchestras as well as libraries of expensive books, greenhouses for exotic plants, kennels of pedigree dogs, and collections of antiques, firearms, and scientific instruments.

In the face of the commercialization of agriculture and inflation of prices, European aristocrats converted their remaining legal rights (called *seigneurial dues*, from the French *seigneur*, for "lord") into money payments and used them to support an increasingly expensive lifestyle. Peasants felt the squeeze as a result. French peasants, for instance, paid a wide range of dues to their landlords—including payments to grind grain at the lord's mill, bake bread in his oven, and press grapes at his winepress—and various inheritance taxes on the land. In addition, peasants had to work on the public roads without compensation for a specified number of days every year. They also paid taxes to the government on salt, an essential preservative, and on the value of their land; customs duties if they sold produce or wine in town; and the tithe on their grain (one-tenth of the crop) to the church.

In Britain, the landed gentry could not claim these same onerous dues from their tenants, but they tenaciously defended their exclusive right to hunt game. The game laws kept the poor from eating meat and helped protect the social status of the rich. The gentry enforced the game laws themselves by hiring gamekeepers who hunted down poachers and even set traps for them in the forests. According to the law, anyone who poached deer or rabbits while armed or disguised could be sentenced to death. After 1760, the number of arrests for breaking the game laws increased dramatically. In most other countries, too, hunting was the special right of the nobility and a cause of deep popular resentment.

Even though Enlightenment writers sharply criticized nobles' insistence on special privileges, most aristocrats maintained their marks of distinction. The male court nobility continued to sport swords, plumed hats, makeup, and powdered hair; middle-class men wore simpler and more somber clothing. Aristocrats had their own seats in church and their own quarters in the universities. Frederick II ("the Great") of Prussia (r. 1740–1786) made sure that nobles dominated both the army officer corps and the civil bureaucracy. Catherine II of Russia (r. 1762–1796) granted the nobility vast tracts of land, the exclusive right to own serfs, and exemption from personal taxes and corporal punishment. Her Charter of the Nobility of 1785 codified these privileges in exchange for the nobles' political subservience to the state. In many countries, including Spain and France, the law prohibited aristocrats from engaging directly in retail trade. In Austria, Spain, the Italian states, Poland-Lithuania, and Russia, most nobles consequently cared little about Enlightenment ideas; they did not read the books of the philosophes and feared reforms that might challenge their dominance of rural society.

In France, Britain, and the western German states, however, the nobility proved more open to the new ideas. Among those who personally corresponded with Rousseau, for example, half were nobles, as were 20 percent of the 160 contributors to the *Encyclopedia*. It had not escaped their notice that Rousseau had denounced inequality. In his view, it was "manifestly contrary to the law of nature . . . that a handful of people should gorge themselves with superfluities while the hungry multitude goes in want of necessities."

The Middle Class and the Making of a New Elite

The Enlightenment offered middle-class people an intellectual and cultural route to social improvement. The term *middle class* referred to the middle position on the social ladder; middle-class families did not have legal titles like the nobility above them but did not work with their hands like the peasants, artisans, or workers below them. Most middle-class people lived in towns or cities and earned their living in the professions—as doctors, lawyers, or lower-level officials—or through investment in land, trade, or manufacturing. In the eighteenth century, the ranks of the middle class—also known as the *bourgeoisie*, after *bourgeois*, the French word for "city dweller"—grew steadily in western Europe as a result of economic expansion. In France, for example, the overall population grew by about one-third in the 1700s, but the bourgeoisie nearly tripled in size. Although middle-class people had many reasons to resent the nobles, they also aspired to be like them.

Nobles and middle-class professionals mingled in Enlightenment salons and joined the new Masonic lodges and local learned societies. The members of Masonic lodges were known as *freemasons* because that was the term given to apprentice masons when they were deemed "free" to practice as masters of their guild. Although not explicitly political in aim, the lodges encouraged equality among members, and both aristocrats and middle-class men could join. Members wrote constitutions for their lodges and elected their own officers, thus promoting a direct experience of constitutional government.

Freemasonry arose in Great Britain and spread eastward: the first French and Italian lodges opened in 1726; Frederick II of Prussia founded a lodge in 1740; and after 1750, freemasonry spread in Poland, Russia, and British North America. In France, women set up their own Masonic lodges. Despite the papacy's condemnation of freemasonry in 1738 as subversive of religious and civil authority, lodges continued to multiply throughout the eighteenth century because they offered a place for socializing outside of the traditional channels and a way of declaring one's interest in the Enlightenment and reform. In short, freemasonry offered a kind of secular religion. After 1789 and the outbreak of the French Revolution, conservatives would blame the lodges for every kind of political upheaval, but in the 1700s many high-ranking nobles became active members and saw no conflict with their privileged status.

Shared tastes in travel, architecture, and the arts helped strengthen the links between nobles and members of the middle class. "Grand tours" of Europe often led upper-class youths to the recently discovered Greek and Roman ruins at Pompeii, Herculaneum, and Paestum in Italy. The excavations aroused enthusiasm for the neoclassical style in architecture and painting, which began pushing aside the rococo and the long dominant baroque. Urban residences, government buildings, furniture, fabrics, wallpaper, and even pottery soon reflected the neoclassical emphasis on purity and clarity of forms. The English potter Josiah Wedgwood (1730–1795) almost single-handedly created a mass market for domestic crockery by appealing to middle-class desires to emulate the rich and royal. His designs of special tea sets for the British queen, for Catherine the Great of Russia, and for leading aristocrats allowed him to advertise his wares as fashionable. By 1767, he claimed that his Queensware pottery had "spread over the whole Globe," and indeed by then his pottery was being marketed in France, Russia, Venice, the Ottoman Empire, and British North America.

■ **Neoclassical Style**

In this Georgian interior of Syon House on the outskirts of London, various neoclassical motifs are readily apparent: Greek columns, Greek-style statuary on top of the columns, and Roman-style mosaics in the floor. The Scottish architect Robert Adam created this room for the duke of Northumberland in the 1760s. Adam had spent four years in Italy and returned in 1758 to London to decorate homes in the "Adam style," meaning the neoclassical manner. (Fotomas Index, UK.)

This period also supported artistic styles other than neoclassicism. Frederick II of Prussia built himself a palace in the earlier rococo style, gave it a French name, *Sans-souci* ("worry-free"), and filled it with the works of French masters of the rococo. The new emphasis on emotion and family life was reflected in a growing taste for moralistic family scenes in painting. The paintings of Jean-Baptiste Greuze (1725–1805), much praised by Diderot, depicted ordinary families at moments of domestic crisis. Such subjects appealed in particular to the middle-class public, which now attended the official painting exhibitions in France that were held regularly every other year after 1737. Court painting nonetheless remained much in demand. Marie-Louise-Elizabeth Vigée-Lebrun (1755–1842), who painted portraits at the French court, reported that in the 1780s "it was difficult to get a place on my waiting list. . . . I was the fashion."

Although wealthy nobles still patronized Europe's leading musicians, music, too, began to reflect the broadening of the elite, and the spread of Enlightenment ideals as classical forms replaced the baroque style. Complex polyphony gave way to melody, which made music more accessible to the ordinary listener. Professional orchestras now played for large audiences of well-to-do listeners in sizable concert halls. The public concert gradually displaced the private recital, and a new attitude toward "the classics" developed: for the first time in the 1770s and 1780s, concert groups began to play older music rather than simply playing the latest commissioned works. This laid the foundation for what we still call *classical* music today, that is, a repertory of the greatest music of the eighteenth and early nineteenth centuries. Because composers now created works that would be performed over and over again as part of a classical repertory, rather than occasional pieces for the court

628 CHAPTER 15 • THE PROMISE OF ENLIGHTENMENT

or noble patrons, they deliberately attempted to write lasting works. As a result, the major composers began to produce fewer symphonies: the Austrian composer Franz Joseph Haydn (1732–1809) wrote more than one hundred symphonies, but his successor Ludwig van Beethoven (1770–1827) would create only nine.

The two supreme masters of the new musical style of the eighteenth century show that the transition from noble patronage to classical concerts was far from complete. The Austrians Haydn and Wolfgang Amadeus Mozart (1756–1791) both wrote for noble patrons, but by the early 1800s their compositions had been incorporated into the canon of concert classics all over Europe. Incredibly prolific, both excelled in combining lightness, clarity, and profound emotion. Both also wrote numerous Italian operas, a genre whose popularity continued to grow: in the 1780s, the Papal States alone boasted forty opera houses. Haydn spent most of his career working for a Hungarian noble family, the Eszterházys. Asked why he had written no string quintets (at which Mozart excelled), he responded simply: "No one has ordered any."

Interest in reading, like attending public concerts, took hold of the middle classes. Shaped by coffeehouses, Masonic lodges, and public concerts more than by formal schooling, the new reading public fed a frenzied increase in publication. By the end of the eighteenth century, six times as many books were being published in the German states, for instance, as at the beginning. One Parisian author commented that "people are certainly reading ten times as much in Paris as they did a hundred years ago." Provincial towns in Britain, France, the Dutch Republic, and the German states published their own newspapers; by 1780, thirty-seven English towns had local newspapers. Newspapers advertised arithmetic, dancing, and drawing lessons—and abortifacients and cures for venereal disease. Lending libraries multiplied, and, in England especially, even small villages housed secular book clubs. Women benefited as much as men from the spread of print. As one Englishman observed, "By far the greatest part of ladies now have a taste for books."

The novel had become a respectable and influential genre. Among the most widely read novels were those of the English printer and writer Samuel Richardson (1689–1761). In *Clarissa Harlowe* (1747–1748), a long novel in eight volumes, Richardson tells the story of a young woman from a heartless upper-class family who is torn between her family's choice of a repulsive suitor and her attraction to Lovelace, an aristocratic rake. Although she runs off with Lovelace to escape her family, she resists his advances; after being drugged and raped by Lovelace—despite the frantic pleas of readers of the first volumes to spare her—Clarissa dies of what can only be called a broken heart. One woman complained to Richardson, "I verily believe I have shed a pint of tears, and my heart is still bursting." Richardson claimed that he wrote *Clarissa* as a kind of manual of virtuous female conduct, yet critics nonetheless worried that novels undermined morals with their portrayals of low-life characters, the seductions of virtuous women, and other examples of immoral behavior.

Although he himself grew up reading novels with his father, Rousseau discouraged novel reading in *Émile*. Still, he helped change attitudes in the new elite toward children by offering an educational approach for gently drawing the best out of children rather than repressing their natural curiosity and love of learning. Paintings now showed individual children playing at their favorite activities rather than formally posed with their families. Books about and for children became popular. *The Newtonian System of the Universe Digested for Young Minds*, by "Tom Telescope," was published in Britain in 1761 and reprinted many times. Children's toys, jigsaw puzzles, and clothing designed for children all appeared for the first time in the 1700s. At the same time, however, the Enlightenment's emphasis on reason, self-control, and childhood innocence made parents increasingly anxious about their children's sexuality. Moralists and physicians wrote books about the evils of masturbation, "proving" that it led to physical and mental degeneration and even madness. One English writer linked masturbation to debility of body and of mind; infertility; epilepsy; loss of memory, sight, and hearing; distortions of the eyes, mouth, and face; a pale, sallow, and bluish complexion; wasting of the limbs; idiotism; and death itself. While the Enlightenment thus encouraged excessive concern about children being left to their own devices, it nevertheless taught the middle and upper classes to value their children and to expect their improvement through education.

Life on the Margins

Even more than worrying about their children, the upper and middle classes worried about the increasing numbers of poor people. Although booming foreign trade—French colonial trade, for example, increased tenfold in the 1700s—fueled a dramatic economic expansion, the results did not necessarily trickle all the way down the social scale. The population of Europe grew by nearly 30 percent, with especially striking gains in England, Ireland, Prussia, and Hungary. (See "Taking Measure," page 630.) Even though food production increased, shortages and crises still occurred periodically. Prices went up in many countries after the 1730s and continued to rise gradually until the early nineteenth century; wages in many trades rose as well, but less quickly than prices. Peasants who produced surpluses to sell in local markets and shopkeepers and artisans who could increase their sales to meet growing demand prospered. But those at the bottom of the social ladder—day laborers in the cities and peasants with small holdings—lived on the edge of dire poverty, and when they lost their land or work, they either migrated to the cities or wandered the roads in search of food and work. In France alone, 200,000 workers left their homes every year in search of seasonal employment elsewhere. At least 10 percent of Europe's urban population depended on some form of charity.

The growing numbers of poor people overwhelmed local governments and created fears about rising crime. In some countries, beggars and vagabonds had been locked up in workhouses since the mid-1600s. The expenses for running these

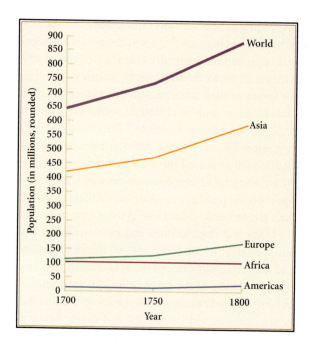

■ TAKING MEASURE
**World Population Growth,
1700–1800**

*Asia had many more people than
Europe, and both Asia and Europe were growing much more
rapidly in the 1700s than Africa
or the Americas. The population
stagnation in Africa has been the
subject of much scholarly controversy. What are the advantages of
a growing population? What are
the disadvantages?*
(Adapted from Andre Gundar Frank,
Reorient: Global Economy in the Asian Age
[Berkeley: University of California Press,
1998].)

overcrowded institutions increased 60 percent in England between 1760 and 1785.
After 1740, most German towns created workhouses that were part workshop, part
hospital, and part prison. Such institutions also appeared for the first time in Boston,
New York, and Philadelphia. To supplement the inadequate system of religious charity, offices for the poor, public workshops, and workhouse-hospitals, the French government created *dépôts de mendicité*, or beggar houses, in 1767. The government sent
people to these new workhouses to labor in manufacturing, but most were too weak
or sick to work, and 20 percent of them died within a few months of incarceration.

Those who were able to work or keep their land fared better: an increase in literacy, especially in the cities, allowed some lower-class people to participate in new
tastes and ideas. One French observer insisted, "These days, you see a waiting-maid
in her backroom, a lackey in an ante-room reading pamphlets. People can read in
almost all classes of society."◆ In France, however, only 50 percent of men and
27 percent of women could read and write in the 1780s (although that was twice
the rate of a century earlier). Literacy rates were higher in England and the Dutch
Republic, much lower in eastern Europe. About one in four Parisians owned books,
but the lower classes overwhelmingly read religious books, as they had in the past.

Whereas the new elite might attend salons, concerts, or art exhibitions, peasants
enjoyed their traditional forms of popular entertainment, such as fairs and festi-

---

◆ For a primary source that shows the impact of Enlightenment ideas on one French artisan, see Document
48, Jacques-Louis Ménétra, *Journal of My Life*.

vals, and the urban lower classes relaxed in cabarets and taverns. Sometimes pleasures were cruel. In Britain, bullbaiting, bearbaiting, dogfighting, and cockfighting were all common forms of entertainment that provided opportunities for organized gambling. Even "gentle" sports frequented by the upper classes had their violent side, showing that the upper classes had not become so different as they sometimes thought. Cricket matches, whose rules were first laid down in 1744, were often accompanied by brawls among fans (not unlike soccer matches today, though on a much smaller scale). Many Englishmen enjoyed what one observer called a "battle royal with sticks, pebbles and hog's dung."

As population increased and villagers began to move to cities to better their prospects, sexual behavior changed, too. The rates of births out of wedlock soared, from less than 5 percent of all births in the seventeenth century to nearly 20 percent at the end of the eighteenth. Historians have disagreed about the causes and meaning of this change. Some detect in this pattern a sign of sexual liberation and the beginnings of a modern sexual revolution: as women moved out of the control of their families, they began to seek their own sexual fulfillment. Others view this change more bleakly, as a story of seduction and betrayal: family and community pressure had once forced a man to marry a woman pregnant with his child, but now a man could abandon a pregnant lover by simply moving away.

Increased mobility brought freedom for some women, but it also aggravated the vulnerability of those newly arrived in cities from the countryside. Desperation, not reason, often ruled their choices. Women who came to the city as domestic servants had little recourse against masters or fellow servants who seduced or raped them. The result was a startling rise in abandoned babies. Most European cities established foundling hospitals in the 1700s, but infant and child mortality was 50 percent higher in such institutions than for children brought up at home. Some women tried herbs, laxatives, or crude surgical means of abortion; a few, usually servants who would lose their jobs if their employers discovered they had borne a child, resorted to infanticide. Reformers criticized the harshness of laws against infanticide, but they showed no mercy for "sodomites" (as male homosexuals were called), who in some places, in particular the Dutch Republic, were systematically persecuted and imprisoned or even executed. Male homosexuals attracted the attention of authorities because they had begun to develop networks and special meeting places. The stereotype of the effeminate, exclusively homosexual male seems to have appeared for the first time in the eighteenth century, perhaps as part of a growing emphasis on separate roles for men and women.

Roots of Industrialization

Although it was only starting to take hold, industrialization would eventually transform European society. The process began in England in the 1770s and 1780s and included four interlocking trends: (1) population increased dramatically, by more than 50 percent in England in the second half of the eighteenth century;

(2) manufacturers introduced steam-driven machinery to increase output; (3) they established factories to concentrate the labor of their workers; and (4) the production of cotton goods, which were lighter and more versatile than woolens, increased tenfold. Together these factors sparked the Industrial Revolution, which would change the face of Europe—indeed, of the entire world—in the nineteenth century.

Innovations in the technology of cotton production permitted manufacturers to make use of the growing supply of raw cotton shipped from the plantations of North America and the Caribbean. In 1733, the Englishman John Kay patented the flying shuttle, which weavers operated by pulling a cord that drove the shuttle to either side, enabling them to "throw" yarn across the loom rather than draw it back and forth by hand. When the flying shuttle came into widespread use in the 1760s, weavers began producing cloth more quickly than spinners could produce the thread. The shortage of spun thread propelled the invention of machines to speed the process of spinning: the spinning jenny and the water frame (a power-driven spinning machine) were introduced in the 1760s. In the following decades, water frames replaced thousands of women hand-spinning thread at home. In 1776, the Scottish engineer James Watt developed an improved steam engine, and, in the 1780s, Edmund Cartwright, an English clergyman and inventor, designed a mechanized loom, which when perfected could be run by a small boy and yield fifteen times the output of a skilled adult weaver working a handloom. By the end of the century, all the new power machinery was assembled in large factories that hired semiskilled men, women, and children to replace skilled weavers.

■ Handloom Weaving

This plate from the Encyclopedia *demonstrates handloom weaving of gold-threaded fabrics (tassels, trims, fringes, borders). Fancy threads could not be used on the early mechanical looms, which were suitable only for basic cotton thread. This kind of handloom weaving continued well into the 1800s.* (Stock Montage, Inc.)

Historians have no single explanation for why England led the Industrial Revolution. Some have emphasized England's large internal market, increasing population, supply of private investment capital from overseas trade and commercial profits, or natural resources such as coal and iron. Others have cited England's greater opportunities for social mobility, its relative political stability in the eighteenth century, or the pragmatism of the English and Scottish inventors who designed the necessary machinery. These early industrialists hardly had a monopoly on ingenuity, but they did come out of a tradition of independent capitalist enterprise. They also shared a culture of informal scientific education through learned societies and popular lectures (one of the prominent forms of the Enlightenment in Britain). For whatever reasons, the combination of improvements in agricultural production, growth in population and foreign trade, and willingness to invest in new machines and factories appeared first in this relatively small island.

Although the rest of Europe did not industrialize until the nineteenth century, textile manufacturing—long a linchpin in the European economy—expanded dramatically in the eighteenth century even without the introduction of new machines and factories. Textile production increased because of the spread of the "putting-out" or "domestic" system. Hundreds of thousands of families manufactured cloth in every country from Britain to Russia. Under the putting-out system, manufacturers supplied the families with raw materials, such as woolen or cotton fibers. Working at home in a dimly lit room, a whole family labored together. The mother and her children washed the fibers and carded and combed them. Then the mother and oldest daughters spun them into thread. The father, assisted by the children, wove the cloth. The cloth was then finished (bleached, dyed, smoothed, and so on) under the supervision of the manufacturer in a large workshop, located either in town or in the countryside. This system had existed in the textile industry for hundreds of years, but in the eighteenth century it expanded immensely, drawing in thousands of peasants in the countryside, and it included not only textiles but also the manufacture of such products as glassware, baskets, nails, and guns. The spread of the domestic system of manufacturing is sometimes called *proto-industrialization* to signify that the process helped pave the way for the full-scale Industrial Revolution.

All across Europe, thousands of people who worked in agriculture became part-time or full-time textile workers. Peasants turned to putting-out work because they did not have enough land to support their families. Men labored off-season and women often worked year-round to augment their meager incomes. At the same time, population growth and general economic improvement meant that demand for cloth increased because more people could afford it. Studies of wills left by working-class men and women in Paris at the end of the eighteenth century show that people owned more clothes of greater variety. Working-class men in Paris began to wear underclothes, something rare at the beginning of the century. Men and women now bought nightclothes; before, Europeans had slept naked except in cold weather. And white, red, blue, yellow, green, and even pastel shades of cotton now replaced the black, gray, or brown of traditional woolen dress.

State Power in an Era of Reform

All rulers recognized that manufacturing created new sources of wealth, but the start of industrialization had not yet altered the standard forms of competition between states: commerce and war. The diffusion of Enlightenment ideas of reform had a more immediate impact on the ways European monarchs exercised power than did industrialization. Historians label many of the sovereigns of this time "enlightened despots" or "enlightened absolutists," for they aimed to combine Enlightenment reforms with absolutist powers. Implementation of reforms, such as improvements in the peasantry's condition in Austria, freer markets for grain in France, extension of education in Russia, and new law codes in almost every country, were directly affected by the success or failure in the competition for trade and territory. French losses in the Seven Years' War, for example, prompted the French crown to introduce far-reaching reforms that provoked violent resistance and helped pave the way for the French Revolution of 1789. Reform proved to be a two-edged sword.

War and Diplomacy

Europeans no longer fought devastating wars over religion that killed hundreds of thousands of civilians; instead, professional armies and navies battled for control of overseas empires and for dominance on the European continent. Rulers continued to expand their armies: the Prussian army, for example, nearly tripled in size between 1740 and 1789. Widespread use of flintlock muskets required deployment in long lines, usually three men deep, with each line in turn loading and firing on command. Military strategy became cautious and calculating, but this did not prevent the outbreak of hostilities. The instability of the European balance of power resulted in two major wars, a diplomatic reversal of alliances, and the partition of Poland-Lithuania among Russia, Austria, and Prussia.

The War of the Austrian Succession (1740–1748) broke out when Holy Roman Emperor Charles VI died in 1740 without a male heir. Most European rulers recognized the emperor's chosen heiress, his daughter Maria Theresa, because Charles's Pragmatic Sanction of 1713 had given a woman the right to inherit the Habsburg crown lands. The new king of Prussia, Frederick II, who had just succeeded his father a few months earlier in 1740, saw his chance to grab territory and immediately invaded the rich Austrian province of Silesia. France joined Prussia in an attempt to further humiliate its traditional enemy Austria, and Great Britain allied with Austria to prevent the French from taking the Austrian Netherlands (Map 15.1). The war soon expanded to the overseas colonies of Great Britain and France as well. French and British colonials in North America fought each other all along their boundaries, enlisting Native American auxiliaries. Britain tried but failed to isolate the French Caribbean colonies during the war, and hostilities broke out in India, too.

■ MAP 15.1　The War of the Austrian Succession, 1740–1748

The accession of a twenty-three-year-old woman, Maria Theresa, to the Austrian throne gave the new king of Prussia, Frederick II, an opportunity to invade the province of Silesia. France joined on Prussia's side, Great Britain on Austria's. In 1745, the French defeated the British in the Austrian Netherlands and helped instigate a Jacobite uprising in Scotland. The rebellion failed, and British attacks on French overseas shipping forced the French to negotiate. The peace treaties guaranteed Frederick's conquest of Silesia, which soon became the wealthiest province of Prussia. France came to terms with Great Britain to protect its overseas possessions; Austria had to accept the peace settlement after a formal public protest.

www.bedfordstmartins.com/huntconcise　See the ONLINE STUDY GUIDE for more help in analyzing this map.

Maria Theresa (r. 1740–1780) survived only by conceding Silesia to Prussia in order to split the Prussians off from France. The Peace of Aix-la-Chapelle of 1748 recognized Maria Theresa as the heiress to the Austrian lands, and her husband, Francis I, became Holy Roman Emperor, thus reasserting the integrity of the Austrian Empire. The peace of 1748 failed to resolve the colonial conflicts between Britain and France, and fighting for domination continued unofficially.

In 1756, a major reversal of alliances—what historians call the "Diplomatic Revolution"—reshaped relations among the great powers. Prussia and Great Britain signed a defensive alliance, prompting Austria to overlook two centuries of hostility and ally with France. Russia and Sweden soon joined the Franco-Austrian alliance. When Frederick II invaded Saxony, an ally of Austria, with his bigger and better-disciplined army, the long-simmering hostilities between Great Britain and France over colonial boundaries flared into a general war that became known as the Seven Years' War (1756–1763).

Fighting soon raged around the world (Map 15.2). The French and British battled on land and sea in North America (where the conflict was called the French and Indian War), the West Indies, and India. The two coalitions also fought each other in central Europe. At first, in 1757, Frederick the Great surprised Europe with a spectacular victory at Rossbach in Saxony over a much larger Franco-Austrian army. But in time, Russian and Austrian armies encircled his troops. Frederick despaired: "I believe all is lost. I will not survive the ruin of my country." A fluke of history saved him. Empress Elizabeth of Russia (r. 1741–1762) died and was succeeded by the mentally unstable Peter III, a fanatical admirer of Frederick and things Prussian. Peter withdrew Russia from the war. (This was practically his only accomplishment as tsar. He was soon mysteriously murdered, probably at the instigation of his wife, Catherine the Great.) In a separate peace treaty, Frederick kept all his territory, including Silesia.

The Anglo-French overseas conflicts ended more decisively than the continental land wars. British naval superiority, fully achieved only in the 1750s, enabled Great Britain to rout the French in North America, India, and the West Indies. In the Treaty of Paris of 1763, France ceded Canada to Great Britain and agreed to remove its armies from India, in exchange for keeping its rich West Indian islands. Eagerness to avenge this defeat would motivate France to support the British North American colonists in their War of Independence just fifteen years later.

Although Prussia suffered great losses in the Seven Years' War—some 160,000 Prussian soldiers died either in action or of disease—the army helped vault Prussia to the rank of leading powers. In 1733, Frederick II's father, Frederick William I, had instituted the "canton system," which enrolled peasant youths in each canton (or district) in the army, gave them two or three months of training annually, and allowed them to return to their family farms the rest of the year. They remained "cantonists" (reservists) as long as they were able-bodied. In this fashion, the Prussian military steadily grew in size; by 1740, Prussia had the third or fourth largest army in Europe even though it was tenth in population and thirteenth in land area. Under Frederick II, Prussia's military expenditures rose to two-thirds of the state's revenue. Almost every nobleman served in the army, paying for his own support as an officer and buying a position as company commander. Once retired, the officers returned to their estates, coordinated the canton system, and served as

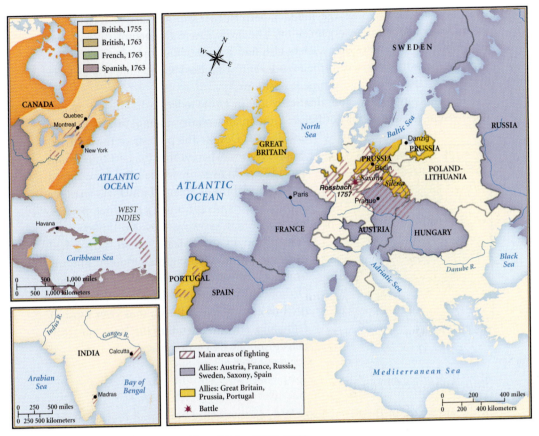

■ MAP 15.2 The Seven Years' War, 1756–1763

In what might justly be called the first worldwide war, the French and British fought each other on the European continent, in the West Indies, and in India. Their international struggle coincided with a realignment of forces within Europe caused by the desire of Austria, France, and Russia to check Prussian growth. Fearing, with reason, a joint Austrian-Russian attack, Frederick II of Prussia invaded Saxony in August 1756. Despite overwhelming odds, Frederick managed time and again to emerge victorious, until the Russians withdrew and the coalition against Prussia fell apart. The treaty between Austria and Prussia simply restored the status quo. The changes overseas were much more dramatic. Britain gained control over Canada and India but gave back to France the West Indian islands of Guadeloupe and Martinique. Britain was now the dominant power on the seas.

www.bedfordstmartins.com/huntconcise   See the ONLINE STUDY GUIDE for more help in analyzing this map.

local officials. In this way, the military permeated every aspect of rural society, fusing army and agrarian organization. The army gave the state great power, but the militarization of Prussian society also had a profoundly conservative effect: it kept the peasants enserfed to their lords, and it blocked the middle classes from access to estates or high government positions.◆

Prussia's power grew so dramatically that in 1772 Frederick the Great proposed the division of large chunks of Polish-Lithuanian territory among Austria, Prussia,

The First Partition of Poland, 1772

and Russia. Despite the protests of the Austrian empress Maria Theresa that the partition would spread "a stain over my whole reign," she agreed to split one-third of Poland-Lithuania's territory and half of its people among the three powers. Austria feared growing Russian influence in Poland and in the Balkans, where Russia had been successfully battling the Ottoman Empire. Conflicts between Catholics, Protestants, and Orthodox Christians in Poland were used to justify this cynical move. Russia took over most of Lithuania, effectively ending the large but weak Polish-Lithuanian commonwealth.

State-Sponsored Reform

In the aftermath of the Seven Years' War, all the belligerents faced pressing needs for more money to fund their growing armies, to organize navies to wage overseas conflicts, and to counter the impact of inflation. To make tax increases more palatable to public opinion, rulers appointed reform-minded ministers and gave them a mandate to modernize government. As one adviser to Joseph II put it, "A properly constituted state must be exactly analogous to a machine . . . and the ruler must be the foreman, the mainspring . . . which sets everything else in motion." Such reforms always threatened the interests of traditional groups, however, and the spread of Enlightenment ideas aroused sometimes unpredictable desires for more change.

Legal reform, both of the judicial system and of the often disorganized and irregular law codes, was central to the work of many reform-minded monarchs. Although Frederick II favored all things French in culture—he insisted on speaking French in his court and prided himself on his personal friendship with Voltaire—he made Prussian justice the envy of Europe. His institution of a uniform civil justice system created the most consistently administered laws and efficient

---

◆ For a primary source that outlines Frederick's political philosophy, see Document 49, Frederick II, "Political Testament."

■ **Dividing Poland, 1772**

In this contemporary depiction, Catherine the Great, Joseph II, and Frederick II point on the map to the portion of Poland-Lithuania each plans to take. The artist makes it clear that Poland's fate rested in the hands of neighboring rulers, not its own people. (Mansell/Time, Inc.)

judiciary of the time. Joseph II of Austria (r. 1780–1790) also ordered the compilation of a unified law code, a project that required many years for completion. Catherine II of Russia began such an undertaking even more ambitiously. In 1767, she called together a legislative commission of 564 deputies and asked them to consider a long document called the *Instruction*, which represented her hopes for legal reform based on the ideas of Montesquieu and the Italian writer Cesare Beccaria. Montesquieu had insisted that punishment should fit the crime; he criticized the use of torture and brutal corporal punishment. In his influential book *On Crimes and Punishments* (1764), Beccaria argued that laws should be printed for everyone to read and administered in rational procedures, that torture should be abolished as inhumane, and that the accused should be presumed innocent until proven guilty. Despite much discussion and hundreds of petitions and documents about local problems, little came of Catherine's commission because the monarch herself—despite her regard for Voltaire and his fellow philosophes—proved ultimately unwilling to see through far-reaching legal reform.

Rulers everywhere wanted more control over church affairs, and they used Enlightenment criticisms of the organized churches to get their way. In Catholic countries, many government officials resented the influence of the Jesuits, the major Catholic teaching order. The Jesuits trained the Catholic intellectual elite, ran a worldwide missionary network, enjoyed close ties to the papacy, and amassed great wealth. Critics mounted campaigns against the Jesuits in many countries, and by the early 1770s the Society of Jesus had been dissolved in Portugal, France, and Spain. In 1773, Pope Clement XIV (r. 1769–1774) agreed under pressure to disband the order, an edict that held until a reinvigorated papacy restored the society in 1814. Joseph II of Austria not only applauded the suppression of the Jesuits but also required Austrian bishops to swear fidelity and submission to him. Under Joseph, the Austrian state supervised seminaries, reorganized diocesan boundaries, abolished contemplative monastic orders, and confiscated their property to pay for education and poor relief.

Enlightened absolutists also tried to gain greater state authority over education, even while extending education to the lower classes. Joseph II launched the most ambitious educational reforms of the period. In 1774, once the Jesuits had been disbanded, a General School Ordinance in Austria ordered state subsidies for local schools, which the state would regulate. By 1789, one-quarter of the school-age children attended school. In Prussia, the school code of 1763 required all children between the ages of five and thirteen to attend school. Although not enforced uniformly, the Prussian law demonstrated Frederick II's belief that modernization depended on education. Catherine II of Russia also tried to expand elementary education—and the education of women in particular—and founded engineering schools.

No ruler pushed the principle of religious toleration as far as Joseph II of Austria, who became Holy Roman Emperor and co-regent with his mother, Maria Theresa, in 1765 and then ruled alone after 1780. In 1781, he granted freedom of religious worship to Protestants, Orthodox Christians, and Jews. For the first time these groups were allowed to own property, build schools, enter the professions, and hold political and military offices. The efforts of other rulers to extend religious toleration proved more limited. Louis XVI signed an edict in 1787 restoring French Protestants' civil rights—but still they could not hold political office. Great Britain continued to deny Catholics freedom of open worship and the right to sit in Parliament. Most European states limited the rights and opportunities available to Jews. In Russia, only wealthy Jews could hold municipal office, and in the Papal States, the pope encouraged forced baptism. The leading philosophes opposed persecution of the Jews in theory but often treated them with undisguised contempt. Diderot's comment was all too typical: the Jews, he said, bore "all the defects peculiar to an ignorant and superstitious nation."

Limits of Reform

When enlightened absolutist leaders introduced reforms, they often faced resistance from groups threatened by the proposed changes. The most contentious area of reform was agricultural policy. Whereas Frederick II and Catherine II reinforced the authority of nobles over their serfs, Joseph II tried to remove the burdens of serfdom in the Habsburg lands. In 1781, he abolished the personal aspects of serfdom: serfs could now move freely, enter trades, or marry without their lords' permission. Joseph abolished the tithe to the church, shifted more of the tax burden to the nobility, and converted peasants' labor services into cash payments.

The Austrian nobility furiously resisted these far-reaching reforms. When Joseph died in 1790, his brother Leopold II had to revoke most reforms to appease the nobles. On his deathbed, Joseph recognized the futility of many of his efforts; as his epitaph he suggested, "Here lies Joseph II, who was unfortunate in all his enterprises." Prussia's Frederick II, like Joseph, encouraged such agricultural innovations as planting potatoes and turnips (new crops that could help feed a growing population), experimenting with cattle breeding, draining swamplands, and clearing forests. But Prussia's noble landlords, the Junkers, continued to expand their estates at the expense of poorer peasants, and Frederick did nothing to ameliorate serfdom except on his own domains.

Reforming ministers also tried to stimulate agricultural improvement in France. Unlike most other western European countries, France still had about 100,000 serfs; though their burdens weighed less heavily than those in eastern Europe, serfdom did not entirely disappear until 1789. A group of economists called the *physiocrats* urged the French government to deregulate the grain trade and make the tax system more equitable to encourage agricultural productivity. In the interest of establishing a free market, they also insisted that urban guilds be abolished because they prevented free entry into the trades. Their proposed reforms applied the Enlightenment emphasis on individual liberties to the economy; Adam Smith took up many of the physiocrats' ideas in his writing in favor of free markets. The French government heeded some of this advice and gave up its system of price controls on grain in 1763, but it had to reverse this decision in 1770 when grain shortages caused a famine.

French reform efforts did not end there. To break the power of the parlements (the thirteen high courts of law that had led the way in opposing royal efforts to increase and equalize taxation), Louis XV appointed a reform-minded chancellor who in 1770 replaced the parlements with courts in which the judges no longer owned their offices and thus could not sell them or pass them on as an inheritance. Justice would then be more impartial. Nevertheless, the judges of the displaced parlements aroused widespread opposition to what they portrayed as tyrannical royal policy. The furor calmed down only when Louis XV died in 1774 and his successor, Louis XVI (r. 1774–1792), yielded to aristocratic demands and restored the old parlements. Louis XV died one of the most despised kings in French history, resented both for his high-handed reforms and for his private vices. Underground pamphlets lampooned him, describing his final mistress, Madame Du Barry, as a prostitute who pandered to the elderly king's well-known taste for young girls. This often pornographic literature linked despotism to the supposedly excessive influence of women at court.

Louis XVI tried to carry out part of the program suggested by the physiocrats, and he chose one of their disciples, Jacques Turgot (1727–1781), as his chief minister. Turgot pushed through several edicts that again freed the grain trade, suppressed many guilds, converted the peasants' forced labor on roads into a money tax payable by all landowners, and reduced court expenses. He also began making plans to introduce a system of elected local assemblies, which would have made government much more representative. Faced with broad-based resistance led by the parlements and his own courtiers, as well as with riots against rising grain prices, Louis XVI dismissed Turgot, and one of the last possibilities to overhaul France's monarchy collapsed.

The failure of reform in France paradoxically reflected the power of Enlightenment ideas; everyone now endorsed Enlightenment ideals but used them for different ends. The nobles in the parlements blocked the French monarchy's reform efforts using the very same Enlightenment language spoken by the crown's ministers. But unlike Austria, the other great power that faced persistent aristocratic resistance to reform, France had a large middle-class public that was increasingly frustrated by the failure to institute social change, a failure that ultimately helped undermine the monarchy itself. Where Frederick II, Catherine II, and even Joseph II used reform to bolster the efficiency of absolutist government, attempts at change in France backfired. French kings found that their ambitious programs for reform succeeded only in arousing unrealistic hopes.

Rebellions against State Power

Although traditional forms of popular discontent had not disappeared, Enlightenment ideals and reforms changed the rules of the game in politics. Governments had become accountable for their actions to a much wider range of people than ever before. In Britain and France, ordinary people rioted when they perceived government as failing to protect them against food shortages. The growth of informed public opinion had its most dramatic consequences in the North American colonies, where a struggle over the British Parliament's right to tax turned into a full-scale war for independence. The American War of Independence showed that once put into practice, Enlightenment ideals could have revolutionary implications.

Food Riots and Peasant Uprisings

Population growth, inflation, and the extension of the market system put added pressure on the already beleaguered poorest classes of people. Seventeenth-century peasants and townspeople had rioted to protest new taxes. In the last half of the eighteenth century, the food supply became the focus of political and social conflict. Poor people living in the villages and the towns believed it was the government's responsibility to ensure that they had enough food, and many governments did stockpile grain to make up for the occasional bad harvest. At the same time, in keeping with Adam Smith's and the French physiocrats' free market proposals, governments wanted to allow grain prices to rise with market demand, because higher profits would motivate producers to increase the supply of food.

Free trade in grain meant selling to the highest bidder even if that bidder was a foreign merchant. In the short run, in times of scarcity, big landowners and farmers could make huge profits by selling grain outside their hometowns or villages. This practice enraged poor farmers, agricultural workers, and city wage workers, who could not afford the higher prices. Lacking the political means to affect policy, they could enforce their desire for old-fashioned price regulation only by rioting. Most did not pillage or steal grain but rather forced the sale of grain or flour at a "just" price and blocked the shipment of grain out of their villages to other markets. Women often led these "popular price fixings," as they were called in France, in desperate attempts to protect the food supply for their children.

Such food riots occurred regularly in Britain and France in the last half of the eighteenth century. One of the most turbulent was the so-called Flour War in France in 1775. Turgot's deregulation of the grain trade in 1774 caused prices to rise in several provincial cities. Rioting spread from there to the Paris region, where villagers attacked grain convoys heading to the capital city. Local officials often ordered merchants and bakers to sell at the price the rioters demanded, only to find themselves arrested by the central government for overriding free trade. The government brought in troops to restore order and introduced the death penalty for rioting.

Frustrations with serfdom and hopes for a miraculous transformation provoked the Pugachev rebellion in Russia beginning in 1773. An army deserter from the southeast frontier region, Emelian Pugachev (1742–1775) claimed to be Tsar Peter III, the dead husband of Catherine II. Pugachev's appearance seemed to confirm peasant hopes for a "redeemer tsar" who would save the people from oppression. He rallied around him Cossacks like himself who resented the loss of their old tribal independence. Now increasingly enserfed or forced to pay taxes and endure army service, these nomadic bands joined with other serfs, rebellious mineworkers, and Muslim minorities. Catherine dispatched a large army to squelch the uprising, but Pugachev eluded them and the fighting spread. Nearly three million people eventually participated, making this the largest single rebellion in the history of tsarist Russia. When

The Pugachev Rebellion, 1773

■ **Russian Peasants**

This engraving from the 1700s shows Russian peasants in their one-room hut. Two or more married brothers, their wives, children, and parents would share the space with poultry and livestock. Cooking took place in one corner, which was always diagonally across from the icon corner (left), where socializing took place. The fathers and younger men slept on benches, the rest of the family in the loft (right). In the winter, everyone slept near the oven. (Fotomas Index, UK.)

Pugachev urged the peasants to attack the nobility and seize their estates, hundreds of noble families perished. Foreign newspapers called it "the revolution in southern Russia" and offered fantastic stories about Pugachev's life history. Finally, the army captured the rebel leader and brought him in an iron cage to Moscow, where he was tortured and executed. In the aftermath, Catherine tightened the nobles' control over their serfs and harshly punished those who dared to criticize serfdom.

Public Opinion and Political Opposition

Peasant uprisings might briefly shake even a powerful monarchy, but the rise of public opinion as a force independent of court society caused more enduring changes in European politics. Across much of Europe and in the North American colonies, demands for broader political participation reflected Enlightenment notions about individual rights. Aristocratic bodies such as the French parlements, which had no legislative role like that of the British Parliament, insisted that the monarch consult them on the nation's affairs, and the new educated elite wanted more influence, too. Newspapers began to cover daily political affairs, and the public learned the basics of political life, despite the strict limits on political participation in most countries.

Monarchs turned to public opinion to seek support against aristocratic groups that opposed reform. Gustavus III of Sweden (r. 1771–1792) called himself "the first citizen of a free people" and promised to deliver the country from "insufferable aristocratic despotism." Shortly after coming to the throne, Gustavus proclaimed a new constitution that divided power between the king and the legislature, abolished the use of torture in the judicial process, and assured some freedom of the press.

In France, both the parlements and the monarch appealed to the public through the printed word. The crown hired writers to make its case; the magistrates of the parlements wrote their own rejoinders. French-language newspapers published in the Dutch Republic provided many people in France with detailed accounts of political news and also gave voice to pro-parlement positions. One of the new French-language newspapers printed inside France, *Le Journal des Dames* ("The Ladies' Journal"), was published by women and mixed short stories and reviews of books and plays with demands for more women's rights.

The Wilkes affair in Great Britain showed that public opinion could be mobilized to challenge a government. In 1763, during the reign of George III (r. 1760–1820), John Wilkes, a member of Parliament, attacked the government in his newspaper, *North Briton*, and sued the crown when he was arrested. He won his release as well as damages. When he was reelected, Parliament denied him his seat, not once but three times.

The Wilkes episode soon escalated into a major campaign against the corruption and social exclusiveness of Parliament, complaints the Levellers had first raised during the English Revolution of the late 1640s. Newspapers, magazines, pamphlets, handbills, and cheap editions of Wilkes's collected works all helped promote his cause. Those who could not vote demonstrated for Wilkes. In one incident, eleven people died when soldiers broke up a huge gathering of his supporters. The slogan "Wilkes and Liberty" appeared on walls all over London. Middle-class voters formed a Society of Supporters of the Bill of Rights, which circulated petitions for Wilkes; they gained the support of about one-fourth of all the voters. The more determined Wilkesites proposed sweeping reforms of Parliament, including more frequent elections, more representation for the counties, elimination of "rotten boroughs" (election districts so small that they could be controlled by one big patron), and restrictions of pensions used by the crown to gain support. These demands would be at the heart of agitation for parliamentary reform in Britain for decades to come.

Popular demonstrations did not always support reforms. In 1780, the Gordon riots devastated London. They were named after the fanatical anti-Catholic crusader Lord George Gordon, who helped organize huge marches and petition campaigns against a bill the House of Commons passed to grant limited toleration to Catholics. The demonstrations culminated in a seven-day riot that left fifty buildings destroyed and three hundred people dead. Despite the continuing limitation on voting rights in Great Britain, British politicians were learning that they could ignore public opinion only at their peril.

Political opposition also took artistic forms, particularly in countries where governments restricted organized political activity. A striking example of a play with a political message was *The Marriage of Figaro* (1784) by Pierre-Augustin Caron de Beaumarchais (1732–1799), a watchmaker, a judge, a gunrunner in the American War of Independence, and a French spy in Britain. *The Marriage of Figaro* was first a hit at court, when Queen Marie-Antoinette had it read for her friends. But when her husband, Louis XVI, read it, he forbade its production on the grounds that "this man mocks at everything that should be respected in government." When finally performed publicly, the play caused a sensation. The chief character, Figaro, is a clever servant who gets the better of his noble employer. When speaking of the count, he cries, "What have you done to deserve so many rewards? You went to the trouble of being born, and nothing more." Two years later, Mozart based an equally famous but somewhat tamer opera on Beaumarchais's story.

Revolution in North America

Oppositional forms of public opinion came to a head in Great Britain's North American colonies, where the result was American independence and the establishment of a republican constitution that stood in stark contrast to most European regimes. The successful revolution was the only blow to Britain's increasing dominance in world affairs in the eighteenth century, and as such it was another aspect of the power rivalries existing at that time. Yet many Europeans saw the American War of Independence, or the American Revolution (1775–1783), as a triumph for Enlightenment ideas. As one German writer exclaimed in 1777, American victory would give "greater scope to the Enlightenment, new keenness to the thinking of peoples and new life to the spirit of liberty."

The American revolutionary leaders had been influenced by a common Atlantic civilization; they participated in the Enlightenment and shared political ideas with the opposition Whigs in Britain. Supporters demonstrated for Wilkes in South Carolina and Boston, and the South Carolina legislature donated a substantial sum to the Society of Supporters of the Bill of Rights. In the 1760s and 1770s, both British and American opposition leaders became convinced that the British government was growing increasingly corrupt and despotic. British radicals wanted to reform Parliament so the voices of a broader, more representative segment of the population would be heard. The colonies had no representatives in Parliament, and colonists claimed that "no taxation without representation" should be allowed. Indeed, they denied that Parliament had any jurisdiction over the colonies, insisting that the king govern them through colonial legislatures and recognize their traditional British liberties. The failure of the "Wilkes and Liberty" campaign to produce concrete results convinced many Americans that Parliament was hopelessly tainted and that they would have to stand up for their rights as British subjects.

The British colonies remained loyal to the crown until Parliament's encroachment on their autonomy and the elimination of the French threat at the end of the Seven Years' War transformed colonial attitudes. Unconsciously, perhaps, the colonies had begun to form a separate nation; their economies generally flourished in the eighteenth century, and between 1750 and 1776 their population almost doubled. With the British clamoring for lower taxes and the colonists paying only a fraction of the tax rate levied on the Britons at home, Parliament passed new taxes, including the Stamp Act in 1765, which required a special tax stamp on all legal

■ **Overthrowing British Authority**
The uncompromising attitude of the British government went a long way toward dissolving long-standing loyalties to the home country. During the American War of Independence, residents of New York City pulled down the statue of the hated George III. (Lafayette College Art Collection, Easton, PA.)

IMPORTANT DATES

1740–1748	War of the Austrian Succession: France, Spain, and Prussia versus Austria and Great Britain	**1776**	American Declaration of Independence from Great Britain; James Watt improves the steam engine, making it suitable for new industrial projects; Adam Smith's *The Wealth of Nations*
1751–1772	*Encyclopedia* published in France		
1756–1763	Seven Years' War fought in Europe, India, and the American colonies	**1781**	Joseph II of Austria undertakes wide-reaching reform; Immanuel Kant's *The Critique of Pure Reason*
1762	Jean-Jacques Rousseau's *The Social Contract* and *Émile*		
1764	Voltaire's *Philosophical Dictionary*	**1785**	Catherine the Great's Charter of the Nobility grants nobles exclusive control over their serfs in exchange for subservience to the state
1770	Louis XV of France fails to break the power of the French law courts		
1772	First partition of Poland	**1787**	Delegates from the states draft a new United States Constitution
1773	Pugachev rebellion of Russian peasants		

documents and publications. After violent rioting in the colonies, the tax was repealed, but in 1773 a new Tea Act revived colonial resistance, which culminated in the so-called Boston Tea Party of 1773. Colonists dressed as Indians boarded British ships and dumped the imported tea (by this time an enormously popular beverage) into Boston's harbor. The British government tried to clamp down on the unrest, but British troops in the colonies soon found themselves fighting locally organized militias.

Political opposition in the American colonies turned belligerent when Britain threatened to use force to maintain control. In 1774, the First Continental Congress convened, composed of delegates from all the colonies, and unsuccessfully petitioned the crown for redress. The next year the Second Continental Congress organized an army with George Washington in command. After actual fighting had begun, in 1776, the congress proclaimed the Declaration of Independence. An eloquent statement of the American cause written by Thomas Jefferson, a delegate from Virginia, the Declaration of Independence was couched in the language of universal human rights, which enlightened Europeans could be expected to understand. George III denounced the American "traitors and rebels." But European newspapers enthusiastically reported on every American response to "the cruel acts of oppression they have been made to suffer." Two years after the Declaration was issued, France boosted the American cause by entering on the colonists' side in 1778. Spain, too, saw an opportunity to check the growing power of Britain, though without actually endorsing American independence out of fear of the response of its Latin American colonies. Spain declared war on Britain in 1779; in 1780, Great Britain declared war on the Dutch Republic in retaliation for Dutch support of the rebels. The worldwide conflict that resulted was more than Britain could handle. The American colonies achieved their independence in the peace treaty of 1783.

The newly independent states still faced the challenge of republican self-government. The Articles of Confederation, drawn up in 1777 as a provisional constitution, proved weak because they gave the central government few powers. In 1787, a constitutional convention met in Philadelphia to draft a new constitution. It established a two-house legislature, an indirectly elected president, and an independent judiciary. The Constitution's preamble insisted explicitly, for the first time in history, that government derived its power solely from the people and did not depend on divine right or on the tradition of royalty or aristocracy. The new educated elite of the eighteenth century had now created government based on a "social contract" among male, property-owning, white citizens. It was by no means a complete democracy, and women and slaves were excluded from political participation. But the new government represented a radical departure from European models. In 1791, a Bill of Rights was appended to the Constitution outlining the essential rights (such as freedom of speech) that the government could never overturn. Although slavery continued in the American republic, the new emphasis on rights helped fuel a movement for its abolition in both Britain and the United States.

Interest in the new republic was greatest in France. The United States Constitution and various state constitutions were published in French with commentary by leading thinkers. Even more important in the long run were the effects of the American war. Dutch losses to Great Britain aroused a widespread movement for political reform in the Dutch Republic, and debts incurred by France in supporting the American colonies would soon force the French monarchy to the edge of bankruptcy and then to revolution. Ultimately, the entire European system of royal rule would be challenged.

Conclusion

The American Revolution was the most profound practical result of the general European movement known as the Enlightenment. When Thomas Jefferson looked back many years later on the Declaration of Independence, he said he hoped it would be "the signal of arousing men to burst the chains under which monkish ignorance and superstition had persuaded them to bind themselves." What began

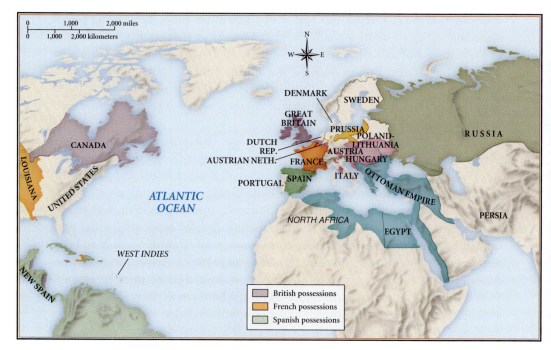

■ **MAPPING THE WEST Europe and the World, c. 1780**

Although Great Britain lost control over the British North American colonies, which became the new United States, European influence on the rest of the world grew dramatically in the eighteenth century. The slave trade linked European ports to African slave-trading outposts and to plantations in the Caribbean, South America, and North America. The European countries on the Atlantic Ocean benefited most from this trade. Yet almost all of Africa, China, Japan, and large parts of India still resisted European incursion, and the Ottoman Empire, with its massive territories, still towered over most European countries.

as a cosmopolitan movement of a few intellectuals in the first half of the eighteenth century reached a relatively wide audience among the educated elite of men and women. The spirit of reform swept from the salons and coffeehouses into the halls of government. Reasoned, scientific inquiry into the causes of social misery and laws defending individual rights and freedoms gained adherents everywhere.

For most Europeans, however, Enlightenment remained a promise rather than a reality. Rulers such as Catherine the Great had every intention of retaining their full, often unchecked, powers, even as they corresponded with leading philosophes, announced support for their causes, and entertained them at their courts. Moreover, would-be reformers often found themselves thwarted by the resistance of nobles, by the priorities rulers gave to waging wars, or by popular resistance to deregulation of trade that stripped away protection against the uncertainties of the market. Yet even the failure of reform contributed to the ferment in Europe after 1770. Peasant rebellions in eastern Europe, the "Wilkes and Liberty" campaign in Great Britain, the struggle over reform in France, and the revolution in America all occurred at about the same time, and their conjunction convinced many Europeans that the world was in fact changing. Just how much it had changed, and whether the change was for better or for worse, would become more evident in the next decades.

Suggested References for further reading and online research appear on page SR-23 at the back of the book.

www.bedfordstmartins.com/huntconcise   See the ONLINE STUDY GUIDE to assess your mastery of the material covered in this chapter.

The French Revolution and Napoleon

1789–1815

O N OCTOBER 5, 1789, A CROWD OF SEVERAL THOUSAND WOMEN marched in a drenching rain twelve miles from the center of Paris to Versailles. They demanded the king's help in securing more grain for the hungry and his reassurance that he did not intend to resist the emerging revolutionary movement. Joined by thousands of men who came from Paris to reinforce them, the next morning they broke into the royal family's private apartments. To prevent further bloodshed— two of the royal bodyguards had already been killed and their heads paraded on pikes—the king agreed to move his family and his government back to Paris. A dramatic procession guarded by thousands of ordinary men and women made its slow way back to Paris. The people's proud display of cannons and pikes underlined the fundamental transformation that was occurring. Ordinary people had forced the king of France to respond to their grievances. The French monarchy was in danger, and if such a powerful and long-lasting institution could come under fire, then could any monarch of Europe rest easy?

Although even the keenest political observer did not predict its eruption in 1789, the French Revolution had its immediate origins in a constitutional crisis provoked by a growing government deficit, traceable to French involvement in the American War of Independence. The constitutional crisis came to a head on July 14, 1789, when armed Parisians captured the Bastille, a royal fortress and symbol

■ **Fall of the Bastille**

The Bastille appears in all its imposing grandeur. The event depicted here is the surrender of the prison's governor, Bernard René de Launay. Because so many of the besieging citizens were killed (only one defender died), popular anger ran high, and de Launay became a sacrificial victim. As a hastily formed citizens' guard marched him off to city hall, crowds taunted and spat at him. When he lashed out at one of the men nearest him, he was immediately stabbed and shot. A pastry cook cut off the governor's head, which was promptly displayed as a trophy on a pike held high above the crowd. Royal authority had been successfully challenged and even humiliated.

(Château de Versailles, France/Bridgeman Art Library, NY.)

a Versaille a Versaille. du 5. Octobre 1789.

■ **Women's March to Versailles, October 5, 1789**

This anonymous engraving shows a crowd of armed women marching to Versailles to confront the king. The sight of armed women frightened many observers and demonstrated that the Revolution was not only men's affair. Notice the middle-class woman in a hat at the far left. She is obviously reluctant to join in but is being pulled along by the market women in their simple caps.
(Musée de la Ville de Paris/Musée Carnavalet, Paris/Giraudon/Art Resource, NY.)

of monarchical authority in the center of the capital. The fall of the Bastille, like the women's march to Versailles three months later, showed the determination of the common people to put their mark on events.

The French Revolution first grabbed the attention of the entire world because it seemed to promise universal human rights, constitutional government, and broad-based political participation. In the words of its most famous slogan, it pledged "Liberty, Equality, and Fraternity" for all. The revolutionaries used a blueprint based on the Enlightenment idea of reason to remake all of society and politics: they executed the king and queen, established a republic for the first time in French history, abolished nobility, and gave the vote to all adult men. Even as the Revolution promised democracy, however, it also inaugurated a cycle of violence and intimidation. When the revolutionaries encountered resistance to their programs, they set up a government of terror to compel obedience. Some historians therefore see in the French Revolution the origins of modern *totalitarianism*—that is, governments that try to control every aspect of life, including daily activities, while limiting all forms of political dissent.

The Revolution might have remained a strictly French affair if war had not involved the rest of Europe. After 1792, huge French republican armies, fueled by patriotic nationalism, marched across Europe, promising liberation from traditional monarchies but often delivering old-fashioned conquest and annexation. French victories spread revolutionary ideas far and wide, from the colonies in the Caribbean, where the first successful slave revolt established the republic of Haiti, to Poland and Egypt. The army's success ultimately undermined the republic and made possible the rise of Napoleon Bonaparte, a remarkable young general from Corsica, an island off Italy, who brought France more wars, more conquests, and a form of military dictatorship.

Bonaparte ended the French Revolution even while maintaining some of its most important innovations. He transformed France from a democratically elected republic to an empire with a new aristocracy based on military service. Although he tolerated no opposition at home, he prided himself on bringing French-style liberation to peoples elsewhere. Yet he also continued the revolutionary policy of conquest and annexation; by 1812, he ruled over an empire bigger than any Europe had seen since Roman times. Eventually, resistance to the French armies and the ever-mounting costs of military glory toppled Napoleon I, but not before he had established himself as an almost mythic figure. Reformer, revolutionary, dictator, and empire-builder: Napoleon played all the roles and has remained a figure of controversy right down to the present. The French Revolution produced many surprises; Napoleon Bonaparte was the most astonishing of them.

The Revolution of Rights and Reason

Between 1787 and 1789, revolts in the name of liberty broke out in the Dutch Republic, the Austrian Netherlands (present-day Belgium and Luxembourg), and Poland as well as in France. At the same time, the newly independent United States of America prepared a new federal constitution. Historians have sometimes referred to these revolts as the *Atlantic revolutions* because so many protest movements arose in countries on both shores of the North Atlantic in the late 1700s. These revolutions were the product of long-term prosperity and high expectations: Europeans in general were wealthier, healthier, more numerous, and better educated than they had ever been before; and the Dutch, Belgian, and French societies were among the wealthiest and best educated within Europe. Most scholars agree, however, that the French Revolution differed greatly from the others. Not only was France the richest, most powerful, and most populous state in western Europe, but its revolution was also more violent, longer lasting, and ultimately more influential.

Protesters in the Low Countries and Poland

Political protests in the Dutch Republic attracted European attention because Dutch banks still controlled a hefty portion of the world's capital at the end of the eighteenth century, even though the Dutch Republic's role in international politics had diminished. Government-sponsored Dutch banks owned 40 percent of the British national debt, and by 1796, they held the entire foreign debt of the United States. Relations with the British deteriorated during the American War of Independence, however, and by the middle of the 1780s, agitation in favor of the Americans had boiled over into an attack on the stadholder, the prince of Orange, who favored close ties with Great Britain and had kinglike powers.

Building on support among middle-class bankers, merchants, and writers who favored the American cause, the Dutch Patriots, as the protesters called themselves, soon gained a more popular audience by demanding political reforms and organizing armed citizen militias of men, called Free Corps. Parading under banners that read "Liberty or Death," they forced local officials to set up new elections to replace councils that had been packed with Orangist supporters through patronage or family connections. The future American president John Adams happened to be visiting Utrecht when such a revolt occurred. He wrote admiringly to Thomas Jefferson that "in no instance, of ancient or modern History, have the People ever asserted more unequivocally their own inherent and unalienable Sovereignty." In 1787, the Free Corps took on the troops of the prince of Orange and got the upper hand. In response, Frederick William II of Prussia, whose sister had married the stadholder, intervened with tacit British support. Thousands of Prussian troops soon occupied Utrecht and Amsterdam, and the House of Orange regained its former position.

Internal social divisions paved the way for successful outside intervention. Many of the Patriots from the richest merchant families feared the growing power of the Free Corps. The Free Corps wanted a more democratic form of government and encouraged the publication of pamphlets and cartoons attacking the prince and his wife, the rapid spread of clubs and societies made up of common people, and crowd-pleasing public ceremonies, such as parades and bonfires, which sometimes turned into riots. In the aftermath of the Prussian invasion in September 1787, the Orangists got their revenge: lower-class mobs pillaged the houses of prosperous Patriot leaders, forcing many to flee to the United States, France, or the Austrian Netherlands. Those Patriots who remained nursed their grievances until the French republican armies invaded in 1795.

The Austrian Netherlands experienced unrest, too. The Belgians of the ten provinces there might have remained tranquil if Austrian emperor Joseph II had not tried to introduce Enlightenment-inspired reforms. Joseph abolished torture, decreed toleration for Jews and Protestants (in this resolutely Catholic area), and suppressed monasteries. His reorganization of the administrative and judicial systems eliminated many offices that belonged to nobles and lawyers, sparking resistance among the upper classes in 1788. They claimed that they wanted only to defend historic local liberties against an overbearing government. Their resistance galvanized democrats, who wanted a more representative government and organized clubs to give voice to their demands. By late 1789, each province had separately declared its independence, and the Austrian administration had collapsed. Delegates from the various provinces declared themselves the United States of Belgium, a clear reference to the American precedent.

Once again, however, internal squabbling doomed the rebels. In the face of increasing democratic ferment, aristocratic leaders drew to their side the Catholic clergy and peasants, who had little sympathy for the democrats of the cities. Every Sunday in May and June 1790, thousands of peasant men and women, led by their priests, streamed into Brussels carrying crucifixes, nooses, and pitchforks to intimidate the democrats and defend the church. Faced with the choice between the Austrian emperor and "our current tyrants," the democrats chose to support the return of the Austrians under Emperor Leopold II (r. 1790–1792), who had succeeded his brother.

A reform party calling itself the Patriots also emerged in Poland, which had been shocked by the loss of a third of its territory in the First Partition of 1772. The Patriots sought to overhaul the weak commonwealth along modern western European lines and looked to King Stanislaw August Poniatowski (r. 1764–1795) to lead them. A nobleman who owed his crown to the dubious honor of being Catherine the Great's discarded lover but who was also a favorite correspondent of the Parisian salon hostess Madame Geoffrin, Poniatowski saw in moderate reform the only chance for his country to escape the consequences of a century's misgovernment and cultural decline. Ranged against the Patriots stood most of the aristocrats and the formidable Catherine the Great, determined to uphold imperial Russian influence.

Watchful but not displeased to see Russian influence waning in Poland, Austria and Prussia allowed the reform movement to proceed. In 1788, the Patriots got their golden chance. Bogged down in war with the Ottoman Turks, Catherine could not block the summoning of a reform-minded parliament, which with King Stanislaw's aid outmaneuvered the antireform aristocrats. Amid much oratory denouncing Russian overlordship, the parliament enacted the constitution of May 3, 1791, which established a hereditary monarchy with somewhat strengthened authority, at last freed the two-house legislature from the individual veto power of every aristocrat, granted townspeople limited political rights, and vaguely promised future Jewish emancipation. Abolishing serfdom was hardly mentioned. Modest though they were, the Polish reforms did not endure. Catherine II could not countenance the spread of revolution into eastern Europe and within a year engineered the downfall of the Patriots and further weakened the Polish state.

Origins of the French Revolution, 1787–1789

Many French enthusiastically greeted the American experiment in republican government and supported the Dutch, Belgian, and Polish patriots. But they did not expect the United States or the Dutch Republic to provide them a model. Montesquieu and Rousseau, the leading political theorists of the Enlightenment, taught that republics suited only small countries, not big ones like France. Moreover, the French monarchy on the surface seemed as strong as ever. After suffering humiliation at the hands of the British in the Seven Years' War (1756–1763), the French had regained international prestige by supporting the victorious Americans, and the monarchy had shown its eagerness to promote reforms. In 1787, for example, the French crown granted civil rights to Protestants. Yet by the late 1780s, the French monarchy faced a serious fiscal crisis caused by a mounting deficit. It soon provoked a constitutional crisis of epic proportions.

France's fiscal problems stemmed from its support of the Americans against the British in the American War of Independence. About half of the French national budget went to paying interest on the debt that had accumulated. In contrast to Great Britain, which had a national bank to help raise loans for the government, the French government lived off relatively short-term, high-interest loans from private sources including Swiss banks, government annuities, and advances from tax collectors. For years the French government had been trying unsuccessfully to modernize the tax system to make it more equitable. The peasants bore the greatest burden of taxes, whereas the nobles and clergy were largely exempt. Tax collection was also far from systematic: private contractors collected many taxes and pocketed a large share of the proceeds. With the growing support of public opinion, the bond and annuity holders from the middle and upper classes now demanded a clearer system of fiscal accountability.

Faced with a mounting deficit and growing criticism of Queen Marie-Antoinette's personal spending, Louis XVI (r. 1774–1792) tried every available avenue to raise funds. In 1787, he submitted proposals for reform to an Assembly of Notables, a group of handpicked nobles, clergymen, and officials. When it refused to cooperate, the king presented his proposals for a more uniform land tax to his old rival the parlement of Paris. When it too refused, he ordered the parlement judges into exile in the provinces. Overnight, the judges (members of the nobility because of the offices they held) became popular heroes for resisting the king's "tyranny"; in reality, however, the judges, like the notables, wanted reform only on their own terms. Louis finally gave in to demands that he call a meeting of the Estates General, which had last met 175 years before.

The calling of the Estates General electrified public opinion. Who would determine the fate of the nation? There were three estates, or orders, in the Estates General. The deputies in the First Estate represented some 100,000 clergy of the Catholic church, which owned about 10 percent of the land and collected its own taxes (the tithe) on peasants. The deputies of the Second Estate represented the nobility, about 400,000 men and women who owned about 25 percent of the land, enjoyed many tax exemptions, and collected seigneurial dues and rents from their peasant tenants. The deputies of the Third Estate represented everyone else, at least 95 percent of the nation. In 1614, at the last meeting of the Estates General, each order had voted separately, and either the clergy or the nobility could therefore veto

REVEIL DU TIERS ETAT.

Ma sainte, il étoit tems que je me réveillas, car l'oppression de mes fers me donnions le cochemar un peu trop fort.

■ The Third Estate Awakens

This print, produced after the fall of the Bastille (notice the two heads raised on pikes outside the prison), shows a clergyman (First Estate) and a nobleman (Second Estate) alarmed by the awakening of the commoners (Third Estate). The Third Estate breaks the chains of oppression and arms itself to battle for its rights. The message is that social conflicts lay behind the political struggles in the Estates General. (Musée Carnavalet/Photo Bulloz.)

www.bedfordstmartins.com/huntconcise   See the ONLINE STUDY GUIDE for more help in analyzing this image.

any decision of the Third Estate. Before the elections to the Estates General in 1789, the king agreed to double the number of deputies for the Third Estate (making them equal in number to the other two combined), but he left it to the Estates General to decide whether the estates would continue to vote separately by order rather than by individual head. Voting by order would conserve the traditional powers of the clergy and nobility; voting by head would give the Third Estate an advantage because many clergymen and even some nobles sympathized with the Third Estate.

As the state's censorship apparatus broke down, pamphleteers by the hundreds denounced the traditional privileges of the nobility and clergy and called for voting by head rather than by order. In the winter and spring of 1789, thousands of men (and a few women by proxy) held meetings to elect deputies and write down their grievances. The effect was immediate. Although educated men dominated the meetings at the regional level, the humblest peasants also voted in their villages and burst forth with complaints, especially about taxes. As one villager lamented, "The last crust of bread has been taken from us." The long series of meetings raised expectations that the Estates General would help the king to solve all the nation's ills.

These new hopes soared just at the moment France experienced an increasingly rare but always dangerous food shortage. (See "Taking Measure," below.) Bad weather damaged the harvest of 1788, causing bread prices to rise in many places in the spring and summer of 1789 and threatening starvation for the poorest people. A serious slump in textile production had been causing massive unemployment since 1786. Hundreds of thousands of textile workers were out of work and hungry, adding another volatile element to an already tense situation.

When some twelve hundred deputies journeyed to the king's palace of Versailles for the opening of the Estates General in May 1789, many readers avidly followed the developments in newspapers that sprouted overnight. Although most nobles insisted on voting by order, the deputies of the Third Estate refused to proceed on that basis. After six weeks of stalemate, on June 17, 1789, the deputies of the Third Estate took unilateral action and declared themselves and whoever would join them the "National Assembly," in which each deputy would vote as an individual. Two days later, the clergy voted by a narrow margin to join them. Barred from their meeting hall on June 20, the deputies met on a nearby tennis court and swore an oath not to disband until they had given France a constitution that reflected their newly declared authority. This "tennis court oath" expressed the determination of the Third Estate to carry through a constitutional revolution.

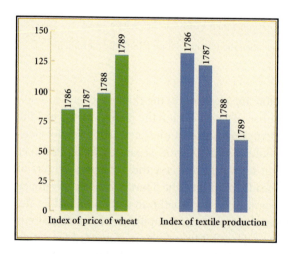

■ **TAKING MEASURE**
Wheat Prices and Textile Production in France, 1786–1789
This chart, comparing yearly averages against an index set at 100 (based on the average of all four years), shows the dramatic change over time in wheat prices and textile production.
The price of wheat steadily increased in the years just prior to the French Revolution, while the production of textiles dramatically declined. What would be the consequences of this movement in opposite directions? Which groups in the French population would be especially at risk?
(From Ernest Labrousse et al., *Historie économique et sociale de la France* [Paris: Presses Universitaires de France, 1970], 553.)

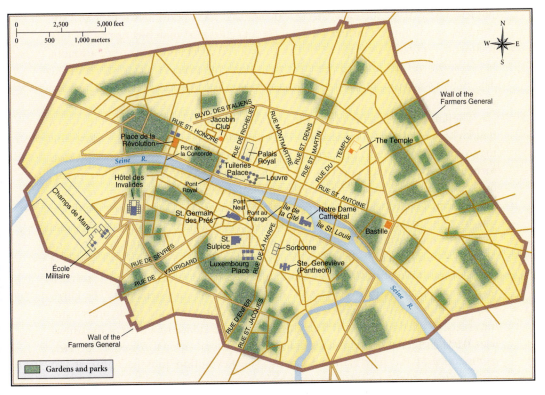

■ **MAP 16.1 Revolutionary Paris, 1789**

The French Revolution began with the fall of the Bastille on July 14, 1789. The huge fortified prison was located in a working-class neighborhood on the eastern side of the city. Before attacking the Bastille, crowds had torn down many of the customs booths located in the wall of the Farmers General (the private company in charge of tax collection) and had taken the weapons stored in the Hôtel des Invalides, a veterans' hospital on the western side of the city where the upper classes lived. In other words, the crowds had roamed throughout the city.

www.bedfordstmartins.com/huntconcise   See the ONLINE STUDY GUIDE for more help in analyzing this map.

At first Louis appeared to agree to the new representative assembly, but he also ordered thousands of soldiers to march to Paris. The deputies who supported the new National Assembly feared a plot by the king and high-ranking nobles to arrest them and disperse the assembly. "Everyone is convinced that the approach of the troops covers some violent design," one deputy wrote home. Their fears were confirmed when on July 11 the king fired Jacques Necker, the Swiss Protestant finance minister and the one high official regarded as sympathetic to the deputies' cause.

The popular reaction in Paris to Necker's dismissal and the threat of military force changed the course of the French Revolution. When the news spread, the common people in Paris began to arm themselves and attack places where either grain or arms were thought to be stored (Map 16.1). A deputy in Versailles reported home: "Today all of the evils overwhelm France, and we are between despotism, carnage, and famine." On July 14, 1789, an armed crowd marched on the Bastille, the fortified prison (see page 653) that symbolized royal authority. After a chaotic battle in which one hundred armed citizens died, the prison officials surrendered. The angry crowd shot and stabbed the governor of the prison and flaunted his head on a pike.

The fall of the Bastille (an event now commemorated as the French national holiday) set an important precedent. The common people showed themselves willing to intervene violently at a crucial political moment. All over France, food riots turned into local revolts. Local governments were forced out of power and replaced by committees of "patriots" loyal to the revolutionary cause. The patriots relied on newly formed National Guard units composed of civilians. One of their first duties was to calm the peasants in the countryside, who feared that the beggars and vagrants crowding the roads might be part of an aristocratic plot to starve the people by burning crops or barns. In some places, the Great Fear (the term used by historians to describe this rural panic) turned into peasant attacks on aristocrats or on seigneurial records of peasants' dues kept in the lord's château. The king's government began to crumble. One of Louis XVI's brothers and many other leading aristocrats fled into exile. In Paris, the marquis de Lafayette, a hero of the American War of Independence and a noble deputy in the National Assembly, became commander of the new National Guard. The Revolution thus had its first heroes, its first victims, and its first enemies.

From Monarchy to Republic

Until July 1789, the French Revolution followed a course much like that of the protest movements in the Low Countries. Unlike the Dutch and Belgian uprisings, however, the French Revolution did not come to a quick end. The French revolutionaries first tried to establish a constitutional monarchy based on the Enlightenment principles of human rights and rational government. This effort failed when the king attempted to raise a counterrevolutionary army. When war broke out in 1792, new tensions culminated in a second revolution on August 10, 1792, that deposed the king and established a republic in which all power rested in an elected legislature.

Before drafting a new constitution, the deputies of the National Assembly had to confront growing violence in the countryside, as peasants refused to pay seigneurial dues to their landlords and in some places took matters into their own hands and attacked lords' castles and records. In response to peasant unrest, on the night of August 4, 1789, noble deputies announced their willingness to give up their tax exemptions and seigneurial dues. By the end of the night, amid wild enthusiasm, dozens of deputies had come to the podium to relinquish the tax exemptions of their own professional groups, towns, or provinces. The National Assembly decreed the abolition of what it called "the feudal regime"—that is, it freed the few remaining serfs and eliminated all special privileges in matters of taxation, including all seigneurial dues on the land (a few days later, the deputies insisted on financial compensation for some of these dues, but most peasants refused to pay). Peasants had achieved their goals. The Assembly also mandated equality of opportunity in access to official posts. Talent, rather than birth, was to be the key to success. Enlightenment principles were beginning to become law.

Three weeks later, the deputies drew up a Declaration of the Rights of Man and of the Citizen as a preamble to the constitution. In words reminiscent of the American Declaration of Independence, whose author Thomas Jefferson was in Paris at the time, it proclaimed, "Men are born and remain free and equal in rights."◆ The Declaration granted freedom of religion, freedom of the press, equality of taxation, and equality before the law. By pronouncing all "men" free and equal, the Declaration immediately created new dilemmas. Did women have equal rights with men? What about free blacks in the colonies? How could slavery be justified if all men were born free? Did religious toleration of Protestants and Jews include equal political rights? Women never received the right to vote during the French Revolution, though Protestant and Jewish men did. Women were theoretically citizens under civil law but without the right to full political participation.

Some women did not accept their exclusion, viewing it as a betrayal of the promised new order. In addition to joining demonstrations, such as the march to Versailles in October 1789, women wrote petitions, published tracts, and organized political clubs to demand more participation. In her Declaration of the Rights of Women of 1791, Olympe de Gouges (1748–1793) played on the language of the official Declaration to make the point that women should also be included. In Article I, she announced, "Woman is born free and lives equal to man in her rights." Unresponsive to such calls for women's equality, the National Assembly gave voting rights only to white men who passed a test of wealth. The Constitution defined them as the "active citizens"; all others were "passive."

Despite these limitations, France became a constitutional monarchy in which the king served simply as the leading state functionary. A one-house legislature was responsible for making laws. The king could hold up enactment of laws but could not veto them absolutely. The deputies abolished all the old administrative divisions of the provinces and replaced them with a national system of eighty-three regional departments (*départements*) with identical administrative and legal structures (Map 16.2). All officials were elected; no offices could be bought and sold. The deputies also abolished the old taxes and replaced them with new ones that were supposed to be uniformly levied. The National Assembly had difficulty

---

◆ For the complete text of the Declaration of the Rights of Man and of the Citizen, see Document 50.

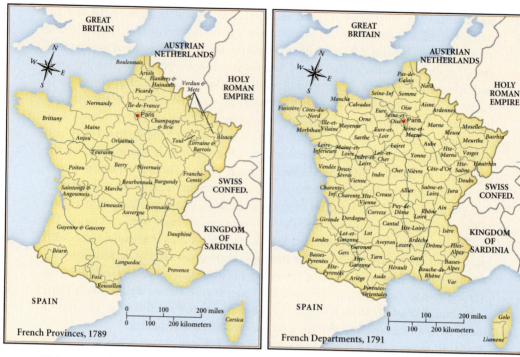

■ **MAP 16.2 Redrawing the Map of France, 1789–1791**

Before 1789, France was divided into provinces, each with its own administration. Some provinces had their own law codes. The new National Assembly determined to install uniform administrations and laws for the entire country. Discussion of the administrative reforms began in October 1789 and was completed on February 15, 1790, when the Assembly voted to divide the provinces into eighty-three departments with names based on their geographical characteristics: Basses-Pyrénées for the Pyrenees mountains, Haute-Marne for the Marne River, and so on. By eliminating the old names of provinces, with their historical associations, and supplanting them with geographical ones, the Assembly aimed to show that reason would now govern all French affairs.

collecting taxes, however, because many people had expected a substantial cut in the tax rate. The new administrative system survived, nonetheless, and the departments are still the basic units of the French state today.

When the deputies turned to reforming the Catholic church, they created enduring conflicts. Motivated partly by the ongoing financial crisis, the Assembly confiscated all the church's property and promised to pay clerical salaries in return. A Civil Constitution of the Clergy passed in July 1790 set pay scales for the clergy and provided that the voters elect their own parish priests and bishops just as they elected other officials. The impounded church property served as a guarantee for the new paper money, called *assignats*, issued by the government. The *assignats* soon became subject to inflation because the government began to sell the church lands to the highest bidders in state auctions. The sales increased the landholdings of wealthy city dwellers and prosperous peasants but cut the ground out from under the *assignats*.

Convinced that monastic life encouraged idleness and a decline in the nation's population, the deputies also outlawed any future monastic vows and encouraged monks and nuns to return to private life on state pensions. Many monks took the opportunity, but few nuns did. For nuns, the convent was all they knew. As the Carmelite nuns of Paris responded, "If there is true happiness on earth, we enjoy it in the shelter of the sanctuary."

Faced with resistance to these changes, in November 1790 the National Assembly required all clergy to swear an oath of loyalty to the Civil Constitution of the Clergy. Pope Pius VI in Rome condemned the constitution, and half of the French clergy refused to take the oath. The oath of allegiance permanently divided the Catholic population, which had to choose between loyalty to the old church and commitment to the Revolution with its "constitutional" church. The revolutionary government lost many supporters by passing laws against the clergy who refused the oath and by forcing them into exile, deporting them forcibly, or executing them as traitors. Riots and demonstrations led by women greeted many of the oath-taking priests who showed up to replace those who refused.

The reorganization of the Catholic church offended Louis XVI, who was reluctant to recognize the new limits on his powers. On June 20, 1791, the royal family escaped in disguise from the Tuileries palace in Paris and fled to the eastern border of France, where they hoped to gather support from Austrian emperor Leopold II, the brother of Marie-Antoinette. The plans went awry when a postmaster recognized the king from his portrait on the new French money, and the royal family was arrested at Varennes, forty miles from the Austrian border. The National Assembly tried to depict this incident as a kidnapping, but the "flight to Varennes" touched off demonstrations in Paris against the royal family, whom some now regarded as traitors. Cartoons circulated depicting the royal family as animals being returned "to the stable."

The Constitution finally completed in 1791 provided for the immediate election of a new Legislative Assembly. In a rare act of self-denial, the deputies of the National Assembly declared themselves ineligible for the new Assembly. Those who had experienced the Revolution firsthand departed from the scene, opening the door to men with little previous experience in national politics. The status of the king might have remained uncertain if war had not intervened, but by early 1792 everyone seemed intent on war with Austria. Louis and Marie-Antoinette hoped that war would lead to the definitive defeat of the Revolution, whereas the deputies who favored a republic believed that war would reveal the king's treachery and lead to his downfall. On April 21, 1792, Louis declared war on Austria. Prussia immediately entered on the Austrian side. Thousands of French aristocrats, including two-thirds of the army officer corps, had already emigrated, including both the king's brothers, and they were gathering along France's eastern border in expectation of joining Leopold's counterrevolutionary army.

When fighting broke out in 1792, all the powers expected a brief and relatively contained war. Instead, it would continue despite brief interruptions for the next twenty-three years. War had an immediate radicalizing effect on French politics. When the French armies proved woefully unprepared for battle, the authority of the Legislative Assembly came under fire. In June 1792, an angry crowd invaded the hall of the Assembly in Paris and threatened the royal family. In response, Lafayette left his command on the eastern front and came to Paris to insist on punishing the demonstrators. His appearance only fueled distrust of the army commanders, which increased to a fever pitch when the Prussians crossed the border and advanced on Paris. The Prussian commander, the duke of Brunswick, issued a manifesto— the Brunswick Manifesto—announcing that Paris would be totally destroyed if the royal family suffered any violence.

The ordinary people of Paris did not passively await their fate. Known as *sans-culottes* ("without breeches")—because men who worked with their hands wore long trousers rather than the knee breeches of the upper classes—they had followed every twist and turn in revolutionary fortunes. Political clubs had multiplied since the founding in 1789 of the first and most influential of them, the Jacobin Club, named after the former monastery in Paris where the club first met. Every local district in Paris had its club, where men and women listened to the news of the day and discussed their opinions. Faced with the threat of military retaliation and frustrated with the inaction of the Legislative Assembly, on August 10, 1792, the *sans-culottes* organized an insurrection and attacked the Tuileries palace, where the king resided. The Legislative Assembly ordered new elections, this time by universal male suffrage (no wealth qualifications as in the Constitution of 1791), for a National Convention that would write a new constitution.

When it met, the Convention abolished the monarchy and on September 22, 1792, established the first republic in French history. The republic would answer only to the people, not to any royal authority. Violence soon exploded again when early in September 1792 the Prussians approached Paris. Hastily gathered mobs stormed the overflowing prisons to seek out traitors who might help the enemy. In an atmosphere of near hysteria, eleven hundred inmates were killed, including many ordinary and completely innocent people. The princess of Lamballe, one of the queen's favorites, was hacked to pieces and her mutilated body displayed beneath the windows where the royal family was kept under guard. These "September massacres" showed the dark side of popular revolution, in which the common people demanded instant revenge on supposed enemies and conspirators.

The National Convention faced a dire situation. It needed to write a new constitution for the republic while fighting a war with external enemies and confronting increasing resistance at home. The Revolution had divided the population: for some it had not gone far enough toward providing food, land, and retribution against enemies; for others it had gone too far by dismantling the church and the monarchy. The French people had never known any government other than monarchy.

Only half the population could read and write at even a basic level. In this situation, symbolic actions became very important. Any public sign of monarchy was at risk, and revolutionaries soon pulled down statues of kings and burned reminders of the former regime.

The fate of Louis XVI and the future direction of the republic divided the deputies elected to the National Convention. Most of the deputies were middle-class lawyers and professionals who had developed their ardent republican beliefs in the national network of Jacobin Clubs. After the fall of the monarchy in August 1792, however, the Jacobins divided into two factions. The Girondins (named after a department in southwestern France, the Gironde, which provided some of its leading orators) met regularly at the salon of Jeanne Roland, the wife of a minister. They resented the growing power of Parisian militants and tried to appeal to the departments outside of Paris. The Mountain (so called because its deputies sat in the highest seats of the Convention), in contrast, was closely allied with the Paris militants.

The first showdown between the Girondins and the Mountain occurred during the trial of the king in December 1792. Although the Girondins agreed that the

■ **The Guillotine**

Before 1789, only nobles were decapitated if condemned to death; commoners were usually hanged. J. I. Guillotin, a professor of anatomy and a deputy for the Third Estate in the National Assembly, first proposed equalization of the death penalty. He also suggested that a mechanical device be constructed for decapitation, leading to the instrument's association with his name. The Assembly decreed decapitation as the death penalty in June 1791. Another physician, A. Louis, actually invented the guillotine. Its use began in April 1792 and did not end until 1981, when the French government abolished the death penalty. Although it was invented to make death equal and painless, the guillotine disturbed many observers; its mechanical operation and efficiency—the executioner merely pulled up the blade by a cord and then released it—seemed somehow inhuman. Nonetheless, the guillotine fascinated as much as it repelled. Reproduced in miniature, painted onto snuffboxes and china, worn as jewelry, and even serving as a toy, the guillotine became a part of popular culture, celebrated as the people's avenger by supporters of the Revolution and vilified as the preeminent symbol of the Terror by opponents. (Musée Carnavalet/Photo Bulloz.)

king was guilty of treason, many of them argued for clemency, exile, or a popular referendum on his fate. After a long and difficult debate, the Convention supported the Mountain and voted by a very narrow majority to execute the king. Louis XVI went to the guillotine on January 21, 1793, sharing the fate of Charles I of England in 1649. "We have just convinced ourselves that a king is only a man," wrote one newspaper, "and that no man is above the law."

Terror and Resistance

The execution of the king did not end the new regime's problems. The continuing war required even more men and money, and the introduction of a national draft provoked massive resistance in some parts of France. In response to growing pressures, the National Convention set up a highly centralized government designed to provide food, direct the war effort, and punish counterrevolutionaries. Thus began "the Terror," in which the guillotine became the most terrifying instrument of a government that suppressed almost every form of dissent. The leader of this government, Maximilien Robespierre, aimed to create a "Republic of Virtue," in which the government would teach, or force, citizens to become virtuous republicans through a massive program of political re-education. These policies only increased divisions, which ultimately led to Robespierre's fall from power and to a dismantling of government by terror.

Robespierre and the Committee of Public Safety

The conflict between the Girondins and the Mountain did not end with the execution of Louis XVI. Militants in Paris agitated for the removal of the deputies who had proposed a referendum on the king, and in retaliation the Girondins set up a special commission to investigate the situation in Paris, ordering the arrest of various local leaders. In response, Parisian militants organized an armed demonstration and invaded the National Convention on June 2, 1793, forcing the deputies to decree the arrest of their twenty-nine Girondin colleagues.

Setting the course for government and the war increasingly fell to the twelve-member Committee of Public Safety, set up by the Convention on April 6, 1793. When Robespierre (1758–1794) was elected to the committee three months later, he became in effect its guiding spirit and the chief spokesman of the Revolution. A lawyer from northern France known as "the incorruptible" for his stern honesty and fierce dedication to democratic ideals, Robespierre remains one of the most controversial figures in world history because of his association with the Terror. In September 1793, again in response to popular pressure, the deputies of the Convention voted to "put Terror on the agenda." Robespierre took the lead in implementing this decision. Although he originally opposed the death penalty and the war, he was convinced that the emergency situation of 1793 required severe measures, including death for those, such as the Girondins, who opposed the committee's policies.

Like many other educated eighteenth-century men, Robespierre read the classics of republicanism from the ancient Roman writers Tacitus and Plutarch to the Enlightenment thinkers Montesquieu and Rousseau. But he took them a step further. He spoke eloquently about "the theory of revolutionary government" as "the war of liberty against its enemies." He defended the people's right to democratic government, while in practice he supported many emergency measures that restricted their liberties. He personally favored a free market economy, as did almost all middle-class deputies, but in this time of crisis he was willing to enact price controls and requisitioning. The Convention had organized paramilitary bands called "revolutionary armies" to hunt down hoarders and political suspects, and on September 29, 1793, it established a General Maximum on the prices of thirty-nine essential commodities and on wages. In a speech to the Convention, Robespierre explained the necessity of a government by terror: "The first maxim of your policies must be to lead the people by reason and the people's enemies by terror . . . without virtue, terror is deadly; without terror, virtue is impotent." *Terror* was not an idle term; it seemed to imply that the goal of democracy justified what we now call totalitarian means—that is, the suppression of all dissent.

Through a series of desperate measures, the Committee of Public Safety set the machinery of the Terror in motion. It sent deputies out "on mission" to purge unreliable officials and organize the war effort. In the first universal draft of men in history, every unmarried man and childless widower between the ages of eighteen and twenty-five was declared eligible for conscription. Revolutionary tribunals set up in Paris and provincial centers tried political suspects. In October 1793, the Revolutionary Tribunal in Paris convicted Marie-Antoinette of treason and sent her to the guillotine. The Girondin leaders and Madame Roland were also guillotined, as was Olympe de Gouges. The government confiscated all the property of convicted traitors.

The Terror won its greatest success on the battlefield. As of April 1793, France faced war with Austria, Prussia, Great Britain, Spain, Sardinia, and the Dutch Republic—all fearful of the impact of revolutionary ideals on their own populations. To face this daunting coalition of forces, the French republic tapped a new and potent source of power, nationalist pride, in decrees mobilizing young and old alike: "The young men will go to battle; married men will forge arms and transport provisions; women will make tents and clothing and serve in hospitals; children will make bandages." Forges were set up in the parks and gardens of Paris to produce thousands of guns, and citizens everywhere helped collect saltpeter, a rock salt used to make gunpowder. By the end of 1793, the French nation in arms had stopped the advance of the allied powers, and in the summer of 1794 it invaded the Austrian Netherlands and crossed the Rhine River. The army was ready to carry the gospel of revolution and republicanism to the rest of Europe.

The Republic of Virtue, 1793–1794

The program of the Terror went beyond pragmatic measures to fight the war and internal enemies to include efforts to "republicanize everything"—in other words, to effect a cultural revolution. Refusing to tolerate opposition, the republic left no stone unturned in its endeavor to get its message across. Songs—especially the new national anthem, "La Marseillaise" (named after the soldiers from the city of Marseille who first sang it)—placards, posters, pamphlets, books, engravings, paintings, sculpture, even everyday crockery, chamberpots, and playing cards conveyed revolutionary slogans and symbols. Foremost among them was the figure of Liberty (an early version of the Statue of Liberty now in New York harbor), which appeared on coins and bills, letterheads and seals, and as statues in festivals. Hundreds of new plays were produced and old classics revised. To encourage the production of patriotic and republican works, the government sponsored state competitions for artists. Works of art were supposed to "awaken the public spirit and make clear how atrocious and ridiculous were the enemies of liberty and of the Republic."

At the center of this elaborate cultural campaign were the revolutionary festivals modeled on Rousseau's plans for a civic religion. The festivals first emerged in 1789 with the spontaneous planting of liberty trees in villages and towns. The Festival of Federation on July 14, 1790, marked the first anniversary of the fall of the Bastille. Under the Convention, the well-known painter Jacques-Louis David (1748–1825), who was a deputy and an associate of Robespierre, took over festival planning. David aimed to destroy the mystique of monarchy and to make the republic sacred. His Festival of Unity on August 10, 1793, for example, celebrated the first anniversary of the overthrow of the monarchy. In front of the statue of Liberty built for the occasion, a bonfire consumed the crowns and scepters of royalty while a cloud of three thousand white doves rose into the sky.

Some hoped the festival system would replace the Catholic church altogether. They initiated a campaign of de-Christianization that included closing churches (Protestant as well as Catholic), selling many church buildings to the highest bidder, and trying to force even those clergy who had taken the oath of loyalty to abandon their clerical vocations and marry. Great churches became storehouses for arms or grain, or their stones were sold off to contractors. The medieval statues of kings on the façade of Notre Dame cathedral were beheaded. Church bells were dismantled and church treasures melted down for government use.

In the ultimate step in de-Christianization, extremists tried to establish a Cult of Reason to supplant Christianity. In Paris in the autumn of 1793, a goddess of Liberty, played by an actress, presided over a Festival of Reason in Notre Dame cathedral. Local militants in other cities staged similar festivals, which alarmed deputies in the Convention, who were wary of turning rural, devout populations against the republic. The Committee of Public Safety halted the de-Christianization campaign, and Robespierre with David's help tried to institute an alternative, the Cult of the Supreme Being, in June 1794. Neither cult attracted many followers.

In principle, the best way to ensure the future of the republic was through the education of the young. The deputy Georges-Jacques Danton (1759–1794), Robespierre's main competitor as theorist of the Revolution, maintained that "after bread, the first need of the people is education." The Convention voted to make primary schooling free and compulsory for both boys and girls. It took control of education away from the Catholic church and tried to set up a system of state schools at the primary and secondary levels, but it lacked trained teachers to replace those the Catholic religious orders provided. As a result, opportunities for learning how to read and write may have diminished. In 1799, only one-fifth as many boys enrolled in the state secondary schools as had studied in church schools ten years earlier.

Although many of the ambitious republican programs failed, almost all aspects of daily life became politicized, even colors. The tricolor—the combination of red, white, and blue that was to become the flag of France—was devised in July 1789, and by 1793 everyone had to wear a cockade (a badge made of ribbons) with the colors. Using formal forms of speech—*vous* for "you"—or the title *Monsieur* or *Madame* might identify someone as an aristocrat; true patriots used the informal *tu* and *Citoyen* or *Citoyenne* ("Citizen") instead. Some people changed their names or gave their children new kinds of names. Biblical and saints' names, such as Jean,

■ The Revolutionary Tricolor
This painting by an anonymous artist probably shows a deputy wearing the uniform prescribed for those sent to supervise military operations. His dress prominently displays the revolutionary tricolor—red, white, and blue—both on his official sash and on the trim of his hat. Plumes had once been reserved for nobles; now nonnobles could wear them on their hats, but they still signaled dignity and importance. Dress became a contested issue during the Revolution, and successive governments considered prescribing some kind of uniform, at least for deputies in the legislature.
(Louvre/Reunion des Musées Nationaux.)

Pierre, Joseph, or Marie, gave way to names recalling heroes of the ancient Roman republic (Brutus, Gracchus, Cornelia), revolutionary heroes, or flowers and plants. Such changes symbolized adherence to the republic and to Enlightenment ideals rather than to Catholicism.

Even the measures of time and space were revolutionized. In October 1793, the Convention introduced a new calendar to replace the Christian one. Year I dated from the beginning of the republic on September 22, 1792. Twelve months of exactly thirty days each received new names derived from nature—for example, Pluviôse (roughly equivalent to February) recalled the rain (*la pluie*) of late winter. Instead of seven-day weeks, ten-day *décades* provided only one day of rest every ten days and pointedly eliminated the Sunday of the Christian calendar. The five days left at the end of the calendar year were devoted to special festivals called *sans-culottides*. The calendar remained in force for twelve years despite continuing resistance to it. More enduring was the new metric system based on units of ten that was invented to replace the hundreds of local variations in weights and measures. Other countries in Europe and throughout the world eventually adopted the metric system.

Successive revolutionary legislatures had also changed the rules of family life. The state took responsibility for all family matters away from the Catholic church: birth, death, and marriage registration now happened at city hall, not the parish church. Marriage became a civil contract and as such could be broken. The new divorce law of September 1792 was the most far-reaching in Europe: a couple could divorce by mutual consent or for reasons such as insanity, abandonment, battering, or criminal conviction. Thousands of men and women took advantage of the law to dissolve unhappy marriages, even though the pope had condemned the measure. (In 1816, the government revoked the right to divorce.) In one of its most influential actions, the National Convention passed a series of laws that created equal inheritance among all children in a family, including girls. A father's right to favor one child, especially the oldest male, was considered aristocratic and hence antirepublican.

Resisting the Revolution

By intruding into religion, culture, and daily life, the republic inevitably provoked resistance. Shouting curses against the republic, uprooting liberty trees, carrying statues of the Virgin Mary in procession, hiding a priest who would not take the oath, singing a royalist song—all these expressed dissent with the new symbols, rituals, and policies. Many women, in particular, suffered from the hard conditions of life that persisted in this time of war, and they had their own ways of voicing discontent. Long bread lines in the cities exhausted the patience of women, and police spies reported their constant grumbling, which occasionally turned into spontaneous demonstrations or riots over high prices or food shortages. Other forms of

■ **Anti-Robespierre Satire**

In The Purifying Pot of the Jacobins *(1793), the anonymous artist makes fun of the Jacobin Club's penchant for constantly examining the political correctness of its members. The Robespierre-like inquisitor uses a magnifying glass to check for loyalty, symbolized by the red cap of liberty worn by militant revolutionaries, and carries a knife in his pocket. Those who failed the test suffered harsh, sometimes fatal consequences.* (Art Resource, NY.)

resistance were more individual. One young woman, Charlotte Corday, assassinated the outspoken deputy Jean-Paul Marat in July 1793. Corday fervently supported the Girondins, and she considered it her patriotic duty to kill the deputy who, in the columns of his paper *The Friend of the People,* had constantly demanded more heads and more blood. Marat was immediately eulogized as a great martyr: Corday went to the guillotine vilified as a monster but confident that she had "avenged many innocent victims."

Organized resistance broke out in many parts of France. The arrest of the Girondin deputies in June 1793 sparked in several departments insurrections that if coordinated might have threatened the central government in Paris. But the army promptly dispatched the rebels. After the government retook the city of Lyon, one of the centers of the revolt, the deputy on mission ordered sixteen hundred houses demolished. Special courts sentenced almost two thousand people to death. The name of the city was changed to Ville Affranchie (Liberated Town).

In the Vendée region of western France, resistance turned into full-scale civil war. Between March and December 1793, peasants, artisans, and weavers joined under noble leadership to form a "Catholic and Royal Army." One rebel group explained its motives: "They [the republicans] have killed our king, chased away our priests, sold the goods of our church, eaten everything we have and now they want to take our bodies [in the draft]." The uprising took two different forms: in the Vendée itself, a counterrevolutionary army organized to fight the republic; in nearby Brittany, resistance took the form of guerrilla bands, which united to attack a target and then quickly melted into the countryside. Great Britain provided money and underground contacts for these attacks.

For several months in 1793, the Vendée rebels stormed the largest towns in the region. Both sides committed atrocities. At the small town of Machecoul, for example, the rebels massacred five hundred republicans, including administrators and National Guard members; many were tied together, shoved into freshly dug graves, and shot. By the fall, however, republican soldiers had turned back the rebels. A republican general wrote to the Committee of Public Safety claiming, "There is no more Vendée, citizens, it has perished under our free sword along with its women and children. . . . Following the orders that you gave me I have crushed children under the feet of horses, massacred women who at least . . . will engender no more brigands." "Infernal columns" of republican troops marched through the region to restore control, military courts ordered thousands executed, and republican soldiers massacred thousands of others. In one especially gruesome incident, the deputy Jean-Baptiste Carrier supervised the drowning of some two thousand Vendée rebels, including a number of priests. Barges loaded with prisoners were floated into the Loire River near Nantes and then sunk. Controversy still rages about the rebellion's death toll. Estimates of rebel deaths alone range from about 20,000 to 250,000 and higher. Many thousands of republican soldiers and civilians also lost their lives. Even the low estimates reveal the carnage of this catastrophic confrontation between the republic and its opponents.

The Fall of Robespierre and the End of the Terror, 1794–1799

In an atmosphere of fear of conspiracy that these outbreaks fueled, Robespierre tried simultaneously to exert the Convention's control over popular political activities and to weed out opposition among the deputies. The Convention cracked down on popular clubs and societies in the fall of 1793. First to be suppressed were women's political clubs. Founded in early 1793, the Society of Revolutionary Republican Women played a very active part in *sans-culottes* politics. The society urged harsher measures against the republic's enemies and insisted that women have a voice in politics even if they did not have the vote. The Convention abolished women's political clubs in order to limit agitation in the streets. The deputies called on biological arguments about natural differences between the sexes to bolster their case. As one argued, "Women are ill suited for elevated thoughts and serious meditations."

■ **A Women's Club**

In this gouache by the Lesueur brothers, The Patriotic Women's Club, *the club president urges members to contribute funds for poor patriot families. Women's clubs focused on philanthropic work but also discussed revolutionary legislation and the debates in the National Assembly. The colorful but sober dress indicates that the women are middle class.*

(Musée de la Ville de Paris/Musée Carnavalet, Paris/Giraudon/Art Resource, NY.)

In the spring of 1794, the Committee of Public Safety moved against its critics among leaders in Paris and deputies in the Convention itself. First, a handful of men labeled "ultrarevolutionaries"—in fact a motley collection of local Parisian politicians—were arrested and executed. Next came the other side, the "indulgents," so called because they favored moderation of the Terror. Included among them was the deputy Danton himself, once a member of the Committee of Public Safety and a friend of Robespierre despite the striking contrast in their personalities. Danton was the Revolution's most flamboyant orator and, unlike Robespierre, was a high-living, high-spending, excitable politician. At every turning point in national politics, his booming voice had swayed opinion in the National Convention. Now, under government pressure, the Revolutionary Tribunal convicted him and his friends of treason and sentenced them to death.

With the arrest and execution of these leaders in Paris, the prophecies of doom for the Revolution seemed about to be realized. "The Revolution," as one of the Girondin victims of 1793 had remarked, "was devouring its own children." Even after the major threats to the committee's power had been eliminated, the Terror continued and even worsened. A law passed in June 1794 denied the accused the right of legal counsel, reduced the number of jurors necessary for conviction, and allowed only two judgments: acquittal or death. The category of political crimes expanded to include "slandering patriotism" and "seeking to inspire discouragement." Ordinary people risked the guillotine if they expressed any discontent. The rate of executions in Paris rose from five a day in the spring of 1794 to twenty-six a day in the summer. The political atmosphere darkened even though the military situation improved. At the end of June, French armies decisively defeated the main Austrian army and advanced through the Austrian Netherlands to Brussels and Antwerp. The emergency measures for fighting the war were working, yet Robespierre and his inner circle had made so many enemies that they could not afford to loosen the grip of the Terror.

The Terror hardly touched many parts of France, but overall, the experience was undeniably traumatic. Across the country, the official Terror cost the lives of at least 40,000 French people, most of them living in the regions of major insurrections or near the borders with foreign enemies, where suspicion of collaboration ran high. As many as 300,000 people—one out of every fifty French people—went to prison as suspects between March 1793 and August 1794. The toll for the aristocracy and the clergy was especially high. Many leading nobles perished under the guillotine, and thousands emigrated. Thirty thousand to forty thousand clergy who refused the oath emigrated, at least two thousand (including many nuns) were executed, and thousands were imprisoned. The clergy were singled out in particular in the civil war zones: 135 priests were massacred at Lyon in November 1793 and 83 shot in one day during the Vendée revolt. Yet many victims of the Terror were peasants or ordinary working people.

The final crisis of the Terror came in July 1794. Conflicts within the Committee of Public Safety and the National Convention left Robespierre isolated. On July 27, 1794 (the ninth of Thermidor, Year II, according to the revolutionary calendar), Robespierre appeared before the Convention with yet another list of deputies to be arrested. Many feared they would be named, and they shouted him down and ordered him arrested along with his followers on the committee, the president of the Revolutionary Tribunal in Paris, and the commander of the Parisian National Guard. An armed uprising led by the Paris city government failed to save Robespierre when most of the National Guard took the side of the Convention. Robespierre tried to kill himself with a pistol but only broke his jaw. The next day he and scores of followers went to the guillotine.

The men who led the attack on Robespierre in Thermidor (July 1794) did not intend to reverse all his policies, but that happened nonetheless because of a violent backlash known as the "Thermidorian Reaction." Newspapers attacked the Robespierrists as "tigers thirsting for human blood." The new government released hundreds of suspects and arranged a temporary truce in the Vendée. It purged Jacobins from local bodies and replaced them with their opponents. It arrested some of the most notorious "terrorists" in the National Convention, such as Carrier, and put them to death. Within the year, the new leaders abolished the Revolutionary

Tribunal and closed the Jacobin Club in Paris. Popular demonstrations met severe repression. In southeastern France, in particular, a "White Terror" replaced the Jacobins' "Red Terror." Former officials and local Jacobin leaders were harassed, beaten, and often murdered by paramilitary bands who had tacit support from the new authorities. Those who remained in the National Convention prepared yet another constitution in 1795, setting up a two-house legislature and an executive body—the Directory—headed by five directors.

The Rise of Napoleon Bonaparte

Between 1795 and 1799, the republic endured in France, but it directed a war effort abroad that would ultimately bring to power the man who would dismantle the republic itself. The story of the rise of Napoleon Bonaparte (1769–1821) is one of the most remarkable in Western history. It would have seemed astonishing in 1795 that the twenty-six-year-old son of a Corsican noble would within four years become the supreme ruler of France and one of the greatest military leaders in world history. In 1795, he was a penniless artillery officer, only recently released from prison as a presumed Robespierrist. Continuing warfare, the upheavals caused in the rest of Europe by the impact of the French Revolution, and political divisions within the revolutionary leadership gave Bonaparte the opportunity to change the course of history.

Revolution on the March

The powers allied against France had squandered their best chance to defeat France in 1793, when the French armies verged on chaos because of the emigration of noble army officers and the problems of integrating new draftees. At that moment, Prussia, Russia, and Austria were preoccupied once again with Poland. "I shall fight Jacobinism, and defeat it in Poland," vowed Catherine the Great in 1792. She abolished Poland's constitution of May 3, 1791, and joined with Prussia in gobbling up generous new slices of Polish territory in the Second Partition of 1793 (Map 16.3). When Tadeusz Kościuszko (1746–1817), an officer who had been a foreign volunteer in the War of American Independence, tried to lead a nationalist uprising, Catherine's army struck again. This time, Russia, Prussia, and Austria wiped Poland completely from the map in the Third Partition of 1795. "The Polish question" would plague international relations for more than a century as Polish rebels flocked to any international upheaval that might undo the partitions.

While Russia, Prussia, and Austria feasted on Poland, France regrouped. Because of the new national draft, the French had a huge and powerful fighting force of 700,000 men by the end of 1793. But the army faced many problems in the field. As many as a third of the recent draftees deserted before or during battle. Uniforms fashioned out of rough cloth constricted movements, tore easily, and retained the

■ MAP 16.3 The Second and Third Partitions of Poland, 1793 and 1795

In 1793, after Russian armies invaded Poland, Russia and Prussia agreed to another partition of Polish territories. Prussia took over territory that included 1.1 million Poles while Russia gained 3 million new inhabitants. Austria gave up any claims to Poland in exchange for help from Russia and Prussia in acquiring Bavaria. When Kościuszko's nationalist uprising failed in 1794, Russia, Prussia, and Austria agreed to a final division. Prussia absorbed an additional 900,000 Polish subjects, including those in Warsaw; Austria incorporated 1 million Poles and the city of Cracow; Russia gained another 2 million Poles. The three powers determined never to use the term "Kingdom of Poland" again.

damp of muddy battlefields, exposing the soldiers to the elements and the spread of disease. At times, the soldiers were fed only moldy bread, and if their pay was late, they sometimes resorted to pillaging and looting. Generals might pay with their lives if they lost a key battle and their loyalty to the Revolution came under suspicion. France nevertheless had one overwhelming advantage: its soldiers, drawn largely from the peasantry and the lower classes of the cities, fought for a revolution that they and their brothers and sisters had helped make. The republic was their government, and the army was in large measure theirs, too; many officers had risen through the ranks by skill and talent rather than by inheriting or purchasing their positions. One young peasant boy wrote to his parents, "Either you will see me return bathed in glory, or you will have a son who is a worthy citizen of France who knows how to die for the defense of his country."

When French armies invaded the Austrian Netherlands and crossed the Rhine in the summer of 1794, they proclaimed a war of liberation. These promises profoundly divided European opinion. In 1789, many had greeted events with unabashed enthusiasm. The English Unitarian minister Richard Price had exulted, "Behold, the light . . . after setting AMERICA free, reflected to FRANCE, and there kindled into a blaze that lays despotism in ashes, and warms and illuminates EUROPE." Democrats and reformers from many countries flooded to Paris to witness events firsthand. Supporters of the French Revolution in Great Britain, like

■ The English Reaction to the French Revolution

In this caricature, James Gillray, a supporter of the Tories in Britain, satirizes the French version of liberty but also subtly mocks the British upper classes. He portrays French liberty as a creature (is it man or woman?) who has only onions to eat but still sings the praises of French freedom and plenty. The British figure is a fat magistrate who complains that high taxes will cause slavery and starvation, while he stuffs himself on the British national dish of roast beef. Gillray produced thousands of political caricatures. (British Museum.)

the earlier reformers of the 1760s and 1770s, joined constitutional and reform societies that sprang up in many cities. The most important of these societies, the London Corresponding Society, founded in 1792, corresponded with the Paris Jacobin Club and served as a center for reform agitation in England. Pro-French feeling ran even stronger in Ireland. Catholics and Presbyterians, both excluded from the vote, came together in 1791 in the Society of United Irishmen, which eventually pressed for secession from England.

European elites became alarmed when the French abolished monarchy and nobility and encouraged popular participation in politics. The British government, for example, quickly suppressed the corresponding societies and harassed their leaders, charging that their ideas and their contacts with the French were seditious. In the United States, opinion fiercely divided on the virtues of the French Revolution. In Sweden, King Gustavus III (r. 1771–1792) was assassinated by a nobleman who claimed that "the king has violated his oath . . . and declared himself an enemy of the realm." The king's son and heir, Gustavus IV (r. 1792–1809), was convinced that the French Jacobins had sanctioned his father's assassination. Although just across the border from France, Spain's royal government suppressed all news from France, fearing that it might ignite the spirit of revolt. This fear was not misplaced because even in Russia, for instance, 278 outbreaks of peasant unrest occurred between 1796 and 1798. One Russian landlord complained, "This is the self-same . . . spirit of insubordination and independence, which has spread through all Europe."

Middle-class people near the northern and eastern borders of France reacted most positively to the French invasion. In the Austrian Netherlands, Mainz, Savoy, and Nice, French officers organized Jacobin Clubs that attracted middle-class locals. The clubs petitioned for annexation to France, and French legislation was then introduced, including the abolition of seigneurial dues. Despite resistance, especially in the Austrian Netherlands, these areas remained part of France until 1815, and the legal changes were permanent. Like Louis XIV a century before, most deputies in the National Convention considered the territories annexed in 1794 within France's "natural frontiers"—the Rhine, the Alps, and the Pyrenees.

The Directory government that came to power in 1795 was torn between defending the new frontiers and launching a more aggressive policy of creating semi-independent "sister" republics wherever the armies succeeded. Aggression won out. When Prussia declared neutrality in 1795, French armies swarmed into the Dutch Republic, abolished the stadtholderate, and—with the revolutionary penchant for renaming—created the new Batavian Republic, a satellite of France. The French set up a Cisalpine Republic when Bonaparte defeated the Austrian armies in northern Italy in 1797. After the French attacked the Swiss cantons in 1798, they set up the Helvetic Republic and curtailed many of the Catholic church's privileges. They conquered the Papal States in 1798 and installed a Roman Republic; the pope fled to Siena.

As the French conquered more and more territory, "liberated" people in many places began to view them as an army of occupation. In the German Rhineland, for example, gangs of bandits preyed on the French and on Jews. One German traveler reported, "It is characteristic of the region in which the bandits are based that these two nations [the French and the Jews] are hated. So crimes against them are motivated not just by a wish to rob them but also by a variety of fanaticism which is partly political and partly religious." Because the French offered the Jews religious toleration and civil and political rights wherever they conquered, anti-French groups sometimes attacked Jews.

Revolution in the Colonies

The revolution that produced so much upheaval in continental Europe had repercussions in France's Caribbean colonies. These colonies were crucial to the French economy. Twice the size in land area of the neighboring British colonies, they also produced nearly twice as much revenue in exports. The slave population had doubled in the French colonies in the twenty years before 1789. St. Domingue (present-day Haiti) was the most important French colony. Occupying the western half of the island of Hispaniola, it was inhabited by approximately 465,000 slaves, 30,000 whites, and 28,000 free people of color, whose primary job was to apprehend runaway slaves and ensure plantation security.

Despite the efforts of a Paris club called the Friends of Blacks, most French revolutionaries did not consider slavery a pressing problem. As one deputy explained, "This regime [in the colonies] is oppressive, but it gives a livelihood to several million Frenchmen. This regime is barbarous but a still greater barbarity will result if you interfere with it without the necessary knowledge."

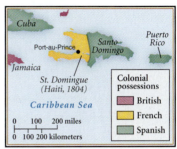

St. Domingue on the Eve of the Revolt, 1791

In August 1791, slaves in northern St. Domingue, inspired by the slogan "Listen to the voice of Liberty which speaks in the hearts of all," organized a large-scale revolt. To restore authority over the slaves, the Legislative Assembly in Paris granted civil and political rights to the free people of color. This action infuriated white planters and merchants, and in 1793 they signed an agreement with Great Britain, now France's enemy in war, declaring British sovereignty over St. Domingue. To complicate matters further, Spain, which controlled the rest of the island and had entered on Great Britain's side in the war with France, offered freedom to individual slave rebels who joined the Spanish armies as long as they agreed to maintain the slave regime for the other blacks.

The few thousand French republican troops on St. Domingue were outnumbered, and to prevent complete military disaster, the French commissioner freed all the slaves in his jurisdiction in August 1793 without permission from the government in Paris. In February 1794, the National Convention formally abolished slavery and granted full rights to all black men in France's colonies. These actions had the desired effect. One of the ablest black generals allied with the Spanish, the ex-slave François-Dominique Toussaint L'Ouverture (1743–1803), changed sides and committed his troops to the French. The French eventually appointed Toussaint governor of St. Domingue as a reward for his efforts.

The vicious fighting and flight of whites left the island's economy in ruins. In 1800, the plantations produced one-fifth of what they had in 1789. In the zones Toussaint controlled, army officers or government officials took over the great estates and kept all the freed people working in agriculture under military discipline. The former slaves were bound to their estates like serfs and were forced to work the plantations in exchange for an autonomous family life and the right to maintain personal garden plots.

Toussaint remained in charge until 1802, when Napoleon sent French armies to regain control of St. Domingue. They arrested Toussaint and transported him to

■ **Toussaint L'Ouverture**
The leader of the St. Domingue slave uprising appears in his general's uniform, sword in hand. This portrait appeared in one of the earliest histories of the revolt, Marcus Rainsford's Historical Account of the Black Empire of Hayti *(London, 1805). Toussaint, a former slave who educated himself, fascinated many of his contemporaries in Europe as well as the New World by turning a chaotic slave rebellion into an organized and ultimately successful independence movement.* (North Wind Picture Archives.)

France, where he died in prison. His arrest prompted the English romantic poet William Wordsworth (1770–1850) to write of him:

> *There's not a breathing of the common wind*
> *That will forget thee; thou hast great allies;*
> *Thy friends are exultations, agonies,*
> *And love, and man's unconquerable mind.*

Toussaint became a hero to abolitionists everywhere, a potent symbol of black struggles to win freedom.♦ Napoleon attempted to reimpose slavery, but the remaining black generals defeated his armies, which had been weakened by yellow fever, and in 1804 proclaimed the Republic of Haiti.

♦ For a set of primary sources that illuminate Toussaint's revolutionary principles and actions, see Document 51, Toussaint L'Ouverture, "Revolution in the Colonies."

The End of the French Republic

Toussaint had followed with interest Napoleon's rise to power in France; he once wrote to Bonaparte, "From the First of the Blacks to the First of the Whites." Like Toussaint, Napoleon Bonaparte made the most of the opportunities afforded by war. The Directory regime installed in 1795 had tenuously held on to power while trying to fend off challenges from the remaining Jacobins and the resurgent royalists. Bands of young men dressed in knee breeches and rich fabrics picked fights with known Jacobins and disrupted theater performances with loud antirevolutionary songs. All over France, people banded together and petitioned to reopen churches closed during the Terror. If necessary, they broke into a church to hold services with a priest who had been in hiding or with a lay schoolteacher who was willing to say Mass. Amid increasing political instability, generals in the field became practically independent, and the troops felt greater loyalty to their units and generals than to the republic. As one army captain wrote, "In a conquering people the military spirit must prevail over other social conditions." Military victories had made the army a parallel and rival force to the state.

Thanks to some early military successes and links to Parisian politicians, Bonaparte was named commander of the French army in Italy in 1796. His astounding success in the Italian campaigns of 1796–1797 launched his meteoric career. With an army of fewer than fifty thousand men, he defeated the Piedmontese and the Austrians. He negotiated with the Austrians himself, and in quick order he established client republics dependent on his own authority. He molded the army into his personal force by paying the soldiers in cash taken as tribute from the newly conquered territories. He mollified the Directory government by sending home wagonloads of Italian masterpieces of art, which were added to Parisian museum collections (most are still there) after being paraded in victory festivals.

In 1798, the Directory set aside its plans to invade England, gave Bonaparte command of the army raised for that purpose, and sent him across the Mediterranean Sea to Egypt, away from the Parisian centers of power. The French had encouraged the Irish to time a rebellion to coincide with their planned invasion, and when the French went elsewhere, the British mercilessly repressed the revolt. Thirty thousand people were killed. Twice as many regular British troops (seventy thousand) as fought in any of the major continental battles against Napoleon were required to put down the rebellion.

The Directory government hoped that French occupation of Egypt would strike a blow at British trade by cutting the route to India and thus compensate France for its losses there years before. Once the army disembarked in Egypt, however, the British admiral Horatio Nelson destroyed the French fleet while it was anchored in Aboukir Bay. In the face of determined resistance and an outbreak of the bubonic plague, Bonaparte's armies retreated from a further expedition in Syria. But the French occupation of Egypt lasted long enough for that largely Muslim country to experience the same kinds of Enlightenment-inspired legal reforms that had been introduced in Europe: the French abolished torture, introduced equality before the law, eliminated religious taxes, and proclaimed religious toleration.◆

Even the failures of the Egyptian campaign did not dull Bonaparte's luster. Bonaparte had taken France's leading scientists with him on the expedition, and his soldiers had discovered a slab of black basalt dating from 196 B.C. written in both hieroglyphic and Greek. Called the *Rosetta stone* after a nearby town, it enabled scholars to finally decipher the hieroglyphs used by the ancient Egyptians. When his army was pinned down after its initial successes, Napoleon slipped out of Egypt and made his way secretly across the Mediterranean to southern France.

In October 1799, Bonaparte arrived in Paris at just the right moment. The war in Europe was going badly. The departments of the former Austrian Netherlands had revolted against new conscription laws. Deserters swelled the ranks of the rebels in western France. A royalist army had tried to take the city of Toulouse in the southwest. And many government leaders wanted to revise the Constitution of 1795. Disillusioned members of the government saw in Bonaparte's return an occasion to overturn the Constitution of 1795.

On November 9, 1799 (18 Brumaire, Year VIII, by the revolutionary calendar), the conspirators persuaded the legislature to move out of Paris to avoid an imaginary Jacobin plot. But when Bonaparte stomped into the meeting hall the next day and demanded changes in the Constitution, he was greeted by cries of "Down with the dictator." His quick-thinking brother Lucien, president of the Council of Five Hundred (the lower house), saved Bonaparte's coup by summoning troops guarding the hall and claiming that the deputies had tried to assassinate the popular general. The soldiers ejected the deputies, and a hastily assembled rump legislature voted to abolish the Directory and establish a new three-man executive called the consulate.

Bonaparte became First Consul, a title revived from the ancient Roman republic. He promised to be a man above party and to restore order to the republic. A new constitution was submitted to the voters. Millions abstained from voting, and the government falsified the results to give an appearance of even greater support to the new regime. Inside France, political apathy had overtaken the original enthusiasm for revolutionary ideals. Bonaparte's coup d'état appeared to be just the latest in a long line of upheavals in revolutionary France. Within the year, however, he had effectively ended the French Revolution and set France on a new course toward an authoritarian state.

Napoleon had no long-range plans to establish himself as emperor and conquer most of Europe. The deputies of the legislature who engineered the coup d'état of November 1799 picked him as one of three provisional consuls only because he

---

◆ For a primary source that shows Napoleon's invasion from a native perspective, see Document 52, Abd al-Rahman al-Jabartî, "Napoleon in Egypt."

■ **Napoleon as Military Hero**

In this painting from 1800–1801, Napoleon Crossing the Alps at St. Bernard, *Jacques-Louis David reminds the French of Napoleon's heroic military exploits. Napoleon is a picture of calm and composure while his horse shows the fright and energy of the moment. David painted this propagandistic image shortly after one of his former students went to the guillotine on a trumped-up charge of plotting to assassinate the new French leader. The former organizer of republican festivals during the Terror had become a kind of court painter for the new regime.*

(© Photo RMN/Herve Lewandowski.)

was a famous general. Still, the constitution of 1799 made Bonaparte the First Consul with the right to pick the Council of State, which drew up all laws. He quickly exerted control by choosing men loyal to him. Government was no longer representative in any real sense: the new constitution eliminated direct elections for deputies and granted no independent powers to the three houses of the legislature. Bonaparte and his advisers chose the legislature's members out of a small pool of "notables." Almost all men over twenty-one could vote in the plebiscite (referendum) to approve the constitution, but their only option was to choose *Yes* or *No*.

Emperor Napoleon I, r. 1804–1814

Napoleon left an indelible stamp on French institutions and political life. He reconciled with the Catholic church and with exiled aristocrats willing to return to France. He sped up the centralization of political power and ensured order by suppressing political dissent. He supervised the unification of France's many law codes into one Napoleonic Code that has remained in force to this day. Yet his fame and much of his power rested on his military conquests. His military prowess brought him to the heights of power, but as a consequence, he could not survive defeat on the battlefield.

The Authoritarian State

Bonaparte's most urgent task was to reconcile to his regime Catholics who had been alienated by revolutionary policies. Though nominally Catholic, Napoleon held no deep religious convictions. "How can there be order in the state without religion?" he asked cynically. "When a man is dying of hunger beside another who is stuffing himself, he cannot accept this difference if there is not an authority who tells him: 'God wishes it so.'" In 1801, a concordat with Pope Pius VII (r. 1800–1823) ended a decade of church-state conflict. The pope validated all sales of church lands, and the government agreed to pay the salaries of bishops and priests who would swear loyalty to the state. Catholicism was officially recognized as the religion of "the great majority of French citizens." (The state also paid Protestant pastors' salaries.) The pope thus brought the huge French Catholic population back into the fold, and Napoleon gained the pope's support for his regime.

Napoleon continued the centralization of state power that had begun under the absolutist monarchy of Louis XIV and resumed under the Terror. As First Consul, he appointed prefects who directly supervised local affairs in every *département*, or region. He created the Bank of France to facilitate government borrowing and relied on gold and silver coinage rather than paper money. He also frequently made ends meet by exacting tribute from the territories he conquered.

Napoleon promised order and an end to the upheavals of ten years of revolutionary turmoil, but his regime severely limited political expression. He never relied on mass executions to achieve control, but he refused to allow those who opposed him to meet in clubs, influence elections, or publish newspapers. A decree reduced the number of newspapers in Paris from seventy-three to thirteen (and then finally to four), and the newspapers that remained became government mouthpieces. Government censors had to approve all operas and plays, and they banned "offensive" artistic works even more frequently than their royal predecessors. The minister of police, Joseph Fouché, a leading figure in the Terror of 1793–1794, could impose house arrest, arbitrary imprisonment, and surveillance of political dissidents. Political contest and debate shriveled to almost nothing. When a bomb attack on Napoleon's carriage failed in 1800, Fouché suppressed evidence of a royalist plot and instead arrested hundreds of former Jacobins. More than one hundred of them were deported and seven hundred imprisoned.

Napoleon's intention to eliminate the republic became clear in 1802. He named himself First Consul for life, and in 1804, with the pope's blessing, he crowned himself emperor. Plebiscites approved these decisions, but no alternatives were offered. Napoleon's charismatic personality dominated the new imperial regime. He worked hard at establishing his reputation as an efficient administrator with broad intellectual interests. He met frequently with scientists, jurists, and artists, and stories abounded of his unflagging energy. He worked constantly, whether on military campaigns or on state affairs, taking only a few minutes for each meal. "Authority," declared his adviser Sieyès, "must come from above and confidence from below."

As emperor, Napoleon cultivated personal symbolism to enhance his image as a hero. His face and name adorned coins, engravings, histories, paintings, and public monuments. His favorite painters embellished his legend by depicting him as a warrior-hero of mythic proportions. In his imperial court, Napoleon staged his entrances carefully to maximize his personal presence: his wife and courtiers were dressed in regal finery, and he was announced with great pomp—but he usually arrived dressed in a simple military uniform with no medals.

Believing that "what is big is always beautiful," Napoleon embarked on ostentatious building projects that would outshine even those of Louis XIV. Government-commissioned architects built the Arc de Triomphe, the Stock Exchange, fountains, and even slaughterhouses. Most of his new construction reflected his neoclassical taste for monumental buildings set in vast empty spaces. Old, winding streets with their cramped houses were demolished to make way for Napoleon's grand designs.

Napoleon did not rule alone. He relied on men who had served with him in the army. His chief of staff Alexandre Berthier, for example, became minister of war, and the chemist Claude Berthollet, who had organized the scientific part of the expedition to Egypt, became vice president of the Senate in 1804. Napoleon's bureaucracy was based on a patron-client relationship, with Napoleon as the ultimate patron. Some of Napoleon's closest associates married into his family.

Combining aristocratic and revolutionary values in a new social hierarchy that rewarded merit and talent, Napoleon used the Senate to dispense his patronage and personally chose as senators the nation's most illustrious generals, ministers, prefects, scientists, rich men, and former nobles. Intending to replace both the old nobility of birth and the republic's strict emphasis on equality, in 1802 he took a step toward creating a new nobility by founding a Legion of Honor. (Members of the legion received lifetime pensions along with their titles.) By 1814, the legion had thirty-two thousand members, 95 percent of them military men.

In 1808, Napoleon introduced a complete hierarchy of noble titles, ranging from princes down to barons and chevaliers. All Napoleonic nobles had served the state. Titles could be inherited but had to be supported by wealth—a man could not be a duke without a fortune of 200,000 francs, or a chevalier without 3,000 francs. To go along with their new titles, Napoleon gave his favorite generals huge fortunes, often in the form of estates in the conquered territories.

Napoleon's own family reaped the greatest benefits. He made his older brother, Joseph, ruler of the newly established kingdom of Naples in 1806, the same year he installed his younger brother Louis as king of Holland. He proclaimed his twenty-three-year-old stepson Eugène de Beauharnais viceroy of Italy in 1805 and established his sister Caroline and brother-in-law General Murat as king and queen of Naples in 1808, when he moved Joseph to the throne of Spain. Napoleon wanted to establish an imperial succession, but he lacked an heir. In thirteen years of marriage, his wife Josephine had borne no children, so in 1809 he divorced her and in 1810 married the eighteen-year-old Princess Marie-Louise of Austria. The next year she gave birth to a son to whom Napoleon immediately gave the title "king of Rome."

The New Paternalism

Because Napoleon shared the rewards of rule with his own family, it is perhaps not surprising that he brought a familial model of power to his empire, instilling his personal version of paternalism. The prime mover of this system was the new Civil Code. The revolutionary governments had tried to unify and standardize France's multiple legal codes; Napoleon finally succeeded because he personally presided over the commission that drafted the new code, completed in 1804. Called the Napoleonic Code as a way of further exalting his image, it defined and ensured property rights, guaranteed religious liberty, and established a uniform system of law that provided equal treatment for all adult males and affirmed the right of men to choose their professions.

The code sharply curtailed women's rights in almost every aspect of public and private life. One of the leading jurists remarked, "There have been many discussions on the equality and superiority of the sexes. Nothing is more useless than such disputes. . . . Women need protection because they are weaker; men are free because they are stronger." The law obligated a husband to support his wife, but he alone controlled any property held in common. A wife could not sue in court, sell or mortgage her own property, or contract a debt without her husband's consent.

The Civil Code modified even those few revolutionary laws that had been favorable to women, and in some instances it denied women rights they had exercised under the monarchy. Divorce was still possible, but a wife could petition for divorce only if her husband brought his mistress to live in the family home. In contrast, a wife convicted of adultery could be imprisoned for up to two years. The code's framers saw these discrepancies as a way to reinforce the family and make women responsible for private virtue, while leaving public decisions to men. The French code was imitated in many European and Latin American countries and in the French colony of Louisiana, where it had a similar negative effect on women's rights. Not until 1965 did French wives gain legal status equal to that of their husbands.

The Civil Code not only reasserted the old regime's patriarchal system of male domination over women but also insisted on a father's control over his children, which revolutionary legislation had limited. For example, children under age sixteen who refused to follow their fathers' commands could be sent to prison for up to a month with no hearing of any sort. At the same time, the code required fathers to provide for their children's welfare. Napoleon himself encouraged the foundation of private charities to help indigent mothers, and one of his decrees made it easier for women to abandon their children anonymously to a government foundling hospital. Napoleon hoped such measures would discourage abortion and infanticide, especially among the poorest classes in the fast-growing urban areas.

In periods of economic crisis, the government opened soup kitchens, but in time-honored fashion it also arrested beggars and sent them to newly established workhouses. For prostitutes, whose numbers had increased because of migration from the countryside to the cities and wartime upheavals, the Napoleonic state developed a novel paternalist approach. The authorities arrested prostitutes who worked on their own, but they tolerated brothels, which could be supervised by the police, and required the women working in them to have monthly medical examinations for venereal disease.

Napoleon took little interest in girls' education, believing that they should spend most of their time at home learning religion, manners, and such "female occupations" as sewing and music. For boys, by contrast, the government set up a new system of *lycées*, state-run secondary schools in which boys wore military uniforms and drumrolls signaled the beginning and end of classes. (Without the military trappings, the lycées are now coeducational and still the heart of the French educational system.)

The new paternalism extended to relations between employers and employees. The state required all workers to carry a work card attesting to their good conduct, and it prohibited all workers' organizations. The police considered workers without cards as vagrants or criminals and could send them to workhouses or prison. After 1806, arbitration boards settled labor disputes, but they took employers at their word while treating workers as minors, demanding that foremen and shop super-intendents represent them. Occasionally strikes broke out, led by secret, illegal jour-neymen's associations, yet many employers laid off employees when times were hard, deducted fines from their wages, and dismissed them without appeal for being absent or making errors. These limitations on workers' rights won Napoleon the support of French business.

Napoleon continued the central government's patronage of science and intel-lectual life but once again put his own distinctive paternalist stamp on these ac-tivities. He closely monitored the research institutes established during the Rev-olution, sometimes intervening personally to achieve political conformity. An impressive outpouring of new theoretical and practical scientific work rewarded the state's efforts. Experiments with balloons led to the discovery of laws about the ex-pansion of gases, and research on fossil shells prepared the way for new theories of evolutionary change later in the nineteenth century.

Napoleon aimed to modernize French society through science, but he could not tolerate criticism. He considered most writers useless or dangerous, "good for nothing under any government." Some of the most talented French writers of the time had to live in exile. The best-known expatriate was Germaine de Staël (1766–1817), known as Madame de Staël, the daughter of Louis XVI's chief min-ister Jacques Necker. When explaining his desire to banish her, Napoleon exclaimed, "She is a machine in motion who stirs up the salons." While exiled in the German states, Madame de Staël wrote a novel, *Corinne* (1807), whose heroine is a brilliant woman thwarted by a patriarchal system, and *On Germany* (1810), an account of the important new literary currents east of the Rhine. Her books were banned in France.

Although Napoleon restored the strong authority of state and religion in France, many royalists and Catholics still criticized him as an impious usurper. François-René de Chateaubriand (1768–1848) admired Napoleon as "the strong man who has saved us from the abyss," but he preferred monarchy. In his view, Napoleon had not properly understood the need to defend Christian values against the Enlight-enment's excessive reliance on reason. Chateaubriand wrote his *Genius of Chris-tianity* (1802) to draw attention to the power and mystery of faith. He warned, "It is to the vanity of knowledge that we owe almost all our misfortunes.... The learned ages have always been followed by ages of destruction."

"Europe Was at My Feet": Napoleon's Military Conquests

Building on innovations introduced by the republican governments before him, Napoleon revolutionized the art of war with tactics and strategy based on a highly mobile army. Napoleon attributed his military success "three-quarters to morale" and the rest to leadership and superiority of numbers at the point of attack. Con-

■ **Germaine de Staël**

One of the most fascinating intellectuals of her time, Anne-Louise Germaine de Staël seemed to irritate Napoleon more than any other person did. Daughter of Louis XVI's Swiss Protestant finance minister, Jacques Necker, and wife of a Swedish diplomat, Madame de Staël frequently criticized Napoleon's regime. She published best-selling novels and influential literary criticism, and whenever allowed to reside in Paris she encouraged the intellectual and political dissidents from Napoleon's regime.
(Photographie Bulloz.)

scription provided the large numbers: 1.3 million men of ages twenty to twenty-four were drafted between 1800 and 1812, another million in 1813–1814. Military service was both a patriotic duty and a means of social mobility. The men who rose through the ranks to become officers were young, ambitious, and accustomed to the new ways of war. Consequently, the French army had higher morale than the armies of other powers, most of which rejected conscription as too democratic and continued to restrict their officer corps to the nobility. Only in 1813–1814 did French morale plummet, as the military tide turned against Napoleon.

When Napoleon came to power in 1799, desertion was rampant, and the generals competed with one another for predominance. Napoleon united all the armies into one Grand Army under his personal command. By 1812, he commanded 700,000 troops. In any given battle, between 70,000 and 180,000 men, not all of them French, fought for France. Life on campaign was no picnic, yet Napoleon inspired almost fanatical loyalty. A brilliant strategist who carefully studied the demands of war, he outmaneuvered nearly all his opponents. He gathered the largest possible army for one great and decisive battle and then followed with a relentless pursuit to break enemy morale altogether. He fought alongside his soldiers in some sixty battles and had nineteen horses shot from under him. One opponent said that Napoleon's presence alone was worth 50,000 men.

One of Napoleon's greatest advantages was the lack of coordination among his enemies. Britain dominated the seas but did not want to field huge land armies. On the European continent, the French republic had already established satellite regimes in the Netherlands and Italy, which served as a buffer against the big powers to the east—Austria, Prussia, and Russia. By maneuvering diplomatically and militarily, Napoleon could usually take these on one by one. After reorganizing the French armies in 1799, for example, Napoleon won striking victories against the Austrians at Marengo and Hohenlinden in 1800, forcing them to agree to peace terms. Once the Austrians had withdrawn, Britain agreed to the Treaty of Amiens in 1802, effectively ending hostilities in Europe. Napoleon considered the peace with Great Britain merely a truce, however, and it lasted only until 1803. When the attempt to retake St. Domingue failed, Napoleon abandoned his plans to extend his empire to the Western Hemisphere. As part of his retreat, he sold the Louisiana Territory to the United States in 1803.

France's Retreat from America

When war resumed in Europe, the British navy once more proved its superiority by defeating the French and their Spanish allies in a huge naval battle at Trafalgar in 1805. France lost many ships; the British lost no vessels, but their renowned admiral Lord Horatio Nelson died in the battle. On land, however, Napoleon remained invincible. In 1805, Austria took up arms again when Napoleon demanded that it declare neutrality in the conflict with Britain. Napoleon promptly captured 25,000 Austrian soldiers at Ulm in Bavaria in 1805. After marching on to Vienna, he again trounced the Austrians, who had been joined by their new ally, Russia. The battle of Austerlitz, often considered Napoleon's greatest victory, was fought on December 2, 1805, the first anniversary of his coronation.

After maintaining neutrality for a decade, Prussia declared war on France. In 1806, the French promptly destroyed the Prussian army at Jena and Auerstadt. In 1807, Napoleon defeated the Russians at Friedland. Personal negotiations between Napoleon and the young tsar Alexander I (r. 1801–1825) resulted in a humiliating settlement imposed on Prussia, which paid the price for temporary reconciliation between France and Russia. The Treaties of Tilsit turned Prussian lands west of the Elbe River into the kingdom of Westphalia under Napoleon's brother Jerome, and Prussia's Polish provinces became the duchy of Warsaw. Alexander recognized Napoleon's conquests in central and western Europe and promised to help him against the British in exchange for Napoleon's support against the Turks. Neither party kept the bargain. Napoleon once again had turned the divisions among his enemies in his favor.

Wherever the Grand Army conquered, Napoleon's influence soon followed. By annexing some territories and setting up others as satellite kingdoms with much-reduced autonomy, Napoleon attempted to colonize large parts of Europe. He brought the disparate German and Italian states together to rule them more effectively and to exploit their resources for his own ends. In 1806, he established the Confederation of the Rhine, which soon included almost all the German states except Austria and Prussia. The Holy Roman Emperor gave up his title, held since the thirteenth century, and became simply the emperor of Austria. Napoleon established three units in Italy: the territories directly annexed to France and the satellite kingdoms of Italy and Naples. Italy had not been so unified since the Roman Empire.

Consolidation of German and Italian States, 1812

Napoleon forced French-style reforms on both the annexed territories, which were ruled directly from France, and the satellite kingdoms, which were usually ruled by one or another of Napoleon's relatives but with a certain autonomy. Napoleon brought in French experts to work with handpicked locals to abolish serfdom, eliminate seigneurial dues, introduce the Napoleonic Code, suppress monasteries, subordinate church to state, and extend civil rights to Jews and other religious minorities. Reactions to these innovations were mixed. Napoleon's chosen rulers often made real improvements in roads, public works, law codes, and education. Yet tax increases and ever-rising conscription quotas also fomented discontent. The annexed territories and satellite kingdoms paid half the French war expenses. Napoleon's brother Louis would not allow conscription in his kingdom of the Netherlands because the Dutch had never had compulsory military service. In 1810, Napoleon annexed the satellite kingdom because his brother had become too sympathetic to Dutch interests.

Napoleon's victories forced defeated rulers to rethink their political and cultural assumptions. After suffering a crushing military defeat in 1806, Prussian king Frederick William III (r. 1797–1840) appointed a reform commission, and on its recommendation he abolished serfdom. Peasants gained their personal independence from their noble landlords, who could no longer sell them to pay gambling debts, for example, or refuse them permission to marry. Yet the lives of the former serfs remained bleak; they were left without land, and their landlords no longer had to care for them in hard times. The king's advisers also overhauled the army to make the high command more efficient and to open the way to the appointment of middle-class officers. Prussia instituted these reforms to try to compete with the French, not to promote democracy. As one reformer wrote to Frederick William, "We must do from above what the French have done from below."

Reform received lip service in Russia. Tsar Alexander I had gained his throne after an aristocratic coup deposed and killed his autocratic and capricious father, Paul (r. 1796–1801), and in the early years of his reign the remorseful young ruler created Western-style ministries, lifted restrictions on importing foreign books, and founded six new universities. There was even talk of drafting a constitution. But none of these efforts reached beneath the surface of Russian life, and by the second decade of his reign Alexander began to reject the Enlightenment spirit that his grandmother Catherine the Great had instilled in him.

Napoleon's Fall

Napoleon's empire ultimately failed because it was based on a contradiction: Napoleon tried to reduce almost all of Europe to the status of colonial dependents even though Europe had long consisted of independent states. His actions resulted instead in a great upsurge of the nationalist feeling that has dominated European politics to the present.

The one power always standing between Napoleon and total dominance of Europe was Great Britain. The British ruled the seas and financed anyone who would oppose Napoleon. In an effort to bankrupt this "nation of shopkeepers" by choking its trade, Napoleon inaugurated the Continental System in 1806. It prohibited all commerce between Great Britain and France, as well as between Great Britain and France's dependent states and allies. At first the system worked: British exports dropped 20 percent in 1807–1808, and industrial production declined 10 percent; unemployment and a strike of sixty thousand workers in northern England resulted. The British retaliated by confiscating merchandise on ships, even those of powers neutral in the wars, that sailed to or from ports from which the British were excluded by the Continental System.

In the midst of continuing wars, however, the system proved impossible to enforce, and widespread smuggling brought British goods into the European market. British industrial growth continued despite some setbacks. Calico-printing works, for example, quadrupled their production, and imports of raw cotton increased 40 percent. At the same time, French and other continental industries benefited from the temporary protection from British competition. By 1814, the Italian city of Bologna had five hundred factories and Modena four hundred. The French suffered their greatest commercial losses in the port cities, whose trade with the Caribbean colonies had been disrupted by war and Haitian independence.

Smuggling British goods was only one way of opposing the French. Almost everywhere in Europe, resistance began as local opposition to French demands for money or for draftees, but it eventually prompted that patriotic defense of the nation known as nationalism. In southern Italy, gangs of bandits harassed the French army and local officials; thirty-three thousand Italian bandits were arrested in 1809 alone. But resistance continued through a network of secret societies, called the *carbonari* ("charcoal-burners"), which got its name from the practice of marking each new member's forehead with a charcoal mark. Throughout the nineteenth century, the *carbonari* played a leading role in Italian nationalism. In the German states, intellectuals wrote passionate defenses of the virtues of the German nation and of the superiority of German literature. One of the greatest writers of the age, Friedrich Schiller (1759–1805), typified the turn in German sentiment against French revolutionary politics:

> Freedom is only in the realm of dreams
> And the beautiful blooms only in song.

The German states experienced a profound artistic and intellectual revival, which eventually connected with anti-French nationalism. This renaissance included a resurgence of intellectual life in the universities, a thriving press, and the multiplication of Masonic lodges and literary clubs.

No nations bucked under Napoleon's reins more than Spain and Portugal. In 1807, Napoleon sent 100,000 troops through Spain to invade Portugal, Great Britain's ally. The royal family fled to the Portuguese colony of Brazil, but fighting continued, aided by a British army. When Napoleon got his brother Joseph named king of Spain in place of the senile Charles IV (r. 1788–1808), the Spanish clergy and nobles raised bands of peasants to fight the French occupiers. Even Napoleon's taking personal command of French forces failed to quell the Spanish, who for six years fought a war of national independence that pinned down some 250,000 French soldiers. Germaine de Staël commented that Napoleon "never understood that a war might be a crusade. . . . He never reckoned with the one power that no arms could overcome—the enthusiasm of a whole people."

More than a new feeling of nationalism was aroused in Spain. Peasants hated French requisitioning of their food supplies and sought to defend their priests against French anticlericalism. Spanish nobles feared revolutionary reforms and were willing to defend the old monarchy in the person of the young Ferdinand VII, heir to Charles IV, even while Ferdinand himself was congratulating Napoleon on his victories. The Spanish Catholic church spread anti-French propaganda that equated Napoleon with heresy. As the former archbishop of Seville wrote to the archbishop of Granada in 1808, "You realize that we must not recognize as king a free-mason, heretic, Lutheran, as are all the Bonapartes and the French nation." In this tense atmosphere, the Spanish peasant rebels, assisted by the British, countered

▪ Napoleon's Mamelukes Massacre the Spanish

In one of the paintings he produced to criticize Napoleon's occupation of Spain, Second of May 1808 at the Puerta del Sol *(1814), Francisco Goya depicts the brutal suppression of the Spanish revolt in Madrid against Napoleon. Napoleon used Mamelukes, Egyptian soldiers descended from freed Turkish slaves. For the Spanish Christians—and for European viewers of the painting—use of these mercenaries made the event even more horrifying. Europeans considered Muslims, and Turks in particular, as menacing because the Europeans had been fighting them for centuries.* (Museo del Prado, Madrid.)

every French massacre with atrocities of their own. They tortured their French prisoners (boiling one general alive) and lynched collaborators.

Despite opposition, Napoleon ruled over an extensive empire by 1812 (see "Mapping the West," page 700). He controlled more territory than any European ruler had since Roman times. Only two major European states remained fully independent—Great Britain and Russia—but once allied they would successfully challenge his dominion and draw many other states to their side. Britain sent aid to the Portuguese and Spanish rebels, while Russia once again prepared for war. Tsar Alexander I made peace with the Ottoman Turks and allied himself with Great Britain and Sweden. In 1812, Napoleon invaded Russia with 250,000 horses and 600,000 men, including contingents of Italians, Poles, Swiss, Dutch, and Germans. This daring move proved to be his undoing.

Napoleon followed his usual strategy of trying to strike quickly, but the Russian generals avoided confrontation and retreated eastward, destroying anything that might be useful to the invaders. In September, on the road to Moscow, Napoleon finally engaged the main Russian force in the gigantic battle of Borodino. French casualties were 30,000 men, including 47 generals; the Russians lost 45,000. Once again the Russians retreated, leaving Moscow undefended. Napoleon entered the deserted city, but the victory turned hollow because the departing Russians had set the wooden city on fire. Within a week, three-fourths of it had burned to the ground. Still Alexander refused to negotiate, and French morale plunged with worsening problems of supply. Weeks of constant marching in the dirt and heat had worn down the foot soldiers, who were dying of disease or deserting in large numbers.

In October, Napoleon began his retreat; in November came the cold. Napoleon himself reported that on November 14 the temperature fell to 24 degrees Fahrenheit. A German soldier in the Grand Army described trying to cook fistfuls of raw bran with snow to make something like bread. For him the retreat was "the indescribable horror of all possible plagues." Within a week, the Grand Army lost 30,000 horses and had to abandon most of its artillery and food supplies. Russian forces harassed the retreating army, now more pathetic than grand. By December, only 100,000 troops remained, one-sixth the original number, and the retreat had turned into a rout: the Russians had captured 200,000 soldiers, including 48 generals and 3,000 other officers.

Napoleon had made a classic military mistake that would be repeated by Adolf Hitler in World War II: fighting a war on two distant fronts simultaneously. The Spanish war tied down 250,000 French troops and forced Napoleon to bully Prussia and Austria into supplying soldiers of dubious loyalty for the Moscow campaign. They deserted at the first opportunity. The fighting in Spain and Portugal also worsened the already substantial logistical and communications problems involved in marching to Moscow.

Napoleon's humiliation might have been temporary if the British and Russians had not successfully organized a coalition to complete the job. Napoleon still had resources at his command; by the spring of 1813 he had replenished his army with another 250,000 men. With British financial support, Russian, Austrian, Prussian, and Swedish armies met the French outside Leipzig in October 1813 and defeated Napoleon in the Battle of the Nations. One by one, Napoleon's German allies deserted him to join the German nationalist "war of liberation." The Confederation of the Rhine dissolved, and the Dutch revolted and restored the prince of Orange. Joseph Bonaparte fled Spain, and a combined Spanish-Portuguese army under British command invaded France. In only a few months, the allied powers crossed the Rhine and marched toward Paris. In March 1814, the French Senate deposed Napoleon, who abdicated when his remaining generals refused to fight. Napoleon

	IMPORTANT DATES		
1787	Prussian invasion stifles Dutch Patriot revolt	1795	Third (final) Partition of Poland
1788	Beginning of resistance of Austrian Netherlands against reforms of Joseph II; opening of reform parliament in Poland	1799	Napoleon Bonaparte comes to power in a coup
		1801	Napoleon signs a concordat with the pope
1789	French Revolution begins	1804	Napoleon crowns himself emperor of France and issues new Civil Code
1791	Beginning of slave revolt in St. Domingue (Haiti)		
1792	Beginning of war between France and the rest of Europe; second revolution of August 10 overthrows French monarchy	1805	British naval forces defeat the French at the battle of Trafalgar; Napoleon wins his greatest victory at the battle of Austerlitz
		1812	Napoleon invades Russia
1793	Second Partition of Poland by Austria and Russia; Louis XVI of France executed for treason	1815	Napoleon defeated at Waterloo and exiled to island of St. Helena, where he dies in 1821
1794	France annexes the Austrian Netherlands; abolition of slavery in French colonies; Robespierre's government by terror falls		

went into exile on the island of Elba off the Italian coast. His wife, Marie-Louise, refused to accompany him. The allies restored to the throne Louis XVIII (r. 1814–1824), the brother of Louis XVI (whose son was known as Louis XVII even though he died in prison in 1795 without ever ruling).

Napoleon had one last chance to regain power because Louis XVIII lacked a solid base of support. The new king tried to steer a middle course through a charter that established a British-style monarchy with a two-house legislature and guaranteed civil rights. But he was caught between returning émigré nobles who demanded a complete restoration of their lands and powers and those who had supported either the republic or Napoleon during the previous twenty-five years. Sensing an opportunity, Napoleon escaped from Elba in early 1815 and, landing in southern France, made swift and unimpeded progress to Paris. Although he had left in ignominy, now crowds cheered him and former soldiers volunteered to serve him. The period known as the "Hundred Days" (the length of time between his escape and his final defeat) had begun. Louis XVIII fled across the border, waiting for help from France's enemies.

Napoleon quickly moved his reconstituted army into present-day Belgium. At first it seemed that he might succeed in separately fighting the two armies arrayed against him—a Prussian army and a joint force of Belgian, Dutch, German, and British troops led by Sir Arthur Wellesley (1769–1852), duke of Wellington. But the Prussians evaded him and joined with Wellington at Waterloo. Completely routed, Napoleon had no choice but to abdicate again. This time the victorious allies banished him permanently to the remote island of St. Helena, far off the coast of West Africa, where he died in 1821 at the age of fifty-two.

Conclusion

The cost of Napoleon's rule was high: 750,000 French soldiers and 400,000 others from annexed and satellite states died fighting for the French between 1800 and 1815. The losses among those attempting to stop Napoleon were at least as high, but no military figure since Alexander the Great in the fourth century B.C. had made such an impact on world history. Napoleon's plans for a united Europe, his insistence on spreading the legal reforms of the French Revolution, his social welfare programs, and even his inadvertent awakening of national sentiment set the agenda for European history in the modern era.

The revolutionary cataclysm permanently altered the political landscape of Europe. The French executed their king as a traitor and set up Europe's first republic with universal male suffrage and a written guarantee of "the rights of man." Ordinary people marched in demonstrations, met in clubs, and in the case of men, voted in national elections for the first time. They got their first taste of democracy. But the ideals of universal education, religious toleration, and democratic participation could not prevent the institution of new forms of government terror to persecute, imprison, and kill dissidents. The French revolutionary experiment thus led to democracy *and* to a kind of totalitarianism. The French used the new spirit of national pride to inspire a huge citizen army, but the army conquered other peoples and gave a leading general the chance to take power for himself. Napoleon in turn created yet another new form of rule with a long history in the modern era: a police state in which the generals played a leading political role. Napoleon suppressed all other meaningful political participation and offered in its place law and order and modernization from above. Like many other authoritarian rulers after him, however, Napoleon could not maintain his position once he lost in battle.

As events unfolded between 1789 and 1815, the French Revolution became *the* model of modern revolution and in the process set the enduring patterns of all modern politics. Republicanism, democracy, terrorism, nationalism, and military dictatorship all took their modern forms during the French Revolution. Even the terms *left* and *right* got their political meaning in this period: "the left" was a

■ MAPPING THE WEST Europe under Napoleonic Domination, 1812

In 1812, Napoleon had at least nominal control of almost all of western Europe. Even before he made his fatal mistake of invading Russia, however, his authority had been undermined in Spain and seriously weakened in the Italian and German states. His efforts to extend French power sparked resistance almost everywhere. As Napoleon insisted on French domination, local people began to think of themselves as Italian, German, or Dutch. Thus Napoleon inadvertently laid the foundations for the nineteenth-century spread of nationalism.

reference to deputies who favored extensive change and sat together in seats to the speaker's left in 1789; deputies who preferred a more cautious and conservative stance sat as a group to the speaker's right. The breathtaking succession of regimes in France between 1789 and 1815 inevitably raised disturbing questions about the relationship between rapid political change and violence. Do all revolutions in the name of democracy inevitably degenerate into wars of conquest or terror? Is a regime democratic if it does not allow poor men, women, or blacks to vote? Is a militaristic, authoritarian style of government the only answer to divisive political conflicts in a time of war? The French Revolution and its aftermath—the era of Napoleon—raised these questions and many more.

Suggested References for further reading and online research appear on page SR-25 at the back of the book.

www.bedfordstmartins.com/huntconcise   See the ONLINE STUDY GUIDE to assess your mastery of the material covered in this chapter.

Industrialization and Social Ferment

1815–1850

A POPULAR GERMAN LITHOGRAPH published around 1830 shows two drunken workingmen standing in front of a water pump in Berlin. In the lithograph's caption, one says, "What'd you think, Schulze, what if that were Kümmel [the Berlin liqueur made with caraway]?" His comrade responds, "Yeah, that would be my first wish if I could wish three times." "So, and the second?" "That all [water] pumps were full of Kümmel."* The lithograph captures the new preoccupation with lower-class behavior in this time of social change and political upheaval. As industrialization spread across western Europe, peasants and workers streamed into the cities, creating unprecedented social problems. The population of Berlin, for example, more than doubled between 1819 and 1849, reaching 412,000. Already by 1840, more than half the residents of Berlin had been born outside the city. Many feared that the flood of newcomers would encourage the spread of disease, crime, and social unrest.

Although the people of Europe longed for peace and stability in the aftermath of the Napoleonic whirlwind, they lived in a world that was deeply unsettled

*Translation from Mary Lee Townsend, *Forbidden Laughter: Popular Humor and the Limits of Repression in Nineteenth-Century Prussia* (Ann Arbor: University of Michigan Press, 1992), 10.

■ Drink and the Working Class
In his lithograph Two Drunken Day Laborers *(c. 1830), the German artist Franz Burchard Dörbeck calls attention to the propensity of the working classes to drink. Lithography (from the Greek* lithos, *"stone") was invented by a German engraver in 1798, but its use spread across Europe only in the nineteenth century. The artist used a greasy crayon to trace an image on a flat stone. The grease attracted ink; the blank areas repelled it. The inked stone was embedded in a printing press that could produce thousands of identical images. By creating pictures of every class in society and their problems, and by publishing their images in daily and weekly newspapers, artists enlightened a mass audience about social and political problems created by industrial and urban growth.* (Stadtmuseum Berlin; photo: Hans-Joachim Bartsch, Berlin.)

by two parallel revolutions: the French Revolution and the Industrial Revolution. Even as restored monarchs tried to limit challenges to their rule, the French Revolution and its Napoleonic sequel created new expectations for constitutional government, democracy, and national self-determination. At the same time, the Industrial Revolution spread from Great Britain to continental Europe in the form of factories and railroads. Industrialization produced new social problems that reinforced demands for political change. Under the impact of the French and Industrial Revolutions, new ideologies emerged. Conservatism, nationalism, liberalism, socialism, and communism each offered their adherents a doctrine that explained social change and advocated a political program to confront it.

Social ferment bubbled up in a variety of forms. Painters, poets, and musicians advocated the new style of romanticism. While novelists depicted the social types created by economic change, middle-class men and women joined together in reform societies to urge specific programs for fighting prostitution, assisting poor mothers, encouraging temperance (abstention from alcohol), or abolishing slavery. Despite these efforts at reform, the most unfortunate sometimes pulled up stakes and emigrated to other places, such as the United States. Between 1815 and 1850, more than five million Europeans left their home countries for new lives overseas. For those who stayed behind, revolution remained an ever-present option. Political revolts shook Spain, Italy, Russia, Greece and almost all of Latin America in the 1820s. In 1830, a wave of liberal and nationalist revolutions washed over France, Belgium, Poland, and some of the Italian states. In 1848, yet another French Revolution sparked uprisings in much of Europe. Social ferment threatened to transform into cataclysmic upheaval.

The "Restoration" of Europe

When Napoleon went off to his permanent exile on St. Helena, those allied against him breathed a collective sigh of relief. Revolution, it seemed, had finally been defeated. Some of the returning rulers so detested French innovations that they tore French plants out of their gardens and threw French furniture out of their palaces. Even as Napoleon had made his last desperate bid for power in the Hundred Days between his escape from Elba and his final defeat, his enemies were meeting in the Congress of Vienna (1814–1815) to decide the fate of postrevolutionary Europe. Many of Europe's rulers hoped to nullify revolutionary and Napoleonic reforms and "restore" their old regimes; the Congress of Vienna settled the boundaries of European states, determining who would rule each nation. The congress also established a new framework for international relations based on periodic meetings—congresses—between the major powers. This congress system, or "concert of Europe," helped prevent another major war until the 1850s, and no conflict comparable to the Napoleonic wars would occur again until 1914.

The Congress of Vienna, 1814–1815

The Vienna settlement produced a new equilibrium that relied on cooperation among the major powers while guaranteeing the status of smaller states. In addition to determining the boundaries of France, the congress had to decide the fate of Napoleon's duchy of Warsaw, the German province of Saxony, the Netherlands, the states once part of the confederation of the Rhine, and various Italian territories. All had either changed hands or been created during the wars. These issues were resolved by face-to-face negotiations among representatives of the five major powers: Austria, Russia, Prussia, Britain, and France. With its aim to arrange a long-lasting, negotiated peace endorsed by all parties—both winners and losers—the Congress of Vienna provided a model for the twentieth-century League of Nations and United Nations.

Austria's chief negotiator, Prince Klemens von Metternich (1773–1859), took the lead in negotiations. A well-educated nobleman who spoke five languages, Metternich served as a minister in the Austrian cabinet from 1809 to 1848. Although his penchant for womanizing made him a security risk in the eyes of the British Foreign Office (he even had an affair with Napoleon's younger sister), he worked with the British prime minister Robert Castlereagh (1769–1822) to ensure a moderate

■ **The Congress of Vienna**

An unknown French engraver caricatured the efforts of the diplomats at the Congress of Vienna, complaining that they used the occasion to divide the spoils of European territory. At the far left stands Metternich preparing to take Venice and Lombardy (northern Italy).

(Historisches Museum der Stadt Wien.)

agreement that would check French aggression yet maintain France's great-power status. Metternich and Castlereagh believed that France must remain a major player so that no one European power might dominate the others. In this way, France could help Austria and Britain counter the ambitions of Prussia and Russia. When the French army failed to oppose Napoleon's return to power in the Hundred Days, the allies took away all territory conquered by France since 1790 and required France to pay an indemnity and support an army of occupation until it was paid.

The goal of the congress was to achieve postwar stability by establishing secure states with guaranteed borders (Map 17.1). Where possible, the congress simply re-

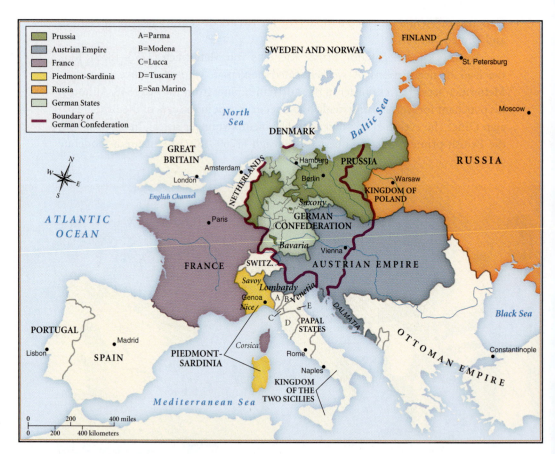

■ **MAP 17.1 Europe after the Congress of Vienna, 1815**

The diplomats meeting at the Congress of Vienna could not simply "restore" Europe to its prerevolutionary borders. Too much had changed since 1789. France was forced to return to its 1790 borders, and Spain and Portugal regained their former rulers. The Austrian Netherlands and the Dutch Republic were united in a new kingdom of the Netherlands, the German states were joined in a Germanic Confederation that built upon Napoleon's Confederation of the Rhine, and Napoleon's Grand Duchy of Warsaw became the kingdom of Poland with the tsar of Russia as king.

stored traditional rulers, as in Spain and the Italian states. The great powers decided to turn Napoleon's duchy of Warsaw into a new Polish kingdom but made the tsar of Russia its king. (Poland would not regain its independence until 1918.) The former Dutch Republic and the Austrian Netherlands, both annexed to France, now united as the new kingdom of the Netherlands under the restored stadholder. Prussia gained territory in Saxony and on the left bank of the Rhine to compensate for its losses in Poland. To make up for its losses in Poland and Saxony, Austria reclaimed the Italian provinces of Lombardy and Venetia and the Dalmatian coast. Austria now presided over the German Confederation, which replaced the defunct Holy Roman Empire and also included Prussia.

The lesser powers were not forgotten. The kingdom of Piedmont-Sardinia took Genoa, Nice, and part of Savoy. Sweden obtained Norway from Denmark but had to accept Russia's conquest of Finland. Finally, various international trade issues were also resolved. At the urging of Great Britain, the congress agreed to condemn in principle the slave trade, abolished by Great Britain in 1807. In reality, however, the slave trade continued in many places until the 1840s.

To impart spiritual substance to this very calculated settlement of political affairs, Tsar Alexander proposed a Holy Alliance that would ensure divine assistance in upholding religion, peace, and justice. Prussia and Austria signed the agreement, but Great Britain refused to accede to what Castlereagh called "a piece of sublime mysticism and nonsense." Pope Pius VII also refused on the grounds that the papacy needed no help in interpreting the Christian truth. Despite the reassertion of traditional religious principle, the congress had in fact given birth to a new diplomatic order: in the future, the legitimacy of states depended on the treaty system, not on divine right.

The Emergence of Conservatism

The French Revolution and Napoleonic domination of Europe had shown contemporaries that government could be changed overnight, that the old hierarchies could be overthrown in the name of reason, and that even Christianity could be written off or at least profoundly altered with the stroke of a pen. The potential for rapid change raised many questions about the proper sources of authority. Kings and churches could be restored and former revolutionaries locked up or silenced, but the old order no longer commanded automatic obedience. The old order was now merely *old*, no longer "natural" and "timeless." It had been ousted once and therefore might fall again. People insisted on having reasons to believe in their "restored" governments. The political doctrine that justified the restoration was *conservatism*.

Conservatives benefited from the disillusionment that permeated Europe after 1815. In the eyes of most Europeans, Napoleon had become a tyrant who ruled in his own interests. Conservatives believed it was crucial to analyze the roots of such tyranny so established authorities could use their knowledge of history to prevent its recurrence. They saw a logical progression in recent history: the Enlightenment based on reason led to the French Revolution, with its bloody guillotine and horrifying Terror, which in turn spawned the authoritarian and militaristic Napoleon. Conservative intellectuals therefore either rejected Enlightenment principles or at least subjected them to scrutiny and skepticism.

The most influential spokesman of conservatism was Edmund Burke (1729–1799), the British critic of the French Revolution. He argued that the revolutionaries erred in thinking they could construct an entirely new government based on reason. Government, Burke said, had to be rooted in long experience, which evolved over generations. All change must be gradual and must respect national and historical traditions.

Like Burke, later conservatives believed that religious and other major traditions were an essential foundation for any society. Conservatives blamed the French Revolution's attack on religion on the skepticism and anticlericalism of such Enlightenment thinkers as Voltaire, and they defended both hereditary monarchy and the authority of the church, whether Catholic or Protestant. The "rights of man," according to conservatives, could not stand alone as doctrine based simply on nature and reason. The community, too, had its rights, more important than those of any individual, and established institutions best represented those rights. The church, the state, and the family would provide an enduring social order for everyone. Faith, sentiment, history, and tradition must fill the vacuum left by the failures of reason and excessive belief in individual rights. Across Europe, these views were taken up and elaborated by government advisers, professors, and writers. Not surprisingly, they had their strongest appeal in ruling circles and guided the politics of men such as Metternich in Austria and Alexander I in Russia.

The restored monarchy in France provided a major test for conservatism because the returning Bourbons had to confront the legacy of twenty-five years of upheaval. Louis XVIII (r. 1814–1824) tried to ensure a measure of continuity by maintaining Napoleon's Civil Code. He also guaranteed the rights of ownership to church lands sold during the revolutionary period and created a parliament composed of a Chamber of Peers nominated by the king and a Chamber of Deputies elected by very restricted suffrage (fewer than 100,000 voters in a population of 30 million, or about 3 percent). In making these concessions, the king tried to follow a moderate course of compromise, but the Ultras (ultraroyalists) pushed for complete repudiation of the revolutionary past. When Louis returned to power after Napoleon's final defeat, armed royalist bands attacked and murdered hundreds of Bonapartists and former revolutionaries. In 1816, the Ultras insisted on abolishing divorce and set up special courts to punish opponents of the regime. When an assassin killed Louis XVIII's nephew in 1820, the Ultras demanded even more extreme measures.

The Revival of Religion

The experience of revolutionary upheaval and nearly constant warfare prompted many to renew their religious faith once peace returned. In France, the Catholic church sent missionaries to hold open-air "ceremonies of reparation" to express repentance for the outrages of revolution. In Rome, the papacy reestablished the Jesuit order, which had been disbanded during the Enlightenment. In the Italian states and Spain, governments used religious societies of laypeople to combat the influence of reformers and nationalists such as the Italian *carbonari*.

Revivalist movements, especially in Protestant countries, could on occasion challenge the status quo, not support it. In parts of the Protestant German states and Britain, religious revival had begun in the eighteenth century with the rise of Pietism and Methodism, movements that stressed individual religious experience rather than reason as the true path to moral and social reform. The English Methodists followed John Wesley (1703–1791), who preached an emotional, morally austere, and very personal "method" of gaining salvation. The Methodists, or Wesleyans, gradually separated from the Church of England and in the early decades of the nineteenth century attracted thousands of members in huge revival meetings that lasted for days. Shopkeepers, artisans, agricultural laborers, miners, and workers in cottage industry, both male and female, flocked to the new denomination. Even though Methodist statutes of 1792 had insisted that "none of us shall either in writing or in conversation speak lightly or irreverently of the government," Methodists fostered a sense of democratic community with their hostility to elaborate ritual and their encouragement of popular preaching. Methodist women traveled on horseback to preach in barns, town halls, and textile dye houses. Methodist Sunday schools that taught thousands of poor children to read and write eventually helped create greater demands for working-class political participation.

The religious revival was not limited to Europe. In the United States, the second "Great Awakening" began around 1790 with huge camp meetings that brought together thousands of people, many of them Methodist. (The original Great Awakening took place in the 1730s and 1740s, sparked by the preaching of George Whitefield, a young English evangelist and follower of John Wesley.) During this period, Protestant sects began systematic missionary activity in other parts of the world, with British and American missionary societies taking the lead in the 1790s and early 1800s. In the British colony of India, Protestant missionaries argued for the reform of Hindu customs. *Sati*—the burning of widows on the funeral pyres of their husbands—was abolished by the British administration of India in 1829. Missionary activity by Protestants and Catholics would become one of the arms of European imperialism and cultural influence in the nineteenth century.

Political Challenges to the Conservative Order

The conservative Vienna settlement disappointed all those who dreamed of constitutional freedoms and national independence, and within a few years, discontent rose to the surface. The Vienna powers joined together to confront these challenges, and they succeeded in areas where they were able to intervene militarily, most notably Spain and the Italian states. In Greece and Latin America, however, revolts for national independence succeeded. The Greeks eventually obtained European support because they wanted freedom from Europe's traditional enemy, the Ottoman Turks. The Latin Americans won their independence because Napoleon's occupation had undermined the authority of the Spanish and Portuguese rulers.

When Ferdinand VII regained the Spanish crown in 1814, he created opposition with extreme measures to restore the powers of the prerevolutionary nobility, church, and monarchy. He had foreign books and newspapers confiscated at the frontier and allowed the publication of only two newspapers. In 1820, disgruntled soldiers demanded that Ferdinand proclaim his adherence to the Constitution of 1812, which he had abolished in 1814. When the revolt spread, Ferdinand convened the *cortes* (parliament), which could agree on practically nothing. Ferdinand bided his time, and in 1823 a French army invaded with the consent of the other Vienna powers and restored him to power. His government then tortured and executed hundreds of rebels; thousands were imprisoned or forced into exile.

Hearing of the Spanish uprising, rebellious soldiers in the kingdom of Naples joined forces with the *carbonari* and demanded a constitution. When a new parliament met, it, too, broke down over internal disagreements. The promise of reform sparked rebellion in the northern Italian kingdom of Piedmont-Sardinia, where rebels urged Charles Albert, the young heir to the Piedmont throne, to fight the Austrians for Italian unification. He vacillated; but in 1821, after the rulers of Austria, Prussia, and Russia met and agreed on intervention, the Austrians defeated the rebels in Naples and Piedmont (see Map 17.1). Liberals were arrested in many Italian states, and the pope condemned the secret societies as "at heart only devouring wolves." Despite the opposition of Great Britain, which condemned the "indiscriminate" suppression of revolutionary movements, Metternich convinced the other powers to agree to his muffling of the Italian opposition to Austrian rule.

Aspirations for constitutional government surfaced in Russia when Alexander I died suddenly in 1825. On the December day that the troops assembled in St. Petersburg to take an oath of loyalty to Alexander's brother Nicholas as the new tsar, rebel officers insisted that the crown belonged to another brother, Constantine, who they hoped would be more favorable to constitutional reform. Constantine, though next in the line of succession after Alexander, had refused the crown. The soldiers nonetheless raised the cry "Long live Constantine, long live the Constitution." (Some troops apparently thought that "the Constitution" was Constantine's wife.) Soldiers loyal to Nicholas easily suppressed the Decembrists (so called after the month of their uprising), who were so outnumbered that they had no realistic chance to succeed. The subsequent trial, however, made the rebels into legendary heroes. For the next thirty years, Nicholas I (r. 1825–1855) used a new political police, the Third Section, to spy on potential opponents and stamp out rebelliousness.

The Ottoman Turks faced growing nationalist challenges in the Balkans, but the European powers feared that supporting them would encourage a rebellious spirit at home. The Serbs revolted against Turkish rule and won virtual independence by 1817. A Greek general in the Russian army, Prince Alexander Ypsilanti, tried to lead a revolt against the Turks in 1820 but failed when the tsar, urged on by Metternich, disavowed him. Metternich feared rebellion even by Christians against their Turkish rulers. A second revolt, this time by Greek peasants, sparked a wave of atrocities in 1821 and 1822. The Greeks killed every Turk who did not escape. In retaliation the Turks hanged the Greek patriarch (head of the Greek Orthodox church), and in the areas they still controlled they pillaged churches, massacred thousands of men, and sold the women into slavery.

Nationalistic Movements in the Balkans, 1815–1830

Western opinion turned against the Turks; Greece, after all, was the home of Western civilization. While the great powers negotiated, Greeks and pro-Greece committees around the world sent food and military supplies; a few enthusiastic European and American volunteers even joined the Greeks. The Greeks held on until the great powers were willing to intervene. In 1827, a combined force of British, French, and Russian ships destroyed the Turkish fleet at Navarino Bay; and in 1828, Russia declared war on the Turks and advanced close to Istanbul. The Treaty of Adrianople of 1829 gave Russia a protectorate over the Danubian principalities in the Balkans and provided for a conference among representatives of Britain, Russia, and France, all of whom had broken with Austria in support of the Greeks. In 1830, Greece was declared an independent kingdom under the guarantee of the three powers; in 1833, the son of King Ludwig of Bavaria became Otto I of Greece. Nationalism, with the support of European public opinion, had made its first breach in Metternich's system.

■ Greek Independence

From 1836 to 1839, the Greek painter Panagiotis Zographos worked with his two sons on a series of scenes depicting the Greek struggle for independence from the Turks. Response was so favorable that one Greek general ordered lithographic reproductions for popular distribution. In this way, nationalistic feeling could be encouraged even among people not directly touched by the struggle. Here Turkish sultan Mehmet the Conqueror, exulting over the fall of Constantinople in 1453, views a row of Greeks under the yoke, a sign of submission.
(Collection, Visual Connection.)

Across the Atlantic, national revolts also succeeded after a series of bloody wars of independence. Taking advantage of the upheavals in Spain and Portugal that began under Napoleon, restive colonists from Mexico to Argentina rebelled. Their leader was Simon Bolívar (1783–1830), son of a slave owner, who was educated in Europe on the works of Voltaire and Rousseau. Although Bolívar fancied himself a Latin American Napoleon, he had to acquiesce to the formation of a series of independent republics between 1821 and 1823, even in Bolivia, which is named after him. At the same time, Brazil (then still a monarchy) separated from Portugal (Map 17.2). The United States recognized the new states, and in 1823 President James Monroe (1758–1831) announced his Monroe Doctrine, closing the Americas to European intervention—a prohibition that depended on British naval power and British willingness to declare neutrality.

■ MAP 17.2 Latin American Independence, 1804–1830

The French lost their most important re-maining American colony in 1804 when St. Domingue declared its independence as Haiti. But the impact of the French Revo-lution did not end there. Napoleon's occu-pation of Spain and Portugal seriously weakened the hold of those countries on their Latin American colonies. Despite the restoration of the Spanish and Portuguese rulers in 1814, most of their colonies suc-cessfully broke away in a wave of rebellions between 1811 and 1830. Meanwhile, a re-volt in Spain in 1820–1823 led to a consti-tutional regime. The Spanish general sent to suppress the revolt in Mexico ended up joining the rebels' cause and helping them establish independence in 1821.

The Advance of Industrialization and Urbanization

French and English writers of the 1820s introduced the term *Industrial Revolution* to capture the drama of contemporary economic change and to draw a parallel with the French Revolution. But we should not take the comparison too literally. Unlike the French upheaval, the Industrial Revolution did not have definite dates that marked its beginning or ending. From their first appearance in Great Britain in the second half of the eighteenth century, steam-driven machinery, large factories, and a new working class spread slowly to the rest of Europe and eventually to the rest of the world. Still, historians have shown that industrialization and its corollary ur-banization accelerated quite suddenly in the first half of the nineteenth century and touched off loud complaints about their effects. Contemporaries did not fully un-derstand the link between industrial and urban growth, and even today, scholars debate the connection. Population growth did not just change life in the cities; it produced new tensions in the countryside, too.

The Rise of the Railroad

Steam-driven engines took on a dramatic new form in the 1820s when the English engineer George Stephenson perfected an engine to pull wagons along rail tracks. Suddenly, railroad building became a new industry. (See "Taking Measure," page 715.) The idea of a railroad was not new: iron tracks had been used since the seventeenth century to haul coal from mines in wagons pulled by horses. A railroad system of transport, however, developed only after Stephenson's invention of a steam-powered locomotive. In 1830, the Liverpool and Manchester Railway line opened to the cheers of crowds and the congratulations of government officials, including the duke of Wellington, the hero of Waterloo and now prime minister. In the excitement, some of the dignitaries gathered on a parallel track. When another engine approached at high speed, most of the gentlemen scattered to safety, but former cabinet minister William Huskisson fell and was hit. In a few hours he died, the first official casualty of the newfangled railroad.

Railroads were dramatic and expensive—the most striking symbol of the new industrial age. One German entrepreneur confidently predicted, "The locomotive is the hearse which will carry absolutism and feudalism to the graveyard." Placed on the new tracks, steam-driven carriages could transport people and goods to the cities and link coal and iron deposits to the new factories. In the 1840s alone, railroad track mileage more than doubled in Great Britain, and British investment in railways jumped tenfold. The British also began to build railroads in India. Canal building waned in the 1840s: the railroad had won out.

Britain's success with rail transportation led other countries to develop their own projects. Railroads grew spectacularly in the United States in the 1830s and 1840s. Belgium, newly independent in 1830, opened the first continental European railroad with state bonds backed by British capital in 1835. By 1850, France had 2,000 miles of railroad and the German states nearly twice as many; Great Britain had 6,000 miles and the United States 9,000 miles. In all, the world had 23,500 miles of track by midcentury.

Railroad building spurred both industrial development and state power (see "Mapping the West," page 752). Governments everywhere participated in the construction of railroads, which depended on private and state funds to pay for the massive amounts of iron, coal, heavy machinery, and human labor required to build and run them. One-third of all investment in the German states in the 1840s went into railroads. Demand for iron products accelerated industrial development. Until the 1840s, cotton had led industrial production; between 1816 and 1840, cotton output more than quadrupled in Great Britain. But from 1830 to 1850, Britain's output of iron and coal doubled. Similarly, Austrian output of iron doubled between the 1820s and the 1840s.

Steam-powered engines made Britain the world leader in manufacturing. By midcentury, more than half of Britain's national income came from manufacturing and trade. The number of steamboats in Great Britain increased from two in 1812 to six

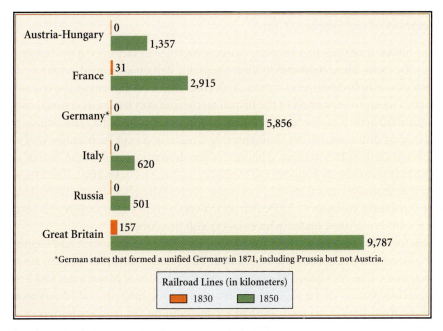

■ TAKING MEASURE Railroad Lines, 1830–1850

Great Britain quickly extended its lead in building railroads. The extension of commerce and, before long, the ability to wage war would depend on the development of effective rail networks. These statistics might be taken as predicting a realignment of power within Europe after 1850. What do the numbers say about the relative positions of Germany and Austria-Hungary and of Germany and France?

(From B. R. Mitchell, *European Historical Statistics, 1750–1970* [New York: Columbia University Press, 1975], F1.)

hundred in 1840. Between 1840 and 1850, steam-engine power doubled in Great Britain and increased even more rapidly elsewhere in Europe, as those adopting British inventions strove to catch up. The power applied in German manufacturing, for example, rose from 60,000 to 360,000 hp (units horsepower) during the 1840s but still amounted to only a little more than a quarter of the British figure.

Although Great Britain consciously strove to protect its industrial supremacy, thousands of British engineers defied laws against the export of machinery or the emigration of artisans. The best known of them, John Cockerill, set up a machine works in Belgium that was soon selling its products as far east as Poland and Russia. Cockerill claimed to know about every innovation within ten days of its appearance in Britain. Only slowly, thanks to such pirating of British methods and to new technical schools, did most continental European countries begin closing the gap. Belgium became the fastest-growing industrial power on the continent: between 1830 and 1844, the number of steam engines in Belgium quadrupled, and Belgians exported seven times as many steam engines as they imported. Even so, by 1850, continental Europe still lagged almost twenty years behind Great Britain in industrial development.

Formation of the Working Class

Steam-driven machines first brought workers together in factories in the textile industry. By 1830, more than one million people in Britain depended on the cotton industry for employment, and cotton cloth constituted 50 percent of the country's exports. The rapid expansion of the British textile industry had as its colonial corollary the destruction of the hand manufacture of textiles in India. The British put high import duties on Indian cloth entering Britain and kept such duties very low for British cloth entering India. The figures are dramatic: in 1813, the Indian city of Calcutta exported to England £2,000,000 of cotton cloth; by 1830, Calcutta was importing from England £2,000,000 of cotton cloth. When Britain abolished slavery in its Caribbean colonies in 1833, British manufacturers began to buy raw cotton in the southern United States, where slavery still flourished.

Factories drew workers from the urban population surge, which had begun in the eighteenth century and now accelerated. The reasons for urban growth are not entirely clear. The population of such new industrial cities as Manchester and Leeds increased 40 percent in the 1820s alone. Historians long thought that factory workers came from the countryside, pushed off the land by the field enclosures of the 1700s. But recent studies have shown that the number of agricultural laborers actually increased during industrialization in Britain, suggesting that a growing birthrate created a larger population and fed workers into the new factory system.

The new workers came from several sources: families of farmers who could not provide land for all their children, soldiers demobilized after the Napoleonic wars, artisans displaced by the new machinery, and children of the earliest workers who had moved to the factory towns. A system of employment that resembled family labor on farms or in cottage industry also developed in the new factories. Entire families came to toil for a single wage, although family members performed different tasks. Workdays of twelve to seventeen hours were typical, even for children, and the work was grueling. Community ties remained important as workers migrated from rural to urban areas to join friends and family from their original villages.

As urban factories grew, their workers gradually came to constitute a new socioeconomic class with a distinctive culture and traditions. Like *middle class*, the term *working class* came into use for the first time in the early nineteenth century. It referred to the laborers in the new factories. In the past, workers had labored in isolated trades: water and wood carrying, gardening, laundry, and building. In contrast, factories brought people together with machines, under close supervision by their employers. They soon developed a sense of common interests and organized societies for mutual help and political reform. From these would come the first labor unions.

Fearing their displacement by machines, bands of handloom weavers wrecked factory machinery and burned mills in the Midlands, Yorkshire, and Lancashire. To restore order and protect industry, the British government sent in an army of twelve thousand regular soldiers and made machine wrecking punishable by death. The rioters were called *Luddites* after the fictitious figure Ned Ludd, whose signature appeared on their manifestos. (The term is still used to describe those who resist new technology.)

Other British workers focused their organizing efforts on reforming Parliament, whose members were chosen in elections dominated by the landowning elite. One reformer complained that the members of the House of Commons were nothing but "toad-eaters, gamblers, public plunderers, and hirelings." Reform clubs held large open-air meetings, and ordinary people eagerly bought cheap newspapers that clamored for change. In August 1819, sixty thousand people attended an illegal meeting held in St. Peter's Fields in Manchester. When the local authorities sent the cavalry to arrest the speaker, panic resulted; eleven people were killed and many hundreds injured. Punsters called it the Battle of Peterloo or the Peterloo Massacre. An alarmed government passed the Six Acts, which forbade large political meetings and restricted press criticism, suppressing the reform movement for a decade.

Despite striking industrial growth, factory workers remained a minority everywhere. In the 1840s, factories in England employed only 5 percent of the workers; in France, 3 percent; in Prussia, 2 percent. Many peasants kept their options open by combining factory work with agricultural labor. They worked in agriculture during the spring and summer and in manufacturing in the fall and winter. Unstable industrial wages made such arrangements essential. Some new industries idled periodically: for example, iron forges stopped for several months when the water level in streams dropped, and blast furnaces shut down for repairs several weeks every year. In hard times, factory owners simply closed their doors until demand for their goods improved.

In addition, workers, both men and women, continued to toil at home in putting-out, or cottage, industries. In the 1840s, for example, two-thirds of the manufacturing workers in Prussia and Saxony labored at home for contractors or merchants who supplied raw materials and then sold the finished goods. Even without mechanization, some of the old forms of putting-out work changed, however. Tailoring, for example, had been the province of male artisans preparing entire garments in small shops but was now broken up into piecework that was farmed out to women working at home for much lower "piece rates."

Even though factories employed only a small percentage of the population, they attracted much attention because they created unheard-of riches and new forms of poverty all at once. "From this filthy sewer pure gold flows," wrote the French aristocrat Alexis de Tocqueville after visiting the new English industrial city of Manchester in the 1830s. "Here humanity attains its most complete development and its most brutish, here civilization works its miracles and civilized man is turned almost into a savage." Studies by physicians set the life expectancy of workers in Manchester at just seventeen years in 1840 (partly because of high rates of infant mortality), compared to the average in England of forty years. Visitors invariably complained about the smoke and soot. One American visitor to Britain in the late 1840s described how "in the manufacturing town, the fine soot or *blacks* darken the day, give white sheep the color of black sheep, discolor the human saliva, contaminate the air, poison many plants, and corrode monuments and buildings."

Authorities worried in particular about the effects on families. A doctor in the Prussian town of Breslau (population 111,000 in 1850), for example, reported that in working-class districts "several persons live in one room in a single bed, or per-haps a whole family, and use the room for all domestic duties, so that the air gets vitiated [polluted]. . . . Their diet consists largely of bread and potatoes." In Great Britain, the Factory Act of 1833 outlawed the employment of children under the age of nine in textile mills (except in the lace and silk industries) and limited the workdays of children ages nine to thirteen to nine hours a day and those ages thir-teen to eighteen to twelve hours. Adults worked even longer hours. When investi-gating commissions showed that women and young children, sometimes under age six, were hauling coal trucks through low, cramped passageways in coal mines, the British Parliament passed a Mines Act in 1842 prohibiting the employment of women and girls underground. In 1847, the Central Short Time Committee, one of Britain's many social reform organizations, successfully pressured Parliament to limit the workday of women and children to ten hours. Countries in continental Europe followed the British lead, but since most did not insist on government inspection, enforcement was lax.

The advance of industrialization in eastern Europe was slow, in large part be-cause serfdom still survived there, hindering labor mobility and tying up invest-ment capital: as long as peasants were legally tied to the land as serfs, they could not migrate to the new factory towns, and landlords felt little incentive to invest their income in manufacturing. The problem was worst in Russia, where industri-alization had hardly begun and would not take off until the end of the nineteenth century. Nevertheless, even in Russia signs of industrialization could be detected: raw cotton imports (a sign of a growing textile industry) increased sevenfold be-tween 1831 and 1848, and the number of factories doubled along with the size of the industrial workforce.◆

Urbanization and Its Consequences

Industrial development spurred urban growth wherever factories were located in or near cities, yet cities grew even with little industry. Here, too, Great Britain led the way: half the population of England and Wales lived in towns by 1850, while

---

◆ For a primary source that illustrates the advance of industrialization in eastern Europe, see Document 53, "Factory Rules in Berlin."

in France and the German states the urban population was only about a quarter of the total. Both old and new cities teemed with growing population in the 1830s and 1840s. In the 1830s alone, London grew by 130,000 people; Paris expanded by 120,000 between 1841 and 1846, Vienna by 125,000 between 1827 and 1847, and Berlin by 180,000 between 1815 and 1848.

Massive rural emigration, rather than births to women already living in cities, accounted for this remarkable increase. Europe's population grew by nearly 100 percent between 1800 and 1850, yet agricultural yields increased only by 30 to 50 percent. City life and new factories beckoned those faced with hunger and poverty, including emigrants from other lands: thousands of Irish emigrated to English cities, Italians went to French cities, and Poles flocked to German cities. Since the construction of new housing could not keep up with population growth, overcrowding was inevitable. In Paris, 30,000 workers lived in lodging houses, eight or nine to a room, with no separation of the sexes. In 1847 in St. Giles, the Irish quarter of London, 461 people lived in just twelve houses. Men, women, and children huddled together on piles of filthy rotting straw or potato peels because they had no money for fuel to keep warm.

Severe crowding worsened already dire sanitation conditions. Residents dumped refuse into streets or courtyards, and human excrement collected in cesspools under apartment houses. At midcentury, London's approximately 250,000 cesspools were emptied only once or twice a year. Water was scarce and had to be fetched daily from nearby fountains. Despite the diversion of water from provincial rivers to Paris and a tripling of the number of public fountains, Parisians had enough water for only two baths annually per person (the upper classes enjoyed more baths; the lower classes, fewer). In London, private companies that supplied water turned on pumps in the poorer sections for only a few hours three days a week. In rapidly growing British industrial cities such as Manchester, one-third of the houses contained no latrines. Human waste ended up in the rivers that supplied drinking water. The horses that provided transportation inside the cities left droppings everywhere, and city dwellers often kept chickens, ducks, goats, pigs, geese, and even cattle, as well as dogs and cats, in their houses. The result was a "universal atmosphere of filth and stink."

Such conditions made cities prime breeding grounds for disease; those with 50,000 people or more had twice the death rates of rural areas. In 1830–1832 and again in 1847–1851, devastating outbreaks of cholera swept westward from Asia across Europe (touching the United States and South America as well in 1849–1850). Today we know that a waterborne bacterium causes the disease, but at the time no one understood the disease and everyone feared it. The usually fatal disease induced violent vomiting and diarrhea and left the skin blue, eyes sunken and dull, and hands and feet ice cold. While cholera particularly ravaged the crowded, filthy neighborhoods of rapidly growing cities, it also claimed many rural as well as some well-to-do victims. In Paris, 18,000 people died in the 1832 epidemic and 20,000 in that

FATHER THAMES INTRODUCING HIS OFFSPRING TO THE FAIR CITY OF LONDON.

■ Lithograph of London

This English lithograph draws attention to the connection between contaminated water supplies—in this case the Thames River in London—and epidemic disease. Notice that diphtheria, scrofula, and cholera are cited at the bottom of the print. The title, Father Thames Introducing His Offspring to the Fair City of London, *is particularly jarring. A monsterlike figure drags a dead body out of the slime and presents it to the fair maiden who represents London. The subtitle, "A Design for a Fresco in the New Houses of Parliament," challenges the political leadership to recognize the social problems festering nearby.* (Hulton Getty/Liaison Agency.)

www.bedfordstmartins.com/huntconcise   See the ONLINE STUDY GUIDE for more help in analyzing this image.

of 1849; in London, 7,000 died in each epidemic; in Russia, the epidemic was catastrophic, claiming 250,000 victims in 1831–1832 and a million in 1847–1851.

Rumors and panic followed in the epidemics' wakes. In Paris in April 1832, a crowd of workers attacked a central hospital, believing the doctors were poisoning the poor but using cholera as a hoax to cover up the conspiracy. Eastern European peasants burned estates and killed physicians and officials. Although devastating, cholera did not kill as many people as tuberculosis, Europe's number-one deadly disease. But tuberculosis took its victims one by one and therefore had less impact on social relations.

Raging epidemics spurred a growing concern for public health. When news of the cholera outbreak in eastern Europe reached Paris in 1831, the city set up commissions in each municipal district to collect information about lower-class housing and sanitation. In Great Britain, reports on sanitation conditions among the working class led to the passage of new public health laws.

But government intervention did little to ease the social tensions inspired by rapid urban growth. The middle and upper classes lived in large apartments or houses with more light, more air, and more water than lower-class dwellings. The lower classes lived nearby, however, sometimes in the cramped upper floors of the same apartment houses. Reformers believed that overcrowding among the poor led to sexual promiscuity and illegitimacy. They depicted the lower classes as dangerously lacking in sexual self-control. A physician visiting Lille, France, in 1835 wrote of "individuals of both sexes and of very different ages lying together, most of them without nightshirts and repulsively dirty. . . . The reader will complete the picture."

Officials collected statistics on illegitimacy that seemed to bear out these fears: one-quarter to one-half of the babies born in the big European cities in the 1830s and 1840s were illegitimate, and alarmed medical men wrote about thousands of infanticides. Between 1815 and the mid-1830s in France, 33,000 babies were abandoned at foundling hospitals every year; 27 percent of births in Paris in 1850 were illegitimate, compared with only 4 percent of rural births. Sexual disorder seemed to go hand in hand with drinking and crime. Beer halls and pubs dotted the urban landscape. One London street boasted twenty-three pubs in three hundred yards. Police officials estimated that London had 70,000 thieves and 80,000 prostitutes. In many cities, nearly half the urban population lived at the level of bare subsistence, and increasing numbers depended on public welfare, charity, or criminality to make ends meet. A Swiss pastor said of the workers, "Their hearts seethe with hatred of the well-to-do; their eyes lust for a share of the wealth about them; their mouths speak unblushingly of a coming day of retribution."

New Ideologies

A host of new political doctrines offered competing solutions to the new social tensions created by rapid urban growth and the spread of industry. Although traditional ways of life still prevailed in much of Europe, new modes of thinking about changes in the social and political order arose in the 1820s and 1830s. This was an era of "isms"—conservatism, liberalism, socialism, nationalism, and romanticism. The French Revolution had caused people to ask questions about the best possible form of government, and its effects had made clear that people acting together could change their political system. The events of the 1790s and the following decades, however, also produced enormous differences of opinion over what constituted the ideal government. Similarly, the Industrial Revolution posed fundamental questions about changes in society and social relations: How did the new social order differ from the earlier one, which was less urban and less driven by commercial concerns? Who should control this new order? Should governments try to moderate or accelerate the pace of change? Answers to these questions about the social and political order were called *ideologies*, a word coined during the French Revolution. An *ideology* is a coherent set of beliefs about the way a society's social and political order should be organized. New political and social movements organized around these ideologies.

Liberalism

As an ideology, liberalism traced its origins to the writings of John Locke in the seventeenth century and the Enlightenment philosophy of the eighteenth. The adherents of *liberalism* defined themselves in opposition to conservatives on one end of the political spectrum and revolutionaries on the other. Unlike conservatives, liberals supported the Enlightenment ideals of constitutional guarantees of personal liberty and free trade in economics, believing that greater liberty in politics and economic matters would promote social improvement and economic growth. For that reason, they also generally applauded the social and economic changes produced by the Industrial Revolution, while opposing the violence and excessive state power promoted by the French Revolution. The leaders of the rapidly expanding middle class composed of manufacturers, merchants, and professionals favored liberalism.

The foremost exponent of early-nineteenth-century liberalism was the English philosopher and jurist Jeremy Bentham (1748–1832). He called his brand of liberalism *utilitarianism* because he held that the best policy is the one that produces "the greatest good for the greatest number" and is thus the most useful, or utilitarian. Bentham's criticisms spared no institution; he railed against the injustices of the British parliamentary process, the abuses of the prisons and the penal code, and the educational system. In his zeal for social engineering, he proposed elaborate schemes for managing the poor and model prisons that would emphasize rehabilitation through close supervision rather than corporal punishment.

Bentham and many other liberals joined the abolitionist, antislavery movement that intensified between the 1790s and 1820s. Agitation by such groups as the London Society for Effecting the Abolition of the Slave Trade succeeded in gaining a first victory in 1807 when the British House of Lords voted to abolish the slave trade. The abolitionists' efforts finally bore fruit in 1833 when Britain abolished slavery in all its colonies.

British liberals pushed for two major reforms in addition to the abolition of slavery: expansion of the electorate to give representation to a broader segment of the middle class and repeal of the Corn Laws or tariffs on foreign grain. They gained their first goal in the Reform Bill of 1832. When the Tories in Parliament resisted the proposed extension of the right to vote, liberals and their supporters organized mass demonstrations. In this "state of diseased and feverish excitement" (according to its opponents), the Reform Bill passed after the king threatened to create enough new peers to obtain its passage in the House of Lords. Although the number of male voters increased by about 50 percent, only one in five Britons could now vote, and voting still depended on holding property. Nevertheless, the bill gave representation to new cities in the industrial north for the first time and set a precedent for further widening suffrage.◆

When landholders in the House of Commons thwarted efforts to lower grain tariffs, two Manchester cotton manufacturers set up an Anti–Corn Law League. The league denounced the landlords as "a bread-taxing oligarchy" and "blood-sucking vampires" and attracted working-class backing by promising lower food prices. The league established local branches, published newspapers and the journal *The Economist* (founded in 1843 and now one of the world's most influential periodicals), and campaigned in elections. They eventually won the support of the Tory prime minister Sir Robert Peel, whose government repealed the Corn Laws in 1846.

Liberalism had less appeal in continental Europe because industrial growth was slower and the middle classes smaller than in Britain. French liberals agitated for greater press freedoms and a broadening of the vote. Liberal reform movements also grew up in the pockets of industrialization in Prussia and the Austrian Empire. Some state bureaucrats, especially university-trained middle-class officials, favored economic liberalism. Hungarian count Stephen Széchenyi (1791–1860) personally campaigned for the introduction of British-style changes. He introduced British agricultural techniques on his own lands, helped start up steamboat traffic on the Danube, encouraged the importation of machinery and technicians for steam-driven textile factories, and pushed the construction of Hungary's first railway line, from Budapest to Vienna.

In the 1840s, however, Széchenyi's efforts paled before those of the flamboyant Magyar nationalist Lajos Kossuth (1802–1894). After spending four years in prison for sedition, Kossuth grabbed every opportunity to publicize American democracy and British political liberalism, all in a fervent nationalist spirit. In 1844, he founded the Protective Association, whose members bought only Hungarian products; to Kossuth, boycotting Austrian goods was crucial to ending "colonial dependence" on Austria. Born of a lesser landowning family without a noble title, Kossuth did not hesitate to attack "the cowardly selfishness of the landowner class."

Even in Russia, signs of liberal, even socialist, opposition appeared in the 1830s and 1840s. Small "circles" of young noblemen serving in the army or bureaucracy met in cities, especially Moscow, to discuss the latest Western ideas and to criticize the Russian state: "The world is undergoing a transformation, while we vegetate in

---

◆ For a primary source that argues for the bill and reveals liberal principles, see Document 54, T. B. Macaulay, "Speech on Parliamentary Reform."

our hovels of wood and clay," wrote one. Out of these groups came such future revolutionaries as Alexander Herzen (1812–1870), described by the police as "a daring free-thinker, extremely dangerous to society." Tsar Nicholas I (r. 1825–1855) banned Western liberal writings as well as all books about the United States. He sent nearly ten thousand people a year into exile in Siberia as punishment for their political activities.

Socialism and the Early Labor Movement

Socialism took up where liberalism left off: socialists believed that the liberties advocated by liberals benefited only the middle class, the owners of factories and businesses, not the workers. They sought to reorganize society totally rather than to reform it piecemeal through political measures. Many were utopians who believed that ideal communities are based on cooperation rather than competition. Like Thomas More, whose book *Utopia* (1516) gave the movement its name, the utopian socialists believed that society would benefit all its members only if private property ceased to exist.

Socialists criticized the new industrial order for dividing society into two classes: the new middle class, or *capitalists*, who owned the wealth; and the working class, their downtrodden and impoverished employees. Such divisions tore the social fabric, and, as their name suggests, the socialists aimed to restore harmony and cooperation through social reorganization. Three early socialists helped instigate the movement: Robert Owen, Claude Henri de Saint-Simon, and Charles Fourier. Robert Owen (1771–1858) founded British socialism. A successful Welsh-born manufacturer, Owen bought a cotton mill in New Lanark, Scotland, in 1800 and began to set up a model factory town, where workers labored only ten hours a day (instead of seventeen, as was common). He moved to the United States in the 1820s to establish in Indiana a community he named New Harmony. The experiment collapsed after three years, a victim of internal squabbling. Nonetheless, Owen's experiments and writings inspired the movement for producer cooperatives (businesses owned and controlled by their workers), consumer cooperatives (stores in which consumers owned shares), and a national trade union.

Claude Henri de Saint-Simon (1760–1825) and Charles Fourier (1772–1837) were Owen's contemporaries in France. Saint-Simon was a noble who had served as an officer in the War of American Independence and lost a fortune speculating in national property during the French Revolution. Fourier traveled as a salesman for a Lyon cloth merchant. Both shared Owen's alarm about the effects of industrialization on social relations. Saint-Simon coined the terms *industrialism* and *industrialist* to define the new economic order and its chief animators. He believed that work, the central element in the new society, should be controlled not by politicians but by scientists, engineers, artists, and industrialists. To correct the abuses of the new industrial order, Fourier urged the establishment of communities that were part garden city and part agricultural commune; all jobs would be rotated to max-imize happiness. The emancipation of women was essential to Fourier's vision of a harmonious community: "The extension of the privileges of women is the fundamental cause of all social progress."

Women participated actively in the socialist movements of the day, even though socialist men often shared the widespread prejudice against women's political ac-tivism. In Great Britain, many women joined the Owenites and helped form coop-erative societies and unions. They defended women's working-class organizations against the complaints of men in the new societies and trade unions. As one woman wrote, "Do not say the unions are only for men . . . 'tis a wrong impression, forced on our minds to keep us slaves!" As women became more active, Owenites agitated for women's rights, marriage reform, and popular education. In 1832, Saint-Simonian women founded a feminist newspaper in France, *The Free Woman*. Some followers of Saint-Simon's brand of socialism developed a quasi-religious cult with elaborate rituals and a "he-pope" and "she-pope," or ruling father and mother. They lived and worked together in cooperative arrangements and scandalized some by advocating free love.

The French activist Flora Tristan (1801–1844) devoted herself to reconciling the interests of male and female workers. She had seen the "frightful reality" of London's poverty and made a reputation reporting on British working conditions. Tristan published a stream of books and pamphlets urging male workers to address women's unequal status, arguing that "the emancipation of male workers is *impos-sible* so long as women remain in a degraded state." She advocated a Universal Union of Men and Women Workers.

Even though most male socialists ignored Tristan's plea for women's participa-tion, like her they also worked to found working-class associations. The French socialist Louis Blanc (1811–1882) explained the importance of working-class associations in *Organization of Labor* (1840), which deeply influenced the French labor movement. Similarly, Pierre-Joseph Proudhon (1809–1865) urged workers to form producers' associations so that the workers could control the work process and eliminate profits made by capitalists. His 1840 book *What Is Property?* argues that property is theft: labor alone is productive, and rent, interest, and profit are unjust.

After 1840, some socialists began to call themselves "communists," emphasiz-ing their desire to replace private property by communal, collective ownership. The Frenchman Étienne Cabet (1788–1856) first used the word *communist*. In 1840, he published *Travels in Icaria*, a novel describing a communist experiment in which a popularly elected dictatorship efficiently organized work, reduced the workday to seven hours, and made work tasks "short, easy, and attractive."

Out of the churning of socialist ideas of the 1840s emerged two men whose collaboration would change the definition of socialism and remake it into an ideology that would shake the world for the next 150 years. Karl Marx (1818–1883) and Friedrich Engels (1820–1895) were both sons of prosperous German-Jewish families that had converted to Christianity. Marx studied philosophy at the University of Berlin, edited a liberal newspaper until the Prussian government suppressed it, and then left for Paris, where he met Engels. While working in the offices of his wealthy family's cotton manufacturing interests in Manchester, England, Engels had been shocked into writing *The Condition of the Working Class in England in 1844* (1845), a sympathetic depiction of industrial workers' dismal lives. In Paris, where German and eastern European intellectuals could pursue their political interests more freely than at home, Marx and Engels organized a Communist League, in whose name they published the *Communist Manifesto* (1848). It eventually became the touchstone of Marxist and communist revolution all over the world.◆

Negligible as was Marx's and Engels's influence in the 1840s, they had already begun their lifework of scientifically understanding the "laws" of capitalism and fostering revolutionary organizations. Their principles and analysis of history were in place: communists, the *Manifesto* declared, must aim for "the downfall of the bourgeoisie [capitalist class] and the ascendancy of the proletariat [working class], the abolition of the old society based on class conflicts and the foundation of a new society without classes and without private property." Marx and Engels embraced industrialization because they believed it would eventually bring on the proletarian revolution and lead inevitably to the abolition of exploitation, private property, and class society.

Socialism accompanied, and in some places incited, an upsurge in working-class organization in western Europe. In 1824, the British government repealed laws prohibiting labor unions, though it maintained restrictions on strikes. Other European rulers forbade unions, though they tolerated cooperatives and societies for mutual aid. Working-class organization struck fear in the hearts of many in the upper classes. A British newspaper exclaimed in 1834, "The trade unions are, we have no doubt, the most dangerous institutions that were ever permitted to take root."

Many British workers joined in the Chartist movement, which aimed to transform Britain into a democracy. In 1838, political radicals drew up the People's Charter, which demanded universal manhood suffrage, vote by secret ballot, equal electoral districts, annual elections, and the elimination of property qualifications for and the payment of stipends to members of Parliament. Chartists denounced their opponents as seeking "to keep the people in social slavery and political degradation." Many women took part by founding female political unions, setting up Chartist Sunday schools, organizing boycotts of unsympathetic shopkeepers, and

---

◆ For an original source that reflects Marx and Engels's historical vision, see Document 55, Friedrich Engels, "Draft of a Communist Confession of Faith."

joining Chartist temperance associations. Nevertheless, the People's Charter refrained from calling for woman suffrage because the movement's leaders feared that doing so would alienate potential supporters.

The Chartists organized a massive campaign during 1838 and 1839, with large public meetings, fiery speeches, and torchlight parades. Presented with petitions for the People's Charter signed by more than a million people, the House of Commons refused to act. In response to this rebuff from middle-class liberals, the Chartists allied themselves in the 1840s with working-class strike movements in the manufacturing districts and associated with various European revolutionary movements. But at the same time, they—like their British and continental allies—distanced themselves from women workers. Chartists complained that working-women undermined men's manhood, taking men's jobs and turning the men into "women-men" or "eunuchs." Continuing agitation and organization prepared the way for a last wave of Chartist demonstrations in 1848.

Nationalism

Nationalists could be liberals, socialists, or even conservatives. *Nationalism* holds that all peoples derive their identities from their nations, which are defined by common language, shared cultural traditions, and sometimes religion. When such "nations" do not coincide with state boundaries, as they often did not in the nineteenth and twentieth centuries, nationalism can produce violence and warfare as different national groups compete for control over territory.

The French showed the power of national feeling in their revolutionary and Napoleonic wars, but they also provoked nationalism in the people they conquered. Once Napoleon and his satellite rulers departed, nationalist sentiment turned against other outside rulers—the Ottoman Turks in the Balkans, the Russians in Poland, and the Austrians in Italy. Intellectuals took the lead in demanding unity and freedom for their peoples. They collected folktales, poems, and histories and prepared grammars and dictionaries of their native languages (Map 17.3). Students, middle-class professionals, and army officers formed secret societies to promote national independence and constitutional reform.

Nationalist aspirations were especially explosive for the Austrian Empire, which included a variety of peoples united only by their enforced allegiance to the Habsburg emperor. The empire included three main national groups: the Germans, who made up one-fourth of the population; the Magyars of Hungary (which included Transylvania and Croatia); and the Slavs, who together formed the largest group in the population but were divided into different nationalities such as Poles, Czechs, Croats, and Serbs. The empire also included Italians in Lombardy and Venetia and Romanians in Transylvania. Efforts to govern such diverse peoples preoccupied Metternich, chief minister to the weak Habsburg emperor Francis I (r. 1792–1835). As a conservative, Metternich believed that the experience of the

■ MAP 17.3 Languages of Nineteenth-Century Europe

Even this detailed map of linguistic diversity understates the number of different languages and dialects spoken in Europe. In Italy, for example, few Italians spoke Italian as their first language. Instead, they spoke local dialects such as Piedmontese or Ligurian, and some might speak better French than Italian if they came from the regions bordering France. The map does underline the inherent contradictions of nationalism in eastern Europe, where many linguistic regions incorporated other languages and the result was constant conflict. But even in Spain, France, and Great Britain, linguistic diversity continued right up to the beginning of the 1900s.

French Revolution proved the superiority of monarchy and aristocracy as forms of government and society. His domestic policy aimed to restrain nationalist impulses, and with the help of a secret police set up on the Napoleonic model, he largely succeeded until the 1840s. He insisted, for example, that "the Lombards [northern Italians] must forget that they are Italians."

The new Germanic Confederation set up by the Congress of Vienna had a federal assembly, but it largely functioned as a tool of Metternich's policies. The only sign of resistance came from university students, who formed nationalist student societies, or *Burschenschaften*. In 1817, they held a mass rally at which they burned books they did not like, including Napoleon's Civil Code. One of their leaders, Friedrich Ludwig Jahn, spouted such xenophobic (antiforeign) slogans as "If you let your daughter learn French, you might just as well train her to become a whore." Metternich was convinced that the *Burschenschaften* in the German states and the *carbonari* in Italy were linked in an international conspiracy. In 1820, when a student assassinated the playwright August Kotzebue because he ridiculed the student movement, Metternich convinced the leaders of the biggest German states to pass the Karlsbad Decrees dissolving the student societies and more strictly censoring the press. No evidence for a conspiracy was found.

Tsar Alexander faced similar problems in Poland, his "congress kingdom" (so called because the Congress of Vienna had created it), which in 1815 was one of Europe's most liberal states. The tsar reigned in Poland as a limited monarch, having bestowed a constitution that provided for an elected parliament, a national army, and guarantees of free speech and a free press. But by 1818, Alexander had begun retracting his concessions. Polish students and military officers responded by forming secret nationalist societies to plot for change by illegal means. In 1830, they rebelled against Alexander's successor Nicholas I. In reprisal, the tsar abolished the Polish constitution and ordered thousands of Poles executed or banished.

Most of the ten thousand Poles who fled took up residence in western European capitals, especially Paris, where they campaigned for public support. Their intellectual leader was the poet Adam Mickiewicz (1798–1855), whose mystical writings portrayed the Polish exiles as martyrs of a crucified nation with an international Christian mission. Mickiewicz formed a Polish Legion to fight for national restoration, but rivalries and divisions prevented united action until 1846, when Polish exiles in Paris tried to launch a coordinated insurrection for Polish independence. Plans for an uprising in the Polish province of Galicia in the Austrian Empire collapsed, however, when peasants instead revolted against their noble Polish masters. Slaughtering some two thousand aristocrats, a desperate rural population served the Austrian government's end by defusing the nationalist challenge.

One of those most touched by Mickiewicz's vision was Giuseppe Mazzini (1805–1872), a fiery Italian nationalist and republican journalist. Exiled in 1831 for his opposition to Austrian rule in northern Italy, Mazzini founded Young Italy, a secret society that attracted thousands with its message that Italy would touch off a European-wide revolutionary movement. In the 1830s and 1840s, nationalism spread among the many different peoples of the Austrian Empire. During the revolutions of 1848, however, it would become evident that these different ethnic groups disliked each other as much as they disliked their Austrian masters.

In most of the German states, economic unification took a step forward with the foundation in 1834, under Prussian leadership, of the *Zollverein*, or "customs union." Economist Friedrich List argued that the elimination of tariffs within the borders of the union would promote industrialization and cooperation and enable the union to compete with the rest of Europe. German nationalists sought a government uniting German-speaking peoples, but they could not agree on its boundaries. Austria was not part of the Customs Union. Would the unified German state include both Prussia and the Austrian Empire? If it included Austria, what about the non-German territories of the Austrian Empire? And could the powerful and conservative kingdom of Prussia coexist in a unified German state with other, more liberal but smaller states? These questions would vex German history for decades to come.

In Russia, nationalism took the form of opposition to Western ideas. Russian nationalists, or "Slavophiles" (lovers of the Slavs), opposed the "Westernizers," who wanted Russia to follow Western models of industrial development and constitutional government. The Slavophiles favored maintaining rural traditions infused by the values of the Russian Orthodox church. Only a return to Russia's basic historical principles, they argued, could protect the country against the corrosion of rationalism and materialism. Slavophiles sometimes criticized the regime, however, because they believed the state exerted too much power over the church. The conflict between Slavophiles and Westernizers continues to shape Russian cultural and intellectual life to the present day.

The most significant nationalist movement in western Europe could be found in Ireland. The Irish had struggled for centuries against English occupation, but Irish nationalists developed strong organizations only in the 1840s. In 1842, a group of writers founded the Young Ireland movement that aimed to recover Irish history and preserve the Irish Gaelic language (spoken by at least one-third of the peasantry). Daniel O'Connell (1775–1847), a Catholic lawyer and landowner who sat in the British House of Commons, hoped to force the British Parliament to repeal the Act of Union of 1801, which had made Ireland part of Great Britain. In 1843, London newspapers reported "monster meetings" that drew crowds of as many as 300,000 people in support of repeal of the union. In response, the British government arrested O'Connell and convicted him of conspiracy. More radical leaders, who preached insurrection against the English, replaced him.

Romanticism

More an artistic movement than a true ideology, *romanticism* glorified nature, emotion, genius, and imagination. It proclaimed these as antidotes to the Enlightenment and to classicism in the arts, challenging the reliance on reason, symmetry, and cool geometric spaces. Classicism idealized models from Roman history; romanticism turned to folklore and medieval legends. Classicism celebrated orderly, crisp lines; romantics sought out all that was wild, fevered, and disorderly. Chief among the arts of romanticism were poetry, painting, and music, which captured the deep-seated emotion characteristic of romantic expression. George Gordon, Lord Byron (1788–1824), explained his aims in writing poetry:

> *For what is Poesy but to create*
> *From overfeeling, Good and Ill, and aim*
> *At an external life beyond our fate,*
> *And be the new Prometheus of new man.*

Prometheus was the mythological figure who brought fire from the Greek gods to human beings. Byron did not seek the new Prometheus among the men of industry; he sought him within his own "overfeeling," his own intense emotions.◆

Romantic poetry elevated the wonders of nature almost to the supernatural. Nature, wrote the English poet William Wordsworth (1770–1850), "to me was all in all." It allowed him to sing "the still, sad music of humanity." Like many poets of his time, Wordsworth greeted the French Revolution with joy; in his poem "French Revolution" (1809), he remembered his early enthusiasm: "Bliss was it in that dawn to be alive." But gradually he became disenchanted with the revolutionary experiment and celebrated British nationalism instead; in 1816, he published a poem to commemorate the "intrepid sons of Albion [England]" who died at the battle of Waterloo.

Their emphasis on authentic self-expression at times drew romantics to exotic, mystical, or even reckless experiences. Such transports drove one leading German poet to the madhouse and another to suicide. Some romantics depicted the artist as possessed by demons and obsessed with hallucinations. The aged German poet Johann Wolfgang von Goethe (1749–1832) denounced the extremes of romanticism, calling it "everything that is sick." In his epic poem *Faust* (1832), the retelling of a sixteenth-century legend, Faust offers his soul to the devil in return for a chance to taste all human experience—from passionate love to the heights of power—in his effort to reshape nature for humanity's benefit. Faust's striving leaves a wake of suffering and destruction. Goethe did not make the target of his warning explicit, but the French revolutionary legacy and industrialization both seemed to be releasing "faustian" energies that could be destructive.

Romanticism in painting also often expressed anxiety about the coming industrial order while idealizing nature. These concerns came together in an emphasis on natural landscape. The German romantic painter Caspar David Friedrich (1774–1840) depicted scenes—often in the mountains, far from any factory—that

◆ For a primary source that reveals the romantic vision, see Document 56, Victor Hugo, "Preface to *Cromwell.*"

■ **Caspar David Friedrich,**
Wanderer above the Sea of Fog
(1818)
*Friedrich, a German romantic painter,
captured many of the themes most
dear to romanticism: melancholy, isolation, and individual communion
with nature. He painted trees reaching
for the sky and mountains stretching into the distance. Nature to
him seemed awesome, powerful, and
overshadowing of human perspectives.
The French sculptor David d'Angers
said of Friedrich, "Here is a man
who has discovered the tragedy of
landscape."*
(Co Elke Walford, Hamburg/Hamburger
Kunsthalle.)

captured the romantic fascination with the sublime power of nature. His melancholy individual figures look lost in the vastness of an overpowering nature.
Friedrich hated the new modern world and considered industrialization a disaster.
The English painter Joseph M. W. Turner (1775–1851) depicted his vision of nature
in mysterious, misty seascapes, anticipating later artists by blurring the outlines of
objects. The French painter Eugène Delacroix (1798–1863) chose contemporary as
well as medieval scenes of great turbulence to emphasize light and color and break
away from what he saw as "the servile copies repeated *ad nauseam* in academies of
art." Critics denounced the new techniques as "painting with a drunken broom." To
broaden his experience of light and color, Delacroix traveled in the 1830s to North
Africa and painted many exotic scenes in Morocco and Algeria.

Architects of the period sought to recapture a preindustrial world. When the
British Houses of Parliament were rebuilt after they burned down in 1834, the architect Sir Charles Barry constructed them in a Gothic style reminiscent of the
Middle Ages. This medievalism was taken even further by A. W. N. Pugin, who
prepared the Gothic details for the Houses of Parliament. In his polemical book
Contrasts (1836), Pugin denounced modern conditions and compared them unfav-
orably with those in the 1400s. To underline his view, Pugin wore medieval clothes
at home.

The towering presence of the German composer Ludwig van Beethoven (1770–1827) in early-nineteenth-century music helped establish the direction for musical romanticism. His music, according to one leading German romantic, "sets in motion the lever of fear, of awe, of horror, of suffering, and awakens just that infinite longing which is the essence of Romanticism." Beethoven's symphonies conveyed the impression of growth, a metaphor for the organic process with an emphasis on the natural that was dear to the romantics. For example, his Sixth Symphony, the *Pastoral* (1808), used a variety of instruments to represent sounds heard in the country. Some of his work was explicitly political; his Ninth Symphony (1824) employed a chorus to sing the German poet Friedrich Schiller's verses in praise of universal human solidarity.

If any common political thread linked the romantics, it was support for nationalist aspirations, especially through the search for the historical origins of national identity. The Polish composer and pianist Frédéric Chopin (1810–1849) became a powerful champion for the cause of his native land with music that incorporated Polish folk rhythms and melodies. English poet Lord Byron died fighting for Greek independence. Romantic nationalism permeated *The Betrothed* (1825–1827), a novel by Alessandro Manzoni (1785–1873) that constituted a kind of bible for Italian nationalists. The career of the writer Sir Walter Scott (1771–1832) incorporated many of the strands of romanticism. He translated Goethe and published Scottish ballads that he heard as a child. After achieving immediate success with his poetry, he switched to historical novels, but he also wrote a nine-volume life of Napoleon and edited historical memoirs. His novels are almost all renditions of historical events, from *Rob Roy* (1817), with its account of Scottish resistance to the English in the early eighteenth century, to *Ivanhoe* (1819), with its tales of medieval England. The influence of Scott's historical novels was immense. One contemporary critic claimed that *Ivanhoe* was more historically true than any scholarly work: "There is more history in the novels of Walter Scott than in half of the historians."

Reform or Revolution?

Europeans faced a daunting set of challenges in the 1830s and 1840s: the settlement devised by the Congress of Vienna was cracking under the pressure of unsatisfied nationalist and democratic aspirations, and industrialization and urbanization had produced dangerous social tensions made vivid by an outpouring of government reports, medical accounts, and novelistic depictions. Reformers of various stripes organized to meet these challenges, as well as new problems appearing in overseas colonies. Their efforts failed to stem the tide of revolution, which rose again in 1830 and 1848 and threatened to wash away the conservative regimes of the Vienna settlement.

Depicting and Reforming the Social Order

Lithographs, poetry, painting, and even booklets of jokes helped drive home the need for social reform, but novels proved to be the art form best suited to portraying the new society created by industrialization and urbanization. Thanks to increased literacy, the spread of reading rooms and lending libraries, and serialization in newspapers and journals, novels reached a large reading public and helped shape public awareness. Unlike the fiction of the eighteenth century, which had focused on individual personalities, the great novels of the 1830s and 1840s specialized in the description of social life in all its varieties. Manufacturers, financiers, starving students, workers, bureaucrats, prostitutes, underworld figures, thieves, and aristocratic men and women filled the pages of works by popular writers such as Honoré de Balzac and Charles Dickens. Pushing himself to exhaustion and a premature death to get out of debt, the French writer Balzac (1799–1850) cranked out ninety-five novels and many short stories. He aimed to catalog the social types that could be found in French society. Many of his characters, like himself, were driven by the desire to climb higher in the social order.

The English author Charles Dickens (1812–1870) worked with a similar frenetic energy and for much the same reasons. When his father was imprisoned for debt in 1824, the young Dickens took a job in a shoe-polish factory. In 1836, he published a series of literary sketches of daily life and then produced a series of novels that appeared in monthly installments and attracted thousands of readers. In them he paid close attention to the distressing effects of industrialization and urbanization. In *The Old Curiosity Shop* (1841), for example, he depicts the Black Country, the manufacturing region west and northwest of Birmingham, as a "cheerless region," a "mournful place," in which tall chimneys "made foul the melancholy air." In addition to publishing such enduring favorites as *Oliver Twist* (1838) and *A Christmas Carol* (1843), he ran charitable organizations and pressed for social reforms. For Dickens, the ability to portray the problems of the poor went hand in hand with a personal commitment to reform.

Novels by women often revealed the bleaker side of women's situations. *Jane Eyre* (1847), a novel by the English writer Charlotte Brontë, describes the difficult life of an orphaned girl who becomes a governess, the only occupation open to most single middle-class women. Although in an economically weak position, Jane Eyre refuses to achieve respectability and security through marriage, the usual option for women. The French novelist George Sand (Amandine-Aurore Dupin, 1804–1876) took her social criticism a step further. She announced her independence in the 1830s by dressing like a man and smoking cigars. Like many other women writers of the time, she published her work under a male pseudonym while creating female characters who prevail in difficult circumstances through romantic love and moral idealism. Sand's novel *Indiana* (1832), about an unhappily married

■ **George Sand**

This lithograph (1842) by Alcide Lorentz shows George Sand in one of her notorious masculine costumes. Sand published novels, plays, essays, travel writing, and an autobiography. She actively participated in the revolution of 1848 in France, writing pamphlets in support of the new republic. Disillusioned by the rise to power of Louis-Napoleon Bonaparte, she withdrew to her country estate and devoted herself exclusively to her writing.
(The Granger Collection.)

woman, was read all over Europe. Her notoriety made the term *George-Sandism* a common expression of disdain for independent women.

Although women's professional opportunities were severely limited, they took a prominent role in charitable and reform work. Catholic religious orders, which by 1850 enrolled many more women than men, ran schools, hospitals, leper colonies, insane asylums, and old-age homes. New Catholic orders, especially for women, were established, and Catholic missionary activity overseas increased. Protestant women in Great Britain and the United States established Bible, missionary, and female reform societies by the hundreds. Many societies dedicated themselves to reforming prostitutes and castigating their male clients. As a pamphlet of the Boston Female Moral Reform Society explained, "Our mothers, our sisters, our daughters are sacrificed by the thousands every year on the altar of sin, and who are the agents in this work of destruction: Why, our fathers, our brothers, and our sons."

Religiously motivated reformers first had to overcome the perceived indifference of the working classes; less than 10 percent of the workers in the cities attended religious services. To combat such indifference, British religious groups launched the Sunday school movement, which reached its zenith in the 1840s. By 1851, more than half of all working-class children between five and fifteen were attending Sunday school, even though very few of their parents regularly went to religious services. The Sunday schools taught children how to read at a time when few working-class children could go to school during the week.

Catholics and Protestants alike promoted the temperance movement to fight the "pestilence of hard liquor." The first societies had appeared in the United States as early as 1813, and by 1835 the American Temperance Society claimed 1.5 million members. The London-based British and Foreign Temperance Society, established in 1831, matched its American counterpart in its opposition to all alcohol. Temperance advocates saw drunkenness as a sign of moral weakness and a threat to social order. Industrialists pointed to the loss of worker productivity, and efforts to promote temperance often reflected middle- and upper-class fears of the lower classes' lack of discipline. One German temperance advocate insisted, "One need not be a prophet to know that all efforts to combat the widespread and rapidly spreading pauperism will be unsuccessful as long as the common man fails to realize that the principal source of his degradation and misery is his fondness of drink." Yet temperance societies also attracted working-class people who shared the desire for respectability.

Social reformers saw education as one of the main prospects for uplifting the poor and the working class. In addition to setting up Sunday schools, British churches founded organizations such as the British and Foreign School Society. More secular in intent were the Mechanics Institutes, which provided education for workers in the big cities. In 1833, the French government passed an education law that required every town to maintain a primary school, pay a teacher, and provide free education to poor boys. As the law's author, François Guizot, argued, "Ignorance renders the masses turbulent and ferocious." Girls' schools were optional, although hundreds of women taught at the primary level, most of them in private, often religious schools. By the late 1830s, 60 percent of children attended primary school in France, still less than in Protestant Prussia, where 75 percent of children went to school. Popular education remained woefully undeveloped in most of eastern Europe. Peasants were specifically excluded from the few primary schools in Russia, where Tsar Nicholas I blamed the Decembrist uprising of 1825 on education.

Above all else, the elite sought to impose discipline and order on working people. Popular sports, especially blood sports such as cockfighting and bearbaiting, suggested a lack of control, and long-standing efforts in Great Britain to eliminate these recreations now gained momentum through organizations such as the Society for the Prevention of Cruelty to Animals. By the end of the 1830s, bullbaiting had been abandoned in Great Britain. "This useful animal," rejoiced one reformer in 1839, "is no longer tortured amidst the exulting yells of those who are a disgrace to our common form and nature." Other blood sports died out more slowly, and efforts in other countries generally lagged behind those of the British.

When private charities failed to meet the needs of the poor, governments often intervened. Great Britain sought to control the costs of public welfare by passing a

■ **Bearbaiting**
This colored engraving (1821) of Charley's Theater in London shows that bearbaiting did not attract only the lower classes, as reformers often implied. Top hats were most often worn by middle-class men, who seem to be enjoying the spectacle of dogs taunting the bear as much as the working-class men present. At this time, bearbaiting, like bullbaiting, began to come under fire as cruel to animals. (Mary Evans Picture Library.)

new poor law in 1834, called by its critics the "Starvation Act." The law required that all able-bodied persons receiving relief be placed in workhouses, with husbands separated from wives and parents from children. Workhouse life was designed to be as unpleasant as possible so that poor people would move on to regions of higher employment. British women from all social classes organized anti–poor law societies to protest the separation of mothers from their children in the workhouses.

Many women viewed charitable work as the extension of their domestic roles: they promoted virtuous behavior and morality and thus improved society. In one widely read advice book, Englishwoman Sarah Lewis suggested in 1839 that "women may be the prime agents in the regeneration of mankind." But women's social reform activities concealed a paradox. According to the set of beliefs that historians call the doctrine or ideology of domesticity, women should live their lives entirely within the domestic sphere; they should devote themselves to the home. The English poet Alfred, Lord Tennyson, captured this view in a popular poem published in 1847: "Man for the field and woman for the hearth; / Man for the sword and for the needle she. . . . All else confusion." Many believed that maintaining proper and distinct roles for men and women was critically important to maintaining social order in general.

Most women had little hope of economic independence. The notion of a separate, domestic sphere for women prevented them from pursuing higher education,

■ **Life as a Married Couple**
This lithograph by Honoré Daumier, titled All That One Would Want *(1846), shows a wife following meekly behind her husband. Daumier is criticizing the provision of Napoleon's Civil Code that required wives to go to live wherever their husbands chose. He published no fewer than four thousand prints and caricatures criticizing the social inequalities worsened by economic development. He satirized landlords, judges, lawyers, politicians, and even King Louis-Philippe himself. In the early 1830s, Daumier's political satires landed him in prison for six months. His work always took the side of the lowly and downcast and poked fun at the high and mighty.* (Jean-Loup Charmet.)

work in professional careers, or participation in politics through voting or holding office, all activities deemed appropriate only to men. Laws everywhere codified the subordination of women. Many countries followed the model of Napoleon's Civil Code, which classified married women as legal incompetents along with children, the insane, and criminals. In Great Britain, which had no national law code, the courts upheld the legality of a husband's complete control.

Distinctions between men and women were most noticeable in the privileged classes. Whereas boys attended secondary schools, most middle- and upper-class girls still received their education at home or in church schools, where they were taught to be religious, obedient, and accomplished in music and languages. As men began to wear practical clothing—long trousers and short jackets of solid, often dark colors, no makeup (previously common for aristocratic men), and simply cut hair—women continued to dress for decorative effect, now with tightly corseted waists that emphasized the differences between female and male bodies. Middle- and upper-class women had long hair that required hours of brushing and pinning up, and they wore long, cumbersome skirts. Advice books written by women detailed the tasks that such women undertook in the home: maintaining household accounts, supervising servants, and organizing social events.

Scientists reinforced stereotypes. Once considered sexually insatiable, women were now described as incapacitated by menstruation and largely uninterested in sex, an attitude that many equated with moral superiority. Thus was born the

"Victorian woman," a figment of the largely male medical imagination. Physicians and scholars considered women mentally inferior. In 1839, Auguste Comte, an influential early French sociologist, wrote, "As for any functions of government, the radical inaptitude of the female sex is there yet more marked . . . and limited to the guidance of the mere family."

Abuses and Reforms Overseas

Despite such attitudes, British women played a major role in the antislavery movement; as many as 350,000 women signed one major petition to Parliament demanding the abolition of slavery. Reformers gained one of their major objectives when Britain abolished slavery in its colonies in 1833. British missionary and evangelical groups condemned the conquest, enslavement, and exploitation of native African populations and successfully blocked British annexations in central and southern Africa in the 1830s. The new Latin American republics abolished slavery in the 1820s and 1830s after they defeated the Spanish with armies that included many slaves. In France, the government of Louis-Philippe (r. 1830–1848) took strong measures against clandestine slave traffic, virtually ending French participation during the 1830s. Slavery was abolished in the remaining French Caribbean colonies in 1848.

Slavery did not disappear immediately just because the major European powers had given it up. The transatlantic trade in slaves did not seriously diminish until 1850 (see Figure 14.1, page 575). Human bondage continued unabated in Brazil, Cuba (still a Spanish colony), and the United States. Some American reformers supported abolition, but it remained a minority movement. Like serfdom in Russia, slavery in the Americas involved a quagmire of economic, political, and moral problems that worsened over time.

As Europeans turned their interest away from the plantation colonies of the Caribbean toward colonies in Asia and Africa, they developed new forms of colonial rule. Colonialism became *imperialism*—a term first coined in the mid-nineteenth century. Colonialism most often led to the establishment of settler colonies, direct rule by Europeans, slave labor from Africa, and wholesale destruction of indigenous peoples. In contrast, imperialism usually meant more indirect forms of economic exploitation and political rule. Europeans still derived economic profit from their colonies, but now they also aimed to reform colonial peoples in their own image—when doing so did not conflict too much with their economic interests.

In the 1830s and 1840s, France and Britain continued to extend their influence across the globe. Using the pretext of an insult to its envoy, France invaded the north African country of Algeria in 1830 and after a long military campaign established political control over most of the region in the next two decades. By 1850, more than seventy thousand French, Italian, and Maltese colonists had settled there, often confiscating the lands of native peoples. The new French administration of the colony made efforts to balance native and settler interests, however, and eventually France would not only incorporate Algeria into France but also try to assimilate its native population to French culture. France also imposed a protectorate government over the South Pacific island of Tahiti.

Although the British granted Canada greater self-determination in 1839, they extended their dominion elsewhere by annexing Singapore (1819), an island off the Malay peninsula, and New Zealand (1840). They also increased their control in India through the administration of the East India Company, a private group of merchants chartered by the British crown. The British educated a native elite to take over much of the day-to-day business of administering the country and used native soldiers to augment their military control. By 1850, only one in six soldiers serving Britain in India was European.

The East India Company also tried to establish a regular trade with China in opium, a drug long known for its medicinal uses but increasingly bought in China as a recreational drug. The Chinese government did its best to keep the highly addictive drug away from its people, both by forbidding Western merchants to venture outside the southern city of Guangzhou (Canton) and by banning the export of precious metals and the import of opium. These measures failed. By smuggling opium grown in India into China and bribing local officials, British traders built up a flourishing market. When in 1839 the Chinese authorities expelled British merchants from southern China, Britain retaliated by bombarding Chinese coastal cities, beginning the First Opium War. In 1842, it dictated to a defeated China the Treaty of Nanking, by which the British forced the opening of four more Chinese ports to Europeans,

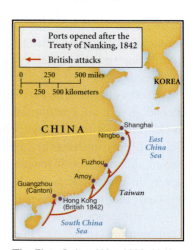

The First Opium War, 1839–1842

took sovereignty over the island of Hong Kong, received a substantial war indemnity, and were assured of a continuation of the opium trade. In this case, reform took a backseat to economic interest, despite the complaints of religious groups in Britain.

The Revolutions of 1830 and 1848

Imperialist ventures abroad continued even as the revolutionary legacy revived again in Europe, first in 1830 and then in a more widespread series of upheavals in 1848. Given its revolutionary past, it is not surprising that France took the lead. In 1830, a revolution overthrew the French king, Charles X (r. 1824–1830), the younger brother and successor to Louis XVIII. Charles X brought about his own downfall by pushing through a Law of Indemnity in 1825 to compensate nobles for the loss of their lands during the revolution of 1789. At the same time, he insisted on a Law of Sacrilege imposing the death penalty for such offenses as stealing religious objects from churches. He then dissolved the legislature, removed many wealthy and powerful voters from the rolls, and imposed strict censorship. Spontaneous demonstrations in Paris led to fighting on July 26, 1830. After three days of street battles in which 500 citizens and 150 soldiers died, a group of moderate liberal leaders, fearing the reestablishment of a republic, agreed to give the crown to Charles X's cousin Louis-Philippe, duke of Orléans.

Charles X went into exile in England, and the new king extended political liberties and voting rights. Although the number of voting men nearly doubled, it remained minuscule—approximately 170,000 in a country of 30 million, between 5 and 6 percent. Such reforms did little for the poor and working classes, who had manned the barricades in July. Dissatisfaction with the 1830 settlement boiled over in Lyon in 1831, when a silk-workers' strike over wages turned into a rebellion that died down only when the army arrived. Revolution had broken the hold of those who wanted to restore the pre-1789 monarchy and nobility, but it had gone no further this time than installing a more liberal, constitutional monarchy.

The success of the July Revolution in Paris ignited the Belgians, whose country had been annexed to the kingdom of the Netherlands in 1815. Differences in traditions, language, and religion separated the largely Catholic Belgians from the Dutch. King William of the Netherlands appealed to the great powers for help, but Great Britain and France opposed intervention and invited Russia, Austria, and Prussia to a conference that guaranteed Belgium independence in exchange for its neutrality in international affairs. Belgian neutrality would remain a cornerstone of European diplomacy for a century. After much maneuvering, the crown of the new kingdom of Belgium was offered to a German prince, Leopold of Saxe-Coburg, in 1831. Belgium, like France and Britain, now had a constitutional monarchy.

Political tensions boiled to the surface again in the late 1840s when crop failures across Europe threatened the food supply and food prices shot skyward. In the best of times, urban workers paid 50 to 80 percent of their income for a diet consisting largely of bread; now even bread was beyond their means. Overpopulation hastened famine in some places, especially Ireland, where an airborne blight destroyed the staple crop, potatoes, in 1846, 1848, and 1851. Out of a population of 8 million, as many as 1 million people died of starvation and disease. Corpses lay unburied on the sides of roads, and whole families were found dead in their cottages, half-eaten by dogs. Hundreds of thousands emigrated to England, the United States, and Canada.

High food prices also drove down the demand for manufactured goods, resulting in increased unemployment. Industrial workers' wages had been rising—in the German states, for example, wages rose an average of 5.5 percent in the 1830s

■ **The Potato Blight and Irish Famine**

Daniel McDonald's painting The Discovery of the Potato Blight *(1852) shows a family
digging potatoes only to find the crop rotted from blight. Potato blight spelled disaster for
thousands of families. The airborne blight spores landed on the potato plants and killed the
leaves, which fell to the ground. Spores washed into the earth and infected the underground
tubers. A crop could look normal yet be infected.*

and 10.5 percent in the 1840s—but the cost of living rose about 16 percent each
decade, canceling out wage increases. Seasonal work and regular unemployment
were already the norm when the crisis of the late 1840s intensified the uncertainties of urban life. "The most miserable class that ever sneaked its way into history"
is how Friedrich Engels described underemployed and starving workers in 1847.

The specter of hunger tarnished the image of established rulers and amplified
voices critical of them. Louis-Philippe's government had blocked all moves for electoral reform, and in February 1848, a banquet campaign sponsored by the political opposition turned into a revolution. At first the police and the army dispersed
the demonstrators who took to the streets on February 22, 1848. The next day,
however, forty or fifty people died when panicky soldiers opened fire on the crowd.
On February 24, faced with fifteen hundred barricades and a furious populace,
Louis-Philippe abdicated and fled to England. A hastily formed provisional
government declared France a republic once again.

The new republican government issued liberal reforms—an end to the death penalty for political crimes, the abolition of slavery in the colonies, and freedom of the press—and agreed to introduce universal adult male suffrage despite misgivings about political participation by peasants and unemployed workers. To address the gnawing problem of unemployment, the government allowed Paris officials to organize a system of "national workshops" to provide those out of jobs with construction work. When women protested their exclusion, the city set up a few workshops for women workers, albeit with wages lower than men's. To meet a mounting deficit, the provisional government then levied a 45 percent surtax on property taxes, alienating peasants and landowners.

The establishment of the republic politicized many segments of the population. Scores of newspapers and political clubs revived grassroots democratic fervor; meeting in concert halls, theaters, and government auditoriums, clubs became a regular attraction for the citizenry. Women also formed clubs, published women's newspapers, and demanded representation in national politics. Street-corner activism alarmed middle-class liberals and conservatives. To maintain control, the republican government paid some unemployed youths to join a mobile guard with its own uniforms and barracks. Tension between the government and the workers in the national workshops rose; the communist Étienne Cabet led one demonstration of 150,000 workers. Class warfare loomed like a thunderstorm on the horizon.

Faced with rising radicalism in Paris and other big cities, the voters elected a largely conservative National Assembly in April 1848, which immediately appointed a five-man executive committee to run the government and deliberately excluded known supporters of workers' rights. Suspicious of all demands for rapid change, the deputies dismissed a petition to restore divorce and voted down women's suffrage, 899 to 1. When the numbers enrolled in the national workshops in Paris rocketed from a predicted 10,000 to 110,000, the government ordered the workshops closed to new workers, and on June 21 it directed that those already enrolled move to the provinces or join the army.

The workers of Paris responded to these measures on June 23 by taking to the streets in the tens of thousands. In the June Days, as the following week came to be called, the government summoned the army, the National Guard, and the newly recruited mobile guard to fight the workers. Provincial volunteers came to help put down the workers, who had been depicted to them as lazy ruffians intent on destroying order and property. One observer breathed a sigh of relief: "The Red Republic [red being associated with demands for socialism] is lost forever; all France has joined against it. The National Guard, citizens, and peasants from the remotest parts of the country have come pouring in." The republic's army crushed the workers; more than 10,000, most of them workers, were killed or injured, 12,000 were arrested, and 4,000 eventually were convicted and deported.

When the National Assembly adopted a new constitution calling for a presidential election in which all adult men could vote, the electorate chose Louis-Napoleon Bonaparte, nephew of the dead emperor. Bonaparte got more than

5.5 million votes out of some 7.4 million cast. He had lived most of his life outside of France, and the leaders of the republic expected him to follow their tune. In uncertain times, the Bonaparte name promised something to everyone. Even many workers supported him because he had no connection with the blood-drenched June Days.

In reality, Bonaparte's election spelled the end of the Second Republic, just as his uncle had dismantled the first one, established in 1792. In 1852, on the forty-eighth anniversary of Napoleon I's coronation as emperor, Louis-Napoleon declared himself Emperor Napoleon III (r. 1852–1870). (Napoleon I's son died and never became Napoleon II, but Napoleon III wanted to create a sense of legitimacy and so used the Roman numeral III.) Political division and class conflict had proved fatal to the Second Republic. Although the revolution of 1848 never had a period of terror like that in 1793–1794, it nonetheless ended in similar fashion, with an authoritarian government that tried to play monarchists and republicans off against each other.

The Parisian uprising soon sparked other revolts. Italian nationalists hoped to unite a diverse collection of territories. In January 1848, a revolt had already broken out in Palermo, Sicily, against the Bourbon ruler. When news came of the revolution in Paris, a huge nationalist demonstration in Milan quickly pitted Austrian forces against armed demonstrators. In Venice, an uprising drove out the Austrians. Peasants in the south of Italy occupied large landowners' estates, while across central Italy revolts mobilized the poor and unemployed against local rulers. But class tensions and regional differences stood in the way of national unity. Property owners, businessmen, and professionals wanted liberal reforms and national unification under a conservative regime; intellectuals, workers, and artisans dreamed of democracy and social reforms. Some nationalists

The Divisions of Italy, 1848

favored a loose federation; others wanted a monarchy under Charles Albert of Piedmont-Sardinia; still others urged rule by the pope. A few shared Mazzini's vision of a republic with a strong central government. Many leaders of national unification spoke Italian only as a second language; most Italians spoke regional dialects.

As king of the most powerful Italian state, Charles Albert played a central role. After some hesitation caused by fears of French intervention, he led a military campaign against Austria. It soon failed, partly because of dissension over goals and tactics among the nationalists. Although Austrian troops defeated Charles Albert in the north in the summer of 1848, democratic and nationalist forces prevailed at

Revolutions of 1848			
1848		**November**	Insurrection drives the pope out of Rome
January	Uprising in Palermo, Sicily	**December**	Francis Joseph becomes Austrian emperor; Louis-Napoleon elected president in France
February	Revolution in Paris; proclamation of republic		
March	Insurrections in Vienna, German cities, Milan, and Venice; autonomy movement in Hungary; Charles Albert of Piedmont-Sardinia declares war on Austrian Empire	**1849**	
		February	Rome declared a republic
		April	Frederick William of Prussia rejects crown of united Germany offered by Frankfurt parliament
May	Frankfurt parliament opens	**July**	Roman republic overthrown by French intervention
June	Austrian army crushes revolutionary movement in Prague; June Days end in defeat of workers in Paris	**August**	Russian and Austrian armies combine to defeat Hungarian forces
July	Austrians defeat Charles Albert and Italian forces		

first in the south. In the fall, the Romans drove the pope from the city and in February 1849 declared Rome a republic. For the next few months republican leaders, such as Mazzini and Giuseppe Garibaldi (1807–1882), congregated in Rome to organize the new republic. These efforts faltered in July when foreign powers intervened. The new president of republican France, Louis-Napoleon Bonaparte, sent an expeditionary force to secure the papal throne for Pius IX (r. 1846–1878). Mazzini and Garibaldi fled. Although revolution had been defeated in Italy, the memory of the Roman republic and the commitment to unification remained, and they would soon emerge again with new force.

News of the revolution in Paris also provoked popular demonstrations in the German states. "My heart beat with joy. The monarchy had fallen. Only a little blood had been shed for such a high stake, and the great watchwords Liberty, Equality, Fraternity were again inscribed on the banner of the movement." So responded one Frankfurt woman to Louis-Philippe's overthrow. The Prussian army's efforts to clear the square in front of Berlin's royal palace on March 18, 1848, provoked panic and street fighting around hastily assembled barricades. The next day the crowd paraded wagons loaded with dead bodies under

The German States, 1848

King Frederick William IV's window, forcing him to salute the victims killed by his own army. In a state of near collapse, the king promised to call an assembly to draft a constitution and adopted the German nationalist flag of black, red, and gold.

The goal of German unification soon took precedence over social reform or constitutional changes within the separate states. In March and April 1848, most of the German states agreed to elect delegates to a federal parliament at Frankfurt that would attempt to unite Germany. Local princes and even the more powerful kings of Prussia and Bavaria seemed to totter. In Bavaria, students marched to the "Marseillaise" and called for a republic. Yet the revolutionaries' weaknesses soon became apparent. The eight hundred delegates to the Frankfurt parliament had little practical political experience: "a group of old women," one socialist called them; a "Professors Parliament" was the common sneer. These delegates had no access to an army, and they dreaded the demands of the lower classes for social reforms. Unemployed artisans and workers smashed machines; peasants burned landlords' records and occasionally attacked Jewish moneylenders; women set up clubs and newspapers to demand their emancipation from "perfumed slavery."

The advantage lay with the princes, who retained legal authority and control over the armed forces. The most powerful German states, Prussia and Austria, expected to determine whether and how Germany should unite. While the Frankfurt parliament laboriously prepared a liberal constitution for a united Germany—one that denied self-determination to Czechs, Poles, and Danes within its proposed German borders—the Prussian king Frederick William IV (r. 1840–1860) recovered his confidence. First his army crushed the revolution in Berlin in the fall of 1848. Prussian troops then intervened to help other local rulers put down the last wave of democratic and nationalist insurrections in the spring. In April 1849, when the Frankfurt parliament finally concluded its work, offering the emperorship of a constitutional, federal Germany to the king of Prussia, Frederick William contemptuously refused this "crown from the gutter."

By the summer of 1848, the Austrian Empire, too, had reached the verge of complete collapse. Just as Italians were driving the Austrians out of their lands in northern Italy and Magyar nationalists were demanding political autonomy for Hungary, on March 13, 1848, in Vienna, a student-led demonstration for political reform turned into rioting, looting, and machine-breaking. Metternich resigned, escaping to England in disguise. Emperor Ferdinand promised a constitution, an elected parliament, and the end of censorship. Beleaguered authorities in Vienna could not refuse Magyar demands for home rule, and Széchenyi and Kossuth both became ministers in the new Hungarian government. The Magyars were the largest ethnic group in Hungary but still did not make up 50 percent of the population, which included Romanians, Slovaks, Croats, and Slovenes, who preferred Austrian rule to domination by local Magyars.

The ethnic divisions in Hungary foreshadowed the many political and social divisions that would doom the revolutionaries. Fears of peasant insurrection

■ **Revolution of 1848 in Eastern Europe**
This painting by an unknown artist shows Ana Ipatescu leading a group of Romanian revolution-
aries in Transylvania in opposition to Russian rule. The Transylvanian provinces of Moldavia and
Walachia had been under Russian domination since the 1770s and occupied directly since 1829. In
April 1848, local landowners began to organize meetings. Paris-educated nationalists spearheaded
the movement, which demanded the end of Russian control and various legal and political re-
forms. By August the movement had split between those who wanted independence only and those
who pushed for the end of serfdom and for universal manhood suffrage. In response, the Russians
invaded Moldavia and the Turks moved into Walachia. By October, the uprising was over. Russia
and Turkey agreed to control the provinces jointly. (The Art Archive.)

prompted the Magyar nationalists around Kossuth to abolish serfdom. This measure alienated the largest noble landowners. In Prague, Czech nationalists convened
a Slav congress as a counter to the Germans' Frankfurt parliament and called for a
reorganization of the Austrian Empire that would recognize the rights of ethnic minorities. Such assertiveness by non-German peoples provoked German nationalists
to protest on behalf of German-speaking people in areas with a Czech or Magyar
majority.

The Austrian government slowly took advantage of these divisions. To quell
peasant discontent and appease liberal reformers, it abolished all remaining peasant obligations to the nobility in March 1848. Rejoicing country folk soon lost

interest in the revolution. Class conflicts flared in Vienna, where the middle classes had little sympathy for the starving artisans and workers. The new Hungarian government alienated the other nationalities when it imposed the Magyar language on them. Similar divisions sapped national unity in the Polish and Czech lands of the empire.

Military force finally broke up the revolutionary movements. The first blow fell in Prague in June 1848; General Prince Alfred von Windischgrätz, the military governor, bombarded the city into submission when a demonstration led to violence (including the shooting death of his wife, watching from a window). After another uprising in Vienna a few months later, Windischgrätz marched 70,000 soldiers into the capital and set up direct military rule. In December, the Austrian monarchy came back to life when the eighteen-year-old Francis Joseph (r. 1848–1916), unencumbered by promises extracted by the revolutionaries from his now-feeble uncle Ferdinand, assumed the imperial crown after intervention by leading court officials. In the spring of 1849, General Count Joseph Radetsky defeated the last Italian challenges to Austrian power in northern Italy, and his army moved east, joining with Croats and Serbs to take on the Hungarian rebels. In August, the Austrian army teamed up with Tsar Nicholas I, who marched into Hungary with more than 300,000 Russian troops. Hungary was put under brutal martial law. Széchenyi went mad, and Kossuth found refuge in the United States. Social conflicts and ethnic divisions weakened the revolutionary movements from the inside and gave the Austrian government the opening it needed to restore its position.

Aftermath to 1848

The revolutionaries of 1848 failed to achieve most of their goals, but their efforts left a profound mark on the political and social landscape. Between 1848 and 1851, the French served a kind of republican apprenticeship that prepared the population for another, more lasting republic after 1870. No French government could henceforth rule without extensive popular consultation. In Italy, the failure of unification did not stop the spread of nationalist ideas and the rooting of demands for democratic participation. In the German states, the revolutionaries of 1848 turned nationalism from an academic idea into a popular movement. The very idea of a Frankfurt parliament and the insistence on brandishing a German national flag at demonstrations showed that German nationalism had become a practical reality. The initiation of artisans, workers, and journeymen into democratic clubs increased political awareness in the lower classes and helped prepare them for broader political participation. Almost all the German states had a constitution and a parliament after 1850. The spectacular failures of 1848 thus hid some important successes.

The absence of revolution in 1848 was just as significant as its presence. No revolution occurred in Great Britain, the Netherlands, or Belgium, three places where industrialization and urbanization had developed most rapidly. In Great

Britain, the prospects for revolution actually seemed quite good: the Chartist movement took inspiration from the European revolutions in 1848 and mounted several gigantic demonstrations to force Parliament into granting all adult males the vote. But Parliament refused and no uprising occurred, in part because the government had already proved its responsiveness. The middle classes in Britain had been co-opted into the established order by the Reform Bill of 1832, and the working classes had won parliamentary regulation of children's and women's work.

The other notable exception to revolution among the great powers was Russia, where Tsar Nicholas I maintained a tight grip through police surveillance and censorship. The Russian schools, limited to the upper classes, taught Nicholas's three most cherished principles: autocracy (the unlimited power of the tsar), orthodoxy (obedience to the church in religion and morality), and nationality (devotion to Russian traditions). These provided no space for political dissent. Social conditions also fostered political passivity: serfdom continued in force, and the slow rate of industrial and urban growth created little discontent.

For all the differences between countries, some developments touched them all. European states continued to expand their bureaucracies. For example, in 1750 the Russian government employed approximately 10,500 functionaries; a century later it needed almost 114,000. In Great Britain, a swelling army of civil servants produced parliamentary studies on industrialization, foreign trade, and colonial profits, while new agencies such as the British urban police forces (10,000 strong in the 1840s) intruded increasingly in ordinary people's lives. States wanted to take children out of the fields and factories where they worked with their families and educate them. In some German cities, the police reported people who cleared snow off their roofs after the permitted hour or smoked in the street. A few governments even prescribed the length of sermons.

Although much had changed, the aristocracy remained the dominant power almost everywhere. As army officers, aristocrats put down revolutionary forces. As landlords, they continued to dominate the rural scene and control parliamentary bodies. They also held many official positions in the state bureaucracies. One Italian princess explained, "There are doubtless men capable of leading the nation . . . but their names are unknown to the people, whereas those of noble families . . . are in every memory." Aristocrats kept their authority by adapting to change: they entered the bureaucracy and professions, turned their estates into moneymaking enterprises, and learned how to invest shrewdly.

The reassertion of conservative rule hardened gender definitions. Women everywhere had participated in the revolutions, especially in the Italian states, where they joined armies in the tens of thousands and applied household skills toward making bandages, clothing, and food. Schoolgirls in Prague had thrown desks and chairs out of windows and helped build students' barricades. Many women in Paris had supported the new republic and seized the occasion of greater political openness to demand women's rights, only to experience isolation as their claims were

IMPORTANT DATES

1814–1815	Congress of Vienna
1820	Revolt of liberal army officers against the Spanish crown; Karlsbad Decrees abolish German student societies and tighten press censorship
1824	Ludwig van Beethoven, Ninth Symphony
1825	Russian army officers demand constitutional reform in the Decembrist uprising
1830	Manchester and Liverpool Railway opens in England; Greece gains independence from Ottoman Turks; France invades and begins conquest of Algeria; rebels overthrow Charles X of France and install Louis-Philippe; beginning of cholera epidemic in Europe
1832	British Parliament passes Reform Bill; Johann Wolfgang von Goethe, *Faust*
1833	Factory Act regulates work of children in Great Britain; abolition of slavery in the British Empire
1834	German customs union (*Zollverein*) established under Prussian leadership
1839	Beginning of Opium War between Britain and China
1846	Famine strikes Ireland; Corn Laws repealed in England; peasant insurrection in Austrian province of Galicia
1847	Charlotte Brontë, *Jane Eyre*
1848	Last great wave of Chartist demonstration in Britain; Karl Marx and Friedrich Engels, *The Communist Manifesto*; revolutions of 1848 throughout Europe; abolition of slavery in French colonies; end of serfdom in Austrian Empire
1851	Crystal Palace exhibition in London

denied by most republican men. Men in the revolutions of 1848 almost always defined universal suffrage as a male right. When workingmen gained the vote and women did not, the notion of separate spheres penetrated even into working-class life: political participation became one more way to distinguish masculinity from femininity. As conservatives returned to power, all signs of women's political activism disappeared. The French feminist movement, the most advanced in Europe, fell apart after the June Days when the increasingly conservative republican government forbade women to form political clubs and arrested and imprisoned two of the most outspoken women leaders for their socialist activities.

In May 1851, Europe's most important female monarch presided over a mid-century celebration of peace and industrial growth that helped dampen the still-smoldering fires of revolutionary passion. Queen Victoria (r. 1837–1901), who herself promoted the notion of domesticity as women's sphere, opened the international Exhibition of the Works of Industry of All Nations in London on May 1.

■ **The Crystal Palace**

This color lithograph (1851) by George Baxter provides a good view of the exterior of the main building for the Exhibition of the Works of Industry of All Nations in London. Sir Joseph Paxton (1801–1865) designed the gigantic building. It stood 1,848 feet long by 456 feet wide by 135 feet high; 772,784 square feet of ground-floor area covered no less than 18 acres.

(© The Bridgeman Art Library International Ltd.)

A monument of modern iron and glass architecture had been constructed to house the display; the building was more than a third of a mile long and so tall that it was erected over the trees of its Hyde Park site. Soon people referred to it as the "Crystal Palace"; its nine hundred tons of glass created an aura of fantasy, and the abundant goods from all nations inspired satisfaction and pride. One German visitor described it as "this miracle which has so suddenly appeared to dazzle the inhabitants of our globe." In the place of revolutionary fervor, the Crystal Palace offered a government-sponsored spectacle of what industry, hard work, and technological imagination could produce.

Conclusion

Many of the six million people who visited the Crystal Palace display had not forgotten the threat of disease, fears of overpopulation, popular resentments, and political upheavals that had been so prominent in the 1830s and 1840s. Even though industrial growth brought railroads, cheaper clothing, and access to exhibitions like the Crystal Palace, it also produced urban overcrowding and miserable working

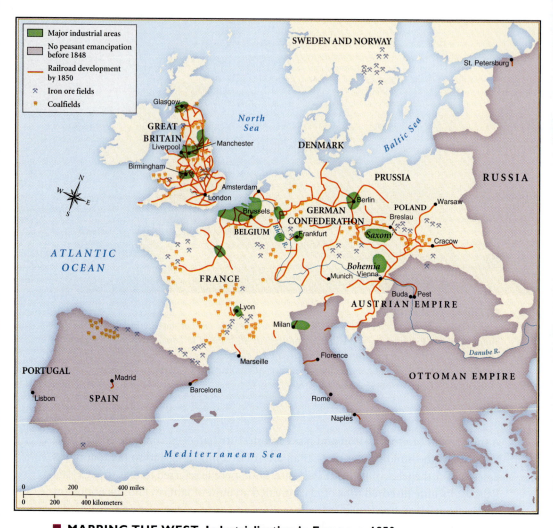

Legend:
- Major industrial areas
- No peasant emancipation before 1848
- Railroad development by 1850
- Iron ore fields
- Coalfields

■ **MAPPING THE WEST** Industrialization in Europe, c. 1850

Industrialization first spread across northern Europe in a band that included Great Britain, northern France, Belgium, the northern German states, the region around Milan in northern Italy, and Bohemia. Much of Scandinavia and southern and eastern Europe did not participate in this first phase of industrial development. Although railroads were not the only factor in promoting industrialization, the map makes clear the interrelationship between railroad building and the development of new industrial sites of coal mining and textile production.

conditions. The Crystal Palace presented the rosy view, but the housing shortages, inadequacy of water supplies, and recurrent epidemic diseases had not disappeared. Social reform organizations still drew attention to prostitution, child abandonment, alcohol abuse, and other problems associated with burgeoning cities.

Although the revolutions of 1848 brought to the surface the profound tensions within a European society in transition toward industrialization and modernization, they did not definitively resolve those tensions. Industrialization and urbanization continued, workers developed more extensive organizations, and liberals, conservatives, and socialists fought over the pace of reform. The revolutions made their most striking impact negatively rather than positively: confronted with the menace of revolution, elites sought alternatives that would be less threatening to the established order and still permit some change. This search for alternatives became immediately evident in the question of national unification in Germany and Italy. National unification would hereafter depend on what the Prussian leader Otto von Bismarck would call "blood and iron," not speeches and parliamentary resolutions.

Suggested References for further reading and online research appear on page SR-26 at the back of the book.

www.bedfordstmartins.com/huntconcise   See the ONLINE STUDY GUIDE to assess your mastery of the material covered in this chapter.

Constructing the Nation-State

c. 1850–1880

I N 1859, THE NAME VERDI SUDDENLY APPEARED scrawled on walls across the disunited cities of the Italian peninsula. The graffiti seemed to celebrate the composer Giuseppe Verdi, whose operas thrilled crowds of Europeans. Verdi was a particular hero among Italians, however, for his stories of downtrodden groups struggling against tyrannical government seemed to refer specifically to their plight. As his operatic choruses thundered out calls to rebellion in the name of the nation, Italian audiences were sure that Verdi meant for them to throw off Austrian and papal rule and unite in a new version of the ancient Roman Empire. Yet the graffiti was doubly political, a call to arms in the days before mass media. For VERDI also formed an acronym for *Vittorio Emmanuele Re* ("king") *d'*Italia, and in 1859 it summoned Italians to unite immediately under Victor Emmanuel II, king of Sardinia and Piedmont—the one leader with a nationalist, modernizing profile. The graffiti did its work, for the very next year Italy united as a result of warfare, popular uprisings, and hard bargaining by political realists.

In the wake of the failed revolutions of 1848, European statesmen and the politically conscious public increasingly rejected the politics of idealism in favor of *Realpolitik*—a politics of tough-minded realism aimed at strengthening the state and tightening social order. Claiming to distrust the romanticism and high-minded ideologies of the revolutionaries and hoping to control nationalism, Realpolitikers believed in playing power politics, strengthening the national economy, and using violence to attain their goals. Two particularly skilled practitioners of Realpolitik, the Italian Camillo di Cavour and the Prussian Otto von Bismarck, succeeded in

■ **Aïda Poster**

Aïda, *Giuseppe Verdi's opera of human passion and state power, became a staple of Western culture. As the opera played across Europe, it brought Europeans into a common cultural orbit. Written to celebrate the opening of the Suez Canal,* Aïda *also celebrated Europe's better access to Asian resources provided by the new waterway. As the poster shows, the opera ushered in another wave of Egyptomania—the craze for Egyptian styles and objects.* (Madeline Grimoldi.)

755

unifying Italy and Germany, respectively, not by consensus but by war and diplomacy. Most leading figures of these decades, enmeshed like Verdi's operatic heroes in violent political maneuverings, advanced state power by harnessing the forces of nationalism and liberalism that had led to earlier romantic revolts.

Many ingredients went into making modern nation-states and empires during these momentous decades. Continued economic development was crucial, and entrepreneurs produced a host of new inventions, new procedures, and new ways of doing business. A growing sense of national identity and common purpose was forged by both culture and government policy. As productivity and wealth increased, governments took vigorous steps to improve the urban environment, monitor public health, and promote national sentiment. State support for cultural developments ranging from public schools to opera productions helped establish a common fund of knowledge and even shared political beliefs. Authoritarian leaders such as Bismarck and the new French emperor Napoleon III believed that a better quality of life would not only calm revolutionary impulses and build state power but also keep political liberals at bay.

Culture also built a sense of belonging. Reading novels, attending art exhibitions, keeping up-to-date at the newly fashionable world's fairs, and attending theater and opera created a greater sense of being French or German or British but also of being European. Cultural works increasingly rejected romanticism, featuring instead realistic aspects of ordinary people's lives. Artists painted nudes in shockingly blunt ways, eliminating romantic hues and poses. Verdi's celebrated opera *La Traviata* showed a frolicking courtesan menacing a middle-class family. The Russian author Leo Tolstoy depicted the bleak life of soldiers in the Crimean War that erupted in 1853 between the Russian and Ottoman Empires, while his countryman Fyodor Dostoevsky wrote of criminals and murders in urban neighborhoods.

Realpolitik cared less for the costs than for the outcomes of state building. Advancing state power entailed intensifying colonization and stamping out resistance to global expansion. At home it uprooted neighborhoods in favor of constructing public buildings, roads, and parks. The process of nation building was often brutal, bringing war, arrests, protests, and outright civil war—all of these the centerpieces of Verdi's operas as well. As the wars of German unification drew to a close in 1871, an uprising of Parisians threw the new terms of national and industrial growth into question as citizens challenged the central government's intrusion into everyday life and its failure to count the costs. For the most part, the powerful Western state did not take shape automatically during these years. Instead, its growth occasioned warfare, dislocation, new inroads on the lives of people around the world, shrewd policy, and heated debate. Realpolitik produced all of these, as well as a general climate of modern opinion that valued realism and hard facts.

The End of the Concert of Europe

The revolutions of 1848 had weakened the concert of Europe, driving out its architect Metternich and allowing the forces of nationalism to flourish. It became more difficult for countries to control their competing ambitions and act together. In addition, the dreaded resurgence of Bonapartism in the person of Napoleon III (Louis-Napoleon, the nephew of Napoleon I) added to the volatility in international politics as France sought to reassert itself. One of Napoleon's targets was Russia, formerly a mainstay of the concert of Europe. From Russia's pursuit of further expansion, France helped engineer the Crimean War of 1853–1856. Taking a huge toll in human life, the war weakened Russia and Austria and made way for a massive shift in the distribution of European power.

Napoleon III and the Quest for French Glory

Louis-Napoleon Bonaparte encouraged the resurgence of French grandeur and the cult of his famous uncle as part of nation building. "There are certain men who are born to serve as a means for the march of the human race," he wrote. "I consider myself to be one of these." In deft political coups Louis-Napoleon converted himself from president of the Second Republic to emperor. Repressing opposition in towns and cities, he declared himself Emperor Napoleon III (r. 1852–1870) and proclaimed the Second Empire on December 2, 1852, anniversary of Napoleon I's own ascension to power.

Napoleon III acted as Europe's schoolmaster, showing its leaders how to combine economic liberalism and nationalism with authoritarian rule. Cafés where men might discuss politics were closed, and a rubber-stamp legislature (the *Corps législatif*) reduced representative government to a façade. Imperial style replaced republican rituals. Napoleon's opulent court dazzled the public, and the emperor cultivated a masculine image of strength and majesty by wearing military uniforms (like his namesake) and by conspicuously maintaining mistresses. Napoleon's wife, Empress Eugénie, however, followed middle-class conventions such as separate spheres for men and women by serving as a devoted mother to her only son and supporting many volunteer charities. The authoritarian, apparently old-fashioned order imposed by Napoleon satisfied the many peasants who opposed urban radicals as they went to the polls.

Yet Napoleon III was simultaneously a modernizer, and he promoted a strong economy, public works programs, and jobs, which lured the middle and working classes away from radical politics. International trade fairs, artistic expositions, and the magnificent rebuilding of Paris helped sustain French prosperity as Europe recovered from the hard times of the late 1840s. Empress Eugénie wore lavish gowns, encouraging French silk production and keeping Paris at the center of the lucrative

■ **Napoleon III and Eugénie Receive the Siamese Ambassadors**
At a splendid gathering of their court, Emperor Napoleon III, Empress Eugénie, and their son and heir greet ambassadors from Siam, whose exoticism and servility before the French imperial family are the centerpiece of this depiction. Amid the grandeur of the Napoleonic dynasty, the West towers above the East. (Giraudon/Art Resource, NY.)

fashion trade. The regime also reached a free-trade agreement with Britain and backed an innovative investment bank—the Crédit Mobilier. Such new institutions led the way in financing railroad expansion, and railway mileage increased fivefold during Napoleon III's reign. During the economic downturn of the late 1850s, he wooed support by allowing for working-class organizations and introducing democratic features into his governing methods. Although some historians have judged Napoleon III to be enigmatic and shifty because of these abrupt changes, his maneuvers were pragmatic responses to the fluid conditions.

On the international scene, Napoleon III's main goals were to overcome the containment of France imposed by the Congress of Vienna, realign continental politics to benefit France, and acquire international glory like a true Bonaparte. To realign European politics, Napoleon pitted France first against Russia in the Crimean War, then against Austria in the War of Italian Unification, and finally against Prussia in the Franco-Prussian War of 1870. Beyond Europe, Napoleon's army continued to enforce French rule in Algeria and Southeast Asia and tried to install Habsburg emperor Francis Joseph's brother Maximilian as ruler of Mexico and ultimately of all Central America—an assault that ended in 1867 with Maximilian's execution. Napoleon's foreign policy transformed relations among the great powers by causing a breakdown in the international system of peaceful diplomacy established at the Congress of Vienna. While his encouragement of projects like the Suez Canal to connect the Mediterranean and the Red Seas proved visionary, this push for worldwide influence eventually destroyed him: the French overthrew him after Prussia easily defeated his army in 1870.

The Crimean War, 1853–1856: Turning Point in European Affairs

Napoleon first flexed his diplomatic muscle in the Crimean War (1853–1856), which began as a conflict between the Russian and Ottoman Empires but ended as a war with long-lasting consequences for much of Europe. While professing to uphold the concert of Europe, Russia continued to build state power by making further inroads into Asia and the Middle East. In particular, Tsar Nicholas I wanted to absorb much of the Ottoman Empire, fast becoming known as "the sick man of Europe" because of its disintegrating authority. Napoleon III maneuvered Tsar Nicholas to be more aggressive, and amid this increasing belligerence war erupted in October 1853 between the two eastern empires (Map 18.1).

Behind the widening war lay the question of Europe's balance of power. To protect its Mediterranean routes to East Asia, Britain prodded the Ottomans to stand up to Russia. The Austrian government still resented its dependence on Russia in putting down Hungarian revolutionaries in 1849 and felt threatened by continuing Russian expansion into the Balkans. This anxiety helped Napoleon III gain a promise of Austrian neutrality during the war, thus fracturing the conservative Russian-Austrian coalition that had quashed French ambitions since 1815. In the fall of 1853, the Russians blasted the wooden Turkish ships to bits at the Ottoman port of Sinope on the Black Sea; in 1854, France and Great Britain, enemies in war for more than a century, declared war on Russia to defend the Ottoman Empire's sovereignty and territories.

■ **MAP 18.1 The Crimean War, 1853–1856**

The most destructive war in Europe between the Napoleonic Wars and World War I, this conflict drew attention to the conflicting ambitions around territories of the declining Ottoman Empire. Importantly for state building in these decades, it fractured the alliance of conservative forces from the Congress of Vienna, allowing Italy and Germany to come into being as unified states and permitting Napoleon III to pursue his ambitions for France.

www.bedfordstmartins.com/huntconcise
See the ONLINE STUDY GUIDE for more help in analyzing this map.

Faced with attacking the massive Russian Empire, the allies settled for limited military goals focused on capturing the Russian naval base at Sevastopol on the Black Sea in the Crimea. Even so, the Crimean War was spectacularly bloody. British and French troops landed in the Crimea in September 1854 and waged a long siege of the fortified city, which fell after a year of savage and costly combat. Generals on both sides demonstrated their incompetence, and governments failed to provide combatants with even minimal supplies, sanitation, or medical care. The war claimed a massive toll. Three-quarters of a million men died, more than two-thirds from disease and starvation.

In the midst of this unfolding catastrophe, Alexander II (r. 1855–1881) ascended the Russian throne after the death of his father, Nicholas I, in 1855. With casualties mounting, the new tsar sued for peace. As a result of the Peace of Paris, signed in March 1856, Russia lost the right to base its navy in the Straits of Dardanelles and the Black Sea, which were declared neutral waters. Moldavia and Walachia (which soon merged to form Romania) became autonomous Turkish provinces under the victors' protection.

Some historians have called the Crimean War one of the most senseless conflicts in modern history because competing claims in southeastern Europe could have been settled by diplomacy had it not been for Napoleon III's driving ambition. Yet the war was full of consequence. New technologies were introduced into warfare: the railroad, shell-firing cannon, breech-loading rifles, steam-powered ships, and the telegraph. The relationship of the home front to the battlefront was beginning to change with the use of the telegraph and increased press coverage. Home audiences received news from the Crimean front lines more rapidly and in more detail than ever before. However, reports of incompetence, poor sanitation, and the huge death toll outraged the public. One admirable figure rose above the carnage—Florence Nightingale. She seized the moment to escape the confines of middle-class domesticity by organizing a battlefield nursing service to care for the British sick and wounded. Through her tough-minded organization of nursing units, she improved the sanitary conditions of the troops both during and after the war and pioneered nursing as a profession. Finally, the war accomplished Napoleon III's goal of severing the alliance between the Habsburgs and Russia, the two conservative powers on which the Congress of Vienna peace settlement had rested since 1815. It thus ended Austria's and Russia's grip on European affairs and undermined their ability to contain the forces of liberalism and nationalism.

Spirit of Reform in Russia

Defeat in the Crimean War not only thwarted Russia's territorial ambition but also forced Russia on the path of reform. Hundreds of peasant insurrections had erupted during the decade before the Crimean War. Serf defiance ranged from malingering while at forced labor to boycotting vodka to protest its heavy taxation. "Our own and neighboring households were gripped with fear," one aristocrat reported, because everyone expected "a serf rising at any minute." Although economic development spread in parts of eastern Europe, the Russian economy stagnated compared with western Europe. Old-fashioned farming techniques led to depleted soil and food shortages, and the nobility was often contemptuous of ordinary people's suffering. Nonetheless, through sympathetic portrayals of serfs and frank depiction of brutal masters, such as in novelist Ivan Turgenev's *A Hunter's Sketches* (1852), a spirit of reform grew. A Russian translation of Harriet Beecher Stowe's antislavery novel *Uncle Tom's Cabin* (1852) also appeared in the 1850s and struck a responsive chord. When Russia lost the Crimean War, the educated public, including some government officials, found the poor performance of serf-conscripted armies a disgrace and the system of serf labor an intolerable liability.

Confronted with the need for change, Alexander proved more flexible than his father Nicholas I. Well educated and more widely traveled, he ushered in what came to be known as the age of Great Reforms, granting Russians new rights from above as a way of ensuring that violent action from below would not force change. The most dramatic reform was the emancipation of the serfs—almost 50 million people—beginning in 1861.♦ By the terms of emancipation, communities of former serfs, headed by male village elders, received grants of land. The community itself, called a *mir*, had full power to allocate this land among individuals and to direct their economic activity. Thus, although emancipation partially laid the groundwork for a modern labor force in Russia, communal landowning and decision making prevented unlimited mobility and the development of a pool of free labor. The condition attached to these so-called land grants was that peasants were not *given* land along with their personal freedom: they were forced to "redeem" the land they farmed by paying the government through long-term loans, which in turn compensated the original landowners. With much land and the best of it going to the nobility, most peasants ended up owning less land than they had tilled as serfs. These conditions, especially the huge burden of debt and communal regulations, blunted Russian agricultural development for decades. But idealistic reformers believed the emancipation of the serfs, once treated by the nobility practically as livestock, produced miraculous results. As one of them put it, "The people are without any exaggeration transfigured from head to foot. . . . The look, the walk, the speech, everything is changed."

Local administration, the judiciary, and the military were also reformed. The government compensated the nobility for loss of peasant services and set up *zemstvos*—regional councils through which aristocrats could direct neglected local matters such as education, public health, and welfare. Aristocratic dominance

---

♦ For the text of his emancipation proposal, see Document 57, Alexander II, "Address in the State Council."

■ **Emancipation of the Russian Serfs**
The Crimean War came as a harsh warning that the Russian Empire sorely needed social reform in an age of growing state power. The plight of tens of millions of serfs was often dire compared to the condition of western Europeans, and the emancipation of 1861 was seen as key to stabilizing both state and society. (Hulton Getty/Liaison Agency.)

assured that *zemstvos* would remain a conservative structure, but they became a countervailing political force to the distant central government, especially as some nobles profited from the relaxation of censorship and of restrictions on travel to see how the rest of Europe was governed. Simultaneously, judicial reform gave all Russians, even former serfs, access to modern civil courts, rather than leaving them at the mercy of a landowner's version of justice or secret, blatantly preferential practices. The Western principle of equality of all persons before the law, regardless of social rank, was introduced in Russia for the first time. Military reform followed in 1874 when the government ended the twenty-five-year period of conscription, substituting a six-year term and attention to education, efficiency, and humane treatment of recruits to make the Russian army more competitive with those in western Europe.

Alexander's reforms assisted modernizing and market-oriented landowners just as enclosures and emancipation had done much earlier in western Europe. At the same time, the changes diminished the personal prerogatives of the nobility, leaving their authority weakened and sparking intergenerational conflict. "An epidemic seemed to seize upon [noble] children . . . an epidemic of fleeing from the parental roof," one observer noted. Rejecting aristocratic leisure, youthful rebels from the upper class valued practical activity and sometimes identified with peasants and workers. Some formed communes where they hoped to do humble manual labor; others turned to higher education, especially the sciences. Rebellious daughters of the nobility flouted parental expectations by cropping their hair short, wearing black, and escaping from home through phony marriages so they could study in European universities. This repudiation of traditional society led Turgenev to label radical youth as *nihilists* (from the Latin for "nothing"), a term that meant a lack of belief in any values whatsoever.

The atmosphere of reform also produced resistance among Russian-dominated nationalities, including an uprising by aristocratic and upper-class nationalist Poles in 1863. By 1864, Alexander II's army regained control of the Russian section of Poland, having used reforms to buy peasant support in defeating the rebels. In the Caucasus and elsewhere, Alexander responded to nationalist unrest with repression and programs of intensive Russification—a tactic meant to reduce the threat of future rebellion by national minorities within the empire by forcing them to adopt Russian language and culture. In this era of the Great Reforms, the tsarist regime only partially succeeded in developing the administrative, economic, and civic institutions of the nation-state elsewhere.

War and Nation Building

With the concert of Europe a thing of the past, politicians in the German and Italian states used the opportunity to unify their countries quickly and violently through warfare. When disunity threatened, the United States also waged a bloody civil war to ensure its borders. Historians sometimes treat the rise of powerful nation-states such as Italy, Germany, and the United States as part of an inevitable process, but millions of individuals in these states and elsewhere maintained a local or some other complex sense of identity in the midst of national unification.

Cavour, Garibaldi, and the Process of Italian Unification

Despite the failure of the revolutions of 1848 in the Italian states, the issue of *Risorgimento* (literally meaning "rebirth" but associated with the movement for Italian unification) continued to percolate, aided by the disintegration of diplomatic stability across Europe. This time the clear leader of Risorgimento would be the kingdom of Piedmont-Sardinia, in the economically modernizing north of Italy. The kingdom rallied to the operas of Verdi, but it was fortified with railroads, a modern army, and the support of France against the Austrian Empire, which still dominated the peninsula.

The architect of the new Italy was the pragmatic Camillo di Cavour (1810–1861), prime minister of the kingdom of Piedmont-Sardinia from 1852 until his death. A rebel in his youth, the young Cavour had conducted agricultural experiments on his aristocratic father's land. He organized steamship companies, played the stock market, and inhaled the heady air of modernization during his travels to Paris and London. Cavour thus made economic development rather than democratic uprising the means to achieve a united Italy. As prime minister to the capricious and scheming king, Victor Emmanuel II (r. 1861–1878), he capitalized on favorable conditions to develop a healthy Piedmontese economy, a modern army, and a liberal political climate as the foundation for Piedmont's control of the unification process (Map 18.2).

■ **MAP 18.2 Unification of Italy, 1859–1870**

The many states of the Italian peninsula had different languages, ways of life, and economic inter-
ests. In the north, the Kingdom of Sardinia, which included the commercially advanced state of
Piedmont, had much to gain from a unified market and a more extensive pool of labor. Although
King Victor Emmanuel's and Garibaldi's armies unified these states into a single country, it would
take decades to construct a culturally, socially, and economically connected nation.

To unify Italy, however, Piedmont would have to confront Austria, which governed the provinces of Lombardy and Venetia and exerted strong influence over most
of the peninsula. Cavour turned for help to Napoleon III, who at a meeting in the
summer of 1858 promised French assistance in exchange for the city of Nice and the
region of Savoy. Napoleon III expected that France rather than Austria would influence the peninsula thereafter. Sure of French help, Cavour provoked the Austrians
to invade northern Italy in April 1859, and using the newly built Piedmontese rail-

road to move troops, the French and Piedmontese armies achieved rapid victories at Solferino and Magenta. The cause of Piedmont now became the cause of nationalist Italians everywhere, even those who had supported romantic republicanism in 1848. Political liberals in Tuscany and other central Italian states rose up on the side of Piedmont. Suddenly fearing Piedmontese force, Napoleon independently signed a peace treaty with Habsburg emperor Francis Joseph. Its terms gave Lombardy but not Venetia to Piedmont, and the rest of Italy remained disunited.

Napoleon's plans for controlled liberation of Lombardy and Venetia and a partitioned Italy were derailed as support for Piedmont continued to swell inside Italy and as a financially strapped Austria stood by helplessly. Ousting their rulers, citizens of Parma, Modena, Tuscany, and the Papal States (except Rome, which French troops had occupied) elected to join Piedmont. In May 1860, Giuseppe Garibaldi (1807–1882), a committed republican, inspired guerrilla fighter, and veteran of the revolutions of 1848, set sail from Genoa with a thousand red-shirted volunteers (many of them teenage boys) to liberate Sicily, where peasant revolts against landlords and the corrupt government were under way. In the autumn of 1860, the forces of King Victor Emmanuel of Piedmont-Sardinia and Garibaldi finally met in Naples. Although some of his supporters still clamored for social reform and a republic, Garibaldi threw his support to the king. In 1861, the kingdom of Italy was proclaimed with Victor Emmanuel as king.

Exhausted by a decade of overwork, Cavour died within months of leading the unification, leaving lesser men to organize the new Italy. Consensus among Italy's elected political leaders was often elusive once the war was over, and admirers of Cavour, such as Verdi (who had been made senator), fled the heated political scene. The wealthy commercial north and impoverished agricultural south remained at odds, as they do even today. Italian borders did not yet seem final because Venetia and Rome remained outside them,

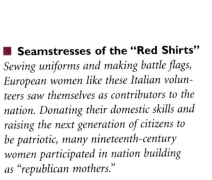

■ **Seamstresses of the "Red Shirts"**
Sewing uniforms and making battle flags, European women like these Italian volunteers saw themselves as contributors to the nation. Donating their domestic skills and raising the next generation of citizens to be patriotic, many nineteenth-century women participated in nation building as "republican mothers."

under Austrian and French control, respectively. But the legend of an Italian struggle for freedom symbolized by the figure of Garibaldi and his Red Shirts sentimentalized the economic and military Realpolitik that had made unification possible.

Bismarck and the Realpolitik of German Unification

The most momentous act of nation building for the future of Europe and of the world was the creation of a united Germany in 1871. This, too, was the work of Realpolitik, undertaken once the concert of Europe was smashed and the champions of the status quo were defeated. Employing the old military order to wage war, yet with the support of economic modernizers who saw profits in one huge national market, the Prussian state brought a vast array of cities and kingdoms under its control within a single decade. From then on, Germany prospered, continuing to consolidate its economic and political might.

The architect of a unified Germany was Otto von Bismarck (1815–1898), the Prussian minister-president. Bismarck came from a traditional *Junker* (Prussian landed nobility) family on his father's side; his mother's family included high-ranking bureaucrats and literati of the middle class. At university, the young Bismarck had gambled and womanized, interested only in a course on the economic foundations of politics. After failing in the civil service, he worked to modernize operations on his landholdings while leading an otherwise loutish life, but his marriage to a pious Lutheran woman gave him new purpose. In the 1850s, his diplomatic service to the Prussian state made him increasingly angry at Habsburg domination of German affairs and the roadblock it created to the full flowering of Prussia.

In 1862, William I (king of Prussia, r. 1861–1888; German emperor, r. 1871–1888) appointed Bismarck prime minister in hopes that he would quash the growing power of the liberals in the Prussian parliament. The liberals, representing the prosperous professional and business classes, had gained parliamentary strength at the expense of conservative landowners during the decades of industrial expansion. Indeed, the liberals' wealth was crucial to the Prussian state's ability to augment its power. Desiring Prussia to be like western Europe, Prussian liberals advocated the extension of political rights and increased civilian control of the military. William I, along with members of the traditional Prussian elite such as Bismarck, rejected the western European model. Bismarck simply rammed through programs to build the army and thwart civilian control. "Germany looks not to Prussia's liberalism, but to its power," he preached. "The great questions of the day will not be settled by speeches and majority decisions—that was the great mistake of 1848 and 1849—but by blood and iron."

After his triumph over the parliament, Bismarck led Prussia into a series of wars, against Denmark in 1864, against Austria in 1866, and, finally, against France in 1870. Using war as a political tactic, he kept the disunited German states from choosing Austrian leadership and instead united them around Prussia. Bismarck drew Austria into a joint war with Prussia against a rebellious Denmark in 1864 over Denmark's proposed incorporation of the provinces of Schleswig and Holstein, with their partially German population. Their joint victory resulted in an agreement that Prussia would administer Schleswig, and Austria, Holstein. Such an arrangement stretched Austria's geographic interests far from its central European base.

Austria proved weaker than Prussia, as the Habsburgs dealt with lagging economic development, a swelling national debt, and the restless national minorities within its borders. Bismarck encouraged Habsburg pretensions to its former grandeur and influence and simultaneously fomented disputes over the administration of Schleswig and Holstein, goading Austria into declaring war on Prussia itself. In the summer of 1866, Austria went to war with the support of most small states in the German Confederation. Within seven weeks, the modernized Prussian army, using railroads and breech-loading rifles against the outdated Austrian military, had won decisively. Victory allowed Bismarck to drive Austria from the German Confederation, create a North German Confederation led by Prussia, and coordinate economic and political programs (Map 18.3).

To bring the remaining German states into the rapidly developing nation, Bismarck next moved to entrap France in a war with Prussia. During the Austro-Prussian War, Bismarck had suggested to Napoleon III that his neutrality would bring France territory, thus heating up nationalist sentiments in both France and Germany. The atmosphere became even more charged when Spain proposed a minor Prussian prince to fill its vacant throne. This candidacy threatened the French with Prussian rulers on two of their borders and inflated Prussian pride. Bismarck used the occasion to stir up nationalist journalism in both countries by editing a diplomatic communication (the Ems telegram) to make it look as if the king of Prussia had insulted France. Release of the revised version to journalists inflamed the French public into demanding war. The parliament gladly declared it on July 19, 1870, setting in motion the alliances Prussia had created with the other German states. The Prussians captured Napoleon III with his army on September 2, 1870, and the Second Empire fell two days later. With Prussian forces still besieging Paris, in January 1871 in the Hall of Mirrors at Versailles, King William of Prussia was proclaimed the *kaiser* of a new, imperial Germany. The terms of the peace signed in May 1871 required France to cede the rich industrial provinces of Alsace and Lorraine to Germany and to pay a multi-billion-franc indemnity. Without French protection for the papacy, Rome became part of Italy. Germany was now poised to dominate continental politics.

Prussian military might served as the foundation for German state building, and a complex constitution ensured the continued political dominance of the aristocracy and monarchy. The kaiser, who remained Prussia's king, controlled the military and appointed Bismarck to the powerful position of imperial chancellor. The German states balanced monarchical authority somewhat through the *Bundesrat*, a body composed of representatives from each state. The *Reichstag*, an assembly

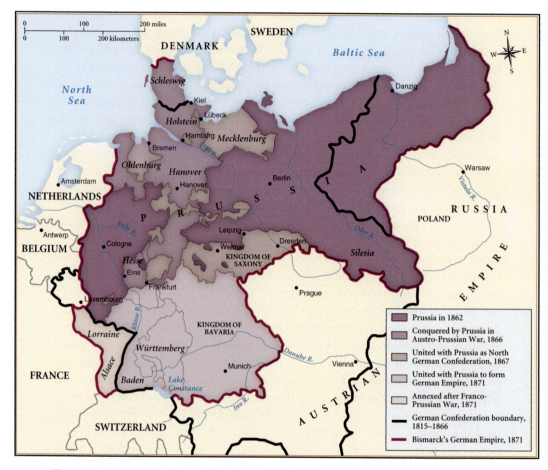

■ MAP 18.3 Unification of Germany, 1862–1871

In a complex series of diplomatic maneuvers, Bismarck welded disunited kingdoms and small states into a major continental power independent of the other dominant German dynasty, the Habsburg monarchy. Prussia's use of force unified Germany politically, and almost immediately that unity unleashed the new nation's economic potential. An aristocratic and agrarian elite remained firmly in power, but a rapidly growing working class would soon become a political force to be reckoned with.

elected by universal male suffrage, ratified all budgets. In framing this constitutional settlement, Bismarck accorded rights such as suffrage in the belief that the masses would uphold autocracy out of their fear of "the domination of finance capital"— shorthand for "liberal power." He balanced this move, however, with an electoral system in which votes from the upper classes counted more than votes from the lower classes. He had little to fear from liberals, who, dizzy with German military success, came to support the blend of economic progress, constitutionalism, and militaristic nationalism that Bismarck represented.

■ **Emperor William I of Germany, 1871**

The defeat of France in the Franco-Prussian War of 1870–1871 ended with the proclamation of the king of Prussia as emperor of a unified Germany. Otto von Bismarck, who had orchestrated the wars of unification, appropriately appears in this artistic rendering as the central figure attired in heroic white. The event in the French palace of Versailles symbolized the militaristic and antagonistic side of state building, especially the Franco-German rivalry that would disastrously motivate European politics in the future. (AKG London.)

Francis Joseph and the Creation of the Austro-Hungarian Monarchy

There was no blueprint for nation building. Just as the Crimean War left Russia searching for solutions to its social and political problems, so the confrontation with Cavour and Bismarck left the Habsburg Empire at bay. At first, the Habsburg Empire emerged from the revolutions of 1848 and 1849 renewed by the ascension of Francis Joseph (r. 1848–1916), who favored absolutist rule. A tireless worker, Francis Joseph enhanced his authority through stiff, formal court ceremonies, playing to the popular fascination with the trappings of power. Although the emperor stubbornly resisted change, official standards of honesty and efficiency improved, and the government promoted local education. The German language was used by the administration and taught by the schools, but the government respected the rights of national minorities—Czechs and Poles, for instance—to receive education and to communicate with officials in their native tongues. Above all, the government abolished most internal customs barriers, freed trade with Germany, fostered a boom in private railway construction, and attracted foreign capital. The capital city of Vienna underwent extensive rebuilding, and people found jobs as industrialization progressed.

In a fast-paced age, the absolutist emperor could not match Bismarck in advancing modernization and the power of the state. Prosperous liberals resented the swarm of police informers, the nearly free hand of the Catholic church in education and in civil institutions such as marriage, and their own lack of representation in such important policy matters as taxation and finance. Funds for modernizing the military dried up. After Prussia's victory over Francis Joseph's scaled-back armies in 1866, the most disaffected but wealthy part of the empire, Hungary, became the key to stability, even to the empire's existence. The leaders of the Hungarian agrarian elites forced the emperor to accept a "dual monarchy"—that is, Magyar home rule over the Hungarian kingdom. This agreement restored the Hungarian parliament and gave it control of internal policy (including the right to decide how to treat Hungary's national minorities). Although the Habsburg emperor Francis Joseph was crowned king of Hungary and Austro-Hungarian foreign policy was coordinated from Vienna, the Hungarians mostly ruled themselves after 1867 and hammered out common policies such as tariffs in acrimonious negotiations with Vienna.

The Austro-Hungarian Monarchy, 1867

The dual monarchy of Austria-Hungary, or Austro-Hungarian monarchy as the new arrangement was also called, was designed specifically to address Hungarian demands, but in so doing it strengthened the voices of Czechs, Slovaks, and at least half a dozen additional national groups in the Habsburg Empire wanting the same kind of self-rule. Czechs who helped the empire advance industrially failed to gain Hungarian-style liberties, and for some of the dissatisfied ethnic groups, Pan-Slavism—that is, the transnational loyalty of all ethnic Slavs—became a rallying cry as the various Slav peoples saw themselves as linked through a common heritage. Instead of looking toward Vienna, they turned to the largest Slavic country—Russia—as a focal point for potential national unity. As the nation-state grew in strength, transnational movements like Pan-Slavism would emerge to provide alternative allegiances for those not recognized as equal citizens in their home countries.

Political Stability through Gradual Reform in Great Britain

In contrast to the turmoil in continental Europe, Britain appeared the epitome of liberal progress. By the 1850s, the monarchy symbolized domestic tranquility and propriety. Unlike their predecessors, Queen Victoria (r. 1837–1901) and her hus-

■ **Queen Victoria and Prince Albert**

In the mid-nineteenth century, rulers started using the new photographic technology to portray themselves as respectable and distinguished figures. Queen Victoria and her husband were expert publicists, often posing as an ordinary middle-class couple and the epitome of domestic order in marked contrast to their often dissolute royal predecessors. Photos of them were sold or given away on small cards called cartes de visites, *which many leaders used to spread their fame.*
(The Royal Archives © Her Majesty Queen Elizabeth II.)

band, Prince Albert, were considered models of morality, British stability, and middle-class virtues. Britain's parliamentary system incorporated new ideas and steadily brought more men into the political process. Economic prosperity further fortified peaceful political reform except for Ireland's continued suffering and thwarted demands for justice. Smooth governmental decision making was fostered by an ever-changing and focused party system: the Tory party evolved into the Conservatives, many of whose policies favored the aristocracy. Nonetheless, the Conservatives still went along with the developing liberal consensus around economic development and representative government. The Whigs changed names, too, and became the Liberals. In 1867, the Conservatives, led by Benjamin Disraeli, passed the Second Reform Bill, which made a million more men eligible to vote.

Political parties supported reforms because pressure groups now influenced the party system. The Law Amendment Society and the Social Science Association, for example, lobbied for laws to improve social conditions, and women's groups advocated the Matrimonial Causes Act of 1857, which facilitated divorce, and the Married Women's Property Act of 1870, which allowed married women to own property and keep the wages they earned. Dissension over new policies was papered over by plush ceremonies that united critics and activists and, more important, different social classes. Whereas previous monarchs' sexual infidelities had incited mobs to riot, the monarchy of Queen Victoria and Prince Albert, with its newly devised celebrations of royal marriages, anniversaries, and births, drew respectful crowds. Promoting the monarchy in this way was so successful that the term *Victorian* came to symbolize almost the entire century and could refer to anything from manners to political institutions. Yet Britain's politicians were as devoted to Realpolitik as were those in Germany, Italy, or France, especially using violence to expand their overseas empire. The violence was far beyond the view of most British people, however, allowing them to imagine their nation as peaceful, advanced, and united.

Civil War and Nation Building in the United States and Canada

In North America, increasing nationalism and powerful economic growth characterized the nation-building experience. The United States entered a midcentury period of upheaval with a more democratic political culture than existed in Europe. Almost universal white male suffrage, a rambunctiously independent press, and mass political parties endorsed the accepted view that sovereignty derived from the people.

The United States continued to expand its territory to the west (Map 18.4). In 1848, victory in a war with Mexico almost doubled the size of the country: Texas was officially annexed, and large portions of California and the American Southwest extended the borders of the United States into former Mexican land. Politicians and ordinary citizens alike favored banning the native Indian peoples from these western lands. Complicating matters, however, was the question of whether the U.S. West would be settled by free white farmers or whether southern slaveholders could bring in their slaves.

The issue polarized the country. In the North, the new Republican party emerged to demand "free soil, free labor, free men," although few Republicans endorsed the abolitionist demand to end slavery. With the 1860 election of Republican Abraham Lincoln to the presidency, most of the slaveholding states of the South seceded to form the Confederate States of America. Between 1861 and 1865, the United States was torn apart by civil war between North and South.

Under Lincoln's leadership, the North fought to restore the Union. Lincoln did not initially aim to abolish slavery, but in January 1863 his Emancipation Proclamation came into force as a wartime measure, officially freeing all slaves in the Confederate states and turning the war into a fight not only for the Union but also for liberation from slavery. After the summer of 1863, the superior industrial strength and military might of the North overpowered and physically destroyed much of the South. By April 1865, the North had prevailed even though a Confederate sympathizer had assassinated Lincoln. Distancing the United States still further from the colonial plantation model, constitutional amendments ended slavery and promised free African American men full political rights.

■ MAP 18.4 United States Expansion, 1850–1870

Like Russia, the United States expanded into adjacent regions to create a continental nation-state, conquering indigenous peoples and taking over their territories. The United States' treatment of those whose lands it took was different from Russia's, however. Native American peoples were herded into small confined spaces called reservations so that settlers could acquire thousands of square miles for farming and other enterprises. Gradually some Native Americans acquired the right to vote, and the U.S. government granted full citizenship for all in 1925.

Northerners hailed their victory as the triumph of American values, but racism remained entrenched throughout the United States. By 1871, northern interest in promoting African American political rights was waning, and southern whites began regaining control of state politics, often by organized violence and intimidation. The end of northern occupation of the South in 1877 put on hold for nearly a century the promise of rights for blacks.

The North's triumph had profound effects elsewhere in North America. It allowed the reunited United States to contribute to Napoleon III's defeat in Mexico in 1867. The United States also demanded the annexation of Canada in retribution for Britain's partiality to the Confederacy because of British dependence on cotton. To head off this threat, the British government allowed Canadians to form a united, self-governing dominion. According dominion status answered Canadian appeals for home rule and lessened domestic opposition to Britain's control of Canada.

Industry and Nation Building

Behind the growing power of European states lay the often dramatic development of economic and technological power. Industry turned out a cornucopia of products that improved people's material well-being. Paris, Vienna, and other cities experienced a frenzy of building, and the wages of many workers increased. Unpredictable downturns in business, however, threatened both entrepreneurs and the working class. Businesspeople sought remedies in further innovation, in new managerial techniques, and in revolutionizing marketing, most visibly in the development of the department store. Governments played their part by changing business law and supporting the drive for global profits. The steady advance of industry and the rise of a consumer economy further transformed the work lives of millions of people.

Industrial Innovation

Industrial, technological, and commercial innovation transformed nineteenth-century Europe. New products ranging from the bicycle, typewriter, and telephone to the internal combustion engine provided dizzying proof of industrial progress. Many independent tinkerers and inventor-manufacturers created new products, and sophisticated engineers—for example, Karl Benz of Germany and Armand Peugeot of France—invented revolutionary technologies such as the gasoline engine. Electricity began to provide the power to light everything from private drawing rooms to government office buildings. To fuel industrial growth, the leading industrial nations mined and produced massive quantities of coal, iron, and steel during the 1870s and 1880s. Production of iron increased from 11 million to 23 million tons. Steel output in the industrial nations grew just as impressively, increasing from 500,000 to 11 million tons in the 1870s and 1880s. Manufacturers used the metal to build the more than 100,000 locomotives that pulled trains during these years—trains that transported two billion people annually.

Historians used to contrast a "second" Industrial Revolution, with its concentration on heavy industrial products, to the "first" Industrial Revolution of the eighteenth and early nineteenth centuries, in which innovations in textile making and the use of steam energy predominated. But many historians now believe this distinction applies mainly to Britain. In countries where industrialization came later, the two stages occurred simultaneously. Numerous textile mills were installed on the European continent later than in Britain, for instance, at the same time as blast furnaces were constructed. Industrialization led to the decline of cottage production in traditional crafts like weaving. But home industry—or outwork—persisted in garment making, metalwork, and "finishing trades" such as porcelain painting and button polishing. The coexistence of home and factory enterprise continued through all the changes in manufacturing, to the present day.

Industrial innovations also transformed agriculture. Chemical fertilizers boosted crop yields, and reapers and threshers mechanized harvesting. In the 1870s, Sweden produced a cream separator, a first step toward mechanizing dairy farming. Wire fencing and barbed wire replaced wooden fencing and stone walls, both of which were labor-intensive to create. Refrigeration, developed during this period, allowed fruits, vegetables, and meat to be transported without spoiling, thus diversifying and increasing the urban food supply. Tin from colonial trade facilitated large-scale commercial canning, which made many foods available year-round to people in the cities.

During these decades, Britain's rate of industrial growth slowed as its entrepreneurs remained wedded to older, successful technologies. Two countries began surpassing Britain in research, technical education, innovation, and rate of growth: Germany and the United States. Profiting from the acquisition of resource-rich Alsace and Lorraine, German businesses invested in research and began to mass-produce goods that other countries had originally manufactured. Germany also spent as much money on education as on its military in the 1870s and 1880s. This investment resulted in highly skilled engineers and technical workers whose productivity enabled Germany's electrical and chemical engineering capabilities to soar. The United States began an intensive exploitation of its vast natural resources, including coal, ores, gold, and oil. Whereas German accomplishments rested more on state promotion of industrial efforts, U.S. growth often involved innovative entrepreneurs, such as Andrew Carnegie in iron and steel and John D. Rockefeller in oil.

Most other countries trailed the three leaders in the pervasiveness of industry. French industry grew steadily, but French businesses remained smaller than businesses in Germany and the United States. Although France had some huge mining, textile, and metallurgical establishments, many French businessmen retired early to imitate the still-enviable aristocratic way of life. Industrial development in Spain, Austria-Hungary, and Italy was primarily a local phenomenon. Austria-Hungary had densely industrialized areas around Vienna and in Styria and Bohemia, but the rest of the country remained tied to traditional, unmechanized agriculture. Italy's economy continued to industrialize in the north while remaining rural and agricultural in the south. The Italian government spent more on building Rome into a grand capital than it invested in economic growth. A mere 1.4 percent of Italy's 1872 budget went to education and science, compared with 10.8 percent in Germany. The commercial use of electricity helped Scandinavians, who were poor in coal and ore, to industrialize in the last third of the nineteenth century. Sweden and Norway became leaders in the use of hydroelectric power and the development of electrical products. Russia's road to industrialization was torturous, slowed partly by its relatively small urban labor force. Many Russian peasants who may have wished to take advantage of the opportunities of industrialization were tied to the *mir*, or landed community, by the terms of the serf emancipation. By the end of the century, however, the burgeoning of the railroads combined with growth in metallurgical and mining operations lifted Russia toward industrial development.

Facing Economic Crisis

Although innovations and business expansion often conveyed a sense of optimism, economic health was far from steady. Sharp downturns occurred in the business cycle throughout these decades, and within two years of the end of the Franco-Prussian War, prosperity abruptly gave way to a severe economic depression in many industrial countries. The crisis of 1873 was followed by almost three decades of economic fluctuations, most alarmingly a series of sharp downturns whose severity varied from country to country. People of all classes lost their jobs or businesses and faced consequences ranging from long stretches of unemployment to bankruptcy. Economists of the day were stunned by the relentlessness and pervasiveness of the slump. Because economic ties bound industrialized western Europe to international markets, recession affected the economies of such diverse regions as Australia, South Africa, California, Newfoundland, and the West Indies.

By the 1870s, industrial and financial setbacks—not agricultural ones, as in the past—were sending businesses into long-term tailspins in a climate of innovation and fundamentally new economic problems. First, the start-up costs of new enterprises skyrocketed. Textile mills had required relatively modest amounts of capital in comparison with factories producing steel and iron. Industrialization had become what modern economists call *capital-intensive* rather than *labor-intensive:* industrial growth required the purchase of expensive machinery, not merely the hiring of more workers. Second, the distribution and consumption of goods were inadequate to sustain industrial growth, in part because businessmen kept wages so low despite rising productivity that workers could afford little besides food. Industrialists had made their fortunes by emphasizing production, not consumption. The series of slumps refocused entrepreneurial policy on finding ways to enhance sales and distribution and to control markets and prices.

New laws and institutions helped raise capital. Development of the limited-liability corporation protected businesspeople from personal responsibility for the firm's debt and thus encouraged their investment. Before limited liability, business owners drew the necessary capital primarily from their own family assets, and financial backers were individually responsible for a firm's financial difficulties. In one case in England, a former partner who failed to have his name removed from a legal document after leaving the business remained responsible to creditors when the company went bankrupt. He lost everything he owned except a watch and the equivalent of $100. Public financing in stocks also helped raise vast amounts of new capital. Early stock exchanges had dealt mainly in government bonds and in government-sponsored enterprises such as railroads. By the end of the century, stock markets traded heavily in industrial corporate stock, thus raising money from a larger pool of private capital than before.

In another adaptive move, firms in the same industry banded together in cartels and trusts to control prices and competition. Cartels flourished particularly in

German chemical, iron, coal, and electric industries. For example, the Rhenish-Westphalian Coal Syndicate, founded in 1893, eventually dominated more than 95 percent of coal production in Germany. Although business owners continued to advocate free trade, cartels broke with free-trade practices by restricting output and setting prices. Smaller businesses trying to compete and consumers had no effective means of resisting these new business techniques. Trusts appeared first in the United States. In 1882, John D. Rockefeller created the Standard Oil Trust by acquiring stock from many different oil companies and placing it under the direction of trustees. The trustees then controlled so much of the companies' stock that they could set prices for the entire industry and even dictate to the railroads the rates for transporting the oil.

Like the practices of cartels and trusts, government imposition of tariffs expressed declining faith in classical liberal economics. Much of Europe had adopted free trade after midcentury, but during the recessions of the 1870s, huge trade deficits—caused when imports exceed exports—had soured many Europeans on the concept. A country with a trade deficit had less capital available to invest internally; fewer jobs were created, and the chances of social unrest increased. Farmers in many European countries were hurt when improvements in transportation made it possible to import perishable food, such as cheaper grain from the United States and Ukraine. With broad popular support, governments approved tariffs throughout these decades to prevent competition from foreign goods.

Revolution in Business Practices

Industrialists tried to minimize the damage of economic downturns by revolutionizing the everyday conduct of their businesses in offices. A generation earlier, a factory owner was directly involved in every aspect of his business and often learned to run the firm through trial and error. In the late 1800s, industrialists began to hire managers to run their increasingly complex day-to-day operations. Managers who specialized in sales and distribution, finance, and the purchase of raw materials made decisions and oversaw the implementation of their policies. Simultaneously the emergence of a "white-collar" service sector of office workers meant the employment of secretaries, file clerks, and typists to guide the flow of business information. Banks that accepted savings from the general public and that invested those funds heavily in business needed tellers and clerks; railroads, insurance companies, and government-run telegraph and telephone companies all needed armies of white-collar employees.

Workers with mathematical skills and literacy acquired in the new public primary schools staffed this service sector, which provided clean work for educated, middle-class women. Whether to help pay the growing cost of raising and educating children or to support themselves, unmarried and a greater number of married women of the respectable middle class took jobs despite the dominant ideology of

■ **Crespin and Dufayel Department Store**

The department store marked the definitive transition of European society from one of subsistence and scarcity to one of relative abundance. Centralizing the sale of all varieties of goods, department stores displayed more consumer items than any single person could possibly use. This particular Parisian department store is relatively subdued in its displays, but others ran sales and so seductively arranged goods that Europe's uninitiated consumers were often tempted into irrational purchasing. (Jean-Loup Charmet.)

domesticity. Employers, as one put it, found in the new women workers a "quickness of eye and ear, and the delicacy of touch" essential to office work. By hiring women for newly created clerical jobs, business and government contributed to a dual labor market in which certain categories of jobs were predominantly male and others were overwhelmingly female. White-collar work gradually became ghettoized around cheap female labor. In the absence of competition, businesses in the service sector saved significantly by paying women chronically low wages—much less than they would have had to pay men for the same work.

Finally, the rise of consumer capitalism transformed the scale of consumption the way industrial capitalism had transformed the scale of production. The principal institution of this change was the department store. Founded after midcentury in the largest cities, department stores gathered such an impressive variety of goods in one place that consumers popularly called them "marble palaces" or "the eighth wonder of the world." Created by daring entrepreneurs, department stores eventually replaced the single-item stores that people entered knowing clearly what they wanted to purchase. Instead, these modern palaces sought to stimulate consumer whims and desires with lavish displays spilling over railings and counters in glorious disarray. Shoppers no longer bargained rationally over prices; now they reacted to sales, a new marketing technique that could incite a buying frenzy. Because most men lacked the time for shopping expeditions, department stores appealed mostly to women, who came out of their domestic sphere into a new public role. Attractive salesgirls, another variety of service workers, were hired to inspire customers to buy. Glossy mail-order catalogs brought to rural households both necessities and exotic items from the faraway dream world of the city.

Establishing Social Order

This age of nation building and economic expansion disturbed everyday life, often bringing chaos and sometimes dramatic public protest. Thus government officials developed mechanisms to forge internal social unity and order, hoping to offset the violence and economic change by which the nation-state was expanding. Confronted with growing populations and crowded cities, governments throughout Europe intervened to preserve social peace by attending to public health and safety. Many liberal theorists advocated a laissez-faire government that left social and economic life largely to private enterprise. Nevertheless, confident in the benefits of European institutions in general, bureaucrats and reformers paid more attention to citizens' lives and, with the help of missionaries and explorers, spread European influence to the farthest reaches of the globe.

Bringing Order to the Cities

European cities became the backdrop for displays of state power and national solidarity; thus efforts to improve sanitation and control disease redounded to the state's credit. Governments focused their refurbishing efforts on their capital cities, although many noncapital cities acquired handsome parks, widened streets, and erected stately museums and massive city halls. In 1857, Francis Joseph ordered the destruction of the old Viennese city walls and their replacement with concentric boulevards lined with major public buildings such as an opera house and government offices. Opera houses and government buildings were tangible displays of national wealth and power, and the broad boulevards allowed crowds to observe royal pageantry. These wide roads were also easier for troops to navigate than the twisted, narrow medieval streets that in 1848 had concealed insurrectionists in cities such as Vienna and Paris—an advantage that convinced some otherwise reluctant officials to approve the expense. Impressive parks and public gardens showed the state's control of nature while they helped order people's leisure time.

One effect of refurbished cities was to highlight class differences. Construction first required destruction; buildings and entire neighborhoods of housing for the poor disappeared, and thousands of city dwellers were dislocated. The boulevards often served as boundaries marking rich and poor sections of the city. In Paris, the process of urban change was called *Haussmannization,* named for the prefect Georges-Eugène Haussmann, who implemented a grand design that included eighty-five miles of new city streets, many lined with showy dwellings for the wealthy. Tens of thousands of poor people lost their homes when old buildings were torn down. Improved architectural taste including "Victorian" ornamentation, many believed, would blot out the ugliness of commerce and industry. Moreover, the size and spaciousness of the many new banks and insurance companies built in London "help[ed] the impression of stability," as an architect put it, and this would foster social order.

Amid signs of economic prosperity, the devastation caused by repeated epidemics of diseases such as cholera debilitated city dwellers and gave the strong impression of social decay. Poor sanitation allowed typhoid bacteria to spread through sewage and into water supplies, infecting rich and poor alike. In 1861, Britain's Prince Albert reputedly died of typhus, commonly known as a "filth disease." Unregulated urban slaughterhouses and tanneries; heaps of animal excrement in chicken coops, pigsties, and stables; human waste alongside buildings; open cesspools; and garbage everywhere facilitated the spread of disease. The stench, diseases, and "morbid air" of cities indicated such a degree of failure, disorder, and danger that sanitation became a government priority.

Scientific research, increasingly undertaken in public universities and hospitals, provided the means to promote public health and control disease. France's Louis Pasteur, whose three young daughters had died of typhus, advanced the germ theory of disease. Seeking a method to prevent wine from spoiling, Pasteur began his work in the mid-1850s by studying fermentation. He found that the growth of living organisms caused fermentation, and he suggested that certain organisms—bacteria and parasites—might be responsible for human and animal diseases. Pasteur further demonstrated that heating foods such as wine and milk to a certain temperature, a process soon known as *pasteurization,* killed these organisms and made food safe. In the mid-1860s, English surgeon Joseph Lister applied the germ theory in medicine. He connected Pasteur's theory of bacteria to infection and developed antiseptics for treating wounds and preventing puerperal fever, a condition that was caused by the dirty hands of physicians and midwives and that killed innumerable women after childbirth.

Governments undertook projects to improve sewer and other sanitary systems, and citizens prized such urban improvements, often attributing them to national superiority. In Paris, huge underground collectors provided a watertight terminus for accumulated sewage. In addition, Haussmann piped in water from uncontaminated sources in the countryside to provide each household with a secure supply. Such ventures were imitated throughout Europe: the Russian Empire's port city Riga (now in Latvia), for example, organized its first water company in 1863. Improved sanitation testified to progress and a more active role for the state. Shopkeepers agitated for paved streets to end the difficulties of transporting goods along

■ **Vienna Opera House**
The era of nation building saw the construction of architectural monuments in the center of capital cities to display cultural power and to bring music, art, and science to the people. Vienna's center was rebuilt around imposing façades like that of the Imperial Opera House, which opened in 1869. (Hulton Getty/Liaison Agency.)

muddy or flooded roadways. When public toilets for men became a feature of modern cities, women petitioned governments for similar facilities. On the lookout for disease and sanitary dangers, the average person became more aware of smells and the foul air that had been an accepted part of daily life for thousands of years. To show that they were becoming more "civilized," the middle and lower-middle classes bathed more regularly. Middle-class concerns for refinement and health mirrored the quest of governments for order.

Expanding the Reach of Bureaucracy

Central to enacting new programs to build social order and enhance the nation was an expansion of state bureaucracies. The nation-state required citizens to follow a growing catalog of regulations as government authority reached further into the realm of everyday life. The regular censuses that Britain, France, and the United States had begun early in the nineteenth century became routine in most other countries as well. Censuses provided the state with personal details of citizens' lives such as age, occupation, marital status, residential patterns, and fertility. Governments used these data for a variety of endeavors, ranging from setting quotas for military conscription to predicting needs for new prisons. Reformers like Florence Nightingale, who gathered medical and other statistics to support sanitary reform, believed that such quantitative information made government less susceptible to corruption, special deals, and inefficiency. In 1860, Sweden introduced taxation based on income, which opened an area of private life—one's earnings from work or investment—to government scrutiny.

To bring about their vision of social order, most governments, including those of Britain, Italy, Austria, and France, also expanded their regulation and investigation of prostitution. Venereal disease, especially syphilis, was a scourge that, like typhus, infected individuals and whole families. Officials blamed prostitutes, not their clients, for its spread. The police picked up suspect women and turned them over to public health doctors, who examined them for syphilis. If necessary, they were incarcerated for mandatory treatment. As states began monitoring prostitution and other social matters like public health and housing, they had to add departments and agencies. In 1867, Hungary's bureaucracy handled fewer than 250,000 individual cases, ranging from health to poverty issues; twenty years later it handled more than a million. Eager to acquire these jobs, the middle classes lobbied to eliminate the aristocrats' stranglehold on the top positions and to end the practice of dispensing civil service jobs as rewards for political loyalty. In Britain, a civil service law passed in 1870 required competitive examinations to ensure competency in government posts—an idea in the air since the West had become familiar with the Chinese examination system in the sixteenth and seventeenth centuries.

Schooling and Professionalizing Society

As governments imposed new standards of competency, they became more knowledge based and professional. Growing numbers of middle-class doctors, lawyers, managers, professors, and successful journalists found their positions enhanced by the prestige of science, information, and regulation. Governments began to allow professional people to influence policy and to determine rules specifying who would and would not be admitted to "the professions." Such legislation had both positive and negative effects: groups could set their own standards, but some otherwise qualified people were prohibited from working because they lacked the established credentials. The German medical profession, for example, was granted authority to control licensing, which led to more rigorous university training for future doctors but also pushed midwives out of medicine and caused the arrest of healers not trained in medical school. Science, too, became the province of the trained specialist rather than the amateur genius. Scientists were likely to be employed by universities and institutes, funded by the government, and provided with equipment and assistants. Like other members of the middle class, professors of science were intensely patriotic, often interpreting their work as part of an international struggle for prestige and excellence.

Bureaucrats and professionals called for radical changes in the scope, curriculum, and personnel of schools—from kindergarten to university—to make the general population more fit for citizenship and useful in fostering economic progress. Ongoing expansion of the electorate along with lower-class activism prompted one British aristocrat to exclaim, "We must now educate our masters!" The growth of commerce and the state was partly behind a craze for learning, which made traveling lecturers, public forums, reading groups, and debating societies popular among the middle and working classes. Governments also introduced compulsory schooling to reduce illiteracy (more than 65 percent in Italy and Spain in the 1870s and even higher in eastern than in western Europe; see "Taking Measure," below). Even a few hours of lessons each day were said to teach important social habits and the responsibilities of citizenship, along with practical knowledge.

Accomplishing this goal was not easy. Initially, various religious denominations had supervised schools and charged tuition, making primary education an option chosen only by prosperous or religious parents. After the 1850s, many leaders felt that liberal rationalism should supplant religiosity as a guiding principle. In 1861, an English commission on education concluded that, instead of the Bible, "the knowledge most important to a labouring man is that of the causes which regulate the amount of his wages, the hours of his work, the regularity of his employment, and the prices of what he consumes." Supplanting religion was one challenge and enforcing school attendance another. Although the Netherlands, Sweden, and Switzerland had functioning primary-school systems before midcentury, rural

■ **TAKING MEASURE Decline of Illiteracy, 1850–1900**

The development of mass politics and the consolidation of the nation-state depended on building a cohesive group of citizens concerned with the progress of the nation. Increasing literacy was thus a national undertaking but one with national variations ranging from the low levels of illiteracy in Prussia to the high levels in Austria-Hungary and Russia. Even in regions of high illiteracy, however, governments successfully got people reading.

(Theodore Hamerow, *The Birth of New Europe: State and Society in the Nineteenth Century* [Chapel Hill: University of North Carolina Press, 1983], 169.)

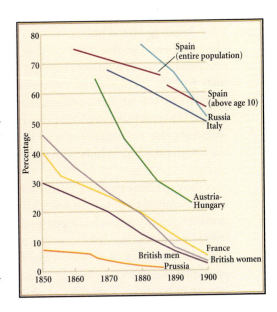

parents depended on their children to perform farm chores and believed that boys and girls would gain useful knowledge in the fields or the household. Urban home-makers needed their children to help with domestic tasks such as fetching water, disposing of waste, tending the younger children, and scavenging for household necessities such as stale bread from bakers or soup from local missions. Secondary and university education was even more of a luxury, and Russia and some other countries saw modern subjects such as science and technology as potentially subversive.

Nonetheless, primary-school systems grew, women's education developed, and the secondary school became more systematized, reflecting the demands of both an industrial society and a bureaucratic state. In Prussia, secondary schools (*Gymnasia*) offered a liberal arts curriculum that trained students for a variety of careers. In the 1860s, however, new *Realschulen*, less prestigious at the time, em-phasized math, science, and modern languages for those who would not attain a Gymnasium degree or go on to attend the university. Reformers pushed for more advanced and more complex courses for young women. In France and Russia, for example, government leaders themselves saw that "public education has had in view only half the population—the male sex," as the Russian minister of education wrote to Tsar Alexander II in 1856. Both Napoleon III and Alexander II sponsored secondary- and university-level courses for women as part of their programs to control the modernization of society. Reformers from across the political spec-trum concurred that women who knew some science, history, and literature would rear their children better and prove more interesting wives. Even so, higher educa-tion for women remained a hotly contested issue because religion, sewing, deport-ment, and writing appeared more than adequate.

Education, however, opened professional doors to young women, who in the 1860s began to attend universities in Zurich and Paris, where medical training was open to them. Despite criticism that they would undermine the system of sepa-rate spheres, women doctors thought their practice of medicine would protect fe-male patients' modesty and bring feminine values to health care. In Britain, the founders of two women's colleges, Girton (1869) and Newnham (1871) at Cam-bridge University, believed that exacting standards in women's higher education would provide an example of a modern curriculum, reward merit, and thus raise the low standards of scholarship prevalent in the men's colleges of Cambridge and Oxford.

The expanding need for instructed citizens offered opportunities for large num-bers of women to enter teaching, a field once dominated by men. Hundreds of women founded nurseries, kindergartens, and primary schools based on the En-lightenment idea that developmental processes start at an early age. In Italy, women founded schools as a way to expand knowledge and teach civics lessons, thus providing a service to the fledgling state. Yet the idea of women teaching also aroused intense opposition: "I shudder at philosophic women," wrote one critic of female kindergarten teachers. Seen as radical because it enticed middle-class women out of the home, the cause of early childhood education, or the "kindergarten movement," was as controversial as most other educational reforms.

Spreading Western Order beyond the West

In an age of nation building and industrial development, colonies took on new importance, adding a political dimension to the economic role that global trade already played in national prosperity. After midcentury, Great Britain, France, and Russia revised their colonial policies by instituting direct rule, expanding colonial bureaucracies, and in many cases providing a wider array of social and cultural services such as schools. For instance, in the 1850s and 1860s provincial governors and local officials promoted the extension of Russian borders to gain control over nomadic tribes in central and eastern Asia. As in areas like Poland and the Ukraine, they instituted educational and religious policies that they felt essential to social order.

    Great Britain, the era's mightiest colonial power, made a dramatic change of course toward direct political rule during these decades. Before the 1850s, British liberals desired commercial gain from colonies, but believing in laissez-faire, they kept political involvement in colonial affairs minimal. In India, for example, an East India trading company ruled on Britain's behalf, and many regional rulers awarded the company commercial advantages. Since the eighteenth century, the East India Company had expanded its dominion over various kingdoms on the Indian subcontinent whenever a regional throne fell vacant and had built railroads throughout the countryside. Gradually the British bureaucratic and economic presence expanded, allowing some Indian merchants to grow wealthy and send their children to British schools. Other local men enlisted in the British-run Indian army, despite resistance to British institutions.

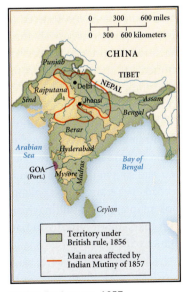

    In 1857, Indian troops, both Muslim and Hindu, violently rebelled against this expanded presence and its disregard for local beliefs. Ignoring the Hindu ban on beef and the Muslim prohibition on pork, the British had forced Indian soldiers to use cartridges greased with cow and pig fat. The infuriated soldiers stormed and conquered Delhi and declared the independence of the Indian nation—an uprising that became known as the Sepoy Mutiny. Simultaneously the Rani Lakshmibai, widow of the ruler of the state of Jhansi in central India, led a separate military revolt when the East India Company tried to take over her lands after her husband died. Brutally

Indian Resistance, 1857

put down by the British, the Sepoy Mutiny and the Jhansi revolt gave birth to Indian nationalism. They also persuaded the British government to issue the Government of India Act of 1858, by which Britain took direct control of India.♦ In 1876, the British Parliament declared Queen Victoria the empress of India.

A system of rule emerged in which close to half a million Indians governed a region the British called *India* under the supervision of a few thousand British men. Indians also collected taxes and distributed patronage. Colonial rule meant both blatant domination and more subtle intervention in everyday life. British policy forced the end to indigenous production of finished goods such as cotton textiles that would compete with Britain's own manufactures. Instead, the British wanted cheaper raw materials such as wheat, cotton, and jute to supply their industries. Enclaves of British civil servants enforced segregation and an inferior status on all classes of Indians. Simultaneously, however, ordinary Indians benefited in some places from improved sanitation and medicine. After the British attack on their practices, some upper-class Indians rejected Indian customs such as infanticide, child marriage, and *sati*—a widow's self-immolation on her husband's funeral pyre. British notions of a scientific society also proved attractive to some, and the unity that British rule brought to what were once small localities and princedoms with separate allegiances promoted nationalism.

French political expansion was similarly a matter of push, pull, and paradox. The French government pushed to establish its dominion over Cochin China (modern southern Vietnam) in the 1860s. But missionaries in the area, ambitious French naval officers stationed in Asia, and even some local peoples pulled the French government to make successive attacks in the region. Like the British, the French brought improvements, such as the Mekong Delta project that increased the amount of cultivated land and spurred rapid growth of the food supply. Sanitation and public health programs proved a mixed blessing because they led to population growth that strained other resources. Furthermore, landowners and French imperialists siphoned off most of the profits from economic improvement. The French also undertook a cultural mission to transform cities, such as Saigon, with tree-lined boulevards and other signs of Western urban life. French literature, theater, and art diverted not only colonial officials but also upper-class Indochinese.

Strategic commercial and military advantages remained an important motivation for some European overseas ventures in this age of Realpolitik. The Crimean War had shown the great powers that the Mediterranean basin was pivotal and thus needed to be tamed. Napoleon III, remembering his uncle's campaign in Egypt, took an interest in building the Suez Canal, which would connect the Mediterranean with the Red Sea and the Indian Ocean and thus dramatically shorten the route to

---

♦ For an autobiographical account of Indian life in the British colony, see Document 58, Krupa Sattianadan, "Saguna: A Story of Native Christian Life."

Asia. The canal was completed in 1869, and as canal fever spread, Verdi composed the opera *Aïda* (set in ancient Egypt) in celebration.

Great Britain and France were especially eager to do business with Egypt, where the combined value of imports and exports had jumped from 3.5 million Egyptian pounds in 1838 to 21 million in 1880 (and would grow to 60 million in 1913). European capital investment in the region also rose, first in ventures such as the Suez Canal in the 1860s and then in the laying of thousands of miles of railroad track and the creation of telegraph systems. Improvement-minded rulers in Asia and Africa paid dearly in 12 percent interest rates for modernization. The completion of harbors, dams, canals, and railroads increased the Middle East's desirability as a market for European exports and as an intermediate stop on the way to trade with Asia. Having invested in the Suez Canal and in other commercial development, the British and French soon took over the Egyptian treasury to secure their own financial investments, and after invading Egypt in 1882, the British effectively took over the government. Despite heated parliamentary opposition at home, Britain reshaped the Egyptian economy from a system based on multiple crops that maintained the country's self-sufficiency to one that emphasized the production of a few crops—mainly cotton, raw silk, wheat, and rice—that were especially useful to European manufacturing. Colonial powers, local landowners, and moneylenders profited from these agricultural changes, while the bulk of the rural population barely eked out an existence.

The rest of the Mediterranean and the Ottoman Empire felt the heightened presence of the European powers. Driving into the North African hinterland, the French army occupied all of Algeria by 1870, and the number of European immigrants reached one-quarter million by then. There was also a pull: French rule in Algeria as elsewhere was aided by the attraction of European goods, technology, and institutions to the local peoples. Merchants and local leaders cooperated in building railroads, sought bank loans and trade from the French, and sent their children to European-style schools. Many local peoples, however, resisted the invasions and died from European-spread diseases. By 1872, the native population in Algeria had declined by more than 20 percent from five years earlier. As a further guarantee of their Mediterranean claims, the French occupied neighboring Tunisia in 1881. Elsewhere, businessmen from Britain, France, and Germany flooded Asia Minor with cheap goods, driving artisans from their trades and into low-paid work building railroads or processing tobacco. Instead of basing wage rates on gender (as they did at home), Europeans used ethnicity and religion, paying Muslims less than Christians, and Arabs less than other ethnic groups. Such practices, as well as contact with European technology and nationalism, planted the seeds for anticolonial movements.

The vastness of China allowed it to escape complete takeover, but traders and Christian missionaries from European countries, carrying their message of Christian salvation, made inroads for the Western powers. Directing the Christian message to a population that had almost doubled during the preceding century and now numbered about 430 million, missionaries spread Christianity among people already disturbed by demographic growth, defeat in the Opium War, and economic pressures from European trade. These contacts with the West had helped generate the mass movement known as the Taiping (Heavenly Kingdom). Its millions wanted an end to the ruling Qing dynasty, the elimination of foreigners, more equal treatment of women, and land reform. By the mid-1850s, the Taiping controlled half of China. The Qing regime, its dynasty threatened, promised the British and French greater influence in exchange for aid. The result was a bloody civil war that lasted until 1864 with some 30 million to 60 million Chinese killed (compared with 600,000 dead in the United States' Civil War). When peace finally came, Western governments controlled much of the Chinese customs service and had almost unlimited access to the country.

Japan alone was able to escape European domination. Through Dutch traders at Nagasaki, the Japanese had become keenly aware of industrial, military, and commercial innovations of European society. By 1854, when Americans claimed to be opening Japan to trade, contacts with Europe had already given the Japanese a healthy appetite for Western goods and knowledge and an interest in superior Western weaponry. Trade agreements with the United States and European nations followed. In 1867, the ruling Tokugawa shogun (the dominant military leader) abdicated under pressure from reformers, who subsequently restored the emperor to full power. The goal of the Meiji Restoration (1868) was to establish Japan as a modern, technologically powerful state free from Western control. The word *Meiji*, chosen by the new emperor to name his reign, meant "enlightened rule," and the regime professed to combine "Western science and Eastern values" as a way of "making new"—hence, a combination of *restoration* and innovation.

The Culture of Social Order

The complex reactions of artists and writers to the rising nation-state and its expanding reach ushered in an age of realism in the arts in the 1850s to 1870s. After 1848, many artists and writers expressed profound grievances, notably about political repression, economic growth, and the effect of enfranchising working-class men. To many artists, daily life, infused with commercial values and organized by government officials, seemed tawdry and hardly bearable. Unlike the romantics of the first half of the century, artists of the second half often had difficulty depicting heroic ideals. "How tired I am of the ignoble workman, the inept bourgeois, the stupid peasant, and the odious priest," wrote the French novelist Gustave Flaubert, frustrated by his inability to romanticize these figures as previous generations had done. Such disenchantment promoted the literary and artistic style called *realism*. In contrast, intellectuals proposed theories called *positivism* and *Darwinism*, which appraised social change and even political upheaval as part of human progress.

Realism, positivism, and Darwinism shared a claim to look at society with an objective eye and to depict social order starkly.

The Arts Confront Social Reality

The quest for national power enlisted culture in its cause. The reading public devoured biographies of political leaders, past and present, and credited heroes with creating the triumphant nation-state. As literacy spread, readers of all classes responded to the mid-nineteenth-century novel and to an increasing number of artistic, scientific, and natural history exhibitions. Whether reading the same novels or attending musical events together, citizens were schooled in a common artistic style called *realism*.

A well-financed press and commercially minded publishers produced an age of best-sellers out of the craving for realism. The novels of Charles Dickens appeared in serial form in magazines and periodicals, and each installment attracted eager buyers for the latest plot twist. His characters came from contemporary English society and included starving orphans, grasping lawyers, heartless bankers, and ruthless opportunists. *Bleak House* (1852) used dark humor to portray the judicial bureaucracy's intrusion into private life; *Hard Times* (1854) depicted the grinding poverty and ill health of workers. The novelist George Eliot (the pseudonym of Mary Ann Evans) examined contemporary moral values and deeply probed private, "real-life" dilemmas in works such as *The Mill on the Floss* (1860) and *Middlemarch* (1871–1872). Depicting rural society—high and low—Eliot allowed Britons to see one another's predicaments, wherever they lived. She knew the pain of ordinary life from her own experience: she was a social outcast because she lived with a married man. Despite her fame, she was not received in polite society. These popular novels showed a hard reality and thus helped form a shared culture among people in distant parts of a nation much as state institutions did.

French writers also scorned dreams of political utopias and ideals of transcendent beauty. In *Madame Bovary* (1857), Gustave Flaubert told the story of a bored doctor's wife who, full of romantic longings and eager for distraction, has one love affair after another and becomes so hopelessly indebted that she commits suicide. Serialized in a Paris journal, *Madame Bovary* scandalized French society for its frank picture of women's sexuality. The poet Charles-Pierre Baudelaire, called "Satanic" by his critics, wrote explicitly about sex; in *Les Fleurs du mal* ("Flowers of Evil," 1857), he expressed sexual passion, described drug- and wine-induced fantasies, and spun out visions condemned as perverse. French authorities fought this violation of social convention, successfully prosecuting Flaubert and Baudelaire on obscenity charges. The issue was social and artistic order: "Art without rules is no longer art," the prosecutor maintained.

During the era of the Great Reforms, Russian writers debated whether western European values were insidiously transforming Russian culture. Rather than dividing the nation, this discussion about Russian culture united people around a national issue. From one viewpoint, Ivan Turgenev created a powerful novel of Russian life, *Fathers and Sons* (1862), a story of nihilistic children rejecting the older, romantic generation's spiritual values and espousing science instead. Popular in the West, Turgenev aroused anger in Russian readers for the way he criticized both romantics and the new generation of hardheaded "materialists." From another point of view, Fyodor Dostoevsky in *The Possessed* (1871–1872) and other works showed the dark, ridiculous, and neurotic side of nihilists, thus holding up Turgenev as a soft-headed romantic. Dostoevsky's highly intelligent characters in *Notes from the Underground* (1864) and *Crime and Punishment* (1866) are often personally tormented and condemned to lead absurd, even criminal lives. He used these antiheroes to emphasize spirituality and traditional Russian values, but with a "realistic" spin by planting such values in ordinary people.

Unlike writers, visual artists across Europe depended on government commissions and government-sponsored exhibitions and drew a more limited set of buyers. Prince Albert of England was an active patron of the arts, purchasing works for official collections and for himself until his death in 1861. Having artwork chosen for display at government-sponsored exhibitions (called *salons* in Paris, the center of the art world) was the best way for an artist to gain prominence and earn a living. Officially appointed juries selected works of art to be exhibited and then chose prizewinners from among them. Hundreds of thousands of people from all classes attended these exhibitions.

After 1848, artists began rejecting romantic conventions idealizing ordinary folk and grand historic events. Instead, Gustave Courbet, for example, portrayed weary laborers at backbreaking work because he believed an artist should "never permit sentiment to overthrow logic." The city, artists found, had become a visual spectacle, a place of great destruction but also of wide new boulevards where urban residents performed as part of the cityscape. Artists' canvases showed the renovated city as a stage for individual ambition and display. *Universal Exhibition* (1867) by Édouard Manet used the World's Fair of 1867 as the background; figures from all social classes in the foreground were separated from one another by the planned urban spaces as they promenaded, gazing at the Paris scene and watching one another to learn the new social rules of modern life. Manet also broke with romantic conventions of the nude. His *Olympia* (1865) depicted a white courtesan lying on her bed, attended by a black woman. This disregard for the classical traditions of showing women in mythical or idealized settings was too much for the critics: "A sort of female gorilla," one wrote of *Olympia*. "Her greenish, bloodshot eyes appear to be provoking the public," wrote another. Shocking at first, graphic portrayals that shattered comforting illusions became a feature of modern art.

Artistic realism faced a challenge from photography—a challenge that found its response in the 1860s to 1890s in a new style called *impressionism*. Manet coined the term to reflect the artist's attempt to capture a single moment by focusing on

■ **Gustave Courbet,**
Wrestlers (1850)
Courbet painted his dirty, grunting
wrestlers in the realist style, which
rejected the hazy romanticism of
revolutionary Europe. These mus-
cular men summed up the resort
to physical struggle during these
state-building decades and con-
veyed the art world's recognition
that Realpolitik had taken over
the governance of society.
(Museum of Fine Arts, Budapest/The
Bridgeman Art Library, NY.)

the ever-changing light and color found in everyday vision. Using splotches and dots, impressionists moved away from the precise realism of earlier painters: Claude Monet, for example, was fascinated by the way light transformed an object, and he often portrayed the same place—a bridge or a railroad station—at different times of day. Dutch-born Vincent Van Gogh used vibrant colors in great swirls to capture sunflowers, corn stacks, and the starry evening sky. Such distortions of reality made the impressionists' visual style seem outrageous to those accustomed to realism, but others enthusiastically greeted impressionism's luminous quality as more real than realism. Industry contributed to the new style, as factories produced a range of pigments that allowed artists to use a wider, more intense spectrum of colors.

In both composition and style, impressionists borrowed heavily from Asian art and architecture, knowledge of which rapidly infiltrated Europe as the West extended its reach. The concept of the fleetingness of situations came from a centuries-old and well-developed Japanese concept—*mono no aware* (serenity before and sensitivity to the fleetingness of life). The color, line, and delicacy of Japanese art (which many impressionists collected) is evident, for example, in Monet's later paintings of water lilies, his studies of wisteria, and even his re-creation of a Japanese garden at his home in France as the subject for artistic study. Similarly, the American expatriate Mary Cassatt used the two-dimensionality of Japanese art in her *In the Loge* (1879) and other paintings. Other artists, such as Edgar Degas, imitated Asian art's use of wandering and conflicting lines to orchestrate space on a canvas, and Van Gogh filled the background of portraits with copies of intensely colored Japanese prints.

As art departed from photographic realism, it nonetheless kept commenting on the changing economic scene, especially the fact that a growing segment of service workers did less physical work and had more energy for leisure. The works of French painter Georges Seurat, for example, depicted the newly created parks with their walking paths and Sunday bicyclists; white-collar workers carrying books or newspapers paraded in their store-bought clothing. Degas focused on portraying women—from ballet dancers to laundry women—in various states of exertion and fatigue. Van Gogh, avoiding the intense colors he typically used for the countryside, depicted the bleak outskirts of cities, where industries were often located and where the desperately poor lived.

Unlike most of the visual arts, opera was commercially profitable, accessible to most classes of society, and thus effective artistically for reaching the nineteenth-century public. Verdi used musical theater to contrast noble ideals with the corrosive effects of power, love of country with the inevitable call for sacrifice and death, and the lure of passion with the need for social order. The German composer Richard Wagner, the most flamboyant and musically innovative composer of this era, hoped to revolutionize opera by fusing music and drama to arouse the audience's fear, awe, and engagement. A gigantic cycle of four operas, *The Ring of the Nibelungen* (1854–1874), reshaped ancient German myths into a modern, nightmarish allegory of a world doomed by its obsessive pursuit of money and power and redeemable only through unselfish love. Another of his operas, *The Master Singer of Nürnberg* (1867), was a nationalistic tribute to German culture, and like the arts elsewhere, helped unite isolated individuals into a public with a shared, if debated, cultural experience.

Religion and Secular Order

Organized religion formed one bulwark of traditional social and political order after the revolutions of 1848, but the expansion of state power set the stage for clashes over influence. Should religion have the same hold on government and public life as in the past, thus competing with the national loyalty? The views were mixed and would remain so. In the 1850s, many politicians supported religious institutions and attended public church rituals because they were another source of order. Simultaneously, some nation builders, intellectuals, and economic liberals rejected the competing worldviews and competition for jurisdiction of established churches, particularly Roman Catholicism. Bismarck was one of these. Believing that the church impeded the growth of nationalist sentiment, in 1872 he mounted a full-blown *Kulturkampf* (culture war) against Catholic influence. The government expelled the Jesuits in 1872, increased state power over the clergy in Prussia in 1873, and introduced obligatory civil marriage in 1875. Bismarck, however, overestimated his ability to manipulate politics, for both conservatives and Catholics objected to religious repression in the name of state building.

The Catholic church felt assaulted on two fronts: by the growth of rationalism, which supplanted religious faith for many people, and by state building in Italy and Germany, which competed for people's traditional loyalty. In addition, nation building had resulted in the extension of liberal rights to Jews, whom many Christians considered enemies. Provocatively attacking reform and changing values, Pope Pius IX (r. 1846–1878) issued *The Syllabus of Errors* (1864), which put the church and the pope at odds "with progress, with liberalism, and with modern civilization." In 1870, the First Vatican Council approved the dogma of papal infallibility. This teaching proclaimed that the pope spoke divinely revealed truth on issues of morality and faith. Eight years later, a new pontiff, Leo XIII (r. 1878–1903), began the process of reconciliation with modern politics by encouraging up-to-date scholarship in Catholic institutes and universities and by accepting aspects of democracy. Leo's ideas marked a dramatic turn, ending the Kulturkampf and fortifying beleaguered Catholics across Europe.

Religious doctrine continued to have powerful popular appeal, but the place of organized religion in society was changing. Church attendance declined among workers and artisans, but many people in the upper and middle classes and most of the peasantry remained faithful. The Orthodox church of Russia and eastern Europe with its Pan-Slavic appeal fostered nationalism among oppressed Serbs and became a rallying point. Women's spirituality intensified, and Roman Catholic and Russian Orthodox religious orders of women increased in size and number. Men, by contrast, were falling away from religious devotion. In 1858, an outburst of popular religious fervor, especially among women, followed a young peasant girl's visions of the Virgin Mary at Lourdes in southern France. Bernadette Soubirous said that Mary told her to drink from the ground, at which point a spring appeared. Crowds besieged the area to be cured of ailments by the waters of Lourdes. In 1867, less than ten years later, a railroad track was laid to Lourdes to enable millions of pilgrims to visit the shrine on church-organized trips. The Catholic church thus showed that it was not passé and was willing to use modern means, such as railroads, medical verification of miraculous cures, and journalism, to make Lourdes itself the center of a brisk commercial as well as religious culture.

Almost contemporaneously with Bernadette's vision, the English naturalist Charles Darwin published *On the Origin of Species* (1859), a challenge to the Judeo-Christian worldview that humanity was a unique creation of God. Darwin argued that life had taken shape over countless millions of years before humans existed and that human life was the result of this slow development, or evolution. As a young scientist on an expedition to South America, Darwin theorized that because of evolution, species of animals varied from one tropical island to another even though climate and other natural conditions were roughly the same: new biological forms arise from older ones as the most fit forms survive and reproduce. Instead of the Enlightenment vision of nature and society as harmonious, Darwin saw the constant turmoil of all species, including humans, struggling to survive. In this fight, only the hardiest prevail and in the selection of sexual partners pass their natural strength to the next generation. In a perpetual challenge to meet the forces of nature, Darwin suggested, some species die out and those with better-adapted characteristics survive in a new environment.

Darwin's theories angered adherents of traditional Christianity because the idea of evolution undercut the story of creation described in Genesis. According to the biblical account, God miraculously brought the universe and all life into being in six days. According to Darwin, life developed from lower forms through a primal battle for survival and through the sexual selection of mates—processes that Darwin called *natural selection.* An eminently respectable Victorian gentleman, Darwin announced that the Bible gave a "manifestly false history of the world."

Darwin's theories also undermined certain liberal, secular beliefs. Enlightenment principles, for example, glorified nature as tranquil and noble and viewed human nature as essentially rational. The theory of natural selection—survival of the fittest—suggested a different kind of human society, one based in a hostile environment where combative individuals and groups constantly fight one another.♦

Darwin's findings and other innovative biological research influenced contemporary beliefs about society. In the 1860s, working in obscurity on pea plants in his monastery garden, Gregor Mendel discovered the principles of heredity from which the science of genetics later developed. Investigation into the female reproductive cycle led German scientists to discover the principle of spontaneous ovulation—the automatic release of the egg by the ovary whether sexual intercourse took place or not. This discovery caused theorists to conclude that men had aggressive and strong sexual drives because reproduction depended on their sexual arousal. In contrast, the spontaneous and cyclical release of the egg independent of arousal indicated that women were passive and lacked sexual feeling.

Darwin added to the social commentary. The legal, political, and economic privilege of white European men in the nineteenth century, he maintained, naturally derived from their being more highly evolved than white women or people of color. Despite his belief in a common ancestor for people of all races, Darwin held that people of color, or "lower races," were far behind whites in intelligence and civilization. As for women, "the chief distinction in the intellectual powers of the two sexes," Darwin declared, "is shewn by man's attaining to a higher eminence in whatever he takes up." A school of Social Darwinism, derived from this Darwinist

---

♦ For an excerpt from Charles Darwin's *The Descent of Man,* see Document 59.

thought, arose to lobby for public policy based on a vulgarized version of evolution and natural selection.

From Natural Science to Social Science

Darwin's thought accelerated the search for alternatives to the religious understanding of social order as being divinely ordained. Simultaneously the theories of the French social philosopher Auguste Comte, whose ideas formed the basis of a "positive science" of society and politics, also inspired a host of reform organizations. *Positivism* claimed that careful study of facts would generate accurate, or "positive," laws of society. Comte's *System of Positive Politics, or Treatise on Sociology* (1851) proposed that social scientists construct knowledge of the political order as they would construct understanding of the natural world—by means of informed investigation. This idea inspired people to believe they could solve the problems spawned by economic and social change. Comte also promoted women's participation in reform because he deemed "womanly" compassion and love and scientific public policy to be equally fundamental to social harmony. Positivism led not only to women's increased social and political activism but to the growth of the social sciences.

■ **Darwin Ridiculed, c. 1860**

Charles Darwin's theories claimed that humans evolved from animal species and rejected the long-standing explanation of a divine human origin. His scientific ideas so diverged from people's beliefs that cartoonists lampooned both the respectable Darwin and his theory. Despite the controversy, evolution withstood the test of further scientific study.

(Hulton Getty/Liaison Agency.)

www.bedfordstmartins.com/huntconcise
See the ONLINE STUDY GUIDE for more help in analyzing this image.

For a time, the influential English philosopher John Stuart Mill became an enthusiast of Comte, whose theories led Mill to espouse widespread reform and mass education and to support the complete enfranchisement of women. Mill's political treatise *On Liberty* (1859) couched his aspiration for general social improvement in a concern that superior people not be brought down or confined by the will of the masses. Influenced by his wife, Harriet Taylor Mill, he notoriously advocated the extension of rights to women and introduced a woman suffrage bill into the House of Commons after her death. The bill's defeat prompted Mill to publish *The Subjection of Women* (1869), a work recapitulating his studies with his wife. Translated into many languages and influential in eastern Europe, Scandinavia, and the Western Hemisphere, *The Subjection of Women* presented the family as maintaining an older kind of politics devoid of modern concepts of rights and freedom. Mill also proposed that women's voluntary obedience and love in marriage made each woman deceptively appear "not a forced slave, but a willing one." Critiquing the century's basic beliefs about men's and women's roles, *The Subjection of Women* became a respected guide for a growing women's movement committed to expanding liberal rights.

The more progressive side of Mill's social thought was soon lost in the flood of Social Darwinist theories. Even before *Origin of Species*, Herbert Spencer's *Social Statics* (1851) advocated the study of society but also promoted laissez-faire and unadulterated competition, claiming that the "unfit" should be allowed to perish in the name of progress. Spencer's opposition to public education, social reform, and any other attempt to soften the harshness of the struggle for existence struck a receptive chord among the middle and upper classes and contributed to the surge of Social Darwinism in the next decades. The influence of Darwinism and Mill's liberalism, like that of the arts, religion, and science, would serve to shape the public, setting the subjects and terms of social and political thought. In an age of nation building, culture often enhanced the political call for realistic, hardheaded thinking about social order.

Contesting the Order of the Nation-State

By the end of the 1860s, the unchecked growth of the state and the ongoing process of economic change had led to palpable tensions in European society. New theories of work life and politics appeared—most notably those of economist and philosopher Karl Marx (1818–1883), who advocated socialism. Protests abounded over the terms of work and especially against the upheavals in everyday life caused by the expanding power of the state as it ripped apart cities for improvements and sent workers scurrying for new places to live. In France, anger at defeat in the Franco-Prussian War and at economic hardship made these tensions erupt into a bitter though brief civil war. In the spring of 1871, the people of Paris—blaming the centralized state for the French surrender to the Germans—declared Paris a *commune,* a community of equals without bureaucrats and pompous politicians. Marx's books analyzing the growth of capitalism and national politics—as well as analysis of the Paris Commune—provided workers with a popular and politically galvanizing account of events. From the 1870s on, these two phenomena—the writings of Karl Marx and the fury of working people—renewed fear among the middle classes that both nation-state and industrial society might be violently destroyed.

Changes in Worklife and the Rise of Marxism

Changes in technology and management practices eliminated outmoded jobs and often made the work of those who survived job cuts more difficult. Workers complained that new machinery sped up the pace of work to an unrealistic level. For example, new furnaces at a foundry in suburban Paris required workers to turn out 50 percent more metal per day than they had produced using the old furnaces. Stepped-up productivity demanded much more physical exertion to tend and repair machines, often at a faster pace, but workers did not receive additional pay for their extra efforts. Workers also grumbled about the proliferation of managers; many believed that foremen, engineers, and other supervisors interfered with their work. For women, supervision sometimes brought on-the-job harassment, as in the case of female workers in a German food-canning plant who kept their jobs only in return for granting sexual favors to the male manager.

As new machines replaced old, managers established formal skill levels, from the most knowledgeable machinist to the untrained carrier of supplies. On the one hand, the introduction of machinery "deskilled" some jobs—traditional craft ability was not a prerequisite for operating many new machines. Employers could increasingly use untrained workers, often women, and pay them less than they paid skilled workers. On the other hand, inventions always demanded new skills, especially for those who had to understand work processes or repair machinery. Employers began to use the concept of skill (based in the old craft traditions) to segment the labor force, but sometimes the designations were arbitrary. Already prevalent in such trades as garment making, the trend toward breaking down and separating work processes into discrete tasks continued. For example, builders employed excavators, scaffolders, and haulers to do the "dirty work," hiring fewer highly paid carpenters. Those filling unskilled jobs could not count on regular employment and spent much of their time searching out temporary jobs. On the other end of the scale, foremen were no longer the most skilled workers but instead were supervisors chosen, as one worker complained, for the "pushing powers . . . of driving fellow men."

Many in the urban labor force continued to do outwork at home. Every branch of industry—from metallurgy to toy manufacturing to food processing—employed women at home, and their work was essential to the family economy. They painted tin soldiers, wrapped chocolate, made cheese boxes, decorated porcelain, and polished metal. Factory owners liked to employ outworkers because low piece rates made them desperate for work under any conditions and they were willing to work extremely long days. A German seamstress at her new sewing machine reported that she "pedaled at a stretch from six o'clock in the morning until midnight. . . . At four o'clock I got up and did the housework and prepared meals." Owners could lay off women at home during slack times and rehire them whenever needed with little fear of organized protest. Although joblessness and destitution always threatened, some city workers prospered in comparison to those left behind in rural areas, despite the decline of traditional artisanal work.

By and large, the urban working class was better informed, more visible, and more connected to the progress of industry and the nation-state. After a period of repression in the 1850s, workers' organizations slowly reemerged as a political force in the West, many of them influenced either by the ideas of former printer Pierre-Joseph Proudhon (1809–1865) or by anarchist thought. In the 1840s, Proudhon had coined the explosive phrase "Property is theft," suggesting that ownership robbed propertyless people of their rightful share of the earth's benefits. He opposed the centralized state and proposed that society be organized instead around natural groupings of men (but not women, who should work in seclusion at home for their husbands' comfort) in artisans' workshops. These workshops and a central bank crediting each worker for his labor would replace government and would lead to a *mutualist* social organization. Anarchism maintained that the existence of the state was the root of social injustice. According to Russian nobleman and anarchist leader Mikhail Bakunin (1814–1876), the slightest infringement on freedom, especially by the central state and its laws, was unacceptable. The political theory of *anarchism* thus advocated the destruction of all state power.

As workers' movements revived, Marx constantly battled mutualism and anarchism. These doctrines, he insisted, were emotional and wrongheaded, lacking the sound, scientific basis of his own theory, subsequently called *Marxism*. Marx's analysis, expounded most notably in *Das Kapital* ("Capital"), adopted the liberal idea, dating back to John Locke in the seventeenth century, that human existence was defined by the requirement to work as a way of fulfilling basic needs such as food, clothing, and shelter. Published between 1867 and 1894, *Das Kapital* was based on mathematical calculations of production and profit that would justify Realpolitik for the working classes. Marx held that the fundamental organization of any society, including its politics and culture, derived from the relationships arising from work or production. This idea, known as *materialism,* meant that the foundation of a society rested on class relationships—such as those between serf and medieval lord, slave and master, or worker and capitalist. Marx called the class relationships that developed around work the *mode of production*—for instance, feudalism, slavery, or capitalism. Rejecting the liberal focus on individual rights, he emphasized the unequal class relations caused by feudal lords, slaveholders, and the capitalists or bourgeoisie—that is, those who took control of the "means of production" in the form of the capital, land, tools, or factories necessary to fulfill basic human needs. Workers' awareness of their oppression would produce class consciousness among those in the same predicament and ultimately lead them to revolt against their exploiters. Capitalism would be overthrown by these workers—the *proletariat*—and an era of socialism would ensue. Tough-minded theories that social conflict was necessary for progress were common to Marx and Darwin.

The Paris Commune versus the French State

The conditions of working-class life remained harsh, and a wave of strikes erupted in the late 1860s. In France alone, 40,000 workers participated in strikes in 1869, followed by more than 85,000 in 1870. The strikers included artisans and industrial workers who felt overworked and underpaid because of the continuing pace and expense of technological innovation. In the 1870s, three decades of economic boom and bust would open to aggravate the situation. More often than not, the strikes focused on economic issues. But at times, such as in the Paris Commune, protesters questioned the system as a whole.

The bloody and bitter struggle over the Paris Commune developed using mutualist and socialist political ideas that churned to the surface in Paris as the Franco-Prussian War ended. The Haussmannization of Paris, which had displaced workers from their homes in the heart of the city, embittered many Parisians against the state. As the Prussians pressed on to Paris in 1870, the besieged Parisians demanded new republican liberties, new systems of work, and a more balanced distribution of power between the central government and localities. By the winter of 1870–1871, the Parisian population was suffering from the harsh weather and a Prussian siege that deprived them of sufficient food to feed more than 2 million people. As Parisians demanded to elect their own local officials to handle the emergency, the temporary republican government replacing the fallen Napoleon III sent the army into Paris in mid-March. For Parisians, this decision revealed the utter despotism of the centralized government, and they declared themselves a self-governing commune on March 28, 1871. Other French municipalities would do the same in an attempt to form a decentralized state of independent, confederated units.

In the Paris Commune's two months of existence, its forty-member council, its National Guard, and its many other improvised offices found themselves at cross-purposes. Trying to maintain "communal" instead of "national" values, Parisians quickly developed a wide array of political clubs, local ceremonies, and self-managed, cooperative workshops. Women workers, for example, banded together to make National Guard uniforms on a cooperative rather than a profit-making basis. Beyond liberal political equality, the Commune proposed to liberate the worker and ensure "the absolute equality of women laborers." Thus a *commune* in contrast to a *republic* was meant to entail a social revolution. But Communards often disagreed on what specific route to take to change society: mutualism, anti-clericalism, feminism, international socialism, and anarchism were but a few of the proposed avenues to social justice.

In the meantime, the provisional government at Versailles struck back to reinstitute national order. It quickly stamped out similar uprisings in other French cities. On May 21, the army entered Paris. In a week of fighting, both Communards and the army set the city ablaze (the Communards did so to slow the progress of government troops). Both sides executed hostages, and in the wake of victory the army shot tens of thousands of citizens found on the streets. Just to be in the city meant treason: Parisian insurgents, one citizen commented, "deserved no better judge than a soldier's bullet." The Communards had fatally promoted a kind of antistate in an age of growing national power. Soon a different interpretation of the Commune emerged: it was the work of the *pétroleuse*, or "woman incendiary"—a case of women run mad, crowding the streets in frenzy and fury. Within a year, writers were blaming the burning of Paris on women—"shameless slatterns, half-naked women, who kindled courage and breathed life into arson." Revolutionary men often became heroes in the history books, but women in political situations were characterized as "sinister females, sweating, their clothing undone, [who] passed from man to man."

Defeat in the Franco-Prussian War, the Commune, and the civil war were all horrendous blows from which the French state struggled to recover. Key to restoring order in France after 1870 were instilling family virtues, fortifying religion, and claiming that the Commune had resulted from the collapsed boundaries between the male political sphere and the female domestic sphere. Karl Marx

■ Woman Incendiary

The Paris Commune galvanized women activists, many of whom hoped to reform social conditions. After the fall of the Commune, women Communards were denigrated as half-clothed degenerates as a way of underscoring the disorderliness of the Commune's resistance to the state.
(Jean-Loup Charmet.)

IMPORTANT DATES			
1850s–1860s	Positivism and Darwinism become popular in social and political thought	1868	The Meiji Restoration begins in Japan
1850s–1870s	Realism in the arts	1869–1871	Women's colleges founded at Cambridge University
1852	The Second Empire begins in France	1870	Bismarck manipulates the Ems telegram and sparks the Franco-Prussian War
1854–1856	Britain and France clash with Russia in the Crimean War	1871	Franco-Prussian War ends; German Empire proclaimed at Versailles; Parisians form Commune in March to oppose the central government; the French army crushes the Commune in May
1857	Sepoy Mutiny in India		
1860s–1890s	Impressionism flourishes in the arts; absorption of Asian influences		
1861	Victor Emmanuel declared king of a unified Italy; abolition of serfdom in Russia	1872	Bismarck begins the Kulturkampf against Catholic influence
1861–1865	Civil War in the United States	1873	Extended economic recession begins; the impact is global
1867	Second Reform Bill, increasing the ranks of male voters, passed by English Parliament; Austro-Hungarian monarchy established	1876	Queen Victoria declared empress of India

disagreed: he analyzed the Commune as a class struggle of workers attacking bourgeois interests, which were embodied in the centralized state. Executions and deportations by the thousands nearly shut down the French labor movement and kept fear of workers smoldering across Europe.

Conclusion

Throughout modern history, the development of nation-states and the economic prosperity on which they depended has been neither inevitable nor uniform nor peaceful. This was especially true in the nineteenth century, when ambitious politicians, resilient monarchs, and determined bureaucrats transformed very different countries into various kinds of states by a variety of methods and policies. Nation building was most dramatic in Germany and Italy, where states unified through military force and where people of many political tendencies ultimately agreed that national unity trumped most other causes. Compelled by military defeat to shake off centuries of tradition, the Austrian and Russian monarchs instituted reforms as

Ottoman Empire
Occupied by Austria-Hungary
Independent or autonomous
Autonomous Ottoman province

■ **MAPPING THE WEST** Europe and the Mediterranean, c. 1880

European nation-states consolidated their power by building unified state structures and by developing the means to foster social and cultural integration of the diverse peoples within their borders. They also were rapidly expanding outside their boundaries, extending the economic and political reach of the nation-state. North Africa and the Middle East—parts of the declining Ottoman Empire—had particular appeal for their resources and for their potential for further European settlement. They were one gateway to the rest of the world.

a way of keeping their systems viable. In eastern Europe, the middle class was far less powerful than in western Europe, and reform came from above to preserve autocratic power rather than from popular agitation to democratize it.

After decades of romantic fervor, hardheaded realism in politics and the industrial economy became a much-touted norm, often with unexpected consequences. Darwin and Marx breathed the air of realism, and their theories were disturbing to those who maintained an Enlightenment faith in social and political harmony. Realist novels and art jarred polite society; like the operas of Verdi, they also portrayed dilemmas of the times. The internal policies of the growing state apparatus that were meant to bring order often brought disorder. When the ordinary people of the Paris Commune rose up to protest the loss of French power and prestige but also to defy the trend toward economic modernity and state building, their actions raised difficult questions. How far should the power of the state extend in both domestic and international affairs? Would nationalism be a force for war or for peace? As these issues ripened, the next decades would see continued economic advance, growing competition for global power, and unprecedented changes that ultimately would lead to war.

Suggested References for further reading and online research appear on page SR-28 at the back of the book.

www.bedfordstmartins.com/huntconcise　　See the ONLINE STUDY GUIDE to assess your mastery of the material covered in this chapter.

Empire, Modernity, and the Road to War

c. 1880–1914

I N THE FIRST DECADE OF THE TWENTIETH CENTURY, a wealthy young Russian man traveled from one country to another to find relief from neurasthenia, a common malady in those days. Its symptoms included fatigue, lack of interest in life, depression, and sometimes physical sickness. In 1910, the young man encountered Sigmund Freud, a Viennese physician whose unconventional treatment—eventually called *psychoanalysis*—took the form of conversations about the patient's dreams, sexual experiences, and everyday life. Over the course of four years, Freud uncovered his patient's deeply rooted fear of castration disguised as a phobia for wolves—thus the name Wolf-Man by which the young man is known to us. Often building his theories from information about colonized peoples and cultures, Freud worked his cure, as the Wolf-Man himself put it, "by bringing repressed ideas into consciousness." Freud's theories laid the groundwork for an understanding of the human psyche that has endured, with modifications and some controversy, to our own time.

The Wolf-Man is evocative of the age. Born into a family that owned vast estates, he reflected the growing prosperity of Europeans, albeit on a grander scale

■ **Pablo Picasso, *Les Demoiselles d'Avignon* (1907)**

The work of Spanish artist Pablo Picasso has become emblematic of modernity. Drawing on images from around the colonized world, modernist painters drew special inspiration from the art of Africa by imitating the clean lines and elongated limbs of its wooden statuary. In Les Demoiselles d'Avignon *("The Young Ladies of Avignon"), Picasso also borrowed the facial structure of African masks for his depiction of a group of prostitutes. ("Avignon" does not refer to the French town but to Avignon Street in a notorious section of Barcelona.) In addition to such imperial borrowings, modernists broke with harmonious melodies in music and pleasing depictions of the natural world. To many in polite society, modernism was jolting and shocking, an unwelcome reflection of growing violence among nations, the oppression of empire, and escalating militarism.*

(Picasso, Pablo. *Les Demoiselles d'Avignon*. Paris [June–July 1907]. Oil on canvas, 8′ × 7′8″. The Museum of Modern Art, New York. Acquired through the Lillie P. Bliss Bequest. Photograph © The Museum of Modern Art, New York © 2001 Estate of Pablo Picasso/Artists Rights Society, NY.)

than most. Countless individuals seemed, like him, anguished and mentally disturbed. Suicide was not uncommon. The Wolf-Man's own sister and father died from intentional drug overdoses. Throughout European society people engaged in agonized questioning about family life, gender relationships, empire, religion, and the consequences of technology and progress. Conflict rattled Europe and the rest of the world as an array of powers, including Japan, fought their way into even more territories and took political control. Every sign of imperial wealth brought on an apparently irrational sense of Europe's decline. The British writer H. G. Wells saw in this era "humanity upon the wane . . . the sunset of mankind."

Governments expanded the male electorate during this period in the hope of making politics more harmonious and manageable. Ethnic chauvinism, anti-Semitism, and militant nationalism, however, increased the violence of political rhetoric. Women suffragists along with politically disadvantaged groups such as the Slavs and Irish demanded full rights, but the liberal ethos of tolerance was swept away by a wave of political assassinations and public brutality. As the race for worldwide empire continued—most notably in an intense contest among the European powers for control of Africa and its vast natural wealth—colonized peoples developed a variety of liberation movements, many of them matching the progressive values but also the violence of the colonizing powers. While the great powers fought to dominate people around the world, the competition for empire fueled an arms race that threatened to turn Europe, the "most civilized" continent in the world according to its leaders, into a savage battleground.

Those were just some of the conflicts associated with *modernity*—a term often used to describe the accelerated pace of life, the rise of mass politics, and the decline of a rural social order that were so visible in the West from the late nineteenth century on. *Modernity* also refers to the response of artists and intellectuals to this rapid change. The celebrated "modern" art, music, science, and philosophy of this period still resonate for their brilliant, innovative qualities. Yet these same innovations were often considered offensive at the time: cries of outrage at the new music echoed in concert halls, and educated people were shocked at Freud's ideas that sexual drives motivate even the smallest children. Every advance in science and the arts had consequences that undermined middle-class faith in artistic and scientific progress.

When the heir to the Austro-Hungarian throne was assassinated in June 1914, few gave any thought to the global significance of the event, least of all Wolf-Man, whose treatment with Freud was just ending and who viewed that fateful day of June 28 simply as the day he "could now leave Vienna a healthy man." Yet the assassination was the catalyst for an eruption of political and societal discord that had been simmering for several decades, as the nations of Europe lurched from one diplomatic crisis to another. The consequences of the resulting war—World War I—like the insights of Freud, would shape modern life.

The Challenge of Empire

The quest for empire remained intense and became increasingly paradoxical. In a climate of ongoing boom and bust, colonies provided crucial markets for some businesses. Late in the century, for example, French colonies bought 65 percent of France's exports of soap, and imperialism provided huge numbers of jobs to people in European port cities. Yet Europeans did not benefit uniformly from the search for new markets, which often proved more costly than profitable. Whether they benefited or not, taxpayers in all parts of a nation paid for colonial armies, increasingly costly weaponry, and colonial administrators. As politicians debated the economic value of colonies, imperialism intensified distrust in international politics though empire-building was meant to ensure great-power status. Countries vied with one another for a share of world influence. In securing India's borders, for example, the British faced Russian expansion in Afghanistan and along the borders of China. Bringing conflict around the world, imperial competition made areas of Europe, such as the Balkans, more volatile than ever as states sought status and national security in the control of disputed territory.

Motives for imperialism were equally paradoxical. Goals such as fostering national might, boosting national loyalty, and the centuries-old effort to Christianize peoples often proved unattainable or difficult to measure. Governments worried that imperialism—because of its expense and the constant possibility of war— might weaken rather than strengthen them. The French statesman Jules Ferry (1832–1893) argued that France "must keep its role as the soldier of civilization." But it was unclear whether imperialists should emphasize soldiering—that is, conquest and conflict—or the more encompassing goal of exporting culture and religion.◆ Hoping to Christianize colonized peoples, European missionaries ventured to newly secured areas of Africa and Asia. A woman missionary working among the Tibetans reflected a common view when she remarked that the native peoples were "going down, down into hell, and there is no one but me . . . to witness for Jesus amongst them." Europeans were confident of their religious and cultural superiority. In the judgment of many, Asians and Africans—variously characterized as lying, lazy, self-indulgent, or irrational—were a class beneath Europeans. One English official pontificated that "accuracy is abhorrent to the Oriental mind." Viewing other races as "degenerate" prompted missionaries and other "civilizers" to turn a blind eye toward the most brutal military measures against the growing local resistance to imperialism.

◆ For a source that reveals Europeans' passionate debate over imperialism, see Document 60, Jules Ferry, "Speech before the French National Assembly."

Scramble for Africa

After the British takeover of the Egyptian government in the 1880s, European influence turned into direct control as one sub-Saharan African territory after another fell to European military force (Map 19.1). The centuries-old slave trade had drastically diminished by this time, and Europeans' principal objective was expanding trade in Africa's raw materials, such as palm oil, cotton, diamonds, cocoa, and rubber. Additionally, with its industrial and naval supremacy and its empire in India, Britain hoped to keep the southern and eastern coasts of Africa secure for stopover ports on the route to Asia. The British, French, Belgians, Portuguese, Italians, and Germans jockeyed to dominate peoples, land, and resources—"the magnificent cake of Africa," as King Leopold II of Belgium (r. 1865–1909) put it. Driven by insatiable greed, Leopold claimed the Congo region of central Africa, thereby initiating competition with France for that territory and inflicting on local African peoples unparalleled acts of cruelty. German chancellor Otto von Bismarck, who saw colonies mostly as political bargaining chips, sent out explorers in 1884 and established German control over Cameroon and a section of East Africa. Faced with competition, the British poured millions of pounds into preserving their position by dominating the continent "from Cairo to Cape Town," as the slogan went, and the French cemented their hold on large portions of western Africa.

Technological development of powerful guns, railroads, steamships, and medicines were central to the expansion of Western domination. The gunboats that forced the Chinese to open their borders to opium played a part in forcing African ethnic groups to give up their independence. Quinine and guns were also an important factor in African conquest. Before the development of medicinal quinine in the 1840s and 1850s, the deadly tropical disease malaria had threatened to decimate any European party embarking on exploration or military conquest, giving Africa the nickname "White Man's Grave." The use of quinine, extracted from cinchona bark from the Andes, to treat malaria sent death rates among missionaries, adventurers, traders, and bureaucrats plummeting. While quinine saved white lives, technology to take lives was also advancing. Improvements to the breech-loading rifle and the development of the machine gun, or "repeater," between 1862 and the 1880s dramatically increased firepower. Europeans carried on a brisk trade selling inferior guns to Africans on the coast, but peoples of the interior used bows and

■ **MAP 19.1 Africa, c. 1890**

The scramble for Africa entailed a real reversal of European trading practices, which until approximately 1880 generally were limited to the coastline. The effort to conquer, economically penetrate, and rule the interior would result in a map of the continent (see Map 19.2) that made sense only to the imperial powers, for it divided ethnic groups and created colonial entities that had nothing to do with Africans' sense of geography, patterns of settlement, or political organization.

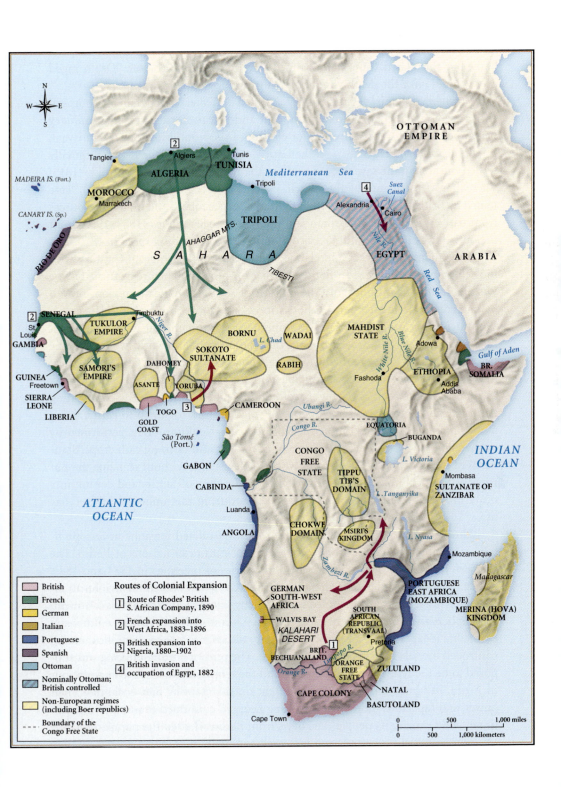

OTTOMAN EMPIRE

Tangier

MADEIRA IS. (Port.)

Algiers   Tunis

TUNISIA

ALGERIA

MOROCCO

Marrakech

CANARY IS. (Sp.)

Mediterranean Sea

Tripoli

Suez Canal

Alexandria   Cairo

RIO DE ORO

S   A   H   A   R   A

AHAGGAR MTS.

TRIPOLI

TIBESTI

EGYPT

ARABIA

Red Sea

SENEGAL

St. Louis

GAMBIA

Timbuktu

TUKULOR EMPIRE

Niger R.

BORNU

WADAI

L. Chad

MAHDIST STATE

White Nile R.

Blue Nile R.

Adowa

Gulf of Aden

GUINEA

Freetown

SIERRA LEONE

LIBERIA

SAMORI'S EMPIRE

DAHOMEY

ASANTE   **YORUBA**

SOKOTO SULTANATE

RABIH

Fashoda

ETHIOPIA

Addis Ababa

BR. SOMALIA

TOGO

GOLD COAST

São Tomé (Port.)

CAMEROON

Ubangi R.

Congo R.

EQUATORIA

BUGANDA

INDIAN OCEAN

GABON

CABINDA

Luanda

CONGO FREE STATE

TIPPU TIB'S DOMAIN

L. Victoria

L. Tanganyika

Mombasa

SULTANATE OF ZANZIBAR

ATLANTIC OCEAN

ANGOLA

CHOKWE DOMAIN

MSIRI'S KINGDOM

L. Nyasa

Mozambique

Zambezi R.

Madagascar

GERMAN SOUTH-WEST AFRICA

WALVIS BAY

KALAHARI DESERT

SOUTH AFRICAN REPUBLIC (TRANSVAAL)

Pretoria

PORTUGUESE EAST AFRICA (MOZAMBIQUE)

MERINA (HOVA) KINGDOM

BRIT. BECHUANALAND

Limpopo R.

ORANGE FREE STATE

Orange R.

ZULULAND

CAPE COLONY

NATAL

BASUTOLAND

Cape Town

Legend

- British
- French
- German
- Italian
- Portuguese
- Spanish
- Ottoman
- Nominally Ottoman; British controlled
- Non-European regimes (including Boer republics)
- --- Boundary of the Congo Free State

Routes of Colonial Expansion

1. Route of Rhodes' British S. African Company, 1890
2. French expansion into West Africa, 1883–1896
3. British expansion into Nigeria, 1880–1902
4. British invasion and occupation of Egypt, 1882

0   500   1,000 miles

0   500   1,000 kilometers

arrows. Muslim slave traders and European Christians alike crushed African resistance with blazing gunfire: "The whites did not seize their enemy as we do by the body, but thundered from afar," claimed one local African resister. "Death raged everywhere—like the death vomited forth from the tempest."

Nowhere did this destructive capacity have greater effect than in southern Africa, where farmers of European descent and prospectors, rather than military personnel, battled African peoples for control of the frontier regions of Transvaal, Natal, the Orange Free State, and the Cape Colony. Although the Dutch originally settled the area in the seventeenth century, the British had gained control by 1815. Thereafter, descendants of the Dutch, called *Boers* (Dutch for "farmers"), were joined by British immigrants in their fight to wrest farmland and mineral resources from natives. British businessman and politician Cecil Rhodes (1853–1902), sent to South Africa for his health just as diamonds were being discovered in 1870, cornered the diamond market and claimed a huge amount of African territory with the help of official charters from the British government, all before he turned forty. Pushing hundreds of miles into the interior of southern Africa (a region soon to be named Rhodesia after him), Rhodes moved into gold mining, too. His ambition for Britain and for himself was boundless: "I contend that we are the finest race in the world," he explained, "and that the more of the world we inhabit the better it is." Europeans credited China and India with a scientific and artistic heritage, but Africans were seen as valuable only for manual labor despite their many accomplishments such as dyeing, road building, and architecture. By confiscating Africans' land, Europeans forced native peoples to work for them to earn a living and to pay the taxes they imposed. Subsistence agriculture, often performed by women and slaves, thus declined in favor of mining and farming cash crops. Standards of living dropped for Africans who lost their lands without realizing the Europeans were claiming permanent ownership. Systems of family and community unity provided support networks for Africans during this upheaval in everyday life.

Almost immediately, the scramble for Africa escalated tensions in Europe itself, prompting Bismarck to call a conference of European nations at Berlin. The fourteen nations at the conference, held in a series of meetings in 1884 and 1885, decided that their settlements along the African coast guaranteed their rights to internal territory. This agreement led to the strictly linear dissection of the continent; geographers and diplomats cut across indigenous boundaries of African culture and ethnic life (Map 19.2). The Berlin conference also banned the sale of alcohol and controlled the sale of arms to native peoples. The purpose of the meeting was supposed to be the reduction of bloodshed and the tempering of European ambitions in Africa, but European leaders were intent on maintaining and expanding their power, and rapacious individuals like King Leopold continued to plunder the continent and terrorize its people. The news from Berlin whetted the popular appetite for more imperialist ventures and increased competition among a greater number of nations for colonies.

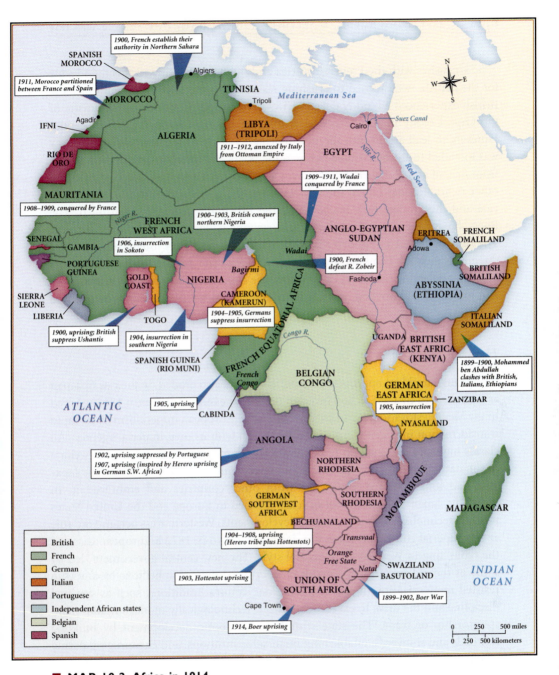

Map labels (clockwise and by region):

1900, French establish their authority in Northern Sahara

SPANISH MOROCCO

1911, Morocco partitioned between France and Spain

MOROCCO

IFNI

Agadir

RIO DE ORO

MAURITANIA

1908–1909, conquered by France

SENEGAL

GAMBIA

PORTUGUESE GUINEA

SIERRA LEONE

LIBERIA

1900, uprising; British suppress Ushantis

1906, insurrection in Sokoto

FRENCH WEST AFRICA

Niger R.

GOLD COAST

TOGO

NIGERIA

1900–1903, British conquer northern Nigeria

1904, insurrection in southern Nigeria

Algiers

TUNISIA

Tripoli

ALGERIA

LIBYA (TRIPOLI)

1911–1912, annexed by Italy from Ottoman Empire

Mediterranean Sea

Suez Canal

Cairo

EGYPT

Nile R.

Red Sea

1909–1911, Wadai conquered by France

Wadai

Bagirmi

CAMEROON (KAMERUN)

1904–1905, Germans suppress insurrection

SPANISH GUINEA (RIO MUNI)

FRENCH EQUATORIAL AFRICA

French Congo

Congo R.

1905, uprising

CABINDA

ATLANTIC OCEAN

ANGOLA

1902, uprising suppressed by Portuguese
1907, uprising (inspired by Herero uprising in German S.W. Africa)

ANGLO-EGYPTIAN SUDAN

1900, French defeat R. Zobeir

Fashoda

BELGIAN CONGO

NORTHERN RHODESIA

GERMAN SOUTHWEST AFRICA

1904–1908, uprising (Herero tribe plus Hottentots)

BECHUANALAND

SOUTHERN RHODESIA

Transvaal

Orange Free State

1903, Hottentot uprising

UNION OF SOUTH AFRICA

Cape Town

1914, Boer uprising

Natal

SWAZILAND

BASUTOLAND

1899–1902, Boer War

ERITREA

Adowa

FRENCH SOMALILAND

BRITISH SOMALILAND

ABYSSINIA (ETHIOPIA)

ITALIAN SOMALILAND

1899–1900, Mohammed ben Abdullah clashes with British, Italians, Ethiopians

UGANDA

BRITISH EAST AFRICA (KENYA)

GERMAN EAST AFRICA

1905, insurrection

ZANZIBAR

NYASALAND

MOZAMBIQUE

MADAGASCAR

INDIAN OCEAN

Legend:

- British
- French
- German
- Italian
- Portuguese
- Independent African states
- Belgian
- Spanish

0   250   500 miles
0   250   500 kilometers

■ MAP 19.2 Africa in 1914

Uprisings intensified in Africa in the early twentieth century as Europeans tried both to consolidate their rule through bureaucratization and military action and to extract more wealth from the Africans. While the Europeans were putting down rebellions against their rule, a pan-African movement arose, attempting to unite Africans as one people. As in Asia and the Middle East, the more the colonial powers tried to impose their will, the greater the political forces—including the force of political ideas—that took shape against them.

www.bedfordstmartins.com/huntconcise   See the ONLINE STUDY GUIDE for more help in analyzing this map.

Skirmishes with the French in Africa and the Boer War turned this mood sour for the British. Accustomed to crushing resistance to their imperial ambitions, the British experienced a bloody defeat in 1896, when Cecil Rhodes, prime minister of the Cape Colony in southern Africa, directed his right-hand man, Dr. Leander Jameson, to lead a raid into the neighboring territory of the Transvaal. The foray was intended to stir up trouble between the Boers and the more recent immigrants from Britain and elsewhere who had come to southern Africa in search of gold and other riches. Rhodes hoped the raid would justify a British takeover of the Transvaal and the Orange Free State, which the Boers independently controlled. The Boers, however, easily routed the raiders, striking a blow at British imperial pride. The British did not accept defeat: for the next three years they fought the Boer War directly against the Transvaal and the Orange Free State. Britain finally annexed the area after defeating the Boers in 1902, but the cost of war—in money, destruction, and loss of life—horrified many Britons and caused them to see imperialism as a burden.

Imperial Newcomers

Europeans' confident approach to imperialism was also eroded by the rise of Japan as a power. Led by the Satcho Hito clan, whose accession to power in 1868 ushered in the Meiji Restoration, Japan escaped the "new" European imperialism by its rapid transformation into a modern industrial nation with its own imperial agenda. "All classes high and low shall unite in vigorously promoting the economy and welfare of the nation," ran one of the first pronouncements of the new regime. The Japanese had long acquired knowledge from other countries and embraced it. In the 1870s, Japanese government officials traveled to Europe and the United States to study technological and industrial developments. Western dress became the rule at the imperial court, and when fire destroyed Tokyo in 1872 a European directed the rebuilding in Western architectural style. The new central government, led by some of the old *samurai*, or warrior elite, crushed massive rebellions by any who resisted modernization. It also merged older samurai traditions, such as spiritual discipline and the drive to excel, with a large, technologically modern military and sponsorship of trade. The state stimulated economic development by building railroads and shipyards, establishing financial institutions, and encouraging daring innovators like Iwasaki Yataro, founder of the Mitsubishi firm, to develop heavy industries such as mining and shipping. In Japan, unlike the rest of Asia, the adaptation of Western-style enterprises became a patriotic goal.

Like its Western models, Japan started intervening in nationalist and imperialist struggles elsewhere in Asia. This interference ultimately provoked war with its traditionally more powerful neighbors China and Russia. The Japanese had started building an empire by invading the Chinese island of Formosa (present-day Taiwan) in 1874 and in 1894 by sparking the brief Sino-Japanese War, which in 1895 ended

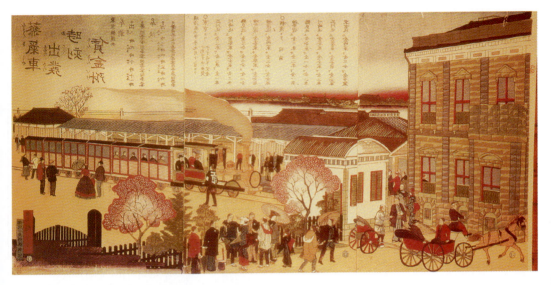

■ **Modernization in Japan**

Japan modernized with breathtaking speed. As this view of a railroad station indicates, Japan borrowed from the West but did not abandon its own culture. In this woodcut by Ando Hiroshige II—son of an artist imitated by many in the West—many of the Japanese wear Western-style clothes and others continue to wear traditional styles. Notice, too, the native cherry trees and the portrayal of traditional modes of transportation. The train schedule appears across the top.
(Laurie Platt Winfrey Inc.)

China's domination of Korea. Japan's growing imperial ambitions soon clashed with those of the great powers. Russian expansion to the east and south in Asia, the building of the Trans-Siberian Railroad through Manchuria, and sponsorship of anti-Japanese groups in Korea so angered the Japanese that they attacked tsarist forces at Port Arthur in 1904 (Map 19.3). The conservative Russian military proved inept in the ensuing year-long Russo-Japanese War: in an astonishing display of poor leadership, Russia's Baltic Fleet sailed halfway around the globe only to be completely destroyed in the battle of Tsushima Straits (1905). Opening an era of Japanese domination in East Asian politics, the victory was the first by a non-European nation over a European great power in the modern age. As one English general ominously observed of the Russian defeat: "I have today seen the most stupendous spectacle it is possible for the mortal brain to conceive—Asia advancing, Europe falling back." Japan went on to annex Korea in 1910 and to eye other areas in which to challenge the West.

There were other troublesome newcomers to the imperial table. Almost simultaneously, Spain lost Cuba, Puerto Rico, and the Philippines as a result of its defeat in the Spanish-American War of 1898. Urged on the United States by the expansionist-minded Theodore Roosevelt (1858–1919), then assistant secretary

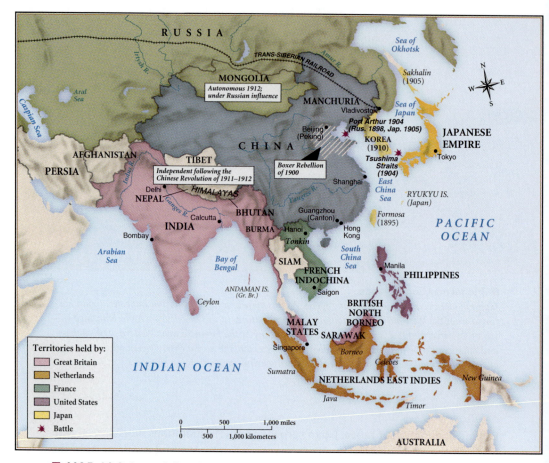

■ MAP 19.3 Imperialism in Asia, 1894–1914

Most of the modernizing states converged on Asia. The established imperialists came to blows in East Asia as they struggled for influence in China and encountered a formidable new rival— Japan. Simultaneously, liberation movements like that of the Boxers in China were taking shape, committed to throwing off restraints imposed by foreign powers. In 1911, Sun Yat-Sen overthrew the Qing dynasty and started the country along a different course.

of the navy, and the inflammatory daily press, this war revealed the fragility of established European empires and the unpredictability of imperial fortunes. Even the triumphant United States, encouraged by the British poet Rudyard Kipling (1865–1936) to "take up the white man's burden" by bringing the benefits of Western civilization to those liberated from Spain, had to wage a bloody war against the Filipinos, who wanted independence, not another imperial ruler. Reports of American brutality in the Philippines further disillusioned the European public, who liked to imagine native peoples joyously welcoming the bearers of civilization.

Emerging powers had an emotional stake in gaining colonies. In the early twentieth century, Italian public figures aimed to restore Italy to its ancient position of world domination by conquering Africa. After its disastrous war against Ethiopia in 1896, Italy won a costly victory over Turkey in Libya. But these wars roused Italian hopes for national grandeur only to dash them. Germany likewise demanded an end to the virtual British-French monopoly of colonial power. Foremost among the new competitors for empire, German bankers and businessmen were ensconced throughout Asia, the Middle East, and Latin America. Colonial skirmishes Germany had once ignored became matters of utmost concern. Germany, too, instead of winning unalloyed glory, met humiliation and constant problems, especially in its dealings with Britain and France. As Italy and Germany aggressively pursued new territory, the rules set for imperialism at the Berlin conference a generation earlier gave way to increasingly heated rivalry and nationalist fury.

Growing Resistance to Colonial Domination

The Japanese military victory over two important dynasties—the Qing in China and the Romanov in Russia—within a single decade had repercussions in the colonies. Uprisings began in China after its 1895 defeat by Japan forced the ruling Qing to grant more economic concessions to Western powers. Humiliated by these events, peasants organized into secret societies to restore Chinese integrity. One organization, based on beliefs in the spiritual values of boxing, was the Society of the Righteous and Harmonious Fists (or Boxers), whose members maintained that ritual boxing would protect them from a variety of evils, including bullets. Encouraged by the Qing ruler and desperate because of worsening economic conditions, the Boxers rebelled in 1900, massacring the missionaries and Chinese Christians to whom they attributed China's troubles.◆ The colonial powers put down the Boxer Rebellion and forced the Chinese to pay a huge indemnity, to destroy many of their defensive fortifications, and to allow more extensive foreign military occupation. The Boxer Rebellion thoroughly discredited the Qing dynasty; in 1911 a successful group of revolutionaries overthrew the dynasty and the next year declared China a republic. Their leader, Sun Yat-Sen (1866–1925), who had been educated in Hawaii and Japan, combined Western concepts with traditional Chinese values, including revival of the Chinese tradition of correctness in behavior between governors and the governed and modern economic reform. Sun's stirring leadership and the changes brought about by China's revolution seriously threatened Western channels of trade and domination.

In 1885, the Indian elite founded the Indian National Congress, which challenged Britain's right to rule, but the Japanese victory over Russia stimulated

◆ For a statement of beliefs distributed by the Boxers at the height of their rebellion, see Document 61, the I-ho-ch'uan (Boxers), "The Boxers Demand Death for All 'Foreign Devils.'"

Indian politicians to take a more radical course. An anti-British Hindu leader, B. G. Tilak (1856–1920), preached noncooperation: "We shall not give them assistance to collect revenue and keep peace. We shall not assist them in fighting beyond the frontiers or outside India with Indian blood and money." Tilak promoted Hindu customs, asserted Hindus' distinctiveness from British ways, and inspired violent rebellion in his followers. This brand of nationalism broke with that based on assimilating to British culture and promoting gradual change. Trying to repress Tilak, the British sponsored the Muslim League, a rival nationalist group favored for its restraint and its potential to divide Muslim nationalists from Hindus in the Congress. Facing political activism on many fronts, however, Britain made two concessions: voting rights based on property ownership and Indian representation in ruling councils. Because the independence movement had not fully reached the masses, these small concessions allowed the British to maintain power by appeasing influential dissidents among the upper and middle classes. But Britain's hold on India was weakening.

Revolutionary nationalism also was sapping the Ottoman Empire, which for centuries had controlled much of the Mediterranean. In the nineteenth century, several rebellions had plagued Ottoman rule, and more erupted early in the twentieth century because of growing resistance to the empire and to European

■ **Boxer Rebellion**

The Boxers sought to fortify the Chinese government against the many powers threatening its survival. They used brightly colored placards to spread information about their mission and its importance and to build support. The placards also depicted battles with imperialist forces and showed Boxer triumphs over foreign missionaries and other menacing groups.

(Photo courtesy Thames and Hudson, Ltd., London.)

influence. Sultan Abdul Hamid II (r. 1876–1909) tried to revitalize the multieth-nic empire by using Islam to counteract the rising nationalism of the Serbs, Bul-garians, and Macedonians. Instead, he unwittingly provoked the burgeoning of Turkish nationalism in Constantinople itself. Turkish nationalists rejected the sul-tan's pan-Islamic solution and built their movement on the uniqueness of their culture, history, and language, changing the word *Turk* from one of derision to one of pride and purging their language of words from Arabic and Persian. The events of 1904–1905 electrified these nationalists with the vision of a modern Turkey becoming "the Japan of the Middle East," as they called it. In 1908, a group called the Young Turks took control of the government in Constantinople. Their triumph motivated others in the Middle East and the Balkans to demand an end to Ottoman domination in their regions as well. But the Young Turks, often aided by European powers with financial and political interests in the region, brutally tried to repress the uprisings in Egypt, Syria, and the Balkans that their own suc-cess had encouraged.

Modern Life in an Age of Empire

Advancing empire not only made the world an interconnected marketplace but transformed everyday culture and society. Success in manufacturing and foreign ventures created millionaires, and consumers in the West could purchase goods that poured in from around the world. Many Europeans grew healthier, partly because of improved diet and partly because of the efforts of reformers who sponsored government programs aimed at promoting the fitness necessary for citizens of im-perial powers. Opportunities for mobility arose as Europeans opened up the globe. Working people's experience of the internationalizing force of imperialism was different from that of the middle class: increasingly from the mid-nineteenth century on, millions facing political or economic insecurity migrated to the United States, Canada, Australia, Argentina, Brazil, and Siberia and, as frequently, from country to city and back.

Growing European power was nonetheless accompanied by hazards to social norms and stability. Prosperity for global and industrial entrepreneurs contributed to social mixing, challenging the position of established groups such as the landed nobility. Even as Western ideals of a comfortable family life flourished because of Europe's improved standard of living, these norms were challenged: a falling birthrate, a rising divorce rate, and growing activism for marriage reform provoked intense debate by the turn of the century. Homosexuality became acknowledged as a way of life and the topic of politics. Middle-class women took jobs and became active in public to such an extent that some feared the disappearance of distinct gender roles. Discussions of gender roles and private life contributed to rising social tensions while they also fueled the optimism of reformers that Western society was making constant progress.

Life in the "Best Circles"

Profits from empire and industrial expansion swelled the ranks of the upper class, or "best circles," so called at the time because of their members' wealth, education, and social status. Many people in the best circles came from the aristocracy, which retained much of its power and was still widely emulated. Increasingly, however, aristocrats had to socialize with new millionaires from the bourgeoisie. In fact, the very distinction between aristocrat and bourgeois became blurred, as monarchs gratefully bestowed aristocratic titles on millionaire industrialists and business-people. Moreover, down-at-the-heels aristocrats were only too willing to offer their children in marriage to families from the newly rich. Such arrangements brought much-needed infusions of funds to old, established families and the cachet of an aristocratic title to upstart families. Thus Jeanette Jerome, daughter of a wealthy New York financier, married England's Lord Randolph Churchill (their son Winston later became England's prime minister). Even millionaires without official connections to the aristocracy discarded the modest ways of a century earlier to build palatial country homes and villas, engage in conspicuous displays of wealth, and wall themselves off from the poor in suburbs or new sections of town. To justify their success, the wealthy often appealed to Social Darwinist principles, which assured them that their accumulation of money demonstrated the natural superiority of the rich.

Upper-class men bonded around hunting, their favorite leisure activity, which was reshaped by imperial contact. For centuries, fox and bird hunting had been aristocratic pastimes in parts of Europe; now, big-game hunting in Asia and Africa became the rage. European hunters forced native Africans, who traditionally depended on hunting for income or food and for group unity, to work as guides, porters, and domestics on hunts. By mastering foreign games like polo (an Asian sport) or activities like big-game hunting, Europeans demonstrated that they could conquer not only territory but less tangible things like culture. Collectors on the hunts brought exotic specimens back to Europe for zoological exhibits, natural history museums, and traveling displays, all of which flourished during this period.

Members of the upper class did their best to exclude others by controlling their children's social lives, especially by monitoring girls' sexual activity and relationships with the lower classes. Upper-class men had liaisons with lower-class women—a double standard judged promiscuity normal for men and immoral for women—but few thought of marrying them. Parents still arranged many marriages directly, and visiting days brought eligible young people together to help ensure correct matrimonial decisions.

Ritualistic visits filled the everyday lives of upper-class women. Instead of working for pay, upper-class women devoted themselves to having children, directing staffs of servants, and maintaining standards of etiquette and social conduct. Furnishings in fashionable homes displayed imperial motifs in these decades:

■ **Lord and Lady Curzon on a Tiger Shoot**

Big-game hunting became the imperial sport of choice, and real adventurers came to see fox hunting and other traditional pastimes of the elites as effeminate if not decadent. European hunters took the sport over from local Africans and Asians who previously had depended on the hunt for their livelihood. Now these Africans and Asians served the European amateurs, many of whom were in wretched physical shape. Some women enjoyed hunting, too. As a gesture of chivalry, men would let a woman deliver the coup de grâce, *or death shot, if a tiger materialized during a hunt.*
(India Office Library/British Library.)

Persian-inspired designs in textiles, Oriental carpets, wicker furniture, and Chinese porcelains. With the importation of azaleas, rhododendrons, and other plants from around the world, private gardens replaced parks and lawns and became another responsibility. Being an active consumer of fashionable clothing was also a time-consuming female activity. In contrast to men's plain garments, upper-class women's clothing was elaborate, ornate, and dramatic, featuring constricting corsets, long voluminous skirts, bustles, and low-cut necklines for evening wear. Women took their roles seriously by keeping detailed accounts of their expenditures and monitoring their children's religious and intellectual development. In addition, they tried to offset the drabness of industrial life with the rigorous practice of art and music. One Hungarian observer wrote, "The piano mania has become almost an epidemic in Budapest as well as Vienna." Some upper-class women were also quite active outside the home, engaging in religious and philanthropic activities to aid lower-class women and children.

Although middle-class professionals could sometimes mingle with people at the apex of society, especially in charity work, their lives remained more modest. They employed at least one servant, which created the illusion of leisure for busy middle-class women performing the onerous duties of maintaining a home. Professional men working at home did so from the best-appointed room. Middle-class domesticity substituted cleanliness and polish for upper-class conspicuous consumption. The soap and tea used in middle-class homes were becoming signs— along with hard work—of a sense of racial superiority over the colonized peoples who actually produced those goods.

The "Best Circles" Transformed

Despite the well-being of the middle and upper classes, urgent concerns over population, marriage, and sexuality clogged the agendas of politicians and reformers from the 1880s on. (See "Taking Measure," below.) The staggering population increases of the eighteenth century had continued through the nineteenth. At the turn of the twentieth century, cities looked chaotic, as population soared and changed the urban landscape. Germany increased in size from 41 million people in 1871 to

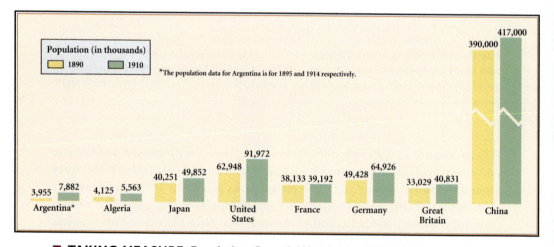

■ **TAKING MEASURE** Population Growth Worldwide, 1890–1910

Countries in the West were undergoing a demographic revolution in these decades as birthrates declined sharply. Nevertheless, population in many countries soared because of improved health, and nations such as Argentina and the United States received vast numbers of immigrants. Exceptions were China and other regions suffering the effects of imperialism, and France, where growth stagnated because the French had drastically curtailed reproduction early in the nineteenth century.

(B. R. Mitchell, *International Historical Statistics: Africa, Asia, and Oceania, 1750–1993*, 3d ed. [London: Macmillan Reference, 1998], 3, 56, 57; Mitchell, *International Historical Statistics: The Americas, 1750–1993*, 4th ed. [London: Macmillan Reference, 1998], 6, 24; Mitchell, *International Historical Statistics: Europe, 1750–1993*, 4th ed. [London: Macmillan Reference, 1998], 4, 8.)

64 million in 1910; tiny Denmark, from 1.7 million in 1870 to 2.7 million in 1911. Such growth resulted from improvements in sanitation and public health that extended longevity and reduced infant mortality. To cope with their burgeoning populations, Berlin, Budapest, and Moscow were torn apart and rebuilt, following the lead of Vienna and Paris. The German government pulled down eighteenth-century Berlin and reconstructed the city with new roadways and mass-transport systems that helped push the capital city's population to over 4 million. Rebuilding for population growth was not confined to the capitals of the most powerful states: Balkan cities such as Sofia, Belgrade, and Bucharest gained tree-lined boulevards, public buildings, and improved sanitation.

While the absolute size of the population was rising in much of the West, the birthrate (measured in births per thousand people) was falling because of urbanization and industrialization. The birthrate had been decreasing in France since the eighteenth century; other European countries began experiencing the decline late in the nineteenth century. The Swedish rate dropped from 35 births per thousand people in 1859 to 24 per thousand in 1911; even populous Germany went from 40 births per thousand in 1875 to 27 per thousand in 1913. In an age of agricultural industrialization, farm families needed fewer hands, and individual couples increasingly practiced birth control to limit family size. Abstinence was a common method, but the spread of new birth-control practices that would encompass most of the globe by the end of the twentieth century mainly accounted for modern Europe's ebbing birthrate. In cities, pamphlets and advice books for those with enough money and education spread information about coitus interruptus—the withdrawal method of preventing pregnancy. Technology also played a role in curtailing reproduction: condoms, improved after the vulcanization of rubber in the 1840s, proved fairly reliable in preventing conception. In the 1880s, Aletta Jacobs (1851–1929), a Dutch physician, opened the first birth-control clinic, which specialized in promoting the new, German-invented diaphragm. Abortions were also legion.

The wider use of birth control stirred controversy. Critics accused middle-class women, whose fertility was falling most rapidly, of holding a "birth strike." Anglican bishops, meeting early in the twentieth century, deplored family limitation, especially by artificial means, as "demoralizing to character and hostile to national welfare." Politicians worried about a crisis in masculinity that would undermine military strength. In the United States, Theodore Roosevelt, now president, blamed middle-class women's selfishness for the population decline, calling it "one of the most unpleasant and unwholesome features of modern life." The "quality" of those being born worried activists and politicians: if the "best" classes had fewer children, they asked, what would society look like when peopled mostly by the "worst" classes? The decline in fertility, one German nationalist warned, would make the country a "conglomerate of alien peoples, above all Slavs and probably East European Jews as well." The Social Darwinist focus on national peril in a menacing world merged the

■ **A Large German Family**

Improved medicine, hygiene, and diet at the turn of the century helped more people survive in-
fancy and childhood. Thus in many cases family size grew larger, as this photo from a working-
class apartment suggests. Even opponents of birth control were appalled that lower-class families
were becoming larger than families in the "best circles," where limitation of childbirth was increas-
ingly practiced. (AKG London.)

debate on gender and family issues with anxieties over class and race, inflaming the
political climate.

Reformers focused on improving both the conditions within marriage and the
quality of children born. The fear that one's nation or "race" was being polluted by
the presence of "aliens," the mentally ill, and the severely disabled gave rise to *eu-*
genics, a pseudoscience popular among wealthy, educated Europeans at the turn of
the century. As a famed Italian criminologist put it, such classes were not people
but "orangutans." Eugenicists favored increased fertility for "the fittest" and limitations on the fertility of "degenerates," leading even to their sterilization or elimination. Women of the better classes, reformers felt, would be more inclined to reproduce if the shackles in the traditional system of marriage were removed and wives
gained the legal right to their wages and to their own property. Sweden, which made
men's and women's control over property equal in marriage, allowed women to
work without their husbands' permission. Other countries, among them France
(1884), legalized divorce and made it less complicated, and thus less costly, to ob-

tain. Reformers had good reason to believe that these legal changes would result in an upswing of the birthrate. Given the existing constraints of motherhood—no financial resources to leave the home, no legal rights to their own children, little recourse in the event of an abusive or miserable marriage—women were reluctant to have more than two or three, if any, children. Divorce would allow unhappy couples to separate and undertake a new, more loving, and thus more fertile marriage. By the early twentieth century, several countries had passed legislation that provided government subsidies to needy mothers.

The conditions of marriage, motherhood, and other aspects of women's lives varied throughout Europe: women could get university degrees in Austrian universities long before they could at Oxford or Cambridge. A greater number of legal reforms occurred in western Europe, however. In much of rural eastern Europe, the father's power over the extended family remained almost dictatorial. According to a survey of family life in eastern Europe in the early 1900s, fathers married off their children so young that 25 percent of women in their early forties had been pregnant more than ten times. Yet reform of everyday customs occurred, as community control gave way to individual practice in places, even though the pace of such change was slower than it was in western Europe. For instance, in some Balkan villages, a kind of extended-family system called the *zadruga* survived from earlier times: all the nuclear families shared a common great house, but now individual couples developed a degree of privacy by building one-room sleeping dwellings surrounding the great house. Among the middle and upper classes of eastern Europe, many grown children were coming to believe they had a right to select a marriage partner, not just to accept the spouse their parents chose for them for economic or social reasons.

The spread of empire and rapid social change set the stage for even bolder behaviors among some middle-class women. Adventurous women traveled the globe to promote Christianity, make money, or obtain knowledge of other cultures. The increasing availability of white-collar jobs for the educated meant that more European women could afford to adopt an independent way of life. So-called new women dressed more practically, wearing fewer petticoats and looser corsets, biked and hiked through city streets and down country lanes, lived apart from the family in women's clubs or apartments, and supported themselves. Italian educator Maria Montessori, for example, went to medical school and secretly gave birth to an illegitimate child. Artists such as the German painter Gabriele Münter lived openly with their lovers. The growing number of women living on their own and freely moving in public challenged accepted views of women's economic dependence and relative seclusion in the traditional middle-class family. The "new woman," German philosopher Friedrich Nietzsche wrote, had led to the "uglification of Europe."

Not just gendered behavior but sexual identity fueled discussion. Among books in the new field of "sexology," which studied sex scientifically from a clinical and medical point of view, *Sexual Inversion* (1894) by Havelock Ellis was

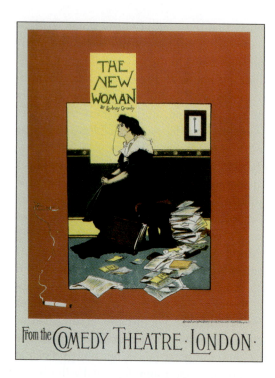

■ **Sydney Grundy, *The New Woman* (1900)**
By the opening of the twentieth century, the "new woman" had become a much-discussed phenomenon. Artists painted portraits of this independent creature, while playwrights such as Henrik Ibsen and novelists such as Nobel Prize winner Sigrid Undset depicted her ambition to throw off the wifely role—or at least to shape that role more to her own personality. The new woman was also well educated: she had been to university, or wrote as a journalist, or entered professions such as law and medicine.
(Jean-Loup Charmet.)

popular. Ellis, a British medical doctor, postulated a new personality type—the homosexual—identifiable by such traits as effeminate behavior and a penchant for the arts in males and physical passion for members of their own sex in both males and females. Homosexuals joined the discussion, calling for recognition that they composed a legitimate and natural "third sex" and were not just people behaving sinfully. The press provoked debate on the other side: in the spring of 1895, reporters covered the trial of Irish playwright Oscar Wilde, who was sentenced to two years in prison for indecency—a charge that referred to his sexual affairs with young men. After Wilde's conviction, one newspaper rejoiced, "Open the windows! Let in the fresh air!" Between 1907 and 1909, German newspapers also publicized the courts-martial of men in Kaiser William II's closest circle who were condemned for homosexuality and transvestitism. Amid growing concern over population and family values, the public received assurances from the government itself that William's own family life "provides the entire country with a fine model." Sexuality thus took on patriotic overtones: the accused homosexual elite in Germany were said by journalists to be out to "emasculate our courageous master race." Although these cases paved the way for growing sexual openness in the next generations, sexual issues would simultaneously become regular weapons in politics.

Working People's Strategies

For centuries, working people had migrated from countryside to city and from country to country to make a living. By the end of the nineteenth century, empire and economic change were spurring millions more to migrate. Older port cities of Europe, such as Riga, Marseille, and Hamburg, offered jobs in industry and global trade; new colonies provided land, posts for soldiers and administrators, and the possibility of unheard-of wealth in diamonds, gold, and other natural resources.

Some Europeans moved far beyond their national borders. In parts of Europe, the land simply could not produce enough to support a rapidly expanding population: Sicilians by the hundreds of thousands left the eroded soil of their island to find work in the industrial cities of northern Europe or the United States. The British Isles, especially Ireland, yielded one-third of all European emigrants between 1840 and 1920, first because of the potato famine and then because of uncertain farm tenancy and periodic economic crisis. Between 1886 and 1900, half a million Swedes out of a population of 4.75 million quit their country (Figure 19.1). Millions of rural Jews, especially in eastern Europe, left their villages for economic reasons. Russian Jews fled in the face of vicious anti-Semitism. Russian mobs attacked Jewish communities, destroying homes and businesses and even murdering some Jews.

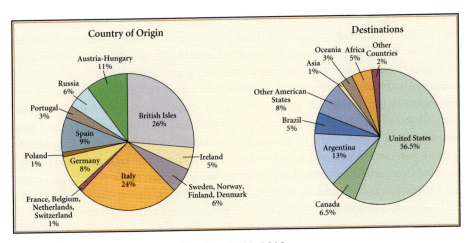

■ FIGURE 19.1 European Emigration, 1881–1910

The suffering caused by economic change and by political persecution motivated people from almost every European country to leave their homes for greater security elsewhere. North America attracted nearly two-thirds of these migrants, many of whom followed reports of vast quantities of available land in Canada and the United States. Both countries were known for following the rule of law and for economic opportunity in urban as well as rural areas.

(Data adapted from Walter F. Willcox, ed., *International Migrations*. Volume I: Statistics [New York: Gordon and Breach Science Publishers, rep. 1969], 242–47.)

Commercial and imperial prosperity determined destinations. As news of opportunity reached Europe, most migrants went to North and South America, Australia, and New Zealand. The railroad and steamship made journeys across and then out of Europe more affordable, more comfortable, and faster, even though most migrants sailed in steerage, with few amenities. Once established elsewhere, migrants frequently sent money back home and thus remained part of the family economy. Nationalist commentators in Slovakia, Poland, Hungary, and other parts of eastern and central Europe bemoaned the loss of ethnic vigor, but peasants themselves welcomed the arrival of "magic dollars" from their kin. Migrants appreciated the chance to begin anew without the deprivation and social constrictions of the old world. One settler in the United States was relieved to escape the meager peasant meal of rye bread and herring: "God save us from . . . all that is Swedish," he wrote home sourly.

Migration out of Europe often meant the end of the old ways of life. Men and women seeking employment had to learn new languages and civic practices and compete for jobs in unfamiliar, growing cities, where they formed the cheapest pool of labor, often in factories or sweatshops. Women who stayed at home working, however, tended to associate with others like themselves, preserving traditional ways. More insulated at home, they might never learn the new language or put away their peasant dresses. Their husbands and children were more likely than they to put the past behind them as they faced the challenges of the factories and schools of the new world.

Internal migration from rural areas to European cities—more common than international migration—accelerated urbanization. The most urbanized countries were Great Britain and Belgium, followed by Germany, France, and the Netherlands. In Russia, only 7 percent of the population lived in cities of 10,000 or more; in Portugal the figure was 12 percent. Cities of more than 100,000 grew the most, but every urban area attracted migrants seeking employment. Nevertheless, more people lived in rural areas with under 2,000 people than lived in towns and cities, and migration back to rural areas occurred at harvest time. Temporary migrants to the cities worked as masons, drivers of horse-drawn cabs, or factory hands to supplement declining income from agriculture. In the winter, those remaining on the land turned to cottage industry, making bricks, pottery, sieves, shawls, lace, locks, and samovars. To maintain their status as independent artisans, handweavers sent their wives and daughters to towns to work in factories.

Toward National Fitness: Reforming the Working Class, Expanding Sports and Leisure

Two phenomena softened the upheavals of migration and the stresses of economic modernization. One was the rise of middle- and upper-class reform organizations and charities to improve urban conditions. The other was the emergence of competitive sports and the growing interest in healthy recreation. Influenced by Social

Darwinist thought, which associated moral behavior and physical fitness with national strength, governments generally endorsed both phenomena.

Settlement houses, clinics, and maternal and child wellness societies seemed to spring up overnight in cities. Young men and women, often from universities, flocked to staff these new organizations. Reformers eagerly took up residence in settlement houses in poor neighborhoods to study and help the people. Believing in the scientific approach to solving social problems, they sought the causes of social ills and their solutions. One group devoted to this enterprise was the Fabian Society in London, a small organization established in 1884. Committed to a socialism based on reform and state planning rather than revolution, the Fabians helped found the Labour Party in 1893 as a way of making social improvement a political issue. Religious fervor often added a moral component to reform efforts: some Protestants and Catholics countered growing secularization through increased missionary efforts abroad and among the urban poor at home. In the 1890s, Pope Leo XIII called for a more active ministry among the working classes. In response, the church in Hungary, for example, channeled some of its efforts away from its traditional constituency in villages and toward ministering to workers in cities.

Impelled as well by a Social Darwinist fear that Europeans would lack the fitness to survive in a competitive world, philanthropists and government agencies intervened more and more in the lives of working-class families. They sponsored health clinics and milk centers to provide good medical care and food for children, and they instructed mothers in child-care techniques, including breast-feeding—an important way, reformers maintained, to promote infant health. Some schools distributed free lunches, medicine, and clothing. Some professionals began to make birth-control information available in the belief that small families were more likely to survive the rigors of urban life. But some reformers believed that the sexual exploitation of women would increase if the likelihood of pregnancy were overcome so easily. On the downside, government officials and private reformers deemed themselves the overseers of working-class families and entered apartments without being invited. Such intrusions pressured poor, overworked mothers to conform to standards for their children—such as finding them respectable shoes and other clothing—that they often could not afford.

The fear that women were not producing healthy enough children and were stealing jobs from men led reformers to push for protective legislation. Such legislation barred women across Europe from night work and from pottery and other "dangerous" trades, allegedly for health reasons even though medical statistics demonstrated that women became sick on the job less often than men. The new laws assigning some jobs to women and others to men did not prevent women from earning their livelihood, but they made the task harder by limiting women's access to well-paying jobs.

Also serving to enhance national fitness, as well as providing some release from the stresses of daily life, were competitive sports and healthy leisure-time activities. As nations competed for territory and economic markets, male athletes banded

■ **Anglo-Indian Polo Team**
Team sports underwent rapid development during the imperial years, as spectators rooted for the
success of their football team in the same spirit they rooted for their armies abroad. Some educa-
tors believed that team sports formed the male character so that men could be more effective sol-
diers against peoples of other races. Thus this mixed team of polo players was uncharacteristic. In
cricket, soccer, and other sports, city challenged city, nation challenged nation, and race often chal-
lenged race. (Hulton Getty Collection/Liaison Agency.)

together to organize team sports that eventually replaced village games. Soccer,
rugby, and cricket drew mass followings and helped to integrate migrants as well as
people from the lower and upper classes into a common national culture. Large audiences drawn from all classes backed their favorite teams, and competitive sports
began to be seen as valuable promoters of national strength and spirit. Newspapers
reported the results of all sorts of contests, including the Tour de France bicycle race,
sponsored by tire makers who wanted to prove the superiority of their products.

Team sports further differentiated male and female spheres and thus promoted
social order based on distinctions between the sexes. Some team sports for women
emerged—soccer, field hockey, and rowing—but women generally were encouraged to engage in individual sports. "Riding improves the temper, the spirits and
the appetite," wrote one sportswoman. "Black shadows and morbid fancies disappear from the mental horizon." Rejecting the idea of women's natural frailty, reformers introduced exercise and gymnastics into schools for girls, often with the
idea that they would strengthen young women for motherhood and thus help build
the nation-state. So-called Swedish exercises for young women spread through
respectable homes across Europe, while more cosmopolitan women practiced
yoga.

The middle classes believed their leisure pursuits should not only be fun but also hone mental and physical skills. Thus mountain climbing became a popular middle-class hobby. Working-class people adopted middle-class habits by joining clubs for bicycling, touring, and hiking. Laborers and their families also sought the benefits of fresh air and exercise by visiting the beach, taking the train into the countryside, and enjoying day trips on river steamships. Clubs that sponsored trips often had names such as "The Patriots" or "The Nationals," again associating physical fitness with national strength. The new emphasis on healthy recreation gave individuals a greater sense of individual freedom and power and thereby fostered a sense of citizenship based less on constitutions and rights than on an individual nation's exercise of raw power. A farmer's son in the 1890s boasted that with a bicycle "I was king of the road, since I was faster than a horse."

Sciences of the Modern Self

Scientists and Social Darwinists found cause for alarm not only in the condition of the working class but also in modern society's complaints about fatigue and irritability. Such illnesses originated in the "nerves," they reasoned, which were overstimulated by the pace and demands of urban living. A rash of books in the 1890s expounded on the subject of nervous illness. The most widely translated of them, *Degeneration*, written by Hungarian-born physician Max Nordau (1849–1923), blamed overstimulation for both individual and national deterioration. According to Nordau, increasingly bizarre modern art, male lethargy, and female hysteria were all symptoms of overstimulation and signs of a general downturn in the human species. The Social Darwinist prescription for curing such mental decline was imperial adventure, renewed virility, and increased childbearing.

Some researchers attempted to quantify and classify mental characteristics. Scientific study of the origins of criminal traits created the field of criminology. The French psychologist Alfred Binet (1857–1911) designed intelligence tests that he claimed could measure the capacity of the human mind more accurately than schoolteachers could. In Russia, physiologist Ivan Pavlov (1849–1936) proposed that conditioning mental reflexes—that is, causing a subject to associate a desired response with a previously unrelated stimulus—could modify behavior. His experiments, especially his success in changing the behavior of a dog, formed the basis of modern psychology.

Sigmund Freud (1856–1939) devised an approach to modern anxieties that, he claimed, avoided traditional moral evaluations of human behavior. He became convinced that the human psyche was far from rational. Dreams, he explained in *The Interpretation of Dreams* (1900), reveal a repressed part of personality—the "unconscious"—where all sorts of desires are more or less hidden. Freud also believed that the human psyche is made up of three competing parts: the *ego*, the part that is most in touch with external reality; the *id* (or libido), the part that governs instinctive drives and sexual energies; and the *superego,* the part that serves as the force of conscience. Like Darwin's ideas, Freud's notions challenged the widespread liberal beliefs in a unified, rational self that acts in its own interest and, by implication, in the certainty of progress. ◆

Freud shocked many of his contemporaries by insisting that all children have sexual drives from the moment of birth. He also believed that many of these sexual impulses have to be repressed for the individual to attain maturity and for society to remain civilized. Attaining one's adult sexual identity is always a painful process because it depends on repressing infantile urges, which include bisexuality and incest. Thus the Wolf-Man's nightmare of white wolves outside his window symbolized his unresolved sexual feelings for members of his family. Freud claimed that certain aspects of gender roles—such as motherhood—are normal and that throughout their lives women in general achieve far less than men do. At the same time, he believed that adult gender identity results not from anatomy alone (motherhood is not the only way to be female) but from inescapable mental processing of life experiences as well. He thus made gender more complicated than simple biology would suggest. Finally, Freud's psychoanalytic theory maintained that girls and women have powerful sexual feelings, an assertion that broke with ideas of women's passionlessness.

The influence of psychoanalysis became pervasive in the twentieth century, offering paradoxes and representing another turn toward global thinking. Two mainstays of psychoanalysis—free association of ideas and interpretation of dreams—derived from African and Asian influences on Freud's thought: the "talking cure," as it was quickly labeled, gave rise to a general acceptance of talking out one's problems. As psychoanalysis became a respected means of recovering mental health, terms such as *neurosis, unconscious,* and *libido* came into widespread use and could apply to anyone, not just the mentally ill. By way of paradox, psychoanalysis reflected the many contradictions at work in turn-of-the-century Europe. For example, Freud attributed girls' complaints about unwanted sexual advances or abuse to fantasies caused by "penis envy." This idea led members of the new profession of social work to believe that most claims of such abuse were not true. So on the one hand, Freud was a meticulous scientist, examining symptoms, urging attention to the most minute evidence from everyday life, and demanding that sexual life be regarded with a rational rather than a religious eye. But on the other hand, he was a pessimistic visionary who abandoned the optimism of the Enlightenment and pre-Darwinian science and instead theorized that humans are motivated by irrational drives toward death and destruction and that these drives shape society's collective mentality. Freud would later interpret the devastation of World War I as bearing out his bleak conclusions.

◆ For an excerpt from Freud's best-known work, see Document 62, Sigmund Freud, *The Interpretation of Dreams.*

■ **Freud's Office**

Sigmund Freud's therapy room, where his patients experienced the "talking cure," was filled with imperial trophies such as Oriental rugs and African art objects. Freud himself was fascinated by cures brought about through shamanism, trances, and other practices of non-Western medicine as well as through drug-induced mental states. In 1938, Freud fled to England to escape the Nazis. This photo shows his office in London. (Mary Evans Picture Library/Sigmund Freud copyrights.)

Modernity and the Revolt in Ideas

Although the intellectuals and artists who participated in the turmoil and triumph of turn-of-the-century society did not know it at the time, their rejection of accepted beliefs and artistic forms announced a new era. Scientific theories that time is relative and that energy and mass are interchangeable rocked established truths about time, space, matter, and energy. Philosophers emphasized the role of the irrational and accidental in everyday life. Art and music became unrecognizable. Artists and musicians who deliberately produced shocking, lurid works were, like Freud, heavily influenced by advances in science, critical thinking, and empire. Amid contradictions such as the blending of the scientific and the irrational, "West" and "non-West," intellectuals and artists helped launch the disorienting revolution in ideas and creative expression that we now identify collectively as *modernism*.

The Challenge to Positivism

Late in the nineteenth century, at the height of empire-building and reform efforts, many philosophers and social thinkers rejected the century-old belief that scientific methods would lead to the discovery of enduring social laws. This belief, called *positivism,* had emphasized the permanent nature of fundamental laws and had motivated reformers' attempts to perfect legislation based on studies of society. Challenging positivism, the philosophers Wilhelm Dilthey (1833–1911) in Germany and John Dewey (1859–1952) in the United States declared that because human experience is ever changing, theories and standards cannot be constant or enduring. Just as scientific theory was modified over time, so must social theories and practice react pragmatically to the immediate conditions at hand. In the same vein, German political theorist Max Weber (1864–1920) maintained that the sheer numbers involved in policymaking would often make decisive action by bureaucrats impossible—especially in times of crisis, when a charismatic leader might usurp power because of his ability to make flexible and instinctive decisions. Thus the development of impartial forms of government such as bureaucracy carried the potential for undermining the rule of law. Turn-of-the-century thinkers called *relativists* and *pragmatists* influenced thinking about society throughout the twentieth century.

The most radical scholar was the German philosopher Friedrich Nietzsche (1844–1900), who early in his career developed the challenging distinction between the "Apollonian," or rational, side of human existence and the "Dionysian" side, with its expression of more primal urges. Nietzsche believed that people generally cling to rational, Apollonian explanations of life because Dionysian ideas about nature, death, and love such as those found in Greek tragedy are too disturbing. He maintained that all assertions of scientific fact and theory are mere illusions, that knowledge of nature has to be expressed in mathematical, linguistic, or artistic representation. Truth, Nietzsche insisted, thus exists only in the representation itself, for humans can never experience unfiltered knowledge of nature or reality. This aspect of Nietzsche's philosophy would lead to the late-twentieth-century school of thought called *postmodernism.*

Much of Nietzsche's writing took the form of aphorisms—short, disconnected statements of truth or opinion—a form that broke with the logical rigor of traditional Western philosophy. Nietzsche used aphorisms to convey the impression that his ideas were a single individual's unique perspective, not universal truths that thinkers since the Enlightenment had claimed were attainable. Influenced by a range of Asian philosophies, Nietzsche was convinced that late-nineteenth-century Europe was witnessing the decline of dogmatic truth, most notably in religion—hence his announcement that "God is dead, we have killed him." Far from arousing dread, the death of God, according to Nietzsche, would give birth to a joyful quest for new "poetries of life" to replace worn-out religious and middle-class rules. Not the rule-bound bourgeois but the untethered "superman" was Nietzsche's highly influential model. On his death, however, Nietzsche's sister edited his diatribes against middle-class values into attacks on Jews. She revised his complicated concepts about each individual's "will to power" and the "superman" so as to appeal to nationalists and to justify violent anti-Semitism and competition for empire.

Revolutionizing Science

While philosophers questioned the ability of science to provide timeless truths, scientific inquiry itself flourished, and the scientific method gained authority in history, psychology, and other fields beyond the traditional sciences. Many people still held positivist assumptions. Technological breakthroughs and improvements in hygiene earned science public prestige. Around the turn of the century, however, discoveries by pioneering researchers shook the foundations of traditional scientific certainty and challenged accepted knowledge about the nature of the universe.

In 1896, Antoine Becquerel (1852–1908) discovered radioactivity and suggested the mutability of elements by the rearrangement of their atoms. French chemist Marie Curie (1867–1934) and her husband, Pierre Curie (1859–1906), isolated the elements polonium and radium, which are more radioactive than the uranium Becquerel used. From these and other discoveries, scientists concluded that atoms are composed of subatomic particles moving about a core. Instead of being solid, as scientists had believed since ancient times, atoms are largely empty space and act not as a concrete substance but as an intangible electromagnetic field. German physicist Max Planck (1858–1947) announced his influential quantum theorem in 1900; it demonstrated that energy is emitted in irregular packets, not in a steady stream.

Scientists had already demonstrated that light has a uniform velocity regardless of the direction it travels from the earth and that the speed of light is unrelated to the motion of the earth. Thus older theories of light on which scientists had relied were no longer tenable. It was in this unsettled situation that physicist Albert Einstein (1879–1955) published his special theory of relativity. On his own, working in a Swiss patent office, he proclaimed in his 1905 paper that space and time are not absolute categories but instead vary according to the vantage point of the observer. Only the speed of light is constant. That same year, he also suggested that the solution to problems in Planck's quantum theorem lay in considering light both as little packets *and* as waves. These theories continued to undercut Newtonian physics as well as commonsense understanding.

Einstein later proposed yet another blurring of two distinct physical properties, mass and energy. He expressed this equivalence in the formulation $E = mc^2$, or energy equals mass times the square of the speed of light. In 1916, his general theory of relativity connected the force, or gravity, of an object with its mass and postulated a fourth mathematical dimension to the universe. Much more lay ahead, once Einstein's theories of energy were developed: television, nuclear power, and, within forty years, nuclear bombs.

The revolutionary findings of Planck, Einstein, and others were not accepted immediately because power and time-honored beliefs were at stake. Einstein like Planck struggled against mainstream science and its professional institutions. Marie Curie faced such resistance that even after she became the first person ever to

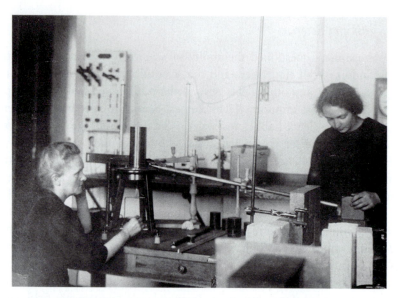

■ **Marie Curie and Her Daughter**
Recipient of two Nobel Prizes, Marie Curie came from Poland to western Europe to study science. Curie's extraordinary career made her the epitome of the new womanhood; her daughter Irene Joliot-Curie followed her into the field and also won a Nobel Prize. Both women died of leukemia caused by their exposure to radioactive materials. Today a reconstruction of the Curie laboratory as a museum contains a display indicating the intense radioactivity remaining in the scientific instruments they used a century ago. (ACJC—Archives Curie et Joliot-Curie.)

receive a second Nobel Prize (1911), the prestigious French Academy of Science turned down her candidacy for membership that year. Traditionalists, however, eventually gave way, and Max Planck institutes were established in German cities, streets across Europe were named after Marie Curie, and Einstein's name became synonymous with genius. These scientists achieved what historians call a *paradigm shift*—that is, in the face of staunch resistance they transformed the foundations of science and came themselves to supersede other names.

Modern Art

Conflicts between traditional values and new ideas also raged in the arts, as artists distanced themselves from classical Western realism and from the conventions of polite society. Modernism in the arts not only fractured traditional standards but ushered in competing artistic styles and disagreement about art's relationship to society. Some modern artists tried both to challenge and to comfort urbanites caught up in the rush of modern life. Abandoning the soft colors of impressionism as too subtle for a dynamic industrial society, a group of Parisian artists exhibiting in 1905 combined blues, greens, reds, and oranges so intensively that they were called *fauves,* or "wild beasts." A leader of the short-lived fauvism, Henri Matisse (1869–1954) soon struck out in a new direction, targeting the expanding class of white-collar workers. Matisse dreamed of "an art . . . for every mental worker, be he businessman or writer, like an appeasing influence, like a mental soother, something like a good armchair in which to rest from physical fatigue."

In the work of the French artist Paul Cézanne (1839–1906), one of the most powerful and enduring trends in modern art took shape. Emphasizing structure, Cézanne used rectangular daubs of paint to capture a geometric vision of dishes, fruit, drapery, and the human body. Accentuating the lines and planes found in nature, Cézanne's art, like science, was removed from the realm of ordinary perception. Following in Cézanne's footsteps, Spanish artist Pablo Picasso (1881–1973) initiated *cubism,* a style whose radical emphasis on planes and surfaces portrayed people as bizarre, inhuman, almost unrecognizable forms. Picasso's painting *Les Demoiselles d'Avignon* (1907) depicted the bodies of the *demoiselles,* or young ladies (prostitutes in this case), as fragmented and angular, with their heads modeled on African masks (see page 805). Continuing along the path of impressionism and fauvism, Picasso's work showed the profound influences of African, Asian, and South American arts, but his interpretation of these influences was less decorative and more brutal than those by Matisse, for example. Like explorers, botanists, and foreign journalists, he was bringing knowledge of the empire into the imperial homeland, this time in a distinctly disturbing form.

Across Europe, political critique also shaped art. "Show the people how hideous is their actual life, and place your hands on the causes of its ugliness" was the anarchist challenge at the time. Picasso, who had spent his youth in the heart of working-class Barcelona, a hotbed of anarchist thought, aimed to replace middle-class sentimentality in art with truth about industrial society. In 1912, Picasso and the French painter Georges Braque (1882–1963) devised a new kind of collage that incorporated bits of newspaper, string, and other artifacts. The effect was a canvas that appeared to be cluttered with refuse. The newspaper clippings Picasso included described battles and murders, suggesting the shallowness of Western pretensions to high civilization. In eastern and central Europe, artists criticized the growing nationalism that determined official purchases of sculpture and painting: "The whole empire is littered with monuments to soldiers and monuments to Kaiser William of the same conventional type," one German artist complained. Such groups as the Berlin Secession and the Vienna Workshop were at the forefront of depicting psychological complexity in experimental form.

Scandinavian and eastern European artists produced anguished works. Like the vision of Freud, their style of portraying inner reality—called *expressionism*—broke with middle-class optimism. Norwegian painter Edvard Munch (1863–1944) aimed "to make the emotional mood ring out again as happens on a gramophone." His painting *The Scream* (1895) used twisting lines and a depiction of tortured skeletal human form to convey the horror of modern life that many artists perceived. The German avant-garde artist Gabriele Münter (1877–1962) and Russian painter Wassily Kandinsky (1866–1944) opened their "Blue Rider" exhibit in Munich featuring "expressive" work that made use of geometric forms and striking colors. Artists of the Blue Rider group imitated the paintings of children and the mentally ill to achieve their depiction of psychological reality. Kandinsky, who employed these forms and colors to express an inner, spiritual truth, is often credited with producing the first fully abstract paintings. The expressionism of Austrian painter Oskar Kokoschka (1886–1980) was even more intense, displaying ecstasy, horror, and hallucinations. As a result, his work—like that of other expressionists and cubists before World War I—was a commercial failure in an increasingly complex marketplace that featured not only museum curators but professional dealers and art "experts." Trade in art became professionalized, as had medicine and government work before it, even as modern artists sought to shatter traditional norms.

Only one innovative style emerged an immediate commercial success: *art nouveau* ("new style") won approval from government, critics, and the masses. Creating everything from dishes and advertising posters to streetlamps and even entire buildings in this new style, designers manufactured beautiful things for the general public. As one French official said about the first version of art nouveau coins issued in 1895, "Soon even the most humble among us will be able to have a masterpiece in his pocket." Adapted from Asian design, the organic and natural elements of art nouveau were meant to offset the fragmentation of factory and office work with images depicting the unified forms of nature. The impersonality of machines was replaced by intertwined vines and flowers and the softly curving bodies of female nudes that would psychologically soothe the individual viewer—an idea that directly contrasted with Picasso's artistic vision. Gustav Klimt (1862–1918), son of a Czech goldsmith, flourished in Viennese high society because his paintings captured the psychological essence of dreamy, sensuous women, their bodies Eastern-inspired mosaics liberally dotted with gold. Art nouveau was the notable exception to the public outcries over innovations in the visual arts.

Musical Iconoclasm

"Astonish me!" was the motto of modern dance and music, both of which shocked audiences in the concert halls of Europe. American dancer Isadora Duncan (1877–1927) took Europe by storm at the turn of the century when, draped in a flowing garment, she danced barefoot in the first performance of modern dance. Drawing on sophisticated Japanese practices, hers was nonetheless called a primitive style that "lifted from their seats people who had never left theater seats before except to get up and go home." Similarly, experimentation with forms of bodily expression animated the Russian Ballet's performance in 1913 of *Rite of Spring* by Igor Stravinsky (1882–1971), the tale of an orgiastic dance to the death performed

■ **Léon Bakst, _Nijinsky in "L'Après-Midi d'un Faune"_ ("Nijinsky in 'The Afternoon of a Faun,'" 1912)**

Theater sets, costume designs, and performance itself resonated with the experimental climate of early-twentieth-century Europe. Léon Bakst, a Russian painter and set designer, used art nouveau style to capture the faunlike character of ballet star Vaslav Nijinsky. Yet on the eve of World War I, Nijinsky was part of a revolution in ballet that introduced jerky, awkward, pounding movements to indicate the primal nature of dance. (Wadsworth Atheneum, Hartford. The Ella Gallup Sumner and Mary Catlin Sumner Collection Fund.)

to ensure fertile soil and a bountiful harvest. The choreography of its star, Vaslav Nijinsky (1890–1950), created a scandal. Nijinsky and the troupe struck awkward poses and danced to rhythms intended to sound primitive. At the work's premiere in Paris, one journalist reported that "the audience began shouting its indignation.... Fighting actually broke out among some of the spectators." Such controversy made _Rite of Spring_ a box-office hit, although its choreographer was called a "lunatic" and the music itself "the most discordant composition ever written."

Music had been making this turn for several decades. Having heard Asian musicians at international expositions, French composers such as Claude Debussy (1862–1918) transformed their style to reflect non-European musical patterns and themes. The twentieth century opened with _Scheherazade_ by Frenchman Maurice Ravel (1875–1937) and _Madame Butterfly_ by the Italian composer Giacomo Puccini (1858–1924), both with non-Western subject matter. Using non-Western tonalities, sound became jarring to many listeners. Austrian composer Richard Strauss (1864–1949) upset convention by using several keys simultaneously in his compositions. Like the fragmented representation of reality in cubism, atonality or several tonalities at once distorted familiar harmonic patterns for the audience. Strauss's operas *Salome* (1905) and *Elektra* (1909) reflected modern fascination with violence and obsessive passion. A newspaper critic claimed that Strauss's dissonant works "spit and scratch and claw each other like enraged panthers." The Hungarian pianist Béla Bartók (1881–1945) incorporated folk melodies into his compositions in order to elevate Hungarian ethnicity above the Habsburg Empire's multinationalism. His music disturbed some audiences because of its nationalism and others because of its dissonance.

The early orchestral work of Austrian composer Arnold Schoenberg (1874–1951), who also wrote cabaret music to earn a living, shocked even Strauss. In *Theory of Harmony* (1911), Schoenberg proposed eliminating tonality altogether; a decade later he devised a new twelve-tone scale. "I am aware of having broken through all the barriers of a dated aesthetic ideal," Schoenberg wrote of his music. But new aesthetic models distanced artists like Schoenberg from their audiences, separating high from low culture even more and ending the support of many in the upper classes, who found this music not only incomprehensible but unpleasant. The artistic elite and the social elite parted ranks. "Anarchist! Nihilist!" shouted Schoenberg's audiences, showing their contempt for modernism and bringing the language of politics into the arts.

Politics in a New Key

The political atmosphere grew charged alongside the modernist disturbances in intellectual life, even though the advance of liberal opinions opened the door to expanded political representation and growing tolerance. Networks of communication, especially the development of journalism, enhanced the trend toward universal male suffrage in Europe, leading to the creation of mass politics. Working-class people seemed to come into their own: even high-ranking politicians such as William Gladstone, the prime minister of Great Britain, had to campaign by railroad to win their support. Simultaneously, however, political activists were no longer satisfied with the liberal rights sought by reformers a century earlier. Militant nationalists, anti-Semites, socialists, suffragists, and others demanded changes that challenged liberal values. Traditional elites, resentful of the rising middle classes and urban peoples, aimed to stem constitutional processes and the development of modern life. Mass politics soon threatened social unity, especially in central and eastern Europe, where governments often answered reformers' demands with refusal and repression.

Mass Politics and the Growing Power of Labor

Mass politics was a combination of the right to vote accorded to men across Europe before World War I and the rise of popular activism, especially among working people. In the fall of 1879, William Gladstone (1809–1898), leader of the British Liberals, whose party was then out of power, waged an experimental electoral campaign across the country. Speaking before thousands of workingmen and -women, he urged greater self-determination in India and Africa and advocated a way of life based on "honest, manful, humble effort" in the middle-class tradition of "hard work." Newspapers around the country highlighted his trip, further fueling public interest in politics. Gladstone's Liberals won the election, and he became prime minister—testimonial to the trend toward expanded participation in political life. The Reform Act of 1884 doubled the British electorate, to around 4.5 million men, enfranchising many urban workers and artisans and thus diminishing traditional aristocratic influence in the countryside. This move reflected the universal manhood suffrage already granted in France and in Germany; the rest of Europe would follow suit before World War I.

Journalism helped elite politicians forge a broad national community of up-to-date citizens by providing ready access to information (and misinformation) about politics and world events. The invention of mechanical typesetting and the production of newsprint from wood pulp lowered the costs of printing; the telephone allowed reporters to communicate news to their papers almost instantly. Once philosophical and literary in content, daily newspapers now emphasized the sensational, using banner headlines and gruesome or lurid details—particularly about murders, sexual scandals, and sagas of the empire—to sell papers as well as political points of view. In the hustle and bustle of industrial society, one editor wrote, "you must strike your reader right between the eyes." Elites grumbled that the sensational press was another sign of social decay. But for up-and-coming people from the working and middle classes it provided an entrée into politics and an avenue to success. As London, Paris, Vienna, Berlin, and St. Petersburg became centers not only of politics but of news, a number of European politicians got their start working for daily newspapers.

Working-class solidarity in neighborhoods, shop-floor activism, the development of labor unions, and the rise of worker or socialist parties formed the other side of mass politics. Community bonds forged by homemakers and neighborhood groups were a necessary precondition for collective worker action. School officials or police looking for truant children and delinquents met a phalanx of housewives ready to hide the children or to lie for their neighbors. When landlords evicted tenants, women would gather in the streets and return household goods as fast as they were removed from the rooms of ousted families. Meeting on doorsteps or at fountains, laundries, pawnshops, and markets, women initiated rural newcomers into urban ways and developed class unity. Conditions of economic life also led workers to organize formal unions, which attracted the allegiance of millions. Unions demanded a say in working conditions and aimed, as one union's rule book put it, "to ensure that wages . . . always follow the rises in the price of basic commodities." Despite worker turbulence of the Paris Commune, strong unions even appealed to some industrialists because a union could make strikes more predictable (or even prevent them), present demands more coherently, and provide a liaison for labor-management relations.

From the 1880s on, the pace of collective action for more pay, lower prices, and better working conditions accelerated. In 1888, for example, hundreds of young women who made matches, the so-called London matchgirls, struck to end the fining system, under which they could be penalized an entire day's wage for being a minute or two late to work. This system, the matchgirls maintained, helped companies reap profits of more than 20 percent. Newspapers and philanthropists picked up the strikers' story, helping them win their case. Soon after, London dockworkers and gasworkers protested their precarious working conditions. Across Europe, the number of strikes and demonstrations rose from 188 in 1888 to 289 in 1890. Housewives, who often demonstrated in support of strikers, carried out their own protests against high food prices. In keeping with centuries of women's protest, they confiscated merchants' goods and sold them at what they considered a just price. "There should no longer be either rich or poor," argued organized Italian peasant women. "All should have bread for themselves and for their children. We should all be equal." Fearing threats to industrial and agricultural productivity, governments increasingly responded with force, even though most strikes were about the conditions of everyday life for workers and not about political revolution.

From unions soon evolved working-class political parties. Craft-based unions of skilled artisans, such as carpenters and printers, were the most active and cohesive, but from the mid-1880s on, a *new unionism* attracted transport workers, miners, matchgirls, and dockworkers. These new unions were nationwide groups with salaried managers who could plan massive general strikes across the trades, focusing on such common goals as the eight-hour workday, and thus paralyze an entire nation. Large unions of the industrialized countries of western Europe, like cartels and trusts, increasingly influenced business practices. They were joined by working-class parties: the Labour Party in England, the Socialist Party in France, and the Social Democratic Parties of Sweden, Hungary, Austria, and Germany—most of them inspired by Marxist theories. Germany was home to the largest socialist party in Europe after 1890.

Workingwomen joined these parties, but in much smaller numbers than men. Not able to vote in national elections and usually responsible for housework in addition to their paying jobs, women had little time for party meetings. Furthermore, their low wages hardly allowed them to survive, much less to pay party or union dues. Many workingmen opposed their presence, fearing women would dilute the union's masculine camaraderie. Contact with women would mean "suffocation," one Russian workingman believed, and end male union members' sense of being "comrades in the revolutionary cause." The shortage of women's voices in unions and political parties paralleled women's exclusion from government; it helped make the middle-class belief in separate spheres part of a working-class ideology that glorified the heroic struggles of a male proletariat against capitalism. Marxist leaders continued to maintain that injustice to women was caused by capitalism and would disappear in socialist society. As a result, although the new political organizations encouraged women's support, they downplayed women's concerns about lower wages and sexual coercion.

Socialist parties attracted workingmen because they promised the triumph of new male voters who could become a powerful collective force in national elections. Those who accepted Marx's assertion that "workingmen have no country," however, wanted an international movement that could address workers' common interests. In 1889, some four hundred socialists from across Europe (joined by many on-lookers and unofficial participants) met in Paris to form the Second International, a federation of working-class organizations and political parties replacing the First International, founded by Marx before the Paris Commune. Growing strength, especially electoral victories, raised issues for socialists. Some felt uncomfortable sitting with the upper classes in parliaments. Others worried that their participation in cabinets would produce reform but compromise their ultimate goal of revolution. Often these deputies refused seats in the government. Between 1900 and 1904, the Second International wrestled with the issue of reformism—that is, whether socialists should employ evolutionary tactics rather than pushing for a violent revolution to overthrow governments.

European leaders watched with dismay the rise of working-class political power late in the century. Some trade union members, known as *syndicalists,* along with anarchists kept Europe in a panic with their terrorist acts. Anarchism flourished in the less industrial parts of Europe—Russia, Italy, and Spain, where many rural people looked to the possibility of life without the domination of large landowners and government. Many advocated extreme tactics, including physical violence and even murder. "We want to overthrow the government . . . with violence since it is by the use of violence that they force us to obey," wrote one Italian anarchist. In the 1880s, anarchists bombed stock exchanges, parliaments, and businesses and by the 1890s were assassinating heads of state: Spanish premier Antonio Canovas del Castillo in 1897, Empress Elizabeth of Austria-Hungary in 1898, King Umberto of Italy in 1900, and President William McKinley of the United States in 1901, to name a few famous victims. Syndicalists advocated the use of direct action, such as general strikes and sabotage, to bring industry and government under the control of labor unions by paralyzing the economy.

But much worker organization was also sociable, intertwining community solidarity with activities of everyday life. The gymnastic and choral societies that had once united Europeans in nationalistic fervor now served working-class goals. Songs emphasized worker freedom, progress, and eventual victory. Socialist gymnastics, bicycling, and marching societies rejected competition and prizes as middle-class preoccupations, but they valued physical fitness for helping workers in the "struggle for existence"—a reflection of Darwinian thinking about "survival of the fittest." Workers also held festivals and gigantic parades, most notably on May 1, proclaimed by the Second International as a labor holiday. Like religious processions of an earlier time, parades were rituals that fostered unity. European governments at the time could not discriminate among the various worker organizations and frequently prohibited such public gatherings, fearing they were tools for agitators.

Another group of working-class parties operated in exile. The Russian government, for instance, outlawed political parties until 1905 and persecuted activists. The foremost Russian activist, V. I. Lenin (1870–1924), migrated to western Europe after his release from confinement in Siberia and earned his reputation among Russian Marxists there with his hard-hitting journalism and political intrigue. Lenin advanced the theory that a highly disciplined socialist elite would lead a lightly industrialized Russia immediately into socialism. Outmaneuvering the Mensheviks, who dominated Russian Marxism, Lenin's Bolsheviks, so named after the Russian word for "majority" (which they had briefly formed), constantly struggled to suppress other groups. Neither of these factions, however, had as large a constituency within Russia as the Socialist Revolutionaries, whose objective was to politicize peasants rather than industrial workers as the prelude to a populist revolution. All these groups prepared for the revolutionary moment through study, propaganda efforts, and organizing—not through the electoral politics successfully employed elsewhere in Europe. Whether operating in representative or authoritarian countries, working-class organizations caused the upper and middle classes grave anxiety. Despite growing acceptance of representative institutions and despite the spread of education, many in the "best circles" still believed that they alone should hold political power.

Rights for Women and the Battle for Suffrage

Singly or in groups, women continued to agitate against their exclusion from benefits of liberalism such as parliamentary representation. They usually could not vote, exercise free speech, or own property if married. Laws in France, Austria, and Germany curtailed women's political activism, including their attendance at political meetings. Influenced by the cultural ideal of *Bildung*—the belief that education can strengthen character and that individual development has public importance—German women sought better education for themselves and more opportunity to teach, instead of agitating for political reform. In several countries, women continued to monitor the regulation of prostitution. Their goal was to prevent prostitutes from being imprisoned on suspicion of having syphilis when men with syphilis faced no such incarceration. Other women took up pacifism as their special cause. Many of them were inspired by Bertha von Süttner's popular book, *Lay Down Your Arms* (1889), which emphasized the terror inflicted on women and families by the ravages of war. (Later von Süttner would influence Alfred Nobel to institute a peace prize and then win the prize herself in 1903.)

By the 1890s, however, many activists had concluded that only the right to vote would correct the problems caused by male privilege, which they were combating in piecemeal fashion. Thus, major suffrage organizations with millions of activists, paid officials, and permanent offices emerged out of the earlier reform groups and women's clubs. Using skills gained from their charity work and from this organizing, British suffrage leader Millicent Garrett Fawcett (1847–1929) and other women pressured members of Parliament for the vote, recruited members, and participated in national and international congresses on behalf of suffrage. Similarly, American Susan B. Anthony (1820–1906) traveled throughout the United States, organized suffrage societies, edited a newspaper, raised money for the movement, and founded the International Woman Suffrage Association in 1904. The leadership argued that men had promised to protect disfranchised women but that this system of male chivalry had led to exploitation and abuse. Power and privilege—no matter how couched in expressions of goodwill—worked to the detriment of those without them. "So long as the subjection of women endures, and is confirmed by law and custom, . . . women will be victimized," a leading suffragist claimed. Other activists believed that women had the attributes needed to counterbalance masculine qualities in the running of society. The characteristics that came from mothering should shape a country's destiny as much as qualities that stemmed from work in industry and trade, they asserted.

Women's rights activists were predominantly, though not exclusively, from the middle class. Enjoying conveniences like freestanding stoves, running water, and household help, they had more time than workingwomen to be activists, and a higher level of education allowed them to read the works of feminist theorists such as Harriet Taylor and John Stuart Mill. Many were influenced by such works as Norwegian playwright Henrik Ibsen's *A Doll's House* (1879), whose heroine Nora leaves a loveless and oppressive marriage. Olive Schreiner's *The Story of an African Farm* (1889) was equally influential. Her heroine rejects the role of submissive wife and describes the British Empire as a "dirty little world, full of confusion." Some working-class women also participated, although many distrusted the middle class and saw suffrage for women as less important than economic concerns. Textile workers in Manchester, England, for example, put together a vigorous suffrage movement connecting the vote to improved working conditions. Socialists and suffragists, however, usually differed over issues of class and gender.

In 1906 in Finland, suffragists achieved their first major victory when the Finnish parliament granted women the vote. But the failure of parliaments elsewhere in Europe to enact similar legislation provoked some suffragists to violence. Part of the British suffragist movement adopted a militant political style. Emmeline Pankhurst (1858–1928) and her daughters had founded the Women's Social and Political Union (WSPU) in 1903 in the belief that women would accomplish nothing unless they threatened men's property. In 1907, WSPU members began to stage parades in English cities, and in 1909 they began a campaign of violence, blowing up railroad stations, slashing works of art, and chaining themselves to the gates of Parliament. Easily disguising themselves as ordinary shoppers, they carried little hammers in their muffs to smash the plate-glass windows of department stores and

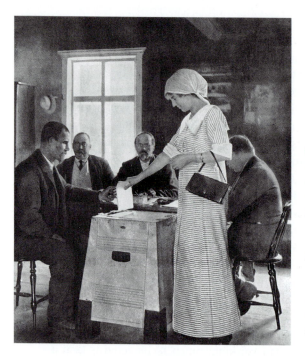

■ **Woman Suffrage in Finland**
In 1906, Finnish women became the first women in Europe to receive the vote in national elections when the socialist party—usually opposed to feminism as a middle-class rather than a working-class project—supported woman suffrage. The Finnish vote elated activists in the West, now linked by many international organizations and ties, because it showed that more than a century of lobbying for reform could lead to gains.
(Mary Evans Picture Library.)

shops. Parades and demonstrations made suffrage a public spectacle, provoking violent attacks on the marchers by outraged men. Arrested for disturbing the peace, the marchers went on hunger strikes in prison. Like striking workers, these women were willing to use confrontational tactics to obtain rights. As politicians continued to deny women the vote, militant suffragists added to the tensions of conflict-ridden urban life.◆

Liberalism Modified

Governments in western Europe, where liberal institutions seemed well entrenched, sought to control the conflicts of the late nineteenth century with pragmatic policies that often (and paradoxically) struck at liberalism's very foundations. Some ended laissez-faire in trade by instituting protective tariffs; some politicians and reformers decided that government needed to intervene in more than economic matters and expand social welfare legislation. In 1905, the British Liberal Party won a solid majority in the House of Commons and seemed determined to enact social legislation to gain working-class support. "We are keenly in sympathy with the

---

◆ For a primary source that explains the goals and defends the strategies of militant suffragists, see Document 63, Emmeline Pankhurst, "Speech from the Dock."

representatives of Labour," one Liberal politician announced. "We have too few of them in the House of Commons." The British government initiated a system of relief for the unemployed in the National Insurance Act of 1911, provided new taxes on the wealthy to fund the system, and eliminated the veto power of the House of Lords.

A modified liberalism advanced in Britain on social issues, but the Irish question tested British commitment to such values as self-determination and individual rights. British political reforms armed disaffected Irish tenant farmers with the secret ballot, making them less like colonized peoples than before. The political climate in Ireland was explosive mainly because of the repressive tactics of absentee landlords, many of them English and Protestant. These landlords evicted unsuccessful and prosperous tenants alike so they could raise the rents of newcomers. But Irish tenants elected a solid bloc of nationalist representatives to the British Parliament. The Irish members of Parliament, voting as a group, had sufficient strength to defeat legislation proposed by either the Conservatives or the Liberals. Irish leader Charles Parnell (1846–1891) demanded support for home rule—allowing Ireland to have its own parliament—in return for Irish votes. The House of Lords vetoed the bills.

Parnell's leadership ended because of scandal in his personal life, but in the 1890s, new groups formed to foster Irish culture. In 1901, the circle around the modernist poet William Butler Yeats (1865–1939) and the charismatic patriot and actress Maud Gonne (1865–1953) founded the Irish National Theater. Gonne took Irish politics into everyday life by opposing British efforts to woo the young. Every time an English monarch visited Ireland, he or she held special receptions for children. Gonne and other Irish volunteers sponsored competing events, handing out candies and other treats for patriotic youngsters. Speaking Gaelic instead of English, singing Gaelic songs, using Catholicism as a rallying point, and generally reconstructing an "Irish way of life," the promoters of Irish culture threw into question the educated class's preference for everything English. This cultural agenda took political shape with the founding in 1905 of Sinn Fein ("Ourselves Alone"), a group that strove for complete Irish independence. In 1913, Parliament approved home rule for Ireland, but the outbreak of World War I prevented the legislation from taking effect and cut short dreams of independence.

Liberal Italian nation-builders, left with a towering debt from unification and with massive pockets of discontent, drifted more rapidly from liberalism's moorings. With little money being spent on education and sanitary improvements, the average Italian feared the devastating effects of national taxes and the military draft on the family economy. Corruption plagued Italy's constitutional monarchy, which had developed neither the secure parliamentary system of England nor the authoritarian monarchy of Germany to guide its growth. To forge a national consensus in the 1890s, prime ministers used patriotic rhetoric, bribes to gain support from the press, and imperial adventure, culminating in a second thwarted attempt to conquer Ethiopia in 1896. Riots and strikes, followed by armed government re-pression, erupted, until Giovanni Giolitti, who served as prime minister for three terms between 1903 and 1914, adopted a policy known as *trasformismo* (from the word for "transform"), by which he used bribes, public works programs, and other benefits to localities to influence their deputies in parliament. Political opponents called Giolitti the "Minister of the Underworld" and accused him of preferring to buy the votes of local bosses instead of spending money to develop the Italian econ-omy. He hoped to appease unrest in the industrializing cities of Turin and Milan and in the depressed agrarian south by instituting social welfare programs and, in 1912, nearly complete manhood suffrage.

Anti-Semitism, Nationalism, and Zionism in Mass Politics

In the two decades leading up to World War I, anti-Semitism and nationalism suggested pat answers to complex questions. Leaders invoked these concepts to maintain interest-group support, to direct hostility away from themselves, and to win elections. The public responded vehemently, coming to see Jews as villains re-sponsible for the perils of modern society and the nation-state as the hero in the struggle to survive. In both republics and monarchies, anti-Semitism and nation-alism played key roles in mass politics by providing a focus for the creation of a radical right increasingly committed to combating the radical left of social democ-racy. Adopting the imperiled nation as its theme and using the Social Darwinist category of race to identify threats to the nation, the right fundamentally changed the older notion of nationalism based on liberal ideas of rights. Liberals had hoped that voting by the masses would make politics more harmonious as parliamentary debate and compromise smoothed out class differences. But anti-Semites and nationalists, scorning tolerant liberal values as effete, often preferred fights in the street to consensus-building in parliaments.

The most notorious instance of anti-Semitism occurred in France, where the political compromise that had created the Third Republic after the French defeat in the Franco-Prussian War produced institutional fragility. An alliance of busi-nessmen, shopkeepers, professionals, and rural property owners backed republican government, but destabilizing economic downturns, widespread corruption, at-tempted coups, and the politics of anti-Semitism threatened political chaos at every turn. The press attributed failures of almost any kind to Jews, and despite an ex-cellent system of primary education promoting literacy and rational thinking, the public was quick to agree. The clergy and monarchists also contributed to the be-lief that the republic was backed by a conspiracy of Jews.

Amid rising anti-Semitism, a French army captain, Alfred Dreyfus (1859–1935), was charged with spying for Germany in 1894. A Jew, Dreyfus had attended the elite École Polytechnique in Paris and become an officer in the French military, whose upper echelons were traditionally aristocratic, Catholic, and monarchist. Dreyfus's conviction and harsh exile to Devil's Island failed to stop the espionage, but the republican government adamantly upheld his guilt. Then several newspapers received proof that the army had used perjured testimony and fabricated documents to convict Dreyfus. In 1898, the celebrated French novelist Émile Zola published "J'accuse" ("I accuse") on the front page of a Paris daily. Zola cited a list of military lies and cover-ups perpetrated by highly placed government officials to create an illusion of Dreyfus's guilt. The article was explosive because it named names and endorsed a liberal government based on truth and tolerance. "I have but one passion, that of Enlightenment," wrote Zola. "J'accuse" led to public riots, quarrels among families and friends, and denunciations of the army, eroding public confidence in the republic and in French institutions. The government finally pardoned Dreyfus in 1899, ousted from office the aristocratic and Catholic officers held responsible, and ended religious teaching orders to ensure a public school system that was secular and that taught liberal values of toler-ance. Nonetheless, the Dreyfus Affair made anti-Semitism a standard tool of politics by producing hate-filled slogans that would shape the mainstream of politics.

The ruling elites in Germany also used anti-Semitism as a political weapon to garner support from those who feared the consequences of Germany's sudden and overwhelming industrializa-tion. Bismarck had pursued a culture war against Catholics and then in 1882–1884

■ **Public Opinion in the Dreyfus Affair: "Ah! The Dirty Beast!"**

The French army used forged documents and perjured testimony to convict Captain Alfred Dreyfus of espionage. In a climate of escalating anti-Semitism, the conviction of a Jew struck many in the public as yet another narrow escape for the country. Only intense detective work by pro-Dreyfus activists and lobbying by Dreyfus's family convinced republican leaders that the system of equal rights was imperiled not by Dreyfus but by the bigotry of the army and those right-wing politicians who had trumped up the case against him.

(Photothèque des Musées de la Ville de Paris.)

turned his attention to wooing the working classes with an array of social programs such as accident and disability insurance. Outlawing the Social Democrats, he next used high tariffs to forge a conservative alliance of agricultural and industrial magnates. The agrarian elites, unlike French conservatives, still controlled the highest reaches of government and influenced the kaiser's policy. But the basis of their power was rapidly eroding, as agriculture, from which they drew their fortunes and social prestige, declined as a percentage of Germany's gross national product. As new opportunities lured rural people away from the land and as industrialists grew wealthier than they, the agrarian elites came to loathe industry and the working class. As a Berlin newspaper noted, "The agrarians' hate for cities . . . blinds them to the simplest needs and the most natural demands of the urban population."

Conservatives and a growing radical right claimed that Jews, who made up less than 1 percent of the German population, were responsible for the disruption of traditional society and charged them with being the main beneficiaries of economic change. In the 1890s, nationalist and anti-Semitic pressure groups flourished, spewing diatribes against Jews and "new women" but also against Social Democrats, whom they branded as internationalist, socially destructive, and unpatriotic. In the 1890s, the new Agrarian League played to the fears of small farmers by accusing Jews of causing agricultural booms and busts. Other parties directed hate-filled speeches against an array of groups. Expressions of extremist hatred and violent feelings of nationalism rather than rational programs to meet problems of economic change became regular features of campaigns.

People in Austria-Hungary—the Dual Monarchy—also expressed their political and economic discontent in militantly nationalistic and anti-Semitic terms, but nationalism there felt the presence of many competing ethnic groups.

Principal Ethnic Groups in Austria-Hungary, c. 1900

From 1879 to 1893, Austrian prime minister Count Edouard von Taaffe favored Catholics and the Slavic parties in order to break the growing power of liberals. But every favor to one group brought protest from the others. Foremost among the nationalists were the Hungarians, who wanted autonomy for themselves while forcibly imposing Hungarian language and culture on all other ethnic groups in Hungary. The demands for greater Hungarian influence (or *Magyarization,* from Magyars, the principal ethnic group) stemmed from Budapest's importance as a thriving industrial city and the massive export of Hungarian grain from the vast estates of the Hungarian nobility, which balanced the monarchy's foreign trade deficit. Political chaos ensued from Magyar domination, as

Slovaks, Romanians, and Ruthenians protested horrendous labor conditions and tens of thousands of others demanded the vote. In the face of this resistance, Hungarians intensified Magyarization, even decreeing that all tombstones be engraved in Magyar.

Hungarian policies changed the course of Habsburg politics by arousing other nationalists to intensify their demands for rights. Croats, Serbs, and other Slavic groups in the south organized and called for equality with the Hungarians. The central government gave more privileges to the Czechs and allowed them to increase the proportion of Czech officials in the government simply because growing industrial prosperity in their region gave them more influence. But every step toward recognition of Czech ethnicity provoked outrage from the traditionally dominant ethnic Germans, causing more tensions in the empire. When in 1897 Austria-Hungary decreed that government officials in the Czech region of the empire would have to know Czech as well as German, the Germans rioted.

Tensions mounted as politicians in Vienna linked the growing power of Hungarian and Czech politicians to Jews. A prime instigator of this "politics of the irrational"—as historians often label this ultranationalist and anti-Semitic phenomenon—was Karl Lueger (1844–1910), whose newly formed Christian Social Party attracted members from among the aristocracy, Catholics, artisans, shopkeepers, and white-collar workers. Lueger used hatred to appeal to those groups for whom modern life meant a loss of privilege and security. In 1895, he was elected mayor of Vienna after using rough language and verbal abuse against Jews and ethnic groups in his campaign. Lueger's ethnic nationalism and anti-Semitism destabilized the multinational coexistence on which Austria-Hungary was based. By the turn of the century, Jewishness became a symbol that politicians often harped on in their election campaigns, calling Jews the "sucking vampire" of modernity and blaming them for the tumult of migration, social dislocation, and just about anything else that other people did not like. Politics became a thing not of parliaments but of the streets, inflaming the atmosphere with racism.

The prevailing view in the West that a Jewish identity was inferior to a Christian one provoked varying responses from Jews themselves. Jews in western Europe had responded to the spread of legal tolerance by adopting liberal political and cultural values, intermarrying with Christians, and in some cases converting to Christianity—a practice known as assimilation. Many Jews also favored the German Empire because classical German culture seemed more appealing than the Catholic ritual promoted by Austria-Hungary. By contrast, Jews in Russia and Romania were increasingly singled out for persecution, legally disadvantaged, and forced to live in ghettos. If Jews wanted refuge, the cities of central and eastern Europe provided the best opportunity to succeed. They often adopted the cosmopolitan culture of Vienna or Magyar ways in Budapest. Despite escalating anti-Semitism, the celebrated composer Gustav Mahler, the budding writer Franz Kafka, and the pioneer of psychoanalysis Sigmund Freud were shaped in the crucible of Habsburg society. By

1900, Jews were both prominent in cultural and economic affairs in cities across the continent and discriminated against, even victimized, elsewhere.

Most Jews, however, were not so accomplished or prosperous as these cultural giants, and pogroms and economic change brought their escalating migration to the United States and other countries. Amid this vast migration and continued persecution, a spirit of Jewish nationalism arose, as Jews began organizing resistance to pogroms and anti-Semitic politics, and intellectuals drew upon Jewish folklore, philology, and history to establish a national identity. In the 1880s, the Ukrainian physician Leon Pinsker, seeing the Jews' lack of national territory as fundamental to the persecution heaped on them, advocated the migration of Jews to Palestine. Strongly influenced by Pinsker, Theodor Herzl (1860–1904) called not simply for migration but for the creation of a Jewish nation-state. A Hungarian-born Jew, Herzl experienced anti-Semitism firsthand as a Viennese journalist and writer in Paris during the Dreyfus Affair. With the support of poorer eastern European Jews, he succeeded in calling the first International Zionist Congress (1897), which endorsed settlement in Palestine and helped gain financial backing from the Rothschild banking family. By 1914, some 85,000 Jews had resettled in Palestine.

Tempests in the Russian Empire

Nonetheless, European domestic politics remained explosive and nowhere more so than in Russia, where anti-Semitism escalated and internal affairs were in disarray. Russia was almost the only European country without a constitutional government, and reform-minded Russian youth increasingly turned to revolutionary, even terrorist groups for solutions to political and social problems. Writers fueled an intense debate over Russia's future. Novelist Leo Tolstoy, author of the epic *War and Peace* (1869), opposed the revolutionaries' desire to overturn the social order and believed that Russia above all required spiritual regeneration. In his novel *Anna Karenina* (1877), Tolstoy tells the story of an impassioned, adulterous love affair but also weaves in the spiritual quest of Levin, a former "progressive" landowner who, like Tolstoy himself, eventually rejects modernization and idealizes the peasantry's tradition of stoic endurance. Radicals, however, sought to change Russia by violent action rather than by spiritual uplift, and in 1881, one of them killed Tsar Alexander II in a bomb attack. His death failed to provoke the peasant uprising the terrorists expected because peasants thought the assassination of the "tsar liberator" was directed against them.

Alexander III (r. 1881–1894), rejecting the liberal reforms that his father had proposed on the eve of his assassination, unleashed a new wave of oppression against religious and ethnic minorities and gave the police almost unchecked power. Intensified Russification aggravated old grievances among oppressed nationalities such as the Poles; it also turned the once-loyal German middle and upper classes of the Baltic provinces against Russian rule, with serious long-term consequences. But the major victims were the five million Russian Jews, confined to the eighteenth-century Pale of Settlement (the name for the restricted territory in which they were permitted to live), against whom local officials instigated new pogroms. Distinctive language, dress, and isolation in ghettos made Jews easy targets in an age when the Russian government was enforcing cultural uniformity and national identity. Government officials also encouraged people to blame Jews for escalating taxes and living costs—though the true cause was the policy of raising taxes to force the peasantry to pay for industrialization and reform.

When Alexander III's son Nicholas II took the throne in 1894, the empire was trapped in the contradictions of European modernity. Taught as a child to hate Jews, Nicholas II (r. 1894–1917) stepped up the persecutions, and in his reign many high officials eagerly endorsed anti-Semitism to gain his favor. Pogroms became a regular feature of the Easter holiday in Russia, and Nicholas increasingly limited where Jews could live and how they could earn a living. He supported even more severe Russification and further restrictions on the empire's many minorities such as the Poles, Ukrainians, and Tatars—giving the impression that Russia enjoyed a uniform national culture. Simultaneously, Russians settled much of Siberia, and the government sponsored industrialization, especially the growth of transport and industry. Industrialization, however, produced onerous taxes and urban unrest as Marxist and union activists incited workers to demand better conditions. In 1903, skilled workers led strikes in Baku, where Armenians and Tatars united in a demonstration that showed how urbanization and Russification could actually facilitate political action that challenged the autocratic regime.

In the context of Russia's trouncing in the Russo-Japanese War, the situation exploded into revolution. One Sunday in January 1905, a crowd gathered outside the tsar's Winter Palace in St. Petersburg to try to make Nicholas aware of brutal working conditions. Instead of allowing the demonstration to pass, troops guarding the palace shot into the crowd, killing hundreds and wounding thousands. News of "Bloody Sunday" prompted turmoil across Russia, as workers struck over wages, hours, and factory conditions and demanded political representation in the government. They rejected the leadership of both Social Democrats and Social Revolutionaries and instead organized their own councils, called *soviets*. In February, Grand Duke Sergei, the tsar's uncle, was assassinated; in June, sailors on the battleship *Potemkin* mutinied; in October, a massive railroad strike brought rail transportation to a halt and the Baltic states and Transcaucasia rebelled; and in November, uprisings broke out in Moscow. Professionals and the upper classes joined the assault on autocracy, demanding a

The Russian Revolution of 1905

constitutional monarchy and a representative legislature. They believed the reliance on censorship and the secret police that was characteristic of Romanov rule had relegated Russia to the ranks of the most backward states.

Impelled by the continuing violence, the tsar created a representative body— the Duma. Although very few could vote for representatives to the Duma, its mere existence, coupled with the right of public political debate, liberalized government and allowed people to present their grievances to a responsive body. Political parties took shape, and the Revolution of 1905 drew to an end. But people soon wondered whether anything had really changed. From 1907 to 1917, the Duma convened, but twice when the tsar disliked its recommendations, he sent the delegates home and forced new elections. Prime Minister Pyotr Stolypin (1863–1911), a successful administrator and landowner, was determined to eliminate one source of discontent by ending the *mir* system of communal farming, canceling the peasants' burden of redemption payments, and making loans available to peasants for the purchase of land. Although these reforms did not eradicate rural poverty, they did allow people to move to the cities in search of jobs, and they created a larger group of independent peasants. However, Stolypin took stern steps against political groups, urged more pogroms, and stepped up Russification. The industrial proletariat also grew, and another round of strikes broke out, culminating in a general strike in St. Petersburg in 1914. Despite the creation of the Duma and other reforms, the imperial government and the conservative nobility had no solution to the ongoing social turmoil and felt little inclination to share power. Their ineffectual response to the Revolution of 1905 would foster an even greater revolution in 1917, while ongoing domestic conflicts opened one of the roads to war.

Roads to World War I

Unsettled internal politics made the international scene increasingly dangerous, while imperial rivalries intensified antagonisms among European states. After centuries of global expansion, imperial adventure soured for Britain and France as the twentieth century opened, and being an imperial power proved difficult for such newcomers as Italy and Germany. As a result of imperial competition, one British economist wrote in 1902, "Diplomatic strains are of almost monthly occurrence between the Powers." Western nationalism in its many varieties swelled. In the spring of 1914, U.S. president Woodrow Wilson sent his trusted adviser Colonel Edward House abroad to assess the tensions among the European powers. "It is militarism run stark mad," House reported. Government spending on what people called the "arms race" stimulated European economies; but arms were not stockpiled only for economic growth. Europe was jittery, as it waged a growing number of wars to keep colonial peoples in line. In German East Africa, for example, colonial forces countered native resistance in 1905 with a scorched-earth policy, which eventually killed more than 100,000 Africans (see Map 19.2). The French closed the University of

Hanoi, executed Indochinese intellectuals, and deported thousands of suspected nationalists to maintain a tenuous grip on Indochina (see Map 19.3). A French general stationed there noted "the growing hatred that our subjects show toward us more and more." By 1914, the air was even more charged, with militant nationalism in the Balkan states and conflicts in domestic politics also setting the stage for war. Although historians have long debated whether World War I could have been avoided, they have had to content themselves with tracing the steps Europeans took along the road toward mass destruction.

Competing Alliances and Clashing Ambitions

As the twentieth century opened, an alliance system first established by Bismarck to ensure the peaceful consolidation of the new German Empire and to maintain European stability was changing rapidly. Anxious about the Balkans and Russian leadership of the Slavs, Austria-Hungary had entered a defensive alliance with Germany in 1879. The Dual Alliance, as it was called, offered protection against Russia, which appeared to threaten Hungarian control of its Slavic peasantry. In 1882, Italy joined this partnership (henceforth called the Triple Alliance), largely because of Italy's imperial rivalries with France, but Bismarck also signed the Reinsurance Treaty (1887) with Russia to stifle Habsburg illusions about having a free hand against rivals for Slavic loyalty. Bismarck intended these alliances to show that Germany was now a "satisfied" nation and one that hoped to prevent further destabilizing wars.

Bismarck's delicate alliance started unraveling, however, when a blustering but deeply insecure young kaiser, William II, mounted the German throne in 1888. Advisers flattered the twenty-nine-year-old into thinking that his own personal talent made Bismarck a hindrance, even a rival. William II (r. 1888–1918) dismissed Bismarck in 1890 and, because he ardently supported German nationalism and thus the alliance with a supposedly kindred Austria-Hungary, let the alliance with Russia lapse, driving the Russians to ally with the French. Next, Germany under William II became "dissatisfied" with its international status and inflamed rather than calmed the diplomatic atmosphere. Convinced of British hostility toward France and emboldened by Germany's growing industrial might, the kaiser used the opportunity presented by the defeat of France's ally Russia in the Russo-Japanese War to contest French claims in Morocco, brashly landing his own ship in Morocco in 1905 to challenge personally French predominance. To resolve what became known as the First Moroccan Crisis, an international conference met in Spain in 1906. Instead of awarding Germany new territory, the powers supported French rule. The French and British military, faced with German aggression in Morocco, drew closer together. When the French finally took over Morocco in 1911, Germany triggered the Second Moroccan Crisis by sending a gunboat to the port of Agadir and demanding concessions from the French (see Map 19.2). This time no power—not even

Austria-Hungary—backed the German move or acknowledged this dominant country's economic might.

William's brazen diplomatic demands were predicated on imperial rivalry between France and Britain, which seemed to preclude an alliance between these traditional enemies. Constant rivals in Africa, Britain and France had edged to the brink of war in 1898 at Fashoda in the Sudan (see Map 19.2). The French government, however, backed away, and both nations were frightened into getting along for mutual self-interest. To prevent another Fashoda, they entered into secret agreements, the first of which (1904) guaranteed British claims in Egypt and French claims in Morocco. This agreement marked the beginning of the British-French alliance called the *Entente Cordiale*. After the Moroccan incident, the British and French made binding military provisions for the deployment of their forces in case of war, strengthening the Entente Cordiale. Thus two opposing alliance systems were now in place.

Smarting from its setbacks on the world stage, Germany refocused on its role in continental Europe. German statesmen began envisioning the creation of a *Mitteleuropa* that included central Europe, the Balkans, and Turkey under their sway. Russia, however, saw itself as the protector of Slavs in the region and wanted to replace the Ottomans as the dominant Balkan power, especially after Japan had crushed its hopes for expansion to the east. In 1877–1878, in the Russo-Turkish War, Russia had helped Bulgaria, Bosnia-Herzegovina, Serbia, and Montenegro in their revolts against the declining Ottoman Empire. Although Bulgarian independence was rolled back by the great powers, Serbia and Montenegro became fully independent. Austria's swift annexation of Bosnia-Herzegovina during the Young Turk revolt in 1908 enraged not only the Russians but the Serbs as well, because these southern Slavs wanted Bosnia as part of an enlarged Serbia. The Balkans thus whetted many appetites, and the region was ripe for war (Map 19.4).

Even without the greedy eyes cast on the Balkans by outside powers, the situation would have been extremely complex given the tensions created by political modernity and the lure of national independence. By the early twentieth century, the Balkan states, composed of several ethnicities as well as Orthodox Christians, Roman Catholics, and Muslims, sought more Ottoman and Habsburg territory that included their own ethnic group—a complicated desire given the mixed ethnicities of every region. In the First Balkan War, in 1912, Serbia, Bulgaria, Greece, and Montenegro joined forces to gain Macedonia and Albania from the Ottomans. The victors divided up their booty but soon turned against one another. Serbia, Greece, and Montenegro contested Bulgarian gains in the Second Balkan War in 1913. Much to Austrian dismay, these allies won a quick victory, though Austria-Hungary managed in the peace terms to prevent Serbia from annexing parts of Albania. Grievances between the Serbs and the Habsburgs, who feared that any disturbance in the Balkan balance of power would encourage ethnic rebellion at home, now seemed irreconcilable, and angry Serbs looked to Russia for help.

■ MAP 19.4 The Balkans, 1908–1914

Balkan peoples—mixed in religion, ethnicity, and political views—were successful in developing and asserting their desire for independence, especially in the First Balkan War, which claimed territory from the Ottoman Empire. Their increased autonomy sparked rivalries among them and continued to attract attention from the great powers. Three empires in particular—the Russian, Ottoman, and Austro-Hungarian—simultaneously sought greater influence for themselves in the region, which became a powder keg of competing ambitions.

The Race to Arms

In the nineteenth century, global rivalries and aspirations for national greatness made constant readiness for war seem increasingly necessary. On the seas and in foreign lands, the colonial powers battled to establish control, and they developed railroad, telegraph, and telephone networks everywhere to link their conquests and to move troops as well as commerce. Governments began to conscript ordinary citizens for periods of two to six years into large standing armies, in contrast to smaller eighteenth-century forces that had served the more limited military goals of the time. By 1914, escalating tensions in Europe boosted the annual intake of conscripts: Germany, France, and Russia called up 250,000 or more troops each year; Austria-Hungary and Italy, about 100,000. Per capita expenditures on the military rose in all the major powers between 1890 and 1914; the proportion of national budgets devoted to defense in 1910 was lowest in Austria-Hungary at 10 percent and highest in Germany at 45 percent.

The modernization of weaponry also transformed warfare. Swedish arms manufacturer Alfred Nobel (1833–1896) patented dynamite and developed a kind of gunpowder that improved the accuracy of guns and produced a less cloudy battlefield environment by reducing smoke from the process of firing. The industrial revolution in chemicals affected long-range artillery, which by 1914 could fire on targets as far as six miles away. Greater accuracy and heavy firepower made military offensives more difficult to win than in the past because neither side could overcome such weaponry. Military leaders devised strategies to protect their armies from overwhelming firepower. In the Russo-Japanese War, Chinese defenders dug trenches and strung barbed wire in an attempt to hold on to Port Arthur. In that conflict and in the Boer War, new weapons were used, including howitzers, Mauser rifles, and Hotchkiss machine guns. Munitions factories across Europe manufactured ever-growing quantities of these weapons.

Naval construction also played a major role in nationalist politics. To defend against more powerful, accurate weaponry, ships were made of metal rather than wood after the mid-nineteenth century. In 1905, the English launched the HMS *Dreadnought*, a warship with unprecedented firepower and the centerpiece of a program to update the British navy by constructing at least seven battleships per year. Germany followed British naval building step by step and made itself a force to be feared not just on land but also at sea. Grand Admiral Alfred von Tirpitz (1849–1930) encouraged the insecure William II to see the navy as the essential ingredient needed to make Germany a world power and oversaw an immense buildup of the fleet. Tirpitz admired the American naval theorist Alfred Thayer Mahan (1840–1914) and planned to build bases as far away as the Pacific, following Mahan's conclusion that command of the seas had historically been the key factor in determining international power. The German drive to build battleships further motivated Britain to ally with France in the Entente Cordiale. Britain raised its naval spending from $50 million per year in the 1870s to $130 million in 1900; Germany, from $8.75 million to $37.5 million; France, from $37 million to $62.5 million. The Germans announced the fleet buildup as "a peaceful policy," but, like the British buildup, it led only to a hostile international climate and intense competition in weapons manufacture.

Military policy was made with the use of public relations campaigns and an eye on internal politics. When critics of the arms race suggested a temporary "naval holiday" to stop British and German shipbuilding, British officials opposed the moratorium by warning that it "would throw innumerable men on the pavement." Colonial leagues, nationalist organizations, and other patriotic groups lobbied for military spending, while enthusiasts in government publicized large navies as beneficial to international trade and domestic industry. To enlarge the German fleet, Tirpitz made sure the German press connected the buildup to the cause of national power and pride. The press accused Social Democrats, who wanted an equitable tax system more proportionate to wealth, of being unpatriotic. The Conservative Party in Great Britain, eager for more battleships, made popular the slogan "We want eight and we won't wait." The remarks of one military leader typified the sentiments of the time, even among the public at large. When asked in 1912 about his predictions for war and peace, he responded enthusiastically, "We shall have war. I will make it. I will win it."

1914: War Erupts

June 28, 1914, began as an ordinary day for Austria's Archduke Francis Ferdinand and his wife, Sophie, as they ended a state visit to Sarajevo in Bosnia. Wearing full military regalia, the archduke was riding in a motorcade to bid farewell to various officials when a group of young Serb nationalists threw bombs in an unsuccessful assassination attempt. The full danger did not register, and after a stop the archduke and his wife set out again. In the crowd was another nationalist, Gavrilo Princip, who for several weeks had traveled clandestinely to reach this destination, dreaming of reuniting his homeland of Bosnia-Herzegovina with Serbia and smuggling weapons with him to accomplish his end. The unprotected and unsuspecting couple became Princip's victims, as he shot both dead.

■ **Archduke Francis Ferdinand and His Wife in Sarajevo, June 1914**
Archduke Francis Ferdinand, heir to the Austro-Hungarian monarchy, was a thorn in the side of many politicians because he did not want to favor Hungarian interests over other ethnic interests in his kingdom. His own family life was also unusual for royalty in those days: his wife, Sophie, and he had married for love and did not like to be apart. They were traveling together to Bosnia in 1914. The double assassination was the immediate prelude to the outbreak of World War I. (Mary Evans Picture Library.)

Some in the Habsburg government saw an opportunity to put down the Serbians once and for all. Evidence showed that Princip had received arms and information from Serbian officials who directed a terrorist organization from within the government. Endorsing a quick defeat of Serbia, German statesmen and military leaders urged the Austrians to be unyielding and reiterated promises of support in case of war. The Austrians sent an ultimatum to the Serbian government, demanding public disavowals of terrorism, suppression of terrorist groups, and the participation of Austrian officials in an investigation of the crime. The ultimatum was severe. "You are setting Europe ablaze," the Russian foreign minister remarked of the humiliating demands made upon a sovereign state. Yet the Serbs were conciliatory, accepting all the terms except one—the presence of Austrian officials in the investigation. Kaiser William was pleased: "A great moral success for Vienna! All reason for war is gone." His relief proved unfounded. Confident of German backing, Austria-Hungary used the Serbs' resistance to that one demand as the pretext for declaring war against Serbia on July 28.

Complex and ineffectual maneuvering now consumed statesmen, some of whom tried very hard to avoid war. The tsar and the kaiser sent pleading letters to one another not to start a European war. The British foreign secretary proposed an all-European conference, but to no avail. Germany displayed firm support for Austria in hopes of convincing the French and British to shy away from the war. The failure of either France or Britain to fight, German officials believed, would keep Russia from mobilizing. At the same time, German military leaders had become fixed on fighting a short, preemptive war that would provide territorial gains leading toward the goal of a *Mitteleuropa*. Furthermore, martial law would justify the arrest of the leadership of the German Social Democratic Party, which posed a threat to conservative rule.

The European press caught the war fever of the expansionist, imperialist, and other pro-war organizations, even as many governments were torn over what to do. Likewise, military leaders, especially in Germany and Austria-Hungary, promoted mobilization rather than diplomacy in the last days of July. The Austrians declared war and then ordered mobilization on July 31 without fear of a Russian attack. They did so in full confidence of German military aid, because as early as 1909 the German chief of staff Helmuth von Moltke had promised that his government would defend Austria-Hungary, believing Russia would not dare intervene. But Nicholas II ordered the Russian army to mobilize in defense of Russia's Slavic allies, the Serbs. Encouraging the Austrians to attack Serbia, the German general staff mobilized on August 1.

German strategy was based on the Schlieffen Plan, named after its author, Alfred von Schlieffen, a former chief of the general staff. The plan outlined a way to combat antagonists on two fronts by concentrating on one foe at a time. First would come a rapid and concentrated German blow to the west against Russia's

IMPORTANT DATES

1870s–1914	Vast emigration from Europe continues; the new imperialism	**1903**	Emmeline Pankhurst founds the Women's Social and Political Union to fight for woman suffrage in Great Britain
1882	Triple Alliance formed among Germany, Austria-Hungary, and Italy	**1904–1905**	Japan defeats Russia in the Russo-Japanese War
1882–1884	Bismarck sponsors social welfare legislation in Germany	**1905**	Revolution erupts in Russia; violence forces Nicholas II to establish an elected body, the Duma; Albert Einstein publishes his special theory of relativity
1884	Reform Act doubles the size of the male electorate in Britain		
1884–1885	European nations carve up Africa at the Berlin conference	**1906**	Women receive the vote in Finland
1889	Socialists meet in Paris and establish the Second International	**1907**	Pablo Picasso launches cubism with his painting *Les Demoiselles d'Avignon* and other works
1894–1899	Dreyfus Affair lays bare anti-Semitism in France		
1899–1902	Boer War fought between Dutch descendants and the British in South African states	**1908**	Young Turks revolt against rule by the sultan in the Ottoman Empire
1900	Sigmund Freud publishes *The Interpretation of Dreams*	**1911–1912**	Revolutionaries overthrow the Qing dynasty and declare China a republic
1901	Irish National Theater established by Maud Gonne and William Butler Yeats	**1914**	Assassination of the Austrian archduke Francis Ferdinand and his wife by a Serbian nationalist precipitates World War I

ally France, which would lead to France's defeat in six weeks; accompanying that strike would be a light holding action to the east. With France beaten, German armies in the west would then be deployed against Russia, which, German war planners believed, would be slow to mobilize. The attack on France was to proceed through Belgium, whose neutrality was guaranteed by the European powers. Events did not occur as the Germans hoped. The Belgian government rejected an ultimatum to allow the uncontested passage of the German army through the country, and Germany's subsequent violation of Belgium's neutrality brought Britain into the war on the side of Russia and France, which already was mobilizing in support of its ally Russia.

■ MAPPING THE WEST Europe at the Outbreak of World War I, August 1914

All the powers expected a great, swift victory when war broke out. Sharing borders, many saw a chance to increase their territories; and as rivals for trade and empire, they were almost all convinced that war would bring them many advantages. But if the European powers appeared well prepared and invincible at the start of the war, relatively few would survive the conflict intact.

Conclusion

Rulers soon forgot their last-minute hesitation in the general celebration that erupted with the war. "Old heroes have reemerged from the books of legends," wrote a Viennese actor after watching the troops march off. "A mighty wonder has taken place, we have become *young*." Both sides exulted, believing in certain victory and a resolution to tensions ranging from the rise of the working class to political problems caused by global imperial competition.

Imperialism and the arms race had stimulated militant nationalism and brought many Europeans to favor war over peace. The crisis of modernity had helped blaze the path to war. Facing continuing violence in politics, incomprehensibility in the arts, and problems in the industrial order, Europeans had come to believe that war would set events back on course and save them from the perils of modernity. "Like men longing for a thunderstorm to relieve them of the summer's sultriness," wrote one Austrian official, "so the generation of 1914 believed in the relief that war might bring." Such a possibility caused Europeans to rejoice. But instead of bringing the refreshment of summer rain, war opened an era of political turmoil, widespread suffering, massive human slaughter, and even greater doses of modernity.

Suggested References for further reading and online research appear on page SR-30 at the back of the book.

www.bedfordstmartins.com/huntconcise   See the ONLINE STUDY GUIDE to assess your mastery of the material covered in this chapter.

War, Revolution, and Reconstruction

1914–1929

J ULES AMAR FOUND HIS TRUE VOCATION in World War I. A French expert on making industrial work more efficient, Amar switched focus after 1914 as hundreds of thousands of men returned from the battlefront missing body parts. Plastic surgery developed rapidly, as did the construction of masks and other devices to hide deformities. Amar, who designed artificial limbs and appendages in these traumatic years, sought to devise prostheses that would allow the wounded soldier to return to normal life by "mak[ing] up for a function lost, or greatly reduced." So the arms that he designed used hooks, magnets, and other mechanisms with which the veteran could hold a cigarette, play a violin, and most important work with tools such as typewriters. Mangled by the weapons of modern technological warfare, the survivors of World War I would be made whole, it was thought, by technology such as Amar's.

Amar dealt with the human tragedy of the "Great War," so named by contemporaries because of its staggering human toll—forty million wounded or killed in battle. The Great War was also what historians call a "total war," meaning one built on full mobilization of soldiers, civilians, and the technological capacities of the most highly industrialized nations. The Great War did not settle problems or restore social order as the European powers hoped it would. Instead, the war produced political cataclysm, overturning the Russian, German, Ottoman, and Austro-Hungarian Empires. The crushing burden of war on the European powers

■ **Grieving Parents**
Before World War I, the German artist Kaethe Köllwitz gained her artistic reputation with wood-cuts of handloom weavers whose livelihoods were threatened by industrialization. From 1914 on, she depicted the suffering and death that swirled around her and never with more sober force than in these two monuments to her son Peter, who had died on the western front in the first months of battle. Today one can still travel to his burial place in Vladslo, Belgium, to see this father and mother mourning their loss, like millions across Europe in those heartbreaking days.
(The John Parker Picture Library.)

accelerated the rise of the United States, while service in the war intensified the demands of colonized peoples for autonomy.

For all the vast changes that the Great War ushered in, it also hastened transformations under way before it started. Nineteenth-century optimism, already on the decline, gave way to postwar cynicism. Many Westerners turned their backs on politics and attacked life with frenzied gaiety in the Roaring Twenties, snapping up new consumer goods, drinking in entertainment provided by films and radio, and enjoying personal freedoms that Victorianism had forbidden. Others found reason for hope in the new political systems the war made possible: Soviet communism and Italian fascism. Modern communication technologies such as radio gave politicians the means to promote a mass politics that ironically was often antidemocratic, militaristic, and eventually totalitarian.

Seen as a solution to the conflicts of modernity, a war that was long anticipated and even welcomed in some quarters destabilized Europe and the rest of the world far into the next decades. From statesmen to ordinary citizens, many Europeans like Amar would devote their peacetime efforts to making war-ravaged society function normally, while others saw that task as utterly futile, given the globally transformative force of the Great War.

The Great War, 1914–1918

When war erupted in August 1914, the ground had been prepared with long-standing alliances, the development of strategies for war, and the buildup of military technologies such as heavy artillery, machine guns, and the airplane. Seeing precedents in Prussia's rapid victories in the 1860s and 1870 and the swift blows that Japan dealt Russia in 1904–1905, most people felt that the conflict would be short and decisive. But the unforeseen happened: the war lasted for more than four years, and it was a total war, mobilizing entire societies and producing the unprecedented horror that made it "great."

Blueprints for War

World War I pitted two sets of opponents formed roughly out of the alliances developed during the previous fifty years. On one side stood the Central Powers (Austria-Hungary and Germany), which had evolved from Bismarck's Triple Alliance. On the other side stood the Allies (France, Great Britain, and Russia), which had emerged as a bloc from the Entente Cordiale between France and Great Britain and the 1890s treaties between France and Russia. In 1915, Italy, originally part of the Triple Alliance, joined the Allies in hopes of postwar gain. The two sides expanded globally almost from the start: in late August 1914, Japan, eager to extend its empire into China, went over to the Allies; in the fall the Ottoman Empire united with the Central Powers against its traditional enemy, Russia (see Map 20.1).

The same ferocious hunger for power, prestige, and prosperity that had inspired imperialism motivated the antagonists. Germany aspired to a far-flung empire to be gained by annexing Russian territory and incorporating parts of Belgium, France, and Luxembourg. Some German leaders wanted to annex Austria-Hungary as well. Austria-Hungary hoped to retain its great-power status in the face of competing nationalisms within its borders. Among the Allies, Russia wanted to reassert its status as a great power and as the protector of the Slavs by adding a reunified Poland to the Russian Empire and by taking formal leadership of other Slavic peoples. France, too, craved territory, especially the return of Alsace and Lorraine, taken after the Franco-Prussian War, to secure its boundaries with Germany. Britain sought to cement its hold on Egypt and the Suez Canal, as well as to secure the rest of the British world empire. By the Treaty of London (1915), France and Britain promised Italy territory in Africa, Asia Minor, the Balkans, and elsewhere in return for joining the Allies.

The colonial powers enlisted or conscripted tens of thousands of colonized men into their military forces. Britain deployed Indian regiments in western Europe in the first days of the war and enlisted Arabs against the Turks. France relied heavily on Senegalese and North African recruits, promising them French citizenship for their service. Germany used colonial soldiers in Europe and later in Africa and Asia.

From the start, machine guns and rifles, airplanes, battleships, submarines, and motorized transport—cars and railroads—were at the disposal of the armies. As the war proceeded, chlorine gas, tanks, bombs, and other new technologies would develop. The war itself became a lethal testing ground, as both new and old weapons were used, often ineffectively. Despite the availability of the new, more lethal technology, an old-fashioned vision of warfare made many officers unwilling to abandon sabers, lances, bayonets, and cavalry charges. Officers on both sides believed in a "cult of the offensive": they were sure that spirited attacks and high troop morale would be decisive. They were mistaken. In the face of massive firepower, the "cult of the offensive" would cost millions of lives.

Battlefronts

The first months of the war crushed hopes for a quick victory. All the major armies mobilized rapidly. Guided by the Schlieffen Plan (see page 858), the Germans quickly reached Luxembourg and Belgium and expected unchallenged passage through them and into France. Tricked by German diversionary tactics, the main body of French troops attacked the Germans in Alsace and Lorraine instead of meeting the invasion from the north. The Schlieffen Plan disintegrated when the Belgians unexpectedly resisted, slowing the German advance and allowing British and French troops to reach the northern front. In September, British and French armies engaged the Germans along the Marne River in France. Neither side could defeat the other, and the number of casualties was shocking: in the first three months of

■ **The Toll of Trench Warfare**

On both sides, the war took an enormous toll in male lives, leaving politicians and citizens alike concerned about society's future. Depictions of bodies shattered by heavy firepower, however, rarely reached the home front, so the illusions that the war was about individual prowess and that individual soldiers had a fighting chance of survival remained intact. Troops from the colonies were often depicted as bringing an innate savagery to the battlefront, although these soldiers had even less chance of surviving because usually they were placed in the front lines.

(Left: Imperial War Museum, London; right: Robert Hunt Library.)

war, more than 1.5 million men fell on the western front alone. Firepower turned what was supposed to be an offensive war of movement into a stationary, defensive impasse along a line stretching from the North Sea through Belgium and northern France to Switzerland. Deep within parallel trenches dug along this western front, soldiers lived a nightmarish existence (Map 20.1).◆

On the eastern front, the "Russian steam-roller"—so named because of the number of men mobilized, some twelve million in all—drove far more quickly than expected into East Prussia. The Russians believed that no army could withstand their massive numbers, no matter how ill equipped and poorly trained Russian forces were. The Germans, however, crushed the tsar's army in East Prussia and turned south to Galicia. Victory boosted German morale and made heroes of the military leaders Paul von Hindenburg (1847–1934) and Erich Ludendorff (1865–1937). But despite heartening victories, by year's end German triumphs in the east had failed to knock out the Russians and also had undermined the

◆ For German and British accounts of the experience of the battlefront, see Document 64, Fritz Franke and Siegfried Sassoon, "Two Soldiers' Views of the Horrors of War."

■ MAP 20.1 The Fronts of World War I, 1914–1918

Fighting on all fronts destroyed portions of Europe's hard-won industrial and agricultural capacity. Because the western front remained relatively stationary, the devastation of land and resources in northern and eastern France was especially intense. Men engaged in trench warfare developed an intense camaraderie based on their mutual suffering and deprivation.

Schlieffen Plan, which called for only a light holding action in the east until the western front had been won.

War at sea proved equally indecisive. Confident in Britain's superior naval power, the Allies blockaded ports to prevent supplies from reaching Germany and Austria-Hungary. William II and his advisers planned a massive submarine, or

U-boat (*Unterseeboot*, "underwater boat"), campaign against Allied and neutral shipping around Britain and France. In May 1915, German submarines sank the British passenger ship *Lusitania* and killed 1,198 people, including 124 Americans. Despite U.S. outrage, Woodrow Wilson (1856–1924; president 1913–1921) maintained a policy of U.S. neutrality; Germany, unwilling to provoke Wilson further, called off unrestricted submarine warfare. In May 1916, the navies of Germany and Britain finally clashed in the North Sea at the inconclusive battle of Jutland, which demonstrated that the German fleet could not master British seapower (see Map 20.1).

Ideas of a negotiated peace were discarded: "No peace before England is defeated and destroyed," the kaiser railed against his cousin King George V. "Only amidst the ruins of London will I forgive Georgy." French leadership called for a "war to the death." General staffs continued to prepare fierce attacks several times a year. Indecisive campaigns opened with heavy artillery pounding enemy trenches and gun emplacements. Troops then scrambled "over the top" of their trenches, usually to be mowed down by machine-gun fire from defenders secure in their own trenches. On the western front, throughout 1915 the French assaulted the enemy in the north to drive the Germans from industrial regions, but they accomplished little, and casualties of 100,000 and more during a single campaign became commonplace. On the eastern front, Russian armies captured parts of Galicia in the spring of 1915 and lumbered toward Hungary. The Central Powers struck back in Poland later that year, bringing the front closer to Petrograd (formerly St. Petersburg), the Russian capital.

The next year was even more disastrous. To cripple French morale, the Germans launched massive assaults on the fortress at Verdun, firing as many as a million shells in a single day. Combined French and German losses totaled close to a million men. Nonetheless, the French held. Hoping to relieve their allies, the British unleashed an artillery pounding of German trenches in the Somme River region in June 1916. In several months of battle at the Somme, 1.25 million men were killed or wounded, but the final result was stalemate. By the end of 1916, the French had absorbed more than 3.5 million casualties. To help the Allies engaged at Verdun and the Somme, the Russians struck again, driving once more into the Carpathians, recouping territory, and menacing the Habsburg Empire. Only the German army stopped the Russian advance.

Had military leaders thoroughly dominated the scene, historians judge, all armies would have been demolished in nonstop offensives by the end of 1915. Yet ordinary soldiers in this war were not automatons in the face of what seemed to them suicidal orders. For long periods of time, some battalions experienced hardly any casualties. These low rates stemmed from agreements among troops to avoid battles. Enemies facing each other across the "no man's land" separating the trenches frequently ate their meals in peace even though the trenches were within hand grenade reach. Throughout the war, soldiers on opposing sides fraternized. During pauses in the fighting, they played an occasional game of soccer, shouted to each other across the battlefield, exchanged mementos, and made gestures of agreement not to fight. One British veteran of the trenches explained to a new recruit that the Germans "don't want to fight any more than we do, so there's a kind of understanding between us. Don't fire at us and we'll not fire at you." Burying enemy dead in common graves with their own fallen comrades, many ordinary soldiers came to feel more warmly toward enemies who shared the trench experience than toward uncomprehending civilians back home.

Newly forged bonds of male camaraderie alleviated some of the misery of trench life and aided survival. The sharing of the danger of death and the deprivations of front-line experience weakened traditional class distinctions. Some upper-class officers and working-class draftees became friends in that "wholly masculine way of life uncomplicated by women," as one soldier put it. Soldiers picked lice from one another's bodies and clothes, revered section leaders who tended their blistered feet, and came to love one another, sometimes even passionately. Positive memories of this front-line sense of community survived the war and influenced postwar politics.

Troops of colonized soldiers from Asia and Africa had different experiences, especially because they were often put in the very front ranks where the risks were greatest. European observers noted that these soldiers suffered particularly from the rigors of a totally unfamiliar climate and strange food as well as from the ruin inflicted by Western war technology. Yet, like class divisions, racial barriers sometimes fell—for instance, whenever a European understood enough to alleviate the distress that cold inflicted. The perspectives of colonial troops changed, too, as they saw their "masters" completely undone and "uncivilized." When fighting did break out, trenches became a veritable hell of shelling and sniping, flying body parts, rotting cadavers, and blinding gas. Some soldiers were reduced to hysteria or were shell-shocked by the violence of battle. Alienation and cynicism helped others to cope: "It might be me tomorrow," a young British soldier wrote his mother in 1916. "Who cares?" Soldiers who had gone to war to escape ordinary life in industrial society learned, as one German put it, "that in the modern war . . . the triumph of the machine over the individual is carried to its most extreme form." They took this hard-won knowledge into battle, pulling their comrades back when an offensive seemed lost or too costly.

The Home Front

World War I was taking place off the battlefield, too. Even before the war reached the stage of catastrophic impasse, it was "total." Total war meant the indispensable involvement of civilians in war-related industry: manufacturing shells and machine guns, poisonous gases, bombs and airplanes, and eventually tanks. The increased production of coffins, canes, wheelchairs, and the artificial limbs devised by the likes of Jules Amar was also a wartime necessity. Civilians had to work overtime for, believe in, and sacrifice for victory. To keep the war machine operating smoothly, governments oversaw factories, transportation systems, and resources ranging from food to coal to textiles. Before the war, such tight government control would have outraged many liberals, but now it was accepted as a necessary condition for victory.

At first, political parties put aside their differences. Many socialists and working-class people who had criticized the military buildup announced their support for the war. For decades, socialist parties had preached that "the worker has no country" and that nationalism was mere ideology meant to keep workers disunited and subject to the will of their employers. In August 1914, however, the socialist rank and file, along with most of the party leaders, became as patriotic as the rest of society. Feminists divided over whether to maintain their traditional condemnation of militarism or to support the war. Although many feminists actively opposed the conflict, Emmeline Pankhurst and her daughter Christabel were among those who became militant nationalists, even changing the name of their suffrage paper to *Britannia*. Parties representing the middle classes shelved their distrust of the socialists and working classes. In the name of victory, national leaders wanted to end political division of all kinds: "I no longer recognize [political] parties," William II declared on August 4, 1914. "I recognize only Germans."

Governments mobilized the home front with varying degrees of success. All countries were caught without ready replacements for their heavy losses of weapons and military equipment and soon also felt the shortage of food and labor. War ministries set up boards to allocate labor on the home front and the

■ **War Propaganda, 1915**

"Never Forget!" screams the headline of this propaganda poster depicting an assaulted woman in despair. Intended to incite sentiment against the Germans, the poster suggests what German passage through neutral Belgium came to be called—"the rape of Belgium." Propaganda offices for the Allies sent out reports of women attacked and children massacred as the German armies moved through Belgian territories.

(Mary Evans Picture Library.)

battlefront and give industrialists financial incentives to encourage productivity. Emergency measures in several countries allowed the drafting of both men and women for military or industrial service, further blurring distinctions between military and civilian life. In Russia, however, the bureaucracy only reluctantly and ineffectively cooperated with industrialists and other groups that could aid the war effort. Desperate for factory workers, the Germans forced Belgian citizens to move to Germany, housing them in prison camps. In the face of rationing, municipal governments set up canteens and day-care centers. Rural Russia, Austria-Hungary, Bulgaria, and Serbia, where youths, women, and old men struggled to sustain farms, had no such relief programs.

Governments throughout Europe passed sedition laws that made it a crime to criticize official policies. To ensure civilian acceptance of longer working hours and shortages of consumer goods, governments created propaganda agencies to tout the war as a patriotic mission to resist villainous enemies. British propagandists fabricated atrocities that the German "Huns" supposedly committed against Belgians, and German propaganda warned that French African troops would rape German women if Germany was defeated. In Russia, Nicholas II changed the German-sounding name of St. Petersburg to the Russian Petrograd in 1914.

Playing on fears and arousing hatred, propaganda rendered a compromise peace unlikely. Nonetheless, some individuals sought to shatter the nationalist consensus supporting the war. In 1915, activists in the international women's movement met in The Hague, site of late-nineteenth-century peace conferences, in their own effort to end the war. "We can no longer endure . . . brute force as the only solution of international disputes," declared Dutch physician Aletta Jacobs. Despite their lack of success, many spent the remainder of the war urging statesmen to work out a peace settlement. In Austria-Hungary, nationalist groups agitating for ethnic self-determination hampered the empire's war effort. The Czechs undertook a vigorous anti-Habsburg campaign at home, while exiled politicians in Paris established the Czechoslovak National Council to lobby Western governments for recognition of Czech rights. In the Balkans, Croats, Slovenes, and Serbs formed a committee to plan a South Slav state carved from Habsburg possessions and other Balkan territory. The Allies encouraged such independence movements as part of their strategy to defeat the Habsburgs.

The war upset the social order as well as the political one. In the war's early days, many women had lost their jobs when luxury shops, textile factories, and other nonessential establishments closed. With men at the front, many women headed households with little support and few opportunities to work. But governments and businesses soon recognized the amount of labor it would take to wage technological war. As more and more men left for the trenches, women who had lost their jobs in nonessential businesses as well as many low-paid domestic workers took over higher-paying jobs in formerly restricted munitions and metallurgical

■ **German Welder Being Trained**
As men were siphoned off to the battle-front in World War I, women took their places in factories and transportation and service industries—working over-time to supply the insatiable needs of modern, technological warfare. Women thus gained higher pay and learned new productive skills such as welding. A new working-class woman emerged from the experience of war.
(Ullstein Bilderdienst.)

industries. In Warsaw, they drove trucks, and in London, they worked as streetcar conductors. Some young women nursed the wounded near the front lines.♦

Women's assumption of men's jobs looked to many like the reversal of traditional gender roles. From the start, a steady flood of wounded and weakened men returned home to women who had adapted resourcefully and taken full charge. Workingmen commonly protested that women, in the words of one metalworker, were "sending men to the slaughter." Men feared that when the war was over women would remain in the workforce, robbing them of their role as breadwinner. Many people, even some women, objected to women's loss of femininity. "The feminine in me decreased more and more, and I did not know whether to be sad or glad about this," wrote one Russian nurse about learning to wear rough male clothing near the battlefield. Others criticized young female munitions workers for squandering their pay on ribbons and jewelry and echoed other prewar gender tensions.

♦ For an interview with a French female factory worker, see Document 65, L. Doriat, "Women on the Home Front."

Although many soldiers from different social backgrounds felt bonds of solidarity in the trenches, wartime conditions increasingly pitted civilians against one another or against the government. Workers toiled longer hours eating less, while many in the upper classes bought abundant food and fashionable clothing on the black market (outside the official system of rationing). Governments allowed many businesses high rates of profit, a step that resulted in a surge in the cost of living and thus contributed to social strife. Shortages of staples like bread, sugar, and meat grew worse as the brutal "turnip winter" of 1916–1917—when turnips were often the only available food—progressed. A German roof workers' association pleaded for relief: "We can no longer go on. Our children are starving." Civilians in occupied areas and in the colonies suffered the most oppressive working conditions. The combatants deported or conscripted able-bodied people in territories they occupied. The French forcibly transported some 100,000 Vietnamese to work in France for the war effort. Africans also faced grueling forced labor along with skyrocketing taxes and prices. All such actions, like increasing class divisions, led to further politicization.

1917–1918: Protest, Revolution, and War's End

By 1917, the situation was becoming desperate, and discontent on the home front started shaping the course of the war. Neither patriotic slogans before the war nor propaganda during it had prepared people for wartime suffering. Cities across Europe experienced civilian revolt; soldiers mutinied, and nationalist struggles continued to plague Britain and Austria-Hungary. Soon revolution was sweeping Europe, toppling the Russian dynasty for good.

War Protest

On February 1, 1917, the German government, hard-pressed by public clamor over mounting casualties and by the military's growing control over decision making, resumed unrestricted submarine warfare. The military made the irresistible promise to end the war in six months by cutting off imported food and military supplies to Britain and thus forcing the island nation to surrender before the United States could come to its rescue. The British responded by mining harbors and the seas and by developing the convoy system of shipping, in which a hundred or more warships and freighters traveling the seas together could drive off the submarines. The Germans' submarine gamble failed to thwart the British. Moreover, unrestricted submarine warfare brought the United States into the war in April 1917, after German U-boats had sunk several American ships.

Political opposition increased in Europe, and deteriorating living conditions sparked outright revolt by civilians. "We are living on a volcano," warned an Italian politician in the spring of 1917. High prices and food shortages plagued everyday life. Food shortages in the cities of Italy, Russia, Germany, and Austria provoked riots by women who were unable to feed their families. As inflation mounted, tenants conducted rent strikes, factory hands and white-collar workers alike walked off the job, and female workers protested the skyrocketing cost of living and their fatigue from overwork. Amid protest, the new emperor of Austria-Hungary secretly asked the Allies for a negotiated peace to avoid a total collapse of his empire. In the summer of 1917, the German Reichstag made peace overtures. Woodrow Wilson further weakened civilian resolve in Germany and Austria-Hungary in January 1918 by issuing his Fourteen Points, a blueprint for a new international order that held out the promise of a nonvindictive peace settlement to war-weary citizens of the Central Powers. The Allies, too, faced dissent. In the spring of 1917, French soldiers mutinied against further bloody and fruitless offensives. In Russia, wartime protest turned into outright revolution.

Revolution and Civil War in Russia

Of all the warring nations, Russia sustained the greatest number of casualties—7.5 million by 1917. Slaughter on the eastern front drove hundreds of thousands of peasants into the Russian interior, bringing hunger, homelessness, and disease. In March 1917, crowds of workingwomen swarmed the streets of Petrograd demanding relief from harsh conditions, and soon factory workers and other civilians joined them. Russia's comparative economic underdevelopment made the demands of the war impossible to meet. Instead of remaining loyal to the tsar, many in the army were embittered by the massive casualties caused by their inferior weapons and their leaders' foolhardy tactics.

Since the Revolution of 1905, the masses had become politicized and increasingly willing to protest the government's incompetence, in particular Nicholas II's ineptitude. Unlike other heads of state, Nicholas failed to unify the bureaucracy and his peoples in a concerted wartime effort. Grigori Rasputin, a combination of holy man and charlatan, held Nicholas and his wife, Alexandra, in his thrall by claiming to control the hemophilia of their son and heir. Rasputin's disastrous influence on state matters led educated and influential leaders to withdraw their support. When riots erupted in March 1917, Nicholas abdicated, and the three-hundred-year-old Romanov dynasty came to an end.

Politicians from the old Duma formed a new ruling entity called the Provisional Government. At first, hopes were high that under the Provisional Government, as one revolutionary poet put it, "our false, filthy, boring, hideous life should become a just, pure, merry, and beautiful life." Composed essentially of moderates, the Provisional Government had to pursue the war successfully, manage internal affairs better, and set government on a firm constitutional footing to establish its credibility. However, it did not rule alone, for the Russian Revolution felt the tug of many different political forces. Spontaneously elected soviets—councils of workers and soldiers—competed with the government for political support. Born during the Revolution of 1905, the soviets campaigned to end the deference society usually paid the wealthy and officers, urged respect for workers and the poor, and temporarily gave an air of celebration and carnival to this political cataclysm. The peasantry, another force competing for power, began to confiscate gentry estates and withhold produce from the market because of the lack of consumer goods for which to exchange food. Urban food shortages intensified.

In hopes of further destabilizing Russia, in April 1917 the Germans provided safe rail transportation for Lenin and other prominent Bolsheviks to return from exile through German territory. Lenin had devoted his entire existence to bringing about socialism through the force of his small band of Bolsheviks, and as a political exile he had no parliamentary experience. Upon his return to Petrograd, Lenin issued the April Theses, a radical document that called for Russia to withdraw from

■ **Lenin Addressing the Second All-Russian Congress of Soviets**
In the spring of 1917, the German government craftily let Lenin and other Bolsheviks travel from their exile in Switzerland back to the scene of the unfolding revolution in Russia. A committed revolutionary instead of a political reformer, Lenin used oratory and skillful maneuvering to convince many in the soviets to follow him in overthrowing the Provisional Government, taking Russia out of the war, and implementing his brand of communism. (Novosti, London.)

the war, for the soviets to seize power on behalf of workers and poor peasants, and for all private land to be nationalized. The Bolsheviks aimed to supplant the Provisional Government with the slogans "All power to the soviets" and "Peace, land, and bread."

Time was running out for the Provisional Government, which saw a battlefield victory as the only way to ensure its position. On July 1, the Russian army attacked the Austrians in Galicia but was defeated once again (see Map 20.1). The new prime minister, the Socialist Revolutionary Aleksandr Kerensky (1881–1970), used commanding oratory to arouse patriotism but lacked the political skills to fashion an effective wartime government. In November 1917, the Bolshevik leadership, urged on by Lenin, seized power on behalf of a congress of soviets while simultaneously asserting its own right to form a government. When elections for a constituent assembly in January 1918 failed to give the Bolsheviks a plurality, the party used troops to disrupt the assembly and took over the government by force. They seized town and city administrations, closing down the *zemstvos* (local councils) and other institutions in the countryside where opposition support was keen. In the winter of 1918–1919, the Bolshevik government, observing Marxist doctrine, abolished private property and nationalized factories in order to restore production, which had fallen off precipitously. The Provisional Government had allowed both men and women to vote in 1917; Russia was thus the first great power to legalize universal suffrage—a hollow privilege once the Bolsheviks limited electoral slates to candidates from the Communist Party.

The Bolsheviks asked Germany for peace and agreed to the Treaty of Brest-Litovsk (March 1918), which placed vast regions of the old Russian Empire under German occupation (Map 20.2). The treaty partially realized the German ideal of a central European region, or *Mitteleuropa,* under German control. Because the loss of millions of square miles put Petrograd at risk, the Bolsheviks relocated the capital to Moscow and formally adopted the name *Communists* (taken from Marx's writings) to distinguish themselves from the socialists and social democrats who had voted for the disastrous war in the first place. Lenin agreed to the catastrophic terms of the treaty not only because he had promised to bring peace to Russia but also because he believed that the rest of Europe would soon rebel against war and overthrow the capitalist order.

Resistance to Bolshevik policies mushroomed into a civil war in which the pro-Bolsheviks (or "Reds") faced an array of antirevolutionary forces (the "Whites"). On the White side, the tsarist military leadership, composed of many landlords and supporters of aristocratic rule, fielded whatever troops it could muster. Dispossessed businessmen and the liberal intelligentsia soon lent their support. Many non-Russian nationality groups, formerly incorporated into the empire through force, Russification, and other bureaucratic efforts, fought the Bolsheviks because they saw their chance for independence. Before World War I ended, Russia's former allies, notably the United States, Britain, France, and Japan, landed troops in the coun-

■ **MAP 20.2 The Russian Civil War, 1917–1922**

Nationalists, aristocrats, middle-class citizens, and property-owning peasants tried to combine their interests to defeat the Bolsheviks, but they failed to create an effective political consensus. The result was more suffering for ordinary people, whose produce was confiscated to fight the civil war. The Western powers and Japan also sent in troops to put down this revolution that so threatened the economic and political order.

try both to block the Germans and to stop Bolshevism. To compete effectively with the Bolsheviks, the counterrevolutionary groups desperately needed a strong leader and unified goals. Instead, the groups competed with one another: the pro-tsarist forces, for example, alienated those aspiring to nation-state status, such as the Ukrainians, Estonians, and Lithuanians. Ultimately, without a common purpose or unified command, the opponents of revolution could not win.

The civil war shaped communism. Leon Trotsky (1879–1940), Bolshevik commissar of war, built the highly disciplined Red Army by ending democratic procedures, such as the election of officers, that had originally attracted soldiers to Bolshevism. Lenin and Trotsky introduced the policy of war communism, whereby urban workers and troops moved through the countryside, brutally confiscating grain from the peasantry to feed the army and workforce. The Cheka (secret police) set up detention camps for political opponents and black marketeers and shot many of them without trial. The expansion of the size and strength of the Cheka and the Red Army—the latter would eventually number five million men—accompanied the expansion of the bureaucracy, making government more authoritarian and undermining the promise of Marxism that revolution would bring a "withering away" of the state.

As the Bolsheviks clamped down on opposition during the bloody civil war, they organized their supporters to foster revolutionary Marxism across Europe. In March 1919, they founded the Third International, also known as the Comintern (Communist International) for the explicit purpose of replacing the old International with a centralized organization dedicated to preaching communism. By mid-1921, the Cheka had shored up Bolshevism in Russia, and the Red Army had secured the Crimea, the Caucasus, and the Muslim borderlands. When the Japanese withdrew from Siberia in 1922, the civil war ended in central and east Asia. The Bolsheviks were now in charge of a state as multinational as the old Russian Empire had been (see Map 20.2).

The Russian Revolution led by the Bolsheviks promised bold experiments in social and political leadership. The revolution turned out the inept Romanovs and the privileged aristocracy, but the civil war turned Russia into a battlefield stalked by disease, hunger, and death. Moreover, the brutal way in which the Bolsheviks came to power—by crushing their opponents—ushered in a political style and direction far different from earlier socialist hopes.

Ending the War: 1918

Having pulled Russia out of World War I, the Bolsheviks left the rest of Europe's leaders confronting a new balance of forces. Facing war protest as well, these leaders also were left fearing that communism might lie in their future.

In the spring of 1918, the Central Powers made one final attempt to smash through the Allied lines, but the offensive ground to a bloody halt within weeks. By then, the British and French had started making limited but effective use of tanks supported by airplanes. Although the first tanks were cumbersome, their ability to withstand machine-gun fire made offensive attacks possible. In the summer of 1918, the Allies, now fortified by the Americans, pushed back the Germans all along the western front and headed toward Germany. The German armies, suffering more than two million casualties between spring and summer, rapidly disintegrated.

By October 1918, the desperate German command helped create a civilian government, hoodwinking inexperienced politicians to take responsibility for the defeat and to sue for peace. Deflecting blame from the military, generals proclaimed themselves still fully capable of winning the war. Weak-willed civilians, they claimed, had dealt the military a "stab in the back" that forced a surrender. Amid this blatant political deceit, naval officers called for a final sea battle, sparking mutiny against what the sailors saw as a suicide mission. The sailors' revolt spread to the workers, who demonstrated in Berlin, Munich, and other major German cities. The uprisings provoked Social Democratic politicians to declare a German republic in an effort to prevent revolution. On November 9, 1918, Kaiser William II fled as Germans declared a republic and the Central Powers collapsed on all fronts. Since the previous winter, Austria-Hungary had kept many combat divisions at home simply to maintain civil order. At the end of October, Czechs and Slovaks had declared an independent state, and the Croatian parliament simultaneously announced Croatia's independence.

Finally, on November 11, 1918, at 5:00 A.M., an armistice was signed. The guns fell silent on the western front six hours later. In the course of four years, European civilization had been sorely tested, if not shattered. Conservative figures put the battlefield toll at a minimum of ten million deaths and thirty million wounded, incapacitated, or eventually to die of their wounds. In every European combatant country, industrial and agricultural production had plummeted, and much of the reduced output had been put to military use. Asia, Africa, and the Americas, which depended on European trade, also felt the painful impact of Europe's declining production. From 1918 to 1919, the weakened global population suffered an influenza epidemic that left at least twenty million more dead.

Moral questioning accompanied the suffering. Soldiers returning home in 1918 and 1919 flooded the book market with their memoirs, trying to give meaning to their experiences. Whereas many had begun by emphasizing heroism and glory, others were cynical and bitter by war's end. They insisted the fighting had been meaningless. Total war had drained society of resources and population and had inadvertently sown the seeds of future catastrophes.

The Search for Peace in an Era of Revolution

Amid the quest for peace, revolutionary fervor swept the continent of Europe, especially in the former empires of Germany and Austria-Hungary. Until 1921, the triumph of socialism seemed plausible, as many of the newly independent peoples of eastern and central Europe fervently supported socialist principles. The revolutionary mood captured workers and peasants in Germany, too. In contrast, many liberal and right-wing opponents hoped for a political order based on military authority of the kind they had relied on during the war. Faced with a volatile mix of revolution and counterrevolution, diplomats from around the world arrived in Paris in January 1919 to negotiate the terms of peace, often without recognizing the magnitude of the changes brought about by war.

Europe in Turmoil

Urban people and returning soldiers ignited the protest that swept Europe in 1918 and 1919. In January 1919, the red flag of socialist revolution flew from city hall in Glasgow, Scotland, while in cities of the collapsing Austro-Hungarian Empire workers set up councils to direct factory production and to influence politics. Many soldiers did not disband at the armistice but formed volunteer armies, making Europe ripe not for parliamentary politics but for revolution by force.

Germany was politically unstable, partly because of the shock of defeat. Independent socialist groups and workers' councils vied with the dominant Social Democrats for control of the government, and workers and veterans took to the streets to demand food and back pay. Whereas in 1848 revolutionaries had marched to city hall or the king's residence, these protesters took over newspapers and telegraph offices, thus controlling the flow of information. Some were inspired by one of the most radical socialist factions, the Spartacists, led by cofounders Karl Liebknecht (1871–1919) and Rosa Luxemburg (1870–1919). Unlike Lenin, the two Spartacist leaders favored political uprisings that would give workers political experience and thus eliminate the need for an all-knowing party leadership. They argued for *direct* worker control of institutions, but they shared Lenin's dislike for parliamentary politics.

Social Democratic leader Friedrich Ebert (1871–1925), who headed the new government, shunned revolution and supported the creation of a parliamentary republic. Splitting with his former socialist allies, he called on the German army and the Freikorps—a roving paramilitary band of students, demobilized soldiers, and others—to suppress the workers' councils and demonstrators. He thus gave official credence to the idea that political differences could be settled with violence. "The enthusiasm is marvelous," wrote one young soldier. "No mercy's shown. We shoot even the wounded. . . . We were much more humane against the French in the field." Protest continued even as a constituent assembly meeting in the city of Weimar in February 1919 approved a constitution and founded a parliamentary republic. This time the right rebelled, for the military leadership dreamed of a restored monarchy: "As I love Germany, so I hate the Republic," wrote one officer. Facing a military coup by Freikorps officers, Ebert called for a general strike that abruptly averted a takeover by showing the lack of popular support for a military regime. In so doing, the Weimar Republic had set the dangerous precedent of relying on street violence, paramilitary groups, and protests to solve political problems.

Revolutionary activism surged and was smashed. Late in the winter of 1919, leftists proclaimed soviet republics—governments led by workers' councils—in Bavaria and Hungary. These soon fell before the assault of the volunteer armies and troops. The Bolsheviks tried to establish a Marxist regime in Poland in the belief that its people wanted a workers' revolution. Instead, the Poles resisted and drove the Red Army back in 1920, while the Allied powers rushed supplies and advisers to Warsaw (see Map 20.2). Though this and other revolts failed, they provided further proof that total war had loosened political and social order.

The Paris Peace Conference, 1919–1920

As political turmoil engulfed peoples from Berlin to Moscow, the Paris peace conference opened in January 1919. Visions of communism spreading westward haunted the assembled statesmen, but the desperation of millions of war-ravaged citizens, the status of Germany, and the reconstruction of a secure Europe topped their agenda. Leaders such as French premier Georges Clemenceau needed to satisfy their angry citizens, who demanded revenge or, at the very least, compensation for their suffering. France had lost 1.3 million people—almost an entire generation; and more than a million buildings, six thousand bridges, and thousands of miles of railroad lines and roads had been destroyed while the war was fought on French soil. Great Britain's representative, Prime Minister David Lloyd George, caught the mood of the British public by campaigning in 1918 with such slogans as "Hang the kaiser." Italians arrived on the scene demanding the territory promised to them in the 1915 Treaty of London. Meanwhile, U.S. president Woodrow Wilson, head of the new world power that had helped achieve the Allied victory, had his own agenda. His Fourteen Points, on which the truce had been based, was steeped in the language of freedom and called for open diplomacy, arms reduction, an "open-minded" settlement of colonial issues, and the self-determination of peoples.

The Fourteen Points did not represent the mood of the victors, however. Allied propaganda had made the Germans seem like inhuman monsters, and many citizens demanded a harsh peace. Moreover, some military experts feared that Germany was using the armistice only to regroup for more warfare. Indeed, Germans widely refused to admit that their army had lost the war. Eager for army support, Ebert had given returning soldiers a rousing welcome: "As you return unconquered from the field of battle, I salute you." Thus, conservative leaders among Wilson's former allies campaigned to make him look naive and deluded. "Wilson bores me with his Fourteen Points," Clemenceau complained. "Why, the good Lord himself has only ten."

Nevertheless, Wilson's Fourteen Points appealed to European moderates and persuaded Germans that the settlement would not be vindictive. His commitment to *settlement* as opposed to *surrender* contained tough-minded stipulations, for Wilson wisely recognized that Germany was still the strongest state in Europe. He merely pushed for a treaty that balanced the strengths and interests of various European powers. Economists and other specialists accompanying Wilson to Paris agreed that, harshly dealt with and humiliated, Germany might soon become vengeful and chaotic.

After six months, the statesmen and their teams of experts produced the Peace of Paris (1919–1920), composed of a cluster of individual treaties. These treaties shocked the countries that had to accept them, and in retrospect historians see how they destabilized eastern and east-central Europe (Map 20.3). The treaties separated Austria from Hungary, reduced Hungary by almost two-thirds of its inhabitants and three-quarters of its territory, broke up the Ottoman Empire, and treated Germany severely. They replaced the Habsburg Empire with a group of small, internally divided, and relatively weak states: Czechoslovakia, Poland, and the Kingdom of the Serbs, Croats, and Slovenes, soon renamed Yugoslavia. After a century and a half of partition, Poland was reconstructed from parts of Russia, Germany, and Austria-Hungary; one-third of its population was ethnically non-Polish. The statesmen in Paris also created a Polish Corridor that connected Poland to the Baltic

■ MAP 20.3 Europe and the Middle East after the Peace Settlements of 1919–1920

The political landscape of central, east, and east-central Europe changed dramatically as a result of the Russian Revolution and the Peace of Paris. The Ottoman, German, Russian, and Austro-Hungarian Empires were either broken up altogether into multiple small states or territorially reduced in size. The settlement left resentments among Germans and Hungarians and created a group of weak, struggling nations in the heartland of Europe. The victorious powers took over much of the oil-rich Middle East.

www.bedfordstmartins.com/huntconcise   See the ONLINE STUDY GUIDE for more help in analyzing this map.

Sea and separated East Prussia from the rest of Germany. Austria and Hungary were both left reeling at their loss of territory and resources. Many of the new states became rivals and were for the most part politically and economically weak.

The Treaty of Versailles with Germany was the centerpiece of the Peace of Paris, however. France recovered Alsace and Lorraine, and the victors would temporarily occupy the left, or western, bank of the Rhine and the coal-bearing Saar basin. Wilson accepted his allies' expectations that Germany would pay substantial reparations for civilian damage during the war. The specific amount was set in 1921 at the crushing sum of 132 billion gold marks. Germany also had to reduce its army, almost eliminate its navy, stop manufacturing offensive weapons, and deliver a large amount of free coal each year to Belgium and France. Furthermore, it was forbidden to have an air force and had to give up its colonies. The average German saw in these terms an unmerited humiliation that was compounded by Article 231 of the treaty, which described Germany's "responsibility" for damage "imposed . . . by the aggression of Germany and her allies." The outraged German people interpreted this as a "war guilt" clause, which allowed the victors to collect reparations from economically viable Germany rather than from decimated Austria. War guilt made Germany an outcast in the community of nations.

Besides redrawing the map of Europe, the Peace of Paris set up an organization called the League of Nations, whose responsibility for maintaining peace—a principle called *collective security*—was to replace the divisive secrecy of prewar power politics. As part of Wilson's vision, the league would guide the world toward disarmament, arbitrate its members' disputes, and monitor labor conditions around the world. Returning to prewar isolationism, the United States Senate, in a humiliating defeat for the president, failed to ratify the peace settlement and refused to join the league. Moreover, both Germany and Russia initially were excluded from the league and were thus blocked from acting in legal concert with other nations.

The covenant, or charter, of the League of Nations organized the administration of the colonies and territories of Germany and the Ottoman Empire—such as Togo, Cameroon, Syria, and Palestine—through a system of mandates (see "Mapping the West," page 905). The European powers exercised political control over mandated territory, but local leaders retained limited authority. The league covenant justified the mandate system as providing governance by "advanced nations" over territories "not yet able to stand by themselves under the strenuous conditions of the modern world." However, colonized and other people of color who had served on the battlefield began to challenge the claims of their European masters. They had seen how savage and degraded these people who claimed to be racially superior, politically more advanced, and leaders of global culture could be. "Never again will the darker people of the world occupy just the place they had before," the African American leader W. E. B. Du Bois predicted in 1918. The mandate system continued the practice of apportioning the globe among European powers, but like the Peace of Paris it aroused anger and resistance.

Economic and Diplomatic
Consequences of the Peace

The financial and political settlement in the Peace of Paris had repercussions in the 1920s and beyond. Western leaders worried deeply about two intertwined issues in the aftermath of the war. The first was economic recovery. France, the hardest hit by wartime destruction and billions of dollars in debt to the United States, estimated that Germany owed it at least $200 billion. The British, by contrast, worried about maintaining their empire and restoring trade with Germany, not about exacting huge reparations. Nevertheless, both France and Britain depended on some monetary redress to pay their war debts to the United States because Europe's share of world trade had plunged during the war.

Germany claimed that the demand for reparations strained its government, already beset by political upheaval. But hardship was not the result of the Peace of Paris alone. The kaiser had refused to raise taxes, especially on the rich, to pay for the war, so the new German republic had to pay reparations and to manage the staggering war debt. As an experiment in democracy, the Weimar Republic needed to woo the citizenry, not alienate it by hiking taxes. In 1921, when Germans refused to present a realistic payment scheme, the French occupied several cities in the Ruhr until a settlement was reached.

Embroiled with powers to the west, the German government deftly sought economic and diplomatic relations in eastern Europe. It reached an agreement to foster economic ties with Russia, desperate for western trade, in the Treaty of Rapallo (1922). Its relations with powers to the west, however, continued to deteriorate. In 1923, after Germany defaulted on coal deliveries, the French and Belgians sent troops into the Ruhr basin, planning to use its abundant resources to recoup their wartime expenditures. Urged on by the government, Ruhr citizens fought back, shutting down industry by staying home from work. The German government printed trillions of marks to support the workers and to pay its own war debts with practically worthless currency. Soon Germany was in the midst of a staggering inflation that demoralized its citizens and gravely threatened the international economy: at one point a single U.S. dollar cost 4.42 trillion marks, and wheelbarrows of money were required to buy a turnip. The spirit of the League of Nations demanded a resolution to this economic chaos through negotiations. The Dawes Plan (1924) and eventually the Young Plan (1929) reduced payments to the victors and restored the value of German currency. Nonetheless, the inflation had wreaked enduring psychological havoc, wiped out people's savings, and ruined those living on fixed incomes.

A second burning issue in addition to economic recovery involved ensuring that peace would last. Statesmen recognized that peace demanded disarmament, a return of Germany to the fold, and security for the new countries of eastern Europe. It took hard diplomatic bargaining outside the league to produce two plans in Germany's favor. At the Washington Conference in 1921, the United States, Great Britain, Japan, France, and Italy agreed to reduce their number of battleships and to stop constructing new ones for ten years. Four years later, in 1925, the league sponsored a meeting of the great powers, including Germany, at Locarno, Switzerland. The Treaty of Locarno provided Germany with a seat in the League of Nations as of 1926. In return, Germany agreed not to violate the borders of France and Belgium and to keep the nearby Rhineland demilitarized (unfortified by troops).

To the east, the door seemed open to a German attempt to regain territory lost to Poland, to form a merger with Austria, or to launch aggression against the states spun off from Austria-Hungary (see Map 20.3). To meet the threat, Czechoslovakia, Yugoslavia, and Romania formed the "Little Entente" in 1920–1921. This was a collective security agreement to protect themselves from their two powerful neighbors, Germany and Russia, and to guard against Hungarian expansionism. Then, between 1924 and 1927, France allied itself with the Little Entente and with Poland. The major European powers, Japan, and the United States also signed the Kellogg-Briand Pact (1928), which formally rejected international violence. The nations failed, however, to commit themselves to concrete action to prevent its outbreak.

The publicity and planning that yielded the international agreements during the 1920s sharply contrasted with old-style diplomacy, which was conducted in secret and subject to little public scrutiny or democratic influence. The development of a system of collective security and the new openness suggested a diplomatic revolution that would promote peace in international relations. Despite this promise, openness allowed diplomats of the era to feed the press reports calculated to arouse the masses. For example, much of the German populace was lashed into a nationalist frenzy by the press and opposing parties whenever Germany's diplomats, who were successfully working to undo the Treaty of Versailles, seemed to compromise. Although international meetings such as the one at Locarno appeared to promote the goal of collective security, they also exposed the diplomatic process to the nationalist press and to demagogues who could rekindle political hatreds.

A Decade of Recovery: Europe in the 1920s

The 1920s was devoted to coming to terms with the cultural and political legacy of the war. The wartime spirit endured in words and phrases from the battlefield that punctuated everyday speech. Before the war, the word *lousy* had meant "lice-infested," but English-speaking soldiers returning from the trenches now applied it to anything bad. Raincoats became *trenchcoats*, and terms like *bombarded* and *rank and file* entered peacetime usage. Maimed, disfigured veterans were present everywhere. Some used prostheses designed by Jules Amar; others without limbs were sometimes carried in baskets—hence the expression *basket case*. They overflowed hospitals and mental institutions, and family life centered on their care. Total war had generally strengthened military values, authoritarian government, and a

■ **Otto Dix, *The Sleepwalkers* (1928)**

Artists in the defeated countries were especially attuned to the tragic absurdity of the war. The German ex-soldier Otto Dix sketched smashed faces and corpses in varying states of decay, depicting people who survived as grotesque or benumbed "sleepwalkers" who picked their way through the postwar wreckage. The simple horror of death and disfigurement made painted whores of those seeking a return to ordinary life.

("The Sleepwalkers" by Otto Dix from *The Nature of War* by John Keegan and Joseph Darracott [Holt, Rinehart and Winston, 1981]. Private Collection, Essen.)

controlled economy. A key question facing society was how to restore civilian government. Although contemporaries referred to the 1920s as the "Roaring Twenties" and the "Jazz Age," the sense of cultural release masked the serious problem of restoring social stability and implementing democracy. Four autocratic governments—in Germany, Austria-Hungary, Russia, and the Ottoman Empire—had collapsed as a result of the war, but how newly empowered citizens would act politically remained a burning question.

Changes in the Political Landscape across Europe

The threat of revolution coexisted with a sense of democratic rebirth because of the collapse of autocratic government and the extension of suffrage to women, widely granted at the war's end. Woman suffrage resulted in part from decades of activism; more immediately, many governments gave women the vote to reward them for their war efforts and to make revolution less tempting. In the first postwar elections, women were voted into parliaments, and the impression grew that they had also made extraordinary gains in the workplace. French men pointedly denied women the vote, insisting they would use their vote to bring

Women Gain Suffrage in the West	
1906	Finland
1913	Norway
1915	Denmark, Iceland
1917	Netherlands, Russia
1918	Czechoslovakia, Great Britain (limited suffrage)
1919	Germany
1920	Austria, United States
1921	Poland
1925	Hungary (limited suffrage)
1945	Italy, France
1971	Switzerland

back the rule of kings and priests. (Only at the end of World War II would France and Italy extend suffrage to women.) Governments continued building the welfare state by expanding payments to families with children and insurance programs for workers. New government benefits attested to a spreading belief that more evenly distributed wealth—sometimes referred to as *economic democracy*—was important to social stability in postwar society.

The slow trend toward economic democracy was not easy to maintain, however, because the cycles of boom and bust that had characterized the late nineteenth century reemerged. A short postwar boom prompted by rebuilding war-torn areas and filling consumer needs unsatisfied during the war was followed by an economic downturn that was most severe between 1920 and 1922. Skyrocketing unemployment led some to question the effectiveness of their governments and the fairness of society. By the mid-1920s, many of the economic opportunities for women had disappeared, and they made up a smaller percentage of the workforce than in 1913.

Hard times especially corroded the new republics of eastern Europe, which were unprepared for independence in the sophisticated world market. None but Czechoslovakia had a mature industrial sector, and agricultural techniques were often primitive. The development of Poland exemplified the postwar political landscape in eastern Europe. Nationalism was increasingly defined in ethnic terms, and the reunified Poland consisted of one-third Ukrainians, Belorussians, Germans, and other ethnic minorities—many of whom had grievances against the dominant Poles. Moreover, varying religious,

Polish	German
Czech	Latvian
Slovak	Lithuanian
Belorussian	Magyar (Hungarian)
Ukrainian	Romanian

National Minorities in Postwar Poland

dynastic, and cultural traditions divided the Poles, who for 150 years had been split among Austria, Germany, and Russia. Polish reunification occurred without a common currency, political structure, or language—even the railroad tracks were not a standard size.

With practically no economic or other support from the Allies, a constitutional government nonetheless took shape in this new Poland. Under a constitution that professed equal rights for all ethnicities and religions, the new democratic government, run by the Sejm (parliament), tried to legislate the redistribution of large estates to the peasantry, but declining crop prices and overpopulation made life in the countryside difficult. Urban workers were better off than the peasantry (two-thirds of the population lived by subsistence farming) but worse off than laborers across Europe. The economic downturn brought strikes and violence in 1922–1923, and the inability of coalition parliaments to effect economic prosperity led to a coup in 1926 by strongman Jozef Pilsudski. Economic hardship and strong-arm solutions went hand in hand in east-central Europe.

Germany was a different case. The industrially sophisticated Weimar Republic confronted daunting challenges to making Germany democratic, even after putting down the postwar revolution. Although the German economy picked up and Germany became a center of experimentation in the arts, political life remained precarious because so many people felt nostalgia for imperial glory and loathed the Versailles treaty's restrictions. On the surface, Weimar's political system—a bicameral parliament and a chancellor responsible to the lower house—appeared similar to the parliamentary system in Britain and France, but extremist politicians heaped daily abuse on parliamentary politics. Anyone who cooperated with the parliamentary system, wrote the wealthy newspaper and film magnate Alfred Hugenberg, "is a moral cripple." Right-wing parties favored violence rather than consensus building, and nationalist thugs murdered democratic leaders and Jews.

Support for the far right came from wealthy landowners and businessmen, white-collar workers whose standard of living had dropped during the war, and members of the lower-middle and middle classes hurt by inflation. Bands of disaffected youth and veterans proliferated, among them a group called Brown Shirts led by ex-soldier and political newcomer Adolf Hitler (1889–1945). In the wake of the Ruhr occupation of 1923, Ludendorff and Hitler launched a coup d'état from a beer hall in Munich. Government troops suppressed the Beer Hall Putsch, but Hitler spent less than a year in jail and Ludendorff was acquitted. For conservative judges as for former aristocrats and most of the prewar bureaucrats who remained in government, such men were national heroes.

In France and Britain, parties of the right had less effect than elsewhere because parliamentary institutions were better established and the upper classes were not plotting to restore an authoritarian monarchy. In France, politicians from the conservative right and moderate left successively formed coalitions and rallied general support to rebuild war-torn regions and to force Germany to pay for the reconstruction. Hoping to stimulate population growth after the devastating loss of life, the French parliament made distributing birth-control information illegal and abortion a severely punished crime.

Britain encountered postwar boom and bust and continuing strife in Ireland. Ramsay MacDonald, elected the first Labour prime minister in 1924, represented the newly formed political ambitions of the working masses. Like other postwar British leaders, he had to swallow the paradoxical fact that although Britain had the largest world empire, many of its industries were obsolete or in poor condition. A showdown came in the ailing coal industry, where prices fell and wages plummeted once the Ruhr mines reopened to offer tough competition to British mines. On May 3, 1926, workers launched a nine-day general strike against wage cuts and danger-ous conditions in the mines. The strike provoked unprecedented middle-class re-sistance. University students, homemakers, and businessmen shut down the strike by driving trains, working on docks, and replacing workers in other jobs. Thus cit-izens from many walks of life revived the wartime spirit to defend the declining economy.

In Ireland, the British government met bloody confrontation over the contin-uing failure to implement home rule. Irish republicans had attacked government buildings in Dublin on Easter Monday 1916 in an effort to wrest Irish independence from Brit-ain. The ill-prepared Easter Uprising was easily defeated, and many participants were executed. The severe punishment only intensified demands for home rule, and in January 1919, republican leaders announced Ireland's independence from Britain and created a separate parliament. The British government refused to recognize the par-liament and sent in the Black and Tans, a volun-teer army of demobilized soldiers so called for the color of their uniforms. Terror reigned in Ire-land, as both the pro-independence forces and the Black and Tans waged guerrilla warfare, tak-ing hostages, blowing up buildings, and even shooting into crowds at soccer matches. By 1921,

The Irish Free State and Ulster, 1921

public outrage forced the British to negotiate a treaty. It reversed the Irish declara-tion of independence and made the Irish Free State a self-governing dominion owing allegiance to the British crown. Northern Ireland, a group of six northern counties containing a majority of Protestants, gained a separate status: it was self-governing but still had representation in the British Parliament. Incomplete in-dependence and the rights of religious minorities remained contentious issues.

European powers encountered rebellion in overseas empires as well. Colonized peoples who had fought in the war expected more rights and even independence. Indeed, European politicians and military recruiters had actually promised the vote and many other reforms in exchange for support. But colonists' political activism, now enhanced by increasing education, trade, and experience with the West, mostly met a brutal response. Fearful of losing India, British forces massacred protesters at Amritsar in 1919 and put down revolts against the mandate system in Egypt and Iran in the early 1920s. The Dutch jailed political leaders in Indonesia; the French punished Indochinese nationalists. For many Western governments, maintaining empires abroad was crucial to ensuring democracy at home, for any hint of declining national prestige fed antidemocratic forces.

Reconstructing the Economy

New worldwide economic competition was as big a challenge to recovery as were global political struggles. During the war, the European economy had lost many of its international markets to India, Canada, Australia, Japan, and the United States. Nonetheless, the war had forced European manufacturing to become more efficient and had expanded the demand for automotive and air transport, electrical products, and synthetic goods. The prewar pattern of mergers and cartels continued after 1918, giving rise to gigantic food-processing firms such as Nestlé in Switzerland and petroleum enterprises such as Royal Dutch Shell. Owners of these large manufacturing conglomerates wielded more financial and political power than entire small countries. By the late 1920s, Europe had overcome the wild economic swings of the immediate postwar years and was enjoying renewed economic prosperity.

Despite this growth, the United States had become the trendsetter in economic modernization. Many European businessmen made pilgrimages to Henry Ford's Detroit assembly line, which by 1929 produced a Ford automobile every ten seconds. Ford touted this miracle of productivity as resulting in a lower cost of living and increased purchasing power for workers. Indeed, whereas French, German, and British citizens in total had under two million cars, some seventeen million cars were on U.S. streets in 1925.

Scientific management, sometimes called the science of work, also aimed to raise productivity. American efficiency expert Frederick Taylor (1856–1915) developed methods to streamline workers' tasks and motions for maximum productivity. European industrialists adopted Taylor's methods during the war and after, but they were also influenced by European psychologists who emphasized the mental aspects of productivity and the need for a balance of work and leisure activities, such as moviegoing and sports, for both workers and managers. In theory, increased productivity not only would produce prosperity for all but also would bind workers and management together, avoiding Russian-style worker revolution. In practice, streamlining did help reduce working hours in many industries, a result that encouraged union leaders to embrace modernization and the "cult of efficiency." For many workers, however, the emphasis on efficiency seemed inhuman; in some workplaces, the restrictions on time and motion were so severe that workers were allowed to use the bathroom only on a fixed schedule. "When I left the factory, it followed me," wrote one worker. "In my dreams I was a machine."

The managerial sector in industry had expanded during the war and continued to do so thereafter. Workers' initiative became devalued; managers alone were considered to be creative and innovative. Managers reorganized work procedures and classified workers' skills. They categorized as "female jobs" work that required less skill and therefore deserved lower wages, thus adapting the old segmentation of the labor market to the new working conditions. Because male workers' jobs were increasingly threatened by labor-saving machinery, unions usually agreed to hold down women's wages to keep women from competing with men for scarce high-paying jobs. Like the managerial sector, union bureaucracy had ballooned during World War I to help monitor labor's part in the war. Union bureaucrats became specialists: negotiators, membership organizers, educators and propagandists, and political liaisons. Playing a key role in politics, unions could mobilize masses of people, as they demonstrated when they blocked coups against the Weimar government in the 1920s and organized the 1926 general strike in Great Britain.

Restoring Society

With combined joy and trepidation, postwar society met the returning millions of brutalized, incapacitated, and shell-shocked veterans. Many veterans harbored hostility toward civilians, who had rebelled against wartime conditions, these soldiers charged, instead of patriotically enduring them. The places the veterans returned to differed from the homes they had left. Veterans often had no jobs. Some soldiers found that their wives and sweethearts had abandoned them—a wrenching betrayal of those who had risked their lives to protect the homeland.

The war had blurred class distinctions, giving rise to expectations that life would be fairer. The massive battlefield casualties had fostered social mobility, making it possible for commoners to move into the ranks of officers, positions often monopolized by the prewar aristocracy. Members of all classes had rubbed shoulders in the trenches. The identical, evenly spaced crosses in military cemeteries implied that all the dead were equal, as did the mass "brothers' graves" at the battlefront, in which rich and poor lay side by side in a single burial pit. On the home front, middle-class daughters worked outside the home, and their mothers did their own housework because their former servants could earn more money working in factories. Women of all classes had cut their hair, wore sleeker clothes, smoked, and had money of their own.

United by patriotism when the war erupted, civilians, especially women, sometimes felt estranged from these returning warriors, who had inflicted so much death and had lived daily with filth, rats, and decaying animal and human flesh. Civilian anxieties were often valid. Tens of thousands of German, central European, and Italian soldiers refused to disband; a few British veterans even vandalized university classrooms and assaulted women streetcar conductors and factory workers. Women who had served at the front could empathize with the soldiers' woes. But many suffragists in England, for instance, who had fought for an end to separate spheres before the war, now embraced gender segregation, so fearful were they of returning veterans.

Fearing the spread of Bolshevism, governments tried to make civilian life as comfortable as possible to reintegrate men into society and prevent revolution. Politicians believed in the stabilizing power of traditional family values and supported social programs such as pensions, benefits for out-of-work men, and housing for veterans to alleviate their pent-up anger. The new housing—"homes for heroes," politicians called the program—was a vast improvement over nineteenth-century working-class tenements. In Vienna, Frankfurt, Berlin, and Stockholm, modern housing projects provided common laundries, day-care centers, and rooms for group socializing. They featured gardens, terraces, and balconies to provide a soothing, country ambiance that offset the hectic nature of industrial life. Inside they boasted modern kitchens, indoor plumbing, central heating, and electricity. Imitating the clean lines of East Asian and African dwellings to create a sense of modernity, domestic architects avoided ornate moldings, plasterwork, and curlicues—now seen as "old-fashioned." Some architects, such as the Swiss-born French architect Le Corbusier (1887–1965), favored "high-rise" apartments that

■ **Le Corbusier's Paris of the Future**
While the war profoundly disillusioned many in the West, peace aroused utopian hopes for a better future. For modern architects like Swiss-born Le Corbusier (1887–1965), the "future city" and the "radiant city" would organize space, and thus life, for ordinary people. Horizontal windows, roof gardens, and very plain façades were hallmarks of this new design—a radical break with ornate prewar styles in building. (Fondation Le Corbusier/A.D.A.G.P.)

adapted the principles of New York's skyscrapers to the domestic environment and satisfied the criterion of urban planning that called for an efficient use of space.

Despite government efforts to restore traditional family values, war had dissolved many middle-class conventions, among them attempts to keep unmarried young men and women apart. Freer relationships and more open discussions of sex characterized the 1920s. Middle-class youth of both sexes visited jazz clubs and attended movies together. Revealing bathing suits, short skirts, and body-hugging clothing emphasized women's sexuality, seeming to invite men and women to join together and replenish the postwar population. Still, the context for sexuality remained marriage. In 1918, British scientist Marie Stopes published the best-seller *Married Love,* and in 1927, the wildly successful *Ideal Marriage: Its Physiology and Technique* by Dutch author Theodor van de Velde appeared. Both described sex in rhapsodic terms and offered precise information about birth control and sexual physiology. Changing ideas about sex were not limited to the middle and upper classes. One Viennese reformer described working-class marriage as "an erotic-comradely relationship of equals" rather than the economic partnership of past centuries. The flapper, a sexually liberated workingwoman, vied with the dedicated housewife to represent the ordinary woman in the public's eyes. Meanwhile, such writers as the Englishman D. H. Lawrence and the American Ernest Hemingway glorified men's sexual vigor in, respectively, *Women in Love* (1920) and *The Sun Also Rises* (1926). Mass culture's focus on heterosexuality encouraged the return to traditional social norms after the gender disorder that troubled the prewar and war years.

As images of men and women changed, people paid more attention to bodily improvement. The increasing use of toothbrushes and toothpaste, safety and electric razors, and deodorants reflected new standards of personal hygiene and grooming. For Western women, a multi-billion-dollar cosmetics industry sprang up almost overnight. Women went to beauty parlors regularly to have their short hair cut, set, dyed, conditioned, straightened, or curled. They also tweezed their eyebrows, applied makeup, and even submitted to cosmetic surgery. Ordinary women painted their faces as formerly only prostitutes had done and competed in beauty contests that judged physical appearance. Instead of wanting to look plump and prosperous, people aimed to become thin and tan. The proliferation of boxers, hikers, gymnasts, and tap dancers spurred people to exercise and to participate in amateur sports. Modern industry encouraged consumers' new focus on personal health, which coincided with the need for a physically fit workforce.

The strong economic upturn encouraged people to buy more and more consumer goods. Thanks to the gradual postwar increase in real wages, middle- and upper-class families snapped up sleek modern furniture, washing machines, and vacuum cleaners. Other modern conveniences such as electric irons and gas stoves appeared in better-off working-class households. Installment buying, popularized from the 1920s on, helped people finance these purchases. Housework became more mechanized, and family intimacy increasingly depended on machines of mass communication such as radios and phonographs, and on automobiles. These new products that transformed private life also brought unforeseen changes in the public world of culture and mass politics.

Mass Culture and the Rise of Modern Dictators

Wartime propaganda had aimed to unite all classes against a common enemy. In the 1920s, the merging of diverse groups into a homogeneous Western culture, increasingly seen as a "mass culture," continued. The homogenizing instruments—primarily radio, film, and newspapers—expanded their influence in the 1920s. Some intellectuals urged elites to form an experimental avant-garde and distance themselves from "the drab mass of society." Others wanted to use modern media and art to reach out to and even control the masses. The mass media had the potential for creating an informed citizenry and thus enhancing democracy. Paradoxically, in the troubled postwar climate, they also provided the tools for dictatorship. They made it possible for authoritarian rulers—Benito Mussolini, Joseph Stalin, and Adolf Hitler—to control the masses in unprecedented ways.

Culture for the Masses

An array of media had received a big boost from the war. Bulletins from the battlefront had whetted the public's craving for news and real-life stories, and sales of nonfiction books soared. After years of deprivation, people felt driven to achieve material success, and they devoured books that advised how to do so. Henry Ford's biography, a story of social mobility and technological accomplishment, became a best-seller in Germany. With postwar readers avidly pursuing practical knowledge, institutes and night schools became popular, and school systems promoted reading in geography, science, and history. Photographs, the radio, and movies also contributed to the formation of national culture.

In the 1920s, filmmaking changed from an experimental medium to a thriving international business, in which large corporations set up theater chains and marketed films worldwide. The war years, when the U.S. film industry began to outstrip the European, gave rise to specialization: directors, producers, marketers, photographers, film editors, and many others subdivided the process. A "star" system turned film personalities into celebrities, promoted by professional publicity and living like royalty. Films of literary classics and political events developed people's sense of a common heritage. Thus the British government sponsored documentaries that articulated national goals, and Bolshevik leaders backed the innovative work of director Sergei Eisenstein (1898–1948), whose films *Potemkin* (1925) and *Ten Days That Shook the World* (1927–1928) presented a Bolshevik view of history to Russian and international audiences.

Films incorporated familiar elements from other cultural forms to cement viewer loyalty. The piano accompaniment that went along with the action of silent films derived from music halls; comic characters, farcical plots, and slapstick humor were borrowed from street or burlesque shows and from trends in postwar living. The popular comedies of the 1920s poked fun at men's and women's feckless attempts to achieve emotional intimacy or featured the flapper and made her more visible to the masses. Lavish movie houses attracted some 100 million weekly viewers, most of them women. As the popularity of films and books crossed national borders, cosmopolitanism and culture for an international audience flourished.

Cinematic portrayals also played to postwar fantasies and fears. In Germany, where filmmakers used expressionist sets and costumes to make films frightening, the influential hit *The Cabinet of Doctor Caligari* (1919) depicted events in an insane asylum as horrifying symbols of state power. Popular detective and cowboy films portrayed heroes who could restore wholeness to the disordered world of murder, crime, and injustice. Depictions of the plight of gangsters appealed to veterans, whose combat experiences had raised questions about the value of life in the modern world. Charlie Chaplin (1889–1977), an English comedian, actor, and producer, created the character of the "Little Tramp," who won international popularity as the defeated hero, the anonymous modern man, trying to preserve his dignity in a mechanized world.

Film remained experimental well into the 1920s, but radio was even more so. Developed from Guglielmo Marconi's wireless technology introduced at the turn of the century, radio broadcasts in the first half of the 1920s were heard by mass audiences in public halls (much like movie theaters) and featured orchestras and song followed by audience discussion. The radio quickly became an affordable consumer item, and public concerts and lectures could then penetrate the individual's private living space. (See "Taking Measure," page 896.) Specialized programming for men (such as sports reporting) and for women (such as advice on home management) soon followed. By the 1930s, radio allowed politicians to reach the masses wherever they might be—even alone at home.

Cultural Debates over the Future

Cultural leaders in the 1920s had different visions of the future. Some were obsessed by the negative implications of the horrendous experience of war. Others—like modernists before the war—held high hopes for creating a fresh future that would bear little relation to the past.

The vision of those haunted by the war was bleak or violent. This outlook was especially a theme in German art. Kaethe Köllwitz (1867–1945), whose son died in the war, portrayed in her woodcuts bereaved parents, starving children, and other heartwrenching, antiwar images (see page 863). Other artists used satire, irony, and

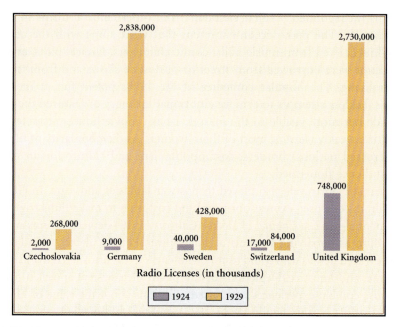

■ **TAKING MEASURE The Growth of Radio, 1924–1929**
The spread of radio technology, like the earlier development of printing, advanced the cultural and political unity of nation-states. The most rapid diffusion of radios occurred in the most industrially and commercially developed societies. At first, governments both programmed and taxed radios. Because of this centralized control and the paperwork it created, historians can compare the country-by-country use of radio in Europe and in much of the rest of the world.

flippancy to express postwar rage and revulsion at civilization's apparent failure. George Grosz (1893–1959), stunned by the carnage like so many other German veterans, joined Dada, an artistic and literary movement that had emerged during the war. Dadaists produced works marked by nonsense, incongruity, and shrieking expressions of alienation. Grosz's paintings and cartoons of maimed soldiers and brutally murdered women reflected his psychic wounds and his self-proclaimed desire "to bellow back." In the postwar years, the modernist desire to shock audiences intensified. Avant-garde portrayals of seediness and perversion in everyday life flourished in cabarets and theaters in the 1920s and reinforced veterans' visions of civilian decadence.

The art world itself became a battlefield, especially in defeated Germany, where art mirrored the Weimar Republic's contentious politics. Popular writers such as Ernst Jünger glorified life in the trenches and called for the militarization of society to restore order. Erich Maria Remarque cried out for an end to war in his controversial novel *All Quiet on the Western Front* (1928). This international best-seller depicted the life shared by enemies on the battlefield, thus aiming to dampen the national hatred stoked by wartime propaganda.

Poets reflected on postwar conditions in more general terms, using styles that rejected the comforting rhymes or accessible metaphors of earlier verse. T. S. Eliot, an American-born poet who for a time worked as a banker in Britain, portrayed postwar life as petty and futile in "The Waste Land" (1922) and "The Hollow Men" (1925). The Irish nationalist poet William Butler Yeats joined Eliot in mourning the replacement of traditional society, with its moral conviction and religious values, by a new, superficial generation gaily dancing to jazz and engaging in promiscuous sex and vacuous conversation. Yeats's "Sailing to Byzantium" (1928) starts:

> *That is no country for old men. The young*
> *In one another's arms, birds in the trees*
> *—Those dying generations*

Both poets had an uneasy relationship with the modern world and at times advocated authoritarianism rather than democracy.

The postwar arts produced many a utopian fantasy turned upside down; *dystopias* of life in postrevolutionary, traumatized Europe proliferated. In expressionist and bizarre stories, Franz Kafka, an employee of a large insurance company in Prague, showed the world as a vast, impersonal machine. His novels *The Trial* (1925) and *The Castle* (1926) evoked the hopelessness of individuals confronting a relentless, machinelike society in which they are minor cogs; his portrayal of postwar civilian life seemed to capture the helplessness that soldiers had felt at the front. As the old social order collapsed under the weight of political and technological innovation, other writers depicted the complex, sometimes nightmarish inner life of individuals. French author Marcel Proust, in his multivolume novel *Remembrance of Things Past* (1913–1927), explored the workings of memory, the passage of time, and sexual modernity through the life of his narrator. At the beginning of the first volume, the narrator is obsessed with his mother's absence as he tries to fall asleep at night. He witnesses progressively disturbing obsessions, such as violent sexuality and personal betrayals of love. The haunted inner life analyzed by Freud was infiltrating fiction: for Proust redemption lay in producing beauty from the raw material of life, not in promoting outmoded conventions of decency and morality.

The Irish writer James Joyce and the English writer Virginia Woolf shared Proust's vision of an interior self built on memories and sensations. Joyce in *Ulysses* (1922) and Woolf in *Mrs. Dalloway* (1925) illuminated the fast-moving inner lives of their characters in the course of a single day. In one of *Ulysses'* most celebrated passages, a long interior monologue traces a woman's lifetime of erotic and emotional sensations. Woolf believed that the war dissolved the solid society from which absorbing stories and fascinating characters were once fashioned. Her characters experience fragmented conversations, momentary sensations, and incomplete relationships.

The other view of the future focused not on the interior life of traumatized society but on the promise of technology. Avant-garde artists before the war had celebrated the new, the futuristic, the utopian. After the war, like Jules Amar crafting prostheses for shattered limbs, they were optimistic that technology could make an entire society whole. The aim of art, observed one of them, "is not to decorate

■ **Virginia Woolf**
Along with Marcel Proust and James Joyce, Virginia Woolf represented the peak of literary modernism with its emphasis on interior states of mind and disjointed, dreamlike slices of reality. Woolf's novels and essays also captured the unappreciated centrality of women, who provided an array of personal services to their more highly valued husbands. Woolf boldly announced that for a woman to be as creative as a man, she needed to be partially relieved of the burdens of family and to have "a room of [her] own."
(Gisele Freund/Photo Researchers, Inc.)

our life but to organize it." German architects and artists influenced by the Bauhaus school of design (after the idea of a craft association, or *Bauhütte*) created streamlined office buildings and designed functional furniture, utensils, and decorative objects, many of them inspired by forms from "untainted" East Asia and Africa. Russian artists, temporarily entranced by the Communist experiment, optimistically wrote novels about cement factories and created ballets about steel—an element common to artificial limbs and to advanced, utopian design.

Artists fascinated by technology and machinery were drawn to the most modern of all countries: the United States. Hollywood films, glossy advertisements, and the bustling metropolis of New York tempted careworn Europeans. They were especially attracted to jazz, the improvisational music emanating from Harlem. African American jazz musicians showed a resiliency of spirit, and performers such as Josephine Baker (1906–1976) and Louis Armstrong (1900–1971) became international sensations when they toured Europe's capital cities. Like jazz, the skyscrapers rising in New York provided Europeans with a potent example of avant-garde expression that rejected a terrifying past and boldly embraced the future.

The Communist Utopia

Communism also promised a shining future and a modern, technological culture. But the Bolsheviks encountered powerful obstacles to consolidating their rule. In the early 1920s, peasant bands called Green Armies revolted against the policy of war communism that permitted the government to seize agricultural produce. Industrial production stood at only 13 percent of prewar levels; the civil war had produced still more casualties; shortages of housing affected everyone; and millions of refugees clogged the cities and roamed the countryside. In the early spring of 1921, workers in Petrograd and sailors at the nearby naval base at Kronstadt revolted. They protested their short rations and the privileged standard of living that Bolshevik supervisors enjoyed, and they called for "soviets without Communists"— that is, a return to the early Bolshevik promise of a worker state.

The government had many of the rebels shot, but the Kronstadt revolt pushed Lenin to institute reform. His New Economic Policy (NEP) returned parts of the economy to the free market. This temporary compromise with capitalist methods allowed peasants to sell their grain freely and to profit from free trade in consumer goods. The state still controlled large industries and banking, but the NEP encouraged people to produce, sell, and even, in the words of one leading Communist, "get rich." Consumer goods and more food to eat soon became available. Some peasants and merchants did indeed get rich, but many more remained impoverished. The rise of "NEPmen," who bought and furnished splendid homes and who cared only about conspicuous consumption, belied the Bolshevik goal of a classless utopia.

Protest erupted within Communist ranks. At the 1921 party congress, a group called the Worker Opposition objected to the party's usurpation of economic control from worker organizations and pointed out that the NEP was an agrarian program, not a proletarian one. In response to such charges of growing bureaucratization, Lenin suppressed the Worker Opposition faction and set up procedures for purging dissidents. Bolshevik leaders also tightened their grip on politics by making the Communist revolution a cultural reality that would inform people's daily lives and reshape their thoughts. Party leaders invaded the countryside to set up classes in a variety of political and social subjects, and volunteers harangued the public about the importance of literacy—only 40 percent on the eve of World War I. To facilitate social equality between men and women, which was part of the Marxist vision of the future, the state made birth control, abortion, and divorce readily available. The commissar for public welfare, Aleksandra Kollontai (1872–1952), promoted birth-control education and the establishment of day care for children of working parents.

The bureaucracy swelled to bring modern culture to every corner of life. *Hygiene* and *efficiency* became watchwords, as they were in the rest of Europe. Such agencies as the Zhenotdel (Women's Bureau) sought to teach women about their rights under communism and about modern sanitary practices. Efficiency experts aimed to replace tsarist backwardness with technological modernity based on American techniques. The short-lived government agency Proletkult tried to develop proletarian culture through such undertakings as workers' universities, a workers' encyclopedia, a workers' theater, and workers' publishing. Russian artists experimented with blending high art and technology in mass culture, and composers punctuated their music with the sound of train or factory whistles. The poet Vladimir Mayakovsky edited a journal advocating utilitarian art, wrote verse praising his Communist passport and essays promoting toothbrushing, and staged uproarious farces for ordinary citizens.

■ **El Lissitzky, *Beat the Whites with the Red Wedge* (1919)**
Russian artist El Lissitzky traveled Europe to bring news of Soviet experimentation. In particular, the Soviets were taken with the new physics, and their works of art surrounded the viewer with geometric forms. But abstract art was also political: in this 1919 painting, the "red" wedge uses the force of physical principles to defeat the objectively greater counterrevolutionary power of the "whites."
(David King Collection.)

As with war communism, many resisted the reshaping of culture to "modern" or "Western" standards. Bolsheviks threatened everyday customs and the distribution of power within the family. As Zhenotdel workers moved into the countryside, for example, they attempted to teach women to behave as men's equals. Peasant families were still strongly patriarchal, however, and Zhenotdel activists threatened gender relations. In Islamic regions incorporated from the old Russian Empire into the new Communist one, Bolsheviks urged Muslim women to remove their veils and change their way of life, but fervent Muslims often attacked both Zhenotdel workers and women who followed their advice.

In the spring of 1922, Lenin suffered a debilitating stroke, and in January 1924, amid ongoing cultural experimentation, factional fighting, and repression, the architect of the Bolshevik Revolution died. The party congress declared the day of his death a permanent holiday, changed the name of Petrograd to Leningrad, and elevated the deceased leader into a secular god. After Lenin's death, no one was allowed to criticize anything associated with his name, a situation that paved the way for abuses of power by later Communist leaders.

Joseph Stalin (1879–1953), who held the powerful position of general secretary of the Communist Party, led the deification of Lenin. Organizing the Lenin cult and dealing with thousands of local party officials gave Stalin the opportunity to dispense an enormous amount of patronage, and his welding in 1924 of Russian and non-Russian regions into the Union of Soviet Socialist Republics gave him a claim to executive accomplishment. Wary of Stalin's growing influence and ruthlessness, Lenin in his last will and testament had asked that "the comrades find a way to remove Stalin." Stalin, however, discredited Leon Trotsky, his chief rival, and prevented Lenin's will from being publicized. Bringing in several hundred thousand new party members who owed their positions in government and industry to him, Stalin by 1928–1929 was advancing toward complete dictatorship in the USSR.

Fascism on the March in Italy

Political chaos and postwar discontent brought Benito Mussolini (1883–1945) to power in Italy. Like the Bolsheviks, he promised an efficient utopia. Italian ire was first aroused when the Allies at Paris refused to honor the territorial promises of the Treaty of London. Domestic unrest swelled when peasants and workers protested their economic plight, made worse by the slump of the early 1920s. Since the late nineteenth century, many Europeans had come to blame parliaments for their ills. So Italians were responsive when Mussolini, a socialist journalist who turned to the radical right, built a personal army (the Black Shirts) of veterans and the unemployed to overturn parliamentary government. In 1922, his supporters, known as Fascists, started a march on Rome, forcing King Victor Emmanuel III (r. 1900–1946) to make the dynamic Mussolini prime minister.

The Fascist movement flourished in the soil of poverty, social unrest, and wounded national pride. It attracted to its bands of Black Shirts many young men who felt cheated of glory by the Allies and veterans who missed the vigor of military life. The *fasces*, an ancient Roman symbol depicting a bundle of sticks wrapped around an ax with the blade exposed, served as the movement's emblem; to Mussolini's supporters it represented both unity and force. Unlike Marxism, fascism scoffed at coherent ideology: "Fascism is not a church," Mussolini announced upon taking power in 1922. "It is more like a training ground." Fascism was thus defined by its political grounding in an instinctual male violence and its opposition to the "antinationalist" socialist movement and parliamentary rule.◆

Mussolini consolidated his power by making criticism of the state a criminal offense and by violently steamrolling parliamentary opposition. Fascist bands demolished socialist newspaper offices, attacked striking workers, used their favorite tactic of forcing castor oil (which causes diarrhea) down the throats of socialists, and even murdered certain powerful opponents. Yet this brutality and the sight of the Black Shirts marching through the streets like disciplined soldiers signaled to many Italians that their country was ordered and modern. Large landowners and businessmen approved Fascist attacks on strikers and financially supported the movement. Their generous funding allowed Mussolini to build a large staff by hiring the unemployed and thus fostering the belief that Fascists could spark the economy when no one else could.

In addition to violence, Mussolini used mass propaganda and the media to foster support for a kind of military campaign to remake Italy. Peasant men huddled around radios to hear him call for a "battle of wheat" to enhance farm productivity. Peasant women, responding to his praise of maternal duty, adored him for appearing to value womanhood. In the cities, the government launched avant-garde architecture projects, designed new statues and public adornments, and used public

---

◆ For a primary source that details Mussolini's political theory, see Document 66, Benito Mussolini, "The Doctrine of Fascism."

■ **Mussolini and the Black Shirts**
For movements like fascism, the best society was one controlled by militarized politics that killed its critics and political opponents. Fascism saw parliamentary democracies as effeminate and doomed in the modern world, which would need dictators and obedient warriors to make it strong, efficient, and machinelike. Thus, in the name of promoting state power, Mussolini gained adherents both within and outside of Italy. (Farabolafoto.)

relations promoters to advertise its achievements. Mussolini claimed that he made the trains run on time, and this one triumph of modern technology fanned people's hopes that he could restore order out of wartime and postwar chaos.

Mussolini added a strong dose of traditional values and prejudices to his modern order. Although he was an atheist, he recognized the importance of Catholicism to most Italians. In 1929, the Lateran Agreement between the Italian government and the church made the Vatican a state under papal sovereignty. The government recognized the church's right to determine marriage and family doctrine and endorsed its role in education. In return, the church ended its criticism of Fascist tactics. Mussolini also introduced a "corporate" state that denied individual political rights in favor of duty to the state. Corporatist decrees in 1926 organized employers, workers, and professionals into groups or corporations that would settle grievances and determine conditions of work. These decrees outlawed

IMPORTANT DATES			
1914, August	World War I begins	**1919**	Constitution for German republic drawn up at Weimar
1914–1925	Suffrage for women expands	**1919–1920**	Paris Peace Conference redraws the map of Europe
1916	Irish nationalists stage Easter Uprising against British rule	**1922**	By Anglo-Irish treaty of 1921, Ireland is split in two: the independent Irish Free State in the south and British-affiliated Ulster in the north; Fascists march on Rome; Mussolini becomes Italy's prime minister; T. S. Eliot publishes "The Waste Land"; James Joyce publishes *Ulysses*
1917, March	Revolution in Russia overturns tsarist autocracy		
1917, April	The United States enters World War I		
1917, November	Bolshevik Revolution in Russia		
1918, March	Russia signs Treaty of Brest-Litovsk and withdraws from the war	**1924**	Lenin dies; Stalin and Trotsky contend for power
1918, November	Revolutionary turmoil throughout Germany; the kaiser abdicates; armistice ends fighting of World War I	**1924–1929**	Period of general economic prosperity and stability
1918–1922	Civil war in Russia	**1929, October**	Stock market crash in United States

independent labor unions and peasant groups, effectively ending societal and workplace activism. Mussolini drew more applause from business leaders when he announced cuts in women's wages; and then late in the 1920s he won the approval of civil servants, lawyers, and professors by banning women from those professions. Mussolini did not want women out of the workforce altogether but aimed to confine them to low-paying jobs as part of his scheme for reinvigorating men.

Mussolini's admirers were numerous across the West and included Adolf Hitler, who throughout the 1920s had been building a paramilitary group of storm troopers and a political organization called the National Socialist German Workers' Party, or Nazis. During his brief stint in jail for the Beer Hall Putsch in 1923, Hitler wrote *Mein Kampf* ("My Struggle," 1925), which articulated both a vicious anti-Semitism and a political psychology for manipulating the masses. Hitler was fascinated by the dramatic success of the Fascists' march on Rome, by Mussolini's legal accession to power, and by his ability to thwart socialists and trade unionists. However, the austere conditions that had allowed Mussolini to rise to power in 1922 no longer existed in Germany. Although Hitler was welding the Nazi Party into a strong political instrument, the Weimar parliamentary government was actually working as the decade wore on.

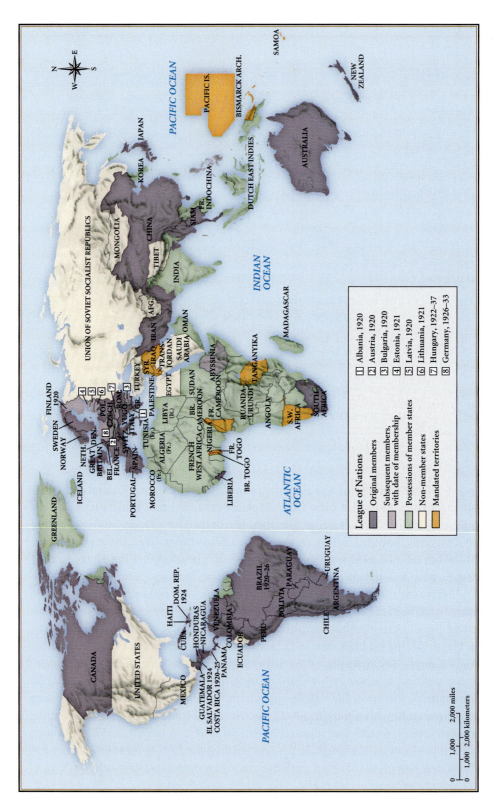

League of Nations

- Original members
- Subsequent members, with date of membership
- Possessions of member states
- Non-member states
- Mandated territories

1 Albania, 1920
2 Austria, 1920
3 Bulgaria, 1920
4 Estonia, 1921
5 Latvia, 1920
6 Lithuania, 1921
7 Hungary, 1922–37
8 Germany, 1926–33

■ **MAPPING THE WEST** Europe and the World in 1929
The map reflects the partitions and nations that came into being as a result of war and revolution, while it obscures the increasing movement toward throwing off colonial rule. The year 1929 was the true high point of empire: the desire for empire would diminish after 1929 except in Italy, which still craved colonies, and in Japan, which continued searching for land and resources to fuel its rapid growth.

Conclusion

The year 1929 was to prove just as fateful as 1914 had been. In 1914, an orgy of death had begun, leading to tens of millions of casualties, the destruction of major dynasties, and the collapse of aristocratic classes. For four years, war promoted the free play of military technology, virulent nationalism, and the control of everyday life by bureaucracy. While dynasties collapsed, the centralization of power increased the scope of the nation-state. The Peace of Paris in 1919 left Germans bitterly resentful, and in eastern and central Europe it created new states built on principles of nationalist ethnic unity—a settlement that, given the intense intermingling of ethnicities, religions, and languages in the area, failed to guarantee a peaceful future.

War furthered the development of mass society. It leveled social classes on the battlefield and in the graveyard, standardized political thinking through wartime propaganda, and extended many political rights to women for their war effort. Peacetime turned improved techniques of wartime production toward churning out consumer goods and technological innovations like air transport, cinema, and radio transmission for greater numbers of people. Modernity in the arts intensified after the war, probing the nightmarish battering endured by all segments of the population.

By the end of the 1920s, the legacy of war had so militarized politics that strongmen had come to power in Hungary, Poland, Romania, the Soviet Union, and Italy, and Adolf Hitler was waiting in the wings in Germany. Many Westerners were impressed by the tough, modern efficiency of the Fascists and Communists, who made parliaments and citizen rule seem out-of-date, even effeminate. Fascist and Communist commitment to violence, compared to that in the war, seemed so tame. When the U.S. stock market crashed in 1929 and economic disaster circled the globe, authoritarian solutions and militarism continued to look appealing. What followed was a series of catastrophes even more devastating than World War I.

Suggested References for further reading and online research appear on page SR-32 at the back of the book.

www.bedfordstmartins.com/huntconcise See the ONLINE STUDY GUIDE to assess your mastery of the material covered in this chapter.

21

An Age of Catastrophes
1929–1945

WHEN ETTY HILLESUM MOVED TO AMSTERDAM in the early 1930s to attend law school, an economic depression gripped the world. A resourceful young Dutch woman, Hillesum pieced together a living as a housekeeper and part-time language teacher. The pressures and pleasures of everyday life blinded her, however, to Adolf Hitler's spectacular rise to power in Germany on a platform demonizing her fellow Jews for the economic slump. World War II ruptured her world. The German conquest of the Netherlands in 1940 led to persecution of Dutch Jews and brought Hillesum to the shattering realization, noted in her diary: "What they are after is our total destruction." The Nazis started relocating Jews to camps in Germany and Poland. Hillesum went to work for Amsterdam's Jewish Council, which was compelled by the Nazis to organize the transportation of Jews to the east. Changing from self-absorbed student to heroine, she did what she could to help other Jews and minutely recorded the deportation. "I wish I could live for a long time so that one day I may know how to explain it." When she was taken prisoner, she smuggled out letters describing the brutal treatment in the transit camps. Etty Hillesum never fulfilled her ambition to become a professional writer: she died in the Auschwitz death camp in November 1943.

The U.S. stock market crash of 1929 opened a horrific era in world history. During the Great Depression of the 1930s, suffering was global, intensifying social grievances throughout the world. In Europe, many people turned to military-style

■ **Nazis on Parade**
By the time Hitler came to power in 1933, Germany was mired in economic depression. Hated by Communists, Nazis, and conservatives alike, the German republic had few supporters. To Germans still reeling from their defeat in World War I, the Nazis looked as though they would restore national power by defeating enemies both within and beyond Germany's borders. Hitler took his cue from Mussolini by promising an end to democracy and tolerance. (Hugo Jaeger/LIFE/Time Pix.)

www.bedfordstmartins.com/huntconcise   See the ONLINE STUDY GUIDE for more help in analyzing this image.

strongmen for answers. Adolf Hitler roused the German masses to rededicate themselves to national greatness. Authoritarian, militaristic, and fascist regimes spread to Portugal, Spain, Poland, Hungary, Japan, China, and elsewhere, trampling on representative institutions. Joseph Stalin oversaw the Soviet Union's rapid industrialization and justified the killing of millions of citizens as being necessary for Soviet growth.

The international scene became doubly menacing because elected leaders in the democracies reacted cautiously to the depression and to fascist aggression. In an age of new mass media, civilian leaders appeared weak and fearful of conflict, while dictators in uniform looked bold and decisive. The German invasion of Poland in 1939 finally roused the democracies, and World War II erupted in Europe. By the end of 1941, the war had spread to the rest of the world with the United States, Great Britain, and the Soviet Union allied in combat against Germany, Italy, and Japan. Tens of millions would perish in this war because technology and ideology had become more deadly than they had been just two decades earlier. Half the dead were civilians, among them Etty Hillesum, whose only "crime" was being a Jew.

The Great Depression

The depression triggered by the U.S. stock market crash of 1929 threw millions out of work and brought suffering to rural and urban folk alike. The whole world felt the depression's impact as commerce and investment in industry fell off, social life and gender roles were upset, and the birthrate plummeted. From peasants in Asia to industrial workers in Germany and the United States, the lives of large segments of the global population were ravaged.

Economic Disaster

In the 1920s, U.S. corporations and banks as well as millions of individual Americans had optimistically invested their money in the stock market or, more often, borrowed money to invest. Taking advantage of easy credit, they bought shares in popular new companies, confident that these investments would yield endless profits. Then, in an attempt to stabilize the market, the Federal Reserve Bank—the nation's central bank, which controlled financial policy—tightened the availability of credit. Brokers demanded that their clients immediately repay the money they had borrowed to buy stock. When millions of shares of stock were sold to pay brokerage bills, the market collapsed. Between early October and mid-November 1929, the value of businesses listed on the U.S. stock market dropped from $87 billion to $30 billion.

The crash spawned a global depression because the United States, a leading international creditor, had financed the relative economic growth of the previous five years. Suddenly strapped for credit, U.S. financiers cut back on loans and called

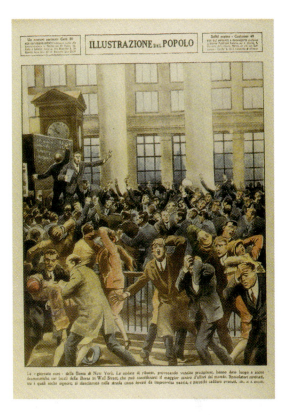

ILLUSTRAZIONE DEL POPOLO

■ **Italian Newspaper Depicts Crash on Wall Street**
The collapse of the U.S. stock market was felt around the world, from Italian cities to the Asian countryside. Credit, the lifeblood of business, dried up. Governments greatly increased import tariffs to protect their nations' industries, thereby curtailing trade. At first, they also cut back on aid to unemployed people, reducing consumer purchasing, worsening financial hardship, and inflicting psychological pain. (Mary Evans Picture Library.)

in debts, undermining banks and industry at home and abroad. The recent U.S. lead in industrial production and the rise of Japanese manufacturing compounded the collapse in Europe. A decline in consumer buying and overproduction further eroded the European economy, from the aging industries of Britain to the fledgling factories of eastern Europe.

The Great Depression left no sector of the world economy unscathed, and government actions worsened the economic catastrophe. To spur their economies, governments used standard tools such as budget cuts and high tariffs against foreign goods, but these policies further dampened trade and spending in the great industrial powers. (See "Taking Measure," page 910.) Great Britain, with its textile, steel, and coal industries near ruin because of out-of-date technology and foreign competition, had close to 3 million unemployed in 1932. By 1933, almost 6 million German workers, about one-third of the workforce, were unemployed, and many Germans were underemployed. France had a more self-sufficient economy, but big businesses such as the innovative Citroën car manufacturer began to fail, and by the mid-1930s more than 800,000 French people had lost their jobs.

In the agricultural sector, prices had been declining for several years because of abundant harvests and technological innovation. The onset of economic

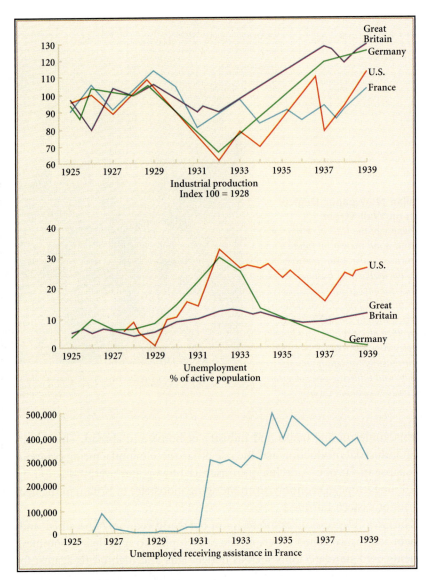

■ **TAKING MEASURE** Industrial Production and Unemployment, 1925–1939

The depression had many dimensions, both measurable and psychological. A calamitous fall in production in the most advanced industrial countries—Germany and the United States—was accompanied by rising unemployment. Whatever the resistance to providing government assistance, the trend toward the welfare state continued, moving from veterans' and old-age pensions to unemployment compensation, as the case of France demonstrates. Although less-industrialized countries around the world experienced smaller cuts in production, for them even the smallest decline was a setback on the road to modernizing their economies.

(Data adapted from V. R. Berghahn, *Modern Germany: Society, Economy, and Politics in the Twentieth Century*, 2d ed. [New York: Cambridge University Press, 1987], 284, and *Atlas Historique, histoire de l'humanité de la préhistoire à nos jours* [Paris: Hachette, 1987].)

depression forced creditors to foreclose on farms and confiscate equipment. Millions of small farmers had no money to buy the chemical fertilizers and motorized machinery they needed to remain competitive; they, too, went under. In eastern and southern Europe, peasants who had pressed for the redistribution of land after World War I could not afford to operate their newly acquired farms. In Poland, many of the 700,000 new landowners fell into debt trying to make their farms viable. Eastern European governments often ignored the farmers' plight—a situation that increased tensions in rural society.

Social Effects of the Crash

Life during the Great Depression was not uniformly bleak. Despite the slump, modernization proceeded. Bordering English slums, one traveler in the mid-1930s noticed, were "filling stations and factories that look like exhibition buildings, giant cinemas and dance halls and cafés, bungalows with tiny garages, cocktail bars, Woolworth's [and] swimming pools." Municipal and national governments continued road construction and sanitation projects. Running water, electricity, and sewage pipes were installed in many homes for the first time. New factories manufactured synthetic fabrics, electrical products such as stoves, and automobiles—all of them in demand. With government assistance, industry developed in eastern Europe. In Romania, for example, industrial production increased by 55 percent between 1929 and 1939.

Throughout the 1930s, the majority of Europeans and Americans had jobs, and people with steady employment benefited from a drastic drop in prices. Despite the depression, many service workers, managers, and business leaders enjoyed considerable prosperity. People with jobs, however, worried about becoming unemployed and having to scrape, like thousands of others, for a bare existence. In towns with heavy industry, sometimes more than half the population was out of work. In England in the mid-1930s, close to 20 percent of the population lacked adequate food, clothing, or housing. In a 1932 school assignment, a German youth wrote: "My father has been out of work for two and a half years. He thinks that I'll never find a job." Thus, despite the prosperity of many people, a dark cloud of fear and resentment settled over Western society.

The economic catastrophe upset social life and strained gender relations. Women often found low-paying jobs doing laundry and cleaning houses. Unemployed men sometimes stayed home all day, increasing the tension in small, overcrowded apartments. Men who stayed home sometimes took over the housekeeping chores but often felt that this "women's work" demeaned their masculinity. As many women became breadwinners, men could be seen standing on street corners begging—a rearrangement of gender expectations that fueled discontent. Young men in cities faced severe unemployment. Some loitered in parks, intruding in areas usually frequented by mothers and their children and old people. As the percentage of farmworkers in the western European population decreased, rural men also faced the erosion of patriarchal authority, once central in overseeing farm labor and allocating property among inheritors. Demagogues everywhere berated parliamentary politicians for their failure to stop the collapse of traditional values. The climate was thus primed for Nazi and fascist politicians who promised to restore prosperity and male dignity.

Politicians of all stripes forecast national collapse as declining birthrates (after a brief postwar upturn) combined with the economic decline. In difficult economic times, people chose to have fewer children. There were other reasons, too, for falling birthrates. Mandatory education and more years of required schooling, enforced more strictly after World War I, resulted in greater expenses for parents. Working-class children no longer earned wages to supplement the family income; instead, they cost the family money while they went to school. As family-planning centers opened, knowledge of birth control spread to the working and lower-middle classes, who continued the half-century-long trend of cutting family size.

Many politicians used the population "crisis" to gain votes by igniting racism: "superior" peoples were selfishly failing to breed, they charged, and "inferior" peoples were poised to take their place. This racism took a violent form in eastern Europe, where the rural population was growing because of increased life expectancy despite an overall drop in the birthrate. The population increase compounded the burdens of eastern European farm families, who faced an unprecedented struggle for survival. Throughout eastern Europe, peasant political parties blamed Jewish bankers for farm foreclosures and Jewish civil servants (of whom there were actually very few) for new taxes and inadequate relief programs. Thus population issues along with economic misery fueled ethnic hatred and anti-Semitism.

Global Dimensions of the Crash

The effects of the depression extended beyond the West, further accelerating the pace of change and spread of discontent in the European colonial empires. World War I and postwar investment had generated economic development, a rising population, and explosive urban growth in Asia, Africa, and Latin America. Between 1920 and 1940, Shanghai ballooned from 1.7 million to 3.75 million residents, Calcutta from 1.8 million to 3.4 million. The depression, however, cut the demand for copper, tin, and other raw materials and for the finished products made in urban factories beyond the West. It drove down the price of foodstuffs such as rice and coffee, and this proved disastrous to people who had been forced to grow a single cash crop. However, the economic picture was uneven in the colonies as well as in Europe. Established industrial sectors of the Indian economy, for instance, gained strength. In textiles, India achieved virtual independence from British cloth.

Economic distress added to smoldering grievances. Millions of African and Asian colonial troops fought for Britain and France in World War I, but after the war these countries gave little back to their colonial populations. In fact, the League of Nations charter pointedly omitted any reference to the principle of racial equality demanded by people of color at the Paris Peace Conference. Their resolve fortified by these slights and by the model of Japan's and their own growing industrial competence, colonial peoples focused on winning independence.

In the 1930s, upper-class Indians who had organized to gain rights from Britain in the late nineteenth century were joined by millions of working people, including hundreds of thousands of returning soldiers. The charismatic Mohandas K. Gandhi (1869–1948) emerged as the leader for Indian independence. Of privileged birth and trained in England as a Western-style lawyer, Gandhi embraced Hindu self-denial, rejecting the elaborate trappings of British life in favor of simple clothing made of thread he had spun. His followers called him "Mahatma," a Hindu term meaning "great-souled." Gandhi advocated *civil disobedience*—the deliberate but peaceful breaking of the law. He claimed that his tactics were modeled on British suffragists' tactics and on the teachings of Jesus, Buddha, and other spiritual leaders. Boycotting British-made goods and disobeying

■ **An Historic Act of Civil Disobedience**

Mohandas Gandhi used nonviolent resistance to challenge British rule. Because of the British government's monopoly on salt, Indians were prohibited from gathering this natural product and every Indian family had to pay a tax on salt. In 1930, Gandhi led his supporters on a 200-mile march to India's salt flats to protest the hated salt tax and to extract salt from seawater. Gandhi was arrested and jailed, but his followers continued their march to the sea.

(© Bettmann/Corbis.)

British laws, he aimed to end the Indians' traditional deference toward the British. British officials jailed Gandhi repeatedly and tried to split the independence movement by encouraging the rival Muslim League and fomenting Hindu-Muslim antagonism.

In the Middle East, Westernizer Mustafa Kemal (1881–1938), known as Atatürk ("first among Turks"), led the Turks to found the independent republic of Turkey in 1923 and to craft a capitalist economy. In an effort to nationalize and modernize Turkish culture, Kemal moved the national capital from Constantinople to Ankara in 1923, changed the ancient Greek *Constantinople* to the Turkish *Istanbul* in 1930, mandated Western dress for men and women, introduced the Latin alphabet, and abolished polygamy. In 1936, women received the vote and became eligible to serve in the Turkish parliament. Also in the Middle East, Persia loosened the European grip on its economy, forced the negotiation of oil contracts, updated its government, and in 1935 changed its name to Iran. In 1936, Britain agreed to end its military occupation of Egypt (though not the Suez Canal), fulfilling the promise of self-rule granted in 1922.

France made fewer concessions to colonized peoples. The French were obsessed by rising trade barriers in Europe and by their own population decline. Their trade with their colonies increased as their trade with Europe lagged, and the demographic surge in Asia and Africa bolstered French optimism. One French official remarked: "One hundred and ten million strong, France can stand up to Germany." Western-educated native leaders, however, contested their people's subjection. In 1930, the French government crushed a peasant uprising that Ho Chi Minh, founder of the Indochinese Communist Party, led.

Preoccupied with their empires, Britain and France let totalitarian forces spread unchecked throughout Europe during the crisis-ridden 1930s.

Totalitarian Triumph

Representative government collapsed in many countries under the sheer weight of social and economic crisis. After 1929, Italy's Benito Mussolini, the Soviet Union's Joseph Stalin, and Germany's Adolf Hitler were able to mobilize vast support for their violent regimes. Overlooking the brutal side of modern dictatorship, many people admired Mussolini and Hitler for the discipline they brought to social and economic life. In an age of crisis, utopian hopes led many to support political violence. Unity and obedience—not freedom and civil rights—were seen as keys to rebirth. The common use of violence has led scholars to apply the term *totalitarianism* to the Fascist, Nazi, and Communist regimes of the 1930s. The term refers to highly centralized systems of government that attempt to control society and ensure conformity through a single party and police terror. Forged in the crucible of war and its aftermath, totalitarian regimes broke with liberal principles and eventually waged war on their own citizens.

The Rise of Stalinism

In the 1930s, Joseph Stalin led the astonishing transformation of the USSR from a rural society into a formidable industrial power. Having taken firm control against Lenin's express wishes, Stalin ended the New Economic Policy (NEP), Lenin's temporary compromise between Marxism and capitalism, with the first of several five-year plans presented in 1929. Outlining a program for massive increases in the output of coal, iron ore, steel, and industrial goods, Stalin warned that without an end to Soviet backwardness "the advanced countries . . . will crush us." He thus established central economic planning—a policy used on both sides in World War I and increasingly favored by economists and industrialists around the world. Between 1928 and 1940, the number of Soviet workers in industry, construction, and transport grew from 4.6 million to 12.6 million. From 1927 to 1937, production in metallurgy and machinery rose 1,400 percent. Stalin's first five-year plan helped make the USSR a leading industrial nation.

Central planning led to the creation of a new elite of bureaucrats and industrial officials. Mostly party officials and technical experts, these managers dominated Soviet workers by limiting their ability to change jobs or move from place to place. Nonetheless, skilled workers as well as bureaucrats benefited substantially from the redistribution of privileges that accompanied industrialism and central planning. Compared with people working the land, both managers and workers in industry had better housing and higher wages, and Communist officials enjoyed additional perquisites such as country homes and luxurious vacations.

Unskilled workers faced a grim plight, often with real dedication. Newcomers from the countryside were herded into barracklike dwellings, even tents, and subjected to dangerous factory conditions. Many took pride in the skills they acquired: "We mastered this profession—completely new to us—with great pleasure," a female lathe operator recalled. More often, however, workers lacked the technical education and even the tools necessary to accomplish goals prescribed by the five-year plan. Because fulfilling the plan had top priority as a measure of progress toward the Communist utopia, official lying about productivity became ingrained in the economic system. Acceptance of grim conditions and fierce determination turned the Soviet Union from an illiterate peasant society into an advanced industrial economy in a single decade. Intense suffering was tolerated because Soviet workers believed in the ethos of "constant struggle, struggle, and struggle" to achieve a Communist society, in the words of one worker: "Man himself is being rebuilt."

In country and city alike, work was politicized. Stalin demanded more grain from peasants (who had prospered under NEP), both to feed the urban workforce and to export as a way to finance industrialization. Peasants resisted government demands by cutting production or withholding produce from the market. Faced with such recalcitrance, Stalin announced a new revolutionary challenge: "liquidation of the kulaks." The name *kulak* ("fist") was a derogatory term for prosperous peasants, but Stalin applied it to anyone who opposed his plans to end independent farming. In the winter of 1929–1930, party workers scoured villages for produce and forced villagers to identify the kulaks in their midst. Propaganda units instilled hatred for anyone connected with kulaks. One Russian remembered believing they were "bloodsuckers, cattle, swine, loathsome, repulsive: they had no souls; they stank." As "enemies of the state," whole families and even entire villages were robbed of their possessions, left to starve, or even murdered outright. Confiscated kulak land formed the basis of the *kolkhoz*, or collective farm, where peasants were to create a Communist agricultural system using cooperative farming and modern machinery.

Once work life was politicized, economic failure took on political meaning and ushered in violent purges. The inexperience of factory workers, farmers, and party officials with advanced industrialization often meant an inability to meet quotas. In the face of the murder of farmers and the experiment with collectivization, Soviet citizens starved as the grain harvest declined from 83 million tons in 1930 to 67 million in 1934. Stalin blamed failure on "wreckers," saboteurs of communism. To rid society of these villains, he instituted *purges*—state violence in the form of widespread arrests, imprisonment in labor camps, and executions. The purges touched nearly all segments of society, but "bourgeois" engineers were the first group condemned for causing low productivity. Trials of prominent figures followed. In 1934, Sergei Kirov, the popular first secretary of the Leningrad Communist Party, was murdered. Stalin used Kirov's death (which he may have instigated) as the pretext to try former Bolshevik leaders. Between 1936 and 1938, a series of "show trials" for alleged conspiracy to overthrow Soviet rule again targeted prominent Bolsheviks. Tortured and coerced to confess in court, most of those found guilty were shot.

The spirit of purge swept society. One woman poet described the scene: "Great concert and lecture halls were turned into public confessionals. . . . People did penance for [everything]. . . . Beating their breasts, the 'guilty' would lament that they had 'shown political short-sightedness' and 'lack of vigilance' . . . and were full of 'rotten liberalism.' " In 1937 and 1938, military leaders were arrested and executed without public trials; in some ranks every officer was killed. From industry and education to the party and the army, not even the Soviet power structure escaped the great purges. Simultaneously, the government developed a system of prison camps stretching several thousand miles from Moscow to Siberia. Called the *Gulag*—an acronym for the administrative arm of the camps—the system held millions of prisoners under lethal conditions. A million people died annually as a result of the harsh conditions. Insufficient food and housing, twelve- to sixteen-hour workdays at mining and other crushing labor, and regular beatings and murder of prisoners rounded out Gulag life, which became another aspect of Soviet violence.

Some historians have seen the purges as a clear-headed attempt by Stalin to eliminate barriers to total control; others, as the machinations of a psychopath. More recently, historians have judged the purges as resulting from power struggles among party officials and fueled by those looking for a quick route to the top. Still other interpretations see many of the denunciations and confessions as sincere expressions of workers' commitment to rooting out enemies of their proletarian utopia. Despite this historical controversy, there is no question about the outcome: ongoing arrests, incarcerations, and executions removed rivals to Stalin's power.

The 1930s also marked a sharp reversal of revolutionary experimentation in social life. Sexual freedom was forced into retreat. Much like the rest of Europe, the Soviet Union experienced a rapid decline in its birthrate in the 1930s. This drop, combined with the need to replace the millions of people lost since 1914, motivated Stalin to end the reproductive freedom of the early revolutionary years. Birth-control information and abortions became difficult to obtain. Lavish wedding ceremonies came back into fashion; divorce became difficult to obtain; and the state criminalized homosexuality. Whereas Bolsheviks had once derided the family as a "bourgeois" institution, propaganda now referred to the family unit as a "school for socialism." Nevertheless, women made gains. More and more women in rural areas learned to read and had access to health-care facilities. As the purges continued, positions in the lower ranks of the party opened to women, and women increasingly were accepted into the professions. The stress on women, particularly those in the industrial workforce, increased, however. In addition to working long hours in factories, they also waited in long lines to obtain scarce consumer goods, and they performed all household and child-care tasks under harsh conditions.

Cultural life was similarly paradoxical under Stalin. Stalinism brought avant-garde experimentation to an end, but modernist artists and intellectuals continued to promote their ability to mobilize the masses through appeals to the unconscious and the emotions in their works. Stalin endorsed this role, calling artists and writers "engineers of the soul," but he controlled their work through the Union of Soviet Writers. The union assigned housing, office space, supplies, equipment, and secretarial help and even determined the types of books authors could write. In return, the "comrade artist" adhered to the official style of "socialist realism," derived from the 1920s focus on the common worker as a type of social hero. Some artists, such as the poet Anna Akhmatova (1889–1966), refused to accept this system.

> *Stars of death stood above us, and Russia,*
> *In her innocence, twisted in pain*
> *Under blood-spattered boots . . .*

wrote Akhmatova in those years. Many others, including the composer Sergei Prokofiev (1891–1953), found ways to accommodate their talents to the state's demands. Prokofiev composed scores for the delightful *Peter and the Wolf* and for Sergei Eisenstein's 1938 film *Alexander Nevsky*, a work that transparently compared Stalin to the towering medieval rulers of the Russian people. Aided by adaptable artists, workers, and bureaucrats, Stalin stood triumphant as the 1930s drew to a close.

■ **N. J. Altman, *Anna Akhmatova* (1914)**

This modernist painting portrays the poet when she was a centerpiece of literary salon life in Russia and the subject of several avant-garde portraits. In the 1930s and 1940s, Akhmatova gave poetic voice to Soviet suffering, recording in her verse ordinary people's endurance of purges, deprivation, and warfare. As she encouraged people to resist the Nazis during World War II, Stalin allowed her to revive Rus-sian patriotism instead of socialist internationalism.

(State Russian Museum, St. Petersburg/The Bridgeman Art Library.)

Hitler's Rise to Power

Hitler ended German democracy. Since the early 1920s, he had been trying to rouse the German people to crush the fragile Weimar Republic. In his coup attempt, in his influential book *Mein Kampf* ("My Struggle," 1925), and in his leadership of the Nazi Party, he drummed a message of anti-Semitism and the rebirth of the German "race." When the Great Depression struck Germany, his party began to outstrip its rivals in elections thanks in part to massive support from businessmen such as film and press mogul Alfred Hugenberg. Hugenberg's newspapers relentlessly slammed the Weimar government, blaming it for the disastrous economy and inflaming wounded German pride over the defeat in World War I. Parliamentary government practically ground to a halt in the face of economic crisis. The Reichstag failed to approve emergency plans to improve the economy, and Hitler's followers made parliamentary government look even more inept by rampaging through the streets and attacking Jews, Communists, and Social Democrats. By targeting all these as a single, monolithic group of "Bolshevik" enemies, the Nazis won wide approval.

As a result of the depression, media publicity, and its own street tactics, Hitler's National Socialist German Workers' Party (NSDAP)—the Nazi Party—which had received little more than 2 percent of the vote in 1928, won almost 20 percent in the Reichstag elections of 1930 and more than doubled its representation in 1932.

Many of Hitler's supporters, like Stalin's, were young and idealistic. In 1930, 70 percent of Nazi Party members were under forty, a stark contrast to the image of Weimar politicians as aged and ineffectual. Although businessmen provided substantial sums of money, Germans of every class supported the Nazis. The largest number of supporters came from the industrial working class, which had the most voters, but white-collar workers and members of the lower middle class joined the party in percentages out of proportion with their numbers in the population.

Hitler's modern propaganda techniques also served him well. His propaganda chief, Joseph Goebbels, released thousands of recordings of Hitler's speeches while circulating Nazi mementos widely among the citizenry.◆ Teenagers painted their fingernails with swastikas, a symbol used by the Nazis, and soldiers flashed metal match covers with Nazi insignia. Nazi rallies were masterpieces of political display. Hitler mesmerized the crowds as their *Führer*, or leader—a strong, superior being. Frenzied and inspirational, he seemed neither a calculating politician nor a rational bureaucrat but "the creative element," as one poet put it. In actuality, however, Hitler viewed the masses as tools. In *Mein Kampf* he explained his philosophy of how to deal with them:

> The receptivity of the great masses is very limited, their intelligence is small. In consequence of these facts, all effective propaganda must be limited to a very few points and must harp on those in slogans until the last member of the public understands what you want him to understand.

With Hitler, as with Stalin, mass politics reached terrifying and cynical proportions.

Nazi success along with Communist electoral strength in the 1932 Reichstag elections made the leader of one of those parties the logical choice as chancellor. Germany's conservative elites—from the military, industry, and the state bureaucracy—loathed the Communists and favored Hitler as a common type they thought they could easily manipulate. In January 1933, he was invited to become chancellor.

The Nazification of German Politics

Hitler took office amid jubilation in Berlin. Tens of thousands of storm troopers (SA or *Sturmabteilung*) holding blazing torches paraded through the streets. Millions of Germans celebrated Hitler's ascent to power. One recalled: "My father went down to the cellar and brought up our best bottles of wine. . . . And my mother wept for joy."

Within a month of Hitler's taking power, the elements of Nazi political domination were in place. In February 1933, the Reichstag building was gutted by fire. Hitler blamed the Communists and used the fire as the excuse for suspending civil rights, imposing censorship of the press, and prohibiting meetings of the opposition.

◆ For a primary source that reveals Hitler's remarkable talent to shape public opinion, see Document 67, Joseph Goebbels, "Nazi Propaganda Pamphlet."

■ **Toys Depicting Nazis**

As a totalitarian ideology, Nazism permeated everyday life. Nazi insignia decorated clothing, dishes, cigarette lighters, and even toys. Men and women became husbands and wives in accordance with Nazi rules and sent their children to Nazi clubs and organizations. Nazi songs, Nazi parades and festivals, and Nazi radio filled leisure hours. (Imperial War Museum, London.)

He had always claimed that *all* political parties except the NSDAP were his enemies. "Our opponents complain that we National Socialists, and I in particular, are intolerant and intractable," he declared. "They are right, we are intolerant! I have set myself one task, namely to sweep those parties out of Germany."

Storm troopers' political violence became a way of life. At the end of March, intimidated Reichstag delegates let pass the Enabling Act, which suspended the constitution for four years and allowed Nazi laws to take effect without parliamentary approval. Solid middle-class Germans approved the Enabling Act as a way to advance the creation of a *Volksgemeinschaft* ("people's community") of like-minded, racially pure Germans—"Aryans" in Nazi terminology. Heinrich Himmler headed the elite SS (*Schutzstaffel*) organization that protected Hitler, and he commanded the government's political police system. The Gestapo, an internal security police force organized by Hermann Goering, also enforced complete obedience to Nazism. These organizations had vast powers to arrest, execute, or imprison people in concentration camps, the first of which opened at Dachau near Munich in March 1933. The Nazis filled it and later camps with socialists, homosexuals, Jews, and others said to interfere with the *Volksgemeinschaft*. As one Nazi leader proclaimed:

[*National socialism*] *does not believe that one soul is equal to another, one man equal to another. It does not believe in rights as such. It aims to create the German man of strength, its task is to protect the German people, and all . . . must be subordinate to this goal.*

Hitler deliberately blurred authority in the government and party so that confusion and bitter competition reigned. He thus prevented the emergence of coalitions against him and allowed himself to arbitrate the confusion, often with violence. When Ernst Roehm, leader of the SA and Hitler's long-time collaborator, called for a "second revolution" to end the corrupt influence of the old business and military elites on the Nazi leadership, Hitler ordered Roehm's assassination. The bloody "Night of the Long Knives" (June 30, 1934), during which hundreds of SA leaders and innocent civilians were killed, enhanced Hitler's support among conservatives. Nazism's terroristic politics remained as the foundation of Hitler's "Third Reich"—a German empire succeeding the empires of Charlemagne and William II.

New economic and social programs, especially those that put people back to work, also bolstered Hitler's regime. Economic revival built popular support, strengthened military industries, and provided the basis for German expansion. The Nazi government pursued *pump priming*—that is, stimulating the economy through government spending on tanks and airplanes and the Autobahn highway system. From farms to factories, the government demanded high productivity, and unemployment declined from a peak of almost 6 million in 1932 to 1.6 million by 1936. When labor shortages began to appear in some areas, the government conscripted single women into service as farmworkers and domestics. The Nazi Party closed down labor unions. Government bureaucrats classified jobs, determined work procedures, and set pay levels, rating women's jobs lower than men's regardless of the level of expertise required. Imitating Stalin, Hitler announced a four-year plan in 1936 with the secret aim of preparing Germany for war by 1940, and he instituted central planning. His programs produced large deficits, which the spoils of future conquests were supposed to eliminate.

Hitler exercised unprecedented power over the workings of everyday life, especially gender roles. In June 1933, a bill took effect that encouraged "Aryans" (individuals whom the Nazis defined as racially pure Germans) to marry and have children. The bill provided for loans to "Aryan" newlyweds, but only to those couples in which the wife left the workforce. The loans were forgiven on the birth of a couple's fourth child. Nazi marriage programs enforced a nineteenth-century ideal of femininity; women were supposed to be subordinate so men would feel tough and industrious despite military defeat and economic depression.

Nazism impoverished ordinary life. Although 70 percent of households had "people's radios" by 1938, the programming that was broadcast was severely censored. Books like Remarque's *All Quiet on the Western Front* were banned, and in May 1933 a huge book-burning ceremony rid libraries of works by Jews, socialists, homosexuals, and modernist writers out of favor with the Nazis. Modern art in museums and in private collections was destroyed or confiscated, and laws took jobs from Jews and women and bestowed them on Nazi Party members. In the Hitler Youth organization, which boys and girls over age ten had to join, children learned to report to Nazi authorities any adults they suspected of disloyalty to the regime, even their own parents. Germans boasted that they could leave their bicycles

outdoors at night without fear of robbery, but their world was filled with informers—some 100,000 of them on the Nazi payroll. In general, the improved economy
led many to believe that Hitler was working an economic miracle while restoring
pride in Germany and the harmonious community of an imaginary past. For hundreds of thousands if not millions of Germans, however, Nazi rule in the 1930s
brought anything but community.

Nazi Racism

The Nazis defined Jews as an inferior "race" dangerous to the superior "Aryan" or
Germanic "race" and responsible for most of Germany's problems, including the
defeat in World War I and the intensity of the depression. Hitler attacked many ethnic and social groups, but he propelled the nineteenth-century politics of anti-
Semitism to new and frightening heights. In the rhetoric of Nazism, Jews were "ver-
min," "abscesses," "parasites," and "Bolsheviks," whom the Germans would have to
eliminate to create a true *Volksgemeinschaft*. By defining the Jews as evil financiers
and businessmen and as working-class Bolsheviks, Hitler fashioned an enemy for
many segments of the German population to hate.

Nazi policy was called "racial," and it led to laws against "non-Aryans"—a group
that, like "Aryans," was never defined. Racial classifications were made to appear
scientific, however, by lists of physical and other characteristics that the Nazis
claimed determined a person's "race." In 1935, the government enacted the
Nuremberg Laws, legislation that specifically deprived Jews of citizenship, defined
Jewishness according to a person's ancestry, ended special consideration for Jewish
war veterans, and prohibited marriage between Jews and other Germans. Women
whom the Nazis defined as "Aryan" faced increasing difficulty obtaining abortions
or birth-control information, but both were readily available to the outcast groups,
including Jews, gypsies, Slavs, and people with mental or physical disabilities. In the
name of improving the "Aryan" race, German doctors helped organize the T4 project, which used carbon monoxide poisoning and other means to kill large numbers
of people—200,000 with disabilities and the elderly—late in the 1930s, preparing
the way for the even larger mass exterminations that would occur later.

Jews were forced into slave labor, evicted from their apartments, and prevented
from buying most clothing and food. In 1938, a Jewish teenager, reacting to the harassment of his parents, killed a German official. In retaliation, Nazis attacked some
two hundred synagogues, smashed the windows of Jewish-owned stores, ransacked
apartments of known or suspected Jews, and threw more than twenty thousand
Jews into prisons and camps. The night of November 9–10 became known as
Kristallnacht, the "Night of Broken Glass." Faced with relentless persecution, which
some historians have called a "social death," by the outbreak of World War II in
1939 more than half of Germany's 500,000 Jews had emigrated. The confiscation
of the emigrants' property enriched their neighbors and individual Nazis; the payment of enormous emigration fees helped finance Germany's revival.

Democracies on the Defensive

Nazism, communism, and fascism offered bold new approaches to modern politics and new kinds of economic and social policies. Their leaders' energetic, military style of mobilizing the masses made the representative governments and democratic values of the United States, France, and Great Britain seem to be the effeminate, decadent systems of declining peoples. During the 1930s, democracies were on the defensive in a variety of arenas—economic, political, and cultural.

Confronting the Economic Crisis

As the depression wore on, some governments undertook notable experiments to solve social and economic crises and still maintain democratic politics. In the early days of the slump, U.S. president Herbert Hoover (1874–1964) opposed direct federal help to the unemployed and in the summer of 1932 even ordered the army to use tanks to break up a march of unemployed World War I veterans in Washington, D.C. With unemployment close to fifteen million, Franklin Delano Roosevelt, the wealthy, patrician governor of New York, defeated Hoover in the fall presidential election, promising innovation. Roosevelt (1882–1945) pushed through a torrent of legislation, known as the "New Deal," some of it inspired by the central control of the economy achieved during World War I: relief for businesses, price supports for hard-pressed farmers, and public works programs for unemployed youth. The Social Security Act of 1935 set up a fund to which employers and employees contributed. It provided retirement benefits for workers, unemployment insurance, and payments to dependent mothers, their children, and people with disabling physical conditions.

Roosevelt's New Deal advanced the trend toward the *welfare state*—a society in which the government guarantees a certain level of economic well-being for individuals and businesses—not only in the United States but elsewhere across the West. The New Deal angered businesspeople and the wealthy, who considered it "socialist." But even as the depression remained severe, Roosevelt (quickly nicknamed FDR) maintained widespread support. Like other successful politicians of the 1930s and thereafter, he made expert use of the mass media, especially in his "fireside chats" broadcast by radio to the American people. In sharp contrast to Mussolini and Hitler, however, Roosevelt aimed in his public statements to sustain—not to denounce—faith in democratic rights and popular government. Eager to separate themselves from Hoover's position, First Lady Eleanor Roosevelt (1884–1962) rushed to greet the next group of veterans marching on Washington and the president received a delegation of veterans at the White House. The Roosevelts insisted that justice and human rights must not be surrendered in difficult times. "We Americans of today . . . are characters in the living book of democracy," FDR told a group of teenagers in 1939. "But we are also its author." Lynchings, racial violence, and harsh discrimination continued to cause enormous suffering in the

■ **Fireside Chat with FDR**

President Franklin Delano Roosevelt was a master of words, uttering many memorable phrases that inspired Americans during the depression and World War II. Here he addresses the nation on August 23, 1938, over a radio hookup while Eleanor Roosevelt and his mother, Sarah, observe. Although Roosevelt was disabled by polio, wore leg braces, and could not walk unassisted, the press never showed or mentioned Roosevelt's impairment, even on the rare occasions when he used crutches or a wheelchair in public. (© Hulton Getty/Liaison Agency.)

United States during the Roosevelt administration, nor did the economy fully recover. But the president's media success and bold programs kept the masses committed to a democratic future.

Sweden also developed a coherent program for solving economic and population problems that reconceived the government's role in promoting social welfare and economic democracy. Sweden industrialized later than western Europe and the United States but had a tradition of community responsibility for working through social and economic difficulties. Sweden succeeded in turning its economy around in the 1930s and instituted central planning of the economy and social welfare programs. It also devalued the currency to make Swedish exports more attractive on the international market. Thanks to pump-priming programs, Swedish productivity rose 20 percent between 1929 and 1935, a time when other democracies were still experiencing decline.

Sweden addressed the population problem with government programs but without racist and antidemocratic coercion. Alva Myrdal (1902–1986), a leading member of Sweden's parliament, believed fertility rates reflected economic conditions and individuals' sense of their personal well-being. Acting on her advice to promote "voluntary parenthood," the government of Sweden started a loan program for married couples in 1937 and introduced prenatal care, free childbirth in a hospital, a food relief program, and subsidized housing for large families. By the end of the decade, almost 50 percent of all Swedish mothers were receiving government aid. Long a concern of feminists and other social reformers in Sweden, care of families became integral to the tasks of the modern state, which now saw itself as responsible for citizen welfare in hard times.

Because the United States, the most powerful democracy, had withdrawn from world leadership by refusing to participate in the League of Nations, Britain and France had greater responsibility for international peace and well-being than their postwar resources could sustain. When the Great Depression hit, Britain was already mired in economic difficulties. Faced with falling government revenues, Prime Minister Ramsay MacDonald, though leader of the Labour Party, reduced payments to the unemployed, and Parliament effectively denied unemployment insurance to women even though they had contributed to the unemployment fund. To protect jobs, the government imposed huge protective tariffs that actually discouraged a revival of international trade and did not relieve British misery. Only in 1933, with the economy continuing to worsen, did the government begin to take effective steps with massive programs of slum clearance, new housing construction, and health insurance for the needy.

Depression struck later in France, but the country endured a decade of public strife in the 1930s due to severe postwar demoralization, stagnant population growth, and wage cuts. Deputies with opposing views on the economic crisis frequently came to blows in the Chamber of Deputies, and governments were voted in and out with dizzying rapidity. Parisians took to the streets to protest the government's belt-tightening policies, and right-wing paramilitary groups mushroomed, attracting the unemployed, students, and veterans to the cause of ending representative government. In February 1934, the paramilitary groups joined Communists and other outraged citizens in riots around the parliament building. "Let's string up the deputies," chanted the crowd. "And if we can't string them up, let's beat in their faces, let's reduce them to a pulp." Hundreds of demonstrators were wounded and killed, but the antirepublican right lacked both substantial support outside Paris and a leader like Hitler or Mussolini capable of unifying its various groups.

Shocked into action by the force of fascism, French liberals, socialists, and Communists established an antifascist coalition known as the Popular Front. Until that time, such a merging of groups had been impossible in democratic countries because of Stalin's strict opposition to Communist collaboration with liberals and socialists, who disavowed Communist-style revolutions. As fascism spread throughout Europe, however, Stalin reversed course and allowed Communists to join such efforts. For just over a year in 1936–1937 and again very briefly in 1938, the French

Popular Front formed a government, with the socialist leader Léon Blum (1872–1950) as premier.

Like the American New Dealers and the Swedish Social Democrats, the French Popular Front instituted long-overdue reforms. Blum extended family subsidies and welfare benefits, and he appointed women to his government (though women in France still were not allowed to vote). In June 1936, the government guaranteed workers two-week paid vacations, a forty-hour workweek, and the right to collective bargaining. Working people would long remember Blum as the man who improved their living standards and provided them with benefits and vacations.

During its brief life, the French Popular Front offered the masses a youthful but democratic political culture. "In 1936 everyone was twenty years old," one man recalled, evoking the atmosphere of idealism. Local cultural centers sprang up, and to express their opposition to fascism, citizens celebrated Bastille Day and other democratic holidays with new enthusiasm. But despite this support from workers, the Popular Front governments were politically weak. Fearing for their investments, bankers and industrialists greeted Blum's appointment by sending their capital out of the country, leaving France financially strapped. "Better Hitler than Blum" was the slogan of the upper classes. Blum's government fell when it also lost the left by refusing material support in the fight against fascism in Spain. As in Britain, memories of World War I caused leaders to block crucial support to foreign democratic forces, such as the republicans in Spain, and to keep domestic military budgets small. The collapse of the antifascist Popular Front in late June 1937 showed the difficulties that pluralistic and democratic societies faced in crisis-ridden times.

Fledgling democracies in central Europe, hit hard by the depression, also fought the twin struggle for economic survival and representative government, but less successfully. In 1932, Engelbert Dollfuss (1892–1934) came to power in Austria, dismissing the parliament and ruling briefly as a dictator. Despite his authoritarian stance, Dollfuss would not submit to the Nazis, who assassinated him in 1934. In Hungary, where outrage over the Peace of Paris remained intense, a crippled economy resulted in right-wing general Gyula Gömbös (1886–1936) taking over in 1932. Gömbös reoriented his country's foreign policy toward Mussolini and Hitler. He stirred up anti-Semitism and ethnic hatreds and left considerable pro-Nazi feeling after his death in 1936. In democratic Czechoslovakia, the Slovaks, who were both poorer and less educated than the urbanized Czechs, built a strong Slovak Fascist Party. In Poland, Romania, Yugoslavia, and Bulgaria, ethnic tensions simmered, and the appeal of fascism grew as the Great Depression lingered.

Cultural Visions in Hard Times

Just as culture had been mobilized during World War I, cultural leaders now mobilized to meet the crisis of economic hard times and political menace. Some empathized with the situations of factory workers, homemakers, and shopgirls struggling to support themselves or their families; others, with the ever-growing numbers of the unemployed and destitute. In 1931, French director René Clair's film *À nous la liberté* ("Give Us Liberty") related prison life to work on a factory assembly line. In 1936, Charlie Chaplin's film *Modern Times* showed the Little Tramp again, this time as a factory worker so molded by his monotonous job that he assumes that anything he can see, even a coworker's body, needs mechanical adjustment. This sympathetic and humorous representation of the modern factory and hard times made Chaplin a hit even in the Soviet Union.

Media sympathy poured out to victims of the crisis. Women were portrayed alternately as the cause of and as the cure for society's problems. *The Blue Angel* (1930), a German film starring Marlene Dietrich, showed how a vital, modern woman could destroy men—and civilization; it depicted a woman's power to dominate over the ineffectuality of an impractical professor. In contrast, heroines in comedies and musicals behaved bravely, pulling their men out of the depths of despair and setting things right. For example, in *Keep Smiling* (1938) and other films, the British comedienne Gracie Fields portrayed spunky working-class women who remained cheerful despite hard times.

Techniques of modern art, such as montage, which overlaid two or more photos or parts of photos, were used to grab visual and psychic attention in the cultural battles of the 1930s. Some intellectuals turned away from experimentation with nonrepresentational forms as they drove home their antifascist, pacifist, or pro-

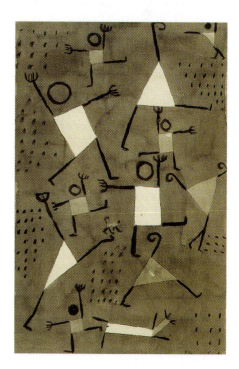

■ **Paul Klee, *Dancing with Fear* (1938)**
Swiss-German artist Paul Klee (1879–1940) explored modern art's ability to evoke universal truths behind surface reality. Delightful shapes and colors often marked his work, although he was always concerned with how technology would affect people's values. As the danger of Nazism's triumph mounted, Klee grew depressed and produced dark visions of fear and death.
("Tanze vor Angst," 1938, 90 [G 10] by Paul Klee. Paul-Klee-Stiftung, Kunstmuseum Bern, photo: Peter Lauri. © ARS, New York.)

worker beliefs. Popular Front writers created realistic studies of human misery and the threat of war that haunted life in the 1930s. The British writer George Orwell described his experiences among the poor of Paris and London, wrote investigative pieces about the unemployed in the north of England, and published an account of atrocities committed by both sides during the Spanish Civil War (1936–1939). Politicized, art reaffirmed Western values such as rationalism, rights, and concern for the poor. German writer Thomas Mann, a Christian, went into exile when Hitler came to power and began a series of novels based on the Old Testament hero Joseph to convey the struggle between humanist values and barbarism. The fourth volume, *Joseph the Provider* (1944), eulogized Joseph's welfare state, in which the granaries were full and the rich paid taxes so the poor might live decent lives. In *Three Guineas* (1938), one of her last works, the English writer Virginia Woolf rejected experimental form for a direct attack on militarism, poverty, and the oppression of women, claiming they were interconnected parts of a single, devastating ethos undermining Europe in the 1930s.

While writers rekindled moral concerns, scientists in research institutes and universities continued to point out limits to human understanding—limits that seemed at odds with the megalomaniacal pronouncements of dictators. Astronomer Edwin Hubble in California determined in the early 1930s that the universe was an expanding entity. Czech mathematician Kurt Gödel maintained that any mathematical system contains some propositions that are undecidable. The German physicist Werner Heisenberg developed the "uncertainty," or "indeterminacy," principle in physics. Scientific observation of atomic behavior, according to this theory, actually disturbs the atom and thereby makes precise formulations impossible. Even scientists, Heisenberg asserted, had to settle for statistical probability.

Religious leaders helped foster a spirit of resistance to dictatorship among religious people. The Swiss theologian Karl Barth encouraged rebellion against the Nazis, teaching that the faithful had to take seriously scriptural justifications of resistance to oppression. Pope Pius XI in his 1931 social encyclical (a letter addressed to the world on social issues), condemned the failure of modern societies to provide their citizens with a decent life and supported government intervention to create better moral and material conditions. The encyclical, *Quadragesimo Anno*, seemed to some an endorsement of the heavy-handed intervention of the fascists, but German Catholics frequently opposed Hitler, and religious commitment inspired many other individuals to oppose the rising tide of fascism.

The Road to World War II

In the wake of economic catastrophe, Hitler, Mussolini, and Japan's military leaders marched the world toward another catastrophic war. Each of these leaders believed that his nation was destined to rule a far larger territory. At first, many ordinary citizens and statesmen in Britain and France hoped that sanctions imposed by the League of Nations would work to contain aggression. Others, believing that the powers had rushed into World War I, counseled the appeasement of Mussolini and Hitler. The widespread desire for peace in the 1930s sprang from fresh and painful memories: the destruction of World War I and the economic turmoil of the Great Depression. But it left many people blind to Japanese actions in China, Hitler's expansionist goals, and the fascist attack on the Spanish republic. So brutal were the interwar years that some historians claim that along with World War I and World War II, they make up a "Thirty Years' War" of the twentieth century.

Japan, Germany, and Italy Strike

Japan's military leaders chafed to control more of Asia and saw China, the Soviet Union, and the other Western powers as obstacles to the empire's prosperity and the fulfillment of its destiny. Renewed military vigor was seen as key to pulling agriculture and small business from the depths of economic depression. The Japanese army took the lead. In September 1931, a train in the Chinese province of Manchuria blew up. Japanese officers used the explosion, which they had set, as an excuse to invade Manchuria, set up a puppet government, and push farther into China. The Japanese public agreed with journalistic calls for aggressive expansion to restore Japan's economy and boost the nation's prestige, and businessmen wanted new markets and resources for their burgeoning but wounded industries. Advocating Asian conquest as part of Japan's "divine mission," the military extended its influence in the government. By 1936–1937, Japan was spending 47 percent of its budget on arms.

The situation in East Asia had international repercussions. Japanese aggression compounded the effect of the growing international market in Japanese goods. The League of Nations condemned the invasion but imposed no sanctions that would have put economic teeth into its condemnation. Nevertheless, the rebuff outraged the Japanese public and goaded the government to ally with Hitler and Mussolini. In 1937, Japan attacked China again, justifying its offensive as a first step toward liberating the region

The Road to World War II	
1929	Global depression begins with U.S. stock market crash
1931	Japan invades Manchuria
1933	Hitler comes to power in Germany
1935	Italy invades Ethiopia
1936	Civil war breaks out in Spain; Hitler remilitarizes the Rhineland
1937	Japan invades China
1938	Germany annexes Austria; European leaders meet in Munich to negotiate with Hitler
1939	Germany seizes Czechoslovakia; Hitler and Stalin sign nonaggression pact; Germany invades Poland; Britain and France declare war on Germany

from Western imperialism. Hundreds of thousands of Chinese were massacred in the "Rape of Nanjing"—an atrocity so named because of the brutality toward girls and women and the grim acts of torture perpetrated by the Japanese. President Roosevelt immediately announced an embargo on the U.S. export of airplane parts to Japan and later enforced stringent economic sanctions on the crucial raw materials that drove Japanese industry. But the Western powers, including the Soviet Union, did not effectively resist Japan's territorial expansion in Asia and the Pacific.

Like Japanese leaders, Mussolini and Hitler called their countries "have-nots." Mussolini threatened "permanent conflict" to expand Italy's borders, and Hitler's agenda included breaking free from the Versailles treaty's military restrictions and providing the "Aryans" with *Lebensraum* (living space) in which to thrive. Nazi plans called for territory to be seized from the "inferior" Slavic peoples and Bolsheviks, who would serve as slaves to the "Aryans" or would be moved to Siberia. Both dictators portrayed themselves as peace-loving men who resorted to extreme measures only to benefit their countries and humanity. Their anticommunism appealed to statesmen across Europe.

In the autumn of 1933, Hitler announced Germany's withdrawal from the League of Nations. In 1935, Hitler loudly rejected the clauses of the Treaty of Versailles that limited German military strength; he reintroduced military conscription and publicly started rearming, although Germany had been rearming in secret for years. Mussolini also chose 1935 to invade Ethiopia, one of the very few African states not overwhelmed by European imperialism. The attack was intended to demonstrate his regime's youth and vigor and to raise Italy's standing among the colonial powers. "The Roman legionnaires are again on the march," one soldier exulted. Although the poorly equipped Ethiopians resisted, their capital, Addis Ababa, fell in the spring of 1936. The League of Nations voted sanctions against Italy, but Britain and France opposed an embargo with teeth in it— one on oil—and thus kept the sanctions from being effective while also suggesting a lack of resolve to fight aggression.

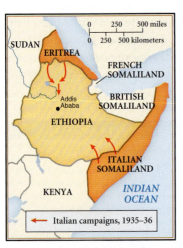

The Ethiopian War, 1935–1936

Profiting from the diversion of Italy's attack on Ethiopia, in March 1936 Hitler had defiantly sent his troops into what was supposed to be a permanently demilitarized zone in the Rhineland. The inhabitants greeted the Germans with wild enthusiasm. The French, whose security was most endangered by this action, protested to the League of Nations instead of countering with an invasion of their own as they had done in the Ruhr in 1923. The British accepted the fait accompli. The two dictators thus appeared as powerful military heroes forging, in Mussolini's muscular phrase, a "Rome-Berlin Axis." Next to them, the politicians of France and Great Britain looked timid.

The Spanish Civil War, 1936–1939

In what seemed like an exception to the trend toward authoritarian government, Spanish republicans overthrew their king in 1931. Nonetheless, large landowners and the Catholic clergy, who had the impoverished peasantry at their mercy, continued to dominate without modernizing the rural economy. The republicans hoped to modernize Spain by promoting industry and efficient, independent farming, but the government they established failed to enact land redistribution, which might have ensured popular loyalty and diminished the power of landowners and the church. This failure was all the more damaging because the antimonarchist forces included a mutually hostile array of liberals, anarchists, Communists, and other splinter groups constantly vying for power and harassing one another. In contrast, wealthy right-wing forces from the large landowners and clergy acted in concert.

In 1936, pro-republican forces temporarily banded together in a Popular Front coalition to win elections and prevent the republic from collapsing under the weight of internal squabbling and growing monarchist opposition. With the Popular Front victory, euphoria swept Spain as coveted municipal jobs were doled out and unemployment abated. The right recovered and revolted under the leadership of General Francisco Franco (1892–1975), who had the support of a host of right-wing groups, including the fascist Falange Party. The military uprising led to the Spanish Civil War (Map 21.1), which pitted the republicans, or Loyalists, against the fascist Falangists and the powerful forces of the authoritarian right.

The struggle became a rehearsal for World War II when Hitler and Mussolini sent military personnel in support of the right and Franco to test new weapons and

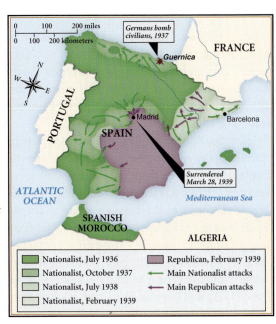

■ **MAP 21.1 The Spanish Civil War, 1936–1939**
Pro-republican and antirepublican forces fought one another to determine whether Spain would be a democracy or an authoritarian state. Germany and Italy sent military assistance, notably airplanes to experiment with bombing civilians, while volunteers from around the world arrived to fight for the losing cause of the republic. Defeating these ill-organized groups, General Francisco Franco instituted a pro-fascist government that sent many to jail and into exile.

Germans bomb civilians, 1937

Guernica

FRANCE

PORTUGAL

Madrid

Barcelona

SPAIN

Surrendered March 28, 1939

ATLANTIC OCEAN

Mediterranean Sea

SPANISH MOROCCO

ALGERIA

- ▇ Nationalist, July 1936
- ▇ Nationalist, October 1937
- ▇ Nationalist, July 1938
- ▇ Nationalist, February 1939
- ▇ Republican, February 1939
- ← Main Nationalist attacks
- ← Main Republican attacks

■ The Spanish Republic Appeals for Aid

The government of the Spanish republic sent out modern advertising and propaganda to attract support from the remaining democracies—especially Great Britain and France. Antiwar sentiment remained high among the British and French, however. Thus, despite the horrifying and deliberate bombing of civilians by Franco's German allies, aid for the republic failed to arrive.

(Imperial War Museum, London.)

to practice new tactics, particularly the terror bombing of civilians. In 1937, low-flying German planes attacked the town of Guernica, mowing down civilians in the streets. This gratuitous slaughter inspired Pablo Picasso's memorial mural to the dead, *Guernica* (1937), in which the intense suffering is starkly displayed in monochromatic grays and whites to capture a sense of moral decay as well as physical death.

The Spanish Republic appealed everywhere for assistance but received little official response except for brief support from the Soviet Union. While Britain and France again showed their war-wariness by refusing to provide aid, a few thousand volunteers from a variety of countries—students, journalists, writers (George Orwell was one), and artists—fought for the republic. As these volunteers put it, "Spain was the place to stop fascism." Republican ranks again splintered into competing groups of liberals, Trotskyites, anarchists, and Communists. In this bitter contest, both sides committed widespread atrocities against civilians. The aid Franco received ultimately proved decisive, and his troops defeated the republicans in 1939. The ensuing dictatorship remained in place until 1975.

Hitler's Conquest of Central Europe, 1938–1939

The fall of central Europe that ultimately led to World War II began with Hitler's annexation of Austria in 1938 (Map 21.2). Many Austrians actually wished for such a merger, or *Anschluss*, after the Paris peace settlement stripped them of their empire. So Hitler's troops entered Austria as easily as tourists, and Austrian enthusiasm made the Anschluss appear to support the Wilsonian idea of "self-determination." The annexation began the unification of "Aryan peoples" into one greater German nation, and it marked the first step in Hitler's planned takeover of the resources of central and eastern Europe. Austria was declared a German province, the Ostmark, and Hitler's thugs ruled once-cosmopolitan Vienna. An observer later commented on the scene: "University professors were obliged to scrub the streets with their naked hands, pious white-bearded Jews were dragged into the synagogue by hooting youths and forced to do knee-exercises and to shout 'Heil Hitler' in chorus."

With Austria firmly in his grasp, Hitler turned to Czechoslovakia and its rich resources. Overpowering this democracy did not appear as simple a task as seizing Austria. Czechoslovakia had a large army and formidable border defenses and armament factories, and most Czech citizens were prepared to fight for their country. However, Hitler gambled correctly that the other Western powers would not interfere, especially as the Nazi propaganda machine poured tremendous abuse on Czechoslovakia for allegedly "persecuting" the German minority. By October 1, 1938, he warned, Czechoslovakia would have to grant autonomy (amounting to Nazi rule) to the German-populated border region, the Sudetenland, or face German invasion.

As the October deadline approached, the British prime minister Neville Chamberlain (1869–1940), Mussolini, and the French premier Edouard Daladier (1884–1970) met with Hitler in Munich and agreed not to oppose Germany's claim to the Sudetenland. The strategy of preventing a war by making concessions for legitimate grievances (in this case, the alleged affront to Germans in the Peace of Paris) was called *appeasement*. At the time, it was widely seen as a positive act, and the agreement between Germany and Great Britain—the Munich Pact—prompted Chamberlain to announce that he had secured "peace in our time."◆ Stalin, excluded from the Munich conference, learned from the deliberations that the democracies were not going to fight to protect eastern Europe.

Having portrayed himself as a man of peace, Hitler waited until March 1939 to invade Czechoslovakia. Britain and France responded by promising military support to Poland, Romania, Greece, and Turkey in case of Nazi invasion. In May 1939, Hitler and Mussolini countered this agreement by signing a pledge of offensive and defensive support called the Pact of Steel.

◆ For the speech in which Chamberlain defined and defended the policy of appeasement, see Document 68, Neville Chamberlain, "Speech on the Munich Crisis."

■ MAP 21.2 The Growth of Nazi Germany, 1933–1939

German expansion was rapid and surprising, as Hitler's forces and Nazi diplomacy brought about the annexation of the new states of central and eastern Europe. Though committed to defending the sovereignty of these states through the League of Nations, French and British diplomats were more interested in satisfying Hitler because they believed that doing so would prevent his claiming even more of Europe. They were mistaken, and Hitler proceeded to acquire the human and material resources of adjacent countries to support the Third Reich.

www.bedfordstmartins.com/huntconcise   See the ONLINE STUDY GUIDE for more help in analyzing this map.

Historians have sharply criticized the Munich Pact because it bought Hitler time to build his army and seemed to give him the green light for further aggression. Some historians believe that a confrontation might have stopped Hitler and that even if war had resulted, the democracies would have triumphed. According to proponents of this view, each military move by Germany, Italy, and Japan should have been met with stiff opposition, and the Soviet Union should have been made a partner to this resistance. Others counter that appeasement provided France and Britain precious time to beef up their own armies, which the Munich crisis prompted them to do, and to prepare their citizens for another war.

On August 23, 1939, to the astonishment of public opinion in the West, Germany and the USSR signed a nonaggression agreement. Despite Hitler's ambition to wipe the Bolsheviks off the face of the earth, Stalin needed time to reconstitute his military because he had destroyed his officer corps in the purges. The Nazi-Soviet Pact provided that if one country became embroiled in war, the other country would remain neutral. Moreover, the two dictators secretly agreed to divide Poland and the Baltic states—Latvia, Estonia, and Lithuania—at some future date. The Nazi-Soviet Pact ensured that if war came, the democracies would be fighting a Germany with no fear of attack on its eastern borders. Believing that Great Britain and perhaps even France would not fight because his aggression had met no resistance so far, Hitler now aimed his forces at Poland.

World War II, 1939–1945

The global catastrophe that quickly came to be called the Second World War opened when Hitler launched an all-out attack on Poland on September 1, 1939. In contrast to 1914, no jubilation in Berlin accompanied the invasion. Two days later, when Britain and France declared war, the mood in other capitals was similarly grim. Japan, Italy, and the United States did not join the battle immediately; their later participation spread the fighting throughout the world. By the time World War II ended in 1945, many Europeans were starving, much of the European continent lay in ruins, and unparalleled atrocities and genocide had killed 6 million Jews and countless others.

The German Onslaught

German ground forces quickly defeated the ill-equipped Polish troops by launching an overpowering *Blitzkrieg* ("lightning war"). The Germans concentrated airplanes, tanks, and motorized infantry to encircle Polish defenders and capture the capital, Warsaw, with overwhelming speed. Allowing the German army to conserve supplies, Blitzkrieg lulled Germans at home into believing that the human costs of gaining Lebensraum for the full flowering of the "Aryan race" would be low. On September 17, 1939, Soviet forces invaded Poland from the east. By the end of the month, the Polish army was in shambles, and the victors had divided Poland according to the Nazi-Soviet Pact. Hitler sold the war within the Third Reich as one of self-defense, especially from what Nazi propagandists called the "warlike menace" of world Jewry.

Hitler ordered an attack on France for November 1939, but his generals, who feared that Germany was ill prepared for total war, were able to postpone the offensive until the spring of 1940. In April 1940, the Blitzkrieg crushed Denmark and Norway; the battles of Belgium, the Netherlands, and France followed in May and June. On June 5, Mussolini, eyeing future spoils for Italy, invaded France from the southeast, as the French defense rapidly collapsed. Nor could the British army, allied with the French, withstand the German onslaught. Trapped on the beaches of Dunkirk in northern France, 370,000 British and French soldiers were rescued in a heroic effort by an improvised fleet of naval ships, fishing boats, and pleasure craft. The dejected French government surrendered on June 22, 1940, leaving Germany to rule the northern half of France, including Paris. In the south, known as Vichy France after the spa town where the government sat, Germany allowed the reactionary and aged World War I hero Henri Philippe Pétain to govern. Stalin used the diversion in western Europe to annex the Baltic states.

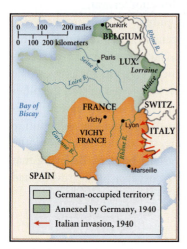

The Division of France, 1940

Britain now stood alone. Blaming Germany's rapid victories on Chamberlain's policy of appeasement, the British swept him out of office and installed as prime minister Winston Churchill (1874–1965), an early advocate of resistance to Hitler. After Hitler ordered the bombardment of Britain in the summer of 1940, Churchill rallied the nation by radio—now in more than nine million British homes—to protect the ideals of liberty with their "blood, toil, tears, and sweat." In the battle of Britain, or Blitz as the British called it, the German air force (*Luftwaffe*) bombed public buildings and monuments, harbors and weapons depots, and industry. Using the wealth of their colonies, the British poured resources into anti-aircraft weapons, a highly successful code-detecting group called Ultra, and development of Britain's advantage in radar. At year's end, the British air industry was outproducing the Germans by 50 percent.

By the fall of 1940, German air losses forced Hitler to abandon his plan for a naval invasion of Britain. Forcing Hungary, Romania, and Bulgaria to join the Axis, Hitler gained access to more food and oil. He then made his fateful decision to attack what he called the "center of judeobolshevism"—the Soviet Union. In June 1941, the German army crossed the Soviet border, as Hitler promised to "raze Moscow and Leningrad to the ground." Deployed along a 2,000-mile front, three million German and other Axis troops quickly penetrated Soviet lines. Stalin disappeared for several days but then rallied to direct the defense. By July, the German army had rolled to within 200 miles of Moscow and eventually reached its suburbs. Using a strategy of rapid encirclement, German troops killed, captured, and wounded more than half the 4.5 million Soviet soldiers defending the borders. Then Hitler blundered. Considering himself a military genius and the Slavic people inferior, he proposed attacking Leningrad, the Baltic states, and the Ukraine simultaneously, ignoring his generals' recommendation to concentrate on Moscow. Carrying out Hitler's cumbersome strategy cost the German forces precious time. Driven by Stalin, local party members, and rising patriotic resolve, the Soviet people fought back. The onset of winter turned Nazi soldiers to frostbitten wretches because Hitler had feared that equipping his army for the harsh Russian winter would suggest to the German people that a prolonged campaign lay in store. His ill-supplied armies succumbed to the weather and disease.

War Expands: The Pacific and Beyond

As the German army stalled in the Soviet Union, a dramatic attack ignited war in the Pacific. On December 7, 1941, Japanese planes bombed American naval and air bases at Pearl Harbor in Hawaii and then decimated a fleet of U.S. airplanes in the Philippines. President Roosevelt summoned Congress to declare war on Japan. The outbreak of war in Europe had intensified U.S.-Japanese competition, as Japan had taken control of parts of the British Empire, bullied the Dutch in Indonesia, and invaded Indochina to procure raw materials for its industrial and military expansion. The militarist Japanese government decided to settle matters with the West once and for all. By spring 1942, the Japanese had conquered Guam, the Philippines, Malaya, Burma, Indonesia, Singapore, and much of the southwestern Pacific.

On December 11, 1941, Hitler declared war on the United States—an appropriate enemy, he proclaimed, as it was "half Judaized and the other half Negrified." Mussolini followed suit. The United States was not prepared for a prolonged struggle. Isolationist sentiment remained strong. U.S. armed forces numbered only 1.6 million, and no plan existed for producing the necessary guns, tanks, and airplanes. Also working against war-preparedness was U.S. ambivalence toward the Soviet Union even in the face of Hitler's attack, and Stalin himself reciprocated the mistrust. Nevertheless, Hitler's four enemies came together in the Grand Alliance of Great Britain, the Free French (an exile government led by General Charles de Gaulle and based in London), the Soviet Union, and the United States. Given the urgency of war and the partners' competing interests, the Grand Alliance and a larger coalition with twenty other countries—known collectively as the Allies—had much internal strife to overcome in their struggle against the Axis—Germany, Italy, and Japan.

The Holocaust

As the German army swept through eastern Europe, it slaughtered Jews, Communists, Slavs, and others whom the Nazis deemed "racial inferiors" and enemies. In Poland, the SS murdered hundreds of thousands of Polish citizens or relocated them to forced labor camps. Across Europe, the German army rounded up civilians to work on farms and in labor camps throughout the Reich—all to power the voracious Nazi war machine. Herded into urban ghettos and living on minimal rations, eastern European Jews became special targets of SS violence. Around captured Soviet towns, Jews were usually shot in pits, some of which they had been forced to dig themselves. After shedding their clothes and putting them in orderly piles for later Nazi use, ten thousand or more at a time were killed, often with the help of anti-Semitic villagers. However, the "Final Solution"—the Nazis' diabolical plan to exterminate all of Europe's Jews—was not yet fully under way.

In addition to the massacres, a bureaucratically organized and efficient technological system for rounding up Jews and transporting them to extermination sites had taken shape by the fall of 1941. On the eve of war in 1939, Hitler had predicted "the destruction of the Jewish race in Europe." Although no clear order written by Hitler exists, he discussed the Final Solution's progress, issued oral directives for it, and from the beginning made lethal anti-Semitism a basis for Nazism. Modern social and legal science and technology, managed by efficient scientists, doctors, lawyers, and government workers, also made the Holocaust work. Six camps in Poland were developed specifically for the purposes of mass murder, although some, like Auschwitz-Birkenau, served as both extermination and labor camps. Using techniques developed in the T4 project in the late 1930s, the camp at Chelmno first gassed Christian Poles and Soviet prisoners of war. Specially designed crematoria for the mass burning of corpses started functioning in 1943. By then, Auschwitz had the capacity to burn 1.7 million bodies per year. About 60 percent of new arrivals—particularly children, women, and old people—were selected directly for murder in the gas chambers. The other 40 percent labored until they were utterly used up; then they, too, were sent to their deaths.

Extermination camps received their victims from across the European continent. In the ghettos in various European cities, councils of Jewish leaders, such as the council in Amsterdam where Etty Hillesum worked, were ordered to identify those to be "resettled in the east." For weakened, poorly armed ghetto inhabitants, open resistance meant certain death. When Polish Jews rose up against their Nazi captors in Warsaw in 1943, they were mercilessly butchered. The Nazis took pains to cloak their true purposes in the extermination camps. Bands played when trainloads of victims arrived; some were given postcards with reassuring messages to mail home. Those not chosen for immediate murder had their heads shaved, were showered and disinfected, and were then given prison garments. So began life in "a living hell," as one survivor wrote.♦

Overworked inmates usually took in less than five hundred calories per day, leaving them vulnerable to typhus and other diseases that swept through the camps. The brutality of mentally disturbed and criminal prison guards and of inhumane medical experiments failed to crush everyone's spirit: women observed religious

---

♦ For more survivor accounts, see Document 69, Sam Bankhalter and Hinda Kibort, "Memories of the Holocaust."

■ **Persecution of Warsaw Jews**
Hitler was determined to exterminate Jews, Slavs, gypsies, homosexuals, and others he deemed
"undesirable," and he often enlisted community leaders to cooperate in deportation and even exe-
cutions. In the 1930s, people fled Germany and then countries the Nazis conquered. In the city of
Warsaw, where Jews were crowded into ghettos and deprived of food and fuel, a Jewish uprising
brought massive retaliation. (© Bettmann/Corbis.)

holidays, celebrated birthdays, and re-created other sustaining aspects of domestic
life. Prisoners forged new friendships that helped in the struggle for survival. Thanks
to those sharing a bread ration and doing him favors, wrote the Auschwitz survivor
Primo Levi, "I managed not to forget that I myself was a man." By the end of the
war in 1945, six million Jews, the vast majority from eastern Europe, along with an
estimated five million to six million gypsies, homosexuals, Slavs, and others were
murdered.

Societies at War

Even more than World War I, World War II depended on industrial productivity
geared totally toward war and mass murder. The Axis countries remained at a
disadvantage throughout the war despite their vast conquests. Although the war
accelerated economic production some 300 percent between 1940 and 1944 in all
belligerent countries, the Allies produced more than three times the Axis output in
1943. Even with its territory occupied and many of its cities besieged, the Soviet
Union increased its production of weapons. Both Japan and Germany made the

most of their lower capacity, most notably in the strategy of Blitzkrieg. Hitler had to avoid imposing wartime austerity because he had come to power promising to end economic suffering, not increase it. The use of millions of slave laborers and assets from occupied areas helped, but both Japan and Germany underestimated the resources and morale of their enemies.

Allied governments were overwhelmingly successful in generating civilian participation, especially among women. In the Axis countries, where government policy particularly exalted motherhood, women avoided paid work even though they were desperately needed in offices and factories. In contrast, women constituted more than half the Soviet workforce by war's end. They dug massive antitank trenches around Moscow and other threatened cities, and 800,000 volunteered for the military, even serving as pilots. As the Germans invaded, Soviet citizens moved entire factories eastward.

Governments used propaganda to mobilize loyalty; even more than in World War I, propaganda saturated society in movie theaters and on the radio. Accustomed to listening to politicians on the air, people were glued to their radios for war news. Films depicted aviation heroes and infantrymen as well as the workingwomen and wives left behind. Government agencies monitored filmmaking and allocated supplies to approved films. In the United States, military leaders loaned authentic props only if they could censor the scripts.

Just as governments sought to mobilize culture between 1939 and 1945, they organized many aspects of everyday life. Bureaucrats regulated the production and distribution of food, clothing, and household products, all of which were rationed and generally of low quality. They gave hints for preparing meals without meat, sugar, fat, and other staples and exhorted women and children to embrace deprivation so their fighting men would survive. Governments hired economists, statisticians, and other specialists to influence civilian thought and behavior. With governments standardizing such items as food, clothing, and entertainment, World War II furthered the development of mass society.

On both sides, propaganda and government policies promoted racial thinking. Since the early 1930s, the German government had drawn ugly caricatures of Jews, Slavs, and gypsies. Similarly, Allied propaganda during the war depicted Germans as sadists and perverts and the "Japs" as uncivilized, insectlike fanatics. The U.S. government forced citizens of Japanese origin into internment camps. In the Soviet Union, Muslims and minority ethnic groups were uprooted and relocated as potential Nazi collaborators. Simultaneously, colonized peoples were drawn into the war through conscription into the armies and forced labor. Some two million Indian men served the Allied cause, as did several hundred thousand Africans. As the Japanese swept through the Pacific and parts of East Asia, they, too, conscripted men into their army. Both sides bombarded colonized societies with propaganda, as radio stations and newspapers proliferated during the war. This propaganda, in the context of forced labor, politicized colonized peoples to seek postwar liberation.

From Resistance to Allied Victory

Professional armies ultimately defeated the Axis powers, but civilian resistance in Nazi-occupied areas also contributed to the Allied triumph. General Charles de Gaulle (1890–1970) directed the Free French government and its forces from England; some 20 percent of these French troops were colonized Asians and Africans. Other French resisters fought in Communist-dominated groups, some of whom gathered information to aid a planned Allied landing on the French coast. Rural partisans plotted assassinations of German officers and civilian collaborators and bombed bridges, rail lines, and military facilities in German-occupied areas. The spirit of resistance produced heroes such as Swedish diplomat Raoul Wallenberg (1912–1947?), whose dealings with Nazi officials saved thousands of Hungarian Jews.

Ordinary people fought back through everyday activities. Homemakers circulated newsletters urging demonstrations at prisons where civilians were detained and in marketplaces where food was rationed. In central Europe, hikers smuggled Jews and others through dangerous mountain passes. Danish villagers created vast escape networks. Resisters played on stereotypes of femininity: women often carried weapons to assassination sites in the correct belief that the Nazis were not likely to suspect or search them; they also seduced and murdered enemy officers. Other actions subtly undermined the demands of fascist leaders. Couples in Germany and Italy limited family size in defiance of pro-birth policies. German teenagers danced the forbidden American jitterbug, thus defying the Nazis and forcing the police to monitor their groups. Resistance underscored the importance of the liberal ideal of individual political action and courage.

Amid civilian resistance, Allied forces started tightening a noose around the Axis in mid-1942 (Map 21.3). A major turning point came in August when the German army began a siege on Stalingrad, a city whose capture would give access to Soviet oil and cut access to the Soviet Union's interior. Months of ferocious fighting ended when the Soviet army captured the ninety thousand German survivors in February 1943. Allied victories in North Africa in 1942 were followed in July 1943 by an Allied landing in Sicily. However, the Germans came to their ally's aid and fought bitterly for the peninsula of Italy until April 1945, when Allied forces finally triumphed. After Italy's liberation, partisans shot Mussolini and his mistress and hanged their dead bodies for public display.

The victory at Stalingrad marked the beginning of the costly Soviet drive westward—during which the Soviets bore the brunt of the Nazi war machine. As Stalin pressed for the opening of a western front, Roosevelt, Churchill, and Stalin met at Teheran, Iran, in November and December 1943 to coordinate their efforts. On June 6, 1944, the combined Allied forces under the command of U.S. General Dwight Eisenhower landed on the heavily fortified beaches of Normandy, France, and then fought their way through the German-held territory of western France. In late July, Allied forces broke through German defenses and a month later helped

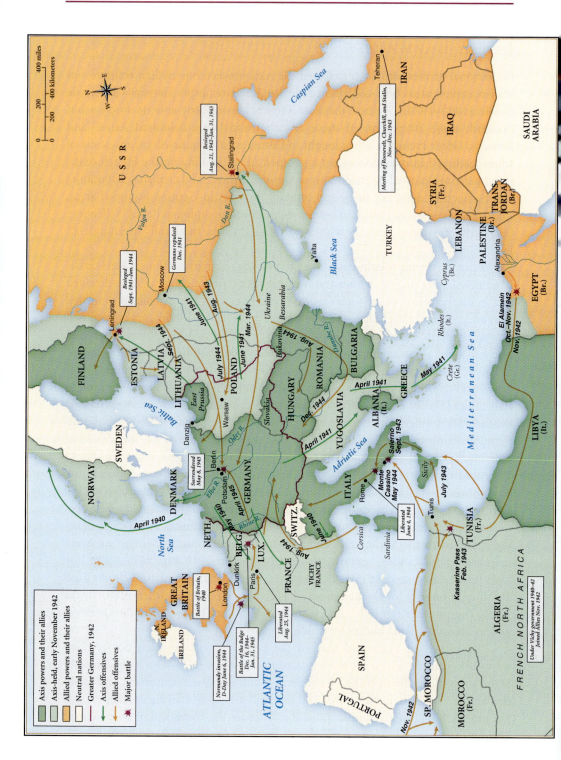

400 miles
400 kilometers

Caspian Sea

IRAN

IRAQ

SAUDI
ARABIA

Besieged
Aug. 21, 1942–Jan. 31, 1943

Stalingrad

Meeting of Roosevelt, Churchill, and Stalin,
Nov.–Dec. 1943

Teheran

SYRIA
(Fr.)

TRANS
JORDAN
(Br.)

LEBANON
(Fr.)

PALESTINE
(Br.)

USSR

Volga R.

Don R.

Besieged
Sept. 1941–Jan. 1944

Germans repulsed
Dec. 1941

Moscow

Leningrad

Aug. 1943

June 1941

July 1944

June 1941

Aug. 1944

Mar. 1944

Sept. 1941

Ukraine

Bessarabia

Bukovina

Danube R.

Black Sea

Yalta

TURKEY

Cyprus
(Br.)

Mediterranean Sea

Alexandria

El Alamein
Oct.–Nov. 1942

Nov. 1942

EGYPT
(Br.)

FINLAND

ESTONIA

LATVIA

LITHUANIA

East
Prussia

Danzig

Warsaw

POLAND

SWEDEN

NORWAY

Baltic Sea

DENMARK

April 1940

Surrendered
May 8, 1945

Berlin

Potsdam

April 1945

Elbe R.

May 1940

Oder R.

Rhine R.

GERMANY

SWITZ.

NETH.

BELG.

LUX.

FRANCE

VICHY
FRANCE

June 1940

Aug. 1944

Slovakia

HUNGARY

Dec. 1944

April 1941

YUGOSLAVIA

ROMANIA

BULGARIA

April 1941

ALBANIA
(It.)

GREECE

May 1941

Crete
(Gr.)

Rhodes
(It.)

Adriatic Sea

ITALY

Rome

Monte
Cassino
May 1944

Salerno
Sept. 1943

Liberated
June 4, 1944

Corsica

Sardinia

Sicily

July 1943

Tunis

TUNISIA
(Fr.)

Kasserine Pass
Feb. 1943

LIBYA
(It.)

FRENCH NORTH AFRICA

ALGERIA
(Fr.)

Under Vichy government 1940–42
Joined Allies Nov. 1942

North
Sea

GREAT
BRITAIN

Battle of Britain,
1940

London

Dunkirk

Paris

Normandy invasion,
D-Day June 6, 1944

Battle of the Bulge
Dec. 16, 1944–
Jan. 31, 1945

Liberated
Aug. 25, 1944

N.
IRELAND

IRELAND

ATLANTIC
OCEAN

SPAIN

PORTUGAL

SP. MOROCCO

MOROCCO
(Fr.)

Nov. 1942

Legend:

- Axis powers and their allies
- Axis-held, early November 1942
- Allied powers and their allies
- Neutral nations
- Greater Germany, 1942
- Axis offensives
- Allied offensives
- Major battle

■ **Battle of Leningrad**

In the face of Nazi invasion, Soviet citizens reacted heroically, moving entire factories to the interior of the country and building fortifications. Nowhere was their resolve so tested as in Leningrad (now St. Petersburg). For more than two years, the German army besieged the city, causing the deaths of hundreds of thousands. Before the Allied landing at Normandy in 1944, the people of the USSR bore the brunt of Nazi military might in Hitler's attempt to defeat what he called "judeo-bolshevism." (Sovfoto.)

liberate Paris, where rebellion had erupted against the Nazis. British, Canadian, U.S., and other Allied forces then fought their way eastward to join the Soviets in squeezing the Third Reich to its final defeat.

In July 1944, a group of German military officers, fearing their country's military humiliation, attempted to assassinate, but only wounded, Hitler. As the Allies advanced, Hitler maintained that Germans were proving themselves unworthy of his greatness and deserved to perish in a cataclysmic conflagration. He refused all negotiations that might have spared Germans further death and destruction. Soviet

■ **MAP 21.3 World War II in Europe and North Africa**

The Axis and Allied powers waged war in Africa and Europe, inflicting massive loss of life and destruction of property on civilians, armies, and all the infrastructure—including factories, equipment, and agriculture—needed to wage total war. The war swept the European continent as well as areas in Africa colonized by or allied with the major powers. Ultimately, the Allies crushed the Axis by moving from east, west, and south to inflict a total defeat.

armies took Poland, and then, facing more than twice as many troops as on the western front, Stalin's forces withstood a fierce German defense in Hungary during the winter of 1944–1945. Hitler's refusal to surrender resulted in massive bombing of Germany. As the Soviet army took Berlin, Hitler committed suicide with his wife, Eva Braun. Although many German soldiers remained committed to the Third Reich, Germany finally surrendered on May 8, 1945.

After the German surrender, the Allies were able to focus solely on the war in the Pacific (Map 21.4). In 1940 and 1941, Japan had ousted the Europeans from many of their colonial holdings in Asia. In 1942, the Allies turned the tide, despite their diminished forces, destroying some of Japan's formidable naval power in battles at Midway Island and Guadalcanal. Unlike the United States, Japan lacked the capacity to recoup losses of ships or manpower. The Allies stormed one Pacific island after another, gaining bases from which to cut off the import of supplies and to launch bombers toward Japan itself. Despite these losses and the firebombing of Tokyo, the Japanese ruled out surrender and resorted instead to *kamikaze* tactics, in which pilots deliberately crashed their planes into American ships, killing themselves in the process.

Meanwhile, a U.S.-based international team of more than 100,000 scientists, technicians, and other workers had developed the atomic bomb. The Japanese practice of dying almost to the man rather than surrender caused Allied military planners to calculate that defeating Japan with conventional weapons might cost hundreds of thousands of Allied lives and take many more months. Thus, on August 6 and 9, 1945, the U.S. government unleashed its new atomic weapons on Hiroshima and Nagasaki, respectively, instantly killing 140,000 people and causing tens of thousands of later deaths from burns, wounds, and other afflictions. Hardliners in the Japanese military wanted to continue the war, but on August 14, 1945, Japan surrendered.

An Uneasy Postwar Settlement

The shape of the postwar settlement was a major Allied concern throughout the war. The aftermath of World War II, however, was unlike the aftermath of World War I. There was neither a celebrated peace conference nor a definitive, formal agreement among all the Allies about the final resolution of the war. The victorious Allies distrusted one another in varying degrees, and the United States and the Soviet Union were poised on the brink of another war.

Wartime agreements among members of the Grand Alliance about the future reflected ongoing differences that roused intense postwar debate. In 1941, Roosevelt and Churchill had forged the Atlantic Charter, which condemned aggression, reaffirmed the ideal of collective security, and endorsed the right of all peoples to choose their governments. Not only had the Allies come to focus on these points, but so had colonized peoples to whom, Churchill had said, the charter was not meant to

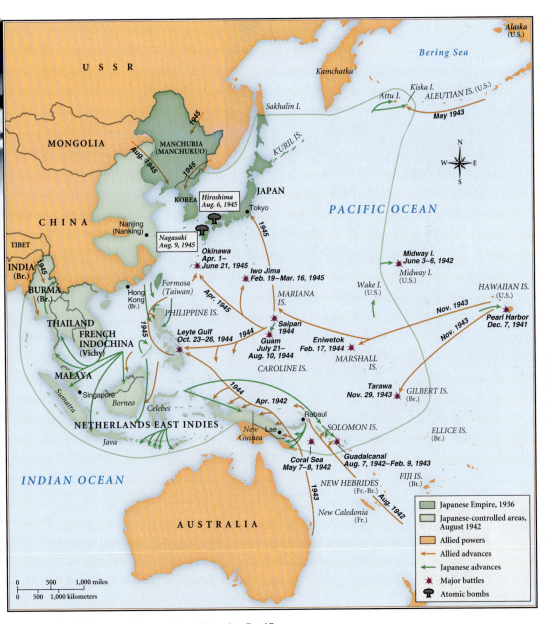

MAP 21.4 World War II in the Pacific

As in Europe, the early days of World War II gave the advantage to the Axis, as Japan took the offensive in conquering islands in the Pacific and territories in Asia—many of them colonies of the European states. Britain countered by mobilizing a vast Indian army. After the disastrous losses at Pearl Harbor and in the Philippines, the United States gradually gained the upper hand by costly assaults, island by island. The Japanese strategy of fighting to the last person instead of surrendering when a loss was in sight was one factor in the decision to drop the atomic bomb in August 1945.

■ **Hiroshima Victim**
In early August 1945, the United States dropped atomic bombs on Hiroshima and Nagasaki, Japan, killing tens of thousands outright and leaving tens of thousands more to die of their wounds. A few days later, Japan surrendered. Controversy still swirls around the decision to drop the bomb. People who see it as a racist act point out that no atomic weapons were dropped on Germany. People who see it as a justified act of warfare point out that Japan's no-surrender policy increased the likelihood of countless more casualties. (Gamma Liaison.)

apply. In October 1944, Churchill and Stalin had agreed on the postwar distribution of territories. The Soviet Union would control Romania and Bulgaria, Britain would control Greece, and together they would oversee Hungary and Yugoslavia. These agreements were at odds with Roosevelt's preference for collective security, self-determination, and open doors in trade. In February 1945, the "Big Three"— as Roosevelt, Churchill, and Stalin were known—had met in the Crimean town of Yalta. There Roosevelt had advocated the formation of the United Nations organization to replace the League of Nations as a global peace mechanism, and he had supported future Soviet influence in Korea, Manchuria, and the Sakhalin and Kurile Islands. At their last meeting, at Potsdam, Germany, in the summer of 1945, the Allied leaders had agreed to give the Soviets control of eastern Poland, to cede a large stretch of eastern Germany to Poland, and to adopt a temporary four-way occupation of Germany that would include France as one of the supervising powers. But as victory unfolded, the Allies scrambled to outmaneuver one another.

IMPORTANT DATES

1929	U.S. stock market crashes; global depression begins; Soviet leadership initiates war against the kulaks	**1938**	Virginia Woolf publishes *Three Guineas*
1930	Nationalist ruler Mustafa Kemal changes the name of Turkey's capital from Constantinople to Istanbul; French crush peasant uprising led by Ho Chi Minh, founder of the Indochinese Communist Party; Marlene Dietrich stars in *The Blue Angel*	**1939**	Germany invades Poland; World War II begins; Spanish Civil War ends
		1940	France falls to the German army
		1940–1941	British air force fends off German attacks in the battle of Britain
1930s	Movement for Indian independence; Sweden constructs welfare state	**1941**	Germany invades USSR; Japan attacks Pearl Harbor; United States enters the war
1933	Hitler comes to power in Germany	**1941–1945**	The Holocaust
		1944	Allied forces land at Normandy, France
1936	Show trials start in the USSR; Stalin purges top Communist Party officials and military leaders; Spanish Civil War begins	**1945**	Germany surrenders; United States drops atomic bombs on Hiroshima and Nagasaki; World War II ends

The Great Depression had inflicted global suffering. The Second World War left fifty million to sixty million people dead, an equal number of refugees without homes, and probably the most tragic moral legacy in human history. Peacemaking proved a long and bitter process that did not end in 1945. Forced into armies or into labor camps for war production, colonial peoples in Asia and Africa were in full rebellion or close to it. For the second time in three decades, they had seen Europeans killing one another, slaughtered by the very technology that Europeans had insisted made European civilization superior to theirs. Deference to Europe was virtually finished; independence was only a matter of time.

Western values at home were imperiled as well. Rational, democratic Europe had succumbed to permanent wartime values. It was this debased Europe that George Orwell captured in his novel *1984* (1949). Poor food and worn clothing, grimy streets and dwellings, people prematurely aged and careworn—all characterized London of the 1940s and Orwell's fictional state, Oceania. Orwell had worked for Britain's wartime Ministry of Information (called the Ministry of Truth in the novel) churning out propaganda and doctored news for wartime audiences. Propagandists had chosen their words carefully. Information and truth hardly mattered: *disengagement* replaced *retreat*, *battle fatigue* substituted for *insanity*, and *liberating*

Percent of population killed
- Over 10%
- 5–10%
- 1–5%
- Under 1%

- ■ Military dead
- ▲ Civilian dead
- ✦ City substantially damaged

FINLAND
■ 79,047

NORWAY
■ 4,780

SWEDEN

ESTONIA

LATVIA

LITHUANIA

Leningrad

North Sea

Baltic Sea

IRELAND

GREAT BRITAIN
■ 271,311
▲ 60,595

DENMARK
■ 4,339

Königsberg

USSR
■ 14,500,000
▲ Over 7,000,000

Coventry

London

Caen

Rotterdam

Düsseldorf

Dortmund

NETH.
■ 13,700
▲ 236,300

Hamburg

Bremen

Hanover

Berlin

Warsaw

POLAND
■ 850,000
(169,822 as Allies)
▲ 5,778,000

Kiev

BELG.
■ 9,561
▲ 75,000

Cologne

GERMANY
■ 2,850,000
▲ 2,300,000

Dresden

Frankfurt

Würzburg

CZECHOSLOVAKIA
■ 6,683
▲ 310,000

FRANCE
■ 210,671
▲ 173,260

SWITZ.

Munich

AUSTRIA
■ 380,000
▲ 145,000

HUNGARY
■ 750,000

ROMANIA
■ 519,822
▲ 465,000

Ploesti

Milan

Genoa

Bologna

YUGOSLAVIA
▲ 1,700,000

Black Sea

SPAIN
■ 4,500 (For Axis)
7,500 (For Allies)
▲ 10,000
(in concentration camps)

Corsica

ITALY
■ 279,820
▲ 17,400 (as Allies)

BULGARIA
■ 18,500
▲ 1,500

Sardinia

GREECE
■ 16,357
▲ 155,300

0   200   400 miles
0   200   400 kilometers

■ MAPPING THE WEST Europe at War's End, 1945

All of Europe was severely shocked during the age of catastrophe, but wartime damage left scars that would last for decades. Major German cities were bombed to bits. The Soviet Union suffered an unimaginable toll of perhaps 25 million deaths due to the war alone. Everything from politics to family life needed rebuilding. The chaos fueled postwar tensions stemming both from the quest to punish those held responsible for such suffering and from the Allied powers' manipulation of recovery assistance to gain political advantage in the cold war.

(From *The Hammond Atlas of the Twentieth Century* [London: Times Books, 1996], 102.)

a country could mean invading it and slaughtering its civilians. Millions rejoiced at the demise of Nazi evil in 1945, but Orwell saw as part of the war's legacy the end of prosperity, the deadening of creativity, and the intrusion of big government into everyday life. For Orwell, bureaucratic intrusion would intensify from the perpetuation of conflict, and fresh conflict was indeed brewing even before the war ended. As Allied powers competed for territory, a new struggle—known as the *cold war*—was beginning.

Conclusion

The Great Depression produced social dislocation and fear—conditions in which dictators were able to thrive because of their promises to restore national greatness and economic prosperity. Enticed by the mass media, people turned from representative institutions toward dynamic, if brutal, leaders. Memories of World War I permitted Hitler and Mussolini to menace Europe unimpeded throughout the 1930s. When a coalition formed to stop them, it was an uneasy one among the imperial powers France and Britain, the Stalinist Soviet Union, and the industrial giant the United States.

The brutal war—waged against civilians as well as armies—taught these powers different lessons and raised different expectations. The United States, Britain, and France emerged from the conflict convinced that at least some citizen well-being would be necessary to prevent a recurrence of fascism. Soviet citizens hoped that their lives would become easier and less restricted. The devastation of the USSR's population and resources, however, made Stalin increasingly obsessed with national security and reparations. Britain and France confronted the final eclipse of their imperial might, underscoring Orwell's insight that the war had transformed society irrevocably. The militarization of society and the deliberate murder of millions of innocent citizens like Etty Hillesum left a permanent blight on the European legacy. Nonetheless, competing visions of how to deal with Germany and eastern Europe and vast arsenals of sophisticated weaponry led the former Allies to threaten one another—and the world—with yet another war.

Suggested References for further reading and online research appear on page SR-34 at the back of the book.

www.bedfordstmartins.com/huntconcise   See the ONLINE STUDY GUIDE to assess your mastery of the material covered in this chapter.

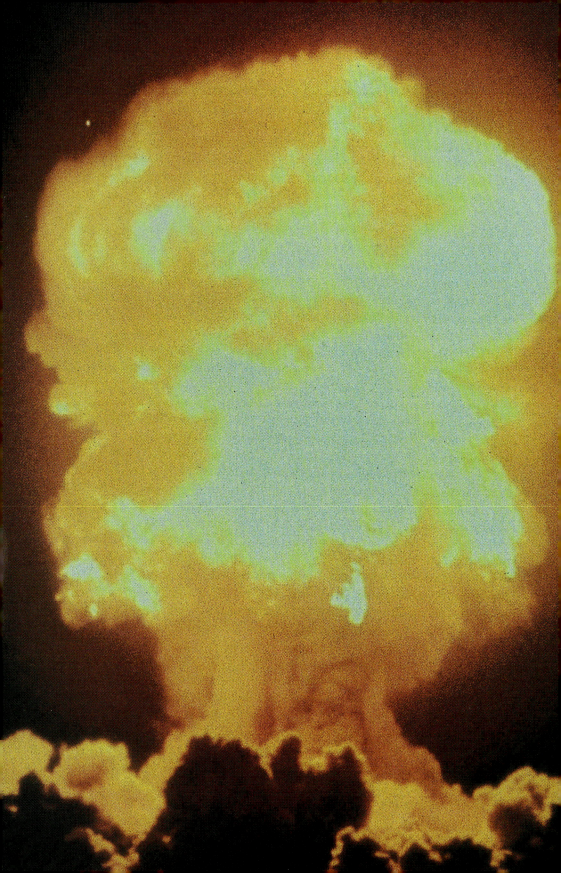

The Atomic Age

c. 1945–1960

I N LATE AUGUST 1949, THE SOVIET UNION DETONATED its first atomic bomb. Two days after President Harry S. Truman announced the news of this test, Billy Graham, a young Baptist minister, based his sermon at a revival meeting on the fearsome event. Graham warned that U.S. officials believed "we have only five to ten years and our civilization will be ended." He announced that Russia had aimed bombs to strike New York, Chicago, and Los Angeles, where the revival was taking place. "Time is desperately short. . . . Prepare to meet thy God," he warned. People flocked to hear Graham, launching the evangelist's astonishing career of spiritual and political influence in the United States and around the globe.

Graham's message—"We don't know how soon, but we do know this, that right now the grace of God can still save a poor lost sinner"—captured the extremes of postwar sentiment in an atomic age. On the one hand, the postwar situation was tragic. Fifty million people had died globally; Europe and Japan were prostrate and their peoples starving; evidence of genocide and other inhumanity was everywhere; the menace of nuclear annihilation loomed. It was to this menace that Graham referred. The old international order was gone, replaced by the rivalry of the United States and the Soviet Union for control of a devastated Europe, whose political and economic systems had collapsed. The nuclear arsenals of these two "superpowers"— a term coined in 1947—grew massively in the 1950s, but they were enemies who did not fight outright. Thus their terrifying rivalry was called the *cold war*. The cold war divided the West and caused acute anxiety, even for someone like Graham from the victorious and wealthy United States.

■ **The Atomic Age**
The dropping of atomic bombs on Hiroshima and Nagasaki in 1945 was followed by several decades of increasingly powerful detonations for testing purposes. The Soviet Union used underground testing, while the United States carried out atmospheric tests in the Pacific region. Protests against testing arose in the 1950s, many of them citing the hazards of radioactivity and the growing threat of nuclear annihilation. Simultaneously, nuclear power was converted to peacetime use, notably serving both as a source of energy and as a therapy for cancer. (Mark Meyer/Liaison Agency.)

On the other hand, the defeat of Nazism inspired an upsurge of hope, a revival of religious feeling like Graham's, and a new commitment to humanitarian goals. Heroic effort had defeated fascism, and that defeat raised hopes that a new age would begin. Atomic science promised advances in medicine, and nuclear energy was trumpeted as a replacement for coal and oil. The creation of the United Nations heralded an era of international cooperation. Around the globe, colonial peoples won independence from European masters, while in the United States the civil rights movement gained new momentum. The welfare state expanded, and by the end of the 1950s economic rebirth, stimulated in part by the cold war, had made much of Europe more prosperous than ever before. An "economic miracle" had occurred.

Extremes of hope and fear infused the atomic age, as society, culture, and the international order were transformed. Gone was the definition of a West comprising Europe and its cultural offshoots, such as the United States, and an East comprising Asian countries, such as India, China, and Japan. During the cold war, *West* came to stand for the United States and its client countries in western Europe, while *East* meant the Soviet Union and its tightly controlled bloc in eastern Europe. Still another terminology arose in the 1950s. The *first world* was the capitalist bloc of countries; the *second world*, the socialist bloc; and the *third world*, the countries emerging from imperial domination. As the world's people redefined themselves politically and culturally, the superpowers took the world to the brink of nuclear disaster when the United States discovered Soviet missile sites on the island of Cuba. From the dropping of the atomic bomb on Japan in 1945 to the Cuban missile crisis of 1962, Graham's dread that "we are moving madly toward destruction" gripped much of the world.

World Politics Transformed

The turmoil of wartime ended the global leadership of Europe. Many countries lay in ruins by the summer of 1945, and conditions would deteriorate before they got better. Bombed and bankrupt, victorious Britain could not feed its people. In contrast, the United States, whose territory was virtually untouched in the war, emerged as the world's sole economic giant, and the Soviet Union, despite suffering immense destruction, retained formidable military might. Having occupied Europe as part of the victorious alliance against Nazism and fascism, the two superpowers used Germany—at the heart of the continent and its politics—to divide Europe in two. By the late 1940s, the USSR imposed Communist rule throughout most of eastern Europe and in the 1950s quashed rebellions against its dominance. Western Europeans found themselves at least partially constricted by the very U.S. economic power that helped them rebuild, as the United States maintained air bases and nuclear weapon sites on their soil. The age of bipolar world politics had begun, with Europe as its testing ground.

Europe Prostrate

In contrast to World War I, when devastation was limited to the front lines around the trenches, armies in World War II had fought a war of movement that leveled thousands of square miles of territory. Across the continent, whole cities were clogged with rubble; homeless survivors wandered the streets. In Sicily and on the Rhine River, almost no bridge remained standing; in the Soviet Union, seventy thousand villages and more than a thousand cities lay in shambles. Everywhere people were suffering. In the Netherlands, the severity of Nazi occupation now brought the Dutch population close to death, relieved only by a U.S. airlift of food. In Britain, basic commodities were difficult to obtain, and many died in the bitterly cold winter of 1946–1947 because of a shortage of fuel. Italian bakers sold bread by the slice. When Allied troops passed through German towns, the famished inhabitants lined the roads in hopes that someone would toss them something to eat. "To see the children fighting for food," one British soldier noted, "was like watching animals being fed in a zoo." There were no uprisings as after World War I. Until the late 1940s, people were exhausted by the struggle for bare survival.

The tens of millions of refugees suffered the most. Many had been inmates of prisons and death camps; others, especially ethnic Germans, had fled westward to escape the victorious but destructive Red Army as it pushed toward Berlin. Native Germans in the Western-occupied zones viewed refugees as competitors for food and work. Many refugees ultimately found homes in countries that experienced little or no war damage, such as Denmark, Sweden, Canada, and Australia. Following the exodus of refugees from the east, western Europe became one of the world's most densely populated regions (Map 22.1).

The USSR drove many people from eastern Europe, yet it lobbied hard for the repatriation of several million Soviet prisoners of war and forced laborers—the first signal of Stalin's determination to revive Communist orthodoxy, which had weakened during the war. The Allies transported the majority of the Russian refugees back to the Soviet Union, where exile or execution for being "contaminated" by Western ideas awaited. As stories of executions filtered out, the Allies slowed the process, leaving hundreds of thousands of Soviets to join the ocean of refugees in western Europe.

Survivors of the concentration camps also discovered that their suffering had not ended with Germany's defeat. Many returned diseased and disoriented, while others often had no home to return to, for property had been confiscated and entire communities destroyed. Moreover, anti-Semitism had become official policy under the Nazis. In the summer of 1946, a vicious crowd in Kielce, Poland, rioted against returning Jewish survivors, killing at least 40 of the 250. Elsewhere in eastern Europe, such violence was common. Meanwhile, some officials across Europe even denied that unprecedented atrocities had been committed and wanted to refuse Jews any help. The U.S. government, fearing anti-Semitic backlash, let only about 12,000 Jews

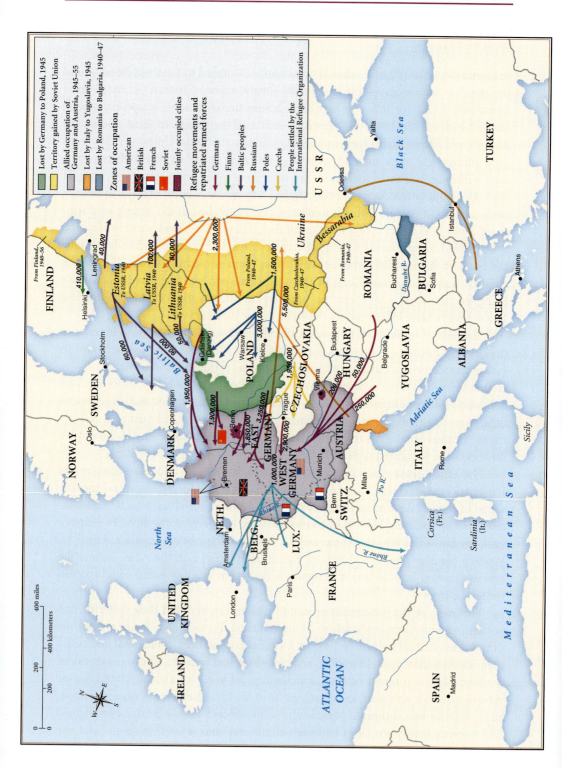

Legend:

Lost by Germany to Poland, 1945
Territory gained by Soviet Union
Allied occupation of Germany and Austria, 1945–55
Lost by Italy to Yugoslavia, 1945
Lost by Romania to Bulgaria, 1940–47
Jointly occupied cities

Zones of occupation
American
British
French
Soviet

Refugee movements and repatriated armed forces
Germans
Finns
Baltic peoples
Russians
Poles
Czechs
People settled by the International Refugee Organization

■ **MAP 22.1 The Impact of World War II on Europe**
European governments, many of them struggling to provide food and other necessities for their populations, found themselves responsible for hundreds of thousands, if not millions, of new refugees. Simultaneously, millions of prisoners of war, servicemen, and slave laborers were returned to the Soviet Union, many of them by force. This situation unfolded amid political instability and even violence.

into the country. Many survivors crammed into the port cities of Italy and other Mediterranean countries, eventually to escape Europe for Palestine, where Zionists had been settling for half a century. As they had in the 1930s, the British balked at this vast migration to the Middle East, for they saw their interests threatened by likely Arab-Jewish conflict over control of the region. Unwilling or unable to help Hitler's most abused victims, many European countries had simply lost the capacity for moral and economic leadership.

New Superpowers: The United States and the Soviet Union

Only two powerful countries were left in 1945: the United States and the Soviet Union. The United States was now the richest country in the world. Its industrial output had increased a remarkable 15 percent annually between 1940 and 1944, a rate of growth that was reflected in workers' wages. By 1947, the United States controlled almost two-thirds of the world's gold bullion and more than half of its commercial shipping, up from almost one-fifth of the total in the 1930s. With continued spending on industrial and military research, a confident mood swept the United States at the end of the war. Casting aside the post–World War I policy of nonintervention, Americans embraced their position as global leaders. Many had learned about the world while tracking the war's progress; hundreds of thousands of soldiers, government officials, and relief workers had direct experience of Europe, Africa, and Asia. Although some feared a postwar depression and many shared Billy Graham's worries about nuclear annihilation, a wave of suburban housing development and consumer spending kept the economy buoyant. Temporarily reversing the trend toward a lower birthrate, a "baby boom" exploded from the late 1940s through the early 1960s in response to economic abundance.

The Soviets also emerged from the war with a well-justified sense of accomplishment. Withstanding horrendous losses, they had resisted the most massive onslaught ever launched against a modern nation. Instead of the international isolation dealt Russia after World War I, Soviet leadership expected equality in decision making with the United States, and indeed many Europeans and Americans had great respect for the Soviet contribution to Hitler's defeat. Ordinary Soviet citizens believed that a victory that had cost the USSR as many as 25 million lives would bring improvement in everyday conditions and a continuation of the war's relatively relaxed politics. "Life will become pleasant," one writer prophesied. "There will be much coming and going, and a lot of contacts with the West." The Stalinist goals of industrialization and defense against Nazism had been won, and thus many Soviets expected an end to decades of hardship.

Stalin took a different view and moved ruthlessly to reassert control. In 1946, his new five-year plan set increased production goals and mandated more stringent collectivization of agriculture. Stalin cut back the army by two-thirds to beef up the labor force and also turned his attention to the low birthrate, a result of wartime male casualties and women's long, arduous working days, which discouraged them from adding child care to their already heavy responsibilities. He introduced an intense propaganda campaign emphasizing that workingwomen should hold down jobs and also fulfill their "true nature" by producing many children.

Origins of the Cold War

In the immediate postwar years, the United States and the Soviet Union engaged in a cold war that would afflict the world for more than four decades. Because no peace treaty officially ended the conflict with Germany as a written record of contest and compromise or of things gone wrong (as in the Peace of Paris), the origins of the cold war remain a matter of debate. Some historians point to consistent U.S., British, and French hostility that began with the Bolshevik Revolution and continued through the war. Others stress Stalin's aggressive policies, notably the Nazi-Soviet alliance in 1939 and his quick claims on the Baltic states and Polish territory when World War II broke out.

During the war, suspicion ran deep. Stalin felt that Churchill and Roosevelt were deliberately letting the USSR bear the brunt of Hitler's onslaught on Europe as part of their anti-Communist policy. Some Americans believed that dropping the atomic bomb on Japan would also frighten the Soviets from land grabs, and the new U.S. president, Harry Truman, was far tougher than Roosevelt toward the Soviet Union. Given what Stalin interpreted as a menace from the West and his own country's exhausted condition, he saw the USSR as needing not just a temporary military occupation but a permanent "buffer zone" of European states loyal to the USSR as a safeguard. Across the Atlantic, Truman saw the initial Soviet occupation of eastern Europe as heralding an era of Communist expansion. By 1946, members of the U.S. State Department were describing Stalin as prepared to continue the centuries-old Russian thirst for "world domination."

The cold war thus became a series of moves and countermoves in the shared occupation of the rich European heartland by two very different countries—the United States and the Soviet Union. In line with its geopolitical needs, the USSR proceeded to repress democratic, coalition governments of liberals, socialists, Communists, and peasant parties in central and eastern Europe between 1945 and 1948. It imposed Communist rule almost immediately in Bulgaria and Romania.

The Cold War, to 1962			
1945–1949	USSR establishes satellite states in eastern Europe	1950–1954	U.S. senator Joseph McCarthy leads hunt for American Communists
1947	Truman Doctrine announces U.S. commitment to contain communism; U.S. Marshall Plan provides massive aid to rebuild Europe	1953	Stalin dies
		1955	USSR and Eastern bloc countries form military alliance, the Warsaw Pact
1948–1949	Soviet troops blockade Berlin; United States airlifts provisions to Berliners	1956	Khrushchev denounces Stalin in "secret speech" to Communist Party Congress; Hungarians revolt unsuccessfully against Soviet domination
1949	Western democracies form North Atlantic Treaty Organization (NATO); Soviet bloc establishes Council for Mutual Economic Assistance (COMECON); USSR tests its first nuclear weapon	1959	Fidel Castro comes to power in Cuba
		1961	Berlin Wall erected
		1962	Cuban missile crisis
1950–1953	Korean War		

In Romania, Stalin cited citizen violence in 1945 as the excuse to demand an ouster of all non-Communists from the civil service and cabinet. In Poland, the Communists fixed the election results of 1945 and 1946 to create the illusion of approval for communism. Nevertheless, the Communists had to share power between 1945 and 1947 in partnership with the popular Peasant Party of Stanisław Mikołajczyk, which had a large constituency of rural workers and peasant landowners.

The United States put its new interventionist spirit to work. It acknowledged Soviet influence in areas the Soviet Union occupied but worried that Communist power would spread to western Europe. The difficult conditions of postwar life made Communist programs promising better conditions increasingly attractive to workers, while Communist leadership in the resistance gave the party a powerful allure. U.S. and British concern mounted when Communist insurgents threatened to overrun the right-wing monarchy the British had installed in Greece in 1944. In March 1947, Truman reacted to the Communist threat by announcing what quickly became known as the *Truman Doctrine*, the countering of political crises with economic and military aid. The president requested $400 million in military aid for Greece and for Turkey, where the Communists were also pressuring. Fearing that Americans would balk at backing Greece, U.S. congressmen would agree to the program only if Truman would "scare hell out of the country," as one put it. Truman thus publicized a massive aid program as necessary to fortify the world against a tide of global Soviet conquest. The show of American support convinced the Communists to back off, and in 1949 the Greek rebels declared a cease-fire.

"The seeds of totalitarian regimes are nurtured by misery and want," the president warned in the same speech that introduced the Truman Doctrine.♦ His linkage of poverty to the rise of dictatorship led to the *Marshall Plan*, a program of massive U.S. economic aid to Europe named after Secretary of State George C. Marshall. The Marshall Plan claimed that it was not directed "against any country or doctrine but against hunger, poverty, desperation, and chaos." Stalin, however, saw it as a U.S. political ploy that caught him without similar economic aid to offer to his client countries in eastern Europe. By the early 1950s, the United States had sent Europe more than $12 billion in food, equipment, and services.

The Soviet Union reacted by suppressing the remaining coalition governments, notably in Hungary and Poland, and assuming political control in central and eastern Europe. Czechoslovakia, which by eastern European standards had prospered under a Communist-led coalition, welcomed the Marshall Plan as the beginning of East-West rapprochement. This illusion ended, however, during a purge of non-Communist officials that began in the autumn of 1947. By June 1948, the socialist president, Edouard Beneš, had resigned and been replaced by a Communist figurehead. Nonetheless, the populace remained so passive that Communist leaders called the takeover "like cutting butter with a knife." The Soviet Union had successfully created a buffer of satellite states in eastern Europe directed by "people's governments."

Yugoslavia after the Revolution, 1948

The only exception to the Soviet sweep in eastern Europe came in Yugoslavia, under the Communist ruler Tito (Josip Broz). During the war, Tito led the powerful anti-Nazi Yugoslav "partisans." After the war, he drew on support from Serbs, Croats, and Muslims to mount a Communist, but not a Soviet, revolution. Eager for Yugoslavia to develop industrially rather than simply serve Soviet needs, he remarked: "We study and take as an example the Soviet system, but we are developing socialism in our country in somewhat different forms." Stalin was furious, for commitment to communism meant obedience to him. Nonetheless, Yugoslavia emerged from its Communist revolution as a culturally diverse federation of six republics and two independent provinces within Serbia. Holding these groups together until his death in 1980, Tito's forceful personality and strong organization also held the Soviets at bay.

♦ For a primary source that elucidates U.S. cold war tactics and the fears and perceptions underlying them, see Document 70, National Security Council, "Paper Number 68."

The Division of Germany

The cold war became most menacing in the superpowers' struggle for control of Germany. The terms of the agreements reached at Yalta provided for Germany's occupation by troops divided among four zones, each of which was controlled by one of the four principal victors in World War II—the United States, the Soviet Union, Britain, and France (Map 22.2). However, the superpowers disagreed on fundamental matters in German history. Many in the United States had come to believe that there was something inherently wrong with the character of Germans, who had provoked two world wars and the Holocaust. After the war, the U.S. occupation forces undertook a reprogramming of German cultural attitudes by controlling the press and censoring the content of all media in the U.S. zone to ensure that they did not express fascist or authoritarian values. In contrast, Stalin believed that Nazism was merely another form of advanced capitalism, and he therefore confiscated and redistributed the estates of wealthy Germans.

A second disagreement over Germany's economic potential led to the partition of Germany. According to the American vision of economic coordination, surplus produce from the Soviet-occupied areas would feed urban populations in the Western-controlled zones; in turn, industrial goods would be sent to the USSR. The Soviets upset this plan and, following the Grand Alliance agreement that the USSR receive reparations from German resources, immediately sent equipment and dismantled industries to the Soviet Union. They transported skilled workers, engineers, and scientists to the USSR to work as virtual slave laborers. Meanwhile, the three Western Allies agreed to merge their zones into a West German state. Instead of continuing to curtail German power as wartime agreements called for, the United

■ **MAP 22.2 Divided Germany and the Berlin Airlift, 1946–1949**

Berlin, controlled by the United States, Great Britain, France, and the Soviet Union, was deep in the Soviet zone of occupation and became a major point of contention among the former allies. When the USSR blockaded the western half of the city, the United States responded with a massive airlift. To stop movement between the two zones, the USSR built a wall in 1961 and used troops to patrol it.

States embarked on an economic buildup under the Marshall Plan to make the Western zone a buffer against the Soviets. By 1948, notions of a permanently weakened Germany had come to an end.

Stalin struck back at the Marshall Plan on July 24, 1948, when Soviet troops blockaded Germany's capital, Berlin. Like Germany as a whole, the city had been divided into four occupation zones, even though it was located more than one hundred miles deep into the Soviet zone and was thus cut off from Western territory (see Map 22.2). Expecting the West to capitulate, the Soviets declared Berlin part of their zone of occupation and refused to allow vehicles to travel through the entire Soviet zone, including Berlin. Instead, the United States responded decisively, flying in millions of tons of provisions to the stricken city. During the winter of 1948–1949, the Berlin airlift—Operation Vittles, as U.S. pilots called it—even funneled coal to the city to warm some two million isolated Berliners. Cold war culture increasingly centered on heroic deeds enacted in Berlin long after the end of the blockade in May 1949, as the divided city became the symbol of the cold war.

The division of Germany and the new bipolarity led to the formation of competing military alliances. The United States, Canada, and their European allies in western Europe and Scandinavia formed the North Atlantic Treaty Organization, or NATO, in 1949. NATO provided a unified military force for the member countries. In 1955, after the United States forced France and Britain to invite West Germany to join NATO, the Soviet Union retaliated by establishing with its satellite countries the military organization commonly called the Warsaw Pact, which included Albania, Bulgaria, Czechoslovakia, East Germany, Hungary, Poland, and Romania. These two massive regional alliances formed the military muscle for the new cold war politics and definitively replaced the individual might of the European powers (Map 22.3).

■ **MAP 22.3 European NATO Members and the Warsaw Pact in the 1950s**

The two superpowers intensified their rivalry by creating large military alliances: NATO, formed in 1949, and the Warsaw Pact, formed in 1955 after NATO invited West German membership. The United States and Canada also were NATO members. International politics revolved around these two alliances, which faced off in the heart of Europe. Military planners on both sides devised war games to plan strategies for fighting a massive war in central Europe over control of Germany.

www.bedfordstmartins.com/huntconcise   See the ONLINE STUDY GUIDE for more help in analyzing this map.

The Political and Economic Recovery of Europe

The ideological clash between East and West served as a background to a remarkable recovery that took place between 1945 and 1960. The first order of business on the political front was a highly charged eradication of the Nazi past. Simultaneously, western Europe revived its democratic political structures, its individualistic culture, and its productive capabilities. Eastern Europe restlessly endured a far less prosperous and far more repressive existence under Stalinism, although the conditions of everyday life improved as peasant societies were forced to modernize. By 1960, people across the continent had escaped the poverty of the depression and war to enjoy a higher standard of living—an "economic miracle" it was even called—than ever before in human history. As governments took increasing responsibility for the health and well-being of citizens, the atomic age also became the age of the welfare state.

Dealing with the Nazi Past

In May 1945, Europeans lived under a complex system of political jurisdiction: local resistance leaders, Allied armies of occupation, international relief workers, and the remnants of bureaucracies often worked at odds to restore society. Amid confusion, starvation, and a thriving black market, the goals of feeding civilians, dealing with the tens of millions of refugees, purging Nazis, and setting up new governments all competed for attention. Occupying armies that covered much of the continent were often a law unto themselves: the Soviets were especially feared for inflicting rape and robbery. Distributing food and clothing, other armed forces tried to instill order. The desire for revenge against Nazis hardened with the discovery of the death camps' skeletal survivors and the remains of the millions murdered there. Swift vigilante justice by civilians released pent-up rage and aimed to punish collaborators for their complicity in the Holocaust and other occupation crimes. Villagers often shaved the heads of women suspected of associating with Germans and made them parade naked through the local streets. Members of the resistance summarily executed tens of thousands of Nazi officers and collaborators on the spot. These became the founding acts of a reborn European political community.

Allied representatives undertook a more systematic "denazification," including official investigations of suspected local collaborators. The trials conducted at Nuremberg, Germany, by the victorious Allies in the fall of 1945 used the Nazis' own documents to provide a horrifying panorama of crimes by Nazi leaders. Although international law lacked a precedent for defining genocide as a crime, the judges at Nuremberg found sufficient cause to sentence half of the twenty-four defendants to death, among them Hitler's closest associates, and the remainder to prison terms. The Nuremberg trials introduced current notions of prosecution for crimes against humanity and an international politics based on demands for human rights.

■ The Punishment of Collaborators

Women who had romantic involvements with Germans were called "horizontal" collaborators to suggest that they were traitorous prostitutes. With heads shaved and often stripped of their clothing, they were forced to parade through cities and towns enduring verbal and other abuse. The public shaming of these women, a vivid part of the memory of the war, served as the background for the film Hiroshima Mon Amour, *which gripped audiences late in the 1950s.*
(Robert Capra/Magnum Photos Inc.)

Allied prosecution of Nazi and fascist leadership never succeeded completely because some of the leaders most responsible for war crimes disappeared. Many Germans were skeptical about denazification. As women in Germany endured starvation and savage rape and, in addition, performed the arduous labor of clearing rubble, the belief took hold that Germans were the main victims of the war. German civilians also interpreted the trials of Nazis as the characteristic retribution of victors rather than the well-deserved punishment of the guilty. Allied officials themselves, eager to restore government services and pursue the cold war, often relied on the expertise of high-ranking fascists and Nazis. The Nazi past haunts European debates, cultural life, and politics to this day, yet political expediency led Westerners at the time to forgive some Nazis quite easily.

Rebirth of the West

Against all political and economic odds, western Europe revived. Reform-minded civilian governments reflected the coalitions that had opposed the Axis. They conspicuously emphasized democracy to show their rejection of the totalitarian regimes that had earlier attracted so many Europeans—with such dire consequences. Rebuilding devastated towns and cities spurred industrial recovery, while bold projects for economic cooperation like the European Common Market and the conversion of wartime technological know-how to peacetime use produced a brisk trade in consumer goods and services in western Europe by the late 1950s.

Resistance leaders had the first claim on office in postfascist western Europe. In France, the leader of the Free French, General Charles de Gaulle, governed briefly as chief of state; he quit over limitations on the president's power that were reminiscent of the Third Republic. The French approved a constitution in 1946 that established the Fourth Republic and finally granted the vote to French women. Meanwhile, Italy replaced its constitutional monarchy with a full parliamentary system that also allowed women the vote for the first time. As in France, a resistance-based socialist government initially governed. Then late in 1945, this was replaced by a coalition headed by the conservative Christian Democrats, descended from the traditional Catholic centrist parties of the prewar period.

It was the Communist Party, however, that seemed to attract the most vocal loyalty of a consistently large segment of the western European population. Symbol of the common man, the ordinary Soviet soldier was a hero to many western Europeans outside occupied Germany, as were the resistance leaders—most of them Communist until late in the war when the impending Nazi collapse lured mainline politicians to join the anti-Nazi bandwagon. People still remembered the common man's plight in the depression of the 1930s. Thus, in Britain, despite the successes of Winston Churchill's Conservative Party leadership, the Labour government of Clement Attlee appeared more socialist by fulfilling promises that it would share prosperity equitably among the classes through expanded social welfare programs and the nationalization of key industries.

In West Germany, however, communism had no appeal. In 1949, centrist politicians helped create a new state, the German Federal Republic, whose constitution aimed to prevent the emergence of a dictator and to guarantee individual rights. West Germany's first chancellor was the seventy-three-year-old Catholic anti-Communist Konrad Adenauer, who allied himself with the economist Ludwig Erhard. Committed to the free market, Erhard had stabilized the postwar German currency so that commerce could resume. The economist and the politician successfully guided Germany away from both fascism and communism and restored the representative government that Hitler had overthrown.

Paradoxically, given U.S. leadership in the fight against fascism, postwar politics in the United States most imperiled individual freedom and democracy. The 1949 explosion of the Soviet atomic bomb and the successful Communist revolution in China brought to the fore Joseph McCarthy, a U.S. senator facing a reelection struggle in 1950. McCarthy warned of a great conspiracy to overthrow the United States. As during the Soviet purges, people were called before congressional panels to confess, testify against friends, think about whether they had ever had Communist thoughts or sympathies. The atmosphere was electric with fear because only five years before, the mass media had run glowing stories about Stalin and the Soviet system. By 1952, more than six million people had been investigated or imprisoned or had lost their jobs. McCarthy had books like Thomas Paine's *Common Sense*, written in the eighteenth century to support the American Revolution, removed from government shelves, and he personally oversaw book burnings. Although the Senate finally voted to censure McCarthy in the winter of 1954, the assault on freedom had been devastating and anticommunism dominated political life.

Given the incredible devastation, the economic rebirth of western Europe was even more surprising than the revival of democracy. In the first weeks and months after the war, the job of rebuilding often involved menial physical labor that mobilized entire populations. With so many men dead, wounded, or detained as prisoners of war, German housewives, called "women of the ruins," earned their living clearing rubble by hand. Initially governments diverted labor and capital into rebuilding infrastructure—transportation, communications, industrial capacity. However, the scarcity of goods sparked unrest and made communism attractive politically because it proclaimed less interest in the revival of big business than in the ordinary person's standard of living. But as the Marshall Plan sustained the initial recovery with American dollars, food and consumer goods became more plentiful, and demand for automobiles, washing machines, and vacuum cleaners boosted economies. The growth in production of all kinds wiped out most unemployment. Labor-short northern Europe even arranged for "guest" workers to migrate from Sicily and other impoverished regions to help rebuild cities. The outbreak of war in Korea in 1950 further encouraged the astonishing rates of economic growth. (See "Taking Measure," page 965.)

The postwar recovery also featured the adaptation of wartime technology to consumer industry and the continuation of military spending. Civilian travel expanded as nations organized their own air systems based on improved airplane technology. Developed to relieve wartime shortages, synthetic goods such as nylon now became part of peacetime civilian life. Factories churned out a vast assortment of plastic products, ranging from pipes to household goods and rainwear. In the climate of cold war, governments ordered bombs, fighter planes, tanks, and missiles; and they also continued to sponsor military research. The cold war ultimately prevented a repeat of the 1920s, when reduced military spending threw people out of jobs and thus fed the growth of fascism.

International cooperation and planning that led to the creation of the Common Market and ultimately the European Union of the 1990s provided a final ingredient in recovery. The Marshall Plan demanded as the condition for assistance that recipients undertake far-reaching economic cooperation. In 1951, Italy, France, Germany, Belgium, Luxembourg, and the Netherlands formed the European Coal and Steel Community (ECSC). This organization managed coal and steel production and prices and, most important, arranged for West German output to benefit western Europe. According to the ECSC's principal architect, Robert Schuman, the

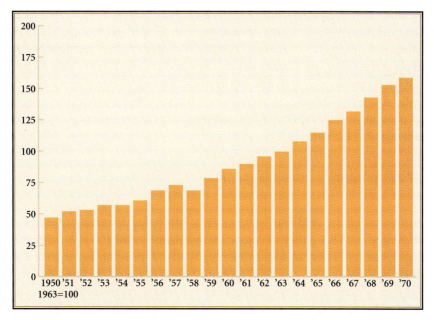

■ **TAKING MEASURE** World Manufacturing Output, 1950–1970

During the "long boom" from the 1950s to the early 1970s, the world experienced increased industrial output, better agricultural production, and rising consumerism. This era of prosperity resulted not only from the demand generated by the need to rebuild Europe but also from the adaptation of war technology to peacetime uses. The General Agreement on Trade and Tariffs (GATT) was also implemented after the war, lowering tariffs and thus advancing trade.
(*Hammond Atlas of the Twentieth Century* [London: Times Books, 1987], 127.)

economic unity created by the organization would make another war "materially impossible." Simply put, the bonds of common productivity and trade would keep France and Germany from another cataclysmic war.

In 1957, "the Six," as the ECSC members were called, took another major step toward regional prosperity when they signed the Treaty of Rome. The treaty provided for a trading partnership called the European Economic Community (EEC), known popularly as the Common Market. The EEC reduced tariffs among the six partners and worked to develop common trade policies. According to one of its founders, the EEC aimed to "prevent the race of nationalism, which is the true curse of the modern world." Increased cooperation produced great economic rewards for the six members. Britain pointedly refused to join the partnership; membership would have required that it surrender certain imperial trading rights. Since 1945, British statesmen had shunned the developing continental trading bloc because, as one of them put it, participation would make it "just another European country." As a result, Britain continued its relative decline. By contrast, the Italian economy, which had also lagged behind that of France and Germany, boomed. The future lay with the soaring prosperity of a new western Europe joined in the Common Market.

Behind the move to the Common Market stood the use of economic planning and coordination by specialists during wartime. Called *technocrats* after 1945, specialists were to base decisions on expertise rather than on personal interest; those working for the Common Market were to disregard the self-interest of any one nation and thus reduce the potential for irrationality and violence in politics, both domestic and international. However, some critics insisted, some even today, that expert planning diminished democracy by putting massive control in the hands of bureaucracy, not legislatures.

The Welfare State: Common Ground East and West

On both sides of the cold war, governments intervened forcefully to ameliorate social conditions. This policy of intervention became known as the *welfare state*, indicating that states were no longer interested solely in maintaining order and augmenting their power. Because the European population had declined during the war, almost all countries now desperately supported reproduction with direct financial aid. Imitating the sweeping Swedish programs of the 1930s, nations expanded or created family allowances, health-care and medical benefits, and programs for pregnant women and new mothers. The French gave larger allowances for each birth after the first; for many French families this allowance provided as much as a third of the household income.

Britain's maternity benefits and child allowances, announced in a wartime report, favored women who did not work outside the home and provided little coverage of any kind to workingwomen. The West German government passed strict legislation that discouraged employers from hiring women. In fact, West Germans bragged about removing women from the workforce, claiming it distinguished democratic practices from Communist ones that were said to demand women's work outside the home. One result of the cutback in pensions and benefits to married women was their high rate of poverty in old age.

In eastern Europe and the Soviet Union, where wartime loss of life had been enormous, women worked nearly full-time and usually outnumbered men in the workforce. Child-care programs, family allowances, and maternity benefits were designed to encourage pregnancies by such women. The scarcity of consumer goods, the housing shortages, and the lack of household conveniences in the Eastern bloc, however, discouraged workingwomen from having large families. Because women had sole responsibility for onerous domestic duties on top of their paying jobs, their already heavy workload increased with the birth of each additional child.

Across Europe, welfare-state programs aimed to improve people's health. State-funded medical insurance, subsidized medical care, or nationalized health-care systems covered health-care needs in industrial nations except in the United States. The combination of better material conditions and state provision of health care dramatically extended life expectancy and lowered rates of infant mortality. Contributing to the overall progress, the number of medical doctors and dentists more than doubled between the end of World War I and 1950, and vaccines greatly reduced the death toll from such diseases as tuberculosis, diphtheria, measles, and polio. In England, schoolchildren on average stood an inch taller than children of the same age a decade earlier. As people lived longer, governments began to establish programs for the elderly. All in all, per capita expenditures on civilian well-being shot up after the war. Belgium, for example, which had spent $12 per capita in 1930, led western European countries with $148 per capita in 1956; Britain, which had led in 1930 with welfare expenditures of $59, now lagged behind with $93 because of its near-bankrupt condition.

State initiatives in other areas played a role in the higher standard of living. A growing network of government-built atomic power plants brought more thorough electrification of eastern Europe and the Soviet Union. Governments legislated better conditions and more leisure time for workers. Beginning in 1955, Italian workers received twenty-eight paid holidays annually; in Sweden workers received twenty-nine vacation days, and the number grew in the 1960s. Planning also helped provide a more varied diet and more abundant food, with meat, fish, eggs, cheese, milk, and fresh fruit supplementing the traditional grain-based foods. Housing shortages posed a daunting challenge after three decades of economic depression and destructive war. Postwar Europeans often lived with three generations sharing one or two rooms. Eastern Europeans faced the worst conditions, whereas Germans and Greeks fared better because only 20 to 25 percent of their prewar housing had been lost. To rebuild, governments sponsored a postwar housing boom. New cities formed around the edges of major urban areas in both East and West. Many buildings went up slapdash, and restored towns took on an undistinguished look and a constantly deteriorating condition. Westerners labeled many Eastern bloc apartments "environmentally horrible." Housing shortages persisted, but the modernized appearance of many European cities suggested that the century's two cataclysmic wars had swept away much of the old Europe.

Recovery in the East

To create a Soviet bloc according to Stalin's prewar vision of industrialization, Communists revived the crushing methods that had served before to transform peasant economies. In eastern Europe, Stalin enforced collectivized agriculture and badly needed industrialization through the nationalization of private property. In Hungary, for example, Communists seized and reapportioned all estates over twelve hundred acres. Having gained support of the poorer peasants through this redistribution, Communists later pushed them into cooperative farming. The process of collectivization was brutal and slow everywhere, and rural people looked back on the 1950s as "dreadful." But others felt that ultimately their lives and their children's

■ Postwar Housing in Poland

Wartime devastation worsened the shortage of housing that had begun with the diversion of re-sources to fight World War I and had increased during the depression of the 1930s, when housing construction almost halted. In the post–World War II years, shortages were so grave that slapdash, cheap buildings with far less than one room per person went up from England to eastern Europe and the Soviet Union. Not until the 1960s did the Soviets begin building anywhere near the million or more housing units needed each year. (Sovfoto.)

lives had improved. "Before we peasants were dirty and poor, we worked like dogs. . . . Was that a good life? No sir, it wasn't. . . . I was a miserable sharecropper and my son is an engineer," said one Romanian peasant.

An admirer of American industrial know-how, Stalin prodded all the socialist economies in his bloc to match U.S. productivity. The Soviet Union formed regional organizations, instituting the Council for Mutual Economic Assistance (COMECON) in 1949 to coordinate economic relations among the satellite countries and Moscow. Modernization of production in the Eastern bloc opened new technical and bu-reaucratic careers, and modernizers in the satellite states touted the virtues of steel plants and modern transport. The terms of the COMECON relationship thwarted development of the satellite states, for the USSR was allowed to buy goods from its clients at bargain prices and sell to them at exorbitant ones. Nonetheless, these for-merly peasant states became oriented toward technology and bureaucratically directed industrial economies. People moved to cities where they received better education, health care, and, ultimately, jobs, albeit at the price of repression. The Catholic clergy, which often protested the imposition of communism, was crushed. Old agrarian elites, professionals, intellectuals, and other members of the middle class were discriminated against, imprisoned, or executed. Prisoners in East German camps did hard labor in uranium and other dangerous mines.

Science and culture were the building blocks of Stalinism in the satellite countries as well as in the USSR. State-instituted programs aimed to build loyalty to the modernizing regime: citizens found themselves obliged to attend adult education classes, women's groups, and public ceremonies. An intense program of Russification and de-Christianization forced students in eastern Europe to read histories of the war that ignored native resistance and gave the Red Army sole credit for fighting the Nazis. Stalinists replaced national symbols with Soviet ones. For example, the Hungarians had to accept a new flag with a Soviet red star beaming rays onto a hammer and sickle; Hungary's national colors were reduced to a small band on the flag. Utter historical distortion, revivified anti-Semitism, and rigid censorship resulted in what one staunchly socialist writer characterized as "a dreary torrent of colorless, mediocre literature." In the USSR itself, Stalin also instituted new purges to ensure obedience and conformity. Marshall Zhukov, a popular leader of the armed forces, was shipped to a distant command, while Anna Akhmatova, the great poet whose popular writing had emphasized perseverance and individual heroism

■ Re-Creating Hungarian Youth

People across Europe focused on the well-being of young people after World War II, and regimes in the Soviet sphere took steps to provide education in Communist ways. Youth groups like those in the early Stalinist USSR served this end, and vivid posters in the Soviet realist style carried inspirational messages. "Forward for the Congress of the Young Fighters of Peace and Socialism," exhorts this poster informing Hungarian youth about a conference to be held in June 1950.

(Magyar Nemzeti Múzeum, Budapest [Hungarian National Museum].)

during the war, died confined to a crowded hospital room because she refused to glorify Stalin in her postwar poetry.

In March 1953, Stalin died. As people openly mourned this man they considered their savior from backwardness and Nazism, troubles already loomed in the empire he ruled so tyrannically. Political prisoners in the labor camps who had started rioting late in the 1940s now pressed their demands for reform. Consumer goods were much scarcer than in the West because of the government's high military spending and the enormous cost of recovery. Amid deprivation and discontent, Soviet officials enjoyed country homes, luxury goods, and plentiful food, but many of them had come to distrust Stalinism and were ready for some changes. A power struggle ensued within the Communist leadership, and protests took place throughout the Soviet bloc. In response, the government freed some prisoners of the Gulag labor camp and beefed up production of consumer goods—a policy called "goulash communism" because in part it resulted in more food for ordinary people.

The old ways could not hold. In 1955, Nikita Khrushchev, an illiterate coal miner before the revolution, outmaneuvered other rivals to emerge the undisputed leader of the Soviet Union, but he did so without the usual executions. The next year he attacked Stalinism. At a party congress, Khrushchev denounced the "cult of personality" Stalin had built about himself and announced that Stalinism did not equal socialism. The "secret speech"—it was not published in the USSR but became widely known—sent tremors through Communist parties around the world. In this climate of uncertainty, protest erupted once more in early summer 1956, when discontented Polish railroad workers struck for better wages. Popular support for their cause ushered in a more liberal Communist program. Inspired by the Polish example, Hungarians rebelled against forced collectivization in October 1956—"the golden October," they would call their uprising. As in Poland, economic issues, especially announcements of reduced wages, sparked some of the first outbreaks of violence, but the protest soon targeted the entire Communist system. Tens of thousands of protesters filled the streets of Budapest and succeeded in returning a popular hero, Imre Nagy, to power. When Nagy announced that Hungary might leave the Warsaw Pact, Soviet troops moved in, killing tens of thousands and causing hundreds of thousands more to flee to the West. Nagy was hanged. The U.S. refusal to intervene showed that, despite a rhetoric of "liberation," it would not risk World War III by militarily challenging the Soviet sphere of influence.

The failure of eastern European uprisings overshadowed significant changes—called a climate of "thaw"—in Soviet policy. In the process of defeating his rivals, Khrushchev ended the Stalinist purges and reformed the courts (which came to function according to procedures, not like the stage for show trials of the past). The gates of the Gulag opened, and the secret police lost many of its arbitrary powers. A new sense of security acquired from increased productivity, military buildup, and stunning successes in aerospace development were also part of the thaw. In 1957, the Soviets successfully launched the first artificial earth satellite, *Sputnik*, and in 1961 they put the first cosmonaut, Yuri Gagarin, in orbit around the earth. The Soviets' edge in space technology shocked the Western bloc and motivated the creation of the U.S. National Aeronautics and Space Administration (NASA).

Soviet successes indicated that the USSR was on the way to achieving Stalin's goal of modernization. Nevertheless, Khrushchev continued to fear and bully dissidents. For example, he forced Boris Pasternak to refuse the 1958 Nobel Prize in literature because his novel *Doctor Zhivago* (1957) cast doubt on the glory of the revolution and affirmed the value of the individual. Yet under the thaw, Khrushchev himself made several trips to the West and was more widely seen by the public than Stalin had been. More confident and more affluent, the Soviets took steps to reduce their diplomacy's paranoid style and concentrated their efforts on spreading socialism in the emerging nations of Asia, Africa, and Latin America.

Decolonization in a Cold War Climate

World War II dealt the final blow to the ability of European powers to maintain their vast empires. The Western powers attempted to stamp out nationalist groups that had strengthened during the war and to reimpose their control—with fatal results. As before, colonized peoples had been on the front lines defending the West; and as before, they had witnessed the full barbarism of Western warfare. Excluded from victory parades and other ceremonies so the powers could maintain the illusion of Western supremacy, adult men in the colonies still did not receive the political rights promised them. Instead, people in Asia, Africa, and the Middle East, often led by individuals steeped in Western values and experienced in war, embraced the cause of independence and often clashed with the West in bloody warfare.

The path to achieving independence was paved with difficulties. In Africa, a continent whose peoples spoke more than five thousand languages, the European conquerors' creation of convenient administrative units such as "Nigeria" and "Rhodesia" had obliterated living arrangements that had relied on ethnic ties and local cultures. In addition, religion played a divisive role in independence movements. In India, Hindus and Muslims battled one another even though they shared the goal of eliminating the British. In the Middle East and North Africa, pan-Arab and pan-Islamic movements might seem to have been unifying forces. Yet many Muslims were not Arab, not all Arabs were Muslim, and Islam itself encompassed many competing beliefs and sects. Differences among religious beliefs, ethnic groups, and cultural practices—many of them invented or promoted by the colonizers to divide and rule—overlapped and undermined political unity. Despite these complications, peoples in what was coming to be called the third world succeeded in throwing off the imperial yoke while they offered a new battlefield for cold war competition between the United States and the Soviet Union.

The End of Empire in Asia

At the end of World War II, leaders in Asia began to mobilize the mass discontent that had intensified during the war and, often facing stiff resistance from white settlers, were able to drive out foreign rulers. Declining from an imperial power to a small island nation, Britain was the biggest loser. In 1947, it parted with India, the "jewel" of its empire. The British had promised in the 1930s to grant India its independence, but they postponed it when war broke out. Some two million Indian men were mobilized, anchoring the war in the Middle East and Asia. Local industry became an important wartime supplier, and Indian business leaders bought out British entrepreneurs short of cash. During this period of economic prosperity for some people, however, food shortages drove many others to overcrowded cities, and political fissures between Hindus and Muslims, long encouraged by the British, widened.

The British faced the inevitable after the war and decreed that two countries should emerge from the old colony, so great was the mistrust between the parties of the Indian National Congress and Muslim League. Thus, in 1947, India was created for Hindus and Pakistan for Muslims. Yet during the independence year, political tensions exploded among opposing members of the two religions. Hundreds of thousands were massacred in the great shift of populations between the two nations. In 1948, a radical Hindu assassinated Gandhi, who though a Hindu himself had continued to champion religious reconciliation. Confronting nationalist movements elsewhere, Britain retained control of Hong Kong; but before two decades of the postwar era had passed, almost half a billion Asians had gained their freedom from the rule of fifty million British (see "Mapping the West," page 989).

In 1949, a Communist takeover in China brought in a government led by Mao Zedong that was no longer the plaything of the traditional colonial powers. Mao Zedong (1893–1976) led his army of Communists to victory over Jiang Jieshi's unpopular, corrupt Nationalist government, which the United States had bankrolled. Chinese communism in the new People's Republic of China emphasized above all the welfare of the peasantry rather than the industrial proletariat and was thus distinct from Marxism and Stalinism. Mao instituted social reforms such as civil equality for women but at the same time copied Soviet collectivization, rapid industrialization, and brutal repression of the privileged classes. Although China began to distance itself from the USSR in the mid-1950s, the Western bloc saw only monolithic red from Leningrad to Beijing.

The United States and the Soviet Union were deeply interested in East Asia, the United States because of the region's economic importance and the USSR because of its shared borders. Thus the Communist Chinese victory spurred both superpowers to increase their involvement in Asian politics. They faced off indirectly in Korea, which had been split at the thirty-eighth parallel after World War II. In 1950, the North Koreans, supported by the Soviet Union, invaded the U.S.-backed South.

The United States maneuvered the UN Security Council into approving a "police action" against the North, and its forces quickly drove well into North Korean territory, where they were met by the Chinese rather than the Soviet army. After two and a half years of stalemate, the opposing sides finally agreed to a settlement in 1953: Korea would remain split at its prewar border, the thirty-eighth parallel.

The United States lost more than 50,000 men in the Korean War and increased its military spending from $10.9 billion in 1948 to almost $60 billion in 1953 to hold the line on Communist expansion. Communist potential in decolonizing areas led the American secretary of state, John Foster Dulles, to characterize Asian countries as a row of dominoes: "You knock over the first one and what will happen is that it will go over [to communism] very quickly." The expansion of the cold war to Asia prompted the creation of an Asian counterpart to NATO.

The Korean War, 1950–1953

Established in 1954, the Southeast Asia Treaty Organization (SEATO) included Pakistan, Thailand, the Philippines, Britain, Australia, New Zealand, France, and the United States. One side effect was the rapid reindustrialization of Japan to provide the United States with supplies.

The cold war spread to Indochina, where nationalists had been struggling against the postwar revival of French imperialism. Their leader, the European-educated Ho Chi Minh, preached both nationalism and socialism and built a powerful organization, the Viet Minh, to fight colonial rule.◆ He advocated the redistribution of land held by big landowners, especially in the rich agricultural area in southern Indochina where some six thousand owners possessed more than 60 percent of the land. Viet Minh peasant guerrillas ultimately forced the technologically advanced French army to withdraw from the country after the bloody battle of Dien Bien Phu in 1954. Later that year the Geneva Convention carved out an independent Laos and divided Vietnam into North and South, each free from French control. The Viet Minh was ordered to retreat to an area north of the seventeenth parallel. But the superpowers' intervention undermined the peace treaty while risking the nuclear brink and subjecting native peoples to the force of their military

---

◆ For a primary source that reveals the goals and motives of the Viet Minh, see Document 71, Ho Chi Minh, "Declaration of Independence of the Republic of Vietnam."

Indochina, 1954

might. In fighting to prevent national liberation in the name of fighting communism, the United States in particular was acquiring a reputation as an "imperialist" power of the old school, nowhere more so than in Vietnam.

The Struggle for Identity in the Middle East

The power of oil and the ability of small countries to see the opportunity for maneuvering between antagonists in the cold war gave new impetus to independence struggles in the Middle East. As in the rest of the world after the war, Middle Eastern peoples renewed their commitment to independence and resisted attempts by the major powers to regain imperial control. Weakened by the war, British oil companies wanted to tighten their grip on profits, as the value of oil soared. The cold war gave Middle Eastern leaders an opening to bargain with the superpowers, playing them off one against another, especially over resources to reestablish war-torn economies. The legacy of the Holocaust, however, complicated the political scene as the Western powers' commitment to secure a Jewish homeland in the Middle East further stirred up Arab determination to regain control of the region.

When World War II broke out, 600,000 Jewish settlers and twice as many Arabs lived, in intermittent conflict, in British-controlled Palestine. In 1947, an exhausted Britain ceded the area to the United Nations to work out a settlement between the Jews and the Arabs. In the aftermath of the Holocaust, the UN voted to partition Palestine into an Arab region and a Jewish one (Map 22.4). Conflicting claims, however, led to war, and Jewish military forces prevailed. On May 14, 1948, the state of Israel came into being. "The dream had come true," Golda Meir, the future president of Israel, remembered, but "too late to save those who had perished in the Holocaust." Israel opened its gates to immigrants, driving its ambitions against those of its Arab neighbors.

One of those neighbors, Egypt, had gained its independence from Britain at the end of the war. Britain, however, retained its control of Middle Eastern oil and its dominance of Asian shipping through the Suez Canal, which was owned by a British-run company. In 1952, Colonel Gamal Abdel Nasser became Egypt's president on a platform of economic modernization and true national independence. A prime goal was reclaiming the Suez Canal, "where 120,000 of our sons had lost their

MAP 22.4 The Partition of Palestine and the Creation of Israel, 1947–1948

The creation of the Jewish state of Israel in 1948 against a backdrop of ongoing wars among Jews and indigenous Arab peoples made the Middle East a powder keg. The struggle for resources and for securing the borders of viable nation-states was at the heart of these bitter contests, threatening to pull the super-powers into a third world war.

lives in digging it [by force]," he stated. In July 1956, Nasser nationalized the canal. Britain, supported by Israel and France, attacked Egypt, bringing the Suez crisis to a head while the Hungarian revolt was in full swing. The British branded Nasser another Hitler, but American opposition made the British back down. Nasser's triumph inspired confidence that the Middle East could confront the West and win.

New Nations in Africa

In sub-Saharan Africa, nationalist leaders roused their people to challenge Europeans' increasing demand for resources and labor, which resulted in poverty for African peoples. "The European Merchant is my shepherd, and I am in want," went one African version of the Twenty-third Psalm. Disrupted in their traditional agricultural patterns, many Africans flocked to shantytowns in cities during the war, where they kept themselves alive through scavenging, craft work, and menial labor for whites. At war's end, Kwame Nkrumah led the diverse inhabitants of the British-controlled West African Gold Coast in Gandhian-style passive resistance. After years of arresting and jailing the protesters, the British withdrew, allowing the state of Ghana to come into being in 1957. Nigeria, the most populous African region, became independent in 1960 after the leaders of its many regional groups and political organizations reached agreement on a federal-style government. In these and other African states where the population was mostly black, independence came less violently than in mixed-race territory (Map 22.5).

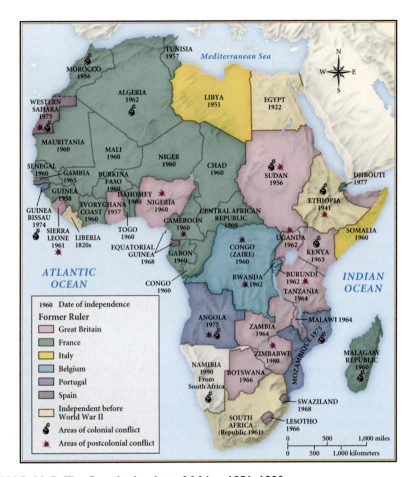

■ **MAP 22.5 The Decolonization of Africa, 1951–1990**
*The liberation of Africa from European rule was an uneven process, sometimes occurring peace-
fully and at other times demanding armed struggle to drive out European settlers, governments,
and armies. After liberation, the difficult process of nation building—forming governments, educating children, providing social services—began. Creating national unity also proved challenging,
except in places where the struggle against colonialism had already brought people together.*

The eastern coast and southern and central areas of Africa had numerous
European settlers who violently resisted independence movements. In British East
Africa, where white settlers ruled in splendor and where blacks lacked both land
and economic opportunity, violence erupted in the 1950s. African men formed rebel
groups named the Land Freedom Army but known as "Mau Mau." With women
serving as provisioners, messengers, and weapon stealers, Mau Mau bands, composed mostly of war veterans from the Kikuyu ethnic group, tried to recover land

from whites. In 1964, after the British had slaughtered some ten to fifteen thousand Kikuyus, Kenya gained formal independence.

France—though eager to regain its great-power status after its humiliating defeat and occupation in World War II—easily granted certain demands for independence, such as those of Tunisia, Morocco, and West Africa, where there were fewer settlers, more limited economic stakes, and less military involvement. Elsewhere, French struggles against independence movements were prolonged and bloody. The ultimate test of the French empire came in Algeria. When Algerian nationalists rebelled against the restoration of French rule in the final days of World War II, the French army massacred tens of thousands of protesters. The liberation movement resurfaced with ferocious intensity as the Front for National Liberation in 1954. In response, the French dug in, sending in more than 400,000 troops. Neither side fought according to the rules of warfare: the French tortured natives, while Algerian women, shielded by gender stereotypes, planted bombs in European cafés and carried weapons to assassination sites.

Shedding its colonies at a rapid rate, France drew the line at Algeria. "The loss of Algeria," warned one statesman, "would be an unprecedented national disaster."

■ **Jomo Kenyatta, First President of the New Kenyan Nation**
Educated in England, Kenyatta wrote Facing Mount Kenya, *a work that explained Kikuyu life as a distinct culture to Westerners. After a costly struggle during which he was imprisoned by the British, Kenyatta became president (1964–1978) of the new republic of Kenya. He stifled political debate by outlawing opposition parties. His one-party government brought social calm, which made Kenya a good place for Western investment.*
(© Bettmann/CORBIS.)

Although many agreed, the Algerian War also threatened social stability as protests in Paris greeted reports of the army's barbarous practices. The French military and settlers in Algeria met the antiwar movement with terrorism against citizens in France. They threatened coups, set off bombs, and assassinated politicians in the name of Algérie Française (French Algeria).

France's Fourth Republic collapsed over Algeria, and in 1958, Charles de Gaulle came back to power. In return for leading France out of its Algerian quagmire, de Gaulle demanded the creation of a new republican government—the Fifth Republic—one with a strong president who could choose the prime minister and exercise emergency power. As his plans actually to decolonize Algeria unfolded, terrorism against him escalated. But by 1962, de Gaulle had negotiated independence with the Algerian nationalists. Hundreds of thousands of *pieds noirs* ("black feet"), as the French condescendingly called Europeans in Algeria, as well as their Arab supporters fled to France. The Dutch and Belgian empires also disintegrated. Violent resistance to the reimposition of colonial rule led to the establishment of the large independent states of Indonesia and Zaire.

As independent nations emerged from colonialism and as continental Europe received immigrants from former colonies, structures arose to promote international security and worldwide deliberations that included voices from the new states. The United Nations convened for the first time in 1945, and one notable change ensured it a greater chance of success than the League of Nations: both the United States and the Soviet Union were active members from the outset. The charter of the UN outlined a collective global authority that would adjudicate conflicts and provide military protection if any members were threatened by aggression. In 1955, Achmed Sukarno, who succeeded in wrenching Indonesian independence from the Dutch, sponsored the Bandung Convention of nonaligned nations to set a common policy for achieving modernization and facing the major powers. Both the UN and the meetings of emerging nations began shifting global issues away from those of the Western powers. Human rights and economic inequities among developing countries and the West nudged their way into public consciousness.

Cultural Life on the Brink of Nuclear War

Both the Holocaust and the cold war shaped postwar leisure and political culture, as the responsibility for Nazism, the cause of ethnic and racial justice, and the merits of the two superpowers set people against one another. Yet this was a time of intense self-scrutiny as Europeans debated decolonization and the Americanization that seemed to accompany the influx of U.S. dollars, consumer goods, and cultural media. While Europeans examined their past and grew prosperous, the cold war menaced. In October 1962, the world held its breath while the leaders of the Soviet Union and the United States provoked the real possibility of nuclear conflagration over the issue of missiles on the island of Cuba.

Restoring "Western" Values

After the depravity and inhumanity of Nazism, cultural currents in Europe and the United States reemphasized universal values and spiritual renewal. Some, like Billy Graham, saw the churches as central to the restoration of values through an active commitment to "re-Christianizing" Europe and the United States. Their success was only partial, however, as the trend toward a more secular culture continued. Thus, in the early postwar years people in the U.S. bloc emphasized the triumph of a Western heritage, a Western civilization, and Western values over fascism, and they characterized the war as one "to defend civilization [from] a conspiracy against man." This definition of *West* often emphasized the heritage of Greece and Rome and the rise of national governments in England, France, and western Europe as they encountered "barbaric" forces, be they nomadic tribes, Nazi armies, Communist agents, or national liberation movements in Asia and Africa. University courses in Western civilization flourished after the war to reaffirm those values. At the same time, the postwar renewal of humanitarianism pushed issues of cultural pluralism and human rights to the forefront of culture.

Memoirs of the death camps and tales of the resistance became compelling reading material. Rescued from the Third Reich in 1940, Nelly Sachs won the Nobel Prize in literature in 1966 for her poetry about the Holocaust. Anne Frank's *Diary of a Young Girl* (1947), the poignant record of a teenager hidden with her family in the back of an Amsterdam warehouse, was emblematic of the survival of Western values in the face of Nazi persecution. Confronted with the small miseries of daily life and the grand evils of Nazism, Anne never stopped believing that "people are really good at heart."

Histories of the resistance also tapped into the public's need for inspiration after an orgy of savagery. Governments erected permanent plaques at spots where resisters had been killed; their biographies filled magazines and bookstalls; organizations of resisters commemorated their role in winning the war. Although resistance efforts were publicized, discussion of collaboration threatened to open old wounds. French filmmakers, for instance, avoided the subject for decades after the war. Many a politician with a Nazi past moved into the new cultural mainstream even as the stories of resistance took on mythical qualities.

By the end of the 1940s, existential philosophy became the rage among the cultural elites and students and in universities. It explored the meaning (or lack of meaning) of human existence in a world where evil flourished. Two of its leaders, Albert Camus and Jean-Paul Sartre, had written for the resistance during the war, although Nazi censors had also allowed the production of Sartre's plays. Existentialists confronted the question of what "being" was about, given what they perceived as the absence of God and the breakdown of morality. Their answer was that "being," or existing, was not the automatic process either of God's creation or of birth into the natural world. One was not born with spiritual goodness in the image

■ Zbigniew Cybulski, the Polish James Dean

Zbigniew Cybulski depicted a tortured young resistance fighter in Andrzej Wajda's film Ashes and Diamonds *(1958). On the last day of World War II, Cybulski's character is supposed to assassinate a Communist resistance leader, and his ambivalence about this act plays out amid the chaos in Poland at war's end. Like existentialist philosophers and other cinema directors at the time, Wajda captured the debate over human values and the interest in young heroes of the postwar era.* (Photofest.)

of a creator; instead, through action and choice, one created an "authentic" existence. Camus's novels, such as *The Stranger* (1942) and *The Plague* (1947), dissected the evils of a corrupt political order and pondered human responsibility in such situations. Sartre's writings emphasized political activism and resistance under totalitarianism. Despite the fact that they had never confronted the enormous problems of making choices while living under fascism, young people in the 1950s found existentialism compelling and made it the most fashionable philosophy of the day.

In 1949, Simone de Beauvoir, Sartre's lifetime companion, published the twentieth century's most important work on the condition of women, *The Second Sex*. Beauvoir believed that most women had failed to take the kind of action necessary to lead authentic lives. Instead, they lived in the world of "necessity," devoting themselves exclusively to reproduction and motherhood. Failing to create an authentic self through considered action and accomplishment, they had become its opposite—an object or "Other." Moreover, instead of struggling to define themselves and assert their freedom, women passively accepted their own "Otherness" and lived as defined by men. Beauvoir's book was a smash hit, in large part because people thought Sartre had written it.♦ Both were celebrities, for the media spread the new commitment to humane values just as it had spread support for Nazism or for its wartime enemies.

While Europeans debated decolonization among peoples of color in Africa and Asia, intellectuals spawned new theories of what liberation would mean for people of color. The first half of the century had witnessed the rise of pan-Africanism, but it was in the 1950s and 1960s that the immensely influential writing of Frantz Fanon, a black psychiatrist from the French colony of Martinique, began analyzing liberation movements. He called the mental functioning of the colonized person "traumatized" by the violence and the brutal imposition of a culture other than one's own as the only standard of value. Ruled by guns, the colonized person knew only violence and would thus naturally decolonize by means of violence. Translated into many languages, Fanon's *Black Skin, White Masks* (1952) and *The Wretched of the Earth* (1961) posed the question of how to "decolonize" one's mind.

Simultaneous with decolonization, in the 1950s the commitment to the civil rights cause embodied in such long-standing organizations as the National Association for the Advancement of Colored People (NAACP, founded 1909) intensified. In principle, African Americans had fought in the war to defeat the Nazi idea of white racial superiority and now hoped to advance that ideal in the United States. In 1954, the U.S. Supreme Court declared segregated education unconstitutional in *Brown v. Board of Education*, a case initiated by the NAACP. On December 1, 1955, in Montgomery, Alabama, Rosa Parks, a part-time secretary for the local branch of the NAACP, boarded a bus and took the first available seat in the so-called white section at the front of the bus. When a white man found himself without a seat, the driver screamed at Parks, "Nigger, move back." Sitting in the front violated southern laws, which encompassed a host of inequitable, even brutal policies toward African Americans. Parks confronted that system through the studied practice of civil disobedience, and her action led to a boycott of public transportation that pushed the civil rights movement into the African American community as a whole.

The culture of rights and human values generated further organizing. A variety of civil rights groups boycotted discriminatory businesses, "sat in" at segregated facilities, and registered black voters disfranchised by local regulations. Many talented leaders emerged, foremost among them Martin Luther King Jr., a minister from Georgia whose oratorical power galvanized activists to Gandhian nonviolent resistance despite brutal white retaliation. For a few years, the postwar culture of nonviolence would shape the civil rights movement. Soon, however, the voices of

---

♦ For an excerpt, see Document 72, Simone de Beauvoir, *The Second Sex*.

thinkers like Fanon would merge with those of the civil rights movement to revolutionize thinking about race and rights.

Rising Consumerism and Shifting Gender Norms

Government spending on reconstruction, productivity, and welfare helped prevent the kind of social, political, and economic upheaval that had followed World War I. Nor did the same tensions prevail among men and women. A rising birthrate, bustling youth culture, and upsurge in consumerism edged out wartime behavior. Because of the decisive result of World War II, men returned from World War II much less frustrated than they had been in the 1920s. Nonetheless, the war affected men's roles and sense of themselves. Young men who had missed World War II adopted the rough, violent style of soldiers, and roaming gangs posed as tough military types. While Soviet youth admired aviator aces, elsewhere groups such as the "teddy boys" in England (named after their Edwardian style of dressing) and the gamberros in Spain took their cues from new forms of pop culture in music and film.

The leader of rock-and-roll style and substance was the American singer Elvis Presley. Sporting slicked-back hair and an aviator-style jacket, Presley bucked his hips and sang sexual lyrics to screaming and devoted fans. In a German nightclub late in the 1950s, members of a group of Elvis fans called the Quarrymen performed, fighting and yelling at one another as part of their show. They would soon become known as the Beatles. Young American film stars, like James Dean in *Rebel without a Cause* and Marlon Brando in *The Wild One,* created the beginnings of a conspicuous postwar youth culture.

The rebellious and rough masculine style appeared also in literature such as James Watson's autobiography explaining how he and Francis Crick had discovered the structure of the gene. Portraying himself as a fanatic bad boy in his 1968 book *The Double Helix,* Watson described how he had rifled people's desk drawers (among other dishonest acts) to become a scientific hero. In the revival of West German literature, Heinrich Böll published *The Clown* (1963), a novel whose young hero takes to performing as a clown and begging in a railroad station. Böll protested that West Germany's postwar goal of respectability had allowed the resurgence of precisely those groups of people who had produced Nazism. Across the Atlantic, the American "Beat" poets, who looked dirty, bearded, and sometimes crazy, like prisoners or labor-camp survivors, critiqued traditional ideals of the upright and rational male achiever.

Both elite and popular culture revealed that two horrendous world wars had weakened the Enlightenment view of men as rational, responsible breadwinners. The 1953 inaugural issue of the American magazine *Playboy* ushered in a widely imitated depiction of a changed male identity. *Playboy* differed from typical pornographic magazines: along with pictures of nude women, it featured serious articles, especially on the topic of masculinity. This segment of the media presented modern man as sexually aggressive and independent of dull domestic life—just as he had been in the war. Breadwinning for a family only destroyed a man's freedom and sense of self. The notion of men's liberty had come to include not just political and economic rights but freedom of sexual expression.

In contrast, Western society promoted a postwar model for women that differed from their wartime experience as essential workers and heads of families in the absence of their men. Instead, postwar women were made to symbolize the return to normalcy—a domestic, nonworking norm. Late in the 1940s, the fashion house of Christian Dior launched a clothing style called the "new look." It featured a pinched waist, tightly fitting bodices, and full skirts. This restoration of the nineteenth-century female silhouette invited a renewal of clear gender roles. Women's magazines publicized the "new look" and urged a return to domesticity and thus normalcy. Even in the hard-pressed Soviet Union, recipes for homemade face creams passed from woman to woman, and beauty parlors did a brisk business. New

The "New Look"
Immediately after the war, the French fashion industry swung into action to devise styles for the return to normal life in the West. Cinched or corseted waists and ample skirts brought to mind the nineteenth century rather than the depression and war years, when some women had started regularly wearing trousers. The elegant middle-class Western lifestyle implied by the "new look" contrasted sharply with the conditions facing most women in the Soviet Union, who had to work to rebuild their devastated country. (Liaison Agency.)

household products such as refrigerators and washing machines raised standards for women's accomplishment in the home by giving them the means to be "perfect" housewives.

However, "new look" propaganda did not mesh with reality. Dressmaking fabric was still being rationed in the late 1940s; even in the next decade women could not get enough of it to make voluminous skirts. In Europe, where people had barely enough to eat, the underwear needed for "new look" contours simply did not exist. Consumers had access only to standardized undergarments available with ration tickets. European women continued to work outside the home after the war; indeed, mature women and mothers were working more than ever before—especially in the Soviet bloc. The female workforce was going through a profound revolution as it gradually became less youthful and more populated by wives and mothers who would work outside the home all their lives despite being bombarded with images of nineteenth-century middle-class femininity.

The advertising business presided over the creation of cultural messages as well as over the rise of a new consumerism that accompanied recovery. Guided by marketing experts, western Europeans were imitating Americans by driving some forty million motorized vehicles, including motorbikes, cars, buses, and trucks. The demand for cars made the automobile industry a leading economic sector. The number of radios in homes grew steadily—for example, by 10 percent a year in Italy between 1945 and 1950—and the 1950s marked a high tide of radio influence. The development of television in the 1920s and 1930s was interrupted by the war, but peacetime saw its rapid spread in the United States, which had twenty million sets by 1953. Only in the 1960s did television become an important consumer item for most Europeans, however. In the 1950s, radio was still king.

The Culture of Cold War

Radio was at the center of the cold war. As superpower rivalry heated up, radio's propaganda function remained at the fore. During the late 1940s and early 1950s, the Voice of America, with its main studio in Washington, D.C., broadcast in thirty-eight languages from one hundred transmitters and provided an alternative source of news for people in eastern Europe. The Soviet counterpart broadcast in Russian around the clock but initially spent much of its wattage jamming U.S. programming. Russian programs stressed a uniform Communist culture and values; the United States, by contrast, emphasized diverse programming and promoted debate about current affairs.

Its issues and events conveyed by radio and other media, the cold war acquired a far-reaching emotional impact. The public heard reports about nuclear buildups or tests of emergency power facilities that sent them scurrying for cover; in school, children rehearsed for nuclear war, and families built bomb shelters in their backyards. Books like George Orwell's *1984* (1949) were claimed by ideologues on both sides as vindicating their beliefs. Ray Bradbury's popular *Fahrenheit 451* (1953), whose title indicated the temperature at which books would burn, condemned cold war curtailment of intellectual freedom. In the USSR, official writers churned out spy stories, and espionage novels topped best-seller lists in the West. *Casino Royale* (1953) by the British author Ian Fleming introduced James Bond, who survived tests of wit and physical prowess at the hands of Communist and other political villains. Soviet pilots would not take off for flights when the work of Yulian Simyonov, the Russian counterpart of Ian Fleming, was playing on radio or television. Reports of Soviets and Americans—fictional or real—facing one another down became part of everyday life.

Culture as a whole came under the cold war banner, as people debated the "Americanization" they saw taking place in Europe. While many Europeans were proponents of American business practices, the Communist Party in France led a successful campaign to ban Coca-Cola for a time in the 1950s. Both sides tried to win the war by pouring vast sums of money into high culture, though the United States did it by secretly channeling government money into foundations to award fellowships to artists and writers or promote favorable journalism around the world. As leadership of the art world passed to the United States, art became part of the cold war. *Abstract expressionism*, practiced by American artists such as Jackson Pollock, produced abstract works by dripping, spattering, and pouring paint. In contrast, abstract works such as those of Pablo Picasso still had elements of realism. Abstract expressionists spoke of the importance of the artist's self-discovery, spiritual growth, and sensations in the process of painting. "If I stretch my arms next to the rest of myself and wonder where my fingers are, that is all the space I need as a painter," commented Dutch-born Willem de Kooning on his relationship with his canvas. Said to exemplify Western "freedom," such painters were given shows in Europe and awarded commissions at the secret direction of the U.S. Central Intelligence Agency (CIA).

The USSR openly promoted an official Communist culture. When a show of abstract art opened in the Soviet Union, Khrushchev yelled that it was "dog shit." Pro-Soviet critics in western Europe saw U.S.-style abstract art as "an infantile sickness" and supported socialist realist art with "human content," showing the condition of the workers and the oppressed races in the United States. In Italy, the *neorealist* technique was developed by filmmakers such as Roberto Rossellini in *Open City* (1945) and Vittorio De Sica in *The Bicycle Thief* (1948). Such works challenged Hollywood-style sets and costumes by using ordinary characters living in devastated, impoverished cities. By depicting stark conditions, neorealist directors conveyed their distance both from middle-class prosperity and from fascist bombast. "We are in rags? Let's show everyone our rags," said one Italian director. Seen or unseen, the cold war entered the most unsuspected aspects of cultural life.

■ **Mark Rothko, *Light Red over Black* (1957)**
Lithuanian-born Mark Rothko spread large, luminous fields of color across his canvases in an attempt to capture universal spiritual values. Usually his paintings contained only two or three of these fields, prompting the viewer to experience long periods of contemplation. Rothko belonged to a school of artists who aimed in the 1950s to reach enduring truths with such primal or "primitive" forms.
(Tate Gallery, London/Art Resource, NY.)

Kennedy, Khrushchev, and the Atomic Brink

It was in this pervasive climate of cold war that John F. Kennedy became U.S. president in 1960. Kennedy represented American affluence and youth but also the nation's commitment to cold war. Kennedy's media advisers and ghostwriters recognized how perfect a match their articulate, good-looking president was to the power of television. A war hero and early fan of the fictional cold war spy James Bond, Kennedy intensified the arms race and escalated the cold war. In 1959, a revolution in Cuba had brought to power Fidel Castro, who allied his government with the Soviet Union. In the spring of 1961, Kennedy, assured by the CIA of success, launched an invasion of Cuba at the Bay of Pigs to overthrow Castro. The invasion failed miserably and humiliated the United States. A few months later, Kennedy had a chilling meeting with Khrushchev in Vienna, at which the Soviet leader brandished the specter of nuclear holocaust over the continuing U.S. presence in Berlin.

In the summer of 1961, East German workers, supervised by police and the army, stacked bales of barbed wire across miles of the city's east-west border to begin construction of the Berlin Wall. The divided city had served as an escape route by which some three million people had fled to the West. Kennedy responded

IMPORTANT DATES			
1945	Cold war begins	1955	Soviet Union establishes the Warsaw Pact
1947	India and Pakistan win independence from Britain; U.S. President Harry Truman announces the "Truman Doctrine"	1956	Egyptian leader General Abdel Nasser nationalizes the Suez Canal; uprising in Hungary against USSR
1948	State of Israel established	1957	Boris Pasternak publishes *Doctor Zhivago*; USSR launches *Sputnik*; European Economic Community formed
1949	Mao Zedong leads Communist revolution in China; Western allies establish NATO; Simone de Beauvoir publishes *The Second Sex*		
1950	Korean War begins	1958	Fifth Republic begins in France
1952	Samuel Beckett publishes *Waiting for Godot*	1961	East German workers begin to construct the Berlin Wall
1953	Stalin dies; Korean War ends; first issue of *Playboy*	1962	United States and USSR face off in the Cuban missile crisis
1954	*Brown v. Board of Education* prohibits segregated schools in the United States; Vietnamese forces defeat the French at Dien Bien Phu		

at home with a call for more weapons and an enhanced civil defense program. In October 1962, matters came to a head when the CIA reported the installation of Soviet medium-range missiles in Cuba. Kennedy now responded forcefully, calling for a blockade of ships headed for Cuba and threatening nuclear war if the missiles were not removed. For several days, the world stood on the brink of nuclear disaster. Then, between October 25 and 27, Khrushchev and Kennedy negotiated an end to the crisis. Kennedy spent the remainder of his short life working to improve nuclear diplomacy; Khrushchev did the same. The two leaders, who had looked deeply into the nuclear future, clearly feared what they saw.

Conclusion

World War II began the atomic age and transformed international power politics. Two superpowers, the Soviet Union and the United States, each controlling atomic arsenals, replaced the former European leadership and engaged in a menacing cold war. The cold war saturated everyday life, giving birth to cold war religion in the

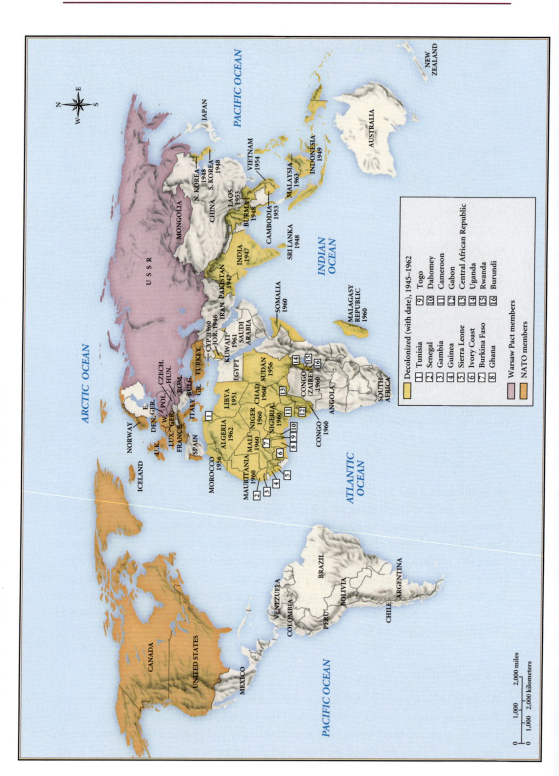

PACIFIC OCEAN

NEW ZEALAND

JAPAN

N
W   E
S

ARCTIC OCEAN

USSR

MONGOLIA

N. KOREA
1948
S. KOREA
1948
CHINA

VIETNAM
1954

LAOS
1953

BURMA
1948

CAMBODIA
1953

AUSTRALIA

INDONESIA
1949

MALAYSIA
1963

SRI LANKA
1948

INDIA
1947

IRAN   PAKISTAN
1947

JOR. 1946
CYP. 1960

TURKEY

SAUDI
ARABIA

KUWAIT
1961

SOMALIA
1960

INDIAN
OCEAN

MALAGASY
REPUBLIC
1960

NORWAY

ICELAND

U.K.   DEN.
E.
GER.
W. POL.
LUX. GER. CZECH.
FRANCE   HUN.
SPAIN   ITALY BULG.
GR.   ROM.

EGYPT

LIBYA
1951

SUDAN
1956

CONGO
(ZAIRE)
1960

ANGOLA

SOUTH
AFRICA

MOROCCO
1956

ALGERIA
1962

MALI
1960

NIGER
1960

CHAD
1960

NIGERIA
1960

CONGO
1960

MAURITANIA
1960

ATLANTIC
OCEAN

1

13

14   15
16

7
6   8 9 10
11
12

5
2   3   4

Decolonized (with date), 1945–1962

1 Tunisia	9 Togo	13 Central African Republic
2 Senegal	10 Dahomey	14 Uganda
3 Gambia	11 Cameroon	15 Rwanda
4 Guinea	12 Gabon	16 Burundi
5 Sierra Leone		
6 Ivory Coast		
7 Burkina Faso		
8 Ghana		

Warsaw Pact members
NATO members

ATLANTIC
OCEAN

PACIFIC OCEAN

CANADA

UNITED STATES

MEXICO

VENEZUELA
COLOMBIA

BRAZIL

PERU

BOLIVIA

CHILE

ARGENTINA

0   1,000   2,000 miles
0   1,000 2,000 kilometers

■ **MAPPING THE WEST The Cold War World, c. 1960**

Superpower rivalry resulted in the division of much of the industrial world into cold war alliances. The United States and the Soviet Union also vied for the allegiance of the newly decolonized countries of Asia and Africa by providing military, economic, and technological assistance. Wars such as those in Vietnam and Korea were also products of the cold war.

preachings of the Reverend Billy Graham and to a secular culture of bomb shelters, spies, and witch-hunts. The postwar reconstruction of Europe created a cold war division into an Eastern bloc dominated by the Soviets and a freer West mostly allied with the United States.

Yet both halves of Europe recovered almost miraculously. Eastern Europe, where wartime devastation was greatest, experienced less prosperity, while in western Europe wartime technology served as the basis for new consumer goods and improved health. Western Europe formed a successful Common Market that would become the foundation for the trend toward European unity. Yet as a result of the war, Germany recovered as two countries, not one, and the former European powers shed their colonies. Newly independent nations emerged in Asia and Africa, opening the possibility for a more equitable distribution of global power.

As the West as a whole grew in prosperity, its cultural life focused on eradicating the evils of Nazism and on surviving the atomic rivalry of the superpowers. In the midst of consumerism and a heated cold war culture, many came to wonder whether cold war was really worth the threat of nuclear annihilation.

Suggested References for further reading and online research appear on page SR-36 at the back of the book.

www.bedfordstmartins.com/huntconcise   See the ONLINE STUDY GUIDE to assess your mastery of the material covered in this chapter.

Challenges to the Postindustrial West

1960–1980

I N JANUARY 1969, JAN PALACH, a twenty-one-year-old philosophy student, drove to a main square in Prague, doused his body with gasoline, and set himself ablaze. In his coat—deliberately put to one side—was a paper demanding an end to Soviet-style repression in Czechoslovakia. It promised more such suicides unless the government lifted state censorship. The manifesto was signed: "Torch No. 1." Across a stunned nation, black flags were flown, close to a million people flocked to Palach's funeral, and shrines to his memory seemed to spring up overnight. For the next few months, as repression continued, more Czech youth followed Palach's grim example and became torches for freedom.

In an age of conspicuous technological growth, Jan Palach's self-immolation was a primal and horrifying scene. It was part of a massive uprising of youth, women, minorities, and many others in the 1960s and 1970s against repression, war, inequality, and technology itself. From Czechoslovakia to the United States and around the world, protests arose against the way in which industrial nations in general and the superpowers in particular were directing society. Political repression outraged these activists, and they objected to the human consequences of technology's dizzying pace. Technological advances, reformers believed, had given enormous power to a handful of financiers, managers, and bureaucrats—the new (but unelected) leaders of "postindustrial society." The term *postindustrial* indicated the emergence of the service sector—including finance, engineering, and health care—as the dominant force in the economy in the West, replacing heavy industry. Many of the protesters were being educated to enter this service elite. As critics, however,

■ **Shrine to Jan Palach**

Jan Palach was a martyr to the cause of an independent Czechoslovakia free to pursue a non-Soviet destiny. His self-immolation for that cause roused the nation. Makeshift shrines that sprang up throughout the 1970s and 1980s served as rallying points that ultimately contributed to the overthrow of Communist rule. (© Mark Garanger/Corbis.)

991

they saw mindless bondage resulting from work in which the majority of people merely watched over an ever-growing number of machines.

While reformers questioned the values of technological society, whole nations challenged the superpowers' monopoly of international power. An agonizing war in Vietnam sapped the resources of the United States, and China confronted the Soviet Union with increasing confidence. The oil-producing states of the Middle East formed a cartel and reduced the flow of oil to the leading industrial nations in the 1970s. The resulting price increases helped bring on a recession in the West. Other third-world countries resorted to terrorism to achieve their ends, and all the wealth and military might of the superpowers could not guarantee that they would emerge victorious in this age of increasingly global competition. Nor during these decades could the superpowers prevent the erosion of their legitimacy—an erosion often brought on by the individual acts of citizens like the human torches.

The Technology Revolution

Three decades after World War II, continuing technological advances steadily boosted prosperity and changed daily life in industrial countries. In Europe and the United States, people awoke to instantaneous radio and television news, worked with computers, and used revolutionary contraceptives to control reproduction. Satellites orbiting the earth reported weather conditions, relayed telephone signals, and collected military intelligence. Household gadgets from electric popcorn poppers and portable radios to automatic garage door openers made life more pleasant. The reliance on machines led one scientist and philosopher, Donna Haraway, to insist that people were no longer self-sufficient individuals but rather *cyborgs*, humans who needed machines to sustain ordinary life processes. However, as with the invention of textile machinery and the railroads in the eighteenth and nineteenth centuries, the full range of social implications—positive and negative—would not take shape all at once.

The Information Age: Television and Computers

Information technology catalyzed social change in these postindustrial decades just as innovations in textile making and the spread of railroads had in the nineteenth century. Its ability to convey knowledge, culture, and politics globally appeared even more revolutionary. In the first half of the twentieth century, mass journalism, film, and radio had begun to forge a more homogeneous society based on shared information and images; in the last third of the century, television, computers, and telecommunications made information more accessible and, some critics said, culture more standardized.

Americans embraced television in the 1950s; after the postwar recovery, it was Europe's turn. Between the mid-1950s and the mid-1970s, Europeans rapidly adopted television as a major entertainment and communications medium. In 1954, 1 percent of French households had television; by 1974, almost 80 percent did. With the average viewer tuning in about four and a half hours a day, the audience for newspapers and theater declined. "We devote more . . . hours per year to television than [to] any other single artifact," one sociologist commented in 1969. As with radio, European governments funded television broadcasting with tax dollars and controlled TV programming to avoid what they perceived as the substandard fare offered by American commercial TV; instead, they featured drama, ballet, concerts, variety shows, and news. In Europe at least, the welfare state assumed a new obligation—to fill citizens' leisure time—and gained more power to shape daily life.

With the emergence of communications satellites and video recorders in the 1960s, state-sponsored television encountered competition. Satellite technology allowed for the transmission of sports broadcasts and other programming to a worldwide audience. Feature films on videotape became readily available to television stations (though not yet to individuals) and competed with made-for-television movies and other programs. The competition increased in 1969 when Sony Corporation introduced the first affordable color videocassette recorder to the consumer market. What statesmen and intellectuals considered the junk programming of the United States—soap operas, game shows, sitcoms—arrived dubbed in the native language, amusing a vast audience with the joys, sorrows, tensions, and aspirations of daily life. Critics charged that both state-sponsored and commercial television avoided extremes to keep sponsors happy, instead spoon-feeding audiences only "official" or "moderate" opinions.

■ **Venice Skyline**
Television swept Europe in the 1960s and 1970s, increasingly uniting people by means of the daily news, theater, films, and game shows. Satellite transmission allowed programming to cross national boundaries, further linking the peoples and cultures of the Common Market. In divided Germany, the exchange of programming bridged even the Berlin Wall and was an early contributor to the erosion of cold war divisions.
(Tom Bross/Stock Boston.)

They complained that, although TV provided more information than had ever been available before, the resulting shared culture represented the lowest common denominator.

East and west, television exercised a powerful political and cultural influence. Even in one rural area of the Soviet Union, over 70 percent of the inhabitants watched television regularly in the late 1970s; the rest continued to prefer radio. Educational programming united the far-flung population of the USSR by broadcasting shows designed to advance Soviet culture. At the same time, with travel impossible or forbidden to many, shows about foreign lands were among the most popular—as were postcards from these lands, which became household decorations. Heads of state could usually preempt regular programming. In the 1960s, French president Charles de Gaulle addressed his fellow citizens frequently, employing the grandiose gestures of an imperial ruler to stir patriotism. As electoral success in Western Europe increasingly depended on cultivating a successful media image, political staffs came to rely on media experts as much as they did policy experts.

Just as revolutionary, the computer reshaped work in science, defense, and ultimately industry. Computers had evolved dramatically since the first electronic computer, Colossus, which the British used in 1943 to decode Nazi military and diplomatic messages. Awesome in its day, Colossus was primitive by later standards—gigantic, slow, able only to decode, and noisy. With growing use in civilian industry and business after the war, computing machines shrank from the size of a gymnasium in the 1940s to the size of an attaché case in the mid-1980s. They also became far less expensive and fantastically more powerful than Colossus, thanks to the development of sophisticated digital electronic circuitry implanted on tiny silicon chips, which replaced the clumsy vacuum tubes used in 1940s and 1950s computers. Within a few decades the computer could perform hundreds of millions of operations per second, and the price of the integrated circuit at the heart of computer technology would fall to less than a dollar, allowing businesses and households access to computing ability at a reasonable cost.

Computers changed the pace and patterns of work not only by speeding up and easing tasks but also by performing many operations that workers had once done themselves. Garment workers, for example, no longer painstakingly figured out how to arrange patterns on cloth for maximum efficiency and economy. A computer specified instructions for the optimal positioning of pattern pieces, and trained workers, usually women, followed the machine's directions. By the end of the 1970s, the miniaturization of the computer had made possible a renewal of the eighteenth-century-style "cottage industry." As in earlier times, people could work in the physical isolation of their homes but be connected to a central mainframe.

Did computers transform society for the better? Whereas the Industrial Revolution had seen physical power replaced by machine capabilities, the information revolution witnessed brainpower augmented by computer technology. Many believed computers would profoundly expand mental life, providing, in the words of one scientist, "boundless opportunities . . . to resolve the puzzles of cosmology, of life, and of the society of man." Others maintained that computers programmed people, reducing human capacity for inventiveness, problem solving, and initiative. As the 1970s closed, such predictions were still untested as this information revolution moved toward a more dramatic unfolding in the 1980s and 1990s.

The Space Age: Science and Satellites

When the Soviets launched the satellite *Sputnik* in 1957, they ignited competition with the United States that was quickly labeled the "space race." U.S. president John F. Kennedy became determined to beat the Soviets in space by putting a man on the moon by the end of the 1960s. Throughout the decade, increasingly complex space flights tested humans' ability to survive the process of space exploration, including weightlessness. Astronauts walked in space, endured weeks (and, later, months) in orbit, docked with other craft, fixed satellites, and carried out experiments for the military and private industry. Meanwhile, a series of unmanned rockets filled the earth's gravitational sphere with weather, television, intelligence, and other communications satellites. In July 1969, a worldwide television audience watched as U.S. astronauts Neil Armstrong and Edwin "Buzz" Aldrin walked on the moon's surface—the climactic moment in the space race.◆

The space race also drove Western cultural developments. Astronauts and cosmonauts were perhaps the era's most admired figures: Yuri Gagarin, Neil Armstrong, and Valentina Tereshkova—the first woman in space—topped the list. A new fantasy world developed. Children's toys and games increasingly had space-related themes. Films such as *2001: A Space Odyssey* portrayed space explorers answering questions about life that were formerly the domain of church leaders. Likewise, in the internationally popular television series *Star Trek*, members of the starship *Enterprise*'s diverse crew wrestled with the problems of maintaining humane values against less-developed, often menacing civilizations. In the Eastern bloc, Polish author Stanislaw Lem's novel *Solaris* (1971) similarly portrayed space-age individuals engaged in personal quests and likewise drew readers and ultimately viewers into a futuristic fantasy.

This space age grew out of cold war concerns, but it also offered the possibility of more global political cooperation: the diffusion of rocket technology, for example, resulted from international efforts. From the 1960s on, U.S. spaceflights often involved the participation of other countries such as Great Britain and the Netherlands.

◆ For two sources that capture the mood of the astronauts and their audience, see Document 73, The *New York Times* and Neil Armstrong and Edwin Aldrin, "The First Men Walk on the Moon."

■ **Valentina Tereshkova, Russian Cosmonaut**
People sent into space were considered heroes personifying modern values of courage, strength, and well-honed skills. Insofar as the space age was part of the cold war race for superpower superiority, the USSR held the lead during the first decade. The Soviets trained both women and men, and the 1963 flight of Valentina Tereshkova—the first woman in space—supported Soviet claims of gender equality in contrast to the U.S. program. (Archive Photos.)

In 1965, an international consortium headed by the United States launched the first commercial communications satellite, *Intelsat I*, and by the 1970s more than four hundred stations worldwide and some 150 countries worked together to maintain global satellite communications.

Lunar landings and experiments in space advanced pure science despite space-race hype. Astronomers, for example, previously dependent on remote sensing for their work, used mineral samples from the moon to calculate the age of the solar system more precisely. Unmanned spacecraft provided data on cosmic radiation, magnetic fields, and infrared sources. Although the media touted the human conquerors of space, breakthroughs in space exploration and astronomy were dependent on a range of technology including the radiotelescope, which depicted space by receiving, measuring, and calculating nonvisible rays. These findings reinforced the "big bang" theory of the origins of the universe, first posited in the 1930s by American astronomer Edwin Hubble and given crucial support in the 1950s by the discovery of a low level of radiation permeating the universe in all directions. Based on the work of Albert Einstein and Max Planck, the "big bang" theory explains the development of the universe from a condition of extremely high density and temperature some ten billion years ago. Nuclei emerged when these conditions dissipated in a rapid expansion of space— the so-called big bang.

Revolutions in Biology, Reproductive Technologies, and Sexual Behavior

Sophisticated technologies extended to the life sciences, bringing dramatic new health benefits and ultimately changing reproduction itself. In 1952, scientists Francis Crick, an Englishman, and James Watson, an American, discovered the configuration of DNA, the material in a cell's chromosomes that carries hereditary information. Apparently solving the mystery of the gene and thus of biological inheritance, they showed how the "double helix" of the DNA molecule splits in cellular reproduction to form the basis of each new cell. This genetic material, biologists concluded, provides a chemical pattern for an individual organism's life. Beginning in the 1960s, genetics and the new field of molecular biology progressed rapidly. Growing understanding of nucleic acids and proteins advanced knowledge of viruses and bacteria that effectively ended the ravages of polio, tetanus, syphilis, tuberculosis, and such dangerous childhood diseases as mumps and measles in the West.

In the wake of this biological revolution came questions about the ethics of humans' tampering with the natural processes of life. For example, understanding how DNA works allowed scientists to bypass natural animal reproduction by means of a process called *cloning*—obtaining the cells of an organism and dividing or reproducing them (making an exact copy) in a laboratory. Ethicists and politicians questioned whether scientists *should* interfere with so basic and essential a process as reproduction. Similarly, the possibility of genetically altering species and even creating new ones (for instance, to control agricultural pests) led to concern about how such actions would affect the balance of nature. In a related medical field, Dr. Christiaan Barnard of South Africa performed the first successful human heart transplant in 1967, and U.S. doctors later developed an artificial heart. These medical miracles, however, prompted questions and even protests. For example, given the shortage of reusable organs, what criteria should doctors use to select recipients? Commentators also debated whether the enormous cost of new medical technology to save a few people would be better spent on helping the many who lacked even basic medical and health care.

Technology also influenced the most intimate areas of human relations—sexuality and procreation. In traditional societies, community and family norms dictated marital arrangements and sexual practices, in large part because too many or too few children threatened the crucial balance between population size and agricultural productivity. As Western societies industrialized and urbanized, however, not only did these considerations become less urgent but the growing availability of reliable birth-control devices permitted young people to begin sexual relations earlier, with less risk of pregnancy. In the 1960s, these trends accelerated, as the birth-control pill, first produced in the United States and tested on women in developing areas, came on the Western market. By 1970, its use was spreading around the world. Millions sought out voluntary surgical sterilization through tubal liga-tions and vasectomies. New techniques brought abortion, traditionally performed by amateurs, into the hands of medical professionals, making it a safe procedure for the first time.

Childbirth and conception itself were similarly transformed. Whereas only a small minority of Western births took place in hospitals in 1920, more than 90 per-cent did by 1970. Obstetricians now performed much of the work midwives had once done. As pregnancy and birth became a medical process, innovative new procedures and equipment made it possible to monitor women and fetuses throughout pregnancy, labor, and delivery. The number of medical interventions rose: cesarean births increased 400 percent in the United States in the 1960s and 1970s, and the number of prenatal visits per patient in Czechoslovakia, for ex-ample, rose 300 percent between 1957 and 1976. In 1978, the first "test-tube baby," Louise Brown, was born to an English couple. She had been conceived when her mother's eggs were fertilized with her father's sperm in a laboratory dish and then implanted in her mother's uterus—a complex process called *in vitro fertilization*. If a woman could not carry a child to term, a laboratory-fertilized embryo could be implanted in the uterus of a surrogate, or substitute, mother. Researchers even began working on an artificial womb to allow for reproduction entirely outside the body—from storage bank to artificial embryonic environment.

A host of controversies—and some tragedies—accompanied these break-throughs. In the early 1960s, a West German drug firm, without prior testing, dis-tributed the tranquilizer thalidomide, claiming that it safely prevented miscarriages. Pregnant women used the drug widely, with unforeseen results: thousands of chil-dren were born with physical and mental disabilities. The Catholic church firmly opposed all mechanical and chemical means of birth control as a sinful interven-tion in a sacred process. Many Catholics and others maintained that life begins at conception, and they branded abortion as murder. In vitro fertilization also stirred disapproval, appearing to some as "playing God" with human life.

Often publicizing these controversies, the expanding media helped democra-tize knowledge of birth-control procedures after World War II and made public dis-cussions of sexual matters explicit, technical, and widespread. Popular use of birth control allowed Western society to be saturated with highly sexualized music, lit-erature, and journalism without a corresponding rise in the birthrate—evidence of the increasing separation of sexuality from reproduction. Abundant statistical sur-veys showed that regular sexual activity began at an ever-younger age, and people talked more openly about sex—another component of cultural change. Finally, in a climate of increased publicity to sexuality, more open homosexual behavior be-came apparent, along with continued efforts to decriminalize it across the West. The Western media announced the arrival of a "sexual revolution." From the late nineteenth century to the 1960s, however, sexual revolution had been trumpeted with each advance in birth-control technology, showing once again the social and political impact of technological transformation.

■ **Children Disabled by Thalidomide**

In the last third of the century, the increasingly destructive side effects of some powerful medicines became apparent. Women who had taken the tranquilizer thalidomide during their pregnancies gave birth to children with severe disabilities. In the race to profit from scientific and technological developments, companies sometimes ignored the consequences for human beings.
(Deutsche Press Agentur/Archive Photos.)

Postindustrial Society and Culture

Reshaped by soaring investments in science and the spread of technology, Western countries in the 1960s started on what social scientists labeled a *postindustrial* course. Instead of being centered on manufacturing and heavy industry, postindustrial society emphasized the distribution of such services as health care and education. The service sector was the leading force in the economy, and this meant that intellectual work, not industrial or manufacturing work, had become primary. Moreover, all parts of society and industry interlocked, forming a system constantly in need of complex analysis. These characteristics of postindustrial society would carry over from the 1960s and 1970s into the next century.

Multinational Corporations

One of the major innovations of the postindustrial era was the rise of multinational corporations. These companies produced for a global market and conducted business worldwide, but unlike older kinds of international firms, they established major factories in countries other than their home base. For example, of the five hundred largest businesses in the United States in 1970, more than one hundred did over a quarter of their business abroad. IBM, for example, operated in more than one hundred countries. Although U.S.-based corporations led the way, Volkswagen, Shell, Nestlé, Sony, and other European and Japanese multinationals also had a broad global scope.

Some multinational corporations had bigger revenues than entire nations. They appeared to burst the bounds of the nation-state as they set up shop in whatever part of the world offered cheap labor. Their interests differed starkly from those of ordinary people with a local or national outlook. In the first years after the war, multinationals preferred European employees, who constituted a highly educated labor pool, had a strong consumer tradition, and eagerly sought secure work. Then, beginning in the 1960s, multinationals moved more of their operations to the emerging economies of formerly colonized states as labor costs, taxes, and regulations increased at home. Although multinational corporations provided jobs in developing areas, profits usually enriched foreign stockholders and thus looked like imperialism reborn.

Many European firms believed that they could stay competitive only by expanding or forming mergers or becoming partners with government in doing business. In France, for example, a massive glass conglomerate merged with a metallurgical company to form a new group specializing in all phases of construction—a wise move given the postwar building boom. European firms increased their investment in research and used international cooperation to produce major new products. This new emphasis on research was a crucial ingredient in postindustrial society. Ventures like the British-French Concorde supersonic aircraft, which, beginning with its first flight in 1976, flew from London to New York in under four hours, and the Airbus, a more practical series of passenger jets inaugurated in 1972 by a consortium of European firms, attested to the strong relationship among government, business, and science (Map 23.1). European firms now commanded large enough research budgets to compete successfully with U.S.-based multinational giants. Whereas U.S. production had surpassed the combined output of West Germany, Great Britain, France, Italy, and Japan in the immediate postwar years, by the mid-1970s the situation was reversed.

The New Worker

In its formative stage, industrial production had depended on workers who often labored to exhaustion and lived in a state of poverty that sometimes led to violence. This scenario changed fundamentally in postwar Europe with the reduction of the blue-collar workforce—a new development resulting from resource depletion in coal mines, the substitution of oil for coal and of plastics for steel, the growth of off-shore manufacturing, and the automation of industrial processes. Within firms,

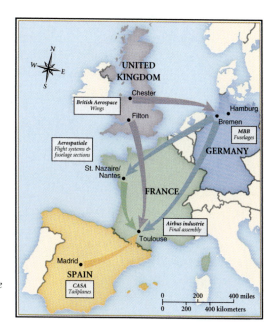

■ MAP 23.1 The Airbus Production System

The international consortium Airbus played an important role in the economic and industrial integration of Europe. It also advanced the revitalization of the individual national economies by establishing new manufacturing centers away from capital cities and by modernizing older ones. Its formation presaged the international mergers and cooperative production that would characterize the late twentieth and early twenty-first centuries. Today Airbus is a global enterprise with parts and service centers around the world, including the United States, China, and India.

the relationship of workers to bosses shifted, as managers started grouping workers into teams that set their own production quotas, organized and assigned tasks, and competed with other teams to see who could produce more. As blue-collar positions disappeared and workers gained responsibilities that had once been managerial prerogatives, union membership declined.

In both U.S.-led and Soviet-bloc countries, a new working class consisting of white-collar service personnel emerged. Its rise undermined old social distinctions based on the way one worked: those who performed service work or had managerial functions were not necessarily better paid than blue-collar workers. The ranks of service workers swelled with researchers, health-care and medical workers, technicians, planners, and government functionaries. Employment in traditional parts of the service sector—banks, insurance companies, and other financial institutions—also surged because of the vast sums of money needed to finance technology and research. Entire categories of employees, such as flight attendants, devoted much of their skill to the psychological well-being of customers. The consumer economy provided more jobs in restaurants and personal health, fitness, and grooming, and in hotels and tourism. By 1969, the percentage of service-sector employees had passed that of manufacturing workers in several industrial countries: 61.1 percent versus 33.7 percent in the United States and 48.8 percent versus 41.1 percent in Sweden. (See "Taking Measure," page 1002.)

Postindustrial work life had some different ingredients in the Soviet bloc. Late in the 1960s, Communist leaders announced a program of "advanced socialism"—

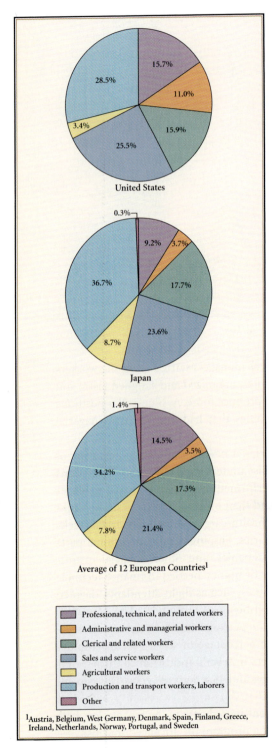

15.7%

28.5%

11.0%

3.4%

15.9%

25.5%

United States

0.3%

9.2% 3.7%

36.7%

17.7%

8.7%

23.6%

Japan

1.4%

14.5%

3.5%

34.2%

17.3%

7.8%

21.4%

Average of 12 European Countries[1]

- Professional, technical, and related workers
- Administrative and managerial workers
- Clerical and related workers
- Sales and service workers
- Agricultural workers
- Production and transport workers, laborers
- Other

[1]Austria, Belgium, West Germany, Denmark, Spain, Finland, Greece, Ireland, Netherlands, Norway, Portugal, and Sweden

■ **TAKING MEASURE** Postindustrial Occupational Structure, 1984

Striking changes occurred in the composition of the workforce in the postwar period. Agriculture continued to decline in importance as a source of jobs, and by the 1980s the percentage of agricultural workers in the most advanced industrial countries had fallen below 10 percent. The most striking development was the expansion of the service sector, which came to employ more than half of all workers. In the United States, the agricultural and industrial sectors, which had dominated a century earlier, now offered less than a third of all jobs.

(*Yearbook of Labour Statistics* [Geneva: International Labour Office, 1992], Table 2.7.)

more social leveling, greater equality of salaries, and nearly complete absence of private production. The percentage of farmers remained higher in the Soviet bloc than in Western Europe. Despite the stated goals of "advanced socialism," a huge difference between professional occupations and those involving physical work remained in socialist countries, where less mobility existed between the two classifications than in Western nations. Much as in the U.S.-led bloc, however, gender helped to shape the workforce into two groups: generally, men earned higher pay for better jobs, and women were relegated to lower paying lesser jobs. Somewhere between 80 and 95 percent of women worked in socialist countries, but they generally held the most menial and worst-paying jobs.

As the postwar boom accelerated, West Germany and other Western nations absorbed immigrant, or "guest," laborers. Coming from Turkey, Greece, southern Italy, Portugal, and North

Africa, these workers collected garbage, built roads, held factory jobs, and cleaned homes. In an environment where desirable work usually required mental operations performed in clean settings, these jobs appeared especially lowly. Males predominated among migrant workers. Female migrants who worked performed similar chores for less pay. Migrants' menial work often was "off the books," so they were cut off from social security and other employee benefits.

Farm life was updated, even bureaucratized. By the 1970s, one could travel for miles in Europe without seeing a farmhouse. Small landowners sold family plots to farmers engaged in *agribusiness*. Governments, farmers' cooperatives, and planning agencies took over decision making from the individual farmer; they set production quotas and handled an array of marketing transactions. In the 1960s, agricultural output rose an average of 3 percent per year in Greece and Spain and 2.5 percent in the Netherlands, France, and Great Britain. Genetic research and the skyrocketing use of machinery contributed to growth. Between 1965 and 1979, the number of tractors in Germany more than tripled from 384,000 to 1,340,000. But bureaucracy played its part, too. For example, in the 1970s a French farmer, Fernande Pelletier, made a living on her hundred-acre farm in southwestern France in the new setting of international agribusiness. Advised by a government expert, Pelletier produced whatever foods might sell competitively in the Common Market—from lamb and veal to foie gras and walnuts—and joined with other farmers in her region to buy heavy machinery and to sell her products. Agricultural solvency required as much managerial and intellectual effort as did success in the industrial sector.

The Boom in Education and Research

Education and research were key to running postindustrial society and offered the means by which nations could maintain their economic and military might. In the West, common sense, hard work, and creative intuition had launched the earliest successes of the Industrial Revolution. By the late twentieth century, success in business or government demanded humanistic or technological expertise and ever-growing staffs of researchers. As one French official put it, "the accumulation of knowledge, not of wealth, . . . makes the difference" in the quest for power.

Investment in research was essential to military and industrial leadership. The United States funneled more than 20 percent of its gross national product into research in the 1960s, in the process siphoning off many of Europe's leading intellectuals and technicians in a so-called brain drain. Complex systems—for example, nuclear power generation with its many components, from scientific conceptualization to plant construction to the publicly supervised disposal of radioactive waste—required intricate professional oversight. Scientists and bureaucrats frequently made more crucial decisions than did elected politicians in the realm of space programs, weapons development, and economic policy. Soviet-bloc nations proved less adept at linking their considerable achievements in science to actual applications because of bureaucratic red tape. In the 1960s, some 40 percent of Soviet-bloc scientific findings became obsolete before the government approved them for application to technology.

The new criteria for success fostered unprecedented growth in education, especially in universities, scientific institutes, and other postsecondary institutions. The number of university students in Sweden rose by about 580 percent and in West Germany by 250 percent between 1950 and 1969. Great Britain established a new network of polytechnic universities to encourage the technical research that elite universities often scorned. France set up administrative schools for future high-level bureaucrats. By the late 1970s, the Soviet Union had built its scientific establishment so rapidly that the number of its advanced researchers in the natural sciences and engineering surpassed that of the United States. Meanwhile, institutions of higher learning added courses in business and management, information technology, and systems analysis.

In principle, education made the avenues to success more democratic by basing them on talent instead of wealth. In fact, societal leveling did not occur in most Western European universities, and instruction often remained rigid and old-fashioned. Although eighteenth-century Europeans had pioneered educational reform, students in the 1960s reported that teachers lectured even young children, who spoke in class only to echo the teacher or to recite homework memorized the night before. At the university level, as one angry student put it, the professor was "a petty, threatened god" who puffed himself up "on the passivity and dependence of students." Such judgments would provoke young people to rebel late in the 1960s against the traditional authority of teachers, officials, and parents.

A Redefined Family and a Generation Gap

Just as education changed dramatically to meet the needs of postindustrial society, the contours of the family and the nature of parent-child relationships shifted from what they had been a century earlier: family roles were transformed, and the relationship between parents and children—long thought to be natural and unchangeable—looked alarmingly different. Even though television and media commentators often delivered messages about what the family should be, technology, consumer goods, and a constant flow of guest laborers and migrants from the former colonies made for enormous variety in what households actually were. Households were now headed by a single parent, by remarried parents merging two sets of unrelated children, by unmarried couples cohabitating, or by traditionally married parents who had fewer children. Households of same-sex partners also became more common. At the end of the 1970s, the marriage rate had fallen 30 percent in the West from its 1960s level. Despite a rising divorce rate, the average marriage lasted one-third longer than it had a century earlier because of increased longevity.

After almost two decades of baby boom, the birthrate dropped significantly. On average, a Belgian woman, for example, bore 2.6 children in 1960 but only 1.8 by the end of the 1970s. Although the birthrate fell, the percentage of children born outside of marriage soared.

Daily life within the family changed. Technological consumer items saturated domestic space, as radio and television often formed the basis of the household's common social life. Machines such as dishwashers, washing machines, and clothes dryers became more affordable and more widespread, reducing (in theory) the time women had to devote to household work and raising standards of cleanliness. More middle-class women worked outside the home during these years to pay for the prolonged economic dependence of children. To advance in a knowledge-based society, postwar youth did not enter the labor force in their teens but instead attended school and required their parents' support. Whereas the early modern family organized labor, taught craft skills, and monitored reproductive behavior, the modern family seemed to have a primarily psychological or postindustrial mission. Parents were to provide emotional nurture while their children learned intellectual skills in school. They could also count on psychologists, social workers, and other social service experts to provide counseling and assistance. Television programs portrayed a variety of family experiences on soap operas and sit-coms and gave viewers an opportunity to see how other families dealt with the tensions of modern life.

Most notably, postindustrial society transformed teenagers' lives. A century earlier, teens had been full-time wage earners; now most were students, financially dependent on their parents into their twenties. Amid the new tensions caused by this prolonged childhood, youth simultaneously gained new roles as consumers. Advertisers and industrialists saw the baby boomers as a multi-billion-dollar market and wooed them with consumer items associated with rock music—records, portable radios, stereos. Replacing romantic ballads, rock music celebrated youthful rebellion against adult culture in biting, critical, and often explicitly sexual lyrics. Sex roles for the young did not change, however. Despite the popularity of a few individual women rockers, promoters focused on men, whom they depicted as surrounded by worshiping female "groupies." The new models for youth were themselves the products of advanced technology and savvy marketing for mass consumption. The Beatles were a little-known English bar band in 1962 when they hired a new manager, Brian Epstein. Epstein remade their image and their music, booking them in major theaters throughout Europe and the United States; by the mid-1960s, public appearances of the Beatles summoned thousands of fans whose hysteria intensified during the group's performances. The mixture of high-tech music, pop-star marketing, and the youthful hysteria of fans contributed to a sense that there was a unique youth culture and a growing "generation gap."

■ **Rolling Stones Tour Europe**
The Rolling Stones took the youth revolution in music to a new level of raw energy and social critique. Much like the modernist avant-garde early in the twentieth century, they were dissonant and shocking. Unlike modernists, however, the Stones were commercially successful, all of them becoming multimillionaires, international celebrities, and role models to youth around the world.
(Dominique Berretty.)

Art, Ideas, and Religion in a Technocratic Society

Cultural trends evolved with technology itself. Like modernists in the past, a new generation of artists addressed growing consumerism and technology with their art. Even as colonies continued officially to rip away from the old imperial powers, their influence on the Western mind remained powerful, leading musicians, scholars, and religious leaders to turn in their direction. At the same time, many of these intellectuals enjoyed increasing international recognition and—like the multinationals they often criticized—global markets.

The "pop art" movement, spearheaded by Richard Hamilton (b. 1922) of Britain and Robert Rauschenberg (b. 1925) of the United States, expanded artistic boundaries as it mocked mass culture. Pop art featured images from everyday life and employed the glossy techniques and products of what these artists called "admass," or mass advertising, society. "There's no reason," they maintained of modern society's commercialism, "not to consider the world as one gigantic painting." Rauschenberg made collages from comic strips, magazine clippings, and fabric to fulfill his vision that "a picture is more like the real world when it's made out of the real world." By the early 1960s, the movement had become a financial success, attracting such maverick American artists as Jasper Johns (b. 1930) and Andy Warhol (1927?–1987), who advanced the parody of modern commercialism. Warhol showed, for example, how the female body, the classic form that attracted nineteenth-century male art buyers, was used to sell everything mass culture had to offer in the 1960s and 1970s. Swedish-born artist Claes Oldenburg (b. 1929) depicted the grotesque aspects of ordinary consumer products in *Giant Hamburger with Pickle Attached* (1962) and *Lipstick Ascending on Caterpillar Tractor* (1967). "High" art picked up "low" objects such as scraps of metal, cigarette butts, dirt, and even excrement: the Swiss sculptor Jean Tinguely (1925–1991) used rusted parts of old machines to make moving fountains. His partner Niki de Saint Phalle (b. 1930) then constructed huge, exuberant figures—many of them inspired by the folk traditions of the Caribbean and Africa—to decorate them. These colorful fountains adorned main squares in Stockholm, Montreal, Paris, and other cities.

■ **Niki de Saint Phalle,** *Fontaine Stravinsky* **(1983)**
Niki de Saint Phalle's exuberant and playful art, seen in the fountains of Paris and cities around the world, captured the accessibility of pop art. Her other work drew inspiration from Caribbean and African styles and celebrated women of decolonizing countries. Living during the rebirth of activism, de Saint Phalle lined up suspended bags of paint and machine-gunned them to create a spattered canvas—her answer to the alleged "macho" style of abstract expressionists like Jackson Pollock. (Barbara Alper/Stock Boston.)

The American composer John Cage (1912–1992) had been working to the same ends when he added sounds produced by such everyday items as combs, pieces of wood, and radio noise into his musical scores. Buddhist influence led Cage also to incorporate silence in music and to compose by randomly tossing coins and then choosing notes by the corresponding numbers in the ancient Chinese *I Ching* ("Book of Changes")—moves that continued the trend away from classical melody that had begun with modernism. Other composers, called *minimalists*, simplified music by featuring repetition and sustained notes as well as by rejecting the "masterpiece" tradition of lush classical compositions. Some stressed modern technology; they introduced tape recordings into vocal pieces and used computers and synthesizers both to compose and to perform their works. German composer Karlheinz Stockhausen (b. 1928) incorporated electronic music into classical composition in 1953, as did Cage soon after. Influenced by his own travels, Stockhausen continued the modern style of fully exploring non-Western tonalities in such 1970s pieces as *Ceylon*. While this music echoed the electronic and increasingly interconnected state of human society, its appeal remained limited and concert audiences diminished. At the same time, improved recording technology and mass marketing brought music of all varieties to a wider home audience than ever before.

The Information Age influenced social science as much as it did art and music. The social sciences reached the peak of their prestige during these decades, often because of their increasing use of statistical models and predictions. Sociologists and psychologists produced empirical studies that purported to demonstrate rules for understanding individual, group, and societal behavior. Simultaneously, the social sciences undermined some of the foundations for the belief that individuals had true freedom and for the assertion that Western civilization was more sophisticated or just than non-Western societies. French anthropologist Claude Lévi-Strauss (b. 1908) developed a theory called *structuralism*. The theory insisted that all societies function within controlling structures—kinship and exchange, for example—that operate according to coercive rules similar to those of language. Structuralism challenged existentialism's tenet that humans could create a free existence, and it shook the social sciences' faith in the triumph of rationality. In the 1960s and 1970s, the findings of the social sciences generally paralleled concerns that technology was creating a society of automatons and that complex managerial systems would eradicate individualism and human freedom.

Debates about free will coincided with new Christian preachings about the changing times. Responding to what he saw as a crisis in faith caused by affluence and secularism, Pope John XXIII (r. 1958–1963) in 1962 convened the Second Vatican Council, known as Vatican II.◆ The council modernized the liturgy, democratized many church procedures, and at the last session in 1965 renounced church

---

◆ For the text of Pope John XXIII's proclamation, see Document 74, "Vatican II."

doctrine that condemned the Jewish people as guilty of killing Jesus. The Catholic church thus opened itself to some new influences. Although Pope John's successor, Paul VI (r. 1963–1978), kept Catholic opposition to artificial birth control alive, he also became the first pontiff to visit Africa, Asia, and South America, and encouraged Catholicism in the Soviet bloc, strengthening religion as a primary focal point for anticommunism there.

Simultaneously, a Protestant revival occurred in the United States, and growing numbers of people joined sects that stressed the literal truth of the Scripture. In Western Europe, however, Christian churchgoing remained at a low ebb. In the 1970s, for example, only 10 percent of the British population went to religious services—about the same number that attended live soccer matches. The composition of the Western religious public was also metamorphosing as migrants from the former colonies increased the strength of non-Christian religions such as Islam and Hinduism.

Contesting the Cold War Order in the 1960s

Affluence, scientific sophistication, and military might elevated the United States and the Soviet Union to the peak of their power early in the 1960s. By 1965, however, the six nations of the Common Market had replaced the United States as the leader in worldwide trade and often acted in their own self-interest across the U.S.-Soviet divide. Communist China, along with countries in Eastern Europe, contested Soviet leadership, and many decolonizing regions refused to become pliable allies to the superpowers. The struggle for Indochinese independence had never ended, and by the mid-1960s a devastating war in Vietnam was under way. But in some respects the most serious challenge to the cold war order came from the rising discontent of citizens like Jan Palach. In the 1960s, they rose up in protest against the consequences of technological development, the lack of fundamental rights, and the prospect of nuclear holocaust latent in the cold war.

Cracks in the Cold War Consensus

In the summer of 1963, less than a year after the shock of the Cuban missile crisis, the United States and the Soviet Union signed a test-ban treaty outlawing the testing of nuclear weapons in the atmosphere and in the seas. The agreement suggested that the superpowers would reduce international tensions to focus on domestic politics. The new Soviet middle class of bureaucrats and managers demanded a better standard of living and a reduction in cold war animosity. In Western European countries, voters elected politicians who promoted an increasing array of social programs designed to ensure economic democracy. A significant minority shifted their

votes away from the conservative Christian Democratic coalitions to Socialist, Labor, and Social Democratic parties in hopes of placing more attention on ordinary
people's needs during rapid change than on the cold war.

Germany and France took different roads to skirting the cold war. In Germany,
Social Democratic politicians had enough influence to shift money from defense
spending to domestic programs. Willy Brandt, the Socialist mayor of West Berlin,
became foreign minister in 1966 and pursued an end to frigid relations with Communist East Germany. This policy, known as *Ostpolitik,* unsettled cold war thinking. It gave West German business leaders what they wanted: "the depoliticization
of Germany's foreign trade," as one industrialist put it, and an unlocking of Soviet-
bloc consumerism. To break the cold war stranglehold, French president Charles
de Gaulle poured more money into French nuclear development, withdrew French
forces from NATO, and signed trade treaties with the Soviet bloc. However, he also
protected France's good relations with Germany to prevent further encroachments
from the Soviet bloc. At home, de Gaulle's government mandated the cleaning of
all Parisian buildings and sponsored the construction of modern housing. With his
haughty and stubborn pursuit of French grandeur, de Gaulle offered the European
public an alternative to superpower toadying.

Brandt's Ostpolitik and de Gaulle's assertiveness had their echoes in the Soviet
bloc. Pushing de-Stalinization, Khrushchev took the dangerous course of trying to
reduce Communist officialdom's privileges, and he sanctioned the publication of dissident Aleksandr Solzhenitsyn's *One Day in the Life of Ivan Denisovitch* (1962), which
revealed firsthand the terrible conditions in the labor camps. Khrushchev's blunders—
notably his humiliation in the Cuban missile crisis, his ineffectual schemes to improve
Soviet agriculture, and his inability to patch the rift with China—led to his ouster in
1964. Nevertheless, the new leadership of Leonid Brezhnev and Alexei Kosygin continued attempts at reform, encouraging plant managers to turn a profit and allowing
the production of televisions, household appliances, and cheap housing to alleviate
the discontent of a better-educated citizenry. The government also loosened restrictions to allow cultural and scientific meetings with Westerners, another move that
relaxed the cold war atmosphere in the mid-1960s. The Soviet satellites in Eastern
Europe grasped the economic opportunity presented by Moscow's relaxed posture.
Poland allowed private farmers greater freedom to make money, and Hungarian leader
János Kádár introduced elements of a market system into the national economy.

In the arts, Soviet-bloc writers continued for a time to thaw the frozen mono-
lith of socialist realism. Ukrainian poet Yevgeny Yevtushenko exposed Soviet complicity in the Holocaust in *Babi Yar* (1961), a passionate protest against the slaughter
of tens of thousands of Jews near Kiev during World War II. Challenging the cele-
bratory nature of socialist art, East Berlin writer Christa Wolf showed a couple tragically divided by the Berlin Wall in her novel *Divided Heaven* (1965). But repression
returned later in the 1960s. The Soviet government took to bulldozing outdoor art
shows, forcing visual artists to hold exhibitions in secret in their apartments and

■ **Hagop Hagopian, *No to the Neutron Bomb!* (1977)**

In an era of ongoing cold war, culture continued to be on the front line, with the Soviets persecuting those who produced abstract or critical art. Artists were adept, however, at incorporating Soviet icons in work critical of the regime. They might, for instance, depict Lenin's portrait but with citizens turning their back on it instead of being inspired by it. Or, as in this painting, they bravely critiqued the course of the arms race.

(The Jane Voorhees Zimmerli Art Museum. Rutgers, The State University of New Jersey. The Norton and Nancy Dodge Collection of Nonconformist Art from the Soviet Union. Photo: Jack Abraham.)

even to turn their living spaces into a new kind of art known as "installations"—the arrangement of everyday objects in large spaces. Dissident artists depicted Soviet citizens as worn and tired in grays and other monochromatic color schemes instead of the brightly attired and heroic figures of socialist realism. Dissident writers relied on the underground *samizdat* system of distribution: uncensored publications were reproduced by hand and carefully passed from reader to reader.

Even in the United States, other issues challenged the cold war for front-page attention. The assassination of President John F. Kennedy in November 1963 shocked the nation and the world. Only momentarily did it quiet escalating demands for civil rights for African Americans and other minorities. White segregationists reacted with extraordinary violence to sit-ins at lunch counters, efforts to register black voters, and freedom marches. This violent racism was a weak link in the American claim to moral superiority in the cold war. In response to the murders and destruction, Kennedy had introduced civil rights legislation and forced the desegregation of schools and universities. In a massive rally in Washington, D.C., in August 1963, hundreds of thousands of marchers assembled around the Lincoln Memorial, where they heard the electrifying words of African American minister Martin Luther King Jr.:

> *I have a dream that . . . all of God's children, black men and white men, Jews and Gentiles, Protestants and Catholics, will be able to join hands and sing in the words of the old Negro spiritual, "Free at last! Free at last! Thank God Almighty, we are free at last!"*

Lyndon B. Johnson (1908–1973), Kennedy's successor, steered the Civil Rights Act through Congress in 1964. This legislation forbade segregation in public facilities and created the Equal Employment Opportunity Commission (EEOC) to fight job discrimination based on "race, color, national origin, religion, and sex." Southern conservatives had tacked on the provision against sex discrimination in the vain hope that it would doom the bill. Modeling himself on his hero Franklin Roosevelt, Johnson envisioned a "Great Society," in which new government programs would improve the chances of the forty million Americans living in poverty. He sponsored myriad reform projects, among them Project Head Start for disadvantaged pre-school children and the Job Corps for training youth. Black novelist Ralph Ellison called Johnson "the greatest American president for the poor and the Negroes."

Vietnam and Turmoil in Asia

During the 1960s, third-world nations increasingly distanced themselves from the superpowers. Many were still tied by technical systems such as radio and telephone networks and by trade to their former rulers; where the cold war was concerned, however, they sought to be nonaligned. Communist China's independent way was the biggest surprise to both the Soviet Union and the United States. Mao Zedong, ever hostile to Western capitalism, also detested Soviet leadership and its stagnating bureaucracy. In 1966, Mao unleashed the Cultural Revolution, a movement to remake individual personality according to his own vision of an ever-evolving socialism. As economic goals lost their importance, China's youth were empowered to haul away people of every class for "reeducation"—which translated to personal humiliation and millions of deaths.

Both superpowers had interests in East and Southeast Asia, but they often failed to see the complex changes under way in the region. American policymakers, for example, did not detect the growing dispute between the two Communist giants because they had an inflexible vision of monolithic communism. While China plunged into Mao's bloody cultural and economic experiments, the peoples of Southeast Asia were coming to grips with decades of demographic upheaval. Despite war and nationalist revolution, the region's population more than tripled between 1920 and 1970, reaching 370 million by the end of the 1970s. Like the 85 percent of third-world leaders who rose from the military, most East and Southeast Asian rulers were dictators, lacking the expertise to make their countries economically sound in the face of soaring population.

Superpower intervention in this unstable part of the world was loaded with risk, and nowhere was this truer than in the U.S. intervention in Vietnam (Map 23.2). After the Geneva settlement in 1954, the United States escalated its commitment to the corrupt and incompetent leaders in non-Communist South Vietnam. North Vietnam, China, and the Soviet Union backed the rebel Vietcong, as the South Vietnamese Communists came to be called. The strength of the Vietcong seemed to grow daily, and by 1966, the United States had more than a half-million soldiers in South Vietnam. Before the war ended in 1975, the United States would drop more bombs on North Vietnam than the Allies had launched on both Germany and Japan during World War II. Television reports carried the optimistic predictions of Johnson's advisers of imminent victory despite mounting U.S. casualties. But after decades of anticolonial struggle, the insurgents rejected a negotiated peace. North Vietnam's leaders calculated that the United States would give in first as the American public recoiled from the horrors of televised slaughter, including scenes of children burned alive by U.S. chemical weapons. Confronting growing antiwar sentiment and increasing military costs, President Johnson announced in March 1968 that he would not run for president again. The U.S. superpower was tarnished, irreparably it seemed at the time; so, too, was the Soviet Union.

■ **MAP 23.2 The Vietnam War, 1954–1975**

The local peoples of Southeast Asia had long resisted incursions by their neighbors. Since the end of the nineteenth century, they also had resisted French rule, never more fiercely than in the war that liberated them after World War II. Though poorly equipped in comparison with the French, the Vietnamese triumphed in the battle of Dien Bien Phu in 1954. Then the Americans became involved, trying to halt what they saw as the tide of Communist influence behind the Vietnamese liberation movement. The ensuing war in Vietnam in the 1960s and 1970s spread into neighboring countries, making the region the scene of vast destruction.

The Explosion of Civic Activism: Civil Rights, Student Protests, and the Women's Movement

In the midst of cold war, technological transformation, and bloody conflict, a new social activism emerged in the West. Students, blacks and other racial minorities, Soviet-bloc citizens, women, environmentalists, and homosexuals sometimes brought their societies to the brink of revolution in their fiery protests.

The U.S. civil rights movement expanded its bold activism. In 1965, César Chávez led Mexican American migrant workers in the California grape agribusiness to strike for better wages and working conditions. Deeply religious and ascetic, Chávez helped Hispanic Americans define their identity and struggle against deportation, inferior schooling, and discrimination. Meanwhile, the African American civil rights movement took a dramatic turn as urban riots erupted across the United States in the summer of 1965. Frustrated and angry, activists transformed their struggle into a militant celebration of their race under the banner "Black is beautiful." The issue they faced was one they felt they had in common with decolonizing people: how to shape an identity different from that of white oppressors. Some urged a push for "black power" to reclaim rights instead of begging for them nonviolently. Turning from the nonviolence of Martin Luther King Jr., formerly pacifist black leaders turned their rhetoric to violence: "Burn, baby, burn" chanted rioters who destroyed the grim inner cities around them.

As a result of the new turn in black activism, white American university students who had participated in the early stages of the civil rights movement found themselves excluded from leadership positions. Many soon joined the swelling protest against technological change, consumerism, and the Vietnam War. European youth caught the fever. In the mid-1960s, university students in Rome occupied an administration building after right-wing opponents assassinated one of their number during a protest against the 200-to-1 student-teacher ratio. Prague students held carnival-like processions, commemorated the tenth anniversary of the 1956 Hungarian uprisings, and took to chanting "The only good Communist is a dead one." The "situationists" in France called on students to wake up from the slumbering pace of mass society and student life by jolting individuals to action with shocking graffiti and street theater.

Students attacked the traditional university curriculum and flaunted their own countercultural values. They questioned how studying Plato or Dante would help them after graduation. "How to Train Stuffed Geese" was French students' satirical version of teaching methods inflicted on them. "No professors over forty" and "Don't trust anyone over thirty" were powerful slogans of the day. Long hair, communal living, and a repudiation of personal hygiene announced students' rejection of middle-class values, as did their denunciation of sexual chastity. With the widespread use of the pill, abstinence became unnecessary as a method of birth control, and students made the sexual revolution explicit and public with open promiscuity. Marijuana use became common among student protesters, and amphetamines and barbiturates became part of the drug culture, which had its own rituals, songs, and gathering places. Scorned by students, businesses nonetheless made billions of dollars selling blue jeans, dolls dressed as "hippies," natural foods, and drugs, as well as packaging and managing the stars of the counterculture.

Women's activism erupted across the political spectrum. Those in the civil rights and student movements soon realized that protest organizations devalued women just as society at large did. Male activists adopted the leather-jacketed machismo style of their film and rock heroes, but women in the movements were often judged by the status of their male-protester lovers. "A woman was [expected] to 'inspire' her man," African American activist Angela Davis complained, noting that women aiming for equality were often accused of "want[ing] to rob [male protesters] of their manhood." A speaker in Frankfurt, West Germany, interrupted a student meeting, demanding "that our problems be discussed substantively. It is no longer enough that women are occasionally allowed to say a few words." More politically conventional middle-class women eagerly responded to the international best-seller *The Feminine Mystique* (1963) by American journalist Betty Friedan. Pointing to the stagnating talents of many housewives, Friedan helped organize the National Organization for Women (NOW) in 1966 "to bring women into full participation in the mainstream of American society now." Working for reproductive rights, women in France helped end the ban on birth control in 1965. In Sweden, they lobbied to make tasks both at home and in the workplace less gender-segregated.

■ Gay Activists in London

The reformist spirit of the 1960s and 1970s changed the focus of homosexuals' activism. Instead of concentrating mostly on legal protection from criminal prosecution, gays and lesbians began affirming a special and positive identity. As other groups who had endured discrimination began making similar affirmations, "identity politics" was born. Critics charged that traditional universal values were sufficient and that homosexuals and others constituted "special-interest" groups. Gays, women, and ethnic or racial minorities countercharged that the universal values first put forth in the Enlightenment seemed to apply only to a privileged few.

(© Hulton Getty/Liaison Agency.)

Women also took to the streets on behalf of such issues as abortion rights and the decriminalization of gay and lesbian sexuality. Many flouted social conventions in their attire, language, and attitudes. Renouncing brassieres, high-heeled shoes, cosmetics, and other adornments, they spoke openly about taboo subjects such as their sexual feelings and even announced that they had resorted to illegal abortions. This brand of feminist activity was meant to shock polite society—and it did. At a Miss America contest in 1968, women protesters crowned a sheep the new beauty queen. West German women students tossed tomatoes at male protest leaders in defiance of standards for ladylike behavior. Many women of color, however, broke with feminist solidarity and spoke out against the "double jeopardy" of being "black and female."

1968: Year of Crisis

The West seethed with protest and calls for reform, which erupted in 1968. In January, on the first day of Tet, the Vietnamese New Year, the Vietcong and the North Vietnamese attacked more than one hundred South Vietnamese towns and American bases, inflicting heavy casualties. The Tet offensive, as it came to be called, caused many Americans to conclude that the war might be unwinnable and gave the antiwar movement crucial momentum. Then, on April 4, 1968, Martin Luther King Jr. was assassinated by a white racist, and more than a hundred cities in the United States erupted in violence as African Americans vented their anguish and rage. On campuses, strident confrontation over the intertwined issues of war, technology, racism, and sexism closed down classes. At the same time, student dissent was escalating in France where in January, students had gone on strike, shockingly invading administration offices to protest their inferior education and status. When later students at the prestigious Sorbonne in Paris took to the streets, police assaulted them. The Parisian middle classes reacted with unexpected sympathy to the student uprising because of their own resentment of bureaucracy. They were also horrified at seeing the elite and brutal police force, the CRS, beating middle-class students and passersby who expressed their support. French workers joined in: some nine million went on strike, occupying factories and calling not only for higher wages but also for "participation" in everyday decision making. To some, the revolt of youth and workers looked as if it might spiral into another French revolution. The normally decisive president Charles de Gaulle seemed paralyzed at first, but he soon sent tanks into Paris. Although demonstrations continued throughout June, the student movement in France at least had been closed down.◆

◆ For a set of firsthand accounts of the wave of rebellion that swept college campuses throughout Europe and the United States in 1968, see Document 75, "Student Voices of Protest."

In Prague, the 1968 revolt began within the Czechoslovak Communist Party itself. In the autumn of 1967 at a party congress, Alexander Dubček, head of the Slovak branch of the party, had called for more social and political openness. Attacked as an inferior Slovak by the leadership, Dubček nonetheless struck a chord among frustrated party officials, technocrats, and intellectuals; Czechoslovaks began to dream of creating a new society—one based on "socialism with a human face." Party officials elevated Dubček to the top position, where he quickly changed the Communist style of government, ending censorship, instituting the secret ballot for party elections, and allowing competing political groups to form. The "Prague Spring" had begun—"an orgy of free expression," one Czech journalist called it. People bought uncensored publications, packed uncensored theater productions, and engaged in almost nonstop political debate.

The Polish, East German, and Soviet regimes threatened the reform government daily. When Dubček failed to attend a meeting of Warsaw Pact leaders, Soviet

■ **Prague Spring**
When the Soviets and other Warsaw Pact members cracked down on the Czech dissidents, they met determined citizen resistance. People refused aid of any kind to the invaders. Indeed, despite dejection at the repression of Dubček's government, protest was ongoing until the final fall of Communist rule two decades later. (Prache-Levin/Sygma.)

threats became intense. Finally in August 1968, Soviet tanks rolled into Prague in a massive show of antirevolutionary force. Citizens tried to halt the return to Communist orthodoxy by using free expression as sabotage. They painted graffiti on tanks and confused invading troops by removing street signs. Illegal radio stations broadcast testimonials of resistance, and merchants refused to sell food or other commodities to Soviet troops. As the Soviets gradually removed reformers from power, Jan Palach and other university students immolated themselves, and protest of one type or another never stopped. In November 1968, the Soviets announced the Brezhnev Doctrine: reform movements, a "common problem" of all socialist countries, would face swift repression.

Protest in 1968 challenged the political direction of Western societies, including superpower dominance. Whether burning draft cards in the United States or scribbling graffiti on public buildings in Europe, activists made all government open to question and would continue to do so into the 1970s. Yet change did not necessarily occur in the way reformers had hoped. Governments turned to conservative solutions, while some disappointed reformers considered more violent measures.

The Erosion of Superpower Mastery in the 1970s

The 1970s brought an era of *détente*—a lessening of cold war tensions—as the United States pulled out of the Vietnam War and as the superpowers negotiated to limit the nuclear arms race. Despite this relaxation in the cold war, the superpowers appeared to lose their dominance. By the early 1970s, student protest evolved into ongoing reform movements, while other groups, such as those favoring Basque independence in Spain and Catholic rights in Northern Ireland, took violent action. This violence affected the superpowers as it threw their allies off balance. Although the United States and the Soviet Union still controlled the balance of power, their grip was also loosening because of their own internal corruption, the challenge of terrorism, and competition from the oil-producing states, Japan, and the Common Market.

The Superpowers Tested

As the 1970s opened, both superpowers faced daunting internal and external challenges to their dominance, but the United States was the most visibly shaken. Elected in 1968 to replace Johnson, the conservative Richard Nixon promised to bring peace to Southeast Asia. In 1970, however, he ordered U.S. troops to invade Cambodia, the site of North Vietnamese bases (see Map 23.2). Campuses erupted again in protest, and on May 4 the National Guard killed four students and wounded eleven others at a demonstration at Kent State University in Ohio. Nixon called the victims "bums," and a growing reaction against the counterculture made many Americans agree with him that the guardsmen "should have fired sooner and longer." Mired in turmoil, the United States and North Vietnam agreed to peace in January 1973 but continued to support the hostilities. In 1975, South Vietnam collapsed under a determined North Vietnamese offensive, and Vietnam was forcibly reunified. The United States reeled from the conflict, suffering loss of young lives, turbulence at home, vast military costs, and a weakening of its reputation around the world.

Simultaneously, the United States pulled off a foreign policy triumph when Henry Kissinger, Nixon's secretary of state and a believer—like Bismarck—in Realpolitik, decided to take advantage of the ongoing conflict between China and the USSR. In 1972, Kissinger's efforts to bring the United States and China closer resulted in Nixon's visiting the *other* Communist power. Within China, the meeting helped stop the brutality and excesses of the Cultural Revolution and helped advance the careers of Chinese pragmatists interested in technology, trade, and relations with the West. Fearful of the Chinese diplomatic advantage, the Soviets made their own overtures to the U.S.-led bloc. In 1972, the superpowers signed the Strategic Arms Limitation Treaty (SALT I), which set a cap on the number of antimissile defenses each country could have. In 1975, in the Helsinki accords on human rights, the Western bloc officially acknowledged Soviet territorial gains in World War II in exchange for the Soviet bloc's guarantee of basic human rights.

Despite these successes, the enigmatic Nixon focused on reelection at any price. His reelection committee paid several men—caught in the act and arrested—to wiretap the telephones at Democratic Party headquarters in Washington's Watergate office building. Not only did the presidential office work against free elections, but after his landslide victory in 1972 Nixon himself attempted to cover up the truth about the Watergate break-in. Between 1968 and 1972, Nixon had forged a powerful conservative consensus; in the summer of 1974, however, the Watergate scandal forced Nixon to resign in disgrace—the first U.S. president ever to do so.

The Soviet leadership also met mounting criticism as it intensified repression. By the early 1970s, the hard-liner Brezhnev had eclipsed Kosygin's influence in the Soviet Union and freely clamped down on critics. After the events in Czechoslovakia in 1968, the Soviet dissident movement was at a low ebb. "The shock of our tanks crushing the Prague Spring . . . convinced us that the Soviet colossus was invincible," explained one pessimistic liberal. Other voices persisted, however. In 1974, Brezhnev expelled Solzhenitsyn from the USSR after the publication of the first volume of *Gulag Archipelago* (1973–1976) in the U.S.-led bloc. Composed from myriad biographies, firsthand reports, and other sources of information about prison camp life, Solzhenitsyn's story of the Gulag (the Soviet system of internment and forced-labor camps) documented the brutal conditions Soviet prisoners endured under Stalin and his successors.

The Kremlin persecuted many ordinary people who did not have Solzhenitsyn's international reputation. Soviet psychologists, complying with the government, certified the "mental illness" of people who did not play by the rules; thus dissidents wound up as prisoners in mental institutions. The crudest Soviet persecutions, however, involved anti-Semitism: Jews were subject to educational restrictions (especially in university admissions), severe job discrimination, and constant assault on their religious practice. A commonplace accusation by Soviet officials was that Jews were "unreliable, they think only of emigrating. . . . It's madness to give them an education, because it's state money wasted." Ironically, even dissidents blamed Jews for the Bolshevik Revolution and for the terror of Stalinist collectivization. As attacks intensified in the 1970s, Soviet Jews sought to emigrate to Israel or the United States, often unsuccessfully.

Dissent persisted in satellite states, and repression prompted some people to flee. In an open letter to the Czechoslovak Communist Party leadership, playwright Václav Havel accused Marxist-Leninist rule of making people materialistic, not socialist, and indifferent to civic life. In 1977, Havel, along with a group of fellow intellectuals and workers, signed Charter 77, a public protest against the Communist regime. The police imprisoned and tormented many of the charter's signatories, including Havel. By this time, the brain drain of Eastern European intellectuals had become significant. The modernist composer Gyorgy Ligeti had left Hungary in 1956, after which his work was celebrated in concert halls and in films such as *2001: A Space Odyssey* (1968). From exile in Paris, Czech writer Milan Kundera enthralled audiences with *The Book of Laughter and Forgetting* (1978) and other novels that chronicled the lives of tortured characters caught in the grim realities of Communist institutions. The presence of these exiles and escapees in the United States and Western European capitals helped erode any lingering support for communism.

The West, the World, and the Politics of Energy

While the superpowers wrestled with internal political embarrassments and the intricacies of nuclear diplomacy, other nations were developing new economic muscle. Since 1960, the six Common Market countries, led by West Germany, had surpassed the United States in percentage of gross world product. This achievement made the Common Market a countervailing economic power to the Soviet Union and the United States. A partial slowdown in the mid-1960s brought rising unemployment, the use of pump-priming techniques to stimulate industrial investment, and layoffs of foreign "guest" laborers and married women in favor of native-born men. Offsetting the slowdown, the opening of Eastern European markets helped bolster Western European prosperity; by the end of the decade, Western European exports to the Soviet bloc totaled some $45 billion annually, producing a burden of debt that Communist countries could ill afford. In 1973, Britain joined the Common Market, followed by Ireland and Denmark (see "Mapping the West," page 1027). The market's exports now amounted to almost three times those of the United States.

The United States faced still other challenges to its power to dominate the international economy, from Japan as well as from the effects of its own policies. Rising purchases of military and imported goods brought inflation and made the United States a debtor nation. Dollars flooded the international currency markets. In 1971, the Bretton Woods currency system, created during World War II to maintain stable international markets, collapsed. As Common Market countries united to prevent financial chaos, they forced the United States to relinquish its single-handed direction of Western economic strategy. Thanks to massive U.S. expenditures in the Korean and Vietnam Wars, Japan emerged as a manufacturing and exporting giant. Even without oil and other key natural resources, Japan experienced an astonishing 11 percent rate of economic growth in the 1960s and had become the world's largest shipbuilder by the 1970s.

Not only Japan but the Middle East's oil-producing nations also dealt Western dominance a critical blow. Tensions between Israel and the Arab world provided the catalyst. On June 5, 1967, Israeli forces, responding to Palestinian guerrilla attacks, seized Gaza and the Sinai peninsula from Egypt, the Golan Heights from Syria, and the West Bank from Jordan. Although Israel won a stunning victory in this Six-Day War, the Arab humiliation led the Arab states to try to forge a common political and economic strategy. In 1973, Egypt and Syria attacked Israel on Yom Kippur, the most holy day in the Jewish calendar, but Israel, with material assistance from the United States, stopped the assault. Having failed militarily, the Arab nations turned decisively to economic clout. The Organization of Petroleum Exporting Countries (OPEC), a relatively loose consortium before the Yom Kippur War, quadrupled the price of its oil and imposed an embargo, cutting off all exports of oil to the United States in retaliation for its support of Israel. For the first time since imperialism's heyday, the *producers* of raw materials—not the industrial powers—controlled the

Israel after the Six-Day War, 1967

flow of commodities and set prices to their own advantage. The West became mired in an oil crisis.

Throughout the 1970s, oil-dependent Westerners watched in astonishment as OPEC upset the balance of economic power. Instead of being controlled by the Western powers, the oil-producing nations helped provoke an economic recession by restricting the flow of oil and charging more for it (Figure 23.1). These actions caused unemployment to rise by more than 50 percent in Europe and the United

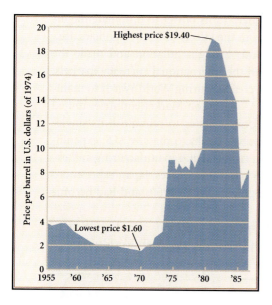

■ FIGURE 23.1 Fluctuating Oil Prices, 1955–1985

Colonization allowed the Western imperial powers to obtain raw materials at advantageous prices. Even with decolonization, European and American firms often had such deep roots in newly independent economies that they were able to set the terms for trade. The OPEC oil embargo and price hikes of the 1970s were signs of change, which included decolonized countries' exercise of control over their own resources. OPEC's action not only led to a decade of painful economic downturn but also encouraged some European governments to improve public transportation and to impose policies designed to make individual consumers reduce their dependence on oil.

States and the inflation rate to soar because of energy prices. By the end of 1973, the inflation rate jumped to over 8 percent in West Germany, 12 percent in France, and 20 percent in Portugal. Eastern-bloc countries, dependent on Soviet oil, fared little better. Skyrocketing interest rates in the U.S.-led bloc discouraged both industrial investment and consumer buying. With prices, unemployment, and interest rates soaring—the unusual combination of economic conditions was dubbed *stagflation*—Westerners were forced to realize that both energy resources and economic growth had limits.

Political Alternatives in Hard Times: Environmentalism, Feminism, and Terrorism

The unprecedented economic situation and the changing global balance of power inspired new waves of citizen activism ranging from reform to the most violent terrorism. On the reform end, a sense of limits to global resources encouraged the formation of environmental political parties. An escapee from Nazi Germany, E. F. "Fritz" Schumacher, produced one of the bibles of the environmental movement, *Small Is Beautiful* (1973), which spelled out how technology and industrialization threatened the earth and its inhabitants. Environmentalists like Schumacher and the American Rachel Carson, author of *Silent Spring* (1962), advocated the immediate rescue of rivers, forests, and the soil from the ravages of factories and chemical farming. These attitudes challenged almost two centuries of faith in industrial growth and in the infinite ability of humanity to extract progress from the natural world.

Initially the environmental movement had its greatest political effect in West Germany. As student protest subsided in the 1970s, environmentalism united members of older and younger generations around the 1960s political tactic called *citizen initiatives*, in which groups of people blocked everything from public transportation fare increases to plans for urban growth. Taking their cue from Chancellor Willy Brandt's Ostpolitik, citizen initiative groups targeted nuclear power and nuclear installations and attracted tens of thousands to demonstrations in the 1970s. Then, in 1979, the Green Party was founded in West Germany, and across Europe Green Party candidates forced other politicians to voice concern for the environment. In the Soviet bloc, Communist commitment to industrial development blinded governments to environmental destruction and to the effects of pollution on people; citizen protest continued to focus on basic needs and individual freedom.

Feminist activism made real gains in the 1970s. Environmental parties attracted many women angered by the birth of "thalidomide babies" and concerned about the chemical contamination of their families' food. Men could escape to the moon or into their careers, a West German ecologist maintained, but not women, "who must give birth to children, willingly or unwillingly, in this polluted world of ours." Other women's activism had notable successes in the 1970s. In Catholic Italy, feminists won the right to divorce, to gain access to birth-control information, and to obtain legal abortions. The demand for these rights as well as for equal pay, job opportunities, and protection from rape, incest, and battering framed the major legal struggles of thousands of women's groups in the 1970s.

Activism ranged from individual to international efforts. In the U.S.-led bloc, personal change also became a goal for women. Consciousness-raising sessions in which groups of women shared individual experiences with marriage, with children, and in the workforce alleviated some of the isolation women felt at home. Soviet-bloc women, who often formed the majority of the workforce and shouldered responsibility for all domestic work, received inspiration from feminist stories spread through the *samizdat* network. At the other extreme were international meetings begun in 1977, when fifteen thousand activist women from around the globe poured into Houston, Texas, to mark the International Year of Women. The meeting brought together Westerners interested in political and economic rights and cultural equality and third-world women who called for an end to violence, starvation, and disease. The utter poverty afflicting women in less-developed countries called into question the commonality on which Western feminist politics was based. The issue of sexual orientation also challenged many mainstream activists in Houston, as lesbians exposed the greater privileges heterosexual women enjoyed. Organization, raised consciousness, and some economic gains backed women's entry into local and national government from the 1970s on.

Terrorist bands took a radically different path, responding to the conservative political climate and worsening economic conditions with kidnappings, bank robberies, bombings, and assassinations. Disaffected and well-to-do youth, steeped in the most extreme theories of society's decay, often joined these groups. Eager to bring down the Social Democratic coalition that led West Germany throughout the 1970s,

Nationalist Movements of the 1970s

the Baader-Meinhof gang assassinated prominent businessmen as well as judges and other public officials. Practiced in assassinations of public figures and random shootings of pedestrians, Italy's Red Brigades kidnapped and then murdered the head of the dominant Christian Democrats in 1978. Advocates of independence for the Basque nation in northern Spain assassinated Spanish politicians and police.

In Britain, nationalist and religious violence in the 1970s pitted the Catholics in Northern Ireland against the dominant Protestants. Catholics experienced job discrimination and a lack of civil rights. Demonstrators urged union with the Irish Republic, and with protest escalating, the British government sent in troops. On January 30, 1972, which became known as "Bloody Sunday," British troops fired at demonstrators and killed thirteen, setting off a cycle of violence that left five hundred dead within the year. Protestants fearful of losing their dominant position combated a reinvigorated Irish Republican Army (IRA), which carried out bombings and assassinations to achieve the union of the two Irelands in order to end the oppression of Catholics.

Terrorists failed in their goal of overturning the existing democracies, and, sorely tried as it was, parliamentary government scored some important successes in the 1970s. The Iberian peninsula, suffering under dictatorship since the 1930s, regained its freedom and set out on a course of greater prosperity. The death of Spain's Francisco Franco ended more than three decades of dictatorial rule. Franco's handpicked successor, King Juan Carlos (b. 1938), surprisingly steered his nation to Western-style constitutional monarchy, facing down threatened military coups. Portugal and Greece also ousted right-wing dictators, thus paving the way for their integration into Western Europe and for substantial economic growth.

Yet the dominance of the West was deteriorating. In 1976, Jimmy Carter, a wealthy farmer and governor of Georgia, narrowly won the U.S. presidential election (the first after the Watergate scandal) by selling himself as an outsider to Washington corruption. Carter could do little to return the economy to its pre-Vietnam and pre–oil embargo prosperity or stem global terrorism. His administration faced an insurmountable crisis late in the 1970s when students, clerics, shopkeepers, and unemployed men in Iran began a religious agitation that brought to power Ayatollah Ruhollah Khomeini, a fundamentalist Muslim leader. From exile in Paris, Khomeini had rallied the impoverished people and discontented Shi'ite Muslims

■ **Soldiers and Civilians in Northern Ireland**

Separatist, civil rights, and terrorist movements made everyday life unpredictably dangerous in the last third of the century as activists increasingly directed their violence against ordinary people. The world wars had often targeted civilians, and those leading internal struggles did so even when the declared wars were over. In Belfast, Northern Ireland, British troops fought to put down the Irish Republican Army and restore unity. Civilians were often drawn into the conflict. Only late in the 1990s did both sides call a halt to the killing and agree to negotiate.
(Brian Aris/Camera Press London.)

of Iran with audiotaped messages calling for a transformation of the region into a truly Islamic society and the renunciation of Western ways advocated by the deposed shah. In the autumn of 1979, revolutionary supporters of Khomeini took hostages at the American embassy in Teheran and would not release them. The paralysis of the United States in the face of Islamic militancy along with soaring inflation following another round of OPEC price hikes suggested that the 1980s and 1990s might cripple the West even more.

Conclusion

The 1960s and 1970s left the West with a sense of emergency. In these decades, an unprecedented level of technological development transformed businesses, the nature of warfare, the exploration of space, and the functioning of government. It also had an enormous impact on everyday life. Work changed as society reached a stage called *postindustrial*, in which the service sector predominated. New patterns of

IMPORTANT DATES			
c. 1960	"Pop art" movement begins to win mainstream support	**1968**	"Prague Spring" reform movement in Czechoslovakia against communism; student uprisings throughout Europe and the United States
1962–1965	Vatican II reforms Catholic ritual and dogma		
1963	U.S. civil rights leader Martin Luther King Jr. leads March on Washington; U.S. president John F. Kennedy assassinated; Betty Friedan publishes *The Feminine Mystique*	**1969**	U.S. astronauts walk on the moon's surface
		1972	SALT I treaty between the United States and Soviet Union
		1973	North Vietnam and the United States sign treaty ending war in Vietnam; OPEC raises price of oil and imposes oil embargo on the West
1964	Nikita Khrushchev ousted in the USSR, replaced by Leonid Brezhnev and Alexei Kosygin		
1965	International consortium led by the United States launches *Intelsat I*, the first commercial communications satellite; Christa Wolf publishes *Divided Heaven*	**1973–1976**	Aleksandr Solzhenitsyn publishes *Gulag Archipelago*
		1974	Watergate scandal forces resignation of U.S. president Richard Nixon
1966	Willy Brandt becomes West German foreign minister and develops Ostpolitik, a policy designed to bridge tensions between the two Germanys	**1977**	Feminists gather in Houston to mark the first International Year of Women
		1978	Birth of the first "test-tube baby"
1967	South Africa's Dr. Christiaan Barnard performs first successful human heart transplant; Israel expands its territory in the Six-Day War	**1979**	Environmentalists found the Green Party in West Germany; Iranians take U.S. hostages in Teheran

family life, new relationships among the generations, and revised standards for sexual behavior also characterized these years. Optimism about the potential of humans to perpetuate progress and affluence abounded. Yet technological change produced stubborn problems: concentrations of bureaucratic and industrial power, social inequality, environmental degradation, even uncertainty about humankind's future.

A surge of rebellion among youth, ethnic and racial minorities, and women condemned these conditions along with the threats posed by the continued cold war. By the end of the 1970s, war in Vietnam, protests throughout the Soviet bloc, the power of oil-producing states, and the growing political force of Islam had weakened superpower preeminence. The U.S.-led bloc also confronted terrorism, and the Soviet Union, long able to repress dissent in a growing economy, was put-

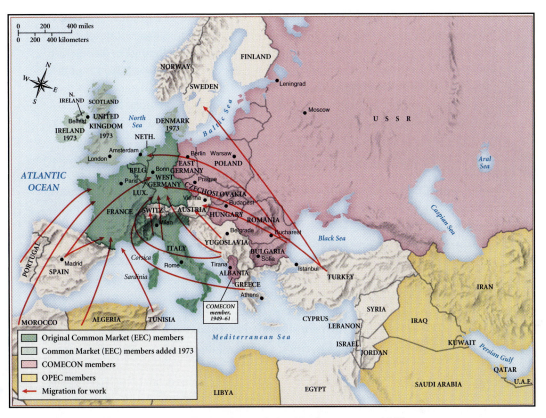

■ MAPPING THE WEST Europe and the Mediterranean, 1980

Despite the continuation of the cold war and the division of Europe into two antagonistic blocs, the superpowers' grip diminished during the 1960s and 1970s. Within the Soviet bloc, several governments introduced features of a market economy, and communications technology brought news of life in the U.S.-led bloc. U.S. allies protested American policies in Vietnam, and anti-American elements were very much in evidence in the uprisings of 1968. Mediterranean countries played their role in the West's transformation during these decades, not only during the oil embargo but in sending tens of thousands of migrants to work in labor-short Europe and often to settle there permanently.

ting more resources into military buildup than it could ultimately support. While the superpowers faltered, society approached the global age—one prepared by the array of technology of the 1960s and 1970s.

Suggested References for further reading and online research appear on page SR-37 at the back of the book.

www.bedfordstmartins.com/huntconcise See the ONLINE STUDY GUIDE to assess your mastery of the material covered in this chapter.

The New Globalism:
Opportunities and Dilemmas
1980 to the Present

I NSTEAD OF MAKING UP PATRIOTIC "LETTERS TO THE EDITOR" as was the custom under communism, in the mid-1980s the Soviet magazine *Ogonyok* ("Small Fires") began printing actual reports from readers. A woman identifying herself as a "mother of two" protested that the cost-cutting policy of reusing syringes in hospitals was spreading AIDS. "Why should little kids have to pay for the criminal actions of our Ministry of Health?" she asked. Other readers complained of corrupt factory managers, of "the radioactive sausages" foisted on the public after the disastrous explosion at the Chernobyl nuclear power plant, and of endless lines at nearly empty grocery stores. Sales of *Ogonyok* soared from a few hundred thousand copies to four million, and the experiment in printing real letters flooded the offices with hundreds of thousands of pieces of mail. The *Ogonyok* example was not unique: all across the Soviet bloc people were exploring political participation and resistance. They wrote, picketed, and protested; in so doing, they created an unprecedented public activism that, with incredibly little bloodshed, toppled the Soviet empire in 1989 and ended the cold war.

The collapse of communism in Europe had some unexpected negative repercussions, including the eruption of ethnic violence in the region, the deterioration of everyday life, and the decline of public services. The last result was part of a general trend in the West, as advanced industrial economies questioned the century-long trend toward the welfare state. Government support for citizens' health,

■ **Europeans React to 9/11 Terror**
On September 11, 2001, terrorists killed thousands of people from dozens of countries in airplane attacks on the World Trade Center in New York. Globally, people expressed their shock and sorrow in vigils, and like this British tourist in Rome, they remained glued to the latest news. Terrorism, which had plagued Europeans for several decades, easily traveled the world in these days of more open borders, economic globalization, and cultural exchange, finally reaching the sole superpower left after the collapse of the Soviet Union. Led by the United States, an international coalition took shape to attempt to eliminate this destructive by-product of a shrinking globe. (© Corbis.)

housing, and social security diminished, although governments increased subsidies and incentives for businesses facing global competition from the rising economic power of Japan, China, and other Asian countries. International business mergers accelerated from the 1990s on, and the Internet connected enterprises around the world in a matter of seconds, providing a force for international unity that offset competition.

The end of the cold war thus hastened the arrival of the "global age"—marked by the national and international migration of millions of people; the further expansion of markets; the lively cultural exchange of popular music, books, films, and television entertainment; and worldwide awareness of AIDS, environmental degradation, genocide, and terrorism. The end of superpower rivalry eased the way for this global exchange. It also resulted in the unprecedented dominance of the United States in world affairs. Nevertheless, new forces arose to compete with the West, in particular the economic power of the "Asian tigers" and the cultural might of Islam. As the twentieth century drew to a close, many observers equated globalism first and foremost with the revolutionary power of the Internet. Whatever the meaning of these many new phenomena, there was no question that people living in the twenty-first century would face extraordinary opportunities and dilemmas that had worldwide resonance.

Global Challenges

The end of the cold war ushered in many challenges. First, the health of the world's peoples and of the environment encountered a three-pronged attack from nuclear disaster, acid rain, and surging population. Second, economic prosperity and physical safety continued to elude great masses of people, especially in the southern half of the globe. Third, more states than ever before exercised economic and political power, especially through multinational organizations such as the World Bank and the World Trade Organization, but at the same time allegiance to nonstate and transnational ideas such as Islamic fundamentalism and ethnic autonomy called into question not only national borders but the concept of the nation-state itself.

Pollution and Population

Whereas industrialization and population growth had once seemed positive developments, people became aware of their downside. Despite the spread of ecological awareness, technological development continued to threaten the environment. The dangers were laid bare in 1986 when an explosion in the reactor at the nuclear power plant at Chernobyl, in the Soviet Union north of Kiev, blew the roof off the containment building and spewed radioactive dust into the atmosphere. The reactor, like most in the USSR, had minimal safety features. Many plant workers died within the year from the effects of radiation; others perished more slowly. Levels of radioactivity rose hundreds of miles in all directions, contaminated meat and produce across Europe had to be destroyed, and by the 1990s cancer rates in the region were soaring, particularly among children.

Other environmental problems also had devastating global effects. Pollutants from automobile exhausts and the burning of high-sulfur coal mixed with atmospheric moisture to produce acid rain, a poisonous brew that contaminates drinking water and destroys vegetation when it falls to earth as rain or snow. In Eastern Europe, the unchecked use of high-sulfur coal produced acid rain that ravaged forests and air pollution that inflicted ailments such as chronic bronchial disease on children. In South America, rain forests were cut down at an alarming rate to open land for cattle grazing or for cultivation of cash crops. Clearing the forests threatened both the global oxygen supply and the biological diversity of the entire planet.

By the late 1980s, scientists determined that the use of chlorofluorocarbons (CFCs), chemicals used in aerosols and refrigerants, had blown a hole in the earth's atmospheric ozone layer. Part of the blanket of gases surrounding the earth, ozone prevents harmful ultraviolet rays from reaching the planet. Simultaneously, emissions from automobiles and industry were adding to the density of gases in the thermal blanket. The result was *global warming*, an increase in the temperature of the earth's atmosphere. Changes in temperature and dramatic weather cycles of drought or drenching rain indicated that a *greenhouse effect* might be permanently warming the earth.

The global public stepped up pressure on governments to check pollution. The affluent West possessed the resources to begin to undo some of the damage accompanying industrialization. Automobile manufacturers in Western Europe and the United States began building cars with lower carbon monoxide emissions, and industrialists scaled back on factory pollution of air and waterways. Consumers began recycling newspaper, glass, aluminum cans, and plastic containers. Municipal governments in Europe turned some streets into automobile-free pedestrian zones, established "green" areas, and even banned cars altogether when ozone levels reached a danger point. European countries and Japan led the world in providing efficient public transportation, thus reducing the number of polluting automobiles on the streets.

Nations with less-developed economies struggled with the pressing issue of surging population. By 1995, Europe was actually experiencing negative growth (more deaths than births), and the less industrially developed countries accounted for 98 percent of all population growth—in part because of the spread of Western medicine. By late 1999, the globe's population had reached 6 billion, and a doubling was forecast for 2045. (See "Taking Measure," page 1032.) In nonindustrial countries, life expectancy rose by an average of sixteen years between 1950 and 1980. By this measure of social health, the superpowers did not fare particularly well. Life expectancy in the Soviet Union fell steadily in the 1970s to 1990s, from a peak of

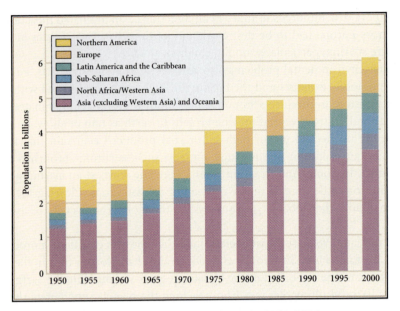

Population in billions

- Northern America
- Europe
- Latin America and the Caribbean
- Sub-Saharan Africa
- North Africa/Western Asia
- Asia (excluding Western Asia) and Oceania

1950 1955 1960 1965 1970 1975 1980 1985 1990 1995 2000

▪ **TAKING MEASURE** World Population Growth, 1950–2000

In the twenty-first century, a major question is whether the global environment can sustain billions of people indefinitely. In the early modern period, local communities lived in accordance with unwritten rules that worked to balance population size with the productive capacities of individual farming regions. Centuries later, the need for balance had reached global proportions. As fertility dropped around the planet because of contraception, population continued to grow because of improved health. The political, social, and environmental results remain unclear.

seventy years in the mid-1970s to fifty-three for Russian men in 1995. By 1995, the United States had fallen from the top twenty in longevity for both women and men. Meanwhile, fertility rates, which had been dropping in the West for decades, were also declining in the less-developed world by 1995, as some 58 percent of couples were estimated to use birth control. Demographers hoped the slowdown in population increase signaled an alternative to ongoing, calamitous growth. Nonetheless, migration and urbanization worsened the problems of nations lacking the resources to care for their swelling numbers.

Despite the spread of Western medicine in the form of vaccines and drugs for diseases such as malaria and smallpox into the less-developed world, half of all Africans did not have access to safe drinking water. Drought and poverty, along with the maneuvers of politicians in some cases, spread famine in regions such as Sudan. Critics said these conditions were the result of a growing divide not between East and West but among countries of the wealthy North and the far poorer South. Medical practice in the industrialized nations focused on high-tech solutions to health problems. Specialists performed heart bypass surgery, transplanted organs, and treated cancer with radiation and chemotherapy. Preventive care for the masses received less attention. Instead, a disproportionate amount of expensive and high-tech hospital services went to the upper classes, especially men. At the other end of the scale, the unemployed suffered more chronic illnesses than people who were better off, but they received less care. The distribution of health services became a hotly debated issue in the general argument of whether technological solutions could remedy global problems.

North versus South?

During the 1980s and 1990s, world leaders tried to address the growing economic schism between the earth's northern and southern regions. Southern peoples—except for Australians and New Zealanders—suffered lower living standards and greater health problems than northerners. Recently emerging from colonial rule and economic exploitation by the North, citizens of the South could not yet count on their new governments to provide welfare services or public education. International organizations such as the World Bank and the International Monetary Fund provided loans for economic development, but the conditions tied to those loans, such as cutting government spending, led to the criticism that underprivileged southerners would gain no real benefit if education and health care had to be cut. Some twenty-first-century leaders advocated that wealthy countries simply acknowledge centuries of imperial pillage and give the South the money it needs.

Southern regions encountered various barriers to economic development. In Latin America, some nations grappled with government corruption, multi-billion-dollar debt, widespread crime, and grinding poverty. Mexico and some other countries, however, began to strengthen their economies by marketing their oil and other natural resources more effectively. Sub-Saharan Africa suffered from drought, famine, disease, and civil war. In Rwanda, for example, military rule, ideological factionalism, and ethnic antagonism produced a lethal mixture of conflict and genocide in the 1990s. Millions perished; others were left starving and homeless. Although African countries began turning away from military dictatorship and toward parliamentary government, global economic advance was uneven in Africa, and the scourge of AIDS made matters worse.

Emerging economies in the Southern Hemisphere as a whole, however, continued to increase their share of gross domestic product during the 1980s and 1990s, and some achieved political gains as well. In South Africa, black peoples began winning the struggle for political rights. In 1990, the moderate government of F. W. de Klerk released the African political leader Nelson Mandela (b. 1918), imprisoned for almost three decades because of his antiapartheid activism. De Klerk's government followed Mandela's release with the gradual end of segregation in parks and on beaches and in 1993 agreed to a democratic constitution that granted the vote to the nonwhite majority while guaranteeing the civil liberties of whites and other minorities. The next year, Mandela became South Africa's president in a landslide electoral victory, formalizing the institution of a multiracial democracy attractive to international business. In India, Rajiv Gandhi (1944–1991), the grandson of India's first prime minister, Jawaharlal Nehru, worked for education, women's rights, and an end to bitter local rivalries. His assassination in 1991 by Tamil nationalists raised questions about whether India would have the strong leadership necessary to attract investment and continue modernization. The answer was soon obvious as India forged ahead in communications and other high-tech industries.

Islam Confronts the West

The Iran hostage crisis, which began in 1979, showed religion, nationalism, and the power of oil uniting to make the Middle East an arbiter of international order. The region's charismatic leaders—in the 1980s, Iran's Ayatollah Khomeini, Libya's Muammar Qaddafi, and Iraq's Saddam Hussein; in the 1990s, Osama bin Laden—variously promoted a pan-Arab or pan-Islamic world order that gathered increasing support. Khomeini's program of "Neither East, nor West, only the Islamic Republic" had wide appeal. Turning from the Westernization encouraged by the shah, his regime required women to cover their bodies almost totally in special clothing, restricted their access to divorce, and eliminated a range of other rights. Islamic revolutionaries believed these restrictions would restore the pride and Islamic identity that imperialism had stripped from Middle Eastern men. Khomeini won widespread support among Shi'ite Muslims. Even though Shi'ites constituted the majority in many Middle Eastern countries, they had long been ruled by Sunni Muslims. The tables turned in Iran when Khomeini proclaimed the ascendancy of the Shi'ite clergy in revolutionary Iran's Islamic society.

Power in the Middle East remained fragmented, however, and Islam did not achieve its unifying goals (Map 24.1). Instead, war plagued the region. The refusal of the Iranian Shi'ites to release the hostages seized in 1979 at the U.S. embassy contributed to the collapse of the Carter presidency and the election of Ronald Reagan in 1980 (the hostages were freed soon after his inauguration in January 1981). Meanwhile, in September 1980, Iraq's president, Saddam Hussein, launched an attack on Iran. He feared that Iraq's Shi'ite minority might rebel against his Sunni regime, and he sought to deflect their aggression into a patriotic crusade against the non-Arab Iranians. The Iraqi leader also coveted oil-rich territory in Iran. Eight years of combat, however, led only to stalemate and massive loss of life on both sides.

The Soviet Union became entangled with Islamic forces in Afghanistan when it supported a coup by a Communist faction against Afghanistan's Communist government in 1979. The factionalism provided an opening for stiff resistance by Afghanis who saw their traditional way of life being threatened by communism's modernizing thrust. By 1980, tens of thousands of Soviet troops were fighting in Afghanistan, using the USSR's most advanced missiles and artillery in an ultimately unsuccessful effort to overcome Muslim leaders. After the withdrawal of Soviet

■ **Muslims at Prayer in Marseille, France**

As migration increased during the 1980s and 1990s, Europe became more ethnically and racially diverse than it had been for centuries. In most European countries, immigrants eventually could become citizens. Switzerland and Germany used the criterion of common ancestry to determine who would have political and civil rights. Cultural exchange and interaction accelerated during these decades, and debates over cultural values and cultural identity multiplied.

(Steve McCurry/Magnum Photos, Inc.)

forces in 1989 and the collapse of the USSR in 1992, power in Afghanistan remained contested until the late 1990s, when the Islamic fundamentalist Taliban party succeeded in imposing a strict regime.

As the Soviet bloc fell apart in 1989–1992, Saddam Hussein was the first to test the post–cold war waters. At the end of the Iran-Iraq war in 1988, Iraq staggered under a heavy debt and a lowered standard of living. Hussein viewed the annexation of neighboring Kuwait, whose 600,000 citizens enjoyed the world's highest per capita income, as a solution to Iraq's troubles. In 1990, Iraqi forces invaded the oil-rich country. Much to Hussein's surprise, the deployment of Iraqi troops on the Saudi Arabian border galvanized a UN coalition (joined by the USSR) to stop the Iraqi invasion. A multinational force led by the United States pummeled the Iraqi army. Iraq's defeat in 1991 heightened pressure on Middle Eastern leaders to negotiate peaceful solutions to their disputes.

Nevertheless, some leaders willingly resorted to violence and international terrorism to advance their causes. Hopes for peace among Palestinians and Israelis

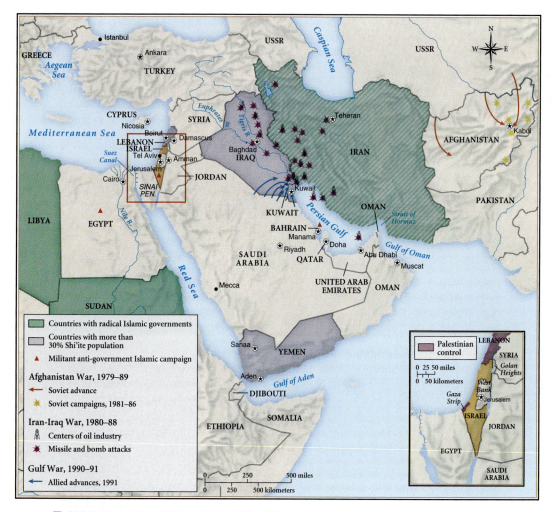

■ MAP 24.1 The Middle East, 1980–1991

Tensions among states in the Middle East, especially the ongoing conflict between Palestinians and Israelis, increased in the 1980s. As Islam took center stage in politics, Middle Eastern populations divided over such issues as the extent of religious determination of state policies, the role of religion in everyday life, and access to human rights including freedom of speech and of movement. Conflicts erupted around some of these questions because, as elsewhere, politicians exploited people's fears and emotions in their pursuit of power. In the 1990s, the increasing demands of globalization pulled some citizens in the direction of secularization, high-tech international partnerships, and a reduction in the costly politics of violence. In 2001, however, violence escalated among Arabs and Israelis, bringing the region to the breaking point.

dimmed after 2000, as peace talks broke down and armed clashes escalated. An unprecedented act of terrorism against the United States occurred on September 11, 2001, when militants from Arab countries hijacked planes and flew them into the Twin Towers of the World Trade Center in New York City and the Pentagon on the outskirts of Washington, D.C. Inspired by the radical leader Osama bin Laden, who sought to end the presence of U.S. armed forces in Saudi Arabia and other areas important to Islam, the hijackers had trained in bin Laden's terrorist camps in Afghanistan and learned to pilot planes in the United States. The loss of more than three thousand lives—not only Americans but people from dozens of other countries—led to a "war against terrorism." The administration of U.S. president George W. Bush forged a multinational coalition with the vital cooperation of dissidents within Afghanistan and predominantly Islamic countries such as Pakistan. The coalition enjoyed quick successes against the terrorists in Afghanistan and brought to an end the harsh Taliban rule, but it became clear that terrorist cells existed throughout the world and that terrorism would pose one of the most frightening global challenges of the twenty-first century.

The Rise of the Pacific Economy

From the last third of the twentieth century and into the twenty-first, an incredible global diffusion of industry and technology took place, especially in Asia. Just as economic change in the early modern period had redirected European affairs from the Mediterranean to the Atlantic, so explosive productivity from Japan to Singapore in

the 1980s began to transfer economic power from the Atlantic region to the Pacific. In 1982, the Asian Pacific nations accounted for 16.4 percent of global gross domestic product, a figure that had doubled since the 1960s. More surprising, by the mid-1990s China was achieving economic growth rates of 8 percent and more, and Japan had developed the second largest national economy after the United States.

South Korea, Taiwan, Singapore, Hong Kong, and China were popularly called the "Asian tigers" because of the ferocity of their growth. Japan, however, led the charge. Investment in high-tech consumer industries drove the Japanese economy. In 1982, Japan had 32,000 industrial robots in operation, Western Europe had 9,000, and the United States had 7,000. In 1989, the Japanese government and private businesses in Japan invested $549 billion to modernize Japan's industrial capacity—a full $36 billion more than U.S. public and private investment combined. Such spending paid off handsomely: buyers around the world snapped up automobiles, televisions, videocassette recorders, and

"Tigers" of the Pacific Rim, c. 1985

computers from Japanese or other Asian Pacific companies. By the end of the 1980s, Japan was home to the world's eight largest banks and to a brokerage house that was twenty times larger than its nearest American competitor. As the United States poured vast sums into its cold war military budget, Asian Pacific investors purchased U.S. government bonds, thus financing America's ballooning national debt. Forty years after its defeat in World War II, Japan was bankrolling its former conqueror.

Despite rising national prosperity in Asia, many individual Asian workers, particularly outside of Japan, saw only modest gains. Women in South Korea and Taiwan labored in sweatshops to produce clothing for J. C. Penney, Calvin Klein, and other U.S.-based companies. Using the lure of a low-paid, docile female workforce, Asian governments were able to attract foreign electronics and other industries. Educational standards rose, however, and these women gained access to birth control and medical care. Despite the persistent grip of authoritarian governments, some of the "Asian tigers" ranked high in human development by UN standards.

In Japan, too, results were mixed: workers were expected to subordinate their personal interests to those of the business firm, just as Japanese businesses followed the dictates of the national government. The rewards for this discipline were great, and for a time Japanese ideas about business and management were touted as offering a model that the West should follow. Then dissatisfaction with Japan's patriarchal political elite developed. In 1989, Japanese women led the way in voting out of office a prime minister who kept a mistress. Women also entered the parliament and cabinet, long a bastion of elderly men. In 2002, the women of Japan threatened the downfall of another prime minister, who had dismissed a woman minister of foreign affairs. Government attempts to maintain cultural homogeneity brought charges of racism from abroad, as hundreds of thousands of non-Japanese who illegally entered Japan to perform the menial labor shunned by native workers experienced considerable discrimination. Critics began to express concern about environmental deterioration, the quality of life in Japan's overcrowded cities, and the growing menace of domestic terrorism.

In the 1990s and early twenty-first century, mounting economic difficulties plagued Japan and the other "Asian tigers." Financial scandals and widespread corruption, which the government refused to address, destabilized the Japanese economy. The stock market plunged, as did the value of the yen. Domestic consumers cut back, and some investors sent their money abroad for higher returns. From 1997 on, Japan's depressed economy menaced the region and the world. A severe business crisis struck the Pacific Rim as currency speculation and irresponsible and corrupt financial practices—"crony capitalism"—brought down the Thai currency in 1997 and then toppled politicians and industrial leaders in Indonesia, South Korea, and elsewhere in the region; by 2001 recession had spread to Europe and the United States. Many Asian leaders, notably the Japanese, seemed reluctant to take corrective action despite the growing realization that in the "global age" worldwide industrial and financial health was affected by economic conditions everywhere.

The Welfare State in Question

As the 1980s opened, stagflation and the realignment of global economic power forced non-Communist governments in the West to put their economic houses in order. The unprecedented mix of the energy crisis, soaring unemployment, and double-digit inflation sparked the election of conservative politicians, who maintained that decades of supporting a welfare state were at the heart of economic problems. Across the West, tough times intensified feelings that the unemployed and new migrants were responsible for the downturn. Nineteenth-century emphases on competitiveness, individualism, and revival of privilege for the "best circles" replaced the twentieth-century trend toward advancing economic democracy to combat totalitarianism.

Thatcher Reshapes Political Culture

More than anyone else, Margaret Thatcher (b. 1925), the outspoken leader of Britain's Conservative Party from 1979 to 1990, reshaped the West's political and economic ideas. Coming to power amid continuing economic decline, revolt in Northern Ireland, and labor unrest, the combative prime minister eschewed the politics of consensus building. Believing that only a resurgence of private enterprise could revive the sluggish British economy, she lashed out at union leaders, Labour politicians, and people who received welfare-state benefits as enemies of British prosperity. Her anti-welfare-state policies struck a revolutionary chord. She called herself "a nineteenth-century liberal," referring to the economic individualism

■ **Margaret Thatcher**
As British prime minister for more than a decade, Margaret Thatcher profoundly influenced European history by cutting back the welfare state. Thatcher believed, and convinced others, that the welfare state did not advance society and made citizens lazy by rewarding those who were not contributing to the nation. Her tenure in office encouraged other politicians from Ronald Reagan to Helmut Kohl to execute similar cuts in programs. More than any other head of state, she set the general course in domestic policy for the late twentieth century.
(Stuart Franklin/Sygma.)

of that age. In her view, business leaders and entrepreneurs were the key members of society. Although immigrants often worked for the lowest wages and contributed to profits, she characterized as inferior the unemployed and immigrants from Britain's former colonies, saying that neither group contributed to national wealth. Under Thatcher, even workers blamed labor leaders or newcomers for Britain's trauma.

The policies of "Thatcherism" were based on *monetarist* or *supply-side* theories associated most prominently with U.S. economist Milton Friedman. Monetarists contend that inflation results when government pumps money into the economy at a rate higher than a nation's economic growth rate. They advocate a tight rein on the money supply to keep prices from rising rapidly. Supply-side economists maintain that the economy as a whole flourishes when business prosperity "trickles down" throughout the society. To implement such theories, the British government cut income taxes on the wealthy to spur new investment and pushed up sales taxes to compensate for the lost revenue. The result was an increased burden on working people, who bore the brunt of the sales tax. Thatcher also vigorously pruned government intervention in the economy: she sold publicly owned businesses and utilities such as British Airways; refused to prop up "outmoded" industries such as coal mining; and slashed education and health programs. These economic policies came to be known as *neo-liberalism.*

In the first three years of Thatcher's government, the British economy responded poorly to her shock treatment. The quality of universities, public transportation, highways, and hospitals deteriorated, and leading scholars and scientists left Britain in a renewal of the brain drain. In addition, social unity fragmented—in 1981, blacks and Asians rioted in major cities—and Thatcher's popularity sagged. A turning point came in March 1982, when Argentina invaded the British Falkland Islands in the South Atlantic. Thatcher invoked patriotism to unify the nation and refused to surrender the distant islands without a fight. The gamble paid off, as the prime minister's public support soared. When inflation eventually dissipated, historians and economists debated whether the change resulted from Thatcher's policies or from the lack of spending power that burdened the poor and unemployed. In any case, Thatcher's program became the standard. Britain had been one of the pioneers of the welfare state, and now it pioneered in changing course. By the twenty-first century even the Labour government of Tony Blair (b. 1953) had adopted a neo-liberal program.

The Reagan Revolution and Its Aftermath

Moved by the same social and political vision as Thatcher, Ronald Reagan (b. 1911; president, 1981–1989) worked a similar revolution. The former actor was at his best in carefully planned television appearances. During these, Reagan vowed to promote the values of the "moral majority," which included commitment to Bible-based religion, dedication to work, sexual restraint, and unquestioned patriotism. Chastising so-called spendthrift and immoral "liberals," he introduced "Reaganomics"—a program of whopping income tax cuts combined with massive reductions in federal spending for student loans, school lunch programs, and mass transit. Like Thatcher, Reagan believed that tax cuts would lead to investment and reinvigorate the economy; federal outlays for welfare programs, which he felt only encouraged sloth, would generally be unnecessary thereafter.

In foreign policy, Reagan spent most of his time in office preoccupied with the Communist threat. The long-time cold warrior labeled the Soviet Union an "evil empire" and demanded huge military budgets to counter the Soviet arms buildup of the 1970s. Reagan announced the Strategic Defense Initiative, known popularly as "Star Wars," a costly plan to put lasers in space to defend the United States against a nuclear attack.

The combination of tax cuts and military expansion had pushed the federal budget deficit to $200 billion by 1986. Critics held Reaganomics accountable for the escalating violence and drug use in schools across the country and the growing numbers of homeless Americans sleeping on the streets. Although Reagan's administration spent less of the gross national product on the military than Eisenhower's had (7.5 percent as opposed to 10 percent), it did so at a time when the United States faced stiff competition from such global powers as Japan and West Germany.

The election of Democrat Bill Clinton (b. 1946) as U.S. president in 1992 did not fundamentally change the move away from the welfare state and toward neoliberalism. As in Britain, an ethic of *workfare* (a term suggesting that people receiving government benefits should work for them) continued in the United States, and the goal of competitiveness in an increasingly global economy justified crumbling urban schools and the statistical decline in real wages for the lower and middle segments of society. In fact, the U.S. economy as a whole soared in the 1990s, lifting people in the professions and top management to ever greater wealth. Seen from this vantage point, the cuts in social programs were a real success. Other people attributed rising wealth to technology's boosting productivity and streamlining business processes.

Alternatives to Thatcherism

Other Western European leaders found retrenchment of the welfare state in the face of stagflation necessary, but did so without Thatcher's politically divisive rhetoric. West German leader Helmut Kohl (b. 1930), who took power in 1982, reduced welfare spending, froze government wages, and cut corporate taxes. By 1984, the inflation rate was only 2 percent, and West Germany had acquired a 10 percent share of world trade. Unlike Thatcher, Kohl did not fan class and racial hatreds. The politics of divisiveness was particularly unwise in Germany, where terrorism on the left and on the right continued to flourish. Moreover, the legacy of Nazism loomed menacingly. "Let's gas 'em," said unemployed German youth of immigrant Turkish workers. The revival of Nazi rhetoric appalled many in Germany's middle class rather than gaining their support. This divisiveness would become even more menacing a few years later when Germany faced the economic problems posed by the reunification of the country.

France took a different political path, though by 1981 stagflation had put more than 1.5 million people out of work and reduced the economic growth rate to an anemic 1.2 percent. The French elected a socialist president, François Mitterrand (1916–1996), who nationalized banks and certain industries and stimulated the economy by wage increases and social spending—the opposite of Thatcherism. Museums, libraries, and other new public buildings arose; new subway lines opened; and public transportation improved. Financial leaders reacted by sending capital abroad, and in Mitterrand's second term, conservatives captured the majority of seats in the assembly, which entitled them to choose the prime minister. When the conservative prime minister Jacques Chirac succeeded Mitterrand as president, neo-liberal policies came into their own as a respected way of ensuring prosperity. Even the selection of socialist prime minister Lionel Jospin in 1997 did not turn back the clock: by 2002, under Jospin there had been greater privatization of publicly owned companies and the consequent accomplishment of more business mergers than ever before. Repercussions similar to those elsewhere in Europe emerged, as the politically racist National Front leader Jean-Marie Le Pen won 17 percent of the vote in the first round of balloting in the 2002 presidential elections. Le Pen promised to deport African and Muslim immigrants and cut France's ties with nonwhite nations.

Meanwhile, a cluster of smaller states without heavy defense commitments enjoyed increasing prosperity, though many slashed away at welfare programs. In Spain, tourist dollars helped rebuild the southern cities of Granada and Córdoba, and the country joined the Common Market in 1986. In Ireland, a surge of investment in education for high-tech jobs combined with low wages to bring much new business to the country in the 1990s. Prosperity and the increasingly unacceptable death toll led to a political rapprochement between Ireland and Northern Ireland in 1999. Austria prospered, too, in part by reducing government pensions and aid to business. Austrian chancellor Franz Vranitsky summed up the changed focus of government in the 1980s and 1990s: "In Austria, the shelter that the state has given to almost everyone—employee as well as entrepreneur—has led . . . a lot of people [to] think not only what they can do to solve a problem but what the state can do. . . . This needs to change." The century-long growth of the welfare state seemed to be over by the 1990s, but the future mission of government was unclear.

Almost alone, Sweden maintained a full array of social programs for everyone. The government also offered each immigrant a choice of subsidized housing in neighborhoods inhabited primarily by Swedes or primarily by people from the immigrant's native land. Such programs were expensive: the tax rate on income over

$46,000 was 80 percent. Despite a highly productive workforce, Sweden dropped from fourth to fourteenth place among nations in per capita income by 1998. Although the Swedes reduced their costly dependence on foreign oil by cutting consumption in half between 1976 and 1986, their welfare state came to seem extreme to many citizens. As in politics elsewhere, immigrants were cast as the major threat to the country: "How long will it be before our Swedish children will have to turn their faces toward Mecca?" ran one politician's campaign speech in 1993.

The Collapse of Soviet Communism

The most consequential event of the 1980s and 1990s was the breakup of the Soviet bloc in 1989 followed by the collapse of the USSR itself in the 1990s. Emblematic of other trends, the end of bipolarity hastened globalization, while socialist collapse undermined the largest single system providing government benefits to citizens. But what most struck people at the time was the suddenness of it all, for throughout the 1980s U.S.-bloc analysts erroneously reported that the Soviet empire was in robust health. Yet protest by workers, artists, and others had never really stopped across the Soviet realm despite repression of the Prague Spring. CIA reports to the contrary, the Soviet economy was not robust but deteriorating, even with steps toward economic reform in Poland and Hungary. Communications, international trade, and democratic movements were pulling apart a vast region that communism had structured for almost half a century. Ironically, the triumph of democracy in the former Soviet empire opened an era of painful adjustment, uncertainty, and violence for hundreds of millions of people.

Rebellion in Poland, Reform in the Soviet Union

Dissent against Soviet rule reached crisis stage in the summer of 1980, when Poles reacted furiously to government-increased food prices by going on strike. As the protest spread, workers at the Gdańsk shipyards, led by electrician Lech Walesa, created an independent labor movement called Solidarity. The organization soon embraced much of the adult population, including a million members of the Communist Party. The Catholic church, long in the forefront of opposition to socialist secularization, and intellectuals supported Solidarity workers as they occupied factories in protest against inflation, the scarcity of food, and other deteriorating conditions of everyday life. Solidarity members waved Polish flags and paraded giant portraits of the Virgin Mary and Pope John Paul II (b. 1920)—a Polish native.

Having achieved mass support at home and worldwide sympathy through media coverage, Solidarity leaders insisted that the government recognize the organization as an independent union—a radical demand under communism. As food became scarce and prices rose, tens of thousands of women marched in the streets crying, "We're hungry!" The Communist Party teetered toward collapse until the police and the army, with Soviet support, imposed a military government and in the winter of 1981 outlawed Solidarity. Reporters and dissidents, using global communications, kept Solidarity alive as a force both inside and outside of Poland. Stern and puritanical, General Wojciech Jaruzelski took over as the head of Poland's new regime in 1981, but the general could not push repression too far: he needed new loans from the U.S.-led bloc to keep the sinking Polish economy afloat. Instability in Poland set the stage for communism's downfall.

The rise of Solidarity exposed the economic woes of people living in the Soviet bloc. Years of stagnant and then negative growth led to a deteriorating standard of living. After working a full day, Soviet homemakers stood in long lines to obtain basic commodities; housing and food shortages necessitated a three-generation household in which grandparents took over tedious homemaking tasks from their working children and grandchildren. "There is no special skill to this," a seventy-three-year-old grandmother and former garbage collector remarked: "You just stand in line and wait." Even so, they often went away empty-handed, as basic household supplies like soap disappeared instantly from stores. One cheap and readily available product—vodka—often formed the center of people's social lives. Alcoholism reached crisis levels, diminishing productivity and tremendously straining the nation's morale.

Economic stagnation had many other ramifications. Ordinary people decided not to have children, and fertility fell below replacement levels throughout the Soviet bloc, except in Muslim areas of Soviet Central Asia. The country was forced to import massive amounts of grain because 20 to 30 percent of the grain produced in the USSR rotted before it could be harvested or shipped to market, so great was the inefficiency of the state-directed economy. Industrial pollution, spewed out by enterprises interested only in meeting production quotas, reached scandalous dimensions. A massive and privileged party bureaucracy hobbled industrial innovation and failed to achieve socialism's professed goal of a decent standard of living for working people. To match American military growth, the Soviet Union diverted 15 to 20 percent of its gross national product (more than double the U.S. proportion) to armaments. As this combustible mix of problems heated up, a new generation was coming of age that had no memory of World War II or Stalin's purges. One Russian observer found members of the younger generation "cynical but less afraid." "They believe in nothing," a mother said of Soviet youth in 1984.

In 1985, a new leader, Mikhail Gorbachev (b. 1931), opened an era of unexpected change. The son of peasants, Gorbachev had risen through the party ranks as an agricultural specialist and had traveled abroad to gain a firsthand glimpse of life in the West. He quickly proposed several unusual programs. The first, *perestroika* ("restructuring"), aimed to reinvigorate the Soviet economy by improving productivity, increasing the rate of capital investment, encouraging the use of up-to-date technology, and gradually introducing such market features as prices and profits. The second, a policy called *glasnost* (usually translated as "openness" or

■ **The Gorbachevs and Reagans at the Reagans' Ranch**

Ronald Reagan raised the temperature of the cold war with a massive arms buildup in the 1980s that caused the U.S. budget deficit to soar. When Mikhail Gorbachev came to power in the USSR, he changed course, encouraging freer speech, seeking innovation in the economy, and reducing cold war tensions. The two leaders' regular meetings helped slow the arms race.

(Ruelas, L.A. Daily News/Sygma.)

"publicity"), called for disseminating "wide, prompt, and frank information" and allowing Soviet citizens new measures of free speech.♦ When officials complained that glasnost threatened their status, Gorbachev replaced more than a third of the party's leadership in the first months of his administration. The pressing need for glasnost became most evident after the Chernobyl catastrophe in 1986, when bureaucratic cover-ups delayed the spread of information about the accident, with lethal consequences for people living near the plant.

After Chernobyl, even the Communist Party and Marxism-Leninism were opened to public criticism and contestation. Party meetings suddenly witnessed complaints about the highest leaders and their policies. Television shows such as *The Fifth Wheel* adopted the outspoken methods of American investigative reporting; one program showed an interview with an executioner of political prisoners and exposed the plight of Leningrad's homeless children. Political factions arose

---

♦ For a pair of newspaper articles that illustrate Gorbachev's revolutionary policies, see Document 76, "Glasnost and the Soviet Press."

across the political spectrum. In the fall of 1987, one of Gorbachev's erstwhile allies, Boris Yeltsin, quit the governing Politburo after denouncing perestroika as inadequate for real reform. Yeltsin's political daring, which in the past would have consigned him to oblivion (or Siberia), inspired others to organize in opposition to the crumbling ruling orthodoxy. By the spring of 1989, in remarkably free balloting, not a single Communist was chosen for office in Moscow's local elections.

Glasnost and perestroika dramatically affected superpower relations as well. Recognizing how severely the cold war arms race was draining Soviet resources, Gorbachev almost immediately began scaling back missile production. His unilateral actions gradually won over Ronald Reagan. Beginning in 1985, the two leaders initiated a personal relationship and began defusing the cold war. "I bet the hard-liners in both our countries are bleeding when we shake hands," said the jovial Reagan at the conclusion of one meeting. In early 1989, Gorbachev at last withdrew Soviet forces from the debilitating war in Afghanistan, and by the end of the year the United States started to cut back its own vast military buildup.

The Revolutions of 1989

Tremors shook the Communist world in the spring of 1989. Inspired by Gorbachev's visit to China's capital, Beijing, thousands of students massed in Tiananmen Square to demand democracy. They used telex machines and electronic mail to rush their messages to the international community, and they effectively conveyed their goals through the cameras that Western television trained on them. China's aged Communist leaders, while pushing economic modernization and even allowing market operations, refused to consider the introduction of democracy. As workers began joining the Democracy forces, the government crushed the movement and executed as many as a thousand rebels.

Despite the setback to the forces of democracy in China, the spirit of revolt advanced in Eastern Europe in 1989 and brought decades of Communist rule to an end. Indeed, the year 1989 has been designated the twentieth century's *annus mirabilis* ("year of miracles") because of the sudden and unexpected disintegration of Communist power throughout the region (Map 24.2). Events in Poland took a dramatic turn first. In June, the Polish government, weakened by its own bungling of the economy and lacking Soviet support for further repression, held free parliamentary elections. Solidarity candidates drove out the Communists, and by early 1990 Walesa became president, hastening Poland's rocky transition to a market economy.

As it became evident that the Soviet Union would not intervene in Poland, the fall of communism repeated itself in country after country. In Hungary, which had experimented with "market socialism" since the 1960s, popular demands for liberalization led the parliament to dismiss the Communist Party as the official ruling institution. In Czechoslovakia, which after 1968 had been firmly restored to Soviet-style rule, people watched the progress of glasnost expectantly. Although they could

■ **MAP 24.2 The Collapse of Communism in Europe, 1989–1991**

In one form or another, resistance to communism had been continuous since the 1940s; thus, the 1989 overthrow of Communist governments in the USSR satellite countries in Eastern Europe occurred with surprising rapidity. In 1991, Communist Yugoslavia began to break up into individual states composed of competing ethnicities and religions. Then the USSR itself fell apart, as the Baltic states seceded, followed by the official dissolution of the rest of the USSR on January 1, 1992.

see Gorbachev on television calling for free speech, he never mentioned reform in Czechoslovakia. Demonstrators protested in the streets for democracy, but the government cracked down by turning the police on them. The turning point came in November 1989 when Alexander Dubček, leader of the Prague Spring of 1968, addressed crowds in Prague's Wenceslas Square with a call for the ouster of Stalinists from the government. Almost immediately, the Communist leadership resigned. Capping the country's "velvet revolution," as it became known because of its lack of bloodshed, the formerly Communist-dominated parliament elevated dissident playwright Václav Havel to the presidency.

The most potent symbol of a divided Europe—the Berlin Wall—stood in the midst of divided Germany. East Germans had attempted to escape over the wall for decades, despite their country's reputation as having the most dynamic economy in the socialist world. In the summer of 1989, crowds of East Germans flooded the borders of the crumbling Soviet bloc, and hundreds of thousands of urban protesters at home rallied throughout the fall against the regime. On November 9, an ambiguous statement from the East German government encouraged guards to allow free passage across the wall. Protest turned to festive holiday: West Berliners handed out bananas, a consumer good that had been in short supply in the Eastern zone, and that fruit became the unofficial symbol of reunion. Almost immediately, Berliners released years of frustration at their division by assaulting the wall with sledgehammers and bringing home chunks as souvenirs. The government finished its complete destruction in the fall of 1990.◆

Almost as soon as the Berlin Wall tumbled, the world's attention fastened on the political drama in Romania. Since the mid-1960s, Nicolae Ceauşescu had ruled as the harshest dictator in Communist Europe since Stalin. In the name of modernization, he destroyed whole villages; to build up the population, he outlawed contraceptives and abortion, a restriction that led to the abandonment of tens of thousands of children. Most Romanians lived in utter poverty as Ceauşescu channeled almost all the country's resources into building himself an enormous palace in Bucharest. Yet, in early December 1989, an opposition movement rose up. Most of the army turned against the government and crushed the forces loyal to Ceauşescu. On Christmas Day, viewers watched on television as the dictator and his wife were tried by a military court and then executed.

■ **Destroying the Berlin Wall**

The most disturbing symbol of the cold war, the Berlin Wall came down in 1989 as dramatically as it had gone up in 1961. The next decade saw not only the reunification of Germany but the massive rebuilding of Berlin as the nation's capital.

(© Reuters Newmedia Inc./Corbis.)

◆ For an interview with one of the grassroots organizers against Soviet control, see Document 77, Cornelia Matzke, "Revolution in East Germany: An Activist's Perspective."

The collapse of communism in Europe paved the way for the reunification of Germany. Chancellor Helmut Kohl of West Germany based the campaign for re-unification on the promise of a more comfortable way of life. A shrewd politician, Kohl acted on what he called his "grass-roots instinct that the East Germans wanted their microwaves now, and not in three years." Full political union took place on October 3, 1990, far earlier than anyone had expected at the end of 1989. The re-alities of unification, however, did not live up to the dream. East German industry passed into the hands of West German managers, whose efficiencies in downsizing the workforce caused unemployment to soar, especially among women and youth. Many social services, such as day-care centers that allowed women to work to sup-port their families, closed down. Social tensions flared, leading to violent attacks or hateful rhetoric against immigrants. Amid these stresses, the economy declined late in the 1990s relative to other countries in Europe, and its health became a major issue in the 2002 elections. Throughout the former Soviet bloc, the transition to democracy and free markets gave rise simultaneously to economic upheaval, expressions of wide-ranging discontent, and hope for a better future.

The Breakup of Yugoslavia and the Soviet Union

After a few euphoric months, the problems of post-Communist life intensified, as first Yugoslavia and then the Soviet Union itself fell apart. The Soviet empire, like the Russian empire from which it grew, had held together more than one hundred ethnic groups, and the five republics of Soviet Central Asia were home to fifty mil-lion Muslims. Similarly in Yugoslavia, Communist rulers had enforced unity among religious and ethnic groups, but in 1990 the Serb Communist Slobodan Milosevic won the presidency of his republic and began to assert Serb ascendancy. In the spring of 1991, Slovenia and Croatia seceded, but the Croats soon lost almost a quarter of their territory to the Serb-dominated Yugoslav army (Map 24.3). An even more devastating civil war engulfed Bosnia-Herzegovina, where the republic's Mus-lim majority tried to create a multiethnic state. Many Bosnian Serb men formed a guerrilla army, backed by the covert support of Milosevic's government, and gained the upper hand; the Muslim Bosnians were prevented by a UN arms embargo from equipping their forces adequately to resist. Late in the 1990s, the Serb forces started attacking people of Albanian ethnicity living in the Yugoslav province of Kosovo. From 1997 to 1999, hundreds of thousands of Albanian Kosovars fled their homes as Serb militias and the Yugoslav army began attacking the civilian population. NATO pilots bombed the region in an attempt to drive back the army and Serb militias. Amid incredible violence and suffering, UN peacekeeping forces stepped in to enforce an interethnic truce.

During the 1990s, civilians died by the tens of thousands as Yugoslav republics broke away and as Serbs pursued a policy they called "ethnic cleansing"—that is, genocide—against the other nationalities. They raped women to leave them

■ **MAP 24.3 The Former Yugoslavia, c. 2000**
*After a decade of destructive civil war, UN forces and UN-brokered agreements attempted to
protect civilians in the former Yugoslavia from the brutal consequences of post-Communist rule.
Ambitious politicians, most notably Slobodan Milosevic, used the twentieth-century Western
strategy of fostering ethnic and religious hatred as a powerful tool to build support for themselves
while making those favoring peace look softhearted and unfit to rule.*

pregnant with Serb babies. Men and boys were often taken away and massacred.
Military units destroyed libraries and museums, architectural treasures like the
Mostar Bridge, and cities rich with medieval history such as Dubrovnik. Ethnic
cleansing thus entailed destroying actual people as well as all traces of their complex cultural past. Many in the West explained violence in the Balkans as part of
"age-old" blood feuds manifesting the backwardness of an almost "Asian" society.
Others saw ethnic rivals' use of genocide to achieve national power as a thoroughly
modern phenomenon of the West in the twentieth century. Driven from office,
Milosevic was handed over in 2001 to an international tribunal to be tried for crimes
against humanity.

■ **Yugoslavia in 1990, before Destruction of the Mostar Bridge (top) and after (bottom)**
In modern history, the construction of a nation-state has depended on the growth of institutions, such as armies and bureaucracies, and the promotion of a common national culture. In an effort to dominate Bosnia and Croatia, Serbs destroyed non-Serb architecture, books, and such ancient symbols as the Mostar Bridge. (Top: Sygma. Bottom: Stephane Cardinale/Sygma.)

In the USSR, Gorbachev announced late in 1990 that there was "no alternative to the transition to the market," but his plan was too little, too late and satisfied no one. Perestroika failed to improve the Soviet economy: people confronted soaring prices, unemployment, and even greater scarcity of goods than they had endured in the past. The Russian parliament's election of Boris Yeltsin as president of the Russian Republic over a Communist candidate provoked a coup attempt in August 1991 by antireform hard-liners that included the powerful head of the Soviet secret police, or KGB. While they held Gorbachev, who held the title of President of the Congress of People's Deputies, under house arrest, Yeltsin, standing atop a tank outside the Russian Republic's parliament building, called for mass resistance. Hundreds of thousands of residents of Moscow and Leningrad filled the streets, and units of the army defected to protect Yeltsin's headquarters. People used fax machines and computers to coordinate internal resistance and send messages to the rest of the world. The coup was in complete disarray in the face of citizen determination not to allow a return of Stalinism or any form of Soviet orthodoxy.

The Soviet Union disintegrated. People tore down statues of Soviet heroes; Yeltsin outlawed the party newspaper, *Pravda*, and sealed the KGB files. The Soviet parliament suspended operations of the Communist Party itself. One republic after another followed the lead of the Baltic states, which declared their independence in September 1991. Ethnic conflict erupted. In the Soviet republic of Tajikistan, native Tajiks rioted against Armenians living there; in Azerbaijan, Azeris and Armenians clashed over contested territory; and in the Baltic states, anti-Semitism revived as a political tool. The USSR finally dissolved on January 1, 1992. Twelve of the fifteen former Soviet republics banded together as the Commonwealth of Independent States (Map 24.4).

Politics and the conditions of everyday life continued to deteriorate. The coup and drive for dissolution of the USSR so tainted Gorbachev's regime that he ceded power to Yeltsin. But increasingly plagued by corruption, the Russian economy plunged into an ever-deepening crisis. Yeltsin's political allies bought up national resources, stripped them of their value, and sent billions of dollars out of the country. Ethnic and religious battles continued, and the military attacked Muslim dissenters in the province of Chechnya, leaving massive casualties on both sides. In Russia, the political right appealed to nationalist sentiments and won increasing support. As members of the so-called Russian mafia interfered in the economy and assassinated legitimate entrepreneurs and anyone who criticized them, Western powers reduced their aid to rebuild Russian infrastructure. People took drastic steps to stay alive. Hotel lobbies became clogged with women turning to prostitution because they were the first people fired as industry privatized and service jobs were cut back. Ordinary citizens stood on the sidewalks of major cities selling their household possessions. A low point was reached in August 1998 with the crash of the Soviet stock market and the devaluation of the ruble. Investors around the world lost amounts equivalent to millions of dollars.

There were, of course, many pluses to the end of communism. People were able to travel freely, and the media were more open than ever before in Russian history. Some people, many of them young and highly educated, profited from contacts with technology and business. However, their frequent emigration to more prosperous parts of the world further depleted Russia's human resources. "I knew in my heart that it would collapse," said one ex-dissident, commenting sadly on the exodus of youth from his country, "but it never crossed my mind that the future would look like this."

■ **MAP 24.4 Countries of the Former Soviet Union, c. 2000**
Following an agreement of December 1991, twelve of the republics of the former Soviet Union formed the Commonwealth of Independent States (CIS). Dominated by Russia and with Ukraine often disputing this domination, the CIS worked to bring about common economic and military policies. As nation-states dissolved rapidly in the late twentieth century, regional alliances and coordination were necessary to meet the political and economic challenges of the global age.

In May 2000, Vladimir Putin, former head of the security services (the successor organization to the KGB), became president of Russia. Putin argued that the free market and democracy would have to fit with Russian "realities," notably the tradition of a paternalistic state. Attacking corruption and building a string of alliances in the West, Putin seemed to offer a steadier hand, especially over the massive Soviet-era arsenal of nuclear weapons and in the escalating fight against terrorists—many of them operating on Russia's doorstep in Afghanistan, Tajikistan, and Uzbekistan.

Global Culture and Western Civilization at the Dawn of a New Millennium

As the final years of the twentieth century unfolded, thinkers began to debate the future. On the one side was a view that the end of the cold war meant "an end of history" because the great ideological struggles were over and Western values had triumphed. Attached to this view was a related one: the rest of the world was absorbing Western cultural values rapidly as it developed technologically and adopted more and more features of representative government and human rights. An opposing view predicted a "clash of civilizations" in which the increasing incompatibility of religions and cultures would lead to global strife. According to this scenario, Islam, as it gathered more than one billion followers, would confront Western values rather than absorb them, and citizens of the growing number of small states populated by different ethnic and racial groups would simply refuse to live under a common national umbrella.

The actual movement of peoples and cultures in the late twentieth century suggests that neither view holds. International migration, the movement of disease, the information revolution, and the global sharing of culture have produced neither a successful Western homogenization nor a convincing argument for the cultural purity of any group: "Civilizations," as Nobel Prize winner Amartya Sen wrote after the terrorist attacks of September 11, 2001, "are hard to partition . . . given the diversities within each society as well as the linkages among different countries and cultures." In the 1980s and 1990s, Western society changed as rapidly as it had changed hundreds of years earlier when it came into intense contact with the rest of the globe. Moreover, national boundaries in the traditional European center of the West were weakening politically and economically with the growing strength of the European Union and the simultaneous splintering of large nations into small states based on claims to ethnic uniqueness. Culture ignored national boundaries as East, West, North, and South became saturated with one another's cultural products. Some observers even labeled the new millennium an era of "denationalization." But there is no denying that even while the West absorbed peoples and cultures, it continued to exercise not only economic but also cultural influence over the rest of the globe. Long acknowledged, this power was also debated and contested.

Redefining the West: The Impact of Global Migration

The movement of people globally was massive in the last third of the twentieth century and into the twenty-first. Uneven economic development, political persecution, and warfare (which has claimed as many as 100 million victims worldwide since 1945) sent tens of millions in search of safety and opportunity. In the 1970s alone, more than 4.7 million people moved to the United States. By 1982, France had about 4.5 million foreign residents, and by 2001 six million Muslims. Other parts of the world were as full of people on the move as the West. The oil-producing nations of the Middle East employed millions of foreign workers, who generally constituted one-third of the labor force. Singapore and Nigeria were home to millions of foreign-born inhabitants. Ongoing violence in Africa sent Rwandans, Zairians, and others to South Africa as its government became dominated by blacks. War in Afghanistan made Iran one of the most popular asylums, with close to 2 million refugees in 1995.

Migrants often earned desperately needed income for family members who remained in the native country, and in some cases they propped up the economies of entire nations. In the southern African country of Lesotho, where the soil had been ruined by overuse during colonial rule, between 40 and 50 percent of national income came from migrant workers, particularly from those who toiled in the mines of South Africa. In countries as different as Yugoslavia, Egypt, Spain, and Pakistan, money sent home from abroad constituted up to 60 percent of national income. In places where immigration was restricted, millions of people nevertheless successfully crossed borders: from Mexico and China to the United States, over unguarded African frontiers, between European states. Unprotected by law, such migrants risked exploitation and abuse of their human rights. Those at greatest risk were Eastern European and Asian prostitutes, many of whom were coerced into international sex rings that controlled their passports, wages, and lives. Foreign workers were a convenient scapegoat for native peoples suffering from economic woes such as unemployment caused by downsizing. Political parties with racist programs came to life in Europe, where unemployment was in double digits at various times in the 1980s and 1990s.

Among migrants to the West, women had little to say in decisions about leaving home; a patriarchal head of the household generally made such choices. Once abroad, migrant women suffered the most from unstable working conditions and usually obtained more menial, lower-paying jobs than migrant men or native Europeans. They also were more likely than men to be refused political asylum. Rape and other violence against them, even during civil war, were classified as part of everyday life, not politics. The offspring of immigrants also had a difficult time adjusting to their new surroundings. Young people generally struggled for jobs, and unemployment hit them especially hard because "whites" and "real" citizens received preference. They also struggled with questions of identity, often feeling torn between two cultures. Young black immigrants in particular began to forge an international or transnational identity, one that combined elements of African, Caribbean, American, and European cultures. As tens of millions of people migrated in the 1980s and 1990s, belief in a national identity based on a single, unique culture began losing ground.

Uncertain Borders of the Nation-State

The Western nation-state had been an increasingly powerful source of identity for five hundred years, never more so than in the twentieth century. By the twenty-first century, however, the nature of European national borders was changing through the force of mass migration, international cooperation, technology, and transnational allegiances. Regional alliances like NATO and the Warsaw Pact had appeared to override national interests, but nothing compared with the turn-of-the-millennium merging of individual nation-states into the European Union (Map 24.5). In 1992, the twelve countries of the EC ended national distinctions in the spheres of business activity, border controls, and transportation. Citizens of EC member countries carried a common burgundy-colored passport, and governments, whether municipal or national, had to treat all member nations' firms the same. In 1994, by the terms of the Maastricht Treaty, the EC became the European Union, and on January 1, 2002, citizens of twelve EU countries (Britain, Denmark, and Sweden declined to participate) shed their national currencies for the euro (the European Currency Unit or ECU). Using the euro for the first time, an Irish architect enthused, gave "a sense of Europe coming together as one." Common policies governed everything from the number of American soap operas aired on television to pollution controls on automobiles.◆

Some national leaders had opposed tighter integration as an infringement on national sovereignty. In the 1980s, Margaret Thatcher, Britain's then prime minister, warned that terrorists would pass freely across borders, objected to the use of a common currency, and criticized moves toward closer pan-European unity, but her forceful opposition seemed so out of step with the times that her own party forced her resignation in 1991. Despite warnings of an emerging "Eurospeak" and a dull standardization of culture, countries continued to join the original twelve. Sweden, Finland, and Austria joined the EU in 1995; Turkey and Cyprus were officially scheduled for entry. Most former Communist-run nations also sought inclusion. As union tightened, a highly advanced industrial megastate complete with its own bureaucracy overlaid the traditionally distinct individual nations of the Western heartland.

◆ For a source that encapsulates proponents' arguments for a truly unified Europe, see Document 78, François Mitterrand, "Speech to the European Parliament."

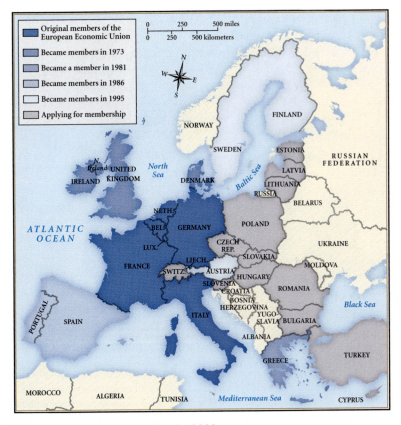

■ MAP 24.5 The European Union in 2000

The European Union appeared to increase the economic health of its members despite the rocky valuation of the common currency—the euro. The EU decidedly helped end the traditional warfare member nations had waged against one another for centuries, and common passports, common business laws, and borders open to member countries facilitated trade and the migration of workers. Many critics feared the further loss of cultural distinctiveness among peoples in an age of mass communications if the economic union turned into a political one. Other skeptics predicted "Americanization" if political cooperation among European countries was lacking.

Rapid technological change in electronic communications also made traditional national borders appear easily permeable, if not obsolete. In 1969, the U.S. Department of Defense developed a computer network to carry communications in case of nuclear war. This system and others like it in universities, government, and business grew into an unregulated system of more than ten thousand networks globally. These came to be known as the *Internet*—shorthand for *internetworking*. By 1995, users in more than 137 countries were connected to the Internet, creating new "communities" based on business needs, shared cultural interests, or other factors that transcended common citizenship in a particular nation-state.

■ **Euro Currency**

People in twelve countries of the European Union confronted a common currency—the euro—on January 1, 2002. These residents at a German senior citizens' home learn to recognize the different denominations and value of the new currency. The shift from a national to an international currency concerned many citizens, but most quickly realized that a common currency would inhibit great fluctuation in prices from country to country while also allowing shoppers to cross borders freely and compare costs. A less tangible benefit was the common European identity that the euro promoted. (© AFP/Corbis.)

Communicating over the Internet allowed users often to escape censorship and other forms of state regulation. A global marketplace emerged, offering goods and services ranging from advanced weaponry to organ transplants. While enthusiasts claimed that electronic communication could promote world democracy, critics charged that communications technology favored elites and disadvantaged those without computer skills. Yet these skills advanced so quickly that in 2001 Estonia, Hungary, and the Czech Republic as well as Morocco, India, and the Philippines were successfully luring businesses to employ their citizens as help-desk and call-center service workers. The Internet allowed the service industry to globalize (see "Mapping the West," page 1066).

Internet and other communications technology promoted business mergers and the rise of "global cities" in the 1990s. Access to almost up-to-the-minute information on inventory, wages, costs, and transportation worldwide allowed businesses to move in and out of countries rapidly in response to changes in economic and political conditions. As a result, workers in one country were pitted against workers in a similar job category on the other side of the globe. Global corporations neither inspired nor displayed national loyalty. Moreover, high technology consigned people without modern skills to minimum-wage jobs as clerks and fast-food attendants. "Global cities," such as New York, Hong Kong, Tokyo, and London, swelled in the 1990s; their postmodernist architecture soared to new heights. In these cities, high-level information specialists—lawyers, accountants, financiers, and a variety of analysts—formed a decision-making loop in the technological network. Their financial power changed the complexion of most cities, making them unaffordable to low-level information managers and service workers.

Disease also operated on a global terrain. In the early 1980s, the spread of a global epidemic disease, acquired immune deficiency syndrome (AIDS), challenged Western values and Western technological expertise. An incurable, virulent killer

■ **Hong Kong Skyline**

The 1980s saw Hong Kong, Singapore, China, and other Pacific economies soar and develop the most modern technological capabilities. Skylines changed, reshaped by mountainous glass and steel skyscrapers, and cities like Hong Kong came to symbolize everything postmodern. No longer could the East be used as an exotic foil to help those in the West lay claim to a superior civilization.
(Jane Tyska/Stock Boston.)

that shuts down the body's immune system, AIDS initially afflicted heterosexuals in central Africa; the disease later turned up in Haitian immigrants to the United States and in homosexual men worldwide. At the turn of the twenty-first century, no cure had been discovered, though protease-inhibiting drugs helped alleviate the symptoms. The mounting death toll prompted some to liken AIDS to the bubonic plague that had decimated Europe in the fourteenth century and it reinforced negative stereotypes about some of the most vulnerable victims. As millions contracted the disease in Africa, treatment was not forthcoming there because the ill were too poor to pay for the necessary drugs. The Ebola virus and dozens of other diseases also smoldered, deadly and incurable.

The Global Diffusion of Culture

Culture has long transcended political boundaries; archaeologists point to cultural diffusion as a constant feature of human history. In the ancient world, the Romans studied the work of Greek philosophers. In the eighteenth and nineteenth centuries, Western scholars immersed themselves in Asian languages. In the postwar period, new forms of transportation and communication vastly accelerated cultural exchange. Tourism, for instance, became the largest single industry in Britain and in many other Western countries by the early 1990s. Throngs of visitors from Japan and elsewhere testified to the powerful hold of the West on the world's imagination. The Chinese students demonstrating in Tiananmen Square had rallied around their own representation of the Statue of Liberty (which itself was a gift from France to the United States). In Japan, businesspeople wore Western-style clothing, and sports fans watched soccer, baseball, and other Western sports and used English sports terminology.

Remarkable innovations in communications have also integrated cultures and made the earth seem a much smaller place with a distinctly Western flavor. Videotapes and satellite-beamed telecasts carry American television shows to Hong Kong and Japanese movies to Europe and North America. American rock music sells briskly in Russia and elsewhere in the former Soviet bloc. When more than 100,000 Czechoslovakian rock fans, including President Václav Havel, attended a Rolling Stones concert in Prague in 1990, it was clear that despite a half-century of supposedly insular Communist culture, Czechs and Slovaks had been tuned in to the larger world. Sports stars like the Brazilian soccer player Pelé and the American basketball hero Michael Jordan became better known to countless people than their own national leaders. In today's world, millions of people anywhere on the planet might be spectators at a "live" event, whether a World Cup competition or an Academy Awards broadcast from Hollywood.

The political power of the United States and the Western presence in the global economy have given Western culture an edge. U.S. success in "marketing" culture, along with the legacy of British imperialism, has helped to make English the dominant international language. Many English words—for example, *stop, shopping, parking, okay, weekend,* and *rock*—have infiltrated dozens of non-English vocabularies. English is the official language of the European Union and of the new Central European University in Budapest. Unofficially, it is the language of travel. In the 1960s, French president de Gaulle, fearing corruption of the French language, banned new words such as *computer* in government documents; but such a directive could not stop the influx of English into scientific, technical, diplomatic, and daily life. Germany, the Netherlands, and other European countries with polyglot traditions rapidly assimilated new words.

As it had been doing for centuries, the West continued to devour material from elsewhere—Hong Kong films, African textiles, Indian music, Latin American pop culture. Publishers successfully marketed written works by major non-Western artists and intellectuals, and Hollywood made many of their novels into internationally distributed films. Some of this literature won both popular and critical acclaim and exerted a strong influence on European and North American writers. The lush, exotic fantasies of Colombian-born Nobel Prize winner Gabriel García Márquez, for example, attracted a vast Western readership. His novels, including *One Hundred Years of Solitude* (1967) and *Love in the Time of Cholera* (1988), portray people of titanic ambitions and passions who endure war and all manner of personal trials. Another Nobel Prize recipient who won high regard in the West was Egyptian writer Naguib Mahfouz. Having immersed himself in his youth in great Western literature, Mahfouz authored more than forty books. His celebrated *Cairo Trilogy,* written in the 1950s, describes a middle-class family—from its practice of Islam and seclusion of women to the business and cultural life of men in the family. British colonialism forms the trilogy's backdrop; it impassions the protagonists and shapes their lives and destinies. In the eyes of many Arab observers, Mahfouz was a "safe" choice for the Nobel Prize, not only because he produced a literature about the history of colonialism but also because he had adopted a European style. "He borrowed the novel from Europe; he imitated it," charged one fellow Egyptian writer. "It's not an Egyptian art form. Europeans . . . like it very much because it is their own form." The globally read Egyptian Nawal el-Saadawi was also accused of producing exotic accounts of women's oppression to appeal to Western feminists. Thus, although non-Western literature reshaped Western taste, it sometimes provoked charges of inauthenticity in its authors' homelands.

Immigrants to Europe described how the experience of Western culture felt to the refugee. The popular writer Buchi Emecheta in her novel *In the Ditch* (1972) and her autobiography *Head above Water* (1986) explored her experiences as a newcomer to Britain. Her *Joys of Motherhood* (1979) was an imaginary foray back in time to probe the nature of mothering under colonial rule in her native Lagos in West Africa. While critiquing colonialism and the welfare state from a non-Western perspective, Emecheta, like many writers and politicians from less-developed countries, felt the lure of Western education and Western values. International conflict around artistic expression became dangerous. Salman Rushdie (b. 1947), also an immigrant to Great Britain (from India), produced the novel *The Satanic Verses* (1988), which ignited outrage among Muslims around the world because it appeared to blaspheme the prophet Muhammad. From Iran, the Ayatollah Khomeini promised both a monetary reward and salvation in the afterlife to anyone who would assassinate the writer. In a display of Western cultural unity, international leaders took bold steps to protect Rushdie until the threat was lifted a decade later.

The mainstream became fraught with conflict as groups outside the accepted circles engaged in artistic production. From within the West, novelist Toni Morrison, who in 1993 became the first African American woman to win the Nobel Prize for literature, described the nightmares, daily experiences, and dreams of the descendants of men and women who had been brought as slaves to the United States. But many parents objected to the inclusion of Morrison's work in high school and college curricula. Critics charged that, unlike Shakespeare's universal Western truth, the writing of African Americans, Native Americans, and women represented only a partial vision, not great literature. Eastern-bloc writers who found success in the West were also criticized. Milan Kundera left Czechoslovakia in 1975 after Communist police harassed him for his rebellious writing. Settling in Paris, Kundera produced *The Book of Laughter and Forgetting* (1979) and *The Unbearable Lightness of Being* (1984). In these works, he dwelt on the importance of remembering the oppressive climate of the Eastern bloc instead of following a natural tendency to forget or to search for material ease. He and other dissident writers who were often wildly successful in the United States and Western Europe met with suspicion and criticism from their colleagues who

■ **Toni Morrison Receiving the Nobel Prize**

The first African American woman to receive the Nobel Prize for literature, Toni Morrison used her literary talents to depict the condition of blacks under slavery and after emancipation. Morrison also published cogent essays on social, racial, and gender issues in the United States.

(Pressens Bild/Gamma Liaison.)

remained behind. In the land of prosperous book contracts, charged one Polish critic, writing was not literature but merely a "line of business."

Some writers and artists chose not to leave the Communist world, and they survived by creating acceptable art, even if the government did not embrace it wholeheartedly. East German writer Christa Wolf explored subjects, such as individuality, personal guilt, and the search for self-identity, that went against the grain of East Germany's Communist ideology. In such works as *The Quest for Christa T.* (1970), she touched on themes that appealed deeply to Westerners in the 1970s and 1980s. Others in the Communist world mixed global cultures no matter how dangerous or unpopular. The acclaimed composer Sofia Gubaidulina (b. 1931)—a Tatar, granddaughter of a teacher of Islam, and herself a Christian strongly influenced by Asian mysticism—created music with electronic guitars, tam-tams, and accordion along with screams and whispers. Her music was tonal and atonal, like the chant of monks and like Wagner—a collage of sound and music from everywhere. Her music, however, lacked the harshness of modernists from the middle of the century and represented a turn toward accessibility in classical music.

Some called such hyper-mixing of influences *postmodernism*, and one definition of *postmodernism* referred to multiplicity without a central unifying theme or privileged canon. Striking examples of postmodern art abounded in Western society, including the AT&T building in New York City, the work of architect Philip Johnson. The structure itself, designed in the late 1970s, looked sleek and modern, but its entryway was a Roman arch, and its cloud-piercing top suggested the eighteenth-century Chippendale style. The blueprints of Johnson and other postmodernists recalled the human past and drew from cultural styles that spanned millennia and continents without valuing one style above others. The Guggenheim Museum in Bilbao, Spain, opened in 1997 and designed by the American architect Frank Gehry, was similarly bizarre by classical or even modern standards as it represented forms, materials, and perspectives that by rules of earlier decades did not belong together. These were aesthetic examples of the postmodern, which also gave rise to films and novels without the unity of a single narrative or plot.

Other intellectuals defined *postmodernism* in political terms as an outgrowth of the demise of the eighteenth-century ideals of human rights, individualism, personal freedom, and their guarantor—the Western nation-state. A structure like the Bilbao Guggenheim was just an international tourist attraction that had no Spanish roots or purpose; consumption, global technology, mass communications, and international migration made citizenship, nationalism, and rights irrelevant to its meaning. It was a rootless structure, unlike the Louvre in Paris or the Prado in Madrid. Moreover, the end of formal imperialism meant an end to the white privilege behind modern civil rights as defined in the eighteenth century. The 1982 American film *Blade Runner*, for example, depicted a dangerous, densely packed, multiethnic Los Angeles patrolled by police with high-tech gear—a metropolis with no place for national or personal identity or human rights. For postmodernists of

■ **Christo and Jeanne-Claude,** *Umbrellas* **(1984–1991)**

Attuned to global differences and similarities in landscape, environment, and ways of life, the artists Christo and Jeanne-Claude created an art that enhanced people's sensual experience of the everyday world. Their installation of umbrellas in California (top) and Japan (bottom) featured colors that complemented distinctive rural terrain, just as their wrapping of the Reichstag in Berlin (1971–1995) had enhanced urban architecture. As global citizens, they recycle the vast quantities of materials once their works are dismantled, and they pay for their projects themselves.

(Top: Christo and Jeanne-Claude: *The Umbrellas, Japan-USA*, 1984–1991. California site. Photo: Wolfgang Volz. © Christo 1991. Bottom: Christo and Jeanne-Claude: *The Umbrellas, Japan-USA*, 1984–1991. Ibaraki, Japan site. Photo: Wolfgang Volz. © Christo 1991.)

IMPORTANT DATES			
1979	Islamic revolution in Iran; Prime Minister Margaret Thatcher begins dismantling the welfare state in Britain and introduces neo-liberalism	1990–1991	War in the Persian Gulf
		1991	Civil war erupts in the former Yugoslavia
1980	An independent trade union, Solidarity, organizes resistance to Polish communism	1992	Soviet Union is dissolved
		1993	Toni Morrison becomes the first African American woman to win the Nobel Prize for literature
Early 1980s	AIDS epidemic strikes the West; rise of the Pacific economy	1994	Postapartheid elections held in South Africa
1981	Ronald Reagan becomes U.S. president	1997	Collapse of Thai currency and upset of the "Asian tigers"
1985	Mikhail Gorbachev comes to power in the USSR	1999	World population reaches six billion
1986	Explosion at Soviet nuclear power plant at Chernobyl; Spain joins the Common Market	2000	Vladimir Putin becomes president of Russia
		2001	Terrorist attack on the United States and declaration of a "war against terrorism"
1989	Chinese students revolt in Tiananmen Square and government suppresses them; fall of the Berlin Wall	2002	Euro currency goes into circulation in the European Union
1990s	Internet revolution		

a political bent, computers had replaced the autonomous, free self and bureaucracy had rendered representative government obsolete.

A third definition of *postmodernism* investigated the "unfreedom" or irrationality that shaped human life. French psychoanalyst Jacques Lacan (1901–1981), who deeply influenced Western literary criticism in the 1980s and 1990s, maintained that people operate in an unfree, predetermined world of language with its own patriarchal laws. In becoming social, communicating beings, we must bow to these laws already implanted in us at birth. Another prominent French thinker, Michel Foucault (1926–1984), professed to deplore the easy acceptance of such liberal ideas as the autonomous self, the progressive march of history, and the advance of freedom. The sexual revolution, he insisted, was not liberating at all; rather, sexuality was merely a way in which humans exercised power over one another and through which society, by allowing sexual expression, actually controlled individuals. Freedom, in the opinion of these postmodern intellectuals, had lost credibility: even in the most intimate part of human experience, individuals were locked in a grid of social and individual constraints. For some people struggling with the legacy of colonialism, racism, and sexism, the message that the image of the rational and superior West was illusory actually provided hope.

Conclusion: The Making of the West Continues

Although some postmodernists proclaimed an end to centuries of faith in progress, they themselves worked within the modern Western tradition of constant criticism and reevaluation. Moreover, said their critics, the daunting problems of contemporary life—population explosion, resource depletion, North-South inequities, global pollution, ethnic hatred, and global terrorism—demanded the exercise of humanistic values and the renewal of a rational commitment to progress now more than ever. Postmodernists and other philosophers countered with the question of "unintended consequences"—that is, the question of whether one could begin to know the consequences of an act. Who would have predicted, for example, the human misery resulting from the fall of the Soviet empire?

The years since 1980 proved both sides correct. The collapse of communism signaled the eclipse of an ideology that was perhaps noble in intent but deadly in practice. Events in South Africa and Northern Ireland, for example, indicated that certain long-feuding groups were wearying of conflict and groping for peace, even as other peoples took up arms against their neighbors. Yet the unintended consequences of communism's fall were bloodshed, sickness, and hardship, and the global age ushered in by the Soviet collapse brought "denationalization" to many regions of the world. Instead of being advocates for peace, prosperous militants from Saudi Arabia, Egypt, Indonesia, and the Philippines have unleashed unprecedented terrorism on the world, while many in Africa and Asia also face disease and the dramatic social and economic change associated with the global age.

Western traditions of democracy, human rights, and economic equality have much to offer. Given that these were usually intended only for certain people, global debates about their value abound. The nation-state, which protected those values for privileged Westerners, is another legacy that must be rethought in an age of transnationalism, when more people than ever are demanding the dignity of citizenship without its being pegged to a single ethnicity. At the same time, the West faces questions of its own cultural identity—an identity made from the far-flung cultural, natural, and human resources of Asia, Africa, and the Western Hemisphere.

■ **MAPPING THE WEST The World at the Start of the New Millennium**
By the twenty-first century, the Internet had transformed communications and economic organiza-
tion into an interconnected global network. People in the so-called North had greater access to this
network in 1999 and for the most part enjoyed greater wealth than people in the South. Despite
globalization, historians still find local and national conditions of political, social, and economic
life important in telling the full story of peoples and cultures.
(From **www.mids.org** [Austin: Matrix Information and Directory Services, Inc.].)

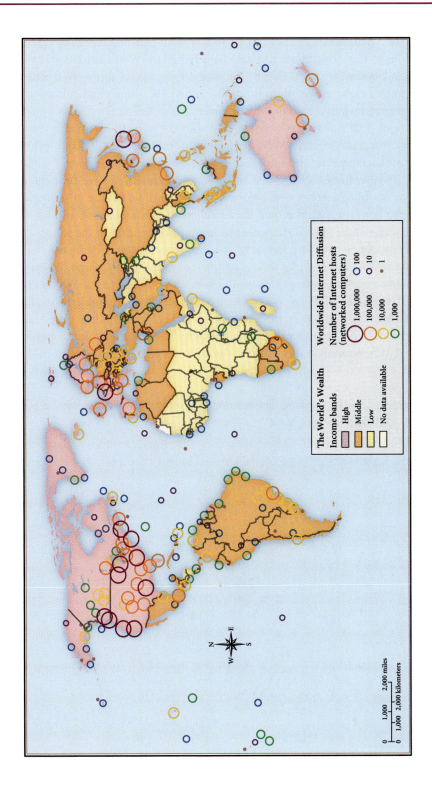

Non-Westerners have challenged, criticized, refashioned, and made enormous contributions to Western culture; they also have served the West's citizens as slaves, servants, and menial workers. One of the greatest challenges to the West and to the world in this global millennium is to determine how peoples and cultures can live together on terms that are fair for everyone.

A final challenge to the West is living with the inventive human spirit. In the past five hundred years, the West has benefited from its scientific and technological advances. Longevity and improved material well-being have spread around the world, while communication and information technology have brought people closer to one another than ever before. At the same time, the use of technology allowed the last century to become the bloodiest in human history, and the searing events of September 11, 2001, showed technology once again in the service of mass murder. War, genocide, and terrorism are among technology's hallmarks, and even now the world's leaders urge their scientific communities to search for ever more destructive weapons, posing perhaps the greatest challenge to the West and to the world. The making of the West has been a constantly inventive undertaking but also an often tragic one. What mixture of peoples and cultures will face the paradoxical challenge of technology to protect the creativity of the human race in our current century? What opportunities will they seize to forge our common global future?

Suggested References for further reading and online research appear on page SR-39 at the back of the book.

www.bedfordstmartins.com/huntconcise   See the Online Study Guide to assess your mastery of the material covered in this chapter.

Suggested References

CHAPTER 1
Foundations of Western Civilization, to 500 B.C.

Making Civilization, to 1000 B.C.

Archaeological excavation and new scientific techniques for analyzing organic materials are improving understanding of the long period in the Stone Age during which human life changed radically from that of hunters and gatherers to that of settled agriculturists. Because recent wars have drastically limited archaeological exploration in Mesopotamia (present-day Iraq), scholars must concentrate on studying already excavated material and texts to understand the complex social and economic history of the region in early times. Recent translations and analysis of Mesopotamian myths have made this literature more accessible.

Ancient Near Eastern sites: http://www-oi.uchicago.edu/OI/DEPT/RA/ABZU/ABZU.HTML

Banning, E. B. "The Neolithic Period: Triumphs of Architecture, Agriculture, and Art," *Near Eastern Archaeology* 61 (1998): 188–237.

Barber, Elizabeth Wayland. *Women's Work: The First 20,000 Years. Women, Cloth, and Society in Early Times.* 1994.

Crawford, Harriet. *Sumer and the Sumerians.* 1991.

*Dalley, Stephanie, trans. *Myths from Mesopotamia: Creation, the Flood, Gilgamesh, and Others.* 1991.

Ehrenberg, Margaret. *Women in Prehistory.* 1989.

Fagan, Brian M. *People of the Earth: An Introduction to World Prehistory.* 9th ed. 1997.

Kuhrt, Amélie. *The Ancient Near East, c. 3000–330 B.C.* Vol. 1. 1995.

Mieroop, Marc van de. *The Ancient Mesopotamian City.* 1997.

Oates, Joan. *Babylon.* Rev. ed. 1986.

Phillipson, David W. *African Archaeology.* 2d ed. 1993.

Postgate, J. N. *Early Mesopotamia: Society and Economy at the Dawn of History.* 1994.

Snell, Daniel C. *Life in the Ancient Near East, 3100–332 B.C.E.* 1997.

Wenke, Robert J. *Patterns in Prehistory: Humankind's First Three Million Years.* 4th ed. 1999.

Early Civilizations in Egypt, the Levant, and Anatolia, c. 3100–1000 B.C.

Archaeology continues to uncover the best evidence for the civilizations of the Bronze Age, from sub-Saharan Africa to southwest Asia. Publications on every aspect of ancient Egyptian life continue to pour out, while studies of the Levant emphasize the interaction of its various cultures in trade and in war.

Aldred, Cyril. *The Egyptians.* Rev. ed. 1984.

Aubet, Maria Eugenia. *The Phoenicians and the West: Politics, Colonies, and Trade.* 1993.

---

*Primary sources are indicated with an asterisk.

Bryce, Trevor. *The Kingdom of the Hittites*. 1998.

Kendall, Timothy. *Kerma and the Kingdom of Kush, 2500–1500 B.C.: The Archaeological Discovery of an Ancient Nubian Empire*. 1997.

*Lesko, Barbara S., ed. *Women's Earliest Records: From Ancient Egypt and Western Asia*. 1989.

Meeks, Dimitri, and Christine Favard-Meeks. *Daily Life of the Egyptian Gods*. Trans. G. M. Goshgarian. 1996.

Miller, J. Maxwell, and John H. Hayes. *A History of Ancient Israel and Judah*. 1986.

*Moran, William L., ed. *The Amarna Letters*. 2002.

Redford, Donald B., ed. *The Oxford Encyclopedia of Ancient Egypt*. 2000.

Robins, Gay. *Women in Ancient Egypt*. 1993.

Royal tomb of the sons of Pharaoh Ramesses II: http://www.kv5.com

Tyldesley, Joyce. *Hatshepsut: The Female Pharaoh*. 1996.

Virtual Museum of Nautical Archaeology (including the Uluburun shipwreck): http://nautarch.tamu.edu/ina/vm.htm

Wildung, Dietrich, ed. *Sudan: Ancient Kingdoms of the Nile*. Trans. Peter Der Manuelian and Kathleen Guillaume. 1997.

Shifting Empires in the Ancient Near East, to 500 B.C.

Recent scholarship on the Near East takes an integrative approach to archaeological and textual evidence and extends chronological coverage down to the eve of Alexander the Great's conquest in the late fourth century B.C. Women's history and the significance of Persian religion for later faiths have also been active fields of study.

Brosius, Maria. *Women in Ancient Persia (559–331 B.C.)* 1996.

Cohn, Norman. *Cosmos, Chaos, and the World to Come: The Ancient Roots of Apocalyptic Faith*. 1993.

Cook, J. M. *The Persian Empire*. 1983.

Finegan, Jack. *Archaeological History of the Ancient Near East*. 1979.

Kuhrt, Amélie. *The Ancient Near East, c. 3000–330 B.C.* Vol. 2. 1995.

Lloyd, Seton. *The Archaeology of Mesopotamia: From the Stone Age to the Persian Conquest*. Rev. ed. 1984.

Nigosian, S. A. *The Zoroastrian Faith: Tradition and Modern Research*. 1993.

Persepolis and Ancient Iran: http://www-oi.uchicago.edu/OI/MUS/PA/IRAN/PAAI/PAAI_Persepolis.html

Greek Civilization, to 750 B.C.

Intensive study of Cretan civilization has raised many questions about traditional interpretations of it as more peaceful than its Mediterranean neighbors. Controversy also persists about the causes of the tumult of the period 1200–1000 B.C., as in the work of Robert Drews. Research on the Dark Age by Sarah Morris and others emphasizes that the period was not as dark as sometimes asserted, because Greece remained in contact with the Near East.

Aegean Bronze Age: http://devlab.dartmouth.edu/history/bronze_age

Ancient Olympic Games: http://olympics.tufts.edu/

Chadwick, John. *The Mycenaean World*. 1976.

Crete: http://harpy.uccs.edu/greek/crete.html

Dickinson, Oliver. *The Aegean Bronze Age*. 1994.

Drews, Robert. *The End of the Bronze Age: Changes in Warfare and the Catastrophe, ca. 1200 B.C.* 1993.

Farnoux, Alexandre. *Knossos: Searching for the Legendary Palace of King Minos*. Trans. David J. Baker. 1996.

Hall, Jonathan M. *Ethnic Identity in Greek Antiquity*. 2000.

Hanson, Victor Davis. *The Other Greeks: The Family Farm and the Agrarian Roots of Western Civilization*. 1995.

Morris, Sarah P. *Daidalos and the Origins of Greek Art*. 1992.

Murray, Oswyn. *Early Greece*. 2d ed. 1993.

Mycenae: http://harpy.uccs.edu/greek/mycenae.html

Osborne, Robin. *Greece in the Making, 1200–479 B.C.* 1996.

Sanders, N. K. *The Sea Peoples: Warriors of the Ancient Mediterranean, 1250–1150 B.C.* Rev. ed. 1985.

Swaddling, Judith. *The Ancient Olympic Games*. 1980.

Remaking Greek Civilization, c. 750–500 B.C.

The Greek city-state did not spring up in a cultural vacuum, but the scarcity of contemporary sources makes it difficult to know which influences mattered most. See, for example, the differing approaches of Morris and Starr. Recent research argues for a greater role for individual entrepreneurs in what is usually regarded as state-initiated colonization in the Archaic period (see Robin Osborne's article in the Fisher and van Wees collection). Another trend is to lessen the focus on Athens and Sparta in scholarship on the emerging Greek city-state and bring in as many other places as possible.

*Barnes, Jonathan. *Early Greek Philosophy*. 1987.

Boardman, John. *The Greeks Overseas: Their Early Colonies and Trade*. New ed. 1980.

Burke, Paul F., Jr. *Olympians: The Gods and Goddesses of Ancient Greece*. 2001.

Burkert, Walter. *The Orientalizing Revolution: The Near Eastern Influence on Greek Culture in the Early Archaic Age*. Trans. Margaret E. Pinder and Walter Burkert. 1992.

Cartledge, Paul. *Spartan Reflections*. 2001.

Fisher, Nick, and Hans van Wees, eds. *Archaic Greece: New Approaches and Evidence*. 1998.

Garlan, Yvon. *Slavery in Ancient Greece*. Rev. ed. Trans. Janet Lloyd. 1988.

Halperin, David M. *One Hundred Years of Homosexuality and Other Essays on Greek Love*. 1990.

Hurwitt, Jeffrey M. *The Art and Culture of Early Greece, 1100–480 B.C.* 1985.

Kennell, Nigel M. *The Gymnasium of Virtue: Education and Culture in Ancient Sparta*. 1995.

McGlew, James F. *Tyranny and Political Culture in Ancient Greece*. 1993.

Morris, Ian. *Burial and Ancient Society: The Rise of the Greek City-State*. 1987.

Ober, Josiah, and Charles W. Hedrick, eds. *The Birth of Democracy: An Exhibition Celebrating the 2500th Anniversary of Democracy*. 1993.

Starr, Chester. *Individual and Community: The Rise of the Polis, 800–500 B.C.* 1986.

CHAPTER 2
The Greek Golden Age, c. 500–400 B.C.

Clash between Persia and Greece, 499–479 B.C.

Recent scholarship emphasizes how the ancient Greeks tried to understand their own identity by contrasting themselves with others, especially the non-Greek-speaking peoples ("barbarians") of the Near East. It also stresses the differing approaches to war characteristic of the Greek city-states and the Persian Empire.

Georges, Pericles. *Barbarian Asia and the Greek Experience: From the Archaic Period to the Age of Xenophon*. 1994.

Green, Peter. *The Greco-Persian Wars*. 1996.

Hall, Edith. *Inventing the Barbarian: Greek Self-Definition through Tragedy*. 1991.

Lazenby, J. F. *The Defence of Greece, 490–479 B.C.* 1993.

Olmstead, A. T. *History of the Persian Empire*. 1948.

Smith, John Sharwood. *Greece and the Persians*. 1990.

Athenian Confidence in the Golden Age, 479–431 B.C.

In addition to placing ancient Athenian government in the context of political theory on democracy, scholars are increasingly exploring its significance for modern democratic government. Online resources are now available and important for studying the full context of Golden Age Athenian history.

Athenian democracy: http://www.perseus.tufts.edu/~hartzler/agora/site/demo/index.html

Camp, John M. *The Athenian Agora: Excavations in the Heart of Classical Athens.* 1986.

Loomis, William T. *Wages, Welfare Costs, and Inflation in Classical Athens.* 1998.

Ober, Josiah, and Charles W. Hedrick, eds. *The Birth of Democracy: An Exhibition Celebrating the 2500th Anniversary of Democracy.* 1993.

———. *Demokratia: A Conversation on Democracies, Ancient and Modern.* 1996.

Parthenon: http://www.perseus.tufts.edu/cgi-bin/architindex?lookup=Athens,+Parthenon

Pollitt, J. J. *Art and Experience in Classical Greece.* 1972.

Samons, Loren J., III, ed. *Athenian Democracy and Imperialism.* 1998.

Thorley, John. *Athenian Democracy.* 1996.

Tradition and Innovation in Athens's Golden Age

After long neglect, historians have begun seriously discussing the meaning of the customs of Greek daily life and religion. Fierce debates have ensued about how to measure and evaluate the difference between the Greeks' habits and understandings and contemporary Western mores. James Davidson, for example, rebuts the popular view that Greeks considered sex a game of aggressive domination with winners and losers; that is a modern, not an ancient, idea.

Cartledge, Paul. *Aristophanes and His Theatre of the Absurd.* 1990.

Cohen, Edward E. *The Athenian Nation.* 2000.

Davidson, James. *Courtesans and Fishcakes: The Consuming Passions of Classical Athens.* 1998.

Easterling, P. E., and J. V. Muir, eds. *Greek Religion and Society.* 1985.

Ferguson, John. *Morals and Values in Ancient Greece.* 1989.

Fisher, N. R. E. *Slavery in Classical Greece.* 1995.

Garland, Robert. *Daily Life of the Ancient Greeks.* 1998.

———. *Religion and the Greeks.* 1994.

Garner, Richard. *Law and Society in Classical Athens.* 1987.

Goldhill, Simon. *Reading Greek Tragedy.* 1986.

Greek daily life: http://www.museum.upenn.edu/Greek_World/Daily_life/index.html

Hanson, Victor Davis. *The Other Greeks: The Family Farm and the Agrarian Roots of Western Civilization.* 1995.

Kerferd, G. B. *The Sophistic Movement.* 1981.

Lefkowitz, Mary R., and Maureen B. Fant, eds. *Women's Life in Greece and Rome: A Source Book in Translation.* 1982.

Morris, Ian, ed. *Classical Greece: Ancient Histories and Modern Archaeologies.* 1994.

Parker, Robert. *Athenian Religion: A History.* 1996.

Patterson, Cynthia B. *The Family in Greek History.* 1998.

Sealey, Raphael. *Women and Law in Classical Greece.* 1990.

The End of the Golden Age, 431–404 B.C.

The Spartan victory in the Peloponnesian War in 404 B.C. ended the Golden Age of Athens. Controversy continues to this day over how to explain the Athenian defeat: was it caused by political disunity and failure of leadership at Athens or by Sparta's success in winning Persian financial support? Deciding the issue is difficult because our best source for the war, Thucydides, unfortunately breaks off in 411 B.C. At least Strassler's wonderfully helpful edition of that author now allows easy access to what we do have.

Kagan, Donald. *The Archidamian War.* 1974.

———. *The Fall of the Athenian Empire.* 1987.

———. *The Outbreak of the Peloponnesian War.* 1969.

———. *The Peace of Nicias and the Sicilian Expedition.* 1981.

Lazenby, J. F. *The Spartan Army.* 1985.

Strassler, Robert B., ed. *The Landmark Thucydides: A Comprehensive Guide to the Peloponnesian War.* 1996.

CHAPTER 3
From the Classical to the Hellenistic World, c. 400–30 B.C.

The Decline of Classical Greece, c. 400–350 B.C.

Fortunately, we have good ancient sources on which to base our history of the frequent wars and shifting alliances among Greek city-states in the fourth century B.C. Moreover, the works of Plato and Aristotle, unlike those of many ancient authors, have survived well enough that we can study their thought in detail.

Adcock, F. E. *The Greek and Macedonian Art of War.* 1957.

Barnes, Jonathan. *Aristotle.* 1982.

Garnsey, Peter. *Ideas of Slavery from Aristotle to Augustine.* 1996.

Gosling, J. C. B. *Plato.* 1973.

Greek archaeology: http://archnet.uconn.edu/regions/europe.php3

Hornblower, Simon. *The Greek World, 479–323 B.C.* 1983.

McKechnie, Paul. *Outsiders in the Greek Cities in the Fourth Century B.C.* 1989.

Strauss, Barry S. *Athens after the Peloponnesian War: Class, Faction, and Policy, 403–386 B.C.* 1986.

Tritle, Lawrence A., ed. *The Greek World in the Fourth Century: From the Fall of the Athenian Empire to the Successors of Alexander.* 1997.

The Rise of Macedonia, 359–323 B.C.

In 1977, Manolis Andronicos greatly enhanced our knowledge of ancient Macedonia by discovering the rich tombs of the royal family in the time of Philip, Alexander, and the successor kings, but dispute still rages over the identification of who was buried where. Scholars also are energetically debating Alexander's character. A. B. Bosworth, for example, sees him as a natural-born killer, and John Maxwell O'Brien sees him as undone by alcoholism.

Andronicos, Manolis. *Vergina: The Royal Tombs and the Ancient City.* 1989.

Borza, Eugene N. *In the Shadow of Olympus: The Emergence of Macedon.* 1990.

Bosworth, A. B. *Alexander and the East: The Tragedy of Triumph.* 1996.

———. *Conquest and Empire: The Reign of Alexander the Great.* 1988.

Ellis, J. R. *Philip II and Macedonian Imperialism.* 1976.

Ginouvès, René, ed. *Macedonia: From Philip II to the Roman Conquest.* 1994.

Green, Peter. *Alexander of Macedon, 356–323 B.C. A Historical Biography.* 1991.

Hamilton, J. R. *Alexander the Great.* 1973.

Macedonian royal tombs at Vergina:
   http://alexander.macedonia.culture.gr/2/21/211/21117a/e211qa07.html

O'Brien, John Maxwell. *Alexander the Great, the Invisible Enemy: A Biography.* 1992.

*Roisman, Joseph. *Alexander the Great: Ancient and Modern Perspectives.* 1995.

The Hellenistic Kingdoms, 323–30 B.C.

Recent research, especially that of Susan Sherwin-White and Amélie Kuhrt, stresses the innovative responses of the successor kings to the challenges of ruling multicultural empires. Underwater archaeology has begun to reveal ancient Alexandria in Egypt, whose harbor district has sunk below the level of today's Mediterranean Sea.

Bowman, Alan K. *Egypt after the Pharaohs: 332 B.C.–A.D. 642.* 1986.

Cartledge, Paul, and Antony Spawforth. *Hellenistic and Roman Sparta: A Tale of Two Cities.* 1989.

Chauveau, Michel. *Egypt in the Age of Cleopatra.* Trans. David Lorton. 2000.

Empereur, Jean-Yves. *Alexandria Rediscovered.* 1998.

Grainger, John D. *Seleukos Nikator: Constructing a Hellenistic Kingdom.* 1990.

Grant, Michael. *From Alexander to Cleopatra: The Hellenistic World.* 1982.

Green, Peter. *Alexander to Actium: The Historical Evolution of the Hellenistic Age.* 1990.

Hölbl, Günther. *A History of the Ptolemaic Empire.* 2001.

Ptolemaic Egypt: http://www.houseofptoley.org

Sherwin-White, Susan, and Amélie Kuhrt. *From Samarkhand to Sardis: A New Approach to the Seleucid Empire.* 1993.

Shipley, Graham. *The Greek World after Alexander, 323–30 B.C.* 2000.

Tarn, W. W. *Hellenistic Civilisation.* 3d ed. Rev. G. T. Griffith. 1961.

Hellenistic Culture

Modern scholarship has rejected the old view that Hellenistic culture was decadent and "impure" because it mixed Greek and Near Eastern tradition and therefore was less valuable and interesting than Classical Greek culture. Instead, scholars now tend to identify the imaginative ways in which Hellenistic thinkers and artists combined the old and the new, the familiar and the foreign. Studying Hellenistic philosophers for the intrinsic interest of their ideas has become common, for example, as opposed to seeing them merely as inferior successors to Plato and Aristotle.

Ancient Alexandria in Egypt: http://pharos.bu.edu/Egypt/Alexandria

Cartledge, Paul, et al., eds. *Hellenistic Constructs: Essays in Culture, History, and Historiography.* 1997.

Collins, John J. *Between Athens and Jerusalem. Jewish Identity in the Hellenistic Diaspora.* 2d ed. 2000.

Green, Peter, ed. *Hellenistic History and Culture.* 1993.

Gruen, Erich S. *Heritage and Hellenism: The Reinvention of Jewish Tradition.* 1998.

Hellenistic artifacts: http://www.museum.upenn.edu/greek_World/Land_time/Hellenistic.html

Koester, Helmut. *Introduction to the New Testament.* Vol. 1, *History, Culture, and Religion of the Hellenistic Age.* 1982.

Long, A. A. *Hellenistic Philosophy: Stoics, Epicureans, Sceptics.* 2d ed. 1986.

Martin, Luther. *Hellenistic Religions: An Introduction.* 1987.

Mikalson, Jon D. *Religion in Hellenistic Athens.* 1998.

Momigliano, Arnaldo. *Alien Wisdom: The Limits of Hellenization.* 1975.

Phillips, E. D. *Greek Medicine.* 1973.

Pollitt, J. J. *Art in the Hellenistic Age.* 1986.

Pomeroy, Sarah B. *Women in Hellenistic Egypt: From Alexander to Cleopatra.* Rev. ed. 1990.

Ridgway, Brunilde Sismondo. *Hellenistic Sculpture I: The Styles of ca. 331–200 B.C.* 1990.

Schäfer, Peter. *Judeophobia: Attitudes toward the Jews in the Ancient World.* 1997.

Sharples, R. W. *Stoics, Epicureans, and Sceptics: An Introduction to Hellenistic Philosophy.* 1996.

*Snyder, Jane M. *The Woman and the Lyre: Women Writers in Classical Greece and Rome.* 1989.

Walbank, F. W. *The Hellenistic World.* Rev. ed. 1992.

White, K. D. *Greek and Roman Technology.* 1984.

Witt, R. E. *Isis in the Greco-Roman World.* 1971.

CHAPTER 4
The Rise of Rome, c. 753–44 B.C.

Social and Religious Traditions

Historians have long appreciated that to understand Roman history one must understand Roman values. Recent scholarship emphasizes how those values related to religion. In addition, study of legends about the foundation of Rome shows how Romans much later in the republic relied on those stories to define their national identity.

Beard, Mary, et al. *Religions of Rome.* 2 vols. 1998.

Bradley, Keith. *Slavery and Society at Rome.* 1994.

Daily life (and more): http://vroma.rhodes.edu/~bmcmanus/romanpages.html

Earl, Donald. *The Moral and Political Tradition of Rome.* 1967.

Gardner, Jane. *Women in Roman Law and Society.* 1986.

Miles, Gary B. *Livy: Reconstructing Early Rome.* 1992.

Potter, T. W. *Roman Italy.* 1987.

Rawson, Beryl, ed. *The Family in Ancient Rome: New Perspectives.* 1986.

Tellegen-Couperus, Olga. *A Short History of Roman Law.* 1993.

Williams, Craig A. *Roman Homosexuality: Ideologies of Masculinity in Classical Antiquity.* 1999.

From Monarchy to Republic, c. 753–287 B.C.

Instead of seeing early Rome as shaped largely by Etruscan influence, contemporary scholarship stresses the Romans' own efforts at shaping their state and culture, as clearly explained in T. J. Cornell's book. Recent interpretation of the struggle of the orders has concentrated on the effects of the overlapping interests of patricians and plebeians rather than merely on the division between the orders.

Boëthius, Axel. *Etruscan and Early Roman Architecture.* 2d ed. 1978.

Bonfante, Larissa, ed. *Etruscan Life and Afterlife: A Handbook of Etruscan Studies.* 1986.

Brunt, P. A. *Social Conflicts in the Roman Republic.* 1971.

Cornell, T. J. *The Beginnings of Rome: Italy and Rome from the Bronze Age to the Punic Wars (c. 1000–264 B.C.).* 1995.

Crawford, Michael. *The Roman Republic.* 2d ed. 1993.

Ladder of offices (*cursus honorum*): http://vroma.rhodes.edu/~bmcmanus/romangvt.html

MacNamara, Ellen. *The Etruscans.* 1991.

Timeline of Roman history: http://acs.rhodes.edu/~jruebel/timeline

Watson, Alan. *International Law in Archaic Rome: War and Religion.* 1993.

———. *Rome of the XII Tables: Persons and Property.* 1975.

Wiseman, T. P. *Remus: A Roman Myth.* 1995.

Consequences of Roman Imperialism, Fifth to Second Centuries B.C.

Scholarly debate about the causes and effects of Roman imperialism remains vigorous. Interpretations now tend to stress a multiplicity of causes and the complicated ways in which conquered peoples responded to and resisted Roman power, even after their defeat. Continuing archaeological excavation at Carthage has revealed much about the history of that extremely successful Phoenician foundation.

Alcock, Susan. *Graecia Capta: The Landscapes of Roman Greece.* 1993.

Astin, Alan E. *Cato the Censor.* 1978.

Badian, E. *Publicans and Sinners: Private Enterprise in the Service of the Roman Republic.* 1972.

———. *Roman Imperialism in the Late Republic.* 2d ed. 1968.

Conte, Gian Biagio. *Latin Literature: A History.* Trans. Joseph B. Solodow. Rev. Don Fowler and Glenn W. Most. 1994.

Errington, R. M. *The Dawn of Empire: Rome's Rise to World Power.* 1972.

Etruscan realistic portraiture (second century B.C.):
http://www.worcesterart.org/Collection/Ancient/1926.19.html

Gabba, Emilio. *Republican Rome: The Army and the Allies.* Trans. P. J. Cuff. 1976.

Goldsworthy, Adrian. *The Punic Wars.* 2000.

Gruen, Erich S. *The Hellenistic World and the Coming of Rome.* 2 vols. 1984.

Harris, William V. *War and Imperialism in Republican Rome, 327–70 B.C.* 1985.

Lancel, Serge. *Carthage: A History.* Trans. Antonia Nevill. 1995.

Nicolet, Claude. *The World of the Citizen in Republican Rome.* 1980.

Ogilvie, R. M. *Roman Literature and Society.* 1980.

Salmon, E. T. *Roman Colonization under the Republic.* 1970.

Sekunda, Nicholas, et al. *Caesar's Legions: The Roman Soldier, 753 B.C. to 117 A.D.* 2000.

Strong, Donald. *Roman Art.* 2d ed. 1988.

Taylor, Lilly Ross. *Roman Voting Assemblies: From the Hannibalic War to the Dictatorship of Caesar.* 1966.

Toynbee, J. M. C. *Roman Historical Portraits.* 1978.

Upheaval in the Late Republic, c. 133–44 B.C.

Only with the history of the late republic do the surviving written sources become more than scanty. Contemporary documents such as the many letters and speeches of Cicero and the memoirs of Caesar supplement the ancient narrative accounts (which date to the later period of empire). Arguments about the failure of the republic now tend to reject the traditional view that destructive rivalries were based more on family and group loyalties than on political differences. Instead, deep divisions about political issues are seen to be primary, in addition to the emergence of new forms of elite competition.

Beard, Mary, and Michael Crawford. *Rome in the Late Republic.* 1985.

*Bradley, Keith R. *Spartacus and the Slave Wars: A Brief History with Documents.* 2001.

Greenhalgh, Peter. *Pompey the Republican Prince.* 1982.

———. *Pompey the Roman Alexander.* 1981.

Keaveney, Arthur. *Sulla: The Last Republican.* 1982.

Meier, Christian. *Caesar: A Biography.* Trans. David McLintock. 1995.

Roman archaeological sites: http://www.ukans.edu/history/index/europe/ancient_rome/E/Roman/RomanSites*Topics/Archaeology.html

Shotter, David. *The Fall of the Roman Republic.* 1994.

Southern, Pat. *Cleopatra.* 1999.

Stockton, David. *The Gracchi.* 1979.

Ward, Allen. *Marcus Crassus and the Late Roman Republic.* 1977.

CHAPTER 5
The Roman Empire, c. 44 B.C.–A.D. 284

Creating "Roman Peace"

For decades, scholars have debated Augustus's motives in contriving the principate and how to evaluate his rule. Whether they label him tyrant or reformer, all agree that he was a brilliant visionary. Recent research on the ways Augustus and his successors communicated the meaning of empire to the public stresses the role of grandiose and often violent spectacles.

Auguet, Roland. *Cruelty and Civilization: The Roman Games.* 1972.

Bradley, Keith. *Slavery and Society at Rome.* 1994.

Conlin, Diane Atnally. *The Artists of the Ara Pacis: The Process of Hellenization in Roman Relief Sculpture.* 1997.

Futrell, Alison. *Blood in the Arena: The Spectacle of Roman Power.* 1997.

Galinsky, Karl. *Augustan Culture.* 1996.

Henig, Martin, ed. *A Handbook of Roman Art: A Comprehensive Survey of All the Arts of the Roman World.* 1983.

Horace's country house: http.//www.humnet.ucla.edu/horaces-villa/contents.html

Jackson, Ralph. *Doctors and Diseases in the Roman Empire.* 1988.

Potter, D. S., and D. J. Mattingly, eds. *Life, Death, and Entertainment in the Roman Empire.* 1999.

Roman emperors: http://www.roman-emperors.org

Southern, Pat. *Augustus.* 1998.

Wallace-Hadrill, Andrew. *Augustan Rome.* 1993.

Wiedemann, Thomas. *Emperors and Gladiators.* 1995.

Zanker, Paul. *The Power of Images in the Age of Augustus.* Trans. Alan Shapiro. 1988.

Maintaining "Roman Peace"

The avoidance of civil war was the foremost marker of the period of "Roman peace" in the late first and second centuries. As various scholarly studies show, this interlude was made possible both by the devotion to duty of emperors such as Aurelius and by the general prosperity that emerged during the absence of war in imperial territory.

Garnsey, Peter, and Richard Saller. *The Roman Empire: Economy, Society, and Culture.* 1987.

Johnston, David. *Roman Law in Context.* 1999.

Köhne, Eckart, and Cornelia Ewigleben. *Gladiators and Caesars: The Power of Spectacle in Ancient Rome.* 2000.

Lintott, Andrew. *Imperium Romanum: Politics and Administration.* 1993.

Mattern, Susan. *Rome and the Enemy: Imperial Strategy in the Principate.* 1999.

Roman towns and monuments:
http://www.ukans.edu/history/index/europe/ancient_rome/E/Roman/home.html

Treggiari, Susan. *Roman Marriage: Iusti Coniuges from the Time of Cicero to the Time of Ulpian.* 1991.

Webster, Graham. *The Roman Imperial Army of the First and Second Centuries A.D.* 3d ed. 1985.

Wiedemann, Thomas. *The Julio-Claudian Emperors, A.D. 14–70.* 1989.

The Emergence of Christianity

Few fields in ancient history generate as much scholarly activity as does the study of early Christianity, and the disputes over how to understand it are lively. The significance of the role of women is especially controversial. The sources are relatively plentiful, compared with those for other periods in Greek and Roman history, but their meaning is hotly contested because both the authors and their interpreters usually have particular points of view.

Clarke, Andrew D. *Serve the Community of the Church: Christians as Leaders and Ministers.* 2000.

Doran, Robert. *Birth of a World View: Early Christianity in Its Jewish and Pagan Contexts.* 1999.

Kraemer, Ross Shephard. *Her Share of the Blessings: Women's Religion among Pagans, Jews, and Christians in the Greco-Roman World.* 1992.

MacMullen, Ramsay. *Christianizing the Roman Empire (A.D. 100–400).* 1984.

Meeks, Wayne A. *The First Urban Christians: The Social World of the Apostle Paul.* 1983.

Riley, Gregory J. *The River of God: A New History of Christian Origins.* 2001.

Schurer, Emil. *The History of the Jewish People in the Age of Jesus Christ (175 B.C.–A.D. 135).* Rev. ed. 4 vols. 1973, 1979, 1986.

Stambaugh, John E., and David L. Balch. *The New Testament in Its Social Environment.* 1986.

Torjesen, Karen Jo. *When Women Were Priests: Women's Leadership in the Early Church and the Scandal of Their Subordination in the Rise of Christianity.* 1993.

Witt, R. E. *Isis in the Greco-Roman World.* 1971.

The Crisis of the Third Century

Unfortunately, our sources become fragmentary during the period when the empire was in danger of splitting into pieces. The fundamental problem remained what it had always been: the Roman monarchy's propensity to generate civil war and the inevitably disastrous effects on the economy. Hence, scholarly study of the crisis must always begin with military and political history.

Elton, Hugh. *Frontiers of the Roman Empire.* 1996.

————. Military Aspects of the Collapse of the Roman Empire:
    http://www.unipissing.ca/department/history/orb/milex.htm

Grant, Michael. *The Collapse and Recovery of the Roman Empire.* 1999.

Isaac, Benjamin. *The Limits of Empire: The Roman Army in the East.* 1989.

MacMullen, Ramsay. *Roman Government's Response to Crisis, A.D. 235–337.* 1976.

CHAPTER 6

The Transformation of the Roman Empire, A.D. 284–c. 600

Reorganizing the Empire

In addition to trying to reconcile the sources' sometimes conflicting information about the events of the late third and fourth centuries, scholars continue to debate the personalities and motives of Diocletian and Constantine. Understanding these emperors is challenging because their religious sensibilities, markedly different from those of most modern believers, so deeply influenced their political actions.

Barnes, Timothy D. *Constantine and Eusebius.* 1981.

Bowersock, G. W., Peter Brown, and Oleg Grabar, eds. *Late Antiquity: A Guide to the Postclassical World.* 1999.

Corcoran, Simon. *The Empire of the Tetrarchs: Imperial Pronouncements and Government,* A.D. *284–324.* Rev. ed. 2000.

Diocletian's biography: http://www.roman-emperors.org/dioclet.htm

Elsner, Jaś. *Imperial Rome and Christian Triumph: The Art of the Roman Empire,* A.D. *100–450.* 1998.

Harl, Kenneth W. *Coinage in the Roman Economy, 300* B.C. *to* A.D. *700.* 1996.

Salzman, Michele Renee. *On Roman Time: The Calendar of 354 and the Rhythms of Urban Life in Late Antiquity.* 1990.

Southern, Pat, and Karen R. Dixon. *The Late Roman Army.* 1996.

Whittaker, C. R. *Frontiers of the Roman Empire: A Social and Economic Study.* 1994.

Williams, Stephen. *Diocletian and the Roman Recovery.* 1985.

Christianizing the Empire

Recent research has deepened our appreciation of the complexity of the religious transformation of the Roman Empire and the emotional depths that the process reached for polytheists and Christians. People's ideas about the divine changed, as well as their ideas about themselves, even at the most intimate levels and activities of human life.

Bowersock, G. W. *Julian the Apostate.* 1978.

———. *Martyrdom and Rome.* 1995.

Brown, Peter. *Augustine of Hippo.* 1967.

———. *The Body and Society: Men, Women, and Sexual Renunciation in Early Christianity.* 1988.

Drake, H. A. *Constantine and the Bishops: The Politics of Intolerance.* 2000.

Early Christian literature: http://www.ocf.org/OrthodoxPage/reading/St.Pachomius/Welcome.html

Herrin, Judith. *The Formation of Christendom.* Rev. ed. 1989.

MacMullen, Ramsay. *Christianity and Paganism in the Fourth to Eighth Centuries.* 1997.

McLynn, Neil B. *Ambrose of Milan: Church and Court in a Christian Capital.* 1994.

Raven, Susan. *Rome in Africa.* New ed. 1984.

Rousseau, Philip. *Pachomius: The Making of a Community in Fourth-Century Egypt.* 1985.

Rousselle, Aline. *Porneia: On Desire and the Body in Antiquity.* Trans. Felicia Pheasant. 1988.

Wills, Garry. *Saint Augustine.* 1999.

Germanic Kingdoms in the West

Debate still thrives over how to categorize the social and cultural transformation of the Roman world in the fourth and fifth centuries after the large-scale incursions of Germanic peoples. It is becoming increasingly clear that those people underwent a process of ethnogenesis (developing a separate ethnic identity) in constructing their new kingdoms on imperial territory in western Europe, but it is less clear how to measure the extent of the trauma inflicted on Romans and Roman culture.

Barnwell, P. S. *Emperor, Prefects, and Kings: The Roman West, 395–565.* 1992.

Burns, Thomas. *Barbarians within the Gates of Rome: A Study of Roman Military Policy and the Barbarians, ca. 375–425* A.D. 1994.

*Drew, Katherine Fischer. *The Laws of the Salian Franks.* 1991.

Geary, Patrick J. *Before France and Germany: The Creation and Transformation of the Merovingian World.* 1988.

———. *The Myth of Nations: The Medieval Origins of Europe.* 2001.

Heather, Peter. *The Goths and Romans.* 1996.

King, Anthony. *Roman Gaul and Germany.* 1990.

Matthews, John. *Western Aristocracies and Imperial Court,* A.D. *364–425.* 1975.

Wolfram, Herwig. *The Roman Empire and Its Germanic Peoples.* Trans. Thomas Dunlap. 1997.

The Byzantine Empire in the East

Scholars today recognize the "Byzantine Empire" as the continuation of the eastern Roman Empire, emphasizing the challenge posed to its rulers in trying to maintain order and prosperity for their distinctly multicultural and multilingual population. The story of the Byzantine emperors poses provocative questions because the inclusiveness of their regimes was made possible by a political rigor that some would say approached tyranny.

Bowersock, G. W. *Hellenism in Late Antiquity.* 1990.

Byzantine history: http://thoughtline.com/byznet/

Cameron, Averil. *The Mediterranean World in Late Antiquity,* A.D. *395–600.* 1993.

Cavallo, Guglielmo, ed. *The Byzantines.* 1997.

Haldon, John. *Byzantium: A History.* 2000.

Rice, Tamara Talbot. *Everyday Life in Byzantium.* 1967.

Women in Byzantine history bibliography: http://www.wooster.edu/Art/wb.html

CHAPTER 7
The Heirs of the Roman Empire, 600–750

Byzantium: A Christian Empire under Siege

Ousterhout and Brubaker, and Weitzmann, concentrate on religion, culture, and the role of icons. Treadgold and Whittow tend to stress politics and war.

The Byzantine Studies Page: http://www.bway.net/~halsall/byzantium.html

*Geanakoplos, Deno John, ed. and trans. *Byzantium: Church, Society, and Civilization Seen through Contemporary Eyes.* 1986.

Haldon, J. F. *Byzantium in the Seventh Century: The Transformation of a Culture.* 1990.

Norwich, John Julius. *Byzantium: The Early Centuries.* 1989.

Ousterhout, Robert, and Leslie Brubaker. *The Sacred Image East and West.* 1995.

Treadgold, Warren. *A History of the Byzantine State and Society.* 1997.

Weitzmann, Kurt. *The Icon: Holy Images, Sixth to Fourteenth Century.* 1978.

Whittow, Mark. *The Making of Byzantium, 600–1025.* 1996.

Islam: A New Religion and a New Empire

The classic (and as yet unsurpassed) discussion is in Hodgson. Crone's book is considered highly controversial; Kennedy's is useful to consult for basic facts.

Ahmed, Leila. *Women and Gender in Islam: Historical Roots of a Modern Debate.* 1992.

Crone, Patricia. *Meccan Trade and the Rise of Islam.* 1987.

Hodgson, Marshall G. S. *The Venture of Islam: Conscience and History in a World Civilization.* Vol. 1, *The Classical Age of Islam.* 1974.

Islamic Sourcebook: http://www.fordham.edu/halsall/islam/islamsbook.html

Kennedy, Hugh. *The Prophet and the Age of the Caliphates: The Islamic Near East from the Sixth to the Eleventh Century.* 1986.

Lapidus, Ira. *A History of Islamic Societies.* 1988.

*Lewis, Bernard, ed. and trans. *Islam: From the Prophet Muhammad to the Capture of Constantinople.* 2 vols. 1987.

Ruthven, Malise. *Islam in the World.* 1984.

Waddy, Charis. *Women in Muslim History.* 1980.

The Western Kingdoms

Wood and Geary provide complementary guides to the Merovingian world. Goffart suggests important ways to read primary sources from the period. Recent keen historical interest in the role of the cults of the saints in early medieval society is reflected in Van Dam.

*Bede. *A History of the English Church and People.* Trans. Leo Sherley-Price. 1991.

Charles-Edwards, T. M. *Early Christian Ireland.* 2001.

Collins, Roger. *Early Medieval Spain: Unity in Diversity, 400–1000.* 1983.

Fouracre, Paul. *The Age of Charles Martel.* 2000.

*Fouracre, Paul, and Richard A. Gerberding, eds. *Late Merovingian France: History and Hagiography, 640–720.* 1996.

Geary, Patrick. *Before France and Germany: The Creation and Transformation of the Merovingian World.* 1988.

Goffart, Walter. *The Narrators of Barbarian History (A.D. 550–800): Jordanes, Gregory of Tours, Bede, and Paul the Deacon.* 1988.

*Gregory of Tours. *The History of the Franks.* Trans. Lewis Thorpe. 1976.

Gregory of Tours: http://www.unipissing.ca/department/history/4505/show.htm

Van Dam, Raymond. *Saints and Their Miracles in Late Antique Gaul.* 1993.

Wood, Ian. *The Merovingian Kingdoms, 450–751.* 1994.

CHAPTER 8

Unity and Diversity in Three Societies, 750–1050

Byzantium: Renewed Strength and Influence

Recent studies of Byzantium stress the revival in the arts and literature, but Garland is interested in the place of women in politics, while Treadgold looks at political and military developments more generally. Almost nothing was available in English on eastern Europe and Russia until the 1980s.

Byzantine art: http://gallery.sjsu.edu/artH/byzantine/mainpage.html

Davies, Norman. *God's Playground: A History of Poland.* Vol. 1. 1982.

Fine, John V. A., Jr. *The Early Medieval Balkans: A Critical Survey from the Sixth to the Late Twelfth Century.* 1983.

Franklin, Simon, and Jonathan Shepard. *The Emergence of Rus, 750–1200.* 1996.

Garland, Lynda. *Byzantine Empresses: Women and Power in Byzantium, A.D. 527–1204.* 1999.

Manteuffel, Tadeusz. *The Formation of the Polish State: The Period of Ducal Rule, 963–1194.* Trans. A. Gorski. 1982.

*Psellus, Michael. *Fourteen Byzantine Rulers: The Chronographia.* Trans. E. R. A. Sewter. 1966.

Safran, Linda, ed. *Heaven on Earth: Art and the Church in Byzantium.* 1991.

Treadgold, Warren. *The Byzantine Revival, 780–842.* 1988.

Wilson, N. G. *Scholars of Byzantium.* 1983.

From Unity to Fragmentation in the Islamic World

The traditional approach to the Islamic world is political (Kennedy). Glick is unusual in taking a comparative approach. The newest issue for scholars is the role of women in medieval Islamic society (Spellberg).

Ashtor, E. *A Social and Economic History of the Near East in the Middle Ages.* 1976.

Glick, Thomas. *Islamic and Christian Spain in the Early Middle Ages: Comparative Perspectives on Social and Cultural Formation.* 1979.

Kennedy, Hugh. *The Prophet and the Age of the Caliphates: The Islamic Near East from the Sixth to the Eleventh Century.* 1986.

Makdisi, George. *The Rise of Colleges.* 1981.

Spellberg, Denise. *Politics, Gender, and the Islamic Past.* 1994.

The Creation and Division of a New Western Empire

Huge chunks of the primary sources for the Carolingian world are now available in English translation, thanks in large part to the work of Paul Dutton. Hodges and Whitehouse provide the perspective of archaeologists. The Carolingian renaissance is increasingly recognized as a long-term development rather than simply the achievement of Charlemagne.

Carolingian studies: http://orb.rhodes.edu/encyclop/religion/hagiography/carol.htm

*Dutton, Paul Edward. *Carolingian Civilization: A Reader.* 1993.

*———. *Charlemagne's Courtier: The Complete Einhard.* 1998.

*Einhard and Notker the Stammerer. *Two Lives of Charlemagne.* Trans. Lewis Thorpe. 1969.

Hodges, Richard, and David Whitehouse. *Mohammed, Charlemagne, and the Origins of Europe.* 1983.

McKitterick, Rosamond. *Carolingian Culture: Emulation and Innovation.* 1994.

Nelson, Janet. *Charles the Bald.* 1987.

Riche, Pierre. *Daily Life in the World of Charlemagne.* Trans. J. A. McNamara. 1978.

The Emergence of Local Rule in the Post-Carolingian Age

Historians used to lament the passing of the Carolingian Empire. Recently, however, they have come to appreciate the strengths and adaptive strategies of the post-Carolingian world. Duby speaks of the agricultural "takeoff" of the period, while Head and Landes explore new institutions of peace.

Duby, Georges. *The Early Growth of the European Economy: Warriors and Peasants from the Seventh to the Twelfth Century.* Trans. H. B. Clark. 1974.

Fell, Christine E., Cecily Clark, and Elizabeth Williams. *Women in Anglo-Saxon England, and the Impact of 1066.* 1984.

Frantzen, Allen. *King Alfred.* 1986.

Head, Thomas, and Richard Landes, eds. *The Peace of God: Social Violence and Religious Response in France around the Year 1000.* 1992.

Jones, Gwyn. *A History of the Vikings.* Rev. ed. 1984.

Lawson, M. K. *Cnut: The Danes in England in the Early Eleventh Century.* 1993.

Medieval and Renaissance manuscripts: http://www.columbia.edu/cu/libraries/indiv/rare/images

Medieval studies: http://argos.evansville.edu

Medieval studies: http://www.georgetown.edu/labyrinth/labyrinth-home.html

Reuter, Timothy. *Germany in the Early Middle Ages, c. 800–1056.* 1991.

Sweeney, Del, ed. *Agriculture in the Middle Ages: Technology, Practice, and Representation.* 1995.

*Whitelock, Dorothy, ed. *English Historical Documents.* Vol. 1. 2d ed. 1979.

Wilson, David. *The Vikings and Their Origins: Scandinavia in the First Millennium.* 1970.

CHAPTER 9
Renewal and Reform, 1050–1200

The Commercial Revolution

The idea of a commercial revolution in the Middle Ages originated with Lopez. Little discusses some religious consequences. Hyde explores the society and government of the Italian communes. Moore looks at the cultural and political "revolution" wrought by the cities.

Epstein, Steven. *Wage Labor and Guilds in Medieval Europe.* 1991.

Hyde, J. K. *Society and Politics in Medieval Italy: The Evolution of Civil Life, 1000–1350.* 1973.

Little, Lester K. *Religious Poverty and the Profit Economy in Medieval Europe.* 1978.

Lopez, Robert S. *The Commercial Revolution of the Middle Ages, 950–1350.* 1976.

*Lopez, Robert S. and Irving W. Raymond, eds. *Medieval Trade in the Mediterranean World.* 1955.

Moore, R. I. *The First European Revolution, c. 970–1215.* 2000.

Church Reform and Its Aftermath

The Investiture Conflict, which pitted the pope against the emperor, has been particularly important to German historians. Blumenthal gives a useful overview. The consequences of church reform and the new papal monarchy included both the growth of canon law (see Brundage) and the crusades (see Erdmann and Riley-Smith). Glick looks at Jewish-Christian relations.

Blumenthal, Uta-Renate. *The Investiture Controversy: Church and Monarchy from the Ninth to the Twelfth Century.* 1991.

Brundage, James A. *Medieval Canon Law.* 1995.

Crusades: http://orb.rhodes.edu/bibliographies/crusades.html

Duby, Georges. *Medieval Marriage: Two Models from Twelfth-Century France.* Trans. Elborg Forster. 1978.

Erdmann, Carl. *The Origins of the Idea of Crusade.* Trans. Marshall W. Baldwin and Walter Goffart. 1977.

Glick, Leonard B. *Abraham's Heirs: Jews and Christians in Medieval Europe.* 1999.

*Peters, Edward, ed. *The First Crusade: The Chronicle of Fulcher of Chartres and Other Source Materials.* 1971.

Riley-Smith, Jonathan. *The Crusades. A Short History.* 1987.

———. *The First Crusaders, 1095–1131.* 1997.

*Tierney, Brian, ed. *The Crisis of Church and State, 1050–1300.* 1964.

The Revival of Monarchies

The growth of monarchical power and the development of state institutions are topics of keen interest to historians. Clanchy points to the use of writing and record keeping in government. Hudson explores the growth of royal institutions of justice. Fuhrmann looks at the German experience.

Clanchy, Michael T. *From Memory to Written Record, 1066–1307.* 2d ed. 1993.

Douglas, David C. *William the Conqueror: The Norman Impact upon England.* 1967.

Dunbabin, Jean. *France in the Making, 843–1180.* 1985.

Fuhrmann, Horst. *Germany in the High Middle Ages, c. 1050–1200.* Trans. T. Reuter. 1986.

Hallam, Elizabeth M. *Domesday Book through Nine Centuries*. 1986.

Hudson, John. *The Formation of the English Common Law: Law and Society in England from the Norman Conquest to Magna Carta*. 1996.

*Otto of Freising. *The Deeds of Frederick Barbarossa*. Trans. C. C. Mierow. 1953.

*Suger. *The Deeds of Louis the Fat*. Trans. Richard C. Cusimano and John Moorhead. 1992.

New Forms of Scholarship and Religious Experience

The new learning of the twelfth century was first called a "renaissance" by Haskins. Clanchy's more recent study looks less at the revival of the classics, stressing instead the social and political context of medieval teaching and learning. Recent research on religious developments includes discussions of women in the new monastic movements of the twelfth century (Venarde) and challenges to old views about the Cistercian order (Berman). *The Little Flowers of Saint Francis* gives a good idea of Franciscan spirituality.

Abelard's *History of My Calamities*: http://www.fordham.edu/halsall/basis/abelard-histcal.html

Benson, Robert L., and Giles Constable, eds., with the assistance of Carol Lanham. *Renaissance and Renewal in the Twelfth Century*. 1982.

Berman, Constance Hoffman, *The Cistercian Evolution: The Invention of a Religious Order in Twelfth-Century Europe*. 2000.

Clanchy, Michael. *Abelard: A Medieval Life*. 1997.

Constable, Giles. *The Reformation of the Twelfth Century*. 1996.

Ferruolo, Stephen C. *The Origins of the University: The Schools of Paris and Their Critics, 1100–1215*. 1985.

Haskins, Charles Homer. *The Renaissance of the Twelfth Century*. 1927.

Hildegard of Bingen: http://www.uni-mainz.de/~horst/hildegard/links.html

Hildegard von Bingen: Ordo virtutum, Deutsche Harmonia Mundi CD, 77394 (music from Hildegard's *Scivias* and the expanded play at its end).

Letters of Abelard and Heloise. Trans. Betty Radice. 1974. Includes *History of My Calamities*.

The Little Flowers of Saint Francis. Trans. L. Sherley-Price. 1959.

Murray, Alexander. *Reason and Society in the Middle Ages*. 1978.

Southern, R. W. *Scholastic Humanism and the Unification of Europe*. Vol. 1, *Foundations*. 1995.

Venarde, Bruce L. *Women's Monasticism and Medieval Society: Nunneries in France and England, 890–1215*. 1997.

CHAPTER 10

An Age of Confidence, 1200–1340

War, Conquest, and Colonization

Apart from Robert Bartlett's pathbreaking study, the many fronts of war during this period are usually explored separately. Although the Fourth Crusade has long been of interest to historians (W. B. Bartlett), only recently were the Northern Crusades brought to the center of scholarly discussion by Christiansen. Boyle's discussion of the Mongol conquests is already a classic; Morgan's study rightly classifies the Mongols among the "Peoples of Europe."

Bartlett, Robert. *The Making of Europe: Conquest, Colonization, and Cultural Change, 950–1350*. 1993.

Bartlett, W. B. *An Ungodly War: The Sack of Constantinople and the Fourth Crusade*. 2000.

Boyle, John A. *The Mongol World Empire, 1206–1370*. 1977.

Christiansen, Eric. *The Northern Crusades*. 2d ed. 1997.

Costen, Michael. *The Cathars and the Albigensian Crusade*. 1999.

Larner, John. *Marco Polo and the Discovery of the World*. 1999.

Morgan, David. *The Mongols.* 1986.

*Polo, Marco. *The Travels.* Trans. Ronald Latham. 1958.

Politics of Control

Clanchy documents the growth of monarchical power; Moore and Jordan connect powerful monarchies to the politics of persecutions. Jones considers how and why the Italian communes eventually adopted one-man rule. O'Callaghan shows how even representative institutions were initially tools of powerful kings.

Clanchy, Michael T. *England and Its Rulers, 1066–1272.* 2d ed. 1998.

*Fourth Lateran Council: http://abbey.apana.org.au/councils/ecum12.htm

Jones, Philip J. *The Italian City-State: From Commune to Signoria.* 1997.

Jordan, William Chester. *The French Monarchy and the Jews: From Philip Augustus to the Last Capetians.* 1989.

Moore, R. I. *The Formation of a Persecuting Society: Power and Deviance in Western Europe, 950–1250.* 1987.

O'Callaghan, Joseph F. *The Cortes of Castile-León, 1188–1350.* 1989.

Religious and Cultural Life in an Age of Expansion

Bynum and Rubin are interested in the religious lives and beliefs of the laity rather than of religious professionals. Duby places Gothic architecture in a wide cultural framework, while Kessler and Zacharias explore the connections between religion and art.

Bynum, Caroline Walker. *Holy Feast and Holy Fast: The Religious Significance of Food to Medieval Women.* 1987.

*Dante. *The Divine Comedy.* Many editions; recommended are translations by Mark Musa, John Ciardi, and Robert Pinsky.

Duby, Georges. *The Age of the Cathedrals: Art and Society, 980–1420.* Trans. Eleanor Levieux and Barbara Thompson. 1981.

Kessler, Herbert L. and Johanna Zacharias. *Rome 1300: On the Path of the Pilgrim.* 2000.

Rubin, Miri. *Corpus Christi: The Eucharist in Late Medieval Culture.* 1991.

*Thomas Aquinas: http://www.newadvent.org/summa/

CHAPTER 11

Crisis and Renaissance, 1340–1500

A Multitude of Crises

The plague has always been a subject of great interest to historians (Horrox), and the work of Jordan shows that its ravages were clearly linked to the earlier Great Famine. Froissart thought that the Hundred Years' War was a chivalric venture, but Allmand shows how it helped create two modern states.

Allmand, Christopher. *The Hundred Years' War: England and France at War, c. 1300–1450.* 1988.

The Black Death. Ed. and trans. Rosemary Horrox. 1994.

*Froissart, Jean, *Chronicles.* Trans. Geoffrey Brereton. 1968.

Inalcik, Halil. *The Ottoman Empire: The Classical Age, 1300–1600.* Trans. Norman Itzkowitz and Colin Imber. 1973.

Jordan, William Chester. *The Great Famine: Northern Europe in the Early Fourteenth Century.* 1996.

Nirenberg, David. *Communities of Violence: Persecution of Minorities in the Middle Ages.* 1996.

Oatley, Francis. *The Western Church in the Later Middle Ages.* 1979.

Plague and public health in Renaissance Europe: http://jefferson.village.virginia.edu/osheim/intro.html

New Forms of Thought and Expression: The Renaissance

The old association between the Renaissance and the history of Florence is slowly giving way to a wider view (see Kirkpatrick, Welch, and the anthology edited by Elmer). In addition to the study of great artists and writers, recent scholars (such as Jardine) have turned their attention to the ways in which a market for cultural goods such as books and manuscripts was created by savvy, prestige-seeking consumers.

Blockmans, Wim, and Walter Prevenier. *The Promised Lands: The Low Countries under Burgundian Rule, 1369–1530.* Trans. Elizabeth Fackelman. Ed. Edward Peters. 1999.

Eisenstein, Elizabeth L. *The Printing Press as an Agent of Change: Communications and Cultural Transformations in Early-Modern Europe.* 1980.

Herlihy, David, and Christiane Klapisch-Zuber. *Tuscans and Their Families: A Study of the Florentine Catasto of 1427.* 1978.

Jardine, Lisa. *Worldly Goods.* 1996.

Kirkpatrick, Robin. *The European Renaissance, 1400–1600.* 2002.

Renaissance art links: http://www.lincolnu.edu/~kluebber/euroart.htm

*The Renaissance in Europe: An Anthology. Eds. Peter Elmer, Nicholas Webb, and Roberta Wood. 2000.

Welch, Evelyn. *Art in Renaissance Italy, 1350–1500.* 1997.

On the Threshold of World History

The traditional view of "Europe discovering the world" has been replaced by a more nuanced and complex discussion that includes non-European views and uses Asian, African, and Mesoamerican sources.

Epstein, Steven A. *Speaking of Slavery: Color, Ethnicity, and Human Bondage in Italy.* 2001.

*The Log of Christopher Columbus. Ed. Robert H. Fuson. 1987.

Russell-Wood, A. J. R. *A World on the Move: The Portuguese in Africa, Asia, and America, 1415–1808.* 1992.

Subrahmanyam, Sanjay. *The Career and Legend of Vasco da Gama.* 1997.

CHAPTER 12
Struggles over Beliefs, 1500–1648

The Protestant Reformation

While continuing to refine our understanding of the leading Protestant reformers, recent scholars have also offered new interpretations that take into consideration the popular impact of the reformers' teachings.

Bainton, Roland. *Women of the Reformation in Germany and Italy.* 1971.

Blickle, Peter. *The Revolution of 1525.* 1981.

Bouwsma, William J. *John Calvin: A Sixteenth-Century Portrait.* 1988.

Brady, Thomas A. *Turning Swiss: Cities and Empire, 1450–1550.* 1985.

Carney, Jo Eldridge, ed. *Renaissance and Reformation,1500–1620: A Biographical Dictionary.* 2001.

*Essential Works of Erasmus. Ed. W. T. H. Jackson. 1965.

*Hillerbrand, Hans J., ed. *The Protestant Reformation.* 1969.

Hsia, R. Po-chia. *The World of the Catholic Renewal.* 1997.

Luther's writings in English: http://history.hanover.edu/early/luther.htm

Oberman, Heiko A. *Luther: Man between God and Devil.* 1990.

Scribner, R. W. *For the Sake of Simple Folk: Popular Propaganda for the German Reformation.* 1981.

State Power and Religious Conflict, 1500–1618

The personalities of rulers such as Charles V, Philip II, and Elizabeth I remain central to the religious and political conflicts of this period. Recent scholarship also highlights more structural factors, especially in the French Wars of Religion and the rise of the Dutch Republic.

Cameron, Euan, ed. *Early Modern Europe: An Oxford History.* 1999.

*Guicciardini, Francesco. *The History of Italy.* Trans. Sidney Alexander. 1969.

Holt, Mack P. *The French Wars of Religion, 1562–1629.* 1995.

Israel, Jonathan. *The Dutch Republic: Its Rise, Greatness, and Fall, 1477–1806.* 1995.

Kamen, Henry. *Philip of Spain.* 1997.

Mattingly, Garrett. *The Defeat of the Spanish Armada.* 2d ed. 1988.

Richardson, Glenn. *Renaissance Monarchy: The Reigns of Henry VIII, Francis I, and Charles V.* 2002.

Strong, Roy. *The Cult of Elizabeth: Elizabethan Portraiture and Pageantry.* 1977.

The Thirty Years' War and the Balance of Power, 1618–1648

As ethnic conflicts erupt again in Eastern Europe, historians have traced their roots back to the intertwined religious, ethnic, and dynastic struggles of the Thirty Years' War.

Asch, Ronald G. *The Thirty Years War: The Holy Roman Empire and Europe, 1618–48.* 1997.

Lee, Stephen J. *The Thirty Years War.* 1991.

Parker, Geoffrey. *The Military Revolution: Military Innovation and the Rise of the West, 1500–1800.* 1988.

———, ed. *The Thirty Years' War.* 2d ed. 1997.

*Rabb, Theodore K., ed. *The Thirty Years' War.* 2d ed. 1972.

Economic Crisis and Realignment

Painstaking archival research has enabled historians to reconstruct the demographic, economic, and social history of this period. Recently, attention has focused more specifically on women, the family, and the early history of slavery.

Ashton, Trevor H., ed. *Crisis in Europe.* 1965.

Braudel, Fernand. *The Mediterranean and the Mediterranean World in the Age of Philip the Second.* 2 vols. Trans. Siân Reynolds. 1972–1973.

De Vries, Jan. *The Economy of Europe in an Age of Crisis, 1600–1750.* 1982.

Parry, J. H. *The Age of Reconnaissance.* 1981.

Wiesner, Merry E. *Women and Gender in Early Modern Europe.* 1993.

A Clash of Worldviews

The transformation of intellectual and cultural life has long fascinated scholars. Recent works have developed a new kind of study called "microhistory," focused on one person (like Ginzburg's Italian miller) or a series of individual stories (as in Roper's analysis of witchcraft in the German states).

Baroque architecture: http://www.lib.virginia.edu:80/dic/colls/arh102/index.html

*Drake, Stillman, ed. *Discoveries and Opinions of Galileo.* 1957.

The Galileo Project: http://riceinfo.rice.edu/Galileo

Ginzburg, Carlo. *The Cheese and the Worms: The Cosmos of a Sixteenth-Century Miller.* Trans. John and Anne Tedeschi. 1992.

Jacob, James. *The Scientific Revolution.* 1998.

Roper, Lyndal. *Oedipus and the Devil: Witchcraft, Sexuality, and Religion in Early Modern Europe.* 1994.

Skinner, Quentin. *The Foundations of Modern Political Thought.* Vol. 2, *The Age of Reformation.* 1978.

Thomas, Keith. *Religion and the Decline of Magic.* 1971.

Zagorin, Perez. *Francis Bacon.* 1998.

CHAPTER 13
State Building and the Search for Order, 1648–1690

Louis XIV: Model of Absolutism

Recent studies have examined Louis XIV's uses of art and imagery for political purposes and have also rightly insisted that absolutism could never be entirely absolute because the king depended on collaboration and cooperation to enforce his policies. Some of the best sources for Louis XIV's reign are the letters written by important noblewomen. The Web site of the Château of Versailles includes views of rooms in the castle.

Beik, William. *Absolutism and Society in Seventeenth-Century France: State Power and Provincial Aristocracy in Languedoc.* 1985.

*———. *Louis XIV and Absolutism: A Brief Study with Documents.* 1999.

Burke, Peter. *The Fabrication of Louis XIV.* 1992.

Collins, James B. *The State in Early Modern France.* 1995.

*Forster, Elborg, trans. *A Woman's Life in the Court of the Sun King: Elisabeth Charlotte, Duchesse d'Orléans.* 1984.

Ranum, Oreste. *The Fronde: A French Revolution, 1648–1652.* 1993.

*Sévigné, Madame de. *Selected Letters.* Trans. Leonard Tancock. 1982.

Versailles: http://www.chateauversailles.fr

Absolutism in Central and Eastern Europe

Too often central and eastern European forms of state development have been characterized as backward in comparison with those of western Europe. Now historians emphasize the patterns of ruler-elite cooperation shared with western Europe, but they also underscore the weight of serfdom in eastern economies and political systems.

Barkey, Karen. *The Ottoman Route to State Centralization.* 1994.

Dukes, Paul. *The Making of Russian Absolutism, 1613–1801.* 1990.

Friedrich, Karin. *The Other Prussia: Royal Prussia, Poland and Liberty, 1569–1772.* 2000.

Kivelson, Valerie A. *Autocracy in the Provinces: The Muscovite Gentry and Political Culture in the Seventeenth Century.* 1996.

Vierhaus, Rudolf. *Germany in the Age of Absolutism.* Trans. Jonathan B. Knudsen. 1988.

Wilson, Peter H. *German Armies: War and German Politics, 1648–1806.* 1998.

Constitutionalism in England

Although recent interpretations of the English revolutions emphasize the limits on radical change, Hill's portrayal of the radical ferment of ideas remains fundamental.

Carlin, Norah. *The Causes of the English Civil War.* 1999.

Cust, Richard, and Ann Hughes, eds. *The English Civil War.* 1997.

*Graham, Elspeth, et al., eds. *Her Own Life: Autobiographical Writings by Seventeenth-Century English Women.* 1989.

*Haller, William, and Godfrey Davies, eds. *The Leveller Tracts, 1647–1653.* 1944.

Hill, Christopher. *The World Turned Upside Down: Radical Ideas during the English Revolution.* 1972.

Israel, Jonathan, ed. *The Anglo-Dutch Moment: Essays on the Glorious Revolution and Its World Impact.* 1991.

Mack, Phyllis. *Visionary Women: Ecstatic Prophecy in Seventeenth-Century England.* 1992.

Manning, Brian. *Aristocrats, Plebeians, and Revolution in England, 1640–1660.* 1996.

Constitutionalism in the Dutch Republic and the Overseas Colonies

Studies of the Dutch Republic emphasize the importance of trade and consumerism. Recent work on the colonies has begun to explore the intersecting experiences of settlers, Native Americans, and African slaves.

*Campbell, P. F., ed. *Some Early Barbadian History.* 1993.

Delâge, Denys. *Bitter Feast: Amerindians and Europeans in Northeastern North America, 1600–64.* Trans. Jane Brierley. 1993.

*Foster, William C., ed. *The La Salle Expedition to Texas: The Journal of Henri Joutel, 1684–1687.* Trans. Johanna S. Warren. 1998.

Israel, Jonathan. *Dutch Primacy in World Trade, 1585–1740.* 1989.

Merrell, James Hart. *Into the American Woods: Negotiators on the Pennsylvania Frontier.* 1999.

Price, J. L. *The Dutch Republic in the Seventeenth Century.* 1998.

Schama, Simon. *The Embarrassment of Riches: An Interpretation of Dutch Culture in the Golden Age.* 1988.

Thornton, John. *Africa and Africans in the Making of the Atlantic World, 1400–1800.* 1992.

The Search for Order in Elite and Popular Culture

Historians do not always agree about the meaning of popular culture: was it something widely shared by all social classes, or was it a set of activities increasingly identified with the lower classes, as Burke argues? The central Web site for Dutch museums allows the visitor to tour rooms and see paintings in scores of Dutch museums, many of which have important holdings of paintings by Rembrandt and Vermeer.

Burke, Peter. *Popular Culture in Early Modern Europe.* 1978.

Davis, Natalie Zemon. *Women on the Margins: Three Seventeenth-Century Lives.* 1995.

DeJean, Joan E. *Tender Geographies: Women and the Origins of the Novel in France.* 1991.

Dobbs, Betty Jo Teeter, and Margaret C. Jacob. *Newton and the Culture of Newtonianism.* 1994.

Dutch museums: http://www.hollandmuseums.nl

Elias, Norbert. *The Civilizing Process: The Development of Manners.* Trans. by Edmund Jephcott. 1978.

*Fitzmaurice, James, ed. *Margaret Cavendish: Sociable Letters.* 1997.
Todd, Janet M. *The Secret Life of Aphra Behn.* 1997.

CHAPTER 14
The Atlantic System and Its Consequences, 1690–1740

The Atlantic System and the World Economy

It is easier to find sources on individual parts of the system than on the workings of the interlocking trade as a whole, but work has been rapidly increasing in this area. Dunn's book nonetheless remains one of the classic studies of how the plantation system took root. Eze's reader should be used with caution, as it sometimes distorts the overall record with its selections.

Blackburn, Robin. *The Making of New World Slavery: From the Baroque to the Modern, 1492–1800.* 1997.

Dunn, Richard S. *Sugar and Slaves: The Rise of the Planter Class in the English West Indies, 1624–1713.* 1972.

*Eze, Emmanuel Chukwudi, ed. *Race and the Enlightenment: A Reader.* 1997.

Jordan, Winthrop D. *The White Man's Burden: Historical Origins of Racism in the United States.* 1974.

Mintz, Sidney W. *Sweetness and Power: The Place of Sugar in Modern History.* 1985.

Morgan, Philip D. *Slave Counterpoint: Black Culture in the Eighteenth-Century Chesapeake and Low Country.* 1998.

Northrup, David. *Africa's Discovery of Europe.* 2002.

Slave movement during the eighteenth and nineteenth centuries:
    http://dpls.dacc.wisc.edu/slavedata/

Smith, Alan K. *Creating a World Economy: Merchant Capital, Colonialism, and World Trade, 1400–1825.* 1991.

New Social and Cultural Patterns

Many of the novels of the period provide fascinating insights into the development of new social attitudes and customs. In particular, see Daniel Defoe's *Robinson Crusoe* (1719) and *Moll Flanders* (1722); the many novels of Eliza Heywood; and Antoine François Prévost's *Manon Lescaut* (1731), a French psychological novel about a nobleman's fatal love for an unfaithful woman, which became the basis for an opera in the nineteenth century.

Artwork of Boucher, Chardin, and Watteau:
    http://mistral.culture.fr/lumiere/documents/peintres.html

De Vries, Jan. *European Urbanization, 1500–1800.* 1984.

Earle, Peter. *The Making of the English Middle Class: Business, Society, and Family Life in London, 1660–1730.* 1989.

Handel's Messiah: The New Interactive Edition (CD-ROM). 1997.

Raynor, Henry. *A Social History of Music, from the Middle Ages to Beethoven.* 1972.

Roche, Daniel. *The People of Paris: An Essay in Popular Culture in the Eighteenth Century.* Trans. Marie Evans. 1987.

Consolidation of the European State System

Studies of rulers and states can be supplemented by work on "political arithmetic" and public health.

Aspromourgos, Tony. *On the Origins of Classical Economics: Distribution and Value from William Petty to Adam Smith.* 1996.

Black, Jeremy, ed. *Britain in the Age of Walpole.* 1984.

Brewer, John. *The Sinews of Power: War, Money, and the English State, 1688–1783.* 1990.

Brockliss, Laurence, and Colin Jones. *The Medical World of Early Modern France.* 1997.

Campbell, Peter R. *Power and Politics in Old Regime France, 1720–1745.* 1996.

Frey, Linda, and Marsha Frey. *Societies in Upheaval: Insurrections in France, Hungary, and Spain in the Early Eighteenth Century.* 1987.

Hughes, Lindsey. *Russia in the Age of Peter the Great.* 1998.

Lawrence, Susan C. *Charitable Knowledge: Hospital Pupils and Practitioners in Eighteenth-Century London.* 1996.

Raeff, Marc. *Understanding Imperial Russia: State and Society in the Old Regime.* Trans. Arthur Goldhammer. 1984.

The Birth of the Enlightenment

The definitive study of the early Enlightenment is the book by Hazard, but many others have contributed biographies of individual figures or, more recently, studies of women writers.

Besterman, Theodore. *Voltaire.* 1969.

Grendy, Isobel. *Lady Mary Wortley Montagu.* 1999.

Hazard, Paul. *The European Mind: The Critical Years, 1680–1715.* 1990.

*Hill, Bridget, ed. *The First English Feminist: Reflections upon Marriage and Other Writings by Mary Astell.* 1986.

*Jacob, Margaret C. *The Enlightenment: A Brief History with Selected Readings.* 2000.

Rothkrug, Lionel. *The Opposition to Louis XIV: The Political and Social Origins of the French Enlightenment.* 1966.

Smith, Hilda L. *Reason's Disciples: Seventeenth-Century English Feminists.* 1982.

CHAPTER 15

The Promise of Enlightenment, 1740–1789

The Enlightenment at Its Height

The interpretive study by Gay remains useful even though it is over thirty years old. Starobinski's intellectual biography of Rousseau shows the unities in the life and work of this enduringly controversial figure. Much more emphasis has been placed in recent studies on the role of women; on this point see Goodman and Landes. Equiano, an ex-slave, offers one of the earliest firsthand views of the experience of slavery. Voltaire's *Candide* is an accessible introduction to the thought of the philosophes.

*Equiano, Olaudah. *The Interesting Narrative and Other Writings.* Ed. Vincent Carretta. 1995.

Gay, Peter. *The Enlightenment: An Interpretation.* 2 vols. 1966, 1969.

Goodman, Dena. *The Republic of Letters: A Cultural History of the French Enlightenment.* 1994.

Griswold, Charles. *Adam Smith and the Virtues of Enlightenment.* 1999.

Jacob, Margaret C. *Living the Enlightenment: Freemasonry and Politics in Eighteenth-Century Europe.* 1991.

Landes, Joan B. *Women and the Public Sphere in the Age of the French Revolution.* 1988.

McMahon, Darrin M. *Enemies of the Enlightenment: The French Counter-Enlightenment and the Making of Modernity.* 2001.

Starobinski, Jean. *Jean-Jacques Rousseau: Transparency and Obstruction.* Trans. Arthur Goldhammer. 1988.

*Voltaire. *Candide.* Ed. and trans. Daniel Gordon. 1999.

Voltaire Foundation: http://www.voltaire.ox.ac.uk

Society and Culture in an Age of Enlightenment

Recent work has drawn attention to the lives of ordinary people. The personal journal of the French glass-worker Ménétra is a rarity: it offers extensive documentation of the inner life of an ordinary person during the Enlightenment. Ménétra claimed to have met Rousseau. Even if not true, the claim shows that Rousseau's fame was not limited to the upper classes.

Darnton, Robert. *The Great Cat Massacre and Other Episodes in French Cultural History.* 1984.

Gullickson, Gay L. *Spinners and Weavers of Auffay: Rural Industry and the Sexual Division of Labor in a French Village, 1750–1850.* 1986.

Hull, Isabel V. *Sexuality, State, and Civil Society in Germany, 1700–1815.* 1996.

Jarrett, Derek. *England in the Age of Hogarth.* 1986.

McManners, John. *Death and the Enlightenment.* 1981.

*Ménétra, Jacques Louis. *Journal of My Life.* Trans. Arthur Goldhammer. Introd. Daniel Roche. 1986.

Mozart Project: http://www.mozartproject.org/

Stone, Lawrence. *The Family, Sex, and Marriage in England, 1500–1800.* Abridged ed. 1979.

Trumbach, Randolph. *Sex and the Gender Revolution.* 1998.

State Power in an Era of Reform

Biographies and general histories of this period tend to overemphasize the individual decisions of rulers. Although these are incontestably important, side-by-side reading of Büsch, Frederick II's writings on war, and Showalter's book on the wars themselves offers a broader view that puts Frederick II's policies into the context of military growth and its impact on society.

Blanning, T. C. W. *Joseph II.* 1994.

Büsch, Otto. *Military System and Social Life in Old Regime Prussia, 1713–1807: The Beginnings of the Social Militarization of Prusso-German Society.* Trans. John G. Gagliardo. 1997.

Cronin, Vincent. *Catherine, Empress of All the Russias.* 1996.

*Frederick II, King of Prussia. *Frederick the Great on the Art of War.* Ed. and trans. Jay Luvaas. 1999.

Showalter, Dennis E. *The Wars of Frederick the Great.* 1996.

Szabo, Franz A. J. *Kaunitz and Enlightened Absolutism, 1753–1780.* 1994.

Venturi, Franco. *The End of the Old Regime in Europe, 1768–1776: The First Crisis.* Trans. R. Burr Litchfield. 1989.

Rebellions against State Power

Exciting work has focused on specific instances of riot and rebellion. One of the most interesting studies is Thompson's work on the British repression of poaching and its significance for British social and political history. Palmer's overview remains valuable, especially for its comparative aspects.

Alexander, John T. *Autocratic Politics in a National Crisis: The Imperial Russian Government and Pugachev's Revolt, 1773–1775.* 1969.

Palmer, R. R. *The Age of Democratic Revolution: A Political History of Europe and America, 1760–1800.* Vol. 1, *The Challenge.* 1959.

*Rakove, Jack N. *Declaring Rights: A Brief History with Documents.* 1998.

Thomas, P. D. G. *John Wilkes: A Friend to Liberty.* 1996.

Thompson, E. P. *Whigs and Hunters: The Origin of the Black Act.* 1975.

Wood, Gordon S. *The Radicalism of the American Revolution.* 1992.

CHAPTER 16
The French Revolution and Napoleon, 1789–1815

The Revolution of Rights and Reason

In the 1950s and 1960s, historians debated vehemently about whether the French Revolution should be considered part of a more general phenomenon of Atlantic revolutions, as Palmer argues. The most influential book on the meaning of the French Revolution is still the classic study of Tocqueville, who insisted that the Revolution continued the process of state centralization undertaken by the monarchy. Among the most important additions to the debate have been new works on women, Jews, Protestants, and slaves.

*Baker, Keith Michael, ed. *The Old Regime and the French Revolution. University of Chicago Readings in Western Civilization,* vol. 7. 1987.

Chartier, Roger. *The Cultural Origins of the French Revolution.* Trans. Lydia G. Cochrane. 1991.

*Hunt, Lynn, ed. *The French Revolution and Human Rights: A Brief Documentary History.* 1996.

Lefebvre, Georges. *The Coming of the French Revolution.* Trans. with a new preface, R. R. Palmer. 1989.

*Levy, Darline Gay, Harriet Branson Applewhite, and Mary Durham Johnson, eds. *Women in Revolutionary Paris, 1789–1795.* 1979.

Palmer, R. R. *The Age of the Democratic Revolution: A Political History of Europe and America, 1760–1800.* Vol. 2, *The Struggle.* 1964.

Polasky, Janet L. *Revolution in Brussels, 1787–1793.* 1987.

Tocqueville, Alexis de. *The Old Regime and the French Revolution.* Trans. Stuart Gilbert. 1955. Originally published 1856.

Terror and Resistance

The most controversial episode in the French Revolution has not surprisingly provoked conflicting interpretations. Soboul offers the Marxist interpretation, which Furet specifically opposes. Very recently, interest has shifted from these broader interpretive issues back to the principal actors themselves: Robespierre, the Jacobins, and women's clubs have all attracted scholarly attention.

Desan, Suzanne. *Reclaiming the Sacred: Lay Religion and Popular Politics in Revolutionary France.* 1990.

Furet, François. *Interpreting the French Revolution.* Trans. Elborg Forster. 1981.

Godineau, Dominique. *The Women of Paris and Their French Revolution.* Trans. Katherine Streip. 1998.

Haydon, Colin, and William Doyle, eds. *Robespierre.* 1999.

Hunt, Lynn. *Politics, Culture, and Class in the French Revolution.* 1984.

Soboul, Albert. *The Sans-Culottes: The Popular Movement and Revolutionary Government, 1793–1794.* Trans. Remy Inglis Hall. 1980.

Sutherland, D. M. G. *France, 1789–1815: Revolution and Counterrevolution.* 1986.

The Rise of Napoleon Bonaparte

In the past, controversy about the Revolution in France raged while its influence on other places was relatively neglected. This imbalance is now being redressed in studies of the colonies and the impact of the revolutionary wars on areas from Egypt to Ireland. Recent work pays close attention to the social background of soldiers as well as their experiences in warfare.

Beaucour, Fernand Emile, Yves Laissus, and Chantal Orgogozo. *The Discovery of Egypt.* Trans. Bambi Ballard. 1990.

Blanning, T. C. W. *The French Revolutionary Wars, 1787–1802.* 1996.

Censer, Jack R., and Lynn Hunt. *Liberty, Equality, Fraternity: Exploring the French Revolution* (includes a CD-ROM of images and music). 2001.

Elliot, Marianne. *Partners in Revolution: The United Irishmen and France.* 1982.

Forrest, Alan I. *The Soldiers of the French Revolution.* 1990.

James, C. L. R. *Black Jacobins: Toussaint L'Ouverture and the San Domingo Revolution.* 2d ed. 1989.

Emperor Napoleon I, r. 1804–1814

Much has been written about Napoleon as a military leader, but only recently has his regime within France attracted interest. Historians now emphasize the mixed quality of Napoleon's rule. He carried forward some revolutionary innovations and halted others.

Alexander, R. S. *Napoleon.* 2001.

*Arnold, Eric A., Jr., ed. *A Documentary Survey of Napoleonic France.* 1994.

*Brunn, Geoffrey, ed. *Napoleon and His Empire.* 1972.

Crook, Malcolm. *Napoleon Comes to Power: Democracy and Dictatorship in Revolutionary France, 1795–1804.* 1998.

Ellis, Geoffrey James. *Napoleon.* 1996.

Gates, David. *The Napoleonic Wars, 1803–1815.* 1997.

Kafker, Frank A., and James M. Laux. *Napoleon and His Times: Selected Interpretations.* 1989.

Lyons, Martyn. *Napoleon Bonaparte and the Legacy of the French Revolution.* 1994.

Napoleon Foundation: http://www.napoleon.org

Simms, Brendan. *The Impact of Napoleon: Prussian High Politics, Foreign Policy, and the Crisis of the Executive, 1797–1806.* 1997.

Wilson-Smith, Timothy. *Napoleon and His Artists.* 1996.

CHAPTER 17
Industrialization and Social Ferment, 1815–1850

The "Restoration" of Europe

New visions of diplomacy are emerging in recent scholarship, but internal affairs are relatively understudied. As a consequence, Artz's book is still a good introduction.

Artz, Frederick B. *Reaction and Revolution, 1814–1832.* 1934.

Colley, Linda. *Britons: Forging the Nation, 1707–1837.* 1992.

Di Scala, Spencer. *Italy: From Revolution to Republic, 1700 to the Present.* 2d ed. 1998.

Johnson, Paul. *The Birth of the Modern: World Society, 1815–1830.* 1991.

Laven, David, and Lucy Riall, eds. *Napoleon's Legacy: Problems of Government in Restoration Europe.* 2000.

Schroeder, Paul W. *The Transformation of European Politics, 1763–1848.* 1994.

Seward, Desmond. *Metternich: The First European.* 1991.

The Advance of Industrialization and Urbanization

Because the analysis of industrialization occupied a central role in Marxism, the spread of industrialization has elicited much more historical interest than the process of urbanization. Some of the best recent work on urbanization, such as Kudlick's book on cholera, combines an interest in urban history with an interest in the history of public health. The *Spartacus Internet Encyclopedia* has an excellent section on the textile industry and its transformation.

Engerman, Stanley. "Reflections on 'The Standard of Living Debate.'" In John A. James and Mark Thomas, eds., *Capitalism in Context: Essays on Economic Development and Cultural Change in Honor of R. M. Hartwell.* 1994.

Hobsbawm, E. J. *The Age of Revolution, 1789–1848.* 1996.

Kudlick, Catherine J. *Cholera in Post-Revolutionary Paris: A Cultural History.* 1996.

Mokyr, Joel, ed. *The British Industrial Revolution: An Economic Perspective.* 2d ed. 1999.

More, Charles. *Understanding the Industrial Revolution.* 2000.

Pinkney, David H. *Decisive Years in France, 1840–1847.* 1986.

*Pollard, S., and C. Holmes, eds. *Documents of European Economic History.* Vol. 1, *The Process of Industrialization, 1750–1870.* 1968.

Spartacus Internet Encyclopedia, British History 1700–1950:
http://www.spartacus.schoolnet.co.uk/Britain.html

Thompson, Victoria Elizabeth. *The Virtuous Marketplace: Women and Men, Money and Politics in Paris, 1830–1870.* 2000.

New Ideologies

Ideologies are too often studied in an exclusively national context, so broader generalizations are difficult. The works by Clark and Taylor show how gender entered into working-class organization and socialist ideology.

Beecher, Jonathan. *Charles Fourier: The Visionary and His World.* 1986.

Berlin, Sir Isaiah. *The Roots of Romanticism.* 1999.

Clark, Anna. *The Struggle for the Breeches: Gender and the Making of the British Working Class.* 1995.

*Hugo, Howard E., ed. *The Romantic Reader.* 1957.

Kramer, Lloyd S. *Nationalism: Political Cultures in Europe and America, 1775–1865.* 1998.

*Marx, Karl, and Frederick Engels. *The Communist Manifesto: With Related Documents*, ed. John E. Toews. 1999.

Romantic chronology: http://english.ucsb.edu:591/rchrono/

Sewell, William H., Jr. *Work and Revolution in France: The Language of Labor from the Old Regime to 1848.* 1980.

Taylor, Barbara. *Eve and the New Jerusalem: Socialism and Feminism in the Nineteenth Century.* 1983.

Thompson, E. P. *The Making of the English Working Class.* 1964.

Wright, Beth S. *Painting and History during the French Restoration: Abandoned by the Past.* 1997.

Reform or Revolution?

Interest in the revolutions of 1848 has revived of late, perhaps because the recent upsurge of ethnic violence in the Balkans has prompted scholars to look again at this critical period. Not to be overlooked is the excellent treatment of the Irish famine by O'Grada. The Web site Gallica, produced by the National Library of France, offers a wealth of imagery and information on French cultural history.

Davidoff, Leonore, and Catherine Hall. *Family Fortunes: Men and Women of the English Middle Class, 1780–1850.* 1987.

The Dickens Project: http://humwww.ucsc.edu/dickens/index.html

Evans, R. J. W., and Hartmut Pogge von Strandmann, eds. *The Revolutions in Europe, 1848–1849: From Reform to Reaction.* 2000.

Gallica: Images and Texts from Nineteenth-Century French-Speaking Culture: http://gallica.bnf.fr/

Lincoln, W. Bruce. *Nicholas I: Emperor and Autocrat of All the Russias.* 1978.

O'Grada, Cormac. *The Great Irish Famine.* 1989.

Roberts, James S. *Drink, Temperance, and the Working Class in Nineteenth-Century Germany.* 1984.

Rodner, William S. *J. M. W. Turner: Romantic Painter of the Industrial Revolution.* 1997.

Sperber, Jonathan. *The European Revolutions, 1848–1851.* 1994.

Townsend, Mary Lee. *Forbidden Laughter: Popular Humor and the Limits of Repression in Nineteenth-Century Prussia.* 1992.

*Walker, Mack, ed. *Metternich's Europe.* 1968.

CHAPTER 18
Constructing the Nation-State, c. 1850–1880

The End of the Concert of Europe

The inglorious Crimean War has often been left behind in historiography despite its impact on European politics. Much of the best new literature focuses not only on political changes but on the war's social impact in Russia. Engel and the Kingston-Mann and Mixter anthology give searching looks at Russian peasant life in this age of transition.

Edgerton, Robert B. *Death or Glory: The Legacy of the Crimean War.* 1999.

Engel, Barbara Alpern. *Between the Fields and the City: Women, Work, and Family in Russia, 1861–1914.* 1994.

Hazareesingh, Sudhir. *From Subject to Citizen: The Second Empire and the Emergence of Modern French Democracy.* 1998.

Kingston-Mann, Esther, and Timothy Mixter, eds. *Peasant Economy, Culture, and Politics of European Russia, 1800–1921.* 1991.

*Seacole, Mary. *Wonderful Adventures of Mrs. Seacole in Many Lands.* 1857.

Wortman, Richard S. *Scenarios of Power: Myth and Ceremony in Russian Monarchy.* 2000.

War and Nation Building

Nation building has produced a varied literature ranging from biographies to studies of ceremonials and the presentation of royalty as celebrities and unifying figures. Two Web sites show the complexities of this process. Brown University's Victorian Web demonstrates the connections among royalty, politicians, religion, and culture. Bucknell University's Russian Studies site opens to the strains of the Russian national anthem, composed in the reign of Nicholas I to foster reverence for the dynasty and homeland.

Blackbourn, David. *Fontana History of Germany, 1780–1918: The Long Nineteenth Century.* 1997.

Breuilly, John. *The Formation of the First German Nation-State, 1800–1871.* 1996.

DiScala, Spencer. *Italy: From Revolution to Republic, 1700 to the Present.* 1995.

Homans, Margaret. *Royal Representations: Queen Victoria and British Culture, 1837–1876.* 1998.

Russian studies: http://www.departments.bucknell.edu/Russian/

Smith, Paul. *Disraeli: A Brief Life.* 1996.

The Victorian Web: http://landow.stg.brown.edu/victorian/victov.html

Industry and Nation Building

Industry advanced on every front, from the development of new products and procedures to the reorganization of work life and consumption. Trebilcock's classic work on the creation of an economic infrastructure contrasts with more recent studies (such as Rappaport's) on the impact of consumers and taste in driving economic change.

Coffin, Judith. *The Politics of Women's Work: The Paris Garment Trades, 1750–1915.* 1996.

Crossick, Geoffrey, and Serge Jaumin, eds. *Cathedrals of Consumption: The European Department Store, 1850–1939.* 1999.

Franzoi, Barbara. *At the Very Least She Pays the Rent: Women and German Industrialization.* 1985.

Good, David. *The Economic Rise of the Habsburg Empire.* 1984.

Marks, Steven G. *Road to Power: The Trans-Siberian Railroad and the Colonization of Asian Russia, 1850–1917.* 1991.

Rappaport, Erika. *Shopping for Pleasure: Women in the Making of London's West End.* 2000.

Trebilcock, Clive. *The Industrialization of the Continental Powers.* 1981.

Establishing Social Order

Nation building entailed state-sponsored activities stretching from promoting education to rebuilding cities. New histories show the process of creating a sense of nationality through government management of people's environment, so that citizenship became part of seemingly nonpolitical life.

Eley, Geoff, and Ronald Grigor Suny, eds. *Becoming National: A Reader.* 1996.

Hamm, Michael F. *Kiev: A Portrait, 1800–1917.* 1993.

Johanson, Christine. *Women's Struggle for Higher Education in Russia, 1855–1900.* 1987.

Jordan, David. *Transforming Paris: The Life and Labor of Baron Haussmann.* 1995.

Lebra-Chapman, Joyce. *The Rani of Jhansi: A Study in Female Heroism in India.* 1986.

Rotenberg, Robert. *Landscape and Power in Vienna.* 1995.

Slezkine, Yuri. *Arctic Mirrors: Russia and the Small Peoples of the North.* 1994.

Wohl, Anthony. *Endangered Lives: Public Health in Victorian Britain.* 1983.

The Culture of Social Order

Like the biographies of politicians, the lives of artists and intellectuals have proved crucial to understanding this period of realism and Realpolitik. They show artists, intellectuals, and scientists addressing the central issues of their day amid dramatic social change.

Bordenheimer, Rosemarie. *The Real Life of Mary Ann Evans: George Eliot, Her Letters and Fiction.* 1994.

*Darwin, Charles. *Autobiography.* 1969.

Gieson, Gerald L. *The Private Science of Louis Pasteur.* 1996.

Kaufman, Suzanne. "Lourdes, Popular Religion, and Tourism." In Shelley Baranowski and Ellen Furlough, eds. *Being Elsewhere: Tourism, Consumer Culture, and Identity in Modern Europe and North America.* 2000.

Mayr, Ernst. *One Long Argument: Charles Darwin and the Genesis of Modern Evolutionary Thought.* 1991.

*Turgenev, Ivan. *A Hunter's Sketches.* 1852.

Contesting the Order of the Nation-State

The teachings of Karl Marx and the story of the Paris Commune haunted Europeans at the time and have since fascinated historians. The following works capture the fear of the working classes that shaped middle-class thought in the nineteenth century, and they show the energy that working- and middle-class people alike put into politics and into developing political theories, especially in this period of political transformation.

Gullickson, Gay. *Unruly Women of Paris: Images of the Commune.* 1996.

McClellan, David. *Karl Marx: His Life and Thought.* 1978.

Nord, Philip. *The Republican Moment: Struggles for Democracy in Nineteenth-Century France.* 1995.

CHAPTER 19

Empire, Modernity, and the Road to War, c. 1880–1914

The Challenge of Empire

New studies of imperialism show not only increasing conquest and the creation of an international economy but also the social and cultural impulses behind it. The University of Pennsylvania's African studies Web site offers an exciting look at African history, politics, and culture—some of it from this era. Depictions of African art and architecture, such as works confiscated for Western museums, are especially vivid. In the midst of raucous political and social debate, the European powers faced growing resistance to their domination and increasingly serious setbacks. Many historians now judge Europe to have played a less commanding role in the rest of the world than the leading empires claimed.

African Studies Center: http://www.sas.upenn.edu/African_Studies/AS.html

Baumgart, Winfried. *Imperialism: The Idea and Reality of British and French Colonial Expansion.* 1989.

Cohen, Paul A. *History in Three Keys: The Boxers as Event, Experience, and Myth.* 1997.

Crosby, Alfred W. *Ecological Imperialism: The Biological Expansions of Europe, 900–1900.* 1993.

Ferro, Marc. *Colonization: A Global History.* 1997.

Gouda, Frances. *Dutch Culture Overseas: Colonial Practice in the Netherlands Indies, 1900–1942.* 1995.

Hane, Mikiso. *Modern Japan: A Historical Survey.* 1992.

Headrick, Daniel R. *The Tools of Empire: Technology and European Imperialism in the Nineteenth Century.* 1981.

Japanese history: http://www.csuohio.edu/history/japan/ index.html

Kansu, Aykut. *The Revolution of 1908 in Turkey.* 1997.

Meyers, Ramon H., and Mark R. Peattie, eds. *The Japanese Colonial Empire, 1895–1945.* 1984.

*Pruitt, Ida. *A Daughter of Han: The Autobiography of a Chinese Working Woman.* 1945.

Rotberg, R. I. *The Founder: Cecil Rhodes and the Pursuit of Power.* 1988.

Sinha, Mrinalini. *Colonial Masculinity: The "Manly Englishman" and the "Effeminate Bengali" in the Late Nineteenth Century.* 1995.

Wesseling, H. L. *Divide and Rule: The Partition of Africa, 1880–1914.* 1996.

Modern Life in an Age of Empire

Historians are engaged in serious study of the transformations of everyday life that industrial and imperial advance had brought about by the early twentieth century. In particular, personal and domestic life, as seen in the works of Hull, Walkowitz, and Duberman et al., have taken on greater importance as components of social movements and political developments.

Accampo, Elinor A., Rachel G. Fuchs, and Mary Lynn Stewart, eds. *Gender and the Politics of Social Reform in France, 1870–1914.* 1995.

Blakely, Allison. *Blacks in the Dutch World: The Evolution of Racial Imagery in Modern Society.* 1993.

*Bonnell, Victoria, ed. *The Russian Worker.* 1983.

Duberman, Martin, Martha Vicinus, and George Chauncey, Jr. *Hidden from History: Reclaiming the Gay and Lesbian Past.* 1989.

Engelstein, Laura. *The Keys to Happiness: Sex and the Search for Modernity in Fin-de-Siècle Russia.* 1992.

Gillis, John. *A World of Their Own Making: Myth, Ritual, and the Quest for Family Values.* 1996.

Hull, Isabell. *The Entourage of Kaiser Wilhelm II, 1888–1918.* 1982.

MacKenzie, John. *The Empire of Nature: Hunting, Conservation, and British Imperialism.* 1988.

Maynes, Mary Jo. *Taking the Hard Road: Life Course in French and German Workers' Autobiographies in the Era of Industrialization.* 1995.

Moch, Leslie Page. *Moving Europeans: Migration in Western Europe since 1650.* 1993.

Walkowitz, Judith. *City of Dreadful Delight: Narratives of the Sexual Danger in Late-Victorian London.* 1993.

Worobec, Christine D. *Peasant Russia: Family and Community in the Post-Emancipation Period.* 1991.

Modernity and the Revolt in Ideas

Some of the most controversial historiography sees the road to World War I as paved with cultural conflict. Many of the studies here suggest that new forms of art, music, dance, and philosophy were as central to the challenges Europe faced as were ethnic, economic, and international turmoil.

Eksteins, Modris. *Rites of Spring: The Great War and the Birth of the Modern Age.* 1989.

Everdell, William R. *The First Moderns: Profiles in the Origins of Twentieth-Century Thought.* 1997.

Jensen, Robert. *Marketing Modernism in Fin-de-Siècle Europe.* 1994.

Kern, Steven. *The Culture of Space and Time, 1880–1918.* 1983.

*Mann, Thomas. *Buddenbrooks.* 1901.

Nehamas, Alexander. *Nietzsche: Life as Literature.* 1985.

Nineteenth- and twentieth-century philosophy: http://www.epistemelinks.com/index.asp

Silverman, Debora L. *Van Gogh and Gauguin: The Search for Sacred Art.* 2000.

Politics in a New Key

Historians are uncovering the dramatic changes in political life and assessing the consequences of the rise of mass politics across Europe, including the development of suffragist movements. Some studies cited here investigate a second major political phenomenon: the formation of a politics of hatred and the rise of aggressive, warlike nationalism to replace nationalism based on rights and constitutional values.

Burns, Michael. *Dreyfus: A Family Affair.* 1992.

Chickering, Roger. *We Men Who Feel Most German: A Cultural Study of the Pan-German League, 1886–1914.* 1984.

Dennis, David B. *Beethoven in German Politics, 1870–1989.* 1996.

Kent, Susan. *Gender and Power in Britain, 1640–1990.* 1999.

Kornberg, Jacques. *Theodor Herzl: From Assimilation to Zionism.* 1993.

MacKenzie, David. *Violent Solutions: Revolutions, Nationalism, and Secret Societies in Europe to 1918.* 1996.

Schorske, Carl E. *Fin-de-Siècle Vienna: Politics and Culture.* 1981.

Scott, Joan. *Only Paradoxes to Offer: French Feminism and the Rights of Man.* 1996.

Weeks, Theodore R. *Nation and State in Late Imperial Russia: Nationalism and Russification on the Western Frontier.* 1996.

Roads to World War I

The question of why World War I broke out remains widely debated. There are always newcomers to the discussion devoted to assessing the responsibility for the war's beginning, but while these historians fix on a single country, other historians like to look at the full range of diplomatic, military, social, and economic conditions.

Ascher, Abraham. *The Revolution of 1905: Authority Restored.* 1992.

Berghahn, Volker. *Germany and the Approach of War.* 1993.

Cecil, Lamar. *Wilhelm II, Prince and Emperor, 1859–1900.* 1989.

Fenyvesi, Charles. *When the World Was Whole.* 1990.

Ferguson, Niall. *The Pity of War: Explaining World War I.* 1999.

Hoensch, Jorg K. *A History of Modern Hungary, 1867–1986.* 1988.

Lambi, Ivo. *The Navy and German Power Politics.* 1984.

Manning, Roberta. *The Crisis of the Old Order in Russia.* 1982.

Tech, Mikulás, and Roy Porter, eds. *The National Question in Europe in Historical Context.* 1993.

Williamson, Samuel. *Austria-Hungary and the Origins of the First World War.* 1991.

CHAPTER 20

War, Revolution, and Reconstruction, 1914–1929

The Great War, 1914–1918

The most recent histories of the Great War consider its military, technological, psychic, social, and economic aspects. This vision of the war as a phenomenon occurring beyond the battlefield as well as on it characterizes the newest scholarship.

Bourke, Joanna. *Dismembering the Male: Men's Bodies, Britain, and the Great War.* 1996.

*Brittain, Vera. *Testament of Youth.* 1933.

Downs, Laura Lee. *Manufacturing Inequality: Gender Division in the French and British Metalworking Industries, 1914–1939.* 1995.

Echenberg, Myron. *Colonial Conscripts: The "Tirailleurs Sénégalais" in French West Africa, 1857–1960.* 1990.

Ellis, John. *A Social History of the Machine-Gun.* 1986.

*Hasek, Jaroslav. *The Good Soldier Schweik.* 1920.

Leed, Eric J. *No Man's Land: Combat and Identity in World War I.* 1979.

Panchasi, Roxanne. "Reconstructions: Prosthetics and the Rehabilitation of the Male Body in World War I." *Differences.* 1995.

Roshwald, Aviel, and Richard Stites, eds. *European Culture in the Great War: The Arts, Entertainment, and Propaganda, 1914–1918.* 1999.

Schmitt, Bernadotte E., and Harold C. Vederler. *The World in the Crucible, 1914–1919.* 1984.

Winter, Jay, and Jean-Louis Robert, eds. *Capital Cities at War: Paris, London, Berlin, 1914–1919.* 1997.

World War I Documents Archive: http://www.lib.byu.edu/%7Erdh/wwi/

1917–1918: Protest, Revolution, and War's End

Histories of the war's end account for the cataclysmic setting: deprivation, ongoing mass slaughter, and the eruption of revolution. Peacemaking also occurred and that, too, was complex. In all, the violence of the postwar scene has made historians call into question the idea that wars end with an armistice.

Lewis, David Levering. *W. E. B. Du Bois. 2 vols.* 1993–2000.

Neuberger, Joan. *Hooliganism: Crime, Culture, and Power in St. Petersburg.* 1994.

Pipes, Richard. *A Concise History of the Russian Revolution.* 1995.

Schwabe, Klaus. *Woodrow Wilson, Revolutionary Germany, and Peacemaking, 1918–1919: Missionary Diplomacy and the Realities of Power.* 1985.

Smith, Leonard. *Between Mutiny and Obedience: The Case of the French Fifth Infantry Division during World War I.* 1994.

Stites, Richard. *Revolutionary Dreams: Utopian Vision and Experimental Life in the Russian Revolution.* 1989.

Wohl, Robert. *A Passion for Wings: Aviation and the Western Imagination.* 1994.

A Decade of Recovery: Europe in the 1920s

Two themes shape the history of the 1920s: recovery from the trauma of war and revolution and ongoing modernization of work and social life. The great technological innovations of the prewar period, such as films and airplanes, receive sophisticated treatment by historians for their impact on people's imagination. The radio is another phenomenon just beginning to find its historians.

Grossman, Atina. *Reforming Sex: The German Movement for Birth Control and Abortion Reform, 1920–1930.* 1995.

Kah, Douglas, and Gregory Whitehead. *Wireless Imagination: Sound, Radio, and the Avant-Garde.* 1992.

Kent, Susan. *Making Peace: The Reconstruction of Gender in Postwar Britain.* 1994.

Miller, Michael. *Shanghai on the Metro: Spies, Intrigue, and the French between the Wars.* 1994.

Nolan, Mary. *Visions of Modernity: American Business and the Modernization of Germany.* 1994.

Rabinbach, Anson. *The Human Motor: Energy, Fatigue, and the Origins of Modernity.* 1990.

Roberts, Mary Louise. *Civilization without Sexes: Reconstructing Gender in Postwar France, 1917–1927.* 1994.

Schwartz, Vanessa, and Leo Charney, eds. *Cinema and the Invention of Modern Life.* 1995.

Mass Culture and the Rise of Modern Dictators

Mass communications advances in cinema and radio provided new tools for the rule of modern dictators who arose from the shambles of war and revolution. Many of the most interesting recent studies look at the cultural components of the consolidation of dictatorial power, while not forgetting the violence that was a particular feature of authoritarian rule in the postwar twentieth century.

Berghaus, Gunter. *Futurism and Politics: Between Anarchist Rebellion and Fascist Reaction, 1909–1944.* 1996.

De Grazia, Victoria. *How Fascism Ruled Women.* 1994.

Harsch, Donna. *German Social Democracy and the Rise of Nazism.* 1994.

*Kollontai, Alexsandra. *Love of Worker Bees.* 1923.

Lyttleton, Adrian. *The Seizure of Power: Fascism in Italy, 1919–1929.* 1987.

Schnapp, Jeffrey. *Staging Fascism: 18BL and the Theater of Masses for Masses.* 1996.

Tumarkin, Nina. *Lenin Lives! The Lenin Cult in Soviet Russia.* 1997.

CHAPTER 21
An Age of Catastrophes, 1929–1945

The Great Depression

Historians look to the depression as a complex event with economic, social, and cultural consequences, but in addition they see its impact as yet another indication of the tightening of global economic connections. To follow some of the political implications for European empires, see in particular Columbia University's South Asia Web site, which explores Gandhi's economic resistance to British colonialism.

Brown, Ian. *The Economies of Africa and Asia in the Inter-war Depression.* 1989.

Evans, Richard J., and Dick Geary. *The German Unemployed: Experiences and Consequences of Mass Unemployment from the Weimar Republic to the Third Reich.* 1987.

James, Harold. *The German Slump: Politics and Economics, 1924–1936.* 1986.

Johnson, H. Clark. *Gold, France, and the Great Depression, 1919–1932.* 1997.

Roszkowski, Wojciech. *Landowners in Poland, 1918–1939.* 1991.

Rothermund, Dietmar. *The Global Impact of the Great Depression, 1929–1939.* 1996.

South Asia and Gandhi: http://www.columbia.edu/cu/libraries/indiv/area/sarai

Totalitarian Triumph

The vicious dictators Stalin, Hitler, and Mussolini are among the most popular subjects for historians and readers alike. Recent historical works have moved beyond this fascination to study their mobilization of art and the media and to consider people's reactions to totalitarian regimes. Historians are especially intrigued with the mixture of modernism and traditionalism or even antimodernism in the dictators' programs and policies.

Ades, Dawn, et al. *Art and Power: Europe under the Dictators, 1930–1945.* 1995.

Berezin, Mabel. *Making the Fascist Self: The Political Culture of Interwar Italy.* 1997.

Burleigh, Michael. *The Third Reich: A New History.* 2000.

Engel, Barbara Alpern, and Anastasia Posadskaya-Vanderbeck, eds. *A Revolution of Their Own: Voices of Women in Soviet History.* 1998.

Fest, Joachim. *Hitler.* 1974.

Fitzpatrick, Sheila. *Stalin's Peasants.* 1994.

Fritzsche, Peter. *Germans into Nazis.* 1998.

Groys, Boris. *The Total Art of Stalinism: Avant-Garde, Aesthetic Dictatorship, and Beyond.* 1992.

Kaplan, Marion. *Between Dignity and Despair: Jewish Life in Nazi Germany.* 1998.

Koonz, Claudia. *Mothers in the Fatherland: Women, the Family, and Nazi Politics.* 1987.

Kotkin, Stephen. *Magnetic Mountain: Stalinism as Civilization.* 1995.

Petrone, Karen. *Life Has Become More Joyous, Comrades. Celebrations in the Time of Stalin.* 2000.

Democracies on the Defensive

The democracies attacked the depression from a variety of perspectives ranging from state policy to film and the arts, yet another indication of how complex politics can be. Further departures from liberal policies, whether in trade or in the development of the activist welfare state, also have attracted historical study.

Kalvemark, Ann-Sofie. *More Children or Better Quality? Aspects of Swedish Population Policy.* 1980.

Kennedy, David M. *Freedom from Fear: The American People in Depression and War, 1929–1945.* 1999.

Lavin, Maud, et al. *Montage and Modern Life, 1919–1942.* 1992.

Rearick, Charles. *The French in Love and War: Popular Culture in the Era of the World Wars.* 1997.

Richards, Jeffrey, ed. *The Unknown 1930s: An Alternative History of the British Cinema, 1929–39.* 1998.

The Road to World War II

The road to war encircled the globe, involving countries seemingly peripheral to the struggles among the antagonists. The perennial question for many historians is whether Hitler could have been stopped, but with globalization there is new attention to the beginnings of war beyond the West as a prelude to decolonization.

Crozier, Andrew. *The Causes of the Second World War.* 1997.

Iriye, Akira. *The Origins of the Second World War in Asia and the Pacific.* 1987.

Knight, Patricia. *The Spanish Civil War.* 1991.

*Mangini González, Shirley. *Memories of Resistance: Women's Voices from the Spanish Civil War.* 1995.

Watt, D. Cameron. *How War Came: The Immediate Causes of the Second World War.* 1989.

World War II, 1939–1945

In a vast literature, historians have charted the war's innumerable and global horrors. The Holocaust, industrial killing, and the nature of racial thinking have drawn particular attention. The United States Memorial Holocaust Museum provides online exhibits giving the history of the Holocaust in different locations. While looking at the social aspects of war, historians have intently debated the development of the cold war within the "hot" war.

Browning, Christopher. *The Path to Genocide: Essays on Launching the Final Solution.* 1992.

*Dawidowicz, Lucy S., ed. *A Holocaust Reader.* 1976.

Dower, John W. *War without Mercy: Race and Power in the Pacific War.* 1986.

Fussell, Paul. *Wartime: Understanding and Behavior in the Second World War.* 1989.

Holocaust Museum: http://usholocaustmuseum.org

Lewis, Peter. *A People's War.* 1986.

Ofer, Dalia, and Lenore J. Weitzman, eds. *Women in the Holocaust.* 1998.

O'Neill, William L. *A Democracy at War: America's Fight at Home and Abroad in World War II.* 1993.

Rhodes, Richard. *The Making of the Atomic Bomb.* 1986.

*Vassiltchikov, Marie. *Berlin Diaries, 1940–1945.* 1988.

Weinberg, Gerhard. *A World at Arms: A Global History of World War II.* 1994.

CHAPTER 22
The Atomic Age, c. 1945–1960

World Politics Transformed

In the past decade, the opening of Soviet archives and closer research in American records have allowed for more-informed views of the diplomacy and politics of the cold war in Europe and around the world. Although few defend Stalin, we now benefit from balanced assessments of superpower rivalry. Two Web sites contain biographies of the main players, time lines, and miscellaneous details of cold war events.

Cold war: http://history.acusd.edu/gen/20th/coldwarO.html

Cold war: http://library.thinkquest.org/10826.mainpage.htm

Cronin, James. *The World the Cold War Made: Order, Chaos, and the Return of History.* 1996.

Eisenberg, Carolyn Woods. *Drawing the Line: The American Decision to Divide Germany, 1944–1949.* 1996.

Gaddis, John. *We Now Know: Rethinking Cold War History.* 1997.

Hogan, Michael J. *A Cross of Iron: Harry S Truman and the Origins of the National Security State, 1945–1954.* 1998.

*Pasternak, Boris. *Doctor Zhivago.* 1958.

Vadney, T. E. *The World Since 1945.* 1992.

Zubkova, Elena. *Russia after the War: Hopes, Illusions, and Disappointments, 1945–1957.* 1998.

Zubok, Vladislav, and Constantine Pleshakov. *Inside the Kremlin's Cold War: From Stalin to Khrushchev.* 1996.

The Political and Economic Recovery of Europe

Though painstaking and complex, recovery in its material and political forms yielded a distinctly new Europe whose characteristics historians are still uncovering. Because of the opening of the archives, historical attention has focused on charting Soviet occupation, recovery, and Communist takeover.

Herf, Jeffrey. *Divided Memory: The Nazi Past in the Two Germanies.* 1997.

Kenney, Padraic. *Rebuilding Poland: Workers and Communists, 1945–1950.* 1997.

Marrus, Michael. *The Unwanted: European Refugees in the Twentieth Century.* 1985.

Medvedev, Roy. *Khrushchev.* 1983.

Moeller, Robert, ed. *West Germany under Construction: Politics, Society, and Culture in the Adenauer Era.* 1997.

Naimark, Norman M. *The Russians in Germany: A History of the Russian Zone of Occupation, 1945–1949.* 1995.

Pinder, John. *European Community: The Building of a Union.* 1991.

Decolonization in a Cold War Climate

Novelists, philosophers, and historians debate the impact and issues of decolonization. Powerful evocations of the brutality of the process appear most often in novels such as *Cracking India*, recently made into the film *Earth.*

Brown, L. Carl. *International Politics and the Middle East.* 1984.

Dunbabin, J. P. D. *The Post-Imperial Age: The Great Powers and the Wider World.* 1994.

*Fanon, Frantz. *The Wretched of the Earth.* 1961.

Flaghan, Simha. *The Birth of Israel: Myths and Realities.* 1987.

Hargreaves, J. D. *Decolonization in Africa.* 1996.

McIntyre, W. David. *British Decolonization, 1946–1997: When, Why, and How Did the British Empire Fall?* 1999.

*Sidhwa, Bapsi. *Cracking India: A Novel.* 1992.

Cultural Life on the Brink of Nuclear War

Cold war culture, including the growth of consumerism, make the 1950s a fertile field for research, especially as new sources become available. Saunders and other historians have focused on governments' direction of high culture to the point that some artists and writers were made "stars" because of government intervention.

*Beauvoir, Simone de. *The Mandarins.* 1956.

Boyer, Paul. *By the Bomb's Early Light: American Thought and Culture at the Dawn of the Atomic Age.* 1985.

Cohen-Solal, Annie. *Sartre.* 1987.

Heineman, Elizabeth D. *What Difference Does a Husband Make? Women and Marital Status in Nazi and Postwar Germany.* 1999.

Kuisel, Richard. *Seducing the French: The Dilemma of Americanization.* 1993.

Lapidus, Gail. *Women in Soviet Society: Equality, Development, and Social Change.* 1978.

Marcus, Milicent. *Italian Film in the Light of Neorealism.* 1986.

Marling, Karal Ann. *As Seen on TV: The Visual Culture of Everyday Life in the 1950s.* 1994.

McDowell, Colin. *Forties Fashion and the New Look.* 1997.

Poiger, Uta. *Jazz, Rock, and Rebels: Cold War Politics and American Culture in a Divided Germany.* 2000.

Saunders, Frances Stonor. *Who Paid the Piper?* 1999.

Swann, Abram de. *In Care of the State: Health Care, Education, and Welfare in Europe and the United States in the Modern Era.* 1988.

CHAPTER 23

Challenges to the Postindustrial West, 1960–1980

The Technology Revolution

Wartime technological development came to have profound consequences for the peacetime lives of individuals and for society. The following works describe the new technologies and analyze their importance. Authors are divided on whether the new developments should be feared or embraced.

Hecht, Gabrielle. *The Radiance of France: Nuclear Power and National Identity after World War II.* 1998.

Kimbrell, Andrew. *The Human Body Shop: The Cloning, Engineering, and Marketing of Life.* 1997.

Mazlich, Bruce. *The Fourth Discontinuity: The Co-Evolution of Humans and Machines.* 1994.

*Rhodes, Richard, ed. *Visions of Technology: A Century of Vital Debate about Machines, Systems, and the Human World.* 1999.

Singer, Edward Nathan. *The Twentieth Century Revolution in Technology.* 1998.

*Stanworth, Michelle, ed. *Reproductive Technologies: Gender, Motherhood, and Medicine.* 1987.

Postindustrial Society and Culture

Changes in the way people worked became striking in the 1960s, causing social observers to analyze the meaning of the transformation. Many critics agree that technology's creation of a postindustrial workplace changed not only the way people worked but also how they lived in families and interacted with peers.

Bennett, Tony, ed. *Rock and Popular Music: Politics, Policies, Institutions.* 1993.

Evans, Christopher. *The Micro Millennium.* 1979.

Hochschild, Arlie. *The Time Bind: When Work Becomes Home and Home Becomes Work.* 1997.

Proctor, Robert. *Cancer Wars: The Politics behind What We Know and Don't Know about Causes and Trends.* 1994.

Sampson, Anthony. *The New Europeans.* 1968.

Sinfield, Alan. *Literature, Politics, and Culture in Post-War Britain.* 1989.

Contesting the Cold War Order in the 1960s

Historians look to domestic politics, international events, social change, and cultural life to capture the texture of this tumultuous decade. But the momentous changes on so many fronts still need synthetic treatment. A Martin Luther King Web site introduces visitors to the biography, speeches, sermons, and major life events of the slain civil rights leader.

Caute, David. *Sixty-Eight.* 1988.

*Dubček, Alexander. *Hope Dies Last: The Autobiography of Alexander Dubček.* 1993.

Fineberg, Jonathan. *Art since 1940: Strategies of Being.* 1995.

Fink, Carole, et al. *1968: The World Transformed.* 1998.

*Guy-Sheftall, Beverly, ed. *Words of Fire: An Anthology of African-American Feminist Thought.* 1995.

Katsiaficas, George. *The Subversion of Politics: European Autonomous Social Movements and the Decolonization of Everyday Life.* 1997.

*Lévi-Strauss, Claude. *Tristes Tropiques.* 1961.

The Martin Luther King Jr. Papers Project at Stanford University:
    http://www.stanford.edu/group/King

Tarrow, Sidney. *Democracy and Disorder: Protest Politics in Italy, 1965–1975.* 1989.

The Erosion of Superpower Mastery in the 1970s

As the superpowers continued their standoff, historians found that myriad global changes affected their status. Some of the most compelling reading is found in personal testimonies such as Chang's account of Maoism and the Cultural Revolution, while the dissident art of the Soviet Union is striking for its deft and moving critique of life under communism. Many interesting Web sites explore the development of green parties over the past three decades, the most inclusive being that of the global organization with links to green parties of all continents and countries.

Battah, Abdalla M., and Yehuda Lukachs, eds. *The Arab-Israeli Conflict: Two Decades of Change.* 1988.

*Chang, Jung. *Wild Swans: Three Daughters of China.* 1991.

Green parties worldwide: http://www.greens.org

Huelsberg, Werner. *The German Greens: A Social and Political Profile.* 1988.

Koshar, Rudy. *Germany's Transient Pasts: Preservation and National Memory in the Twentieth Century.* 1998.

Laqueur, Walter. *The Age of Terrorism.* 1987.

Olson, James S., and Randy Roberts. *Where the Domino Fell: America and Vietnam, 1945–1990.* 1996.

Rosenfeld, Alla, and Norton T. Dodge. *From Gulag to Glasnost: Nonconformist Art from the Soviet Union.* 1995.

Smith, Dennis B. *Japan since 1945: The Rise of an Economic Superpower.* 1995.

*Solzhenitsyn, Aleksandr Isaevich. *The Gulag Archipelago.* 1973–1976.

Swain, Geoffrey, and Nigel Swain. *Eastern Europe since 1945.* 1993.

CHAPTER 24
The New Globalism: Opportunities and Dilemmas, 1980 to the Present

Global Challenges

Historians see the challenges since the 1980s as enormously diverse, ranging from conditions in the environment to issues of leadership in international affairs to the safety of the world's citizens in a global age. However, as Rives and Yousefi show, challenges such as the globalization of work have benefits as well as costs.

Appleyard, Reginald. *International Migration: Challenges for the Nineties.* 1991.

Feshbach, Murray. *Ecological Disaster: Cleaning Up the Hidden Legacy of the Soviet Regime.* 1995.

Keylor, William R. *The Twentieth-Century World: An International History.* 1992.

*Khadduri, Majid, and Edmund Ghareeb. *War in the Gulf, 1990–1991.* 1997.

Moin, Baqr. *Khomeini: Life of the Ayatollah.* 1999.

Rives, Janet, and Mahmood Yousefi. *Economic Dimensions of Gender Inequality: A Global Perspective.* 1997.

UN population data: http://www.unfpa.org/swp/swpmain.htm

The Welfare State in Question

The transformation of the welfare state involved powerful political personalities and raised fundamental issues about the nature of citizenship. Much cutting-edge history concerns an analysis of citizens' relationships to their states and their relationships to one another in an age of global migration and dramatic economic change. The work of Gilroy in particular has brought these questions to the fore.

Ash, Timothy Garton. *In Europe's Name: Germany and the Divided Continent.* 1993.

Caciagli, Mario, and David I. Kertzer, eds. *Italian Politics: The Stalled Transition.* 1996.

Gilroy, Paul. *"There Ain't No Black in the Union Jack": The Cultural Politics of Race and Nation.* 1987.

Sassen, Saskia. *Globalization and Its Discontents: Essays on the New Mobility of People and Money.* 1998.

Schaller, Michael. *Reckoning with Reagan: America and Its President in the 1980s.* 1992.

Thompson, Juliet S., and Wayne C. Thompson. *Margaret Thatcher: Prime Minister Indomitable.* 1994.

The Collapse of Soviet Communism

Historians will be telling and retelling this story, for the full consequences of communism's collapse are still unfolding. As new archives open, scholars, such as Kligman, focus on recounting some of the most horrendous aspects of Communist rule. Others, like Wachtel, explain the post-Communist situation in terms of very long-standing trends such as the obstacles to creating cultural unity among peoples of the former Yugoslavia.

Funk, Nanette, and Magda Mueller. *Gender Politics and Post-Communism: Reflections from Eastern Europe and the Former Soviet Union.* 1993.

Glenny, Misha. *The Fall of Yugoslavia: The Third Balkan War.* 1996.

*Gorbachev, Mikhail. *Memoirs.* 1996.

Jarausch, Konrad. *The Rush to German Unity.* 1994.

Kazanov, Anatoly M. *After the USSR: Ethnicity, Nationalism, and Politics in the Commonwealth of Independent States.* 1995.

Kligman, Gail. *The Politics of Duplicity: Controlling Reproduction in Ceauşescu's Romania.* 1998.

Sternhal, Suzanne. *Gorbachev's Reforms: De-Stalinization through Demilitarization.* 1997.

Strayer, Robert. *Why Did the Soviet Union Collapse?* 1998.

Wachtel, Andrew B. *Making a Nation, Breaking a Nation: Literature and Cultural Politics in Yugoslavia.* 1998.

Weigel, George. *Witness to Hope: The Biography of Pope John Paul II.* 1999.

Global Culture and Western Civilization at the Dawn of a New Millennium

The fate of cultural identity in an age of globalization engages a wide range of investigation and theorizing. From the nation-state to our individual relationships, as Applegate and Turkle, among others, suggest, long-standing identities are open to rethinking.

Agre, Philip. *Computation and Human Experience.* 1997.

Applegate, Celia. "A Europe of Regions: Reflections on the Historiography of Sub-National Places in Modern Times." *American Historical Review* 104 (1999): 1157–82.

Bales, Kevin. *Disposable People: New Slavery in the Global Economy.* 1999.

Dery, Mark. *Escape Velocity: Cyberculture at the End of the Century.* 1996.

*Emecheta, Buchi. *The Joys of Motherhood.* 1979.

Geddes, Andrew. *Immigration and European Integration.* 2000.

Huntington, Samuel P. *The Clash of Civilizations and the Remaking of the World Order.* 1996.

Iriye, Akira. *Cultural Internationalism and World Order.* 1997.

*Morrison, Toni. *Paradise.* 1998.

Piening, Christopher. *Global Europe: The European Union in World Affairs.* 1997.

Public Broadcasting Service: http://www.pbs.org

Rashid, Ahmed. *Jihad: The Rise of Militant Islam in Central Asia.* 2002.

Redmond, John, and Glenda S. Rosenthal. *The Expanding European Union: Past, Present, Future.* 1998.

Turkle, Sherry. *Life on the Screen: Identity in the Age of the Internet.* 1995.

Index

continued

continued

continued

continued

continued

continued

continued

continued

continued